THE CAMBRIDGE HISTORY OF LATIN AMERICA

VOLUME III

From Independence to c. *1870*

THE CAMBRIDGE HISTORY OF LATIN AMERICA

THE CAMBRIDGE
HISTORY OF
LATIN AMERICA

VOLUME III

From Independence to c. 1870

edited by

LESLIE BETHELL

Reader in Hispanic American and
Brazilian History at University College London

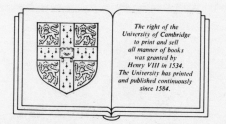

The right of the
University of Cambridge
to print and sell
all manner of books
was granted by
Henry VIII in 1534.
The University has printed
and published continuously
since 1584.

CAMBRIDGE UNIVERSITY PRESS

Cambridge

London   New York   New Rochelle

Melbourne   Sydney

te of the University of Cambridge
gton Street, Cambridge CB2 1RP
ew York, NY 10022, USA
gh, Melbourne 3166, Australia

© Cambridge University Press 1985

First published 1985
Reprinted 1986

Printed in Great Britain at the University Press, Cambridge

Library of Congress catalogue card number: 83–19036

British Library cataloguing in publication data

The Cambridge history of Latin America.
Vol 3: From independence to c.1870
1. Latin America – History
I. Bethell, Leslie
980   F1410

ISBN 0 521 23224 4

SE

CONTENTS

MAPS

GENERAL PREFACE

In the English-speaking and English-reading world the multi-volume Cambridge Histories planned and edited by historians of established reputation, with individual chapters written by leading specialists in their fields, have since the beginning of the century set the highest standards of collaborative international scholarship. *The Cambridge Modern History*, planned by Lord Acton, appeared in sixteen volumes between 1902 and 1912. It was followed by *The Cambridge Ancient History*, *The Cambridge Medieval History* and others. The *Modern History* has now been replaced by *The New Cambridge Modern History* in fourteen volumes, and *The Cambridge Economic History of Europe* has recently been completed. Cambridge Histories of Islam, of Iran and of Africa are published or near completion; in progress are Histories of China and of Judaism, while Japan is soon to join the list.

In the early 1970s Cambridge University Press decided the time was ripe to embark on a Cambridge History of Latin America. Since the Second World War and particularly since 1960 research and writing on Latin American history had been developing, and have continued to develop, at an unprecedented rate – in the United States (by American historians in particular, but also by British, European and Latin American historians resident in the United States), in Europe (especially in Britain and France) and increasingly in Latin America itself (where a new generation of young professional historians, many of them trained in the United States, Britain or Europe, had begun to emerge). Perspectives had changed as political, economic and social realities in Latin America – and Latin America's role in the world – had changed. Methodological innovations and new conceptual models drawn from the social sciences (economics, political science, historical demography, sociology, anthropology) as well as from other fields of historical

ix

research were increasingly being adopted by historians of Latin America.
The Latin American Studies monograph series and the *Journal of Latin
American Studies* had already been established by the Press and were
beginning to publish the results of this new historical thinking and
research.

In 1974 Dr Leslie Bethell, Reader in Hispanic American and Brazilian
History at University College London, accepted an invitation to edit the
Cambridge History of Latin America. For the first time a single editor
was given responsibility for the planning, co-ordination and editing of
an entire History. Contributors were drawn from the United States and
Canada, Britain and Europe, and Latin America.

The Cambridge History of Latin America is the first large-scale, authoritative survey of Latin America's unique historical experience during
almost five centuries from the first contacts between the native American
Indians and Europeans (and the beginnings of the African slave trade) in
the late fifteenth and early sixteenth centuries to the present day. (The
Press has under consideration a separate Cambridge History of the native
peoples of America – North, Middle and South – before the arrival of the
Europeans.) Latin America is taken to comprise the predominantly
Spanish- and Portuguese-speaking areas of continental America south of
the United States – Mexico, Central America and South America –
together with the Spanish-speaking Caribbean – Cuba, Puerto Rico, the
Dominican Republic – and, by convention, Haiti. (The vast territories in
North America lost to the United States by treaty and by war, first by
Spain, then by Mexico, during the first half of the nineteenth century are
for the most part excluded. Neither the British, French and Dutch
Caribbean islands nor the Guianas are included even though Jamaica and
Trinidad, for example, have early Hispanic antecedents and are now
members of the Organisation of American States.) The aim is to produce
a high-level synthesis of existing knowledge which will provide historians of Latin America with a solid base for future research, which
students of Latin American history will find useful and which will be of
interest to historians of other areas of the world. It is also hoped that the
History will contribute more generally to a deeper understanding of Latin
America through its history in the United States and in Europe and, not
least, to a greater awareness of its own history in Latin America.

For the first time the volumes of a Cambridge *History* will be published
in chronological order: Volumes I and II (Colonial Latin America – with
an introductory section on the native American peoples and civilizations

on the eve of the European invasion) appeared in 1984; Volume III (From Independence to *c.* 1870) in 1985; Volumes IV and V (*c.* 1870 to 1930) will be published in 1986; and Volumes VI–VIII (1930 to the present) as soon as possible thereafter. Each volume or set of volumes examines a period in the economic, social, political, intellectual and cultural history of Latin America. While recognizing the decisive impact on Latin America of external forces, of developments within what is now called the capitalist world system, and the fundamental importance of its economic, political and cultural ties first with Spain and Portugal, then with Britain, France and, to a lesser extent, Western Europe as a whole, and finally with the United States, the emphasis of the *History* will be upon the evolution of internal structures. Furthermore, the emphasis is clearly on the period since the establishment of all the independent Latin American states except Cuba at the beginning of the nineteenth century, which, compared with the colonial and independence periods, has been relatively neglected by historians of Latin America. The period of Spanish and Portuguese colonial rule from the sixteenth to the eighteenth centuries is the subject of two of the eight volumes. Six are devoted to the nineteenth and twentieth centuries and will consist of a mixture of general, comparative chapters built around major themes in Latin American history and chapters on the individual histories of the twenty independent Latin American countries (plus Puerto Rico), and especially the three major countries – Brazil, Mexico and Argentina. In view of its size, population and distinctive history, Brazil, which has often been neglected in general histories of Latin America, written for the most part by Spanish Americans or Spanish American specialists, will here receive the attention it deserves.

An important feature of the *History* is the bibliographical essays which accompany each chapter. These give special emphasis to books and articles published during the past 15–20 years, that is to say, since the publication of Howard F. Cline (ed.), *Latin American History: essays in its study and teaching, 1898–1965* (2 vols., published for the Conference on Latin American History by the University of Texas Press, Austin, Texas, 1967), and Charles C. Griffin (ed.), *Latin America: a guide to the historical literature* (published for the Conference on Latin American History by the University of Texas Press, Austin, Texas, 1971); the latter was prepared during 1966–9 and included few works published after 1966.

PREFACE TO VOLUME III

Volumes I and II of *The Cambridge History of Latin America* published in 1984 were largely devoted to the economic, social, political, intellectual and cultural history of Latin America during the three centuries of Spanish and Portuguese colonial rule from the beginning of the sixteenth century to the beginning of the nineteenth century. (The first section of the first of these two, closely integrated, volumes on colonial Latin America surveyed the native American peoples and civilizations on the eve of the European 'discovery', invasion, conquest and settlement of the 'New World' in the late fifteenth and early sixteenth centuries. No attempt, however, was made to present a full-scale account of the evolution of the various indigenous American societies – in isolation from the rest of the world – during the several millennia before their first contact with Europeans. This will form part of a separate Cambridge History of the Native Peoples of North, Middle and South America.)

Volume III of *The Cambridge History of Latin America* is largely devoted to the breakdown and overthrow of Spanish and Portuguese colonial rule in Latin America during the first quarter of the nineteenth century and the history of Latin America during the half century after independence (to *c*.1870). The five chapters in Part One examine the origins of Latin American independence, the revolutions and wars by which mainland Spanish America separated itself from Spain – while at the same time fragmenting into more than a dozen independent republics – and Brazil's relatively peaceful separation from Portugal as a single independent empire, the political, economic and social structures of the new Latin American states, and finally, the international dimension of Latin American independence. Part Two deals separately with the Caribbean from the late eighteenth century to *c*.1870 and consists of two chapters: the first on Haiti, the former French colony of Saint-Domingue which in 1804 became the first independent – and black – Latin American republic, and Santo Domingo which secured its independence from Spain only to be occupied by Haiti for almost a quarter of a century before it, too, became an independent republic (the Dominican Republic); the second on Cuba which, along with Puerto Rico, remained a Spanish colony throughout the period under consideration.

Parts Three and Four of this volume, and in many respects its central core, examine the economic, social and political history of the independent Latin American states from *c*.1820 to *c*.1870. This was in general a period of relatively modest growth for Latin America's export-oriented economies as many recovered from the destruction and dislocation caused by the wars of independence and most were slow to be incorporated into the new international economic order dominated by Britain. Partly as a consequence it was also a period of only limited social change, apart perhaps from the abolition of slavery in many countries (though not, significantly, in Cuba and Brazil). And it was, at least in the Spanish American republics (with the striking exception of Chile), a period of violent political conflict, instability and *caudillismo*. Brazil's fragile political stability – and unity – was seriously threatened in the 1830s, but survived and was consolidated during the middle decades of the century. It was during the post-independence period that Mexico lost half its territory as a result of the secession of Texas (1836) and the war with the United States (1846–8). Besides a number of relatively minor conflicts, there were at the end of the period two major wars between the Latin American states: the Paraguayan War (1865–70) between Brazil, Argentina and Uruguay (the Triple Alliance) and Paraguay, in which Paraguay was crushed and lost territory to Argentina and Brazil, and the War of the Pacific (1879–83) between Chile and an alliance of Peru and Bolivia, as a result of which Chile enlarged its national territory by a third at the expense of Peru and Bolivia. Part Three includes two general chapters on Spanish America after independence – the first on economy and society, the second on politics, ideology and society – followed by six chapters on individual Spanish American countries or groups of countries: Mexico; Central America (Guatemala, El Salvador, Honduras, Nicaragua and Costa Rica); Venezuela, Colombia and Ecuador; Peru and Bolivia; Chile; and the River Plate Republics (Argentina, Uruguay and Paraguay). Part Four consists of two chapters on the Empire of Brazil from 1822 to 1870.

Finally, the volume concludes with a survey in Part Five of Latin

American cultural life – art and architecture, music, theatre and, above all, literature – in the independence and early national periods (the Age of Romanticism).

Most of the historians who contributed chapters to this volume – seven British, four North American (three from the United States, one from Canada) and five Latin American (one each from the Dominican Republic, Mexico, Argentina, Peru and Brazil) – also read and commented on the chapters of their colleagues. I am, however, especially grateful in this respect to David Bushnell, José Murilo de Carvalho, Simon Collier, Malcolm Deas, Richard Graham, Tulio Halperín Donghi and Frank Safford. In addition, Emília Viotti da Costa provided critical assessments of the chapters on Brazil. As in the case of the two volumes on colonial Latin America already published, I am, above all, indebted to my colleague John Lynch for the advice he so generously offered throughout the planning and editing of this volume. I have also received a great deal of encouragement from R. A. Humphreys, who first introduced me to the problems – and pleasures – of Latin American history almost thirty years ago.

At the Cambridge University Press Elizabeth Wetton has been the editor responsible for *The Cambridge History of Latin America* in recent years. Cynthia Postan was the subeditor of this volume. Nazneen Razwi at University College London again offered invaluable secretarial assistance. Ann Hudson prepared the index.

Part One

INDEPENDENCE

1

THE ORIGINS OF SPANISH AMERICAN INDEPENDENCE

Spain was a durable but not a developed metropolis. At the end of the eighteenth century, after three centuries of imperial rule, Spanish Americans still saw in their mother country an image of themselves. If the colonies exported primary products, so did Spain. If the colonies depended upon the merchant marine of foreigners, so did Spain. If the colonies were dominated by a seigneurial elite, disinclined to save and invest, so was Spain. The two economies differed in one activity: the colonies produced precious metals. And even this exceptional division of labour did not automatically benefit Spain. Here was a case rare in modern history – a colonial economy dependent upon an underdeveloped metropolis.

During the second half of the eighteenth century Bourbon Spain took stock of itself and sought to modernize its economy, society and institutions. Reformist ideology was eclectic in inspiration and pragmatic in intent. The starting point was Spain's own condition, especially the decline in productivity. Answers were sought in various schools of thought. The ideas of the physiocrats were invoked to establish the primacy of agriculture and the role of the state; mercantilism, to justify a more effective exploitation of colonial resources; economic liberalism, to support the removal of restrictions on trade and industry. The Enlightenment too exerted its influence, not so much in new political or philosophical ideas as in a preference for reason and experiment as opposed to authority and tradition. While these divergent trends may have been reconciled in the minds of intellectuals, they help to explain the inconsistencies in the formation of policy, as modernity struggled with tradition.

The principal aim was to reform existing structures rather than design new ones, and the basic economic objective was to improve agriculture rather than to promote industry. The great population growth of the eighteenth century pressed relentlessly on land. The number of Spaniards increased by some 57 per cent, from 7.6 million at the beginning of the century to 12 million in 1808. Rising demand for agricultural products, both in Spain and on the international market, pushed up prices and the profits of landowners. At the same time the growth of the rural population caused a greater demand for land, and rents began to rise even higher than prices. Now more than ever it was vital to improve techniques, commercialize production, and remove obstacles to growth. The corn laws of 1765 abolished price ceilings on grain, permitted free trade within Spain and exports except during dearth. In 1788 landowners were given the right to enclose their lands and plough up grazing land. There was a limited distribution of royal, municipal and even church land. And the regulations of *comercio libre* from 1765 removed the worst restrictions on trade with Spanish America.

Economic improvement did not lead to great social change. There was a coincidence of interests between government reformers who wished to increase food supplies, landowners – mainly nobility and clergy – who wanted to maximize profit, and exporters who sought new markets. But an incipient middle sector was only faintly heard. Merchant groups were active in overseas trade, and new industrialists were at work in the provinces of the peninsula. Catalonia had developed a modern cotton and woollen industry which exported to America via Cádiz and was seeking more direct outlets. Merchants and manufacturers wanted to liberalize trade still further and to find in America markets which they could not secure in Spain. They anticipated *comercio libre* and profited from it.

Yet Spain missed the opportunity of fundamental change in the eighteenth century and finally abandoned the path of modernization. Castilians, it seemed, were unwilling to accumulate capital for investment in industry, even in the *fomento de industria popular*, the artisan industries so dear to some reformers, preferring instead to acquire additional land and luxury imports. Prospects of agrarian reform were frustrated by government apathy and the opposition of vested interests; agricultural incomes remained low and hindered the development of a national market for industry. The infrastructure too was badly outmoded. By the 1790s the transport system was unable to meet the demands upon it or to serve the needs of a growing population; transport became a major bottleneck which held back economic growth in the

Castilian heartland and prevented it from developing an industry of its own or becoming a market for the industry of other regions. Catalonia and the other maritime provinces reached their overseas markets and sources of raw materials by sea more easily than they reached Castile by land. Finally, except in the Catalan towns and a few ports of northern Spain, business organization was weak. In spite of state support the record of most commercial companies was unimpressive, suffering as they did from lack of capital and slowness of transactions, especially with America. So retarded was the commercial infrastructure that, although Spain produced a sufficiency of grain, the coastal regions often found it necessary to import supplies while export opportunities were also missed: 'at least 60,000 barrels of flour [are] needed by Cuba, which could and should be sent from Spain; our agriculture would profit to the extent of 20,000, 000 *reales* a year, which the North Americans thus take out of our colony'.[1]

The second half of the eighteenth century, it is true, was a time of modest economic recovery in which Catalan industry and colonial trade played their part. But Spain remained essentially an agrarian economy, and overseas trade was valued above all as an outlet for agricultural production. In the final analysis the modernizing measures of Charles III (1759–88) were designed to revive a traditional sector of the economy, and it was made more apparent than ever that the Hispanic world was constructed not upon a division of labour between metropolis and colonies but upon ominous similarities. Old structures survived, and the reform movement itself collapsed amidst the panic induced by the French Revolution and the subsequent reaction under Charles IV (1788–1808). The success of absolute monarchy depended among other things on the character of the monarch. In the person of Charles IV the crown lost all credibility as an agent of reform. Statesmen gave way to courtiers, and the appointment of Manuel Godoy signalled a reversion to the style of the later Habsburgs; the new First Secretary was a classical *valido*, owing his position not to any qualifications but to royal favour alone. Godoy treated Spanish America as nothing more than a source of bullion and its people as taxpayers.

Meanwhile, if Spanish America could not find an industrial supplier and trading partner in Spain there was an alternative. The British economy during the eighteenth century was undergoing revolutionary

---

[1] *Correo Mercantil*, 25 October 1808, quoted in Gonzalo Anes, *Las crisis agrarias en la España moderna* (Madrid, 1970), 312.

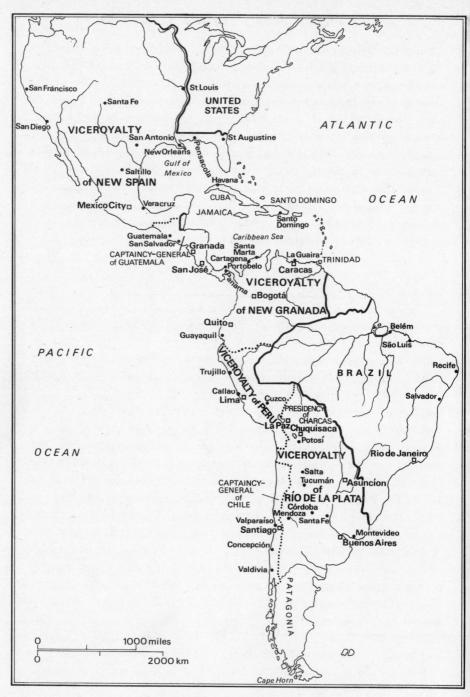

Colonial Spanish America, *c.* 1800

change. And from 1780 to 1800 when the Industrial Revolution became really effective Britain experienced an unprecedented growth of trade, based mainly upon factory production in textiles. It was now that the Lancashire cotton industry underwent great expansion, while iron and steel production also showed an impressive rate of increase. France, the first country to follow Britain's lead, still lagged behind in productivity, and the gap widened during war and blockade after 1789. At this point Britain was virtually without a rival. A substantial proportion – possibly as much as a third – of Britain's total industrial output was exported overseas. About 1805 the cotton industry exported 66 per cent of its final product, the woollen industry 35 per cent, the iron and steel industry 23.6 per cent. And in the course of the eighteenth century British trade had come to rely increasingly on colonial markets. Whereas at the beginning of the eighteenth century 78 per cent of British exports went to the continent of Europe, at the end the protected markets of Britain's European rivals absorbed only 30 per cent, while North America took 30 per cent and 40 per cent went to 'all parts of the world', which meant in effect the British empire, especially the West Indies (25 per cent), and also included the American colonies of Spain. Virtually the only limit on the expansion of British exports to the colonial markets was the purchasing power of their customers, and this depended on what they could earn from exports to Britain. Although Spanish America had only a limited range of commodity exports capable of earning returns in Britain, it had one vital medium of trade, silver. Britain therefore valued her trade with Spanish America and sought to expand it, either through the re-export trade from Spain, or by the channels of contraband in the West Indies and the South Atlantic.

These considerations, of course, did not amount to a policy of British imperialism in Spanish America or an intent to oust Spain by force, either for conquest or for liberation. In spite of the urgings of Spanish American exiles and the promptings of interested merchants, Britain remained aloof. The commercial argument for intervention in Spanish America was rarely regarded as compelling enough to justify fighting for new markets. Until the crisis years of 1806–7, when it appeared that the continent of Europe was being closed to British exports, existing outlets were regarded as adequate. The Spanish American market, though useful in its existing proportions and important enough to be expanded where possible, was never so vital that it was necessary to incorporate it into the British empire. Nevertheless, the market had proved vulnerable to British penetration and the consumers were willing. During times of war with Spain, especially after 1796 when the British navy blockaded Cádiz, British exports supplied the consequent shortages in the Spanish colonies. The invidious contrast between Britain and Spain, between growth and stagnation, between strength and weakness, had a powerful effect in the minds of Spanish Americans. And there was a further psychological refinement. If a world power like Britain could lose the greater part of its American empire, by what right did Spain remain?

The Spanish empire in America rested upon a balance of power groups – the administration, the Church, and the local elite. The administration possessed political though little military power, and derived its authority from the sovereignty of the crown and its own bureaucratic function. Secular sovereignty was reinforced by the Church, whose religious mission was backed by jurisdictional and economic power. But the greatest economic power lay with the elites, property owners in town and country, comprising a minority of *peninsulares* and a greater proportion of creoles (whites born in the colonies). By the eighteenth century local oligarchies were well established through America, based on vested interests in land, mining and commerce, on enduring ties of kinship and alliance with the colonial bureaucracy, with the viceregal entourage and the judges of the *audiencia*, and on a strong sense of regional identity. The weakness of royal government and its need for revenue enabled these groups to develop effective forms of resistance to the distant imperial government. Offices were bought, informal bargains were made. The traditional bureaucracy reflected these conditions, bending to pressure and avoiding conflict, constituting in effect not the agents of imperial centralization but brokers between Spanish crown and American subjects, instruments of bureaucratic devolution rather than a unitary state. The Bourbons found this unacceptable.

Bourbon policy altered relations between the major power groups. The administration itself was the first to disturb the balance. Enlightened absolutism enlarged the function of the state at the expense of the private sector and ultimately alienated the local ruling class. The Bourbons overhauled imperial government, centralized the mechanism of control and modernized the bureaucracy. New viceroyalties and other units of administration were created. New officials, the intendants, were appointed. New methods of government were tried. These were partly administrative and fiscal devices; they also implied closer supervision of the American population. What the metropolis thought was rational development, the local elites interpreted as an attack on local interests. For the intendants replaced *alcaldes mayores* and *corregidores*, officials who had long had been adept at reconciling different interests. They derived their income not from a salary but from entrepreneurship, trading with the Indians under their jurisdiction, advancing capital and credit, supplying equipment and goods, and exercising an economic monopoly in their district. Their financial backers, merchant speculators in the colonies, guaranteed a salary and expenses to ingoing officials, who then forced the Indians to accept advances of cash and equipment in order to produce an export crop or simply to consume surplus commodities. This was the notorious *repartimiento de comercio*, and by it the different interest groups were satisfied. The Indians were forced into producing and consuming; royal officials received an income; merchants gained an export crop; and the crown saved money on salaries. The price, of course, was high in other respects, amounting to abdication of imperial control in face of local pressures. The practice was extensive in Mexico; and in Peru it helped to cause the Indian rebellion of 1780.

Spanish reformers decreed the abolition of the entire system in the interests of rational and humane administration. The Ordinance of Intendants (1784 in Peru, 1786 in Mexico), a basic instrument of Bourbon reform, ended *repartimientos* and replaced *corregidores* and *alcaldes mayores* by intendants, assisted by subdelegates in the *pueblos de indios*. The new legislation introduced paid officials; and it guaranteed the Indians the right to trade and work as they wished.

Enlightened administrative reform did not necessarily work in America. Colonial interests, peninsular and creole alike, found the new policy inhibiting and they resented the unwonted intervention of the metropolis. The abolition of *repartimientos* threatened not only merchants and landowners but also the Indians themselves, unaccustomed to using money in a free market and dependent on credit for livestock and merchandise. How could Indians now be incorporated into the economy? Private capitalists hesitated to step into the place of the old officials and advance credit, fearing it was illegal. So there was confusion, and production and trade were damaged. Some hoped for the suppression of the intendants and the restoration of the *repartimientos*. Others took the law into their own hands. In Mexico and Peru the *repartimientos* reappeared, as the subdelegates sought to increase their income, the landowners to retain their grip on labour and the merchants to re-establish old consumer markets. After a brief flurry, therefore, Bourbon policy was sabotaged within the colonies themselves; local elites responded unfavourably to the new absolutism and they would soon have to decide whether to reach for political power in order to prevent further instalments of enlightened legislation.

As the Bourbons strengthened the administration, so they weakened the Church. In 1767 they expelled the Jesuits from America, some 2,500 in all, the majority of them Americans, who were thus removed from their homelands as well as their missions. The expulsion was an attack on the semi-independence of the Jesuits and an assertion of imperial control. For the Jesuits possessed a great franchise in America, and in Paraguay they had a fortified enclave; their ownership of haciendas and other forms of property gave them independent economic power which was enhanced by their successful entrepreneurial activities. In the long term Spanish Americans were ambivalent towards the expulsion. The Jesuit property expropriated in 1767, the extensive lands and rich haciendas, were sold to the wealthiest groups in the colonies, the creole families who were credit-worthy enough to bid for them. More immediately, however, Spanish Americans regarded the expulsion as an act of despotism, a direct attack upon their compatriots in their own countries. Of the 680 Jesuits expelled from Mexico about 450 were Mexicans. Of the 360 or so expelled from Chile some 58 per cent were Chileans, 25 per cent Spaniards and the rest from other parts of Europe and America. Their life-long exile was a cause of great resentment not only among themselves but also among the families and sympathisers whom they left behind.

'All privileges are odious', said the Count of Campomanes. An essential theme of Bourbon policy was opposition to corporate bodies possessing a special franchise in the state. The embodiment of privilege was the Church, whose *fueros* gave it clerical immunity from civil jurisdiction and whose wealth made it the largest source of investment capital in Spanish America. The power of the Church, though not its doctrine, was one of the principal targets of the Bourbon reformers. They sought to bring the clergy under the jurisdiction of the secular courts and in the process they increasingly curtailed clerical immunity. Then, with the defences of the Church weakened, they hoped to lay hands on its property. The clergy reacted vigorously. While they did not challenge Bourbon regalism, they bitterly resented the infringement of their personal privilege. They resisted Bourbon policy and were supported in many cases by pious laymen. The lower clergy, whose *fuero* was virtually their only material asset, were the more seriously alienated, and from their ranks, particularly in Mexico, many of the insurgent officers and guerrilla leaders would be recruited.

Another focus of power and privilege was the army. Spain had not the resources to maintain large garrisons of regular troops in America, and she relied chiefly on colonial militias, strengthened by a few peninsular units. From 1760 a new militia was created and the burden of defence was placed squarely on colonial economies and personnel. But Bourbon reforms were often ambiguous in their effects. To encourage recruits, militia members were admitted to the *fuero militar*, a status which gave to creoles, and to some extent even to mixed races, the privileges and immunities already enjoyed by the Spanish military, in particular the protection of military law, to the detriment of civil jurisdiction. Moreover, as imperial defence was increasingly committed to the colonial militia, officered in many cases by creoles, Spain designed a weapon which might ultimately be turned against her. Even before this point was reached the militia created problems of internal security.

In Peru, when the Indian rebellion of 1780 broke out, the local militia first stood by and watched, and then suffered severe defeat. As its efficiency and its loyalty were both called into question, the authorities decided that it was too great a risk to employ a militia force consisting of *mestizo* (mixed Indian-Spanish) troops and creole officers, many of whom had their own grievances against Bourbon policy, in a counter-insurgency role among Indians and mixed races. To crush the revolt they sent in regular army units from the coast officered by peninsular Spaniards and composed largely of blacks and mulattos (mixed black-European), with loyal Indian conscripts in support. In the wake of the rebellion Spain took a number of steps to strengthen imperial control. The role of the militia was reduced and responsibility for defence was restored to the regular army. Senior officers in both regular and militia units were now invariably Spaniards. And the *fuero militar* was restricted, especially among non-whites. Thus the militia was prevented from becoming an independent corporation, and the creoles were halted in their progress along the ladder of military promotion. This was a source of grievance, but one which remained muted in the peculiar social structure of Peru. Fear of the Indian and *mestizo* masses was a powerful stimulus to loyalty among creoles and a potent reason for accepting white rule, even if the whites were *peninsulares*.

In Mexico, as in Peru, there were few signs of creole militarism. A military career was not in itself attractive, nor was it made so by the authorities. In fact the militia had its critics. Viceroy Revillagigedo thought it folly to give weapons to Indians, blacks and *castas* (people of mixed race), and he doubted the loyalty of creole officers. Even after 1789, when the militia was in fact expanded, the creoles usually joined for non-military reasons, for offices and titles, and to add prestige to a fortune made in mining or trade. As for the *fuero militar*, no doubt it was useful, but against it had to be weighed the hardships of military service. The lower classes obtained little from army service, though a few saw it as a way to escape the degradation of their caste. This however only reinforced the fears held by creole officers, and by all whites, that the army might be turned against them. If the creoles feared the Indians, the *peninsulares* distrusted the creoles, and for this reason it was rare for a creole to obtain a senior commission, even after 1789 when Spain could spare few regulars from Europe. The lesson which Mexicans learnt was that access to military promotion, as well as to civil office, was increasingly restricted, and that official hostility to corporate privilege appeared to coincide with a reaction against creole influence in government.

While the Bourbons curtailed privilege in Spanish America, so they exerted closer economic control, forcing the local economies to work directly for Spain and diverting to the metropolis the surplus of production and revenue which had long been retained within the colonies. From the 1750s great efforts were made to increase imperial revenue. Two devices were particularly favoured. Royal monopolies were imposed on an increasing number of commodities, including tobacco, spirits, gunpowder, salt and other consumer goods. And the government assumed the direct administration of taxes traditionally farmed out to private contractors. The dreaded *alcabala*, or sales tax, continued to burden all transactions, and now its level was raised in some cases from 4 to 6 per cent, while its collection was more rigorously enforced. The new revenue was not normally expended within America itself on public works and services. It was converted instantly into specie and shipped to Spain, depriving the local economies of vital money supply. In Mexico royal income rose from 3 million pesos in 1712 to 14 million a year by the end of the century. Six million of this went as pure profit to the treasury in Madrid. In good years colonial revenue might represent 20 per cent of Spanish treasury income. This dwindled almost to zero during times of war with Britain, especially in the years 1797–1802 and 1805–8, though even then the crown still received an American revenue indirectly by selling bills of exchange and licences for neutrals – and sometimes for the enemy – to trade with the colonies.

Americans were not consulted about Spanish foreign policy, though they had to pay for it in the form of tax increases and wartime shortages. In addition to the complaints of all consumers, particular economic interests had particular grievances. The mining sectors in Mexico and Peru paid substantial sums in the royal fifth, war taxes on silver, duties on refining and coining, fees on state-controlled supplies of mercury and gunpowder, not to mention war loans and other extraordinary contributions. And from 1796, when war with Britain impeded the supply of mercury from Spain, miners suffered heavy losses. Conditions inherent in Spanish rule, therefore, were seen as obstacles to productivity and profit. Yet Spain valued mining and favoured its interests. From 1776 the state played its part in reducing production costs, halving the price of mercury and gunpowder, exempting mining equipment and raw materials from *alcabalas*, extending credit facilities, and in general improving the infrastructure of the industry. Other sectors were not so privileged. Agricultural interests had various grievances. Ranchers deplored the many taxes on marketing animals and the *alcabalas* on all animal sales and purchases; sugar and spirits producers complained of high duties; and consumers, *peninsulares*, creoles and castes alike, complained about taxes on goods in daily use. Although tax burdens did not necessarily make revolutionaries out of their victims or cause them to demand independence, yet they engendered a climate of resentment and a desire for some degree of local autonomy.

From about 1765 resistance to imperial taxation was constant and sometimes violent. And as, from 1779 and the war with Britain (1779–83), Spain began to turn the screw more tightly, so opposition became more defiant. In Peru in 1780 creole riots were overtaken by Indian rebellion; and in New Granada in 1781 creoles and *mestizos* surprised the authorities by the violence of their protest.[2] From 1796 and a renewed war in Europe tax demands were relentless, and from 1804 they increased still further. Donations were demanded from wealthy families, in Mexico for amounts between 50,000 and 300,000 pesos, in Peru for lesser sums. Grants were made from the military pension funds, from other public

---

[2] See below, 32–4.

funds, from the *consulados* (merchant guilds) and the *cabildos* (municipal councils). No doubt some of these donations were expressions of patriotism on the part of wealthy *peninsulares* and officials, but others were forced and resented. The greatest grievance was caused by the *consolidación* decree of 26 December 1804 which ordered the sequestration of charitable funds in America and their remission to Spain.

As applied in Mexico, the decree attacked Church property where it most hurt. The Church had great capital resources. In particular the chantries and pious foundations possessed large financial reserves, accumulated over the centuries from bequests of the faithful. In putting this capital to work the churches and convents of Mexico acted as informal financial institutions, advancing money to merchants and property owners, indeed anyone wishing to raise a mortgage-type loan to cover purchase of property or other expenditure, the interest rate being 5 per cent a year. Capital rather than property was the principal wealth of the Mexican Church, and church capital was the main motor of the Mexican economy. By this law chantries and pious funds were very much depleted, and this affected not only the Church but the economic interests of the many people who relied on church funds for capital and credit. These included noble *hacendados* and small farmers, urban property owners and rural proprietors, miners and merchants, a variety of social types, Spaniards as well as creoles. Perhaps the greatest hardship was suffered by a large number of medium and small proprietors, who could not assemble capital quickly enough and were forced to sell their property on highly unfavourable terms. Many substantial landowners had difficulty in repaying; a few had their estates seized and auctioned. The clergy were embittered, especially the lower clergy who often lived on the interest of the capital loaned. Bishop Manuel Abad y Queipo, who estimated the total value of church capital invested in the Mexican economy at 44.5 million pesos, or two-thirds of all capital invested, warned the government that resistance would be strong. He went in person to Madrid to request the government to think again; Manuel Godoy, Charles IV's chief minister, gave him no satisfaction, but in due course, following Napoleon's invasion of the peninsula, the hated decree was suspended, first on the initiative of the viceroy (August 1808) and then formally by the supreme junta in Seville (4 January 1809). Meanwhile some 10 million pesos had been sent to Spain, and the officials who collected it, including the viceroy, shared 500,000 pesos in commission. The sequestration of church wealth epitomized Spanish colonial policy in the last decade of empire. If the effects stopped short of catastrophe and rebellion, they were nonetheless ominous for Spain. This careless and ignorant measure alerted the Church, outraged property owners and caused a great crisis of confidence. It was a supreme example of bad government, exposing corruption among Spanish officials in Mexico and misuse of Mexican money in Spain. In enforcing the policy the authorities broke peninsular unity in Mexico and turned many Spaniards against the administration. And to Mexicans this was the ultimate proof of their dependence, as they saw Mexican capital taken out of the Mexican economy and diverted to Spain, to serve a foreign policy in which they had no say and no interest.

The sequestration joined rich and poor, Spaniard and creole, in opposition to imperial interference and support for a greater control over their own affairs. Moreover, it came at a time when increased tax demands could no longer be justified as a measure of increased productivity or expanding trade.

The Bourbon planners sought to apply increased fiscal pressure to an expanding and a controlled economy. And first they undertook the reorganization of colonial trade to rescue it from foreign hands and guarantee exclusive returns to Spain. Spanish exports, carried in national shipping, to an imperial market, this was their ideal. Between 1765 and 1776 they dismantled the old framework of transatlantic trade and abandoned ancient rules and restrictions. They lowered tariffs, abolished the monopoly of Cádiz and Seville, opened free communications between the ports of the peninsula and the Caribbean and its mainland, and authorized inter-colonial trade. And in 1778 *un comercio libre y protegido* between Spain and America was extended to include Buenos Aires, Chile and Peru, in 1789 Venezuela and Mexico. In the literature of the time it was made abundantly clear that the purpose of *comercio libre* was the development of Spain, not America; and it was intended to bind the colonial economy more closely to the metropolis. Gaspar de Jovellanos, one of the more liberal Spanish economists, extolled the decree of 1778 because it gave greater opportunities to Spanish agriculture and industry in a market which justified its existence by consuming Spanish products: 'Colonies are useful in so far as they offer a secure market for the surplus production of the metropolis'.[3]

---

[3] 'Dictamen sobre embarque de paños extranjeros para nuestras colonias', *Obras de Jovellanos* (Madrid, 1952), II, 71.

A colonial compact of this kind demanded that some 80 per cent of the value of imports from America should consist of precious metals, the rest marketable raw materials, and that no processing industry should be permitted in the colonies except sugar mills. According to these criteria, *comercio libre* was a success. Decrees in themselves, of course, could not create economic growth. To some extent *comercio libre* simply followed and gave legal expression to prevailing trends in the Atlantic economy. But whatever the degree of causation, there is no doubt that Spanish agriculture and industry underwent some revival in this period, which was reflected in an expansion of overseas trade. Shipping alone increased by 86 per cent, from 1,272 vessels in 1710–47 to 2,365 in 1748–78. The imports of gold and silver, public and private, rose from 152 million pesos in 1717–38 to 439 million in 1747–78, an increase of 188 per cent; and precious metals came to constitute at least 76 per cent of total imports from the colonies. Cádiz itself, with the advantage of more outlets in America, continued to dominate the trade. It is true that Catalan exports to America, which had helped to prepare the way for *comercio libre*, benefited still more from its application, and the colonial trade of Barcelona experienced further growth, not least in manufactures. But Cádiz was still the first port of Spain; its exports to America moved strongly ahead, and in the period 1778–96 they amounted to 76 per cent of all Spanish exports to America, Barcelona coming second with some 10 per cent. This was the golden age of the Cádiz trade and a time of new growth for Spain. The average annual value of exports from Spain to Spanish America in the years 1782–96 was 400 per cent higher than in 1778.

Even in these years, however, there were ominous signs. Most of the Spanish exports to America were agricultural goods, olive oil, wine and brandy, flour, dried fruits. Even Barcelona, the industrial centre of Spain, exported up to 40 per cent of its total in agricultural products, mainly wines and spirits, while its industrial exports were almost exclusively textiles; all of these commodities were already produced in America itself and could have been further developed there. Spain's export competed with, rather than complemented, American products, and *comercio libre* did nothing to synchronize the two economies. On the contrary, it was designed to stimulate the dominant sector of the Spanish economy, agriculture. The industrial gap left by Spain was filled by foreigners, who still dominated the transatlantic trade. While there is evidence that after mid-century, 1757–76, the proportion of industrial exports (71.84 per cent) over agricultural (28.16 per cent) increased compared with the period 1720–51 (54.43 and 45.57 per cent respectively), a substantial part of the increase could be attributed to foreign products. Much of the Cádiz trade to America was a re-export trade in foreign goods. In 1778 foreign products amounted to 62 per cent of registered exports to America, and they were also ahead in 1784, 1785 and 1787. Thereafter the share of national goods (still predominantly agricultural) was the greater in every year except 1791, and by 1794 the ratio had been reversed. But this improvement in Spain's performance was countered by contraband and by foreign penetration in America itself, while about 75 per cent of total shipping in the colonial trade was of foreign origin.

Spain remained a quasi-metropolis, hardly more developed than its colonies. But what did *comercio libre* do for Spanish America? No doubt it gave some stimulus to a few sectors of colonial production. The natural trade routes of America were opened up, and Spanish American exports to Spain rose substantially after 1782. The exports of hides from Buenos Aires, cacao and other products from Venezuela, sugar from Cuba, all measurably increased. In Mexico a new commercial class was born, and immigrants from Spain began to compete with the old monopolists. In spite of the opposition of traditional interests in Mexico City, new *consulados* were established in Veracruz and Guadalajara (1795). Pressure for growth and development became more urgent: *consulado* reports drew attention to the country's untapped resources and clamoured for more trade, increased local production, greater choice and lower prices. These were not demands for independence, but the *consulados* expressed a common frustration over the obstacles to development and dissatisfaction with the Spanish trade monopoly. As the secretary of the *consulado* of Veracruz wrote in 1817, 'among the motives, real or imagined, invoked by the rebels for lighting the fire of insurrection, one has been the grievance against the scarcity and costliness of goods, national and foreign, supplied by the merchants of the peninsula'.[4] Indeed *comercio libre* left the monopoly legally intact. The colonies were still debarred from direct access to international markets, except by the uncertain ways of contraband trade. They still suffered from discriminatory duties or even outright prohibitions in favour of Spanish goods. The new impulse to Spanish trade soon saturated these limited markets, and the problem

---

[4] Javier Ortiz de la Tabla Ducasse, *Comercio exterior de Veracruz 1778–1821. Crisis de dependencia* (Seville, 1978), 113.

of the colonies was to earn enough to pay for growing import
Bankruptcies were frequent, local industry declined, even agricultur:
products like wine and brandy were subject to competition from in
ports, and precious metals flowed out in this unequal struggle.

The metropolis had not the means or the interest to supply the variou.
factors of production needed for development, to invest in growth, t
co-ordinate the imperial economy. This was true not only of a neglecte
colony like New Granada but even of a mining economy like Peru, wher
agriculture was depressed for lack of manpower, capital and transport
where consumers depended for grain on Chile, and where only it
mineral resources saved it from complete stagnation. Moreover, th
metropolis was concerned primarily with its own trade to the colonie:
and did not consistently promote inter-colonial trade. The Spanisl
empire remained a disjointed economy, in which the metropolis deali
with a series of separate parts often at the expense of the whole. The
Hispanic world was characterized by rivalry not integration, of Chile
against Peru, Guayaquil against Callao, Lima against the Río de la Plata,
Montevideo against Buenos Aires, anticipating as colonies the divisions
of future nations.

The role of America remained the same, to consume Spanish exports,
and to produce minerals and a few tropical products. In these terms
comercio libre was bound to increase dependency, reverting to a primitive
idea of colonies and a crude division of labour after a long period during
which inertia and neglect had allowed a measure of more autonomous
growth. Now the influx of manufactured goods damaged local industries, which were often unable to compete with cheaper and better
quality imports. The textile industries of Puebla and Querétaro, the
obrajes of Cuzco and Tucumán, all were hit by crippling competition
from Europe. Exports from Guayaquil, a traditional source of textiles
for many parts of the Americas, declined from 440 bales in 1768 to 157 in
1788. From this time the textile industry of Quito remained in depression, displaced in Peruvian and other markets by cheaper imports from
Europe. The decline of Quito's textiles was reported with satisfaction by
Archbishop Antonio Caballero y Góngora, viceroy of New Granada
(1782–9), when he observed that agriculture and mining were 'the
appropriate function of colonies', while industry simply provided
'manufactures which ought to be imported from the metropolis'.[5] The

5 'Relación del estado del Nuevo Reino de Granada' (1789), José Manuel Pérez Ayala, *Antonio
Caballero y Góngora, virrey y arzobispo de Sante Fe 1723–1796* (Bogotá, 1951), 360–1.

fact that Spain could not itself produce all the manufactures needed in its dependencies did not, in the minds of Spanish rulers, invalidate their policy. There was, after all, a small industrial sector in Spain, jealous of its interests; to supplement this, Spanish merchants could still make profits from re-exporting the goods of foreign suppliers; and to maintain dependency was regarded as more important than to mitigate its consequences. It was an axiom among Spanish statesmen and officials that economic dependence was a precondition of political subordination, and that growth of manufactures in the colonies would lead to self-sufficiency and autonomy. In deference to imperial definitions, colonial officials often turned their eyes from reality. Antonio de Narváez y la Torre, governor of Santa Marta, reported in 1778 that he had debated whether to establish factories for the manufacture of cotton, as there were abundant local supplies of best quality raw material, but he had decided against it, in the interests of the system by which 'America provides Spain with the raw materials which this vast and fertile country produces, and Spain redistributes them as manufactures made by her artisans and industries; thus everyone is employed according to the character of both countries, and the relations, ties, and mutual dependence of each part of the empire are maintained'.[6] Spanish manufacturers were constantly on the watch for any infringement of this formula. Catalonia in particular, lacking an outlet in the stagnant and isolated Spanish interior, needed the American market, which was an important consumer of its textiles and other goods and a supplier of raw cotton. The textile workshops of Mexico and Puebla were productive enough to alert the Barcelona manufacturers; they frequently complained of the effect of local competition on their exports and sought from the crown 'the strictest orders for the immediate destruction of the textile factories established in those colonies'.[7]

This was a direct conflict of interests, and the response of the imperial government was predictable. A royal decree of 28 November 1800 prohibiting the establishment of manufactures in the colonies was followed by another of 30 October 1801 'concerning the excessive establishment there of factories and machinery in opposition to those which flourish in Spain and which are intended to supply primarily our Americas'. The government explained that it could not allow the extension of industrial establishments even during wartime, for these

[6] Sergio Elías Ortiz (ed.), *Escritos de dos economistas coloniales* (Bogotá, 1965), 25–6.
[7] Antonio García-Baquero, *Comercio colonial y guerras revolucionarias* (Seville, 1972), 83.

diverted labour from the essential tasks of mining gold and silver and producing colonial commodities. Officials were instructed to ascertain the number of factories in their districts and 'to effect their destruction by the most convenient means they can devise, even if it means taking them over by the royal treasury on the pretext of making them productive'.[8] But times were changing, and from 1796–1802, when war with Britain isolated the colonies from the metropolis, local textile manufacturers managed to begin or to renew operations, and from 1804 war gave further opportunities. Juan López Cancelada claimed in Cadiz in 1811 that 'each of the wars which we have had with the English nation has been a cause of increase in the manufactures of New Spain', and he instanced the case of the textile factories of the Catalan Francisco Iglesias in Mexico, which employed more than 2,000 workers.[9] Spanish manufacturers opposed these developments to the bitter end.

The colonies served Spain as mines, plantations and ranches, now as never before, but even in these appropriate functions relations with the metropolis were subject to increasing strain. In the course of the eighteenth century Mexican silver production rose continuously from 5 million pesos in 1702, to 18 million pesos in the boom of the 1770s, and a peak of 27 million in 1804. By this time Mexico accounted for 67 per cent of all silver produced in America, a position which had been brought about by a conjunction of circumstances – rich bonanzas, improved technology, consolidation of mines under larger ownership, lowering of production costs by tax concessions. Then, from the 1780s, the industry received large injections of merchant capital, a by-product of *comercio libre* itself. New merchants entered the field with less capital but more enterprise. As competition lowered profits, the old monopolists began to withdraw their capital from transatlantic trade and to seek more profitable investments, including mining, with results advantageous to the economy and to themselves. Mexico was exceptionally successful. In Upper Peru all was not well with silver mining, but Potosí survived and continued to produce some surplus for Spain. Lower Peru increased its silver output in the late eighteenth century, a modest boom compared with that of Mexico but vital for the colony's overseas trade. Registered silver rose from 246,000 marks in 1777 to a peak of 637,000 marks in 1799 (a mark was worth 8 pesos 4 reales), maintaining a high level until 1812; during this period improved draining techniques, diversion of capital

[8] *Ibid.*, 84.　　　　　[9] Ortiz de la Tabla Ducasse, *Comercio exterior de Veracruz*, 336–9.

from Potosí, a supply of free labour and the support of the mining tribunal, all contributed to higher output.

The late colonial mining cycle, significant though it was for the local economies, did not entirely serve imperial interests. First, the metropolis was placed under more urgent pressure by the colonies to maintain vital supplies of mercury and equipment, which it was patently incapable of doing during wartime, with the result that Spain itself was seen as an obstacle to growth. Secondly, in one of the great ironies of Spanish colonial history, the climax of the great silver age coincided with the destruction of Spain's maritime power and thus of her colonial trade. From 1796 Spain and her merchants had to watch helplessly as the fruits of empire were diverted into the hands of others, as the returns from the mining boom were placed at risk from foreign marauders or reduced by the trade of foreign merchants.

In agriculture, as in mining, it was impossible to reconcile the interests of Spain and those of America. Creole landowners sought greater export outlets than Spain would allow. In Venezuela the great proprietors, producers of cacao, indigo, tobacco, coffee, cotton and hides, were permanently frustrated by Spanish control of the import–export trade. Even after *comercio libre* the new breed of merchants, whether they were Spaniards or Spanish-orientated Venezuelans, exerted a monopoly stranglehold on the Venezuelan economy, underpaying for exports and overcharging for imports. Creole landowners and consumers demanded more trade with foreigners, denounced Spanish merchants as 'oppressors', attacked the idea that commerce existed 'solely for the benefit of the metropolis', and agitated against what they called in 1797 'the spirit of monopoly under which this province groans'.[10] In the Río de la Plata, too, *comercio libre* brought more Spanish merchants to control the trade of Buenos Aires, sometimes in collusion with local agents. But in the 1790s these were challenged by independent *porteño* merchants who exported hides, employed their own capital and shipping and offered better prices to the *estancieros*. These interests wanted freedom to trade directly with all countries and to export the products of the country without restriction. In 1809 they pressed for the opening of the port to British trade, which the Spaniards, Catalans and other peninsular interests strongly opposed. Here, too, there was an irreconcilable conflict of interests. But even within the colony economic interests were not

---

[10] E. Arcila Farías, *Economía colonial de Venezuela* (Mexico, 1946), 368–9.

homogeneous or united in a vision of independence; and growing regionalism, with one province demanding protection for local products and another wanting freedom of trade, created its own divisions. Yet the conviction grew stronger that, whatever the answer to these problems, they could only be resolved by autonomous decisions.

The imperial role of Spain and the dependence of America were put to their final test during the long war with Britain from 1796. In April 1797, following victory over the Spanish fleet at Cape St Vincent, Admiral Nelson stationed a British squadron outside the port of Cádiz and imposed a total blockade. At the same time the Royal Navy blockaded Spanish American ports and attacked Spanish shipping at sea. The results were dramatic. The trade from Cádiz to America, already in recession from 1793, was now completely paralysed. Imports into Veracruz from Spain dropped from 6,549,000 pesos in 1796 to 520,000 pesos in 1797; exports from 7,304,000 pesos to 238,000; and the prices of many European goods rose by 100 per cent. All over the Americas *consulados* reported extreme shortage of consumer goods and vital supplies. And while American interests pressed for access to foreign suppliers, so the Cádiz merchants insisted on clinging to the monopoly. As Spain considered the dilemma, its hand was forced. Havana simply opened its port to North American and other neutral shipping. Spain was obliged therefore to allow the same for all Spanish America or risk losing control – and revenue. As an emergency measure a decree was issued (18 November 1797) allowing a legal and heavily taxed trade with Spanish America in neutral vessels or, as the decree stated, 'in national or foreign vessels from the ports of the neutral powers or from those of Spain, with obligation to return to the latter'.[11] The object was to make neutrals the medium of trade with the Spanish colonies, the better to avoid the British blockade and to supply the lack of Spanish shipping. They became in effect virtually the only carriers, the one life-line linking the Spanish colonies to markets and supplies. The results were as revealing as the previous stoppage. Under neutral trade imports into Veracruz rose from 1,799,000 pesos in 1798 to 5,510,400 in 1799, exports from 2,230,400 to 6,311,500.

These wartime concessions were reluctantly given and quickly revoked. The Spanish government feared that its control was slipping away in favour of the trade and industry of the enemy, for during this

[11] Sergio Villalobos R., *El comercio y la crisis colonial* (Santiago, 1968), 115.

time colonial trade was almost entirely in the hands of foreigners, including indirectly the British, whose goods were introduced by neutrals. Spain was thus left with the burdens of empire without any of its benefits. Naturally, the merchants of Cádiz and Barcelona objected, and in spite of colonial protests the permit was revoked on 20 April 1799. Yet the outcome was still more damaging to Spain, for the revocation was ignored. Colonies such as Cuba, Venezuela and Guatemala continued to trade with neutrals, and North American shipping continued to trade into Veracruz, Cartagena and Buenos Aires. Spanish vessels simply could not make the crossing between Cádiz and America, such was the dominance of British sea power: of the 22 ships which left Cádiz in the twelve months after the order of April 1799 only 3 reached their destination. So it was the neutrals who saved the colonial trade and the neutrals who profited. This commerce also benefited the colonies, providing improved sources of imports and renewed demand for exports. The Spanish government repeated the prohibition of neutral trade by decree of 18 July 1800, but by now Spanish America was accustomed to dealing directly with its customers and suppliers, and the trade with foreigners was irresistible. As the war continued Spain had to accept the facts. In the course of 1801 special permission was given to Cuba and Venezuela to trade with neutrals. And to retain a place for itself Spain was reduced to selling licences to various European and North American companies, and to individual Spaniards, to trade with Veracruz, Havana, Venezuela and the Río de la Plata; many of their cargoes were British manufactures, sailing with British as well as Spanish licences, making returns in gold, silver or colonial produce to Spain, or neutral ports, or even to England.

The Spanish trade monopoly came to an effective end in the period 1797–1801, and the economic independence of the colonies was brought considerably closer. In 1801 Cádiz colonial exports were down 49 per cent on 1799 and imports 63.24 per cent. Meanwhile the trade of the United States with the Spanish colonies was booming, exports rising from 1,389,219 dollars in 1795 to 8,437,659 in 1801, and imports from 1,739,138 dollars to 12,799,888. The peace of Amiens in 1802, it is true, enabled Spain to renew her communications with the colonies, and merchants sought out the ports and markets of America once more. There was a surge of trade, and in the years 1802–4 Cádiz recovered, though 54 per cent of its exports to America were foreign goods. But it was impossible to restore the old monopoly: the colonies had now established active trading links with foreigners, especially with the United States, and realised the obvious advantages which they had so long been denied. The renewal of the war with Britain merely confirmed this.

The last remnants of Spanish sea power were now swept aside. On 5 October 1804, anticipating formal war with Spain, British frigates intercepted a large bullion shipment from the Río de la Plata, sank one Spanish vessel and captured three others carrying about 4.7 million pesos. In the following year at Trafalgar catastrophe was complete; without an Atlantic fleet Spain was isolated from the Americas. Imports of colonial products and precious metals slumped, and in 1805 Cádiz exports went down by 85 per cent on those of 1804. The fabric of Spain's world began to fall apart. Once more the colonies began to protest, their exports blocked and devalued, their imports scarce and expensive. Once more other powers moved in to supplant Spain. The demise of Spain's American trade coincided with a desperate British thrust to compensate for the closure of European markets by Napoleon's continental system. So there was a new urgency to British contraband trade, which earned profits and the sinews of war simultaneously, demonstrating to the colonies, as a Spanish official noted, how 'the English take out of our possessions the money which gives them the power to destroy us'.[12] There was only one way for Spain to counter contraband and that was to admit a neutral trade; in 1805 such a trade was authorized once more, this time without the obligation of returning to Spain. The metropolis was now virtually eliminated from the Atlantic. From 1805 neutral shipping dominated the trade of Veracruz, contributing 60.53 per cent of total imports in 1807 and 95.11 per cent of exports (over 80 per cent silver). In 1806 not a single vessel from Spain entered Havana, and the Cuban trade was conducted by neutrals, foreign colonies and Spanish colonies. In 1807 the metropolis received not one shipment of bullion.

The effect of the wars on Spain was that of a national disaster. A whole range of her agricultural products, together with manufactured goods, were deprived of a vital market, and while this caused recession in the agricultural sector, about one third of the textile industry closed down. Industry and consumers alike felt the shortage of colonial primary products, while the non-arrival of precious metals hit the state as well as merchants. The crown had to seek new sources of income: from 1799 it

---

[12] Antonio de Narváez, Cartagena, 30 June 1805, Ortiz, *Escritos de dos economistas coloniales*, 112.

tried to impose economies on the administration and demanded an annual contribution of 300 million reales; new issues of state bonds were launched, higher import taxes demanded, and finally the fatal *consolidación* was decreed. The future of Spain as an imperial power was now seriously in doubt. The economic monopoly was lost beyond recovery. All that remained was political control, and this too was under increasing strain.

On 27 June 1806 a British expeditionary force from the Cape of Good Hope occupied Buenos Aires. The invaders rightly calculated that they had little to fear from the Spanish viceroy and his forces, but they underestimated the will and ability of the people of Buenos Aires to defend themselves. A local army, augmented by volunteers and commanded by Santiago Liniers, a French officer in the Spanish service, attacked the British on 12 August and forced them to capitulate. The original expedition had been unauthorized but the British government was tempted into following it up and dispatched reinforcements. These captured Montevideo on 3 February 1807. Again local reaction was decisive. The incompetent viceroy was deposed by the *audiencia* and Liniers was appointed captain-general. The creole militias were once more deployed. And the invaders played into their hands. Crossing the River Plate from Montevideo, the British advanced on the centre of Buenos Aires. There they were trapped by the defenders, capitulated and agreed to withdraw.

The British invasions of Buenos Aires taught a number of lessons. Spanish Americans, it seemed, were unwilling to exchange one imperial master for another. Yet Spain could take little comfort from this. Its colonial defences had been exposed and its administration humiliated. The deposition of a viceroy was an unprecedented event with revolutionary significance. It was the local inhabitants, not Spain, who had defended the colony. The creoles in particular had tasted power, discovered their strength and acquired a new sense of identity, even of nationality. Thus, the weakness of Spain in America brought the creoles into politics.

New opportunities in government and commerce drew increasing numbers of Spaniards to America in the second half of the eighteenth century. Some sought jobs in the new bureaucracy, others followed the route of *comercio libre*. Spilling over from northern Spain, the immigrants came to form a successful entrepreneurial class, active in commerce and mining, and constantly reinforced from the peninsula, where population growth

pressed hard on land and employment and produced another justification of empire. Spanish Americans felt they were the victims of an
invasion, a new colonization, a further Spanish onslaught on trade and
office. Yet the facts of demography were on the side of the creoles.
Around 1800 in Spanish America, according to Alexander von Humboldt, in a total population of 16.9 million, there were 3.2 million whites,
and of these only 150,000 were *peninsulares*. In fact the true number of
peninsulares was even lower than this, nearer to 30,000 and not more than
40,000 in the whole of Spanish America. Even in Mexico, the area of
greatest immigration, there were only about 14,000 *peninsulares* in a total
population of 6 million, of whom 1 million were whites. This minority
could not expect to hold political power indefinitely. In spite of increased
immigration, the population trend was against them. Independence had
a demographic inevitability and simply represented the overthrow of a
minority by the majority. But there was more to it than numbers.

All Spaniards might be equal before the law, whether they were
peninsulares or creoles. But the law was not all. Essentially Spain did not
trust Americans for positions of political responsibility; peninsular-born
Spaniards were still preferred in higher office and transatlantic commerce. Some creoles, owners of land and perhaps of mines, had wealth
enough to be classed with *peninsulares* among the elite. But the majority
had only a moderate income. Some were *hacendados* struggling with
mortgages and household expenses; others were managers of estates or
mines, or local businessmen; others scraped a living in the professions;
and some poor creoles merged into the upper ranks of the popular
classes, where they were joined by *mestizos* and mulattos through
marriage and social mobility. First-generation Americans felt the greatest pressure, for they were immediately challenged by a new wave of
immigrants and, being nearest to the Europeans, were more acutely
conscious of their own disadvantage. To the creole, therefore, office was
a need not an honour. They wanted not only equality of opportunity
with *peninsulares*, or a majority of appointments; they wanted them above
all in their own regions, regarding creoles from another country as
outsiders, hardly more welcome than *peninsulares*. During the first half of
the eighteenth century the financial needs of the crown caused it to sell
offices to creoles, and thus their membership of American *audiencias*
became common and at times predominant. In the period 1687–1750 out
of a total of 311 *audiencia* appointees 138, or 44 per cent, were creoles.
During the 1760s the majority of judges in the *audiencias* of Lima,

Santiago and Mexico were creoles. The implications for imperial government were obvious. Most of the creole *oidores* (judges) were linked by kinship or interest to the landowning elite, and the *audiencias* had become a reserve of the rich and powerful families of their region, so that sale of office came to form a kind of creole representation.

The imperial government emerged from its inertia and from 1750 it began to reassert its authority, reducing creole participation in both church and state, and breaking the links between bureaucrats and local families. Higher appointments in the Church were restored to Europeans. Among the new intendants it was rare to find a creole. A growing number of senior financial officials were appointed from the peninsula. Creole military officers were replaced by Spaniards on retirement. The object of the new policy was to de-Americanize the government of America, and in this it was successful. Sale of *audiencia* office was ended, the creole share of places was reduced, and creoles were now rarely appointed in their own regions. In the period 1751–1808, of the 266 appointments in American *audiencias* only 62 (23 per cent) went to creoles, compared with 200 (75 per cent) to *peninsulares*. In 1808 of the 99 men in the colonial tribunals only 6 creoles had appointments in their own districts and 19 outside their districts.

The consciousness of difference between creoles and *peninsulares* was heightened by the new imperialism. As Alexander von Humboldt observed: 'The lowest, least educated and uncultivated European believes himself superior to the white born in the New World'.[13] In the Río de la Plata Félix de Azara reported that mutual aversion was so great that it often existed between father and son, between husband and wife. In Mexico Lucas Alamán was convinced that this antagonism, born of the preference shown to *peninsulares* in offices and opportunities, was the 'cause' of the revolution for independence.

Modern historiography is less certain. It is argued that the function of colonial elites as economic entrepreneurs investing in agriculture, mining and trade tended to fuse the peninsular and creole groups, as did their association in urban and rural occupations. In spite of Bourbon policy, there was still a close connection between local families and the colonial bureaucracy. In Chile the creole elite was closely integrated into kinship and political groups and preferred to manipulate the administration rather than fight it. In Peru there were linked groups of landed,

[13] Alexander von Humboldt, *Ensayo político sobre el reino de la Nueva España* (6th Spanish edn, 4 vols, Mexico, 1941), II, 117.

merchant, municipal and bureaucratic oligarchies, in which *peninsulares* and creoles merged as a white ruling class. In Mexico the nobility – about fifty families – combined a number of roles and offices. One group made its fortunes in overseas trade, invested profits in mines and plantations and acted primarily in the export sector. These were mainly *peninsulares*. Others, the majority of them creoles, concentrated on mining and on agriculture producing for the mining sector. They all spent heavily on conspicuous consumption, military status and the Church. And they preferred to co-opt the imperial bureaucracy by marriage and interest rather than to confront it. They found eventually that there was a limit to their influence, that Spain still thwarted Mexican development, taxed Mexican wealth and gave Mexico inferior government. While this alienated them from Bourbon policy, it did not necessarily make them supporters of independence. Everywhere in Spanish America the wars of independence, when they came, were civil wars between defenders and opponents of Spain, and the creoles were to be found on both sides. In this way functions, interests and kinship are seen as more important than the creole-peninsular dichotomy and as rendering it less significant. The argument is a useful corrective to hyperbole but it is not the whole story.

The evidence of antipathy between creoles and *peninsulares* is too specific to deny and too widespread to ignore. Their rivalry was part of the social tension of the time. Contemporaries spoke of it, travellers commented upon it, officials were impressed by it. The Spanish bureaucracy was aware of the division and so were Americans. In 1781 the *comuneros* of New Granada demanded offices for 'creoles born in this kingdom', and insisted that 'nationals of this America should be preferred and privileged over Europeans'.[14]

In Mexico a closely knit group of peninsular immigrants who made profits in trade, finance and mining sometimes married into local wealth. Their creole heirs often lost the family fortune by investing in land, where low profits, mortgages and extravagant living frustrated their expectations and caused a resentment which, however irrational, was none the less real. In Venezuela the creole aristocracy, the *mantuanos*, were a powerful group of landowners, office-holders and *cabildo* members, who profited from trade expansion under the Bourbons to increase their exports of cacao and other commodities. But economic growth menaced as well as favoured them. Spanish monopoly merchants in

[14] John Leddy Phelan, *The people and the king. The Comunero Revolution in Colombia, 1781* (Madison, 1978), 174, 179–80.

Venezuela tightened their grip on the import–export trade. Moreover, growth brought to the colony swarms of new immigrants, Basques, Catalans and above all Canarians, poor but ambitious men, who soon controlled the Venezuelan end of trade with Spain and the interior, became owners of warehouses, stores, shops and bars. No doubt the antagonism between landowners and merchants could be described as one between producers and purchasers, without invoking the creole–peninsular argument. But the fact remained that the merchants depended upon Spain for their monopoly. The British blockade enabled them to squeeze the creole producers still more, giving them minimal prices for exports and charging high for imports. So they strongly resisted neutral trade, 'as though', complained the Venezuelan producers in 1798, 'our commercial laws have been established solely for the benefit of the metropolis'.[15]

Moreover the new *peninsulares* encroached on the political preserves of the Venezuelan aristocracy. In 1770 the crown declared the principle that European Spaniards had as much right as Americans to hold office in Venezuela. With the backing of the crown, the *peninsulares* now advanced to share *cabildo* posts with Venezuelans and to dominate the newly created *audiencia*. In Venezuela, as elsewhere, there was a Spanish reaction against creole domination in the last decades of empire, and here too office was sought by creoles not simply as an honour but as a means of controlling policy and defending their traditional privileges. The later Bourbons, in favouring *peninsulares* against creoles, in using America as a prize for Spaniards, sharpened existing divisions and increased the alienation of the creoles.

If the creoles had one eye on their masters, they kept the other on their servants. The creoles were intensely aware of social pressure from below, and they strove to keep the coloured people at a distance. Race prejudice created in Americans an ambivalent attitude towards Spain. The *peninsulares* were undoubtedly pure whites, even if they were poor immigrants. Americans were more or less white, and even the wealthiest were conscious of race mixture, anxious to prove their whiteness, if necessary by litigation. But race was complicated by social, economic and cultural interests, and white supremacy was not unchallenged; beyond its defences swarmed Indians, *mestizos*, free blacks, mulattos and slaves. In parts of Spanish America slave revolt was so fearful a prospect that

---

[15] Miguel Izard, *El miedo a la revolución. La lucha por la libertad en Venezuela (1777–1830)* (Madrid, 1979), 127.

creoles would not lightly leave the shelter of imperial government or desert the ranks of the dominant whites. On the other hand, Bourbon policy allowed more opportunities for social mobility. The *pardos* – free black and mulattos – were allowed into the militia. They could also buy legal whiteness through purchase of *cédulas de gracias al sacar*. By law of 10 February 1795 the *pardos* were offered dispensation from the status of *infame*: successful applicants were authorized to receive an education, marry whites, hold public office and enter the priesthood. In this way the imperial government recognized the increasing numbers of the *pardos* and sought to assuage a tense social situation by removing the grosser forms of discrimination. The result was to blur the lines between whites and castes, and to enable many who were not clearly Indian or black to be regarded as socially and culturally Spanish. But the whites reacted sharply to these concessions. The demographic increase of the castes in the course of the eighteenth century, together with growing social mobility, alarmed the whites and bred in them a new awareness of race and a determination to preserve discrimination. This could be seen in the Río de la Plata, in New Granada, and in others parts of Spanish America. But it was Venezuela, with its plantation economy, slave labour force and numerous *pardos* – together forming 61 per cent of the population – which took the lead in rejecting the social policy of the Bourbons and established the climate of the revolution to come.

The whites in Venezuela were not a homogeneous class. At the top were the aristocracy of land and office, owners of slaves, producers of the colony's wealth, commanders of the colony's militia. In the middle was a group of lesser office-holders and clergy. And at the bottom surged the *blancos de orilla*, marginal whites such as shopkeepers and traders, artisans, seamen, service and transport personnel; many of these were identified with the *pardos*, whom they often married. The majority of *peninsulares* and Canarians in Venezuela belonged to these poor whites, and some of the antagonism of creoles towards *peninsulares* may well have been the resentment of patrician landowners towards common immigrants whom they regarded as of low birth. But the *peninsulares* were pure white, while many creoles were not. This simply aggravated sensitivity about race and heightened creole suspicion of *pardos*, Indians and slaves. Imperial policy increased their anger, for they considered it too indulgent towards *pardos* and slaves. The creole elite stubbornly opposed the advance of the *gente de color*, protested against the sale of whiteness, and resisted popular education and the entry of *pardos* to the University. They were concerned among other things at the loss of a dependent labour force in a period of hacienda expansion and export growth. As *pardos* established themselves in artisan occupations, independent subsistence farming and cattle enterprises in the *llanos*, the white landowners sought to keep them in subordination and peonage. They also saw a security risk in the progress of the *pardos* and petitioned, though unsuccessfully, against their presence in the militia. They regarded it as unacceptable 'that the whites of this province should admit into their class a mulatto descended from their own slaves'; and they argued that the establishment of *pardo* militias gave the coloureds an instrument of revolution without noticeably improving imperial defence.[16] These forebodings were intensified by horror of slave agitation and revolt. Again, the creole aristocracy complained that they were abandoned by the metropolis. On 31 May 1789 the Spanish government issued a new slave law, codifying legislation, clarifying the rights of slaves and duties of masters, and seeking to provide better conditions in slave life and labour. But the creole proprietors rejected state intervention between master and slave and bitterly fought this decree on the grounds that slaves were prone to vice and independence and their labour was essential to the economy. In Venezuela – indeed all over the Spanish Caribbean – planters resisted the new law and procured its suspension in 1794. The creoles were frightened men: they feared a caste war, inflamed by French revolutionary doctrine and the contagious violence of Saint-Domingue.

In other parts of Spanish America race tension took the form of direct confrontation between the white elite and the Indian masses, and here too creoles looked to their own defences. In Peru they belonged to a very small minority. In a population of 1,115,207 (1795), 58 per cent were Indians, 20 per cent *mestizos*, 10 per cent free *pardos* and slaves, and 12 per cent whites. This minority, while it controlled the economic and political life of the country, could never forget the surrounding Indian masses nor ignore the succession of rebellions against royal officials and white oppression. In Peru the creoles had no reason to doubt Spanish determination to keep the Indians in subordination; but after the great rebellion of Tupac Amaru they noticed the way in which they themselves were demoted from a security role and their militias demobilized. In Mexico, too, the social situation was explosive, and the whites were always aware of the simmering indignation of the Indians and castes, and of the

[16] Representation dated 28 Nov. 1796, F. Brito Figueroa, *Las insurrecciones de los esclavos negros en la sociedad colonial venezolana* (Caracas, 1961), 22–3.

increasing lawlessness among the lower classes, to control which the military and militia were frequently deployed. Alamán described the Mexican Indians as 'an entirely separate nation; all those who did not belong to them they regarded as foreigners, and as in spite of their privileges they were oppressed by all the other classes, they in turn regarded all the others with equal hatred and distrust'. In 1799 Manuel Abad y Queipo, bishop-elect of Michoacan, remarked on the deep cleavages in Mexican society, where between the Indians and the Spaniards 'there is the conflict of interests and the hostility which invariably prevails between those who have nothing and those who have everything, between vassals and lords'.[17] Traditionally the elite looked to Spain to defend them; property owners depended upon the Spanish authorities against threats from labourers and workers, and against the violence born of poverty and delinquency. But the pent-up anger of the Mexican masses exploded in 1810 in a violent social revolution, which proved to the creoles what they had long suspected, that in the final analysis they themselves were the guardians of social order and the colonial heritage. Given their numerical superiority among the whites, they had to be.

If there was a 'Spanish reaction' in the last decades of imperial rule, there was also a creole backlash. The creoles lost confidence in Bourbon government and began to doubt whether Spain had the will to defend them. Their dilemma was urgent, caught as they were between the colonial government and the mass of the people. The government had recently reduced their political influence, while the masses were a threat to their social hegemony. In these circumstances, when the monarchy collapsed in 1808, the creoles could not allow the political vacuum to remain unfilled, their lives and property unprotected. They had to move quickly to anticipate popular rebellion, convinced that if they did not seize the opportunity, more dangerous forces would do so.

The flaws in the colonial economy and the tensions in colonial society were brought to the surface in riot and rebellion. At one level these were simply responses to Bourbon policy. The development of the colonial economy and the increase of public revenue, two perfectly compatible objects in the eyes of Spanish reformers, were seen by Americans as a

17 Lucas Alamán, *Historia de México* (5 vols., Mexico, 1883–5), I, 67; Manuel Abad y Queipo, 'Estado moral y político en que se hallaba la población del virreinato de Neuva España en 1799', José María Luis Mora, *Obras sueltas* (Mexico, 1963), 204–5.

basic contradiction in imperial policy. Bourbon administration of the Indians was equally inconsistent, to the Indians if not to the crown, torn as it was between the desire to give protection against abuses and an overriding concern to maintain the number of tribute-payers and the supply of labour. The instruments of change were also judged from different standpoints. The advance of the Bourbon state, the end of decentralized government and creole participation, these were regarded by the Spanish authorities as necessary steps towards control and revival. But to the creoles it meant that in place of traditional bargaining by viceroys, who were prepared to compromise between king and people, the new bureaucracy issued non-negotiable orders from a centralized state, and to creoles this was not progress. The movements of protest, therefore, were overt resistance to government innovation, anti-tax riots and risings against specific abuses; they took place within the framework of colonial institutions and society and did not challenge them. But appearances are deceptive. Beneath the surface the rebellions revealed deeply rooted social and racial tension, conflict and instability, which lay silent throughout the eighteenth century and suddenly exploded when tax pressure and other grievances brought together a number of social groups in alliance against the administration and gave the lower sectors an opportunity to rise in protest. While they were not true social revolutions, they exposed veiled social conflicts. This can be seen in the reaction of the leading creoles. After an initial involvement in purely fiscal agitation, they usually saw the danger of more violent protest from below, directed not only against administrative authority but against all oppressors. The creoles then united with the forces of law and order to suppress the social rebels.

The typology of the rebellions was diverse. The two earliest movements, the *comuneros* of Paraguay (1721–35) and the rebellion in Venezuela (1749–52), isolated in time and space from the rest, gave indications of incipient regional awareness and a consciousness that American interests were different from Spanish interests. The rebellion in Quito in 1765, on the other hand, was a simple though violent anti-tax movement in an area of declining industry, a movement which brought into view the latent conflict between Spaniards and Americans and, as the viceroy of New Granada reported, demonstrated the creole 'hatred of taxes, Europeans . . . and any form of subjection'.[18] Tax collectors became more exigent in time of war, not simply to obtain revenue for imperial defence but also to

[18] Joseph Pérez, *Los movimientos precursores de la emancipación en Hispanoamérica* (Madrid, 1977), 64.

finance Spain's war effort in Europe and elsewhere. The war of 1779–83 between Spain and Britain, therefore, weighed heavily on the colonies, as the metropolis endeavoured to force yet greater surpluses from them; resentment grew into rebellion, and soon the Andean provinces of the empire were plunged into crisis.

In 1781 New Granada erupted in a movement which provided a model sequence of Bourbon innovation, colonial resistance and renewed absolutism. The principal cause of outrage was the procedure of the regent and visitor-general, Juan Francisco Gutiérrez de Piñeres, whose ruthless methods and uncompromising demands contrasted harshly with the traditional process of bargain and compromise. He increased the *alcabala* sales tax to 4 per cent, took it out of farm into direct administration and revived an obsolete tax for naval defence. He also reorganized the tobacco and spirits monopolies, increasing the price to the consumer and, in the case of tobacco, restricting production to high quality areas. These burdens fell on a stagnant economy, poor population and, above all, numerous small farmers. After a series of protests and disturbances, serious rebellion broke out on 16 March 1781 centred on Socorro and San Gil. The rebels refused to pay taxes, attacked government warehouses, drove out the Spanish authorities and, in the name of the *común*, proclaimed a group of leaders. The chief of these was Juan Francisco Berbeo, a *hacendado* of modest means and some military experience. And soon a movement which began as a popular and predominantly *mestizo* insurrection came under the command of the creole elite of land and office, who joined it with some trepidation in order to control what they could not prevent.

The *comuneros* were a powerful force, at least in numbers, and a horde many thousands strong marched on Bogotá, together with a band of Indians. They could have broken into the capital and imposed a reign of terror on Spaniards and creoles alike. But Berbeo and his associates were not revolutionaries. The cry of their movement was the traditional one, 'Long live the king and death to bad government'. The tyranny they opposed was that of the Spanish bureaucracy, not the structure of colonial society. Berbeo and the other creoles, therefore, held back the rebel army, preferring to negotiate with Archbishop Caballero y Góngora and indirectly with the elite in Bogotá. This was the traditional way, and the result was a compromise settlement, the capitulations of Zipaquirá (8 June 1781). These provided for the suppression of the tobacco monopoly and of various taxes; the restriction and reduction of the *alcabala* from 4 to 2 per cent; certain administrative reforms favouring local self-government; greater access to office for Americans; and improved conditions for the Indians. In effect the capitulations were negotiated by two men, Berbeo and Caballero, each convinced that it was necessary to concede something in order to avoid a more violent revolution. Berbeo was then appointed *corregidor* of Socorro, assuming that the movement was at an end. But was it?

All social sectors in the colony had some grievance against royal policy, and in the beginning the revolt reflected this. The *comunero* movement was a temporary alliance of patrician and plebeian, white and coloured, in opposition to bureaucratic oppression and fiscal innovation. The leaders were middle-rank property owners in land and business, and they headed the revolt to control it and turn it to their advantage. The creole aristocracy in Bogotá were also allies of a kind; they had tax grievances like everyone else, and they had a particular interest in a certain article of the capitulations, one which had little to do with the motives of the *común*: that, in appointments to offices, 'nationals of this America should be preferred and privileged over Europeans'.[19] This satisfied the creole elite, and they were prepared to make common cause with the authorities if the insurrection went further. For there were indeed other sufferers and other wrongs. The Indians too participated in the rebellion. In Santa Fe and Tunja they demanded restitution of their lands. In the *llanos* of Casanare they rose in revolt against Spanish authority, clergy and whites. Everywhere they objected to the tribute. And the citizens of Bogotá were, if anything, more terrified of the Indians outside the gates than they they were of the *comuneros*. The Indians themselves, enraged by the invasion of their community lands (*resguardos*), were not easy allies of creole *hacendados* and land-hungry *mestizos*, many of whom had profited from the resettlement of the Indians and the auction of their lands. Although the capitulations secured a lowering of tribute and restoration of *resguardos*, they purposely stipulated that the Indians had the right to own and sell the land; this was a gain for creoles and *mestizos*, potential purchasers, rather than for the Indian communities. But the Indians were not the only frustrated *comuneros*. The rebellion also raised the hopes of the poor and dispossessed in the colony. Although they too wanted abolition of monopolies, cheaper consumer goods and freedom of production, theirs was the hatred of the poor

---

[19] Phelan, *The people and the king*, 179–80.

against the rich, of those who had nothing against those who owned all.
In the region of Antioquia *mestizos*, mulattos and other castes rioted,
slaves resisted their masters and demanded freedom. And nearer the
heart of the rebellion a leader emerged who represented the socially
oppressed. José Antonio Galán, a man of the people, a mulatto perhaps
or *mestizo*, saw the capitulations as a betrayal, a device to stop the
comuneros entering Bogotá. He took over the more radical remnants of the
movement and made it, if not a real revolution, a protest with a stronger
appeal to the lower sectors, the castes and perhaps the slaves.

The creoles were outraged and collaborated with the authorities in
suppressing this unauthorized extension of their movement. Former
comunero leaders hunted down Galán, 'the Tupac Amaru of our kingdom', as they now called him, and prevented him from organizing a
second march on Bogotá. As a royal official reported, 'The same captains
of Socorro helped to calm the uneasy situation with promptitude,
solidarity and zeal; and thus they demonstrate their loyalty, obedience
and attachment to the king, and that they were only seeking to free
themselves from oppressions and the intransigence of the regent'.[20] So
the *comunero* leaders were exonerated. As for Galán and his associates,
they were brutally executed, a warning to the creoles and an example to
the people. In the wake of the rebellion, taxes were lowered to old levels,
but the monopolies remained, and if the fiscal regime became blander it
kept the same object in view, and royal revenues continued to rise. Later
the *comunero* movement was considered a lost opportunity on the road to
independence. At the time, however, neither the *comuneros* nor their
opponents regarded it as an independence movement. The authorities
played on the theme of social subversion, and the creoles showed that
they feared the people more than Spain and preferred dependence to
revolution.

This was true elsewhere in Spanish America. The *comunero* movement
spilled over into Venezuela, where it exposed similar divisions in
colonial society and came to grief in similar isolation. Overtly this too
was an anti-tax and anti-monopoly rebellion, and as such it embraced all
sectors of society, resentful of the increased imperial pressure exerted by
the new intendancy and by the abrasive policy of the intendant, José de
Abalos. As the captain general of the *comuneros*, Juan José García de
Hevia, observed, 'Rich and poor, noble and commoner, all complain'.

---

[20] Report dated 2 June 1781, *Archivo del General Miranda* (24 vols., Caracas, 1929–50), XV, 42.

But they did not all react in the same way. The most violent reaction was the armed insurrection of the common people in the Andean provinces, small farmers, artisans, petty traders, labourers in town and country, sometimes joined by Indians. The caudillos of the movement came from a higher social group, who believed they could share in the benefits of the capitulations secured by the creoles of New Granada. But most men of property remained aloof. The rich creoles of Maracaibo were more interested in trade, in the expansion of production and exports, than in the grievances of the poor people of the interior. And when eventually they took notice of the *comuneros*, it was to condemn them and to offer to help repress them 'with their own persons'.[21] The captain-general of Venezuela commended the creole aristocracy to the government for their 'spirit of loyalty and attachment to the king', and their resistance to the claims of the people. In effect, the creoles preferred Spain to anarchy; the social structure itself was the last line of Spanish defences.

This was seen most vividly in Peru, where the different worlds of whites and Indians co-existed in uneasy proximity. Yet rebellion in Peru was not exclusively Indian. There was another movement in the towns, an outburst spreading like an infection from January 1780, directed against internal customs, increased sales taxes and other forms of fiscal pressure. Although Indians from the towns and surrounding sierra joined the protest in their hundreds, more significant was the participation of poorer creoles and *mestizos, cholos* and other castes, resentful of the extension of tribute status to themselves. The principal centres of protest were Cuzco, Arequipa, La Paz and Cochabamba. The rebellion in La Paz called for unity of the kind shown by the North American colonists, 'worthy of memory and of our envy'.[22] But creole discontent was not the same as that of the Indians, and as the tax revolts were overtaken by Indian rebellion, so the majority of creoles held back or withdrew from the urban movements. This was the case in Oruro, where a creole-led revolt in 1781 was overwhelmed numerically by Indians in alliance with *cholos*, until the creoles joined forces with the Spanish authorities to defeat and expel them.

Indian grievances were more serious and their causes more profound, stemming as they did from the tyranny of the *corregidores*, simultaneously

---

[21] Carlos E. Muñoz Oraá, *Los comuneros de Venezuela* (Merida, 1971), 136–7; Pérez, *Los movimientos precursores*, 105.

[22] Boleslao Lewin, *La rebelión de Tupac Amaru y los orígenes de la emancipación americana* (Buenos Aires, 1957), 151.

officials, judges and merchants to the Indians; from the inflexible
demands upon them for tribute, taxes and tithes; from the *reparto*, or
imposition of goods; and from the *mita* system with its inhuman
conditions of forced labour, especially in the mines of Potosí. Among the
many Bourbon expedients two in particular, the raising of the *alcabala*
from 4 to 6 per cent and the establishment of internal customs posts to
ensure collection, weighed heavily on Indian producers and traders as
well as consumers and served to alienate the middle groups of Indian
society and to nurture a rebel leadership. Peru was the scene of recurring
Indian rebellions throughout the eighteenth century, culminating in that
led by José Gabriel Tupac Amaru, an educated *cacique* and a descendant
of the Inca royal family. Tupac Amaru began peaceful agitation for
reform in the 1770s and first sought justice in the Spanish courts. When
this failed, and as visitor-general José Antonio de Areche turned the
screw tighter on Indian Peru, he led his followers into violent insurrection, attacking *corregidores*, sacking *obrajes* and occupying villages. Beginning near Cuzco in November 1780, the movement soon engulfed a great
part of southern Peru, then in a second and more radical phase spread to
the Aymara provinces of Upper Peru. The extended family and kinship
network of Tupac Amaru and its links with regional trade and transport
gave the whole movement a coherent chain of command, a source of
recruitment and continuity of leadership. But the greatest impetus came
from the cause itself.

Tupac Amaru declared war to the death against the Spaniards, and his
stated object was 'to extinguish the *corregidores* . . . to abolish the Potosí
mitas, the *alcabalas*, the internal customs, and many other pernicious
exactions'. He also endeavoured to give his movement a universal
character, appealing across social divisions. He called on the creoles to
join with the Indians 'to destroy the Europeans', and he claimed to stand
for 'the protection, perservation and tranquility of the Europeans'.[23] The
attempt to revive the creole alliance failed. The social policy of Tupac
Amaru was too revolutionary to satisfy more than the dispossessed. He
attacked forced labour and promised to free slaves, or at least those who
joined his forces. He sought to destroy *obrajes* and *repartimientos de
comercio*, while his followers attacked white towns and their inhabitants
indiscriminately. Horrified by the enormity of the rebellion, the creoles
made common cause with Spaniards in defence of their inheritance.

23 *Ibid.*, 402–3, 415–16, 422–3.

Church and state, creole and European, the whole established order closed ranks against Tupac Amaru, and after a violent struggle in which 100,000 lives were lost, most of them Indian, the movement collapsed. The Indian leaders were brutally executed, their followers hunted down, and by January 1782, after a short but severe shock, the Spaniards were again in control. A few institutional reforms were then applied – intendants replaced *corregidores* and *repartimiento* was abolished – but these were designed for imperial strength rather than Indian welfare.

Did Tupac Amaru aspire to independence? The Spanish authorities claimed that he did, and sympathisers in other parts of America saw him as king of Peru. He undoubtedly became more radical once the revolution began, but independence was something else. The documentary evidence is unclear, even suspect. In any case, freedom from Spain was only part of his movement. The real revolution was against the privileges of the whites, creoles as well as Spaniards, and the ultimate aim was to end the subordination of the Indians. These were essentially social objectives. As for independence, it was unlikely that an Indian rebellion would have had the ideas, organization and military resources necessary for such a cause. The Indians also lacked solidarity. During the rebellion of Tupac Amaru at least twenty *caciques*, motivated in part by personal and tribal rivalry or already recruited into the Spanish system, kept their people loyal to the crown and in some cases joined the royalist forces. Indian rebellions lacked a further condition for independence, creole leadership. The creoles were committed to the existing economic structure, and this was based upon Indian labour in the mines, haciendas and workshops. And, outnumbered as they were, they hesitated to put themselves at the head of a movement which they might not be able to control. Independence, when it came, would be on different terms.

The rebellions of the eighteenth century, therefore, were not strictly speaking 'antecedents' of independence. It is true that the Spanish authorities denounced them as subversive, either out of apprehension or for purposes of propaganda. Intendant Abalos argued that the root cause of all the rebellions of 1780–1 was not taxation 'but the hostility of these natives towards Spain and their fervent desire for independence'.[24] This was more than the rebels themselves envisaged. They appealed rather to past utopias, to a pre-Caroline golden age when bureaucratic centralization and tax oppression were unknown. Nevertheless, although the

---

[24] Representation to Charles III, Caracas, 24 Sept. 1781, Muñoz Oraá, *Los comuneros de Venezuela*, 39.

rebels did not formulate ideas of independence, they helped to create a climate of opinion which presented a fundamental challenge to tradition-al rule. They proved in effect that the formula 'Viva el rey y muera el mal gobierno' was obsolete; as a medium of protest it was no longer realistic, discredited not least by the Bourbons themselves, whose policy of centralization invalidated the old distinction between king and govern-ment and made the crown frankly responsible for the actions of its servants. The rebellions moreover underlined the fact that the new government came from outside. In this sense they were a further stage in the development of colonial self-awareness, a brighter if unexplained sign of incipient nationalism, a dramatic defence of identity and interests which were demonstrably different from those of the metropolis. The *comuneros* expressed a belief that New Granada was their country, that it belonged to the people who were born and lived there, and that these natural proprietors were threatened by Spanish intruders. Even the rebellion in Peru emitted a sense of nationality. Tupac Amaru spoke of *paisanos*, *compatriotas*, meaning Peruvians as distinct from European Spaniards. In his proclamation of 16 November 1780, offering freedom to the slaves, he called on *la Gente Peruana* to help him confront the *Gente Europea*, on behalf of the 'common good of this kingdom'.[25] The *Gente Peruana*, whom he also called the *gente nacional*, consisted of whites, *mestizos*, Indians, all the natives of Peru, the only criterion being that they were distinct from the foreigners. These ideas were natural products of colonial experience. They were not, however, representative of the Indian movement as a whole.

Incipient nationalism was a potent influence but not an Indian one. The manifestos of Tupac Amaru expressed creole rather than Indian con-cepts, the ideas of a precocious leader, not of a typical Indian. The Indians and other marginalized elements of colonial society could have little if any sense of national identity, and their closest relations were with the hacienda, the community, or the local administration, not with a wider entity. The expectations of the creoles, on the other hand, reflected a deeper awareness, a developing sense of identity, a conviction that they were Americans, not Spaniards. This presentiment of nationality was far more subversive of Spanish sovereignty and far more conducive to independence than specific demands for reform and change. At the same

[25] *Colección documental de la independencia del Perú* (30 vols., Lima, 1971), II, ii, 272.

time as Americans began to disavow Spanish nationality they were also aware of differences among themselves, for even in the pre-national state the various colonies rivalled each other in their resources and their pretensions. America was too vast a continent and too vague a concept to attract individual loyalty. Men were primarily Mexicans, Venezuelans, Peruvians, Chileans, and it was in their own country, not America, that they found their national home. These countries were defined by their history, administrative boundaries, physical environment, which marked them off not only from Spain but also from each other; they were the homes of societies, each of them unique, and economies, all with different interests.

From what sources was this national consciousness fed? Americans were rediscovering their own lands in a uniquely American literature. Creole writers in Mexico, Peru and Chile expressed and nurtured a new awareness of *patria* and a greater sense of exclusiveness, for as the *Mercurio Peruano* observed: 'It interests us more to know what is happening in our own nation.'[26] Among the first to give cultural expression to Americanism were the creole Jesuits expelled from their homeland in 1767, who became in exile the literary precursors of American nationalism. The Peruvian Jesuit Juan Pablo Viscardo was an ardent advocate of independence, to the cause of which he bequeathed his *Lettre aux Espagnols-Américains*, published in 1799. 'The New World', wrote Viscardo, 'is our homeland, and its history is ours, and it is in this history that we ought to seek the causes of our present situation.'[27] Viscardo's treatise was a call to revolutionary action. The majority of the Jesuit exiles, however, had a different object, to dispel European ignorance of their countries; so they described the nature and history of their homelands, their resources and assets, producing in the process works of scholarship as well as of literature. If it was not yet a national literature, it contained an essential ingredient of nationalism, awareness of the *patria's* historical past. But the real significance of the Jesuit works lay not in direct influence – few of them were published in Spanish in their lifetime – but in the way they reflected the thinking of other less articulate Americans. When the creoles themselves expressed their patriotism it was usually more optimistic than that of the exiles. The pre-independence period saw the birth of a literature of identity in which Americans

[26] R. Vargas Ugarte, *Historia del Perú. Virreinato (Siglo XVIII)* (Buenos Aires, 1957), 36.
[27] Miguel Batllori, *El Abate Viscardo. Historia y mito de la intervención de los Jesuítas en la independencia de Hispanoamérica* (Caracas, 1953), Apéndice, p. viii.

glorified their countries, acclaimed their resources and appraised their peoples. As they instructed their compatriots in their assets, so these authors pointed to American qualifications for office and in effect for self-government. The terms themselves instilled confidence through repetition – *patria*, homeland, nation, our America, we Americans. Although this was still a cultural rather than a political nationalism and was not incompatible with imperial unity, yet it prepared men's minds for independence by reminding them that America had independent resources and the people to manage them.

The new Americanism was a more powerful influence than the Enlightenment. The ideas of the French *philosphes*, their criticism of contemporary social, political and religious institutions, their concern for human freedom, were not unknown in the Hispanic world, though they did not receive universal acceptance, and the majority of people remained Catholic in conviction and devoted to absolute monarchy. The Spanish version of the Enlightenment purged it of ideology and reduced it to a programme of modernization within the established order. As applied to America this meant making the imperial economy a more fruitful source of wealth and power and improving the instruments of control. 'To bring my royal revenues to their proper level', this was how Charles III expressed his colonial policy in 1776, and it had little to do with the Enlightenment. And if in Spain itself only marginal changes occurred after 1765, in Spanish America values and structures remained equally inviolate. In this context it may be questioned whether 'Enlightenment' or even 'reform' are appropriate terms in which to describe Spain's imperial policy or its ideological environment in the period 1765–1810. There was, of course, a sense in which modernization owed something to the thought of the eighteenth century: the value attached to useful knowledge, the attempts to improve production by means of applied science, the belief in the beneficent influence of the state, these were reflections of their time. As Archbishop Viceroy Caballero y Góngora explained to his successor, it was necessary to substitute the useful and exact sciences for pointless speculations, and in a kingdom such as New Granada, with products to exploit, roads to build, mines and swamps to drain, there was more need of people trained to observe and measure than to philosophize. Modernization of this kind was more concerned with technology than with politics. The Spanish 'Enlightenment' in America was really little more than a programme of renewed imperialism.

But Spanish America could also obtain the new philosophy directly from its sources in England, France and Germany. The literature of the Enlightenment circulated with relative freedom. In Mexico there was a public for Newton, Locke and Adam Smith, for Descartes, Montesquieu, Voltaire, Diderot, Rousseau, Condillac and D'Alembert. Readers were to be found among high officials, members of the merchant and professional classes, university personnel and ecclesiastics. Peru was the home of a group of intellectuals, many of them products of the royal college of San Carlos, members of the Economic Society and contributors to the *Mercurio Peruano*, who were acquainted with the writings of Locke, Descartes and Voltaire, and familiar with ideas of social contract, the primacy of reason and the cult of freedom. But what did this mean? The Enlightenment was by no means universal in America nor, once implanted, did it survive intact: its growth was meagre, weakened by conservatism and confined by tradition. Chronologically its impact was late. The revolutions of 1780–1 owed little, if anything, to the thought of the Enlightenment, and it was only between then and 1810 that it began to take root. Diffusion increased in the 1790s: in Mexico the Inquisition began to react, alarmed less by religious heteredoxy than by the political content of the new philosophy, which it regarded as seditious, 'contrary to the security of states', full of 'general principles of equality and liberty for all men', and in some cases a medium for news of 'the frightful and damaging revolution in France'.[28] In general, however, the Enlightenment inspired in its creole disciples not so much a philosophy of liberation as an independent attitude towards received ideas and institutions, a preference for reason over authority, experiment over tradition, science over speculation. No doubt these were enduring influences in Spanish America, but for the moment they were agents of reform, not destruction.

Yet there remained a number of creoles who looked beyond reform to revolution. Francisco de Miranda, who had read the works of the *philosophes* during his army service in Spain in the 1770s, transformed ideology into activism. So, of course, did Simón Bolívar, whose liberal education, wide reading and extensive travels in Europe opened his mind to new horizons, in particular to English political example and the thought of the Enlightenment. Hobbes and Locke, the encyclopaedists and *philosophes*, especially Montesquieu, Voltaire and Rousseau, all left a

[28] M. L. Pérez Marchand, *Dos etapas ideológicas del siglo XVIII en México a través de los papeles de la Inquisición* (Mexico, 1945), 122–4.

deep impression upon his mind and gave him a lifelong devotion to reason, freedom and order. In the Río de la Plata Manuel Belgrano read extensively in the new philosophy. Mariano Moreno, product of the University of Chuquisaca in company with other revolutionaries, was an enthusiastic admirer of Rousseau, whose *Social Contract* he edited in 1810 'for the instruction of young Americans'.

In New Granada a group of educated creoles, politically more advanced than the *comuneros*, were the nucleus of radical opposition to the Spanish regime. Pedro Fermín de Vargas carried enlightenment to the point of subversion. From Zipaquirá, where he was *corregidor*, he fled abroad in 1791–2 in search of foreign aid for his revolutionary schemes. He declared to the British government that Spanish Americans and Indians were treated like foreigners and slaves in their own country and had reached the point of insurrection: 'the population of the country is sufficient to aspire to independence and the kingdom of New Granada is now like an eldest son who needs to emancipate himself'.[29] To finance his flight he sold his books to Antonio Nariño, a wealthy young creole of Bogotá. In 1793 Nariño printed on his own press a translation of the French Declaration of the Rights of Man, a document which had already been prohibited in America by the Inquisition of Cartagena. The edition of a hundred copies was printed only to be destroyed, and its publisher was subsequently exiled for treason. Nariño was a friend of Francisco Javier Espejo, a *mestizo* doctor and lawyer of Quito, and another disciple of the Enlightenment. In a series of satirical publications Espejo savagely criticized the defects of the Quito economy and denounced Spanish rule as their cause. In 1795 he too was jailed on charges of subversion. Although Spanish authorities dealt with this creole opposition as a conspiracy, in fact the events of 1793–5 were examples of propaganda rather than revolution and they were confined to the elite. They had some importance in showing the influence of the French Revolution, but no firm power base.

The conspiracy of Manuel Gual and José María España was more serious, as it frankly sought to establish an independent republic of Venezuela. The two Venezuelans were prompted by a Spanish exile, Juan Bautista Picornell, reader of Rousseau and the Encyclopaedists and a confirmed republican. Recruiting *pardos* and poor whites, labourers and small proprietors, the conspiracy came to the surface in La Guaira in

---

[29] Vargas to British government, 20 Nov. 1799, *Archivo del General Miranda*, xv, 388.

July 1797 with an appeal for equality as well as liberty, for harmony between all classes, the abolition of Indian tribute and of negro slavery, and the establishment of freedom of trade. The conspirators attacked 'the bad colonial government' and invoked the example of the English colonies in North America. The formula of previous risings, 'viva el rey y muera el mal gobierno', they rejected as self-contradictory. Either the king knew what his government was doing and approved, or he did not know and failed in his duty. They wanted a republic, nothing less; but they received little response. Creole property owners collaborated with the authorities in suppressing the men of La Guaira, offering to serve the captain-general 'with their persons and resources'. The movement was doomed by its radicalism.

These men were true precursors of independence, though they were a small minority and ahead of public opinion. The creoles had many objections to the colonial regime, but these were pragmatic rather than ideological; in the ultimate analysis the greatest threat to Spanish rule came from American interests rather than European ideas. Yet the distinction perhaps is unreal. The thought of the Enlightenment was part of the complex of contributing factors, at once an impulse, a medium and a justification of the revolution to come. If the Enlightenment was not an isolated 'cause' of independence, it was part of its history; it provided some of the ideas which informed it and became an essential ingredient of Latin American liberalism in the post-independence period. During the wars of independence and after, men of identical economic interest and social position frequently took opposite political standpoints. Ideas had their own power, convictions their own persuasion.

The Enlightenment was brought into political focus by the revolutions in North America and France. In the years around 1810 the influence of the United States was exerted by its mere existence, and the close example of liberty and republicanism remained an active inspiration in Spanish America, one as yet unsullied by misgivings concerning the policy of this powerful neighbour. As early as 1777 a Spanish version of proclamations of the Continental Congress (1774–5) was in the hands of Dr José Ignacio Moreno, subsequently rector of the Central University of Venezuela and participant in the conspiracy of 1797. The works of Tom Paine, the speeches of John Adams, Jefferson and Washington all circulated in the subcontinent. Many of the precursors and leaders of independence visited the United States and saw free institutions at first hand. It was in New York, in 1784, that Francisco de Miranda conceived the idea of 'the liberty and independence of the whole Spanish American continent'. Bolívar had an enduring respect for Washington and admired, though not uncritically, the progess of the United States, 'land of freedom and home of civic virtue', as he described it. United States trade with Spanish America was a channel not only of goods and services but also of books and ideas. Copies of the Federal Constitution and the Declaration of Independence, in Spanish translation, were carried into the area by United States merchants, whose liberal views coincided with their interest in the growth of a monopoly-free market. After 1810 Spanish Americans would look for guidance to the republican experience of their northern neighbour in their search for the rights of life, liberty and happiness. Constitutions in Venezuela, Mexico and elsewhere would be closely modelled on that of the United States, and many of the new leaders – though not Bolívar – would be profoundly influenced by North American federalism.

The model of revolution offered by France had less appeal. As Miranda observed in 1799, 'We have before our eyes two great examples, the American and the French Revolutions. Let us prudently imitate the first and carefully shun the second.'[30] First impressions had raised greater hopes. Manuel Belgrano described in his autobiography the response of young intellectuals – he was then in Spain – to the events of 1789: 'the ideas of liberty, equality, security and property took a firm hold on me, and I saw only tyrants in those who would prevent a man, wherever he might be, from enjoying the rights with which God and Nature had endowed him'.[31] The Spanish government attempted to prevent French news and propaganda from reaching its subjects, but the barriers were breached by a flood of revolutionary literature in Spain and America. Some read the new material out of curiosity. Others instinctively recognized their spiritual home, embracing the principles of liberty and applauding the rights of man. Equality was another matter. Situated as they were between the Spaniards and the masses, the creoles wanted more than equality for themselves and less than equality for their inferiors. The more radical the French Revolution became and the better it was known, the less it appealed to the creole aristocracy. They saw it as a monster of extreme democracy and anarchy, which, if admitted into America, would destroy the world of privilege they enjoyed. The danger was not remote.

---

30 Miranda to Gual, 31 Dec. 1799, *ibid.*, xv, 404.
31 Manuel Belgrano, *Autobiografía* (Buenos Aires, 1945), 13–18.

In 1791 the French Caribbean colony of Saint-Domingue was engulfed in a massive slave revolt. Saint-Domingue was a prototype, the most productive colony in the New World, its sole function to export sugar and coffee to the metropolis. For this purpose France had established a military and bureaucratic presence, a plantation economy and a slave labour force held down by violence. The social situation was always explosive, not simply because of the merciless exploitation of half a million slaves and the degradation of the free coloureds, but also because of divisions within the white minority. In its spectacle of disintegration, of *grand blanc* against *petit blanc*, white against mulatto, mulatto against black, Saint-Domingue was colonial America in microcosm. The Revolution of 1789 acted as an instant dissolvent, arousing different responses to the opportunity of liberty and equality, and releasing social and racial tensions long suppressed. In the knowledge that the master race was hopelessly divided, the slaves rose in revolt in August 1791, attacked plantations and their owners, and began a long and ferocious struggle for abolition of slavery and independence from France. French policy wavered between abolition decreed by the National Assembly and the attempt of Napoleon to reconquer the island for France and slavery. But in the end France had to admit defeat, and on 1 January 1804 black and mulatto generals proclaimed the new state of Haiti, the first black republic in the Americas.

To Spanish America Haiti was an example and a warning, observed by rulers and ruled alike with growing horror. The creoles could now see the inevitable result of loss of unity in the metropolis, loss of nerve by the authorities, and loss of control by the colonial ruling class. Haiti represented not only independence but revolution, not only liberty but equality. The new regime systematically exterminated the remaining whites and prevented any white from re-establishing himself as a proprietor; it recognized as Haitian any black and mulatto of African descent born in other colonies, slave or free, and these were invited to desert; and it declared war on the slave trade. These social and racial policies branded Haiti as an enemy in the eyes of all colonial and slave regimes in the Americas, and they took immediate steps to protect themselves, none more vigorously than Spain, which in the course of the Haitian revolution had lost the adjacent colony of Santo Domingo. In November 1791, within three months of the outbreak, Spanish colonial authorities were warned to adopt defensive measures against contagion. Haitian blacks were denied entry to Spanish colonies, and even white refugees were suspect.

Venezuela was regarded as particularly vulnerable to penetration, partly because of its proximity, partly because of its own history of slave protest, resistance and escape throughout the eighteenth century. Blacks and mulattos from the French Antilles, fleeing from Napoleon's counter-offensive, made their way via Trinidad to the eastern coasts of Venezuela, to become in the official view a potential fifth column. Alerted by the advance of their own *pardos*, the creoles of Venezuela reacted sharply. The *audiencia* of Caracas sought to protect the institution of slavery against French revolutionary doctrines, 'capable of prejudicing the minds of simple people especially the slaves, who number more than 100,000 in this province alone'. Evidence was at hand. In 1795 a black and *pardo* revolt convulsed Coro, the centre of the sugar-cane industry and the base of a white aristocracy extremely conscious of race and class. The movement was led by José Leonardo Chirino and José Caridad González, free negroes who had travelled about the Caribbean and learnt of events in France and Haiti. They mobilized the slaves and coloured labourers, three hundred of whom rose in May 1795, and proclaimed 'the law of the French, the republic, the freedom of the slaves, and the suppression of the *alcabala* and other taxes'.[32] The rebels occupied haciendas, sacked property, killed landowners and invaded the city of Coro; but they were isolated, easily crushed, and many of them were shot without trial. The Haitian revolution had further repercussions. In May 1799 a corsair expedition from Port-au-Prince sought to collaborate with a rebellion in Maracaibo, where two hundred men of the *pardo* militia set out to kill whites, establish 'the system of liberty and equality' and create a black republic as in Haiti, beginning with the abolition of slavery. It was another failure, but another example of that constant underlying struggle of blacks against whites which characterized the last years of the colonial regime.

Spanish American revolutionaries anxiously disassociated themselves from the Haitian revolution. Miranda in particular was concerned about its effect on his reputation in England: 'I confess that much as I desire the liberty and independence of the New World, I fear anarchy and revolution even more. God forbid that the other countries suffer the same fate as Saint-Domingue, scene of carnage and crimes, committed on the pretext of establishing liberty; better that they should remain another century under the barbarous and senseless oppression of Spain.'[33]

[32] Pedro M. Arcaya, *Insurrección de los negros en la serranía de Coro* (Caracas, 1949), 38.
[33] Miranda to Turnbull, 12 Jan. 1798, *Archivo del General Miranda*, xv, 207.

Miranda argued that it was vital for him to reach Venezuela first, before the Haitians did, and in 1806 he led a tiny expedition to his homeland. Unfortunately for his reputation he stopped to re-group in Haiti, where he was advised not to be content with exhorting the creoles to rise but 'to cut off heads and burn property', and where a rumour started that he planned to use black Haitians.[34] In fact, Miranda was as socially conservative as other creoles and he had no intention of inciting a race war. But the damage was done. At Coro he was met first by a stony silence then by opposition from creole landowners, who denounced him as a 'heretic' and a 'traitor'.

If Haiti was a warning, therefore, it was also an incentive. Spanish Americans, too, would soon be faced with a crisis in the metropolis and a failure of imperial control. Then they would have to fill the political vacuum, and they would seize independence not to create another Haiti but to prevent one.

Crisis came in 1808, the culmination of two decades of depression and war. The modest progress of Bourbon reform in Spain was cut short by the impact of the French Revolution, which drove frightened ministers into reaction and a bewildered king into the arms of Manuel Godoy. As leadership declined from the standards of Charles III and his reforming ministers to those of Charles IV and the court favourite, government was reduced to mere patronage at home and clientage abroad. The Spanish people suffered severe adversity. The great agrarian crisis of 1803 was a time of acute famine, hunger and mortality, proof of how little the Bourbons had done to improve agriculture, trade and communications. Meanwhile, in spite of its efforts to maintain national independence, the government had neither the vision nor the resources to resolve the pressing problems of foreign policy. The French alliance did not save Spain: it merely emphasized her weakness, prolonged her wars and exposed her colonial commerce to British attack. Spanish American visitors to the peninsula in these years were horrified by what they saw, a once powerful metropolis enfeebled to the point of collapse and grateful enough to be a satellite of France. Now more than ever they realized that Spanish interests were not their interests, that America 'needed to be neutral to be happy', as Servando Teresa de Mier put it. Worse was to come. When, in 1807–8, Napoleon decided to reduce Spain totally to his

---

[34] Paul Verna, *Pétion y Bolívar* (Caracas, 1969), 95.

will and invaded the peninsula, Bourbon government was divided against itself and the country left defenceless against attack. In March 1808 a palace revolution forced Charles IV to dismiss Godoy and to abdicate in favour of his son, Ferdinand. The French then occupied Madrid, and Napoleon induced Charles and Ferdinand VII to proceed to Bayonne for discussions. There, on 5 May 1808, he forced both of them to abdicate and in the following month proclaimed Joseph Bonaparte king of Spain and the Indies.

In Spain the people rose and began to fight for their independence. At the end of May 1808 provincial juntas organized resistance to the invader, and in September a central junta was formed which invoked the name of the king, sought to unite the opposition to France and, in January 1809, issued a decree that the dominions in America were not colonies but an integral part of the Spanish monarchy.

These events created in America a crisis of political legitimacy and power. Authority came traditionally from the king; laws were obeyed because they were the king's laws. Now there was no king to obey. This also brought into question the structure of power and its distribution between imperial officials and the local ruling class. The creoles had to decide upon the best way to preserve their heritage and to maintain their control. Spanish America could not remain a colony without a metropolis, or a monarchy without a monarch.

2

THE INDEPENDENCE OF MEXICO AND CENTRAL AMERICA

On the eve of the struggle for independence from Spain the viceroyalty of New Spain (Mexico) constituted a vast area extending from the Caribbean to the Pacific and from the borders of Guatemala and Chiapas to the huge Eastern and Western Internal Provinces, including the territory later incorporated as the south-western United States. The viceroyalty, with a population in 1814 of 6,122,000 (the United States in 1810 had a population of 7,240,000) accounted for over one-third of the total population of the Spanish overseas empire. Mexico City, the viceregal capital, was the largest city in North or South America and, with a population in 1811 of 168,811, after Madrid, the second largest city in the empire.

New Spain was also by far the richest colony of Spain. Its trade through the main port of Veracruz from 1800 to 1809 amounted to an annual average of 27.9 million pesos and in the next decade, between 1811 and 1820, to an annual average of 18 million pesos, divided equally between exports and imports. The colony's total output of goods and services stood in 1800 at approximately 240 million pesos, or roughly 40 pesos *per capita*. This was only half the *per capita* production of the United States, at that time, for example, but considerably more than that of any other American colony, Spanish or Portuguese. Agriculture and live-stock, which employed approximately 80 per cent of the total labour force, produced about 39 per cent of national resources; manufacturing and cottage industries produced about 23 per cent of total output; trade accounted for 17 per cent; mining for 10 per cent; and the remaining 11 per cent came from transportation, government and miscellaneous sources. Economic activity on this scale produced large revenues, directly and indirectly, for the Spanish crown. Between 9 and 10 per cent of New Spain's total product (about 24 million pesos) entered the royal

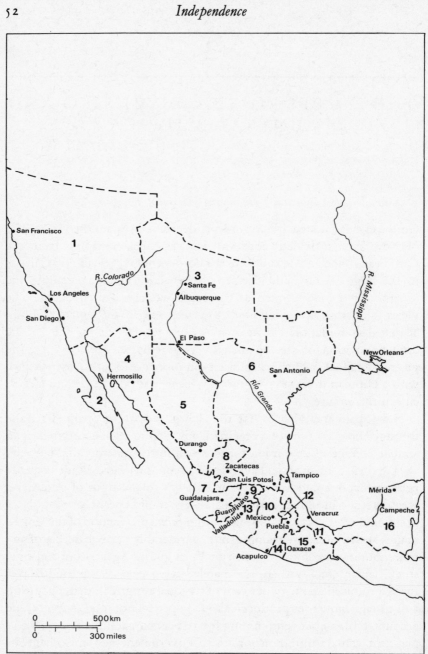

Mexico on the eve of independence.

Key

1. Government of New California

2. Government of Old California

3. Government of New Mexico (an Internal Province of the West)

4. Intendancy of Arizpe (government of Sonora and Sinaloa, Internal Provinces of the West)

5. Intendancy of Durango (government of Nueva Vizcaya, an Internal Province of the West)

6. Intendancy of San Luis Potosí (includes governments of Coahuila, Texas, Nuevo León and Nuevo Santander, the Internal Provinces of the East)

7. Intendancy of Guadalajara

8. Intendancy of Zacatecas

9. Intendancy of Santa Fe de Guanajuato

10. Intendancy of México

11. Intendancy of Veracruz

12. Government of Tlaxcala

13. Intendancy of Valladolid de Michoacán

14. Intendancy of Puebla

15. Intendancy of Antequera de Oaxaca

16. Intendancy of Mérida de Yucatán

treasury or Church coffers, and nearly half of that (12 million pesos) left the colony for the peninsula. The rest was retained for the support of the viceregal regime and for yearly grants (*situados*) to maintain the government and defence of the Caribbean islands, the Floridas, Louisiana and other territories. In addition, Spain imposed a number of economic constraints on the trade of New Spain, the most important being the prohibition on trade with foreign ports, the existence of royal monopolies on tobacco, gun powder, mercury, official paper and a number of other vital commodities, and a large number of duties paid either on the export of Mexican goods or on the import of Spanish or non-Spanish goods through Spain. Exports of colonial products to foreign markets paid duties in Spain of between 15 and 17 per cent, while foreign goods in transit to the colonies paid duties of 36.5 per cent. Spain re-exported at least 90 per cent of the precious metals and agricultural products sent to her from New Spain. The multitude of taxes and trade restrictions has been calculated to have cost New Spain 17.3 million pesos a year in the last twenty years of the colonial regime, or 2.88 pesos per person, which is 7.2 per cent of total colonial income. This was nearly thirty-five times the burden imposed by the British upon the thirteen North American colonies in the last years before the independence of the United States.[1]

All this, the product of recent research, was, of course, only vaguely sensed by Mexicans at the end of the colonial era. And while Spanish economic controls and monopolies were a major source of colonial complaint, equally important were Spanish social and administrative restrictions. The three main ethnic groups – white, *mestizo* or mixed blood and Indian – had different legal and customary status, each possessing a separate set of fiscal obligations, civil rights and social and economic prerogatives. Indians made up 60 per cent of the national population, *castas* 22 per cent, and whites 18 per cent. The whites themselves were dangerously divided between those Spaniards born in America (creoles) who numbered 17.8 per cent of the population and the European-born (called in Mexico *gachupines*) who counted only 15,000, or 0.2 per cent of the total national population. The tiny number of peninsulars made up the administrative elite of the colony because of their control of higher governmental and military positions. The Europeans consisted of about 7,500 military personnel, about 6,000 civil servants and merchants and 1,500 clergy. There were only a handful of European women in the entire colony – only 217 in Mexico City according to the German observer Alexander von Humboldt – since the European immigrants tended to marry the daughters of wealthy creole families. This European elite controlled the government, the army, the

[1] John H. Coatsworth, 'Obstacles to economic growth in nineteenth-century Mexico', *American Historical Review*, 83/1 (1978), 80–100; idem, *From backwardness to underdevelopment: the Mexican economy, 1800–1910* (forthcoming), chap. IV.

church and most external trade, as well as the domestic wine and textile industries.

Next on the social ladder came the mine owners, merchants and the owners of land and other property, most of them creole and constituting the 'natural elite' of the Mexican population. Some of them were bearers of Spanish noble titles. Yet they were excluded from full participation in political power. They also faced the loss of their fortunes by absorption through marriage with peninsular immigrants, through economic stagnation or unfortunate investment, or even by imperial fiat such as the 1804 Decree of Consolidation which, until its annulment in 1808, threatened all property owners by forcing them to pay off their extensive mortgages owed to the church for transfer to Spain to pay for the European wars. Though highly favoured, the Mexican creole elite were anxious about the future of their country and about their status within it.

Further down the social scale were the lawyers and other trained creoles who held most of the lower level governmental and church offices. Indeed, in 1811 a majority, 65 per cent, of the approximately 555 to 600 posts in the viceregal bureaucracy in Mexico City were held by creoles, compared with 35 per cent held by Europeans. Yet, with only rare exceptions, the Spanish-born held the higher positions and the Mexicans were relegated to the lower status offices.[2] In 1808 there were twelve Europeans and five creoles (only three locally born) on the *audiencia* of Mexico City, six Europeans and one creole on the *audiencia* of Guatemala, and four Europeans and three creoles on the *audiencia* of Guadalajara. Similarly, while creoles predominated in the membership of cathedral chapters throughout the country, only one bishop, at the time of independence, was creole. Equally frustrated were the small merchants, middle level *hacendados*, lesser miners, and – of increasing importance after 1810 – lower creole militia officers who hastened to seek upward mobility in the rapidly expanding militia. Taken together these elements formed what can be called the bourgeoisie. Though they were infinitely privileged compared to the vast majority of the population, they still felt themselves to be discriminated against when compared to the peninsular or creole elite. Perhaps the major political tension at work among whites in this society was the unfulfilled aspiration for economic and social advancement among this bourgeoisie which expanded rapidly in size

[2] Linda Arnold, 'Social, economic and political status in the Mexico City central bureaucracy: 1808–1822', paper presented at the V Reunión de Historiadores Mexicanos y Norteamericanos, Pátzcuaro, 1977.

with New Spain's economic growth in the late eighteenth century. This bourgeoisie, furthermore, was politically conscious, particularly those who were acquainted with the kind of ideas advocated by the philosophers of the Enlightenment. Some were even acquainted with the *Historia antigua de México* by the exiled Jesuit Francisco Clavijero and the works of other ideologues of creole identity, or *Mexicanismo* in its incipient form. During the War of Independence these ideas would be transformed by such authors as Fray Servando Teresa de Mier and Carlos María Bustamante into full-fledged anti-Spanish nationalism.

The *castas* and Indians, together 82 per cent of the population, were segregated from the privileged classes by formal legislation and custom as well as by their poverty. Excluded from public or church office by law, theoretically forbidden to live side by side in the same villages, limited in social mobility by prohibitions upon entering the professions, they were the labourers and providers of society, subjected to an oppression that paternal royal laws did nothing to alleviate. The Indians, and *mestizos* living among them, were subject to the payment of tribute and to special codes of law. Once or twice in every generation epidemics carried off between 10 and 50 per cent of the urban poor and uncounted numbers of rural poor. These epidemics were often related to cycles of agricultural failure which resulted in upward spirals in the prices of basic commodities, provoking massive unemployment, rural migration to the cities and outbreaks of social unrest. Statistics concerning increases in the price of maize for the last two decades before independence indicate a serious deterioration in the condition of the poor. In 1790 maize sold at a low of 16 and at a high of 21 reales per *fanega*; in 1811 it sold for 36 reales. A major agricultural crisis swept Mexico from 1808 to 1811, and played a role in sparking the mass rebellion of 1810. Close to half the *per capita* income of the poor was spent in the purchase of maize alone. They lived constantly at the edge of survival. The colonial economy, extractive and mercantilist and based on neo-feudal norms of labour control, guaranteed the continued oppression of the masses in hacienda, mine, or sweatshop (*obraje*). Moreover, the ethnic distinctions of Spanish law, which would continue even after independence and in the face of often contradictory legislation, were the major cause not only of lower-class political unrest in New Spain but also of economic inefficiency and underdevelopment that left Mexico a legacy of unrealized human talent. In some areas of limited labour supply, such as mining centres or northern livestock producing territories, ethnic distinctions were relaxed, but an oversupply of labour kept discrimination in effect in most of New Spain. The rebellions that began in 1810 would seek to correct many of these abuses; at the very least they were a kind of response on the part of the Indians and *castas* to their oppression.

While the uprisings of the lower classes in 1810 and thereafter, particularly under the leadership of the two great heroes of independence, Miguel Hidalgo and José María Morelos, are a distinguishing feature of the Mexican independence struggle, it would not be the lower orders, in Mexico or anywhere else in Spanish America, who determined either the outcome of independence or the form the new states would take. The lower-class uprisings, indeed, served to delay and even obscure the chief source of Mexican dissent, which was creolism, the urge of the white creoles, middle and upper class, and of the white elites associated with Mexico through residence, property ownership, or kinship, if not through birth, to gain control over the economy and the state. Although Hidalgo proclaimed independence in the name of Ferdinand VII, and although Morelos proclaimed independence in opposition to Ferdinand VII, the Mexican bourgeoisie and elite aimed initially at autonomy within the empire.

Educated creoles gradually became conscious of their separateness through their awareness of Mexico's great pre-conquest history as interpreted with pride by Clavijero, their idealization of themselves as the proper heirs either of the Aztecs or else of the first conquerors who they judged had been displaced by royal administrators, and their intense dedication to the proposition that the appearance in Mexico of the Virgin of Guadalupe constituted a mark of divine destiny upon all things Mexican. The creoles thus identified themselves as Americans, distinct from the peninsulars and with differing political objectives. They had become conscious, in short, of their own role as colonial subjects. Meanwhile, members of the domestic elite, even if they did not adopt the ideas of neo-Aztecism and proto-Mexicanism, had serious grievances against the imperial regime which culminated with the Decree of Consolidation of 1804. For the first time since the New Laws of 1542 the elite became aware that an arbitrary act by the peninsula could threaten their very existence. As yet, however, neither the elite nor the creole middle class aspired to outright independence because of their fear of the masses and their dependence upon the traditions of church and state to maintain social order. But they did aspire to autonomy. Signs of this were clearly perceived by two outstanding contemporary observers, the bishop-elect of Michoacán, Manuel Abad y Queipo, and Alexander von Humboldt, although both tended to emphasize the political conflict of creole versus peninsular.

The alliance that was forming between the creole bourgeoisie and property-owning elite broke up in the immediate wake of the collapse of Spain under Napoleonic assault in 1808. The overthrow of Charles IV and his chief minister Manuel Godoy, the accession of Ferdinand VII, followed immediately by the usurpation of the throne by Napoleon's brother Joseph and the imprisonment of Ferdinand VII in France, threw into doubt the fundamental base of the Spanish constitution, the primacy of the sovereign. Mexico City heard of the accession of Ferdinand VII on 9 June 1808; on 16 July it heard of the overthrow of Ferdinand by Napoleon. The next two months witnessed a unique crisis in the colony. Provincial juntas of government sprang up in Spain and competed with each other for Mexico's recognition. The Junta of Oviedo, which had received an initial promise of aid from Britain in the joint struggle against France, and the junta of Seville, both dispatched commissioners to Mexico. The authorities in Mexico City could not immediately decide which of the two juntas was legitimate. The *audiencia* and the absolutist peninsular minority in the capital argued against recognizing any self-proclaimed junta and advocated that Mexico should maintain the incumbent royal officials in office until the emergence of a legitimate home government. Under the leadership of two of its members, José Primo Verdad and Juan Francisco Azcárate, and influenced by the radical thinker, Melchor de Talamantes, a friar from Peru, the *cabildo* (city council) of Mexico City which largely represented the creoles adopted a resolution on 15 July calling upon the viceroy, José de Iturrigaray, to assume direct control of the government in the name of Ferdinand VII and the representatives of the people. The core argument of the city council was that, in the absence or incapacity of the king, 'sovereignty lies represented in all the kingdom and the classes that form it; and more particularly, in those superior tribunals that govern it and administer justice, and in those corporations that represent the public'.[3] The city council thus requested the viceroy to recognize the sovereignty of the nation and to call together in the near future a representative assembly of the cities of New Spain. This constituted a call for autonomous

[3] Representation of Mexico City to Viceroy Iturrigaray, 19 July 1808, Archivo del Ex-Ayuntamiento, Mexico, Historia, en general, vol. 2254, no. 34.

government in the context of a history of three centuries of absolutism. The chief advocates of this plan, in addition to Azcárate, Primo Verdad and Talamantes, were prominent creoles such as the marqués de Uluapa, the marqués de Rayas, the conde de Medina, the conde de Regla, and Jacobo de Villaurrutia, a member of the *audiencia*. Its chief opponents were the majority of the members of the *audiencia* and peninsular *hacendados*, merchants and mine owners. Perhaps the creole proposal would have provoked little result except for the fact that Viceroy Iturrigaray gave every indication of favouring, or at least not opposing, the idea. He called for representatives of the chief corporations in the capital to meet to discuss the future government of New Spain. The absolutist party decided that the only way to avert the danger of New Spain's drifting toward revolution with viceregal connivance was to remove the viceroy.

Legally, in view of the absence of the monarch and the claim by various Spanish juntas to possess authority in his name, the creole (Mexican) proposal was not treasonable. It was a call for the restoration of authority to the city councils, which were in the creole view the original location of authority in Mexico after the Spanish Conquest. Neither Azcárate nor Primo Verdad, authors of the proposal, questioned the king's ultimate authority. Primo Verdad argued that 'authority came to the king from God, but not directly, rather through the people'. Azcárate argued that there existed a pact between the nation and the king; in the king's absence the nation assumed sovereignty, but upon his return, the people's direct exercise of authority would cease automatically.[4] The absolutists, however, viewed it as high treason because it profoundly threatened Spanish dominion. The crux of the matter was whether Mexico was a colony. The autonomists who rejected the idea that their country was a colony, argued that it was one of the kingdoms composing the Spanish monarchy. Like the provinces and kingdoms of the peninsula, Mexico could create a provisional junta to govern in the king's name during the crisis. The absolutists argued that New Spain was not a kingdom like those of the peninsula and that any proposition to establish regional autonomy was illegal. To them, Mexico had to be preserved as a supplier of bullion to the mother country that was now facing extinction from foreign conquest. The *audiencia* thought that the proposal to call an assembly of the cities carried overtones of the French

---

[4] Luis Villoro, *El proceso ideológico de la revolución de independencia* (Mexico, 1967), 37–8.

Estates General of 1789. A fine double standard was at work, and the Mexicans knew it, since the provinces of Spain were already doing what Mexico proposed to do. The wartime government soon to be created in Spain would proclaim Mexico an equal part of the monarchy (along with the rest of the overseas territories), yet Spanish policy required that it should not be equal.

Under Iturrigaray's urgings, a total of four meetings of leading personages from the capital took place in August and September 1808 (although the assembly of the cities was never called). The principal question under debate was which of the two major Spanish juntas should Mexico recognize; in the end, the lack of agreement prevented the recognition of either. The chief effect of the meetings was to convince the peninsulars that the viceroy had hopelessly compromised himself by his willingness to listen to the creoles, and under the leadership of a conservative peninsular *hacendado* and merchant, Gabriel de Yermo, a plot was hatched to overthrow the viceroy. With the support of the *audiencia* and the archbishop, Yermo and a group of peninsulars from the *Consulado*, perhaps three hundred in all, entered the viceregal palace on the morning of 16 September 1808 and arrested the viceroy. In the next few hours the conspirators arrested the most prominent supporters of the provisional government idea – Talamantes, Azcárate, Primo Verdad and a number of other leading creoles. Primo Verdad died after a few days in custody; Talamantes died of yellow fever in a Veracruz prison in 1809, becoming the first martyrs to creolism. Viceroy Iturrigaray was removed from office by the *audiencia* and replaced by the octogenarian retired field marshal, Pedro de Garibay, who the peninsulars hoped would serve as their puppet.

It was now impossible for New Spain to pursue the path toward creole provisional government and independence that was taken by most of the continental South American colonies in the period from 1808 to 1810. The creole autonomists had been routed by the single deft blow of a handful of powerful conservatives. No administrative or other reforms were undertaken by the new viceroy, nor by his successor from July 1809 to May 1810, Archbishop Francisco Javier Lizana y Beaumont, nor by the *audiencia* which briefly ruled in place of a viceroy from May to September 1810. The creation of a unified government in Spain, the Junta Central, its proclamation of equality for Americans and its call for the parliament, or Cortes, to meet with American members included, did little to satisfy the Mexicans. The governments in Mexico City from 1808 to 1810 were largely inept and failed to address the problem of creole and lower class discontent, concentrating instead on the rather slight danger posed by French agents who were being sent to America. The extraordinary and illegal overthrow of a Spanish viceroy by peninsular absolutists had in fact itself done much to weaken the legitimate authority of Spain. Servando Teresa de Mier, in his book *Historia de la revolución de Nueva España* (1813), claimed that Iturrigaray's overthrow justified American independence, for the coup destroyed the social pact that had linked Mexico with the kings of Spain. That question might lie in the realm of philosophy; for the oppressed of New Spain the coup was but another example of the growing despotism of Spain. Indeed, suppression of the autonomist impulse in 1808 exacerbated Mexican grievances and resulted in the uprising of 1810. In May of that year Bishop Abad y Queipo of Michoacán warned that a mass social insurrection was at hand in New Spain and in September, only two days after the arrival in Mexico City of the new viceroy, Francisco Javier Venegas, the revolution began.

In the rich agricultural centre of Querétaro, in the intendancy of Guanajuato, a group of wealthy creoles, including Ignacio Allende, a cavalry officer and son of a wealthy merchant, Juan de Aldama, a militia officer, Mariano Abasolo, another militia officer and Miguel Domínguez, a creole *corregidor* of Querétaro and the highest ranking conspirator, launched a revolutionary conspiracy to overthrow the Spanish absolutists and their *audiencia*. Allende and Abasolo had earlier participated in a plot hatched by two officers, José Mariano Michelena and José María García Obeso, in the city of Valladolid, which had been suppressed on the eve of its proposed starting date, 21 December 1809. By the summer of 1810 the Querétaro plotters had attracted the support of Miguel Hidalgo y Costilla, a non-conformist and free-living parish priest from the small town of Dolores, who soon emerged as the leader of the conspiracy. A creole of brilliant academic achievements, Hidalgo had devoted his energies to the study of Enlightenment texts and to community organization to improve the lives of the Indians and *mestizos* in his parish. Deeply secular in his interests, he had engaged for many years in debate and consideration of the country's social and political problems and commanded a large following of both creoles and Indians. The conspirators planned a mass insurrection based on the Indians who, they thought, would join them in dispossessing the *gachupines* of their wealth and property while simultaneously respecting the wealth and property of the white creoles.

The intendancy of Guanajuato, which comprised most of the geographical region known as the Bajío, was the scene of this conspiratorial activity because of its rather special social makeup. It was a developed and affluent region and consequently the site of acute social pressures. Its economy was based essentially on mining and mining activity stimulated the development of agriculture and manufacturing to supply its needs. Well over half the Indians and *castas* in the region lived outside traditional communities and worked as free labour in mines and haciendas; they were therefore more socially mobile and had greater expectations than the tributaries living in less developed regions. The Bajío's wealth made it less dependent on Mexico City; its affluent creoles, therefore, felt the political discrimination more intensely. Development was restricted by an outmoded corporatist economic structure, provoking vast discontent among Indian, *mestizo* and creole alike. Thus, the Bajío led the way among the various regions of Mexico in nurturing revolutionary conspiracy. The droughts of 1808–9 and the consequent famines of 1810–11 led to great suffering among the *campesinos*, the closing down of some mines owing to the inability to feed the mules, the laying-off of miners and explosive social unrest. The overthrow of Iturrigaray and two years of inept Spanish government had closed all doors to moderate change. It was in the Bajío that pent up rage and unremitting misery exploded.

The rebellion was to commence in early October, but in the first two weeks of September the royalist authorities were informed by various sources of the projected uprising and the *corregidor* Domínguez was seized in Querétaro. When news of the discovery of the plot reached Hidalgo at his home in Dolores he decided to start the revolt at once. Thus, on the morning of 16 September 1810 Hidalgo issued his *Grito de Dolores*, calling upon the Indians and *mestizos* gathered for the Sunday market to join him in an uprising aimed at defending religion, throwing off the yoke of peninsular domination as represented particularly by the men responsible for the removal of Iturrigaray from office, and ending tribute and other degrading marks of subservience. The revolution was begun in the name of Ferdinand VII, and the Virgin of Guadalupe – the ultimate symbol of Mexican piety – was proclaimed the rebellion's guardian and protectress. Later Hidalgo would add other elements to this vague programme. He would call for independence, the abolition of slavery and the return of lands to Indian communities. In the meantime, he never prohibited his followers from looting; in effect he encouraged them to dispossess the Spaniards.

The revolt spread with explosive fury throughout the intendancy of Guanajuato as the tributary population rose spontaneously in what rapidly became a violent war of retribution against the whites, both peninsular and creole, whom the Indians identified as their oppressors. On the first day of the revolt the rebels captured the town of San Miguel el Grande; two days later they entered the rich town of Celaya; and on 23 September, a force of some 25,000, unarmed but enthusiastic, reached the city of Guanajuato, capital of the intendancy. On 28 September the insurgents stormed the fortress-like granary where the Europeans and creoles had taken refuge, massacred its defenders and submitted the city to two days of plunder. Guanajuato's destruction thereafter provided a symbol of rebel ferocity that the royalists could conveniently use in their propaganda. By early October the rebel horde numbered 60,000, and on 17 October it took the city of Valladolid, the diocesan centre where Hidalgo himself had studied. Encouraged by their rapid success, the rebels planned to turn toward the viceregal capital of Mexico City where, in the expected quick blow, they would liberate the colony.

The Hidalgo revolt, although it proclaimed independence as its goal, was unclear in its objectives, lacking a carefully thought out programme and firm leadership. Hidalgo, in calling the oppressed Indians and *castas* to violent revolt, had unleashed forces that he was unable to control and scarcely understood. The revolt was viewed by New Spain's European and creole population as an Indian uprising, a Mexican equivalent of the Peruvian rebellion of Túpac Amaru in 1780. After the massacre at Guanajuato, it seemed clear that this was not a rebellion against political oppression but a race war directed against all whites and men of property. Thus, although its leaders were creole, the Hidalgo uprising attracted no further creole support. Even the survivors of the autonomist movement of 1808, such as Juan Francisco Azcárate, publicly condemned the revolt. The *cabildo* of Mexico City, previously a centre of creole complaints against the European monopoly of offices and commerce, offered the viceregal government its fullest support. The Church responded with interdicts, inquisitorial condemnations and propaganda against the rebels. Viceroy Venegas responded with public proclamations of stern warnings against all who aided the rebels and with plans to reorganize the 22,000 local militia and 10,000 veteran troops. He appointed Brigadier Félix María Calleja, a peninsular, as commander of a newly organized army of the centre, hoping to draw upon Calleja's twenty-one years' experience and personal contact with Mexico and unique combination of skills to muster creole support. To retain or win back the loyalty of the Indians and *mestizos* he decreed the abolition of the tribute on 5 October, an action soon duplicated by the Spanish Cortes. The royal propaganda campaign was extensive and largely convinced even the lower classes in the central region of the country that the rebels were a threat to all elements of the population.

On 28 October 1810 Hidalgo and his followers, now numbering 80,000, drew up outside Mexico City. On 30 October the rebels were engaged by a small royalist force at a pass over the mountains called Monte de las Cruces. The untrained rebels faced disciplined royalist soldiers for the first time and, although their numbers alone permitted them to carry the day and drive the royalists back, it was a pyrrhic victory. Hidalgo lost 2,000 men in battle, but more significantly, he lost an estimated 40,000 men, or half his force, in desertions. The dream of an instant victory was dashed. Hidalgo's army remained camped outside the city for three days, sending demands that the viceroy capitulate, but on 2 November the rebels withdrew up the road toward Querétaro, reluctant to risk total defeat and thereby losing their best chance of victory. On 7 November the rebel forces met Calleja's advancing army near the village of Aculco and there sustained a disastrous defeat that largely spelled the end of their short but terrible uprising. In its wake, Hidalgo and Allende divided their forces, with Hidalgo going to Valladolid and then to Guadalajara and Allende going to Guanajuato. In Valladolid and Guadalajara Hidalgo ordered or permitted the summary executions of over four hundred Europeans, thus revealing a vindictiveness that had not previously existed in his leadership. The atrocities were provoked by Hidalgo's awareness that his movement was rapidly failing. When Allende was driven out of his stronghold of Guanajuato on 24 November the mob massacred 138 European prisoners. General Calleja took reprisals after he entered the city, as did the royalist commander, José de la Cruz, among the villages east of Querétaro. It was estimated that in Hidalgo's revolt 2,000 of New Spain's 15,000 European Spaniards were killed. More creoles were killed, proving that the Indians were not interested in distinguishing between their white oppressors.

Hidalgo and his commanders spent December 1810 and the first half of January 1811 in Guadalajara reorganizing their devastated army. By the middle of January they had amassed a force of 80,000 once again. The unarmed and untrained peasants were thrown against the main royalist army of Calleja at the Bridge of Calderón outside Guadalajara on 17 January. The rebels were routed in their most serious defeat and the leaders fled. In disorganized flight to the comparative safety of the north, Hidalgo was stripped of his military command by his own lieutenants. By mid March General Calleja had regained control of central and western Mexico. Fleeing further northward, Hidalgo and his chief officers were captured in Coahuila in late March. They were transferred to the city of Chihuahua, tried and executed. Hidalgo gave many indications of regret for leading the uprising and is alleged to have signed before his death a general statement abjuring the revolution. He was shot on 30 July, and his head, together with those of three other rebel leaders, was removed, transferred to Guanajuato and displayed on the corner of the city's granary, scene of the greatest of the rebel massacres, for the next ten years.

Hidalgo is remembered in modern Mexico as 'the father of independence' and deified as one of Mexico's greatest national heroes. The day of the *Grito de Dolores*, 16 September, is Mexico's independence day. Yet, Hidalgo's revolt lasted only three months and its impact upon the struggle for independence was largely counter-productive. It submitted the centre of the country to bloodshed and destruction; it forced creoles into the royalist camp in order to defend their lives and property; and it drowned the original object of autonomy in a sea of blood. Hidalgo lost control of his uprising and permitted or condoned extreme savagery. The greatest weaknesses of the uprising were its lack of clear objectives and the terror it provoked among creoles who might have supported a less destructive movement for political reform. General Calleja recognized this in 1811 when he wrote: 'This vast kingdom weighs too heavily upon an insubstantial metropolis; its natives and even the Europeans themselves are convinced of the advantages that would result from an independent government; and if the absurd insurrection of Hidalgo had been built upon this base, it seems to me as I now look at it, that it would have met with little opposition.'[5]

The memory of Hidalgo's bloody revolt prevented many potential supporters from joining the rebels. Yet the rebellion was not snuffed out. General Calleja wrote to the viceroy: 'The insurrection is far from calm;

[5] Hugh Hamill, *The Hidalgo Revolt: prelude to Mexican independence* (Gainesville, Florida, 1966), 220.

it returns like the hydra in proportion to the number of times its head is cut off.'[6] Leadership of the movement passed to the priest, José María Morelos, and to Ignacio López Rayón, who continued to lead the remaining rebel forces in the Bajío. There were a host of lesser rebel leaders as well, some dedicated patriots, others little more than bandit chiefs. Morelos, a far greater leader and more skilled commander than Hidalgo, was eventually acknowledged as the chief leader of the rebellion after Rayón's prestige was shattered in the battle of Zitácuaro in January 1812. Born of a poor *mestizo* family in Michoacán, Morelos had worked in youth as a mule driver. He eventually improved himself by university study, became a priest and was appointed to poor Indian parishes in Michoacán. Closer to the Indians than even Hidalgo, Morelos joined the rebellion in its first weeks. Assigned by Hidalgo to carry the revolt to the south coast, he created an effective and manageably small army which constituted the chief threat to royalist power until 1815. Morelos also made major strides in clarifying the political and social objectives of the rebellion, left so vague under Hidalgo. His programme consisted of independence (declared in 1813), a congressional form of government and social reforms – including the abolition of tribute, slavery, the caste system and legal barriers to lower class advancement, as well as the introduction of an income tax. The most nationalist of the rebel leaders, he dropped the pretence of being loyal to the king's sovereignty and endowed the symbol of the Virgin of Guadalupe with deeper patriotic content. He also advocated distribution of the lands to those who worked them and in a controversial document he appeared to call for the confiscation and redistribution of all property belonging to his enemies, the wealthy. He tempered his social revolution with declarations of the Catholic Church's absolute primacy and right to tithe, and he declared his respect for private property. He openly courted creole support in more moderate proclamations but, like Hidalgo, failed to receive it.

General Calleja very nearly brought the Morelos rebellion to an end in the spring of 1812, when he besieged the rebel forces for 72 days at the town of Cuautla Amilpas, where Morelos had settled to prepare for an assault on Mexico City. But Morelos and his army evacuated the place on 1 May and, despite great losses, the rebel army was not crushed. By November 1812 Morelos had rallied and captured the important

[6] Francisco de Paula de Arrangoiz y Berzábal, *Méjico desde 1808 hasta 1867* (4 vols., Madrid, 1871), I, 137.

southern city of Oaxaca, giving him control of much of the south and placing him at the height of his power. He then devoted the entire summer of 1813 to an attempt to capture Acapulco, which was ultimately successful but largely useless. With its capture in the late summer Morelos's military fortunes began to decline. He departed from Acapulco to organize the rebel congress he had called to meet at Chilpancingo, a decision urged upon him by his civilian political advisers. The Congress of Chilpancingo began its meetings on 14 September 1813 and immediately conferred on Morelos executive power. The real task of the congress was to set up some kind of a formal government that could apply to foreign powers for possible recognition. Morelos's civilian advisers prevailed upon him to accept this, so as to remove the suspicion that he was creating a military dictatorship. On 6 November 1813 the congress declared independence.

Morelos's military power declined rapidly after the declaration of independence. In December 1813 he failed to take the city of Valladolid, which he had wished to establish as the insurgent capital. On 5 January 1814 his retreating army suffered another serious defeat at Puruarán, and one of his chief commanders, Mariano Matamoros, was captured and executed. At the same time, the small Congress of Chilpancingo turned to internal bickering, as Ignacio Rayón contested Morelos's supreme authority. In January the congress was forced to flee from Chilpancingo and thereafter it remained an itinerant body. On 22 January Morelos surrendered the executive power to congress and effectively lost military command as well. Congress placed military authority in the hands of Ignacio Rayón, José María Cos and Juan Nepomuceno Rosains. Meanwhile, the city of Oaxaca returned to royalist hands and Morelos's other chief lieutenant, Hermenegildo Galeana, was killed in a skirmish. Finally, in the summer of 1814 the congress settled in the town of Apatzingán, and there, in October, particularly influenced by Carlos María Bustamante, Andrés Quintana Roo and Ignacio Rayón, proclaimed a formal constitution which was meant to attract the support of liberal elements in Mexico in the wake of the absolutist restoration in Spain. Morelos's influence on the constitution was negligible, though, as a member of congress at that time, he was one of the signers. Indeed, the Constitution of Apatzingán, in creating a three-man executive and prohibiting any governmental official from holding military command, constituted a reaction against Morelos's earlier one-man rule. The constitution failed to have the anticipated propaganda impact, however, since the rebels did not have sufficient access to printing presses to distribute it widely. Indeed, its only widespread distribution came in royalist propaganda that quoted the constitution in order to condemn it.

The rebel congress spent most of 1815 fleeing from place to place to escape the royalist forces, and its security became increasingly uncertain. In September 1815 congress decided to transfer its location to the east coast, which required the entire insurgent government to travel through royalist territory. Morelos was given the job of defending it in its move. On 5 November a royalist detachment of six hundred men caught up with the rebels. Morelos defended the deputies as they escaped in confusion but was himself captured. He was transferred to Mexico City, tried and found guilty. As a priest he was also tried by the Inquisition and formally degraded by an archdiocesan court. On 22 December 1815 he was taken to the small town of San Cristóbal Ecatépec north of Mexico City and executed by firing squad.

Morelos's revolt, supported more by *mestizos* than by Indians, was conducted with greater military skill, organization and political purpose than Hidalgo's uncontrolled uprising of Indians had been. Morelos won many important victories, he clarified the objectives of the revolution, sponsored a declaration of independence, created a congress to regularize his government, conducted war through properly organized and trained revolutionary armies, and demonstrated exceptional talent and selfless dedication to the cause. Yet, like Hidalgo, he also advocated social reforms that were too radical for a large segment of the politically active population. And by the time he took active leadership of the movement he had to face the challenge not only of other ambitious rebel leaders who resisted his leadership – notably Rayón – but also a reorganized and strengthened royalist opposition. After September 1810 the royalists could not be caught by surprise as they had been by Hidalgo.

The royalist leadership of Viceroy Venegas and his chief general and successor, Calleja, was perhaps as brilliant as any New Spain had previously known, although the two men quarrelled bitterly during Venegas's term of office, mainly over Calleja's ambition to eradicate the revolts quickly and by extreme military measures. Venegas was closely associated with the faction of peninsular merchants in Mexico City, since he came as viceroy directly from his previous post as governor of Cádiz, still the main centre of Spanish trade with America. The merchants of Cádiz dominated the government of the Regency and the Cortes which settled there in 1810. There were thus good reasons for creole suspicion of Venegas, but his record as a successful military commander in the peninsular war against Napoleon, particularly his participation in the great Spanish victory at Bailén, as well as his upright and correct conduct as viceroy after 1810, won for him the support of the frightened creole elite. He halted the decline in the prestige of the viceregal office caused by the two and a half year interregnum under Garibay and Lizana from 1808 to 1810. However, a mistake for which the creoles never forgave him – although he was only acting on the orders of the Cádiz government – was his offer of rewards and honours immediately upon his arrival in Mexico City to Gabriel de Yermo and others prominent in the overthrow of Viceroy Iturrigaray. In this he showed that insensitivity toward local feelings for which Spain was notorious. For many years to come creole deputies to the Spanish Cortes would ascribe the desire for independence among Mexicans to this impolitic offer of rewards to the absolutist enemies of Iturrigaray. Many rebels drawn from the ranks of the regional militias would make the same point because of their abiding loyalty to Iturrigaray, who had reorganized the militias and granted them new distinctions.

It was the viceregal government that fought the rebellions in New Spain. Although representing Spain and loyal to the mother country, the viceregal regime made most of the military, political and economic policy, fielded the armies, raised tax revenues, launched propaganda campaigns, organized militias, recruited troops, and even ignored or evaded inconvenient or inappropriate royal orders from Spain. At no time did Spain itself do much of the fighting; for the most part, Mexicans fought Mexicans. The royalist armies that met Hidalgo were 95 per cent Mexican. Of the total military force of 32,000 men in New Spain before the war, veteran Spanish troops numbered only 10,620. An additional 8,448 men came to New Spain in several expeditionary forces from the peninsula betwen 1812 and 1817 to join a military force which had grown to over 85,000 men by 1820. The backbone of the royalist forces remained creole and *mestizo*. The War of Independence was not a lopsided contest with a foregone conclusion; it was, rather, a struggle in which the nation was divided in its loyalties and in which the final outcome was not inevitable; it was a revolutionary civil war.

Viceroy Venegas reorganized the viceregal regime on many fronts and placed it on a war footing. This was no small task for a regime that had been caught by surprise by Hidalgo's *Grito de Dolores*. Yet, by the end of only three months the royalists had succeeded in proving that the revolts could be contained. In the immediate wake of the *Grito* Venegas had reorganized the existing veteran troops into twelve regional commandancies – Mexico City, Guadalajara, Veracruz, Valladolid, Oaxaca, Zacatecas, San Luis Potosí, Puebla, Guanajuato, Sonora, Durango and Mérida – and armies such as Calleja's army of the centre, appointing skilled Spaniards and creoles of high rank to commands. He had immediately moved to create new local militia units and to fill out the rolls of provincial regiments and municipal militias. By April 1811 conscription was in effect to keep these battalions filled, with a resulting impact in lost manpower in the guilds, colleges, government offices and even the university. The Royal and Pontifical University of Mexico had its students enrolled in the Patriotic Battalions, while its main building was taken over to house one of the regiments, causing the effective dissolution of the university. By August 1811 police authorities were drawing up lists of conscripts, and direct levies began among the artisans and the urban lower class. It seems that even tributary Indians, previously exempt from armed service, were also taken. The viceroy was constantly urged on by General Calleja who had the support not only of ultraroyalists and peninsulars but also of many creoles. Calleja urged conscription for all Europeans, something the viceroy refused, and accused the peninsulars living in Mexico of refusing to fight. By May 1812 the feud between Venegas and Calleja was public. After Calleja's costly siege of Morelos at Cuautla Amilpas, which resulted in only limited success, Viceroy Venegas judged Calleja's public opposition to be a threat and disbanded the army of the centre. General Calleja then took up residence in Mexico City, where he was surrounded by both ultraroyalists and creole liberals attempting to win him to their side. This disparate following besieged Spain with requests for Venegas to be replaced by Calleja.

Meanwhile, Viceroy Venegas organized effective counter-insurrectionary techniques for the surveillance and control of the civilian population. Two plots in early 1811 provoked him to create a kind of martial law administration in the capital and chief cities. A plot in April 1811 to kidnap the viceroy and force him to order the release of Hidalgo, who had been captured in Coahuila, revealed the existence of a group of suspicious individuals among the capital's leading creoles. A second conspiracy, uncovered in August 1811, led to the arrest and execution of a number of conspirators. Several ecclesiastics were also implicated, causing disagreement between the civil and ecclesiastical powers over who had authority to try them for treason. Venegas eventually agreed to allow the friars involved to go into exile. The viceroy's suspicion of the clergy, and the complicity of a number of lower ranking clerics in the leadership of the rebellion, led him on 25 June 1812 to publish his famous 'blood and fire' decree abolishing all special immunities for ecclesiastics found guilty of treason. He authorized royal commanders in the field to try all clerical insurgents. This order, a major affront against the tradition of clerical immunity which shocked Spain as well as Mexico, was not put in effect in Mexico City or Guadalajara, but it was implemented elsewhere. The plot of August 1811 led Venegas to create a new Junta of Police and Public Security in Mexico City, which superseded and absorbed an existing body of a similar name that had been created in 1809. This Junta of Security administered both a system of passports and a domestic police system which granted the new police force the power to hear cases and impose penalties in its own district courts. The police system remained in effect until Spain ordered its abolition in 1813, while the passport system remained throughout the War of Independence.

To pay for the expanded military activity the viceregal government resorted initially to a call for voluntary donations and loans from individuals. Until 1812 this elicited huge contributions from the wealthy Europeans and creoles. In February 1812 the first forced loan of the war was instituted. Viceroy Venegas created special taxes on food and a 10 per cent tax on private buildings and residences. Viceroy Calleja created others. One, called a 'forced direct contribution', was a type of income tax applied on a graduated scale against incomes over 300 pesos a year. Other new duties imposed by Calleja included taxes on carriages and horses, increased sales taxes and new levies on corn and other staples. Finally, in 1815 Calleja planned perhaps the most unusual of his new duties – a forced lottery. Apparently, he withdrew his plans for this lottery because of popular discontent, for it seems to have been applied only against public employees.

These new taxes went hand in hand with widespread disruption of supply and revenue caused by the rebellions, resulting in great increases in food costs and a soaring viceregal debt that totalled 49 million pesos in 1813 and 80 million in 1816. Although the new taxes permitted the royal government to keep one step ahead of financial collapse, they also had the effect of depressing production, unsettling private enterprise, increasing the cost and decreasing the profit from productive activities and limiting private funds available for recuperation of mines and farms. Mining Deputations (regional branches of the Mining Tribunal) were forced to pay the cost of quartering troops in the mining centres and were. charged convoy duties for sending silver and gold in heavily guarded convoys. Mine owners and workers abandoned the mining centres, capital fled the industry, credit was unavailable and mercury (necessary for extracting silver) remained in limited supply at a very high cost. As a consequence, the output of minted gold and silver dropped from an annual average of 22.5 million pesos for the decade 1800–9 to an annual average of 11.3 million for the next decade, a decline of almost 50 per cent. The colony's exports and imports declined by more than a third from the first to the second decade of the century. According to contemporaries, agricultural production and domestic industrial output also fell sharply. These consequences were as much due to governmental tax policies and royalist exactions as to the direct effects of the war itself.

Spain also persisted in its dedication to commercial exclusivism in Spanish America, which was politically and economically harmful. The British were very anxious to obtain legal entry into the Mexican market, but all attempts to reach formal agreement with Spain – as, for example, through British mediation in the rebellions in return for permission to trade – came to nothing. Spain rejected outright a British offer to mediate in Mexico on the grounds that no rebel government controlled that region, although from 1811 to 1820 it engaged in periodic negotiations for British mediation in Buenos Aires and New Granada. One side or the other always broke off these discussions, while Spain clung to its trade monopoly long after Spanish shipping had virtually disappeared from the Pacific and the South Atlantic. Direct Spanish trade to Mexico via Cuba continued to the end, though at a reduced level. Unlike Peru, Mexico was never cut off totally from Spanish shipping and, as a consequence, the foreign trade that existed was carried on under cover.

Under Calleja, who became viceroy on 4 March 1813, the conscriptions and taxes continued to increase until by the middle of 1813 New Spain was governed by a military regime in all but name. This was also the period of the greatest danger for the royal regime, for Morelos's rebellion was at its height. Moreover, epidemics raged in Mexico City, Puebla and Veracruz; the epidemic of 1813 killed 20,000 people, or one-eighth of the population, in Mexico City alone. And political confusion caused by the implementation of the Spanish Constitution of 1812 immensely compounded the job of restoring order and reconquering territory.

Perhaps the greatest challenge facing the viceregal government of New Spain besides the rebellions themselves was the liberal reform programme of the Spanish Cortes that governed Spain and the Indies from September 1810 until the restoration of Ferdinand VII in May 1814. The Cortes reforms included the abolition of the Indian tribute and the Inquisition, equality for overseas subjects, sweeping restrictions on the powers of the religious orders and freedom of the press. In 1812 the Cortes capped the reform programme with a written constitution, the first in Spain's history and the fundamental precedent not only for future Spanish constitutions but also for the first constitution of republican Mexico in 1824. The constitution, promulgated in Cádiz in March 1812 and formally proclaimed in Mexico in September, made Spain a limited constitutional monarchy with the king reduced to the status of chief executive. The Cortes and king (or, during his captivity, the Regency representing him) constituted the legislative and executive branches of government; if the king should return from captivity in France he would be required to accept the constitution before he could resume his throne. Viceroys and governors were made 'political chiefs' of their territories. *Deputaciones Provinciales* (Provincial Deputations) were to be elected to share power with the political chiefs, and the hereditary city councils were to be replaced with elected councils. Technically, the viceroy of New Spain was deprived of jurisdiction over those parts of the viceroyalty which already had their own captains general – the Eastern and Western Internal Provinces, New Galicia and Yucatán. *Audiencias* were reduced to the status of courts of law.

The creoles of Mexico responded with enthusiasm to the Cortes and sent a number of distinguished deputies to Cádiz. By 1811 the Mexican representatives had become leaders of the American deputation in the Cortes. A number of them, of whom the most prominent were Miguel Guridi y Alcocer (Tlaxcala), José Miguel Ramos Arizpe (Coahuila), and José Miguel Gordoa (Zacatecas), took an active part in advocating more liberal provisions in the constitution. Other Mexican deputies, however, notably Antonio Joaquín Pérez (Puebla) and José Cayetano de Foncerrada (Michoacán), were among the more prominent conservatives.

Thirteen of the Mexican deputies signed a representation submitted to the Cortes by all the American delegations on 1 August 1811 assessing the causes of the struggles for independence and advocating solutions. Referring to the particular case of Mexico, the deputies argued that Hidalgo's insurrection was caused by Iturrigaray's overthrow by a faction of Europeans who were then rewarded by Viceroy Venegas. Each overseas colony, they declared, ought to have a separate government under the king's suzerainty, a type of commonwealth of autonomous states. This proposal was not acted upon by the Cortes, of course, for although it was dominated by the liberals, the Cortes was also located in the city of Cádiz and virtually dependent on the monopoly merchants to provide the revenues for Spain's national survival. Despite its liberalism, the Cortes remained European in its orientation and continued to view the overseas territories as sources of revenue. The Mexican deputies also participated in a representation to the Cortes signed by all the American and Asian members, which consisted of eleven basic demands for reforms in the overseas territories. These demands included equal proportional representation in the Cortes; free foreign trade; suppression of all state and private monopolies; free mining of mercury; equal rights of Americans to state offices; distribution of half of the administrative posts in each territory to natives of that territory; and restoration of the Jesuit order in America – not one of which was granted by the Cortes.

Absolutist royalists in Mexico viewed the Cortes as a major new threat to Spanish power because it encouraged a political resurgence among the creoles. Consequently, Viceroy Venegas adopted a policy of selective application of Cortes reforms and obstruction of others, a policy Viceroy Calleja continued. The first Cortes decree to provoke the anger of the viceroy was the establishment of the free press, passed by the Cortes in November 1810 and received in Mexico City in January 1811. It declared that, with the exception of publications on religious matters, all persons were free to publish their political ideas without prior approval by state authorities. Venegas, convinced that in the condition of Mexico this decree would encourage the rebellion, simply refused to put it into effect. He persisted in this for two years, making no public statement concerning the law but simply ignoring it. He sought the advice of the ecclesiastical hierarchy and political leaders and a majority of them advised against implementation of the law. In Mexico and Spain creoles protested. Ramos Arizpe, the Cortes deputy, led the fight in Cádiz to have the viceroy ordered to implement the free press. The city council of Mexico City complained of Venegas's delay, calling his actions despotic. All to no avail: the free press was not implemented in Mexico until the arrival of the constitution in September 1812. No authority, not even the Cortes, had the power to force the viceroy to implement the law.

With the proclamation of the liberal constitution in Mexico the creole dissidents rejoiced, assuming that it guaranteed them a greater voice in local decisions. The free press, a major provision of the constitution, could no longer be resisted and automatically went into effect. Among those journalists who appeared in print with their criticisms of the Spanish system were Carlos María Bustamante, who published the journal *El Juguetillo*, and José Joaquín Fernández de Lizardi, the journal *El Pensador Mejicano*. Neither man was yet a declared rebel, though both were highly critical commentators. After three months of a free press, Viceroy Venegas decided he had seen enough. On 5 December 1812 he suspended Article 371 of the constitution – the free press – after consultation with the *audiencia*. When Calleja became viceroy in March 1813 the suspension remained in effect, even though in his first public statement as viceroy he promised to implement the constitution fully. Not until June 1814 did he publish a statement declaring that it was his intention to keep the free press in suspension in order to prevent the insurrection from spreading. Again the Cortes deputies and city councils demanded enforcement, but nothing could move the viceroy. Busta-mante fled into hiding and openly declared his support for the rebels; Fernández de Lizardi went to prison.

The policy of the two viceroys toward the elections called for in the constitution was just as absolutist. When the first parish voting occurred in Mexico City on 29 November 1812 it was to select a group of electors who would then choose the new city council. All the electors chosen were creoles and a number were prominent supporters of the rebels. A group of secret partisans of independence, *Los Guadalupes*, wrote to Morelos that this meant the destruction of the *gachupín* government. On 14 December Viceroy Venegas, alleging that many irregularities had occurred, annulled the election and ordered the hereditary city council to remain in office in Mexico City. It was a viceregal coup, against which the creoles had no recourse. In fact, few irregularities had taken place; Venegas was prompted merely by a rather heavy-handed political expe-diency. When Calleja became viceroy he was less clumsy; he determined to pursue a policy of studied neglect of the constitutional agencies but without provoking the outcries of moderates by arbitrary actions against them. Hence, he ordered the aborted city council election to be com-pleted, and in April 1813 the electors chose a new *cabildo* consisting entirely of creoles of whom the viceroy alleged three-quarters were rebel sympathizers. Elections for the Provincial Deputation and Cortes members followed. Yet, from the time he took office until the abolition of the constitution the next year, Calleja intervened in local elections, attempted to influence their outcome, or, more deftly, refused to be bound by the advice of elected bodies. Although he no longer possessed the title viceroy, he simply functioned as if he did. Nor did he face censure from the Cortes, for a Cortes committee in late 1813 actually recommended that a military regime be established in Mexico in order to oppose the threat of Morelos. Calleja did not require such support, since he already functioned as if he were at the head of a military dictatorship. Calleja's suspicions of the constitutional *cabildo* in Mexico City were confirmed when captured rebel documents revealed the extent of the complicity of some councillors in giving aid to various rebels. The *audiencia* insisted that the elected officials were all advocates of independence. Calleja frequently complained that his attempts to bring suspicious partisans to trial were obstructed by the procedures laid down in the constitution. It was not until after the king's restoration that he felt able to proceed against those liberal creole constitutionalists whom he suspected of treason. During 1815, after the annulment of the constitution, Calleja arrested a number of prominent creole leaders in Mexico City, including four former city councillors and three men who had been elected to the Cortes but barred from taking their seats.

By 1814 disaffection was widespread. Ultraroyalists continued to view the Cortes and constitution of 1812 as the greatest single threat to the maintenance of royal power. In a letter to the Spanish government Calleja announced that he and the *audiencia* had agreed that he should continue to operate as a viceroy, not merely as a superior political chief, that he was the personal representative of the monarch and would act that way. Meanwhile, most creoles recognized that the Cortes was just as imperialist as the governments which had preceded it and that the constitution had not significantly improved their status.

In March 1814, after the collapse of French rule in Spain, Ferdinand VII was released by Napoleon from six years of captivity in France and returned to Spain. On 4 May, he issued a long manifesto at Valencia annulling the constitution of 1812 and all the acts of the Cortes in Cádiz. The royal coup was announced in Mexico in August, where the royal authorities greeted the restoration of absolutism with joy. (The rebels under Morelos responded with the promulgation of their Constitution of

Apatzingán, which they hoped would attract the support of liberal creoles.) By the end of 1814 a series of decrees restored government to the conditions that had prevailed in 1808. The elected bodies were abolished, hereditary city councils returned to office, the *audiencia* and viceroy and captains general had their full authority restored. In 1815 even the Inquisition and the Jesuit order were restored.

Although the precedents established between 1810 and 1814 were of the first importance, the most significant role of the Cortes was as a forum for the expression of American grievances against the *ancien régime*. Few of the Mexican deputies could fail to be affected by the debates of the Cortes, and the political manoeuvrings in the heady atmosphere of free, radical Spain. Most of the Mexicans who served from 1810 to 1814 returned again in 1820 when the Cortes was re-established, and many of the deputies from the latter period, 1820–23, served as ministers and leading figures of the first independent governments in Mexico.

The great convulsion of the Spanish empire from 1808 to 1814 had also been reflected in events in the kingdom of Guatemala (Central America). Governed from Guatemala City by a president-captain general and an *audiencia*, the kingdom of Guatemala consisted of Guatemala, Chiapas (which at independence joined Mexico), El Salvador, Honduras, Nicaragua and Costa Rica. (Panama was the most northerly province of the viceroyalty of New Granada and thus adhered to the mainland of South America at the time of independence, becoming part of the republic of Gran Colombia.) In 1786 intendancies had been created in El Salvador, Honduras, Nicaragua and Chiapas; Costa Rica was an isolated part of the intendancy of Nicaragua; Guatemala remained outside the intendancy system, under the direct administration of the captain general in the capital. The establishment of the system of intendants served to increase the sense of separate identity felt by the constituent parts of the kingdom, particularly El Salvador and Nicaragua. Central America at the beginning of the nineteenth century had a population of about one and a quarter million, of whom well over half were Indians. Most of the remainder were *ladinos*, that is to say *mestizos* or mulattos of many degrees of intermixture. As in New Spain, a handful of whites dominated the government and economy, and of these the European-born were a tiny proportion. Guatemala had also experienced the stirrings of Enlightenment ideas at the close of the eighteenth century, particularly in the University of San Carlos whose graduates made up most of the creole leadership. In 1796 the creole elite had founded a centre for reformist thought, the *Sociedad Económica de Amigos del País*, which, although suppressed from 1800 to 1811, had nonetheless the effect of spreading the new ideas. Representative of this reformist group were the Honduran lawyer, José Cecilio del Valle, the Salvadoran planter and merchant, Juan Bautista Irisarri, and Alejandro Ramírez and Simón Bergaño y Villegas, the editors, and Ignacio Beteta, the publisher of the *Gazeta de Guatemala*.

There was no talk of political independence among the Central American elite; local improvement in trade, navigation and agriculture were the principal desires. The Hidalgo uprising in Mexico caused widespread concern among this class as well as among the royal administrators. Antonio González Mollinedo y Saravia, who served as thirty-fourth president of the *audiencia* of Guatemala from 1801 to 1811, was ordered to Mexico to help suppress the rebellion in 1811 and there lost his life when he was caught by the rebels. He was succeeded by José de Bustamante y Guerra (1811–18), who pursued much the same policy as Viceroy Calleja. Bustamante was similarly placed in the peculiar position of having to govern under the Constitution of 1812 which he personally opposed. Like Venegas and Calleja he implemented only the letter of the constitution and not its spirit. He also obstructed implementation of freedom of the press, while intervening in elections and attempting to stifle the political initiative of elected city councils and Provincial Deputations. He delayed the opening of the two Provincial Deputations until late in 1813. The constitution provoked new liberal–conservative differences and led to the same sort of political ferment as in Mexico. It gave substantial encouragement to the development of a spirit of federalism in Central America. It restored the Economic Society that had been previously suppressed, it created two Provincial Deputations in Guatemala City and León, it brought about elected city councils in the larger cities and it led to the decree establishing a new university in León. Central American deputies participated actively in the debates of the Cortes, generally being viewed as colleagues of the Mexican deputation. The most prominent Central American deputy was Antonio Larrazábal, who in 1811 presented a list of liberal demands on instructions from the *cabildo* of Guatemala City advocating political liberalism, elective and representative offices, relaxation of commercial restrictions, stimulation of production and of educational institutions, a free press and a Central American Junta Superior. Other Central American deputies, such as

Florencio Castillo (Costa Rica), José Ignacio Avila (San Salvador), Manuel de Micheo and José Cleto Montiel (Guatemala), and Mariano Robles and Fernando Antonio Davila (Chiapas), particularly emphasized the demand of their long neglected provinces for improvements to the ports, canals, river systems and the rest of the infrastructure necessary for future internal development, as well as requesting the foundation of new universities and seminaries. The wishes of the creole deputies largely served the interests of the creole elite but, like those of most other American deputies, were phrased in liberal and altruistic terms. The government of Bustamante, meanwhile, sided with the pro-Spanish mercantile interests, with the textile manufacturers and with the small landholders against the interests of the creole elite. Thus the Cortes era provoked the first tentative formulation of political parties in Guatemala, as the wealthy creole elite found its interests opposed by the pro-government party of Europeans and lesser creoles. The Spanish colonial monopoly was the key element in the debate, as Bustamante struggled to resist the flow of inexpensive British cottons from the British foothold at Belize on the east coast of Guatemala. The leaders of the creole aristocratic party were the Aycinena family. Though not advocates of independence, the Aycinenas were enthusiastic supporters of the constitution, and José de Aycinena, former intendant of San Salvador, became a member of the constitutional Council of State of Spain in 1812, the first Guatemalan to achieve so high a position.

While no mass rebellion occurred in Central America, the ferment of the Cortes era helped to provoke four lesser rebellions or conspiracies. Insurrections occurred in November 1811 in San Salvador over the demand to create a separate bishopric there; in Granada in December 1811 over resentment against the political dominance of León and the misrule of the intendant; and in San Salvador again in January 1814 inspired by the Morelos rebellion. Manuel José de Arce, who would later become the first president of the federal Republic of Central America, was the chief figure in the two Salvadoran uprisings. The most important conspiracy occurred in Guatemala City in December 1813, centred on the Bethlemite religious order, but it was discovered before it came to fruition. All these insurrections were rapidly suppressed by Bustamante's government.

Bustamante greeted the overthrow of the Cortes and constitution with as much joy as Calleja, perhaps more, since the Cortes had ordered his removal from office in early 1814. He immediately began a systematic

persecution of the liberal creoles in the Aycinena faction and the city
council of Guatemala City – all those, in fact, who had endorsed the
cabildo's instructions to Larrazábal in 1810. On his recommendation the
king agreed to the removal from office of all the signatories. In Spain
Larrazábal was imprisoned as part of the absolutist reaction. Until 1817
the Aycinenas and others were denied full exercise of citizenship,
removed from the city council, persecuted by suits for back taxes and
denied government protection. This further increased their grievances
against the captain general and the monopoly merchants who were now
ascendant. Even the *Gazeta de Guatemala* ceased publishing in 1816. An
alliance gradually began to form between the leading creole families and
poor creole *letrados*, or professional men, who were denied appointment
because of their politics or because of their place of birth. This alliance of
the 'first families' and poor creole aspirants to office would carry
Guatemala to independence in 1821. Nonetheless, as long as Bustamante
remained in office Guatemala remained under tight control and was
politically quiescent.

In 1818 the incessant complaints of the Aycinena faction, expressed
frequently in correspondence with its Spanish merchant allies in the
peninsula and by José de Aycinena who now sat on the Council of the
Indies, had its effect and Bustamante was replaced as president of the
audiencia and captain general by Carlos Urrutia y Montoya, an elderly and
mild-mannered officer. Even before Urrutia left his previous post in
Santo Domingo members of the creole aristocracy surrounded him, and
by the time of his arrival in Guatemala City he was under their influence.
In office, Urrutia pursued a commercial policy which he thought would
prevent contraband but which actually played into the hands of the
creole elite who advocated more open trade. In 1819 he authorized trade
with British-held Belize. He relaxed Bustamante's coastal defence against
smugglers, thus encouraging not only more smuggling but the first
forays into Central American waters of South American privateers
representing the rebellious governments in Buenos Aires and New
Granada. Furthermore, when the constitution was reproclaimed in 1820
he proved to be friendly toward it.

It is notable that in both Guatemala and Mexico the administrations that
took office after the suppression of the early revolts were politically more
lax; inadvertently they helped to encourage renewed political activity
among the creole dissidents. After the abolition of the constitution,

Viceroy Calleja in New Spain had sworn that he would end the rebellion there even if he had to march at the head of the whole army across the country, laying it waste with fire and sword. As a consequence, he spent most of late 1814 and early 1815 in an effort to suppress the rebellions. He succeeded so well that after the capture and execution of Morelos the rebellions gradually ceased, leaving only a few chieftains like Guadalupe Victoria and Vicente Guerrero in the field either with no followers or else with small bands who turned mainly to cattle theft and robbery and presented no sustained threat to the regime. There were fears by royalist commanders, however, that the guerrillas had merely gone underground, and, given the speed of the rising in 1820 and 1821, those fears appear well grounded. Nonetheless, when Calleja handed his command over to his successor on 16 September 1816 he left behind a defeated and discredited revolution, a large and well-trained army, an organized treasury with new taxes to provide revenue, a reorganized civilian trade under the protection of convoys and a regular mail system. The conservative historian Lucas Alamán concluded that 'if Spain had not lost its dominion over these countries by later events, Calleja would have been recognized as the reconqueror of New Spain and the second Hernán Cortés'.[7] After 27 years of residence and service in New Spain, Calleja left Mexico, urging his successor to continue his methods of pacifying the country.

Juan Ruiz de Apodaca, the new viceroy, thought the best policy to pursue in late 1816 was one of accommodation and the offer of amnesty, hoping that a return to normal political relations between the classes and between Mexico and the mother country would be possible. Apodaca's offer of amnesty to former rebels was readily accepted by many thousands. Until 1820 the only major rebel threat Apodaca had to face was the abortive attempt in 1817 of Javier Mina, a disaffected Spanish liberal, to land an expedition on the coast to fight for independence. Mina was captured and executed. Another preoccupation of the royal regime was the apparent threat of war with the United States over delays in the negotiations between 1817 and 1819 of a treaty for the cession of the Floridas. As captain general of Cuba in 1816, Apodaca had been ordered to place the fleet on a war footing and, as viceroy of Mexico, he was even more concerned. The possibility of North American aggression against the Eastern Internal Provinces or Cuba was a clear danger. The threat of

[7] Lucas Alamán, *Historia de Méjico desde los primeros movimientos que prepararon su independencia en el año de 1808 hasta la época presente* (5 vols., Mexico, 1942), IV, 308.

Anglo-American expansion in Texas had long been recognized and General Calleja, before he became viceroy, had proposed a scheme for settling Mexican militiamen as farmers in the disputed territory. In the Florida treaty, concluded in 1819, the United States recognized a definite border, which Spain, indicating its weakness, considered a great concession. Despite these international complications, however, the situation within Mexico had rapidly stabilized. Apodaca could look with pride on the gradual restoration of normal commerce, the opening of long disused mail routes, the movement of regular silver convoys through former rebel territory, even the opening of abandoned silver mines.

Spain might have restored its control over New Spain but it had not restored the full measure or prestige of its ancient authority. The prestige of the crown had, in fact, been mortally wounded by the long era of the favourite Godoy, by Ferdinand's overthrow of his father Charles IV, by the Napoleonic usurpation, by the Cortes, and by the intransigent absolutism of Ferdinand VII himself after the restoration. The idea of monarchy, however, remained sufficiently attractive for it to form the foundation for the compromise leading to independence for all Mexico, Yucatán, and Central America. The model of the French and North American republics, both of them actual or potential aggressors against the vital interests of Spaniards and Spanish Americans, was enough to frighten most political moderates away from aspirations to republicanism. And the elite of the colonies continued to recognize an essential unity of interest with the monarchical system in the face of other alternatives thus far presented to it. What was needed was a proposal that would both break the colonial dependency on Spain and also guarantee some degree of social stability and protection of property as well as advancement for the aspirants to office. A moderate compromise proposal for independence, different from what Hidalgo, Morelos, or the other earlier rebels had offered was needed. And some catalyst was needed to push the elite and bourgeoisie into a position where they could act together.

That catalyst was provided by the revolution of January to March 1820 in Spain when the large expeditionary force (approximately 14,000 men) gathered at Cádiz under the command of former viceroy Calleja (now captain general of Andalusia), waiting for the order to launch an attempted reconquest of the Río de la Plata, revolted against the absolute regime of Ferdinand VII. Other units of the army across Spain joined the revolt. Though motivated by long-term grievances of the military against the policy of demobilizing the large armed forces after 1814, the revolution of 1820 quickly attracted the support of the growing liberal groups in the peninsula. Support came from such disparate elements as the secret masonic lodges, the so-called *doceañistas* or liberals of the 1812 experiment in Cádiz, the *exaltados* or extreme radicals, the exiled *afrancesados* or former collaborators with the French regime of 1808–14 and other sectors hostile to Ferdinand's despotic absolutism and favouring renovation. Agreeing on almost nothing, the opposition movement coalesced behind the re-establishment of the Constitution of 1812 as their most salient political objective. A frightened king, without military support, had no choice but to accede, submitting himself to the control of a liberal Cortes for the next three years.

The Revolution of 1820 and the failure of the expeditionary force to leave Spain virtually guaranteed the independence of the Río de la Plata and Chile, while the viceroy of Peru, denied royalist reinforcements, foresaw the fall of Spain's most stalwartly loyal colony. The Spanish revolution also gave new life to dissident elements opposed to decrepit absolutism in other parts of Europe, and constitutional systems modelled on Spain's were shortly erected amid revolution and civil war in Portugal and Naples, the two kingdoms most closely linked to Spain by dynastic relations. The effects of Spain's revolution thus swept through Europe and America.

In Spain itself its restoration in the king's name and with his approval, albeit forced, meant that, unlike in 1812, the constitution was fully implemented. For the first time as required by the constitution the king presided over the executive branch. For the next three years Spain endured frequent parliamentary crises since Ferdinand, exercising his constitutional rights to the fullest extent, proceeded to appoint ministers and captains general, in a direct contest with both moderate and radical liberals. Several governments rose and fell during the so-called triennium, while the empire, or what remained of it, was paralysed by political instability. Finally, in early 1823, a French army, dispatched by the Bourbon King Louis XVIII to rescue Ferdinand, invaded Spanish territory and destroyed the liberal system. The ministry fled to Seville, taking with it Ferdinand VII, as a virtual prisoner. The French forces of 100,000 'sons of Saint Louis' were greeted as liberators in many areas by royalist Spaniards. In June 1823 the liberals fell back from Seville to Cádiz, again taking the king with them; some elements even contemplated regicide. Besieged for two months in the port of Cádiz, the traditional bastion of Spanish liberalism, the constitutionalists at last gave up and Ferdinand, for a second time, was restored to the full exercise of his powers. The remainder of his reign, 1823–33, is called the 'ominous decade,' as the king imposed a white terror upon the peninsula, executing and imprisoning leading liberals in a more severe repetition of the 1814 reaction.

The Spanish revolution of 1820 had important political consequences in Mexico as it did in the rest of the Spanish empire. In June 1820 the constitution of 1812 went back into effect and by the middle of August the city councils, Provincial Deputations, and deputies to the Cortes had all been elected. Representatives of both creole elite and bourgeoisie were elected to office; all were autonomists. Viceroy Apodaca placed no impediments on local elections as his predecessors had done, and co-operated fully in implementing the constitution. In a proclamation published in Mexico in July, the king publicly apologized for his abrogation of the constitution in 1814, admitted he had been mistaken and prayed his subjects not to hold his error of judgement against him. This kind of proclamation could only destroy whatever lingering faith in the throne existed among Americans.

The restoration of the constitution provided Mexico (and Central America) with the final evidence of the irrelevance of king and metropolis and thus provoked the final acts of independence. These were not the result of a counter-revolutionary conservatism among the elite, as some historians have argued, for Mexicans in general supported the restored constitution as much as they had in 1812. Rather, it was the political instability, the proof of Spanish duplicity, the continued tension between the old regime and the new liberal system which indicated to Mexicans that Spanish imperial control was now irrelevant to them and to their interests. They continued to support the constitution; indeed many moved towards independence merely because it seemed the only secure path by which to guarantee themselves the privileges granted by the constitution and to protect it from viceregal despotism whittling away its prerogatives. When Mexico, Central America and Yucatán chose independence they did so because the Constitution of Cádiz was guaranteed in the programme of independence. Those elements in Mexican society which advocated moderate reform and constitutional monarchy were now victorious. These goals were conservative when compared with the radical aims of the Hidalgo and Morelos revolutions, but they were not necessarily reactionary. Mexico had already rejected the radicalism of

Indian or *mestizo* revolution. The elite and bourgeoisie recognized that the newly restored Cortes, though it adopted a programme of radical change in peninsular political and economic structures, still took no action to meet the chief complaints of Americans. The Cortes still did not recognize American demands for autonomy and free trade. The Cortes still did not permit equal representation for America since people of African descent were not recognized for electoral purposes. It was thus the constitution that Mexicans supported more than the Cortes; the Cortes government remained an imperialist government.

Dissatisfaction with the actions of the Cortes was increased when fundamental reforms affecting the status of the clergy and the military were introduced, even though they were not immediately implemented in Mexico. In September 1820 the Cortes decreed the suppression of monastic orders and restrictions on the growth of the mendicant orders; suppression of the Jesuits; prohibition on all property entail and on the acquisition of further real estate by civil and ecclesiastical institutions; abolition of the ecclesiastical *fuero*, or immunity from civil prosecution; and abolition of the military *fuero* for militiamen serving in America. These were serious reforms, indeed, and the clergy and militia officers strongly opposed them. The militia, for example, had grown to such a size – 22,000 men in the provincial militia and 44,000 in the urban militia – that its power extended throughout the country and its officers came to exercise regional and local political control. Furthermore, the Cortes had decreed that the militia should be subordinate to local elected civilian juntas and *cabildos* and had even separated command of the troops from the local political chief unless he had also been granted the power of captain general. This opposition encouraged support for independence among the very groups that had previously provided the chief defence of the royal regime.

Thus, there was widespread dissatisfaction with the Spanish colonial regime in Mexico, and its open expression was made possible because Apodaca had implemented the constitutional guarantee of freedom of the press. The drift toward independence, however, was not a counter-revolution designed to forestall implementation of Cortes reforms. Indeed, many of the reforms decreed by the Cortes in late 1820 but not fully implemented in Mexico because of the outbreak of the new revolt, were implemented after independence. These included disbanding the Inquisition, the Jesuits and the Hospitaler orders; confiscating the property of these orders and of the Philippine missions and the Jerusalem

Crusade and of pious funds that paid dividends to exiles; and abolishing property entail. The first independent government went further than the Cortes in proposing such things as the abolition of racial distinctions for citizenship, the opening of government offices to all citizens, and the abolition of slavery. Some officers after independence even voluntarily offered to give up their military *fuero*. The most important proof that the Mexican independence forces did not oppose the constitution is the fact that the programme upon which independence was established, the Plan of Iguala, endorsed the constitution and it remained in force until December 1822. After independence Mexico decreed that all Spanish laws promulgated between the restoration of the Cortes and the proclamation of the Plan of Iguala (which would include the laws of September 1820 directed against the *fuero*, the religious orders and entail) were valid and in effect.

Independence occurred, then, because the restored constitutional regime showed that the Spanish imperial ethos of crown and altar was now defunct, and that Spanish constitutional liberalism was dedicated to maintaining the American territories in colonial dependence. This encouraged the reassertion of all the long-standing complaints against Spanish rule which, if they had been valid under absolutism, were even more deeply felt under liberalism. Furthermore, political turmoil in the peninsula between moderates and radicals, liberals and conservatives, suggested to Mexico that the constitution might be endangered in Spain itself and that some drastic action was necessary to preserve it in Mexico. Given the climate of opinion, the Mexicans needed only an attractive political programme to win them over to the side of independence.

The political plan that made independence a possible alternative for the first time was the work of Agustín de Iturbide and was expressed in the Plan of Iguala which he published in conjunction with the rebel leader, Vicente Guerrero, and proclaimed on 24 February 1821. Iturbide launched a new rebellion against Spain in an act of calculated treason to his oath of loyalty. A long-time royal officer, commander in important royal engagements against the earlier Mexican rebels, he had participated in the defeat of both the Hidalgo and Morelos rebellions. Removed from command in 1816 for alleged misuse of power and improper conduct, he was restored to prominence by Viceroy Apodaca who, in 1820, appointed him commander of the royalist army of the south with a commission to defeat Guerrero who was still active there. By December 1820 he had been converted to the cause of independence, apparently motivated personally by the same anger at the lack of reward for his past services that provoked other creole officers who had participated in the defeat of Hidalgo and Morelos and also the troops in the peninsula itself. Ferdinand VII had refused any special appointments or rewards for either the American or peninsular troops and paid the price for it in military revolt at home and overseas in 1820–1.

Under the terms of the Plan of Iguala New Spain was to become a separate Catholic monarchy, governed under the Constitution of Cádiz until such time as a new Mexican constitution could be written. Ferdinand VII would be invited to assume the throne as emperor, and if he refused his two brothers in turn would be invited. A Mexican Cortes would be called, and in the interim a provisional Sovereign Junta would be formed followed by a Regency. The new government guaranteed the continuation of the Catholic Church, the establishment of independence and the union of Spaniards and Americans. These three guarantees were expressed in terms of 'Religion, Independence, Union'. They would be protected by the Army of the Three Guarantees (*Ejército Trigarante*), composed of rebels as well as any former royalist army members who were prepared to swear their adhesion to the Plan. All persons and property would be respected and protected, the privileges of the clergy would be preserved, and all government, clerical, and military personnel would be guaranteed their positions if they accepted the Plan. As a final gesture to the uncommitted, the Plan of Iguala even praised Spain as a heroic and magnanimous mother country. The membership of the Sovereign Junta as announced in the Plan of Iguala combined both royalists and rebels, with the viceroy being proposed as the chairman (he refused), and with prelates, nobles, officers, city council members, teachers and *audiencia* judges composing the membership.

In the Plan of Iguala Iturbide proposed the political compromise that made independence possible, at one stroke wiping out the objections of both old-time rebels and elite supporters of the royal regime by guaranteeing economic and political stability, a constitutional monarchy, and the preservation of elite privileges, while at the same time promising independence and equality. It offered something for everyone. The elite immediately recognized that Iguala was advantageous and that it fulfilled the aspirations of 1808. The clergy and military were enthusiastic since it guaranteed no deterioration in their condition and held out the hope of rapid advancement. Dedicated rebels, meantime, could now find common cause with their former opponents, recognizing that independence was now achievable and that the new state, even though it would not be a republic as a few of them wished, would nonetheless be reformist. The Plan forged a new, if temporary, alliance of political forces against which the Spanish imperial system could not stand. After eleven years of struggle and confusion Mexico now had a consensus. Central America and Yucatán, in turn, would respond in a similar manner to the Plan of Iguala.

The viceregal regime collapsed only seven months after publication of the Plan of Iguala. The new revolt caught the peninsular royalists by surprise, but there was little they could do to resist it in any case. Within days Iturbide had informed Viceroy Apodaca that the Plan of Iguala would sweep the nation before it, and so it did. Amnestied rebels came out in favour of Iturbide, royalist troops deserted to him, creoles responded to his call with enthusiasm, garrison after garrison capitulated without firing a shot. In June his forces took the rich Bajío section of the kingdom, the heartland of Hidalgo's revolt. In Mexico City the Plan of Iguala was widely distributed and troops there went over in considerable numbers. Viceroy Apodaca, urged on by his officers, suspended several basic constitutional guarantees, in order to resist the rebels. In so doing he provoked further disaffection among creoles who recognized that Iturbide guaranteed the Constitution of Cádiz while the viceroy now threatened it. On these grounds the city council of Mexico City, for example, publicly announced it was withholding its support from the royalist regime. By the end of June the rebels controlled the garrisons of most of the major cities. In July and August most of the others went over, leaving the royalists in control of only Mexico City and Veracruz. On 5 July 1821 a mutiny of peninsular troops deposed Viceroy Apodaca because of his inability to put down the Iturbide revolt, replacing him with Francisco Novella, subinspector general of the Artillery Corps, in an unsuccessful last ditch stand against independence.

At the end of July the man newly appointed by the Cortes as captain general of New Spain, the liberal former minister of war Juan O'Donojú, arrived in Veracruz. Recognizing an accomplished fact, he asked for conferences with Iturbide. Iturbide accepted, designating the village of Córdoba, near Veracruz, as their meeting place. There, on 24 August, Iturbide and O'Donojú signed the Treaty of Córdoba, by which O'Donojú, recognizing the futility of resistance, unilaterally and without the permission of Spain, recognized the independence of the Mexican Empire and placed himself at the head of the royal forces as captain general, agreeing to induce them to surrender. The two men and the Trigarante Army drew up outside Mexico City where on 13 September Novella surrendered to O'Donojú, completing the relatively bloodless Iturbide uprising and the independence process. Iturbide awaited his thirty-eighth birthday on 27 September before making his triumphal entry into Mexico City as head of the new government. He became president of the Regency of the Mexican Empire. The official ideology, not accepted by some emerging political elements, was that this represented the re-establishment of the original Mexican empire subjugated by Spain in 1521.

In Yucatán the re-establishment of the constitution in 1820 had also provoked widespread enthusiasm among creole reformers and autonomists who controlled the elective city councils of Mérida and Campeche and the Provincial Deputation, and of a group of liberals called the Society of San Juan. In June 1820 they induced the octogenarian captain general, Miguel de Castro Araoz, in power since 1815, to resign in favour of Colonel Mariano Carrillo, a liberal and a Mason. Carrillo in turn supplanted the president of the Provincial Deputation with a fellow moderate constitutionalist royalist, Juan Rivas Vertiz. This led to open conflict with more radical reformers which ended with the arrival in January 1821 of the new captain general appointed by the Cortes, Juan María Echeverrí. As late as August 1821 Echeverrí could declare that most Yucatecans did not favour independence despite the advanced state of the Iturbide revolt in Mexico. Meanwhile, the powerful Provincial Deputation, ignoring repeated royal orders from Mexico City and from Spain, had taken steps to disband the tobacco monopoly and to maintain the trade, largely illicit, that had existed during the last six years with Jamaica. Owing to their sense of having accomplished something under the Cortes regime, the Yucatecans remained passive observers of the last phase of the Iturbide revolt. After communication with Mexico City had been broken, they consulted the royal authorities in Guatemala City on civil, judicial, and fiscal matters. Iturbide could not be so easily dismissed, however, and in August a part of the Army of the Three Guarantees was warmly welcomed by the population of Tabasco. After receipt of the news that O'Donojú had signed the Treaty of Córdoba, the Provincial Deputation proposed a meeting of leading figures in Mérida on 15 September. This meeting proclaimed Yucatán independent of Spain, although the Spanish commander, Echeverrí, was retained as chief executive; the government of Iturbide would be recognized if it guaranteed respect for the civil liberties established under the Spanish constitution. With Mexico's promise (in the Plan of Iguala) that it would abide by the Spanish constitution until a Mexican constitution could be written, Yucatán in November joined the independent Mexican Empire, in which it would function as a leading proponent of a federalist constitution, and the peninsular administrators, including Captain General Echeverrí, now quietly departed. In Yucatán, as in Mexico itself, the vital element was support for the Constitution of Cádiz and Iturbide's guarantee of it.

The situation of Central America was remarkably similar, but somewhat more complex. There the re-establishment of the constitution in 1820 provoked an instant revival of constitutionalism as well as the formulation of the first open political factions. The more radical faction was that composed of the Aycinena oligarchy and middle-class elements, an alliance first born out of opposition to the government of Bustamante. It found its voice in the newspaper *El Editor Constitucional*, edited by Pedro Molina. The other, more moderate faction, was represented by José Cecilio del Valle and the newspaper to which he frequently contributed, *El Amigo de la Patria*. The struggle revolved around the issue of free trade, which the most powerful creole merchants favoured and the less well-off merchants opposed. Foreign merchandise, especially British textiles, undercut domestic manufactures produced by small artisans and sold by small retailers. The elections for the *cabildo* of Guatemala City and the Provincial Deputation, held at the end of 1820, were heatedly contested, though in the final analysis neither side carried the day. Furthermore, the full implementation of the constitution served to exacerbate Central American regionalism; Madrid's agreement in May 1821 to permit the establishment of a Provincial Deputation in each intendancy reawakened aspirations for home rule in, for example, Honduras and Chiapas. As in Mexico, Central Americans reacted negatively to the anti-clericalism of the Cortes (particularly with regard to suppression of the Bethlemite order, which had been founded in Guatemala), and to the obvious discrimination of the Cortes toward American interests. In the last months before independence loyalty to Spain rapidly disintegrated.

In March 1821 Captain General Urrutia, owing to illness, delegated his authority to Gabino Gaínza, the army inspector general who had recently arrived from Chile. One month later news arrived of Iturbide's

Plan of Iguala, and Guatemala, like Yucatán, had to determine its stand on the issue. The question became unavoidable when Chiapas decided in late August to subscribe to the Plan, and in so doing permanently transferred its allegiance from Guatemala to Mexico. As in Yucatán, a meeting of leading authorities in the capital was called, and it took place on the same day as the Yucatecan meeting, 15 September 1821. While Molina had actively urged acceptance of independence, the newspaper of Valle had clung to a loyalist position. The meeting was extremely agitated, but several moderates reluctantly accepted independence as an alternative to possible civil war. A declaration of independence, written by Valle, was adopted by twenty-three votes to seven. As in Yucatán, the government remained virtually the same, with the incumbent Spanish official, Gaínza, remaining as chief executive. And as in Mexico and Yucatán, independence was to be based on the precepts of the Constitution of 1812.

The other provinces of Central America were forced by Guatemala City's action to make their own decisions on the question of independence and, just as significantly, on whether they were to remain part of Guatemala or seek total separation. Juntas were chosen to determine what course of action to follow. In San Salvador, where fear of annexation by either Mexico or Guatemala was widespread, the junta, led by liberals José Matías Delgado and Manuel José de Arce, proclaimed on 29 September the independence of the intendancy of El Salvador. In Nicaragua, where similar fears existed, the Provincial Deputation in León proclaimed on 28 September its independence from both Spain and Guatemala. Nicaragua controlled Costa Rica as part of the intendancy, and assumed its declaration of independence applied there. Nonetheless, the Costa Rican town councils met individually and proclaimed independence from Spain, deposing the Spanish governor on 1 November. In Honduras, meanwhile, independence was declared but an open split occurred over whether to join Guatemala or Mexico, with the city of Tegucigalpa favouring Guatemala and the city of Comayagua favouring Mexico.

The confusion in Central America was resolved, at least temporarily, when in an attempt to sway the undecided to join the Mexican Empire, Iturbide threatened to send Mexican troops to Central America. Gabino Gaínza, who had earlier opposed the annexation of Central America by Mexico, now invited the Central American towns to hold open town council meetings (*cabildos abiertos*) to decide upon the incorporation of the entire former kingdom of Guatemala into the Mexican Empire. Although the voting was often irregular, there was a substantial majority, led by conservatives and leading merchants such as Mariano Aycinena and his nephew, Juan José, marqués de Aycinena, Archbishop Ramón Casáus of Guatemala, and Bishop Nicolás García Jerez of Nicaragua, in favour of this move. On 29 December Guatemala City and Quezaltenango united with Mexico, and on 9 January 1822 Gaínza announced the union of all of Central America with Mexico. The union, however, was unacceptable to some Central Americans, notably Delgado and Arce in San Salvador. In June 1822 a small Mexican army under the command of Brigadier General Vicente Filísola arrived in Central America and in the first month of 1823 subdued El Salvador by force. Then the Mexican Empire itself collapsed.

Iturbide had functioned as chief executive and president of the Regency of the new Mexican Empire. After it became clear that Spain would not recognize Mexican independence, much less allow a member of the dynasty to assume the throne, Iturbide's election as emperor was engineered. The army declared his candidacy, and Congress, frightened (and without a quorum), chose him on 19 May 1822. He assumed the title Agustín I. Within a short period he had alienated most elements in the population, and, after he dismissed congress in October 1822, a revolt began under the leadership of two generals, Guadalupe Victoria (soon to be the first president of the republic) and Antonio López de Santa Anna (a future president many times over). By February 1823 the opposition had united in the Plan of Casa Mata, demanding a new congress to take over from the emperor and greater authority for the provincial governments. In March the emperor abdicated. After a year's sojourn in Italy and England, Iturbide returned to Mexico in July 1824 when he was taken prisoner and executed in the state of Tamaulipas. Iturbide's brief career as emperor of Mexico has largely served to cast a shadow over his reputation in Mexican historiography; it should not be forgotten, however, that it was his leadership and his compromise in the Plan of Iguala that made independence possible.

The overthrow of Iturbide ended the ties that had united Central America and Mexico for slightly more than a year. As he prepared to withdraw from Guatemala, General Filísola called on 29 March 1823 for the provinces to send deputies to a Central American congress. Of the former kingdom of Guatemala only Chiapas remained part of Mexico. On 1 July the remaining provinces proclaimed Central American independence under a provisional junta. In Mexico, the fall of Iturbide's empire led to the creation in 1824 of a federal republic with a new constitution partially modelled on the Spanish liberal constitution of 1812. With both Mexico and Central America abandoning centralism and establishing states' rights and regional self-government in federal republics, the long-sought objective of many regions, local autonomy, was at last achieved.

At the conclusion of the independence process Mexico and Central America showed the scars of the long struggle. Loss of life during the Wars of Independence has been estimated to be as high as 10 per cent, or six hundred thousand. Per capita income had fallen from 35–40 pesos in 1810 to 25–30 pesos in 1821; during the last years of the independence struggle there was even a decline in per capita food consumption. Mining production had fallen to less than a quarter, the result of the abandonment of mines and their consequent flooding or deterioration, the flight of capital, and the breakdown of the colonial systems of extraction, mercury supply and refining. Agricultural production had fallen to half of its former level, the result of the disruption of the countryside, the death or departure of *hacendados*, the disappearance of working capital and the destruction of farms, animals and machinery. Industrial output had fallen by two thirds. The continuation of outmoded Spanish laws restricting trade and the perpetuation of labour systems based on ethnic identity and neo-feudalism served to keep the economy backward and to widen the gap between the former viceroyalty and the rapidly developing countries of the North Atlantic. British and North American imports filled the void left by the disappearance of Spanish trade; Mexican and Central American manufactures were unable to compete. Exports – precious metals, cochineal, indigo, vanilla, cotton and hides – were at a value far below imports. The financial weakness of both Mexico and Central America ensured the failure of initial developmental projects. In Mexico the first of a succession of loans from British banking houses was negotiated in 1824. In Central America the first loan was contracted, also with a British banking company, in 1825; its object was chiefly to augment government revenues until a revised tax structure could become operable, but also to encourage the development of an inter-oceanic canal through Nicaragua. Later in 1825 the states of Costa Rica and Honduras attempted to negotiate their own loans with an English firm but the projects were vetoed by Guatemala City. Throughout both

Mexico and Central America, however, loss of confidence, insecurity and uncertainty militated against economic recovery. The rise of uncontrolled militarism, the explosion of regionalism unchecked by central authority, the spread of banditry and political violence – all these indirect effects of the independence struggle continued to haunt the region. The long-term social and economic problems could not be corrected amid the political instability and civil strife that existed for several decades to come. All the other problems the new states inherited – the flight of capital as Spaniards left the region, the disruption of mining, industry and agriculture, massive debts – these could, perhaps, have been solved had there been agreement on the political form the new states were to take. The achievement of Iturbide and the Plan of Iguala was immense – the termination of three centuries of Spanish rule after the failures of the Hidalgo and Morelos revolutions – but it was also limited, for Mexico and Central America now had to begin the process of remaking their own political, economic and social structures.

3

THE INDEPENDENCE OF SPANISH
SOUTH AMERICA

The crisis of the Spanish monarchy in 1808, which left the nation with no government of generally accepted legitimacy, could not help but have a profound impact on the American colonies from New Spain to the Río de la Plata. With hindsight it can be seen to have greatly accelerated those forces, already at work, which eventually produced the separation of the mainland colonies from Spain. At the time, however, outright independence appeared as one of only a number of possible responses, and it still had few proponents. Spanish Americans could accept the rule of Joseph Bonaparte. Alternatively, they could swear obedience either to the provisional authorities thrown up by the Spanish movement of national resistance against the French or else to Ferdinand VII's sister Carlota; the latter had earlier taken refuge in Rio de Janeiro with her husband, Dom João, prince regent of Portugal, and from there offered to rule temporarily on behalf of her brother. Or, again, they could establish native American juntas to rule in the name of the captive Ferdinand exactly as his Spanish provinces had done. In the short run this last alternative amounted to *de facto* autonomy within the framework of a common monarchy, while in the long run it was to prove a transitional stage to complete separation. Autonomy was nowhere sucessfully established before 1810, but that is not sufficient reason to take that year as the start of the independence movement; it is just that until 1810 the autonomists lost all their battles.

Among the collaborators of Joseph I in the mother country there were a number of Spanish Americans, such as the recent director of Madrid's Botanical Garden and future provisional vice-president of Gran Colombia, Francisco Antonio Zea. In the colonies, however, the kind of would-be reformers who sometimes welcomed the French connection in Spain itself were likely to be in the autonomist camp, and those who were looking only to advance their interests by backing an expected winner could hardly take for granted a Napoleonic victory on the American side of the water. There was no French army in the vicinity; instead there was the British navy. Moreover, the revulsion against things French that revolutionary excesses had done so much to spread among Spaniards, and which French intervention in Spain had only reaffirmed, was also felt in Spanish America. Hence Bonapartist intrigues made little headway: at most, certain higher officials briefly toyed with the idea of recognizing Joseph I. But they were always dissuaded by the adamant hostility of the colonial population and by the realization that tampering with dynastic legitimacy could easily endanger the subordination of the colonies to Spain and thus their own position. The most promising situation appeared to be in the Río de la Plata, where the earlier crisis of the British invasions (1806–7) had propelled an officer of French origin, Santiago Liniers, into a position of command as acting viceroy. Liniers was duly visited by a Napoleonic envoy in August 1808; there is no convincing evidence that he allowed himself to be recruited. The French themselves, in any case, soon recognized that Spanish America was a lost cause for Joseph Bonaparte and shifted to a policy of encouraging moves for independence, although the government in Paris was never in a position to do much about the evolving colonial situation.

The Río de la Plata also seemed to offer the best prospects for the Carlotist alternative, which in the end did not work out either. Carlota was in Rio, conveniently close to Buenos Aires, and Buenos Aires was one of the colonial centres most subject to political ferment in the last years of Spanish rule. The British invasions had demonstrated Spain's vulnerability and given to the creoles, who shouldered the main burden of defeating the attackers, a sharply increased sense of importance. Furthermore, as a maritime trading centre, Buenos Aires was open to external influences both intellectual and economic, and the fact that the exports of its immediate hinterland consisted of bulky pastoral commodities made both landed interests and merchant speculators all the more aware of the potential advantages of greater commercial freedom. For various reasons, in fact, there was growing sentiment that the Río de la Plata deserved a larger voice in controlling its affairs; and at first glance the presence of Ferdinand's sister in Brazil offered one way to bring this about. By accepting Carlota's claim to rule the Spanish colonies, a faction of creole business and professional men that included such future leaders of the independence struggle as Manuel Belgrano and Juan José Castelli hoped to fashion an enlightened New World monarchy in which they and others like them might enjoy a real measure of power. Elsewhere, too, Carlota had scattered sympathizers. Yet not even in Buenos Aires did *carlotismo* ever represent more than a further complication in an already confused situation. For one thing, its potential appeal was blunted by fear that Carlota herself was somehow serving as an agent of the Portuguese. For another, Carlota was personally irascible and politically absolutist, whereas her creole supporters were hoping for a moderate and mildly reformist new order. As this inherent contradiction gradually became clear, enthusiasm for her dwindled.

The Carlotist solution could appeal to a band of creole reformists in Buenos Aires only because the existing royal bureaucracy there chose to ignore her theoretically quite respectable pretensions and to give allegiance directly to those other self-appointed inheritors of Ferdinand's mantle who still maintained a precarious foothold in free Spain. By the end of 1808, this meant the *Junta Central* established at Seville. Its claim to rule on a basis of popular sovereignty was in truth revolutionary, even if buttressed with medieval precedents, and would later receive the flattery of imitation on the part of no less revolutionary juntas in the American colonies. But at least it was established in the mother country. Indeed, to accept its authority entailed relatively little disruption in habitual channels of command, and that advantage, combined with the very real enthusiasm aroused by its leadership of the fight against the French, assured it the allegiance of virtually all high officials in the colonies and of the great bulk of *peninsulares*, whether or not they held official position. It could also count on the instinctive loyalty of a large part of the native-born colonial population. Its claim to rule overseas was challenged, however, by others who argued that the American provinces had as much right as the Spanish to create governing bodies in the current emergency – a thesis which found adherents everywhere, although their number and importance varied widely.

The Río de la Plata was the scene of two early, though untypical, moves to create juntas. The governing junta established in Montevideo in September 1808 was headed by the Spanish governor, and its purpose was to withdraw what is now Uruguay from the control not of the junta in Seville but from that of Viceroy Liniers, whom its sponsors accused of Bonapartist leanings. And it dissolved itself as soon as Liniers was replaced, from Seville, by a trustworthy peninsular Spaniard, Baltasar

Hidalgo de Cisneros. While it lasted, the Montevideo junta enjoyed wide local support, mainly because it appealed to feelings of political and commercial rivalry with Buenos Aires.

The attempt to create a junta in Buenos Aires itself on 1 January 1809 was likewise directed against Liniers. One of the prime movers was Martín de Álzaga, the wealthy peninsular merchant who had rallied the *cabildo* against the British invasions and who still led an important faction in local politics. It was a faction identified mainly with the Spanish-born but at the time included such noteworthy creoles as Mariano Moreno, the lawyer who later led the more radical wing of the revolution in the Río de la Plata. Though Álzaga himself was accused even of republicanism by his enemies, the one wholly clear aim of his group was to get rid of Liniers, whether for personal reasons, on suspicion of disloyalty, or to open the way for further political innovations. The attempted coup was thwarted rather easily, since Liniers retained the support of the viceregal bureaucracy and of the creole militia, which was satisfied with the position it had already attained under the aegis of the viceroy. The losers had, however, the satisfaction later in the year of seeing Liniers peacefully step down in favour of the new viceroy, Cisneros. And Cisneros proved to be a prudent and flexible administrator – as he demonstrated in November 1809 by gracefully yielding to the demand to open the port of Buenos Aires to trade with Spain's current ally, Britain.

A less ambiguous, but also unsuccessful, attempt to set up a governing junta had occurred in 1808 in Caracas, capital of the captaincy-general of Venezuela. As in Buenos Aires, there were Spanish-controlled merchant houses oriented to trade with Cadiz and consequently opposed to liberalization of trade. In Venezuela, however, the weight of local influence and opinion was even more decisively in favour of freedom to trade with the outside world. Here the dominant element of society was a 'commercial and agrarian bourgeoisie' – to use the phrase of Germán Carrera Damas[1] – whose leading members were popularly known as *mantuanos*. Within this 'bourgeoisie' there was no absolute functional separation between landowners and merchants. In either capacity, or in both, these were people who depended on the production and export of cacao and other plantation crops, and they were perfectly aware that the Spanish commercial system, despite all temporary exceptions and loopholes, was an impediment to continued growth and prosperity. At the

[1] Germán Carrera Damas, *La crisis de la sociedad colonial* (Caracas, 1976), 80.

same time, again like Buenos Aires, Caracas and the plantation belt of north-central Venezuela lay within easy reach of all manner of external influences, both from Europe and (in this case) from the non-Spanish West Indies and the United States.

Venezuela had even suffered its own invasion of 1806, only the invader was not a foreign power but the Venezuelan-born conspirator and revolutionary agitator, Francisco de Miranda. At that time both *mantuanos* and the population at large rallied to the side of the Spanish authorities against Miranda, whose call for outright independence still appeared too radical. The fear of inadvertently setting off a Haitian-style uprising among slaves and free *pardos*, who together amounted to over half the population of Venezuela, was a particular reason for caution among upper-class creoles. At the same time, fear of the masses was an important reason for not leaving the maintenance of order to the appointed servants of a weakening and seemingly unreliable Spanish government, which had already on various occasions shown itself too willing to encourage the aspirations of the *pardos*.

The Spanish events of 1808 thus caused a profound impression – of alarm and opportunity – in Caracas. The acting captain-general, Juan de Casas, was apparently prepared to consider even the Bonapartist alternative, until he observed the outburst of popular hostility that greeted the arrival of a French mission in Venezuela. At one point he indicated that he might support the setting up of a provisional junta of government in Caracas; but he soon decided that he did not need to go so far. Thus, when the establishment of a junta was formally proposed in November 1808, by a distinguished group of petitioners which included two counts and one marquis, Casas answered with a wave of arrests and confinements. Nobody was severely punished, but one feature of the captain-general's crackdown was a portent of things to come: before moving against *mantuano* malcontents, he was careful to assure himself of support among the *pardos* and to have the *pardo* militia units on alert. Though this did not put an end to scheming among the creoles, the Spanish authorities in Venezuela managed to survive all other threats until April 1810.

Juntistas in Upper Peru (present day Bolivia) had better luck, at least temporarily. In the colonial capital of Chuquisaca a junta of sorts was in fact established in May 1809, and another followed at La Paz not quite two months later. The first of these, to be sure, was the immediate outgrowth of wrangling within the colonial bureaucracy, between the president of Charcas, who had shown interest in, though he did not formally embrace, the *carlotista* option, and the judges of the *audiencia*. The individuals involved were *peninsulares*, fundamentally intent on preserving the traditional relationship between the colonies and Spain, but unable to agree on how best to achieve it. The climax came on 25 and 26 May 1809, when the *audiencia* deposed the president and assumed his powers, pledging due allegiance to Ferdinand in the process. This was not quite the same as setting up a governing junta composed of natives of the region, but the move enjoyed full support from a small band of disaffected professional men – including the Argentine, Bernardo de Monteagudo, who eventually emerged as the right-hand man of the Liberator San Martín – whose underlying objective was some form of American autonomy. These men had, in fact, done what they could to precipitate the crisis, and they now set out to spread the climate of agitation throughout the rest of Upper Peru.

The most striking repercussions were in La Paz, where on 16 July the municipal *cabildo* deposed the local intendant and, for good measure, the bishop, accusing both men of vague treacheries against Ferdinand VII. Shortly afterwards a *junta tuitiva* emerged in control, under the presidency of the *mestizo* and would-be lawyer, Pedro Domingo Murillo. It issued a proclamation that called for a 'new system of government' based on strictly American interests, while bemoaning the past oppression of 'these unfortunate colonies acquired without the least title and kept with the greatest injustice and tyranny'.[2] There was nothing in this or other official documents of the La Paz revolution that unequivocally ruled out a voluntary allegiance to the conveniently captive Ferdinand, but the demand for effective self-government was militantly stated and was not circumscribed, by implication or otherwise, to one passing emergency. In all this the revolutionaries had somewhat exceeded the bounds of discretion. No less unsettling were their call for redress of Indian grievances and their open appeal for the support of the Indian and *mestizo* masses. That appeal struck a number of responsive chords, not all of them favourable to the revolution. Creoles remembered the revolt of Túpac Amaru, led in Upper Peru by Túpac Catari, and most of them were far from eager to run the risk of the same thing happening again.

The seeming radicalism of the La Paz junta not only led to dissension among its initial adherents but intensified the opposition of others who had never sympathized with it. The most effective opposition of all,

2 Carlos Urquizo Sossa (ed.), *Proclama de la junta tuitiva de 1809: esclarecimiento para la historia* (La Paz, 1976), 144–5.

however, came from an external source, the president of Cuzco, José Manuel de Goyeneche. Himself Peruvian-born, Goyeneche was fully committed to the cause of the Spanish central junta, as was the ultra-conservative and exceptionally able viceroy of Peru, José Fernando de Abascal y Sousa. Neither in Cuzco nor in the rest of Peru was there as yet any serious challenge to the political status quo as represented by continued obedience to whatever authorities were ruling in Ferdinand's name in Spain itself. There had been some previous stirrings of discontent and even incipient Peruvian nationalism among the creole intelligentsia, but such sentiments were offset by the fear, as in Upper Peru, of reawakening Indian unrest and by the inherent conservatism of a creole elite whose past glories had been directly related to the privileged situation Peru enjoyed within the Spanish imperial system. Although Peru had lost ground both politically and economically as a result of the imperial reforms and reorganisation of the second half of the eighteenth century, it did not necessarily follow that further changes would be for the better. The colony's relative stagnation made the upper class of Lima, in particular, all the more dependent on the jobs and favours offered by the Spanish state and all the more cautious as a result. As for the Indians, who were a clear majority of the population, they felt the same distrust for the creoles that the creoles felt towards them, and their natural leaders had been mostly eliminated, or intimidated, or simply co-opted. Hence the higher authorities could give full attention to the repression of outbreaks of disorder in neighbouring jurisdictions. It was not long before Goyeneche, with the vigorous support of Viceroy Abascal, moved against La Paz at the head of a force that was small in size but disciplined and well equipped. Its mere approach was sufficient in October 1810 to demoralize the revolutionaries, who were already quarrelling among themselves. There was no need for much fighting. The ringleaders were captured and duly punished; Murillo was one of those put to death. In Chuquisaca, meanwhile, the *audiencia* had consolidated its position, but it was soon having second thoughts and agreed to submit to a new president of Charcas provisionally appointed by Viceroy Cisneros at Buenos Aires.

Even before the end of the La Paz revolution another had broken out in Quito, where the aims of the revolutionaries were less radical than in La Paz but also less ambiguous than in Chuquisaca. The roots of what happened went back to December 1808, when a number of *quiteños* led by the Marquis of Selva Alegre – wealthy landowner and erstwhile patron of

Ecuador's leading intellectual 'precursor' of independence, Eugenio
Espejo – met to plan a response to the Napoleonic conquest of Spain.
They came under suspicion, were arrested, then released for lack of
conclusive evidence. On 10 August 1809, having won over the garrison,
the plotters arrested the president of Quito, Count of Ruiz de Castilla,
and established a governing junta whose president was Selva Alegre,
even though he does not appear to have taken part in the final preparations. Its vice-president was the bishop of Quito, who happened to be a
native of New Granada. Other creole notables gave their endorsement to
the junta, which swore to protect the one true religion and the rights of
the one legitimate monarch, Ferdinand VII.

There is no indication whatever that the marquis, the bishop, or other
leading figures of the Quito nobility and clergy were insincere in
professing allegiance to Ferdinand. Indeed Quito, with a rather preten-
tious upper class that was separated from the Indian and *mestizo* masses
by a deep social gulf and geographically isolated from the centres of new
intellectual currents, seems an unlikely place to have taken the lead in
revolutionary activity of any sort. Yet the very pretentiousness of the
Quito aristocracy, among whom Selva Alegre was far from alone in
holding a Spanish title, presumably made them conscious of their ability
and right to take a larger role in managing their affairs. And the economic
decline of the Ecuadorian highlands, reflecting among other things the
unfavourable effect on local textile manufacturing of the Bourbon
monarchy's commercial reforms, served to promote dissatisfaction.
Under such circumstances the formula offered by the junta – to transfer
power into native hands with minimal disturbance of the traditional
order – had a certain logic in its favour.

Among those leaders of the Quito rebellion who were less socially
prominent but who did most of the actual work, there were some with
more far-reaching, possibly republican, objectives in mind. Hence the
movement contained within itself the potential seeds of tension comparable to that seen in La Paz. Even more serious, and again as in Upper
Peru, there was no lack of outside opposition. The junta claimed
sovereignty over the entire presidency of Quito, but the provinces of
Cuenca and Guayaquil, normally jealous of the capital in any event and
firmly under the control of their peninsular governors, refused to accede.
Naturally Viceroy Abascal of Peru was no more disposed to tolerate the
Quito junta than the one in La Paz, and Viceroy Antonio Amar y Borbón
of New Granada, within whose jurisdiction Quito lay, also made
threatening noises.

Viceroy Amar, however, had first to deal with a demand for setting up a junta in his own capital of Bogotá,[3] which Quito had naturally invited to follow its example. Though in the end he succeeded in heading off the move, he was distracted too long to take effective action against Quito. The same was not true of Abascal, but the counter-revolutionary forces he dispatched never had to do any serious fighting. In October 1809, well before they reached the city itself, the Quito junta simply collapsed, and Ruiz de Castilla resumed his position as president. Selva Alegre, it should be noted, had resigned even earlier, and he and various other aristocratic leaders have been accused by one school of historians of outright disloyalty to the movement they led. That charge remains unproven; but timidity and a lack of true revolutionary commitment were understandably all too evident.[4]

The defeat of the La Paz and Quito juntas did not solve the problem created by the temporary vacancy of the throne. But once again it was events in Spain that brought matters to a head. A succession of French victories eliminated most centres of Spanish national resistance, including Seville. The central junta retreated to Cadiz, where at the end of January 1810 it dissolved itself, giving way to a Council of Regency, one of whose tasks would be to prepare for the opening of a Cortes representing the entire Spanish empire. The change from junta to council made little difference, except for the fact that there was need for an act of recognition of the new body from authorities in the New World, which automatically raised again the question of the colonies' status. Even more important, there seemed now better reason than ever for doubting that full national independence and political stability could be re-established in Spain in the foreseeable future. The result was a new eagerness among creoles to take matters into their hands and a mood of uncertainty among defenders of the existing system.

The first important break came in Caracas, not so much because of the pre-existing climate of agitation there (though another 'conspiracy' had been discovered just a few weeks earlier) as because Venezuela was closest of the mainland colonies to Europe and thus the first to hear the news of developments in Spain. A group of creole notables reacted on 19 April 1810 by deposing the captain-general and establishing a junta in his

[3] Although the colonial name was Santa Fe, this was transformed during the independence period to Santa Fé de Bogotá and ultimately just Bogotá. For convenience, the final designation is used here throughout.

[4] See, for example, Michael T. Hamerly, 'Selva Alegre, president of the quiteña junta of 1809: traitor or patriot?', *Hispanic American Historical Review*, 48/4 (1968), 642–53, and sources cited therein.

place. It was to rule technically in the name of Ferdinand VII – a formula which the revolutionaries swore with varying degrees of sincerity to uphold – but it explicitly denied that the new Spanish Council of Regency could legitimately exercise authority over America. There was no overt opposition from civil or military officials on the spot, and outlying provincial capitals of the captaincy-general of Venezuela mostly followed suit with juntas of their own, semi-autonomous but accepting the general leadership of Caracas. The exceptions were Coro and Maracaibo in the west and Guayana in the east, which proposed to remain loyal to Cadiz. To many people at the far ends of Venezuela, rejecting the authority of Caracas was an added attraction of the loyalist option.

The events in Spain, and now Venezuela, had an unsettling effect on New Granada. Viceroy Amar quickly recognized the Council of Regency, but an important part of the creole population was more convinced than ever of the desirability of establishing American juntas. Because the capital was isolated in the Andean interior, it did not take the lead in the same way as Caracas had. Instead, the first step was taken at Cartagena on the coast, where on 22 May the *cabildo* named two men to share power with the provincial governor in what was at least a quasi-junta. Pamplona and Socorro formed juntas of their own in the first half of July, and Bogotá fell in line on 20 July 1810 with the creation of a governing junta of which Viceroy Amar himself, who this time had peacefully given in to creole pressure, was initially acclaimed president. Over the next few days, however, as all kinds of people took advantage of the change in regime to call for redress against unpopular officials and a number of these were imprisoned, doubts inevitably built up as to the viceroy's reliability. On 25 July he was removed from the junta, still in the name of allegiance to Ferdinand. The news from Bogotá, in turn, triggered off more agitation and the establishment of juntas in other parts of New Granada. And it helped bring matters to a head once more in Quito, where a new junta was installed on 22 September. The president of Quito, Ruiz de Castilla, was made head of it, and in that capacity he lasted considerably longer than Amar at Bogotá; but it also included such prominent creoles and surviving veterans of 1809 as the bishop of Quito and Selva Alegre.

At the other end of South America, the events in Spain produced another series of revolutionary responses. Most important of these was the 'May Revolution' in Buenos Aires, where Viceroy Cisneros reluctantly agreed to the holding of a *cabildo abierto* which on 22 May 1810 commissioned the *cabildo* itself to establish a junta. It did so two days later, making the viceroy its president. Before the junta could begin to function, however, protests broke out, orchestrated by a combination of creole militia leaders and members of the miscellaneous assortment of professional men who since 1808 or even earlier had seen in the crisis of the Spanish monarchy a golden opportunity to effect changes in the colony. Rather easily, these forces carried the day. Thus on 25 May a junta was formally installed which did not include the viceroy and was presided over by Colonel Cornelio Saavedra, a merchant of Upper Peruvian origin but long established in Buenos Aires, whose power base was to be found in the militia units formed to counter the British invasions of 1806–7. The junta proceeded to swear allegiance to Ferdinand though not the Council of Regency and to claim authority over the rest of the viceroyalty.

Much has been written concerning the extent to which the events leading to the establishment of the Buenos Aires junta reflected true currents of popular opinion. Those historians who depict the May Revolution as the work of a mere minority are no doubt correct, but they are belabouring what is obvious and was really inevitable. Most inhabitants of Buenos Aires took no part in any of the proceedings and were not consulted by those who did; nor can it be denied that many were opposed, indifferent, or hesitant to commit themselves. Nevertheless, as Tulio Halperín Donghi points out, the militia organizations that did take part involved a substantial portion of the city's active male population, and the revolution further evoked a positive response from broad popular sectors which ever since the British invasions had been indoctrinated to believe in the brilliant mission and capabilities of Buenos Aires.[5] More problematic was the attitude of the rest of the viceroyalty, where economic and cultural differences and assorted local rivalries, including rivalries with Buenos Aires, precluded any unanimous adherence to the new regime. The junta's call for recognition was eventually heeded by those parts of the viceroyalty that form the present Argentine Republic, though sometimes with hesitation or under compulsion. Montevideo, on the other hand, which in 1808 had set up its own junta in opposition to Buenos Aires, now professed to be satisfied with the Council of Regency and, again, commercial and political rivalry with the viceregal capital was a contributing factor. Paraguay also stood aside, not so much out of

---

[5] Tulio Halperín Donghi, *Politics, economics and society in Argentina in the revolutionary period* (Cambridge, 1975), 155–6, 169, and *passim*.

diehard Spanish loyalism as because of its own resentment of political and commercial subservience to Buenos Aires. And so too, at first, did Upper Peru, where the revolutionaries of 1809 had not yet recovered from Goyeneche's repression – if they were even still alive – and civil and military officials were on the alert to prevent new outbreaks.

Peru itself maintained its position as a bulwark of loyalty, expressed in a new round of declarations of support for whatever authorities were still holding on to some shred of legitimacy at home in Spain and in new *donativos* for Viceroy Abascal to use in the cause of imperial defence. But the captaincy-general of Chile did see fit, with some delay, to follow the example of Buenos Aires. Sparsely populated, isolated and characterized by a static agrarian society in which a few aristocratic families wielded near absolute influence, Chile had not been exactly in the forefront of political and intellectual debate. One of the few Chilean 'precursors' of independence, Fray Camilo Henríquez, later observed that only about six Chileans could read French books and not one could read English, with the result that 'liberal philosophical works were as unknown to them as geography and mathematics'.[6] But Henríquez no doubt exaggerated. And though the extent, or even existence, of serious discontent with Spanish commercial regulations in late colonial Chile is a source of disagreement among historians, there is no doubt that Chileans had been evolving at least a proto-national consciousness. Their first reaction to the Spanish crisis of 1808 had been one of outspoken loyalty to Ferdinand VII, but doubts concerning the advisability of continued subordination to authorities in Spain as against the setting up of a junta in Chile steadily increased and just as steadily heightened existing tensions between creoles and peninsular Spaniards. The *audiencia* sought to reduce tension somewhat in July 1810 by deposing the arbitrary and unpopular captain-general and replacing him with an elderly creole nobleman. The solution was only temporary, however. On 18 September a *cabildo abierto* in Santiago finally gave Chile, too, its own governing junta.

In the traditional historiography of Spanish American independence, the predominant view was that the juntas of 1810 and the movement that developed out of them were integral parts of the same revolutionary process in the western world that produced the Anglo-American Revolution of 1776 and the French Revolution of 1789. It was further assumed that the liberating ideas of the Enlightenment as well as the force of those

---

[6] Raúl Silva Castro (comp.), *Escritos políticos de Camilo Henríquez* (Santiago, 1960), 187.

two examples were necessary, if not quite sufficient, causes for all that happened. This interpretation has been strongly challenged by conservative writers who point out precedents for the ideology of the Spanish American patriots to be found in traditional Hispanic thought. Most frequently cited is the Jesuit Francisco Suárez (1548–1617), best known for his rejection of the divine right of kings and his thesis that civil power is derived from God by way of the people. Thus the right of the American population to set up its own governing bodies in response to the crisis of the Spanish monarchy could as well be justified by reference to Suárez as to Jefferson or Rousseau. In fact, the name of Suárez is conspicuous only by its omission from the propaganda of the revolutionaries. A prior familiarity with the teachings of his school may have facilitated the acceptance of later French and Anglo-Saxon thinkers, but the latter are the authorities cited in practice, alongside the inevitable Greeks and Romans, and admittedly, the replication of juridical arguments used in Spain itself to defend the establishment of a new government by popular initiative following the removal of Ferdinand.[7] The case for minimizing the influence of political ideology in general as a 'cause' of the events in Spanish America in favour of creole-peninsular rivalry, or internal and external economic pressures, is undoubtedly stronger. Nevertheless, ideas were weapons if nothing else, and in that respect the choice of weaponry provided not a few links between the Spanish American revolution and the emerging liberal-democratic currents of western Europe and the United States.

With the Spanish government of national resistance against the French, the creole juntas of 1810 shared not only many of the arguments that served to justify their existence but a common profession of loyalty to Ferdinand VII. Whether sincere or not in that profession, however, the juntas could expect no co-operation either from the authorities in Spain or from loyalist officials still holding command in America. The former were not in a position to do much about the new crop of juntas for the present; the latter sometimes were. At the same time, it is worth noting at the outset that even though the French invasion of Spain had given creole revolutionaries their chance, the international situation offered no hope of outright intervention by foreign powers on their

---

[7] For frequency of authorities cited, cf. Juan Angel Farini, *Gaceta de Buenos Aires 1810–1821: índice general* (Buenos Aires, 1963), and José Ignacio Bohórquez Colorado, 'Indice de la "Gaceta de Colombia"', in *Gaceta de Colombia*, facsimile edn (Banco de la República, Bogotá, 5 vols., 1973–5), v.

behalf such as occurred in the case of the American Revolution. The new governments did evoke considerable sympathy abroad, particularly in the United States, which viewed any movement toward Spanish American autonomy as a flattering imitation of their own example. Even so, sympathy could vary greatly in intensity, and did not in any case automatically lead to action.

In Anglo-America, a bourgeois and Protestant public long exposed to the anti-Spanish Black Legend was somewhat sceptical about developments in Spanish America, and its concrete expectations were limited. As John Adams once observed, the notion that free governments could take root among South Americans was as absurd as to try 'to establish democracies among the birds, beasts and fishes'.[8] Obviously, that was no reason to wish the continuation of the Spanish monarchy which bore a great part of the responsibility for the lack of civic virtue among its subjects; and in due course many Anglo-American spokesmen would be caught up in a spirit of positive enthusiasm for the Spanish American cause. Others would sell supplies or offer services. Official policy, on the other hand, remained cautiously neutral, which meant that even private activities in behalf of the revolutionaries were subject to legal restrictions and intermittent crackdowns. After all, in 1810 the United States was engaged in a bitter controversy with Great Britain, over neutral rights among other issues, and when this led to war in 1812 the government in Washington was even less inclined to abandon neutrality in Spanish America. Or rather, it was only inclined to meddle along its southern and western borders, where its own citizens were encroaching on Spanish territory. The hope of eventually acquiring Florida and Texas by negotiation became a further reason for avoiding overt hostilities with Spain.

In Europe, mainly preoccupied with the wars of Napoleon, the only possible source of assistance to the revolutionaries was Great Britain; and even there conditions were not ideal. Diehard Tories flatly deplored what was happening in Spanish America, and unqualified sympathy was found mainly among radical liberals and some commercial circles. Official policy was again ambivalent. Any loosening of ties between the colonies and Spain enhanced the opportunities for direct British trade with Spanish America, but Spain was an ally against Napoleon in Europe. Moreover, the idea of revolution was not to be encouraged. The

---

[8] *The works of John Adams, second president of the United States*, Charles Francis Adams (comp.), (10 vols., Boston, Mass., 1856), x, 145.

perfect solution, therefore, from the British standpoint, was *de facto* independence for Spanish America within a loose framework of allegiance to the Spanish monarchy. Thus, while merchants with the full knowledge and encouragement of the British government set out to trade with any ports in revolutionary hands, official agents discreetly advised the Spanish Americans against severing all ties with the mother country. The British balanced this advice to the rebels by urging Spain to adopt a conciliatory approach, and almost from the start they offered formal mediation to end the conflict.

The first of the revolutionary governments established in 1810 to face a major challenge was that in Venezuela, where throughout the independence period the struggle was to be waged with greater intensity than in any other area of Spanish America. One reason for this was purely geographic. The nearest of the continental colonies to Spain and directly facing the Spanish Antilles, Venezuela was dangerously exposed to attack. The fact that New Granada to the west was largely in patriot hands gave some protection, and New Granada helped the Venezuelan insurgents recover from their first crushing defeat. The second collapse of Venezuela, however, paved the way for the reconquest of New Granada itself.

One factor which helped precipitate large-scale conflict in Venezuela was the rapid evolution of the revolutionary movement, the first in Spanish America to come out in favour of complete independence. The original Caracas junta made no move to throw off the 'mask of Ferdinand', but it did send missions to Great Britain and the United States to state its case and seek support. It also took such immediately desirable steps as opening the ports to friendly and neutral shipping, prohibiting the slave trade and ending the *alcabala* on basic foodstuffs. It thereby sought to please simultaneously exporters and importers, the British and the popular masses, but its own social orientation was made clear by the terms on which it called for the election of a first Venezuelan congress. Only adult males who were independently employed or who owned property worth at least 2000 pesos could exercise the franchise, and this automatically excluded the vast majority.

Before the congress met (in March 1811), the revolution spawned another deliberative body – the Patriotic Society of Caracas, which gathered together the more militant wing of the 'commercial and agrarian bourgeoisie' as well as token representatives of other social elements, even *pardos*. It quickly became a forum for those like the young Simón Bolívar – one of the wealthiest cacao planters – who had no confidence in Spain's capacity to make changes in her colonial system, even in the seemingly unlikely event that Napoleon should be defeated. This viewpoint (and the Patriotic Society) acquired an additional spokesman when the arch-conspirator Miranda returned home from England in December 1810. Miranda's arrival awakened misgivings among the more moderate creoles, but in fact the idea of full independence made steady progress and was formally declared by congress on 5 July 1811.

The congress next proceeded to draft the liberal constitution of Venezuela's 'First Republic', officially promulgated in December of the same year. A conspicuous feature was its federalist framework, whereby the provinces into which the former Venezuelan colony was subdivided retained authority over their internal affairs but joined together in a federation for handling matters of common interest. In Bolívar's subsequent critique of this constitution federalism was one of the impractical theories that certain 'benevolent visionaries', building 'fantastic republics in their imagination',[9] sought to impose on a country not prepared for them and thereby brought it to the edge of ruin. In reality, the republic that chiefly inspired the constitution-makers was neither fantastic nor imaginary; it was the United States, which Bolívar, too, admired, but because of cultural and historical differences did not consider a proper model for Venezuela. Nor did Miranda wish to follow it in this respect. Both men preferred a more centralized state. However, it was not merely the example of the United States that caused a majority of deputies to vote for federalism. After all, Venezuela, as a political unit of approximately its present size and shape, had only come into existence with the creation of the captaincy-general in 1777, and there had not yet been time for Caracas to overcome the strong particularist tendencies of the other provinces. Moreover, real regional differences in social structure, economy and ethnic composition – between, for example, the slave-worked tropical plantation belt around Caracas, the thinly occupied open range of the Orinoco basin and the western highlands, many of whose closest ties were with Andean New Granada – made some form of federalism intrinsically no more artificial than a unitary structure.

The constitution of 1811 likewise granted legal equality to all men regardless of race, a move that aroused considerable debate but seemed

[9] Simón Bolívar, *Selected writings*, Vicente Lecuna (comp.), and Harold A. Bierck, Jr. (ed.) (2 vols, New York, 1951), I, 19.

an inescapable corollary of the political doctrines to which the founding fathers gave at least lip service. It was expected to please the *pardos*, and it scarcely endangered the rule of the creole elite when the same constitution continued strict occupational and property qualifications for voting. The reforming impulse of the Venezuelan congress was also reflected in the constitutional article which indiscreetly stripped the clergy and the military of their *fueros*. Religious toleration was still rejected, either as objectionable in principle or merely premature, but it was openly discussed, and that in itself had an unsettling effect.

Indeed there were in Venezuela many, native-born as well as European, who felt things had gone much too far. As early as July–August 1811 a serious counter-revolution occurred in Valencia. It was put down, but with difficulty, and the new regime remained incapable of decisive action against the loyalist strongholds farther west in Maracaibo and Coro. In March 1812, following the arrival of reinforcements from Spanish-held Puerto Rico, a small army under the Canarian naval captain, Domingo de Monteverde, began moving from Coro against patriot-held territory. Before Monteverde had advanced very far, he was significantly aided by the hand of nature: on 26 March an earthquake destroyed much of Caracas and other republican-held cities, but barely touched areas loyal to the king. The lesson as to divine preference was clear, and the effect on patriot morale can be imagined. Moreover, the disaster caused economic losses and spread disorganization behind patriot lines.

Continuing social and racial tensions contributed to an increasingly bleak picture. The abolition of the slave trade and the granting of formal equality to free *pardos* made little difference to the structure of society. And the creole upper class, who by virtue of the revolution had acquired a virtual monopoly of political power, used it to defend their interests. Slavery persisted, and runaway slaves were hunted down. A set of ordinances for the *llanos* were drafted which aimed to extend the system of private ownership over both rangeland and wild or half-wild herds at the expense of the undisciplined and largely nonwhite *llaneros*, who would be reduced to the status of a regimented peon class. The *llaneros* were receptive to the call of royalist guerrilla leaders, while elsewhere in Venezuela bands of slaves rose up against their masters in the name of the king.

The appointment of Miranda as supreme commander with dictatorial powers on 23 April 1812 was not enough to stem the tide. He did have a

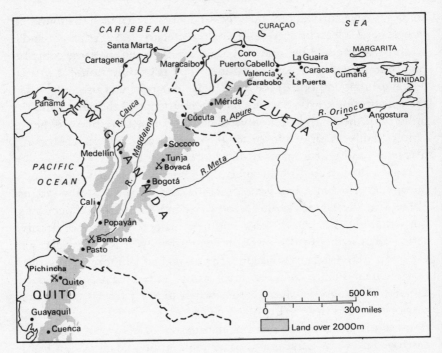

The wars of independence in Spanish South America: the northern theatre

professional military background, it is true, but lack of such qualifications was not the real problem, and he was personally distrusted by many. Monteverde continued to advance, and on 6 July, following an uprising by royalist prisoners, Simón Bolívar was forced to abandon the key fortress of Puerto Cabello. Miranda capitulated on 25 July. He was then prevented from making a safe getaway by a group of his former subordinates, Bolívar among them, who suspected his motives in making the surrender. Imprisoned by Monteverde despite the terms of his surrender, Miranda was shipped off to a Spanish dungeon, where he died in 1816.

Bolívar himself by the end of 1812 was in New Granada, where what Colombian historians once called the *Patria Boba*, or Foolish Fatherland, was in full swing. Its presumed 'foolishness' consisted in large part of an extreme case of internal disunity. In New Granada both difficulties of communication and the social and cultural contrasts between regions were even sharper than in Venezuela, and the capital itself – the smallest and least impressive of the viceregal seats of government – was accessible from the coast only by means of an excruciatingly uncomfortable journey up the Magdalena River and then over Andean trails. In the upland areas adjoining Bogotá, large landed estates alternated with *minifundios* and with the surviving *resguardos*, or communal holdings of Indian villages, which were hard pressed to maintain their integrity against the encroachments of creoles and *mestizos*. Socorro in the north east was still a centre of important craft industries, textiles in particular, and the north western province of Antioquia, as well as the Pacific lowlands, produced the gold that was New Granada's sole important export. Panama, though politically subordinate to New Granada, had almost no contacts with the other provinces, and Cartagena, which served as commercial link between the interior and the outside world, was itself a cultural world apart with a small white upper class presiding over a majority which had a significant Afro-Caribbean component.

Political and other rivalries among the provinces were such that only in November 1811 was it possible to create the United Provinces of New Granada. This was an even weaker federal union than the Venezuelan. Even worse, not all the provinces deigned to join. The most important to hold out was Bogotá itself, now the nucleus of the self-styled State of Cundinamarca. At its head, with semi-dictatorial powers, was the 'precursor', Antonio Nariño, who at the beginning of the independence struggle had been in jail at Cartagena but who eventually returned to his native Bogotá and there took over the government of Cundinamarca. Nariño demanded a unitary regime for New Granada as the only way to put the revolutionary cause on a firm military and political footing. He kept Cundinamarca out of the United Provinces on the ground that their form of union was too weak, thereby weakening it further. Indeed early in 1812 the antagonism between Cundinamarca and the United Provinces degenerated into armed hostilities, which continued on and off until near the end of the *Patria Boba*.

Other regions of New Granada would have none of either faction and gave their loyalty to the Council of Regency in Spain. One of these was Panama, which remained on the sidelines of the struggle until Lima itself declared for independence more than a decade later. Another was Santa Marta, a traditional rival of the patriot-controlled Cartagena, which briefly joined the revolution in 1810, but changed sides before the year was out. Yet another was Pasto in the far south, culturally and economically isolated in its mountain fastness and fanatically steeped in its own variety of popular Catholicism. Popayán, to the north of Pasto, was a disputed area that swung back and forth between loyalist and revolutionary forces. It was in the hope of rolling back one enemy occupation of Popayán and continuing on to Pasto that Nariño, having forged a temporary alliance with the United Provinces, set forth from Bogotá with a small army in September 1813. He retook Popayán but was himself captured not far from his ultimate destination. (Shipped off to a Spanish prison like Miranda, Nariño did live to come home.) Military operations for and against the revolution were mostly limited to these or other regional theatres and were indecisive. Certainly they never distracted the patriots from their own quarrels for very long.

Though New Granada failed to attain organizational unity, its provinces ultimately declared outright independence, albeit in piecemeal fashion. Cartagena led the way on 11 November 1811. Having the one major port, Cartagena also took responsibility for welcoming non-Spanish commerce on a regular basis and abolishing the slave trade. It similarly abolished the Inquisition, for which it had served as one of the three main colonial headquarters. A number of provinces ordered the distribution of the *resguardos* among individual Indians. Though ostensibly designed to give Indians the benefit of private landownership the liquidation of the *resguardos* obviously facilitated their eventual acquisition by non-Indians. It was just as well for the Indians that the new authorities had no real opportunity to implement the measure. In 1814 Antioquia adopted a law of free birth, granting legal freedom to any child born henceforth of a slave mother. This went beyond anything Venezuela had done and in a province whose slave population was scarcely negligible, although it is true that the profitability of slavery in Antioquia's gold mining industry had been on the decline.[10] Notwithstanding this anti-slavery legislation it is clear the social interests represented by the revolutionary leadership in New Granada were generally similar to those behind the Venezuelan First Republic. If no outburst of social and racial conflict occurred to threaten the revolution in New Granada, it was in large part because underlying tensions had not been brought to a head by a process of rapid socio-economic change as in late colonial Venezuela, and because the fitful nature of the independence struggle gave less room for popular participation.

In Venezuela it appeared for a short time as if Monteverde might

---

[10] Alvaro López Toro, *Migración y cambio social en Antioquia durante el siglo diez y nueve* (Bogotá, 1970), 29–30.

succeed in restoring the colonial regime on a solid foundation. But he combined conciliation and retribution in a way that neither destroyed Spain's enemies nor effectively won them over. Typical in this respect is the treatment accorded Simón Bolívar: his estates were sequestered along with numerous others, but he was given his freedom and allowed to leave the colony. Monteverde further antagonized many of Spain's own supporters by his refusal to give more than token acceptance to the Constitution of 1812, adopted by the Cortes of Cádiz and intended to serve as a basis for reuniting European and American Spaniards under a liberal constitutional monarchy, as well as by his tendency to surround himself with nondescript shopkeepers and ex-shopkeepers, particularly Canary Islanders like himself.

Prospects for the revolution started to improve again in January 1813, when Santiago Mariño, who had earlier taken refuge in Trinidad, invaded and established a foothold in eastern Venezuela. A few months later, having obtained the help of the United Provinces of New Granada, Bolívar launched another attack from the west and in the so-called *Campaña Admirable* of 1813 moved quickly towards Caracas, which he entered in triumph on 6 August. In the middle of the campaign, at Trujillo on 15 June, Bolívar proclaimed his 'war to the death', which condemned all peninsular Spaniards who did not actively embrace the revolution while offering amnesty to creole royalists, even those who had taken up arms. Bolívar clearly hoped thereby to bring about a polarization between Spaniards and Americans that would compel the former either to throw in their lot with the insurgents or to abandon Venezuela and would commit the latter ever more firmly to independence. To what extent it accomplished these aims, over and above abetting further atrocities on both sides, is far from clear. But it did faithfully reflect Bolívar's tough-minded approach to the struggle in this new phase. As *de facto* chief of the revolution, thanks to the brilliant success of his *Campaña Admirable*, Bolívar refrained from reinstating the 1812 constitution. The Second Republic was to all intents and purposes a military dictatorship.

In this way Bolívar hoped to avoid the political weaknesses that he personally blamed for the fall of the First Republic. Social and racial conflicts had also contributed to the destruction of the First Republic, and these he did not solve. The revolutionary leadership was looked upon with continuing distrust by the *pardos*. Moreover, Bolívar's reconquest of Caracas still left various regional strongholds in royalist hands, which threatened the restored republic from its flanks while a revival of royalist guerrilla activity gnawed away within. The peninsular small merchant and ex-smuggler, José Tomás Boves, became the most successful of the guerrilla leaders, organizing *pardo* irregulars from whom he obtained absolute loyalty in part because he willingly tolerated the excesses of all kinds that they committed against other whites. He further inspired his men with the promise of creole patriots' property, although the attempt by some historians to portray Boves as pursuing a systematic policy of social levelling and even 'land reform' seems rather questionable.[11] What cannot be denied is the effectiveness of Boves and other leaders of popular royalist guerrillas. Though he too suffered defeats, Boves managed to crush the combined forces of Bolívar and Mariño at the battle of La Puerta on 15 June 1814, which in turn compelled the patriots once more to evacuate Caracas. Boves was killed later in the year during a mopping-up operation in eastern Venezuela, but the Second Republic was over.

For his part Bolívar again moved to New Granada, which had changed little since he left it in 1813. Royalist enclaves remained unsubdued; centralists and federalists were still feuding. By conquering Bogotá in December 1814, he helped settle the latter argument in favour of the federalists, not because he shared their principles but because he owed them a debt for the help the United Provinces had given in 1813. Commissioned next to do something about royalist Santa Marta, he became trapped instead in a quarrel with patriot Cartagena and not long afterwards left in disgust for the West Indies, to devise a new plan of action. He was therefore absent from New Granada when the final disaster occurred.

The defeat of Napoleon's armies in Spain in 1813 and the restoration of Ferdinand VII to the Spanish throne early the following year had meanwhile put Spain in a more favourable position to deal with the rebellion in the American colonies. Despite initial promises to the contrary, the king swept away the apparatus of constitutional monarchy which the Spanish liberals had installed in his absence and in its place he established as nearly absolute a regime as he was able. He and his ministers also solicited a wide range of proposals for the 'pacification of

11 Cf. Germán Carrera Damas, *Boves: aspectos socioeconómicos de su acción histórica* (2nd edn, Caracas, 1968), and Demetrio Ramos, 'Sobre un aspecto de las "tácticas" de Boves', *Boletín de la Academia Nacional de la Historia* (Caracas), 51/201 (1968), 69–73. While Carrera Damas refutes the land-reform thesis, Ramos presents it again in more limited form.

the Indies' which included suggestions for commercial or other concessions to the colonial population, more efficient military repression and
the enlistment of third-party (primarily British) mediation. From the
welter of conflicting ideas no truly coherent policy ever emerged. But
one major expeditionary force did set forth, early in 1815. Consisting of
over 10,000 well-equipped men, it was the largest ever sent by Spain in
the struggle to regain control of its American colonies. The experienced
professional soldier, Pablo Morillo, was its commander and Venezuela
the initial target. Venezuela had been chosen rather than the Río de la
Plata, the preference of the Cadiz merchants with their eyes on the
Buenos Aires market, both because it was more accessible and because in
turn it offered ready access to other strategic theatres. Once the expedition had consolidated royalist control in Venezuela, it was to tackle New
Granada; any troops not then needed in northern South America were to
continue on to Peru (via Panama) or to New Spain.

Though he found on arrival in April 1815 that Boves and company
had largely taken care of the Venezuelan insurgents, Morillo did attempt
to set up an orderly military government for the region. He then entered
New Granada, by way of Santa Marta, with an army of 5,000. He moved
first on Cartagena, which fell not to direct assault but to starvation on 6
December. Morillo's forces next moved inland and occupied Bogotá in
May 1816. The disorganized patriots of New Granada proved no match
for the invaders at any point in the contest, but Morillo was not inclined
toward leniency: starting outside the walls of Cartagena and continuing
after the fall of Bogotá, wholesale executions did away with most of the
top command and many lesser lights of the *Patria Boba*. A few, with
favourable connections or luck, survived with lesser penalties, and
certain others escaped to the eastern *llanos* of New Granada, ultimately to
join forces with similar fugitives from the wreck of patriot Venezuela.
For the most part, however, the viceroyalty of New Granada, including
Quito, was safely in royalist hands by the end of 1816.

Since 1810 developments in Quito had had little direct connection
with those in the rest of the viceroyalty. But Quito could not isolate itself
from the centre of royalist power in Peru. Thus, its second independent
government, organized in September 1810, was overthrown by an army
sent by Viceroy Abascal from Peru, exactly as the first had been in 1809.
This second government did survive longer – roughly two years – and in
that period carried on indecisive conflicts with ultra-royalist Pasto to the
north and with Cuenca and Guayaquil to the south, which again, as in

1809, refused to follow the lead of the capital. Quito experienced some factional struggles among the local nobility, and reached the point of declaring itself an independent constitutional monarchy. It did not achieve much else.

The revolution in the Río de la Plata never succumbed to reconquest or counter-revolution, but it survived only amidst seemingly endless crises of both internal and external origin. It began, as we have already seen, with the establishment in May 1810 of a governing junta at Buenos Aires which was led by the creole militia leader, Cornelio Saavedra. Initially, however, and in the absence of any one leader with the combined military and political stature of Miranda or Bolívar, the most influential single figure was Mariano Moreno, one of the junta's two secretaries, who has been categorized as a 'Jacobin' by both radical admirers and conservative detractors.

The radicalism of the revolution in the Río de la Plata in its early phase did not express itself primarily in legal or institutional innovations. As far as opening the port to trade was concerned, the junta needed only to re-affirm and reformulate what Viceroy Cisneros had done earlier on a provisional basis. The junta affirmed the basic equality between Indians and those of Spanish descent, but a declaration of equality for *pardos* was conspicuously omitted.[12] In Buenos Aires itself, the rhetoric of egalitarianism served mainly to incite popular fervour and to combat the real or alleged privileges of peninsular Spaniards, who began to suffer discrimination in public employment and in the assessment of contributions.

Spaniards and others suspected of disloyalty suffered more than discrimination. The judges of the *audiencia* were sent into exile for presuming to suggest that the junta should recognize the Council of Regency in Spain, and a new supreme tribunal was created in its place. Even harsher treatment was meted out in August 1810 to those implicated in the first overt counter-revolutionary attempt. This occurred in Córdoba, where the claims of the Buenos Aires junta came into conflict with strong loyalist sentiment. Among the promoters of resistance in Córdoba was the hero of the defence of Buenos Aires against the British, Santiago Liniers, who had retired there on being relieved as viceroy in

---

[12] *Registro Nacional de la República Argentina, que comprende los documentos desde 1810 hasta 1891* (14 vols. [of which the first three are titled *Registro Oficial*], Buenos Aires, 1879–91), I, 34. The decree cited here removes Indian militia units from the existing organizations in which they are grouped with *pardos* and provides for them to be grouped instead with white units – precisely to emphasize their superiority to the former and their equality with the latter.

1809. But the junta's response was swift and exemplary, with Moreno one of those insisting that no mercy be shown. Despite his past services, Liniers was summarily shot along with other supposed ringleaders.

Moreno's personal role was most obvious and direct in the field of revolutionary propaganda. Placed in charge of the junta's official newspaper, *Gaceta de Buenos Aires*, he used its pages to prepare opinion to accept more sweeping changes whenever the time was ripe. The articles he wrote himself presented a thinly veiled defence of republican government and independence. Most shocking of all was the publication, in serial instalments, of Moreno's translation of Rousseau's *Social Contract*. He took care to omit the passages on religion, but even with that deletion it was not well received either by devout Catholics or by those who simply felt the revolution was moving too far too fast.

Qualms over the pace of the revolution were especially pronounced in the interior provinces. Although it was soon apparent that the outlying areas of the viceroyalty would have to be brought under the authority of Buenos Aires by force – and Moreno, for one, was glad to accept the challenge – in most of what is now Argentina the new government reached a peaceful accommodation with local oligarchies, or at least with factions of them. But it followed that the same people, or same kinds of people, who dominated provincial society under the old regime continued to do so under the new, and there were few among them who sought anything more radical than greater influence for themselves. They were somewhat uneasy over such developments as the execution of Liniers and the publication of Rousseau. And, when their representatives began to arrive in Buenos Aires to take the places promised them on the junta, they posed an obvious threat to Mariano Moreno and his immediate collaborators. Moreno sought to delay their being seated, but even in Buenos Aires there were some who had misgivings as to the course of the revolution. One of these was the junta's president, Cornelio Saavedra, who still controlled the military apparatus and sided with the provincial delegates. When they were admitted to the junta, in mid-December, Moreno accepted defeat and resigned his office. He received the consolation of a diplomatic assignment to Europe, and this first instance of diplomatic exile was unusually effective, for the displaced junta secretary died en route and was buried at sea.

The departure of Moreno did not end conflict among *morenistas*, *saavedristas* and other factions or sub-factions. The membership of the ruling junta underwent further changes, and in the latter part of 1811 it dissolved entirely, superseded by a First Triumvirate which in due course gave way to a Second Triumvirate – and that, early in 1814, to a Supreme Director. To be sure, the different factions were not concerned exclusively with getting or keeping power. As will be seen below, they kept up the struggle against the declared enemies of the revolution in Upper Peru and Montevideo, although their zeal in combating those enemies did fluctuate. The slave trade was prohibited in April 1812, which was a progressive if hardly radical reform measure and something to please the British. Another measure of the same year invited immigration, but in practice the principal 'immigrants' were British and other foreign merchants who, thanks both to their superior connections abroad and to the use of innovative methods, soon controlled a disproportionate share of the import–export trade. British influence, which was stronger and more direct in the Río de la Plata than in Spanish America as a whole, also contributed to the patriot authorities' failure to lay down the 'mask of Ferdinand' in favour of an outright declaration of independence; for the fiction of allegiance to a captive monarch simplified the task of Great Britain in being simultaneously the ally of Spain against Napoleon in Europe and friend of Spain's rebellious colonies.

The failure to take a frank stand in favour of independence nevertheless seemed reprehensible to some, including the surviving *morenistas* who formed the backbone of the Patriotic Society organized in January 1812 to agitate for more vigorous pursuit of revolutionary political and military objectives. The purpose and, to some extent, the membership of the Patriotic Society overlapped, furthermore, with those of the Lautaro Lodge, a secret society organized on semi-masonic lines. Among the founders of the Lodge was the man who would become Argentina's foremost national hero, José de San Martín, only recently returned from the mother country where he had been serving as a professional officer in the Spanish army. His participation in the Lautaro Lodge and, through it, the larger political scene of the revolution typified the emergence of a new political force: the regular army, whose officers were mostly improvised since the start of the revolution rather than career soldiers such as himself, but who at least were a counter-weight to the largely *saavedrista* urban militia. In any event, the coming together of Moreno's political heirs with San Martín and certain other army leaders associated with the Lautaro Lodge proved too much for the *saavedrista* rump controlling the First Triumvirate, which was overthrown in October 1812. The Second Triumvirate that replaced it was an instrument of the

Lodge, and so in effect was the General Constituent Assembly that began functioning at Buenos Aires in January 1813 as a first national congress.

As the Assembly's official title suggested, it was supposed to adopt a constitution for what used to be the Viceroyalty and was now coming to be called the United Provinces of the Río de la Plata. In practice it never did, and neither did it reach the point of declaring independence, although it made symbolic affirmation of national sovereignty by such acts as the adoption of a distinctive flag, coinage and anthem. It also enacted an ambitious package of reforms including a law of free birth to begin the gradual elimination of slavery, the abolition of legal torture and titles of nobility, the prohibition of founding entails and much else besides. There was also a first dose of anti-clericalism. The abolition of a weakened and widely discredited Inquisition was not really very controversial, but a law prohibiting anyone under 30 years of age from taking vows was a serious blow against the religious orders and was intended to be just that. Even such a measure as the August 1813 decree prohibiting baptism of infants in cold water, though trivial in itself, revealed an undercurrent of hostility toward traditional religious practices. To be sure, the legislative programme of the Assembly had little impact on the basic structure of society, since titles and entails were either nonexistent or strictly unimportant save in the provinces of Upper Peru, and the principle of free birth had less immediate effect on the institution of slavery than the practice – increasingly common – of drafting or confiscating slaves for military service, in return for which they were free if they survived. Yet in its breadth and nuances that programme does tend to justify the Jacobin-sounding designation which the gathering of 1813 has received in Argentine tradition: Assembly of the Year XIII. As the national anthem that it adopted so eloquently states,

> Hear, mortals, the sacred cry:
> Liberty, liberty, liberty;
> Hear the sound of broken chains,
> See noble equality enthroned.

Among the outlying areas of the viceroyalty of the Río de la Plata, Upper Peru was first to receive the concerted attention of the Argentine patriots, and with good reason. It held the silver of Potosí, and its trade was of critical importance to commercial middlemen and tax collectors alike in Buenos Aires. The regional uprisings of 1809 and their harsh aftermath suggested that a liberating army ought to be well received.

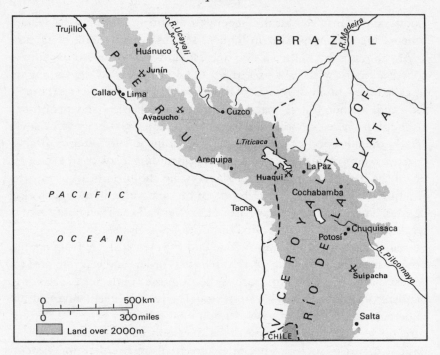

The wars of independence in Spanish South America: the central theatre

Accordingly, one set forth and laboriously climbed into Upper Peru. It was led by a political commissar in the person of Juan José Castelli, a lawyer-member of the Buenos Aires junta and ally of Mariano Moreno who shared the latter's strong commitment to extending the revolution to the farthest limits of the viceroyalty. The revolutionary army won a decisive victory at the battle of Suipacha on 7 November 1810 and entered Potosí soon afterward. In various other places, including Chuquisaca and La Paz, local patriots seized power and quickly established ties with the invaders.

Actually, things had gone too well, so that Castelli and his associates were emboldened to ignore almost every rule of caution. They not only practised undue severity toward defeated loyalists but proved domineering toward those who spontaneously welcomed their arrival. They scandalized the devout by public display of freethinking attitudes. They also made much of the offer of legal equality in appealing for the support of the Indians, which made practical as well as ideological sense in an area of heavy Indian population but was not always appreciated by the whites or even *mestizos*. Nor were the Argentines a match militarily for the experienced loyalist commander, José Manuel de Goyeneche, who, just as in 1809, came over from Peru to restore order. He delivered a crushing defeat to the patriots at Huaqui, near Lake Titicaca, on 20 June 1811. A long retreat followed, in the course of which the Argentines were severely harassed by the very people they had come to liberate. The retreat did not end until the victorious loyalists had penetrated almost to Tucumán.

By 1813 the Argentine patriots were able to retake the initiative and again marched as liberators into Upper Peru. They were led this time by Manuel Belgrano, who was strictly self-taught as a military commander, but was prudent and methodical and avoided the worst of the mistakes committed earlier. By the middle of May he was in Potosí, and both there and elsewhere he made a generally good impression up to the day in November 1813 when, just before his own retreat southward, he tried unsuccessfully to dynamite the Potosí mint. His ultimate failure was due simply to the military superiority of the forces thrown against him, now commanded by the Spanish general, Joaquín de la Pezuela. Yet another invading army was defeated by Pezuela in 1815. Thereafter, the Argentine patriots turned their attention in other directions, leaving the cause of resistance in Upper Peru in the hands of the numerous guerrilla bands that had begun to form as early as 1809 and were never entirely extinguished. These drew on the Indian masses for recruits (as did everyone in that military theatre), but were commonly led by *mestizos* or creoles of non-aristocratic origin. They thrived especially in the mountain valleys just below the *altiplano*, where a succession of *republiquetas* or petty 'republics' rose and fell. Though much reduced in scope after 1816, the guerrillas for all practical purposes constituted the independence movement of what is now Bolivia until the arrival in 1825 of a liberating army from a different, and surprising, direction: Peru (see below).

Although it was not clearly recognized at the time, the abandonment of Upper Peru to local partisans virtually ensured that the region would ultimately be lost to whatever government ruled from Buenos Aires. The *de facto* separation of Paraguay occurred even earlier. When Paraguay held back from recognizing the May 1810 junta, an expedition was organized and despatched under the command of Manuel Belgrano (who later met defeat in Upper Peru). It was twice overcome by Paraguayan militia forces early in 1811. However, once Belgrano withdrew, the Paraguayans set up a junta of their own, in May 1811, by a bloodless coup. They proceeded to enter negotiations with Buenos Aires with a view to finding some basis of co-operation, but in practice Paraguay went its own way, independent of both Madrid and Buenos Aires. By fits and starts – and certainly by the end of 1813 – it succumbed to the firm personal dictatorship of José Gaspar Rodríguez de Francia, a creole intellectual who chose to rule with the support of the Guaraní-speaking *mestizo* masses. Francia distrusted Buenos Aires and set out to isolate Paraguay, not so much from commercial contacts as from the contagion of Argentine political disorders.[13] In this he succeeded, not least because Buenos Aires had greater and nearer problems to worry about than Paraguay's insubordination.

One of the problems that overshadowed Paraguay for the *porteños* (or inhabitants of Buenos Aires) was the situation in Montevideo and its hinterland, the present Uruguay. Here the first effective blow against Spanish domination was struck at the beginning of 1811 by José Gervasio Artigas, scion of a Montevideo family with substantial rural interests and a record of public service. Artigas raised the standard of rebellion in the countryside, where his rapport with gauchos, squatters and middling landowners won him a strong following. He at first acknowledged the supremacy of the Buenos Aires junta. However, he was no unconditional adherent, for he had in mind the establishment of a loose confederation of Río de la Plata provinces, whereas the governments that successively held sway in Buenos Aires could at least agree in rejecting any such arrangement. Artigas also felt aggrieved at what he considered lack of true commitment on the part of Buenos Aires to the liberation of his province, as shown by a willingness to make truces both with the Spanish forces still entrenched in Montevideo and with the Portuguese who saw an opportunity to regain a foothold on the Río de la Plata and sent in a 'pacifying' force in 1811. The Portuguese left again the next year, but only because the British considered this an unnecessary complication and put pressure on them to withdraw. An army from Buenos Aires finally obtained the surrender of Montevideo in 1814, but by then relations with Artigas were definitely broken. Artigas was in fact emerging as a leader of anti-*porteño* federalists in the provinces of the so-called Littoral, along the Paraná River. Forced to deal simultaneously with Artigas and these other dissidents – to say nothing of the continuing problem of Upper Peru – the government in Buenos Aires proved unable

[13] See John Hoyt Williams, 'Paraguayan isolation under Dr. Francia: a re-evaluation', *Hispanic American Historical Review*, 52/1 (1972), 103–9.

to humble Artigas and in February 1815 finally turned Montevideo over to him.

Once in command of the entire *Banda Oriental*, Artigas set to work organizing it under his leadership and reconstructing its war-ravaged economy. In agrarian policy, moreover, he introduced one of the most interesting and original measures of the independence period. The problem he faced was one of depleted herds and vast tracts of land which had been abandoned by their owners. His solution was to confiscate without compensation lands belonging to the 'bad Europeans and worse Americans' who had emigrated (in quite a few cases to Buenos Aires) and to provide for their redistribution, with priority given to 'free blacks, *zambos* of the same class, Indians and poor creoles'.[14] On the basis of this measure Artigas has been acclaimed as South America's first great 'agrarian reformer', and it does reflect a populist bent in social matters as well as the assumption on Artigas's part that the fastest way to get lands back in production was to turn them over to small farmers and ranchers who would exploit them directly. But Artigas never had time to carry out his full programme, since in 1816 he had to cope with a new Portuguese invasion from Brazil. This time the British did not effectively interfere, much less the *porteños*. Moreover, the invaders obtained the support of an appreciable number of Uruguayans who were unhappy with Artigas's agrarian populism and/or convinced that his cause was hopeless. By the beginning of 1820, all the Banda Oriental was under Portuguese control.

The second half decade of the revolution in the Río de la Plata witnessed, on balance, a curtailment of aims and performance that reflected at least in part the existence of widespread dissatisfaction with what had so far been accomplished. Outside Buenos Aires, such dissatisfaction stemmed both from conservative distrust of revolutionary innovations and from local resentment of centralized political control. In Buenos Aires itself, the bulk of the upper class – always hesitant to become identified too closely with the new regime – was thoroughly tired of forced loans and other exactions, tired of political instability, and somewhat disdainful of the civilian and military leaders who since 1810 had made the 'career of the revolution' into a full-time personal vocation.[15]

In both the capital and the interior, the failures of revolutionary leadership in dealing with external foes were a further source of disen-

---

14 Nelson de la Torre, Julio C. Rodríguez and Lucía Sala de Touron, *La revolución agraria artiguista: 1815–1816* (Montevideo, 1969), 167–8.
15 Halperín–Donghi, *Politics, economics and society*, 204–5, 210–13 and *passim*.

chantment. By this time, too, in Spanish America generally the cause of insurrection was approaching its lowest point, while the defeat of Napoleon in Europe ushered in a wave of counter-revolution only one of whose many facets was the restoration of an aggressively reactionary Ferdinand VII in Spain. Hence it now appeared expedient to restrain revolutionary impulses in the Río de la Plata. This was facilitated by the overthrow, in April 1815, of Supreme Director Carlos María de Alvear, who had been another of the founders of the Lautaro Lodge. Though Alvear had lately given his support to desperate schemes for seeking reconciliation with Spain – or, failing that, a British protectorate – he was still heir to the activist tradition of Moreno. He was also perceived, in the interior, as an agent of the most obnoxious variety of *porteño* dictation, and it was there that acts of defiance against his authority began. However, the movement was taken up in Buenos Aires, where much of the army on which Alvear had previously relied as a critical element of support now turned against him.

Alvear was replaced by first one interim Director and then another. Meanwhile a new constituent congress was elected and convened in March 1816 at Tucumán – an obvious concession to provincial discontent. The Congress of Tucumán was a much more conservative body than the Assembly of the Year XIII, and not merely because almost half of its members were priests. It did finally declare the independence of the United Provinces of the Río de la Plata, on 9 July 1816, but this was less a sign of revolutionary militancy than practical recognition of the fact that with absolutism now restored in Spain it was absurd to continue pledging allegiance to Ferdinand. Indeed the same deputies who declared independence were predominantly in favour of constitutional monarchy as a form of government for the new nation. Some felt this could best be achieved by finding a suitable heir to the former Inca emperors, crowning him king of the provinces of the Río de la Plata, and maybe marrying him to a Portuguese princess for added protection. Others hoped for a European prince, and over the next few years feelers were put out in Europe to see if one might be recruited. Nothing came of these schemes, but they did fit the current mood. So did the failure of the new congress to resume the work of reform so dear to its predecessor.

The Congress of Tucumán in May 1816 chose as Supreme Director one of its own members, Juan Martín de Pueyrredón, who shunned liberal innovations as assiduously as did the congress itself. He also worked closely with the congress when in 1817 it moved to Buenos Aires and there began in earnest to draft a constitution, completed in 1819. This first fully-fledged frame of government was both highly centralist, with a national executive who directly named all provincial governors, and socially conservative, featuring limited suffrage and a semi-corporatist parliament. Though ostensibly republican, it could easily have been fitted out, if occasion arose, with a royal chief of state. By this time, however, the vogue for monarchism had begun to recede, so that the continuing efforts to find a monarch did no good for the domestic popularity of Pueyrredón and congress. Neither did their passivity in the face of the Portuguese occupation of Uruguay. At the same time the centralism of the new constitution aroused strong resistance in the other provinces. Faced with rising opposition on almost all sides, Pueyrredón resigned as Supreme Director in June 1819, but his successor was even less able to stem the tide. Early in 1820, the Directorial government and the national congress both dissolved, and the now-independent Argentine nation relapsed into a state of anarchic disunity.

In the larger picture of Spanish American independence, the Pueyrredón administration is remembered chiefly for the support that it gave to the military exploits of José de San Martín even as it was abandoning Artigas to his fate. The son of a Spanish military officer stationed in Argentina, San Martín had achieved some distinction as a Spanish officer himself. However, a combination of liberal sentiments and loyalty to the homeland he left as an adolescent brought him back to America in 1812, where he not only became involved in revolutionary politics through the Lautaro Lodge but devoted his energies and talents to the building up of a more effective military establishment. When he had been home only two years, he was given command of the Army of the North with responsibility for defending the free provinces of the Río de la Plata against the loyalists based in Upper Peru and, eventually, for launching another invasion of those Andean fastnesses. San Martín did not relish the assignment, because he came to feel that the preoccupation with Upper Peru which had characterized the military strategy of the Buenos Aires revolution since 1810 was mistaken. True, Upper Peru was jurisdictionally linked to Buenos Aires, and it lay on the most direct route to Lima, nerve centre of loyalist resistance in South America. On the other hand, experience had demonstrated the difficulty of conquering – and holding – it from the south. To San Martín, it appeared that a better route to Lima lay through Chile, where at the time an indigenous patriot government was hard-pressed by an army sent against it by the viceroy of

Peru, and from there by water to the Peruvian coast. It was a logical strategic assessment, as events would prove. He further believed that the seizure of Lima would indirectly deliver to him the rest of Peru, Upper as well as Lower, which proved to be a rather less logical assumption.

Having arranged his transfer to Mendoza with an appointment as intendant of Cuyo, San Martín took up his duties just as the Chilean patriot regime on the other side of the Andes was collapsing. This did not change his design, since he reasoned that Chile was still likely to provide more willing support to a liberating army than was Upper Peru. He established a good working relationship with Pueyrredón; he also strongly supported the declaration of independence and gave encouragement to ideas of constitutional monarchy. But, above all, he gathered recruits and supplies. Chilean refugees were one source of manpower; another was the slave population of the region, of whose able-bodied male adults the greatest number ended up in San Martín's Army of the Andes.[16] Other slaves were sent to him from Buenos Aires by Pueyrredón, so that when he finally marched about half his infantry was black. Workshops to manufacture powder and even artillery were established in Mendoza, and other surrounding provinces contributed what they could. By the beginning of 1817 all was ready. An army of approximately 5,500 men set off for Chile, through six different Andean passes, in movements carefully orchestrated to alarm and confuse the enemy to the maximum degree.

The Chile that San Martín came to liberate at the beginning of 1817 was in the grip of a royalist counter-revolution which had made a clean sweep of the Chilean *Patria Vieja*, the experiment in self-government launched in September 1810 with the establishment in Santiago of a first ruling junta. Until its collapse in 1814, the *Patria Vieja* had been beset by almost continual conflict between regions and political factions. There was a parallel process of radicalization or 'deepening' of the revolution, but more at the level of rhetoric than of concrete programmes.

The original Chilean junta took such steps as opening the ports to international trade and calling for the election of a congress, which began to function in July 1811. The junta's dominant figure, to the extent that it had one, was Juan Martínez de Rozas, but he soon came in conflict with the congressional majority and reacted by withdrawing to Concepción,

---

[16] José Luis Masini, *La esclavitud negra en Mendoza; época independiente* (Mendoza, 1962), 20–3.

the principal port and population centre of southern Chile as well as his own chief base of support. There he set up a separate and schismatic provincial junta. His place in Santiago was filled by the *Patria Vieja*'s outstanding exponent of revolutionary activism, José Miguel Carrera. Though he belonged to an aristocratic family, as did most actors on the political scene, Carrera cultivated a popular style of politics, frankly bidding for non-aristocratic support; and, as a former creole officer in the Spanish army only recently returned from the peninsula, he enjoyed wide esteem and support among the fledgling military forces of the new regime. This combination of good family connections, popular appeal and military backing proved for a time quite unbeatable.

Carrera first moved to purge the congress of its more conservative elements, thus opening the way for the adoption of a number of progressive measures, among them a law of free birth. Before the end of 1811 he had dissolved congress entirely, making himself dictator, and in the latter capacity he presided over such further innovations as the adoption of a distinctive national flag and the establishment of Chile's first printing press. Yet he did not attempt any reforms that could remotely be termed structural: even the law of free birth had been largely symbolic in Chile, a land of relatively few slaves most of whom were in urban or domestic employment. More important no doubt was the introduction of printing, which led to the birth of political journalism and thereby encouraged the small literate minority to consider a wider range of political options, among which republican government and complete separation from Spain were frankly put forward. Independence was certainly the preference of Carrera personally, as also of Rozas for that matter; but the opportune moment to declare it never arrived. Nor did that shared objective bring Rozas and Carrera together. A local uprising overthrew the Concepción junta in July 1812, after which Carrera sent Rozas into exile.

Carrera could not deal as readily with a more formidable adversary, Viceroy Abascal of Peru, who dispatched a small expeditionary force to Chile early in 1813. Moreover, while Carrera was absent directing an indecisive struggle against the invaders, the junta he had created in Santiago to govern in his absence dismissed him and replaced him with the man who was to become his arch-rival, Bernardo O'Higgins. Son of the former captain-general of Chile and viceroy of Peru, Ambrosio O'Higgins, the new patriot commander was educated partly in England and there had been influenced in favour of Spanish American independence by Francisco de Miranda. In style and temperament, though not ultimate objectives, he was more conservative than Carrera. O'Higgins assumed supreme command, but he was no more successful than Carrera against the army from Peru, now substantially reinforced, and in May 1814 he agreed to a truce which would have allowed Chile limited autonomy under Spanish rule. The truce was never formally ratified. In July of the same year, Carrera staged another coup to re-establish his dictatorship, setting off a round of internecine conflict that further weakened the patriots and thus contributed to the crushing defeat they suffered at the hands of the loyalists in the battle of Rancagua, some 80 kilometres south of Santiago, on 1 and 2 October 1814. Rancagua led to the collapse of the *Patria Vieja*. Carrera, O'Higgins and numerous others took the trail to Mendoza and refuge in Argentina, while the restored Spanish regime imposed harsh repression on those who stayed behind. A few were killed, more confined to the remote islands of Juan Fernández, and many relieved of their properties by confiscation. But the lengths to which repression was carried out stimulated guerrilla resistance and assured San Martín of a heartier welcome when he descended into Chile at the beginning of 1817.

By the time San Martín engaged the enemy on 12 February at Chacabuco, mid-way between Santiago and the main passes from Mendoza, he had assembled roughly 3,500 troops from different bodies of his Army of the Andes, including a substantial number of Chileans. Carrera was not among them, for he had quickly impressed San Martín as troublesome and unreliable, whereas O'Higgins gained the Argentine leader's confidence and became a close collaborator. In fact O'Higgins commanded one of the two patriot divisions at Chacabuco and almost lost the battle through his zeal in launching a frontal attack before the other division completed its flanking movement.[17] But the patriots won and entered Santiago without further opposition. There an improvised assembly offered San Martín the government of Chile, which he immediately declined in favour of O'Higgins.

San Martín's success at Chacabuco still left important enemy forces at large in central Chile. Reinforced from Peru they inflicted on him a serious defeat at Cancha Rayada in March 1818, but on 5 April San Martín won another victory at Maipó, just outside Santiago, which proved decisive. The royalists retained a foothold in southern Chile and

[17] Leopoldo R. Ornstein, 'Revelaciones sobre la batalla de Chacabuco', *Investigaciones y Ensayos* (Buenos Aires), 10/1 (1971), 178–207.

on the island of Chiloé mounted a guerrilla resistance of their own that dragged on for years. They also retained the key coastal fortress at Valdivia, but its supposedly invulnerable defences were overcome in February 1820 by the British naval adventurer Lord Cochrane, who had accepted command of Chile's small but growing sea forces. The elimination of that enemy stronghold was one detail that needed to be taken care of before San Martín could embark on the next stage of his strategic design, which was to liberate Peru.

Another and even more basic prerequisite for the Peruvian campaign was for O'Higgins to create an effective government and source of material support within liberated Chile, particularly as the Argentines were becoming ever more embroiled in domestic troubles and unlikely to give much help. In this matter O'Higgins successfully rose to the challenge: he took control of the administrative apparatus abandoned by the loyalists, collected taxes and seized enemy assets, and vigorously imposed his own authority against all challenges that arose within the patriot camp. The Carrera faction was really not much of a problem, as both José Miguel and two brothers were still in Argentina, where they meddled in Argentine affairs with a view to regaining Chile ultimately. (Instead they were executed by the Argentines.) In any event, the Chilean government functioned well enough to satisfy San Martín's most pressing requirements. When he set sail in August 1820 – with a fleet of 23 ships, including both warships and transports – the expedition had been financed and equipped mainly by Chile and represented an impressive outlay of energy and resources on the part of the Chilean regime. The fleet commander, Cochrane, and most of the higher naval officers were actually foreign mercenaries, but there were still more Chileans than any other nationality on board. The outcome of this expedition will be described below.

The government of O'Higgins had finally declared Chilean independence in February 1818, by which time the gesture was anticlimactic. More daring, in the Chilean context, were certain reforms that O'Higgins adopted, such as the legal prohibition of entailed estates and the abolition of hereditary titles. These measures were taken more or less routinely in most of Spanish America during the independence period, and the fact that in Chile they led to serious resentment suggests the strength of resistance to change in Chilean society. At the same time, those more liberal-minded Chileans who might have welcomed a degree of cautious social innovation were often antagonized by O'Higgins's authoritarian political system and his excessive reliance on a single unpopular adviser, José Antonio Rodríguez Aldea, an ex-royalist. O'Higgins introduced a constitution of sorts in 1818, but it gave him sweeping powers, limited by little more than an advisory senate whose members he named himself. This senate blocked the implementation of the decree on entails, yet it hardly satisfied the criteria of liberal constitutionalism. O'Higgins allowed the 1818 constitution to be replaced with a charter of more conventional republican outline in 1822. However, he manipulated the elections to choose the convention that drafted it, and its terms still seemed calculated to assure his own almost indefinite continuation in office. Thus, it did not quiet all discontent with the political system, which together with lingering resentment over O'Higgins's socio-economic policies and his inability finally to quell loyalist resistance in the south produced a succession of outbreaks and conspiracies in late 1822 and the beginning of 1823. O'Higgins accepted defeat and resigned his powers on 28 January 1823.

The participation of Peruvian forces in suppressing Chile's *Patria Vieja* was just one manifestation of the role played by Peru as the principal base of royalist strength in Spanish South America throughout most of the independence struggle. Quito and Upper Peru had earlier (and more than once) been reconquered from the same direction. Peru's role derived both from the comparative weakness of the revolutionary impulse in Peru itself and from the success of Viceroy José de Abascal in building up his military establishment. Abascal did what he could to enlarge and strengthen the regular forces; he carried out a much greater expansion of the Peruvian militia, whose level of training and equipment left something to be desired but which he clearly saw to be the one means of obtaining a quick and massive increase in troop strength. By 1816 the combined strength, on paper, of army and militia was over 70,000, of whom the vast majority were militia. Effective strength was somewhat less, but so was that of potential adversaries. Naturally, the military importance of Peru was enhanced by its central location, which made it easier for the viceroy to dispatch reinforcements north, east, or south – as required – to beleaguered royalists. His decisiveness in doing so even in theatres within the jurisdiction of the viceroyalties of New Granada and Río de la Plata meant that Lima recovered some of the ground lost through eighteenth-century administrative rearrangements.

This was clearly a source of satisfaction to Peruvian creoles, whose support or at least forbearance was essential. The fact that Peru was safely loyalist also meant that it had a chance to enjoy the benefits of the liberal Spanish constitution of 1812, with its popularly elected municipalities and provincial deputations, relative freedom of the press and other concessions to the spirit of the time. Peru even came to play a significant role in the Cortes of Cádiz, with eight elected deputies present not to mention other Peruvians resident in Spain who were provisionally pressed into service in the revived Spanish parliament pending the arrival of those from home; one Peruvian ultimately served as president of the body. All this, too, was pleasing to most educated creoles, although the failure of the new peninsular regime to offer Spanish America true equality in representation or otherwise inevitably shook the faith of those who had hoped to obtain the solution of colonial grievances through imperial political reform.

The liberal interlude was less pleasing to the ultra-conservative Abascal, who proclaimed the constitution without enthusiasm and enforced it half-heartedly. When in 1814 Ferdinand was re-established on his throne and abolished the constitution, the viceroy lost no time in restoring absolutism in the colony as well. Peruvians discovered further that with or without a constitution their role as defenders of the integrity of the empire was a costly one which had to be paid for through taxes and special contributions; this pleased neither liberals nor absolutists. Some, even in Peru, frankly favoured a revolutionary course, with the result that the viceregal administration could never devote its attention solely to uprisings beyond Peru's borders. There was intermittent concern over conspiracies, real or alleged, in Lima itself, even though none came to fruition, and short-lived disorders occurred here and there in the provinces. Some of the latter were repercussions from the periodic advances of insurgent activity in Upper Peru (as in Tacna in 1811 and 1813), while another at Huánuco in 1812 began as an Indian protest against specific abuses but assumed a larger political character because the Indians were supported by local creole malcontents. It was, of course, no accident that disaffection was more serious in outlying areas, which were both farther from Abascal's vigilance and resentful of their own political and economic subjection to Lima.

The most serious of these provincial uprisings occurred at Cuzco in 1814. It began as a creole and *mestizo* protest against the arbitrary rule of the *audiencia* of Cuzco and, indirectly, the hegemony of Lima; it quickly established a new government, which even the bishop supported. The rebels further enlisted the elderly and opportunistic *cacique*, Mateo García Pumacahua, who had fought years ago for the colonial regime *against* Túpac Amaru and more recently against the insurgents in Upper Peru. He was a valuable acquisition, for the Cuzco revolutionaries would have to confront the implacable hostility of Abascal, and Pumacahua could summon the Indian population of the region to their cause. Yet the more the Indians in fact rallied, the more many creoles had second thoughts, and, though the movement spread to La Paz and Arequipa, it was in the end soundly defeated. From the start, its purpose had been somewhat ambiguous, as the aims of the leaders ranged from personal advancement and redress of particular grievances to the attainment of full independence. In the years following the collapse of the Cuzco rebellion (1814–16) disturbances in the *sierra* and alarms in Lima dwindled just as the independence movement in other colonies gave way to royalist reconquest or entered a period of temporary quiescence.

Abascal went home to Spain in 1816, leaving Peru, safely royalist, in the hands of a new viceroy, Joaquín de la Pezuela, who was another experienced military officer. The treasury, however, was nearly empty, and silver-mining – the one industry to have escaped the general economic decline of the late colonial period – had been hard hit by flooding and wartime dislocations, including interruption of the supply of Spanish mercury used in processing the ore. Militarily, Peru received some modest reinforcements of Spanish regulars after the defeat of Napoleon, but among them were officers of crypto-liberal persuasion whose presence did not make for unity. Meanwhile, as the independence movement regained momentum elsewhere – above all in Chile after 1817 – financial and other pressures on Peru increased once more, at a time when even convinced loyalists were growing weary of the struggle. The independence of Chile entailed other complications such as the interruption of supplies of Chilean grain and the loss of the Chilean tobacco market formerly dominated by producers on the Peruvian north coast, while vessels flying the Chilean flag began carrying out raids on Peruvian ports and Spanish shipping. It is thus hardly surprising that more Peruvians were pondering the possible benefits of changing sides. They showed little inclination to do so precipitously, but San Martín's arrival in September 1820 would at last force the issue and provide the opportunity.

The Argentine liberator (see above) made his initial landing with 4,500 troops at Pisco, roughly 200 kilometres south of Lima. He subsequently moved to Huacho, at a slightly lesser distance north of the capital. In both places he followed for the most part a policy of cautious waiting. He was aware of the Spanish revolution of January 1820 which not only put an end to any serious possibility of reinforcements reaching the royalist forces still active in South America but brought to power a new government that proceeded to restore the constitution and was committed to an attempt to negotiate a settlement of the colonial conflict. He accordingly took advantage of every opportunity – and there were several – to carry out discussions with the other side, and in the course of these he broached the possibility of an agreement to end the war by erecting an independent monarchy under a prince of the Spanish royal family. Though he later said the proposal had been only a negotiating stratagem, there is no doubt that it was in line with what San Martín personally would have liked to see adopted. In the end these negotiations led to no practical result, although in the midst of them the Spanish leadership in Peru did undergo a sudden change, when a military coup deposed the luckless Pezuela as viceroy in favour of José de la Serna.

While exploring the prospects for a negotiated peace, San Martín assumed that the Peruvians themselves would be encouraged by his arrival to declare openly for independence, thus again obviating the need for full-scale offensive action. He did indeed meet a generally favourable reception in the foothold he established, and toward the end of 1820 a string of northern coastal cities came over spontaneously to the patriot side. There was likewise an upsurge of guerrilla resistance in the central *sierra*. Lima, on the other hand, did not change sides. It was only when the Spanish authorities of their own volition withdrew from Lima to the Andean highlands in July 1821 that San Martín entered the city, unopposed, and on 28 July formally proclaimed Peru an independent nation. Since he had no Peruvian equivalent of O'Higgins at his side, he consented forthwith to be its provisional ruler, with the title of Protector.

The royalists' evacuation of Lima was motivated not just by a sense that events were turning against them but by a realistic appreciation that the basic human and material resources of Peru were not to be found in or around the parasitic capital city but principally in the *sierra*. There they would make their stand. For his part, San Martín in Lima found himself hard put to maintain a government, army and civil population of 50,000 when cut off from the highlands. He was forced to levy special contributions that were no more popular than those of the previous regime. For financial as well as political reasons he initiated a harsh programme to expel those peninsular Spaniards who did not actively embrace the new regime, and to confiscate their assets. He thereby antagonized a large part of Lima's creole elite, who in general felt no real commitment to the patriot cause and were linked by multiple family or other associations to the Spaniards. *Limeños* put the chief blame for the 'persecution' of Spaniards on San Martín's principal collaborator in the new regime, the Argentine revolutionary, Bernardo de Monteagudo, but inevitably San Martín's own popularity suffered. He offended the more conservative churchmen by such measures as setting a minimum age for monastic vows, and the powerful landowners of the coastal valleys by drafting their slaves into military service and establishing the principle of free birth. Another set of decrees abolishing Indian tribute, Indian forced labour, and even the use of the term 'Indian', had little practical effect as so much of the Indian population was in Spanish-held areas; but they aroused slight enthusiasm among Peruvian creoles. Moreover, as happened in Chile with O'Higgins, the reforms of San Martín in Peru were uneasily joined with a political programme – in this case, San Martín's support of monarchy as an eventual form of independent government – which tended to alienate some of the very people who should have been most receptive to them.

Meanwhile, San Martín continued to avoid all-out conflict with the enemy. He maintained contact with the highland guerrilla movement but neither gave it effective support nor took decisive action himself, continuing to hope that time would work in his favour even though his lack of a satisfactory resource base and growing disaffection in Lima were reason to doubt that this would be the case. That even he may have come to have doubts is suggested by the eagerness with which he set off to Guayaquil, in July 1822, to confer with his northern counterpart Simón Bolívar, and by his subsequent willingness to abandon the Peruvian theatre entirely and leave the liberation of Peru (and Upper Peru) to Bolívar.

The impasse in Peru was finally broken by the entry of forces from northern South America, where the cause of independence had gradually recovered from the low point of 1816. The principal architect of that recovery was Bolívar, who had wisely left for the West Indies before the final collapse of New Granada. He established himself first in Jamaica, where he published his 'Jamaica Letter' (September 1815), which, in addition to repeating his criticism of the institutions adopted by earlier patriot regimes, declared his unshaken faith in ultimate victory. Next he moved to Haiti, where he succeeded in enlisting the support of President Alexandre Pétion and of certain foreign merchants for his cause. Resupplied in Haiti with men, ships and military equipment, he launched an expedition against the coast of eastern Venezuela in May 1816, the same month in which General Pablo Morillo reconquered Bogotá. He did not succeed and in September was back in Haiti. But, having rebuilt his forces, he returned to Venezuela on 28 December. He never left South America again.

In reality, conditions in Venezuela were increasingly favourable for a resurrection of the patriot cause. It had never been extinguished altogether, since there were always insurgent guerrilla bands in existence in one place or another, and they were particularly strong in an area – the *llanos* – which had been one of the principal recruiting grounds of Boves for his depredations against the Second Republic. In the region of Apure, José Antonio Páez with a band of fellow *llaneros* was gradually expanding his operations against the royalists. Nor is it surprising that more and more *llaneros* (and lower-class Venezuelans generally) were ready to throw in their lot with the patriots. The very success of the royalists meant they now offered more tempting booty. They were also beginning to bear the brunt of class and racial antagonisms, for the arrival of Morillo at the beginning of 1815 to take command of what Boves and other popular guerrilla leaders had regained for the king was only a first step towards the re-establishment of a formal political-military structure. Professional army officers and bureaucrats, peninsular or creole, now took precedence over the Boves-type chieftains and their *pardo* constituencies, who felt slighted. Then, too, there was no lack of conflict between royalist army officers and bureaucrats, arising in large part from the resistance of the latter to the virtually absolute powers which Madrid had entrusted to Morillo and which he left in the hands of an inflexible fellow officer during his absence in New Granada (from which he returned only in December 1816). This in turn weakened the royalist cause; and so did Venezuela's utter lack of resources, after a half-decade of bitter conflict, to support properly either an orderly civil administration or the military machine that was still needed to counter the insurgents.

This is not to say that Bolívar's task was easy. However, on his return at the end of 1816 he succeeded in establishing contact with some of the scattered groups of patriots still active in north-eastern Venezuela, and he kept up pressure on the enemy. At the same time, there was renewed dissension within the patriot camp as well, in particular between Bolívar and General Santiago Mariño, who had also returned from a West Indian sanctuary and resented Bolívar's claim to leadership in a region which had been his personal bailiwick. Partly to avoid friction with Mariño, Bolívar transferred his operations southward to the Orinoco, where on 17 July 1817 the patriots achieved a signal victory: the capture of the city of Angostura. This unimpressive river port became *de facto* capital of the twice-reborn Venezuelan republic. It could be reached by ocean vessels and thus provided an invaluable link with the outside world; it also offered potentially easy communications with existing or future patriot redoubts anywhere on the *llanos* of Venezuela and New Granada that could be reached via the Orinoco and its tributaries.

Bolívar used the Orinoco route to establish connections with Páez, among others. In January 1818 he personally went to call on the *llanero* chieftain, winning from him a slightly less than unconditional recognition as supreme chief, and through Páez he won over the *llaneros*. Bolívar had already issued a decree in October 1817 which promised a share of enemy property to both troops and officers, on a sliding scale by rank; in this he was both ratifying and extending promises informally made by Páez. Bolívar moved to widen his support in still other ways by incorporating the emancipation of slaves among his proclaimed objectives (as he had been doing since his first return to Venezuela in 1816) and by seeing that *pardo* soldiers received their share of promotions. His commitment to abolition had immediate effect only for slaves taken into military service, but it fitted in well with the variety of military populism that Bolívar was now espousing. His efforts to make good on creole promises of equality to *pardos* fitted in too, although there were certain limits. General Manuel Piar, the highest-ranking *pardo*, was executed on shadowy charges of conspiracy when he boldly threatened to raise the race issue again against Bolívar. Naturally, the members of Bolívar's own class kept the largest number of top commands as well as virtually all responsible posts in the civil rump government at Angostura. But Bolívar did not intend the republican cause to be perceived again as only that of a narrow creole elite.

The Liberator was less successful when in 1818 he sought to break out of the *llanos* with an invasion of Andean Venezuela. His *llanero* cavalry was no match for Morillo's veteran infantry in the mountains. But then neither could Morillo make headway against Bolívar and Páez on the plains. Bolívar hoped that he might eventually tip the balance in his favour with the help of the steady trickle of European volunteers – most of them bored or unemployed veterans of the Napoleonic wars – who began arriving through the port of Angostura along with varying amounts of military supplies procured for the republicans by agents abroad. However, Bolívar was not content to occupy himself with purely military preparations. He also summoned an elected congress to meet at Angostura and put the republican regime on a more regular legal basis. This fitted in with still another element of Bolívar's current policy, which was to win the confidence and collaboration of civilian patriots of liberal constitutionalist persuasion, the very kind he had blamed for the failures of the First Republic. In his opening address to the congress on 15 February 1819, the *Discurso de Angostura*, Bolívar emphasized, with Montesquieu, the need to adapt institutions to the particular environment in which they are to function, and he sketched that of Spanish America in bleak terms: 'Subject to the threefold yoke of ignorance, tyranny and vice, the American people have been unable to acquire knowledge, power or virtue. . . .'[18] From this it followed in Bolívar's view that the proper government for such a place as Venezuela, though outwardly republican, should be one in which the disorderly instincts of the populace were checked through a limited suffrage, powerful executive and hereditary senate, with the addition of a 'moral power' composed of eminent citizens having the special function to promote education and good customs. It was a profoundly conservative statement, which summed up the enduring features of Bolívar's political thought. Yet the same address contained a new call for the abolition of slavery and for effective implementation of the soldiers' bonus, suggesting that Bolívar's was a flexible and relatively enlightened brand of conservatism. And he ended with a call for the ultimate union of Venezuela and New Granada.

The Congress of Angostura in due course adopted a constitution that incorporated some, though not all, of Bolívar's political ideas; and it chose to put off the question of slavery until later. The Liberator, meanwhile, had already embarked on the most spectacular of all his military campaigns, which took him from the Venezuelan *llanos* to the heart of New Granada. This strategy involved leaving Caracas a little longer in Morillo's hands, but it took advantage of the fact that in New

---

[18] Bolívar, *Selected writings*, 1, 176.

Granada the enemy was militarily weaker and the state of popular feeling also favourable. The wave of executions, banishments and confiscations there which followed Morillo's reconquest in 1815–16 had not endeared the Spanish cause to the creole upper class, while increased taxation, arbitrary recruitment and labour levies created resentment at other levels of society. At various points guerrilla forces had sprung up, though as yet without really threatening the Spanish regime. The province of Casanare, on the *llanos* of New Granada, had been a haven for republican refugees since the collapse of the *Patria Boba*, and Bolívar (who paid little attention to the theoretical boundary between New Granada and Venezuela) had commissioned one of these men, the ex-law student and now general, Francisco de Paula Santander, to create there an advance base of operations. Santander's success in fulfilling the commission was one more reason for Bolívar's decision to move west.

Even so there were impressive obstacles. The hardships inherent in crossing the flooded Casanare plains in the rainy season were followed by those climbing the eastern range of the Colombian Andes to the barren, 3,900 metre-high *páramo* of Pisba before descending into a series of more hospitable upland valleys. *Llaneros* accustomed to a hot climate could not stand the cold, and British legionaries were not much good when they lost their shoes. But Bolívar's army made the passage and began receiving new recruits and supplies, while sparring with advance detachments of the royalist army commanded by José María Barreiro. The climax came on 7 August 1819 in the battle of Boyacá, just south of Tunja on the road to Bogotá. The combat lasted under two hours and did not involve many men – between them Bolívar and Barreiro had no more than about 5,000 soldiers, with a slight preponderance on the republican side – but the result was a clearcut victory. The royalist army was destroyed, Barreiro himself taken prisoner and the way thrown open for Bolívar to enter Bogotá unopposed three days later. As Spanish authority simply collapsed in most of central New Granada, the patriots acquired a secure reservoir of human and material resources as well as a renewed momentum that would enable them not only to complete the liberation of New Granada but move back toward Andean Venezuela and later still against the royalist strongholds of Quito and Peru.

One more by-product of Boyacá was the formal creation of what historians refer to as Gran Colombia but in its own day was just called Colombia. The union of all the territories of the viceroyalty of New Granada into a single nation was proclaimed by the Congress of

Angostura on 17 December 1819 and was in line not merely with Bolívar's express desire but with a *de facto* situation: with forces drawn from Venezuela and New Granada indiscriminately, Bolívar was moving back and forth between the two, forging a military unity that now needed only to be given political form and legitimacy. Whether the Congress of Angostura was a proper body to bestow such legitimacy is another matter, as it contained only token representation of New Granada and none at all from the Presidency of Quito, still wholly under Spanish rule. But its decree was accepted wherever Bolívar's armies had penetrated. It also adopted a provisional frame of government, pending the election of a Gran Colombian constituent congress which finally met at Cúcuta, on the border between Venezuela and New Granada, in May 1821.

From the liberation of central New Granada in 1819 to the opening of the Congress of Cúcuta there were few spectacular military operations, but a steady consolidation of republican rule in patriot-held territory and a weakening of the enemy's will to fight. Boyacá had been bad enough for royalist morale; then came the Spanish uprising of January 1820 which threw the mother country itself once again into confusion. The revolt of 1820 in Spain led to the restoration of the liberal regime, and, under new instructions, General Morillo sought out Bolívar for the purpose of jointly proclaiming an armistice, which was done at Trujillo (the very spot where Bolívar in 1813 decreed his 'war to the death') on 26 November 1820. Although the new Spanish government hoped this might be a step towards ending the war on a basis of reconciliation between Spaniards and Americans, the fact that Spain was now dealing with the rebels as formal belligerents and equals was in practice an admission of weakness. Morillo himself entered into the truce with genuine reluctance and soon afterward laid down his command. When his successor, Miguel de la Torre, chose to end the armistice ahead of schedule in protest against the patriots' encouragement of growing royalist desertions, Bolívar showed no sign of regret but rather launched his last great campaign on Venezuelan soil. It culminated in the battle of Carabobo, directly south of Valencia, on 24 June 1821. The number of men involved on both sides was roughly twice that at Boyacá, but the result was identical. La Torre's army was destroyed, Caracas was liberated for the last time a few days later, and for most practical purposes Venezuela was now free of Spanish rule.

Bolívar achieved success of a different sort when the Gran Colombian constituent congress, in session at the time of Carabobo, reaffirmed the

Angostura act of union – despite continued lack of Ecuadorian representation – and went on to adopt a rigorously centralist constitution for the new republic. It thus rejected calls for a return to the federalism that Bolívar held responsible for the weakness of earlier patriot regimes. For the rest, the constitution embodied a fairly conventional brand of liberal republicanism, with separation of powers, guarantees of individual rights and assorted borrowings from Anglo-American and European models. Despite the express inclusion of 'extraordinary faculties' for the executive to fall back on in case of emergency – an almost universal device in early as well as later Spanish American constitution-making – the broad powers entrusted to the legislative branch were a source of concern to Bolívar, who for that and other reasons considered the Gran Colombian constitution to have gone decidedly too far in its liberalism. What is more, the Congress of Cúcuta took it upon itself to enact certain other basic reforms, which were likewise of generally liberal tendency. One of these was a law of free birth, giving freedom to all children born in future to slave mothers, though requiring them to work for their mothers' masters until the age of 18. This extended to the whole of the republic the system adopted by Antioquia in 1814 and represented the final implementation, however limited, of Bolívar's promises to end slavery. (It also contained a provision to set up a special fund for buying the freedom of slaves who had the misfortune to be born before the law was issued, but, in practice, no more than a handful were set free by that means.) Another 'reform' of New Granada's *Patria Boba* that was resurrected at Cúcuta and made applicable to the entire republic was the division of Indian communal lands (*resguardos*), but this continued to be little more than a policy objective. A new departure, eventually to prove troublesome, was the law ordering suppression of all male convents with less than eight members and confiscation of their assets which were to be used for public secondary education. This was the first real taste of liberal anti-clericalism, and making schools the beneficiaries of confiscation did not wholly appease the friars or their lay adherents.

The same constituent congress at Cúcuta elected Gran Colombia's first president and vice-president. The only possible choice for president was Bolívar himself: the deputies merely confirmed the supreme authority he already held. For vice-president the choice was less obvious. Francisco de Paula Santander was the eventual winner after a bitter contest with Antonio Nariño, whose recent return from captivity was one more by-product of the Spanish liberal revolt. Santander's success was a tribute to his efficient work as head of the regional administration of New Granada, entrusted to him by Bolívar in 1819, whereas Nariño's past services were offset by the still unburied grudges of his personal and factional enemies.

Vice-President Santander was quickly left in charge of the government as acting chief executive, since Bolívar had no intention of sitting at a desk in Bogotá while there remained Spanish armies in the field. One high-priority target was the Isthmus of Panama, which had always had its revolutionary sympathizers but was isolated from the main centres of patriot activity and, because of its strategic importance, was never without a Spanish garrison. Now it was eyed by Bolívar as a stepping-stone first to Ecuador, where Guayaquil had thrown off Spanish rule by a revolution of its own in October 1820 but where the highlands remained royalist, and then, ultimately, to Peru. There was, however, no need for the invasion he was preparing to take place, since, on 28 November 1821, Panama staged its own uprising. The Isthmians proclaimed their independence and at the same time joined Gran Colombia – on their own initiative, as present-day Panamanians are careful to point out. (The fact that no viable alternative was then available naturally influenced their decision.) Yet, even before the opening of the Panama route to patriot troop movements, Bolívar had sent his most trusted lieutenant, General Antonio José de Sucre, with a small auxiliary force to bolster independent Guayaquil and at the same time to smooth the way for its no less inevitable inclusion in Gran Colombia. Sucre's first foray into the Ecuadorian highlands ended in failure, but in 1822 he took part with Bolívar in a two-pronged campaign against Quito: while the Liberator fought his way through southern New Granada, where Pasto remained fanatically royalist, Sucre was to move inland from Guayaquil. The battle of Bomboná which Bolívar fought on 7 April has been described both as a victory and as a defeat, and it was an expensive one in either case, but he did provide a diversion while Sucre carried out his part of the plan. With additional support from an Argentine–Chilean–Peruvian force supplied by San Martín, he won the decisive battle of Pichincha on a slope overlooking Quito on 24 May. The result was surrender of the Spanish authorities in Quito and, indirectly, of Pasto as well, although the *pastusos* would return to battle in a protracted guerrilla uprising before the region was pacified for good.

Another consequence of Pichincha was the formal incorporation into Gran Colombia of what is now Ecuador. In Quito itself this was really automatic. The situation at Guayaquil was more complex, with Peruvianist, Colombianist and autonomist factions vying for control. The last of these was probably the strongest locally, but Guayaquil had already entrusted the leadership of its military forces to Sucre, and Bolívar, having obtained Quito, did not intend to allow its outlet to the sea a truly free choice. When Guayaquil formally voted to join Colombia on 31 July 1822, it only confirmed a fait accompli.

The future of Guayaquil had not been in question when San Martín met Bolívar in the port city just four days earlier in a conference of which no verbatim record was made and which continues to inspire polemics to this day, mainly between Venezuelan and Argentine historians. The major controversy has centred on the military assistance that San Martín may have requested of Bolívar to complete the liberation of Peru, and the reply given by Bolívar. According to the standard Argentine version, San Martín underscored the need for help in dislodging the royalists from their remaining strongholds and even offered to serve personally under Bolívar's command; Bolívar, it is claimed, proved unco-operative, whereupon San Martín resolved to abandon the Peruvian theatre and leave the glory to his northern counterpart. Venezuelan academicians paint San Martín as relatively unconcerned about the royalist forces in Peru (which seems unlikely), while pointing out correctly that Bolívar did proceed to send reinforcements. It is also perfectly clear that there was not sufficient room in Peru for both liberators. San Martín, who realized that his own effectiveness there had passed its prime, chose to bow out, resigning all powers on 20 September and departing for what ultimately became self-imposed exile in Europe.

Remnants of San Martín's Chilean–Argentine expeditionary force stayed on in Peru after he left, but neither Chile nor Argentina would henceforth make a significant contribution to the struggle for Peruvian independence. Both were too concerned with their own affairs and willing to let Gran Colombia assume the burden. Moreover, the latter was at least outwardly well prepared to assume it. The home front was in the hands of Vice-President Santander, a man who seemed to revel in details of administration and under whom the governmental apparatus somehow functioned. Santander established a good working relationship with the legislative branch, which enjoyed substantial independence but usually in the end gave him what he wanted; it was thus not too difficult for him to live up to the title 'the man of laws', originally bestowed on him by Bolívar. There was dissatisfaction in some quarters over matters of government policy – as Santander and his collaborators continued along the generally liberal path of reform charted by the Congress of Cúcuta – as well as latent regional conflict between Venezuela, New Granada and Ecuador. Yet, for the moment, all this resulted in lively press controversy and congressional debate rather than a breakdown of civil order; and certainly Bolívar's own prestige at home was as high as ever. Accordingly, he could heed the call of Peru without fear of domestic complication.

And the call was not long in coming. Peru itself had no leader to take the place of San Martín: at best there was José de la Riva-Agüero, a *limeño* aristocrat who, unlike most of his class, had long been a partisan of independence and who became president with the help of a military coup. Riva-Agüero, though he had embraced the patriot cause in the first place for largely opportunistic reasons, displayed considerable vigour in raising and reorganizing forces. However, he spent much of his time feuding with the Peruvian congress, and neither he nor it was in a position to finish the war by liberating the *sierra*, still largely dominated by the royalists. Hence, there was much to be said for bringing in someone who had men at his command, a reputation for victory and no prior involvement in Peruvian affairs. Congress added its official invitation to the other entreaties Bolívar had been receiving; and on 1 September 1823 he landed at Callao. Bolívar tried to co-operate with the congress and with the new executive it had established in opposition to Riva-Agüero, even while making overtures to the latter – who soon made himself vulnerable politically by entering into negotiations, not necessarily treasonable, with the Spaniards. Riva-Agüero was then conveniently overthrown by certain of his own followers. Bolívar further began developing a military base in northern Peru, and he took political control openly into his own hands following a mutiny of February 1824 that for a while returned Callao and, indirectly, Lima to the royalists and frightened congress into voting him dictatorial powers.

By mid-1824 Bolívar was ready for the final offensive. Moving south through the *sierra* and obtaining aid from patriot guerrillas, he won a first important victory at Junín on 6 August. Though only a brief cavalry clash, its direct and indirect consequences included the final evacuation of Lima by the royalists. The culmination of the 1824 campaign was the battle of Ayacucho, fought on 9 December by Sucre, since Bolívar was in Lima. It was the last major engagement of the war: Sucre destroyed or captured the entire 7,000-man army led by Viceroy José de la Serna. After this, there was little pretence of further resistance except in Upper Peru, and by the beginning of April 1825 that was finally eliminated thanks to an invasion by Sucre and continued royalist desertions. When a small Spanish detachment still holding out in the fortress of Callao agreed to surrender on 23 January 1826, the war in South America was in fact ended.

One issue that defeat of the royalists did not settle was the future status of Upper Peru, now independent of Spain – and independent of what else? Before the war it had formed part of the viceroyalty of Río de la Plata, but there were also valid reaons, cultural and economic as well as historical, to consider joining it with Peru. However, among the narrow minority of politically conscious inhabitants – those who would staff any new administration – the predominant sentiment was for a separate republic. Bolívar made an effort to delay the decision, but when an Upper Peruvian assembly convoked by Sucre declared full independence in August 1825, he accepted its verdict, particularly as the deputies voted to name the republic Bolívar (soon changed to Bolivia) and invited him to draft a constitution for it.

The text that Bolívar produced in fulfilment of the assembly's request represents a further attempt on his part to combine the appearance and some of the substance of liberal republicanism with safeguards against the spreading disorder that in his view threatened the achievement of the Spanish American liberators. In this connection he had in mind not just disunity in the Río de la Plata and the troubles of Peru, Chile and Mexico, but developments in Gran Colombia, which on the surface remained tranquil but from which he had lately been hearing a growing chorus of complaints. Some of these reflected the discontent of groups adversely affected by measures of the constituent congress or later congresses, such as the friars and the slave-owners, not to mention the textile manufacturers of highland Ecuador who bewailed the lack of a systematically protectionist tariff policy, and the many wealthy citizens who evaded but still denounced an abortive effort to introduce direct taxation. Other grievances involved the dislike of Venezuelans and Ecuadorians for any system in which final authority resided in Bogotá, while still others stemmed from the largely inevitable errors made in organizing a new government. But there was a natural tendency to put the blame on Vice-President Santander and a widespread opinion, which Bolívar shared, that a major source of difficulty had been the attempt of liberal-minded innovators to change too much too soon.

Bolívar concluded that it was necessary to redress the balance in favour of stability and authority; and the Bolivian Constitution was his answer. Its most notorious feature was a president serving for life and with the right to nominate his successor: a constitutional monarch in all but name, with strictly defined legal powers but a fund of personal influence. This invention was supplemented by a complex three-house congress; one element – the Chamber of Censors – was a resurrection of the 'moral power' proposed by Bolívar in 1819 at Angostura, but he did not revive the idea of a hereditary senate. The general tone of the constitution was a slightly implausible blend of Caesarism and aristocracy. In his belief that the framers of independent Latin America's first institutions were often led astray by infatuation with constitutional liberalism of French or Anglo-Saxon origin, Bolívar may well have been correct. What he never offered was a satisfactory alternative.

In Bolivia the new constitution was formally accepted, but with no great enthusiasm. Sucre dutifully agreed to serve as first president, though stating at the outset that he had no intention of serving for life. With even less enthusiasm, and with some question as to the legality of the procedure used, the same constitution was adopted in Peru before the year was out. This was in line with the Liberator's related dream to join Bolivia, Peru and Gran Colombia in a Confederation of the Andes, with some form of his constitutional panacea adopted both by the confederation and by each of its parts. When he finally tore himself away from Peru and Bolivia to go home to Gran Colombia, in the latter part of 1826, one of his motives was to help sway opinion in favour of this scheme. However, even more important was the need to deal with a rapid deterioration of the internal political situation. Since April, Venezuela, under José Antonio Páez, had been in open rebellion, and this had stimulated further defiance of the Santander administration in Ecuador. Bolívar did not exclude the possibility that the crisis was just the opportunity needed in order to impose his new political system, but in reality it proved to be the beginning of the end for Gran Colombia itself. Not only that, but a few months after his own departure from Lima a liberal and nationalist reaction occurred in Peru which led to the fall from power of his Peruvian friends and the revocation there of his Bolivian constitution.

Bolívar's idea of Andean Confederation was soon abandoned for lack of significant support, and the same proved true in the end of his efforts of longer standing to promote a loose league or alliance of all the new

Spanish American states. The latter was an objective eloquently put forward in Bolívar's Jamaica Letter of 1815 and regularly repeated. Bolívar explicitly rejected the possibility of a single huge nation-state, which, as he saw, would have been geographically unwieldy quite apart from whatever conflicting regional interests or feelings of separate identity also stood in the way. To be sure, outright clashes of economic interest among the former Spanish colonies were few, in part because they had more contact with Europe or the United States than with each other. But this relative lack of contact, which did not preclude occasional friction over such matters as the Peruvian tariff on Chilean grain or the pretension of Buenos Aires to control trade and communications via the Paraná River with Paraguay – not that Buenos Aires even recognized Paraguayan autonomy at this stage – was scarcely a favourable condition for the achievement of larger unity. The political rivalry of the former colonial capitals, any one of which would inevitably be restless under the hegemony of another, was no more favourable. Indeed, even before the independence movement began, the various constituent parts of the Spanish empire had already gone far towards developing a proto-national consciousness, based on a sense of their difference not only from the mother country but from each other. The continental scope of the struggle waged in Spanish South America did for a time create new ties, as when Venezuelan soldiers took wives and settled in Ecuador, to which their campaigning had finally brought them, or enriched the speech of Caracas with new expressions learned in Peru.[19] However, the military influx into Peru not just from northern South America but from the Río de la Plata and Chile generated an unstable mixture of gratitude and anti-foreign backlash, which caused trouble first for San Martín and then for Bolívar and had parallels elsewhere too; all too often the liberators of one day came to be perceived as conquerors the next. New Granadan resentment of the predominance of Venezuelans – especially Venezuelans of the lower social orders – among the military leaders of Gran Colombia would likewise be one of the factors contributing to the ultimate failure of that experiment in union.

Though well aware of the difficulties that stood in the way of closer integration, Bolívar hoped to see at least some lasting arrangements of consultation and co-operation among independent territorial units. He was thinking essentially of a *Spanish* American league, as he stressed the

---

[19] Martha Hildebrandt, *La lengua de Bolívar: léxico* (Caracas, 1961), 189–231.

importance of historical and cultural homogeneity. Thus, he invariably excluded the United States and Haiti from his concept of an inter-American system, and he was not at all sure about Brazil which had declared its independence from Portugal in 1822. Bolívar was even somewhat dubious about Argentina which was Spanish American but dominated by a self-centred *porteño* elite, whose lack of genuine American sentiment had previously concerned San Martín. Nevertheless, on the very eve of the battle of Ayacucho in December 1824 Bolívar judged that the time had come for bringing dream to reality. From Lima he sent out invitations to the first international assembly of American states, to be held at Panama. Despite misgivings, he invited Buenos Aires. He did not invite Brazil or the United States, but he hoped that Great Britain – no less culturally alien but Spanish America's leading trade partner and the dominant power politically and militarily – would somehow take his project under its protection. As things turned out, Brazil and the United States were invited anyway by the government of Gran Colombia, but this made little difference. One of the two United States delegates died on the way, the other was unable to leave home in time for the sessions (held during June–July 1826), and neither missed very much. Of the Latin American states, only Mexico, the Central American federation, Gran Colombia and Peru were present. And the agreement that was drawn up for perpetual alliance and military and other co-operation was ratified only by Gran Colombia. An attempt to continue the sessions later in Tacubaya, Mexico, produced even less in the way of concrete results.

The Panama Congress is thus something to be cited as an antecedent of later inter-American collaboration, but indicative of the *lack* of conditions for such collaboration at the time. Not only were the new nations of Spanish America caught up in domestic problems that seemed almost insoluble but there was really little they could do together that they could not do about as well (or badly) on their own. With victory in the independence struggle substantially assured even though Spain had not yet been brought to admit defeat, there was little need for military joint action against the mother country; and meanwhile the possibility that other European powers would effectively intervene on Spain's side, never very serious, had been dispelled by British disapproval. The British themselves were interested only in economic penetration, which the leaders of the new states were generally disposed to welcome. Nor was there any significant prospect of obtaining better terms of trade or investment by presenting a united front in negotiations with the British;

the bargaining position of the war-ravaged ex-colonies *vis-à-vis* the premier trading and industrial power was too weak to begin with. Finally there may have been something to be said for a Spanish American defensive alliance against the expansionist United States, or for that matter Brazil, but it is hard to imagine that this would have produced much practical benefit, for example, for Argentina, in its war with Brazil in 1825–28 over the Banda Oriental (which led to the creation of the modern state of Uruguay), or for Mexico in its war with the United States two decades later.

The emergence of several new Spanish American nations was not, of course, the only result of the long struggle for independence from Spain. There had been considerable loss of life and destruction of property, as well as certain changes, for better or for worse, in the social environment. The demographic impact of the wars was greatest in Venezuela, an area not just bitterly but almost continuously fought over. Recent research, it is true, has cast doubt on the conclusions of those historians who claimed that Venezuela experienced a sharp net decline in population, suggesting that there may have been about as many inhabitants – say, 800,000 – at the end of the independence period as at the beginning.[20] Nor was the loss of such natural increase as might otherwise have occurred due solely to deaths in battle and to the reprisals and counter-reprisals of 'war to the death'. In Venezuela, as in the rest of Spanish America, the opposing sides were not capable of putting really large bodies of men into combat at any one time, and 'war to the death' was never applied with absolute consistency. As in most historical conflicts, both armies and civilian populations suffered substantial losses from disease as well as military action, and there were additional losses from voluntary or forced emigration. Most of the patriots who fled eventually returned, and so did some loyalists; but more of the latter apparently did not.

At the other extreme from Venezuela stood Paraguay, where loss of population was negligible. Furthermore, the demographic impact was uneven in more than regional terms. The once-popular notion that Argentina lacks an appreciable black population because slaves and free *pardos* were systematically drafted in the war of independence and either

---

[20] Cf. John V. Lombardi, *People and places in colonial Venezuela* (Bloomington, Ind., 1976), 59 and *passim*. Lombardi does not give an estimate for the change in population during the independence period but presents great amounts of data, admittedly of sometimes questionable accuracy, for particular places. The most that can be said is that the figures he gives do not appear to support the idea of a drastic general fall in population. See also Miguel Izard, *El miedo a la revolución; la lucha por la libertad en Venezuela (1777–1830)* (Madrid, 1979), 43, 46, 175.

died in battle or failed to return from wherever San Martín took them has also been discredited, but it would appear to contain a kernel of truth, at least for the Cuyo region.[21] (In Gran Colombia, by contrast, Bolívar gave as one reason for drafting slaves precisely the need to *maintain* racial balance by making sure that blacks suffered their proportionate share of casualties.[22]) The clearest case of differential social impact, however, was the effect of emigration on the peninsular minority, whose ranks were seriously depleted even though they nowhere disappeared. Naturally the departure of peninsular Spaniards (and unreconciled creole loyalists) had economic as well as demographic significance. Real estate could not be taken away and was widely confiscated, to be used to finance the new governments and reward deserving patriots; liquid assets were withdrawn more easily. The flight of capital associated with San Martín's harassment of Spanish merchants in Lima created severe problems for San Martín himself and the governments that immediately followed, but it has attracted attention chiefly because of its sudden and massive nature. It was hardly unique.

Another source of decapitalization was the arrival of the English and other foreign merchants who to some extent directly replaced the Spaniards, bearing with them a range of consumer goods that found a greater demand in the newly opened ports of Spanish America than could be paid for out of current export earnings. Moreover, the need to pay for imports with capital assets – including coinage in circulation – was all the greater beause of the impact of the military struggle itself on productive activities. Though Belgrano failed in his attempt to blow up the Potosí mint, mining installations in Upper and Lower Peru suffered severe damage as a result of both intentional sabotage and involuntary neglect at different stages of the conflict. Likewise flocks and herds from Uruguay to Colombia were decimated to provide food and transport for passing armies, with little concern to preserve breeding stock for the future. Even so, beef cattle, horses and other livestock were not completely wiped out, and in due season they could replace their numbers more rapidly and certainly more cheaply than flooded mines could be put back into use or broken machinery repaired. For subsistence farming, the source of livelihood of the great majority of Spanish Americans, the minimum recovery time for abandoned fields or trampled crops was

---

[21] Masini, *La esclavitud negra*, 12–15, 59 and *passim*. Cf. Equipos de Investigación Histórica, *Buenos Aires, su gente 1800–1830* (Buenos Aires, 1976), 89, 194–6, 248.

[22] Bolívar to Santander, 20 April 1820, in *Selected writings*, I, 223.

even shorter. The damage suffered by commercial plantation agriculture
was more complex, for here capital loss and disruption of labour supply
posed special problems. Cacao estates in Venezuela and plantations
producing sugar or other commercial crops in the coastal valleys of Peru
were particularly hard hit by the recruitment of slaves for military service.

There were admittedly a few bright spots in the economic picture, of
which the most obvious was the growth of the Buenos Aires livestock
industry, due to the rising demand for hides and other animal by-
products in industrial countries and to the spread of the integrated meat-
salting plant or *saladero*. The latter had first appeared on the coast of
Uruguay in the late eighteenth century; during the independence period
it took root on the other side of the Río de la Plata. All types of livestock
exports were naturally helped by the increasing ease of commerce with
foreign ports, and Buenos Aires in particular benefited from the fact that
Uruguay was so much more directly affected by military operations. In
Spanish America as a whole, however, the modest success story of rural
Buenos Aires was an unusual, if not quite unique, phenomenon. At the
same time the negative effects of war on so many traditional forms of
production were not offset to any appreciable extent by stimulus given to
new activities. There was increased demand for some craft products such
as cloth for uniforms, and a number of specialized metal foundries,
powder plants and other 'war industries' sprang up; but the economic
and technological repercussions of specifically war-related demand for
goods seem to have been neither profound nor lasting. As a matter of
fact, the demand for war supplies was satisfied in part from external
sources, resulting in a further loss of capital and the accumulation of
foreign debt.

The war effort inevitably created new financial demands upon both
patriot and royalist authorities that ordinary taxes were unable to meet.
Quite apart from the effect on tax yields of any war-related disturbance of
production, the state monopolies suffered from diversion of the operating capital to military or other extraneous expenditures. In Venezuela as
late as 1827 the profits of the tobacco monopoly were barely one-fourth
the pre-war level. Other taxes were simply harder to collect under
wartime conditions, while some, like the tribute, were being ostensibly –
though by no means always in practice – abolished. Only the customs
duties showed a tendency to increase, particularly in a port such as
Buenos Aires, which was continuously under patriot control and whose
immediate hinterland was in relatively sound economic health. But the

net effect everywhere was substantial deficits, to be covered by (among other things) 'extraordinary contributions' and forced loans. In Chile in 1817 voluntary and involuntary domestic loans came to over half of total government income. That was an unusually high figure, but the recourse to loans was universal, and the fact that resident foreign merchants were among the lenders blurred the line between internal debt and the explicitly foreign debts that patriot agents abroad were incurring through purchases on credit and other short-term financial operations even before the new governments were well enough established to be taken seriously on the European bond market.

The first major foreign loans were floated in 1822: £1,000,000 by the Chilean government of O'Higgins, £1,200,000 for Peru and £2,000,000 for Gran Colombia. Gran Colombia borrowed £4,750,000 more in 1824, Peru another £616,000 in 1825. The governments in question did not, of course, receive the full face value of the loans, and of the funds not used merely for consolidation of earlier obligations a major part went to military purchases that were sometimes no longer needed by the time they were made. Moreover, very soon all the loans mentioned were in default, with the result that the financing of the movements for independence left a legacy of diplomatic complications that would take many years to unravel. Such complications did not arise only with European creditors, for the different republics also expected to be repaid for their services in helping to liberate each other. Gran Colombia thus had claims for a 'war debt' to be collected from Peru, which in turn had similar claims to press against Bolivia.

Internal war debts also created problems for the new governments, but equally important was the differential impact of the manner in which money had been raised. Demands particularly for forced loans always hit hardest those whose assets were in liquid form, above all if such persons were in political disfavour, as was the case with peninsular merchants in patriot territory or patriot merchants during any given restoration of Spanish control. Those whose wealth was principally in land enjoyed some built-in protection against forced loans and tended to emerge, on balance, in slightly better condition – unless they happened to provoke outright confiscation of their assets. The church was another net loser from revolutionary financial measures. It, too, provided loans to the contending factions, willingly or otherwise, and it saw its tithe income both declining in total amount and repeatedly retained by the state for military purposes.

This was not the only problem faced by the clergy, whose influence over popular opinion made patriots and royalists alike all the more anxious to manipulate it, not just for financial but also for political advantage. The papacy, by remaining true to its traditional alliance with the Spanish crown and issuing fulminations against the revolutionaries well past the point at which their victory was certain, inevitably saw some weakening of its position in Spanish America. The peninsular clergy, over-represented at the upper levels of the church, also tended to be loyalist. The local clergy, on the other hand, appear to have sided for or against independence on essentially the same lines as the non-clergy. If, as in Pasto, everybody was loyalist, the priests were scarcely an exception. But if, in a given area, the creole elite was predominantly patriot, the same was likely to be true of those creoles who had opted for an ecclesiastical career. Thus, the official gazette of Gran Colombia was within the bounds of permissible exaggeration when it paid tribute to 'this clergy upon whose patriotism has been erected a throne of liberty.'[23] Even so, the papacy's intransigence created problems for the church throughout republican territory by interrupting the normal chain of ecclesiastical command. One problem was the sheer impossibility of obtaining replacements for bishops who died or went into exile. Appropriately enough, the first unequivocal sign that the papacy was prepared to recognize the new order in Spanish America as a fait accompli came in 1827, in the form of the appointment of bishops for vacant Gran Colombian dioceses from a list of names previously approved by Vice-President Santander.

The state of incommunication with Rome was less serious, in the long term, than the beginnings of anti-clerical reform. The abolition of the Inquisition, carried out everywhere during the period, was above all a symbolic gesture in that it did not automatically eliminate existing restrictions on heterodox religious belief; at most it augured laxer enforcement. Far more ominous for the church were such measures as the limitation of religious professions and the suppression of smaller religious houses, of which scattered examples from different parts of Spanish America have already been noted. Others could have been cited, and all of them were just a first instalment of measures designed to restrict ecclesiastical influence. In reality, however, it was scarcely necessary to limit professions by law, as one other development during

23 *Gaceta de Colombia*, 9 February 1823.

the revolutionary period was a spontaneous decline in all kinds of religious vocations. This presumably reflected, in part, the influence of secularizing and irreligious currents of thought from abroad, against which traditionalist spokesmen liked to rail; it also reflects a decline in the attractiveness of clerical careers as against those now available in other fields.

The fact that the military were gaining in numbers and importance *vis-à-vis* the clergy (and almost everyone else) is well known. As long as the independence struggle lasted the reasons were self-evident, and the fact that the military continued to play an enlarged role after independence has mainly to do with the weakness of the institutions of civil government in the new nations. But the military underwent qualitative as well as quantitative changes. As fighting spread, armies grew, and the creole upper class could no longer provide all the officers needed. Thus, whereas the *pardo* militia units of the colonial period had been normally commanded by whites, a select number of *pardos* during the war of independence rose to the top ranks themselves and even began commanding non-*pardos*. Many lower-class creoles or *mestizos* found it easier to rise in military rank on the basis of demonstrated ability. Here the classic example is the *llanero* chieftain, José Antonio Páez, who from a quite modest background rose to the highest military rank and also became the leading political figure in Venezuela, at least in absence of Bolívar. Not only that, but in payment for his services to independence he obtained landed estates that made him one of the country's wealthiest men. He did not obtain (indeed did not really seek) social status as an equal to the surviving members of the *mantuano* elite, but he certainly received their respect.

Both in Venezuela and in other parts of Spanish America, examples such as that of Páez could be multiplied. Nevertheless, they signified a relative increase in ease of upward mobility for particular individuals rather than a change in the structure of society. The one mechanism that could have made the greatest structural difference, which was the confiscation and redistribution of enemy property, did not really do so. Only Artigas in Uruguay unequivocally espoused the division of large estates among small and medium landholders and his agrarian measures proved abortive. More typical was Bolívar's bonus decree of 1817, which assumed that confiscated estates would normally be kept intact and provided only that small claimants, if they wished, could jointly receive a single property; apparently to Bolívar's personal disappointment, the provision turned out to be largely inoperative. As a rule, therefore, new *latifundistas* took the place of the old, or old ones who were also good patriots managed to increase their holdings. Concentration of ownership over the more desirable agricultural and grazing lands was not significantly altered.

The immediate impact of measures affecting slavery was also limited. Although the institution was not yet abolished outright, it declined steadily through the recruitment of slaves for military service, the abolition of the slave trade and the introduction everywhere except Paraguay and Brazilian-occupied Uruguay of the principle of free birth – not to mention the increased opportunities offered to runaway slaves in the confusion of wartime. In Venezuela the slave population fell by about one-third during the struggle, and in some regions the drop was greater. On the other hand, in most of Spanish South America slave labour had been of only limited economic importance; and where it had been significant, as in north-central Venezuela, the new freedmen became either a rural proletariat or a floating population of squatters and drifters. The alarm expressed by their social superiors at the ex-slaves' trouble-making potential reflects some weakening of traditional social controls, but events would prove such fears to have been exaggerated. The blow administered to slavery must still be accounted the most important 'social reform' of the independence period, yet it failed to effect a fundamental redistribution of economic power, and the same could be said of other social and economic innovations that either were decreed by the new governments or came about as unintended by-products of the struggle. The principal means of production in Spanish America continued in the hands of the creole upper class, which by virtue of independence from Spain had now also taken possession of the top level of the political system. This transfer of political power meant that henceforth decisions would be made in terms of national rather than metropolitan interests, or more precisely, national interests as interpreted by the dominant minority. This did not preclude a continuation, in somewhat altered form, of external economic dependency, for the interests of that dominant minority were frequently tied to the production and export of primary commodities. It had, on the contrary, removed those limitations on full incorporation into the world market that were inherent in the Spanish imperial system. Apart from individual exceptions, the incorporation of other social elements into national decision-making would have to wait quite a while longer.

4

THE INDEPENDENCE OF BRAZIL

Portugal at the end of the eighteenth century was a small, economically backward, culturally isolated country on the edge of western Europe, with limited natural resources and only modest military and naval strength, but, at least on the face of it, with one great asset: a world-wide empire stretching across three continents which included the vast and potentially rich colony of Brazil. Portugal's overseas territories in Asia, Africa and America, and above all Brazil, were an important source of crown revenue; income over and above what was necessary to administer and maintain the empire was drawn from taxes on production, consumption and internal trade, from crown monopolies, from voluntary donations (some more voluntary than others) and from duties on imports and exports. Portugal maintained as far as possible a monopoly of trade within its empire and, as well as being the hubs of the trade in Portuguese goods, Lisbon and Oporto were the entrepôts for non-Portuguese goods exported to the colonies and colonial produce imported and re-exported to the rest of Europe. Brazilian re-exports in particular – in the late eighteenth century sugar and cotton, above all – were essential for Portugal's balance of trade. England was Portugal's principal trading partner, supplying Portugal – and indirectly Brazil – with manufactured goods (mainly textiles) in return for wine, olive oil – and Brazilian cotton. (During the first three-quarters of the eighteenth century Brazilian gold had also been a major item in Anglo-Portuguese trade, legal and illegal.) Under treaties going back to the end of the fourteenth century England was also the guarantor of Portugal's independence and the territorial integrity of the Portuguese empire.

During the second half of the eighteenth century, that is to say, during the reigns of José I (1750–77), Maria I (1777–92) and from 1792, when Dona Maria was declared mentally incapable, the Prince Regent João, the future João VI, Portugal, like Spain under the late Bourbons, had taken stock of itself and its empire. Sebastião José de Carvalho e Melo, the Marquês de Pombal, who was in effect prime minister, virtually dictator, throughout the reign of Dom José I, and his successors, notably Martinho de Melo e Castro, Secretary of State for the Navy and Overseas Territories (1770–95), and Rodrigo de Sousa Coutinho, later Conde de Linhares, Secretary of State for the Navy and Overseas Territories (1796–1801) and President of the Royal Treasury (1801–3), were influenced by the 'enlightened' ideas of the time as well as by political and economic realities. They initiated and implemented a series of administrative and economic measures aimed at overcoming Portugal's economic and cultural backwardness and lessening her economic and political dependence on England. Portuguese agriculture was to be modernized; manufacturing, especially the textile industry, developed; education improved; colonial trade expanded; a greater proportion of the profits of empire retained; the balance of trade deficit reduced; and, above all, in a period of rising government expenditure, especially on defence, both in Portugal and in the empire, state revenues increased.

As far as Brazil was concerned this meant in the first place a tightening up, and to some extent a centralization, of administration. The Estado de Grão Pará e Maranhão, a separate state since 1621, was integrated into an enlarged Estado do Brasil in 1774 under a single viceroy (whose seat had been transferred in 1763 from Salvador to Rio de Janeiro). In practice, however, the viceroy had only limited powers outside the captaincy-general of Rio de Janeiro and its subordinate captaincies of Santa Catarina and Rio Grande do Sul. The authority of the governors-general and governors of the eight other captaincies-general who were for the most part directly responsible to Lisbon – Grão Pará (which included the subordinate captaincy of Rio Negro), Maranhão (including Piauí), Pernambuco (including Ceará, Rio Grande do Norte and Paraíba) Bahia (including Sergipe and Espírito Santo), Minas Gerais, São Paulo, Mato Grosso, and Goiás – and of the district (*comarca*) and county (*município*) crown judges (*ouvidores* and *juízes de fora*) who had administrative as well as judicial duties was strengthened, at the expense, for example, of the elected *senados da câmara* (town councils). And methods of tax collection in particular were improved. But there was nothing like the intendancy system introduced into Spanish America. Secondly, strictly within the framework of the mercantilist monopoly, colonial trade was somewhat liberalized. The *frota* (fleet) system between Portugal, Bahia and Rio de

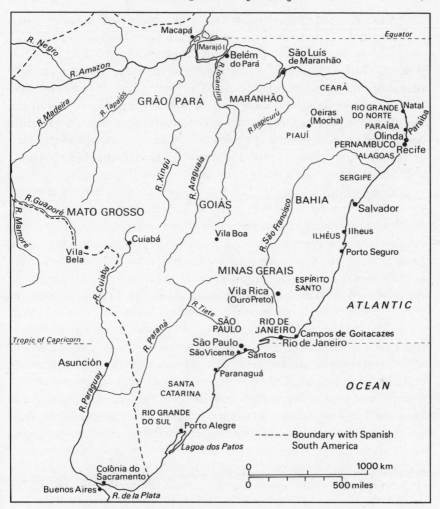

Colonial Brazil, *c.* 1800

Janeiro was ended in 1766; the privileged companies created to trade with Grão Pará and Maranhão and with Pernambuco and Paraíba in 1755 and 1759 (and replacing the fleets to São Luís and Recife) were themselves wound up in 1778–9; some of the state monopolies were abolished. Thirdly, great efforts were made to stimulate production for export, which it was hoped would at the same time widen the market for Portuguese manufactures. (The restrictions on local manufacturing, particularly textiles, were considerably reinforced in, for example, 1785.)

This was a matter of some urgency since after more than a century and a half of growth and prosperity based primarily on plantation agriculture and, during the first half of the eighteenth century, gold and diamond mining, the third quarter of the eighteenth century was for Brazil a period of prolonged economic crisis. The North-East (Pernambuco and Bahia) had lost its virtual monopoly of world sugar production in the middle of the seventeenth century and, though sugar remained Brazil's major cash crop, exports had stagnated somewhat since the 1680s. The production and export of gold and diamonds from Minas Gerais, Goiás and Mato Grosso declined steeply after 1755.

Pombal and his successors failed to regenerate the mining industry of the interior, but by the 1780s, partly as a result of their efforts, coastal Brazil was beginning to experience an agricultural renaissance.[1] This was reinforced in the late eighteenth century by the steady expansion of the market for foodstuffs, including sugar, and raw materials, especially cotton, as a result of population growth, urbanization and the beginnings of industrialization in Western Europe. The French Revolution and its consequences, not least the bloody slave uprising in the French sugar island of Saint Domingue, crippled many of Brazil's competitors and raised world prices for primary produce. Moreover, unlike Spain, which from 1796 until the crisis of 1808 was virtually cut off from its colonies, Portugal until 1807 remained neutral in the wars which followed the French Revolution and the rise of Napoleon, and trade between Portugal and its colonies was not seriously disrupted. The main sugar producing captaincies-general, Bahia and Pernambuco, recovered, albeit temporarily, something like their former prosperity. Increasing quantities of sugar were also exported from the captaincy-general of Rio de Janeiro, where Campos de Goitacazes and the rural hinterland of the capital itself were the centres of production (exports of sugar from Rio doubled between 1790 and 1807), and from São Paulo. Cotton, which was primarily produced in the North (Maranhão and Ceará) and in Pernambuco but now also in Rio de Janeiro, strengthened its position as Brazil's second major export crop. Bahia continued to export tobacco as well as sugar. And in different parts of Brazil new exports emerged; for example, cacao in Pará, rice in Maranhão, Pará and Rio de Janeiro, wheat in Rio Grande do Sul. At the end of the 1790s significant quantities of coffee were for the first time exported from Rio de Janeiro. (Coffee

---

1 For a discussion of the Brazilian economy in the second half of the eighteenth century, and especially the 'agricultural renaissance', see Dauril Alden, *CHLA* II, ch.15.

exports from Rio were to increase sevenfold between 1798 and 1807, signalling the modest beginning of the Brazilian economy's coffee cycle which was to last for more than a century.)

The growth of Brazil's agricultural exports in volume and in value during the last quarter of the eighteenth century, and most dramatically from the mid-1790s, was the biggest single factor behind Portugal's apparent prosperity in the early years of the nineteenth century. J. B. von Spix and C. F. P. von Martius, the German naturalists, described Lisbon as a scene of 'activity and opulence'; it was 'after London . . . the first commercial place in the world'.[2] Portugal's trade with the rest of the world was in surplus in all but two years during the period 1791–1807 and, even more remarkably, with England alone from 1798. Brazilian produce, mainly sugar and cotton, accounted for 80 per cent of the imports from Portugal's colonies and 60 per cent of Portugal's exports and re-exports.[3] As early as 1779 Martinho de Melo e Castro had recognized that 'without Brazil Portugal is an insignificant power'. Twenty-five years later Portugal's dependence on Brazil's resources was greater still. Brazil's economic growth 1780–1800, however, coincided with, and was partly the result of, the Industrial Revolution in Britain and, especially, the unprecedented growth of the British textile and iron and steel industries. The expanding Brazilian market was supplied not with Portuguese but with British manufactures, either as before through the British factory, the community of British merchants in Lisbon, or else on an increasing scale directly smuggled through Brazilian ports, especially Rio de Janeiro, despite all Portugal's efforts, supported by the British merchants resident in Portugal, to prevent unauthorized ships trading with Brazil. From the 1790s Portugal, an underdeveloped dependent metropolis, had an adverse balance of trade with its most important overseas territory. It might be added here that demographic as well as economic forces were also moving against Portugal. At the end of the eighteenth century the population of Brazil (not counting the Indians outside Portuguese control) was more than two million, albeit only 30 per cent white, and growing faster than that of Portugal. Some estimates put it as high as 3–3½ million which was in fact the population of Portugal at the time. Clearly the population of Brazil would soon surpass, if it had

[2] Quoted in Kenneth R. Maxwell, *Conflicts and conspiracies. Brazil and Portugal 1750–1808* (Cambridge, 1973), 234.

[3] For a discussion of Portugal's (and Brazil's) trade in the late eighteenth century, see Andrée Mansuy-Diniz Silva, *CHLA* I, ch.13, Dauril Alden, *CHLA*, II ch.15, and Fernando A. Novais, *Portugal e Brasil na crise do antigo sistema colonial (1777–1808)* (São Paulo, 1979).

not already surpassed, that of Portugal. 'So heavy a branch', wrote Robert Southey in his *Journal of a Residence in Portugal 1800–1*, 'cannot long remain upon so rotten a trunk.'[4]

Some historians have argued that the roots of Brazilian national self-consciousness are to be found in the middle of the seventeenth century in the victory in 1654 over the Dutch, who occupied the North-East for a quarter of a century, or even before, in the exploration of the interior of Brazil by the *bandeirantes* of São Paulo and the early conflicts with Spain in the Río de la Plata. It was, however, during the second half of the eighteenth century that there emerged in Brazil, as in the English and Spanish colonies in the New World, a more acute and more generalized sense of their separate identity among some sectors of the white, American-born colonial oligarchy, which in Brazil consisted primarily of *senhores de engenho* (sugar planters and millowners), cattle barons and other *poderosos da terra*, and, to a lesser extent, mine-owners, merchants, judges and bureaucrats. A minority, though a sizeable minority, of Brazilians now travelled to Europe and were influenced, however indirectly, by the new intellectual climate they encountered there; more Brazilians were educated at Coimbra and other European universities like Montpellier, Edinburgh and Paris; despite the efforts of the Board of Censorship in Lisbon more books were imported into Brazil from Europe (and from North America) and found their way to private libraries; some may even have been read. As a result of the economic, demographic – and intellectual – growth of Brazil in the late eighteenth century voices could be heard for the first time on a significant scale criticizing, first, the mercantilist system and the restrictions it imposed on colonial trade and therefore on agricultural production, secondly, excessive taxation and, thirdly, the limited availability and high price of imported manufactured goods. And the demand for liberalization beyond the limited measures implemented by Pombal and his successors was not confined to the economic sphere. A few liberals – mostly intellectuals, lawyers, bureaucrats and priests, but some landowners and merchants – were prepared to challenge Portuguese absolutism and demand at least a greater degree of political autonomy and Brazilian participation in government.

There was thus in Brazil a growing awareness of conflicts of interest, economic and political, real and potential, with the metropolis, and at the

---

[4] Robert Southey, *Journal of a residence in Portugal 1800–1 and a visit to France 1839*, ed. Adolfo Cabral (Oxford, 1960), 137–9.

same time not only of Portugal's relative economic backwardness *vis-à-vis* its most important colony but also its political and military weakness. The Portuguese crown had a monopoly of political legitimacy and had an important bureaucratic function; it provided, above all, political and social stability. It had, however, little military power. As late as 1800 there were in Brazil only around 2,000 regular troops, *tropas da linha* or *tropa paga*, compared with more than 6,000 in New Spain, for example. Moreover, many of the officers were Brazilian-born, from prominent colonial landed or military families, and the rank and file were mostly recruited in the colony. No wholly European units were stationed in Rio until the 1760s and there were none in Bahia until 1818. Officers in the *milícia*, the reserve army in case of external attack or slave uprising, were mostly landowners and the rank and file theoretically were all the free men in a particular geographic area, except in the major towns where the organization of the militia was based on colour and occupation. The third line *corpos de ordenanças* (territorial units) responsible for internal order and recruitment for the regular army were also dominated by the Brazilian landed class.

Discontent with the economic and political control exercised from Lisbon and hostility between native-born Brazilians and the Portuguese in Brazil, who monopolized so many of the higher offices of state and who dominated the Atlantic trade, was undoubtedly becoming both more extensive and more intensive in the late eighteenth century. But it should not be exaggerated. Brazilians had much closer ties with the metropolis, and much less cause for dissatisfaction, than had the creoles in Spain's American colonies and for many different reasons.

In the first place, the Brazilian oligarchy was for the most part less firmly rooted; Portuguese settlement of Brazil had been a slow, gradual process (the population of the settled areas as late as 1700 was less than half a million) and although there were, of course, particularly in Bahia and Pernambuco, landed families which could trace their origins back to the *donatários* of the sixteenth century, many prominent Brazilian landowners were only first generation Brazilians (or even Portuguese-born but already identifying with Brazil). Secondly, Portuguese colonial rule was by no means as oppressive or as exclusive as Spanish rule; Portugal was a weaker power with more limited financial, military – and human – resources; the Brazilian-born were to be found throughout the middle and lower ranks of the bureaucracy and they even penetrated the ranks of the crown magistrates and governors, not only in Brazil but in other parts of the Portuguese empire such as Goa and Angola and held senior administrative posts in Portugal itself. Much more than Spain, Portugal governed through the local dominant class which was directly involved in at least the implementation if not the formation of policy; entrenched colonial interests were rarely challenged. Thirdly, the family and personal ties which existed between members of the Brazilian and Portuguese elites were sustained and reinforced by their common intellectual formation – predominantly at the university of Coimbra. Unlike Spanish America, Brazil itself had no universities – nor even a printing press – in the colonial period. Fourthly, unlike colonial Spanish America (except Cuba) where native American Indians formed the bulk of the labour force, Brazil was a slave society. Slaves constituted a third or more of the total population and were a characteristic feature of both rural and urban society throughout Brazil. A further 30 per cent of the population was free mulatto or free black. In areas given over to single-crop, export oriented, plantation agriculture like the Mata of Pernambuco, the Recôncavo of Bahia, the coastal region of Maranhão and, increasingly towards the end of the eighteenth century, parts of Rio de Janeiro slaves probably formed the majority of the population. The white minority lived with the fear of social and racial upheaval and was prepared to compromise with the metropolis and accept colonial rule in the interests of social control. Fifthly, the economy of Brazil in the late eighteenth century was, as we have seen, overwhelmingly agricultural and pastoral and, moreover, export oriented. Unlike most Spanish American *hacendados*, *senhores de engenho* and other plantation owners in Brazil had close links with metropolitan merchants, the Atlantic trade and through the metropolitan entrepôts, Lisbon and Oporto, European markets. And the export economy based on agriculture was growing during the last quarter of the eighteenth century, booming even in the 1790s. The planter class was at the same time dependent on the transatlantic slave trade, a predominantly Portuguese enterprise, for their labour supply. And the producers of meat, cereals, hides, oxen and mules in the *sertão* of the North East or in Rio Grande do Sul were in turn heavily dependent on the plantation sector. Compared with colonial Spanish America the domestic economy and internal trade were modest in scale. And Brazil had few, and small, cities; in 1800 only Rio de Janeiro and Salvador had populations of 50,000. Sixthly, Portugal's commercial monopoly was less jealously guarded than Spain's; British manufactures made up the bulk of Portuguese exports to Brazil through Lisbon and, on an increasing scale, directly as well.

Finally, Portugal's reappraisal of its political and economic relations with its colonies and the imperial reorganization which occurred in the second half of the eighteenth century was less far-reaching than Spain's and amounted to less of a direct threat to the colonial status quo and the interests of the colonial elite. On the contrary, many Brazilians profited from the 'agricultural renaissance', the confiscation of Jesuit properties after the expulsion of the Jesuits in 1759 and the expansion of trade, and the growth of the bureaucracy – and the militia – opened up new opportunities for participation in public affairs. The fact is that although Portugal and Brazil did not entirely avoid the 'Democratic Revolution' and the 'crisis of the old colonial system' in the Atlantic world in the second half of the eighteenth century there were only two significant conspiracies (they hardly had time to develop into rebellions) against Portuguese rule in Brazil – the first in Minas Gerais in 1788–9 and the second in Bahia in 1798. (Two other conspiracies – in Rio de Janeiro (1794) and in Pernambuco (1801) – were stifled at birth.)

The *Inconfidência mineira* was by far the most serious of the anti-Portuguese movements of the late eighteenth century. Minas Gerais in the 1780s was one of Brazil's most important and populous captaincies, but one which was undergoing a serious recession as it adjusted to the decline of the mining industry since the mid-1750s and the transition to a mixed agricultural and pastoral economy. It was also a captaincy with a rich intellectual and cultural life. Some of the wealthiest and most influential men in the region – crown judges, *fazendeiros*, merchants, tax farmers, lawyers, priests, regular army officers – were involved in the conspiracy. Most were Brazilian-born, a few were Portuguese. The ideological justification for rebellion was provided by a brilliant generation of intellectuals and poets, many of whom had studied at Coimbra and in France. (An unusually high proportion of the Brazilians educated at Coimbra in the 1770s and 1780s were *mineiros*.) It began as a protest against increasingly oppressive, and clumsily imposed, taxation, especially the collection of arrears in the payment of the royal fifth on gold, the *derrama* (head tax), and a more efficient and less corrupt system of tax collection, but it soon became anti-colonial in character, aiming to end Portuguese rule in Minas Gerais – and Brazil. Its leaders, inspired by the American Revolution, dreamed of a 'republic as free and as prosperous as English America'. The conspiracy, however, failed; it was discovered and the principal conspirators were arrested, tried, banished and, in the case of Joaquim José da Silva Xavier (known as 'Tiradentes', the Toothpuller), hanged. And it is important to remember that the

Inconfidência mineira totally failed to inspire similar movements for political separation from Portugal in São Paulo or Rio de Janeiro, much less in Bahia or Pernambuco.

The conspiracy in Bahia ten years later was a predominantly urban and a much more radical movement aiming at an armed uprising of mulattos, free blacks and slaves. Its leaders were mainly artisans (especially tailors) and soldiers. A small number of young educated white Brazilians, notably Cipriano Barata de Almeida, were also involved. Here the influence of the French Revolution was predominant. The leaders of the rebellion wanted political independence from Portugal, democracy, republican government and free trade but also liberty, equality and fraternity and an end to slavery and all racial discrimination in a captaincy in which one-third of the population were slaves and two-thirds of African origin. (Indeed in the city of Salvador whites were outnumbered 5 to 1.) The dominant class in Bahia was, however, in no mood to listen to demands for political change. The insurrection of *affranchis* (free coloureds) and slaves in Saint Domingue had provided a grim warning to slaveholders throughout the Americas of the consequences of the propagation of ideas of liberalism, egalitarianism and the rights of man in slave societies – and of the challenge to metropolitan control by revolutionary elements among the white population. The sugar boom and overall economic prosperity of the 1790s, which incidentally further strengthened their attachment to slavery and the slave trade, was a further powerful incentive for the Bahia oligarchy to put up with the existing colonial relationship. The 'Tailors' Revolt' was heavily repressed with several dozen arrests and severe punishments; four of the leaders were hung, drawn and quartered; six more were exiled to non-Portuguese Africa.

This is not to say that criticism of the colonial system within the white elite of colonial Brazil had entirely subsided by the 1790s. The economic writings of the reforming bishop of Pernambuco, José Joaquim da Cunha de Azeredo Coutinho (1742–1821), for example, *Memoria sobre o preço do assucar* (1791), *Ensaio economico sobre o commercio de Portugal e suas colonias* (1794) and *Discurso sobre o estado actual das minas do Brasil* (1804) and the *Cartas economico-politicas sobre a agricultura e comercio da Bahia* of João Rodrigues de Brito (1807) serve as a reminder that there remained in Brazil considerable resentment not only at the high level of taxation but also at privileges and monopolies and restrictions on production and trade (especially the role of Portugal as entrepôt) in a period of expanding international markets and the beginnings of the Industrial Revolution.

Whatever the strength of the ties that bound Brazil and Portugal together a fundamental, and eventually irreconcilable, conflict of interest now existed between colony and metropolis. And there was always the danger for Portugal that the demand for a loosening of economic ties would one day lead to the demand for political separation as well.

At this critical juncture Portugal, unlike Spain, was fortunate not only in maintaining its neutrality in the European wars but also in the quality of its political leadership. The contrast between Manuel Godoy, Charles IV of Spain's corrupt and incompetent chief minister from 1792, and Dom Rodrigo de Sousa Coutinho, who came to power in Portugal in 1796, could hardly be sharper. Sousa Coutinho was a determined opponent of all that the French Revolution stood for – the conspiracy of 1798 in Bahia was, as we have seen, firmly repressed – but in, for example, his *Memoria sobre os melhoramentos dos dominios na America* (1798) he recognized the need for enlightened government and political and economic reform to secure the continued loyalty of the Brazilian oligarchy. England had already lost its American colonies; France was struggling to keep Saint Domingue; and there was evidence of growing resistance and revolt among the creoles in different parts of Spanish America. The Portuguese government therefore continued to introduce limited but important measures of economic liberalization (the salt and whaling monopolies were abolished in 1801) and to appoint Brazilians – Manuel Ferreira de Câmara and José Bonifácio de Andrada e Silva, for example – to high positions in the metropolitan and colonial administrations. At the same time Sousa Coutinho was sufficiently intelligent to realize that reform could only delay, and might even precipitate, the inevitable. Moreover, Portugal's future relations with Brazil were somewhat at the mercy of external factors. If Portugal were to be drawn into the war and, in particular, if Napoleon were to invade Portugal (and from 1801 there were hints that he might), Dom Rodrigo before his resignation at the end of 1803 recommended that rather than run the risk of losing Brazil as a result, either through internal revolution or seizure by a colonial rival, the Prince Regent Dom João could and should in the last resort abandon Portugal, move to Brazil and establish 'a great and powerful empire' in South America. Portugal was after all 'neither the best nor the most essential part of the monarchy'.[5]

The idea of transferring the Portuguese court to Brazil was not new. It

---

[5] See Mansuy-Diniz Silva, *CHLA* I, ch.13; Maxwell, *Conflicts and conspiracies*, 233–9; and K. R. Maxwell, 'The Generation of the 1790s and the idea of Luso-Brazilian Empire', in Dauril Alden (ed.), *Colonial roots of modern Brazil* (Berkeley, 1973).

had been canvassed on earlier occasions when the survival of the dynasty
had been in danger, and even in less critical times: for example, in 1738 by
the great eighteenth-century statesman Dom Luís da Cunha, on the
grounds that Brazil's natural resources were greater than Portugal's and
that Rio de Janeiro was better situated than Lisbon to be the metropolis
of a great maritime and commercial empire. There was, of course, bitter
opposition to Dom Rodrigo's proposals of 1803 from vested interests –
mainly merchants in colonial and foreign trade and to a lesser extent
manufacturers – in Lisbon. The British government, on the other hand,
for a mixture of strategic and commercial reasons was in favour of such a
Portuguese move to Brazil in the circumstances of a French invasion. As
early as 1801 Lord Hawkesbury, the British Foreign Secretary, had
instructed the British ambassador in Lisbon to let it be known that if a
decision were made to go to Brazil Britain was ready 'to guarantee the
expedition and to combine with [the Prince Regent] the most efficacious
ways to extend and consolidate his dominions in South America'.[6]

It was after Tilsit (25 June 1807) that Napoleon finally determined to
close the few remaining gaps in his continental system aimed at destroying Britain's trade with Europe. On 12 August 1807 he issued an
ultimatum to António de Araújo de Azevedo, the Portuguese Foreign
Minister: the Prince Regent must close his ports to English ships,
imprison English residents in Portugal and confiscate their property, or
face the consequences of a French invasion. In reply George Canning,
the British Foreign Secretary, through Percy Clinton Sydney Smythe,
the 6th Viscount Strangford, a young Irish peer in charge of the Lisbon
legation at the time, threatened, on the one hand, to capture and destroy
the Portuguese naval and merchant fleets in the Tagus (as he had already
in September destroyed the Danish fleet at Copenhagen) and seize
Portugal's colonies, including Brazil, if Dom João gave in to French
threats, while promising, on the other hand, to renew Britain's existing
obligations to defend the House of Braganza and its dominions against
external attack if he stood firm. And by secret convention in October
1807 Canning offered British protection in the event of the Prince
Regent's deciding to withdraw temporarily to Brazil. From Britain's
point of view, this would be the most satisfactory outcome: not only
would the Portuguese court, the Portuguese fleet and conceivably Brazil

---

6 Quoted in Maxwell, *Conflicts and conspiracies*, 235.

for that matter be kept out of Napoleon's hands, but at a critical time for British trade when British goods were being excluded from Europe and were threatened with exclusion from North America, and British merchants had recently suffered what seemed a major setback on the Río de la Plata (the defeat of the British invasion of 1806–7), it might be expected that Brazil would be opened up to direct British trade. Brazil was itself an important market; it was also a convenient back door to Spanish America.

For a time Dom João tried to satisfy Napoleon by adopting some anti-British measures without totally antagonizing Britain and thus to avoid an agonizing choice. Early in November, however, he learned that General Junot had left Bayonne with 23,000 men and was marching on Portugal. On 16 November Britain tightened the screw when a British fleet under the command of Rear Admiral Sir Sidney Smith arrived off the Tagus. On 23 November news arrived that four days before the French army had actually crossed the Portuguese frontier with Spain and was now only four days' forced march from Lisbon. The next day Dom João took the decision to leave the kingdom he could not retain except as a vassal of France (indeed the survival of the House of Braganza was in serious doubt) and withdraw across the Atlantic to his most important colony. The decision to transfer the court to Brazil was regarded by the local population as a cowardly desertion, an ignominious and disorderly flight, a *sauve-qui-peut*. Certainly it was forced upon Dom João and there were elements of confusion, even farce. But, as we have seen, it was also an intelligent, political manoeuvre which had been long premeditated – and, in the interval between Napoleon's ultimatum and Junot's invasion, carefully planned. Between the morning of 25 November and the evening of 27 November some 10–15,000 people – the Prince Regent Dom João and a dozen members of the royal family (including his mother, the demented Queen Maria, his wife Princess Carlota Joaquina, the daughter of Charles IV of Spain, his sons Dom Pedro (aged nine) and Dom Miguel), the members of the council of state, ministers and advisers, justices of the High Court, officials of the Treasury, the upper echelons of the army and navy, the church hierarchy, members of the aristocracy, functionaries, professional and businessmen, several hundred courtiers, servants and hangers-on, a marine brigade of 1,600 and miscellaneous citizens who managed by various means to secure passage – embarked on the flagship *Principe Real*, eight other ships of the line, eight lesser warships and thirty Portuguese merchant vessels. Also packed on board were the contents of the royal treasury – silver plate, jewels, cash and all moveable assets – government files, indeed the entire paraphernalia of government, a printing press and several libraries including the Royal Library of Ajuda which was to form the basis for the Bibliotheca Publica, later Biblioteca Nacional, of Rio de Janeiro. As soon as the wind was favourable, on 29 November (the day before Junot arrived), the ships weighed anchor, sailed down the Tagus and set out across the Atlantic for Brazil – escorted by four British warships. The head of a European state along with his entire court and government was emigrating to one of his colonies; it was an event unique in the history of European colonialism. Although greatly exaggerating the role he and Admiral Sir Sidney Smith had played in persuading Dom João to leave (the Prince Regent had already embarked when British assistance was offered) Lord Strangford wrote, not entirely without reason, 'I have entitled England to establish with the Brazils the relation of sovereign and subject, and to require obedience to be paid as the price of protection'.[7]

It was a nightmare journey: a storm divided the fleet; the royal party suffered from overcrowding, lack of food and water, lice (the ladies had to cut off their hair) and disease; changes of clothing had to be improvised from sheets and blankets provided by the British navy. Nevertheless, the crossing was successfully accomplished and on 22 January 1808 the royal fugitives arrived in Bahia to a warm reception; it was the first time a reigning monarch had set foot in the New World. Dom João declined an offer to establish his residence in Salvador and after a month left for Rio de Janeiro, arriving on 7 March to another heartwarming welcome, it should be noted, from the local population.

Whatever conclusions are drawn about the political and economic condition of Brazil, its relations with the mother country and the prospects for its future independence before 1808, there is no disputing the profound impact the arrival of the Portuguese court had on Brazil and especially on Rio de Janeiro. The viceregal capital since 1763 and in the late eighteenth century increasingly important economically, Rio de Janeiro overnight became the capital of a worldwide empire stretching as far as Goa and Macao. Between April and October 1808 the major institutions of the absolutist Portuguese state were installed, including the Conselho de Estado, the Desembargo do Paço (the Supreme High

[7] Quoted in Alan K. Manchester, *British preeminence in Brazil. Its rise and decline* (Durham, N.C., 1933), 67.

Court), the Casa de Supplicação (Court of Appeal), the Erário Real (Royal Treasury), the Conselho da Real Fazenda (Council of the Royal Exchequer), the Junta do Comércio, Agricultura, Fábricas e Navigação and the Banco do Brazil. Brazil itself was now governed from Rio, not Lisbon, although the government was, of course, in the hands of the same people, all Portuguese: the Prince Regent, his ministers (notably Dom Rodrigo de Sousa Coutinho, Conde de Linhares, now Minister of Foreign Relations and War and by far the most influential minister until his death in 1812), the Council of State, the higher judiciary and bureaucracy. Significantly, no Brazilians were included. Provincial and local administration were left in the hands of the crown appointed governors of the captaincies and crown judges (many of whom were Brazilians), although the very presence in Rio de Janeiro of the Portuguese king and the Portuguese government in place of the viceroy ensured a degree of increased centralization of power.

The nineteenth-century Portuguese historian, Oliveira Martins, wrote of the events of 1807–8: 'Portugal was [now] the colony, Brazil the metropolis.' Modern Brazilian historians refer to the metropolitanization of the colony. Certainly, the relationship between mother country and colony had been decisively altered. Brazil was no longer strictly speaking a colony. But neither was it independent and in control of its own destiny. The transfer of the Portuguese court to Rio de Janeiro is nevertheless generally regarded as a major stage in the evolution of Brazil towards independence since it would prove impossible, as we shall see, to restore the *status quo ante*.

Of even greater significance perhaps than the establishment of the metropolitan government in Rio – because it would prove even more difficult to reverse – was the ending of the 300-year-old monopoly of colonial trade and the elimination of Lisbon as an entrepôt for Brazilian imports and exports. During his brief stay in Bahia – indeed within a week of his arrival – Dom João had by means of a *Carta Régia* (28 January 1808) opened Brazil's ports to direct trade with all friendly nations. In doing so, he had been advised by, among others, Rodrigo de Sousa Coutinho, Dom Fernando José de Portugal e Castro, the future Marquês de Aguiar, a councillor of state, who had only recently served as viceroy (1801–6) and who would become Minister of the Interior and Finance Minister in the new government in Rio, the Conde de Ponte, governor of the captaincy of Bahia who had only the year before conducted a survey of Bahian planters' views on the economy, and José de Silva Lisboa

(1756–1835), the future visconde de Cairú, a native of Bahia and graduate of Coimbra, a distinguished political economist and author of *Principios de Economia Politica* (1804) which had been greatly influenced by the writings of Adam Smith. The Prince Regent, however, had in fact little alternative – and there is some evidence that the opening of the ports was seen at the time as a temporary measure. The Bahian warehouses were full of sugar and tobacco which could not otherwise be exported; the Portuguese ports were closed as a result of the French occupation and the British blockade. Moreover, government finances were dependent on foreign trade and the duties imports in particular paid. To legalize the existing contraband trade would enable the Portuguese government to control – and tax – it. Britain in any case expected the Portuguese government to open Brazilian ports to direct British trade now that Portugal was occupied by the French. It was part of the secret convention of October 1807, the price of British protection.

Thus, almost accidentally, Dom João on his arrival in Brazil immediately identified with the interests of the big Brazilian landowners and conceded what critics of the old colonial system had most eagerly demanded. (In April he also revoked all the decrees prohibiting manufacturing, especially textile manufacturing, in the colony, exempted industrial raw materials from import duties, encouraged the invention or introduction of new machinery and offered direct subsidies to the cotton, wool, silk and iron industries.) The opening of the ports to foreign trade created a storm of opposition from Portuguese interests in Rio as well as Lisbon, and by decree on 11 June 1808 Dom João in response (but also to facilitate the administration of the customs houses) restricted foreign trade to five ports – Belém, São Luís, Recife, Bahia and Rio de Janeiro – and restricted the Brazilian coastal trade and trade with the rest of the Portuguese empire to Portuguese vessels. He also discriminated in favour of Portuguese shipping by reducing the general tariff on imported goods fixed in January at 24 per cent to 16 per cent in the case of goods brought in Portuguese ships. Nevertheless, the basic principle of open trade had been established.

In practice, at least until the end of the war, direct trade with all friendly nations meant trade with England. As Canning had anticipated Rio de Janeiro became 'an emporium for British manufactures destined for the consumption of the whole of South America'[8] – not only Brazil

---

[8] Quoted in Manchester, *British preeminence*, 78.

itself but the Río de la Plata and the Pacific coast of Spanish America. As early as August 1808 between 150 and 200 merchants and commission agents formed a thriving English community in Rio de Janeiro. One merchant who arrived there in June – John Luccock, a partner in the firm of Lupton's of Leeds, who stayed for ten years and in 1820 published his *Notes on Rio de Janeiro and the southern parts of Brazil*, one of the first comprehensive descriptions of south-central Brazil and especially of the economic transformation which occurred in and around the capital during the years after 1808 – found the city 'heaped high with [British] cloth, ironmongery, clothing and earthenware'.[9] It has been estimated that the total value of all British goods exported to Brazil in 1808 amounted to over £2 million – a figure not equalled for ten years. The number of ships entering Rio in 1808 was more than four times higher than in 1807; most of them were British. Brazilian sugar, cotton and coffee exports which continued to grow after 1808 – and primary commodity prices were at an all-time high for the duration of the war – were also now mainly shipped to Europe in British vessels.

Britain was not satisfied, however, with an open door in Brazil. She wanted the kind of preferential rights she had enjoyed in Portugal for centuries. And Dom João could not refuse these, and other, demands: he was entirely dependent on British troops and arms in the war to defeat the French in Portugal and on the British navy for the defence of Brazil and the rest of Portugal's overseas empire. Lord Strangford, who as British minister had followed the Prince Regent to Rio, finally extracted from him in February 1810, after lengthy negotiations, a Treaty of Navigation and Commerce and a separate Treaty of Alliance and Friendship. The commercial treaty fixed a maximum tariff of 15 per cent ad valorem on British goods, mainly cottons, woollens, linens, hardware and earthenware, imported into Brazil. (A decree of 18 October 1810 lowered duties on Portuguese imports from 16 to 15 per cent, but this could do nothing to restore Portuguese trade with Brazil which collapsed in 1809–13 to some 30 per cent of its 1800–4 level. The only trade to Brazil still dominated by the Portuguese was the trade in slaves from Portuguese Africa. At the same time cheap British imports became even cheaper and to a considerable extent undermined the efforts being made after 1808 to establish Brazilian industries.) Needless to say, Britain did not reciprocate by lowering its virtually prohibitive duties on Brazilian sugar and

[9] See Herbert Heaton, 'A merchant adventurer in Brazil, 1808–1818', *Journal of Economic History*, 6 (1946).

coffee, though not cotton, entering the British market. The Prince Regent in 1810 also formally conceded to British merchants the right to reside in Brazil and to engage in the wholesale and retail trades. Moreover, the British government was given the right to appoint judges conservators, special magistrates responsible for dealing with cases involving British subjects in Brazil.

Under article 10 of the treaty of alliance, the Prince Regent entered into his first treaty engagement for the reduction and eventual abolition of the slave trade. In April 1807, within three weeks of its own abolition, Britain had appealed to Portugal to follow its lead – not surprisingly without success. The new circumstances of the Prince Regent's residence in Brazil presented Britain with a rare opportunity to extract concessions on this front, too. The Prince Regent was obliged as a first step to confine the Portuguese slave trade to his own dominions, that is not allow Portuguese traders to take over the trade from which the British were now obliged to withdraw, and to promise gradually to abolish it. British pressure for the fulfilment of that last commitment would henceforth be unrelenting.

The transfer of the Portuguese court to Rio de Janeiro in 1808 not only opened up Brazil economically but ended Brazil's cultural and intellectual isolation as well. There was an influx of new people and new ideas. In May 1808 a printing press was established in the capital for the first time (followed by new presses in Salvador in 1811 and Recife in 1817); and newspapers and books were published. Public libraries, literary, philosophical and scientific academies, schools and theatres were opened. Between 1808 and 1822, in addition to 24,000 Portuguese émigrés (including the families and retainers of those already there), Rio de Janeiro alone registered 4,234 foreign immigrants, not counting their wives, children and servants. 1,500 were Spanish, especially Spanish American, 1,000 French, 600 English, 100 German, the rest from other European countries and from North America.[10] They were mostly professional men and artisans: doctors, musicians, pharmacists; tailors, shoemakers, bakers, etc. During the period of Dom João's residency the population of the city of Rio de Janeiro doubled from 50,000 to 100,000.

The Portuguese government in Rio also welcomed and facilitated visits – the first since the Dutch occupation of North-East Brazil in the 1630s and 1640s – by distinguished foreign scientists, artists and

---

10 Arquivo Nacional, *Registro de Estrangeiros 1808–1822*, pref. José Honório Rodrigues (Rio de Janeiro, 1960).

travellers. John Mawe, the English naturalist and mineralogist and author of the classic *Travels in the Interior of Brazil* (1812), was the first foreigner to be granted a licence to visit the mining areas of Minas Gerais, then very much in decline. Henry Koster who had been born in Portugal, the son of a Liverpool merchant, went to Pernambuco in 1809 for health reasons and apart from brief visits home remained there until his death in 1820; his *Travels in Brazil* (1816) is regarded as one of the most perceptive descriptions of the Brazilian *Nordeste*. In March 1816 a French artistic mission arrived in Rio. It included the architect Auguste-Henri-Victor Grandjean de Montigny, who designed the Academia de Belas-Artes and many other new and imposing buildings in the capital, and the painters Jean Baptiste Debret (1768–1848) and Nicolas-Antoine Taunay (1755–1838), whose drawings and watercolours are an important record of the landscapes and daily life of Rio in the early nineteenth century, as well as the composer Sigismund von Neukomm (1778–1858), a pupil of Haydn. Two other Frenchmen, Louis-François de Tollenare and the botanist Auguste de Saint-Hilaire, wrote outstanding accounts of their travels in different parts of Brazil between 1816 and 1822. Brazilian geography, natural resources, flora and fauna – and Brazilian Indians – were also studied by a number of remarkable German explorers and scientists – notably Baron von Eschwege, Georg Freyreiss, Frederik Sellow, Maximilian von Wied-Neuwied, Johann Baptist Pohl and the great partnership of Johann Baptist von Spix, zoologist, and Carl Frederick Philip von Martius, botanist – many of whom visited Brazil under the patronage of Princess Leopoldina of Habsburg, the daughter of the Austrian emperor who married Dom João's eldest son, Dom Pedro, in 1817. Princess Leopoldina also brought to Brazil the Austrian painter Thomas Ender (1793–1875). Another notable artist, Johann-Moritz Rugendas (1802–58), first came to Brazil in 1821 with the scientific mission to Mato Grosso and Pará led by Count Georg Heinrich von Langsdorff.

With the liberation of Portugal and the end of the war in Europe it had been generally expected that the Portuguese Prince Regent would return to Lisbon. In September 1814 Lord Castlereagh, the British Foreign Secretary, sent Rear Admiral Sir John Beresford to Rio de Janeiro with two ships of the line and a frigate to conduct Dom João home. On his arrival at the end of December 1814 Beresford put *HMS Achilles* at the Prince Regent's disposal for the return journey. But Dom João had enjoyed his residence in Brazil. Moreover, he was not simply a king in exile; he had brought with him the entire apparatus of the Portuguese state as well as several thousand members of the Portuguese governing class, many though by no means all of whom had put down roots in Brazil and were now reluctant to leave. In the face of conflicting advice Dom João was as usual indecisive. Finally, he listened to Araújo de Azevedo, Conde da Barca, his chief minister (1814–17), and decided to stay in Brazil. And on 16 December 1815 Brazil was raised to the status of kingdom – equal with Portugal. For some historians this, rather than the arrival of the Portuguese court in 1808, marks the end of Brazil's colonial status. Three months later, on the death of his mother, the Prince Regent became King João of Portugal, Brazil and the Algarves. The experiment of a Luso-Brazilian dual monarchy with its centre in the New World was, however, doomed to failure. Dom João was unable to commit himself wholly to Brazil. The Portuguese court and government remained close to the Portuguese community in Brazil and conscious of its interests as well as, ultimately, the interests of Portugal itself. At the same time the demographic and economic trends which so favoured Brazil at the expense of Portugal in the period before 1808 had been reinforced by the differences in their respective fortunes since 1808. The fundamental conflicts between Brazilians and Portuguese had not been and could not be resolved.

In one sense, it is true, the ties between the crown and the Brazilian landowning elite had been strengthened after 1808 as they found a coincidence of interest in open commerce. In particular, both Rio de Janeiro, indeed the centre-south region as a whole, and Bahia under the 'enlightened' governorship of the conde de Arcos (1810–18) had seen their exports of sugar, cotton and, in the case of Rio, coffee grow, although in the post-war period international prices especially of cotton (with the growth of United States production) and sugar (as Cuban production accelerated) began to fall. But royal economic policy was still not entirely free of irritating mercantilist monopolies and privileges as Dom João did what he could to protect the interests of Portuguese merchants resident in Brazil and in Portugal. Moreover, at the back of the Brazilian mind was the possibility of the restoration of Brazil's colonial status and the loss of all the gains since 1808 if Dom João were eventually to return to Lisbon.

On the political side, enlightened absolutism had proved reasonably tolerable to the Brazilian elite, since Dom João now ruled in harmony with their interests and promoted the growth and development of Brazil while at the same time guaranteeing political and social order. Unlike

Spanish America, where after the overthrow of the Spanish monarchy by Napoleon in 1808 there was no king to obey, there had been no crisis of political legitimacy in Brazil. And Brazil had, after all, achieved equal political status in 1815. Moreover, Dom João had made good use of his power to grant non-hereditary titles of nobility – barão, visconde, conde and marquês – and decorations at various levels in the five Orders of Christo, São Bento de Aviz, São Tiago, Tôrre e Espada and Nôssa Senhora da Conceição, to native Brazilians as well as to continental Portuguese (and foreigners), that is to say, offering enhanced social status in return for loyalty to the crown. Below the surface, however, there lurked political aspirations, both liberal and, more strongly, anti-Portuguese. With the absolutist Portuguese government in Rio metropolitan rule was more immediately felt. Avenues to some limited form of political power sharing had been closed; discrimination in favour of the Portuguese, now that there were so many more of them, was more pronounced. The fiscal burden was also greater since the Brazilians alone were obliged to support the court and a larger bureaucracy and military establishment. Moreover, Brazilians were called upon to pay for the dynastic ambitions of Dom João and his wife Carlota Joaquina (as well as the interests of the *estancieiros* of southern Brazil) in the Río de la Plata. The revolutions for independence in Spanish America, and especially the struggle between Artigas and Buenos Aires, had offered a great opportunity for Portugal to regain control of Colônia do Sacramento which had finally been ceded to Spain in 1778 after a century of conflict. As early as 1811 Portuguese troops had crossed the Spanish frontier, but then withdrew. In April 1815 Lord Strangford, who had played a restraining influence, left Rio for London. And soon after Portuguese troops released from the war in Europe began to arrive in Brazil. In June 1816 a Portuguese fleet and 3,500 men left Rio for the Río de la Plata, and in January 1817 General Lecor occupied Montevideo. (In July 1821 the entire Banda Oriental – present-day Uruguay – was incorporated into Brazil as the Cisplatine province.)

There were other examples of the government in Rio apparently sacrificing Brazilian interests to the interests of the Portuguese state, most obviously the Anglo-Portuguese commercial treaty but also the various treaties with England for the suppression of the transatlantic slave trade. For a time the British navy had mistakenly interpreted the treaty of 1810 restricting the Portuguese slave trade to Portuguese territories to mean that the trade was illegal north of the equator, and until 1813 when they were stopped from doing so British warships captured a number of Portuguese slavers. Traders exporting slaves to Bahia and Pernambuco suffered heavy losses and slave prices rose. Then at the Congress of Vienna Portugal did finally agree, by treaty in January 1815, to ban the trade north of the equator in return for a financial indemnity and reiterated its determination to bring about a gradual end to the trade which in February 1815 eight powers (including Portugal) declared 'repugnant to the principle of humanity and universal morality'. Worse was to come from the point of view of the Brazilian slaveholders. In July 1817 the Conde de Palmella, Portugal's minister in London, signed an additional convention to the 1815 treaty giving it teeth: the British navy was given the right to visit and search on the high seas Portuguese vessels suspected of illegal slaving north of the equator and Anglo-Portuguese mixed commissions were to be set up to adjudicate the captures and liberate the slaves. Again Portugal promised to introduce and enforce anti-slave trade legislation and to move towards the final abolition of the entire trade. Diplomatic pressure for further concessions was, however, resisted and the Brazilian slave trade, legal south of the equator, now illegal north, continued to supply the labour needs of Brazil. The trade grew from 15–20,000 per annum at the beginning of the nineteenth century to 30,000 per annum in the early 1820s. Yet for many Brazilians it seemed like the beginning of the end of the slave trade, and the Portuguese had, therefore, sold out a vital Brazilian interest.

Although it undoubtedly existed, and perhaps was growing, Brazilian disaffection from the Portuguese regime now apparently permanently installed in Rio de Janeiro should not be exaggerated. There was still no strong and certainly no widespread demand for political change. The most persistent criticism of Portuguese absolutism and the political system it imposed on Brazil came from Hipólito José da Costa who from June 1808 to 1822 published a highly influential liberal newspaper, the *Correio Brasiliense* – in London. There was only one open rebellion and this as much against political – and fiscal – subordination to Rio de Janeiro as against Portuguese rule as such. Nevertheless, in March 1817 a military revolt which was joined by a few planters and slaveholders facing lower returns from their sugar and cotton exports and higher slave prices, some wealthy merchants, crown judges and priests as well as *moradores* (small, dependent tenant farmers and squatters) and artisans, led to the proclamation of a republic in Pernambuco. The 'organic law' of the republic included religious toleration and 'equality of rights', but defended property and slavery. The revolt spread rapidly to Alagoas, Paraíba and Rio Grande do Norte. But then it faltered. It suffered a good deal of internal factionalism. Britain, having secured the opening of Brazilian ports, favoured the stability and unity of Brazil and refused to encourage it by granting recognition when agents were sent. Two converted merchant ships blockaded Recife from the sea. Finally, an army was gathered together from Bahia, which under governor Arcos remained loyal, and from Rio de Janeiro, and on 20 May 1817 the rebels surrendered. The republic of the north-east had lasted two and a half months. The rest of Brazil had remained quiet. Nevertheless, the revolution of 1817 had revealed the existence of liberal and nationalist ideas, not least within the military. Troops from Portugal were now brought in to garrison the principal cities, and within existing units, in Bahia for example, Portuguese were more often promoted over the heads of Brazilians. With the rapid progress of the revolutions for independence in both southern and northern Spanish South America as a warning, the Portuguese regime showed signs of becoming more repressive. Certainly Thomaz A. Villa Nova Portugal (1817–20) was the most reactionary and pro-Portuguese of all Dom João's chief ministers during his residence in Brazil.

The independence of Brazil was in the event precipitated by political developments in Portugal in 1820–1. On 24 August 1820 a liberal-nationalist revolt erupted in Oporto, followed by another in Lisbon on 15 October. Triggered by the military, they were supported by many sectors of Portuguese society, but especially the bourgeoisie, deeply dissatisfied with political and economic conditions in post-war Portugal. The absolutist King João VI remained in Rio de Janeiro, insensitive it seemed to the problems of Portugal; the roles of metropolis and colony had been reversed. Portugal was governed in the continued absence of Dom João by a Council of Regency presided over by an Englishman, Marshal Beresford, who after the war remained Commander in Chief of the Portuguese Army. Portuguese trade with Brazil had recovered somewhat in the period since the end of the war, but was still far below its pre-1808 level. Landowners, manufacturers, merchants, shippers, indeed most Portuguese, whose economic well-being, as we have seen, had been so heavily dependent before 1808 on Portugal's monopoly position in the trade to and from Brazil, and on the re-export trade in

Brazil's colonial staples, continued to suffer great economic difficulties
(although Portugal's economic decline was not entirely due to the 'loss'
of Brazil). Moreover, without revenue from Brazil and the Brazilian
trade the Portuguese budget was in permanent deficit; civil functionaries
and military personnel went unpaid. At the end of 1820 the liberals
established a *Junta Provisória* to govern in the name of the king whose
immediate return to Lisbon was demanded. João VI would be expected
to adopt the Spanish liberal constitution of 1812 – in force again in Spain
after the liberal Revolution there in January–March 1820 – pending the
formulation of a new Portuguese constitution for which purpose a *Côrtes
Gerais Extraordinárias e Constituintes* was hastily summoned. According
to the instructions of 22 November, the Côrtes was to be elected – for the
entire Portuguese world – on the basis of one deputy for every 30,000
free subjects. (Brazil was allocated some 70–75 seats in an assembly of
over 200.) Provisional *juntas governativas* loyal to the Portuguese revolution were to be set up in the various Brazilian captaincies (now provinces) to supervise the elections to the Côrtes in Lisbon. Behind all these
anti-absolutist, liberal measures, however, there lay also a Portuguese
determination to restore Brazil to its colonial status before 1808.

News of the liberal constitutionalist revolution in Portugal produced
minor disturbances in many Brazilian towns. But, as in Portugal, it was
the military which made the first significant moves against absolutism in
Brazil. On 1 January 1821 Portuguese troops in Belém rebelled and set
up a liberal *junta governativa* for Pará to which Maranhão (3 April) and
Piauí (24 May) later adhered; it immediately declared itself prepared to
organize elections for the Côrtes in Lisbon. On 10 February in Bahia a
similar military conspiracy by liberal troops against their absolutist
officers led to the removal of the governor, the Conde de Palma, and the
establishment of a provisional junta pledged to a liberal constitution for
the United Kingdom of Portugal and Brazil; its members were mostly
Portuguese but it was supported by many prominent Brazilians, if only
to head off the more extreme liberals. In the capital Rio de Janeiro, too,
on 24–26 February a pronunciamento in favour of the constitutionalist
revolution and a gathering of Portuguese troops in the Largo de Rossio
(now the Praça Tiradentes) forced a reorganization of the ministry and
obliged the king himself to approve a future liberal constitution for
Portugal and Brazil; he also decreed, in line with the instructions of the
junta provisória in Lisbon, the establishment of governing provincial
juntas where these did not already exist and the preparation of indirect
elections for the Côrtes.

Serious political conflict arose, however, over the Côrtes' demand that the king return to Lisbon. A Portuguese faction in Rio de Janeiro made up of senior army officers, senior bureaucrats and merchants whose ties were still essentially with Portugal, and who were anxious to recover their monopoly status, naturally favoured the return, although many of them were absolutist or anti-Brazilian more than liberal. On the other hand a 'Brazilian' faction or party now emerged to oppose it. Its main elements were big landowners throughout Brazil, but especially in the captaincies closest to the capital, and Brazilian-born bureaucrats and members of the judiciary. Not all members of the 'Brazilian' party were, however, Brazilian-born. It included those Portuguese whose roots and interests now lay in Brazil: Portuguese bureaucrats who had benefited from the establishment of royal government in Rio, Portuguese merchants who had adjusted to the new economic circumstances of open trade, particularly those in the retail trade in foreign goods and in the internal trade, Portuguese who had invested in land and urban property or who had married into Brazilian families, or who simply now preferred Brazil to Portugal. Many 'Brazilians' though by no means revolutionary and anti-colonialist and certainly not yet nationalist were in favour of a constitution which would reduce the power of the king while at the same time increasing their own power. And it was still not clear that the Côrtes was profoundly anti-Brazilian. It was, however, in the interests of all 'Brazilians' to defend the status quo, to maintain the political equality with the mother country and the economic freedom secured by Brazil since 1808, which would be threatened were Dom João to leave.

The Brazilian dominant class was for the most part conservative, or at most liberal–conservative. It wished to maintain colonial economic and social structures based on the plantation system, slavery and exports of tropical agricultural produce to the European market. But there were liberals, even radical liberals, and some authentic revolutionaries in the city of Rio de Janeiro and in São Paulo as well as in Salvador and Recife, most of them in the professions – especially lawyers and journalists – or artisans – tailors, barbers, mechanics – but also small retailers, soldiers and priests. Most were white, but many were mulatto and free black. They looked for profound changes in politics and society: popular sovereignty, democracy, even a republic; social and racial equality, even land reform and the abolition of slavery. They were ambivalent on the question of whether Dom João should return to Portugal or remain in Brazil.

Dom João faced a difficult dilemma: if he returned he would fall into the hands of the liberals and, possibly, risk the loss of Brazil; if he stayed he would undoubtedly lose Portugal. He considered sending his son Dom Pedro, now 22 years old, to Lisbon, but finally on 7 March 1821 he agreed to return. He had again come under pressure from the military and from the Conde de Palmella, a liberal constitutionalist who won the internal power struggle with Thomaz Villa Nova Portugal, the absolutist first minister, in the court. (Britain also threw its weight behind Dom João's return to Lisbon. Castlereagh hinted that while Britain was obliged to guarantee the Braganzas against external attack this did not extend to internal revolution.) Still Dom João vacillated as the political crisis in Rio de Janeiro deepened. On 21–22 April there were popular demonstrations in the Praça do Comércio demanding a governing junta like those in Pará and Bahia and elections for the Côrtes. Finally, on 26 April Dom João and around 4,000 Portuguese (together with the contents of the Treasury and the Banco do Brasil) set sail for Lisbon after a thirteen-year residence in Brazil, leaving the young Dom Pedro behind in Rio as Prince Regent.

The 'Brazilians' had no alternative now but to organize themselves for the defence of Brazilian interests in the Côrtes. Elections took place for the most part between May and September. They were notable for the fact that almost all those elected were Brazilian-born. And they included several prominent radicals who had participated in the revolution of 1817: for example, Cipriano Barata (Bahia), Muniz Tavares (Pernambuco), Antônio Carlos Ribeiro de Andrada Machado e Silva (São Paulo). The six deputies elected for São Paulo included, besides Antônio Carlos, three others who became distinguished liberal politicians after independence: Padre Diogo A. Feijó, Francisco de Paula Sousa e Melo and Dr Nicolau Pereira de Campos Vergueiro. The elections – and the instructions given to the elected deputies – were also notable for the fact that, apparently, independence for Brazil was not yet regarded as a serious political issue.

The Côrtes had met in Lisbon for the first time at the end of January 1821. The seven deputies from Pernambuco were the first of the Brazilians to arrive – on 29 August; the five from Rio arrived during September and October, those from Maranhão in November, from Bahia on 17 December and the Paulistas, the most formidable group, not until February to May 1822; some, the Mineiros, for example, never arrived. Long before the majority of the Brazilian deputies had taken their seats, however, the Portuguese Côrtes had made its fatal attempt to put back the clock and reduce Brazil to its former colonial status. The Portuguese bourgeoisie in its determination to re-establish its hegemony over Brazil and in particular to deny Britain direct access to Brazil totally failed to recognize the strain put upon the colonial pact by the political, economic and demographic development of Brazil, not least since 1808, and the economic, political and ideological changes which had taken place in Europe and in America which made it unlikely that Portugal alone of European powers would be able to keep its mainland American colonies.

In April 1821 with the news of the constitutional movements in Pará, Bahia and Rio de Janeiro and particularly after the return of Dom João (he arrived in Lisbon on 4 July) the Côrtes, without much success, began bypassing Rio de Janeiro, dealing directly with the different provincial governments in Brazil. An unsuccessful attempt was also made to revoke the trade agreements with Britain; the Portuguese wanted to direct British goods through the metropolis once more and to impose a much higher tariff. Furthermore, in August troop reinforcements were sent to Brazil. Then came what proved to be the decisive moves. On 29 September the Côrtes demonstrated that it intended to govern Brazil by ordering the dismantling of all government institutions established in Rio in 1808 and their transfer back to Lisbon. And on 1 October the appointment of military governors for each province with powers independent of the provincial juntas and directly subject to Lisbon was announced. Finally, on 18 October the Prince Regent himself was ordered to return home. As the Brazilian deputies began at last to arrive during the final months of 1821 and the first half of 1822 they were met – or so they claimed (it could perhaps be argued that they were over-sensitive to their dignity) – with ridicule, insults, threats and a good deal of open antagonism. In the famous words of Manoel Fernandes Thomaz, one of the leaders of the Portuguese liberal revolution, Brazil was a 'terra de macacos, de negrinhos apanhados na costa da Africa, e de bananas'. Not surprisingly, Brazilian demands, presented, for example, by Antô-nio Carlos in March 1822 in the *Apontamentos e Lembranças* of the São Paulo junta, for political and economic equality with Portugal and parallel organs of government with perhaps the seat of the monarchy alternating between Rio de Janeiro and Lisbon, met with little response. It was in any case too late. Events in Brazil were moving inexorably and swiftly towards a final break with Portugal. In October 1822 seven Brazilian deputies – four paulistas, including Antônio Carlos, and three

baianos, including Cipriano Barata – illegally fled Lisbon, first to
London, then to Brazil, rather than swear allegiance to the 1822 Constitution and become members of the Côrtes Ordinárias due to meet for the
first time in December. And the other Brazilian deputies, many of them
radicalized by their unfortunate experience in Lisbon, soon followed.

Brazil had progressed too far since 1808 for anything less than
complete equality with the mother country to be acceptable. The decrees
of late September and early October, news of which arrrived in Rio on 11
December 1821, were the final confirmation of Portuguese intransigence
and determination to reverse all the changes in relations between
Portugal and Brazil since 1808. There followed a major political re-
alignment in Brazil. The 'Portuguese' faction (what was left of it after
Dom João returned to Lisbon) and the 'Brazilian' faction finally – and
permanently – split. The divergent forces within the 'Brazilian' party of
the centre-south – Portuguese-born in Rio de Janeiro with interests in
Brazil, Brazilian conservatives and moderate liberals, especially in São
Paulo and Rio de Janeiro, Brazilian extreme liberals and radicals in Rio
de Janeiro – closed ranks in united resistance to the Portuguese Côrtes.
Since he clearly could not guarantee the continuation of the arrangement
of 1808, the increasingly self-confident Brazilians finally withdrew their
allegiance from King João VI and transferred it to the Prince Regent
Dom Pedro. The battle to keep Dom João in Brazil had been lost in April
1821. The immediate key to the future autonomy of Brazil was now to
persuade Dom Pedro to stay. There was intense political activity in Rio
during the last weeks of 1821 and the first weeks of 1822 as politicians –
and the press – brought pressure to bear on the Prince Regent who, after
some hesitation, finally allowed himself to be won over. In response to a
petition with 8,000 signatures presented by José Clemente Pereira,
himself a Portuguese merchant long resident in Rio, a liberal and the
president of the Senado da Câmara of Rio de Janeiro (which had largely
been ignored by João VI during his residence there), Dom Pedro
announced on 9 January 1822 that he would stay in Brazil. (This episode
is known as *O Fico* from the Portuguese *ficar*, to remain.) The union with
Portugal had not yet been broken, but this significant act of disobedience
by the Prince Regent amounted to a formal rejection of Portuguese
authority over Brazil. A few days later Portuguese troops who refused to
swear allegiance to Dom Pedro were obliged by those who did so – and
who thus formed the nucleus of a Brazilian regular army – to leave Rio de
Janeiro (and fresh troops arriving from Portugal in February were not

allowed to land). On 16 January José Bonifácio de Andrada e Silva (1763–1838), a member of a rich Santos family, educated in Coimbra and for 35 years (until 1819) employed in Portugal as a scientist and royal administrator, now at the age of 58 president of the São Paulo provisional junta, was appointed head of a new 'Brazilian' cabinet. All the other members of the cabinet were Portuguese, it is true, but the appointment was symbolic of the enormous shift which had now taken place in Brazilian politics.

There is some suggestion in the private correspondence between Dom João and Dom Pedro that the former anticipated this course of events when he left Brazil for Portugal and advised his son to throw in his lot with the Brazilians in order that both parts of the empire should at least remain in the hands of the Braganzas with the possibility that one day they might be reunited. For his part Dom Pedro had written bluntly to Dom João in Lisbon, 'Portugal is today a fourth-class state and needful, therefore dependent; Brazil is of the first class and independent.'[11] It may also be that given the threat posed by the Brazilian liberals Dom Pedro, whose political inclinations were decidedly authoritarian, chose to lead rather than be overwhelmed by a movement which was beginning to look more and more like a movement for independence. There is considerable debate among historians about the point at which total political separation from Portugal became the preferred goal of the Brazilians. Until the end of 1821, when the intentions of the Côrtes could no longer be doubted, independence had been the aim of only a radical minority. Even in 1822, it is argued, for some elements in the Brazilian dominant class and, for example, the Brazilian deputies, including the São Paulo group, in Lisbon who constantly emphasized their loyalty to the crown, independence, when it was mentioned at all, still meant autonomy within a dual monarchy and the continuation of some kind of union with Portugal.

At the beginning of 1822 José Bonifácio was unquestionably the dominant figure in the political process in Brazil. His views on social questions were remarkably progressive – he favoured the gradual abolition of the slave trade and even slavery, free European immigration and land reform – but, politically, he was conservative and profoundly hostile to democracy. Once the campaign to keep Dom Pedro in Brazil, which had temporarily and artificially united the Brazilian party, had

---

[11] Quoted by Manoel da Silveira Cardozo in A. J. R. Russell-Wood (ed.), *From colony to nation. Essays on the independence of Brazil* (Baltimore, 1975), 207.

succeeded, José Bonifácio immediately distanced himself not only from the extreme liberals and democrats ('anarquistas e demagogos' he called them), some of whom were republicans, but also many more moderate liberals and set·about rallying support from conservative and liberal-conservative landowners, high ranking bureaucrats and judges (many of them Coimbra-trained) and merchants in Rio de Janeiro, São Paulo and now Minas Gerais for the establishment of an independent monarchy in Brazil. The monarchy he saw as the only means of maintaining political order and social stability – and, it was hoped, territorial unity – in the dangerous period of the transition to independence.

The conflict during the first half of 1822 between José Bonifácio and liberals and radicals like Joaquim Gonçalves Lêdo, Padre Januário da Cunha Barbosa, Domingos Alves Branco Muniz Barreto, José Clemente Pereira and Martim Francisco Ribeiro de Andrada (like Antônio Carlos, the leader of the paulista delegation in Lisbon, a younger brother of José Bonifácio) largely took the form of competition between their respective masonic lodges, the Apostolado and the Grande Oriente, for influence over the young, inexperienced Prince Regent. Insofar as the struggle for power had an ideological element it centred on the question of whether or not a Constituent Assembly should be summoned. On 16 February 1822 José Bonifácio, who was strongly opposed to popular representation in an elected national assembly, persuaded Dom Pedro that a *Conselho de Procuradores da Província* consisting of *homens bons* nominated by means of the traditional procedures was all that was required. It was installed on 2 June, but did not survive. On 3 June despite the opposition of José Bonifácio, Dom Pedro agreed to call a Constituent Assembly. The more extreme liberals then lost the initiative when on 19 June they failed in their efforts to secure direct popular elections for the Assembly. (It was to be elected indirectly on a strictly limited suffrage and in any case did not meet for the first time until 3 May 1823 by which time the leading radicals had been imprisoned or driven into exile.) In the meantime, it had been decided in May 1822 that no further decree of the Portuguese Côrtes would be implemented without the express approval of the Prince Regent. In July more Brazilians were included in José Bonifácio's cabinet. And August saw an increasing number of 'independent' acts by Dom Pedro and the Brazilian government. The final step was taken on 7 September 1822 on the banks of the River Ipiranga, not far from São Paulo. There Dom Pedro received the latest despatches from Lisbon revoking his decrees, charging his ministers with treason and once again demanding his return and the complete subordination of

Brazil to Portuguese rule. At the same time he was advised by José Bonifácio and his wife Princess Leopoldina to break with Portugal once and for all. According to one eye witness (a member of the royal party), in a typically impulsive gesture Dom Pedro grabbed the despatches from the messenger, crumpled them in his hands and ground them under his heel, remarking angrily to those around him, 'From today on our relations with them are finished. I want nothing more from the Portuguese government, and I proclaim Brazil forevermore separated from Portugal.' And then, drawing his sword with a flourish he shouted, 'Long live independence, liberty and the separation of Brazil.' On 12 October, his 24th birthday, Dom Pedro I was acclaimed Constitutional Emperor and Perpetual Defender of Brazil. He was crowned in Rio de Janeiro with, it should be said, much pomp and ceremony on 1 December 1822.

The Brazilian movement for independence from Portugal had drawn its strength from the most important provinces of the centre-south – Rio de Janeiro, São Paulo, Minas Gerais – and especially from the capital, Rio de Janeiro. Pernambuco, where the Brazilian dominant class was anti-Portuguese but remembered the revolution of 1817 and the attempt to establish a republic and where the military garrison, in any case relatively small, proved willing to transfer its allegiance to Dom Pedro, quickly recognized the authority of the independent Brazilian empire. The other provinces of the north-east and the north, where there was still a considerable Portuguese military presence, sizeable Portuguese merchant communities and a good deal of pro-Portuguese sentiment, at least in the coastal cities, remained loyal to the Côrtes in Lisbon. There were fanciful rumours that Portugal might send a punitive expedition and as a first stage of reconquest attempt to separate the north-east and the north, which were closer to Portugal geographically, which were not economically integrated with the centre-south and which in many respects historically had closer ties with Lisbon than with Rio de Janeiro, from the rest of Brazil. If the process of independence were to be completed and consolidated, a long drawn-out civil war avoided and the authority of the new emperor imposed over the whole of the former Portuguese colony, it was imperative to bring the north-east and north, and especially Bahia, by far the most important of the provinces still under Portuguese control, into line as quickly as possible.

At the beginning of 1823 Bahia was bitterly divided, broadly speaking between the Recôncavo and the city of Salvador. This division can be traced back to the appointment of Ignácio Luís Madeira de Mello, a conservative Portuguese colonel, as military governor of the province in February 1822 which was resisted by members of the governing junta, by Brazilian army officers, by the *senhores de engenho* of the Recôncavo and by urban radicals. The resistance was unsuccessful and Madeira de Mello had managed to establish himself in power. In March the Portuguese troops forced to leave Rio in January arrived in Salvador, and they were later further reinforced from Portugal. Madeira de Mello then had at his disposal in Salvador a garrison of 2,000 regular troops plus a militia of 1,500 – the greatest concentration of Portuguese military force in Brazil. But first at Santo Amaro on 22 June, and later at Cachoeira, the conservative sugar barons of the Recôncavo rose in rebellion against the Portuguese attempts to recolonize Brazil. They withdrew their allegiance from João VI and together with a number of Brazilian-born judges set up at Cachoeira an All Bahia Interim Council of Government loyal to Dom Pedro and the government in Rio de Janeiro. The conservative revolutionaries were thus able to head off the more radical opponents of Portuguese colonialism ('demagogues and anarchists', some of whom favoured a separate republic of Bahia) and at the same time guarantee social stability which was increasingly threatened by a series of slave uprisings in the Recôncavo and popular disturbances in the depressed southern areas of the province. The Brazilian military forces, inferior in number, equipment and command, were not, however, strong enough to expel the Portuguese army, although they did begin a seige of the city of Salvador. For his part, Madeira de Mello twice – on 8 November 1822 and 6 January 1823 – failed to break out from Salvador. It was stalemate.

In July 1822, Dom Pedro had appointed a French officer Pierre Labatut as commander of the anti-Portuguese forces in Bahia. Travelling overland from Recife on the final stages of his journey he did not arrive until the end of October, but then with a good deal of energy and professional expertise set about organizing an *Exército Pacificador*. Although Labatut himself was removed by a mutiny in May 1823 and replaced as commander by general José Joaquim de Lima e Silva, he had by the middle of 1823 mobilized a respectable army – at least in terms of numbers: 14,000 men (including 3,000 from Rio and Pernambuco). Madeira de Mello and his troops, nevertheless, still presented a formidable military force to be overcome. Moreover, a Portuguese naval squadron – 1 line of battle ship, 5 frigates, 5 corvettes, 1 brig and 1 schooner – stationed at Bahia gave the Portuguese complete command of the sea.

It was in these circumstances that Dom Pedro turned to Lord Cochrane, the future 10th Earl of Dundonald. Arrogant, ill-tempered, cantankerous, bellicose, Cochrane was one of the most daring and successful frontline frigate captains of his day. He had been struck off the Navy List following a Stock Exchange scandal in 1814, but a few years later began a new career as a mercenary, selling his services to the highest bidder – although usually, it is true, on the side of liberty and national independence. He had already, in 1818, organized the Chilean navy and, with San Martín, had played a major role in securing the independence of Chile and liberating at least the coastal areas of Peru from Spanish rule. Temporarily in semi-retirement on his estate at Quintera in Chile, he now received Dom Pedro's invitation to serve Brazil.

Once again flouting the British Foreign Enlistment Act of 1819, Cochrane accepted the invitation – although only after a certain amount of haggling over rank (he eventually settled for First Admiral and Commander-in-Chief) and emoluments (he indignantly rejected the offer of a Portuguese admiral's pay, which he dismissed as 'notoriously the worst in the world'). Cochrane arrived in Rio de Janeiro on 13 March 1823, bringing with him several other English officers who had served with him in the Pacific, and immediately set about organizing a small Brazilian naval squadron – 9 ships in all – for the blockade of Bahia – in part by encouraging British seamen in Rio at the time to desert their ships. Apart from the flagship, the 74-gun double-decked *Pedro Primeiro* (formerly the *Martim Freitas* and one of the ships which had left Lisbon in November 1807), it was, however, a miserable force. Nevertheless, more out of fear of Cochrane's reputation than the actual force at his command, his arrival persuaded the Portuguese to evacuate Bahia and on 2 July 1823 General Lima e Silva, at the head of a Brazilian army, marched into the city – 'without any disturbance or acts of cruelty or oppression by either party', reported Vice Admiral Sir Thomas Hardy, commander-in-chief of the British South American squadron who, in anticipation of a threat to British lives and property, had moved his flagship *Creole* to Bahia the previous September. In local terms it was essentially a victory for the landowners of the Recôncavo – another conservative revolution.

Once the Portuguese convoy – 13 warships and about 70 transports and merchant vessels carrying 5,000 troops, vast quantities of military stores and a number of leading Portuguese families – had cleared the harbour, Cochrane pursued it relentlessly as far as the Canaries, night after night picking off ships from the rear until less than a quarter remained. Furthermore, the Brazilian frigate *Nitheroy*, commanded by another Englishman, John Taylor, who had served with Nelson at Trafalgar and who had deserted his ship in Rio to join Cochrane earlier in the year, followed the rump of the Portuguese convoy to the mouth of the Tagus and burned another four vessels under the very guns of the *Dom João VI*, the pride of the Portuguese navy.

Cochrane meanwhile had turned his attention to the northern province of Maranhão and on 26 July, largely by bluff, persuaded the small Portuguese garrison at São Luís to surrender. Two days later Maranhão (together with the former sub-captaincy of Piauí) was formally incorporated into the Brazilian empire. On 13 August Cochrane's second-in-command, Captain John Pascoe Grenfell, on board the *Maranhão* (formerly the Portuguese brig *Dom Miguel*), successfully secured the submission of loyalist elements at Belém, again more by the demonstration than the use of force, and the province of Pará (together with the former sub-captaincy of Rio Negro), that is, the whole of Amazonia, became part of the empire. The last Portuguese troops to leave Brazil left Montevideo in March 1824 after the Cisplatine province had also joined the independent Brazilian empire. After his exploits in the north Cochrane had returned to Rio de Janeiro where he was received by Dom Pedro on 9 November 1823 and, among other rewards and decorations, awarded the title Marquês de Maranhão. Though no doubt somewhat exaggerated in British accounts based on his own *Narrative of Services in the Liberation of Chili, Peru and Brazil* (1859) Cochrane and other British naval officers, entirely unofficially, had made a not inconsiderable contribution to the cause of Brazilian independence and, more important, Brazilian unity.[12]

[12] Of those who served with Cochrane, Grenfell became an admiral in the Brazilian navy (he was supreme commander in the war against the Argentine dictator Rosas in 1851–2) and served as Brazilian consul in Liverpool (where he died in 1868). Taylor, who also became an admiral in the Brazilian navy, married a Brazilian and eventually retired to a coffee plantation near Rio de Janeiro. Cochrane's own relations with Brazil were less happy. Not satisfied with the rewards he believed that his services merited and, as always, at loggerheads with his masters – the story of his life – after he had helped put down the republican-separatist revolt in Pernambuco in 1824, Cochrane 'deserted' on board the frigate *Piranga* and sailed to Spithead (where, on 16 June 1825, the Brazilian flag was first saluted in British waters). He then refused to return to Brazil and was dismissed from the Brazilian navy. However, not only was he later reinstated in the British navy – he served, for instance, as commander-in-chief of the North American and West Indian station – but shortly before his death (in 1860) the government of Marquês de Olinda (1857–8), willing to let bygones be bygones, granted him a life pension equal to half the interest on the £100,000 he still claimed from the Brazilian government, and his descendants were eventually paid the sum of £40,000.

By the middle of 1823 Brazil had established her independence from Portugal beyond all doubt, while at the same time avoiding civil war and territorial disintegration. The new Brazilian government, however, was still anxious to secure international recognition of Brazil's *de facto* independence. There were two principal reasons for this: first, to forestall any last ditch attempt by Portugal, once more as a result of the Vilafrancada (May 1823) governed by an absolutist João VI, encouraged and possibly assisted by the reactionary Holy Alliance powers of Europe, to reassert its authority over Brazil in any way; secondly, and ultimately more important, to strengthen the emperor's own authority within Brazil against loyalist, separatist and republican elements. Clearly the attitude of Britain, whose navy commanded the Atlantic, who had emerged from the Napoleonic Wars pre-eminent not only in Europe but in the world at large, and who exercised so much influence in Lisbon, would be decisive. In July 1823 Felisberto Caldeira Brant Pontes (the future Marquês de Barbacena), Dom Pedro's agent in London since July 1821, wrote 'With England's friendship we can snap our fingers at the rest of the world . . . it will not be necessary to go begging for recognition from any other power for all will wish our friendship.'[13]

Although Britain had done nothing to promote it, George Canning, who as a result of Lord Castlereagh's suicide had returned to the Foreign Office only a week after the *Grito de Ipiranga* of 7 September 1822, had been eager to recognize Brazil's independence as quickly as possible: there were particularly strong reasons for doing so (and, incidentally, recognition of Brazil would facilitate the recognition of the new Spanish American republics, at least those whose *de facto* independence from Spain was beyond question and with whom Britain had close commercial ties). In the first place, Portugal was too weak, militarily and financially, to reimpose its rule; Brazil was *de facto* independent, Canning believed, notwithstanding the Portuguese hold on areas of the north-east and the north, from the moment it declared its separation from Portugal. Secondly, Britain already had established relations with Brazil as a result of the Portuguese court's residence there. And Brazil was now Britain's third largest foreign market. By proffering the hand of friendship in her hour of need Britain would consolidate its political and economic ascendancy over Brazil. Thirdly, unlike Spanish America Brazil had retained the monarchy, and Canning was anxious to preserve it as an

---

[13] Quoted in Manchester, *British preeminence*, 193.

antidote to the 'evils of universal democracy' on the continent and as a valuable link between the Old and New Worlds. Any undue delay in recognizing the Brazilian empire might endanger the country's political institutions and undermine its precarious unity. (In March 1824 an armed revolt originating in Pernambuco did, in fact, lead to the establishment of an independent republic, the Confederation of the Equator, in the north-east, but it was defeated after six months.) Finally, Brazil's declaration of independence presented Britain with a unique opportunity to make significant progress on the slave trade question.

In normal circumstances it might have been thought impossible to persuade a newly independent Brazil, one of the greatest importers of African slaves in the New World – 'the very child and champion of the slave trade, nay the slave trade personified' in Wilberforce's eyes – to abolish the trade. But just as Britain had wrung concessions, however limited, from a reluctant Portugal as the price for British support during the war and immediate post-war years so, Canning was quick to realize, Brazil's anxiety for British recognition 'put [her] at our mercy as to the continuation of the slave trade'. In November 1822 Canning and Brant, the Brazilian agent, who had been instructed by Dom Pedro as early as 12 August to negotiate for recognition, discussed unofficially the question of the immediate abolition of the slave trade by Brazil in return for immediate recognition by Britain. Once Brazil's independence had been recognized, and Brazil had abolished the slave trade, Portugal's own excuse for not fulfilling its treaty engagements with Britain to abolish at some future date its trade south as well as north of the equator – the interests of its foremost colony, Brazil – would collapse. In any case, the transportation of slaves to territories outside the Portuguese empire had been prohibited by Portuguese legislation as far back as 1761 as well as by recent Anglo-Portuguese treaties. In the event Canning was restrained from any over-hasty action with respect to Brazil by the ultra Tory members of the Cabinet and by King George IV. Despite the preservation of the monarchy the Brazilian regime was, after all, revolutionary and the crowning of Dom Pedro as emperor had popular, Napoleonic overtones. (In fact the title sprang more from the liberal masonic tradition and in José Bonifácio's eyes it was simply a reflection of the size of Brazil.) Moreover, Britain had to take account of its traditional economic and strategic interests in Portugal. For his part Brant could not deliver the *immediate* abolition of the slave trade. Although Dom Pedro and José Bonifácio both personally abhorred the slave trade – and many

members of the Constituent Assembly which met in May 1823 opposed it
– they dared not alienate the great Brazilian landowners, the main
supporters of the independent Brazilian monarchy, who had no alternative source of labour. The political – and economic – dangers arising
from premature abolition were greater than those that might arise from
non-recognition. The most they could offer, therefore, was gradual
abolition over four or five years in return for immediate British recognition. In the meantime they promised to observe the Anglo-Portuguese
treaties of 1815 and 1817 for the suppression of the trade north of the
equator. Canning, however, was firmly committed to the policy that no
state in the New World would be recognized unless it had already
abolished the slave trade. 'Recognition', he had told the Duke of
Wellington, Britain's representative at the Congress of Verona, 'can only
be purchased by a frank surrender of the slave trade.' He agreed with
Wilberforce that Brazil 'must be purged of its impurity before we take it
into our embraces'.[14]

In September 1823 Portugal requested Britain's good offices in its
relations with Brazil, and Canning agreed. He made it clear, however,
that he was not prepared to wait indefinitely for an acknowledgement by
Portugal of Brazilian independence: to do so would endanger Britain's
commercial interests and its political influence in Brazil. He had in mind
in particular the fact that the Anglo-Portuguese commercial treaty of
1810, which had been accepted by the new Brazilian government, came
up for renewal in 1825 at which time direct negotiations with Brazil
could no longer be avoided. The longer international recognition was
delayed the more difficult it would become to secure from a grateful
Brazil in return not only the continuation of Britain's commercial
privileges in Brazil but also abolition of the Brazilian slave trade. Talks in
London between Brazil and Portugal sponsored by both Britain and
Austria opened in July 1824, were suspended in November and finally
broke down in February 1825. Canning now decided it was time for
Britain to act alone. Sir Charles Stuart, former British minister in Lisbon
during the Peninsular War and ambassador in Paris since 1815, was sent
on a special mission to Rio de Janeiro to negotiate an Anglo-Brazilian
commercial treaty. En route he was successful in persuading a new and
more flexible Portuguese government to accept the inevitable; he was
empowered to negotiate on behalf of Portugal as well.

---

[14] Quoted in Leslie Bethell, *The abolition of the Brazilian slave trade* (Cambridge, 1970), 31.

Stuart arrived in Rio on 18 July and on 29 August signed the treaty by which Portugal recognized the independence of Brazil.[15] In return Brazil agreed to pay Portugal compensation amounting to £2 million. Dom Pedro also pledged himself to defend the territorial integrity of the rest of the Portuguese empire and never to permit any other Portuguese colony – for example, Luanda and Benguela in Portuguese Africa which historically had close ties with Brazil – to unite with the Brazilian empire. (As early as February 1823 José Bonifácio had already told the British chargé in Rio, 'with regard to colonies on the coast of Africa, we want none, nor anywhere else; Brazil is quite large enough and productive enough for us, and we are content with what Providence has given us'.)[16] On the other hand, Dom Pedro retained the right to succeed to the Portuguese throne – leaving open the possibility, as Canning intended, that one day Brazil and Portugal might be peacefully reunited under the House of Braganza.

There was a price to pay for services rendered by Britain in securing Brazil its independence – and for future British friendship and support. In the first place, Britain had throughout all the negotiations since 1822 demanded the abolition of the slave trade in return for the recognition of Brazilian independence, and after a treaty negotiated by Stuart at the time of Portuguese recognition had been rejected by Canning a treaty was finally signed in November 1826 under which the entire Brazilian slave trade would become illegal three years after the ratification of the treaty (i.e. in March 1830). Secondly, an Anglo-Brazilian commercial treaty signed in August 1827 included the continuation of the 15 per cent maximum tariff on British goods imported into Brazil and the right to appoint judges conservators to deal with cases involving British merchants resident in Brazil. The process begun in 1808 whereby Britain successfully transferred its highly privileged economic position from Portugal to Brazil was thus completed.

The separation of Brazil from Portugal, like that of the North American colonies from England and Spanish America from Spain, can to some extent be explained in terms of a general crisis – economic, political and

---

[15] *De facto* recognition by Britain followed in January 1826 when Manuel Rodrigues Gameiro Pessôa was received as Brazilian minister in London. Robert Gordon was sent to Rio de Janeiro as British minister later in the year. The United States, on 26 May 1824, had, in fact, been the first to recognize Brazil. See Stanley E. Hilton, 'The United States and Brazilian independence', in Russell-Wood (ed.), *From colony to nation*.

[16] Quoted in Bethell, *Abolition*, 49–50.

ideological – of the old colonial system throughout the Atlantic world in the late eighteenth and early nineteenth centuries. The independence of Brazil, even more than Spanish American independence, was also the outcome of a chance combination of political and military developments in Europe during the first quarter of the nineteenth century and their repercussions in the New World. The half-century before independence certainly witnessed a growth in colonial self-consciousness and some demand for economic and political self-determination, but for a variety of reasons – the nature of Portuguese colonial rule, the nature of the colonial economy, the overwhelming predominance of slavery, the close ties between the metropolitan and colonial elites – less so in Brazil than in Spanish America. Napoleon's invasion of Portugal and the transfer of the Portuguese court from Lisbon to Rio de Janeiro in 1807–8 can be seen as merely postponing the final confrontation between colony and metropolis which the overthrow of the Spanish monarchy by Napoleon triggered off in Spanish America, but it also brought the Portuguese crown and the Brazilian oligarchy closer together and to a large extent satisfied Brazilian economic and even political grievances. Brazil can be regarded as moving gradually and inevitably towards independence from 1808, but it also has to be recognized that as late as 1820 there was in Brazil no widespread desire for total separation from Portugal. It was the Portuguese revolutions of 1820, the return of the Portuguese court to Lisbon in 1821 and Portugal's determination to reverse the political and economic gains since 1808 which forced the Brazilian dominant class (which included many Portuguese-born) along the road to independence. And in this José Bonifácio de Andrada e Silva, who had spent most of his adult life in Portugal, played a crucial role.

Once decided upon, Brazilian independence was relatively quickly and peacefully established, in contrast to Spanish America where the struggle for independence was for the most part long drawn out and violent. There was little loyalist sympathy and in the last analysis Portugal did not have the financial and military resources to resist it. Moreover, Brazil, unlike Spanish America, did not fragment into a number of separate states. There was no great sense of national identity in Brazil. The centre-south, the north-east and the north were to a large extent different worlds, with their own integrated economies, separated by huge distances and poor communications, though no great geographical barriers. Rio de Janeiro and São Paulo took the lead in the movement for independence, but the other provincial and regional elites whose political, economic and social interests broadly coincided gave their support to the new state with its capital in Rio. Here the availability in Brazil of a prince of the House of Braganza willing to assume the leadership of the independence movement was decisive. Dom Pedro was a symbol of legitimate authority and a powerful instrument of political and social stability and of national unity. The country was also held together by its highly centralized bureaucratic and judicial system. The 'War of Independence' to expel from the north-east and the north the troops which remained loyal to Portugal was short and virtually bloodless, and provided little opportunity for the assertion of separatist tendencies or for that matter the mobilization of popular forces. The Brazilian empire was also fortunate in securing early international recognition of its independence.

The transition from colony to independent empire was characterized by an extraordinary degree of political, economic and social continuity. Pedro I and the Brazilian dominant class took over the existing Portuguese state apparatus which, in fact, never ceased to function. The economy suffered no major dislocation: patterns of trade and investment changed (in particular Britain became Brazil's major trading partner and source of capital), but both the 'colonial' mode of production and Brazil's role in the international division of labour were largely unaffected. There was no major social upheaval: the popular forces which were in any case weak – and divided by class, colour and legal status – were successfully contained; no significant concessions were made to the underprivileged groups in society; above all, the institution of slavery survived (although the slave trade was now under threat). A conservative revolution had been effected. Insofar as the extreme liberalism (and republicanism) of 1789, 1798, 1817, 1821–3 and 1824 had been confronted and defeated it was a counter-revolution.

Nevertheless in 1822–3 Brazilian independence could be said to have been incomplete. The Emperor Pedro I quickly earned the mistrust of the Brazilians, above all by refusing to sever his ties with the Portuguese faction in Brazil and indeed with Portugal. Only with the abdication of Dom Pedro in favour of his 5-year-old Brazilian-born son, the future Dom Pedro II, on 7 April 1831 was the process by which Brazil separated itself from Portugal finally completed.

5

INTERNATIONAL POLITICS AND LATIN AMERICAN INDEPENDENCE

The political and military struggles which resulted in the independence of the Latin American nations were, from the outset, a matter of concern to the whole of the European and Atlantic state system of which the Spanish and Portuguese colonies formed an integral part. This was no new interest. From the sixteenth century the fabulous wealth of the Indies had attracted the envy of other European nations, who aspired both to obtain a share of it for themselves and to deny any advantage from it to their rivals. During the eighteenth century the Family Compact between the Bourbon monarchies of Spain and France emerged as a threat to Britain. But the British offset this advantage quite effectively through an extensive clandestine trade with Spanish America; no serious attempt was made to annex any major Spanish colony to their own empire.

The stately minuet of mercantilist colonial rivalry was, however, disrupted by disturbing developments in the 1790s. The French Revolution introduced new political principles into international relations; the slave rebellion in Saint-Domingue sent a shudder of fear through all the plantation colonies of the New World; Spanish American creole dissidents, of whom Francisco de Miranda was the most outstanding, propagandized throughout Europe in favour of the emancipation of the American colonies from Spanish rule. More specifically, the extreme submission of the weak Spanish monarchy to France, which involved Spain in war against Britain in 1796 and again, after a brief truce, in 1804, led the British government to consider measures against Spain's imperial possessions. Plans for conquest alternated with schemes for liberation; but little was done in either direction until 1806, as Britain's sea-power was adequate to ensure that she, rather than France, was the main beneficiary from Spain's increasingly disrupted colonial commerce.

Even in 1806, neither of the British interventions in South America was the result of a deliberate British policy decision. Miranda may have obtained some verbal commitment from the British Prime Minister, Pitt, before going to the United States to organize an attempt to liberate Venezuela. But Pitt was dead before Miranda reached the West Indies, and, although the Precursor managed to persuade the local British naval commander to support his landing, the new ministry disapproved, and the only further action it authorized was assistance in the evacuation, when the expedition failed to rally popular support among the Venezuelans. Similarly, the invasion of Buenos Aires, undertaken by a British force stationed in South Africa, was totally unauthorized, and the admiral responsible had to face a court-martial. Although public opinion in England demanded the retention of the conquest, the government was unenthusiastic and vacillated between ambitious schemes for further annexations and handing back Buenos Aires in exchange for some gains in Europe. In the end, the measures taken to consolidate British possession were too little and too late. The British force had been ejected before reinforcements arrived, and an attempt at recapture in 1807 was quickly given up in the face of local hostility.

A more urgent problem for Britain in 1807 was the possible fate of Portuguese Brazil. The mother country was being forced by the French emperor to conform to his Continental System and to break its links with its traditional ally and trading partner, Britain. The Portuguese court was placed in an agonizing dilemma when the British government made it clear that, while it could not protect Portugal, it was determined that Brazil would not fall under Napoleon's control. After hesitating until French troops were within sight of Lisbon, the Portuguese royal family finally accepted the British offer of a naval escort to Brazil – a decision that profoundly affected the future of the colony.

Also in 1807, Britain re-appraised her policy towards Spanish America in the light of the experiences of the previous year. Buenos Aires had shown that the colonies would not willingly submit to an exchange from Spanish rule to British; and Miranda's fiasco had demonstrated that the Spanish Americans could not be expected to rise against the Spanish regime unless encouraged by the presence of a sympathetic military force. In the first half of 1808, therefore, increasing French domination of the Spanish government, culminating in Napoleon's deposition of the Spanish royal house and elevation of his brother to the Spanish throne, was countered by British preparations for a liberating expedition to

South America, supplemented by political and propaganda activities in the Spanish colonies. Before the expedition sailed, however, news reached England of Spanish resistance to the Bonapartist usurpation, and the Spanish patriots sought an alliance with Britain against their common enemy. This implied a fundamental reversal of policy. The British army went to the peninsula, instead of to the Spanish colonies, which Britain no longer wished either to conquer or to liberate. Now her policy was to encourage them to give their fullest support to the metropolitan patriots in their struggle against the French invaders.

The French usurpation of the Spanish monarchy was the trigger which set in motion the movements for separation from Spain, though these had much longer-term and more complex origins. As a Mexican patriot put it, 'Napoleon Bonaparte. . . to you Spanish America owes the liberty and independence it now enjoys. Your sword struck the first blow at the chain which bound the two worlds.'[1] This was not, of course, Napoleon's intention. He hoped that the colonies would accept the change of dynasty and sent emissaries with instructions to colonial officials to proclaim Joseph Bonaparte as their king. However, with the exception of a few of the most senior office-holders, who owed their positions to the French influence that had predominated in the Spanish court, colonial opinion reacted with extreme revulsion against the French takeover, and everywhere loyalty to the captive Bourbon monarch Ferdinand VII was effusively proclaimed. France, then, had to change its tack and seek to encourage colonial independence as a means of weakening the Spanish effort in the peninsula. But French propaganda had little effect. It is true that some Spanish American radicals endorsed French revolutionary principles, and that French adventurers exercised some influence from time to time in various provinces. But, when the colonies established autonomous governments in 1810, it was essentially in response to the apparently imminent danger that Napoleon would overrun the peninsula entirely and in order to sever the connection with a metropolitan government which seemed likely to pass under complete French control.

The British policy towards the Spanish empire, like Napoleon's, was subordinated from 1808 to 1814 to the over-riding necessities of the Peninsular War. Little persuasion was needed in 1808 to secure Britain's

---

[1] Carlos María Bustamante, quoted in W. S. Robertson, *France and Latin American independence* (2nd edn, New York, 1967), 71.

political objective of colonial solidarity with the mother country and her new ally in the fight against the French. Economic co-operation was more elusive. Despite Britain's insistence that a share of the colonial trade was necessary to enable her to give effective military assistance in the peninsula, the Spanish patriot government was reluctant to abandon its imperial monopoly, and after 1808, much as in the preceding wartime conditions, British commercial penetration of the Spanish colonies took the form of local temporary permissions to trade or clandestine illegal transactions. Nevertheless, in some of the war years, Latin America was accounting for over a third of Britain's exports, and was thus offsetting to some extent the loss of markets in Europe and the United States.

The Spanish American revolutions of 1810 were an unwelcome development from the point of view of the British government. It could not support the colonial repudiation of metropolitan authority, as the co-operation of the peninsular government was essential in the fight against Napoleon. On the other hand, it would have been imprudent to take Spain's part against the colonists, as this would have endangered Britain's future relations with the emergent states if they succeeded in establishing their independence. 'We ought I conceive neither to encourage the immediate Independence, nor to discourage the eventual Independence, either of the whole, or of any part of Spanish America', advised a British cabinet minister.[2] Britain's policy was to remain neutral between Spain and her colonies, attempting to avoid giving too serious offence to either party – a tightrope she walked remarkably successfully for many years.

In the initial stages this balancing act was made rather easier by the fact that the Spanish American revolutionaries had acted in the name of the Spanish monarchy and continued to recognize the sovereignty of Ferdinand VII, though discountenancing the Regency which claimed to rule on his behalf while he was Napoleon's prisoner. The British government grasped this lifeline. Its first response to the news of the revolution in Venezuela was to point out, in a dispatch that was widely circulated, that the Spanish Regency was still actively waging war against the French, and to stress the importance of Spanish imperial unity in the face of the enemy. However, an accompanying secret dispatch made clear to the governor of Curaçao (who had sent the report of the Caracas revolution) that Britain did not intend to take up arms against the Venezuelans if they

[2] Memorial of Lord Harrowby [1810], British Library, Manuscripts Division, MS Add. 38360 f.301 (Liverpool Papers).

persisted in defying the peninsular government, and that British trade to Venezuela should be encouraged, though without giving any recognition to the new regime.

The arrival of a Venezuelan mission in London in July 1810, seeking diplomatic recognition and military protection, put British policy to an early test. The Foreign Secretary tried to avoid antagonizing Spain by seeing the delegates privately at his home rather than receiving them officially, but he could neither meet their demands nor persuade them to accept the authority of the Spanish Regency. Even this degree of involvement with the revolutionaries led to anger and suspicion on Spain's part, and, as Britain's main objective was to avoid any kind of showdown until Napoleon was defeated, it was necessary to tread very carefully. So, although the British government knew from its contacts with both sides that any reconciliation between Spain and the colonies was extremely unlikely, it continued ostensibly to believe it possible and undertook to mediate between the parties, perhaps more to gain time than in hope of success. Spain was equally insincere in her attitude to mediation, being unwilling to accept Britain's proposals for constitutional and commercial concessions to the colonies so long as she could cherish the hope of some day being able to reduce them to obedience by force. Indeed, the Spanish government, located in Cadiz and very much under the influence of its mercantile interests, insisted on maintaining its monopoly of the colonial trade, and seemed to the British to be more intent on this than on expelling the French invaders from the peninsula. The Spaniards, in turn, viewed British proposals for freeing colonial trade as conceived for Britain's own benefit and wanted Britain to undertake the forcible suppression of the colonial revolts if mediation failed. This Britain could never accept: not only would any such threat have prejudiced the mediation and Britain's posture of neutrality, it would also have caused Spanish American resentment towards Britain, which could have had long-term repercussions. In these circumstances there was no real meeting of minds over mediation; but while the Anglo-Spanish negotiations over the detailed bases of mediation dragged on from 1811 to 1813, an open breach between Britain and Spain was averted.

If the British attitude to the Spanish American revolutions strained Anglo-Spanish diplomatic relations, it made any kind of Anglo-Spanish-American relations very difficult. Representatives sent by the insurgent governments to England had to communicate with the Foreign Secretary through intermediaries, even after some of the South American states had declared their independence from Spain. For example, a delegate from New Granada spent some six months in London, apparently without making any direct contact with the Foreign Office, only seeing a couple of opposition politicians, and having two unofficial interviews with a sympathetic cabinet minister.[3] Nor did Britain send diplomatic representatives to Spanish America. Communications with the insurgent governments were maintained through naval commanders on the South America and West Indies stations, and, in the case of Venezuela and New Granada, through the governors of British or British-occupied colonies such as Jamaica, Trinidad and Curaçao. These officials were instructed to observe strict neutrality and avoid any political involvements, while protecting British commercial interest and, in particular, British subjects and their property, which were finding their way in increasing quantities to South America while conditions in Europe and North America were drastically curtailing normal channels of trade. At times the demands of diplomacy proved a little too exacting for officers from the fighting services. Admiral Sir Sidney Smith espoused rather too warmly the claim of Princess Carlota, wife of the Portuguese Regent, to take over the Spanish colonies on behalf of her brother Ferdinand VII and had to be recalled from Brazil; and a similar fate befell Brigadier Layard, governor of Curaçao, who committed Britain too closely to the patriot government of Venezuela. But these cases were highly exceptional. In the first place, while the sympathies of most naval officers seem to have inclined towards the patriot side, presumably because of their close professional contacts with the mercantile community who favoured the independence movements for the great opportunity they appeared to offer of direct access to new markets, those of most West Indian colonial governors, mindful of the horrors of race war that had overtaken Saint-Domingue and apprehensive of the possible effects on their own slave populations of any subversion of the established order on the Spanish Main, lay with the royalists. In the second place, the British functionaries seldom allowed their partiality for one side or the other to lead them into actions that might prove embarrassing to their home government. Much more typical than the indiscretions of Smith and Layard was the attitude of the authorities in Jamaica, when a royalist expedition from Spain was about to attack Cartagena, in refusing both an offer from the defenders to transfer the port to British control and a request from the Spaniards to supply anchors and cables for their squadron.[4] In the period of the Peninsular War, when the patriots controlled much of Spanish South America for most of the time, neutrality often meant upholding Spanish rights in the face of patriot pressure. But the British effort was little appreciated by the Spaniards who felt entitled to active support from their ally against the rebels and complained that British officials were 'unduly favouring the disaffected provinces'. In a detailed refutation of these allegations, the Foreign Office implied that neutrality was indeed a thankless task, pointing out that 'in various instances such partiality has been shown to the cause of old Spain as to excite very considerable dissatisfaction on the part of the insurgent authorities'.[5]

Britain's sole diplomatic representative in the area was her minister at the Portuguese court in Rio de Janeiro, Lord Strangford, who maintained British influence at a high level until his departure in 1815. Britain considered that by her action in 1807 she had saved Brazil for the Portuguese crown and therefore was entitled to be repaid with special privileges. These were embodied in treaties negotiated by Strangford in 1810, which gave British goods preferential tariff rates and British merchants special legal rights. At the same time the Portuguese bowed to British pressure and agreed to restrict the transatlantic slave trade to Brazil with a view to its gradual abolition. Strangford also, almost inevitably, became involved in the affairs of the Río de la Plata area. Before the revolution of 1810 he negotiated the opening of Buenos Aires to British trade with the viceroy, and thereafter the fact that the revolutionary government professed continued loyalty to Ferdinand VII enabled him to maintain informal relations with it without violating the Anglo-Spanish alliance. More complicated was the situation across the river in the Banda Oriental. Montevideo remained loyal to the Spanish Regency until 1814, but much of the hinterland was in the hands of Uruguayan patriots who refused to accept the authority of the Buenos Aires government. Strangford had to try to uphold British neutrality among these parties and also to restrain the Portuguese, who coveted the adjacent Spanish province, from turning the situation to their own advantage. In 1812 he secured the withdrawal of Portuguese troops, who had gone into the Banda Oriental at the request of the Spaniards in

---

[4] Douglas to Croker, 16 June, 7 November 1815, Public Record Office, London, ADM 1/266–7; Fuller to Bathurst, 10 June 1815, PRO, London, CO 137/149.
[5] Foreign Office to Wellesley, 14 August 1813, PRO, London, FO 72/142 f.126.

Montevideo; but after the royalists were driven out, he was unable to prevent disputes between the patriots of Uruguay and those of Buenos Aires, which eventually gave the Portuguese the excuse to invade the Banda Oriental to restore order in 1816. Strangford had gone by then, but from 1808 to 1815 he had contributed to the reduction of the level of hostilities in the Río de la Plata area and to the enhancement of British prestige in South America.

The one country that might have been in a position to challenge Britain for influence in Latin America at that time was the United States. Untrammelled by European involvements or obligations, linked by proximity and nascent Pan-American sentiments, and with an enterprising merchant fleet as an informal instrument of policy, the young federation was apparently well placed in 1808 to take advantage of the loosening of the imperial chains. But in fact North America remained in the early nineteenth century very much a part of the Atlantic political and economic system and was deeply affected by the Napoleonic wars. Both Britain and France disregarded the rights of neutrals in pursuit of their war aims, and, at the end of 1807, President Jefferson responded to repeated insults to the American flag by imposing an embargo on all exports from American ports, in the hope that the resulting shortages would force the belligerents to respect American vessels. The embargo was a failure as it harmed the United States more than the European powers, but no exploration of new opportunities for trade in the western hemisphere was possible while it persisted. Once it was lifted in 1809, American suppliers found a more convenient market for their agricultural products in the needs of both parties in the Peninsular War. After the revolutions of 1810 and the consequent rise of British influence, there was a brief flurry of United States interest in South America. Some agents were sent out; there were some dealings with Spanish Americans in Washington; and there was even some co-operation with French policy. But America had to subordinate the possible advantages of an active policy in Latin America to the need to avoid antagonizing Spain, with whom a number of border questions were pending, or provoking Britain, still her major trading partner. Finally, the Anglo-American War of 1812–15 directed the energies of the United States away from the southern continent, and, although American frigates achieved occasional successes over British warships in South American waters, the British navy retained sufficient overall control to arrest the development of American commercial relations until the end of the war.

The situation in Latin America in 1815 reflected the fact that international attention had been absorbed in the European wars. In the case of Brazil, the French attack on Portugal had resulted in a decisive act of Anglo-Portuguese co-operation, which retained the colony, apparently securely, in the hands of the Portuguese monarchy. In the case of Spanish America, however, European circumstances dictated that neither France nor Spain was capable of asserting control, while both Britain and the United States had calculated that their interests lay in refraining from any decisive action. The Spanish colonies were thus given the opportunity to determine their own future. That this remained uncertain in 1815 was due more to internal dissension than to European influence.

Although in 1815 the international context changed from one of European war to European peace, the Spanish American question was still viewed by European statesmen very much in terms of its possible impact on their European interests. Of these the most basic was the attempt to restore the *ancien régime* after the unwelcome interlude of the French Revolution and the Napoleonic Wars. Legitimacy and absolutism were seen as safe principles; liberalism as dangerous. The reaction reached an extreme of obscurantism in the Spain of Ferdinand VII, who abrogated the constitution of 1812 and the concessions it made both to peninsular liberalism and to colonial participation, and sent an army to Venezuela and New Granada to start the task of quelling the rebellion by force.

The major European powers also upheld legitimist principles, but did not, in general, support Spain's repressive measures. They believed that the use of force was unlikely to be effective, and that it would only lead to the successful assertion of independence by revolution. This would encourage liberal revolutionaries in Europe to try to subvert the established order which the allied powers were intent on maintaining. They much preferred that Spain should grant concessions to the colonists, which would satisfy their reasonable aspirations and at the same time maintain legitimate authority. Such a policy was also highly compatible with European commercial interests. These were negligible in the case of Austria and Russia. Russia had had ambitious designs in the Pacific for a few years before 1815, but these had been reduced to the more practical and realistic level of retaining her hold on Alaska and securing communications with it.[6] Prussia, however, and other North German states, as

---

[6] See R. H. Bartley, *Imperial Russia and the struggle for Latin American independence 1808–1828* (Austin, Texas, 1978).

well as France, wished to develop South American markets, and Britain had already by 1815 built up a substantial vested interest in the area. The commercial factor grew in importance with patriot success. With the exception of the Río de la Plata, the cause of South American independence was at the nadir in 1816, but thereafter the campaigns of San Martín opened up the trade of Chile and coastal Peru, and a great expansion of direct trade with Europe followed Bolívar's successful campaigns in Gran Colombia and the independence of Mexico in 1821. By 1822 Latin America was absorbing nearly 10 per cent of British exports; British merchants were establishing themselves in the import/ export business in the various ports of the southern continent; and the merchants and financiers of Liverpool and London were committing appreciable amounts of capital in commerical credit and loans to the new governments.

But although the British government was made fully aware of this developing interest, trade does not seem to have been the foremost consideration in British foreign policy. Even after the defeat of Napoleon, Castlereagh continued to be preoccupied with the preservation of European peace, and to regard Spain as an important element in a collective security system designed to prevent any possible re-assertion of French predominance. Accordingly, the arguments in favour of British neutrality between Spain and the colonies which had prevailed during the war continued to be valid. In 1814 the Anglo-Spanish alliance was renewed in a treaty which included a British undertaking to prohibit the supply of armaments to the Spanish American insurgents; and in 1815, when Spain made a new request for mediation, offering exclusive trading rights if Britain succeeded in inducing the colonists to return to their allegiance, Castlereagh answered that Britain did not seek any special privileges and believed that the only feasible basis for mediation was the offer by Spain of substantial concessions to the colonists. The Spanish regime considered that any concessions would be interpreted by the colonists as a sign of weakness and insisted that the mediation should be backed by force. As Spain must have expected, Britain found this quite unacceptable, and the British refusal gave Spain the excuse to turn to the other European powers for the support in her struggle against the colonies that Britain had consistently refused.

Spain may have been encouraged in this course of action by the sympathetic attitude shown by the continental powers in her dispute with Portugal over the occupation of the Banda Oriental. The British government, in fact, shared this sympathy and acceded to a Spanish request to mediate; but Britain regarded the quarrel between Spain and Portugal over Uruguay as an issue quite separate from the dispute between Spain and her colonies. On the wider question, Castlereagh responded to Spain's attempt to appeal to a European forum with a 'Confidential Memorandum' of August 1817 which set out the British view and proposed a joint allied mediation, based on an armistice, a general amnesty and colonial equality and free trade, and specifically ruled out the use of force. Austria and Prussia supported the British position, partly because they saw alignment with Britain as the best means of counteracting the predominance of their powerful neighbour Russia in the alliance. Russia was the most sympathetic of the European monarchies towards Spain, but Tsar Alexander I does not appear to have offered Ferdinand VII direct aid against the colonies, and he seems rather to have urged the necessity of concessions. However, he differed from the other powers in that he proposed that if the concessions were not accepted they should be followed up by economic coercion in some form of boycott; and he did sell eight Russian warships to Spain in 1817. This seems to have encouraged Spain to reject Castlereagh's memorandum and to pin her hopes on the prospect of a new expedition to South America. These hopes were dashed when the Russian ships proved to be unserviceable, and the Portuguese refused to evacuate Montevideo, which was to have been the base for the new attempt at reconquest.

Accordingly, in June 1818, with an eye on the forthcoming Congress of Aix-la-Chapelle, Spain made a new proposal, which accepted an amnesty and equal status for colonists as bases for mediation, but was vague about trade concessions and stipulated that the dignity and rights of the Spanish monarchy must not be compromised, which could be interpreted to rule out any realistic solution. Spain also angled for an invitation to the Congress, but although this was supported by Russia and France, it was vetoed by the others. Indeed, almost the only point on which the five powers were agreed at Aix-la-Chapelle was that they would not use force against the insurgents. France and Russia proposed that the United States should be involved, with the aim of forestalling their expected recognition of the independence of Buenos Aires; and Prussia would have liked representatives from Buenos Aires to be present. There was also disagreement over whether the mediation should be conducted by a committee or by the Duke of Wellington, who was prepared to act only if there was a clear understanding, accepted by

Spain, of the conditions on which the mediation was to proceed. Russia and France proposed the breaking of all communications with the insurgents if the mediation failed, but Britain and Austria opposed, and Castlereagh subsequently was able to convince the Tsar that a commerical boycott was impracticable. Spain was disillusioned by the outcome of the Congress, and even Russian influence in Madrid could not prevent Ferdinand VII from discarding mediation in favour of force. Throughout 1819 Spain concentrated on preparing an expedition against the Río de la Plata, and it was a mutiny among the troops preparing to leave for that destination that triggered off the Liberal Revolution of 1820.

France, isolated after the Tsar changed the Russian stand on economic coercion, played a lone hand for some time after the Congress and incurred the displeasure of both Britain and Spain when it came to light that she had been intriguing with the Buenos Aires patriots for the installation of a scion of the French royal house as monarch of Río de la Plata. While there was general agreement, among British as well as other European statesmen, that monarchy was preferable to republicanism as a form of government for Spanish America, a sentiment that was shared by San Martín and at times by other patriot leaders, the idea of a French monarch, or of any extension of French influence, was greeted with great jealousy and suspicion.

In 1819 Britain made a gesture towards repairing her relations with Spain by passing the Foreign Enlistment Act. This was a somewhat delayed reaction to an accumulation of bitter Spanish recriminations against the activities of patriot agents and their British sympathizers, who had started in 1817 to recruit troops in England and Ireland for service in Venezuela. They also contrived to raise loans and to send armaments, uniforms and other military supplies to aid Bolívar's forces. A Royal Proclamation of 1817 against military service in South America was ineffective; and the government found that, in spite of its undertaking to Spain in the 1814 treaty to prevent the export of arms to the insurgents, it could not prevent munitions being shipped to a neutral port, like the Danish West Indian island of St Thomas, and there re-embarked for Venezuela. Spain continued to complain, and as open recruiting had become a flagrant violation of Britain's professed neutrality, the government felt obliged to bring a bill before Parliament to tighten up the law. This gave the British supporters of the insurgent cause an opportunity to voice anti-Spanish sentiments, to make public their dedication to independence and to express their fears that the bill would antagonize the patriots and risk the loss of the valuable trade already being carried on with them. Some of this opposition may have been whipped up by contractors and financiers with a direct interest in supplying the insurgents, but the measure was genuinely unpopular, and the government had to force it through by appealing to the obligations of national honour. However, by the time it came into effect a British Legion was already in South America and contributing to Bolívar's victories. Moreover, as George Canning had predicted, in dissociating himself from a petition against the bill which he presented to the House of Commons on behalf of the merchants of his Liverpool constituency, the willingness of the Spanish Americans to do business with Britain seemed unaffected.

The preservation of neutrality in the face of a partisan public opinion was a problem which also confronted the United States government in this period. Privateering vessels, carrying the commissions of insurgent states, but fitted out in American ports and manned by American sailors, preyed on Spanish shipping and gave grounds for serious complaint from the Spanish ambassador in Washington. Congress passed a new act in 1817, strengthening the neutrality legislation, but it proved difficult to enforce, as jurors were reluctant to act in opposition to public opinion. On the other hand, a proposal to recognize the independence of Buenos Aires in 1818 was not acted upon, partly because the government did not want to anticipate the possibility of a concerted European move at Aix-la-Chapelle, and thereafter increasing doubts arose about the commitment of the South Americans to democratic and republican government. Moreover, it became more and more necessary to keep on good terms with Spain, which held the key to important American interests. Although the cession of Florida and the settling of the south-western boundary between the United States and the Spanish empire was satisfactorily negotiated in the Adams-Onís treaty of February 1819, Spain managed to delay its ratification for two years, during which time it was vital to maintain neutrality and avoid any anti-Spanish move which might prejudice the successful conclusion of the settlement.

By 1821 the situation had changed significantly. The Liberal Revolution in Spain had both removed the threat of a new armed expedition being sent out from Spain, and offered the possibility that a constitutional government would make the kind of concessions to the colonists that its absolutist predecessor had withheld. However, the new regime soon proved no more willing than the old to grant colonial autonomy, and in the course of 1821 any hope of reconciliation receded as Venezuela was finally liberated, and Mexico, Central America and Peru declared their independence. These developments were, of course, mainly due to events and factors within the Spanish empire. But they also owed something to the fact that Britain was firmly opposed to the interference of any third party in the struggle, and was able to make this view prevail with the other European powers.

In 1822 the outside world began to adjust to the fact that although royalist forces still held the Peruvian sierra and upper Peru, Spanish America had, in effect, succeeded in separating itself from Spain. The United States led the way, perhaps not surprisingly in view of its freedom from the monarchical and legitimist inhibitions of the European powers. In January Congress called on the executive for information, and in March President Monroe responded, recommending that the United States should give *de facto* recognition to the independence of Buenos Aires, Chile, Colombia, Mexico and Peru. The proposal was endorsed by Congress and formally implemented in June when the representative of Gran Colombia was officially received by the president – the first such act of external recognition of any South American country.

The American initiative had rapid repercussions. In April Francisco Antonio Zea, Gran Colombian envoy to Europe, issued from Paris a manifesto to the governments of the European powers, threatening that Colombia would maintain relations only with those countries that recognized its independence and would cut off trade with all others. Although Zea was acting without instructions, and his manifesto was subsequently disavowed by his government, it caused considerable alarm, particularly among the smaller states of North Germany, which could not act in defiance of the legitimist attitude of their powerful neighbours, Austria and Prussia, and which saw their growing economic interests in South America threatened by the favour towards the United States that was implied by Zea's policy. Similar considerations influenced even the British government, which took its first significant step in the direction of acknowledging the *de facto* achievement of Spanish American independence in May 1822, by providing, in a revised navigation law which was then being debated in Parliament, for vessels displaying South American flags to be admitted to British ports, and in doing so, explained its action by reference to United States recognition and Zea's manifesto.

Meanwhile Spain had followed up a strong protest to Washington against recognition with a plea to the European governments not to emulate the example of the United States, especially as Spain was still engaged in negotiating a reconciliation with the colonies, based on liberal principles. Russia, Prussia and Austria assured Spain of their adherence to legitimacy; but Castlereagh in June 1822 foreshadowed a further British move by warning Spain that she could not expect Britain to wait indefinitely, and went on to point out that:

so large a portion of the world cannot, without fundamentally disturbing the intercourse of civilized society, long continue without some recognized and established relations; that the State which can neither by its councils nor by its arms effectually assert its own rights over its dependencies, so as to enforce obedience and thus make itself responsible for maintaining their relations with other Powers, must sooner or later be prepared to see those relations establish themselves, from the over-ruling necessity of the case, under some other form.[7]

A few weeks later, in preparing for the Congress of the European powers which took place at Verona in October and November, Castlereagh drew a distinction between different stages of recognition, which he now regarded 'rather as a matter of time than of principle'. He hoped that the powers might be persuaded to act together in moving from the existing situation of *de facto* commercial relations to a middle position of diplomatic recognition, considering the final *de jure* stage as one which would depend on Spain's renunciation of her rights.

Whether Castlereagh could have won support for his view at Verona as he had done at Aix-la-Chapelle is very doubtful, for Britain had become increasingly distanced from the other Congress powers since 1818. But his suicide ensured that it was never put to the test. Neither Wellington, who went to Verona in his place, and even less Canning, who replaced him at the Foreign Office in September 1822, could command a comparable influence among European statesmen. Indeed, Canning was actively opposed to the Congress system, and while this allowed Britain a free hand to act as she thought best, it reduced her potential influence over the other European powers. Thus, while Britain's intentions towards Spanish America were noted, without eliciting either support or objection, the initiative at the Congress was seized by the French, who showed much more interest in the condition of metropolitan Spain than in that of the Spanish colonies, and prepared the ground for European acquiescence in a French military crusade to

[7] C. K. Webster (ed.), *Britain and the independence of Latin America, 1812–1830* (2nd edn, New York, 1970) II, 388.

destroy Spanish liberalism and return Ferdinand VII to the full exercise
of his powers.

Meantime, Canning had begun to proceed unilaterally with further
steps towards recognition by preparing to send British consuls to the
principal ports and commercial centres in Spanish America, and to order
a naval force to the Caribbean, with the twin objectives of co-operating
with the insurgent governments against pirates who were based in
Spanish colonial waters, and of forcibly demanding restitution of British
vessels and property seized by the royalist authorities. At the end of the
year, however, in face of the imminent danger of French invasion, the
Spanish government showed an uncharacteristic alacrity in redressing
the British grievances, and once again invited Britain's mediation with
the colonists. Canning accordingly called off the naval operations and
delayed the dispatch of the consuls until the Spanish liberal regime had
been completely defeated and Ferdinand VII restored to absolute authority by the action of the French army – which took until the second half of
1823.

The promise of speedy action towards the recognition of the new
Spanish American states in the early stages of Canning's Foreign
Secretaryship thus proved illusory; and the same occurred for very
different reasons in relation to Brazil. The king of Portugal had delayed
returning from Rio de Janeiro to Lisbon until 1821, when it became clear
that if he remained in Brazil the new liberal regime in Portugal would
remove him from the throne. A year later, when the Portuguese government tried to reduce Brazil to its former colonial status, the king's son,
Dom Pedro, who had been left behind as regent in Rio de Janeiro, placed
himself at the head of the colonial separatist movement, and declared
independence in September 1822. Canning saw in this an opportunity to
advance an objective of British policy to which he was personally
committed to a much greater extent than his predecessor. This was the
abolition of the transatlantic slave trade, for which Brazil was now a
major market. Portugal's initial commitment to eventual abolition,
extracted by Britain in 1810, had been followed up by further agreements
in 1815 and 1817. Canning not only wished to ensure that the new state of
Brazil would honour the undertakings of the mother country, but he also
hoped to use the prospect of British recognition as an inducement to
Brazil to abolish the trade completely – a provision which he had already
decided should be a *sine qua non* for the recognition of any of the Spanish
American states.

Unofficial conversations with a Brazilian agent in London in November 1822 suggested that Brazil might agree to abolition in return for immediate British recognition, and Canning felt that such action need not conflict with Britain's obligations to Portugal, or prejudice any subsequent agreement between the crowns of Portugal and Brazil. However, the Brazilian representative turned out not to have authority to conclude such an agreement; the talks were transferred to Rio de Janeiro; and Canning's instructions to his negotiators in February 1823, while urging Brazil towards abolition, did not commit Britain to recognition, possibly because Canning now realized that he could not count on Cabinet approval for his policy. The Brazilian government was anxious to obtain British recognition, believing that 'with England's friendship we can snap our fingers at the rest of the world',[8] but was also aware that the strongest economic interests in the country regarded the slave trade as vital to their prosperity, and it dared not agree to immediate abolition. The possibility of a quick settlement faded; Canning became convinced of the advantages of trying to associate Portugal in the recognition of Brazilian independence; the momentum was lost, and any effective progress was postponed for over a year.

The French invasion of Spain started in April 1823, and by September the country had been completely overrun, and Ferdinand VII freed from the control of the constitutionalists and restored to absolute power. The possibility that this success would be followed by French assistance in the re-imposition of Spanish power in America was naturally a matter of concern to both participants and onlookers. However, although France apparently considered such a course of action on more than one occasion, it never seems to have reached the stage of any serious concerted plan. In spite of a number of vacillations and inconsistencies, the French seem to have reckoned that their main interest in Spanish America was commercial, and that France was likely to be at a disadvantage in this respect if other countries started to extend official recognition and negotiate commercial treaties. France's commitment to legitimacy, which was the whole basis of her restored Bourbon monarchy, inhibited her from acknowledging the independence of the Spanish colonies in advance of the mother country. Hence France's true policy was to persuade Spain to accept the inevitable, and from the middle of 1823 it was intended that the

[8] Quoted in A. K. Manchester, *British preeminence in Brazil: its rise and decline* (2nd edn, New York, 1964), 193.

liberation of Ferdinand VII would be followed by a congress on South America at which the combined pressure of the European powers could be brought to bear on Spain.

But this was by no means self-evident to outside observers, and it was not unreasonable to believe that there was a real threat of French intervention in the Spanish colonies. Canning implied such a belief in warning the French government, a few days before French troops entered Spain, that Britain's neutrality was contingent on the assumption that France would not attempt to take over any part of Spanish America, but he received no reassurance that his assumption was correct. Whether Canning's fears were real, or feigned for diplomatic advantage, has been a matter of much speculation. Whatever the truth, they formed the context in which Canning, in August 1823, sounded out the United States minister in London, Richard Rush, on the possibility of making a joint statement that neither Britain nor the United States believed that Spain could recover her colonies; that each disclaimed annexationist ambitions against them; and that both would oppose the transfer of any portion of the Spanish empire to any other power. Rush, however, was prepared to collaborate with Britain only if she put herself on the same footing as the United States by recognizing the independence of the new states; and Canning had not yet overcome the opposition of a majority of his cabinet colleagues to a policy of recognition, so he dropped the matter in September.

With the collapse of constitutionalist resistance in Spain imminent, Canning then determined to obtain some formal statement of French intentions. The result was a series of talks with the French ambassador, Prince Polignac, in October 1823, which Canning recorded in a document known as the Polignac Memorandum. In these conversations, both parties agreed that the recovery of Spanish authority in the colonies was hopeless, and disavowed any territorial designs on the Spanish empire, or any desire to obtain exclusive commercial privileges there; but Britain warned that any attempt to restrict her existing trade might be met by immediate recognition of the new states, as would any 'foreign interference, by force or by menace'; and France disclaimed 'any design of acting against the Colonies by force of arms'. Moreover, Canning insisted that, in view of her special interests, Britain could not attend any conference on Spanish America 'upon an equal footing with other Powers', and added that the United States ought to participate in any such conference.[9]

---

[9] Webster, *Britain and independence* II, 115–20.

It can scarcely be claimed that the Polignac Memorandum prevented a French intervention, as none was seriously contemplated; indeed it was accepted by the French government without demur, and used by it as an excuse to refuse subsequent requests from the other powers to send forces to Spanish America. Nevertheless, it was a tactical success for Canning and a setback for France, as Polignac was unable to make the agreement conditional on British participation in the proposed conference. Thus, although France succeeded in persuading Ferdinand VII to convoke a meeting, Canning refused to attend, pointing out in reply to Spain's invitation that, although Britain would prefer Spain to give the lead in recognition, she must retain the freedom to act in her own interests as time and circumstances dictated. This decision was bitterly attacked by the continental powers, but Canning was immovable; and the conference, which met on several occasions in 1824 and 1825, was totally ineffective.

Although Canning soon regretted his proposal to Rush for an Anglo-American declaration, the matter did not rest there. When Rush's first report reached Washington, the American administration was on the whole inclined to accept the idea. Secretary of State John Quincy Adams, however, suspected that Canning's real motive in the mutual disavowal of territorial ambitions was to prevent American acquisition of Cuba, and he also felt that it 'would be more candid as well as more dignified to avow our principles explicitly . . . than to come in as a cock-boat in the wake of the British man-of-war'.[10] While the question was still under consideration, Rush reported that Canning no longer seemed interested, perhaps (as was indeed the case) because he was arranging matters directly with France. From these circumstances – the suspicion that France might be contemplating military intervention in Spanish America, the knowledge that Britain was opposed to such intervention, and the pretensions of these and the other European powers to pronounce on the destiny of Spanish America – emerged the passages in the presidential message to the United States Congress of December 1823 that came to be termed the Monroe Doctrine. This emphasized the difference between the European political system and that of America, and stated that any European interference with the object of oppressing or controlling the independent governments in the western hemisphere would be viewed as the manifestation of an unfriendly disposition towards the United States.

[10] Quoted in H. Temperley, *The foreign policy of Canning, 1822–1827* (2nd edn, London, 1966), 123.

The European powers did not react kindly to being told by the United States to keep their hands off the American continent. Moreover, the enunciation of the Monroe Doctrine appeared to synchronize suspiciously with Britain's determination to act independently of the continental powers over Spanish America, and Canning encouraged the belief that he had inspired the American declaration. In fact, however, he saw Monroe's emphasis on the separation of America from Europe as a challenge to Britain's influence, and his subsequent American policy frequently reflected an obsession with United States rivalry.

The free hand which Canning had retained for Britain was exercised as soon as it was clear that Spanish resistance to the French invasion had ceased. In October 1823 consuls were sent to Buenos Aires, Montevideo, Valparaíso, Lima, Panama, Cartagena, Maracaibo, La Guaira, Mexico City and Veracruz. Special commissioners also left for Mexico and Colombia with instructions to ascertain whether their governments had declared independence and were resolved to maintain it; exercised control over their territory and enjoyed the confidence of the population; and had abolished the slave trade. Early in 1824, before any reports were available, the question of the recognition of Spanish American independence was raised in parliament. Canning responded by publishing the Polignac Memorandum and his rejection of the Spanish invitation to the conference, which made clear that the government had the matter under consideration; but it was raised again in June in the form of a petition from London merchants and financiers, urging the government towards immediate recognition. Trade indeed had continued to grow; Latin America was now taking some 15 per cent of British exports, and some millions of pounds had been invested in loans to the new governments and in commercial and mining speculations. This renewed mercantile agitation coincided with favourable reports from the recently-arrived consul in Buenos Aires, and in July the cabinet agreed to authorize the negotiation of a commercial treaty, the conclusion of which would constitute diplomatic recognition. The decision was not made public at the time, however, and negotiations were delayed for several months, while the provincial government of Buenos Aires sought authority to conduct international relations on behalf of the United Provinces of Río de la Plata.

Meanwhile, the commissioners to Mexico and Colombia reported that these countries satisfied the criteria laid down in their instructions, and, although Canning was unhappy about certain aspects of the reports – in particular he wished that the Mexican commissioners had explored more fully the possibility of the revival of a monarchy there – he felt that they gave ample ground for action. In pressing recognition of the new Spanish American states on the cabinet, which he had to do to the point of threatening his resignation, Canning seems to have been concerned less with the actual situation in Spanish America and the pressure from British economic interests than with rivalry with the United States, and, more particularly, with France. The final argument with which he won his point was the refusal of the French government to state when they proposed to withdraw their troops from Spain. It was in reference to this that Canning, in the House of Commons two years later, made his famous claim, 'I resolved that if France had Spain, it should not be Spain "with the Indies". I called the New World into existence to redress the balance of the Old.'[11] British recognition of Spanish America may have been, from Canning's point of view, primarily a calculated act of defiance against the continental powers and their congress system. But he also summed up its significance from the other point of view in his immediate reaction, 'Spanish America is free; and if we do not mismanage our affairs sadly, she is English.'[12] The recognition of the United States had, indeed, come earlier; that of the mother country was not to follow for some years. Each was insignificant in comparison to the recognition of the world's leading naval, commercial and industrial nation. In Colombia the British commissioners reported how the news was received there: 'All the people of Bogotá are half mad with joy . . . exclaiming, "We are now an independent nation!!"'.[13]

Although the United States had begun the process of recognition in 1822, by 1825 it had entered into treaty relations with only Colombia and Central America. It did not take long for Britain to catch up. In the course of 1825 commercial treaties were concluded with the United Provinces of Río de la Plata and with Colombia. These gave a framework of legal protection to British subjects resident in South America, exempted them from military service, forced loans and discriminatory taxation, and secured them the right to practise their Protestant religion. As to trade, Britain sought no preference for her own goods, but simply required that

---

[11] Quoted in Temperley, *Canning*, 381.
[12] Quoted in W. W. Kaufmann, *British policy and the independence of Latin America 1804–1828* (2nd edn, London, 1967), 178.
[13] Webster, *Britain and independence* I, 385.

they should not be charged higher duties than those of the most-favoured-nation. The general basis of commercial and maritime reciprocity on which Britain insisted naturally favoured the established as against the new nations; but the South Americans felt that a treaty with Britain was worth some sacrifice. The Mexicans, on the other hand, seem to have taken an exaggerated view of their country's importance in British eyes and forced concessions on the British negotiators which were unacceptable to the Foreign Office. The draft treaty was thus rejected, and further negotiations took place in Mexico and in London, in which Britain conceded some of the substance of the Mexican objections while retaining her maritime principles, before the treaty was finally ratified in 1827.[14]

These difficulties and delays were partly due to the rivalry for influence in Mexico between British and American diplomatic representatives. The British minister claimed credit for overcoming the American's attempts to prevent the ratification of the British treaty while frustrating the ratification of a commercial treaty between Mexico and the United States and undermining the claims of the United States to leadership of a league of American nations. But there were more basic factors underlying the differences in the development of British and American relations with, in particular, Colombia and Mexico. In 1824 Colombia enquired whether the Monroe Doctrine implied a willingness on the part of the United States to enter into a defensive alliance, and had been told that in case of a threatened intervention the United States would have to act in co-operation with European powers; and a similar probing by Mexico in 1826 revealed that the Monroe Doctrine did not involve any United States commitment towards Latin America. By contrast Colombia appreciated the vigorous British protest against France's action in 1825 in providing a naval escort for Spanish reinforcements to Cuba in violation of the Polignac Memorandum.

Cuba posed another problem for United States relations with Spanish America. Britain, France and the United States were all unwilling to see the island in the hands of one of the others, and were agreed that it was best that it should remain in the possession of Spain. But the United States was reluctant to join in a guarantee which would preclude the possible future accession of Cuba to the American union. Even less was it prepared to allow the island to be liberated from Spanish rule by the

---

[14] See Jaime E. Rodríguez O., *The emergence of Spanish America: Vicente Rocafuerte and Spanish Americanism, 1808–1832* (Berkeley, 1975), 129–42.

forces of Colombia and Mexico, as this would involve the danger of slave insurrection uncomfortably close to America's slave states. Accordingly in 1825 the United States warned both countries not to attack Cuba. Britain, however, took the view that so long as Spain remained at war with the new states they were entitled to invade Spanish territory, but pointed out that the likely consequence of an attack on Cuba was American intervention, which would be unwelcome to Britain and unprofitable to Mexico and Colombia.

This hint was dropped by Britain and acted on by Colombia at the Panama Congress of 1826, an occasion which illustrates both the clarity of British purposes in Latin America and the ambivalence of United States attitudes. Britain readily accepted the invitation to send an observer to this first Pan-American meeting, and had little difficulty in enhancing British influence and in ensuring that any concerted action the Spanish American nations might take would not be prejudicial to British interests. The United States, on the other hand, was not represented. Its Congress was divided over economic relations with Latin America (where the northern states saw commercial opportunities, the south saw only anti-slavery sympathies and competition in primary products), but was agreed that Latin America should not constitute an exception to the general United States policy of no foreign entanglements. Although Congress finally decided to send a delegation to Panama, it acted much too late, and it showed little evidence of 'the avowed pretension of the United States to put themselves at the head of a confederacy of all the Americas, and to sway that confederacy against Europe (Great Britain included)' that Canning apprehended.[15] However much it may have suited Canning's purposes to emphasize it, American rivalry does not in fact appear to have presented any real threat to British hegemony in Latin America, firmly based as it was on economic supremacy backed by naval power.

The progress of Britain and the United States towards regularizing their relations with Spanish America made it necessary for the other European powers, especially those with commercial interests, to reconsider their attitudes. In doing so they were hampered by their legitimist commitment not to act in advance of Spain, and by Ferdinand VII's obstinate refusal to acknowledge the loss of any part of his imperial patrimony, which delayed any Spanish moves towards recognition until

[15] Webster, *Britain and independence* II, 543.

after his death in 1833. France responded to the situation by sending out commercial agents in 1825 on a more official basis than her previous missions, and subsequent pressure from her mercantile community led to the formalizing of consular services. In 1826 vessels showing Spanish American flags were admitted to French ports, and in the following year a commercial agreement was signed with Mexico, which was a 'declaration' rather than a treaty, and enabled the Mexicans to interpret it as an act of recognition and France to claim that it was compatible with her non-recognition policy. The only early political development was the acknowledgement in 1825 of the independence of Haiti in return for an indemnity and trade concessions. As Haiti was a former French colony, this action did not affect the rights of another nation, but it did involve the acceptance of a regime originating in an anti-colonial revolt, and so was felt by legitimists, such as the Austrian Chancellor Metternich, to compromise their sacred precept. Charles X made no further concessions, and it was not until he was overthrown by the July Revolution of 1830 that France accepted the principle of recognition. Thereafter events moved comparatively rapidly, and commercial treaties were negotiated with several Spanish American states over the next few years. But the French action came too late to have any significant impact.

Prussia in the 1820s was developing increasing commercial links with Spanish America, which its government neither authorized nor impeded. After British recognition, economic interests (and, in particular, textile exporters, who valued the Spanish American market) pressed the government to play a more active role. In 1826 commercial agents were exchanged with Mexico, and in 1827 Prussia signed a trade agreement similar to that between Mexico and France. This was followed by the negotiation of a commercial treaty, which in effect acknowledged Mexico's independence, but the Mexican government delayed its ratification until 1831.

Russia and Austria, having little direct business interest in Spanish America, could afford to condemn any dealings with the 'illegitimate' new states, and their attitudes determined the caution and secrecy with which relations were established, not only by Prussia, but also by the minor German states and the smaller European countries. Trade with Spanish America was most crucial to the Hanseatic cities, which were reasonably successful in developing their commercial relations on a semi-official basis, thus avoiding some of the wrath of their more powerful European neighbours. The Netherlands, after being denounced by

Russia for recognizing Colombia, were able to enjoy trading with Mexico by the expedient of sending a consul, but dragged out the negotiation of a treaty until the precedent had been set by Prussia. Sweden was less fortunate, having to give in to Russian pressure to call off a deal for the sale of ships to Mexico. In general, the attitude of the major European powers can be said to have delayed the setting-up of properly regulated relations between the countries of continental Europe and those of Spanish America; but it had probably little more than a marginal effect on the development of trade, which was virtually the only common interest linking the new states with the Old World.

The legitimist considerations which delayed the establishment of relations between the European powers and Spanish America did not operate with the same force in the case of Brazil. The fact that Dom Pedro was heir to the Portuguese throne as well as emperor of Brazil made it easier to envisage a settlement preserving monarchical continuity under the same Braganza dynasty. Moreover, the break was sudden and comparatively peaceful, and, although relations between Portugal and Brazil were far from amicable, there was an absence of the intransigence, embittered by the long war, that characterized Spain's dealings with Spanish America. Bringing the parties together was also facilitated by the fact that direct relations already existed between the European powers and Brazil, deriving from the period when Rio de Janeiro had been the Portuguese seat of government. Britain had a particular interest in the outcome, having a traditional special relationship with Portugal, and trading privileges in Brazil under the treaty of 1810, as well as a concern in the abolition of the slave trade. Austria had dynastic reasons for becoming involved, as Dom Pedro had married an Austrian princess; and Metternich hoped to reconcile these with his legitimist ideology by seeking a solution somewhere between complete separation and complete submission.

Anglo-Austrian mediation talks between Brazil and Portugal began in July 1824, and when, after several meetings, no compromise between Portugal's claims of sovereignty and Brazil's claims of independence emerged, Canning proposed a federal monarchy, with the sovereign residing alternately in Lisbon and Rio de Janeiro. The Portuguese government, under strong anti-British influence, not only made unacceptable counter-proposals but sought support for these both in Brazil and from France, Russia and Prussia behind the backs of the mediating powers, and Canning indignantly suspended the mediation.

But the matter remained of some urgency from the British point of view, as the Anglo-Portuguese commercial treaty of 1810, which still regulated Anglo-Brazilian trade, was due to expire in 1825. Thus Canning decided to try to settle everything by sending a special envoy, Sir Charles Stuart, first to Lisbon and then to Rio de Janeiro. Stuart was greatly assisted by political changes in Lisbon, which brought into office a ministry more friendly to Britain, from which he obtained authority to negotiate Brazilian independence on behalf of the Portuguese crown on the basis of a financial adjustment and some preservation of the Portuguese royal title to Brazil. Stuart left Lisbon in May 1825 and, after considerable haggling over the question of royal titles, secured Brazil's agreement to pay Portugal two million pounds. The settlement, which was signed in July and ratified in November 1825, involved an act of renunciation by the mother country, which conferred *de jure* independence, and opened the way for recognition by even the most doctrinaire of legitimists. Several countries, including Austria, France, Prussia and the Hanseatic cities went beyond this and negotiated commercial treaties between 1826 and 1828, as did the United States, which, although it had led the way in 1824 by recognizing Brazil ahead of Portugal, had been unable to press the Rio government to earlier commercial negotiations.

It was for Britain, however, that the stakes had been highest, and the British now expected to reap the benefit of their diplomatic success. Indeed, Stuart proceeded to try to do this personally. He disregarded his instructions to extend the existing commercial treaty for two years, pending a new agreement which would incorporate a provision for the immediate abolition of the slave trade, and not only negotiated a permanent commercial treaty, but also concluded a slave trade abolition treaty. When his handiwork reached London, Canning rejected both treaties, as they did not conform to British requirements in important respects. A new envoy was sent out, who signed a new anti-slave trade treaty in 1826 which made any Brazilian involvement in the traffic after 1830 equivalent to piracy; and in 1827 he secured a new commercial treaty, which continued Britain's privileged position in Brazilian trade for a further fifteen years.

The abolition of the slave trade, demanded by Britain as the price of recognition, was extremely unpopular in Brazil and contributed significantly to Dom Pedro's loss of support which culminated in his abdication in 1831. The emperor's fall was also partly due to the loss of the Banda Oriental, another development in which Britain played a part. In spite of Spanish protests this area had remained in Portuguese hands and duly passed under Brazilian authority. In 1825 it was claimed by the United Provinces of Río de la Plata, which supported an insurrection in the territory, and war with Brazil ensued. British trade suffered, both from Brazil's blockade of the Río de la Plata and from the fact that the navies of both sides were manned by British sailors enticed from trading vessels by hopes of prize money. Ultimately the local British diplomatic representatives pressed mediation on the two parties, and in 1828 gained acceptance for the independence of the disputed region as the state of Uruguay.

The advantages to be derived from the commercial agreements negotiated in the 1820s and 1830s proved to be significantly less impressive than might have been anticipated from the anxiety with which they had been sought by the rival external powers. In fact, the immediate economic prospects in Latin America had been much exaggerated by the outside world. During the course of the French Revolutionary and Napoleonic Wars in Europe and the Wars of Independence in Spanish America, much of Latin America's trade had already been diverted from the Iberian Peninsula to the more northerly parts of Europe. This process continued after independence, but increases in the overall volume of external trade were modest rather than spectacular. The poverty of the mass of the population limited the demand for European imports; the subsistence nature of much of Latin American agriculture restricted the availability of exportable commodities; and the wars had played havoc with the mining of silver which had traditionally been the continent's main marketable resource. The hopes of rapid development which had generated a speculative boom in the early 1820s had been dashed by 1826, as governments defaulted on loans, mines yielded few bonanzas, revolutions and civil wars threatened foreigners and their property, and the modernizing internationalists who guided the early years of independence on liberal and free trade lines were forced to give way to xenophobic traditionalists who favoured protectionism.

Latin America also receded very rapidly from the forefront of international diplomacy. None of the Latin American countries, preoccupied with their own internal problems and their border disputes with their neighbours, became involved in the balance of power politics of distant Europe. Nor, in general, did the European powers play out their rivalries in Latin America. There were perhaps two exceptions; first the French interventions in Mexico and Buenos Aires in 1838, which probably derived more from France's European need to achieve diplomatic success than from the actual grievances against the Latin American states, and secondly, the Anglo-French involvement in the Río de la Plata in the 1840s, which seems to have stemmed from the desire of both European parties to find an issue over which they could co-operate in order to counteract the effect of their disagreements in other parts of the world. Although the lesson may have been lost on the French, who were to stage a much more ambitious intervention in Mexico in the 1860s, the experience of the 1840s confirmed the truth which the British had learned from their invasion of Buenos Aires in 1806 – that the European nations could not normally deploy their considerable power to political effect on the South American continent.

The limitations of external political influence are well illustrated by Britain's dealings with Brazil in the 1830s and 1840s. Throughout this period Britain was unable to enforce the abolition, of the slave trade to Brazil which she had demanded as the price for her assistance in facilitating international recognition of Brazil's independence. Britain's foreign secretary, Lord Palmerston, was consistently unsuccessful in inducing the Brazilians to make necessary modifications to the Anglo-Brazilian anti-slave-trade treaty and Brazil's own enactment outlawing the traffic. In 1845 one of the few provisions of the treaty which had not been wholly ineffective, the agreement to try slave traders before Anglo-Brazilian mixed commissions, expired, and Brazil would not renew it. The British parliament then passed Lord Aberdeen's Act, whereby Britain unilaterally assumed powers to suppress the Brazilian slave trade, and these were used in 1850 to justify coercive naval action within Brazilian waters. This was the main factor leading to the effective ending of the trade almost immediately. Final abolition, however, also owed a great deal to a change in influential Brazilian opinion on the issue, and to a strengthening of the Brazilian government's authority and its ability effectively to enforce its will.

Another bone of contention was the Anglo-Brazilian commercial treaty, which gave British merchants special protection in Brazilian courts and restricted the level of tariffs that could be charged on British goods, and consequently on those of any other country with a most-favoured-nation agreement. Brazil refused to renew this treaty when it expired in 1842. The loss of the preferential provisions was of little importance, as the British mercantile community no longer needed them;

but the Brazilian government would not even enter into a simple agreement putting Britain on the same footing as other nations unless Britain made concessions which were unacceptable, and British trade thereafter had to continue without treaty regulation. Britain's pre-eminence in Brazilian external commerce thus did not enable her to control Brazil's political decisions.

The expected Anglo-American rivalry never really materialized in South America. It is true that at times concern was expressed over the ability of American shipping to undercut British, but many of the goods carried in American vessels were of British manufacture, and Britain's industrial lead ensured her market dominance until the second half of the nineteenth century. United States diplomatic agents were often envious of the influence apparently enjoyed by their British counterparts, and sometimes they appealed to the State Department for support in trying to undermine it. But Washington, disillusioned by the failure of the new nations to sustain democratic government on the American model, showed little interest.

The story was very different closer to the United States' own borders. There, for a time, Britain tried to compete by supporting the independent republic of Texas, after it had broken away from Mexico in 1836, as a counterpoise to United States predominance in North America. But once Texas had been incorporated into the American union in 1845, Britain offered no resistance to the acquisition of California and other northern provinces of Mexico following the United States–Mexican War of 1846–48.

The one area where genuine Anglo-American rivalry did emerge was the Central American isthmus, and then only in 1848 as a result of the discovery of gold in California, and America's consequent sudden interest in means of transit to the Pacific Coast more convenient than the hazardous pioneer trails through the Great Plains and the Rocky Mountains. Prior to that, the United States government had concerned itself very little with the isthmian area, with the extent of British interests there, or with the various proposals and surveys for inter-oceanic canals that had been made since Central America's independence. The only positive step taken was the conclusion in 1846 of a treaty with New Granada, which included a guarantee of the neutrality of the isthmus of Panama and of New Granada's possession of it. And in this case the initiative came from the Bogotá government, which was fearful of possible European intervention and prepared to offer the removal of discriminatory duties on American trade, which the United States had been unsuccessfully requesting for years. Moreover, when the treaty reached Washington, the American government delayed its ratification for over a year, until the acquisition of California had made the question of isthmian transit one of real significance to the United States.

The development of British interests in Central America before 1848 had little to do with canal projects or United States rivalry, but they did extend beyond the dominance of the export/import trade which characterized Britain's relations with the rest of Latin America. Settlers in British Honduras, who had enjoyed treaty rights to cut wood in Spanish territory, were pressing for the British government to take full responsibility for their settlement now that Spain's interest in the area had ceased, and to recognize the encroachments they had made beyond the treaty boundaries; other British adventurers on the Miskito Shore were urging a revival of the relationship established in the eighteenth century between Britain and the Miskito Indians, whose 'king' had granted them various concessions; and British emigrants from the Cayman Islands, who had settled on virtually uninhabited Roatán and other Bay Islands to which Britain had some traditional claims, were asking for protection against the pretensions of the Central American authorities. Although some local British agents had grandiose ambitions, there is little evidence that the government in London had any concerted plan to use these circumstances to create a sphere of influence in Central America directed against the United States. Nevertheless, when American attention turned towards the isthmus in 1848, Britain was found to hold a dominating position on the Atlantic seaboard of Central America, including the mouth of the San Juan, the only suitable terminal for a canal through Nicaragua, then considered a more promising route than Panama.

There followed a period of frenzied activity, during which local British and American agents contended for diplomatic and strategic advantage in the various Central American states, and when clashes between British officials and American prospectors in transit to California could easily have led to an Anglo-American rupture. But both governments were anxious to avoid this, and in the Clayton-Bulwer Treaty of 1850 they agreed to a compromise, whereby both renounced territorial ambitions in Central America, guaranteed the neutrality of transit routes and pledged co-operation in canal construction. A decade of wrangling over the interpretation and implementation of the treaty ensued, which ended only when Britain agreed to withdraw from the Bay Islands and the Miskito Protectorate, and to settle the boundary of British Honduras with Guatemala. By 1860 Britain had come to recognize that these concessions were necessary to maintain her rights under the 1850 treaty as Central America passed more and more into Washington's sphere of influence.

Because of her naval, commercial and industrial supremacy, Britain was much the most important external influence during the period of Latin America's transition to independence. In the first decade of the nineteenth century, her policy towards the Spanish colonies varied from annexation or emancipation to liberalization within the imperial framework. After the revolutions of 1810, she declared her neutrality and sought to extend this to all other third parties, by expressing her opposition to outside intervention, an opposition which amounted to a prohibition in view of her naval power. This was much less than Spain felt entitled to expect, or than the reactionary European monarchs of post-Napoleonic Europe could have wished; and as independence came to appear inevitable, Britain's relations in Europe became somewhat soured and strained. On the other hand, towards the insurgent colonies, Britain pursued a policy of non-recognition and reconciliation within a monarchical structure, until long after independence had been effectively established. On the whole this was accepted as the best that could be achieved in the circumstances, and Britain emerged on good terms with the new states. Britain's policy not only gave the revolutions a fair chance of success but also enabled British economic interests to capitalize on their already favourable position, while the legitimist policy of the continental monarchies added to the disadvantages of their merchants and manufacturers. Though comparatively free from European entanglements, the United States was still too weak politically and economically to follow an independent line in defiance of Europe and could afford to move only a short step ahead of other powers in supporting the insurgent cause. For half a century after Latin American independence the United States could challenge European nations only in areas in close proximity to her own borders. Nevertheless, apprehensions that America might steal a march on them were an important factor in the policymaking of Britain and other European countries.

The contribution of other nations to Spanish American independence was considerable, possibly even vital; but it consisted essentially in refraining from impeding progress towards emancipation rather than in positively advancing it. By not intervening, the powers left the issue to be decided by the outcome of internal struggles and the interplay of local and metropolitan factors, circumstances which in turn powerfully influenced the shape, condition and character of the new nations when they embarked on independence.

The role of Britain, in particular, in Portuguese America was more positive. Though Brazil's independence was in no way actively promoted by Britain, she was instrumental in the removal of the Portuguese court to South America, an event which created the conditions leading to separation. Moreover, her traditional relationship with Portugal, consolidated while the seat of empire was in Rio de Janeiro, enabled Britain to take a major part in determining the conditions under which Brazil's independence was achieved.

The emergence of the former Spanish and Portuguese colonies as independent nations during the first quarter of the nineteenth century had little impact on world affairs for quite some time. Latin America played no part in the international relations of nineteenth-century Europe, and the European countries found not only that, until the second half of the century at least, the prizes of Latin American trade were less glittering than had been imagined but also that their dominance of external trade gave them little practical influence on the political decision-making of the new Latin American states.

A NOTE ON THE CHURCH AND THE INDEPENDENCE OF LATIN AMERICA[1]

Both sides in the struggle for Spanish American independence (1808–25) sought the ideological and economic support of the Catholic Church. From the beginning the church hierarchy for the most part supported the royalist cause. Under the *patronato real* derived from pontifical concessions to the Habsburgs in the sixteenth century, reinforced by Bourbon regalism in the eighteenth century, bishops were appointed by, dependent on and subordinate to the crown. The overwhelming majority were, in any case, *peninsulares* and identified with the interests of Spain. They also recognized the threat posed by revolution and liberal ideology to the established position of the Church. Bishops whose loyalty to the crown was suspect were either recalled to Spain or effectively deprived of their dioceses, as in the case of Narciso Coll i Prat of Caracas and José Pérez y Armendáriz of Cuzco. Moreover, between the restoration of Ferdinand VII in 1814 and the liberal Revolution in Spain in 1820 the metropolis provided 28 of the 42 American dioceses with new bishops of unquestioned political loyalty. There were, however, a few examples of bishops who clearly sympathized with the patriots – Antonio de San Miguel in Michoacán and José de Cuero y Caicedo in Quito – and some opportunists who had no difficulty coming to terms with the victory of the patriots in their region once it was an accomplished fact.

The lower clergy, especially the secular clergy, were predominantly creole and though divided, like the creole elite as a whole, more inclined, therefore, to support the cause of Spanish American self-rule and eventually independence. There was, moreover, a deep divide, economic and social, between the mass of parish priests and the ecclesiastical hierarchy, and considerable resentment at the virtual monopoly of

[1] The Editor wishes to thank Dr Josep Barnadas and Professor Hans-Jürgen Prien for some of the material used in the preparation of this note.

higher ecclesiastical posts by *peninsulares*. The parish clergy had also been alienated from the Bourbon state by recent attacks on their main, often only, source of income, *capellanías* (chaplaincies or chantries) and other pious endowments, and on the *fuero eclesiástico* which gave them immunity from civil jurisdiction. Some individual priests played outstanding roles in the struggle for Spanish American independence, notably Miguel Hidalgo y Costilla and José María Morelos in New Spain, who so successfully appealed to popular piety, especially that of the Indians, by proclaiming the Virgin of Guadalupe the patron saint of the Spanish American Revolution. In Quito three priests issued the proclamation of independence in 1809 and in 1814 a royalist general listed over 100 priests among the patriots. In Santa Fé de Bogotá three priests were members of the Junta of 1810 and nine participated in the Congress of 1811. By 1815 over 100 priests, including both Hidalgo and Moreles, had been executed in Mexico; many more, seculars and regulars, had been excommunicated. Sixteen priests put their names to the declaration of independence of the Río de la Plata, and thirteen to that of Guatemala. It has been argued that the clergy of Peru showed less enthusiasm for independence, but 26 of the 57 deputies in the Congress of 1822 were priests. At the same time, it is important to note the existence of substantial numbers of loyalist priests who continued to preach obedience to the crown. This was particularly the case in the religious orders where the proportion of *peninsulares* to creoles was higher. And, of course, many of the lower clergy were disposed to adhere to any established authority whatever its political affiliation.

Throughout most of the period of the revolutions and wars for Spanish American independence the papacy maintained its traditional alliance with the Spanish crown – and its opposition to liberal revolution. In his encyclical *Etsi longissimo* (30 January 1816) Pius VII urged the bishops and clergy of Spanish America to make clear the dreadful consequences of rebellion against legitimate authority. Later, however, the Vatican became more politically neutral, partly in response to petitions from Spanish America and concern for the spiritual welfare of the faithful there, and partly because of the anticlerical measures taken by the liberal government in Spain after the Revolution of 1820, culminating in the expulsion of the papal nuncio in January 1823. The pope finally agreed to send a papal mission to the Río de la Plata and Chile. (Among the delegates was the future Pius IX (1846–78), who became therefore the first pope to have visited the New World.) But shortly before it left

Pius VII died (on 28 September 1823, the day that Ferdinand VII was restored to full absolutist power in Spain). Under Pope Leo XII, a strong defender of legitimate sovereignty, Rome's attitude to the Spanish American revolutions for independence hardened once again. His encyclical *Etsi iam diu* (24 September 1824) offered the Spanish king and the royalists in Spanish America the total support of the papacy at the precise moment when they were about to suffer their final defeat. These were political misjudgements not unknown in the history of the papacy and they did not permanently damage the Church. Its problems were much more serious.

The Catholic Church in Spanish America emerged from the struggle for independence considerably weakened. So close had been the ties between crown and church that the overthrow of the monarchy dealt a severe blow to the prestige of the Church throughout Spanish America. In the first place, the intellectual position of the Church was undermined. The same voices of reason that repudiated absolute monarchy also challenged revealed religion, or appeared to do so. In their construction of a new political system the leaders of independence sought a moral legitimacy for what they were doing, and they found inspiration not in Catholic political thought but in the philosophy of the age of reason, particularly in utilitarianism. The influence of Bentham in Spanish America was a specific threat to the Church for it gave intellectual credibility to republicanism and offered an alternative philosophy of life. The Church reacted not by intellectual debate, for which it was ill prepared, but by appeal to the state to suppress the enemies of religion. This then raised the question of the Church's relations with the state.

The position of the Church *vis à vis* the new republican governments was uncertain. Of most immediate concern, some episcopal sees suffered protracted vacancies during the period of the transfer of power, as many bishops, compromised by their adherence to the royalist cause, chose or were forced to return to Spain, and others died and were not replaced. Under pressure from the Holy Alliance powers Rome refused to co-operate with the new rulers of Spanish America, all of whom were at the very least determined to exercise all the rights over the Church previously enjoyed by the Spanish crown and especially the *patronato*, the right to present, in effect to appoint, clergy to the higher ecclesiastical offices, and the more liberal of whom were showing early signs of anticlericalism. There was also a certain amount of papal inertia arising from the fact that the papacy changed hands three times in less than ten years (1823–31). In 1825, for example, archbishop José Sebastián Goyeneche y Barrera of Arequipa was the only legitimate bishop in the entire area comprising the present-day states of Ecuador, Peru, Bolivia, Chile and Argentina. The death of both the archbishop of Guatemala and the bishop of Puebla in 1829 left Mexico and Central America without a single bishop. The following are some of the bishoprics which remained unfilled for long periods: Mexico, 1824–39; Michoacán, 1810–31; Oaxaca, 1828–41; Guatemala, 1830–44; Nicaragua, 1825–49; Caracas, 1817–27; Bogotá, 1818–27; Cuenca, 1814–47; Lima, 1822–34; Trujillo, 1821–36; Concepción, 1817–32; La Plata, 1816–34; Santa Cruz, 1813–35; Asunción, 1820–45; Buenos Aires, 1813–33; Córdoba, 1816–57. Under Pope Gregory XVI (1831–46), however, the dioceses of several countries were gradually reorganized and many vacancies filled. Beginning with New Granada in 1835 political relations were also established with the Spanish American republics.

It is not clear how far ecclesiastical structures below the level of the episcopate had disintegrated. Some clergy died; some returned to Spain. Discipline in many places had been shattered by the factionalism of the wars – and loss of contact with Rome. Generally the religious vocation seems to have become less attractive in the post-revolutionary period. The Church lost perhaps 50 per cent of its secular clergy, and even more of its regulars. In Mexico, for example, the number of the secular clergy fell from 4,229 in 1810 to 2,282 in 1834, and that of regular clergy from 3,112 in 1810 to 1,726 in 1831. In the Franciscan Province of Lima, the average annual number of professions declined from 6.9 in the three decades 1771–1800 to 5.3 (1801–10), 2.3 (1811–20) and none between 1821 and 1837. Within a year of the Republic being proclaimed in Bolivia, 25 of the country's 41 convents had closed their doors – though in this case the hostile legislation of Bolívar and Sucre undoubtedly played a part.

The economic patrimony of the Church which had been seriously weakened by the expulsion of the Jesuits in 1767 and the sequestration and later sale of their considerable estates and which had been threatened by the Consolidation decree of December 1804 for the appropriation of church properties and capital (only partially implemented) was further damaged during the wars of independence. From Mexico to Buenos Aires both royalists and patriots, while protesting their devotion to the Faith, requisitioned from the Church, in a succession of emergency measures, cash, income from tithes, buildings, land and livestock, even at times objects of worship.

The governments of the newly independent Spanish American republics acknowledged Catholicism as the state religion, but at the same time frequently accepted the principle of religious toleration. (Indeed freedom of worship was often guaranteed under the treaties the various Spanish American states signed with Britain in the aftermath of independence.) The Inquisition was invariably abolished – if only as a symbolic act. And Protestantism was brought to Spanish America by the foreign merchants and artisans who settled mainly in the port cities, and by the agents of foreign bible societies. Many liberals, besides asserting the supremacy of the secular state and defending freedom of thought, aimed considerably to reduce the temporal power and influence of the Church which they regarded as the principal obstacle to post-independence economic, social and political modernization. The Church's property, capital, income, educational influence, judicial privileges all came under attack. The Church for its part, as it came under the influence of ultramontane ideas, especially during the papacy of Pius IX, increasingly resisted and mobilized in its own defence the conservative forces in Spanish American society, including popular forces. As a result the conflict between the liberal state and the Catholic Church became a central political issue throughout Spanish America in the middle decades of the nineteenth century – and for some time after – especially in Mexico, where it led to violent confrontation and full-scale civil war in the 1850s and 1860s.

The Catholic Church in Brazil at the beginning of the nineteenth century had neither the institutional strength and political influence nor the economic wealth and judicial privileges of the Church in, for example, Mexico or Peru. Under the *padroado real*, which had been reinforced by Pombaline regalism in the second half of the eighteenth century, Brazil's one archbishop (at Salvador) and six bishops were, like the Spanish American episcopate, appointed by and subordinate to the crown. (The Jesuits, the main opponents of regalism in Brazil as in Spanish America, had been expelled in 1759.) The church hierarchy, however, included many Brazilians, some of whom like José Joaquim da Cunha de Azeredo Coutinho, the bishop of Pernambuco, were prominent defenders of Brazilian landed interests. There was much less of a divide in Brazil, economic, social or ideological, between the hierarchy and the lower clergy. Moreover, the transfer of the Portuguese court from Lisbon to Rio de Janeiro in 1807–8 to a large extent isolated Brazil – and therefore the Church in Brazil – from the extreme political and ideological conflicts which beset Spanish America and the Church in Spanish America in the aftermath of first Napoleon's invasion of the Iberian peninsula and then the restoration of Ferdinand VII in 1814. In the political crisis of 1821–2 the majority of the Brazilian clergy supported the Brazilian faction against the Portuguese and eventually the independence of Brazil under Pedro I. There were, of course, pro-Portuguese elements within the Church, especially in Bahia, Piauí, Maranhão and Pará, some of whom were deported in 1823–4. There were also some extreme liberal and republican priests prominent in, for example, the revolution of 1817 in Pernambuco and, most notably, the independent republic, the Confederation of the Equator, established in the North-East in 1824 led by Frei Joaquim do Amor Divino Caneca, who on the defeat of the Confederation was executed in January 1825. Priests, most of them moderate liberals, played an important role in the politics of the 1820s: in the *juntas governativas* (1821–2), in the Portuguese Côrtes (1821–2), in the Constituent Assembly (1823) and in the first legislature (1826–9) which included more priests (23 out of 100 deputies) than any other social group. One Paulista priest, Diogo Antônio Feijó, who served in all these bodies, went on to become, after the abdication of Dom Pedro I, first Minister of Justice and then Regent for two years (1835–7).

Brazil's transition from Portuguese colony to independent empire was marked by continuity in ecclesiastical as in other matters. The relatively peaceful nature of the movement for independence and the survival of the monarchy ensured that, in contrast to Spanish America, the Church in Brazil – its personnel, its property, its prestige – emerged relatively undamaged, although even in Brazil the first decades of the nineteenth century witnessed a fall in the number of clergy, secular and more particularly regular, as the religious orders entered a period of decline. Its wealth, privileges and influence remained, however, quite modest, and the Church in Brazil, unlike the Church in most Spanish American republics, was not threatened by aggressive liberal anticlericalism in the period after independence. Catholicism remained the state religion, and the transfer of the *padroado*, especially the right to appoint to dioceses, from the Portuguese king to the Brazilian emperor was recognized by Leo XII in the papal bull *Praeclara Portugaliae* (1827). Apart from a dispute which left the important Rio see vacant from 1833 to 1839 there were no serious conflicts between church and state in Brazil until the Brazilian hierarchy came under the influence of ultramontanism in the 1870s.

Part Two

THE CARIBBEAN

6

HAITI AND SANTO DOMINGO, 1790–c.1870[1]

In the late eighteenth century the French colony of Saint-Domingue, the western third of the island of Hispaniola, was the most productive colony in the Antilles. It was also the one afflicted by the most complex economic and social problems. The foundation of Saint-Domingue's economy was sugar, although a certain amount of coffee, cotton and indigo was also produced. Production of sugar dates from the end of the seventeenth century after France had occupied some parts of the island claimed in its entirety by Spain. In the course of the eighteenth century the French planters went on to surpass the production of all the British West Indian colonies put together. By the end of the century, with production costs substantially lower than those of the British plantations, the French could undercut the British in the European sugar market. Their success became yet more marked after the independence of the British North American colonies which, once free of the British colonial monopoly, began to supply themselves with French West Indian products, particularly those of Saint-Domingue. It was precisely from 1783, when the War of American Independence drew to a close, that the French colony's already impressive rate of development accelerated, and the production of sugar reached levels never before attained.

To supply their labour needs, the planters of Saint-Domingue, predominantly white, were importing an average of 30,000 African slaves annually in the years that preceded the French Revolution. Initially the provision of black slaves for the sugar plantations of Saint-Domingue was in the hands of monopoly companies created by the French government during the second half of the seventeenth century. But the planters rebelled against these companies and their monopolies, and both were

[1] Translated from the Spanish by Dr Richard Boulind; translation revised by the Editor. The Editor wishes to thank Dr David Nicholls for help in the final preparation of this chapter.

abolished: the trade in slaves then fell into the hands of merchants based in the most important French ports, who in turn invested the capital they accumulated from the trade in financing a good part of Saint-Domingue's growth. Between 1783 and 1789, for example, the merchants of Bordeaux alone invested about 100 million *livres tournois* in the French colony, in order to increase the production of sugar and of other primary products and to meet the demand of the United States market. The relationship between French merchants and financiers and the planters of Saint-Domingue was never entirely satisfactory, however, because the planters, though prosperous, found themselves ever more dependent upon the capitalists of the metropolis. In Paris many of the dissatisfied planters organized themselves into the famous Club Massiac which conspired to secure a significant degree of political autonomy for Saint-Domingue and a liberalization of trade. There existed in 1789 a spirit of real disaffection from the French colonial system on the part of the great planters, the *grands blancs*, of Saint-Domingue.

Another sector of society – the *affranchis*, or free coloureds (mostly mulatto, some black) – was even more alienated from the French colonial system. During the 1780s the free coloured population had more than doubled, numbering about 28,000 by the time of the French Revolution. Some were now landowners and slave owners, controlling perhaps one-third of the plantations (and the slaves) of the colony. And they resented the antagonism of the 40,000 whites – administrators, soldiers, merchants and planters, but also retail traders and craftsmen (the *petits blancs*) – who could not tolerate the descendants of slaves attaining places of pre-eminence in the economy and society of the colony. A series of discriminatory laws framed for the purpose of restraining the economic and social rise of the *affranchis* had been introduced by the whites during the eighteenth century. The result was incessant enmity between the two groups. In order to defend their rights those rich mulattos who lived in Paris organized the Société des Amis des Noirs, which enjoyed wide prestige among the more liberal groups of the French bourgeoisie. Thus it came about that in 1789, when the Revolution began, a close friendship already existed between some of the most important Revolutionary leaders and representatives of the rich mulattos of Saint-Domingue. They offered 6,000,000 *livres tournois* to help the new French government pay the public debt whose size had helped to trigger off the Revolution. In return for this offer of aid they planned to extort from the National

Assembly a decree which would recognize them as citizens with full rights.

Despite their political indebtedness, the French bourgeoisie hesitated long over granting any concessions to the *affranchis* of Saint-Domingue on the grounds that they might next be called upon to emancipate the almost half a million black slaves who made up 85–90 per cent of the population. The abolition of slavery would inevitably lead to the economic collapse of the colony and in turn the ruin of the French commercial and industrial bourgeoisie, whose prosperity and power was essentially based on the colonies.

The Société des Amis des Noirs which, despite its name, represented the interests of the *gens de couleur* or mulattos only, sent two of its members to England in quest of aid. These members then returned to Saint-Domingue with the idea of seizing by force of arms what was denied to them by France's continued refusal to recognize their rights. Vincent Ogé, the Société's chief envoy, arrived back in Saint-Domingue in October 1790. Together with his brother, and another mulatto named Jean-Baptiste Chavannes, he tried to organize an armed uprising. But the attempt was a failure: the revolt was repressed and Ogé and Chavannes were captured and hanged by the French authorities.

The colony was by now, however, in a state of intense revolutionary ferment. Everyone spoke of the liberties won by the Revolution in France and of the example the United States had set them. The *grand blanc* planters sought autonomy for themselves. The mulattos, fired by the deaths of Ogé and Chavannes, sought equality with the whites and, eventually, independence. Nobody thought or said that the black slaves had any rights, or even deserved any. But day after day they could hear the debates going on among their masters. In the great houses, on the plantations, in the villages, in the markets, the slaves were becoming conscious of their condition and of the possibilities now opening for them to escape from it, following the path blazed for them by the legendary rebel François Macandal in 1758. Little by little the slaves organized themselves. In August 1791, a slave revolt broke out on the plantations in the north of Saint-Domingue – a revolt which was to continue for the next ten years.

Their vital interests menaced by the revolt among their slaves, the white and mulatto landowners arrayed themselves in a common front, for the protection of property, supported by French bayonets. They

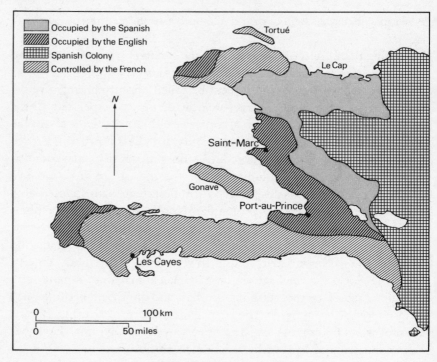

Legend:
- Occupied by the Spanish
- Occupied by the English
- Spanish Colony
- Controlled by the French

N

Tortué

Le Cap

Saint-Marc

Gonave

Port-au-Prince

Les Cayes

0   100 km

0   50 miles

Saint-Domingue, 1794

hastened to call in foreign help, too, when they discovered that Britain was eager to intervene militarily in Saint-Domingue – to turn the conflict to its own advantage and deprive France of its most important West Indian colony. However, there could be no lasting rapprochement between whites and mulattos. In vain did the French government send a high-powered Civil Commission to Saint-Domingue at the end of 1791: the formal alliance that this Commission negotiated between whites and mulattos was soon dissolved by the profound hatred that the two groups entertained for each other.

The divisions between the rival camps now began to come out into the open. The black slaves in revolt looked for and found support in the eastern two-thirds of the island, the Spanish colony of Santo Domingo, where the authorities thought they perceived an opportunity to reconquer the territories in the west that had been lost over a century before, but, despite a *política de tolerancia* after 1700, never formally ceded to France. The mulattos were won over by the French revolutionary government when, on 4 March 1792, a decree recognizing the equality of mulattos with whites was finally issued. For their part, the *grand blanc* settlers sought British help, asking the authorities in Jamaica to send troops to help them put down the blacks and to strengthen their position *vis-à-vis* the mulattos. It was in the midst of this tempestuous situation, that a second French Civil Commission, led by the effectively anti-white Jacobin, Leger-Félicité Sonthonax, arrived, accompanied by six thousand soldiers. His mission was to impose order on the colony.

But imposing order was now the most difficult of tasks: what had started as a slave revolt had already become a civil war – of mulattos against whites, and of planters against the central authorities – and an international war between France, Britain and Spain. Disagreements between the French military commanders and the Civil Commissioners undermined the French position, facilitated the Spaniards' advance across the frontier with an army composed of insurgent blacks and the creole militia of Santo Domingo, and encouraged the British in Jamaica to land troops in the south. The French might have been defeated, had not Sonthonax exceeded his nominal powers and, on 29 April 1793, improvised the astute decision to decree the abolition of slavery in Saint-Domingue. He immediately called on the black rebels, now freemen, to unite with the Army and repel the British military intervention designed to succour the white slave-holding plantation-owners.

This stroke had an important result. One of the principal black revolutionary leaders, Toussaint Louverture, a former *créole* house slave, accepted the call and went over to the side of the French, bringing four thousand men with him. The remaining blacks did not subscribe to Sonthonax's decree and remained in the military service of the Spaniards. For their part, the mulattos also split. Some supported the French government, even though they disagreed with the abolition of slavery. Others supported the *grand blanc* plantation-owners allied to the British.

The French military effort received a major boost from the adherence of leading black and mulatto generals, notably Toussaint, who emerged as the indisputable commander of the French forces in Saint-Domingue; he became brigadier-general in 1796 and major-general in 1797. The Spaniards were driven back across the frontier to their own territory, losing important areas used for rearing the cattle which they had formerly supplied to Saint-Domingue. The British were eventually forced to retreat, after a struggle lasting five years and the loss of more

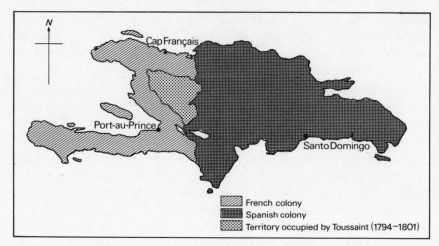

French colony
Spanish colony
Territory occupied by Toussaint (1794–1801)

Territory occupied by Toussaint, 1794–1801

than 25,000 British troops in the campaign. The British left the island in April 1798, following the mission to Saint-Domingue of a special envoy, General Maitland, who signed a secret treaty with Toussaint by which the British relinquished their military occupation in exchange for commercial concessions. Several times during these negotiations Maitland hinted to Toussaint that he should declare his independence, relying on the protection of Britain. Toussaint chose not to take up this option and, in part because of his suspicions of the intentions of the mulattos, preferred to go on governing the colony in the name of France. His authority was accepted by the French governor, General Laveaux, and by the other French officials.

The mulattos, however, felt unable to submit to the government of Toussaint, the black ex-slave. They wanted to establish a government of their own. In February 1799 the chief mulatto general, André Rigaud, and his supporters in the south rebelled against Toussaint, and civil war broke out. In the end, the numerical superiority of the blacks and the brilliant military leadership of Toussaint proved decisive and by August 1800 the mulattos were defeated.

In the meantime Toussaint had been proceeding with the reorganization of the colony and the restoration of its previous economic prosperity. He maintained the plantation system; he returned estates to their previous owners; he forced the ex-slaves to return to their accustomed jobs on the pretext of doing away with vagrancy. He also established relations with the United States which began to supply him with weapons, foodstuffs and other commodities in exchange for the products of the colony. On 12 October 1800 Toussaint, now governor general and commander-in-chief in Saint-Domingue, laid down a code of laws regulating agricultural production. The slaves of 1789 were still to work the plantations, but as wage-earners. Of a plantation's production, one-quarter would remain in the hands of the workers, a half had to be remitted to the public treasury, and the remaining quarter was left for the owner. When the owners saw the production of their plantations being divided amongst their former slaves, they launched an intense propaganda campaign against Toussaint in Cuba, the United States and Europe. In France Napoleon Bonaparte, a man like Toussaint thrown up by the Revolution, seized on these injuries and launched himself into the task of trying to turn back the clock in the colony of Saint-Domingue. He represented the bourgeois interests who had helped him in his rise to power, and who were anxious to gain access to the wealth of Saint-Domingue, which made up two-thirds of France's colonial income. So Napoleon determined to restore absolute control of the colony to metropolitan France.

By a treaty signed in Basle (June 1795) in exchange for the return of territory lost in Europe Spain had submitted to the necessity of ceding the Spanish part of Hispaniola to France. But the French Government had insisted that the colony of Santo Domingo should be handed over only to a French army composed of white soldiers, lest the slave revolution in Saint-Domingue infect the Spanish part of the island. The continuance of war in Europe had prevented the dispatch of such an army. Napoleon now planned to send a force to Santo Domingo and to use it as a base from which to drive Toussaint from power in Saint-Domingue. Toussaint, however, stole a march on the French troops by himself invading the eastern part of the island. He arrived at the old city of Santo Domingo on 26 January 1801, to the consternation of its Spanish residents as well as the many French refugees from revolutionary Saint-Domingue who had crowded into the city. Toussaint proceeded to unify the two parts of the island. He named various officials to run the former Spanish colony and announced several measures designed to transform its economy from one which had hitherto depended almost entirely on ranching into one based on agriculture and producing crops for export. He then returned to the western part of the island to resume the business of reconstruction there. Napoleon, however, having recently also purchased Louisiana from Spain refused to accept the new order established in Hispaniola and launched a huge invasion force to re-impose metropolitan control over both Saint-Domingue and Santo Domingo.

Half of the French fleet arrived in Samaná, one of the bays in the eastern part of the island, on 29 January 1802. The other half appeared off Cap Français on 3 February. Operations then began, with the French forces divided so as to mount attacks from several different quarters. One force marched directly on the city of Santo Domingo, which was captured with little difficulty; other forces landed in other parts of the Spanish half of the island. Part of the fleet attacked Port-au-Prince, while the bulk of the expeditionary force, under the direct command of General Victor-Emmanuel Leclerc, who brought with him his wife, Napoleon's sister Pauline Bonaparte, captured the city of Cap Français, though only after surmounting serious difficulties. On 7 June Toussaint was betrayed and fell into French hands; he died in captivity in France the following year. Blacks and mulattos, however, now united under the leadership of Jean-Jacques Dessalines, a former slave and lieutenant of Toussaint, to initiate the final, bloody steps on the road to independence.

The French – 58,000 men – spent twenty-one months trying to subdue their former slaves. The same men had proved overwhelmingly triumphant in Italy and in Egypt. This time, however, victory was beyond their grasp: the blacks and mulattos of Saint-Domingue had the aid of the most powerful of all allies – yellow fever. According to French army figures, some 50,270 soldiers lost their lives in the campaign, which ended in 1804 with the surrender and flight of the few survivors left under the command of the desperate General Rochambeau after Leclerc himself had succumbed at the end of December 1803. On 1 January 1804 Dessalines and the other victorious black generals proclaimed the independence of Haiti (an Amerindian name for the island of Hispaniola). France had lost its richest colonial possession. Slave-owners throughout the United States, the Caribbean, Spanish America and Brazil felt considerably less secure; slaves everywhere else felt more hopeful. Haiti was Latin America's first independent state and the world's first black republic.

The governor of Santo Domingo, Don Joaquín García y Moreno, had endured since 1795 a long sequence of calamities, as he kept a colony functioning which no longer belonged to Spain but which France refused to occupy until she had assembled sufficient forces. He had no money, since, thanks to British naval activity in the Caribbean, none of the regular subsidy – the *situado* – could get through from Mexico. He had to confront an archbishop whose sole thought was to emigrate as soon as possible, along with all the rest of the secular clergy, so as not to have to co-exist with anti-clerical Frenchmen or with slaves in revolt. He was badgered by thousands of Spanish families who could not emigrate as they wanted to because of the lack of ships to carry them. Nonetheless, refugees crowded the port of Santo Domingo every day, bringing with them their movable property and their slaves, and overloading the local market more than ever by demanding food and articles of primary necessity which simply were not available.

The surrender of Santo Domingo to France in 1795 ranks as one of the great traumas in the history of the Dominican nation. It disrupted the Spanish colonial system and plunged the country into a turbulent torrent of revolutions, wars and invasions which brought it to bankruptcy and set it apart from the general development of the Spanish American colonies. News that the Spanish colony had been ceded to France reached Santo Domingo in October 1795. Those who could not reconcile themselves to the new situation had up to a year to remove themselves to Cuba, Puerto Rico, or Venezuela, where they were to be given facilities to make a fresh start.

For more than a century, the colonists of Santo Domingo had struggled to survive, in face of penetration and usurpation by the French from the west of the island. From the first days of the slave revolt in Saint-Domingue, their aim in fighting had been precisely that of expelling the French from the island altogether. To learn now that they were to be governed by the French was intolerable to the majority of Dominicans who had become intensely pro-Spanish. Many, therefore, now decided to emigrate: between 1795 and 1810 some 125,000 persons are estimated to have left the Spanish sector of the island, leaving its population diminished by two-thirds compared with what it had been before the French Revolution.

During the brief occupation of Dominican territory by Toussaint's troops (1801–2) the rate of emigration by Spanish families accelerated: the population was in fear and trembling at the news of the horrors of the Revolution that French refugees had brought to Santo Domingo. Moreover, Toussaint was resolved to uproot the traditional Dominican labour and agricultural systems, which were based on stock-rearing and on the colony's extensive style of land usage, and which employed only relatively few slaves (under 15,000), whose function was to work as the managers and overseers of the ranches (*hatos*). Toussaint realized that the celebrated indolence of the inhabitants of the eastern part of the island – the subject of much comment by French travellers in the eighteenth century – was a by-product of the ranching economy which for nearly three centuries had underpinned the Spanish colony. He attempted to transform a land devoted to cattle-rearing, where the only cultivation was subsistence farming, into a land intensively exploited for export crops, on the French model of highly capitalized plantations developed in eighteenth-century Saint-Domingue. But the great French invasion led by Leclerc frustrated all his plans, as well as nullifying the abolition of slavery which he had decreed on arriving at Santo Domingo in January 1801. The landowners in the Spanish sector found they preferred to support the French forces Napoleon had sent to reinstate slavery rather than be governed by the black military commanders from Saint-Domingue headed by Paul Louverture, Toussaint's brother. In the event, the Dominicans collaborated with Leclerc and his French troops in order to expel the Haitians. But the Dominicans were destined to pay heavily for this. Once the war in the west had ended with the proclamation of the independence of Haiti in 1804, Dessalines and his staff prepared to punish the Revolution's enemies in the Spanish sector and to drive out the French who had fallen back on Santo Domingo.

Dessalines took over a year to invade, since he needed to consolidate his primacy and organize the new state before he could commit himself to a new military campaign. But one of the decrees issued by the commander-in-chief of the French troops in Santo Domingo, General Jean Louis Ferrand, a decree authorizing the crossing of the frontier by slave-owners seeking slaves for their plantations, finally provoked the invasion in February 1805. One Haitian army marched via the northern, and another via the southern shore of the island, advancing on the city of Santo Domingo. The siege began on 8 March 1805, with the city surrounded by over 21,000 Haitians, and lasted for three weeks. The city was saved from falling into Haitian hands by the desperate defence put up jointly by the French and Spaniards. Above all, however, the Haitians were frustrated by the appearance on 26 March of a squadron of the French navy which was raiding various of the British possessions in the Lesser Antilles, and which Dessalines thought was contemplating a new invasion of Haiti.

The Haitians raised the siege and fell back through the settled area of the interior, sacking the towns of Monte Plata, Cotui and La Vega, and slaughtering the citizens of Moca and Santiago. They left the fields laid waste, the cities ablaze and the churches in ashes behind them. In Moca only two people survived, thanks to corpses having been piled up on those still living in the church where the principal massacre took place. This hecatomb would have important consequences for the relationship of the Dominican and the Haitian peoples for many years to come. At the time, it set off a massive desperate rush to emigrate, as the Dominicans came to the conclusion that their military weakness doomed them to fall into the hands of the Haitians sooner or later and to suffer the fate of the French in the other sector of the island.

Those who remained continued to feel insecure, and this largely counteracted the great efforts the French made in the next three years to reconstruct the country and improve its economy. Nevertheless, the trade in cattle across the frontier was restored, for Haiti never reared sufficient to feed its own population and so needed to buy cattle from Santo Domingo. And partly due to this, a period of tranquillity ensued. The French military government, aware of the strength of pro-Hispanic sentiments amongst the population, set up a paternalistic sort of government which respected traditional laws and customs.

The relative harmony between the French and the Dominicans was shattered in 1808, first by Governor Ferrand's order to the colony's inhabitants to suspend all trade with the Haitians, in particular the commerce in cattle, and secondly, and more seriously by Napoleon's invasion of Spain. The popular uprisings against the French which took place in Madrid on 2 May 1808 were soon common knowledge in the West Indies, especially among the Dominicans living in exile in Puerto Rico, where a rich landowner, Juan Sánchez Ramírez, obtained the governor's support for expelling the French from Santo Domingo. As early as July 1808 it was known in San Juan de Puerto Rico that a governing junta had replaced the deposed Ferdinand VII, and that in the name of Spain it had declared war on France.

Sánchez Ramírez returned to Santo Domingo, and between July and November 1808 devoted himself to organizing a conspiracy and recruiting an army of two thousand men. On 7 November 1808 he arrayed it against six hundred French soldiers in the eastern part of the country. At the famous battle of La Sabana de Palo Hincado the French were annihilated, and the governor lost his life. As soon as news of their defeat reached the city of Santo Domingo the French placed it in a state of siege to resist the attack they thought would follow. But Sánchez Ramírez's troops were not strong enough to seize the city, and the siege dragged on for eight months. Meanwhile, the British in Jamaica had been in contact with the Spaniards in Puerto Rico and, once the siege began, they blockaded the port of Santo Domingo.

When the French, routed by hunger and want, finally surrendered to British naval forces in July 1809, it came as a colossal shock to the Dominicans, who had begun fighting the French over a year before, to see the capital of their country surrendered not to them but to the British. Only after arduous negotiations did the British consent to evacuate the city, but not before removing the bells from the churches and the best guns from the fortifications. Nor did they omit to make the new local authorities deliver enormous loads of caoba wood to pay for the naval blockade. And, as if that were not enough, the Dominicans had to guarantee British vessels free access to the colony, and concede equal treatment with Spanish products and manufactures to British imports.

Ironically, the Dominicans had gone to war against the French to restore Spanish rule to Santo Domingo just as the rest of Hispanic America was preparing to renounce Spanish colonialism. Moreover, the so-called War of Reconquest (1808–9), following two invasions by the Haitians (1801 and 1805), had left the country completely devastated. Economic breakdown was total. The cattle on which Santo Domingo's eighteenth-century prosperity had been founded had been eaten by the clashing armies. In spite of the many efforts made to revive it, at no time in the nineteenth century did stock-rearing succeed in regaining the volume of exports it had attained in the eighteenth. Subsistence agriculture now accounted for most visible activity, and the only surviving money-producing occupations were the cutting and exportation of caoba wood from the south, and the growing and exportation of tobacco from the north of the country. Exports consisted of a few dozen tons of tobacco yearly, some thousands of hides, some caoba wood and a little molasses and rum. Imports were solely what was strictly necessary for an impoverished population amounting to no more than some 75,000 souls, less than 30 per cent of what it had been fifteen years before.

In Haiti independence had not at first altered the existing policy, adopted by Toussaint, of maintaining the plantation system as the basis of the country's economy, with the workers permanently bound to the land.

During the war most of the whites still in the colony had been killed, and Dessalines immediately confiscated the whites' plantations and forbade whites ever to own property in Haiti. In April 1804 he annulled all the sales and donations of land made in any year previous to 1803. The former slaves were forbidden to leave their plantations except with government permission. The measure was unpopular because it signified that the new servile status into which the former slaves had fallen would be maintained indefinitely.

Dessalines was also making himself steadily more unpopular amongst the black masses by trying to break down old loyalties and integrate them into a nation-state. It must be remembered that at the time of independence, the majority of the inhabitants of Haiti had either been born in Africa (*bossals*) or were of the first generation in the New World (*créole*). As soon as they secured the slightest liberty they sought to reconstitute their groups of origin by associating with people of similar linguistic or tribal antecedents. Among mulattos, moreover, Dessalines was unpopular from the beginning, not only because of his colour but because of his land confiscation policies. In October 1806 he was assassinated by enemies who threw his body into the street, where it was torn to pieces by the mob. But during the two years he ruled Dessalines was so effective in confiscating land that by the time of his death the greater part of the land – estimated at between two-thirds and nine-tenths of Haiti's land area – was in the hands of the state.

On the death of Dessalines conflict erupted once more and in 1807 Haiti split into two independent and antagonistic units. In the north the black General Henry Christophe pursued the policies of his predecessor, Toussaint, attempting to preserve the plantations and their labour force intact. But he impressed a new direction on the policy in the interests of increased agricultural production (and exports) and the strength and prosperity of the state. Christophe's solution was to allow his most important generals and officials to lease or manage the plantations: they were obliged to maintain established levels of production and to pay one-quarter of the product to the state, while handing over another quarter in wages to the workers and retaining as much as the whole of the remaining 50 per cent for themselves. In 1811 Christophe reorganized his régime, turning it into a kingdom. His chief comrades in arms – already the recipients of his grants of real estate – now had the chance to acquire numerous titles of nobility as well, the listing and enumerating of which becoming a celebrated diversion of English visitors to Haiti during

Christophe's spectacular reign. Christophe's rule made the kingdom of Haiti one of the most original political experiments in nineteenth-century Latin America, in that it set up an 'African' court and aristocracy in imitation of the contemporary courts of Europe. The architectural marvels Christophe created are rightly famous. He built the palace of Sans Souci at Milot to house and show off the punctilio and ceremonial of his court; to defend his kingdom from the potential French attack which he always thought might again be mounted on his capital city, the former Cap Français, he built the great fortress – the Citadelle – at La Ferrière, fit to rank as one of the wonders of the world.

Christophe succeeded in making the former plantations in the north of Haiti productive again and kept exports at a high level. Most of the rural population remained on the plantations, and the army took on the job of overseeing production so that the freed slaves should not relapse into unproductive idleness. Christophe and his black and mulatto elite were determined that the kingdom of Haiti should avoid the kind of radical changes carried out since the death of Dessalines in the west and south where a republic had been set up in 1807 by those generals – mostly former *affranchis* – who resisted the claims of Christophe, with the mulatto general Alexander Pétion as president.

In the republic the government had begun to sell state land to private individuals and later to distribute parcels of land to officers and men in the army, the amount being related to rank. By this means Pétion turned all the personnel of his army, both mulatto and black, into landowners and automatically won their loyalty. He had already been restoring to their former mulatto owners the great plantations Dessalines had confiscated, thus securing support from this class. By distributing the land to the army Pétion believed that he had insured his republic from any invasion that could be mounted from the north and guaranteed it internal peace. As early as 1809 most of the land in Haiti's south and west had returned to private hands and was farmed by free workers, liberated from the vigilance of the agricultural inspectors of the days of Dessalines.

The immediate result of this policy of parcelling out the land in the republic of Haiti was that most of the new owners of small properties abandoned agriculture for export – especially the growing of sugar-cane or cocoa or indigo which needed complex processes of refining and marketing – in favour of subsistence farming. As a result, production for export – which provided the main revenue of the state – gradually began to decay, in step with the transmutation of many former plantations into small holdings. Only what was needed for feeding a family was grown. Or the plots were simply left uncultivated, since there was nobody to oblige anyone to plant anything. Moreover, as everyone now had property of their own, nobody wanted to work as a labourer for those remaining great landowners who did want to keep sizeable units growing sugar-cane, coffee, cotton or cocoa.

The crop that suffered the most was sugar-cane. Thus, when Pétion died in 1818, sugar production had fallen to a little under 2,000,000 lb a year as against the 60,000,000 lb produced in the time of Toussaint. Indigo was a labour-intensive crop and so ceased to be planted altogether; cotton dwindled to 5 per cent of its former production. Only coffee survived to prevent the total bankruptcy of the republic. The rate of decrease of its production was much slower: in 1818 production had not fallen below a third of its previous level.

In 1818 Pétion was succeeded as president of the republic by his secretary and minister, General Jean-Pierre Boyer. Two years later, in October 1820, King Henry Christophe in the north suffered an apoplectic fit while attending divine service. His illness offered an opening for a conspiracy against him among his own men, wearied by his absolutism and by the enormous labours the king had imposed on the whole population in order to complete the construction of his Citadelle. On discovering the conspiracy Christophe felt disabled and betrayed: he put an end to himself moments before the mob, in open revolt, set fire to his palace of Sans Souci. The rebels in the north of Haiti called in Boyer, who speedily marched in with his army and occupied the city of Cap Haitien – the former Cap Français, in 1820 known as Cap Henry – at the end of October 1820.

The utterly different level of return produced for the respective states by the two contrasting régimes in the north and the south of Haiti now became clearly visible: Boyer entered Christophe's treasury and found in it an accumulation of 150,000,000 francs in gold (45,000,000 Haitian gourdes). Whereas Pétion had created a free peasantry, owning the lands he had distributed, but had weakened the state, Christophe had enriched his state, but returned the masses to bondage. Boyer reunited Haiti. He increased his popularity amongst the black masses of the north by decreeing that all available lands and plantations be distributed among them in the same proportions as Pétion had followed in earlier years in the south of Haiti: that is, by bestowing on each parcels according to his rank, depending on whether he was an army officer, a simple soldier, or a plantation worker. On the economy these measures had the same effects as they had in the south and west.

Whilst Boyer was putting his policy into effect in the north of Haiti, he also had the eastern part of the island in his sights. There, a further twelve years of Spanish administration had not sufficed to rescue the country from the penury to which the War of Reconquest had reduced it, and many in the colony were looking for the political emancipation that other Spanish possessions in the Americas were securing. The independence movement had, in fact, been fermenting ever since the war of 1808–9. Some *criollos* were attracted then by the idea of setting up an independent state as the Haitians had done in 1804. Others were influenced by the move towards independence in Caracas in April 1810, news of which reached Santo Domingo by means of the *Gaceta de Caracas*. This set off several military uprisings, one of them known as the 'Italian Rebellion' because of the country of origin of its principal leaders. Some four months later another rebellion, different in nature, was mounted by four sergeants of French origin who planned a *coup d'état* in order to restore French rule to the colony. The most interesting of these abortive revolts, however, was that of 1812 led by a black group from the environs of the city of Santo Domingo. Some slave and some free, they aimed to bring about an uprising of all the coloured people in the colony, on the Haitian model – slaughtering all the whites.

Dominican society at the beginning of the nineteenth century was, however, very different from that of Haiti. Free mulattos, who felt more affinity with the Spaniards than with the former slaves from whom they had descended, and poor whites made up the bulk of a small population of no more than 75,000 on which the poverty of earlier centuries had inflicted a process of social levelling which had relegated the racial problem to insignificance. In the twenty years since the French Revolution Santo Domingo had been further impoverished by warfare, and decapitated by emigration. The important thing was not to be wholly black – or, at least, not black enough to be taken for a slave or a Haitian. Dominican mulattos had achieved a social ranking quite close to that of whites, though not in all respects equal. As time went by, the term *blanco de la tierra* came into use, signifying a Dominican Spaniard, or a creole ideologically identifying himself with the Spaniards. As in other areas of the Caribbean, the mulatto in Santo Domingo had not the faintest desire to be considered black. That was why the several black, or slave, revolts of the eighteenth and early nineteenth centuries met with no general support among the population.

At the same time the Dominicans' loyalty to Ferdinand VII after his restoration in 1814 soon began to wear thin. The aid that they had hoped to receive from the motherland amounted to little more than the subsidy which was sent from the treasury at Havana: it never exceeded 100,000 pesos a year. This subvention did not amount even to a third of the expenses of the former colony in the years prior to the French Revolution: it scarcely sufficed even to feed and clothe the troops who became increasingly restless as the rewards which the Madrid authorities had promised those who had fought the French never arrived. The rest of the inhabitants of Santo Domingo had to resign themselves to vegetating economically, dependent upon a minuscule trade in caoba wood, tobacco and hides with some of the other West Indian islands, particularly Curaçao and St Thomas.

Of all this Jean-Pierre Boyer, president of Haiti, was aware. He also knew that some Dominican groups favoured union with Haiti in the hope that it would increase the trade in cattle between the two parts of the island. There were rumours in 1820 that some citizens of Santo Domingo, inspired by events elsewhere in the Americas, were planning a *coup d'état* to bring about independence. The same year a subversive manifesto, written and printed in Caracas, circulated in Santo Domingo, calling on the Dominicans to rise up. Communication with Venezuela was frequent, and soldiers, officials and merchants alike were disgusted with Spain's incapacity to improve their condition. The resulting conspiracies served only to encourage Haiti's governing élite, which had never since the times of Toussaint lost its vision of uniting the whole island under one government. For years Henry Christophe sought to entice the inhabitants of the north of Santo Domingo to join his kingdom, but the lively memory of Dessalines' massacres of the Dominicans, in which Christophe and his troops had themselves had a hand, prevented any such move. However, now there was a liberal government in Haiti, presided over by a mulatto who promised to eliminate duties on the cattle trade. Since discontent with Spain was almost universal among the inhabitants of Santo Domingo, the soil was well fertilized for union.

What persuaded Boyer to take immediate action was news that a group of French adventurers were organizing in Martinique a new invasion of Haiti to recover the plantations the whites had lost twenty years earlier. These adventurers planned to attack and occupy the weak Santo Domingo, then ask the French to send troops with which to recover Saint-Domingue itself. Santo Domingo's garrison was in no way strong enough to resist external attack. Moreover, the Haitians suspected that Spain might even be in league with France to help her recover her old colony.

In face of this new threat, to Haitian independence, Boyer set on foot military preparations, meanwhile trying to woo the inhabitants of the eastern sector of the island into rising against Spain and incorporating themselves into the Haitian Republic. In December 1820 news reached Santo Domingo that Boyer's agents were offering military rank, official preferment and land to leaders in the border areas who would back such plans. At the same time, another independence movement was coming to the boil among the bureaucracy, and even among the military, in Santo Domingo itself, where the white creoles were now enthused by the achievements of Simón Bolívar. These two movements – one in the frontier districts in favour of Haiti, and one in the capital with independence as its aim – progressed on parallel but independent lines throughout 1820 and 1821. Finally, on 8 November 1821, a group supporting the Haitians in the frontier town of Beler, led by Major Andrés Amarantes, proclaimed independence and called on the towns of the north of Santo Domingo to unite with the Republic of Haiti. The news reached the leader of the movement in the capital, Don José Núñez de Cáceres, several days later. During the past twelve years Núñez de Cáceres had been the colony's senior official under the Spanish governor, so he had a complete mastery of its administrative and military machinery. He fitted the model of the educated, disaffected creole perfectly: a man relegated to a position of secondary importance under an appointee from Spain and alienated by Spain's total failure to resolve any of the problems of his class or his country.

Since independence plus union with Haiti had been being proclaimed in the frontier areas, Núñez de Cáceres and his group immediately recognized that they had to act fast if they were to succeed with their plans for the independence of Santo Domingo and its union with Gran Colombia as a state within the confederation that Simón Bolívar was trying at this time to bring into being. They boldly brought forward the date of their *coup d'état* and, relying on the support of the troops in the capital, took the Spanish governor, Don Pascual Real, by surprise. At 6 o'clock on the morning of 1 December 1821 they awoke the residents of Santo Domingo by firing off salvos to proclaim the end of Spanish colonial rule in Santo Domingo, and the creation of an 'Independent State of Spanish Haiti'.

The proclamation of the Independent State of Spanish Haiti coincided with the arrival in Santo Domingo of three envoys of President Boyer to tell the Spanish authorities of the Haitian government's decision to support the independence movements in the frontier areas. What had happened was a serious blow to the Haitian government, threatened as it was by a French invasion from Martinique through Santo Domingo which did not now have even the military or diplomatic protection of Spain. At the beginning of January 1822 Boyer therefore secured the authorization of the Haitian senate to march into the eastern sector of the island to defend the frontier towns and achieve the political unity of the island. To avoid bloodshed, Boyer on 11 January 1822 sent a long letter to Núñez de Cáceres to persuade him of the impossibility of having two separate and independent governments in the island.

At the same time he announced that he was marching with an army of twelve thousand men and that no obstacle could halt him. Núñez de Cáceres and the municipality of Santo Domingo had no more than a few dozen undernourished and ill-armed soldiers between them. In face of these tidings they saw no option but to comply with President Boyer's demands; they notified him that all agreed in placing themselves under the protection of the laws of the Republic of Haiti. The leaders of the movement in Santo Domingo had, in fact, sent a messenger to Caracas with the aim of securing an interview with Simón Bolívar and letting him know they had decided to accede to Gran Colombia. But Bolívar was not in Caracas, and Vice-President Páez, who received the Dominican emissary, had no powers to take a decision of this magnitude on his own authority. Boyer arrived in Santo Domingo on 9 February 1822. He was received by the civil and the ecclesiastical authorities in the hall of the Ayuntamiento, and was handed the keys of the city; everyone then proceeded to the cathedral where a Te Deum was sung.

So ended Spanish colonial rule in Santo Domingo. And so, after a brief *independencia efímera*, began Haitian domination of the eastern part of the island which lasted twenty-two years and bound the history of the two peoples, Haitian and Dominican, together for a whole generation. The period of Haitian domination brought the French Revolution to Santo Domingo, since it liquidated the Spanish colonial *ancien régime* and installed an island-wide government which was anti-monarchical, anti-slavery and inspired by the masonic and liberal ideology of the time. At the same time, President Boyer established a political cult of personality

Political divisions of the island, 1822–44

rooted in the principles of the Haitian Constitution of 1816, under which
he was president for life. Haiti during these years, a poor and isolated
land, was a sort of crowned republic in which institutions functioned
only as expressions of the will of the president, whose power in the final
analysis rested upon the army.

Boyer's first public decision, once he had taken possession of Santo
Domingo, in February 1822 was to decree the abolition of slavery in the
eastern sector of the island, and to offer land to all the freemen, so they
could earn their living in liberty farming properties given them by the
state.[2] It was hoped that they might plant coffee, cacao, sugar, cotton,
tobacco and other export crops. However, not only was the Spanish law
of property, in force in the eastern part of the island for three centuries,
different from that of Haiti which originated in French jurisprudence,
but the agrarian system was also completely different. Since the days of
Pétion private ownership of land in Haiti was guaranteed by individual
land-titles issued by the state, while in the Spanish part of the island the

---

[2] Jean-Pierre Boyer, 'Circulaire, en forme d'instruction, du Président d'Haiti, aux colonels Fré-
mont, à Azua; Hogu, à Baní; Prezeau, à Seibé; et aux comandants Isnardy, à Saint-Jean; et Saladin,
à Lamate, sur les devoirs de leurs charges', Santo Domingo, 11 February 1822, in Linstant de
Pradine (ed.), *Recueil général des lois et actes du gouvernement d'Haiti* (Paris, 1851–65), III, 448–56. See
also, Jean Price Mars, *La République d'Haiti et la République Dominicaine* (Port-au-Prince, 1953), I,
198–200, and José Gabriel García, *Compendio de la historia de Santo Domingo* (4 vols., Santo
Domingo, 1968), II, 93–4, who comment upon parts of this circular.

predominant system was that of *terrenos comuneros*. The system of land occupation was entirely irregular owing to the sparseness of the population, the abundance of land and the extensive method by which land was used: it was exploited chiefly for the rearing of cattle and the cutting of timber. A problem thus arose as to the precise ownership of much of the land in the east. Since it could not be immediately resolved, the freedmen had to wait some time before they could receive the lands which Boyer again promised them in a proclamation of 15 June 1822.

Meanwhile, those former slaves who desired to be free of their masters had no other recourse than to enlist in the Haitian army. For this purpose, the so-called 32nd Battalion was created: together with the force of free coloured men known as the 31st Battalion, it constituted the principal military force responsible for the security of the eastern sector.

To resolve the question of which land was available to the state for distribution to the former slaves, Boyer, in June 1822, appointed a special commission. It reported in October that to the state belonged:
(1) land that had been in the hands of the Spanish crown;
(2) the properties of convents, along with their various houses, farms, animals, estates and building sites that pertained;
(3) the buildings and outbuildings of church-run hospitals, together with their estates;
(4) such property of Frenchmen, requisitioned by the Spanish government, as had not been returned to its owners;
(5) the property of persons who had collaborated with the French in the Samaná campaign of 1808, and who had emigrated on board the French squadron;
(6) all the *censos* and ecclesiastical *capellanías* which had fallen in through the passage of time, or had otherwise returned to the treasury of the archdiocese;
(7) lands mortgaged for the benefit of the cathedral.

Boyer submitted the report to the Chamber of Deputies and the Senate; it was approved by both houses on 7 November 1822. The commander-in-chief and governor of Santo Domingo, General J.-M. Borgella, interpreted this as conferring on the report's proposals the force of law. He thenceforth devoted himself to confiscating properties to which the church, in particular, held apparent title, but which had, in fact, been in private hands since the end of the eighteenth century. The owners of these estates and houses were then despoiled by the Haitian governor and their property given to the recently freed slaves, sold at low prices to his own friends, or handed over to the Haitian soldiers, officers and bureaucrats.

To calm the disquiet of the injured parties on 22 January 1823 Boyer appointed a new commission charged with studying the problem and redressing the grievances of inhabitants of the east whose property had now been seized by the state. Before this commission was a gigantic and delicate problem: that of the confused state into which ecclesiastical property had fallen in the 25 years or more since the archbishop and the religious orders left the island as a consequence of the Treaty of Basle. In the intervening years many Dominicans had occupied these lands and buildings, with the blessing of the civil authorities. Under the Spanish land law occupation for as much as twenty years conferred on the occupants property rights.

In a further effort to clarify the situation, on 8 February 1823 Boyer promulgated a decree giving those landowning residents of the Spanish sector who had emigrated up to 9 February 1822, except those who had collaborated with the French in the Samaná conspiracy, four months in which to return to the country to reclaim their properties. The soldiers governing in the east had orders to confiscate the properties of those Dominicans who did not choose to return home. As was to be expected, most of those who had gone abroad stayed there, and their properties (occupied in many cases by their relatives) were, therefore, taken over by the state.

After a full year of Haitian occupation important sections of the Dominican population were extremely discontented. Haitian land policy, in particular, had inflicted heavy damage on the interests of the white landowners. The archbishop of Santo Domingo headed the list of the discontented: ecclesiastical properties had been nationalized; moreover, on 5 January 1823, Boyer had suspended the payment of salaries to the archbishop and other members of the cathedral chapter.

During 1823 several Spanish loyalist conspiracies were discovered. The government also had to suppress an insurrection against the Haitian troops supervising the gangs of workers repairing the road from Santiago to Puerto Plata. The most dangerous conspiracy was hatched in February 1824; however, it was discovered in time, and the government condemned four of its leaders to death; they were hanged in Santo Domingo on 9 March. Then a new group of refugee families sought asylum in Puerto Rico before anything could be done to stop them. However, this latest emigration fitted in well with the government's plans, for it increased the amount of land available for distribution.

In July 1824 Boyer promulgated a law:

to determine which are the movable and the real properties in the eastern sector which appertain to the state, and, with respect to private persons in that sector, to regulate the law affecting landed property, in conformity with the system established in the other parts of the Republic; also to set the remuneration appropriate to the senior clergy of the metropolitan chapter of the cathedral of Santo Domingo, and to provide for the members of religious Orders whose convents have been dissolved.[3]

In the government's view, under this law all residents of the republic would enjoy the right to possess lands of their own, under titles granted to individuals by the state.

To determine which estates were to be incorporated permanently into the patrimony of the state – and their precise boundaries – Boyer decided to carry out a general land survey. And to determine once and for all the true ownership of land Boyer charged his agents to call in the titles to ownership that existed in the Spanish sector, so they could then redistribute them. By this process he would confer on each the amount of land that was due to him, in full possession, and with a new title in place of the old one.

Under the law, no new owner might have less than five *carreaux*, a new-fangled unit equivalent to about five hectares, which the Dominicans, as time went on, came to call the 'boyerana'. On their new estates apart from food for their own subsistence the owners were required to devote themselves mainly to producing crops for export. In the event that an owner did not want to keep the whole estate in production, he was required to grant it or sell it to new owners. Furthermore, rearing pigs or establishing ranches on areas of less than five *boyeranas* – the minimum quantity of land needed if any real profit were to accrue from stock-rearing – was prohibited.

In sum, the law of July 1824 sought to eliminate the system of *terrenos comuneros*, under which landed property in the east was in no way subject to state control; meanwhile it sought to turn every resident of the countryside into a peasant proprietor, occupying land that he owned and was required by law to cultivate. This law was a direct attack on the system of land occupancy peculiar to Santo Domingo: carrying it into effect would mean leaving the great holders of titles to land which had descended from grants made by the Spanish crown in colonial times with

[3] Linstant de Pradine, *Recueil*, IV, 45–50

their estates fragmented, and in part divided among their former slaves and among immigrants from Haiti.

As many of the great landowners had been left deep in debt by the decay of the colony's economy in past years, Boyer planned to woo them by reducing the debts they had contracted when they mortgaged their properties to the church. Church possessions, and the funds from which the church had made loans, were now to belong to the state, and the principal of the loans was now declared reduced to only a third. So as to make it even easier for them to pay off this reduced debt, Boyer gave the landowners three years of grace, within which they could pay off their mortgages by making half-yearly payments to reimburse the state for the principal still owed.

As for members of the monastic orders and the secular clergy attached to the cathedral, the state would compensate all of them with an annual salary of 240 pesos per person, with 3,000 pesos in annual stipend going to the archbishop himself, who had lost the most. Despite this, the archbishop never forgave Boyer for ruining the Dominican church. He never wavered in refusing the stipend assigned and in maintaining an openly hostile attitude to the Haitian government.

To the surprise of Boyer and the other military leaders, the archbishop was not alone in his opposition. He was backed by the peasants themselves, who could see no point in growing cacao, sugar or cotton. They preferred to go on devoting themselves to activities which had proved profitable for decades past – cutting caoba wood in the south, growing tobacco in the central Cibao valley and breeding and rounding up cattle in a large sector of land in the east of the country; there was an assured export market for their products.

By this time the mulatto elite in Haiti was becoming alarmed by the growing penury of the state. On May 1826 Boyer laid before the Haitian Senate an array of laws drafted to reorganize Haiti's agricultural economy on the basic principle that plantation work for peasants was obligatory, and that nobody was to evade it unpunished. The Rural Code, as this package of laws was known, was designed to raise the levels of productivity in the Haitian economy to what they had been in the times of Dessalines. Apart from Government officials, and those who practised a recognized profession, no one was allowed to give up working his land, nor to leave the estate on which he lived and worked, except with the permission of the local Justice of the Peace or the military commandant of the area. Not even permission from the owner of the plantation sufficed to authorize a worker to spend more than a week away from it. Once a farm worker was taken on by a plantation-owner, he was obliged to work for him for at least three years. If he tried to leave before, he was liable to heavy penalties in the form of fines, prison and forced labour. Vagrancy was absolutely prohibited. In order to enforce these measures fully – and many more besides, all intended to bind the worker to the plantation – the army was directed to keep soldiers posted to each plantation to oversee the workers. While employed on this duty they would be maintained by the plantation owner.

In its time, the code was considered to be a masterpiece of Haitian legislation. But despite the enormous advantages the government saw in applying it without delay, the code never took full effect. The workers of rural Haiti simply ignored its existence. In the years since Christophe and Dessalines an independent *minifundista* peasantry had emerged – proprietors of small plots, interested only in subsistence agriculture, with interests utterly opposed to those of the great landowners and, above all, determined not to serve as bondsmen on the great estates. Moreover, the army was in no way a suitable agent for backing up the justices of the peace in their task of imposing the code in the countryside.

For one thing, most of the soldiers were themselves small proprietors of peasant origin. Secondly, in 1825, a year before the code was promulgated, after long and tortuous negotiations, and under threat of bombardment by eleven French warships in the roadstead of Port-au-Prince, the Haitian government had finally agreed to sign a treaty with France under which French settlers were indemnified for their losses in return for French recognition of the independence of Haiti. The terms were harsh but from the army it lifted the burden it had shouldered throughout the generation since the revolution: ever since the 1790s it had stood guard against a French invasion which might some day arrive to reduce everyone to slavery once again. Military discipline was very soon relaxed, and soldiers began to show more interest in their own farms and their own families than in acting as a force to police the plantations. So when the Rural Code was promulgated, the disciplined body required to enforce it was already in decay. The irony in all this was that the code was also intended as an instrument for raising Haiti's export earnings, so she would be able to pay France the 150,000,000 francs (payable in five equal instalments) which the treaty specified as the indemnity required to compensate the former settlers. This, together with certain commercial concessions, had been the condition for France's recognition of Haiti's independence.

The Haitian government was faced with the problem of how to find the money to pay the first instalment of the French indemnity: the coffers of Haiti's treasury were empty. Boyer, therefore, contracted with a French bank for a loan of thirty million francs with which to pay the first instalment, due on 31 December 1825. At the same time, he declared the loan part of the national debt, and promulgated a law which introduced extraordinary taxation to be paid by both parts of the island.

This law provoked enormous antagonism amongst the inhabitants of the eastern sector. The *Ordonnance* of Charles X (April 1825) had clearly stated that it was only the inhabitants of the French sector who were to pay the annual instalments, but the inhabitants of the east were now assessed for a contribution amounting to 458,601 gourdes annually to pay off a debt that they believed was none of their business. Their feelings whipped up by Boyer's political adversaries, the Haitians also largely refused to pay taxes to purchase the independence which they believed they had already won by force of arms in the revolution. In his quest for cash, Boyer was obliged to issue paper money, setting off an inflation which, in less than two years, devalued the Haitian gourde by 250 per cent, and which, with the passage of time, thoroughly discredited it abroad. Likewise, at the end of 1827, Boyer was obliged to seek a new loan from a French bank which exploited Haiti's economic difficulties to exact excessive interest rates and commission charges. Not only had Boyer bankrupted the public treasury; he had henceforth a very vigorous opposition to confront amongst the Haitian mulatto elite, which felt humiliated by the terms of his treaty with France.

During the following years, and especially after 1832, this discontent was expressed in congress by the parliamentary leaders of the opposition and, above all, by the growing number of young lawyers, influenced by the liberal ideas current in the France of Louis Philippe, who desired to alter the system of government that had prevailed in Haiti ever since the foundation of the republic. Political conflict was increasingly accompanied by violence, and in August 1833 the Boyer government expelled the two principal opposition leaders, Hérard Dumesle and David Saint-Preux, from the congress. With opposition to the government becoming more and more general, the opposition deputies were, however, re-elected to congress in 1837, with new support and new lines of attack upon the government. The state of the economy was now causing concern and in June the commission reviewing the nation's finances reported that agricultural production was virtually stagnant. The production of coffee, now Haiti's major crop, had fallen alarmingly for three years: from 48,000,000 lb in 1835 to 37,000,000 lb in 1836, and the 1837 figure promised to be no better. In fact, production in 1837 fell to only 31,000,000 lb, partly as a result of the drought which afflicted the country throughout most of the year.

Meanwhile, in the east anti-Haitian feeling had deepened as a result of the measures the government adopted to Haitianize the Dominican population: obligatory military service for all the men of the island; the prohibition of the use of Spanish in official documents; the requirement that everywhere primary education be conducted in French; restrictions on the celebration of traditional religious festivals; restrictions even on cock-fighting. Instead of renouncing the effort to maintain the union, in June 1830 Boyer had given orders for all the Spanish symbols and coats-of-arms in public thoroughfares, churches and convents to be replaced by those of the republic. As he explained to his military commanders, 'The republic's interest is that the people in the east change their customs and their way of life as soon as possible, so as to adopt those of the republic, so that the union may be made perfect, and the formerly existing difference disappear forthwith.'[4] But, above all, it was Haiti's policy and legislation on land tenure and agricultural organization which kept the spark of opposition alive in the east of the island.

Boyer found that the more he coerced landowners into submitting land titles to the authorities for the latter to delimit the property rightfully theirs under the law of 8 July 1824, the more determined and persistent everyone was in resisting and protesting through those prominent Dominicans who were associated with the Haitian government. In face of such tactics, years went by, making it impossible for Boyer to take over any estates for the nation other than those that had belonged to the church or had been confiscated from émigré Dominicans refusing to return home. For all their insistent demands, by 1834 the Haitian authorities had still not managed to induce the great landowners to hand in their titles. On 7 April of that year, Boyer therefore issued a resolution granting landowners a further period of indulgence in which to submit land titles for confirmation.

This resolution was virtually an ultimatum threatening to extinguish the property rights of all those who did not comply with its stipulations. Its object was to abolish, once and for all, the Dominican land system. The resolution alarmed Santo Domingo's large landowners, who lodged

---

[4] J. P. Boyer, 'Proclamation, en français et en espagnol, au peuple, à l'occasion de la réunion de l'Est à la République', Linstant de Pradine, *Receuil*, III, 452–5.

appeals with the authorities charged with enforcing it. As Boyer aspired to eliminate friction, in August 1834 he felt obliged to proclaim that usufructuary occupiers would have unlimited time to comply with the terms of the resolution of April; among themselves, the actual possessors of land remained deeply distrustful of the government's intentions.

On 16 July 1838 a group of young men in Santo Domingo, some of them merchants or the sons of merchants, met to form a secret society whose purpose was to organize Dominican resistance and cause the secession of the eastern sector from the Republic of Haiti. This society, known as 'La Trinitaria', was led by the merchant Juan Pablo Duarte. By means of an intense propaganda campaign it managed to unite within its ranks the majority of the young men of the city of Santo Domingo whose families had, in one way or another, been injured by the various legal or military decisions of the Haitian government. 'La Trinitaria' united all Dominican opposition to Boyer and created a new revolutionary consciousness amongst the inhabitants of Santo Domingo after years of political lethargy. Thus, between 1838 and 1842, while the Haitians continued their battle in the legislature to compel Boyer to liberalize his regime and improve the conditions under which the Haitian economy laboured, the Dominicans organized a clandestine movement to achieve their independence.

In the west, Haiti's opposition also organized itself – in the so-called Society for the Rights of Man and of the Citizen, led by Hérard Dumesle to fight to oust President Boyer. This society of Haitian liberals did its revolutionary work at the banquets frequently held in the houses of the chief mulatto leaders in the south and west of Haiti, where opposition to Boyer had become traditional and where political liberalism had put down very deep roots. These 'patriotic banquets' were celebrated, for preference, in Jérémie and Les Cayes, at that time centres of anti-government sentiment. The maladministration of the Boyer government was exposed. Above all, opposition leaders promised the peasant proprietors much more profitable markets for their products, and the chance to buy foreign goods at much lower prices.

On 7 May 1842 an earthquake devastated Cap Haitien and Santiago, the two most important cities in the north of the island. One effect of it was to increase the opposition to Boyer, who stood accused of heartlessness in face of his people's misfortune because he had not put in a personal appearance to commiserate with the afflicted. In September 1842 the Society for the Rights of Man and for the Citizen, uniting the leaders of

Haiti's opposition, circulated a manifesto which decried the the evils currently existing, harshly attacked Boyer and denounced the Constitution of 1816 then in force. By 21 November everything was in readiness for the revolt. That day, the conspirators selected General Charles Hérard *l'aîné* to lead them, and awaited the right moment to strike.

The revolt against Boyer broke out on 27 January 1843. The uprising received the name of the 'Reform Movement'. As was to be expected, it rapidly spread throughout the south of Haiti. Boyer ordered the army to mobilize, but the southern population refused to sell or give supplies or food to the government troops. This decided the outcome of the revolution, for it left Boyer without military means to hold Port-au-Prince. On 13 March, at eight o'clock at night, Boyer went on board a British schooner and sailed into exile with all his family. He resigned the power he had exercised for twenty-five years and left the government in the hands of a committee of the Senate, who would hand it over to the revolutionaries.

In the afternoon of 24 March 1843 news of Boyer's fall reached Santo Domingo where the atmosphere was already one of agitation and conspiracy. It acted as a signal for the political groups in opposition to take to the streets, hailing independence and reform for Santo Domingo. After various incidents and disorders had taken place, the pro-Boyer authorities had to capitulate, and on 30 March they handed over the city to a Popular Revolutionary Junta.

During April 1843, as news and instructions from Santo Domingo and from Port-au-Prince reached the various localities in the east, liberal leaders set up popular juntas and committees with the declared intent of defending the Reform Movement. Behind these activities lay a variety of political interests. Boyer's downfall supervened precisely at a time when at least two different separatist movements co-existed in the east. One consisted of Trinitarians and liberals led by Juan Pablo Duarte and supported by the Santanas, a wealthy cattle-ranching family in the east of the country, who looked to independence without any foreign intervention or aid. The other comprised older men, most of whom had occupied administrative posts under the Haitian regime: they sought to end Haitian domination with the aid of France in return for political, tariff and territorial concessions.

Political agitation in favour of the independence of the east grew steadily, and in July 1843 the Haitian Government uncovered a far-reaching plot the Trinitarians had organized to achieve separation.

President Hérard acted quickly to frustrate this movement, and with his army he marched through the towns of the east. In each, he took counter-measures against the Trinitarians, expelling them from the popular juntas and taking the leaders captive before conducting them to Port-au-Prince as hostages. This military sweep left the Trinitarian conspiracy for the time being in disarray, as Duarte had to take refuge in exile, and his colleagues had to operate clandestinely.

Meanwhile, the pro-French group were working underground in deep secrecy in Port-au-Prince, the real centre of political activity. Its principal leaders had been elected deputies to the Constituent Assembly and seized the opportunity to get in touch with the French consul, Pierre Levasseur, whom they pressed to support the old plan for the east to break away and put itself under the protection of France, in return for the surrender to that power of the strategically important north-eastern peninsula of Samaná. With encouragement from Levasseur, they selected 25 April 1844 for the day of their coup against the Haitians. Hearing of this, the Trinitarians secretly planned to declare Dominican independence on 20 February 1844: that is, two months earlier than the date fixed by their rivals. On 1 January 1844 the pro-French group published a manifesto, setting out the reasons inducing them to seek separation from the Haitian Republic, under the protection of France. A fortnight later, January 16, the Trinitarians in their turn brought out their own manifesto, inciting the Dominican population to rebel against the Haitians with a catalogue of the affronts which, in their judgement, the Haitians had inflicted during the previous twenty-two years.

These two manifestos summed up the feelings of the easterners, who continued to see themselves as completely different from the population of western Haiti, in language, race, religion and domestic customs. Both manifestos circulated throughout the country, whipping up antagonism to the Haitians, accused by their authors of the vilest infamies. By the middle of February 1844 the feelings of the eastern population, particularly the people of the city of Santo Domingo, had been raised to fever pitch by the separatist propaganda of the two groups, each of which was manoeuvring to stage its own coup. The Trinitarian coup had to be put off for a week, but finally was launched at midnight on 27 February 1844. Next day the Haitian authorities in Santo Domingo found they had no recourse but to sue for permission to leave.

The Santo Domingo coup of 27 February 1844 elicited an immediate response in Haiti. President Hérard's government, itself in the midst of

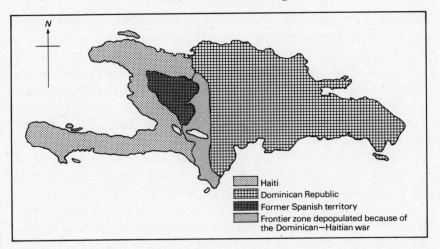

Haiti
Dominican Republic
Former Spanish territory
Frontier zone depopulated because of
the Dominican–Haitian war

Frontiers, 1844–61

the revolution he had triggered, could not tolerate the country splitting in two, with the secession of the east diminishing the resources needed to pay off the remainder of the debt due to France. Hérard therefore determined to put down the Dominican insurgents by force of arms, as he had already done the previous summer.

On 19 March 1844, the Haitian Army, under the personal command of President Hérard, invaded the eastern province from the north and progressed as far as Santiago, but was soon forced to withdraw after suffering heavy losses. Widespread agitation in Port-au-Prince, particularly by former supporters of Boyer, culminated in the overthrow of Hérard and his replacement by the aged black General Philippe Guerrier on 2 May.

General Guerrier now held the commanding position in Haitian politics. But the skein of difficulties enmeshing his government were such as to preclude any opportunity of invading the east of the island again, although he did busy himself with manifestos calling on the Dominicans to reunite with the Republic of Haiti. Philippe Guerrier held power over Haiti for less than a year, for he died at an advanced age in April 1845 and was succeeded by General Jean-Louis Pierrot, who was resolved to revenge the defeat before Santiago and uphold the republic's territorial integrity.

President Pierrot immediately reorganized the army and marched upon the Dominicans once more. But this second campaign found the

Dominicans much better prepared than they had been the year before: after only a few months in power Juan Pablo Duarte had been forced into exile and replaced by Pedro Santana, the Dominican Republic's first military caudillo and the dominant figure in politics for the next twenty years. (He was president 1844–8, 1853–6, 1858–65.) The Haitian offensive of 1845 was stopped on the frontier. On 1 January 1846 Pierrot announced a fresh campaign to put down the Dominicans, but his officers and men greeted this fresh summons with contempt. Thus, a month later – February 1846 – when Pierrot ordered his troops to march against the Dominican Republic, the Haitian army mutinied, and its soldiers proclaimed his overthrow as president of the republic.

The war against the Dominicans had become very unpopular in Haiti. It was beyond the power of the new president, General Jean-Baptiste Riché, to stage another invasion. In any case Pierrot's fall had provoked a revolutionary insurrection among the peasants. Civil war broke out afresh, and for a long time the Haitians were absorbed in their own problems.

Ever since the fall of Boyer in 1843, the chief strength of the peasant movement had lain in Les Cayes, in the south of Haiti. Three black peasant leaders – Jean-Jacques Acaau, D. Zamor and Jean-Claude – denounced the mulatto hegemony in Haitian politics and called first for nationalization and then the distribution of the lands of the rich. Their motley army of peasant irregulars was armed with lances, machetes and pikes, and it was known at the time as *les piquets*. By re-opening the vexed questions of race and colour in Haitian politics it struck terror into the hearts of the mulatto elite, and reinforced the view that the presidency of the republic should be given to a general who was black. The elderly black generals Guerrier, Pierrot and Riché were selected by the mulatto politicians of Port-au-Prince to give Haiti's black masses the feeling that their government represented them. But in fact the mulattos went on pulling the strings from behind the scenes. This was the system known as *la politique de doublure*; that is to say, politics by means of stand-ins, with governments of black soldiers holding the stage, distracting attention from the fact that they were puppets acting at the behest of mulattos.

For some months Acaau and his *piquets* stayed quiet, since Pierrot had made various political concessions. But when Acaau saw Riché, who was a political enemy, elected president, he came out in revolt and Haiti was again plunged into civil war. *Les piquets* were fiercely repressed by the government, and Acaau lost his life, but nevertheless this rebellion

bsorbed Haiti for the next two years, and temporarily distracted the
ttention of her rulers from the Dominican question.

Even though the Dominicans had defeated the Haitians in the 1845
ampaign, their leaders remained convinced that their republic could not
e safe from a fresh Haitian occupation unless they received the co-
peration and protection of a foreign power. So in May 1846 a diplo-
natic mission was despatched to the governments of Spain, France and
Britain to negotiate recognition of the independence of the Dominican
Republic with them and, at the same time, to conclude a treaty of
riendship and protection with whichever power could most effectively
ffer it. The negotiations undertaken by this mission in Europe led to no
mmediate result, since at this time the Spanish government still believed
t might be able to reassert its sovereignty over Santo Domingo.
Accordingly, it refused to recognize Dominican independence and
vould not compromise its stand by agreeing to any sort of protectorate.
For their part, the French government, and later the British government,
onsented only to appoint consuls to represent their interests in Santo
Domingo. Meanwhile, in Haiti, on 27 February 1846, President Riché
lied after only a few days of power and was replaced by an obscure
fficer, General Faustin Soulouque. Politically inexperienced and illiter-
te, Soulouque was viewed as an ideal tool by the Haitian politicians,
vho believed, mistakenly, that they could go on governing the country
hrough him. During the first two years of Soulouque's administration
he conspiracies and opposition he faced in retaining power were so
nanifold that the Dominicans were given a further breathing space in
vhich to continue the re-organization of their country. But, when in
848 France finally recognized the Dominican Republic as a free and
ndependent state and provisionally signed a treaty of peace, friendship,
ommerce and navigation, Haiti immediately protested, claiming the
reaty was an attack upon their own security; they suspected that under it
France was to receive the right to occupy the Bay of Samaná. Moreover,
French recognition of Dominican independence reduced the possibili-
ies of recovering the eastern sector. Haiti would then lose all claim on its
esources, badly needed to pay off the debt they had contracted with
France in 1825, in exchange for French recognition of their own
ndependence. Soulouque decided to invade the east before the French
Government could ratify the treaty. Wasting no time, on 9 March 1849
5,000 men, divided between several army corps commanded by the
nost eminent Haitian officers, crossed the frontier. In an overwhelming

onslaught, the Haitians seized one frontier town after another, up to 21 April when the decisive battle took place. Then, however, Soulouque and his troops tasted defeat and were constrained to retire in haste.

The early campaigns of this War of Independence left the Dominican economy in deep disarray and provoked grave political crises in Santo Domingo. Right from the start, Dominican political and military leaders sought assistance from Spain, from Britain, from France, and from the United States, to defend them against the Haitians. Both France and the United States were eager to take over the peninsula and bay of Samaná, but each wished to prevent the other seizing Samaná first. Britain's interest, on the other hand, was to ensure that neither France nor the United States took over Samaná and to see that the Dominican Republic remained a free country, independent of outside interference. Britain had the biggest stake in the trade with the new republic. (In 1850, she concluded her own treaty of peace, friendship, commerce and navigation with the Dominican Republic and during the next few years through the efforts of her consul, Sir Robert Schomburgk, established a commercial hegemony there.) Britain knew that if either France or the United States came to occupy Samaná and exercise a protectorate, she would lose the advantageous commercial position she enjoyed. Britain therefore worked on the other foreign representatives in Port-au-Prince to persuade Soulouque to sign a truce with the Dominicans which would remain effective for ten years. Though Soulouque, in the event, signed it for only two months, the diplomatic pressure the foreign envoys exerted on him effectively averted any invasion of the Dominican Republic for some years: Soulouque confined his military operations to mobilization on the Haitian side of the frontier. Throughout the years 1851–55, Haiti and the Dominican Republic remained in a state of relative peace along their common border.

Peace between the two countries was then threatened by the Dominicans' initiative in negotiating a treaty of friendship, commerce and navigation with the United States. Its foreseeable consequences included the cession or leasing to the Americans of the peninsula of Samaná. The negotiations were undertaken despite the opposition of the consuls representing Britain and France: they, like the Haitians, viewed any extension of United States influence over the Dominican Republic with alarm. Haiti's fears were understandable: the presence of the United States, a leading pro-slavery power, on Dominican soil would endanger Haiti's own independence.

In November 1855, therefore, Soulouque, who had proclaimed him-
lf emperor of Haiti as Faustin I, in imitation of Dessalines, invaded the
ominican Republic for the second time. There were several battles, the
ost hotly contested of all those in the Dominican–Haitian War, but in
te end, the emperor at their head, the Haitians fled back across the
ontier. The emperor blamed his defeat upon the alleged incompetence
d treasonable conduct of his generals. The most senior of them were
rought before a court-martial, sentenced to death and executed.

Now that Faustin saw that Santo Domingo was not to be reunited
ith Haiti by military means, he essayed a diplomatic manoeuvre to the
me end. In October 1858 he sent Maxime Reybaud, the former consul
f France in Port-au-Prince, to Santo Domingo with instructions to
ropose to the Dominicans that they should reach an entente with the
aitian Government and agree to re-enter a confederation with Haiti, if
nly to avoid annexation by the United States. Otherwise Haiti would
sail them with such overwhelming force that they finally would be
mpelled to submit.

The Dominican government considered these propositions so ex-
emely offensive that President Santana and his ministers expelled
eybaud from the country without giving him any answer at all. But they
mained obsessed with the fear that the emperor was planning a fresh
vasion of Dominican territory, and believed they lacked the resources
confront him in a new campaign, since the new republic's economy
ad already been wrecked by the war with the Haitians.

The emperor did, in fact, want to mobilize his army to invade the
ominican Republic once more. But the Haitian officers were weary of
austin I's tyranny: they perceived that each time war broke out with the
ominicans, he seized the opportunity to assassinate some of them. So,
wards the end of December 1859, under the leadership of General
abre Geffrard, they organized a plot and at the beginning of January
860 the emperor was overthrown and forced into exile. One of the first
ings Geffrard did, on seizing power, was to give the Dominican
overnment notice that his administration would not be planning any
vasion. However, after so many attacks the Dominicans could scarcely
redit this, so they continued with their preparations to confront the
aitians and issued further large quantities of paper money to cover the
osts of military mobilization.

The political and economic problems confronting the Dominican
overnment after the final invasion by Soulouque were so many, and so

serious, that the country's leaders decided they should resurrect the old idea of seeking aid from a foreign power, preferably Spain. Reybaud's mission had had a great deal to do with this decision, for President Santana was thenceforth afraid that Haiti would invade again. Santana seems also to have been pre-occupied with the possibility that the United States might take advantage of his government's weakness to subject the country to a sort of *coup de main* that a group of North Americans had recently inflicted on Nicaragua. The Dominican government was indeed passing through a period when its morale was at its lowest ebb. Though the Haitians had desisted from their previous policy of invading, as Geffrard had announced they would, they were now enticing Dominicans who lived in the border country to re-establish commercial links with Haiti. The market offered by Haiti was so attractive to many residents of the border areas that the Haitians easily found a favourable response, even though, according to many contemporary Dominicans, what Geffrard wanted to achieve through this trade was so to Haitianize the border areas economically as to achieve a piecemeal Haitian predominance there by peaceful means. By May 1860, according to the Dominican Ministry of Finance and Commerce, trade across the border had attained unprecedented proportions.

These, and other, reasons were in President Santana's mind when he took advantage of General Felipe Alfau's proposed recuperative journey to Europe to appoint him the Dominican Republic's Envoy Extraordinary and Minister Plenipotentiary. His mission was to explain to Queen Isabella II of Spain the desperate situation the Dominican Republic found itself in, and to request from her the aid and the arms that were needed for the Dominicans to fortify and hold the harbours and coastal points that the Americans coveted because of their strategic and economic importance. Besides this, he was to negotiate an agreement establishing a Spanish protectorate over Santo Domingo to assist the Dominicans retain their independence from Haiti. On 18 March 1861 the Dominican authorities solemnly proclaimed that the country had been annexed again by Spain. Santo Domingo was to be governed by foreigners once again; and the Dominicans would soon have to resume their long struggle for independence.

However, the Spaniards discovered that the people they had come to govern were no longer quite so Hispanic as they had expected. There were not only racial differences (most of Santo Domingo's population was coloured). After several centuries of colonial isolation followed by

wenty-two years of co-habitation with the Haitians and a further
eventeen years of independence, their customs differed markedly from
hose of Spain. Conflict between Spanish soldiers and officials on the one
and and the Dominican population on the other arose immediately.
acial segregation was imposed; the Spanish Government would not
ecognize the military ranks of the officers of the old republican army;
he paper money was not redeemed immediately; Spanish troops mal-
reated the peasants; the new Spanish archbishop offended the elite by
ersecuting the masonic lodges, estranged the clergy by imposing new
nd strict rules of conduct and discomforted the mass of the laity by
nsisting that it was obligatory to marry in Church; the new judges
rought with them a system of jurisprudence alien to local customs and
onflicting with the Dominicans' traditional laws which, by now, were
ased on the *Code Napoléon* adopted under Haitian influence; freedom to
ell tobacco, the country's chief export crop, was restricted when the
uthorities decided to impose a monopoly favouring Spanish interests;
nerchants resented the imposition of new schedules of import duties
dvantageous to Spanish ships and Spanish goods.

All this created a climate of general discontent which was already
learly evident by the end of 1862, when Spanish officials warned the
panish government in Madrid that rebellion would soon break out.
evolt, in fact, broke out at the beginning of February 1863 and, by the
niddle of that year, grew into a gigantic conflagration. It was stoked by
he Haitian Government which from the beginning had protested
gainst the Spanish annexation and had supplied money, arms and
ictuals to the Dominican rebels. The latter succeeded in taking
antiago, the chief city in the interior of the country, and there set up a
rovisional government to direct the struggle for the restoration of the
epublic.

The installation of this government in Santiago led to nearly two years
f total war, costing Spain more than ten thousand casualties and 33
nillion pesos. The Dominicans themselves lost hundreds of lives, plus
enewed bankruptcy for their economy. Except for Santo Domingo and
ome of the nearby towns, the whole country rose in arms. This was the
Var of the Restoration: it started out as a peasants' revolt, but very soon
ecame a race war and a popular guerrilla war which eventually engaged
he energies of the entire nation.

Geffrard's decision to aid the Dominicans can be readily explained.
he annexation of Santo Domingo by Spain had left Haiti in a most

exposed situation, for she now saw herself encircled by Spain, a slave-owning power, whose possessions in the Antilles – Cuba, Puerto Rico and now Santo Domingo – represented a threat to Haiti's continued independence and all that Haiti stood for. Moreover, the annexation had placed in jeopardy Haiti's continued possession of the territory in the Plaine Centrale that the Haitians had wrested from the Spaniards at the time of Toussaint. The Spaniards claimed the right to recover it forcibly, and under a Royal Order of 14 January 1862, began evicting all the Haitians they found living in the border country. And, since this Order proclaimed Spain's alleged right to various Haitian settlements and territories, the Haitian government could not expect anything less than a Spanish invasion at any moment – to seize land that the Haitians had, for over sixty years, considered to be rightfully theirs. This menace to the Haitians' own security was a powerful motive behind Geffrard's decision to send the Dominicans all the aid he could, no matter what threats the Spaniards uttered.

The war against the Spaniards ended in July 1865 with Dominican independence restored but with the country devastated and disorganized, and most of the peasantry in arms. The Dominican Republic was, for a long time, politically fragmented and unstable because, by the end of the conflict, the country was under the heel of literally dozens of military leaders and guerrilla chiefs, who then began to fight one another for power. The central conflict, as before 1865, was between *santanistas* (who remained a force after Santana's death) and *baecistas* (the politico-military faction around Buenaventura Báez, Santana's great rival from the early days of the republic and twice president before the annexation by Spain). Báez was president for six years (1868–74) and again for two (1876–8), but there were, in fact, twenty-one different governments and no fewer than fifty military uprisings, *coups d'état* and revolutions during the period 1865–79.

After the fall from power of Fabre Geffrard in 1867, Haiti experienced another two years of civil war. President Silvain Salnave (1867–9), though himself a light-skinned mulatto, was largely supported by poor urban blacks (first in Cap Haitien and later in the capital) and the *piquets* of La Grande Anse, and he spent his whole term of office fighting insurgents in different parts of the country; when he was finally forced to flee the capital he was arrested in the Dominican Republic and handed over to the rebels who executed him. Under the government of Nissage Saget (1870–4), a dark-skinned mulatto, there was a return to relative

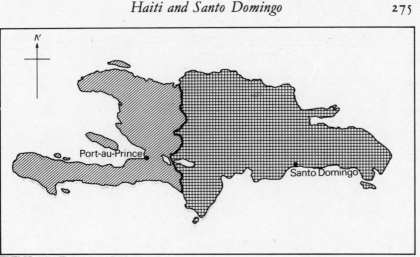

Frontier between Haiti and the Dominican Republic, 1874

political stability, but the elite and the army went on playing politics in an endless struggle between blacks and mulattos. The French debt placed a heavy burden on the Haitian state, depriving it of long-term financing for the constructive activities of its soldiers and its politicians. Peasant landholdings grew ever more fragmented and a *minifundista* peasantry turned in upon itself. The distance separating the black peasantry from the mulatto elite grew. The political hegemony of the mulatto elite which dominated the urban centres survived, however, despite the various *noiriste* movements which shook Haitian society during the second half of the nineteenth century. In one important respect, however, Haitian leaders had changed: they had finally come to recognize their limitations and set aside their pretensions to unify the island of Hispaniola under one government. Uneasily co-existing, the two independent republics – Haiti (with a population of about 1 million) in the western third and the Dominican Republic (with a population of 150,000) in the eastern two-thirds – set out on their very different courses.

7

CUBA FROM THE MIDDLE OF THE EIGHTEENTH CENTURY TO *c*. 1870

The Spanish colony of Cuba in the mid-eighteenth century was a largely forested, half unmapped island. It was known both to Spaniards and their enemies among other European empires primarily as the hinterland to Havana. That famous port had been built in the 1560s in a natural harbour on the north of the island to act as a depot from whence the Spanish treasure fleet could pick up a large naval escort. The few intrepid travellers who penetrated into the interior would have observed that the fauna of Cuba was friendly: there were no snakes, few big reptiles and no large wild animals. The indigenous Indian population – Tainos or Ciboneys – was held to have been absorbed or had died out, though in the unfrequented East of the island a few Taino villages survived. Some 'white' Spanish (or *criollo*) families had some Indian blood – including the Havana grandees, the Recios de Oquendo family.

About half the Cuban population of 150,000 or so lived in the city of Havana, where malaria and yellow fever frequently raged. Most of the rest lived in a few other towns, such as Santiago de Cuba, the seat of an archbishop, Puerto Príncipe, which boasted a bishopric, Sancti Spiritus, Trinidad, Matanzas and Mariel. None of these reached 10,000 in population. Rising above these cities, or near them, were a number of sixteenth-century castles and churches. In Havana three fortresses – la Fuerza, el Morro and la Punta – had all been built to guard the port. Communications were mostly, as elsewhere in the Spanish Americas, by sea. There were few roads. The only substantial employer was the royal dockyard at Havana under the Spanish captain-general and, in order to guarantee to him a ready supply of tropical hardwoods, the felling of all such hardwood trees in the island was supposed to be controlled.

There was little industry in Cuba besides ship repairing, the curing of pork, the salting of beef and the tanning of leather, all of which was done for the benefit of the convoys from Veracruz and Portobelo. There had once in the sixteenth century been a little gold in Cuban rivers, but what there was had been recovered long ago. In Cuba in 1750 there were about a hundred small sugar plantations, mostly close to Havana: the cost of carrying sugar to any other port was prohibitive. They were customarily powered by a handful of oxen. They probably produced about 5,000 tons of sugar a year of which only a tenth was officially exported. In comparison, the territorially much smaller French and English sugar colonies, such as Saint-Domingue or Jamaica, had about six hundred larger plantations which could produce 250 tons of sugar each.

This backwardness in Cuba derived partly from the fact that the island had few rivers suitable to power water mills which were responsible for the wealth of other colonies in the Caribbean. It was partly also because there was no large-scale home market in Spain for such a luxury as sugar.

Tobacco was Cuba's most profitable crop. Much of it was made into snuff, though tobacco planters had already established their *vegas* in the valley of the River Cuyaguateje in West Cuba and begun to plant there the tobacco which later made a 'Havana cigar' the jewel of the smoking world. Not till after 1770 were there any cigar factories in Cuba: cigars were for generations rolled on the spot by the pickers of the tobacco, or the leaf was sent back to Spain to Seville for *cigarros*. Tobacco farms were small in size, as were those which concentrated on bee-keeping for beeswax – another modest export. A few ranches in the savannah of central Cuba produced leather and beef; indeed, prior to the development of snuff, cattle-breeding and the production of hides had been Cuba's main export.

The native Indians of the sixteenth century also passed on to the Spaniards the art of cultivating sweet potato, yam, yucca, pumpkin, maize and various beans, though the colonists avoided vegetables and preferred to import almost everything which they had to eat: bread, for instance, was as a rule made from imported wheat. Wine, too, was imported not made. Fish was not much enjoyed. Coffee had begun to be grown in the French West Indies, but none had yet been introduced into Cuba – or for that matter into any Spanish colony.

Political control of Cuba lay with the captain-general, who himself ultimately depended on the viceroy in Mexico. But Mexico was several weeks away, Spain at least six weeks. The captain-general in Havana also had to share responsibility *de facto* with the commander of the treasure fleet while the latter was in Havana for about six weeks a year. The

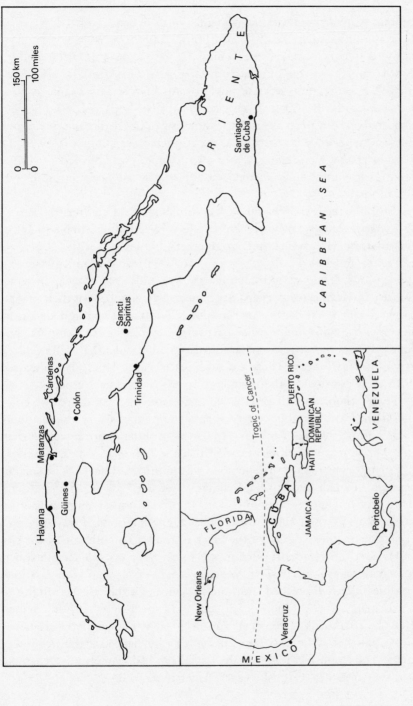

Cuba

captain-general was the father of a small bureaucracy of officials who had been appointed to their posts by the home administrators in Seville. Most of these, like the captain-general himself, were badly paid. All hoped for profit from graft out of their official posts. Treasurers, accountants, judges, naval commissars and port officials of every kind came as poor *peninsulares* to the Spanish empire, as did bishops and priests, and expected one day to return rich to Andalusia or to Castile. But many such persons never in fact returned home and left their families to swell the class of *criollos* who managed the town councils, established prices for most basic commodities, farmed and often eventually became merchants or landowners.

Cuba like the rest of the Spanish empire had by the eighteenth century its own *criollo* aristocracy which consisted of a handful of rich families of whom some – Recio de Oquendo, Herrera, Núñez del Castillo, Calvo de la Puerta and Beltrán de la Cruz – had been in the island for several generations. They would customarily live most of the year in town houses, in Havana (or perhaps Santiago, or Trinidad), visit their plantations or ranches at harvest or times of religious festivals and, as a rule, never visit Spain or any other part of the empire. In this respect they differed from those absentee landlords who enriched themselves in the rest of the Caribbean. These Cuban oligarchs are more to be compared with their cousins on the mainland in this as in other respects.

Three other things distinguished Cuba from many non-Spanish colonies in the Caribbean: the relatively small number of slaves; the relatively large number of free blacks and mulattos; and the importance of urban life. The sugar plantations of the British and French colonies, like those of Portuguese Brazil, had demanded vast numbers of slaves. The smaller number of small-sized Cuban plantations needed fewer. In 1750, there were probably more slaves in Havana in private houses, shipyards or on cattle ranches than there were on sugar plantations. Freed negroes constituted almost a third of the black or mulatto population of the city of Havana. This high proportion was partly the consequence of explicit laws making the purchase of liberty by slaves easier than in, say, British colonies. Partly it derived from the presence of a ruling class willing to emancipate slaves on their death bed – and specially willing to emancipate their bastards. The social and political structure of the island of Cuba, like that of the rest of the Spanish empire, had led to the creation of cities. The English colonies in the Caribbean had scarcely any urban life and that went for English North America as well.

During the second half of the eighteenth century Cuba was transformed into a prosperous sugar colony. These were the four main causes: first, the creation of a new market for sugar at home in Spain and elsewhere – including the newly independent United States of America; secondly the emergence of a class of landlords interested in developing their land and promoting wealth, rather than in preserving status; thirdly, the import of slaves from Africa to Cuba on a far larger scale than before; and finally a series of far-reaching economic reforms introduced by the enlightened ministers of King Charles III, not least the lifting of many of the old bureaucratic restraints on trade. The gradual decline of other islands in the Caribbean as sugar producers also contributed to Cuba's prosperity. More and more investors from outside the Spanish empire put money into Cuba to the benefit both of themselves and of the island, and the colony was quick to introduce new technology in the sugar industry.

The event around which these developments revolved was the British occupation of Havana in 1762. We should not fear to designate turning points in history, if the events really justify it – as these do. The victory of Lord Albemarle's expedition to west Cuba was, of course, first and foremost the conclusion of a victorious war for Britain. Havana had never fallen before to foreign invaders. The British victory was the signal for an immediate descent on the island by merchants of all sorts from all parts of the British Empire – sellers of grain, horses, cloth and woollen goods, iron-ware and minor industrial equipment, sugar equipment and slaves. Before 1762, the Cuban market had been formally closed to foreigners, although much smuggling had occurred.

The chief consequence of Albemarle's victory was that, during the year when the English directed the affairs of Havana, about 4,000 slaves were sold there. This figure was perhaps equivalent to one-eighth of the number of slaves in the island at that time. Earlier applications under Spain to expand the import of slaves had been rejected by the government in Havana on the ground that it would be politically risky to have so many new slaves (*bozales*) in the island. Such fears were now shown to be over-cautious. No great slave revolt followed the sudden increase. When the British left the island after the peace of Paris (1763), slave factors and mercantile relationships with the British islands remained. During the eighteen years following 1763, the number of ships calling per year in Cuba rose from 6 to 200. In particular, there was a steady increase in imports of slaves into Cuba, many of them re-exported from Jamaica.

Slave monopolies granted to particular companies lasted another generation but were evaded. British and North American dealers were a
permanent feature in the Cuban market, and after 1775 Spanish merchants began to go to Africa to bring back slaves to Havana – many of
them being re-sold elsewhere in the empire. In 1778 the Spanish purchased Fernando Po and Annobon from Portugal. In 1789, the Spanish
Government permitted merchants to bring into the empire as many
slaves as they liked – the only regulation being that a third of each
shipload had to be women.

Another immediate consequence of the British conquest was the
disappearance of most old Spanish taxes – *almojarifazgos* (payable on all
goods coming in from Spain); *averia* (payable to the navy); *alcabalas*
(payable on all exports to Spain); and *donativos* (extra levies paid on
demand to help the government in Madrid). Some of these, it is true,
were temporarily restored after the British left. But most restrictions on
trade were abolished for good. In 1765, the right of Spaniards to trade in
the Caribbean was extended to other ports than Cadiz – seven, to begin
with – but that really meant that anyone in Spain who wanted to trade
with Cuba could do so, for the ports included Barcelona, Malaga,
Alicante, Corunna and Santander – a broad spectrum. Commercial
activity within the Spanish empire was free by the time of the War of
American Independence. In 1771 the unstable local copper coinage, the
macuquina, was replaced by the *peso fuerte*. In 1776 Havana became a free
port. Further, the regulation of commerce within the Spanish empire, in
Cuba as in Venezuela, ceased to be the business of the local town council.
The interest of the crown was secured, in the empire as in Spain, by a
general financial commissioner, *intendente*, whose effectiveness was considerable. He enabled the Spanish crown to gain more income from fairer
taxes – an ideal fiscal achievement. In the 1790s duties on the import of
machinery for the production of sugar or coffee were similarly abandoned. Foreign merchants were not only permitted to enter and to settle
in the island but were allowed to buy property; so both British and
United States merchants were soon to be found well-established there.

Francisco de Arango, a planter and lawyer who had fought in the
courts of Madrid, successfully, against the suggestion that the last slave
monopoly (granted to the English firm of Baker and Dawson) should be
renewed, travelled to England with his fellow sugar planter and distant
relation, the conde de Casa Montalvo, to see how the merchants in
Liverpool and London ran their slave trade and how English manufac-

turers worked their factories. On their return to Cuba in 1792 they founded the *Sociedad Económica de Amigos del País*, in Havana, on the model of similar societies elsewhere in Spain and the Spanish empire. That body inspired governmental enquiries and the gathering of both statistics and economic information, and it also led indirectly to the foundation of Cuba's first rudimentary newspaper, *El Papel Periódico*, a daily newssheet from 1793.

Arango and his generation were pioneers of every kind of innovation. They created a public library, built hospitals, a lunatic asylum and free schools (for white children only). In England, Arango had looked at, and been impressed by, a steam engine. One was taken to Cuba in 1794 by the Reinhold firm to be used experimentally in 1797 at the conde de Casa Montalvo's son-in-law's plantation, at Seybabo. Water mills were also used successfully for the first time in west Cuba after French planters and technicians fleeing from the Haitian Revolution had brought to Cuba the idea of the overshot water wheel. Another innovation of the 1790s was a dumb turner which took the place of slaves introducing the cane into the wheel of the mill. A new sugar cane was introduced too in the 1790s – the strong South Sea 'otaheite' strain, while – probably equally important – mangoes were brought to supplement the meagre fruit diet by an English merchant, Philip Allwood, the powerful and controversial representative in Havana of the big Liverpool firm of slave merchants, Baker and Dawson.

By the turn of the eighteenth and the nineteenth century, therefore, Cuba was plainly a very promising part of the Spanish empire, bidding fair, with its plantations spreading far away from Havana, to overtake Jamaica as the biggest producer of sugar in the Caribbean. Spain gave every fiscal encouragement both to those producing and exporting sugar and to those seeking an adequate slave labour force. The export of sugar from Cuba by 1800 already exceeded that of hides, tobacco, cane brandy, wax, coffee and nuts which also came into Spain in ships from Havana. Thus, in the 1770s, Cuba was exporting over 10,000 tons of sugar a year and in the 1790s, just before the outbreak of the Napoleonic Wars, over 30,000 tons. The number of plantations growing sugar increased from about 100 to about 500, and the land planted to sugar cane had increased from 10,000 acres to nearly 200,000. The average size of a sugar plantation in 1762 in Cuba was probably no more than 300 acres; by the 1790s, it was nearly 700. Whereas many old sugar plantations had employed barely a dozen slaves, many new ones of the 1790s employed 100.

As in all progress which involves an increase in the scale of operations, there was an element of suffering. Bigger plantations meant more remote landlords. Mulattos or freed slaves ceased to own sugar mills – as they had occasionally done before 1760. More slaves meant bigger dwelling places, barracks taking the place of huts, and hence fewer private plots on which a slave in the early eighteenth century might have kept a chicken or planted cassava for bread. Small mills vanished, or ceased to make real sugar, producing instead only *raspadura* or rough sugar for consumption by the slaves themselves. Fewer and fewer sugar plantations remained self-sufficient, able to grow maize and vegetables, as well as sugar, burning their own wood or eating their own cattle. Few plantations too troubled about carrying out the Church's regulations that all slaves should be instructed in Christianity. New sugar mills increasingly had lay rather than religious names. Priests turned a blind eye to work on Sundays, and slaves were often buried in unconsecrated ground. Even so, monasteries and even the seminary of Havana in the 1790s had their sugar mills.

Another element had by now also entered Cuban history – and one which has since never been wholly absent: namely, the world sugar market, that is to say, the interests of rich consumers of sugar in other countries. 'I know not why we should blush to confess it', wrote John Adams, 'but molasses was an essential ingredient in American independence'. For two generations before 1775, Massachusetts had drunk, and profited from selling, the best 'Antilles rum'. Jamaica could no longer satisfy the needs of the rum merchants of Massachusetts, since its production was falling, with its soil exhausted. Farmers and planters alike in that era were ignorant of the benefits of fertilizer. North American merchants desired, therefore, to trade with both French and Spanish sugar colonies before the war of independence. British regulations prevented them from doing so. Symbolic of the importance of the Cuban trade in North American eyes was the nomination as first United States commercial representative in Cuba of Robert Smith, the representative in Havana of Robert Morris, the financier of the American Revolution. Most of the increase of sugar production in Cuba was soon being sold in the United States.

The revolution in Haiti (Saint-Domingue) had, if anything, an even greater consequence for Cuba than did the American Revolution. The slave revolt first of all increased the demand for Cuban sugar in such a way as greatly to please Arango and his colleagues. Sugar prices rose so as to increase the tendency, anyway great, of Cuban landowners to turn over their land to sugar cane. But the revolution in Haiti also caused tremors of fear to run through all the plantations of Cuba. Haiti might be ruined commercially after 1791, and that might benefit Cuba economically. But the danger was that the ruin might spread – or be spread. After all, several of the revolutionaries in Saint-Domingue had been Jamaican or had come from elsewhere in the West Indies.

In the event, it was the French planters – those who could do so – who fled from Haiti to Cuba and elsewhere in the still safe Caribbean. And they brought not only terrible stories of murder and revolution but also many useful techniques, to add to those already recently put into use, for the cultivation and processing of sugar. The most important were, first, the so-called 'Jamaican train', by which a long train of copper cauldrons could be heated over a single fire at the same time and at the same temperature and, secondly, the overshot water-wheels which have already been mentioned. Sugar technicians who had worked in Haiti, many born in France, were soon found on the bigger Cuban plantations.

International connections, however, spelled international troubles as well as wealth. The Napoleonic wars not only interrupted trade and delayed the introduction of steam engines for the mills of Cuba on any large scale but also gave the planters an experience of wild fluctuations in sugar prices. In 1807, two-thirds of the sugar harvest went unsold because of a sudden United States suppression of trade with all belligerents. In 1808, the collapse of the Spanish crown before Napoleon left the captain-general, the marqués de Someruelos, with virtually full power in Cuba. The island was in an exposed strategic position. That in turn caused President Jefferson to make the first of many United States bids to protect the island: the United States, he said, would prefer Cuba – and Mexico – to remain Spanish but, should Spain not be able to maintain it herself, the United States would be willing to buy the island. The offer was turned down, but Jefferson continued to toy with the idea while the *cabildo* in Havana, led by Francisco de Arango's cousin, José de Arango, made some moves to suggest annexation to the United States in the face of what some members took to be dangerously liberal tendencies in Spain itself, especially with respect to the abolition of slavery.

The Napoleonic wars were, of course, the midwife of Latin American independence. Cut off from the *madre patria* by the destruction of the Spanish fleet at Trafalgar, enriched by the last thirty years of the Bourbon economic reformation, and politically stimulated by the American, as well as the French, revolutions, *criollos* in South America everywhere began to contemplate political autonomy, even formal independence from Spain. Such ideas, blending with or transforming revolutionary ideas from Haiti, naturally reached Cuba also: a freemason, Ramón de la Luz, organized one of those romantic and ineffective conspiracies which characterized the novels of Stendhal or the history of the Risorgimento in Italy in order to achieve Cuban independence in 1809. These ideas did not prosper, however, for a simple reason: the spectre of Haiti. No sane Cuban planter was ready to risk a serious quarrel with Spain and the Spanish garrison if there were the remotest danger of the opportunity being exploited by leaders of a successful slave revolt. Hence the *junta superior* of Havana rejected the invitation of the *cabildo* of Caracas to take part in the wars of independence. Some physical impediments also restrained Cubans. Cuba was an island and the loyalty to Spain of its cities could easily be maintained by only a few ships of the fleet – should one ever be assembled. Then many royalist refugees fled or emigrated to Cuba from various parts of the Spanish empire on the mainland – strengthening Cuba's reputation as the 'ever faithful island'. Finally, the priests in Cuba, unlike those on the mainland, were mostly Spanish-born, and had no ambition to echo the exploits of the fathers Hidalgo and Morelos in Mexico. Still, it was probably the fear of 'a new Haiti' that most restrained the Cubans: an anxiety given weight by the discovery of another romantic conspiracy – this time led by José Antonio Aponte, a negro carpenter, who planned to burn cane and coffee fields, who apparently made contact with co-religionaries in Haiti and who invoked the African god Chango to help him. A later conspiracy, the *Soles y Rayos de Bolívar* headed by José Francisco Lemus in the 1820s, was much more formidable but, like Aponte's, was also betrayed in the end.

At the same time the Cuban planters were concerned at the threat posed by the British campaign to abolish the slave trade internationally, following the ban on the trade to and from British ports (introduced in 1808). Francisco Arango and others had spoken forcefully against any concessions on this front whilst in Spain in 1812 and 1813, and the first Spanish government after the restoration of Ferdinand VII in 1814 at first resisted British demands. But in 1817 the British were successful in persuading Spain formally to follow their example, and in 1820 Spain legally abolished the slave trade in return for £400,000, to be paid as compensation to slave merchants. Spain also accepted the right of the Royal Navy to stop slave ships and to bring suspected slavers for trial before mixed commissions. This measure naturally led to an increase in slave imports during what seemed in Havana likely to be the last years of the trade. But the ban was not carried out – however much the English began to accustom Cubans to the idea of international intervention in their affairs. The demand for slaves was great and growing and, with ups and downs, the trade survived another fifty years, not least because the government in Madrid was unwilling to antagonize the planters of Cuba by supporting the British whom they believed to be sanctimonious, hypocritical and self-seeking.

As early as 1822, partly in consequence of this British interference, planters in Cuba began to explore again the idea of joining the United States as a new state of the Union. The United States Cabinet discussed the idea but sought to dissuade the Cubans. They preferred the status quo. Yet most leading Americans then supposed that Cuban adhesion to their Union was only a matter of time – a generation at most. Certainly therefore they did not wish to see the independence of the island.

Various schemes for both independence or annexation were widely discussed in the *tertulias* in Havana cafés in the mid-1820s. But, in the event, having lost her mainland American empire, Spain was determined to keep Cuba and Puerto Rico. Forty thousand Spanish troops were stationed in Cuba from the 1820s onwards. They and a network of government spies preserved the island's loyalty. Bolívar once contemplated an invasion of Cuba if the Spaniards did not recognize his new Colombia. The United States were discouraging, and the moment passed.

Cuba's political docility, guaranteed by the Spanish garrison, was the frame for a rapid increase of prosperity based on sugar, as we shall see. By the 1830s Cuba's taxes produced a substantial revenue for the Spanish crown. Cuban revenues were popularly held to account for the salaries of most Spanish ministers. They gave the only guarantee for repayment of debt that could be offered by Spanish governments to London bankers. The captains-general in Cuba profited too – partly from bribes which were the consequence of winking at the slave trade. And this often enabled them to pursue ambitious political programmes at home in Spain on retirement. Had the captains-general fulfilled their obligations and undertaken to abolish the slave trade they would have lost the colony – but to the United States rather than to an independence movement. The old social gap between *criollos* and *peninsulares* persisted. Forbidden to take part in administration – and there was, after all, no politics – the *criollos* grumbled and made money instead. The slightest hint that Spanish control might be relaxed, or that a slave revolt might get out of hand, suggested to Cuba's landowners that the time might come when they should join the North American union. Planters were usually made happy by the determination of successive captains-general, who deported progressive or nationalist writers regularly and who successfully avoided implementing in Cuba the sporadic lurches towards constitutional rule in Spain. The largest sugar mills founded in the 1840s were sometimes exposed to rebellions by slaves. They were put down with a ruthlessness which the planters in Cuba feared would not be approached by the United States government.

In the end, however, the idea of annexation to the Union seized the imagination of a high proportion of prominent Cuban planters led by Carlos Núñez del Castillo, Miguel Aldama, Cristóbal Madán and the Iznaga and Drake families. Their purpose was to join the United States in order to preserve slavery and to safeguard the pursuit of wealth through sugar. They set themselves the task of persuading United States opinion of their point of view. After the entry of Florida, Louisiana, Texas and then (after 1848) California and New Mexico into the Union, Cuba seemed the next obvious candidate. The idea also attracted the new generation of North American politicians, stimulated by these other territorial acquisitions, and intoxicated by the general success and prosperity of the United States. Writers and journalists of the late 1840s had a definite sense that it was 'manifest destiny', in the words of one of them, that the United States should dominate, if not conquer, all the Americas, south as well as north. A campaign urging the United States to buy Cuba was launched. It was evident that many rich Cubans supported the idea, and would do so, if need be, with their money. 'Cuba by geographical position and right . . . must be ours', wrote the editor of the *New York Sun* in 1847; it was 'the garden of the world'.

The annexation of Cuba constituted an important item in the presidential election of 1848. President Polk responded by agreeing to make a formal offer for Cuba to Spain of $100 million. The idea was seriously discussed in Spain but leaked – and uproar ensued. The Spanish government had to reject the idea in order to remain in office. Still, annexationist ideas survived. An expedition of 'liberation' headed by a rebel Spanish general, Narciso López, was prepared in New Orleans in 1849, and eventually set off for Cuba in 1850, with the intention, first, of proclaiming independence from Spain and, then, of joining the Union. The scheme was betrayed, and López was captured and publicly garrotted, though López's flag – a single white star on a red background, the whole set against blue stripes – survived to inspire another generation of more genuine seekers after independence.

Other expeditions followed. The idea of annexation burned increasingly in the minds of the politicians of the U.S. South. The acquisition of Cuba would inevitably strengthen the slave states. For much of the 1850s, Cuban liberation represented one of the dreams of Young America, the proponents of the secession of the South, as indeed it did of romantic revolutionaries in Europe. Garibaldi, Mazzini and Kossuth, for instance, all added their weight to this essentially ambiguous cause. For their part, the planters in Cuba, even after the re-assuring pronouncements of Captain-General Pezuela in 1853, continued to fear that abolitionism might capture the minds of the Spanish officials.

Another offer was made to buy Cuba from Spain by President Pierce in 1854. Again it was rejected by a new government of liberals in Madrid. The Cuban planters were despondent. They feared that Spanish liberalism would be underwritten by English sanctimoniousness and thus permit the establishment of what they termed 'an African republic'. New efforts were made to secure United States interest – and, if necessary, intervention. James Buchanan, ex-secretary of state and minister in London in 1854, believed that, if Spain were to turn down the United States' 'reasonable' offers for Cuba, the United States would be 'justified in wresting it from her'. The Ostend manifesto between Buchanan, Pierce, Soulé (the United States minister in Madrid) and the United States minister in Paris denounced all plans which would lead to Cuba being 'Africanized', but it was disowned in Washington. In New Orleans, meantime, another expedition to liberate Cuba had been assembled under the governor of Louisiana, John Quitman; its members fell out among themselves. In 1857 James Buchanan became president of the United States, and his election owed much to the popularity of the manifesto of Ostend. Buchanan set about seeking to bribe Spanish politicians to sell Cuba – with no more success than had attended the efforts of his predecessors. The United States slid into civil war in 1861 at a moment when the politicians of the South still hoped that they could secure the perpetuation of slavery by acquiring Cuba. The defeat of the South closed that avenue for Cuban planters as it also closed the slave trade. The American Civil War was thus for Cuba the most important event since 1815.

Cuba, in the meantime, had become since the Napoleonic wars the richest colony in the world (which in part explains the limited extent of the psychological or intellectual stock-taking in Spain after the loss of the other provinces of the Spanish empire in the 1820s). Havana, with a population of nearly 200,000, and Santiago de Cuba were, by the 1860s, bustling cosmopolitan cities, while eight other towns had populations of over 10,000. Cuban ports received 3,600 ships a year of which half went to ports outside Havana. As early as 1825 the United States had become a more important trading partner for the colony than Spain; North Americans, merchants as well as politicians, had shown great interest in the island, investing in it and buying increasing percentages of Cuba's export crops.

For a time, coffee had made an effective challenge to sugar as Cuba's main export crop. Coffee had been introduced as early as 1748, but it was never grown on any scale till after the revolution in Haiti which brought to Cuba many experienced coffee growers. Some of those established themselves in Cuba and took full advantage of the tax exemptions which were designed to assist the growing of coffee. Between 1825 and 1845 exports of coffee from Cuba never fell below 12,000 tons, and land sown with coffee was in the mid-1840s slightly larger in extent than that sown with cane. But the rewards of coffee never seriously rivalled sugar, and in the 1850s many cafetals were turned into sugar plantations. The United States' tariffs on coffee imports of 1834, the terrible hurricanes of the 1840s and the beginning of Brazilian competition all damaged Cuban coffee interests. Coffee, however, remained an important crop till the beginning of the wars of independence. In 1860 there were still about 1,000 cafetals, producing 8,000 tons of coffee, mostly in East Cuba. Further hurricanes impoverished many coffee planters and stimulated the sense of deprivation which helped to create the rebellious mood in that region in the late 1860s.

Tobacco had also been a modest, but consistent, rival of sugar. The turning point in its history was the abolition of the royal monopoly of the manufacture of cigars in 1817. In 1821, the old royal tobacco factory – a building of the 1770s – was turned into a military hospital. Afterwards tobacco factories began gradually to be built chiefly by immigrants from Spain, such as Ramón Larrañaga and Ramón Allones. Cuban cigars were increasingly prized – though the majority of tobacco *vegas* continued to be in East Cuba not West, where the best tobacco was already known to be established. Another Cuban export was rum, the best marketed to great effect by Facundo Bacardí, a Catalan immigrant in the 1830s and a millionaire by the 1860s: his light amber product was a great international success.

Sugar remained, however, far and away Cuba's most important crop throughout the nineteenth century. In 1860, about $185 million were invested in sugar, the mills numbered 1,400 and Cuban production already reached some 450,000 tons – a quarter of the world's sugar, far above Jamaica, with only 148,000 tons during the 1850s. Steam-engines from England had been first introduced into sugar plantations during the second decade of the century (four were used in the harvest of 1818), and large steam-powered mills were now producing about 1,000 tons of sugar a year, in comparison with ox-powered mills which still averaged 130 tons only. A series of concessions by the Spanish crown had authorized the outright purchase of all land previously held in usufruct from the crown. The royal approval was also given to the destruction of hardwood forests in the interests of agriculture. A new sugar plantation area opened up in the 1820s and 1830s in Matanzas province at the mouth of the rivers San Juan and Yumurí between Matanzas itself, Colón and Cárdenas, and most of the steam mills were to be found there. The biggest sugar mill in Cuba in 1860 was *San Martín*, in Matanzas. It belonged to a company whose chief investor had apparently been the queen mother of Spain. It employed 800 slaves, planted 1,000 acres and produced 2,670 tons of sugar each year.

As early as 1845 the advanced sugar mills were all linked by private railway to Havana – an innovation which greatly lowered the cost of transporting cane. Cuba had the first railways in Latin America and the Caribbean: that between Havana and Bejucal was opened in 1837, that between Havana and Güines in 1838. In 1830, the average cost of carrying a box containing 3 or 4 cwt of sugar was estimated at $12.50. By train this had dropped after 1840 to $1.25. In the 1820s steam boats appeared too. A regular service plied between Havana and Matanzas as early as any such service in Europe. Steam-powered ships also ran between Havana and New Orleans in the 1830s. Other technological innovations in Cuba in the mid-nineteenth century included the vacuum boiler – first used in Cuba in 1835. The advanced vacuum boiler invented by Charles Derosne in Paris on the basis of the ideas of Norbert Rillieux created what was in effect a 'sugar machine' to co-ordinate all aspects of the manufacturing process. This was first installed in Cuba in 1841, by Derosne in person on the plantation *La Mella*, belonging to Wenceslao

Villa-Urrutia. The result was greatly to reduce the dependence of sugar makers on slaves. The Derosne mills could also produce a new and iridescent white sugar which was much sought after. Finally, in 1850 a centrifugal machine was introduced to Cuba on the mill called *Amistad*, belonging to Joaquín de Ayesterán. This enabled the sugar planter to convert the juice of the sugar cane into a clear, loose, dry and fine sugar in place of old sugar loaves immediately after it left the rollers. These technological developments increased the wealth of those who could afford them but depressed further those planters still using old ox-powered mills and, indeed, helped to drive them into rebellion.

The planters who did enjoy this new wealth were of three sorts: first, those, perhaps of recent Spanish (or Basque) origin, who had made fortunes in trading, particularly slave trading, and had either invested their profits in plantations or had acquired properties by foreclosing on debts. These were the men responsible for putting into effect most of the technological innovations of the age. The best known was Julián de Zulueta, the biggest proprietor in Cuba in the 1860s. Secondly, there were those who derived their sugar plantations from original grants from the Spanish crown in the eighteenth century or earlier, and who were in effect the aristocracy of the island. These families were deeply inter-related and had monopolized municipal government in Havana for a hundred years. Thirdly, there were already a number of foreigners, chiefly Americans, but also Englishmen and Frenchmen – of whom some became hispanicized (or cubanized) after a generation or so on the island. Some of each category became rich on an international level, secured Spanish titles, travelled in Europe or North America and built handsome palaces in Havana where they and their families lived sumptuously. Justo Cantero, a planter in Trinidad, built a house with a Roman bath with two heads of cherubs, one continuously spouting gin (for men) the other eau de cologne (for women).

An essential part of Cuban affairs was the great contribution that fortunes there made to enterprises in Spain. The financial connections are not easy to disentangle. But the relation was close. Juan Güell y Ferrer, for example, invested his Cuban money in Catalan cotton. Pablo de Espalza, another Cuban millionaire, founded the Banco de Bilbao of which he became first president. Manuel Calvo helped to finance the election of King Amadeo of Savoy in 1870. Lists of Cuban slave merchants include many who, like Juan Xifre, helped to finance the first stage of industrialization in Catalonia in the nineteenth century. Meantime captains-general, judges and other officials continued to rely on their stay in Cuba to make fortunes which they then transferred to Spain.

At the other end of the social scale were the slaves. The success of the nineteenth-century sugar economy and the rapid expansion of the slave trade to Cuba had meant that the relative balance between black and white in the island for a time vanished; in the first half of the century there had been a substantial black or mulatto majority. But by the 1860s whites, due to substantial immigration in the middle of the century, had become once more the largest ethnic group. Out of a population of about 1.4 million in 1869, some 27 per cent (360,000) were slaves (compared with 44 per cent in the 1840s). About a third of the slaves worked to a greater or lesser extent in the countryside. Most slaves in the 1860s had been introduced into the island illegally; their importers had contravened the anti-slave trade laws of 1820 and 1845 and had successfully avoided the British navy's anti-slave trade patrols operating under the Anglo-Spanish treaties of 1817 and 1835. Slaves could still purchase their freedom by the old system of *coartación*, or purchase of freedom in instalments; perhaps 2,000 did this every year in the 1850s. Many mothers could buy freedom for their babies for a modest sum. Otherwise a slave had to pay his own market price – $500 or so in the 1830s, $1,000 or so in 1860. In 1860 about 16 per cent (240,000) of the total population were believed to be freed blacks or mulattos, admitted without too many questions into the bureaucracy, or the university.[1]

The immediate consequence of the collapse of annexations with the defeat of the South in the American Civil War was the formation of a pressure group among prominent Cuban planters to secure some at least of the constitutional reforms now being pursued in Spain itself by progressive merchants. Some of the planters concerned were, like Miguel Aldama, ex-annexationists. But they were mostly less rich than those who had favoured annexation – as is evident from the fact that few of those concerned in these schemes, at least in the 1860s, were men who

---

[1] Puerto Rico, for three centuries largely a port of call and military base, also produced sugar by the end of the eighteenth century. Exports grew steadily from the 1820s and reached 105,000 tons in 1870 (only one-seventh of Cuba's sugar exports but by this time slightly more than Brazil's). See Andrés Antonio Ramos, 'The influence of mechanisation in the sugar system of production in Puerto Rico: 1873–1898' (unpublished Ph.D thesis, University of London, 1977), ch.1, The rise and development of the sugar hacienda system in Puerto Rico: 1815–1873. Puerto Rico also produced small quantities of coffee and tobacco. Some moderate-sized haciendas formed, and there was isolated technological innovation. Puerto Rico never had a predominantly slave economy. In 1846, at its peak, the slave population numbered 51,200, 11.5 per cent of the island's population (Ramos, 'The influence of mechanisation', 46), and in 1870 only 39,000. (Editor's note.)

possessed mills with the most advanced sugar technology. (Aldama was an exception.) They desired a reduction of the powers of the captain-general, a constitutional assembly, taxation accompanied by representation – and an extension of the powers of the municipal councils.

This generation of reform-minded planters had also become convinced that with the outbreak of the American Civil War the slave trade would soon be brought to a halt. In 1862 a United States slave captain, Captain Nathaniel Gordon, was hanged for carrying 890 slaves on his ship to Havana – the first such punishment ever for a United States citizen. In the same year the United States and Britain initiated combined operations for the final suppression of the Cuban slave trade. By the time the Spanish government itself introduced new legislation in 1866 the trade had already virtually ceased; the last known importation of slaves into Cuba took place in 1867. Many reformers in Spain and Cuba supported the abolition of the Cuban slave trade in the belief that slavery itself would be preserved in the island. But since the institution of slavery was dependent on the continued importation of slaves – as in Brazil the slave population was never able to reproduce itself naturally – it was realized that one day Cuba would have to face the future without slaves and that alternative sources of labour would have to be found. Some planters were already arguing on economic grounds that in any case contract labour was preferable to slave labour, not least because slave prices had more than doubled during the previous twenty years. Experimental contracts were made with Gallegos, Canary Islanders, Irishmen and Indians from Yucatán. Most satisfactory were the Chinese: some 130,000 were introduced between 1853 and 1872 in conditions even worse than those of the slave trade from Africa, if figures for mortality on the journey mean anything.

The Cuban reformers of the 1860s were on good terms with two enlightened captains-general – Francisco Serrano y Domínguez (1859–62) and Domingo Dulce y Garay (1862–6). It was agreed in 1865 that a Cuban commission should go to Madrid to discuss the island's political future. The next year elections were held for the first time in Cuba, with a high property qualification, it is true, but on the same basis as those which were held in Spain. The *Junta de Información* in Madrid, which also included Puerto Rican representatives, discussed every aspect of constitutional reform as well as the question of slavery. The Cuban members believed they had made some progress by persuading the Spanish government of the need for constitutional change, but all their work was undone by another *coup d'état* in Madrid, bringing the intolerant General

Narváez to power. The reformers returned to Havana with no policy and no future to offer. Constitutional reform within the Spanish empire seemed as closed an avenue as annexation to the Union.

The Cuban reformers who had gone to Madrid were too gentlemanly to contemplate a rebellion for independence. Perhaps they were still affected by the memories of the Haiti rebellion of the 1790s. At all events they could not risk provoking a crisis in which they might lose their slaves immediately, however much they might contemplate the idea of a gradual extinguishing of slave society. This was even more the case with the very rich, the great moguls of nineteenth-century Cuba, who had never contemplated any political innovation other than annexation to the United States. The small number of early trade unionists, especially in the tobacco factories, were interested in higher wages, better working conditions and shorter hours. They had as yet no thoughts about the political future of Cuba save as a Spanish colony which sold both cigars and sugar on a large scale to the United States. The only section of the Cuban community interested in rebellion in the 1860s were the smaller sugar and coffee planters in the east of the island. Impoverished, preoccupied by great world events as only a parochial planter class can be, they had made little money out of recent sugar harvests, since they had resources neither for new machinery nor for new slaves. Their mills were too far from Havana – with no railways and no roads to get to them – to be able easily to command loans from Havana merchants. Some of the planters of the east anticipated the emancipation of slaves by letting them out for wages during the harvest. Some of the families had enough money, true, to send their children to Europe or the United States for education. These returned, however, with their heads full of a spirit of revolution, disturbed by colonial conventions and ashamed of colonial repression. It was among them, particularly among the freemasons, that the spirit of rebellion spread in 1867 and 1868.

Carlos Manuel de Céspedes was a typical small sugar planter of this type, though he was uncharacteristic in one respect: much of his youth had been spent in abortive political activity in Spain. In 1868, he held a public meeting at his farm in Oriente province at which he romantically adjured his hearers to take the road followed elsewhere in Latin America by Bolívar and San Martín. Doubtless little would have come of Céspedes's movement had it not coincided with a major upheaval in Spain: a military rebellion and the flight of Queen Isabel II from Madrid in September 1868. A rebellion in Puerto Rico followed. Then another east Cuban planter, Luis Figueredo, hanged a Spanish tax collector on his farm and invited denunciation as an outlaw. The Cuban rebellion began when Céspedes freed his slaves and founded a small army of 147 men at his estate at La Demajagua on October 10, issuing a declaration, the 'Grito de Yara', which echoed the American Declaration of Independence. This was the beginning of the Ten Years War (1868–78), Cuba's first war of independence.[2]

By 1868 the pattern of future Cuban society had been established as it was to remain. The population of Cuba had assumed most of its modern characteristics – slightly over half Spanish in origin and slightly under half black or mulatto, with a small number of Chinese, Anglo-Saxons, French and others. The proportion has remained much the same since 1868, despite the final eclipse of slavery[3] and a substantial immigration from Spain in the first quarter of the twentieth century. Sugar was very definitely the dominant industry by the 1860s, producing substantial quantities for an ever more voracious world market. That too has remained the case. The whole Cuban economy already revolved, as it has done ever since, around the sugar harvest. There might soon be some changes in the organization of Cuban sugar, characterized by a drop in the number of sugar mills and an increase in the acreage planted with cane, which was occasioned by the availability of cheap steel for longer railway lines and also by the challenge of sugar beet in the 1870s. That, in turn, led to the eclipse of the old *criollo* aristocracy and its substitute after 1900 by companies – themselves substituted by state farms after 1960. But the place of sugar within the national economy has not much varied. Finally, two generations of romantic flirting with the idea of rebellion, in exile or in secret places in Havana, had given to the Cuban national culture an affection (if not an affectation) for heroism and revolt.

---

[2] The formation of the Liberal Reform (later Autonomist) Party in Puerto Rico in 1870 represents the renewal of the political struggle of the *hacendados*, supported by some professionals and artisans, against Spanish colonialism. (Editor's note.)

[3] During the Ten Years War the Spanish Cortes passed the Moret Law (1870), a qualified law of free birth which also freed slaves over 60. (And in 1873 slavery was abolished in Puerto Rico.) A law of 29 July 1880 abolished slavery in Cuba, but instead of indemnity to slave-owners a system of *patronato* (apprenticeship) was to continue until 1888. In the event, the *patronato* was abolished on 7 October 1886 (with only some 25,000 *patrocinados* in Cuba at the time). On the abolition of slavery in Cuba, see Raúl Cepero Bonilla, *Azúcar y abolición* (Havana, 1948); Arthur F. Corwin, *Spain and the abolition of slavery in Cuba, 1817–1886* (Austin, Texas, 1967); Franklin W. Knight, *Slave society in Cuba during the nineteenth century* (Madison, 1970); Rebecca J. Scott, 'Gradual abolition and the dynamics of slave emancipation in Cuba, 1868–86', *Hispanic American Historical Review*, 63/3 (1983), 449–77 and *Slave emancipation in Cuba: the transition to free labour* (forthcoming). (Editor's note.)

Part Three

SPANISH AMERICA AFTER INDEPENDENCE

MEXICO

Mexico • •Veracruz

HAITI   SANTO·DOMINGO
(occupied by Haiti 1822–44)

CUBA   PUERTO RICO (Spanish)
(Spanish)

JAMAICA
(British)

UNITED PROVINCES
of CENTRAL AMERICA

TRINIDAD (British) ·

Caracas
VENEZUELA

NEW GRANADA

•Bogotá

Quito•
ECUADOR

R. Amazon

EMPIRE of
BRAZIL

Salvador
(Bahia)•

Lima•
PERU

•La Paz
BOLIVIA

•Sucre

PARAGUAY

Rio de Janeiro•

Asunción•

ARGENTINE
CONFEDERATION

Santiago•
CHILE

•Buenos
Aires

URUGUAY
•Montevideo

0 _____ 2000 km

0 _____ 1000 miles

Spanish America in 1830

8

ECONOMY AND SOCIETY IN POST-INDEPENDENCE SPANISH AMERICA[1]

In the years between 1808 and 1825 a new relationship was established between the Spanish American economies and the world economy. In comparison with their much fuller incorporation into the expanding international economy which began around the middle of the century and became more pronounced from the 1870s, the changes which accompanied the achievement of political independence may well appear superficial and limited; nevertheless, they constitute a decisive turning-point in the relations between Spanish America and the rest of the world.

The old colonial commercial system had been breaking down since the end of the eighteenth century, but it was only after 1808 that Spain was finally eliminated as the commercial intermediary between Spanish America and the rest of Europe, especially Britain. The special circumstances prevailing both in Europe and the Atlantic economy as a whole at the time had important consequences for Spanish America's future commercial relations. The advance of the French armies into the Iberian peninsula, which triggered off the separation of the American colonies from Spain and Portugal, was intended to complete the closure of continental Europe to British trade. Increasingly isolated from its European markets, Britain was trying, with an urgency bordering on desperation, to replace them. Thus, the opportunity provided by the transfer of the Portuguese court to Rio de Janeiro to trade directly with Brazil for the first time was eagerly accepted. And as, following the overthrow of the Spanish crown in Madrid, the first political upheavals in Spanish America occurred, Rio de Janeiro became not only the entrepôt for an aggressive British commercial drive in Brazil itself but also in Spanish America, especially the Río de la Plata area and the Pacific coast of South America.

[1] Translated from the Spanish by Dr Richard Southern; translation revised by the Editor.

The Río de la Plata was opened to British trade as early as 1809 – by the last Spanish viceroy. The subsequent British expansion into Spanish South America was, however, to depend on the fortunes of revolutionary arms; for even though Royalist administrators eventually showed themselves prepared, as an exceptional measure, to open up their territories to direct trade with Britain, the activities of patriot corsairs made such trade very unattractive. Chile was finally opened up in 1818, Lima not until 1821 – and the rest of Peru even later. In the countries bordering the Caribbean progress was slow and less complete. Venezuela's war of independence lasted for ten years, as did New Granada's. Mexico, with more than half the population and wealth of the Spanish Indies, achieved its independence late (in 1821). Even then it was several years before the Royalists in San Juan de Ulua were eliminated, and this affected Veracruz, the chief Mexican port in the Caribbean. The islands of Cuba and Puerto Rico remained Spanish possessions, but were open to direct trade with foreign countries from 1817, although that trade suffered restrictions aimed at preserving this last colonial market for Spanish products, from textiles to flour. Santo Domingo remained under Haitian occupation until 1844.

The Atlantic coast of South America was therefore the first zone to be incorporated into the new commercial system and the circumstances which impelled Britain rapidly to expand its overseas markets had their earliest and greatest impact there. British merchant adventurers arrived in Rio de Janeiro, Buenos Aires and Montevideo in considerable numbers during the years 1808–12. A few years later Valparaiso became the main port on the Pacific coast of South America, the centre from which British goods were trans-shipped to ports along the coast from La Serena to Guayaquil. The merchant adventurers engaged in the exploration and exploitation of the Latin American market were acting directly for merchants and industrialists in Britain: their task was to find a market as rapidly as possible for the surplus goods which threatened the growth of the British economy. From the outset, they were less concerned with price than with a quick sale and an equally quick return (of which precious metals were easily the most preferred form). To achieve this commercial penetration British goods had often to be offered at prices even lower than had been planned. For example, in 1810, after hearing the news of the liberalization of trade and the outbreak of the revolution in Buenos Aires, many merchant adventurers left London hoping to sell British goods in South America; however, when they arrived in Buenos

Aires, they not only found that there were too many of them, but that they had to face unexpected competition from the shipments of British merchants in Rio de Janeiro. The result was that they had to sell at a loss, thereby hastening the victory of overseas products over those tradition-ally supplied to the Buenos Aires market from the foothills of the Andes or from Peru and Upper Peru. Another consequence was the expansion of the existing consumer market through the inclusion of social groups which had not previously formed part of it.

The opening of Latin American trade to the outside world and the arrival of the British in large numbers also dealt a severe blow to the old style commercial practices which, in Spanish America at least, had been based on a rigid hierarchy. The merchant-exporter in Spain was linked to the Spanish merchant at the Spanish American ports and centres of distribution, and thence to the smaller merchants in the minor centres, and from them to the itinerant peddlers. The system was essentially maintained by *avío* (Mexico) or *habilitación* (Spanish South America), that is to say, the provision of capital by those in the higher levels of the hierarchy to those at the lower level of entrepreneurial activity, and by credit. Very high profit margins were guaranteed at each of these stages, although the profits derived from the provision of credit are not always easily distinguished from commercial activity in the strict sense of the term. The entry of the British, impelled by desperation to make their presence felt, albeit sporadically, at ever lower levels of this commercial system, had a devastating effect. Their preference for quick sales at lower prices, and for the use of cash rather than credit, began to offer at all levels an alternative to a system which conferred its greatest benefits on those at the top.

The peaceful British invasion of Spanish America was facilitated by the long period of political, social and military instability during the wars of independence in which potential local rivals were weakened. The merchant adventurers soon perceived opportunities for excellent profits in the unstable conditions prevailing. Rather than make any attempt to establish regular commercial relations, they employed an opportunistic style of trading. For example, on the Paraná river the Robertson brothers hurried to Santa Fe, to sell Paraguayan *yerba maté*, which scarcity had made much more expensive.[2] Again, in 1821 when San Martín in Chile was preparing his campaign to capture Lima, Basil Hall was secretly

[2] J. P. and W. P. Robertson, *Letters on Paraguay* (London, 1838) I, 358–9.

commissioned by London merchants to take a shipment of goods there before competitors reached it; he was able to 'skim the cream' off that long-isolated market which was the capital of the viceroyalty of Peru.[3]

Although this trade was fatal for local competitors, it was not without risk for British merchant adventurers. They were obliged to be increasingly audacious and very few survived to the end of this phase of exploration and conquest unharmed. This was perhaps inevitable, given the conditions of the period. The needs of the British economy forced the merchants constantly to expand markets whose limits were only apparent when local demand failed to materialize; a process of trial and error ensured that each attempt at expansion ended in failure (because only such failure could bring it to an end); understandably, the embittered reports of the victims accumulated. However, no victim actually reversed the overall advance to which he himself had contributed. Even those who assess the results from a British, rather than a Latin American, point of view find it difficult to argue that the events of this period did not leave a significant legacy for the future. Although British exports to Latin America as a whole no longer accounted for 35 per cent of total British exports, as they had done in 1809 and 1811, nevertheless, with an annual average of around £5 million in the period 1820–50 (roughly half of which went to Spanish America and half to Brazil), they had doubled the averages of the second half of the eighteenth century in terms of value (and multiplied them several times in terms of volume).[4]

During the second quarter of the nineteenth century Britain gradually lost the commercial quasi-monopoly which she had acquired during the wars of independence. This predominance had for a while been threatened by United States competition. Supported by an excellent merchant navy, American merchants spearheaded a more flexible system of trade and navigation. Because they were not serving the needs of an industrial economy like their British competitors, they brought not only United States, but also European, African and Oriental goods to the markets of Latin America (and particularly to those worst supplied by the British, who tended to imitate their Spanish and Portuguese predecessors'

---

3 Samuel Haigh, *Sketches of Buenos Aires, Chile and Peru* (London, 1831), vii.

4 For the figures on British exports to Latin America, 1820–50, see D. C. M. Platt, *Latin America and British trade, 1806–1914* (London, 1973), 31. Whether one concludes, with Professor Platt, that the figures for the three decades following independence are not 'totally out of line' with 'what estimates survive of the colonial trade' depends on whether a doubling of trade is considered to be a significant change. Of course, this change may appear insignificant if it is compared with that which was to occur in the second half of the nineteenth century.

preference for the richest and most densely populated zones). However, an essential element in American exports were 'domestics', a rougher and cheaper cloth than that of Manchester. When the long-term fall in prices caused by the advance of the Industrial Revolution nullified the price advantage, it eliminated an irreplaceable element of the challenge to British predominance. Thereafter, even though American trade was able to obtain local advantages (in Venezuela, for example, it rivalled British trade in the middle of the century), it did not cause London and Liverpool any alarm.

In addition to the North American trade, there was increasingly intensive trade with France, the German states, Sardinia and the old mother countries. However, this appears to have complemented British trade rather than rivalled it. France led in the market for luxury goods, and Germany (as it had before Independence) in semi-luxury goods; this did not affect British dominance in the much wider range of industrial products for popular consumption. France, Sardinia, Spain, Portugal as well as the United States became once again the countries of origin for the growing exports to Latin America of agricultural products (wine, oil and wheat). It could hardly be expected that Britain would preserve the pre-eminence it had achieved through Gibraltar in the export of these products because of the highly exceptional political and military circumstances of the wars of independence.

Britain, then, preserved its leading position as an exporter to Latin America. It was at the same time the principal market for Latin American exports, although there were some important exceptions (like Brazilian coffee) and Britain's position declined more rapidly than in the case of exports to Latin America. This mercantile connection was reinforced by the dominant role of the 'bill on London' in financial transactions between Latin America and the rest of the world.

The increase in British exports to Spanish America after 1808 had a profound impact on the region's balance of trade. Throughout the colonial period (and despite the effects of the so-called Imperial Free Trade established in 1778–82), the value of Spanish American exports had been consistently higher than the value of imports. This was now reversed. Most of the trade gap was, of course, filled by exports of precious metals, which in colonial times had always been the principal item in Spanish American exports – and which dominated Brazilian exports during the first two-thirds of the eighteenth century. However, the Brazilian gold boom now belonged to an irrecoverable past, and although in Spanish America – apart from Upper Peru, the only significant exception – gold and silver mining did not suffer substantial falls in production until the very eve of the crisis of Independence, production fell precipitately during the period of the wars. The substantial export of metal coinage from Spanish America during the second and third decades of the nineteenth century is, therefore, rightly considered as a loss (and even flight) of capital rather than the continuation or renewal of a traditional line of exports.

No doubt there were many causes of this flight of capital. Political instability, which led to the departure of many Spaniards, was one. Certainly the commercial habits of the British conquerors of the Latin American market caused an outflow of precious metals. However, as early as 1813–17, the drive that characterized the first British commercial offensive slackened. And from the early 1820s a more regular system was established throughout most of Latin America underpinned by a series of commercial treaties with the new states which guaranteed freedom of trade and which were imposed (with no possibility of negotiation) as the precondition for British recognition. British merchants began to adopt patterns of trading similar to those of their Spanish predecessors, including the use of credit. Nevertheless, even when at the same time British exports to Latin America declined, the imbalance of trade continued. The fundamental reason appears to be, therefore, the stagnation of Latin American exports. In some spheres of particular significance in international trade (especially mining) these were considerably lower than in the last decades of the colonial period. At the same time, the characteristics of the new commercial system did not favour local capital accumulation. On the contrary, quantities of precious metals accumulated during several decades were actually lost, just at the time when a greater access to the world economy offered opportunities for their investment. Instead they were squandered on imports of consumer goods at a level which Latin America was not able to afford on the basis of its normal flow of exports. Even the reduced level of international trade prevailing in the early 1820s could not be maintained without an increase in production for export, which required massive investment far in excess of the available local capital. It seemed to some at the time (as it did a century later) that if Britain wished to retain and indeed expand its links with the newly independent Latin American states, the commercial relationship would have to be accompanied by a financial relationship which would provide government loans and private investment. This was the proposal for the future of Mexico proposed in 1827 by Sir H. G. Ward, the British chargé d'affaires, a perceptive but by no means disinterested observer: according to him, the first and foremost responsibility of British investors was the outfitting of the mining industry, which in the long term would create the capital necessary for the exploitation of crops in the neglected and depopulated tropical lowlands, thus giving a new impulse to Mexico's exports. In the short term, however, the outfitting of the mining industry was to allow Mexico to continue to pay for its increased imports. It is not surprising that Ward vehemently rejected the alternative solution: to achieve equilibrium by restricting imports and encouraging local production (of textiles, for example).[5]

The investment of capital in Latin America was not the main concern of British merchants anxious as they were to support a reciprocal flow of trade. It appealed more to investors in search of high and quick profits. However, they suffered a swift and harsh disappointment: although the bonds of the new states and the shares of the companies organized in London to exploit the mines of various Latin American countries at first rode easily on the crest of the London stock exchange boom of 1823–5, by 1827 every state except Brazil had ceased to pay interest and amortization on its bonds, and only a few Mexican mining companies had avoided bankruptcy.

For the next quarter of a century (1825–50), the economic relationship between Latin America and the outside world was largely a commercial one; of the financial connection there survived only some mining firms organized as joint-stock companies (whose failure to prosper did not encourage imitators) and a number of committees of disappointed and discontented bondholders, who watched anxiously for a sign of improvement in the Latin American economies in order to press their claims. Even Brazil, which had managed to avoid cessation of payments, would not for many years again have recourse to external credit.

Since the trade imbalance did not disappear immediately, it must, however, be assumed that there was in this period a volume of credit and investment from outside at least sufficient (in the absence of any more effectively institutionalized mechanisms) to maintain some kind of equilibrium. To begin with, from 1820 there was the investment needed to establish the more regular mercantile system which now prevailed

---

[5] H. G. Ward, *Mexico in 1827* (London, 1828), I, 328.

(warehouses, means of transport, etc.), and then there was the investment which was at least partly sumptuary; even in the minor commercial
centres, foreign merchants generally owned the best houses. Other
investment resulted from these merchants managing industrial undertakings or, more often, agricultural properties. However, these investments were only capable of offsetting the trade imbalance between the
Latin American economies and the outside world if it is assumed that,
during this period of consolidation and regularization, the resident
foreign merchants continued to act as agents or partners of merchants or
capitalists in the metropolitan countries. It is not easy to be sure on this
point, but there are examples of this relationship to be found from
Mexico to the Río de la Plata.

For Latin America, independence had redefined the connection with
the metropolis on more favourable terms than in the past. It was not
simply that the commercial connection was no longer accompanied by
direct political domination; this eliminated a fiscal dimension that had
been one of the most onerous elements of the former colonial relationship. The new commercial metropolis had an industrial economy far
more dynamic than that of the former colonial powers and, at least in the
short term, its agents were prepared to sacrifice profit margins to obtain a
greater volume of sales in the new markets. Even when, from the 1820s,
Latin America's trade with Britain came to resemble rather more that of
the late colonial period, the steady advance of the Industrial Revolution
guaranteed that Latin America would benefit in the long term, despite
fluctuations caused by temporary circumstances, from a fall in the price
of British exports. By 1850 the price of the most popular grades of cotton
cloth (which was still the most important article exported to Latin
America) had fallen by three-quarters from its level during the 1810–20
period. The price of other products fell less sharply: woollen cloth,
which did not undergo its technological transformation until around
1850, declined in price by about one-third. Comparison is less easy in the
case of other products – china, porcelain and glass, for example – owing
to changes in the British customs system of classification, but they appear
to have suffered a similar decline and, in any case, they represented a
much smaller proportion of total exports than did textiles. Taking the
picture as a whole, around the middle of the century the price of British
exports, the composition of which was remarkably similar to that
prevailing in the early years of liberalization of trade, appears to have
fallen to about half the level of the period 1810–20.

During these decades the price of primary products also tended to fall, but less markedly. Silver suffered a fall of 6 per cent as against gold, leather from the Río de la Plata region a fall of around 30 per cent, and coffee and sugar a similar decline. Only tobacco suffered a fall of around 50 per cent.[6] It was not until the middle of the nineteenth century that the first signs became evident of a change in Latin America's favourable terms of trade.

Paradoxically, as a result of these favourable terms, the opening up of Latin America to world trade had less profound consequences than had been expected before 1810. Since the level of prices of exportable products did not seem immediately threatened, the effect was more to encourage an increase in the volume of exports than to promote any technological advances in production leading to a reduction of costs. In any case, attempts to develop the export sector were severely restricted by a scarcity of local capital which was aggravated by the war and, as we have seen, by the imbalance in trade in the independence period.

However, the limitations of the transforming impact of the new external connection were principally due to the almost exclusively commercial character of that connection; as we have seen, only exceptionally (during the brief period of optimism that accompanied the boom of 1823–5) was consideration given to capital investment from the metropolis designed to expand and modernize production of goods for export; and we have also observed how the subsequent fortunes of those undertakings were to ensure that they would retain their exceptional character for several decades.

The scarcity of local capital and the reluctance of foreign capitalists to invest in the area were not seen by contemporaries as the principal reasons for the slow growth of the Latin American export economies in the period after independence. Contemporary observers usually drew attention above all to the destruction caused by the wars. In order to appreciate the validity of this point of view, it must be recalled that it was not only resources which were destroyed – that is to say, livestock consumed by the warring armies, mines flooded, money seized from public or private coffers – but also an entire system of economic, juridical and social relationships. Thus, one might include in the inventory of damage the way planters and miners lost control of their slaves in

---

[6] British export prices are based on the real values declared for exports to Buenos Aires, in Public Record Office, London, Customs, Series 6, for the years concerned. For those of leather from the Río de la Plata region, see T. Halperín-Donghi, 'La expansión ganadera en la campaña de Buenos Aires', *Desarrollo económico* (Buenos Aires), (1963), 65. For the prices of Venezuelan coffee, see Miguel Izard, *Series estadísticas para la historia de Venezuela* (Mérida, 1970), 161–3. For those of sugar and tobacco, see M. G. Mulhall, *Dictionary of statistics* (London, 1892), 471–4.

Venezuela, the Upper Cauca in Colombia, or the coast of Peru; the
ending of the *mita* system which forcibly recruited workers in the
highlands of Peru for work in the mines of Upper Peru and the
impossibility of re-establishing this system because of the subsequent
political separation of the two areas; the fluctuations in Chilean wheat
exports to what had become a Peruvian market; the disruption of the
complicated traffic in mules, foodstuffs, liquor and handwoven textiles
throughout the Andes. One might even include the indirect consequences of the wars; besides the destruction of mines in the battle areas
the fall in production of mines elsewhere whose owners, because of the
war, for years neglected to make the necessary investment. Looked at in
this way, the legacy of the war may indeed appear overwhelming,
although difficult to evaluate precisely. Even the actual damage has
never been adequately assessed. Moreover, like the impact of the opening up of Latin America to world trade, the effects of the war were very
unequally distributed over the different regions and sectors of
production.

Opinion in both Spanish America and Europe predicted that mining
products would be most likely to take rapid advantage of the opportunities offered by the opening up of trade, but optimism gradually faded.
Only in Chile would mining production, in the middle of the century,
exceed the volume (in this case small) achieved during the colonial
period. In the rest of Spanish America the most successful mining areas
were those where, after a serious decline, production recovered its pre-
revolutionary level; in many areas, such as New Granada or Bolivia, this
was not to be regained until later, and in some others never.

The reasons for this disappointing performance are complex. In order
to understand them more fully, we must emphasize that the disappointment may be explained in part by the perhaps excessively high hopes
raised, somewhat artificially, in Europe and, by extension, in Spanish
America during the short-lived investment boom which came to an
abrupt end in the crisis of 1825. When considered in the context of the
entire history of mining in Spanish America from its beginning in the
sixteenth century, developments between 1810 and 1850 do not appear to
us to be a consequence of the new socio-economic conditions in which
mining found itself as clearly as they did to contemporary observers.
Whatever the prevailing circumstances, mining went through cycles of
discovery, exploitation and exhaustion. Thus, it is not entirely surprising
that Mexico, or even Peru, which had reached their highest levels of

production in the last decades of the colonial period, should have required a quarter of a century after the return of peace to recover. Similarly it is easier to understand why Chile enjoyed the earliest period of post-independence mining prosperity if it is remembered that its centre was the mine of Chañarcillo, which was only discovered after independence. The recovery of mining in Mexico, as in Bolivia even later, was due not so much to a return to former levels of production in the old mining centres as to the emergence of new centres in Zacatecas and other states. Nevertheless, the disappointment over mining production and exports in the post-independence period still appears justified. It was reasonable to expect that the commercial revolution by stimulating a rise in the volume and value of imports would lend an added urgency to the need for more exports, especially of precious metals. The sluggish response of the mining industry, therefore, requires an explanation that takes into account more than the cycle of bonanza and crisis as determined by the discovery or exhaustion of the richest veins of ore.

Cultural and institutional explanations were for the most part, not surprisingly, proposed by foreigners who had been attracted by the apparently brilliant prospects before 1825: the immorality or frivolity of the ruling classes; the difficulty of finding mine workers with the necessary qualities; the surprising leniency displayed by the ruling classes towards workers during episodes of industrial indiscipline involving foreign entrepreneurs; the rigid character of the laws governing the mining industry; and so on. We will not attempt here to examine the mass of accusations, which reflected above all the profound differences between Spanish Americans and those who were trying to insert themselves into the Spanish American economies. These differences were naturally much sharper where foreigners no longer confined themselves to commerce and moved into productive activities.

Other obstacles to progress in the mining sector were more strictly economic, i.e. the shortage of labour and capital. Both factors were present in varying degrees in all the mining areas of Spanish America. Nevertheless, it seems possible to conclude that the difficulties of recruiting labour have everywhere been exaggerated. There is no doubt that war damage in Mexico, the richest mining zone in the late colonial period, severely hampered post-war reconstruction; however, there is no evidence of a labour shortage as such. After independence, mineworkers received higher monetary wages than the agricultural workers, but this was nothing new, and in any case did not necessarily signify any difference in real wages. Moreover, even though the ending of the *mita* system in mining, referred to above, deprived independent Bolivia of an important source of labour, it is not without significance that the wages of the free workers during the first decades after independence were closer to the wages received by the *mita* workers than to those of the free workers during the colonial period;[7] this does not suggest any shortage of labour. Furthermore, the new mining zones, or those demonstrating the most rapid expansion, do not appear to have found it more difficult than did the older, stagnant zones to recruit the necessary labour; for example, no shortage appears to have impeded the expansion of Chilean mining.

The problem created by the shortage of capital appears to have been more serious. In this sphere, the damage caused by the war seemed less easy to repair. The destruction of the mines and processing plants by actual military operations was very limited even where the mining zone concerned was the theatre of war. The suspension of investment in expansion and maintenance had a more lasting effect, and a concentrated investment of capital became necessary before mining in Spanish America could recover. However, from this point of view, the development of mining up to 1850 does not appear too unsatisfactory: thanks to British and local capital in Mexico and Bolivia, and almost exclusively local capital in Chile and Peru, there was in fact a modest recovery. Nevertheless, we may ask why investment was not more intensive and results more impressive. From the point of view of those responsible for taking the decision to invest, the reasons why this did not occur are quite understandable. Except in Chile, the yield from mining investment was non-existent or very low. In Mexico, for example, there was absolutely no return on the investment made by the British company of Real del Monte, the most important established during the boom which ended in 1825. This was not due to any lack of measures designed to bring the mine out of its stagnation: on the contrary, the company made several costly attempts at improvement; it continued, with even less success, the efforts of the former proprietors to pump water out of the lower levels of the mine, and built an access road for vehicles in an area previously served only by mules. The Real del Monte Company certainly had good reason to complain of its ill fortune: when, after a quarter of a century of investing at a loss, the rights of exploitation were transferred to local entrepreneurs, the latter quickly began to make profits, partly as a result of the very same investments.[8] However, contemporary observers seemed prepared to draw a more precise moral from this experience: H. G. Ward, by no means a disinterested apologist for the British companies established in Mexico, willingly admitted that the decision to invest vast sums in improving production, exploitation and transport had been imprudent. At the other end of Spanish America, John Miers drew a similar conclusion from his experience as an unsuccessful producer of copper in Chile: in his opinion, too, it was necessary to examine carefully the economic impact to be expected from each of the proposed technical improvements; and even investment designed to increase the volume of production without introducing technological innovation ran the risk of being counter-productive.[9] Thus, a conservatism, which reflected the prevailing atmosphere during a period in which there was no technical progress comparable to what was to take place in the second half of the century, led to greater caution where new investment in mining was concerned, except when, as in the case of Chile, exceptionally rich veins of ore guaranteed quick and large profits.

The post-war reconstruction did not lead to the introduction of decisive innovations in the organization of mining operations. In the case of labour there is no doubt that wage-labour now played a dominant role even where it had not done so in the colonial period. This was certainly the case in Bolivia; the picture was slightly different in the gold-mining zone of New Granada, though even there the decline in the importance of slave-labour was clear. However, in the mining areas that had enjoyed the most rapid development during the last years of the colonial period, wage-labour was already dominant. This, of course, concealed even then very different real conditions in the different parts of Spanish America ranging from Mexico, where Humboldt found wage-levels to be higher than those prevailing in Saxony, to the Norte Chico of Chile, where it has been denied, more convincingly than in the case of other zones, that a true wage-labour force existed. These variations continued to exist after the transition to independence, although there is no doubt that the change from stagnation to rapid expansion must have affected the situation of the workers in the Chilean mines.

In colonial times there were similar variations in the way mining itself

8 Robert W. Randall, *Real del Monte, a British mining venture in Mexico* (Austin, Texas, 1972), 81, 100–8, 54–6.
9 John Miers, *Travels in Chile and la Plata* (London, 1826), II, 382–5.

was organized. In Mexico large productive units which financed their expansion from their own profits predominated; they were sometimes even able to invest their profits in the acquisition of agricultural properties which were economically integrated with the mines. In Peru, Bolivia and Chile productive units were smaller and lacked real independence from their suppliers and those who advanced the capital to enable them to continue their activities.[10] (In the case of Upper Peru, the situation of the mining entrepreneurs was further aggravated by the fact that frequently they had to pay high rents to the absentee holders of exploitation rights.) After independence the contrast between Mexico and Peru in this respect continued. As late as 1879, Maurice du Chatenet observed that the majority of the mining entrepreneurs of Cerro de Pasco were not 'rich people, who have capital available . . . [but] have to borrow money from others'. They had to sell their products to their creditors for less than the normal price.[11] Miers had described similar conditions in the Chilean copper-mining zone in the 1820s. However, the prosperity of silver-mining in Chile after 1831 led to the rise of a class of mining entrepreneurs who were not only independent but successful enough for significant amounts of capital to be invested after the middle of the century; the richest entrepreneurs emerged as the proprietors of large urban and rural properties in central Chile. In Bolivia during the same period there were radical changes in the legal framework within which mining activities operated. The newly independent nation cancelled the privileges of the absentee concessionaires and, by granting new concessions, encouraged the rise of larger mining undertakings than those of the colonial period. However, as Bolivian silver mining stagnated in the post-independence period the consequences of these changes were not felt until the last thirty years of the nineteenth century.

The expansion of mining in Spanish America was, therefore, limited almost everywhere by the need for capital, which was never more than partially satisfied. However, another factor limiting the expansion of the Latin American export economies, the level of demand, did not on the whole affect the mining sector. There was, it is true, in the 1820s a boom and a slump in Chilean copper production, which was largely a result of the growth and subsequent catastrophic decline in the demand for

[10] John Fisher, *Minas y mineras en el Perú Colonial, 1776–1824* (Lima, 1977), 101.
[11] Maurice du Chatenet, 'Estado actual de la industria minera en el Cerro de Pasco', *Anales de la Escuela de Construcciones Civiles y de Minas*, First Series, 1 (Lima, 1880), 119.

copper in British India.[12] But throughout the region silver was far more important than any other mineral and the demand for Spanish American silver for coinage was so vast that it was impossible to imagine any limit to the expansion of production. The agricultural sector could not depend on such a steady demand. On the other hand, depending on the commodity concerned, this sector could count on one advantage. This was that it was not so necessary to make a considerable investment before profits could be realized as in the case of a mining industry shattered during the struggle for independence.

The sector of production offering the greatest advantages from minimal investment was stockraising. It was, moreover, influenced, perhaps more than any other sector, by the availability of external markets. From the very beginning of the colonization of Latin America, cattleraising became the way by which land resources could be utilized when other more profitable methods became impossible. The areas over which it spread, without at that time being able to count on satisfactory external markets, were eventually extremely wide: from the north of Mexico to the north-east of Brazil (and, within Brazil, to Minas Gerais once its mining prosperity had ended); from the highlands of New Granada, to the plains of Venezuela and immense areas in Central America to a large part of the Central Valley of Chile as well as the whole of the Río de la Plata region and southern Brazil. In the first half of the nineteenth century a system of exploitation that was still technologically very backward meant it was not necessary (as it was to be later) to limit cattleraising to the most suitable land in these vast areas. The reason why only some of these areas were probably incorporated into the new export economy has less to do, therefore, with production methods than with commerce: it was the ability to channel production into both pre- and post-independence commercial circuits that explains the success of cattleraising in the Río de la Plata area, Venezuela and southern Brazil.

In view of the absence or extreme scarcity of capital and in view of the fact that these were very thinly populated areas in which social discipline was, in several cases, further affected by the disturbed times, the expansion of cattle production was based on extending the available land. However, the difference is striking between the growing prosper-

[12] Report of the British Consul in Valparaiso, Charles R. Nugent, 17 March 1825, in R. A. Humphreys (ed.), *British consular reports on the trade and politics of Latin America* (London, 1940), 96ff.

ity of the cattleraisers of Buenos Aires and the impoverishment of those on the Pacific coast of Central America, as John L. Stephens noted in the middle of the nineteenth century: the reason was, of course, that owners of properties in Central America comparable in area to a European principality had no way to sell their useless wealth, while landowners in the Río de la Plata had free access to the European market.[13] This was because the expansion of imports from abroad consequent upon the liberalization of trade had occurred in the Río de la Plata region earlier and with greater intensity than elsewhere, and it had created the need for a flow of exports which would make a continuing flow of imports possible. In Chile, despite the absence of natural conditions comparable to those of the Río de la Plata region, there was also an expansion of cattleraising for export, although the volume concerned was much smaller. Importers in Buenos Aires, Montevideo and Valparaiso needed goods to send to Europe; their ships needed cargoes for the return journey. They sometimes themselves assumed responsibility for exporting livestock products. What hindered the expansion of exports in other areas less affected by the opening up of trade, therefore, was the absence of a flow of imports and this was especially true, around the middle of the century, of the Pacific coast between Guayaquil and California.

The opening up of trade gave Latin American stockraisers access to a European market which had been from earlier times, and was still, dominated by Russia. This limited the possibilities of Latin American expansion which occurred largely thanks to the extreme abundance and cheapness of land. The long-term decline in the price of leather in the European market dangerously ate into landowners' profit-margins. Hides, of course, maintained their position as the leading export but breeding was maintained and expanded through the diversification of livestock products. Exports of salted meat, which had commenced before the wars of independence, had by 1820 already recovered their prewar level and continued to increase until the middle of the century. Slaves constituted the main market for salted meat (above all, in Cuba and Brazil). Tallow began to make up a higher proportion of exports to Europe from 1830 and, in contrast to leather, enjoyed an almost constant rise in price. Much of the tallow exported was no longer raw but, strictly speaking, grease concentrated by steam; landowners and merchants in the rural areas of the Río de la Plata, for example, had installed 'steam-

13 John L. Stephens, *Incidents of travel in Central America, Chiapas and Yucatan* (New Brunswick, N.J., 1949), I, 300–1.

plants'. Its production, therefore, included a manufacturing stage, although this made but modest demands on numbers and specialization of the labour force or the investment of capital. The production of beef required a much more important manufacturing dimension. The salting-plant, established in or near the port, normally concentrated at least fifty and, in the bigger plants, sometimes several hundred workers, who specialized in widely differentiated tasks, covering the various stages of processing from the slaughter of the animal to the salting and drying of the pieces of meat. In the south of Brazil, these manufacturing enterprises, characterized by many capitalistic traits, used mostly slave-labour, whereas in the Río de la Plata area and in Chile the labourers in the salting-plants were wage-earners who benefited from the high levels of remuneration enjoyed by specialized workers in the Latin American cities at that time.[14]

The labour force required for cattle breeding was also composed of wage-earners; the worker received his wages in money and was not obliged by non-economic pressures or by isolation to spend his wages exclusively on goods acquired from his employer, or from the merchant who owed to that employer his ability to trade on the estancia. This was true of the temporary and specialized workers like horse-breakers, farriers and muleteers, whose wages were in any case higher than those of the permanent workers. However, even though the latter might not have had direct access to the market as consumers (and this is far from evident in all cases), and were the victims of legislative measures that obliged them to be constantly employed, under pain of imprisonment, forced labour or recruitment into the army, this entire apparatus of economic and political control – according to the evidence from all the cattleraising zones – served only to ensure the physical presence of the labour force on the cattle estate; its discipline continued to be less than complete, partly because of the very nature of cattlebreeding and partly because of the scarcity of labour.

Of the various types of livestock raising cattleraising (especially in the half empty areas of Latin America) was by far the most affected by the consequences of the liberalization of trade at the beginning of the nineteenth century. The breeding of sheep, goats and animals native to the Americas was well established in the older, more densely populated

[14] For southern Brazil, see Fernando H. Cardoso, *Capitalismo e escravidão no Brasil meridional: o negro na sociedade escravocrata do Rio Grande do Sul* (São Paulo, 1962). For the Río de la Plata region, see Alfredo J. Montoya, *Historia de los saladeros argentinos* (Buenos Aires, 1956).

and traditional areas, but its transformation did not occur until the second half of the century, when the new commercial pressures had become more intense and spread more evenly over the whole of Spanish America. In the period immediately after independence only Peru experienced a significant expansion in wool exports, both from sheep and Andean camelids. There is no evidence, however, that this was due to an increase in the number of head of wool-bearing animals; it was rather the result of a reorientation towards export overseas of fibres previously utilized by the Andean weaving industry.[15]

Some sectors of agriculture succeeded in taking advantage of the opportunities offered by the liberalization of trade, although none adapted to the prevailing economic conditions as completely as did cattleraising. Temperate crops (cereals, vines and olives) had only limited possibilities for growth because of the lack of additional demand in the European market and high transport costs. Tobacco (which can be produced in both tropical and temperate climates) did not show any significant increase in exports until the middle of the century; and only in Colombia did this process commence as early as the late 1840s. Spain continued to be the chief market for cacao and therefore the change in the structure of foreign trade did not have such a favourable effect on cacao production as it did on other agricultural exports; nevertheless, there was a continued increase in production on the coast of Ecuador, and even in Venezuela, which had been the leading cacao producer in the last years of the colonial period, there was a slight increase in the absolute value of cacao exports, even though its relative proportion of exports declined.

In Venezuela, and to a lesser extent in Ecuador, cacao had been produced by slave labour. It appears that in Ecuador, from the beginning of the post-independence economic reconstruction, the shortage of labour, brought about by manumission and forced recruitment of slaves during the war, though rather less significant here than elsewhere, was filled by Indians from the coast and the highlands. The latter were not organized for production in a unit like the traditional hacienda: they settled on lands belonging to the *hacendado*, to whom they delivered part of their crops and, it seems, also paid rent in the form of labour.[16] In Venezuela the development was more complex: because of the previous

[15] Jean Piel, 'The place of the peasantry in the national life of Peru in the nineteenth century', *Past and Present* 46 (1970), 108–36.

[16] For Venezuela, see John V. Lombardi, *The decline and abolition of Negro slavery in Venezuela, 1820–1854* (Westport, Conn., 1971), *passim*. For Ecuador, see Michael T. Hamerly, *Historia social y económica de la antigua provincia de Guayaquil, 1763–1842* (Guayaquil, 1973), 106ff.

predominance of slave labour, the war had had a more disruptive effect on the labour force in Venezuela than in Ecuador, and during the post-war period there was a sustained and not entirely unsuccessful effort to return some of those slaves to their masters, and to place the emancipated blacks in conditions in many ways comparable to slavery. Nevertheless, the proportion of both slaves and ex-slaves in the labour force declined steadily. In Venezuela they seem to have been replaced by wage-earners more often than by peasants working their lords' lands in return for plots on which they could cultivate their own crops.

That cacao lost its relative importance in Venezuelan agriculture was due, above all, to the expansion of coffee cultivation. Coffee had been grown in Venezuela during the colonial period. It spread rapidly in the post-war period, and reached its highest level of activity in the 1830s. Coffee cultivation, when it spread to new lands, required a delay of three years between the planting of the bushes and the first harvest and therefore the first profits. Expansion was undertaken by landowners who lacked capital, and they were, therefore, obliged to raise money on the market. The law of 10 April 1834, which eliminated the restrictions on contractual freedom imposed by the anti-usury legislation inherited from the colonial period, had as its purpose the creation of a more broadly based money market, and it was, perhaps, too successful. The prosperity of the coffee sector encouraged landowners to raise loans at very high rates of interest, and when that prosperity ended in 1842 they had good reason to regret it. The tension between a chronically indebted landowning class and a mercantile and financial sector intent on collecting its debts was to be a principal factor in the turbulent political history of Venezuela for several decades to come. However, the ending of the coffee boom, following a fall in coffee prices, did not remove coffee from its central place in the export economy of Venezuela. The volume of exports rose by about 40 per cent in the five-year period after the crisis of 1842, compared with the five years before, and this new level was to be maintained until, in 1870, a new and very marked expansion commenced. In the middle of the century coffee accounted for more than 40 per cent of Venezuela's exports, and in the 1870s for over 60 per cent.[17] Unlike Brazil where the expansion of coffee cultivation in this period was almost totally dependent on slave labour, coffee producers in Venezuela generally employed free labour. The increasing financial penury of the

[17] Izard, *Series estadísticas*, 191–3.

landowners, however, led to a decline in the use of wage-labour; arrangements between coffee producer and *conuqueros*, who in return for grants of land worked on the coffee plantations, now became more frequent, and finally became the dominant labour system in the coffee regions of Venezuela.

Thus, despite its need for capital and labour, coffee cultivation in Venezuela found a way of surviving and expanding during the period after independence when plantations worked by slave labour no longer seemed a viable long-term solution. On the other hand, the cultivation of sugar-cane everywhere in Spanish America had been confined within the framework of the plantation employing slave labour (the small sugar-growing areas of Mexico were only partially an exception), and it proved difficult to escape from this system. In the coastal areas of Peru, sugar cultivation in the period after independence depended on the use of slave labour as it had throughout the colonial period. And sugar planters always pointed to the impossibility of increasing the number of slaves as the principal reason for the stagnation of production (until the 1860s). A more satisfactory explanation, however, would seem to be lack of markets.

The one region of Spanish America where tropical agriculture in the form of sugar-cane cultivation enjoyed a spectacular advance was, paradoxically, Cuba which, together with Puerto Rico, remained subject to Spain throughout this period. The brief British occupation of Havana in 1762 is generally considered as the starting-point for a phase of expansion which, despite fluctuations, was to continue for over a century. In the late eighteenth century the Cuban economy, until then diversified but poorly developed, began to be slowly reoriented towards the predominance of sugar, though tobacco and coffee also expanded, and cattleraising by no means disappeared. The Spanish crown partly encouraged this process by liberalizing the laws governing the acquisition and utilization of land. More directly influential, however, were other external changes, notably the end of French rule in Saint-Domingue, which eliminated from the market the biggest sugar producer in the world and caused the migration to Cuba of some of its landowners – with their capital and their slaves.

At the beginning of the nineteenth century the centre of gravity of sugar production shifted from Oriente Province to Havana. The unit of production, the sugar-mill, however, remained relatively small for several decades. The reasons for this were high transport costs and the mill's fuel requirements. There were some big producers who owned several mills, but even they for the most part were dependent on the merchants who had advanced them their initial capital and who continued to provide them with goods and, above all, with slaves. It was, in fact, the continued supply of slaves, most of them directly imported from Africa, which made possible the expansion of Cuban sugar production. In the first decade of the nineteenth century, Britain and the United States had closed their territories to the import of slaves and had forbidden their citizens to engage in the international slave trade. Despite intense international (and especially British) pressure, however, Spain consistently failed to fulfil an early commitment – and later commitments – to terminate the trade. The protection afforded to the slave trade was not the least important motive for the Cuban sugar barons' acceptance of Spanish rule over the island, since an independent Cuba would have been even less able than the decadent Spanish monarchy to resist British demands. In the course of the nineteenth century before the ending of the slave trade in the 1860s – ten years after the final suppression of the Brazilian slave trade in 1850–1 – Cuba was to import hundreds of thousands of slaves. The traffic reached its highest intensity between 1835 and 1840; during those six years, 165,000 Africans were brought to the island, the majority of them destined for the sugar plantations. The slave population grew from under 40,000 in 1774 to almost 300,000 in 1827, when the white population for a time ceased to constitute a majority of the population, to almost 450,000 in 1841.[18]

From the 1840s there was a decline in the import of slaves as British control over the slave trade became more effective. Yet the expansion of sugar cultivation continued for another two decades. It was, in fact, no longer so dependent on vast increases in the size of the slave labour force. The first railway construction began in Cuba as early as 1834, and the first stretch of track was inaugurated in 1838 when neither Spain itself nor independent Spanish America had any railways. The railway not only facilitated communications between the sugar estates and the port, but also made possible the expansion of sugar cultivation which high transport costs had previously prevented; it also freed the estate from its dependence on nearby sources of fuel thus making it possible to grow cane on a much greater proportion of the land of the estate. Later, the

---

[18] Franklin W. Knight, *Slave society in Cuba during the nineteenth century* (Madison, 1970), 22 (Table 1), 86 (Table 8). For further discussion on the Cuban sugar industry and slavery in Cuba, see Thomas, *CHLA* III, chap. 7.

railway was introduced into the estate itself, where it made internal communications cheaper and more efficient, and thus contributed decisively to overcoming the limitations which previously existed on the size of each individual estate.[19]

At the same time the increasing difficulty experienced in renovating the stock of slaves facilitated a parallel transformation in the sugar industry: the more widespread use of steam-driven machinery. This, in turn, made more inevitable the transition from the estate employing a hundred slaves and producing a hundred tons a year to the much bigger estate and the replacement of a significant part of the landowning class. Typically, those who best took advantage of the new opportunities came not from the landowning but from the commercial sector. It was not only a question of a difference of mentality, but of a disparity of resources: few among the old sugar barons were able to make the investments that modernization required. Nevertheless, the expansion of Cuban sugar-cane production, still based as it was on slavery, is the greatest economic success story of the first half of the nineteenth century in Latin America.

Moreover, apart from the small amount of British capital invested in the railways, this success was not due to a fuller incorporation of the Cuban economy into the expanding capital market of Europe. The capital needed for the expansion of sugar production came either from the island itself (with mercantile capital, as we have observed, enjoying a predominant position) or from Spain, or even from the Spaniards who left the continent after independence. (Cuba appears to have been the principal refuge of those fleeing, for example, from Mexico in the 1820s.) In Cuba, as on the mainland, there was an almost total absence of capital from new overseas sources. In contrast to independent Spanish America, Cuba nevertheless achieved an impressive rate of growth during this period.

The exceptional success of the Cuban export economy was the principal factor stimulating the far-reaching transformation of Cuban society, not least the change in the ethnic composition of the population. In continental Spanish America the export economy, which even in the most favoured areas did not expand as quickly as in Cuba, was much less important an influence on social change during the period following

---

[19] For an excellent analysis of this process, see Manuel Moreno Fraginals, *El ingenio: el complejo económico social cubano del azúcar. Vol. I, 1760–1860* (Havana, 1964).

independence. Indeed, for most contemporary observers social change on the contrary created obstacles and limitations to which the export economies had to adapt.

This does not mean that there are no examples of regions in which changes in the texture of society were induced by the growth of production for export. Take, for example, the Norte Chico, in Chile, where a society less rigidly structured than that of central Chile emerged. However, there are few examples as convincing as this and, even here, its impact on Chilean society as a whole was comparatively slight. The other examples of export sector growth, from the considerable success of hides in the Río de la Plata region and Venezuelan coffee to the much more modest success of wool in southern Peru, tend to confirm the view that the effort to expand exports could only achieve success if its protagonists learned to adapt themselves to a social framework which was slowly changing but on which their own influence was marginal. Since throughout most of continental Spanish America, from Mexico to Central America, from New Granada (Colombia) to the Peruvian coast and Bolivia, export sector growth was unexpectedly weak in this period, it is necessary to look to other factors influencing the direction of social change, notably the crisis of the old colonial order (and not only the administrative structure but the set of patterns regulating the relations between social and ethnic groups) and the opening up of Spanish America to world trade, with all that it signified (and not only in the field of commerce).

The Wars of Independence, of course, did a great deal to undermine the *ancien régime* in Spanish America. They were the first wars since the Conquest to affect directly almost all continental Spanish America. They not only led to the destruction of assets, as we have seen, but also to changes in the relations between the different sectors of Spanish American society. The fragmentation of political power, the militarization of society, the mobilization for war of resources and, above all, men meant that the old social order and especially social control of the subordinate classes would never be completely restored on, for example, the plains and in the Oriente region of Venezuela, in the highlands of Peru and Bolivia, and on the plains of Uruguay.

Social relations during and after the Spanish American Wars of Independence were also profoundly affected by a new liberal and egalitarian ideology which rejected the hierarchical society characteristic of the colonial period, and aspired to integrate the different social and ethnic groups into a national society in order to reinforce the political unity of the new states.

Three features of Spanish American society in particular were in conflict with the more liberal and egalitarian tendencies of the early nineteenth century: they were black slavery; legal discrimination, both public and private, against those of mixed race; and the division of society as old as the Conquest itself, into a *república de españoles* and a *república de indios*, the barriers between which, though in fact very easy to cross, were to some extent still in place in 1810.

Slavery was nowhere as central to the relations of production in continental Spanish America at the beginning of the nineteenth century as in Cuba – and, of course, Brazil. Most revolutionary governments had ended the slave trade, in many cases as early as 1810–12. Laws freeing children born to slaves had been introduced in, for example, Chile (1811), Argentina (1813), Gran Colombia (1821), Peru (1821), although these were partly offset by regulations for a period of apprenticeship or forced labour to pay for the costs of upbringing. Laws of free birth were rarely implemented effectively and in any case, except in the long run, did not constitute an attack on the institution of slavery itself. We have already observed that the requirements of war led to the recruitment of slaves, some manumitted, some not. After independence a few countries with only a small number of slaves abolished slavery: Chile (1823), Central America (1824), Mexico (1829). At the same time efforts were also made to revitalize the institution, particularly in areas where it had some importance in production for export. These efforts were frustrated by, above all, the exhaustion of external sources of slaves. The African slave trade was necessary for the maintenance of the slave system, and in continental Spanish America only the Río de la Plata region imported slaves in significant numbers after independence – and then only during the 1820s and 1830s. This led inexorably to the decline, in terms of both quantity and quality, of African slavery, and explains why abolition was eventually decreed in Venezuela, Colombia, Peru and the Argentine provinces in the 1850s without causing significant social and economic disruption.

Less hesitant, and on the whole more successful, was the onslaught on the legal discrimination under which those of mixed race suffered. Its abolition was, it is true, less complete and immediate than the measures announced during the revolutionary period might lead one to suppose;

to cite only one example, in the Río de la Plata region, where egalitarian rhetoric and legislation were very much in evidence during the decade following the Revolution of 1810, *mestizos* and *pardos* were not admitted to the University of Córdoba until the 1850s. Furthermore, when a new state had a financial interest in the maintenance of differential standards, inequalities were more likely to continue: in Peru, for example, the tax paid by the *mestizos* (*contribución de castas*), which brought in considerable revenue, was abolished for a brief period, but then reimposed and survived until the 1850s. However, the system of ethnic castes was undermined nearly everywhere at its very roots when from early in the national period it was no longer obligatory to record a child's racial origin at birth. Even Peru abolished separate registers of baptisms and marriages for *mestizos* and Indians.

The successful abolition of the legal differentiation between the ethnic groups, though not necessarily the ending of inequality in the payment of taxes, becomes more understandable when it is recalled that, in the last years of the colonial period, from Caracas to Buenos Aires, the rise of prosperity at least in urban areas of some people of mixed ethnic origin, even though only an infinitesimal minority, began to affect the ethnic composition of the propertied classes. The war then enabled people of mixed ethnic origin to rise to positions of military and, rather less often, political influence. The Creole elite, still proudly conscious of its own ethnic purity, was nevertheless persuaded that any attempt to embody its prejudices in legal or political discrimination was no longer possible.

The fiscal needs of the new states also contributed to the slowness with which the legal position on the Indians was modified in the half-century following independence. Spain had abolished Indian tribute in 1810. Among the newly independent countries with large Indian populations, it was never reimposed in Mexico, but in Peru and Bolivia, and to a lesser extent in New Granada and Ecuador, despite its legal abolition (in some cases reiterated as, for example, at the Congress of Cúcuta in 1821), tribute continued to be an important source of government revenue, either under its traditional name or disguised by transparent euphemisms.[20]

Relatively little is known of the impact on the Indians of the changes that accompanied the ending of colonial rule. What research there is reveals a picture basically stable but rich in variety and contrasts. This is

[20] Nicolás Sánchez-Albornoz, 'Tributo abolido, tributo impuesto. Invariantes socioeconómicas en la época republicana', *Indios y tributos en el Alto Perú* (Lima, 1978), 187–218.

not surprising in view of the great variety of situations already prevailing before the final crisis of the colonial order: cultural Hispanicization and economic and social integration had of course progressed much further in some areas than in others. The contrast between the centre-north and south in Mexico, a subject which has only recently begun to be investigated, is now as clear as that between the coastal region and highlands of Peru and Ecuador. These differences determined the effect the crisis of independence had on the Indians. And it was the more general changes in the political, social and economic order which accompanied the crisis of emancipation rather than specific changes in the law itself which had the greatest impact. The wave of Indian rebellions in Mexico in the period after independence, for example, was the consequence of the general relaxation of traditional political and social discipline in rural Mexico.

Although the new regimes introduced almost everywhere substantial modifications in the legal status of the Indians, and adopted a concept of the place of the Indian in society substantially different from that prevailing under the *ancien régime*, these specific innovations seem to have had less effect than the general crisis of the old order. The very notion of a separate and parallel *república de indios* was repugnant to the new order and it rejected any alternative method of recognizing, legally and politically, a separate way of life for the Indians. Moreover, the basic institution of the *república de indios*, the Indian community endowed with rights over land, was now considered as an aberration in legal terms, detrimental in economic terms (since it impeded the incorporation of land and labour into a market economy) and disastrous in social and political terms, since it was seen as a formidable obstacle to the assimiliation of the Indian into the new political order. Nevertheless, the Indian community, which had suffered a slow process of erosion even during the colonial period, survived remarkably well in Mexico, Central America and the Andean republics during the first half-century after independence. Its legal dissolution (which would have transformed its members into individual proprietors) had been proposed, for example, by Bolívar in Peru, but it was enacted only occasionally and even then does not appear to have affected the actual functioning of community life. Nor was there any significant erosion on the territorial patrimony which the communities had managed to preserve from the colonial period, in spite of the more favourable ideological climate. This was, no doubt, delayed by the temporary fragility of the new political order and the absence of demographic pressures in this period. Even more decisive was the failure of commercial agriculture to expand significantly. In short, the delayed impact of the new external connection on the complex and loose structures of the Spanish American economies – the effective economic isolation of, for example, the Andean region – is probably the principal explanation for the social stability of those areas inhabited overwhelmingly by Indians.

In vast areas of Spanish America the lack of the stimulus that might have been provided by an expansion of the market weakened the pressures towards further land concentration and the advance of the hacienda at the expense of the Indian communities. Landownership outside the communities remained highly concentrated, of course, though existing landholdings changed hands more frequently in a period of civil war and political upheaval than during the colonial period, and sometimes the largest units were divided. A study of an area near Mexico City shows how a great territorial holding was transformed into the scarcely disguised booty of political and military victory; the first new proprietor was the ephemeral Emperor Agustín de Iturbide, then the estate passed into the hands of Vicente Riva Palacio, who was connected with the liberal faction which emerged for the first time in the following decade. In the long run, however, this booty became less attractive, partly because the weakening of the traditional system of rural labour made the exploitation of these lands less profitable than in the past.[21] In Jiquetepeque on the northern coast of Peru, this period witnessed the consolidation of a class of Creole big landowners, partly recruited from those holding in emphyteusis lands that were formerly ecclesiastical, and partly from among the civilian and military officials of the new republic.[22] In Venezuela, General Páez, among many others, entered into the propertied classes with which he had identified himself politically. In the region of Buenos Aires, so much land was available for cattleraising that it could be divided into huge estates and shared out without much dispute among old and new landowners. Any general conclusion about landholding in the aftermath of independence is, however, highly dangerous in view of the size and diversity of Spanish America and the limited amount of research which has so far been done.

In the cities, the Creole elites were the main beneficiaries of political

---

[21] John M. Tutino, 'Hacienda social relations in Mexico: the Chalco region in the era of Independence', *Hispanic American Historical Review*, 55/3 (1975), 496–528.

[22] Manuel Burga, *De la encomienda a la hacienda capitalista. El valle de Jiquetepeque del siglo XVI al XX* (Lima, 1976), 148ff.

emancipation; they achieved their aim of displacing the Spanish in the top bureaucratic and commercial positions, and at the same time the establishment of independent republican governments increased the opportunities for careers in government and politics. Compared with the pre-revolutionary period the urban elite was, however, weakened by several factors: the elimination of the patrimony and prestige of the Spaniards themselves who had formed such an important part of it; the entry, but not the full integration, of groups of foreign merchants who so often replaced the Spaniards; the upward mobility of individual *mestizos*; and, most important, the replacement of a system of power based on the metropolis and exercised through the cities as political and administrative centres by another system, more locally based, more rural, in which power was exercised by *hacendados* – and caudillos. The urban elites were deprived of part of the material basis of their pre-eminence and also of a large part of its ideological justification. They enjoyed much less of a monopoly of wealth than in the past at a time when wealth was becoming, in comparison with the past, the chief criterion of social differentiation. This led them to regard themselves, even more than in the past, as an educated class, but the justification of a pre-eminent position in society on the basis of education was less and less universally accepted. Its rejection provided an opening – no doubt exaggerated by the urban elites – for an understanding between rural (or urban) political leaders of conservative inclination and an urban popular sector, more numerous, more prosperous and affected to a greater or lesser degree by the egalitarian ideologies diffused by the revolutions for independence.

This leads us to consider a problem which is central to an understanding of what was happening in this phase of the evolution of urban society, in particular in the cities most directly affected by the liberalization of foreign trade. It is usually asserted that this liberalization, by making possible the importation of large quantities of the products of the new industries of Britain and Europe, must have had detrimental effects on those who had hitherto produced these goods locally by craft methods; that is to say, the pauperization of the urban popular sectors was the inevitable consequence of free trade. The counter-argument is that even before 1810 the import of 'luxury' goods (Castilian cloth, metallurgical products, wine) and the inter-regional trade both in these products and in goods for popular consumption had already imposed limitations on the expansion of urban craft industries and that, moreover, the expansion of foreign trade led to a growth of the internal market, which created fresh opportunities for local artisans. Both effects were doubtless felt, and their point of equilibrium was obviously not the same in all Spanish American cities.[23] A more easily defined consequence of the expansion of trade – and the increasing complexity of urban society – was the rise of a more numerous group of retail traders. The increase in the volume of imports did not necessarily lead to the abandonment by the big foreign importers of the Spanish practice of selling direct to the public. However, they were obliged to channel a growing quantity of their retail business towards an increasing number of small shopkeepers. The increase in the consumption of wheat bread led to the replacement of various kinds of maize bread which had been produced in the home by a product often acquired in the shops. And the increased movement of people led to the opening of more inns. Moreover, although the increase in the volume of imported cloth may have adversely affected local producers (who were in fact rarely to be found in the important urban centres), it created a demand for more dressmakers and tailors in the cities where its consumption was concentrated. In general, although it was not universal, there was a growth rather than a decline of the more prosperous sector of the lower classes in the cities of Spanish America in the period following independence. This partly explains the urban elite's often expressed concern for social order which was thought to be threatened, but which nevertheless does not appear to have faced any overt challenge.

There were, nevertheless, few opportunities available to the non-primary sectors of the Spanish American economies for autonomous development in the new post-independence international economic order. Economic dependence – understood, with regard to this period, as above all the acceptance of a place in the international division of labour as defined by the new economic metropolis – imposed rigid limitations on the possibilities for economic diversification in the areas thus incorporated more closely into the world market. Until the end of the period under consideration, the only part of Spanish America that was to create a textile industry capable of transforming its productive processes and competing with overseas imports was, in fact, Mexico. When the causes of Mexico's comparative success are examined, it appears that perhaps the most important factors were the dimensions of

---

[23] For a suggestive examination of these changes in Santiago, Chile, see Luis Alberto Romero, *La Sociedad de la Igualdad. Los artesanos de Santiago de Chile y sus primeras experiencias políticas, 1820–1851* (Buenos Aires, 1978), 11–29.

the market and the existence since the colonial period of an active internal trade, which made production on the scale required by the new technology economically possible. Moreover, in its early stages, there was a mass of skilled artisans concentrated in one urban centre, Puebla, available for employment in the new, more decidedly industrial, phase of textile production in Mexico.[24] Elsewhere the internal market was much more limited – fewer people, often with lower incomes than in Mexico – and it was captured by the foreign merchants, as in the Río de la Plata region, or the market remained small, unintegrated and largely isolated from the outside world, as was the case in almost the entire Andean region. There, the traditional system of textile production – and much else – survived.

In this necessarily brief examination of continuity and change in Spanish American society during the period immediately following independence no mention has so far been made of one factor which might be considered fundamental, that is to say, demographic trends. This omission is partly because very little is known about population trends during this period, but above all because what is known leads to the conclusion that they were not as decisive a factor in the evolution of society as they had been in the colonial period or as they were to be after 1870. In Mexico, following an increase in population in the eighteenth century, the early decades of the nineteenth appear to show a decline in some areas and an overall stagnation. In the rest of Spanish America the trend was clearly upwards, though certainly subject to marked variations from one region to another. Nicolás Sánchez-Albornoz considers it possible to distinguish a more rapid population growth in the regions of more recent Spanish settlement (Cuba, the Antioquia-Cauca region in New Granada, the Río de la Plata area and Venezuela, where the population more than doubled), whether or not these areas were affected by the opening up of overseas trade after independence, and a slower growth in the regions from Mexico through Central America to the Andean backbone of South America populated predominantly by Indians. In the case of Cochabamba (Bolivia), a comparison of the figures for 1793 and 1854 confirms these general conclusions: there was a more rapid growth in the valleys (which expanded their agriculture and attracted immigrants) than in the highlands.[25]

[24] Jan Bazant, 'Evolución de la industria textil poblana', *Historia Mexicana* (Mexico), 13 (1964), 4.
[25] Nicolás Sánchez-Albornoz, *La población de América Latina desde los tiempos precolombinos al año 2000* (2nd edn, Madrid, 1977), 127ff.

The overall increase in the population was based above all on the advance of the agricultural frontier. This advance, although in New Granada or the Río de la Plata region it might take the form of the incorporation of new territories beyond the limits of those previously subject to the political domination of Spain, was almost everywhere based on an expansion into the vast territories which lay between areas of settlement during the colonial period. Cuba and Venezuela offer perhaps the best examples of this process. The connection between the expansion of the frontier and the growth of the agricultural export sector is evident in the case of Cuba, Venezuela or the Río de la Plata region, but less so in New Granada, Chile or – in the minor example just quoted – the valleys of remote Cochabamba. The major urban centres, despite the contrary impressions of contemporary observers, local and foreign, either grew at a slower rate than that of the population as a whole (e.g. Havana or Buenos Aires) or, where the initial urban population was small, at only a slightly higher rate (e.g. Santiago in Chile, or Medellín in Antioquia, Colombia). Some cities remained substantially static during the first half of the nineteenth century, because the slow post-war recovery did not suffice to offset the decline in population caused by the Wars of Independence and their indirect consequences (e.g. Lima and Caracas). Thus, the proportion of the total population of Spanish America living in major cities did not increase, and the opening up of trade appears not to have especially stimulated their growth. Havana, Caracas and Buenos Aires, which were the centres of regions most affected by a vigorous expansion of exports, evinced a relative growth that appears to be lower than the average for Spanish America.

This comparatively slow urban growth, and also the similarity of the rate of growth of the population in the regions which were and which were not incorporated into an expanding economy based on the export of agricultural produce, provide yet another measure of the limited impact of the insertion of Spanish America into the new international economic system, whose nucleus was Britain rather than the old imperial metropolis. From the middle of the nineteenth century, however, there was a gradual transition to a closer and more complex relationship between Spanish America and the outside world than that prevailing in the period immediately after independence.

The third quarter of the nineteenth century was a transition in the economic history of Spanish America between the period of economic stagnation after independence (except in Cuba) and the period of export-led growth from the 1870s or 1880s until the World Depression of the 1930s. The relations between the Spanish American economies and the metropolitan economies were gradually redefined. New opportunities for the export sectors of some continental Spanish American economies, notably Argentina, Peru and Chile, were opened up.

The middle years of the nineteenth century marked, for the economy of Europe, the ending of a period of decline which, after reaching its lowest point in the crisis of 1846, aggravated by the political storms of 1848, yielded place to an impressive wave of expansion destined to last (despite the crisis of 1857 and 1865) until the Great Depression of 1873. During this period the continent of Europe closed the gap with the island that had initiated the Industrial Revolution. Industrial growth contin-ued, in both Britain and Europe, at a faster pace than in the immediate past, and the leading continental European countries introduced, in a more decisive manner than Britain, institutional and organizational innovations: for example, deposit and investment banks, and businesses no longer based on the family, particularly in banking and transport. There was increasing European (and North American) demand for Latin American primary products. The progress of steam navigation was much slower in the South Atlantic and the Pacific than in the North Atlantic, but the establishment of mail-packets was sufficient to ensure a new regularity in the movement of people – and in the flow of informa-tion. (South America was linked to the outside world by telegraph only from the 1870s: the submarine cable reached Rio de Janeiro in 1874.)

Even more important for the future was the re-establishment on a more solid basis of the financial connection which had made only an ephemeral appearance in the early 1820s. A surplus of capital in Europe created a more favourable climate for Latin American loans and invest-ment. It is true that the expansion of external credit was far from achieving the volume that it was to attain in the 1880s, and was channelled in a most uneven manner towards the various Latin American states, which only exceptionally succeeded in establishing the close connections with banking houses of solid repute that would make it possible for investors to enter the Latin American market with greater confidence than in the past (a confidence that was not always well-founded). During the period 1850–73, credits granted to Spanish Ameri-can states were highly speculative in character, and more than one episode before the crisis of 1873 – for example, concerning loans to

Honduras and Paraguay[26] – recalled events of half a century before. Nevertheless, there were signs of the future pattern of financial relations with the metropolis. In some cases (like Peru, as we shall see) credit was linked to the control of the peripheral country's external trade. In others (such as the loans to Argentina and Chile) the granting of credit facilitated the export to the periphery of non-consumer goods. In the 1860s the first foreign private banks specializing in credit for overseas trade and the remittance of funds between Spanish America and Europe were established: the British banks which eventually were to be amalgamated as the Bank of London, Mexico and South America. Of course, bankers from continental Europe also moved into Spanish America, but they did not challenge British hegemony in this field until the 1880s.

Finally, the role of the groups of British merchants established in the ports and commercial centres of Spanish America at the time of the opening up to world trade, and linked to major commercial firms in Britain, began to decline, as did their autonomy. Both the local state and local capitalists became more involved in the growth of the Spanish American economies during this period, but more important for the future was the increasing influence of a new type of business concern, of which the railway company is the best example, metropolitan not only in its origins (even though its capital might not be exclusively metropolitan) but in the headquarters of its management and, above all, in the close connections which it preserved with the metropolitan economy. The new railway company was not only an instrument of mercantile integration between the metropolitan and the neo-colonial economies, which facilitated the concentration of the latter on the sector exporting primary products; from the metropolitan point of view, it fulfilled a more immediately useful function by offering an outlet for metallurgical and engineering products during the construction phase and, in smaller but regular quantities, for those products, and for coal, once the operation of the railways had begun.

The beginnings of railway expansion in continental Spanish America, and especially Argentina, in this period reflects the new relationship between the metropolitan and the peripheral area. In Buenos Aires province the Western railway was begun in 1857 by local capitalists to facilitate the transport of wool. However, this source of capital was soon

---

[26] For Honduras, see D. C. M. Platt, 'British bondholders in nineteenth-century Latin America. Injury and remedy', *Inter-American Economic Affairs*, 14/3 (1960). For Paraguay, see H. G. Warren, *Paraguay and the Triple Alliance. The post-war decade, 1869–1878* (Austin, 1978), 129ff.

found to be insufficient, and eventually the provincial treasury took over the extension of the line before looking to the alternative of handing over the building and operation of the railways to foreign companies. A decade later, local producers and merchants of British origin played an important role in the promotion of the second important railway in Buenos Aires province, the Southern (like the Western at this stage a railway for the transportation of wool) and some of them were to become members of the board of directors of the private company which undertook its management. However, this company was established in London and was responsive from the outset to metropolitan interests; in a few decades the connection, which at first had been so close, between the Southern railway and the economic interests dominant in the region it served had disappeared almost entirely. The line from Rosario to Córdoba, the axis of the future network of the Argentine Central railway, was from the beginning a very different concern. Unlike both the Western and the Southern which served the needs of a productive region already being exploited, this was a line aimed at development, the encouragement of rural industry and commerce; it could not offer quick profits. It was, in fact, built thanks to a state guarantee of minimum earnings by means of a subsidy (in addition to grants of land) paid to the British company which undertook its construction and operation. The metropolitan connection was established, even more overwhelmingly than in the case of the Southern railway, with interests connected to railway building. Connections with local agrarian and commercial interests were developed largely after, and as a consequence of, the building of the railway. These connections were not only less close than in the case of the Southern, but were characterized by an almost permanent antagonism. One reason for this was the conditions offered for the establishment of the line; the guarantee was in proportion to its extension and, even though this encouraged investment, it discouraged those whose objective was an improvement of the service. A second reason was that the railway between Córdoba and Rosario was constructed for the transport of cereals, and from the special characteristics of their storage and transport there arose more serious conflicts of interest between producers and transporters than in the case of wool.[27] Finally, as a consequence of the depression of 1873, the effects of which were felt in Argentina in 1874, the British railway company refused to extend the track, which had

---

[27] Later studies have not superseded H. S. Ferns, *Britain and Argentina in the XIXth Century* (Oxford, 1960), 342ff.

reached, in 1870, as far as Córdoba. The state assumed responsibility for the undertaking, but this decision, which would appear to make the expansion of the railways independent of the metropolis, modified but did not put an end to the external connection. The building of the line was undertaken by a British entrepreneur, Telfener, who had invested his capital in materials for railway construction and who, in this period of economic depression, agreed to advance the necessary funds to the Argentine state.

Argentina, however, though it anticipated future trends in the financial relations between Spanish America and the metropolis, was not typical of the pattern of railway building during this period. In Chile, even though the first railway, in the mining zone of the Norte Chico, was due to the initiative of William Wheelwright, the capital seems to have been raised from local mining entrepreneurs and from the Anglo-Chilean merchants of Valparaíso. In Central Chile, the state played a decisive role from the outset and, although railway building was largely financed through foreign loans, the construction itself was undertaken by an entrepreneur who was certainly foreign (namely the American, Henry Meiggs), but who did not belong to the closely-knit community of entrepreneurs and technicians that was carrying the railway from Britain to South America and the world in general. It was Meiggs who dominated even more completely railway construction in Peru. Here, too, foreign credit provided the basis for the expansion of the railways, not because of any ambition on the part of the metropolis to share in the undertaking, but as an indirect consequence of the monopoly enjoyed by Peru in the guano market. Even in Mexico, which was hampered during this phase of its development by civil war and foreign intervention, the role played by companies based on the metropolis was a secondary one; the main line from Mexico City to Veracruz, inaugurated in 1873, was built and brought into operation by a Mexican private company, with funds in part advanced by the French occupation forces, who needed to expedite its construction for military purposes.[28]

The increasing participation of the metropolitan economies in the peripheral economies through, for example, the incipient banking system and the railway companies, was not only necessary for the expansion of the volume of production in the Spanish American export sectors; it

---

[28] Margarita Urias Hermosillo, 'Manuel Escandón, de las diligencias al ferrocarril, 1833–1862', in Ciro F. S. Cardoso (ed.), *Formación y desarrollo de la burguesía en México. Siglo XIX* (Mexico, 1978), 52.

was no less necessary to enable Spanish America to produce at competitive prices. The advantages as regards the terms of trade which the Spanish American economies had possessed in the preceding period (1808–50) began to become less evident, and by the end of the transitional period (1850–73) they had disappeared or at least sharply declined. The peripheral economies were now no longer growing more slowly than the metropolitan economies, despite the geographical expansion of the metropolitan area in continental western Europe and North America. Within the periphery the Spanish American economies were now competing not only among themselves, or with the old peripheral economies of Eastern Europe, but with new areas, ranging from Canada to Africa and Australia. Without a transfer of capital and technology it was even more difficult to achieve a sustained export boom than in the period immediately after independence.

One obstacle to economic growth in the Spanish American countries during the third quarter of the nineteenth century, and therefore one explanation for the increasing divergence of economic performance between the Spanish American economies, was the continuation, indeed intensification, of political – and military – conflict which destroyed assets and absorbed resources which should have been employed in productive purposes and frightened off foreign capital. Throughout almost the whole of this period, Mexico and, to a somewhat lesser extent, Venezuela, for example, were to be profoundly disturbed by civil wars, the worst since the Wars of Independence. The Mexican civil war was complicated by foreign intervention. Even in Argentina, the minister of finance calculated in 1876 that the cost of the civil wars of the 1850s and 1860s together with the Paraguayan war (1865–70) equalled the total foreign credits received by the Argentine state during this period.

The most highly developed export economy in Spanish America in the two decades after 1850 was the Spanish colony of Cuba; in 1861–4 her exports reached an annual average value of 57 million pesos, and they were not to decline from this level even in the first phase of the Ten Years' War, which began in 1868. At the beginning of the 1870s, therefore, Cuba's exports were almost double those of the independent Spanish American republics that had been most successful in increasing their exports. Argentina, Chile and Peru each had exports of around 30 million pesos, higher than Mexico (with exports worth 24 million pesos in 1870) whose economic stagnation was a reflection both of the effects of the political and military conflicts of the 1850s and 1860s and the decline of its mining sector. There were also significant realignments among the smaller exporters: Uruguay, whose exports were valued at $12\frac{1}{2}$ million pesos, had double the exports of Bolivia and Venezuela (both with around 6 million pesos in value), partly because Montevideo was also the port of shipment for some of Argentina's produce.[29] Bolivia still suffered from the collapse of its mining economy, Venezuela from the social and economic costs of civil war and the gradual fall in the price of coffee, its major export.

The Cuban sugar industry continued its impressive growth in the middle decades of the nineteenth century, but there were problems on the horizon. The decline in the price of sugar, though not so pronounced as it was to be later, had already begun, and expectation of the final abolition of the transatlantic slave trade (it was finally ended in 1865–6) had already led to a marked increase in the price of imported slaves. As a result of this pincer movement there was growing pessimism about the future of the plantation economy: it was now realized that in order to survive sugar cultivation needed to be able to count on alternative sources of labour and capital that would make possible the modernization of the industrial sector. It was doubtful whether both these could be found, and it was increasingly evident that the majority of Cuban planters, even those who had most recently entered the industry and were largely responsible for the recent expansion, could not maintain their dominant position in the face of the introduction of changes that were necessary for the very survival of the sugar-growing sector. The Ten Years' War (1868–78) revealed and aggravated the strains within Cuba's sugar industry, and made it even more certain that the ending of slavery (in the 1880s) and the modernization of the sugar mills would signify the end of the domination of Cuban sugar cultivation by the Cuban and Spanish planters.

The prosperity of the Peruvian export economy, like that of Cuba, was continually accompanied by gloomy forecasts. But this was the only characteristic the two economies had in common. The expansion of Peruvian exports was based on guano; only in the final stage of the guano boom did other products, some of them traditional like sugar and cotton, others new like nitrate, begin to rival guano. And the role played by guano in the Peruvian economy was very different from that played by sugar in Cuba. In the first place, the characteristics of the international guano trade were different: in a context of increasing demand for guano, arising out of the needs of European agriculture, Peru enjoyed through-

[29] For Spanish American exports in this period, see F. Martin, *The Statesman's Yearbook* (London, 1874), *passim*.

out this period a virtual monopoly of supplies. The impact of guano on the Peruvian economy was different too: to export it, all that was needed was collection, which did not require complex techniques and which absorbed above all unskilled labour; furthermore, from the point of view of shipment, its volume was much less than that of sugar of comparable value. Finally, there was a difference in the geographical relationship between the guano-producing area and the core of the Peruvian economy; guano came from a marginal and very small area, consisting of a group of islands a relatively long distance from the coast. All these factors influenced the impact made by the expansion of guano on the Peruvian economy. Its capacity to effect directly transformations in the other sectors, by means of forward and backward linkages, was extremely limited. However, thanks to Peru's monopoly of the supply of guano the Peruvian state was uniquely able to retain a very considerable part of the profits from the export sector, in excess of fifty per cent it appears,[30] a proportion only equalled by Venezuela in the case of petroleum during the Second World War.

Until 1860, the guano trade was in the hands of foreign business concerns, among which the British firm of Antony Gibbs & Sons enjoyed a dominant position. But the royalties obtained by the treasury (in addition to the income derived from the fact that, due to its solvency, Peru again had access to internal and foreign credit) were soon reflected in an increase in public expenditure which was principally channelled into increases in the remuneration of the bureaucracy and the military. Moderate amounts of guano revenue were used for public works and even arms purchases, and the consolidation of the internal debt, which transferred vast resources to private individuals (often with very dubious claims) was, in terms of its political and social impact, an essential aspect of this first phase of the Peruvian guano boom.

The second phase was characterized by the granting of a monopoly of the Peruvian guano trade with the most important market, Britain, to a group of Peruvian concessionaries. The period of expansion had come to an end and the treasury, accustomed to a constant increase in its revenues, began to feel impoverished. It now increasingly had recourse to credits obtained from the guano concessionaries, who had a growing influence in the financial and political life of Peru. In 1869, a government

---

[30] According to the figures given by Shane Hunt in Heraclio Bonilla, *Guano y burguesía en el Perú* (Lima, 1974), 144. For further discussion of the impact of guano on the Peruvian economy, see Bonilla, *CHLA* III, chap. 13.

of conservative tendencies led by General Balta, with more support in the army and the south of Peru than in Lima, broke this financial nexus by transferring the concession for the guano trade to Auguste Dreyfus, a French businessman. Once the concession was obtained, he found no difficulty in obtaining the necessary financial backing in Europe. There was a further increase in both government revenue from guano and credit, and these fresh resources were channelled into an ambitious programme of railway construction, designed to link the southern and central highlands with the Pacific ports. Meanwhile, even though the guano boom had undoubtedly contributed to the recovery of sugar and cotton cultivation in the coastal areas of Peru, it had not succeeded in creating a vigorous group of native capitalists. This was partly, it seems, because the Peruvian group active in the export of guano had only limited financial independence; from the beginning it was dependent on Chilean and British credit. In particular, Peruvian participation in the exploitation of nitrate, which in the far south of Peru and the Bolivian littoral offered an alternative less expensive than guano and which hastened the decline of the latter, was extremely small. From 1874, the end of the guano boom made some painful readjustments necessary and Peru was not well prepared for the very severe trial which the War of the Pacific (1879–83) represented.

Paradoxically, even though the exhaustion of this first cycle of the export trade after independence decisively weakened Peru as it was about to face the challenge of Chile, it was partly the simultaneous exhaustion of their own first export cycle which persuaded Chilean leaders of the urgency of mounting that challenge in order to conquer, along the nitrate-producing coast, a new base for Chile's own exporting capacity and to broaden the fiscal basis of the Chilean state. The expansion of Chilean exports had taken place on a much broader front than that of Peru. In the mining sector the rise of silver was followed by that of copper; in the early 1860s Chile was the biggest exporter of copper in the world. The expansion of mining in Coquimbo and Copiapó, in the Norte Chico, was the result above all of local entrepreneurial activity and investment efforts (though with the usual connections to British mercantile capital, through the Anglo-Chilean firms in Valparaíso). The labour force, though swollen by immigrants from western Argentina, was also predominantly Chilean. This expansion of the northern mining sector was complemented by that of commercial agriculture in the Central Valley, of which the most important export product continued to be, as it had been since colonial times, wheat. From the late 1840s wheat was exported far beyond the traditional, and limited, Peruvian market, to the new markets in the Pacific, namely California and Australia. When the latter quickly became self-sufficient in cereals, the bulk of Chilean exports of flour and wheat were shipped to Argentina, which was to achieve self-sufficiency only in 1870, and to Europe.

The expansion of cereal-growing southwards in Chile began before the building of the longitudinal railway, thanks to the establishment of minor ports such as Constitución and Tomé, which offered an outlet for areas still isolated by land from the nucleus formed by Santiago and Valparaíso. This geographical expansion led to the eviction of the mass of squatters who, as long as the effective ownership of these lands was of no economic interest to the landowning class, had been free to occupy both state-owned and private land. The latter were now claimed more vigorously, and the former soon passed into private hands. Although in the far south there was a significant effort at agricultural colonization, carried out by German immigrants who eventually became proprietors, on the whole this transfer to private ownership benefited the old-established landowners or new owners recruited from the urban upper classes. At the same time this solved the problem of finding a rural labour force; even though the landowners complained at the threat to rural discipline posed by the opening up of new possibilities of employment in mines, public works and the urban areas, there was in fact an increase in the supply of labour. This was reflected in the progressive deterioration of the position of the *inquilinos*, tenant-labourers, whose numbers grew but who had to offer an increased quantity of labour in return for ever-decreasing plots of land.

The existence of an abundant and cheap labour force provided Chilean agriculture with a refuge in the face of increased competition from Argentina, which had more abundant land, and from the United States and Canada which, thanks to mechanization and selection of seeds, were to produce crops at lower costs and also achieve higher quality. This refuge took the form of an archaic system of production, which employed a great deal of labour but which attracted little capital investment, except in irrigation works. However, it was not a very secure refuge: the first casualty was the flour industry, which was complementary to cereal-growing. Chile soon lost the battle with the European and North American producing centres that used the new mills with steel cylinders; thereafter Chilean agriculturists declined to produce the hard wheat these mills required and, as a result, within twenty years Chilean wheat was to be driven out of the international market.

In the mid-1870s this process of involution was only just beginning and was reflected above all in a decline in the volume of agricultural exports and more especially in profits. Not everybody realized this was not merely due to temporary circumstances. In mining, however, there was a complete collapse; at the end of the 1870s Chile, which had enjoyed as a copper producer a position that the country had never attained as a producer of cereals, had been completely driven out of the world market. The reason for this was that the United States, with a new system of mining incorporating new technological processes, began to produce copper at a much lower cost than Chile; the mining entrepreneurs of the Norte Chico had neither the capital nor the access to technological innovations to allow them to compete. There was to be a resurgence of Chilean copper mining in the twentieth century, with the help of those who had indirectly destroyed it in the nineteenth century.

Thus Chile learned that the new world economic climate, even though it opened up fresh opportunities to the peripheral economies, subjected them to a harsher environment, and prosperity did not always survive its rigours. The decline of copper coincided with a resurgence of silver, but the latter, though produced by Chilean mining entrepreneurs, came from the northern littoral which was still Bolivian territory. It was, above all, accompanied by an expansion in the production of nitrate in the Peruvian and Bolivian coastal regions. Paradoxically, however, the War of the Pacific, which gave Chile political control over this area, weakened the predominance of the Chilean and Anglo-Chilean exploiters over the new northern nitrate regions. The victory did not, therefore, bring about the extension to the new territory of the system which had given Chile an ephemeral prosperity in the third quarter of the nineteenth century, and in which the protagonists had been a landowning, mercantile and entrepreneurial class which, though partly foreign in origin, was essentially local. On the contrary, the outcome was to be similar to that of Peru in the case of guano: the principal connection between the nitrate-exporting sector, increasingly controlled from abroad, and the Chilean economy was provided by the state, which received from the taxes on the export of nitrates a very considerable proportion of its increased revenues.[31]

In Argentina a more pronounced tendency towards expansion ensured

[31] For further discussion of the Chilean economy before the War of the Pacific, see Collier, *CHLA* III, chap. 14.

less abrupt transitions between one phase and another of her export sector growth; nevertheless, it is possible to detect in Argentina the same tendencies that we have observed in Chile. In the middle of the nineteenth century the old cattleraising sector, oriented towards the production of hides, tallow and salted beef, appears to have reached its limit owing to the saturation of the European markets. After the middle of the 1850s renewed expansion became possible, firstly as a consequence of the Crimean War which isolated Russian suppliers from western markets, and also in a more permanent way by the progress of the footwear industry, in which mass-production led to an increase in the demand for leather. Nevertheless, the brief period of stagnation was enough to offer decisive encouragement to the expansion of sheepraising; very soon, and until the end of the century, wool was to become the most important livestock product among Argentina's exports.

The expansion of sheepraising which, until the mid-1860s, occurred in a context of rising prices, was facilitated firstly by the extension of the railway, but above all by the increase in immigration (in this case from Ireland and the Basque country). The growing number of immigrants obliged them to accept increasingly unfavourable conditions and it was the sharp decline in agricultural wages which made it possible to maintain and even expand pastoral activity in the hard years that began in 1867. The two most important markets, France and the United States, imposed high duties on the import of wool, while Australian competition depressed the price of Argentine wool, which was of inferior quality owing to the primitive conditions of production and, above all, of storage and marketing.

In these circumstances the pasturing of sheep could no longer provide the main impetus for the expansion of the Argentine export economy. The following decade saw a resurgence of cattleraising in the peripheral lands in the south of Buenos Aires province, where sheep had driven out cattle; and there was a final period of prosperity for the archaic salted beef industry, which still retained its old Cuban market and part of the Brazilian market. Above all, there was also an increase in the production of cereals. In Buenos Aires province this occurred, even in this late period, within the context of the traditional large estate, but in Sante Fe which became the principal cereal-growing province, it was based on centres of agricultural colonization, once again with immigrant farmers. As has been mentioned above, in the mid-1870s, stimulated by rising demand, due to the growth of the cities and the presence in them of an

increasing number of immigrants, Argentina expanded wheat production to the point where it became self-sufficient in cereals.

Also in the 1870s there was a final offensive against the Indians in the
Pampa zone which, by offering fresh booty in land, gave a new lease of
life to the economic formula on which Argentine expansion had been
based: that is, abundant and cheap land, which made it possible to
produce at competitive prices with techniques that required little capital
and comparatively little labour. Labour was scarce in Argentina, and
immigrant labour was never to be as cheap as that available to landowners in rural Chile. Even within the frame of this formula, investment of
capital began to increase, for example in wire fencing and the beginning
of cross-breeding of livestock, which in the 1870s chiefly affected sheep.
However, the Argentine export economy was not to reveal its new
orientation decisively until the 1890s, when cereals and meat were to
become the principal exports, as a result of a transformation no less
profound, albeit less traumatic, than those undergone by the economies
of Peru and Chile.

The redefinition of Spanish America's commercial and financial
relations with the European metropolis was one factor promoting social
transformation during the period 1850–70, but it was by no means the
only factor and what social change there was came slowly. In the first
place, there continued the gradual elimination of slavery throughout
Spanish America. Although in some countries, where there was only a
comparatively small number of slaves – Chile, Central America, Mexico
– slavery had been abolished immediately after independence; in the
countries where there was an economically more significant number of
slaves, abolition did not occur until the middle of the century. Slavery
was abolished in 1846 in Uruguay and in 1853 in the Argentine republic
(except in the province of Buenos Aires, which abolished it only when it
became part of the republic in 1860). It was abolished in Colombia in
1850 and in Peru and Venezuela in 1854. And in 1870 Paraguay became
the last country in continental Spanish America to abolish slavery.
Almost everywhere slavery had been losing its economic significance
principally because the gradual abolition of the Atlantic slave trade and
the various laws of free birth made it increasingly difficult even to
maintain the relatively small existing slave population.

Only Cuba, along with Brazil the last remaining slave society in the
New World, still regarded slavery as essential to agriculture, that is to
say, the sugar industry. And even there, following the ending of the

Cuban slave trade in the mid-1860s, slavery came under threat and among Cuban planters the discussion of possible alternatives became more common. Whereas the alternative preferred by many of them was the immigration of Spanish peasants, which would involve the replacement of the plantation as a productive unit by smaller units worked by tenant farmers or by sharecroppers, the alternative most often adopted in practice was the importation of Chinese coolies, as in Peru, where they were employed in the guano-producing areas and in agriculture in the coastal region. However, Chinese immigration, which was finally ended by British pressure, never contributed a mass of workers comparable in number to those supplied by the African slave-trade.

During the first war of independence in Cuba (1868–78), both sides tried to gain the support of the slaves by offering freedom to those who fought: as the experience of the Wars of Independence in continental Spanish America had demonstrated, slaves were an attractive source of recruits. And in 1870 the Moret Law, passed by the Spanish Cortes, proclaimed the freedom of children born to slaves. Even though these measures did not lead to a very large number of slaves securing their liberty, they helped to consolidate the consensus of opinion with regard to the inevitable and imminent end of slavery. The end came in the 1880s and, along with other factors, forced some painful readjustments on the Cuban sugar industry.

There was during the period 1850–70 further encroachment on the land of the Indian communities, as there had been ever since independence – indeed before. Moreover, legal reforms undermined the juridical basis of the existence of those communities, either by imposing the division of their territorial patrimony among their members, who became proprietors with the right to alienate their property (a right which was not always recognized legally but which could nevertheless be exercised), or by making the usufruct of communal land revert to the state (which could then sell it, along with the other public land, to private owners). Nowhere, however, did these reforms result in a sudden social cataclysm. In Mexico, for example, the effects of the *Ley Lerdo* (1856) and the other laws of the *Reforma* did not come into full effect until the era of Porfirio Díaz (1876–1911); while in the large areas of the Peruvian highlands the legal abolition of the communities was not followed by their effective liquidation until the twentieth century. The reason was that, as always, such liquidations took place above all when the more general transformation of the economy made it profitable to channel the production of the communal lands towards expanding markets, internal or external, and even in such cases it did not always happen. In Guatemala and northern Peru, for example, the economic sector based on the export of agricultural and livestock products required a labour force recruited from the communities, but expanded into land not held by the communities themselves (as in Guatemala), or expanded into a very small area of the communal lands (as in Peru). The consequence was an actual strengthening of the communities since their economic viability was maintained by the labour of those who had migrated. Thus, there did not always occur a linear development from communal to private individual landholding, to the benefit of the hacienda, and where it did take place it was a comparatively slow process: during the period under consideration here the expansion of agriculture for export scarcely affected the communal lands, and thus did not succeed in undermining decisively their social organization.

The beginning of the transformation of Spanish America's external commercial and financial relations and the consequent improvement in the finances of the state in this period contributed to the growth as well as the increased political and social influence of the cities, especially the capitals. There is no doubt that urban growth in the last analysis depended on the expansion of the export sector. In 1870, it is true, Mexico City with about 220,000 inhabitants remained, as it had been at the beginning of the century, the biggest city in Spanish America. But Havana and Buenos Aires had over 200,000 and Buenos Aires was growing much more rapidly than either and was soon to overtake them both. Lima, whose population had just reached 100,000, was now smaller than Montevideo (with an estimated population in 1870 of 125,000) and Santiago (130,000). Bogotá and Caracas, on the other hand, remained stagnant with 50,000 inhabitants each. There were, of course, cases in which urban expansion took place, not in the political centres, but in the centres of the export trade; thus, in Colombia Barranquilla grew faster than Bogotá, and in Ecuador Guayaquil overtook Quito, though the rate of growth of all these cities was small. In Chile, on the other hand, Santiago overtook Valparaíso in this period.[32]

Foreign trade could not directly give employment to a significant number of people; its influence on urban growth was felt through the expansion of the state and the numbers it employed, and the moderniza-

---

[32] For the figures on the populations of cities in this period, see Richard M. Morse, *Las ciudades latinoamericanas.* II *Desarrollo histórico* (Mexico, 1973), *passim.*

tion of transport which, although it diminished the actual number of people employed, tended to urbanize them; thus, railway and tramway workers replaced carters and muleteers. At the same time the process of modernization did not affect other aspects of the life of the cities: the retail trade and domestic service continued to absorb a disproportionate share of the growing number of those employed in cities. Modernization was perhaps superficial, but evident in, for example, the adoption of such innovations as street-lighting by gas and, as a result of growing public and private prosperity, the building of theatres and performances by artists of international repute. As the cities grew, the residential separation of different social groups increased; although in the past there had been no lack of quarters characterized by poverty and crime, the reasons for which rich and poor found it mutually convenient to live close together had weighed more heavily than was now the case in the expanded and renovated cities. The major cities, indeed, grew sufficiently for property speculation to occur. In the 1850s Mexico City witnessed its earliest urban 'colonies'; in Buenos Aires speculative division into lots did not begin until nearly two decades later, but then it grew very swiftly.[33] Simultaneously there occurred the beginnings of public transport; its earliest significant manifestation was the horse-drawn tramcar. Urban growth, by creating a larger potential market, also encouraged the growth of craft industries, and some factories employing a concentrated labour force, such as breweries and cigarette factories. The population attracted to the tertiary sector was, however, more numerous than that employed in the secondary, and the beginnings of a modern proletariat were more often to be found in transport and public services than in industry.

These growing 'bureaucratic-commercial' cities depended for their prosperity on the expansion of the primary exporting sector. Their social structure became more complex, but at the same time more vulnerable to the effects of developments outside Spanish America. Until the mid-1870s, however, this basic fragility and the possible political consequences of the instability of the economic basis of urban expansion did not constitute a cause for alarm. One reason for this was that, through the expansion of the bureaucracy and of public works, the state could indirectly control wider sectors of the urban population than in the past.

[33] María Dolores Morales, 'El primer fraccionamiento de la ciudad de México, 1840–1899', in Cardoso, *Formación y desarrollo*; James R. Scobie, *Buenos Aires, plaza to suburb, 1870–1910* (New York, 1974).

Another factor was the high proportion of foreigners in the urban economy, and no longer only at the upper levels. Although cases such as Buenos Aires and Montevideo, where in the middle of the century the majority of the economically active population was foreign born (and the proportion was to increase subsequently), were far from being typical, in most of the rapidly growing cities the proportion of foreigners in the retail trade and in light industry was considerable.

Quite apart from the peculiar characteristics of this expanding urban society, the reason for the growing weakness of any specifically urban political expression was the peculiar position of the city in the economic and fiscal system consolidated by the steady progress of the sector based on the export of agricultural and livestock products. The prosperity and stability of both the state and the cities were now dependent on the continued growth of the primary export sector of the Spanish American economies.

9

POLITICS, IDEOLOGY AND SOCIETY IN POST-INDEPENDENCE SPANISH AMERICA

To develop valid general statements about Spanish American politics in the half century that followed independence is a formidable task. The countries were diverse in ethnic composition. Bolivia, Peru, Ecuador, Guatemala and (to a lesser degree) Mexico possessed large Indian populations that were only partially assimilated into the dominant Hispanic culture. Elsewhere the *mestizo* was more clearly predominant numerically and almost all of the population was culturally integrated into Hispanic society. These differences had implications for political behaviour. In those societies in which the lower class was largely composed of people culturally distinct from the Hispanic elite, that class was less likely to become actively involved in politics.

The countries also vary greatly geographically. Much of the population of Mexico, Guatemala and the Andean countries was locked into interior highlands, while in Venezuela, Chile and much of the Río de la Plata significant proportions of the population were located in coastal regions. This difference had important implications for the economies, and hence the politics, of these countries. The earlier onset of intensive trade relations with western Europe in the countries with coastal populations and resources enabled their governments, through customs collections, to develop firmer financial bases, and therefore somewhat greater stability, than was often the case in the landlocked countries. Even here, however, there are not simply two patterns. In the 1830s and 1840s Chile's relative stability encompassed the entire area of the republic, while in the Plata region there were only pockets of order. In Venezuela a period of equilibrium in the prosperous 1830s was followed by one of instability with the decline of coffee prices in the 1840s.

The colonial heritage of these countries also varied in important ways. All shared Spanish language and institutions; all had been governed under the same colonial system. Yet the system and its institutions, while recognizably Spanish, were not precisely the same everywhere at the beginning of the republican era. Because of Mexico's political and economic importance throughout almost three centuries of Spanish rule, the Church there had developed an institutional and economic preponderance that was not matched in more recently developed regions such as Venezuela and the Río de la Plata. Generations of wealthy Spaniards and creoles in Mexico had endowed convents and pious foundations with economic resources that made them a major factor in the national economy. Partly for this reason, in Mexico the power and wealth of the Church became a major issue considerably before it developed much significance elsewhere. And the struggle to dismantle church power in Mexico endured for decades and took on a life-and-death intensity. In the Río de la Plata region and Venezuela, on the other hand, the Church had much shallower roots and the powers and privileges of the colonial church were trimmed with relative ease.

Similarly, the Wars of Independence affected these countries in different ways. In Mexico and, to a lesser degree, Peru, a creole officer corps that had been trained and socialized into military careers by the Spanish on the eve of independence remained substantially intact after independence. As a consequence, in Mexico and Peru the professional military tended to play an important part in politics as a self-conscious, more or less coherent interest group. Military leaders in Mexico frequently intervened in the political process to defend the special privileges (*fueros*) that the military had enjoyed under Spanish rule. In Peru the military *fuero* was less an issue. Yet the politics of the military as a corporate group also left an imprint upon the general politics of the nation, while individual military leaders ruled Peru for most of the nineteenth century. Elsewhere the late colonial military was shattered in the Wars of Independence, but with varied results. The substantial group of revolutionary creole officers who emerged to win the independence of Venezuela (and played an important role in liberating New Granada, Ecuador, Peru and Bolivia as well) attempted to assert for the heroes of independence a privileged place like that enjoyed by the Spanish-trained professionals in Mexico. In Venezuela, however, the independence heroes were never able to act effectively as a corporate interest group, though, as in Peru, individual leaders emerged as dominant figures in politics. In New Granada and Chile, the military leaders of independence quickly became subordinated to the interests of a civilian political elite and after 1830 rarely acted as a corporate group. In Argentina the professional military in effect was destroyed in conflict with local militia groups. It is thus difficult to sustain a single simple generalization about the role of the military in politics.

Beyond the problems inherent in the heterogeneity of the countries of Spanish America, generalization is impeded by the paucity of systematic research into the politics of the period after independence. Aside from some notable contributions in the histories of Mexico and Argentina, there has been little analytical work conforming to current canons of historical research. Some of the best work is still at the first stratum of historical research: the analysis of ideas expressed by the elite in printed materials. There is still little analysis of the actual functioning of the political process or of its social connections. And most existing work attempts to deal with politics entirely at the national level, describing primarily the activities of political actors in the national capital. Apart from scattered work in Argentina and Mexico, there are few studies of the political process at the local level, of the groups and interests in play there, or of their connections to national politics. Thus, we have a distorted view of the political process, as we see it primarily through the eyes of a few articulate members of the political elite struggling for possession of the national state. It is well to remember, however, that in this period most of the national states were extremely weak. They could command very limited revenues. And in many cases the national armies were hardly stronger than the forces that could be rallied on an ad hoc basis in the various provinces. In most countries the provinces were effectively controlled by local landowners and merchants, who were often somewhat removed from national politics. Most of the participants in politics were from the upper sectors, but not all members of the upper classes were participants in national politics.

Perhaps the most important theme in the political history of Spanish America in this period is the difficulty encountered in establishing viable new states after the separation from Spain. Most Spanish American states were unable fully to re-establish the legitimacy of authority enjoyed by the Spanish crown before 1808. Formal constitutional systems were enacted, most of which provided for the transfer of power through elections and guaranteed individual liberties. But these formal constitutional provisions frequently proved a dead letter. No political group believed its adversaries would abide by them. Those who held power bent constitutional principles and often harshly repressed those in opposition in order to retain the government. Those out of power believed, generally correctly, that they could not gain possession of the state by means formally prescribed by the constitution, because those who held the government controlled the elections. Opposition politicians, both military and civilian, therefore waited for, and took advantage of, moments of government weakness in order to overthrow the ruling group. Governments were frequently unable to resist these rebellions, often because they were too weak financially to maintain dominant military force or to provide sufficient patronage to buy the allegiance of potential rebels. In few cases were the political elites sufficiently united to enable their countries to escape frequent *coups d'état*, rebellions and civil wars.

A second, related set of themes has to do with the disintegration – in some respects gradual, in others rapid – of Spanish colonial political, social and economic institutions. In political terms, the movement was not merely from monarchy to republic but also from centralized structures of control to the collapse or loosening of these structures, often in the form of federal systems. Along with the weakening of the central state there occurred a sapping of the strength of corporate groups and the caste distinctions that had dominated colonial society and had played important roles in social governance.

This disruption and disintegration of colonial structures was the result not only of the Wars of Independence and subsequent civil conflicts but also of the dominant liberal ideology. Although elements in the political elites strongly disagreed on some issues, there was, broadly speaking, a general acceptance of many aspects of liberal individualist conceptions of society and economy and (to a lesser degree) of liberal ideals of legal equality. Liberal social and economic ideas were associated with the most powerful and economically advanced western nations. Most of Spanish America's political elite ascribed the economic achievements of Great Britain and the United States to their adherence to liberal principles and attributed the economic backwardness of Spanish America to the dominance of illiberal Spanish institutions and policies. In addition, the French Revolution, despite the violence that attended it, had served at least partially to legitimize the liberal ideal of legal equality. Accordingly, the political elites proceeded, with some interruptions and retrogressions, to abolish or weaken the colonial corporate and caste structures most offensive to liberal principles.

In the first decades of the independence era distinctions among castes were abolished in law, if not always in fact. Simultaneously, the first steps were taken toward the abolition of black slavery, a process brought substantially to its conclusion by the middle of the 1850s. Early on in the independence era the elites also proposed, though they did not immediately bring into effect, the division of communally held Indian lands into individual holdings. Such communal holdings were considered inimical to liberal individualist conceptions of society, as well as to liberal economic principles, which held that only an individual property interest and the free play of economic factors (like Indian land and labour) in the marketplace could bring about greater productivity.

Although Spanish American elites often asserted that the division of Indian lands was in the best interests of the Indians themselves, they were also more than dimly aware that Indian lands once divided were likely to fall into the hands of creole landowners. In some places the appropriation of Indian lands resulted from the necessity, or hope, of more effectively mobilizing land and labour for the production of raw materials for export. Although the first steps toward the destruction of Indian communities were taken at the beginning of the period, the process did not reach its culmination until after 1850 when the Spanish American economies were much more closely integrated into the expanding international economy.

Through the interplay of liberal ideologies and economic realities, some corporate groups that had dominated colonial society, notably the colonial guilds of merchants, mining entrepreneurs and artisans, for the most part disappeared. The merchants' and miners' guilds undoubtedly were affected by the collapse of the Spanish state upon which they depended, by the emigration of their Spanish members, and by the fact that to a considerable extent British and other foreign capital and entrepreneurship replaced Spanish capital and enterprise. Artisans' guilds may have been weakened by the gradual decline of handicrafts under the impact of imported manufactures as much as by ideological aversion to guild organization.

The two largest corporate groups of the colonial period, the Church and the military, remained important, if not dominant, even though their structures were also shaken during the independence period. The Church was weakened temporarily by the fact that part of the clergy, particularly among the clerical hierarchy, had defended the royalist cause and by continuing conflict between the new states and the papacy over the right to appoint bishops. Over the longer term it also suffered from seizures of economic resources by the new governments and from the declining attractiveness of ecclesiastical vocations as alternative careers opened up for the creole upper sectors. The professional military also declined in some places because of the inability of the republican governments to support large military establishments, as well as from civilian opposition to large standing armies. Nevertheless, both the Church and the military remained formidable institutions with which the new states had to contend.

Church and military *fueros*, the special juridical privileges enjoyed by clergy and military officers, flew in the face of the liberal ideal of legal equality and also tended to abridge the authority of the state. Furthermore, in various ways the Church obstructed the realization of the liberal economy: Church holidays impeded productivity, and, indeed, the clergy themselves were held to be unproductive. The tithe, collected upon agricultural products, cut farm profits and thus obstructed agricultural development. *Censos* (quitrents) held by the Church on privately-owned property were believed to impede its free circulation in the marketplace. Similarly, Church properties held in mortmain were thought to obstruct the free circulation of property and, according to liberal assumptions, were not worked productively – in these respects being similar to the Indian communal lands. Many civilian politicians therefore came to view Church power and privilege as an important obstacle to economic growth. Finally, many considered the entrenched power of both the Church and the military as a threat to civilian control of the secular state.

Attempts to implant republican systems politically and individualist conceptions juridically and economically were complemented by efforts to create broad-based and practically oriented educational systems. Political elites were worried that the ignorance of the mass of the people, as well as their lack of experience in self-government, might make impossible the foundation of republican governments. It was imperative to establish primary schools in all communities so that the people might be prepared to exercise their functions as citizens. At the same time, though this intention was less explicitly enunciated, primary education under the control of the state (rather than the Church) would serve to inculcate loyalty to the new polities, whose legitimacy was at best uncertain. In addition, basic education was necessary for each person to behave responsibly in an individualistic social system and to maximize his potential in a free economy. Some leaders in all political groups also sought to transform the higher education of the sons of the elite, turning them from the study of useless scholastic formulas and encouraging experimental instruction in the natural sciences, in the hope of creating a new, more practically oriented, economically enterprising elite.

A number of these ideological and institutional changes had their roots in the colonial period, particularly in the period of the so called Bourbon reforms. The decentralization of political structures in the early republican era has been linked by some scholars to the introduction of the intendancy system in the late colonial period. Similarly, under the late Bourbons there occurred some significant alterations of the caste system, with some tendency to increasing incorporation of castes previously discriminated against. Some Bourbon administrators had also advocated the abandonment of the Habsburg policy of holding Indian communities in isolation from Spanish society and had encouraged the integration of the Indians into the society at large. The late Bourbon period also witnessed the undermining of many Indian communities. Under the Bourbons a series of measures attacked the juridical privileges of the Church and attempted to reduce its drag upon the economy. Finally, the first steps to establish public primary schools and to implant practical, scientific instruction at the secondary level had also been taken during the years after 1780.

But if the nineteenth-century liberalization of Spanish America had some roots in the eighteenth century, the process accelerated and broadened with independence. The process fell roughly into three phases. At the dawn of independence, the Spanish American elites, moved by a spirit of optimism about the political and economic possibilities of their new nations, initiated a considerable array of political, juridical, social, economic, fiscal and educational reforms. In some regions, most notably the Río de la Plata, New Granada and Venezuela, this reformist period fell between 1810 and 1827; in Bolivia it was concentrated in the 1820s; in Mexico and Guatemala its zenith occurred in the early 1830s. This reformist burst was followed almost everywhere, however, by a period of pessimism and conservatism, because of deepening economic crisis, early bouts of political instability, and (in some places) social reactions against reforms. This conservative mood, bringing a pause in efforts at institutional change, dominated Spanish America until the middle of the 1840s. Finally, in a number of countries, from the middle of the 1840s to the 1860s, a new generation, charged with a new optimism, encouraged by more favourable economic circumstances, resumed the liberalization process with renewed vigor.

In many respects the institutional changes of the period were more of form than of substance. The new republics, as indicated, often failed to conform to constitutionalist ideals. While upholding the fiction of an individualist society of putatively equal atoms, the elite, as well as others, in fact lived according to the norms established by traditional patron-client relationships in societies marked by great economic and social inequality. Attacks upon ecclesiastical and military privilege hardly dented the political influence of the Church or the power of the military. Many more schools were envisioned by legislators than were actually constructed by villages, and the practical reorientation of the sons of the elite proved a will-o'-the-wisp. Nevertheless, the new forms were believed in, and did not fail to have some influence upon attitudes and behaviour.

Finally the political effects of the region's economic engagement with, and dependence upon, the more developed Atlantic world in the period 1810–70 are too important to go unmentioned. At first, the severe trade imbalances, and consequent monetary and economic constriction, endured by the new Spanish American nations, as well as the mounting external debts of their governments, played an important part in destabilizing these new polities. These problems worked together to create the atmosphere of conservatism that dominated from the end of the 1820s to the middle of the 1840s. The growth of the export economies and the expansion of trade that set in after the middle of the 1840s encouraged a new burst of liberal enthusiasm in many countries. The political effects of increased integration into the international economy varied from country to country. Chile, through its exports and the notable pre-eminence of the port of Valparaiso on the Pacific coast, achieved a prosperity that aided the creation of national unity and a stable state as early as the 1830s. Elsewhere economies that were more or less integrated in the colonial era shattered under the impact of external economic forces. For example, in the late colonial period much of present day Argentina was knitted together economically by the silver trade between Potosí and Buenos Aires. In the independence era this vital economic link disappeared, as Potosí both was cut off from Buenos Aires and declined as a mining centre. Further, as Buenos Aires became an effective exporter of pastoral products and an importer of foreign manufactures, it became politically disengaged from the interior provinces, which were barred from effective exporting by transportation costs and which could offer little of value to Buenos Aires in competition with foreign manufactures. Similarly, in New Granada after independence the improvement of communications with more advanced Atlantic nations, while internal transportation remained backward, encouraged the fragmentation of an inter-regional economy that had flourished in the colonial period. Trade of cotton textiles from Socorro in the eastern part of the country to gold-producing Antioquia in the west diminished as Antioquia's gold increasingly was used to purchase foreign cloth. In a number of Spanish American countries, some regions traded more with the outside world than with other provinces, and political ties were weakened as a consequence.

A deep and abiding problem faced by Spanish American elites was that of constructing political systems that could command effective and enduring authority. In constructing new states, Spanish American leaders were influenced by, and tried somehow to make compatible, a number of conflicting elements. No matter how hostile they had become to Spanish rule during the struggle for independence, they could hardly escape the Spanish political tradition in which they had been nurtured; no matter how much they might formally disavow tradition, it lived on, often in formal institutions and, in any case, informally in modes of political behaviour. But, inevitably, they were strongly influenced by French and British political examples, both directly and through the medium of Spanish liberalism, as well as by North American models. Major political events, particularly in France, from the French Revolution to the Revolutions of 1830 and 1848, clearly affected elite conceptions about proper political modes. Salient European political thinkers, from Montesquieu and Rousseau to Constant and Bentham to Tocqueville, deeply influenced their ideas about the structure of political institutions and the functioning of the political process. One problem confronted by the elite was how to reconcile Spanish political culture with British, French and North American political models. Further, this problem had to be worked out in an economic context that in many places was extremely unfavourable to the maintenance of stable states of any kind.

The first, and most enduring problem was that of reconstructing legitimate authority in the absence of the king. With the removal of the Spanish crown as symbol of authority, could an adequate substitute be found? Furthermore, there was the manner in which the authority of the

Spanish king was conceived. Since the beginning of the sixteenth century, the Spanish monarchs had thoroughly dominated the Cortes the nobility, the Church and the other potential power-holders in Spanish society. Consequently the concepts of representative govern ment and, even more, of popular sovereignty were, at best, weakly developed in Spain, and power was concentrated in the hands of the monarch. The king's power was conceived to be virtually absolute and unrestricted. Could or should the new Spanish American government be constructed along these traditional Spanish authoritarian lines? Or should the Spanish American elite abandon its political tradition in favour of the liberal constitutional models manifested in England English America and (very briefly) in the French Revolution? Finally there was the question of controlling the strongest corporate groups in Spanish American society, the Church and the military. Under the Spanish system, it was the king alone, ultimately, who could command the loyalty and obedience of these corporate bodies. In the absence of the king, would the new states be able to exert equally effective authority over them?

None of these issues was resolved in the first stage of the independence period. The earliest governments (1810–13) appealed to conceptions of popular sovereignty, but also recognized the authority of the captive Ferdinand VII. The problem of adequately symbolizing authority had to be confronted only when the final break with Ferdinand VII came. In any case, in the first stage of independence, despite their formal allegiance to Ferdinand VII, the authority of the various juntas and provisional governments was incomplete at best. In Buenos Aires and Santiago contending groups resorted to *coups d'état*, while in the Río de la Plata New Granada and Venezuela inter-regional civil wars broke out over the efforts of the colonial capitals to control the provinces.

In this early period of disorder, the problem of controlling the established corporate groups emerged almost immediately. In Buenos Aires in particular, but also to a lesser degree in Caracas, Bogotá and Santiago, the militia had played an important role in deposing Spanish administrators. The militia continued to be an important political force making and unmaking governments, a role by no means diminished as its ranks expanded in the struggle against Spanish centres of power. In this period the question at issue was the control of the military in a very direct sense; the question of military *fueros* (privileges) had not yet been raised

Control of, and support by, the Church was equally critical to the survival of the new governments. The earliest creole leaders were solicitous of the Church, generally making few alterations in its status as the official religion. Although the newly constituted governments almost invariably abolished the Inquisition, this was not viewed as an attack upon the Church *per se*, but simply as the elimination of an institution whose excesses were out of keeping with post-Enlightenment western states. In maintaining traditional state protection of the Church creole leaders at the same time claimed the powers of patronage, most particularly the right to present (in effect, to appoint) clergymen for ecclesiastical offices. The new governments claimed this right enjoyed by the Spanish monarchs, on the ground that it was inherent in sovereignty. Papal authorities and the local church hierarchies just as steadfastly denied this claim, arguing that the patronage was granted solely to the Spanish crown. In general, the new governments were only partially successful in controlling the Church and in using its influence to sustain the state. While many in the lower clergy were sympathetic to the new autonomous governments, the Church hierarchy, with certain exceptions, was hostile to the new Spanish American republics. In Venezuela, clerical attacks upon the new republic played a part in its downfall in 1812. Elsewhere, the creole elite was more successful in harnessing the Church to the cause of independence even though the question of state control of ecclesiastical appointments remained unresolved.

While the earliest creole leaders sought to maintain continuity by recognizing Ferdinand VII as the symbolic head of government and by attempting to perpetuate the traditional relationship of state and Church, the political conceptions embodied in the new governments represented clear ruptures with the past. All of the new governments were stamped by the influence of Enlightenment rationalism and most were constructed along the lines of the republican models of the United States and the French Revolution. With the exception of those in the Río de la Plata, almost all of the revolutionary leaders moved quickly to write constitutions, thus expressing the belief that the state must be subject to a written constitution. Implicitly or explicitly these constitutions were based upon the concept of the social contract. The first constitutions (in Venezuela, New Granada and Chile, 1811–12) were proclaimed to be founded upon popular sovereignty, with the law considered the expression of the 'general will' – though usually the 'general will' was interpreted to mean the vote of the majority. The general will was to be exercised, of course, through representative government. Almost all of these earliest

constitutions proclaimed the existence of inalienable natural rights
(liberty, legal equality, security, property); many provided for freedom
of the press; and some attempted to establish jury trials. Almost all
sought to protect these rights through the separation of powers and by
making the executive branch relatively weaker than the legislature.[1]

The early experiments in liberal constitutionalism in Venezuela, New
Granada and Chile collapsed, destroyed by struggles among elite factions
and between rival regions, in the process of which power gravitated into
the hands of a single Supreme Director. Soon afterward creole government itself was annihilated by Spanish forces in all three places. Later
critics, echoing Simón Bolívar in 1819, have tended to emphasize that the
early creole leaders were undone in part by the Enlightenment assumptions that guided them: an excessive optimism about human nature, an
excessive trust in the capacity of laws and constitutions to mould the
behaviour of men, a failure to consider the weight of Spanish tradition
and Spanish colonial history in influencing real political behaviour.
Liberal constitutional principles, including most particularly the separation of powers and constitutional checks upon the power of the executive, flew in the face of Spanish political traditions, in which authority
was concentrated in the hands of the crown, and the realities of Spanish
America at the time. By adopting institutions inspired by Enlightenment
ideas and foreign models, according to this view, creole leaders assured
their own political failure. Such alien institutions were inevitably
doomed to a speedy collapse.

While there is merit in this view, the creation of these institutions may
have been influenced by more than foreign models. The establishment of
constitutionally restricted, weak executives, while taking foreign-in-
spired forms, may also be seen as expressing a local reaction against the
dominance of colonial governors. Similarly, the adoption of the federal
structure, which generally has been attributed to the influence of the
United States' constitution, was also a response to political realities. In
New Granada and Venezuela in 1810–11 and in Mexico in 1822–4, the
various provinces had developed autonomous governments that were
extremely resistant to centralized rule.[2] And in Chile federalism emerged

1 Simon Collier, *Ideas and politics of Chilean independence, 1808–1833* (Cambridge, 1967), 140, 154, 177–
   8, *passim*; Antonio Pombo and José Joaquín Guerra, *Constituciones de Colombia* (4 vols., Bogotá,
   1951), I, 122–9, 144–7, 151–7, 189–90, 246–50, 261–2, 273, 294–303; II, 97–106; Ulises Picon
   Rivas, *Indice constitucional de Venezuela* (Caracas, 1944), 9–15.
2 On Mexico, see in particular Nettie Lee Benson, *La diputación provincial y el federalismo mexicano*
   (Mexico, 1955), 85ff.

temporarily in 1826 in part because of the collapse of the central government in 1824–5.

After 1815 there was a general tendency towards creating governments with strong executives and centralized control of provincial administration. In part this phenomenon was fostered by the mobilization required to defeat the Spanish royalist forces on the battlefield. Many creole leaders also believed stronger, more centralized governments would be necessary to gain the confidence of the European powers, to obtain loans as well as diplomatic recognition. There also was some fear that, even after independence from Spain had been achieved, Spanish American governments would have to be strong if they were to resist intervention by other foreign powers. The reactionary, anti-republican atmosphere of Restoration Europe both reinforced these fears and also subjected Spanish American leaders to more conservative ideological influences than they had known before 1815.

But the tendency to increasing executive power and centralization continued after the Wars of Independence were over, after Spanish American independence had been recognized by the major powers, after the Revolution of 1830 in France. In fact, the tendency to centralization became particularly pronounced between 1826 and 1845. Local conditions, existing before 1825 and continuing through to the 1840s, therefore, played an important role in the centralizing process. At the dawn of independence there had existed a political atmosphere of optimism which had encouraged the utopian constitutional formulations of 1811–12. After 1825, however, continuing political disorder and the onset of economic crisis created an atmosphere of greater pessimism about the social order and the economic and political prospects of Spanish America. During the period from 1820 to 1845 political leaders frequently expressed their fears of the imminence (or the actuality) of anarchy. The great preoccupation of these decades then was the pursuit of political order.

There was, however, some disagreement about how that order was to be achieved. Some, particularly the university educated, looked to various sorts of European constitutional forms as keys to stability. Others, for the most part among the military and the less well educated, preferred to dispense with such constitutional frippery and looked to the use of force, if not terror, as a means of maintaining order.

The desire to establish a stronger constitutional state after 1815 is observable in, for example, the effort, relatively transitory, to erect constitutional monarchies headed by European princes, a pattern most visible in Argentina (1814–18) and Chile (1818). In many cases proponents of monarchy sought to reach accomodation with the reactionary monarchies of post-Napoleonic Europe. In both Argentina and Chile gestures towards monarchy were made in the hope of gaining recognition of their independence and, if possible, protection from external attack. The monarchist schemes of 1814–19 also reflected the conviction of at least some leaders that constitutional monarchy would bolster internal stability. General Manuel Belgrano, in arguing for constitutional monarchy in the 1816 Congress at Tucumán, emphasized both the internal disorder in the Plata region and the dominant political atmosphere in Europe; the adoption of monarchy would be politically advisable as well as diplomatically prudent.

After 1819, when the idea of constitutional monarchy lost its reputability in the Río de la Plata, constitutional monarchy as a means of achieving political stability had important support only in Mexico. There, as early as 1830, Lucas Alamán gave the British envoy to understand that because of Mexico's chronic disorder the idea of importing a European prince was gaining adherents. Such a proposal was publicly discussed in the 1840s, though its proponents probably still were quite few. Finally, between 1864 and 1867 the only actual experiment with rule by a European prince was attempted when Mexican conservatives, in league with Napoleon III, imported Archduke Maximilian of Austria as emperor of Mexico. As in the earlier cases, however, internal political stability was not the only goal in view. For Mexican conservatives the French-backed monarchy was a last gasp effort to recoup declining political strength. For both Mexican conservatives and Napoleon III the experiment ended in ignominious defeat; when Maximilian was executed in 1867, Mexican conservatism as a political movement died with him.

Constitutional monarchy was never a success in Spanish America. In the early stages (1810–30) it was hard to find a generally acceptable European candidate. Because of the intransigence of Ferdinand VII, a candidate closely linked to the Spanish monarchy proved impossible. On the other hand, it was hard to find anyone else acceptable to both England and France – a prerequisite for the success of the measure as a diplomatic gambit. Even if a candidate acceptable to the European powers were found, he would have been an artificial graft (as Maximilian later proved to be), lacking the legitimacy that was supposed to be the key to the success of monarchy. Attempts at homegrown monarchy failed for similar reasons. Belgrano's proposal to enthrone a descendant of the Inca might offer some colour of legitimacy, but was, given creole contempt for the Indian, inherently absurd. Nor would a creole monarch do, as General Agustín Iturbide discovered in Mexico in 1821–2. The elite could hardly accept monarchical or imperial rule by someone already known close at hand as a man of no finer clay than the rest. Most important, perhaps, after the American and French Revolutions the idea of monarchy lost much of its appeal. While the solidity of the British constitutional monarchy was admired everywhere in Spanish America, monarchy as a system represented a remnant of the past. In the optimism of the first years of independence, most in the creole elite preferred to associate themselves with republicanism, a system that seemed to represent the wave of the future. Also, in the early phases, the erection of republics helped to justify the break with Spain. Later, after the early optimism and revolutionary enthusiasm had begun to fade, the now-established republican mode had begun to develop an institutional momentum. After 1820, therefore, most efforts at consolidating central control were at least formally republican in character.

Two basic constitutional formulas stand out in the period from 1819 to 1845: that of centralized republics similar in form to the Spanish Constitution of Cádiz of 1812, and that of the Napoleonic state as advocated by Simón Bolívar. The first type, by far the most common, tended to have broad support among civilian elites, and in particular among lawyers and the university-educated, while the Napoleonic–Bolivarian model tended to have more adherents in the military.

The mark of the Constitution of Cádiz is evident in most of the constitutions of the 1820s and 1830s: in those of Gran Colombia (1821), of New Granada (1830, 1832) and Venezuela (1830); in those of Peru of 1823 and 1828; in the Argentine constitution of 1826, that of Uruguay in 1830, and the Chilean constitution of 1828. The Mexican constitution of 1824 also was heavily influenced by the Spanish constitution but diverged importantly in having a federal structure. Most of these charters created councils of state to advise the president; most provided the executive with only a suspensive veto; most asserted the principle of ministerial responsibility at least by requiring ministers to co-sign all decrees. Many followed the Constitution of Cádiz in attempting to bolster the power of the legislature by instituting a permanent committee of the Congress to act for the legislature when it was out of session. All, with the exception of the Mexican constitution, provided for centrally-appointed provincial officers (variously called intendants, prefects or governors), though in many cases the president had to choose these from panels nominated by provincial bodies. Finally, almost all of these charters created variants of the Spanish *diputación provincial*, an elected body that was to aid the intendant or governor in promoting education and economic development and in assessing and collecting taxes. As in Spain, the presumed functions of these bodies was essentially advisory and administrative, not legislative. In Mexico, however, these *diputaciones provinciales* quickly evolved into full-scale provincial legislatures. In New Granada this evolution was slower and more stunted: until the 1840s their decrees had to be approved by the national legislature. Elsewhere, as in Peru and Uruguay, these bodies either died or never became significant. Thus, following the model of the Spanish constitution of 1812, the creole elite in many places attempted to establish a centralist system, bedizened with the ornaments of constitutionalism.

Spanish American elites were probably attracted to the 1812 Constitution because it represented an effort to do essentially the same thing that they were trying to do: to introduce Anglo-French liberal constitutional ideals into a Spanish political structure. There was, however, one significant difference between the tasks of the constitution-writers of Cádiz and those of the authors of the Spanish American charters of later years. In Cádiz the Spanish liberals were preoccupied with circumscribing the power of an absolutist king, turning him into a constitutional monarch. In Spanish America, however, the same constitutional model was used in an attempt to strengthen, rather than to weaken, central authority as previously constituted in the earliest Spanish American charters. Furthermore, most of the Spanish American constitutions made a significant addition to the Cádiz model, permitting their presidents the use of extraordinary powers in time of external threat or internal disturbance. This escape hatch from the formal constraints of constitutionalism was put to considerable use throughout Spanish America and frequently served to nullify in fact the liberties solemnly proclaimed in the constitutions.

In some countries which opted for the Cádiz model support for centralized authority was not unanimous; elements in the political elite continued to argue for federal structures. In Colombia in 1821, in Chile through the end of the 1820s, and in Mexico and Argentina throughout the period, important political figures supported the federal system, because of regional antagonisms or provincial distrust of the capital but also because they considered the federal structure a barrier against tyranny. In many countries, however, federalists were overwhelmed by those who feared that the federal system would lead (or had led) to anarchy. Usually those who advocated a centralist state were willing to admit the theoretical desirability of federalism from the point of view of liberal constitutionalist principles, but in the same breath they contended the system was 'too perfect', impracticable for Spanish America. The centralist litany held that Spanish rule, by keeping the people ignorant and denying them political experience, had left them unprepared for so extreme a version of democratic republican government. The populace as a whole lacked sufficient enlightenment and civic responsibility (civic virtue) to be able to make wise choices at the local level. Further, there were not enough competent men to fill all of the provincial offices that would be required. Finally, the system, with its multiplication of offices, implied costs which the Spanish American republics could not sustain. Rather than risk the anarchy that surely would follow upon the adoption of the federal system, centralists argued, a little bit of liberty must be sacrificed in order to obtain order. Civic liberties, they contended, would be adequately protected by the division of powers, alternation in office, and other constitutional restraints at the national level, which each of the Cádiz model charters prescribed.

Distrust of the political capacity of the mass of the people was reflected in the property qualifications established in almost all of the centralist constitutions of the 1820s and 1830s. However, as in other cases, it is difficult to discern the degree to which the establishment of property restrictions on suffrage expressed a current of conservatism within Spanish America and to what extent these restrictions were adopted in imitation of European models. European constitutional example, as well as the theories of leading European constitutionalists like Benjamin Constant, provided ample sanction for strict property qualifications of the sort adopted throughout Spanish America.

There were some exceptions to the general tendency to centralization in Spanish America that marked the 1820s and 1830s. But these exceptions were in some cases more or less temporary aberrations, as in the case of the Chilean federalist constitution of 1826–8. And in other cases they were produced by the peculiarities of local political history. For example, as independence from Spain came rather late to Mexico (1821) and to

Peru (1824), they began the sequence of constitutional evolution later than some other regions. Thus, the first Peruvian constitution (1823) corresponded to the earlier constitutions of Venezuela, New Granada and Chile (1811) in establishing a weak, legislature-dominated, plural executive, while the Mexican constitution of 1824 created the federal structure of the 1811 constitutions of Venezuela and New Granada. But both Peru and Mexico rather quickly followed the general tendency to increasing executive power and centralization. The Peruvian constitution of 1823, with its plural executive, was overthrown almost immediately and from that time onward Peru was in the hands of military caudillos operating through a strong presidential regime. In Mexico the federal constitution suffered *de facto* abridgements in 1830–2 and was formally replaced by a centralized system from 1836 through to 1846. The greatest exception to the pattern, Argentina, reflects another kind of local peculiarity. In the Río de la Plata attempts to establish a centralized system culminated in the constitution of 1826. However, the centralist system broke down almost immediately as provincial caudillos and their local backers asserted their independence from Buenos Aires, an independence ratified in the Federal Pact of 1831. During the 1830s and 1840s Juan Manuel de Rosas in Buenos Aires proved able to influence the political direction of the other provinces, but such powers as he had over them were exercised informally and were not recognized in a constitutional system.

While approximations of the Cádiz constitution were most favoured among university-educated politicians between 1820 and 1845, some important elements in the political elite – most notably in the military – believed even this model was not strong enough to provide stable government in Spanish America. Men of this persuasion, of whom Simón Bolívar was the most prominent, shared many of the same assumptions as the proponents of the Cádiz model. They agreed on the danger of anarchy and on the fact that the Spanish American populace lacked the political experience and civic virtue required to sustain a full-blown liberal republic. Yet they differed on the conclusions they drew from these premises. The civilian exponents of the Cádiz constitutions assumed that, while the people could not be trusted, there existed an elite large enough and enlightened enough to run centralized republics. As Fernando de Peñalver, a Venezuelan centralist, explained to his fellow delegates at the Colombian constitutional convention of 1821, 'I do not see virtues in the people, although I see enlightenment in the Congress.'[3] In particular, these centralist republicans believed, along with their federalist peers, in the importance of the principle of alternation in power as a protection against tyranny. Bolívar and other military leaders, on the other hand, did not entirely trust even the elite to conduct politics in an orderly and enlightened manner. They therefore sought to establish a more paternalistic republic, in effect, a constitutional monarchy in republican dress. While Bolívar's constitutional proposals provided for popular elections, much of the power was to be held by men who, once in office, were not subject to elections – most notably a life-president and a hereditary or life-senate. Bolívar hoped that these would provide elements of permanence and continuity that would help to stabilize the new republics.

For Bolívar and others of his inclination, the most appealing constitutional models were those of the British constitutional monarchy and the Napoleonic Consular Constitutions of 1799 and 1802 (which were in part derived from the British model). Generally, the constitutional solutions they supported provided for presidents with long terms of office (eight or ten years, or, in the case of Bolívar's last constitutional schemes, life) and for multiple legislative bodies, one of which would have lifetime or hereditary membership. An early example of a constitutional plan following this model was a proposed outline by Bolívar in 1819 at the Congress of Angostura, which called for a hereditary senate modelled on the British House of Lords and for a strong president. While Bolívar's Angostura plan had a British model, his Bolivian constitution of 1826 was more influenced by the Napoleonic constitutions. The president in effect would be a life consul, with power to designate the vice-president, his successor, as well as the secretaries of state. The president could not be held responsible for the acts of his administration; only the vice-president and the secretaries of state could be impeached. Beyond his extensive appointment powers, the president had the authority freely to adjourn and convoke the legislative bodies. The system was further to be anchored by a chamber of censors (one of three legislative bodies), to be appointed for life, whose duties primarily were to promote and protect the exercise of civic virtue (safeguarding freedom of the press and vigilance against the abuse of authority were two of its jobs).

[3] Colombia, Congreso General, 1821, *Congreso de Cúcuta, 1821: libro de actas* (Bogotá, 1971), 60.

During the 1830s and 1840s the Napoleonic–Bolivarian model was resurrected by several generals who had served under Bolívar and clearly were influenced by him. In 1837 General Andrés Santa Cruz, having temporarily unified Peru and Bolivia in a confederation, promulgated a constitution in which the executive was headed by a protector, with a ten-year term, and in which there was a lifetime senate, whose members were appointed by the protector. In 1843 a similar constitution was proclaimed in Ecuador by another former subordinate of Bolívar, General Juan José Flores, in this case with an eight-year president and the familiar lifetime senate. A modified version of the same constitutional model was implanted by conservative elements in Mexico in 1836.

The constitutions based on the Napoleonic–Bolivarian model were short-lived. In Bolivia and Peru, Bolívar actually succeeded temporarily in imposing his constitution in 1826; but the governments he erected collapsed, and his constitutions were abandoned practically as soon as he removed himself from the scene. When Bolívar attempted to impose his ideas on the Republic of Colombia between 1826 and 1830, he encountered such opposition among the civilian elite that he found it necessary to establish dictatorial rule; the dictatorship in turn provoked an attempt upon his life (September 1828) by younger members of the civilian elite in Bogotá, and Bolívar soon had to admit failure, resigning his office as his enterprise dissolved about him. The Santa Cruz and Flores variations on the Bolivarian constitutions also were short-lived, in each case lasting no more than two years – though that of Santa Cruz was defeated by external intervention from Chile as well as by internal revolt.

The Bolivarian model failed everywhere in part because to many in the civilian elite it smacked too much of monarchy. In addition, by prescribing a life-president and life-censors, Bolívar's scheme violated one of the constitutional principles that university-educated liberals held dear: the principle of alternation in office as a protection against tyranny. Civilians also feared that military leaders would monopolize the presidency. Whether from principle or self-interest, the Bolivarian constitutions were vigorously fought by educated liberals, led in Peru by the priest, Francisco Javier Luna Pizarro, and in Colombia by General Francisco de Paula Santander and a clutch of young lawyers.

Although Bolívar and many among the university-educated were mortal antagonists in the years 1826–30, their differing governmental prescriptions drew on the same body of political thought, most particularly on the doctrines of Benjamin Constant, which were widely circulated in a Spanish translation published in Spain at the time of the liberal revolution of 1820. But liberals tended to emphasize more than Bolívar the individual liberties side of Constant (jury trials, freedom of the press, inviolability of property, restrictions upon the military). Bolívar, on the other hand, stressed the stabilizing elements in Constant, in particular in his conception of the division of powers. Constant conceived of the constitutional monarch as a neutral balance wheel, moderating conflicts among the executive, the representative and judicial powers. Bolívar followed this scheme both in distinguishing the president (constitutional monarch) and the actions of his ministers and in placing the moderating power in the hands of the censors. This Constantian conception of a moderating power was also found in the Mexican centralist constitution of 1836, known as the Seven Laws.

The universal influence of Constant in the 1820s and 1830s is only one indication of the hegemony of moderate European constitutional ideas among Spanish American intellectuals. Whether in Chilean newspapers of the 1820s, the Uruguayan constitutional convention of 1830, or the libraries of New Granadan politicians in the 1840s, the three authors most frequently encountered were Montesquieu, Constant and Bentham. Rousseau, of great help in justifying the establishment of revolutionary governments between 1810 and 1815, was decreasingly relevant to Spanish American concerns after 1820. What most interested the political elite were those works on the practical arts of government, rather than abstract, theoretical treatises on the foundations of sovereignty. Machiavelli figured prominently in libraries of the period. But constitutionalist authors were also consulted as helpful guides. The civilian elite turned to Constant's *Curso de política* for its usefulness in constitution-writing. Of Bentham they read less the philosophical early writings than those works that seemed to offer some guidance in legislation and jurisprudence (the treatises on civil and penal legislation, on judicial evidence, on penal law and the essays on political tactics and parliamentary fallacies). Many other works to which the elites were attracted also were viewed as manuals for the conduct of constitutional government: for example, Cottu on the administration of criminal justice in England and the spirit of English government, Filangieri on legislation, Beccaria and Dumont on criminal punishments, Guizot on the death penalty, Say on political economy. After 1835, Alexis de Tocqueville's *Democracy in America* joined Montesquieu, Constant and Bentham as universally-read authority on the practice of constitutional government. For those of conservative disposition a list of the 1830s or 1840s might also include Chateaubriand, Burke, and Cousin.[4]

Notably missing from the intellectual armature of politicians active between 1820 and 1845 were the extremes of European political thought of the time. In their libraries and public discussions the absolutist royalists, de Maistre and de Bonald, rarely appeared. At the same time, French socialist writings left little imprint on those who dominated politics before 1845. The most notable case of socialist influence in the 1830s is that of the Argentine Esteban Echeverría, who was especially current with Saint-Simonian writings. But Echeverría was really a man of a younger generation not yet contending for power.

Between 1820 and 1845 liberal-to-moderate European constitutionalism thus formed the intellectual stock of educated leaders of all political factions, whether 'extremist' (*exaltado*), moderate, or conservative. There was, of course, some disagreement about aspects of this early nineteenth-century list of political authorities. Bentham and Destutt de Tracy were more widely read than they were accepted. Both were bitterly attacked by political conservatives for their 'materialist' (i.e. sensationalist) philosophies. Yet those conservatives who most objected to Bentham's materialism were nevertheless orthodox liberal constitutionalists. Joaquín Mosquera, a notable anti-Benthamite in New Granada, attacked the English utilitarian partly on the ground that he denied the doctrine of natural rights. Another strong anti-utilitarian, the Peruvian, José María de Pando, was one of the few political intellectuals in Spanish America somewhat influenced by the arch-conservatism of de Bonald and de Maistre. Yet in his constitutional prescriptions even Pando argued not for absolutism but for a decorous, Constantian constitutional monarchy, with guarantees of liberty of the press and trial by jury.[5] Thus, even in a period of marked social and political conservatism, liberal constitutional ideals continued to dominate among the university-educated elite.

Despite an at least intellectual acceptance of constitutionalist ideas by

---

[4] Collier, *Ideas and politics*, 171–6; Juan E. Pivel Devoto, *Historia de los partidos y de las ideas políticas en el Uruguay*, II. *La definición de los bandos (1829–1838)* [the only volume published] (Montevideo, 1956), 53; lists of books in mortuaria, Archivo Nacional de Colombia, Sección República, Notaría 2a, 1840, tomo 43, fos. 57r–58r; 1851, tomo 264, fos. 759r–763v; 1852, tomo 269, fos. 26r–29v; Notaría 3a, 1848, tomo 435, fos. 534v–6r. See also Charles A. Hale, *Mexican liberalism in the age of Mora, 1821–1853* (New Haven, 1968), 55–60, 76, 149–54, *passim*. For sources favoured by an extreme conservative in the 1840s, see Bartolomé Herrera, *Escritos y discursos* (2 vols., Lima, 1929), I, 95–6.

[5] José María de Pando, *Pensamientos y apuntes sobre moral y política* (Cádiz, 1837), 3–5, 14–22, 62, 110–11.

the university-educated, constitutionalist precepts often were not observed in fact. Not everyone active in politics was committed to these ideas. University men predominantly wrote the constitutions and laws, filled most of the seats of the legislatures and held the cabinet posts. But they were not the only political actors, even though they generally had the most to do with the formal aspects of statecraft. Important political roles, as holders of ultimate power, were also played by others – professional military officers, regional caudillos, merchants and landowners – who often knew little of liberal constitutional ideas and cared less. For intellectual politicians the forms of politics, the ideas embodied in laws and constitutions were important. They cared about these ideas and their presumed social consequences, and also these ideas and institutions signified political respectability, in their own eyes as well as in those of civilized Europe. But for those not socialized to European political modes through travel or university education, this sort of consideration had much less weight. Professional military officers were often motivated in politics by concern to protect their reputations, sometimes by a desire to protect the military as an interest group and on occasion by a concern to represent broader social interests. Regional caudillos had to take care to satisfy the local landed oligarchies who often formed the bases of their power. The primary concern of large landowners was to have the support or benevolent neutrality of local officials in their disputes over land tenure. Merchants worried less about the form of government than about whether commercial regulations would be favourable, or at least predictable. Thus, while political ideologies and the institutions they embodied stirred the emotions of educated politicians, to many others they were of little significance.

This lack of concern for constitutional principles was piquantly expressed by Diego Portales, a merchant and dominant political figure in Chile in the 1830s. In 1834 Portales, then governor of Valparaiso, vented his outrage at the opinion of a conservative jurist, Mariano Egaña, that he could not have a dissident arrested without a court order. (Egaña had further enraged Portales by sending along a book on habeas corpus.)[6]

In sum, to follow the opinion of the jurist Egaña, confronting a threat to overthrow authority, the Government ought to cross its arms, unless the suspect was caught in the act. . . . With the men of the law one cannot come to an understanding; and if it's that way, what [expletive] purpose do Constitutions and papers serve, if they are incapable of providing a remedy to an evil that is

---

[6] Raúl Silva Castro (ed.), *Ideas y confesiones de Portales* (Santiago de Chile, 1954), 57–8.

known to exist. . . . In Chile the law doesn't serve for anything but to produce anarchy, the lack of sanctions, licentiousness, eternal law suits. . . . If I, for example, imprison an individual who is conspiring, I violate the law. Damned law, then, if it does not allow the Government to proceed freely in the opportune moment.

University-educated politicians who were nurtured in constitutionalist principles also found themselves betraying these principles in the exercise of power. Vicente Rocafuerte, for example, a leader of the liberal opposition in Mexico in the 1820s and in Ecuador until 1834, once in power and facing armed rebellion in Ecuador in 1835, declared that 'only terror' could reduce the rebels to order and 'conserve the first of all laws which is that of public tranquillity'.

The only course that I have is that they tremble before me. If it were necessary, I will know how to convert myself into a Sylla [Sulla] to save my country from the anarchy that is trying to devour it. A true lover of enlightenment and civilization, I consent to pass for a tyrant.[7]

And, as good as his word, he had dozens of rebels shot.

The frequent breach of proclaimed constitutionalist principles in nineteenth century Spanish America has been the subject of various interpretations. One view is that constitutionalism was necessarily a dead letter because it completely out of keeping with Spanish political traditions.[8] It may also be suggested, however, that, at least in some cases, the violation of constitutional principles was inherent in the task of the educated elite. Their effort to overthrow Spanish social, economic and political institutions and to implant new ones based on British, French and other foreign models was, in effect, revolutionary.[9] Consequently, it is not surprising that in attempting to introduce these changes they frequently resorted to violent measures.

To a considerable degree authority was not successfully embodied in the formal institutions envisioned in Spanish America's many constitutions;

---

[7] Quoted in Richard Pattee, *Gabriel García Moreno y el Ecuador de su tiempo* (Quito, 1941), 56.

[8] Glen Dealy, 'La tradición de la democracia monista en América Latina', *Estudios Andinos*, 4/1 (1974–5), 159–201.

[9] See Ralph Lee Woodward, 'Social revolution in Guatemala: the Carrera revolt', in *Applied enlightenment: 19th century liberalism* (Middle American Research Institute, Publication 23, Tulane University, New Orleans, 1972), 49–53, *passim*. See also Charles Hale's discussion of the contradiction between the liberals' goal of constitutionalism, which implied limited governmental powers, and their desire to break down corporate barriers to individualism, which required a strong state, 'José María Luis Mora and the structure of Mexican liberalism', *Hispanic American Historical Review*, 45/2 (1965), 196–227.

rather it was incarnated in persons. Authority gravitated into the hands of strong leaders, who tended to stand above laws or constitutions. These leaders often were and are thought of as caudillos – men whose force of character enabled them to command the personal loyalty of a substantial band of followers, and who mobilized their adherents to challenge constituted authority or to seize power by violence or the threat of violence.

The term caudillo refers to any kind of pre-eminent leader, and it was used in this sense between 1810 and 1870. Most caudillos, particularly in the first decades of the period, were specifically military leaders who had gained stature during the Wars of Independence. But the term was also applied in these years to other kinds of leaders. In the 1820s, the Peruvian General Agustín Gamarra, himself clearly a caudillo, used the word with reference to the political leadership of a bishop.[10] In current scholarship regarding the nineteenth century the term tends to be used somewhat more narrowly than it was by contemporaries. The caudillo is now generally thought of as one who used violence or the threat of violence for political ends – whether as a professional officer commanding regular army units, or as a militia officer or civilian-on-horseback leading militia or irregular forces into political battle, or (more broadly) as an essentially civilian leader who engaged in violent repression (as in the cases of Dr Francia in Paraguay or Diego Portales in Chile).

Before 1840, most of the men whom we currently think of as caudillos were individuals with some kind of military attainment before their political careers began – soldiers of the independence or provincial militia leaders like Juan Manuel de Rosas, who gained fame as a fighter of Indians. After the 1840s, as the generals of the independence passed from the scene, their roles as military leaders in internal political warfare were partially assumed by men who began their political careers as civilians – by lawyers, journalists, merchants and landowners who were drawn into military leadership by the exigencies of the violent politics of the time.

The caudillo and his band of followers were held together by a network of personal loyalties. What was the basis of these personal attachments? Why did people follow the caudillo? Nineteenth-century writings on this phenomenon, and much of the literature of the twentieth century also, have stressed the personality of the caudillo himself. According to the stereotype, he was a man of great personal magnetism,

---

[10] Gran Mariscal Agustín Gamarra, *Epistolario*, ed. Alberto Tauro (Lima, 1952), 47, 148, 209.

who dominated lesser men by force of will. In the classic nineteenth-century portrait of the caudillo, Domingo Faustino Sarmiento's depiction in 1845 of the Argentine provincial leader Facundo Quiroga, the caudillo is described as saying, 'If I should go into the street and say to the first man I met, "Follow me!", he would follow me without hesitation.' The caudillo's followers responded to him both because they found him attractive and because he intimidated them. The caudillo, again according to the stereotype, was courageous, a man who could command others to perform feats of valour because he himself set the example of bravery and boldness. He also is frequently described as 'telluric', earthy; even if a member of the upper class, he often cultivated a popular style in order to encourage his followers to identify with him personally. Both to demonstrate their virility and to establish their identity with their followers, José Antonio Páez in Venezuela and Juan Manuel de Rosas in Buenos Aires are alleged to have matched their cowboy retinues in feats of horsemanship. While many caudillos affected a common touch, others celebrated themselves with pomp, which may have served to overawe the populace as well as to gratify the leader himself. The caudillo characteristically had an authoritarian personality. Because of his ruthlessness and, even more perhaps, his unpredictability, the caudillo often frightened his followers and his enemies alike.

Many recent treatments, while not denying the personality characteristics of the caudillo, tend to focus instead upon the network of relations between the leader and his adherents. *Caudillismo*, in these accounts, is viewed as a social system, a system structured upon the mutual dependence of the chief and his band. Various kinds of patron–client relationships have been posited. Commonly the caudillo is viewed as handing out largesse to his followers as a reward for faithful service.[11] But more sophisticated interpretations have also noted another kind of patron–client relationship, one in which the caudillo himself was the client of wealthy patrons who 'created and controlled' him as an investment for their own political and/or economic designs.[12] Even in this latter case, of course, one must assume a relationship of mutual dependence, in which neither the caudillo-client nor his wealthy patrons completely controlled the relationship. Most treatments of *caudillismo* as a

---

[11] Eric R. Wolf and Edward C. Hansen, 'Caudillo politics: a structural analysis', *Comparative Studies in Society and History*, 9/2 (1967), 168–79.

[12] Roger M. Haigh, 'The creation and control of a caudillo', *Hispanic American Historical Review*, 44/4 (1964), 481–90. See also Robert L. Gilmore, *Caudillism and militarism in Venezuela, 1810–1910* (Athens, Ohio, 1964), for a well-informed discussion.

patron–client relationship focus on the caudillo as a figure emanating from some regional backwater and assume the network supporting him to be an alliance of local landowners. But not all caudillos emerged from provincial obscurity. Many had as their base of power the support of officers in the national army, or of certain cliques of such officers. Some of the most powerful caudillos, such as General Antonio López de Santa Anna in Mexico, combined the support both of regional oligarchies and of the officers' corps. Finally, one should note that caudillistic patron–client networks often formed elaborate pyramids – in which local *caciques*, with their personal followings, pledged loyalty to regional chieftains, who in turn gave at least temporary and conditional support to caudillos, or other political leaders operating at the national level.

In terms of social classes, the caudillo is frequently thought of as being socially emergent, a man of relatively humble origins whose ambitions for power were prompted in part by a hunger for wealth and social status. Such a conception, of course, nicely fits the idea of a caudillo who is both client to wealthy patrons and patron to followers. One can find many cases of caudillos who fit this description in some degree. But many caudillos, such as Simón Bolívar and General Tomás Cipriano de Mosquera in Colombia, were born to the upper class. Such men were less easily controlled and were viewed as especially unpredictable and therefore intimidating by the upper sectors.

As the caudillo came to power through violence, the legitimacy of his rule was always in question. Consequently he often ruled his domain, local or national, with a sense of insecurity of tenure, knowing that he too might be overthrown by some competing chieftain. Because his *de facto* regime lacked constitutional legitimacy and often met resistance from other caudillos, he often found himself compelled to rule by violence, with little or no attention to constitutional niceties. Not infrequently he seemed to be arbitrary in his political acts. The caudillo's unpredictability was increased by the fact that he ruled according to personal consider-ations. For the caudillo, the primary question was personal loyalty. Those thought to be loyal could depend upon support; those suspected of disloyalty could expect terrible vengeance. On the other hand, the caudillo might make surprising alliances, again often on the basis of personal relations. As ideology was of little concern to most caudillos, they found no difficulty in supporting quite diverse and contradictory causes. In the Río de la Plata caudillos identified themselves variously as unitarians or federalists, often with little sense of the meaning of these terms except as a way of identifying friends and enemies. In Mexico, General Santa Anna threw his weight variously behind liberals or conservatives, depending upon his estimate of the relative strength of their forces. In New Granada, General José María Obando in 1840 waved the banner of federalism in a rebellion launched to defend himself from prosecution (or, in his eyes, persecution) by the national government; in 1853 he considered it impossible to govern as president of a federalist government. Obando's arch-rival, General Tomás Cipriano de Mosquera, on the other hand, moved rather easily from a vigorous centralism in the 1840s to an equally vigorous federalism in the 1850s, following the dictates of his ambition.

Often the personalist leadership of caudillos found expression in rebellion against constituted governments. But in a number of cases a dominant caudillo used his authority to shore up fledgling governmental structures. In Chile caudillistic rebellion and seizure of power characterized the period of the Patria Vieja (1810–14) and the 1820s. But after 1830 a government established through the personal authority of General Joaquín Prieto and his minister Diego Portales ultimately developed institutional strength. By 1851 the Chilean governments were able to sustain their authority without benefit of charismatic leadership. In New Granada the personal authority of General Francisco de Paula Santander in the 1830s and of General Tomás Cipriano de Mosquera in the 1840s helped to support constitutional government which in these years was threatened by only one major caudillistic rebellion. Similarly, in Venezuela the authority of General José Antonio Páez (1830–48) and in the province of Buenos Aires of Juan Manuel de Rosas (1829–52) served to maintain a substantial public order. In much of Spanish America, during much of the time, however, no single caudillo was able to dominate the scene and seemingly interminable series of civil wars or *coups d'état* were staged to determine who should rule. This pattern is most notable in Bolivia, in Peru (1823–45), and in much of the pre-1860 history of the Río de la Plata region.

The sources of *caudillismo* have been the subject of much speculation, but of rather little systematic research. While the full array of hypotheses about the caudillo cannot be presented here, some of the principal explanations can be sketched. Many interpretations emphasize the impact of the Wars of Independence. According to one, the struggle for independence raised military heroes to status and power while the civilian elites and the governing institutions they controlled were correspondingly weakened. The emergence of the caudillo thus can be seen as the result of a 'militarization' of politics between 1810 and 1825.[13] This interpretation has merit for those regions that suffered prolonged periods of violent conflict in the struggle for independence – most notably Venezuela, New Granada, the Río de la Plata and Mexico. But in some regions, such as Central America, there was relatively little military conflict in the process of winning independence, yet caudillos nonetheless emerged in the post-independence period. This fact and the continuation of caudillesque politics for decades after the independence struggle suggest that it is necessary to look beyond the independence period militarization for the sources of caudillismo. The independence wars undoubtedly affected the *forms* that personalist leadership took. But *caudillismo* itself had deeper roots, was the work of more enduring forces.[14]

The most notable beneficiary of independence in Spanish America was the creole upper class. At the end of the colonial period most of its members owned landed property, many could be found in the priesthood, a few engaged in large-scale international commerce. Some also held government positions, but primarily in lesser posts – as lawyers, revenue agents or secondary provincial administrators. With independence, opportunities for careers in government and politics for creoles multiplied, not only because they displaced Spaniards in the highest positions but also because of the very nature of the republican governments that they came to establish. Whereas the colonial system had required only a relatively small corps of judges, provincial administrators, military officers and revenue agents, the new republics demanded all of these and much more: more elaborate systems of appeals courts were established; national legislators, usually in two chambers, and frequently also provincial legislators had to be found; finally, at the highest level there were cabinet and sub-cabinet positions, councils of state, and at least a few diplomatic posts to be distributed.

New political opportunities led to considerable territorial mobility among elements in the creole group. Provincials who came to the capital as legislators often stayed on to educate their families, to enjoy the

<hr />

[13] For example, Asher Christensen, *The evolution of Latin American government* (New York, 1951), and, in a much more sophisticated version, Tulio Halperín Donghi, *The aftermath of revolution in Latin America* (New York, 1973), 1–43.

[14] For further discussion on this point, see below pp.413–20, section on interpretations of political instability in Spanish America during the post-independence period.

cultural ambience and to further their political careers. Provincial families also sent their sons to the capital cities to be educated in the principal secondary schools and universities, not necessarily intending political careers for them – though passage through those institutions provided both the educational certification and the contacts required for such careers. Those who went to be educated in the capital rarely returned to the provinces. One unintended effect of this tendency to converge upon the capital cities was to undermine the development of the provinces by draining off their educated elites.

While ambitious men from the provinces, or from otherwise relatively obscure locations in the upper sectors, entered politics, in some places the richest and traditionally most prestigious families were notably absent from political life. In some cases this was not a matter of choice: men of wealth and social position sometimes were simply displaced by military men who commanded instruments of violence. In other cases the wealthiest men voluntarily removed themselves from the political arena – perhaps as a matter of prudence, perhaps because disorder had brought political careers into discredit, perhaps in distaste for the new social elements that were active in politics. Often, however, men of wealth moved discreetly behind the scenes, directing, or at least influencing, the military caudillos who so much appeared to dominate political life.[15] The withdrawal from overt participation in political office by the richest members of the upper class was perhaps most evident in Argentina and, to a lesser degree, in Mexico. It was, however, far from a universal phenomenon. In Chile, Colombia and Venezuela the wealthiest and most established families were quite prominent in politics through most of the period.

Outside the creole group the political rewards of independence were limited. The creoles were loath to share power with the *mestizos* and others in the nether regions of the colonial social order. Some individual *mestizos* and mulattos did emerge to political prominence during the struggle for independence, largely on the basis of their prowess as leaders of guerrilla or other military forces. But the emergence of these few individuals worried the creoles. Simón Bolívar, for example, was much given to expressing anxiety about a looming 'pardocracy' (rule by the dark-skinned). And the creole elite almost systematically (it now seems in

---

[15] Haigh, 'Creation of a caudillo', 481–90. Haigh's case deals with the northern interior province of Salta in Argentina. A similar argument could be made for the influence of Tomás Manuel de Anchorena and other landed magnates on Juan Manuel de Rosas in Buenos Aires.

retrospect) eliminated from high positions these lower-caste individuals, particularly the mulattos. The two highest-ranking mulatto officers in Venezuela and New Granada, Generals Manuel Piar and José Padilla, were shot for offences that might well have been pardoned in whites. In Mexico the dark-hued insurgent leader, Vicente Guerrero, was detested by the upper classes as uncouth, ignorant and generally unfit; over-thrown as president, he was shot by his opponents.

Although the few prominent mulatto officers were eliminated with some dispatch, the elite faced a much more troublesome problem in the distribution of power between civilian and military creoles. Tulio Halperín Donghi has emphasized that the fight for independence, and in the Río de la Plata for national consolidation, brought the military so much to the fore that the civilian elites who had dominated the colonial regime (civil bureaucrats and ecclesiastical hierarchies) suffered a relative decline in power. Not only were the ranks of the military swollen by the exigencies of war but the structure of civil administration was weakened as the governments lacked revenues. The situation was symbolized by the fact that in many places governments gave first priority to paying the troops, putting civilian bureaucrats on reduced pay. The Church was also debilitated by papal opposition to Spanish American independence, which compromised the Church hierarchy politically, and by conflict over whether appointment of bishops belonged to the nations or reverted to the pope. No new bishops were appointed until 1827. Over the long term the Church also suffered the loss of financial resources that were requisitioned in time of war. Paralleling the decline of the civil and ecclesiastical bureaucracies, in Halperín's view, there occurred a relative loss of power and position by urban merchants, particularly insofar as commerce fell under the domination of foreigners, and a corresponding gain in the power of landowners. Thus, according to Halperín, there occurred both a militarization and a ruralization of power in this period.[16] The following discussion will suggest that this militarization and ruralization thesis, while substantially correct, must be seen not as an absolute but as a change in degree, relative to the colonial order.

For civilian politicians between 1810 and 1830, and in many places long after that, the militarization of politics was an inescapable fact. At the outset the civilian elite was disposed to accept the necessity of military governance, particularly while independence remained

[16] Halperín, *Aftermath of revolution*, 1–43.

insecure. At the end of the 1820s, however, independence now seemed a fact and civilians everywhere in Spanish America began to chafe at military domination and at the excessive size of the armies. The late 1820s and early 1830s, therefore, were marked by civilian efforts both to reduce the numbers of military officers on active duty and to counterbalance the standing army through the creation of provincial militias. These years also were characterized, not surprisingly, by a strong mutual hostility between military men and civilian politicians.

Efforts at civilian control of the military were notably successful in Chile, where Diego Portales, strongly backed by the Santiago aristocracy, created militias with upper-class officers as a counterpoise to the standing army and then encouraged young men of good family to take up professional careers in the regular army itself. In Venezuela in the 1830s some of the heroes of the independence movement rebelled against the loss of military privileges and reduction of the size of the army, but these rebellions were quickly put down by the Venezuelan president, General José Antonio Páez, again with backing from the civilian upper classes. In Argentina, militia forces under Juan Manuel de Rosas succeeded in dismantling the remains of an army of independence already weakened by efforts to dominate the Banda Oriental. In New Granada the problem of managing the military was partly resolved by the breakup of the republic of Gran Colombia, for many of the most troublesome officers were Venezuelans, most of whom returned to their homeland after 1831. Many of the highest New Granadan officers remaining were closely tied to the civilian elite. While some military officers followed General José María Obando into a rebellion that wracked the country from 1839 through 1841, they took up arms on behalf of a general political movement, with both civilian and military adherents, and not in defence of the interests of the military as a corporate group. In all of these countries the reduction of the standing armies was facilitated by the fact that they were substantially *ad hoc* creations, established for the purpose of winning independence, and many of the highest officers were members of landed, upper class families whose social position derived only partly from their military careers and who, therefore, were not averse to retirement from active duty. For others, who were not originally of the upper class, retirement was made attractive through the acquisition of large landholdings granted to them in compensation for their services.

In Mexico, however, the officers who headed the regular army were professional soldiers, men who had been recruited into the Spanish army in the last years of the colonial period. Because of the peculiarities of Mexico's independence, with the royalist army leading the ultimate break with Spain rather than being defeated by insurgent forces, the Spanish-recruited creole professional military hierarchy had remained intact and powerful. And more of them than in some other countries identified strongly with the military career as a source of status and with the army as a corporate group. Consequently, in Mexico the national army retained a strong sense of its corporate interests and acted decisively to defend them until the 1850s. But the political activities of Mexican military officers were hardly confined to the defence of army privileges; in most cases their interventions were acts of political enterprise, reflecting concerns of particular groups but not of army officers as a whole. In Peru and Bolivia remnants of the Spanish-recruited colonial officer class remained in the republican armies and there was a similar identification with the military career as a source of status. In these countries also military officers played a dominant role in politics, rarely, however, acting in defence of corporate interests, usually pursuing individual ambitions.

Cutting back the power of the regular army, even where it proved possible, did not necessarily take the military out of politics. Even where civilian elites were able to establish dominance over the military, almost everywhere they employed generals as the formal heads of state. Civilian politicans felt that only a prestigious general would be sufficiently intimidating to prevent barrack revolts or regional challenges to national authority. Thus, in Chile, where a fortunate combination of upper-class unity and economic prosperity enabled the civilian elite to construct a strong state and to dominate the standing army, two generals presided over the critical first two decades of relatively stable government. In Venezuela also the government of the civilian 'oligarchy' of the 1830s and 1840s was either headed or enforced by General José Antonio Páez and his lieutenant and successor General Soublette. In these countries relations between the civilian elite and the military were relatively untroubled. Elsewhere, where civilian control was much less certain, elites found it necessary to make use of military leaders whom they distrusted, in the knowledge that their countries were not yet ready for outright civilian rule. Thus, in Mexico a succession of civilians of all political persuasions attempted to turn the mercurial General Santa Anna to their uses, with only partial success. In Peru the leader of the liberal faction, Francisco Javier Luna Pizarro, deeply disliked the pre-eminence of military leaders in politics but, recognizing their indispensability, managed the elections of several he thought he could control.

Military leaders were equally important as implements of order in cases where the national state became so weak that political power was fragmented and decentralized. In Argentina the destruction of the national army left the field to local caudillos, whom provincial civilian elites attempted to use as instruments of control but who were themselves not always completely controllable. In Venezuela also locally based caudillos came to the fore, particularly at the end of the 1840s after the demise of the establishment over which General Páez presided. And in Mexico, even though the national army retained ultimate military superiority until its annihilation in the war of 1846, some provincial caudillos, like Juan Alvarez in the region of present-day Guerrero state, were locally dominant. As in Venezuela, the numbers and power of these regional bosses in Mexico increased in the 1850s with the weakening of the war-torn central government. In New Granada, the adoption of federalist government in the 1850s also had the effect of shifting relatively more power into the hands of regional caudillos.

The militarization of politics thus took two basic forms. In Mexico and Peru the dominant caudillos had their bases of support in regular army units, and they attempted to seize control of the national government, acting out of various combinations of individual ambition, corporate interest and upper-class civilian inspiration. At the other extreme, for which the fragmented provinces of Río de la Plata provide the best example, the dominant mode was the caudillo whose base of support was the local militia unit and the backing of the landowners and merchants in the region. In this case the primary function of the caudillo, in the eyes of his upper-class backers, was to keep order in the region and to defend the province from external disruption. Not infrequently, however, the region would serve the caudillo and his backers as a base for an attempt to seize national power. In most countries there were varying combinations of these army-based and regionally based caudillos, their relative importance depending partly on the extent to which the central state could sustain a national army strong enough to dominate the provinces.

Although armed force, either in the hands of national armies or local caudillos, often determined who possessed national or provincial governments, this does not necessarily mean that military figures, national or provincial, determined the direction of politics or of policy, even in those countries where their activities were most evident. Military caudillos, whether ranking generals in the regular army or local figures, often seized power at the behest of civilians or in alliance with them, and, even more commonly, once in power depended upon civilians for political advice and delegated to them the actual work of government. Only exceptionally did a man like New Granada's General Tomás Cipriano de Mosquera make his own policy decisions and actively operate the levers of government.

Caudillos are often depicted as either in alliance with, or created and controlled by, large landowners, whose economic resources and peones provided the essential bases of caudillistic military action. Certainly this was a common pattern, particularly at the provincial level – though one should add that merchants also formed part of these local power elites. But these economic elites were not the only civilian elements linked to caudillos. Often caudillos were allied with the same university-educated lawyer–politicians who so frequently complained of caudillistic military interventions in politics. Both at the local and the national levels university men attached themselves to promising military leaders, and then proceeded to manipulate them. Often these educated men served as secretaries upon whom the caudillos leaned heavily for advice. Sometimes the manipulation occurred at long distance, with intellectual politicians in the capital cities influencing both provincial and national caudillos with a steady flow of newspaper articles and epistolary advice.[17] Finally, once a caudillo was in power, it was to the university men that he must turn to carry on the actual work of government, as well as to defend it in the press. Thus, the caudillos and civilian politicians were linked in a symbiotic relationship marked by mutual suspicion and mutual dependence.[18] The university men often needed the caudillos to carry them to power; the caudillos needed the intellectual and administrative skills of the educated civilians. The character of the relationship between caudillos and intellectual politicians varied a good deal, of course, depending on the relative social position and economic means of both. A wealthy and respected Lucas Alamán might well lecture in a schoolmasterly manner even so powerful a caudillo as General Santa Anna (or an Egaña might so behave toward a Portales); needier and more

[17] Gilmore, *Caudillism*, 54–6; Flora Tristán y Moscozo, *Peregrinaciones de una paría* (Lima, 1946), 261–2; Venezuela, Presidencia, *Pensamiento político venezolano del siglo xix: textos para su estudio* (15 vols., Caracas, 1960–2), XI, 320–33.
[18] Pivel Devoto, *Historia de los partidos y de las ideas políticas*, 9–21, 67; idem, *Historia de los partidos políticos en el Uruguay* (2 vols., Montevideo, 1942), I, 57–9.

obscure men might well adopt a more obsequious posture and bend their political principles more than a little.

Thus, while caudillos in many places determined who would exercise power, it would be misleading to conceive of them as monopolizing power or of the urban elites as completely helpless before them. It would be similarly misleading to suggest that great landowners overwhelmingly dominated the politics of the period. It is true that some *hacendados* could sway elections in their areas or mobilize support for provincial or national caudillos. But this does not mean that landowners always used this power; much less can it be assumed that landowners as a class used this potential in a co-ordinated way. Most *hacendados* simply wanted to be left alone. Generally they did not need the services of the state; if they needed help from provincial authorities, perhaps in a dispute over land, they usually could obtain it by virtue of their own local prominence, without recourse to the national capital. In general, for most landowners, national politics simply meant trouble – seizures of their cattle and forced loans in time of civil war, and rhetoric, agitation and insecurity at other times. Even those landowners who were interested in national politics influenced its course rather little. Insofar as they lived on their haciendas, they were removed from the centre of public events and their relationship to them was necessarily passive. Information on events in the capital was sparse and infrequent. And landowners, in any case, usually had to depend for political instruction and direction on the newspapers and correspondence of professional politicians resident in the capital. By contrast, urban politicians may have lacked the landowners' local influence, and often were in tight financial straits. But as they lived in the nation's nerve centre and their livelihood often depended heavily upon influence with the government, they were both well placed for, and had an interest in, shaping the course of national politics. Thus, the intellectual elite in various ways – as influence-peddlers, journalists, teachers of the sons of the elite and government employees – despite their relative poverty probably had more effective power at the national level than landowners.

The validity of such generalizations, however, varies considerably depending upon the country. In Buenos Aires, in some sense at once a province and a nation in these years, large landowers were sufficiently concentrated regionally to make their influence felt decisively, while their agent, Rosas, effectively removed the intellectual elite from the scene. In a much more geographically fragmented political system, like that of New Granada, landowners were regionally dispersed and most were extremely isolated. The intellectual elite therefore played a much more important role in political organization and mobilization at the national level. To a considerable degree this also seems to have been true of Mexico and Venezuela.

Although in many places the urban elites exercised predominant influence over national politics, it may, nevertheless, be questioned how much effective power this gave them. The national governments were weak and their control over the provinces was incomplete at best. The urban elites therefore directed an apparatus whose actions might often be thwarted at the provincial level by locally dominant landowners and merchants. And, of course, many issues of local importance were settled by provincial elites, without significant involvement of the national government. In this sense one may say that power was ruralized.

Many, if not most, of the political conflicts in Spanish America in the period after independence were fought simply to determine who would control the state and its resources. Nevertheless, there were important political issues which varied in character and significance from country to country. Between 1810 and 1845 the issue of whether the state should have a centralist or federalist structure brought violent conflict to Mexico, Central America and the River Plate region. In Chile and New Granada it was only of temporary significance – in the 1820s in Chile, between 1838 and 1842 in New Granada. Furthermore, where it appeared, the conflict of centralism versus federalism did not always have the same nature or origins. In the Río de la Plata the federalist cause was in some places linked to regional economic interests. In Mexico and Chile, on the other hand, regional economic interests, at least in this period, seem to have been less important in the emergence and growth of federalism. Rather, in these countries, federalism reflected both regional desires for political autonomy and an ideological conviction that the federal system was the best means of protecting individual liberties from state power. In New Granada in the late 1830s federalism was simply a banner raised at an opportune moment by the party out of power to justify its attempt to reconquer control of the state by force of arms. In Peru and Bolivia, also the principal issue may have been less regional interests than who would possess the state. And in the Río de la Plata, while federalism at times may have expressed regional economic interests, the federalist–unitarian struggle also may be described as a series of local battles to determine which caudillos (and segments of local oligarchies) would control particular provinces.

The federalist–centralist conflict tended to be submerged in many places between 1835 and 1845. The forces of centralism had triumphed, definitively in Chile in 1831, temporarily in Mexico (1836–46) and in New Granada (1841–9). In the Río de la Plata, while federalism remained formally triumphant after 1831, Juan Manuel de Rosas moved to centralize power within the federalist framework. Thus, whether through repression or some other resolution of the issue, federalism tended to recede into the background for a time.

Between 1845 and 1870, however, there occurred a second wave of federalism in Mexico, New Granada, Venezuela and, more weakly, Peru. But in this period federalism was much less a source of heated conflict than was the status of the Church. In New Granada and Venezuela an interparty consensus developed in favour of federalism during the 1850s and 1860s. In New Granada liberals of the 1850s supported federalism out of conviction, while conservatives, formerly centralist in inclination, embraced federalism from opportunism. Having lost control of the central government, they concluded that a federal system would best enable them to protect their dominance of regions where conservative strength was greatest. In contrast to the strong emotions and deep commitments generated by questions relating to the Church, positions on the centralist–federalist issue tended to be more rhetorical and tactical.

While there was some variation in the form of political issues, as the federalist question indicates, there was a more or less common theme underlying much political conflict. This theme was the desire of some politicians, university-educated men for the most part, to modernize Spanish America. Particularly among intellectual politicians there was a general belief that Spanish institutions and values were responsible for Spanish American backwardness; they wanted to remodel their societies as much as possible along British, French and North American lines.

As previously indicated, aspects of the modernization process had roots in the Bourbon programme of administrative, economic, fiscal and educational rationalization. In carrying out this programme of rationalization the Bourbons asserted the supremacy of the secular over the ecclesiastical, in particular attempting to reduce the clergy's juridical privileges and tax exemptions and to place church economic resources in the service of the state. The Bourbons also sought to turn university instruction away from scholastic teachings and toward those natural sciences that were thought to be of practical utility.

In addition to pursuing the reform goals associated with the Bourbons, republican politicians of the nineteenth century also sought something that was at most a minor theme under the Spanish Bourbons – the implantation of English and French liberal individualism in social, economic and political institutions and behaviour. The creation of a liberal individualist society meant, in political terms, the establishment of legal equality and the supremacy of the secular state. It also meant guaranteeing freedom of thought. All of these goals – the supremacy of the state, legal equality and freedom of thought – required breaking down the corporate organizations that had dominated colonial society, most particularly the Church and the military. These two institutions challenged the supremacy of the state; their privileges negated legal equality; and their control over their members made impossible the exercise of free thought. The creation of a liberal individualist society meant, in economic terms, the establishment of a free market. To achieve a free market it was necessary to abolish the monopoly privileges stemming from the colonial period, whether those of the government or those that were privately held. For the same reason it was necessary to break up Indian community lands in order to force Indian peasants to operate as individual entrepreneurs under the discipline of market forces. And, it came to be argued, for the nation's economic resources to become fully productive it was necessary to remove the enormous resources held in mortmain by the Church and to free private properties from the burden of perpetual quitrents so that they might circulate freely in the market.

Many aspects of this reform programme had rather generalized support among the educated elite, though there were differences of opinion over the pace at which the reforms should occur. With the exception of the Río de la Plata region and, for a time, Venezuela, there usually tended to be a consensus on economic policy. Between 1820 and 1845 most of those who later became known as conservatives and liberals alike professed Manchesterian liberal economic principles and both varied actual policy from these principles as the occasion demanded. During the late 1820s and early 1830s, when the deluge of British imports had produced heavy trade imbalances, scarcity of circulating media and consequent economic contraction, protection of local manufacturing had adherents among both liberals, like the Mexican Lorenzo Zavala, and men later known as conservatives, like Lucas Alamán in Mexico and Alejandro Osorio in New Granada. At the same time, some men of both political tendencies remained resolutely committed to free trade principles.

This tendency to inter-factional agreement on economic policy, evident between 1825 and 1845, became even more marked after 1845, as most of Spanish America became more fully incorporated into the Atlantic trade system. During the 1830s there had been reason for disagreement: the fact of serious trade imbalances with England and France supported the argument for the protection of native industry, while the hegemony of liberal economic theory encouraged heroic (if misguided) adherence to free trade principles. After 1845, however, fact and theory were no longer so clearly in conflict and tended rather to be mutually reinforcing. Increasing European and North American demand for Spanish America's raw materials enabled more of the countries in the region to bring their external trade into balance, thus seeming to justify the liberal economic faith in free trade. Consequently, during the years 1845 to 1870, in most countries there was a near unanimity on at least the free trade aspects of economic liberalism. (Mexico, where established industrial interests pressed for protection, was an exception to the general pattern.)

Venezuela was one place where disagreement over economic principles for a time became a source of serious political conflict. There coffee planters who had indebted themselves to expand production during years of high prices in the 1830s found themselves unable to repay their creditors when the market declined at the end of the decade. Throughout the 1840s coffee planters campaigned fervently against liberal legislation of 1834 which had freed interest rates from colonial restrictions upon usury and against later laws facilitating the sale of debtors' property. The planters also strayed from liberal economic principles by calling for active government aid for the distressed agricultural sector. Interestingly, this planters' reaction against the effects of economic liberalism provided much of the impetus for the formation of Venezuela's Liberal Party, which in almost every other respect was conventionally liberal. The predictable obverse side of this was that the 'conservative' establishment presided over by Generals Páez and Soublette adhered rigorously to liberal economic principles in defence of the creditor interest.

Like economic policy, fiscal policy generally was not a party or factional issue. Men in all political groups agreed in condemning the tax system inherited from the Spanish as unliberal and irrational, and moved to reform it during the optimism of the early 1820s. When direct taxes introduced during the 1820s and the early 1830s met popular resistance and failed to produce much revenue, almost everyone in the political elite agreed to put them on the shelf. In an atmosphere of fiscal crisis men of all parties agreed to postpone reform to a more favourable occasion. In the period of optimism after 1845, when renewed efforts were made to abolish traditionally established taxes that conflicted with liberal economic principles, such reforms evoked no major conflict.

If elite political groups generally agreed upon economic principles, the same was also true of social policy regarding slavery and Indian communities. In the 1820s, the elites in most countries, in a burst of revolutionary enthusiasm, moved with more or less unanimity to make legislative commitments to the eventual abolition of slavery. But subsequently, through the 1830s and into the 1840s, all parties prudently refrained from hastening the demise of slavery and even took steps to slow its end. While conservative establishments generally presided over attempts to maintain slavery, they faced no serious criticism from liberals. Indeed, Tomás Lander, Venezuela's leading liberal ideologist of the 1830s and 1840s, was an outspoken defender of slavery.

In the latter part of the 1840s attitudes toward slavery changed as some in the younger generation emerging on the political scene at this time attacked the institution as part of their general commitment to ideals of social equality. This new political generation played a prominent role in the abolition of slavery in New Granada in 1850, in Ecuador in 1852, in Argentina in 1853 and in Venezuela and Peru in 1854. However, all political groups apparently recognized that this was an idea whose time had come. Once the young liberals had raised the question forcefully, conservatives made little resistance to abolition and indeed many of them supported it.[19]

A similar tendency to consensus is observable in attitudes toward communal landholding in Indian communities. From the 1820s onward there was a general agreement that communal holdings should be divided among the Indians. Almost all members of the elite considered communal property-holding contrary to liberal economic principles, in that they presumably did not engage the interest of the individual. It was also felt that Indians should be more fully integrated into the dominant

[19] See Halperín, *CHLA* III, ch.8.

society on at least a theoretical or formal basis of equality, something which could not be done as long as they lived apart in communities governed by different principles from the rest of the society. The elite implicitly recognized the unlikelihood that such incorporation would occur on a basis of equality: during the 1820s and 1830s laws breaking up Indian lands placed some checks upon the freedom of the Indians to sell their property, in order to protect them from exploitation. Nevertheless, there was a general belief that the goal of converting Indians to individual property-holders and integrating them into the dominant society was a desirable one. During the initial process of incorporation few voices were raised against it. Only toward the end of the 1840s did a few members of the elite – some conservatives, some liberals – express alarm about potential injury to the Indian peasantry. Only in the 1860s did a somewhat greater number of both liberals and conservatives recognize the devastating results of this reform in depriving the Indians of their land and reducing them to an ever more miserable poverty.[20]

Thus, many aspects of attempts to rebuild Spanish American society and economy in the liberal image did not provoke conflict among the educated political elites. These efforts at liberal reform divided the political elite principally when they impinged upon the power and privileges of the Church. This, of course, they frequently did. For doctrinaire liberals the Church became the principal obstacle to economic, social and political modernization. Its control of substantial properties denied wealth to the state, which desperately needed revenues. Its claims to income from quitrents upon private properties depressed agricultural enterprise. Its juridical privileges both undermined the authority of the state and made a mockery of the principle of legal equality. Its status as a special corporate group encouraged the clergy to identify primarily with the Church, not with the nation. Church discipline denied freedom of thought to the clergy, and the clergy in turn, in the liberal view, attempted to impose thought control on the population at large, condemning books thought to be prejudicial to morals and the faith. Church control of educational institutions also threatened freedom of thought and hampered the introduction of new scientific knowledge. Church opposition to religious toleration hindered the immigration of non-Catholic Europeans, whose skills and capital were desperately needed to build a modern economy.[21]

---

[20] See Halperín, *CHLA* III, ch.8

[21] See, for example, José María Luis Mora, *El clero, la educación y la libertad* (Mexico, 1949), 43–61; idem, *El clero, el estado y la economía nacional* (Mexico, 1959), 22, 27–34.

Confronting liberal efforts to weaken its powers and trim its privileges, the Church could count on various allies. The clergy was able to mobilize elements of the urban lower classes against both religious toleration and the foreign immigrants it was meant to protect. If liberals attempted to end ecclesiastical juridical privileges (*fueros*), the clergy could often depend upon the support of the professional military, whose own special privileges usually were in jeopardy at the same time. Efforts to seize Church economic resources often provoked elements in the upper classes, who viewed such measures as assaults upon property in general. It has been argued that, at least in the early decades of the republican period, large landowners tended to support the Church in political conflicts because they were beholden to ecclesiastical institutions for loans.[22] Whether this was the case or not, it is clear that a substantial proportion of the upper class defended the Church against liberal attack primarily because they viewed the Church as an indispensable instrument of social control.

It would be misleading to give the impression that the issue of the status and power of the Church emerged everywhere simultaneously. On this, as on other issues, each country had its own particular rhythm. In Buenos Aires in the 1820s and Montevideo in the 1830s liberal secularist politicians were able substantially to reduce the powers and privileges of the Church without effective resistance from the clergy. In Mexico and Guatemala, on the other hand, when liberals carried out a frontal assuault upon Church interests in the 1830s, major conflict ensued in both countries, the liberal reformers were defeated, and many of the changes they sought were delayed for decades. Elsewhere the conflict was less dramatic in the early years. In New Granada, the use of Bentham and de Tracy as university texts provoked vigorous denunciations from the clergy and its political supporters in the 1820s and 1830s, but a frontal conflict over the powers and status of the Church was avoided until the 1850s. In Peru and Chile, where liberal forces were weak, liberals even more assiduously avoided confrontation with the Church in the early years of the republican era, deferring serious efforts to trim Church powers and privileges until the 1850s.

Between 1830 and 1845 a relative political stability had prevailed in some parts of Spanish America – most notably in Chile, Venezuela and Buenos Aires, but also to a somewhat lesser degree in New Granada and

---

[22] Michael P. Costeloe, *Church wealth in Mexico: a study of the 'Juzgado de Capellanías' in the archbishopric of Mexico, 1800–1856* (Cambridge, 1967), 28.

Ecuador, where national authority was challenged by only occasional violence. After 1845, however, elite consensus in these countries began to fracture. In the 1840s a new generation of politicians emerged, challenging the persons and policies of those who had held power since the end of the 1820s. Most Spanish American countries had been ruled by the same generation that had made independence. In Mexico, Peru, Venezuela and New Granada presidential power seemed to be the monopoly of the military heroes of Independence, with civilian elites of the same generation collaborating in the organization of politics and the management of government. Men born at the eve of independence, particularly civilians, had cause to wonder when their time might come. Tulio Halperín Donghi has suggested that the fiscal penury endured by almost all Spanish American governments limited their capacity to absorb the younger generations into public posts.[23] Whatever the reason the fact is that in the 1840s the younger generation began, in many places quite consciously, to challenge the existing political establishment which in some places, it should be said, had lost its will or ability to dominate. In Venezuela, by 1844, General Carlos Soublette, who currently governed for the Venezuelan oligarchy, calmly tolerated the mobilization of university students (including two of his sons) in opposition, making little effort to generate support for the established system. In Mexico, disastrous defeat in war with the United States (1846–8) undermined the authority of established politicians in all the major factions and filled the new generation with a sense of the urgency of taking radical measures in order to form a strong, modern state. In New Granada in 1848–9, the government party split, thus opening the way for challenge by a new generation. In Chile, the Portalean system also began to show signs of wear as elements in the governing party began to break away in opposition to President Manuel Montt, thus encouraging a series of liberal rebellions in the 1850s.

Although the political dynamic of the period may be seen as a challenge from a new age-group within the upper social sectors, the struggle also had a class aspect in some places. Historians of the Reforma period in Mexico (1855–76) consider many of the liberal protagonists of this struggle to have been a 'new' generation not merely in the sense of age but also in that of social origin. The new liberal generation that emerged in the 1840s is described as typically composed of mostly ambitious

---

23 Halperín, *Aftermath of revolution*, 127–9.

provincials whose social mobility was made possible by the expansion of secondary education during the early independence period.[24] A similiar generalization might be made about New Granada and, to a lesser degree, Peru and Chile. Young men of such social origins had particular reason to challenge the monopoly of power by established groups and to wish to destroy those remnants of colonial institutions that tended to block social mobility.

Along with young educated provincials, another social group that began to figure prominently between 1845 and 1860 consisted of urban artisans. In New Granada, and to a lesser degree in Mexico, Peru and Chile, this group came into temporary alliance with young upper-sector politicians. Although they collaborated for a time, the two groups seem to have been mobilized for quite different, and even contradictory, reasons. One factor tending from the mid-1840s to energize upper-sector young men was the expansion of Spanish America's external trade. Expanding European demand for Spanish America's tropical products and raw materials created a new ambience of optimism among the upper classes, encouraging a spirit of political regeneration and institutional experimentation. For urban artisans, however, it meant a wave of imported consumer goods that threatened to engulf them. Distressed by increased imports between 1845 and 1855, they briefly found themselves in a paradoxical alliance with young upper-sector politicians, almost all of whom were devout believers in free trade and the expansion of external commerce.

The emerging generation of upper-sector politicians, seeking to develop its own sense of political identity as against the older generation, was receptive to new European influences that had little appeal to the already-formed, established politicians. The impact of these new external influences, along with the dynamic of inter-generational tensions, helped to polarize politics from the middle of the 1840s until 1870, by which time the new generation was thoroughly dominant.

The European political events and ideological currents influencing the new generation varied depending upon local political conditions. In much of Spanish America the powers and privileges of the Church remained a central, and unresolved, problem. Consequently, agitation in France over ecclesiastical issues in the 1830s and 1840s influenced some of these countries after 1845, most particularly Mexico, New Granada,

[24] Justo Sierra, *The political evolution of the Mexican people* (Austin, Texas, 1969), 204; Moisés González Navarro, *Anatomía del poder en México, 1848–1853* (Mexico, 1977), 442–3.

Chile and Peru. The attacks of Michelet and Quinet on the role of the Church in higher education in the 1840s and their book assailing the Jesuits had an impact upon young democrats like Francisco Bilbao (1823–65) in Chile and also served to inflame antagonism toward the Jesuits among the younger generation in New Granada.

In Buenos Aires and Montevideo, where many of the Church's powers and privileges had already been stripped away before 1835, religio-political controversies in Europe were of relatively little concern to young intellectuals. Mazzini's Young Italy, however, had a notable influence among the dissident youth of the Río de la Plata region; one of their intellectual leaders, Esteban Echeverría, for example, proclaimed a Young Argentina. Echeverría and his associates also found some interest in French Socialism, particularly in Saint-Simonian currents. This was much less true in other parts of Spanish America, at least until the European Revolution of 1848.

The inflammation of Church–State issues between 1845 and 1870 in some Spanish American republics, and the new, more fervent spirit with which civilian politicians approached these issues, derived in part from the influence of Lamennais. His criticism of the Church as a political establishment concerned primarily with money, power, and dignities, and his advocacy of a primitive, popular, extra-ecclesiastical Christianity, inspired many in the new generation. He provided them with a rhetoric with which to attack the established Church as part of the old, oppressive order, while claiming adherence to a purer, democratic Christianity. His insistence upon the separation of religion and politics, and therefore upon the separation of Church and State, found echo in Mexico, New Granada, Peru, and Chile. His strongly democratic spirit, with his support of a wide extension of the suffrage, also encouraged the democratic enthusiasms of the new generation, just as his call for administrative decentralization reinforced the federalist political currents in Spanish America. Lamennais's influence, perhaps more than any other, demarcates the generation of the 1840s from its predecessors, who for the most part ignored him. Undoubtedly, Lamennais, like Mazzini, had a special appeal for the younger generation in symbolizing rebellion against established authority.

The European Revolution of 1848 both drew attention to, and crystallized the influence of, utopian Socialist ideas in Spanish America. Shortly after the European revolutions began, aspiring young politicians, influenced by European example, began to reach out to elements in the urban underclasses – principally to the artisan class, not to the very poorest – in an effort to mobilize them politically. In some places such mobilization already had begun to occur even before the Revolution of 1848, most notably perhaps in the agitation carried out in Venezuela by Antonio Leocadio Guzmán in the middle of the 1840s. There were also some precedents in New Granada in the 1830s. But there can be no doubt that the 1848 revolutions stimulated further efforts to mobilize the urban working class. In New Granada an artisans' society formed in 1848 to protest the lowering of tariffs on finishing goods was taken over as a political arm by ambitious liberal university students and young professionals. Reconstituted as the Democratic Society, the artisans' organization helped the liberals gain power in 1849, after which branch societies were established throughout the country to mobilize support for the new government. The New Granadan liberal government made a gesture at socialist forms by decreeing artisans' training shops inspired by the French National Workshops, and young liberals indulged in associational and Christian democratic rhetoric.

In general, however, the new generation was more individualist and liberal than socialist in ideology.[25] Their principal contribution to the artisans' society was a series of unwelcome lectures on the virtues of liberal political economy. The inherent incompatibility between the young upper-class radicals and Bogotá's artisans became evident when the new liberal government failed to provide tariff protection for the artisans' products. A joint military–artisan revolution in 1854 overthrew the liberal government, forcing the young radicals to seek alliance with conservatives in order to suppress the now far-too-popular government established in behalf of the artisans in Bogotá. Although many of their leaders were banished to almost certain death in the jungles of Panama, the artisans remained an element to be contended with in later decades.

Similar efforts to mobilize the urban workers were made by young political aspirants in Peru, where the Progressive Society was established in 1849, and in Chile, where the Society of Equality was formed in 1850. Like the one in New Granada, the Peruvian and Chilean societies attempted rather paternalistically to enlighten the masses in order to mobilize them. Characteristic of this process was the publication by the Chilean society of a periodical, *El amigo del pueblo* (The Friend of the People), in which the *Paroles d'un croyant* of Lamennais was serialized. In

---

[25] See Robert L. Gilmore, 'Nueva Granada's Socialist Mirage', *Hispanic American Historical Review*, 36/2 (1956), 190–211.

both Peru and Chile youthful agitators stimulated popular uprisings during the 1850s. As much as they preached identification with the masses, the young members of the upper class who created these societies could never move beyond their imported rhetoric to a real comprehension of working-class interests. While they attempted to appeal to artisans by supporting model shops patterned after those of France in 1848, in other respects their programmes reflected the concerns of young university graduates anxious to create a political environment favourable to their own emergence. The Peruvian society, for example, like its New Granadan counterpart, particularly emphasized the need for political reforms making possible civilian-controlled government, including reduction of the size of the army and strengthening of the locally based national guard. The Peruvian society also called for the encouragement of immigration, something which could hardly have appealed to its working-class constituency.

The Revolution of 1848 was greeted enthusiastically in New Granada, Peru and Chile, where the new generation had to contend with established government groups that could be viewed as essentially elitist and where, consequently, democratic revolution appealed as a means of political change. In the Río de la Plata, however, the dictatorship of Juan Manuel Rosas in Buenos Aires, like the regimes of lesser caudillos in the provinces, had enjoyed widespread support from the popular classes. In the Plata, therefore, younger intellectual politicians tended to take a more negative view of democratic revolution. In exile in Chile in the 1840s, Domingo Faustino Sarmiento and Juan Bautista Alberdi, even before the European revolutions, expressed the belief that popular sovereignty, in the hands of an ignorant mass, would inevitably lead to dictatorship. While Francisco Bilbao and others in the new generation of Chileans attacked their government as elitist, their Argentine contemporaries resident in Chile defended the Portalean regime as the rule of an enlightened minority, far preferable to the tyranny produced in Argentina by a barbarous majority. The Revolution of 1848, with the subsequent election of Louis Napoleon, served to confirm Sarmiento and Alberdi in their distrust of democracy, at least in countries where the large majority was illiterate. Thus, whereas in parts of Spanish America the new generations tended to a democratic rhetoric (not necessarily democratic practice) even after they became ascendant between 1850 and 1870, in Argentina after the overthrow of Rosas in 1852 the newly dominant intellectual elite tended to a more conservative view of political democracy.

The new generation of liberal politicians that emerged in the 1840s in many respects pursued the same tendencies as their political progenitors, the liberal reformers of the 1820s. But they did so with a new spirit and intensity, in the belief that the earlier generation had failed in its mission to liberalize Spanish American society. Like the liberals of the 1820s, the reformers of 1845–70 affirmed essentially individualist conceptions of state, society and economy. Like their predecessors, they were libertarian constitutionalists, in belief if not in behaviour. But they tended to be more absolute in their individualism, more fervent in their libertarian rhetoric. They called not merely for individual freedoms but for an absolute freedom of conscience, of the press, of education and of commerce – in New Granada even to the extent of sanctioning an absolute freedom of commerce in arms. They called not merely for trial by jury and the abolition of the death penalty but also for constitutional recognition of the right to insurrection. To safeguard these individual freedoms liberals in Mexico, New Granada and Venezuela re-committed themselves to the ideal of federalism looking to the United States as a model, and they resurrected plans of 1825–35 to limit the size of the army and to establish citizens' national guards.

In economic and social policy also the mid-century reformers rededicated themselves to liberal individualism and the ideal of legal equality, both of which they felt had been compromised by their predecessors. They sought to rationalize their countries' economies in accord with nineteenth-century liberal conceptions. This meant abolishing enterprise-constricting taxes that had been allowed to hang on from the colonial period, such as the *alcabala* (sales tax), the tithe and government monopolies. At least during the 1850s they rather dogmatically opposed government intervention in the economy, whether in the form of public enterprise, the extension of monopoly privileges to private enterprise, or protectionist tariffs. Their affirmation of the ideal of legal equality meant the elimination of the juridical privileges of the Church and the military. They also sought the fulfilment of legal equality, as well as of individualist social conceptions, through the abolition of slavery and the incorporation of Indian communities into the dominant, capitalistic, European society. The new generation of reformists recognized that these were themes pursued by the earlier liberals of the 1820s. But they believed that the earlier generation had taken only the first tentative steps toward a necessary elimination of colonial structures. They saw themselves as carrying out a political, economic and social revolution that would bring to completion the movement that had begun in 1810, but had been betrayed during the 1830s.

While the liberals of 1845–70 saw themselves as continuing the work of the reformers of 1810–25, the content and spirit of their enterprise was in some respects different. First, the power and the privileges of the Church came to the fore much more sharply as an issue. The question of the relationship of Church to State had been at issue in the earlier period, but, except in Mexico and Guatemala, it had been a relatively muted one. Between 1845 and 1870 the conflict over the power and privileges of the Church broke into full-scale war, particularly in Mexico and New Granada, and in Ecuador, Peru and Chile, the Church for the first time became a central political issue. Second, in the generation of 1845–70 liberal individualism was in some places – such as New Granada and Chile – combined with an element of French socialist associational rhetoric, though this tendency did not outlast the 1850s. Third, also because of the influence of French socialism and the Revolution of 1848, there was – except in Argentina – a much greater emphasis on the ideal of social democracy than had existed in earlier generations. And along with the emphasis on social democracy, there was a kind of revolutionary fervour that had not been characteristic of the earlier period of reform. One might characterize the reformers of 1810 to 1825 as trying to rationalize the system that they had inherited, in a cool Benthamite spirit. The generation of 1845–70, on the other hand – at least in New Granada, Peru and Chile – conceived themselves more as carrying out a revolution. Or, as Echeverría in the Plata preferred to think of it, a 'regeneration'.

Just as liberalism developed more fervour in the middle of the 1840s, there was a parallel development of a more articulated conservatism. In the 1830s conservative political forces in Spanish America had operated essentially without doctrine. Three of the most successful architects of a conservative order in this decade – Rosas in Buenos Aires, Portales in Chile and General José Antonio Páez in Venezuela – had acted without the aid of any intellectual rationale. In some sense, having the united support of the social establishment and no significant political opposition, they did not need a doctrine. For Portales, statecraft was essentially a practical matter of counterbalancing, if not repressing, threatening forces, in which he felt no need to appeal to broader social or political theories.

In the 1830s the conservatism of the Mexican, Lucas Alamán, resided essentially in a defence of his class: he viewed the political wars of that decade as a battle between 'men of property and respectability', whose social position guaranteed responsible use of power, on the one hand, and a clutch of ambitious social inferiors, who wanted to benefit themselves 'at the nation's cost'. During the 1840s, however, Alamán was sustaining a more explicit conservatism similar to and influenced by Edmund Burke. Alamán now argued explicitly against the liberal tendency to base political thought and action on abstract first principles, emphasizing that political institutions had to be the result of the long historical experience of a given people. The construction of an effective polity could not be the work of a single conception, nor could it 'proceed from theories of speculative legislators, who pretended to subject the human race to imaginary principles that they want to make pass as oracles of incomparable truth'. It had to be 'the result of the knowledge and experience' of centuries. Authority, in effect, had to be based upon tradition. Liberal theories, by destroying the traditional bases of respect for authority, left governmental authorities no 'other means than force to make themselves obeyed'. Alamán, like many other Mexican conservatives, ended by committing himself to the cause of constitutional monarchy.[26]

While Alamán looked to a Burkean tradition and to men of substance as the basis of the political order, the cleric, Bartolomé Herrera, the leading conservative theoretician in Peru, turned to traditional Spanish political thought in making a much more systematic effort to advance a conservative theory of authority. Following sixteenth- and seventeenth-century Spanish scholastic doctrines, Herrera denied the liberal theory of popular sovereignty based upon a social contract, holding that the origin of sovereignty lay in 'divine reason', acting through natural law. Sovereignty had to emanate from eternal principles and therefore could not be based upon the popular will, which is variable and thus often wrong. In Herrera's view the people had neither 'the capacity nor the right to make laws'. The principles upon which laws must be based could be perceived only by 'intellects habituated to conquer the difficulties of mental work'.[27]

[26] José C. Valadés, *Alamán: Estadista e historiador* (Mexico, 1938), 367; Moisés González Navarro, *El pensamiento político de Lucas Alamán* (Mexico, 1952), 59, 86, 116–17, 123–8.

[27] Herrera, *Escritos y discursos*, 1, 63–150; quotations on 131, 137. Similar arguments were made in Mexico by the cleric, Clemente de Jesús Munguía, in his *Del derecho natural* (1849), and by J. J. Pesado in 1857. See González Navarro, *Anatomía del poder*, 374–5; Walter V. Scholes, *Mexican politics during the Juárez regime, 1855–1872* (Columbia, Missouri, 1969), 18–19.

Alamán and Herrera were early and extreme exponents of conservatism. At the end of the 1840s they were joined in political alliance by men who had thought of themselves as moderate liberals, but now began to redefine themselves as conservatives. The European Revolution of 1848 strongly influenced this process. The European revolution was at first greeted with enthusiasm not only by young men but also by moderate liberals of an older generation, who viewed it at first merely as a triumph of the republican ideal. However, as the revolution in France began to take on the character of a socialist revolution, Spanish American moderates recoiled, fearing the impact that European insurrection might have in deranging the lower elements in their own societies. In Mexico, where Indian peasant rebellion already was a concern, Luis Gonzaga Cuevas, a characteristic moderate who evolved into an extreme conservatism, condemned the European revolution as an attack upon property, the very foundation of society. If Mexico were carried along by the 'absurd doctrines' of 1848, Cuevas feared, its small educated class might not be able to repress the ensuing popular disorders. In the context of imminent upheaval, Cuevas, Bernardo Couto and other Mexican moderates were particularly concerned by the intensification of anti-clericalism in Mexico as the Church more than ever appeared indispensable as a bulwark against social disorder. After 1848, therefore, many Mexican moderates joined the country's small group of monarchists in a militant, pro-clerical conservatism.[28]

In other Spanish American countries the ingredients of conservatism were not quite the same. In New Granada conservatives feared not the possibility of peasant rebellion but rather the mobilization of artisans in Bogotá and, after a time, of popular elements in Cali. In Peru and Chile also urban insurrection was more of a threat than the peasantry. Also, outside of Mexico there existed no monarchist movement to serve as the backbone of conservative parties. Nevertheless, with these variations, mid-century conservatism in other parts of Spanish America bore many of the same marks as the Mexican movement. Conservatives for the most part were men who formerly had identified themselves as moderates, who reacted with horror not only at the excesses of Paris but even more at the mouthing of socialist rhetoric by youths in their own countries, and who identified with the Church as the most solid foundation for the defence of the social order.

[28] González Navarro, *Anatomía del poder*, 29–35; Guillermo Prieto, *Memorias de mis tiempos* (Paris–Mexico, 1906), 55, 166–7, 174, 287–9, 332.

In general, conservatives, often with the Spanish clerical writer Jaime Balmes as inspiration, conceived of the Church as central to the stability of society, as well as to the authority of the state. However, conservatives varied in the ways in which they viewed their political ties to the Church. The Church was integral to Herrera's conception of state and society. Many other conservative leaders, however, seem to have thought of the Church in a somewhat more instrumental way, as an institution that was useful as a cohesive social bond, or as a means of political mobilization. Alamán, whose piety cannot be questioned, hinted at this kind of social utility concept of the Church in 1853 when he wrote Santa Anna that 'the Catholic religion [is] . . . the only link that binds all Mexicans when all others have been broken.'[29] An even more clearly instrumental approach to the Church can be seen in one of the founders of New Granada's Conservative Party, Mariano Ospina Rodríguez, who viewed religion as a force for political mobilization. Writing to his fellow conservative, José Eusebio Caro, in 1852, Ospina clinically surveyed the options of conservatives in the choice of 'banners' under which they might organize resistance to a radical-liberal government. Political liberty, he said, was a theme in which intelligent conservatives believed, but it would not serve as a rallying point because the conservative masses did not understand it. Security of person and property were also important to conservatives, but, unfortunately, people motivated only by concern for security would act prudentially and not fight. 'The only conservative banner that has life, and shows resolution and vigor', he concluded, 'is that which acts because of religious sentiments.'[30]

Because of their tendency to use religion as a source of political support, if not as a political weapon, conservatives thrust the Church into the centre of political controversy quite as much as the liberals who sought to reduce ecclesiastical powers and privileges. This occurred at a relatively early point in Mexico, when the government of Anastasio Bustamante (1830–2), in order to shore up a fragile political position, adopted a markedly pro-clerical posture. As a consequence, questions of Church power and privilege, which had played a minor role in Mexican politics up to that point, now came to the fore in opposition politics. Almost immediately after the overthrow of Bustamante those formerly

---

29 As quoted in Hale, *Mexican liberalism*, 32. A similarly instrumental view of religion as protector of property was also espoused by the conservative journal *Omnibus* in 1852. (González Navarro, *Anatomía del poder*, 110.)

30 Mariano Ospina Rodríguez to José Eusebio Caro, Medellín, 22 June 1852, in José Eusebio Caro, *Epistolario* (Bogotá, 1953), 348–52; quotation on p.350.

in opposition carried out a frontal attack on ecclesiastical privilege. Similarly, in New Granada ecclesiastical questions remained more or less dormant after the 1820s until the conservatives in 1842–4 imported the Jesuit order to serve as educational disciplinarians of a potentially rebellious younger generation. The obvious political purpose of this move was not lost upon the student generation of the 1840s, who, once in power in 1849, quickly pressed for and obtained the expulsion of the Jesuits in 1850, which led to a general confrontation with New Granada's clerical hierarchy.

This is not to say that conservative use of the Church as a political ally was the only source of attacks upon ecclesiastical power. In Mexico, in particular, the fiscal penury of the state governments in the 1820s and of the national government in subsequent decades induced both civilian and military politicians to cast an envious eye upon the considerable wealth of the Church. Financial exactions and seizures of church property, particularly in time of internal conflict or foreign war, served to inflame the purely political issue of ecclesiastical privileges in Mexico. In New Granada, seizures of church property also occurred in time of civil war, in 1861. In still other places church property never became a major issue.

Although conservatives and the church hierarchy, as their political positions weakened, tended naturally to reach out to each other, the interests of the ecclesiastical establishment and conservative politicians were by no means identical. Occasionally church leaders found themselves attempting futilely to disengage themselves from the conservative embrace, precisely because this political linkage sometimes brought down upon the Church political attacks that it might otherwise have avoided.

While the conservatives' instrumental use of the Church as a political weapon was partly responsible for attacks upon church powers and privileges at mid-century, attitudes within the Church itself also had an important effect upon the outcome. Under Pius IX the Roman Catholic Church after 1848 became increasingly obdurate in its opposition to liberalism and the pope encouraged (sometimes commanded) a similar intransigence in prelates in Spanish America. In Mexico, in the heat of Puebla's clergy-led rebellion against the government (1855), the archbishop of Mexico reproved the rebels and attempted to conciliate the government; when the pope denounced the liberal constitution of 1857, however, the archbishop accordingly adopted an intransigent position, expelling from the Church all those who adhered to the new constitution. Partly because of the hard line taken by the pope and curia, in countries where issues affecting the status of the Church were raised between 1845 and 1870, as in Mexico and New Granada, the outcome was dramatic and violent confrontation. (Where liberalism was too weak a force to raise these issues until after 1870, as in Bolivia, the process of liberalization, when ultimately undertaken, was relatively smooth and peaceful.)

The intensity of Church–State conflict also depended, however, on the personalities of civilian and clerical leaders. In Mexico, stiff resistance to civil authority on the part of Bishop Munguía of Michoacán in 1851 played an important part in setting off the intense civil–ecclesiastical struggle of the 1850s. In New Granada, Archbishop Mosquera adopted similarly unbending attitudes, thus encouraging polarization. In Peru, on the other hand, Archbishop Goyeneche adopted a conciliatory stance and was able to avoid major conflict. It should be added, however, that the Peruvian prelate did not really face the same kind of challenge as the hierarchies in Mexico and New Granada. In these two countries a broad political movement backed the liberal opposition: in Peru, liberal forces were much weaker and could be controlled by the strong, moderate-centrist leadership of General Ramón Castilla.

In Mexico and New Granada, issues affecting the status of the Church were of central importance between 1845 and 1870; in each the abolition of its juridical privileges, the seizure and sale of its properties, the prohibition of religious orders, the secularization of birth, marriage and death became the foci of political contention. Elsewhere, however, the conflict was less dramatic or the issue was fought over and/or settled at other times. In Peru ecclesiastical privileges were abolished in 1851, but liberals were not able to carry out a total assault like those in Mexico and New Granada. In Central America the liberal attack had begun earlier (1829–38) and had been defeated at least in Guatemala, where conservative, pro-clerical governments dominated until 1870. In Ecuador the Church did not become a source of dramatic conflict until the end of the 1860s, when Gabriel García Moreno instituted a system so extremely pro-clerical as finally to goad liberals into action. In Bolivia and also (with some exceptions) Chile, church issues were kept more or less in abeyance until after 1870. In Buenos Aires, Uruguay and Venezuela, on the other hand, the Church was weaker, and secularizing influences were stronger, so that ecclesiastical privilege and religious orders were removed or reduced easily and early (before 1840).

Apart from the question of the Church, which was an important source of division in Mexico, Guatemala, New Granada, Ecuador and, to a lesser degree, Peru, on many issues there was, among the contending political groups, as much a shifting consensus as conflict. Nevertheless, political elites divided into factions with more or less clear identities. The extent to which these factions could be called political parties prior to 1870 varied from region to region. In countries dominated by violent caudillistic politics, such as the United Provinces of the Río de la Plata, Bolivia, or Peru, there was no place for the development of parties whose purpose was the winning of elections. Elsewhere it is a question of definition.

Certainly there were no political organizations mobilizing large masses of people anywhere in Spanish America before the 1850s – and only rarely then. Throughout the period only a very small number of people were actively engaged in politics. If the existence of parties requires a general consistency of political allegiance over long periods of time, then only a few countries possessed parties before the 1840s. In Chile, despite the shifting commitments of individuals, two general political constellations are observable by the end of the 1820s (the conservative *pelucones, estanqueros* and O'Higginists *versus* the liberal *pipiolos*, federalists and *populares*), though neither existed as a coherent, organized and disciplined group. In New Granada and Uruguay, more or less consistent group loyalties had developed by the end of the 1830s, even though they lacked ideological definition.

In those republics where elections played a significant role in politics, parties in the sense of political groups organized for the purpose of winning elections developed from an early date. Because most national political offices were filled by indirect election, it was crucial to marshal support for certain previously selected electors. Therefore, it was common to distribute printed lists of electors to mobilize the voters of one band or another. This was done in New Granada as early as 1825, in Mexico in 1826 and in Uruguay's first national election in 1830. In New Granada in 1836–8 the names on the lists were being determined by informal, but publicly acknowledged, juntas in both parties.[31] Newspapers were also an important means of mobilizing political forces and

[31] 'El sufragante parroquial', (Bogotá, 1825); Michael P. Costeloe, *La primera república federal de México (1824–1835)* (Mexico, 1975), 73–8; Pivel Devoto, *Historia de los partidos políticos*, I, 37; 'Presidente para 1837. El Jeneral Ciudadano José María Obando', *Constitucional de Cundinamarca*, 15 May 1836; *El Argos*, Bogotá, 15 April 1838; *La Bandera Nacional*, Bogotá, 6 May 1838.

achieving a certain measure of coherence. Through newspapers published in the capital cities, political leaders were able to establish for their adherents in the provinces the political line to be followed. In Venezuela during the 1840s, newspapers, as well as political agents sent out from Caracas, played an important part in mobilizing provincial support.[32] Throughout the 1840s party directorates remained informal, often developing from congressional caucuses or among journalists and others active in politics in the national capital. But, even if informal, they did exist as a means of unifying party action. Not until the beginning of the 1870s, however, were candidates for national office in some countries being selected by party conventions with delegates formally representing all the provinces.

Whether the political groupings be considered as parties or simply as factions, what was the basis of their formation, and how did individuals come to adhere to one group or another? A cynical, and not unreasonable, answer to the first question would be that factions or parties were formed primarily to seize control of the government and the jobs at its disposal. Sustaining this view would not necessarily imply that party choices were accidental. Individuals would attach themselves to political leaders or groups that were more likely to reward them. Often this would mean adhering to leaders and groups with whom they shared regional origin or other personal associations. This way of looking at Spanish American politics in the period has much to recommend it, for there are many instances of political groupings which seem to have at their centre this sort of personal association rather than any ideological consistency. It is particularly true of those groups that formed around caudillos or other dominant individual political leaders (e.g., in Mexico the *jalapeños* and *veracruzanos* who followed Santa Anna, irrespective of ideology, and in New Granada the *caucanos* who formed around General Mosquera, etc.). Such regional or other associational networks clearly also played an important role in cementing political groups otherwise bound by ideological convictions. In New Granada, for example, the Radicals of 1850–80 shared not only standard liberal ideas but also a common generation experience (university students together in the 1840s) and regional background (coming predominantly from the eastern part of the country).

[32] *Pensamiento político venezolano*, XI, 320–33.

In the past most attempts at sociological analysis of the divisions among political elites have viewed the matter in terms of class and economic function. Many appear to have taken Mexico as a model from which to extrapolate. Most sources on Mexican politics, including many more or less contemporary to the events (for example Alamán's history), have described the political battles of 1820–50 as pitting large landowners, the ecclesiastical hierarchy and high-ranking professional military officers against less respectable, socially-emergent elements. The descriptions vary somewhat, depending upon the analyst and the political moment being described. Sometimes government bureaucrats and wealthy merchants and financiers are placed in the conservative alliance. Among those that various authors include in liberal coalitions are young professionals and intellectuals, particularly from the provinces; lower-level military officers; small merchants, artisans, and the petit bourgeoisie in general. With individual variations among these categories, there has been a general agreement upon the validity of a class analysis of Mexican politics in the period, though the most sophisticated descriptions have also introduced regional variables.[33]

In general accounts of Spanish American politics in the nineteenth century the nuances of these statements about Mexico are often stripped away. The usual formulation groups together landowners, military and clergy in a conservative coalition, while professionals and merchants are cast into a liberal bloc. Possibly merchants and professionals have been lumped together, as against landowners and clergy, because of a tendency to apply European categories of bourgeoisie and aristocracy to Spanish America. The idea of a split between an urban bourgeoisie and a rural landowning class has also been reinforced by the fact that in the Río de la Plata region most analysts, following the powerful example of Domingo Faustino Sarmiento's dichotomy between civilization and barbarity, have emphasized a conflict between city and country.

This kind of formulation is increasingly being brought into question.[34] First, insofar as it implies a virtual unanimity within each of these social groups, it is almost certainly wrong. There are, however, a number

[33] Lucas Alamán, *Historia de Méjico* (5 vols., Mexico, 1849–52), v, 823–4, 850–1; Sierra, *Political evolution*, 185–6, 203–5, 226; Costeloe, *La primera república federal*, 74, 85, 169, 185–7, 276, 342; François Chevalier, 'Conservateurs et libéraux au Mexique: essai de sociologie et géographie politiques de l'Indépendance à l'intervention français', *Cahiers d'Histoire Mondiale*, 8 (1964), 457–74.

[34] The following argument is presented at greater length in Frank Safford, 'Bases of political alignment in early republican Spanish America', in Richard Graham and Peter H. Smith (eds.), *New approaches to Latin American history* (Austin, 1974), 71–111.

of other reasons for rejecting *prima facie* this type of general description. The use of such categories as landowner, merchant and professional as ways of dividing social interest groups is implausible, because the upper classes in nineteenth-century Spanish America lacked the specificity of function that this description implies. A single individual was likely to be a large landowner, a merchant and possibly also a university-educated professional or military officer. And if one individual did not fulfil all of these functions, someone else in his immediate family generally supplied the lack. Therefore it is often artificial to divide people politically according to occupation.

Furthermore, even if members of the upper sectors could be divided neatly into economic functional groups, it still would be implausible to see them as in conflict along economic interest group lines. In economies based upon the exportation of agriculturally produced raw materials and the importation of consumer goods for the use of those producing the raw materials, there was a natural identity of interest among the land-owner-producer, the merchant-conveyer and the lawyer who, whether in private practice or public office, attended to the needs of both landowners and merchants. In such a system, of course, there would be temporary conflicts between individual landowners and merchant-creditors. But, except in Venezuela in the 1840s, these disputes did not take on the character of systemic conflict required for them to become political issues. In general an urban-rural upper-class solidarity prevailed. This seems even to have been true in the Río de la Plata, all of the talk of city–country conflict there notwithstanding, for in Buenos Aires the interests of merchants and producers of hides and salted meat were closely meshed, and they often were the same individuals.

Recent studies of various parts of Spanish America have concluded that landowners, merchants and professionals are to be found prominently figuring in almost all political groups. What then can one say about the social characteristics differentiating the contending political groups? First, it cannot be expected that a single principle, or set of principles, of differentiation can be found that will apply accurately to all of the various Spanish American countries, with their differing geographies, ethnic configurations, economic characteristics and colonial traditions. However, several patterns may be posited that are applicable at least to some countries.

If a division between economic functional groups does not hold up well, one can perceive in several countries political divisions in which the distribution of power and status (across occupational lines) played an important role. In Mexico, New Granada and Peru there is a tendency for the affiliations of members of the political elite to correspond roughly to their social location, that is, to their relationship to the structures of economic and political power and of social prestige. This relationship generally was determined in part by regional origins as well as by accidents of birth and social connection within given regions.

Men tended to become conservatives if, in social terms, they were centrally located. This central location might be institutional. Often conservatives were born and raised in towns that had been administratively prominent and/or were educational centres in the colonial period. These places were characterized by a more aristocratic ethos, a more rigid social hierarchy, than the less significant provincial towns. Often the conservative atmosphere of these colonial administrative centres was reinforced by the fact that they were in a state of economic stagnation or decline during the first half of the nineteenth century. Nevertheless, the young men who grew up in them had distinct advantages in entering the political elite, both because of social ties to the hierarchies of civil and ecclesiastical administration and because of access to institutions of higher education that served as conduits to positions of power. Central social location might also be economic. Conservatives also tended to come from towns where there was concentrated economic power. Or their own families were important property owners or were in other ways economically powerful as large merchants or entrepreneurs.

Liberals tended to have more peripheral social locations. They often came from provincial towns that were less significant economically, administratively, or culturally in the colonial period, and where social stratification was less pronounced. They frequently had more limited access to the institutions of higher education that provided channels for entry into the political elite, both through formal training and through social contacts. As young men who journeyed from the provinces to the established cultural centres, often virtually penniless, they suffered a partial or difficult social incorporation into the political elite. Individuals of this sort, who entered the political elite through demonstrated talent, pluck and luck, rather than by birth, were likely to be most sensitive to liberal ideologies of legal equality and individual opportunity and to have no vested interest in the protection of colonial structures of power, privilege and prestige.

There also were peripheral merchants and landowners in the liberal ranks – though they were generally less visible than the professionals because a pronounced political identity could make economic enterprise more hazardous. Typical peripheral merchants might be provincial retailers who possessed limited capital, confronted limited markets and depended upon large merchants in the commercial centres for their supplies of goods and credit. Such men might see themselves as fighting to break through an established commercial structure of oligopoly-controlled trade and credit. However, the motivations of their liberalism might be associated with social opportunity as much as with economic role. Often these provincial merchants were even less privileged versions of the provincials who journeyed to the cultural centres to study law; they were men whose families' economic circumstances did not permit this luxury; thus they too identified strongly with the ideal of equality of opportunity. Many such marginal merchants, however, might be conservative or hostile to all political activity. Peripheral landowners were those holding properties that were relatively marginal either because of modest size or distance from urban markets and that, by the same token, conferred less social distinction than more favourably situated properties. Alternatively, they may have been engaged in export agriculture and thus were more exposed to fluctuations in world markets. Such men, like the peripheral merchants, *might* be, but were not necessarily, attached to liberal political forces.

Many men behaved contrary to the pattern which has been outlined. In particular, socially emergent professionals, whether from the capital city or the provinces, often were co-opted into conservative ranks where they served as political agents (journalists, legislators, etc.). It also should be noted that liberalism was strongest in those provinces that, while less important colonial centres, were not completely marginal in the scheme of republican national politics. They were provinces that could aspire to contend for political influence and power, not regions that were insignificant demographically and economically. Thus, in Mexico, liberalism was a dominant force in such states as Zacatecas, Michoacán, or Jalisco; it was less characteristic of the sparsely populated far north of Mexico which was more removed from national politics and where a few large landowners could dominate politics. Similarly, in New Granada, liberalism was strong in Socorro, which could challenge Bogotá; provinces such as Pasto, the Chocó, or Riohacha, which remained largely outside of the arena of national politics, were ruled by a few entrenched families and remained conservative rather than liberal in inclination.

In Mexico in the 1830s and 1840s it is hard to establish hard-and-fast social identifications of political alignments in part because there were so many political cross-currents, changing individual commitments, shifting factional alliances. Nevertheless it is possible to identify in these years four tendencies whose strength waxed and waned at various moments. At one extreme of the political spectrum were those who after 1830 assumed a centralist and pro-clerical stance and who became identified as conservatives at the end of the 1840s. A large proportion of those publicly identified as conservatives came from the centre of the country – from the upper sectors of Mexico City, the centre of all things; from Puebla, a city of importance as an industrial centre as well as in ecclesiastical administration and education; from Orizaba, closely associated with Puebla. Another city that spawned significant members of the conservative political elite was Campeche in Yucatán, not geographically central, but a town of local importance in the colonial period that was suffering stagnation in the early nineteenth century. Lucas Alamán, widely recognized as the central figure of Mexican conservatism, was the son of a rich mine-owner in Guanajuato, whose family was also closely linked to Spanish administrators there. Other prominent conservatives, like Antonio de Haro y Tamariz and Estevan de Antuñano, were connected with the industrial development of Puebla. Often allied with these civilian conservatives were a number of high-ranking officers in the professional army, particularly those whose military careers began in the Spanish army. While the civilian conservatives were attached to a centralist political system because they thought it more likely to produce order, for the professional military a centralist system was a prerequisite for the budgetary support of a large national army and for the military dominance of that army.

At the other political extreme were the federalists of the 1820s and 1830s or *puros* of the 1840s, who were most firmly committed to a programme of legal equality and the destruction of clerical and military privilege. The leadership of these liberals came predominantly from men with legal or medical professional education, though through the exigencies of civil war some developed military careers. They hailed particularly from provinces encircling the conservative, centralist core area, in an arc running from San Luis Potosí in the north, through Guanajuato and Zacatecas in the north-west to Jalisco and Michoacán in the west to Guerrero and Oaxaca in the south. The provincials' position outside the central structures of power and privilege inherited from the colonial period generally disposed them to the destruction or weakening of these structures. Particularly in provinces to the north and west of Mexico City a class of small farmers created an atmosphere of relative social egaliterianism contrasting with the seigneurial style of the aristocracy of the centre, and provided a substantial base of support for the liberal provincial elites' attacks upon centralist control and clerical privilege.[35]

Between the two poles of the Mexican political spectrum were two mediating groups that often came to power in coalition with one of the extremes. Moderate liberals gathered around Manuel Gómez Pedraza formed one of these intermediary or swing groups. Liberals in principle, they shared the conservatives' distaste for anything smacking too much of the rabble. They alternated between alliances with the conservatives, whose authoritarian centralism they distrusted, and the extreme liberals, whose populist tendencies they disliked. During the 1840s a number of these moderate liberals gravitated into the conservative camp, rallying behind the Church in opposition to *puro* anti-clericalism. The social origins of the moderates tended to be more heterogeneous than those of either extreme, drawing both from the same provincial element that formed the backbone of *puro* liberalism and from the aristocracy of the centre that characterized centralist, pro-clerical conservatism. The other intermediary group was that headed by General Antonio López de Santa Anna, which drew principally upon three clienteles – local supporters from his territorial base in Jalapa and Veracruz, the *agiotistas* (speculators in government bonds), and his following among the professional army, whose interests he often represented.

In New Granada the pattern of political division was sociologically similar to that in Mexico, though somewhat simpler. By the end of the 1830s two parties had emerged, in conflict less over ideology than over control of the government. The party that came to be called conservative at the end of the 1840s had particular strength in the cities of Bogotá, Popayán, Cartagena, and Tunja. All were centres of civil and ecclesiastical administration in the colonial period. In these cities also resided creoles enriched by gold-mining or commerce, or holding large properties worked by Indian peasants or black slaves. All consequently were dominated by social hierarchies headed by civilian and clerical administrators and supported by large property-owners. As centres of concentrated wealth and prestige, they were well endowed with conventual establishments and pious foundations. This meant that they possessed

---

[35] David A. Brading, *Los orígenes del nacionalismo mexicano* (Mexico, 1973), 207–21; Chevalier. 'Conservateurs et libéraux', 457–74.

the most important secondary schools, for in 1821 the properties of understaffed conventual establishments were used to finance *colegios* and universities in these localities. Until mid-century Bogotá, Cartagena and Popayán were the sites of the nation's three universities, and Tunja possessed the best-endowed secondary school. The political establishment ruling from 1837 through the 1840s (ultimately known as conservatives), reinforced the educational advantages of these cities by creating regulations making it impossible for other towns to grant degrees in medicine or law. Consequently, youths growing up in these favoured cities could obtain their university certificate for statecraft much more easily than those from smaller, less educationally endowed towns. The governing elite justified these restriction on the ground that a surplus of young, under-employed lawyers would increase demand for public office and thus create instability.[36]

Liberal strength was most evident in the region of Socorro, in the Caribbean port of Santa Marta and parts of the Upper Magdalena Valley. The Socorro region in the late colonial period was economically of some importance as a supplier of cottage-woven textiles to other parts of the viceroyalty. But Socorro was not an important centre of civil or ecclesiastical administration, and consequently lacked an elaborate social hierarchy or extensive conventional foundations. It was a society of small, independent farmers whose incomes were supplemented by the household weaving of their women, and it was much less aristocratic in social spirit than the administrative centres. The port of Santa Marta was relatively unimportant in the colonial period, for overseas trade was held as the monopoly of Cartagena, the administrative, military and ecclesiastical centre of the Caribbean coast. After 1820, however, under a system of free trade, Santa Marta emerged as New Granada's principal conduit for imported goods, displacing a declining Cartagena. Santa Marta was the seat of a group of emergent, energetic merchants fully committed to the benefits of free enterprise. The Upper Magdalena Valley, producer of tobacco, cinchona bark and cacao, was similarly linked to the expansion of international trade. In the Magdalena Valley as in Socorro small merchants and farmers called for the abolition of the government tobacco monopoly, which constricted individual opportunity and limited production of a potentially important export product but which those established in the government defended on grounds of fiscal

[36] Frank Safford, *The ideal of the practical: Colombia's struggle to form a technical elite* (Austin, Texas, 1976), 107–35.

necessity. In all of these provinces and others, secondary schools were either nonexistent or did not meet government requirements; young men who sought law degrees had, if their parents could afford it, to journey to the established centres, usually to the capital, to make their way. The abolition of restrictions on secondary education was one of the first concerns of the emergent liberal elite after it gained power in 1849.

One region in New Granada, however, fails to conform to the dichotomy of conservative administrative centres *versus* liberal provinces – the gold-mining province of Antioquia. Antioquia, like Socorro and the other liberal provinces, lacked an elaborate ecclesiastical establishment and hence a conventual endowment for secondary education. Like Socorro also, it was characterized by a relatively egalitarian society, compared with Bogotá or Popayán. Yet Antioquia during the 1840s became a bastion of conservatism. Apparently, while not favoured by a colonial institutional inheritance, it became identified with conservatism because of its substantial economic power. Through its gold-mining, it produced the majority of New Granada's foreign exchange in the late colonial period and through the first half of the nineteenth century. Antioqueño merchants, therefore, had a prospering economy to protect, unlike the elites in many other provinces. Thus, they enlisted themselves on the side of order, whatever political form that might take. Like other conservatives they supported the Roman Catholic Church, both out of piety and because it helped to shore up the social order.

The social-location analytical model may be extended to Peru, where a division may be perceived between the conservative Pandos, Pardos and Herreras of Lima and emergent liberals from the provinces, such as Luna Pizarro from Arequipa, Benito Laso from Puno and the Gálvez brothers from Cajamarca. The model works less well in some other places, however. In Buenos Aires it is possible to identify economic power, in the persons of the cattle and salt-meat entrepreneurs, with conservative political forces in the 1820s and 1830s. But the political conservatives who gathered around Juan Manuel de Rosas were no more closely linked to colonial institutional structures than their opponents. In Buenos Aires the conflict seems to have been essentially a struggle between these dominant economic interests, who preferred to do without the nuisance of politics and stood behind Rosas as an agent of order, and a group of educated men who aspired to western liberal political standards. In this sense it was a struggle between 'barbarism' and 'civilization'. A similar struggle between an urban literary elite, attempting to impose something like European political norms, and caudillos with rural ties and little sense of constitutionalism, also marked the politics of Uruguay in the period.

Whatever the political persuasion of members of the Spanish American elite, it is striking how little confidence they showed in their new countries. The largely Spanish-descended elites in no way identified with the *mestizos*, Indians and blacks who formed the lower classes in their countries, and in their own minds they associated themselves more with the European bourgeoisie. Judging the majority of the people in their societies to be backward and ignorant, the elite believed it would be hard to forge a nation from such elements. Partly for this reason almost everywhere in Spanish America the elites enthusiastically encouraged European immigration; they believed immigrants would bring not merely skills and capital but also a more European cast to society. In addition to their distrust of the general population, confidence was further undermined by the chronic political instability of the period, with its attendant insecurity of property in time of civil war. This loss of confidence was reflected in various ways. Some members of the elite emigrated to Europe, and a few more attempted to emigrate without leaving home, seeking to protect their property by becoming recognized as citizens of the United States or of some European power.

Loss of confidence in the new nations was augmented by pressure from foreign powers. Mexico, the Río de la Plata region, New Granada and other areas felt the weight of British and French blockades in the 1830s. Mexico and Central America had to cope with the additional problem of North American aggression. These external forces at once intimidated and seduced the elites. Factions in the elite were often tempted to compromise national independence in order to obtain the aid of an external power. Such was the case of the Uruguayan gentlemen who sought aid from Portuguese Brazil between 1817 and 1825 and of the Argentine *unitarios* exiled in Montevideo who in the late 1830s could not resist alliance with the French against their enemy Rosas in Buenos Aires. (Political factions almost everywhere, of course, also had recourse to aid from neighbouring Spanish American countries.)

On occasion the collapse of confidence in the nation reached such a pitch that elites were willing, in one way or another, to abandon national independence altogether. Lorenzo Zavala in Mexico was so impressed by the economic strength and dynamism of the United States that by 1831 he welcomed North American penetration of Texas as the prelude to a general triumph of liberty in Mexico through the agency of Yankee colonization. Not long afterward Zavala cast his lot with the Yankee state of Texas in its assertion of independence from Mexico. In the following decade the elites in Yucatán, unable to obtain effective help from a collapsed Mexican government in their efforts to dominate Indian rebellion, attempted to annex their province to the United States. More startling and less well known, when in 1857 the United States was pressing New Granada for compensation for the deaths of American citizens in riots in Panama and New Granadan leaders despaired of obtaining British protection, President Mariano Ospina Rodríguez proposed to Washington the annexation of the entire republic of New Granada by the United States. Ospina reasoned that in view of the United States' inexorable expansion, as demonstrated in war with Mexico in 1846–8 and in the filibuster adventures in Nicaragua of the 1850s, New Granada would inevitably be swallowed up sooner or later. Better to get it over with quickly, without unnecessary bloodshed, particularly considering the probability that rule by the United States would bring stability and security of property. A different sort of abdication of independence, but for the same ends, was pursued in the same period by Mexican conservatives who sought to introduce a European monarch to their country.

This fragile sense of the nation was probably greatest in Mexico, most threatened by the United States, and in the Río de la Plata, where the so-called United Provinces could hardly be said to have constituted a nation at all before 1861. A sense of nationhood was probably strongest, on the other hand, in Chile, where national pride was bolstered by triumph in the war against the Peruvian–Bolivian Confederation in 1839, combined with a notable economic prosperity and substantial political order between 1830 and 1850.

Political instability in Spanish America between 1810 and 1870 has invited many explanations. These can be broken down into two general categories, though there are numerous subdivisions within each category. One line of interpretation, taking an extremely long view, tends to emphasize the role of deep-rooted cultural and institutional patterns. Other approaches, which tend to look more closely at events in time, stress the effects of economic and social variables.

Cultural explanations of Spanish American instability have several variants. Earlier in the twentieth century interpretations tended to stress psycho-cultural elements somewhat more than institutions. The Peruvian Francisco García Calderón, under the influence of Miguel de Unamuno and other turn-of-the-century Spanish writers, attributed Spanish American instability to an anarchic, intolerant and exclusivist individualism that was embedded in Spanish culture. At the same time García Calderón noted a seemingly contrary monarchical tradition that, in the republican era, was conducive to presidential dictatorship, which in turn provoked rebellion.[37]

Another exploration of psycho-cultural elements in political instability, a brilliant *tour de force* by the British scholar, Cecil Jane, drew upon the same Spanish sources as García Calderón, but emphasized more the contradictions within Spanish culture. Jane viewed Spaniards and Spanish Americans as idealistic extremists who sought both order and individual liberty in such perfect forms that Spanish American politics swung from one extreme (despotism) to the other (anarchy), rather than finding stability in constitutional compromise between the two contending principles. In the sixteenth and seventeenth centuries, according to Jane, the Hapsburg monarchy managed to embody both of these extreme tendencies, holding them in contradictory, but effective, co-existence. (The Hapsburg monarch proclaimed absolute order but in effect, through inefficiency, permitted much freedom.) Once the king was removed, the extremes found no effective resolution. In the nineteenth century, when conservatives, who embodied the principle of order, were in power, they carried the pursuit of order to such extremes that they inevitably provoked a violent reaction in behalf of liberty. Similarly, when liberals enacted standard western liberal protections of the individual, Spanish Americans did not use these liberties with the responsibility expected by the Englishmen who had developed these liberties, but rather carried them to the extreme of anarchy. The lack of dictatorial restraint brought individualistic chaos, which in turn provoked the resumption of dictatorship.[38]

More recently the cultural mode of explanation has been reformulated in still another way by Richard Morse. Morse, like García Calderón,

---

[37] Francisco García Calderón, *Latin America: its rise and progress* (New York, 1913). Recently an American scholar, Glen Dealy, has not only exhumed the theme of Spanish anarchic individualism to explain the phenomenon of *caudillismo* but has argued that liberal constitutionalism, with its emphasis on tolerance of dissent, was doomed in Spanish America because it was in conflict with the Spanish Catholic 'monist' tradition, which assumes a unified, not a pluralist, society. Dealey, 'La tradición de la democracia monista', 159–201, and idem, *The public man: an interpretation of Latin American and other Catholic countries* (Amherst, Mass., 1977).

[38] Lionel Cecil Jane, *Liberty and despotism in Spanish America* (London, 1929).

is concerned with explaining the tendency to both personalist authoritarianism and anarchy in nineteenth-century Spanish America. Morse sees these characteristics both as being inherent in the Spanish legacy itself and also as being reinforced by the conflict between Spanish traditions and the imported Western liberal constitutional ideals that came into play in Spanish America at the time of independence.

For Morse the key to understanding Spanish American politics lies in the Spanish patrimonial state. He points out that in Spain, as contrasted with other parts of Europe, feudal institutions were weak; the various interest groups (nobility, Church, merchants, etc.) rather than constituting relatively autonomous power centres were heavily dependent upon the state. The state was embodied in the patrimonial power of the king, who was not only the source of all patronage but also the ultimate arbiter of all disputes. The patrimonial ruler (in accord with the Weberian typology):

is reluctant to bind himself by 'law', his rule takes the form of a series of directives, each subject to supersession. . . . Legal remedies are frequently regarded not as applications of 'law', but as a gift of grace or a privilege awarded on the merits of a case and not binding as precedent.[39]

He thus governs in a personalist, potentially arbitrary, manner rather than according to a rule of law.

Thus the organization of power in the system ultimately depended upon the king. Without the presence of the king, the system shattered. Because of the lack of a feudal tradition, Spanish America did not possess the 'underpinning of contractual vassalic relationships that capacitate the component parts of a *feudal* regime for autonomous life'. Most importantly perhaps, the weakness of Spanish feudalism contributed to the weakness of parliamentary traditions. Thus, with the disappearance of the king,

the collapse of the supreme authority activated the latent forces of local oligarchies, municipalities, and extended-family systems in a struggle for power and prestige in the new, arbitrarily defined republics . . . In the absence of developed and interacting economic interest groups having a stake in constitutional process, the new countries were plunged into alternating regimes of anarchy and personalist tyranny. The contest to seize a patrimonial state apparatus, fragmented from the original imperial one, became the driving force of public life in each new country.[40]

[39] Richard M. Morse, 'The heritage of Latin America', in Louis Hartz, *The founding of new societies* (New York, 1964), 157.
[40] *Ibid.*, 162.

In Morse's view, Spanish American political leaders in the nineteenth century were constantly trying to reconstruct the patrimonial authority of the Spanish Crown. But the personalist political leaders (caudillos), while in a number of cases able to establish a temporary charismatic authority, were not able to institutionalize their rule in a generally-accepted 'super-personal legitimacy'. The great exception proving Morse's rule was nineteenth-century Chile, where a unified landowning and commercial elite, under the charismatic leadership of Diego Portales, was able to legitimate a system in which a strong executive could successfully exercise patrimonial power approximating that of the Spanish crown.

One important factor impeding the reconstruction of patrimonial authority along traditional Spanish lines, according to Morse, was the intromission of Western constitutional ideas during the independence era. Anglo-French liberal constitutionalism – with its emphasis on the rule of law, the division and separation of powers, constitutional checks on authority and the efficacy of elections – stood as a contradiction to those traditional attitudes and modes of behaviour which lived in the marrow of Spanish Americans. Because liberal constitutionalism was ill-adapted to traditional Spanish political culture, attempts to erect and maintain states according to liberal principles invariably failed. On the other hand, the authority of imported liberal constitutional ideas, while insufficient to provide a viable alternative to the traditional political model, was often sufficient to undermine the legitimacy of governments operating according to the traditional model. Thus, Spanish America's political instability between 1810 and 1870 was, in Morse's view, aggravated by the tension between traditional political models, to which Spanish American leaders gravitated instinctively, and constitutional principles, which served as a constant criticism of those who used power in the traditional manner. In Morse's interpretation stability could be achieved only when a synthesis could be achieved in which traditional models dominated and constitutional principles became mere window-dressing. This, he contends, was the pattern in the exceptional case of Chile, where the 'structure of the Spanish patrimonial state was re-created, with only those minimum concessions to Anglo-French constitutionalism that were necessary for a nineteenth-century republic which had just rejected monarchical rule'.[41]

41 *Ibid.*, 163–4.

Morse's cultural analysis is in many ways compelling. Reviewing the political history of Spanish America in the fifty years after independence, one can find many examples of behaviour that fit well into his conceptions. On the other hand, the approach has some evident weaknesses. First, like many analyses that emphasize culture as a determining variable, Morse's interpretations, and those that follow him, treat culture in an excessively static manner – as if Spanish culture, once crystallized at some point in the distant past, never underwent significant change afterward. In particular, there is a tendency to underestimate the degree to which imported liberal constitutional ideas came not only to be sincerely believed by the university-educated but even to attain a substantial legitimacy. Liberal constitutionalist ideals failed to achieve the hegemony they enjoyed in British cultures, but they did have a significant effect on modes of political thought and became at least partially incorporated into the political rules. The constitutionalist idea of 'no re-election', for example, was violated frequently, yet the idea had sufficient power to serve as a means of discrediting those who sought to continue themselves in office. And in a number of countries by the end of the period it had become an effective part of the living constitution.

Second, the cultural interpretations of Morse and others in their concentration on concepts of legitimacy and political and social values tend to disregard the role of geographic, economic, and social structural factors in destabilizing political systems, and in permitting their stabilization. For example, Chile's unique stability in the 1830s and 1840s was aided by the singular geographical concentration of its landed and commercial elite. Chile in these years was also enjoying a prosperity that was exceptional by comparison with other Spanish American countries. This prosperity generated funds that enabled the Chilean government to sustain itself against attempted rebellions. In this light, the success of the Portalean system of presidential authoritarianism which after Portales' death became institutionalized may not so much be attributable to its harmony with traditional values and expectations[42] as to the fact that it had the wherewithal to suppress dissidents, something that other, fiscally weakened republics were less able to do. In some circumstances, may not a government be considered 'legitimate' largely because it has the power to maintain itself?

[42] See Francisco Antonio Moreno's application of Morse's interpretations to Portalean Chile in *Legitimacy and stability in Latin America: a study of Chilean political culture* (New York, 1969), 91–127.

In contrast with the cultural interpretations, other analyses emphasize the economic causes of political instability in Spanish America. One variant of such analyses, now of some vintage, stresses conflicts among different regions or social groups that were generated by their differing interests in relation to the international economy. An interpretation of this sort, although unstructured, is implied in the work of Justo Sierra, who contends that several of the rebellions in pre-1850 Mexico were produced by the machinations of coastal merchants who objected to changes in government tariff policies. A much clearer example is Miron Burgin's analysis of Argentine politics in the period, which stresses the conflict of regional economic interests.[43]

Recently there has developed some scepticism about interpretations emphasizing conflicting group or regional interests. While individual merchants or landowners might have civil or private disputes over loans or contracts, almost never were there political conflicts between merchants and landowners as groups, because, in an export economy, their long-term interests tended to coincide. The case of Venezuela in the 1840s is, in this respect, exceptional. Conflicting regional economic interests, while possibly discernible in some cases, were also unlikely to generate major political conflict. In most Spanish American countries transportation was so backward and expensive that the various regions hardly formed part of the same economy and there was little opportunity for their interests to come sharply into conflict. Minor intra-regional conflicts did occur, as different towns in the same region competed for supremacy as ports or political centres. But these intra-regional conflicts were unlikely to cause national government to become unstrung.

In fact, in these unintegrated economies instability was more likely to be caused by *lack* of economic interest than by conflicting economic interests. In a number of countries the regions that most frequently initiated rebellions against the national government were those whose location made it difficult or impossible to participate effectively in the export trade. In these regions the local elites, for lack of economic opportunities in which to invest their energies, turned to politico-military enterprise. In New Granada, the Cauca region, trapped between two looming mountain-ranges and thus unable to export its product effectively, was a seedbed of rebellion throughout the period. Economic stagnation undoubtedly also played a part in the frequent rebellions of Arequipa and Cuzco against authorities in Lima. And parts of the

[43] Sierra, *Political evolution of the Mexican people*, 213, 218–19, 222, 229–30; Miron Burgin, *Economic aspects of Argentine federalism* (Cambridge, Mass., 1946).

Argentine interior probably also fit this pattern. In contrast, those regions that were most effectively integrated into the export economy tended to be the most stable politically. In Argentina, the possibility of profiting from external trade undoubtedly played an important part in unifying the merchants and ranchers of Buenos Aires behind the stern, no-nonsense government of Juan Manuel de Rosas. Realization that the progress of their province lay in international trade and that efforts to dominate the rest of the country had only served to check this economic progress encouraged them to support Rosas in a policy of attending to the province and forgoing political grandeur.

Several interpretations argue that before 1870 limited integration into the international economy and the lack of an integrated national economy delayed the emergence of dominant bourgeoisies that could, in alliance with foreign interests, act effectively to guarantee political order and stability in Spanish America. Because of the character of the hacienda economy, landowners were not cohesive enough to form political alliances that could control the politics of their countries. Consequently, ambitious, socially-emergent caudillos stepped into the power vacuum. However, these caudillos as political entrepreneurs were not able to satisfy more than temporarily the armed bands that followed them, so that their periods of dominance generally were short-lived.[44]

Interpretations of instability that emphasize the lack of a strong, united class committed to sustain the state are complemented by treatments that stress the financial weakness of the new governments. Lack of funds made it difficult for them to retain the loyalty of the armies as well as to co-opt potentially dissident civilian elites through patronage. Like other Spanish American countries, Mexico, for example, was burdened with heavy foreign debts acquired originally in the 1820s. Mexican governments, according to Jan Bazant, faced a choice of either collecting taxes to make payments on the debts, thus courting internal rebellion, or of not paying the foreign creditors, thus inviting the intervention of foreign powers. Hoping to rescue the state from its chronic near-bankruptcy, Mexican leaders were tempted to lay their hands on the great wealth of the Church; but attacks upon Church property also brought rebellion, and, on occasion, the overthrow of the government.[45]

Both the fiscal approach to political instability and the analysis

---

[44] Wolf and Hansen, 'Caudillo politics', 168–79. For further discussion of *caudillismo*, see above, pp 370–5.

[45] Jan Bazant, *Alienation of church wealth in Mexico* (Cambridge, 1971), as elaborated upon by Stephen R. Niblo and Laurens B. Perry, 'Recent additions to nineteenth-century Mexican historiography', in *Latin American Research Review*, 13/3 (1978), 13–15.

pointing to the lack of strong supporting classes are brought together in the interpretation of Tulio Halperín Donghi. Halperín ascribes the financial weakness of the new states partly to the effects of Spanish America's engagement with the Atlantic economy. Acute trade imbalances created currency stringencies and economic contraction, weakening the economic underpinnings of their governments. At the same time their social underpinnings, most particularly the urban bourgeoisie, were weakened by the invasion of foreign merchants and the inability of the state to pay its civilian employees.[46] Possibly Halperín, on the basis of Argentine experience, exaggerates the extent to which Spanish American merchants were undermined, for in some places foreign merchants' control of the markets was only temporary. But an interpretation stressing the commercial situation of the new countries has the advantage of helping to explain not merely the instability of the 1810–70 period when the trade positions of most of them were relatively weak but also the relatively greater political stability of the post-1870 period, when increasing European demand greatly augmented the volume of their exports as well as improving their trade balances.

By contrast with the political instability that characterized most of Spanish America between 1810 and 1870, the decades from 1870 to 1910 were years of political consolidation and centralization, generally under governments of a secular and modernizing but more or less authoritarian and undemocratic cast. In Mexico, the liberal hegemony established by Benito Juárez with the overthrow of Maximilian's imperial government in 1867 evolved into the dictatorship of Porfirio Díaz (1876–1911). In Guatemala the regime of Justo Rufino Barrios (1871–85) provided a similar combination of formal liberalism and authoritarian rule. In Venezuela the comparable anti-clerical, liberal, modernizing dictator was Antonio Guzmán Blanco (1870–88). In Colombia the establishment of authoritarian order was attempted in the 1880s by Rafael Núñez, a man of liberal antecedents who sustained his centralist regime through alliance with the Church and ardently pro-clerical Conservatives. Argentina presented another variation on the same theme, as, under an oligarchy rather than a dictator, it became consolidated politically as a unified nation in the 1870s and enjoyed economic growth unparalleled in Latin America during subsequent decades.

[46] Halperín, *Aftermath of revolution*, 1–43.

From the point of view of the intellectual and cultural historian the Porfiriato and other authoritarian liberal regimes are notable for their abandonment of all but the external trappings of liberal ideology and for the adoption of a more hardheaded, authoritarian political style. These regimes may thus be considered as having returned to something more closely approximating the governing mode of Spanish tradition. Most interpreters of the era of political consolidation after 1870, however, tend to emphasize the economic foundations of the new order. Growing European and North American demand for Latin American raw materials brought a flow of foreign loans and investments in railroads, mines and export agriculture and, in the case of Argentina and Uruguay, European immigrants as well. These foreign inputs, as well as greatly increased returns from exports and customs collections on imports, gave some regimes in the 1870–1910 period the wherewithal to co-opt potential dissidents into government jobs, and placate them with concessions or contracts, and to maintain modernized national armies with which to repress those opponents who could not be bought. Not only were these central governments now fiscally stronger and therefore more able to contain dissent, but the economic opportunities of the era also tended so to absorb the attention of the upper sectors that their interest in politics as a form of economic enterprise greatly subsided. The new era was, for the upper sectors, one of moneymaking more than political conflict, of businesslike practicality rather more than ideological crusading. It was an era of 'order and progress'.

10

MEXICO FROM INDEPENDENCE
TO 1867[1]

The royalist brigadier, Agustín de Iturbide, proclaimed the independence of Mexico on 24 February 1821 at Iguala, a small town in the heart of the southern, tropical *tierra caliente* or 'hot country'. In his manifesto, the Plan of Iguala, Iturbide called for independence, the union of Mexicans and Spaniards and respect for the Roman Catholic Church. The form of government was to be a constitutional monarchy in which the emperor would be chosen from a European, preferably Spanish, dynasty 'so as to give us a monarch already made and save us from fatal acts of ambition', and the national constitution was to be drawn up by a congress. With this the first of his so-called 'three guarantees', Iturbide won the support of the old guerrilla fighters for independence, particularly General Vicente Guerrero who at this time was operating not far from Iguala. The second guarantee offered security to Spanish-born residents of Mexico, and with the third he sought to attract the clerical establishment by promising to preserve ecclesiastical privileges, recently under attack in Spain by the liberal, revolutionary regime. The army would take upon itself the task of 'protecting' the guarantees.

Iturbide's appeal proved remarkably successful. In less than six months, he was master of the country, except for the capital city and the ports of Acapulco and Veracruz. It was at Veracruz that the newly appointed Spanish captain-general, Juan O'Donojú, disembarked on 30 July. He had been instructed to introduce liberal reforms in New Spain but at the same time to ensure that the colony remained within the Spanish empire. His instructions, however, were based on information received in Madrid about events which had taken place in the colony some four or five months previously, and he at once recognized that the

---

[1] The Author and the Editor wish to acknowledge the help of Professor Michael P. Costeloe, University of Bristol, in the final preparation of this chapter.

situation had changed significantly since then. Mexican independence appeared to him already a fact and, wanting to depart as quickly as possible from the yellow fever infested port, he decided to seek a meeting with Iturbide. They met on 24 August in Córdoba, at the foot of the snow-capped Citlaltepetl volcano, and they signed a treaty which recognized 'The Mexican Empire' as a sovereign and independent nation. The treaty paraphrased the Iguala manifesto, but there were several modifications. According to the manifesto, the throne was to be offered to Ferdinand VII, or, in case of his refusal, to a prince of a reigning dynasty. It was assumed that there would be at least one prince willing to accept. The text signed in Córdoba, however, named four specific candidates, all of the Spanish dynasty, and no reference was made to other European royal families. If the four Spaniards were to refuse the throne, the future emperor was to be selected by the Mexican congress. This change is unlikely to have been fortuitous, and it was to have important consequences, especially in the career of the ambitious Iturbide. As the meeting at Córdoba lasted only a few hours, it seems certain that Iturbide had already carefully prepared the long text in advance and was well aware of the implications of the changes made to the original Iguala declaration. O'Donojú, on the other hand, who must have been tired following his long journey from Spain and was possibly ill, overlooked the modification. He signed the document with his constitutional title of Captain General and Superior Political Chief, although to the present day he remains known in Mexico as the last Spanish viceroy. Brigadier Iturbide signed as First Chief of the Imperial Army. Within a few months he was to be Generalísimo.

The acceptance of independence by O'Donojú facilitated the transfer of power in the capital. Having delayed his entrance so that it coincided with his thirty-eighth birthday, Iturbide rode into Mexico City on 27 September. On the next morning, he chose the thirty-eight members of the governing junta stipulated in both the Iguala manifesto and the treaty of Córdoba. In a formal act, this junta then declared the independence of Mexico. With Iturbide acting as its president, the junta consisted of well-known ecclesiastics, lawyers, judges, members of the Mexican nobility and a few army officers, among them Colonel Anastasio Bustamante who, like Iturbide, was a former royalist officer. Old fighters for independence such as Nicolás Bravo, Guadalupe Victoria and Guerrero were not members, but O'Donojú was included in accordance with the agreement reached at Córdoba. It was expected that he would give

Iturbide a helping hand in the transition between the viceroyalty and a future empire under a Spanish prince. In fact, O'Donojú fell ill and died ten days later before being able to appoint the commissioners who were to have gone to Madrid to negotiate a settlement, again as envisaged in the Córdoba agreement. As president of the junta and regent of the empire, Generalísimo Iturbide could still have sent envoys to Madrid but he did not do so.

Not surprisingly, the Spanish attitude towards Mexican independence was hostile from the beginning. Although the greater part of the Spanish army stationed in Mexico swore allegiance to the new nation, a group of royalist diehards withdrew to San Juan de Ulúa, an island fortress in front of Veracruz harbour, and waited there for reinforcements with which to reconquer the country. They were not disavowed by the Madrid government and on 13 February 1822 the Spanish Cortes rejected the Córdoba treaty. The news of this refusal by the mother country to accept Mexico's independence reached Mexico City several months later.

Independence in 1821 did not bring any immediate revolutionary change in the social or economic structure of the country. The first and principal effect was that the political power formerly exercised by the royal bureaucracy was transferred to the army, that is to say, to a coalition of Iturbide's royalist and Guerrero's republican armies.

The second pillar of the new nation was the Roman Catholic Church. Like all the established colonial institutions, it had suffered significant losses in its manpower and material possessions during the decade of war. By 1822 there were ten dioceses but only four had bishops, and from a total of 4,229 in 1810 the secular clergy had decreased to 3,487. The male regulars had decreased from 3,112 in 1810 to approximately 2,000 by the end of 1821 and the number of monasteries from 208 to 153. In sum, the total number of clergy fell from 9,439 to 7,500 and the number of parishes also declined. Church revenues, particularly from tithes, showed a substantial fall. In the archbishopric of Mexico, the tithe income was reduced from 510,081 pesos in 1810 to 232,948 pesos in 1821 and in the dioceses of Michoacán, from 500,000 pesos to 200,000 pesos by 1826.

The tithe figures reflect the general economic decline which had taken place. The statistics provided by the amount of coinage minted indicate that mining decreased by more than a half from a yearly average of 22½ million pesos in 1800–9 to approximately 10 million pesos in 1820 and 1822. (In 1821 only about 6 million pesos were minted.) There is no reliable information available on agriculture and manufacturing. Cereal production may have recovered by 1820, but sugar cane and other farming sectors remained depressed. Manufacturing output may have declined by as much as a half and public finances were reduced by a similar proportion. Government revenues in 1822 amounted to over 9 million pesos but expenditure rose to 13 million pesos, leaving a deficit of 4 million pesos. The public or national debt had shown a marked increase from 20 million pesos in 1808 to 35 million pesos in 1814 and 45 million pesos by 1822.

It was against this background of economic recession and budget deficit that the constitutional congress assembled in the capital on 24 February 1822. To Iturbide's unpleasant surprise, most of the deputies were either 'bourbonists', that is, pro-Spanish monarchists, or republicans. They were in dispute with him over several matters from the very first day and it was against a background of rapidly deteriorating relations between Iturbide and the deputies that the Spanish rejection of the Córdoba agreement became known. Until that moment, Spain, the mother country with which the bonds of kinship and religion remained strong, had still been venerated by almost everyone. Now Spain denied freedom to her daughter country. The ensuing resentment and disappointment quickly gave rise to the feeling that there was no reason why Mexico should not have a monarch of its own choosing. Spain, by its refusal to accept the reality of independence and its rejection of the opportunity to keep Mexico within the Bourbon dynasty, played into the hands of Iturbide. On the night of 18 May 1822, the local army garrison proclaimed him Emperor Agustín I and on the next morning, under considerable military and popular pressure, congress accepted the situation and acknowledged its new monarch. Since Spain had rejected the Córdoba treaty, said deputy Valentín Gómez Farías, a physician and future liberal leader, Mexico was free to determine its own destiny. In the absence of the archbishop who declined to anoint the new ruler, Iturbide was crowned by the president of the congress on 21 July in the capital's magnificent cathedral.

Iturbide's empire was not to last. From the outset, there were basic obstacles to its survival. The Mexican nobility yearned for a European prince and looked with disdain on Iturbide, the son of a merchant; *hacendados* and traders, most of whom were Spanish born, hoped for a European prince to deliver them from forced loans and other fiscal burdens; and finally there was a strong body of republicans which included some prominent journalists, lawyers and progressive clergy. One such cleric was Servando Teresa de Mier who, after an adventurous life in Europe and the United States, had been imprisoned in the dungeons of the San Juan de Ulúa fortress. Its shrewd Spanish commander released him at the end of May and Servando soon occupied a seat in congress. Both within that assembly and in the public arena outside, he was to propagate his republican ideas with great vigour.

It is not surprising, therefore, that Iturbide's fall was even faster than his elevation. The bourbonists charged him with having violated his promise to offer the throne to a European prince. Iturbide's own arbitrary acts encouraged the spread of republican ideas which until then had by and large been restricted to intellectuals. Ambitious army officers were also discontented; while a foreign prince might be tolerable, they found it difficult to accept one of their own kind; if an imported prince was not to be had, then the solution was a republic, which was at least a system in which they could become presidents. Opposition to Iturbide grew and in an atmosphere of restricted freedom of expression, conspiracies mushroomed. By 26 August, just five weeks after his coronation, Iturbide had already imprisoned nineteen members of congress and several army officers. On 31 October, he dissolved the troublesome congress altogether. He weakened his position even further by a series of confiscatory fiscal measures and the merchants who suffered, for the most part Spanish, turned to the bourbonists for support.

The port of Veracruz was especially important to Iturbide's security. It was situated opposite the island fortress of San Juan de Ulúa which remained in Spanish hands.[2] A rebellion might be started there, with Spanish acquiescence if not support, and in the event of failure, rebel leaders could take refuge in the fortress. Distrusting the ambitious young military commander of Veracruz, a twenty-eight-year old colonel, Antonio López de Santa Anna, Iturbide summoned him to Jalapa, a town in the mountains over a hundred kilometres from the port, where he relieved him of his command and ordered him to report to Mexico City. Santa Anna had not the slightest intention of obeying the emperor. After galloping all night, he returned to his barracks the following morning and, before news of his removal reached Veracruz, on the afternoon of the same day, 2 December 1822, he publicly accused Iturbide of tyranny. He proclaimed a republic, calling for the reinstallation of congress and

---

[2] The Spaniards in San Juan de Ulúa did not capitulate until 1825.

the formation of a constitution based on 'Religion, Independence and Union', that is, the same three guarantees of the Iguala manifesto which he claimed had been infringed by the emperor. He also made a bid for the support of influential local Spanish merchants at Veracruz by calling for peace and commerce with the mother country.[3]

Within a few days, however, Santa Anna had changed his mind about his hasty profession of republican faith. In 1822, Mexican republicans did not often use the term 'republic' in their propaganda; instead, they spoke of Liberty, Nation and the Sovereignty of Congress. A decade previously, Hidalgo had not formally proclaimed independence and it had taken several years for the idea of a Mexico not subject to the king of Spain to take root. Now, similarly, the word republic also sounded too revolutionary. Hence Santa Anna revised his position and, four days later, he issued a more moderate and detailed manifesto. This document was probably drawn up by the former minister of the newly independent republic of Colombia to Mexico, Miguel Santa María (a native of Veracruz), who had been expelled by Iturbide for participating in a republican conspiracy and was at that time in Veracruz awaiting a ship to take him home. Without mentioning a republic, the manifesto called for the removal of the emperor. 'The true liberty of the fatherland' meant a republic to the republicans and a constitutional monarchy to bourbonists and Spaniards. Thus both factions were urged to unite against Iturbide. The insistence on the Iguala guarantees had the same purpose: 'independence' was essential to Mexicans, 'union' to Spaniards, and 'religion' to both. It is not known whether Santa Anna was sincere about the republic or whether he had imperial ambitions of his own.

A fortuitous circumstance helped Santa Anna: the inveterate guerrilla fighter, Guadalupe Victoria, who had recently escaped from prison, chanced to be in Veracruz and he signed Santa Anna's manifesto of 6 December 1822. Thus Santa Anna, who had been a royalist officer during the war of independence and until now a supporter of Iturbide, secured the aid of a famous insurgent general who was already suspected of republican inclinations. A few weeks later, Generals Bravo and Guerrero, former comrades-in-arms of Morelos, escaped from Mexico City and once back in their own region of the *tierra caliente*, they declared their support for the Veracruz uprising. 'We are not against the established system of government', they declared: 'we do not intend to

---

[3] The proclamation is reproduced in C. M. Bustamante, *Diario Histórico de México, I, 1822–1823* (Zacatecas, 1896), 16–17.

become republicans; far from that, we only seek our liberty.' Such denials, however, seem to confirm the impression that they were indeed republicans, but their own support was among Indian peasants who were held to be not only religious but also monarchist. Finally, the majority of the army in which the officers – many of them Spaniards by birth – had been royalists and later supporters of Iturbide succumbed to the influence of two former Mexican liberal deputies to the Spanish Cortes, the priest Miguel Ramos Arizpe and José Mariano Michelena. The army 'pronounced' itself against Iturbide. The emperor abdicated on 19 March 1823, and the reassembled congress promptly appointed a provisional triumvirate consisting of Generals Victoria, Bravo and Negrete, the first two of whom were generally thought to be republicans. On 8 April, congress nullified the Iguala manifesto as well as the Córdoba treaty and decreed that Mexico was henceforth free to adopt whatever constitutional system it wished. The republic was a fact.

Thus Santa Anna had unleashed a movement which brought down Iturbide's empire and ended with the establishment of a republic. Even if the new political system was conceived by intellectuals, it was the army which had converted it into reality and at the same time become its master. The speed with which it succeeded pointed the way to future uprisings by dissatisfied military officers.

Bearing in mind Iturbide's past services to the nation's independence, congress did not at first deal with him harshly. He was offered a generous allowance provided that he resided in Italy. But the former emperor was not happy in exile. Misled by rumours of support, he returned in July 1824, landing near Tampico on the Gulf Coast, and unaware that, during his absence, congress had declared him a traitor. He was arrested and executed within a few days of his arrival.

Iturbide's inability to introduce some measure of order into the Treasury had been an important cause of his downfall. The triumvirate applied itself at once to the task of restoring public confidence and the improved atmosphere made it possible to obtain two loans on the London market: 16 million pesos were borrowed at the beginning of 1824 with Goldschmitt and Company and a similar amount with Barclay and Company a few months later.[4] Mexico thereby assumed a burden of 32 million pesos in foreign debt, but because of a low contract price and bankers' deductions, only about 10 million pesos was in fact received.

---

[4] Throughout the period examined in this chapter one peso equalled one U.S. dollar.

The government originally expected to use this money for long-term improvements, but when it finally arrived it was quickly absorbed by current expenses such as salaries of public employees, notably the military. Nevertheless, the proceeds of these loans seem to have been a stabilizing factor in the first years of the republic and in 1823–4 the foreign debt which they entailed did not seem excessive.[5] With British interest in the mineral resources of the country very evident, Mexico was optimistic about its future. During the years 1823 to 1827 the British invested more than 12 million pesos in Mexican mining ventures, especially silver-mining companies. Thus a total of well over 20 million pesos were injected into the ailing economy.

The person who was most instrumental in bringing British capital to Mexico was Lucas Alamán, who from April 1823 was Minister of the Interior and of Foreign Affairs (one of four Cabinet members). The brilliant son of a Mexican mining family which had acquired a Spanish title of nobility, Alamán had returned from a prolonged stay in Europe shortly after Iturbide's fall from power. As Marquis of San Clemente, he had perhaps dreamt of becoming a minister in the court of a Mexican Bourbon monarch, but the end of Iturbide's empire was not followed by any renewal of attempts to offer the throne to a European prince. On the contrary, it meant the end of serious monarchist plans for many years to come. Alamán entered, therefore, into the service of a republican government.

With the republic now taken for granted and monarchism being viewed almost as treason, new labels began to be adopted. Former supporters of a Mexican empire with a European prince at its head became centralist republicans, advocating a strong, centralized régime, reminiscent of the viceroyalty. Most of the republican opponents of Iturbide became federalists, supporting a federation of states on the United States model. The old destructive struggle between royalists and independents, who had in 1821 become bourbonists and republicans respectively and then temporary allies against Iturbide, re-emerged in 1823 under different slogans. After Iturbide's abdication power fell briefly into the hands of the bourbonist faction, but then a perhaps unexpected turn of events had helped the republican cause. Blaming the bourbonists for having overthrown Iturbide, the former emperor's supporters now joined the republicans and the elections for the new constitutional congress produced a majority for the federalists.

---

[5] There was at this time an internal public debt of 45 million pesos.

The constitutional congress met in November 1823 and almost a year later adopted a federal constitution which closely resembled that of the United States. The Mexican constitution of 1824 divided the country into nineteen states which were to elect their own governors and legislatures, and four territories which were to be under the jurisdiction of the national congress. The usual division of powers – executive, legislative and judicial – was retained but in one important respect the Mexican constitution differed from its northern model: it solemnly proclaimed that: 'The religion of the Mexican nation is and shall be perpetually the Catholic, Apostolic, Roman religion. The nation protects it with wise and just laws and prohibits the exercise of any other.'[6] Of the three guarantees in the Iguala manifesto only two remained; independence and religion. The third, union with Spaniards which implied a monarchy with a European prince, had been replaced by the federal republic.

In contrast to the insurgent constitution of Apatzingán in 1814 which specified that the law should be the same for everyone, the 1824 charter did not mention equality before the law. This omission was certainly not intended to safeguard the interests of the small, if not insignificant, Mexican nobility which only comprised a few dozen families. Its significance was much greater because it permitted the continuation of the *fueros* or legal immunities and exemptions from civil courts enjoyed by the clergy and the military. These privileges had, of course, existed before independence but then both the Church and the army had been subject to royal authority on which civil obedience to laws depended and which had not been seriously questioned for three centuries. With the supreme regal authority gone, and in the absence of a strong nobility or bourgeoisie, the vacuum was at once filled by the popular heroes of the victorious army. Freed of royal restraint, the army became the arbiter of power in the new nation. Federalist or centralist, a general was to be president of the republic.

Mexico also adopted the United States practice of electing a president and a vice-president. The two leading executives could be men of different or opposing political parties with the obvious danger of rivalry continuing between them while in office. Indeed, the first president was a liberal federalist, General Guadalupe Victoria, a man of obscure origins, and the vice-president a conservative centralist, General Nicolás Bravo, a wealthy landowner. Both men had been

---

[6] Felipe Tena Ramírez, *Leyes fundamentales de México, 1808–1973* (Mexico, 1973), 168.

guerrilla fighters for independence but by 1824 they belonged to two hostile factions. Political parties were as yet unknown but the two groups used the masonic movement as a focal point for their activities and propaganda. The centralists tended to become masons of the Scottish Rite while the federalists, with the help of the United States minister to the new republic, Joel R. Poinsett, became members of the York Rite. The lodges provided the base from which the conservative and liberal parties would arise almost a quarter of a century later.

President Victoria sought to maintain in his cabinet a balance between the centralists and the federalists in the hope of keeping some semblance of unity in the national government. Nevertheless, the most able of the pro-centralist ministers, Lucas Alamán, was, as early as 1825, quickly forced out of office by federalist attacks. In the following year, after a long and bitterly fought electoral campaign, the federalists gained a significant majority in Congress, particularly in the chamber of deputies. Tension increased in January 1827 with the discovery of a conspiracy to restore Spanish rule. Spain was the only important country not to have recognized Mexican independence and with many wealthy Spanish merchants still resident in the new republic, as well as others who retained their posts in the government bureaucracy, it was not difficult to incite popular hatred against everything Spanish. Mexican nationalism became a convenient and effective weapon used by the federalists to attack the centralists who were widely believed to favour Spain. Fighting on the defensive and using religion as a counter to nationalism, the centralists took revenge for Alamán's dismissal in a campaign against the American minister Poinsett who was a Protestant. As the well-intentional but ineffectual President Victoria was unable to control the ever more aggressive federalists, the centralist leader and vice-president, Bravo, finally resorted to rebellion against the government. Bravo was promptly defeated by his former comrade-in-arms, General Guerrero, and sent into exile. Both had fought the Spaniards side by side under the command of Morelos, but Guerrero had chosen the federalist cause which allowed him to keep control of his native *tierra caliente*.

The main political issue was the forthcoming presidential election, scheduled for 1828. Bravo's revolt spoiled the chances of the centralists who were unable even to present a candidate. Then the federalists split into moderates and radicals. The centralists or conservatives chose to rally behind the moderate candidate, General Manuel Gómez Pedraza, the Minister of War in Victoria's cabinet and a former royalist officer and then supporter of Iturbide. His opponent was General Guerrero, nominally the leader of the federalists but believed by many to be little more than a figurehead controlled by the liberal journalist and former senator for Yucatán, Lorenzo Zavala. Gómez Pedraza was elected president and General Anastasio Bustamante vice-president, but Guerrero refused to recognize the result and, on his behalf, Zavala organized a successful revolution in the capital in December 1828. Mere formalities followed. Guerrero was duly 'elected' in January 1829 and received the office from Victoria on 1 April. Constitutional order had collapsed after only four years.

Guerrero, a popular hero of the war against Spain, was a symbol of Mexican resistance to everything Spanish. The expulsion of Spaniards still living in the republic was quickly decreed[7] and preparations to resist a long-expected Spanish invasion force were begun. Guerrero's minister of finance, Zavala, found the Treasury almost empty and set about raising revenue. Obtaining some funds by selling Church property nationalized by the colonial authorities, he also decreed a progressive income tax, a unique attempt of its kind in this period of Mexico's history. His moves against ecclesiastical property and his well-known friendship with Poinsett made him unpopular with the Church and his attempts at social reform and at seeking support among the lower classes made him hated by all the propertied groups.

The long-awaited invasion by Spanish troops came at the end of July 1829, and it served to cause a temporary lull in the factional political conflict as the nation rallied to the call for unity. General Santa Anna hurried from his Veracruz headquarters to Tampico where the invading force had landed, and he promptly defeated it. He became an instant war hero and the country enjoyed the exhilaration of victory. But the euphoria was brief and with the external threat overcome, the Catholic and conservative faction soon renewed their campaign against the Guerrero administration. It did not yet dare to touch the president, still the hero of independence and now the saviour of the nation from Spanish aggression. Instead, the targets became the Protestant Poinsett and the democrat Zavala. The attacks on them became so fierce that Zavala was obliged to resign on 2 November and Poinsett, an easy, expendable scapegoat, left Mexico soon afterwards.

Deprived of the support of Zavala and Poinsett, Guerrero lost his

---

[7] The expulsion of certain groups of Spaniards had already been decreed in 1827.

office the following month when Vice-president Bustamante led a revolt with the support of General Bravo, already returned from his recent exile. Guerrero retired, unmolested, to his hacienda in the south, far from the central government's control. On 1 January 1830, Bustamante, acting as president, formed his cabinet. In contrast with the governments of 1823–7, which had tried to keep an uneasy balance of federalists and centralists, and with the populist inclined Guerrero régime, the new administration was openly conservative. The leading cabinet member was Alamán, once again occupying the key post of Minister of Internal and Foreign Affairs. He began to implement his political programme at once: opposition was suppressed after years of complete freedom; for the first time since Iturbide's fall, the central government sought to curb the states in several of which new, liberal ideas were rampant; property rights which in the last analysis could be traced to the Spanish conquest were safeguarded, and the Church's privileges were reaffirmed. Alamán evidently had in mind a settlement with Spain and with the Holy See.

Some of these and other developments were not to Guerrero's liking and he again revolted in the south at the head of a band of guerrilla fighters. General Bravo chose to remain loyal to Bustamante and Alamán, and he was appointed to lead the army against Guerrero who was captured in January 1831 and executed by order of the central government a few weeks later.

The cruel treatment of Guerrero requires an explanation. Bravo had been defeated in 1827 but was merely exiled and there were other similar cases. It is reasonable to ask, therefore, why in the case of Guerrero the government resorted to the ultimate penalty. The clue is provided by Zavala who, writing several years later, noted that Guerrero was of mixed blood and that the opposition to his presidency came from the great landowners, generals, clerics and Spaniards resident in Mexico. These people could not forget the war of independence with its threat of social and racial subversion. Despite his revolutionary past, the wealthy creole Bravo belonged to this 'gentleman's club', as did the cultured creole, Zavala, even with his radicalism. Hence Guerrero's execution was perhaps a warning to men considered as socially and ethnically inferior not to dare to dream of becoming president.

The conservative government of Bustamante was not negative and reactionary in everything it did. The country's economy and finances were improved as a result of a variety of measures. Since the end of 1827 when the civil conflict had begun to emerge Mexico had been unable to pay interest on the two foreign loans contracted in London. Now it was agreed with bondholders that the debt arrears, amounting to more than 4 million pesos, should be capitalized. Confidence was thus restored at the price of increasing the capital debt, but there was probably no other solution. Silver-mining remained in a depressed condition as a result of the overexpansion of previous years, and of military and civil disturbances. There was not much that could be done at the time to revive the industry and Alamán turned his attention to other spheres of economic activity. For example, he established a government bank which was to finance the introduction of cotton spinning and weaving machines and he prohibited the import of English cottons. The bank's funds were to come from high protectionist tariffs. Money was lent to Mexican and foreign merchants and financiers interested in becoming manufacturers. Machines were ordered in the United States and the first cotton-spinning mills began to operate in 1833. By this time, the Bustamante–Alamán government was no longer in power, but Alamán had laid the foundations of a revolution in the textile industry which, once started, continued to grow while the governments around it changed. As a result of his initiatives, a decade later Mexico had some fifty factories which could reasonably supply the mass of the population with cheap cotton cloth. The industry was especially prominent in the traditional textile city of Puebla and in the cotton-growing state of Veracruz where water power was abundant. The rate of growth can be seen in the following figures: in 1838, the factories spun 63,000 lb of yarn and in 1844 over 10,000,000 lb: in 1837 they wove 45,000 bolts of cloth and in 1845, 656,500. Thereafter the growth was slow. Alamán did not restrict his attention to textiles but he failed to accomplish any such spectacular results in, for example, agriculture which, although a devout Roman Catholic himself, he had to acknowledge was severely hampered by the ecclesiastical tithe.

Bustamante was not strong enough to impose a permanent centralized republic and rival political groups soon emerged. Francisco García, governor of the silver-mining state of Zacatecas, had carefully developed a powerful civilian militia, and he decided to challenge the pro-clerical regime in the capital. His friend, the senator and former supporter of Iturbide, Valentín Gómez Farías, suggested that the state sponsor an essay competition on the respective rights of Church and State in relation to property. The winning entry, submitted in December 1831 by an impecunious professor of theology, José María Luis Mora, justified the disentailment of ecclesiastical property and thus provided a theoretical basis for an anti-clerical, liberal ideology and movement. The timing was propitious. With the defeat of Guerrero and Zavala, the rights of private property had been definitively safeguarded. Hence there was no real danger that an attack on Church property might develop into a radical assault on property in general. The essence of liberalism lay precisely in the destruction of Church property combined with a strengthening of private property.

Mora was a theoretician rather than a man of action and it fell to Gómez Farías to organize the opposition against Bustamante. Since the Zacatecas militia of volunteers was merely a local force, he needed an ally in the professional army. General Santa Anna had been in revolt against Bustamante since January 1832. His personal ideology was obscure, but in the public mind he was widely associated with Guerrero whom he had consistently supported. Here, therefore, was an opportunity for him to benefit from the unpopularity of Guerrero's execution. Furthermore, as he was still a national hero, having reaped the glory from the defeat of the Spanish invasion of 1829, he could seek to take Guerrero's place as the popular favourite. The combination of Gómez Farías's liberal campaign and Santa Anna's military revolt forced Bustamante to dismiss Alamán and his Minister of War, José Antonio Facio, the two men who were widely held to have been responsible for Guerrero's death. Such cabinet changes were not sufficient and by the end of 1832, Bustamante was obliged to admit defeat. As the new Minister of Finance in the interim administration, Gómez Farías took control of the government in the capital. Zavala, who had returned to Mexico after more than two years in the United States, was not offered a cabinet post; his brand of populism was now replaced by a middle class anti-clericalism and he had to be satisfied with the governorship of the state of Mexico. In March 1833, Santa Anna was elected president and Gómez Farías, vice-president, with their term of office beginning formally on 1 April. Gómez Farías was eager to introduce liberal reforms and Santa Anna, for the time being, preferred to leave the exercise of power to his vice-president while remaining on his Veracruz estate and awaiting the reaction of public opinion.

Freed of presidential restraint, Gómez Farías initiated a broad reform programme, particularly in respect of the Church. The obligation under civil law to pay tithes was removed and payment became entirely voluntary. Then civil enforcement of monastic vows was removed and friars and nuns were permitted to leave the monastery or nunnery at their convenience. All transfers of property belonging to the regular orders since independence were also declared null and void. While the first law affected mainly the bishops and canons, whose income came mostly from the tithe revenues, the last two decrees were intended to bring about the eventual disappearance of the regular orders. The disposal of monastic real estate was already under discussion in congress and the sale of such property was declared illegal to prevent the Church from selling to trusted persons and thus evade the disentailment. Even so, the liberals were not to see the disentailment implemented for many years to come.

Gómez Farías, his cabinet and the liberal congress also attempted to reduce the size of the army and it was not long before senior military officers and the higher clergy were imploring Santa Anna to intervene. At last, when several army officers and their troops revolted in May 1834 and when the rebellion spread, he chose to leave his hacienda and assume his presidential authority in the capital. The consequences were soon apparent. The reforms were repealed and, in January 1835, Gómez Farías was stripped of his vice-presidential office. Two months later, a new congress approved a motion to amend the 1824 constitution with a view to introducing a centralist republic. Well aware that the bastion of federalism was Zacatecas, Santa Anna invaded the state, defeated its militia and deposed Governor García. On 23 October 1835 Congress delivered a provisional centralist constitution which replaced the states by departments, the governors of which would henceforth be appointed by the president of the republic.

Santa Anna was not, however, to complete the establishment of a strong, centralized régime. Not long after the defeat of Zacatecas, an unforeseen and, for Mexico as well as for Santa Anna, a most unwelcome complication arose in the north. The province of Texas resisted the move towards centralism and finally resorted to arms. After colonists had driven out the northern Mexican forces Santa Anna decided to lead in person what he regarded as a mere punitive expedition. Before leaving Mexico City, he told the French and British ministers that if he found that the United States government was aiding the rebels, 'he could continue the march of his army to Washington and place upon its Capitol the Mexican flag'.[8] Santa Anna succeeded in capturing San Antonio at the beginning of March 1836, but was decisively defeated and taken prisoner

[8] W. H. Callcott, *Santa Anna, the story of an enigma who once was Mexico* (Hamden, Conn., 1964), 126.

the following month. By this time, the Texans had already declared their independence. The vice-president of the new Texan republic was none other than the liberal from Yucatán, Lorenzo Zavala, but he died six months later. In the hands of the Texans as a prisoner of war, Santa Anna signed a treaty granting Texas its independence and recognizing the Rio Grande as the boundary between the two countries. He was subsequently released and in February 1837 he returned to Mexico in disgrace, for the Mexican government had meanwhile repudiated the treaty and refused to relinquish its claim to the former province.

To some extent, Mexico managed to balance its defeat in the north with a success on the European diplomatic front: Spain and the Holy See finally recognized the nation's independence at the end of 1836. At about the same time, Congress approved a detailed centralist constitution. In the hope of giving the country much needed stability, this increased the presidential term from four to eight years, and it seemed for a time that a period of peace could be anticipated. The hopes were premature. Bustamante was returned to office as the new president, but those conservatives who remembered his strong régime of 1830–2 were disappointed. The two leading centralists, Santa Anna and Alamán, had been discredited, and without their support or pressure Bustamante showed an increasing inclination to lean towards the federalists who agitated for the return of the 1824 constitution. A conservative politician warned the president that the clergy and the wealthy classes might feel compelled to 'deliver themselves into the hands of General Santa Anna'.

It was a French invasion of Veracruz in 1838, undertaken to exact compensation for damages to French-owned property, which gave Santa Anna the opportunity to regain popular esteem. He marched to Veracruz and his brave conduct once again made him a national hero. The following year, he was appointed interim president while Bustamante left the capital to fight federalist rebels. A few months later, however, he returned the office to its legitimate holder and retired to his rural retreat to wait for favourable developments. He did not have long to wait. Bustamante's popular support was dwindling, and in July 1840 he was captured by federalist army units. They summoned Gómez Farías – who on his return from exile had been in and out of prison – and proclaimed a federal republic. The uprising was suppressed after several days' street fighting and Bustamante was released. In a reaction against the growing chaos, the writer José María Gutiérrez Estrada advocated a monarchy with a European prince as the solution for the ills of Mexico. Gutiérrez Estrada, like Zavala, was a native of Yucatán, although he took the opposite road. While Yucatán, encouraged by the success of Texas, was fighting its own battle against Mexican centralism, he concluded that the centralist republic was too weak to impose order. Although few shared Gutiérrez Estrada's monarchist opinions, Bustamante had clearly lost the support of both radical federalists and extreme conservatives. Santa Anna was also unhappy with the 1836 constitution which had introduced a curious 'supreme conservative power' as a restraint on the power of the president. Finally, Yucatán declared its independence and Bustamante proved unable to bring it back into the republic, either by negotiation or by force of arms. An increase in taxes, tariffs and prices served only to spread the mood of discontent even wider. The country was ripe for another revolution.

Thus, in August 1841, General Mariano Paredes Arrillaga, commander of Guadalajara, called for the removal of Bustamante and amendments to the 1836 constitution to be enacted by a new constitutional congress. He was promptly supported by the army, and Santa Anna stepped in as an intermediary, becoming provisional president in October 1841. Another former royalist officer, General Paredes was known as a conservative and the new situation constituted, in effect, a centralist revolt against centralism. Santa Anna was, however, too shrewd to let himself be tied to any one party. He needed funds for the reconquest of Texas and Yucatán, as well as for his own ostentatious behaviour, and only the Church could provide them. As a way of putting pressure on the clergy, he offered the portfolio of finance to Francisco García, the former liberal governor of Zacatecas whom he himself had deposed in 1835. The elections to the new congress were sufficiently free to produce a majority of federalist or liberal deputies many of whom were young and were to achieve prominence years later. In 1842 they were obliged to labour on the new constitution in the shadow of Santa Anna's presidency. Nevertheless they managed to produce two drafts. Both still recognized the Roman Catholic faith as the only permitted religion and, in order not to annoy Santa Anna, they spoke of departments rather than states. The distinctive feature of the second draft, however, was the inclusion of a declaration of human rights, or 'guarantees'; in particular, it specified that the law should be the same for all and that no special law courts should exist. In other words, immunities from civil law should be abolished and all government monopolies were to end. Moreover, education was to be free.

In December 1842 the army disbanded Congress while it was discussing the constitutional reforms and, in the absence of Santa Anna, acting

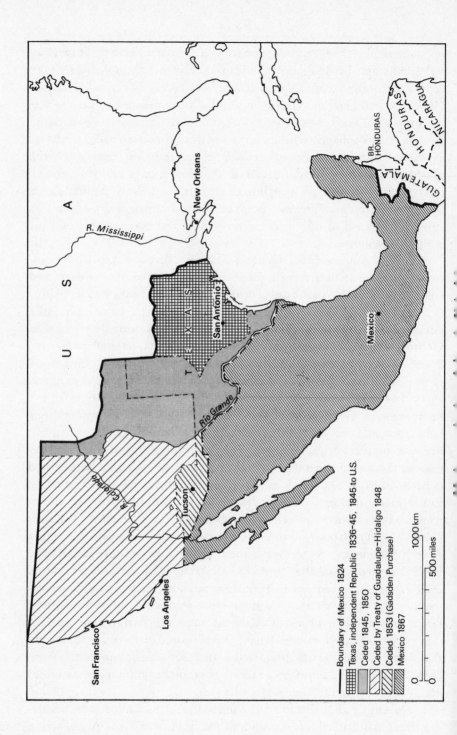

Boundary of Mexico 1824

Texas, independent Republic 1836–45, 1845 to U.S.

Ceded 1845, 1850

Ceded by Treaty of Guadalupe–Hidalgo 1848

Ceded 1853 (Gadsden Purchase)

Mexico 1867

U   S   A

R. Mississippi

New Orleans

TEXAS

San Antonio

Rio Grande

R. Colorado

Tucson

Los Angeles

San Francisco

Mexico

GUATEMALA

BR
HONDURAS

HONDURAS

NICARAGUA

0   500 miles

0   1000 km

President Bravo appointed a committee of leading conservative land-owners, clerics, army officers and lawyers which a few months later had devised a constitution acceptable to Santa Anna. The document was centralist and conservative, and human rights, especially equality, were not mentioned. Presidential powers, however, were enhanced by the omission of the 'supreme conservative power' introduced in the 1836 constitution. The president's power was not to be absolute, for although the authors of the new charter wanted a strong head of state, they did not want a despot.

The new Congress proved little more tractable than the disbanded one and when Santa Anna's fiscal extortions became unbearable, General Paredes, known for his honesty in financial matters, rebelled in Guadalajara. The Chamber of Deputies in the capital showed sympathy with his movement and other army units soon declared their support. Santa Anna was overthrown at the end of 1844, imprisoned and then exiled for life. Congress elected General José Joaquín Herrera, reputed to be a moderate, to the presidency.

This latest round of political upheavals in the capital had taken place against the background of deteriorating relations between Mexico and the United States. In 1843 Great Britain and France had arranged a truce between Mexico and Texas, but the truce did not lead to recognition of Texan independence by the Mexicans. On the contrary, insisting that Texas was still part of Mexico, Santa Anna announced that its annexation by the United States, which was favoured by many Americans, would be tantamount to a declaration of war.

Annexation was in fact approved by the United States Congress in February 1845, and thereafter the pace of events quickened. Mexican public opinion, both conservative and liberal, was inflamed against the aggressive politicians in Washington, but the new president, General Herrera, soon found that the financial and military state of the country made resistance hopeless and that help from Europe would not be forthcoming. Hence he attempted to negotiate a settlement. In the atmosphere of the time such a move was seen as treasonable by the Mexican people. In December 1845 General Paredes rebelled again on the pretext that 'territory of the Republic was to be alienated, staining forever national honour with an everlasting infamy in consenting to deal with the perfidious cabinet of the United States'.[9] He demanded the

[9] T. E. Cotner, *The military and political career of José Joaquín Herrera, 1792–1854* (Austin, Texas, 1949), 146.

removal of Herrera and another extraordinary congress to produce a new constitution. The army units in the capital obeyed the call, Herrera resigned and Paredes became president at the beginning of January 1846. At that time, the 1843 conservative constitution was in force and in seeking to change it, Paredes, a Catholic conservative, was clearly not looking towards a liberal republic. He gave an inkling of his views when he proclaimed: 'We seek a strong, stable power which can protect society; but to govern that society, we do not want either the despotic dictatorship of a soldier or the degrading yoke of the orator.'[10] It soon became apparent that he meant monarchy and, under his protection, Lucas Alamán publicly revived the central idea of Iturbide's Plan of Iguala, that of setting up a Mexican monarchy with a European prince on the throne. Given the international situation, such a monarchy could have been a bulwark against United States expansion, but it should by then have been clear to every educated Mexican that a monarchy had to stand on the shoulders of a strong and numerous nobility. A member of one of the few Mexican noble families, Alamán had overlooked this precondition of a monarchy, although it is possible that he expected it to be supported by European armies. He also seemed to have ignored the fact that the ruling group in Mexico, the army, was republican.

In any event, there was simply no time to import a European prince and thus obtain help against the United States. Hostilities broke out in April 1846 and in two or three months the United States army had defeated the Mexican forces and occupied parts of northern Mexico. Paredes' inability to defend the country and his monarchist sympathies swayed public opinion to the other extreme; perhaps, it was thought, the old federalist Gómez Farías and the once-national-hero Santa Anna, both known to hate the United States, might be more effective. Santa Anna, in his Cuban exile, had foreseen this possible reaction as early as April when he wrote to Gómez Farías, then in exile in New Orleans. As if nothing had happened between them, Santa Anna suggested in his customary verbose style that they should work together; that the army and the people should unite; and that he now accepted the principles of freedom. Possibly thinking that the army needed Santa Anna and that he could get rid of him later, Gómez Farías agreed. It was tacitly understood that Santa Anna would again become president and Gómez Farías vice-president.

[10] J. F. Ramírez, *Mexico during the war with the United States*, ed., W. V. Scholes, trans., E. B. Scherr (Columbia, Missouri, 1950), 38.

Gómez Farías departed for Mexico and at the beginning of August, aided by army units headed by General José Mariano Salas, the capital was taken and the constitution of 1824 restored. The United States government then permitted Santa Anna to pass through the blockade and land at Veracruz – in the belief, perhaps, that with the fall of the extreme anti-American Paredes the war might be stopped or that Santa Anna would make peace on terms favourable to the United States, or that he would simply bring more chaos into the already chaotic Mexico. On 16 September 1846, the two contrasting heroes, Santa Anna and Gómez Farías, rode together through the capital in an open carriage, and their relationship was formalized in December when congress appointed Santa Anna president and Gómez Farías, vice-president.

Santa Anna soon left to lead the army, and Gómez Farías, to satisfy the pressing needs of the army, nationalized ecclesiastical properties to the value of 15 million pesos, approximately one-tenth of the Church's total wealth. As there was no time for their valuation, he then ordered the immediate confiscation and sale of Church assets estimated at 10 million pesos. The Church, of course, protested and a reactionary military revolt began in the capital towards the end of February 1847. Santa Anna returned on 21 March and a week later he repealed both confiscatory decrees but not without first receiving a promise from the Church authorities that they would guarantee a loan of a million and a half pesos. Santa Anna had evidently learned to use the liberals to blackmail the Church. The clergy complied, knowing that the loan would probably never be repaid. They did not have the ready cash, however, and the money was raised by the government selling short-term bonds at a discount to financiers with the guarantee that the Church would redeem them. As Gómez Farías resisted dismissal the vice-presidency was abolished on 1 April. This second partnership of the two leading politicians of the period was to be their last.

On 9 March, while the capital city was the theatre of civil war, the United States forces, under the command of General Winfield Scott, landed near Veracruz, and the port surrendered on 29 March. The invading forces took Puebla in May, and despite many acts of heroism by the city's inhabitants, the capital was occupied on 15 September. The following day, Santa Anna resigned as president (but not as commander-in-chief) and eventually left the country. Mexican resistance ended and the United States army did not proceed further inland. It set up a municipal council in the capital, consisting of prominent liberals, among them Miguel Lerdo who would achieve fame some years later, while it awaited the emergence of a Mexican government with which the peace negotiations could begin. With General Herrera holding together the remnants of the army, a new government was formed in non-occupied Toluca and later Querétaro under the presidency of Manuel de la Peña y Peña, the non-political chief justice of the Supreme Court. Anti-American liberals like Gómez Farías and, among the rising new generation, Melchor Ocampo, also to become famous in later years, would have no part in the new administration. Defeat was generally attributed to the incompetence and treason of Santa Anna. Some Mexicans blamed the 'colossus of the north'. Fifteen prominent men wrote thus in 1848: 'The Mexican Republic, to whom nature has been prodigal, and full of those elements which make a great and happy nation, had among other misfortunes of less account, the great one of being in the vicinity of a strong and energetic people.'[11] Not everybody looked for a scapegoat. One writer complained of 'the iniquitous and shameful rule the Americans have imposed on us', but he added, 'the sad thing about it is that the punishment has been deserved.'[12]

The United States army did its best to shorten the suffering and the humiliation of the Mexican people. The new government was contacted and a peace treaty negotiated and finally signed on 2 February 1848. Mexico forfeited what was already in fact lost: Texas, New Mexico and California. The Mexican negotiators, however, did obtain the return of much that the United States believed it had occupied on a permanent basis, like, for example, Lower California. Even so, the lost provinces amounted to about half of Mexico's territory, although they only contained between one and two per cent of its total population and had then few known natural resources. Hence their loss did not disrupt the Mexican economy, and Mexico was to receive an indemnity of 15 million dollars. Understandably, sections of Mexican society viewed the treaty as ignominious and its signatories as traitors, and some wished to wage a guerrilla war against the invaders. But reason prevailed. A reluctant congress finally ratified the treaty on 30 May and the occupation forces left shortly afterwards, to the mixed joy of the Mexican landed class which was by this time threatened by a social revolution.

[11] Ramón Alcaráz *et al.*, *Apuntes para la historia de la guerra entre México y los Estados Unidos* (Mexico, 848); Eng. trans., *The other side: or notes for the history of the war between Mexico and the United States* (New York, 1850), 1.
[12] Ramírez, *Mexico during the war*, 161.

In 1829, the United States' diplomat, Poinsett, had summed up the situation in the Mexican countryside with the following words:

Here therefore is wanting that portion of a community which forms the strength of every nation, a free peasantry. The Indians cannot as yet be regarded in that light. They are laborious, patient and submissive, but are lamentably ignorant. They are emerging slowly from the wretched state to which they had been reduced . . . At present seven-eighths of the population live in wretched hovels destitute of the most ordinary conveniences. Their only furniture a few coarse mats to sit and sleep on, their food Indian corn, pepper and pulse, and their clothing miserably coarse and scanty. It is not that the low price of labour prevents them from earning a more comfortable subsistence in spite of the numerous festivals in each year but they either gamble away their money or employ it in pageants of the Catholic Church . . . All these evils would be greatly mitigated by education.[13]

The condition of Indian peasants in Mexico remained the same in 1847. The rural areas consisted of haciendas, which may be described as large farming enterprises, settlements or estates, and Indian villages with communal lands. On the hacienda labourers were often bound to the estate by peonage or debt-servitude – a legacy of the colonial period. The peon in debt was not permitted to leave until he had paid it, or unless another *hacendado* paid it for him. In other words, rural labourers were bought and sold for the price of their debt. If a peon in debt fled, he could be hunted down, brought back and punished. This *de facto* peonage was typical of central Mexico. In the isolated Yucatán peninsula and in the thinly populated north legalized servitude still existed.

Melchor Ocampo was the first liberal *hacendado* to write on the sensitive subject of the Mexican rural labour system. In a short article published in 1844, he condemned peonage not only as immoral but as not conducive to progress. Ocampo wrote that he had cancelled the full debt of all his peons four times. If one of his labourers in debt fled from his farm, perhaps to find work with another *hacendado* offering higher wages, he claimed him only if he was guilty of a criminal offence. He ended by exhorting peons not to borrow money and employers to lend only in cases of emergency.

Recent research has shown that not all rural labourers owed money to their employers. On some haciendas, at least, a considerable number of workers owed nothing and there were even some to whom the hacienda owed money. The peons would usually withdraw this from what

---

13 *Diplomatic correspondence of the United States concerning the Independence of the Latin-American Nations,* William R. Manning (ed.) (New York, 1925), III, 1673–6; reproduced in Lewis Hanke (ed.), *History of Latin American civilization,* II *The modern age* (London, 1967), 22–6.

amounted to a savings account to make purchases at the hacienda store. Finally, some *hacendados* either did not bother to denounce indebted fugitives to the authorities or were not successful in bringing them back.[14] Even if they owed nothing, the peons were not entirely free to leave their employment at will. Vagrancy laws, also inherited from the colonial period, made it difficult for landless peons to wander around the country looking for another or better job. It was safer to attach oneself to a hacienda and stay there permanently. Curiously, it was to the peon's advantage to borrow as much and work as little as possible because then he could never be dismissed. This was another feature of the system specifically criticized by Ocampo.

Indians in the villages were better off because they could work as seasonal labourers on the neighbouring hacienda. This was a convenient arrangement because few peasants had enough land to support themselves throughout the year. They were free men, but, on the other hand, if their harvest failed they starved. One advantage of peonage was that the peons could always borrow maize from the *hacendado*.

There were several other rural groups who must be distinguished from peons and village peasants. These were squatters, renters, tenants, or sharecroppers who lived within the bounds of the hacienda, usually in small settlements. Rarely able to pay rent in cash, they were often forced to pay with their own or their sons' labour, and, if they resisted, their animals, perhaps a few head of cattle, might be confiscated. They could also, of course, be evicted although this was probably rare because it was to the landowner's convenience to have them there as potential peons. The *hacendado* was obviously a lord on his territory. The social and ethnic inequalities were accepted by all and peons, peasants and tenants do not seem to have resented their inferior status. Their protests were restricted to the abuses of the powerful against which it was difficult, if not impossible, to find redress through normal channels.

Special conditions prevailed in Yucatán. The local *hacendados* were successfully growing *henequén* – sisal, a fibre-producing agave – for export and had few ties with central Mexico.[15] Quite naturally, Yucatán

[14] See J. Bazant, *Cinco haciendas mexicanas. Tres siglos de vida rural en San Luis Potosí, 1600–1910* (Mexico, 1975), 103–8; *idem, A concise history of Mexico from Hidalgo to Cárdenas 1805–1940* (Cambridge, 1977), 64–6, 88–9; *idem,* 'Landlord, labourer and tenant in San Luis Potosí, northern Mexico, 1822–1910', in *Land and labour in Latin America,* Kenneth Duncan and Ian Rutledge (eds.) (Cambridge, 1977), 59–82.

[15] Howard Cline, 'The henequén episode in Yucatán', *Interamerican Economic Affairs*, 2/2 (1948), 30–51.

embraced federalism and in 1839 rebelled against Mexico with the help of Mayan soldiers, becoming for all practical purposes an independent state. In 1840, the American traveller, John L. Stephens, found the Indian peons submissive and humble. Two years later, after his second visit, he warned:

What the consequences may be of finding themselves, after ages of servitude, once more in the possession of arms and in increasing knowledge of their physical strength is a question of momentous import to the people of that country, the solution of which no man can foretell.[16]

Stephen's forebodings were borne out five years later. In return for the service of Indian peasants as soldiers, the whites had promised to abolish or at least reduce parochial fees, to abolish the capitation tax payable by all Indian adults, and to give them free use of public and communal lands. None of these promises were fulfilled and the Mayas rebelled in the summer of 1847 with the aim of exterminating or at least expelling the white population. The revolt soon developed into full-scale war, known ever since as the War of the Castes. Mexico had just been defeated by the United States and, even had it wished to do so, was unable to send an army to Yucatán to suppress the revolt. In the cruel war which followed, the Indians almost succeeded in driving their enemies into the sea. In their despair, the whites went as far as to offer Yucatán to Great Britain, the United States, or, indeed, any country willing to protect them.

While Yucatán was in the throes of this race war, Indian tribes, forced southward by the expansion of the United States, invaded the sparsely populated regions of northern Mexico, burning haciendas, villages and mining settlements, and indiscriminately killing their inhabitants. Again, the Mexican government was too weak to prevent these incursions.

Social and ethnic revolt took a different form in central Mexico. Here the Indians did not form a compact, linguistic group and nor were they in a clear majority, as were the Mayas in Yucatán. However, deserters from the army, fugitives from justice, vagrants and similar elements, taking advantage of Mexico's military defeat and the chaos which followed, formed armed bands which began to terrorize the countryside. In at least one district, in the mountains of the states of Guanajuato, Querétaro and San Luis Potosí, a revolutionary agrarian movement developed. This so-called Sierra Gorda rebellion sought to give free land to hacienda tenants and peons, but the rebels were not strong enough to attack cities, and

[16] John Lloyd Stephens, *Incidents of travel in Yucatán* (Norman, Oklahoma, 1962), II, 214.

they had to be satisfied with the burning of haciendas. The Mexican
ruling class, demoralized, embittered and divided, watched helplessly as
the remnants of their once great country were beginning to fall apart.

But then the situation began slowly to improve. The United States
military historian, R. S. Ripley, commented in 1849:

The effect of the war upon Mexico has been and will continue to be greatly
beneficial. The first great apparent good is that the prestige of the army . . . has
been entirely swept away. That this has been the case is demonstrated by the
comparative quietude which has existed in Mexico since the conclusion of peace,
and the at least apparent stability of a government administered upon republican
principles.[17]

The main explanation for the improvement, however, was the war
indemnity. President Herrera's government of moderate liberals had no
revenues and no doubt would have collapsed had it not received at the
outset 3 million pesos of the indemnity on account. With this money it
was able to purchase surplus military equipment from the United States
army, re-establish social order in central Mexico and send reinforcements
to the north and to Yucatán. After several years of fighting in Yucatán, in
which the local landowners had enlisted the support of their peons and
also hired United States mercenaries, the insurrection of the Mayan
Indians was gradually quelled. The Yucatán creoles saved their skins and
their property, but lost forever their hope of becoming independent of
Mexico. Moreover, the population of Yucatán had been reduced by
almost half.[18]

Payments on account of the indemnity continued, and Mexico was
able to put its public finances in order. In 1846, the principal of the
foreign public debt was fixed, after protracted negotiations in London, at
51 million pesos. Then the war intervened, and interest on the new
principal was not paid, but in a friendly gesture towards Mexico, the
London committee of bondholders sacrificed the arrears and agreed to a
reduction of the annual interest rate from 5 per cent to 3 per cent.
Thereafter, the fairly reasonable payments were met until 1854. The
economy as a whole also seems to have improved. On the evidence of
coinage figures, silver and gold-mining, the most important industry,
showed some recovery. From a yearly average production of over 20
million pesos before the war of independence which fell to 10 million

17 R. S. Ripley, *The war with Mexico* (1849; New York, 1970), II, 645.
18 The population in 1837 was 582,173; in 1862, 320,212.

pesos in 1822, there was a gradual increase thereafter, reaching almost 20 million pesos a year again in 1848–50, the three years in which the indemnity payments were available. This was followed by a decline to 16 million pesos in 1854 and a rise in the decade 1858–67 to 17,800,000 pesos.

The final months of 1850 saw presidential elections once more in Mexico. Herrera's favourite was his own minister of war, General Mariano Arista, a moderate liberal. Other groups backed their own candidates and although Arista did not receive an absolute majority, he secured a commanding lead. Early in January 1851, the Chamber of Deputies elected him president with the delegations of eight states voting for him as against five who preferred General Bravo. This was the first time since independence that a president had been able not only to complete his term, although not a full one, but also to hand over office to a legally elected successor. The constitutional process was, however, soon to break down once again.

As long as social subversion threatened the established order, liberals and conservatives were willing to unite in mutual self-defence. The conservative, anti-American Alamán had even deplored the withdrawal of the hated Protestant army of occupation which had protected his and everybody else's property against bandits and rebels. The liberal oracle, Mora, had written from Europe to his friends in Mexico that Indian rebellions should be rigorously suppressed. But once the immediate danger was swept away, conservative opposition to the moderate liberal regime had intensified once more. More than one-third of the votes in the elections at the beginning of 1851 went to the conservative Bravo. Moreover, the financial outlook for the new government was far from promising; the funds of the United States indemnity were almost exhausted; government revenues had fallen because of increased contra-band made easier by the closer proximity of the United States border; the size of the army had been reduced, but military expenditure was still enormous because of renewed Indian invasions of northern Mexico (and dismissed officers joined the ranks of the opposition). The budget deficit exceeded 13 million pesos in 1851.[19] The government of General Arista soon came under attack from conservatives, radical liberals and support-ers of Santa Anna. It did not matter that some leading conservatives were tarnished by their past monarchist views, some radical liberals by their

[19] In the period 1821–67 government expenditure averaged $17.5 million, revenue only $10 million a year.

collaboration with the occupation authorities and, of course, Santa Anna by his ineptitude bordering on treason. The tide was moving against the moderate liberals who, in the popular mind, had betrayed the nation by signing the peace treaty and by 'selling' one-half of its territory; they were responsible for the present disaster.

In July 1852, in Guadalajara, José M. Blancarte, a former colonel in the national guard, deposed the state governor, Jesús López Portillo, a moderate liberal, and yet another military revolt spread to other states. It was not immediately clear who was in revolt, whether conservatives or liberals, or both, nor for what purpose. When the dust settled a few months later, it appeared that everybody wanted the return of Santa Anna. Arista resigned and the generals, believing themselves unable to rule, agreed to summon the former dictator, then living in Colombia. On 17 March 1853, Congress duly elected Santa Anna to be president and the government sent for him to return.

In a letter to Santa Anna Alamán explained the conservative programme: full support for the Church; a strong army; the abolition of federalism; and a strong executive subject to certain principles and responsibilities. He did not make clear, however, who was to watch over Santa Anna. Perhaps he viewed Santa Anna's next presidency as a stepping stone to a Bourbon monarchy. The conservatives were not alone in their renewed activity. When Santa Anna landed at Veracruz, he was greeted by Miguel Lerdo de Tejada, who had been sent there as a representative of the radical liberals. As early as 1848, Lerdo had accused the army and the Church of being the cause of Mexico's ruin. Santa Anna asked him to submit his ideas in writing and Lerdo complied with a long letter in which he reiterated his earlier criticisms and ended by proposing various material improvements which the republic badly needed.

Santa Anna took possession of the presidency on 20 April 1853. On this occasion his support was broader than it had been in 1846 when the radical liberals alone of organized political groups had called for his return. Now both conservatives and liberals were bowing to his leadership, each convinced that they could bring him to their side. He formed a mixed cabinet with the conservative Alamán in the Ministry of Internal and Foreign Affairs and the independent liberal, Antonio de Haro y Tamariz, as Minister of Finance. The latter was a particularly important appointment in view of Santa Anna's previous use of liberals to blackmail the Church. Lerdo de Tejada became Under-Secretary of the new Ministry of Development and did much to promote the building of telegraph lines, essential for progress in the mountainous terrain of

Mexico. The 1824 constitution was suspended but nothing was proclaimed in its place. Santa Anna could have reinstated the 1843 centralist constitution but, conservative though it was, it did put severe limits on the power of the president. Among other things, for example, it prohibited the president from selling, giving away, exchanging, or mortgaging any part of the national territory. For reasons known at the time only to himself, such restrictions were not to his liking. He governed, therefore, without a constitution.

During the first months of his government, Santa Anna lost his two most able Ministers: Alamán died in June and Haro resigned in August, after failing in his attempt to cover the budget deficit of 17 million pesos with the issue of bonds guaranteed by Church property. The clergy had protested vehemently against Haro's policy and Santa Anna had to devise another means of finding the money. In March, just a few weeks before he became president, the United States had seized what is now part of southern Arizona. Mexico was powerless to expel the invaders and was strongly invited to sell it to the United States. An agreement was reached towards the end of 1853. From the sale price of 10 million pesos, Mexico was to receive immediately 7 million pesos.[20]

Santa Anna's regime became increasingly reactionary and autocratic. He loved the pageantry and pomp of office but despised the daily work of administration. During his several earlier periods as head of state, he had resolved the problem by leaving the presidential work to a civilian vice-president while reserving affairs of the army and the glory to himself. In 1853, with the country split into two hostile parties and on the brink once more of disintegration, he found that he had to accept the full burden of the presidency. He embellished it, however, with such a variety of titles and prerogatives that he became a monarch in all but name. Iturbide's execution meant that he could never assume the title of emperor but instead he acquired more real power than Iturbide had even imagined. In December 1853, he was granted the right to name his successor and when the sealed envelope was later opened, it was found to contain the name of Iturbide's son. To bolster his authority and prestige, and perhaps also to ease his conscience, Santa Anna did everything he could to appear as heir of the man to whose downfall he had so much contributed. For example, in November 1853 he announced the posthumous award to Iturbide of the title of liberator and had his portrait placed in government buildings.

---

[20] The territory in question is called, in Mexico, La Mesilla; in the United States, the transaction is known as the Gadsden purchase.

In accordance with his reactionary posture, he also granted many concessions to the Church, allowing the reinstatement of the Jesuits and repealing the 1833 law which had removed the civil enforcement of monastic vows. He restricted the press and sent many liberals to gaol and exile. Eventually he went too far. In February 1854, several army officers in the south, led by Colonel F. Villareal, rose in arms and on 1 March, at Ayutla, the revolution was provided with a programme, which was amended ten days later at Acapulco. Its main points were as follows: the removal of Santa Anna; the election of a provisional president by representatives appointed by the commander-in-chief of the revolutionary army; and, finally, a demand for an extraordinary congress to produce a new constitution. Similar appeals had been proclaimed earlier and elsewhere but with little impact. This Ayutla–Acapulco manifesto made no mention of the well-known liberal demands and nobody could have suspected that out of this army uprising with limited objectives liberal Mexico would be born. In Acapulco, the obscure colonel who had launched the revolt at Ayutla was replaced by a retired colonel, Ignacio Comonfort, a wealthy merchant and landowner and a friend of General Juan Alvarez, the *cacique* of the ever rebellious south.

Alvarez had inherited control of the *tierra caliente* from Guerrero who had himself inherited the prestige of Morelos. They had all fought together in the War of Independence. The power of Alvarez, himself a *hacendado*, was based on the support of Indian peasants whose lands he protected. His army was drawn from the Indians and their support was sufficient to keep him in power on the Pacific coast for more than a generation. Eventually, the area under his control was separated from the state of Mexico to form the new state of Guerrero. He had no higher ambition and as long as central governments, liberal or conservative, did not meddle in his domain, his relations with them were good. Certainly, Santa Anna had displeased him when he appointed Alamán to the cabinet because Alamán was widely regarded as the author of Guerrero's execution, but, as the able conservative minister died soon after being appointed, relations between Santa Anna and Alvarez improved.

Then the ageing dictator made a mistake. Perhaps he no longer trusted Alvarez or perhaps he simply wished to pursue his plan to centralize the administration. Whatever the case, he removed some army officers and government officials on the Pacific coast, whereupon they flocked to Alvarez. It was on his hacienda that the revolution was planned. The strategy was to unite the nation against Santa Anna and hence the programme was restricted to generalities. The only indication that the revolution might be liberal in character was the presence of Comonfort, a moderate liberal. Alvarez assumed the leadership but, as had been the case with Guerrero, his views on basic national issues were unknown. The revolt spread irresistibly and in August 1855 Santa Anna relinquished the presidency and sailed into exile. The revolutionary government confiscated his property which had once been worth the enormous sum of one million pesos.[21] Soon a forgotten man, he was not permitted to re-enter the country until 1874 when the then president, Sebastián Lerdo, allowed him to return to Mexico City where he died two years later.

As the capital was in the hands of Alvarez's Indian soldiers it was not surprising that he was elected president by the representatives he had chosen from among the leaders of the revolt and the liberal intellectuals returned from prison and exile. Bravo had recently died leaving him as the sole surviving hero of the War of Independence, and his election thus symbolized the revolutionary tradition of Hidalgo, Morelos and Guerrero. Yet Alvarez had not sought the presidency – he was sixty-five years old – and he did not feel at home in the capital. He must also have resented the way in which he and his Indians were treated by both conservatives and moderate liberals who feared a renewal of race and class war. Instinctively perhaps, they recalled the democratic undercurrent in Morelos's rebellion and Guerrero's association with the radical Zavala. Alvarez now had the opportunity to punish the ruling groups and avenge Guerrero's death but his objective may have been limited to strengthening his hold on the south by enlarging the state of Guerrero and moving its boundaries closer to the capital. Whatever his aims, he ignored Comonfort's advice and, with one exception, appointed to the cabinet radical liberals, or *puros* as they were known. Leaving the Ministry of War to Comonfort himself who, as a moderate, could be expected to hold the army together, Alvarez entrusted the portfolio of Foreign Affairs to Melchor Ocampo and appointed Benito Juárez to the Ministry of Justice, Guillermo Prieto to the Treasury, Miguel Lerdo de Tejada to the Ministry of Development and Ponciano Arriaga to the Ministry of the Interior.

These five ministers belonged to a new generation, untainted by the failures of previous liberal governments. All except one had been born

21 Robert A. Potash; 'Testamentos de Santa Anna', *Historia Mexicana*, 13/3 (1964), 428–40.

during the War of Independence and they only remembered an independent Mexico with its perpetual disorders. Although they dreamed of an orderly regime based on the rule of law, none of them was a systematic thinker or theoretician. This was not perhaps a serious weakness, for Mora had worked out the liberal programme many years before. Apart from Lerdo, they shared one other thing in common; they had all been persecuted by Santa Anna.

Ocampo and Lerdo have already been mentioned above. Both as governor of the state of Michoacán and as a private citizen, Ocampo had acquired a reputation for his attacks on high parochial fees which were one of the main causes of the indebtedness of hacienda peons. Because both birthrate and infant mortality were high, hacienda labourers spent a great deal of their money on baptisms and funerals. In most cases, it was the *hacendado* who paid the actual fees and then charged them to their peons' accounts. Marriage fees were also so high that many couples did not marry. In striking at the root of the problem Ocampo inevitably attracted the hatred of thousands of parish priests whose livelihood depended on the fees, in contrast to the higher clergy, bishops and canons, who lived mainly from the tithe revenues (the payment of which had been voluntary since 1833). Not surprisingly, Ocampo had been exiled from Mexico soon after Santa Anna's rise to his last presidency. In New Orleans, where the liberal exiles gathered, Ocampo befriended the former governor of the state of Oaxaca, Benito Juárez, the only Indian in the group, who had been exiled by Santa Anna for having opposed him in the Mexican–American war. Under Ocampo's influence, Juárez became a radical liberal.

In November 1855 Juárez, the Minister of Justice, produced a law which abolished clerical immunities by restricting the jurisdiction of ecclesiastical courts to ecclesiastical cases. It also proposed to divest the army of some of its privileges. Perhaps thinking that he had done enough to create irreversible changes, or perhaps compelled by the storm of protest raised by the so-called 'Juárez Law', Alvarez appointed Comonfort as substitute president at the beginning of December and resigned a few days later. Short as his presidency had been – only two months – it was decisive for the future of the country.

Comonfort appointed a cabinet of moderate liberals, but it was already too late. In several parts of the country, groups of laymen, army officers and priests had rebelled with the cry of *religión y fueros* (religion and immunities). One armed band called for the repeal of the Juárez Law, the removal of Comonfort and the return to the 1843 conservative constitution. In January 1856, it managed to seize the city of Puebla and establish a government there. Moderate though he was, Comonfort had to suppress the uprising and he forced the surrender of Puebla at the end of March. The local bishop, Labastida, took pains to disassociate himself from the rebels, but Comonfort put the blame on the Church and decreed the attachment of ecclesiastical property in the diocese until the cost of his campaign had been covered. Feeling that the Church should not be blamed for the insurrection, Labastida refused to pay the indemnity with the result that the government expelled him and confiscated the clerical property. In one way or another, Church property was being used to finance rebellion against the government and the answer seemed to be confiscation. But in view of the violent reaction unleashed by the Puebla confiscatory decree, it seemed prudent to try a different, indirect approach which would appear less anti-clerical. This was probably the reasoning behind the disentailment law enacted at the end of June 1856 by Lerdo de Tejada, now Minister of Finance.

Lerdo de Tejada has already been mentioned as the radical liberal who had 'collaborated' with the United States' occupation army in the municipal council of the capital and then with the reactionary Santa Anna in the Ministry of Development. He had been pessimistic about Mexico's ability to carry out a liberal revolution; he believed it would have to be imposed from above or from abroad. But finally, in 1856, he had the opportunity to carry out a programme of radical anti-clericalism. The main feature of the so-called 'Lerdo Law' was that the Church must sell all its urban and rural real estate to the respective tenants and lessees at a discount which would make the transaction attractive to buyers. Should buyers refuse to purchase, the property would be sold by government officials at public auction. The ecclesiastical corporations most affected by the law were the regular orders. The monasteries owned large country estates as well as town houses and the convents possessed the best real estate in the cities. The higher clergy were not to suffer much because its wealth was of a different kind and parish priests were not affected directly because parishes did not generally own any property except the parish house itself.[22] In the villages, however, there were brotherhoods or confraternities devoted to religious purposes, and many of them owned land or property which was now to be disentailed, much to the

---

[22] Parish priests might, of course, have property of their own; but that would not be affected by the law.

grief of villagers and priests alike. At first sight, the law did not look confiscatory: the Church was to be paid either in instalments equal to former rents or in a lump sum equal to the capitalized rent. But there was a loophole. According to the law, the Church in the future would not be able to acquire or own properties. The Church would therefore have no safeguards and hence would face a gradual despoilment. Consequently, the Church authorities protested and refused to comply.

As believers in private property, the liberals also sought the liquidation of the property of civil corporations. This affected in particular the Indian villages, most of which were still large landholders. These villages possessed various types of property including communal pastures, or *ejidos*, which were exempted from disentailment because Lerdo considered them essential for the village. Nevertheless, in actual practice, parts of the *ejidos* began to be sold, despite protests by the peasants.

The Lerdo Law was put into effect at once. As the Church in most cases refused to sell, government officials signed the deeds of sale to the former tenants or lessees and now house or landowners. Many pious tenants refrained from claiming the property which was then purchased by wealthy speculators, some of whom were well-known financiers who specialized in loans to the government and had thus become important holders of government bonds. Whereas they might have been previously connected with conservative regimes, their investments in the disentailed clerical properties tended to make them allies of the liberals. Tenants loyal to the Church ignored the new landlords, continuing to pay their rent to the former ecclesiastical owner, awaiting the day when the house would be returned to the Church. This confused and complex situation regarding the disentailed properties was evident within a few months of the law's implementation and it was clear that it could not be permitted to last indefinitely.

While Lerdo was dealing with Church property, his colleague, José María Iglesias, the new Minister of Justice, was working on a law to limit parochial fees. In general, the 'Iglesias Law' of 11 April 1857 declared as valid the fees charged in the colonial period or at the beginning of independent Mexico and which were evidently low. It then prohibited the collection of parochial fees from the poor who were defined as persons earning the minimum amount necessary for survival. As most parishioners were poor, this meant the end of wealthy curates. The law prescribed severe penalties for those priests who charged the poor for their services or refused to baptize, marry or bury them free of charge.

Again, the Church condemned the law as illegal and immoral, and refused to comply.

In the meantime, approximately 150 deputies in congress, most of whom were young liberals drawn from the professional classes – lawyers, government officials or journalists – were debating the new constitution. Among the older generation there was Valentín Gómez Farías, after Mora's death in Paris in 1850 the patriarch of Mexican liberalism and now seventy-five years old. The issues and problems in 1856 were different from those which Ocampo had faced in 1842 and even more so than those confronting Gómez Farías in 1833. The war with the United States had inevitably left a mark on the mind of most liberals. For example, in 1848 Ocampo described the struggle between the states and the central, federal government, as 'systematic anarchy'.[23] He came to the conclusion that federation, as it had existed in Mexico since the adoption of the 1824 constitution, had made easier the separation of Texas and the temporary secession of Yucatán, and had subsequently been a cause of the defeat and dismemberment of the country. He must have recalled Servando Teresa de Mier's opinion that Mexico needed a strong central government in the first phase of its independence. Perhaps centralism was the right course after all, though not if it meant the domination of the army and the Church. Now that the government was a liberal one, it was advisable to strengthen it, especially since the proximity of the American border weakened the hold of central Mexico on the states to the north, making a further dismemberment of the country possible in the future. Liberals, therefore, became just as centralist as their conservative rivals, although they continued to pay lip service to the federalism with which liberalism had been identified for so many years. The new constitution, approved on 5 February 1857 following almost a year of discussion, kept the federal structure but, characteristically, while the official title of the 1824 document had been the Federal Constitution of the United Mexican States, the new charter was named the Political Constitution of the Mexican Republic.

Now that federalism had lost its meaning, the Church took its place as the main issue between liberals and conservatives. In a radical departure from the 1842 constitutional projects, and even more from the 1824 constitution, the liberals in 1856 wished to introduce full freedom of worship for all religions; in other words, religious toleration. The

---

[23] Moisés González Navarro, *Anatomía del poder en México (1848–1853)* (Mexico, 1977), 378.

proposal turned out to be too advanced. Mexico's population consisted mostly of peasants loyal to their Church, and although the educated classes may have been as liberal as their European counterparts, they could not antagonize the mass of villagers, already stirred by their priests. The Minister of the Interior warned Congress: 'the Indians are excited and for this reason it is very dangerous to introduce a new element which will be exaggerated by the enemies of progress in order to drown us in a truly frightening anarchy'.[24] The proposal was dropped, but, at the same time, the traditional assertion that Mexico was a Roman Catholic nation was also omitted, thus leaving a curious gap in the constitution. Not daring to touch the image, sacred to the common people, of a Catholic Mexico, the delegates nevertheless included in the constitution all the other anti-clerical demands, especially the basic concepts of the 'Juárez Law' (1855) and the 'Lerdo Law'(1856).

The liberals were as anti-militaristic as they were anti-clerical. In this respect, however, they realized that they had to tread carefully because General Comonfort, president and commander-in-chief of the army, was already showing signs of impatience with Congress. Hence the liberal deputies restricted themselves to the abolition of the judicial privileges of the army, thereby confirming what had already been enacted in the Juárez Law.

Finally, the new constitution affirmed complete freedom for all citizens. For the first time since the 1814 Apatzingán constitution, every Mexican, however poor (but excluding vagrants and criminals), was given the right to vote and to be elected, and a declaration of human rights, including the inviolability of private property, was also specified. With its ban on the corporate ownership of real estate, the constitution was more sweeping than the Lerdo Law. Lerdo had exempted village *ejidos* or communal pastures, but the constitution did not mention them, the implication being that they could be disentailed. Their disentailment was, in fact, attempted on the basis of the new constitution, but it had to be halted because of Indian opposition. The liberals could not afford to wage war on two fronts, against the Church and against the Indian peasants. As far as the Church was concerned, they sought to isolate it by gaining allies among all social strata. They succeeded in doing so in urban centres where the middle and some of the upper classes profited by the disentailment of corporate property. In the rural areas where the Church was traditionally strong, they were unable to isolate it, but they

24 Francisco Zarco, *Historia del Congreso Constituyente (1856–1857)* (2nd edn, Mexico, 1956), 630.

did drive a wedge into the hitherto solidly conservative countryside by letting large landowners purchase former ecclesiastical haciendas. Ironically, it was the rural rich, not the rural poor, who tended to support the liberals.

Most liberals saw in the adoption of the constitution of 1857 a realization of their life-long dreams. They were now able to assume a more conciliatory attitude in some respects. For example, a subtle change in public opinion caused the government to reopen the Franciscan monastery in the capital which had been closed some months previously because an alleged conspiracy had taken place within its walls. Moreover, with the resignation of Lerdo at the beginning of the year, the disentailment of property slowed down. The government was ready to negotiate and on 1 May 1857, Comonfort sent his Minister of Justice to Rome. The Holy See appeared ready to accept the disentailment transactions so far implemented, but it demanded that the legal right to acquire and own property should be restored to the Church. Even the conservative Mexican press suggested in August that the disentailment should be legalized through an agreement with Rome.

It seemed obvious that a compromise with both the Church and the conservatives would require the repeal of the more extreme articles of the constitution. Comonfort, elected constitutional president in September with only reluctant support from the radicals who preferred Lerdo, was believed to favour such a course as the only way of avoiding civil war. But compromise was not to prevail. The liberals saw in Comonfort a conservative and the conservatives a liberal, and he was left without support. In the civil war which followed it was the conservatives who took the initiative. Reactionary army units in the capital, led by General Félix Zuloaga, rebelled in December 1857 with the avowed aim of annulling the constitution. While upholding Comonfort's authority, the army took control of the city, dissolved Congress and arrested, among others, the new president of the Supreme Court, Benito Juárez. After some hesitation, Comonfort approved Zuloaga's programme. A month later, Zuloaga took the second step: he removed Comonfort and assumed the presidency himself. Perhaps out of revenge against ungrateful conservatives, Comonfort, in the final moments of his power, managed to release Juárez from prison before leaving the country, unmolested by conservatives and ignored by liberals. Yet his decision to free Juárez rendered an immense service to the liberal cause, as future events were to show.

Juárez fled to Querétaro. From there, he proceeded to Guanajuato and, arguing that the constitutional order had been destroyed, he proclaimed himself president of the republic and appointed a cabinet with Ocampo as its most distinguished member. As head of the Supreme Court – the office of vice-president not having been adopted by the 1857 constitution – he had the constitutional right to the presidential succession in the absence of the legally elected president. Shortly after his arrival at Guanajuato, a resident wrote to a friend in Mexico City: 'An Indian by the name of Juárez, who calls himself president of the republic, has arrived in this city.'[25]

Thus, with a conservative president in Mexico City and a liberal president in Guanajuato, the Three Years War began. In earlier decades, when faced by a counter-revolution, the liberals had submitted to the army virtually without resistance. Now, they still did not have an army of consequence, but they had mass support in cities and parts of the rural areas which made it possible for them gradually to create a new army with former liberal lawyers and journalists as officers. In contrast, since Alamán's death, there had been a curious lack of educated civilians among the conservatives. Events were to reveal that the regular army and the Church were not by themselves strong enough to resist the liberal movement. This was not to be a walkover, as Santa Anna's counter-revolutionary coups had once been.

Following Zuloaga's second coup, some state governors acknowledged him as president, others declared their opposition and some reversed their original stance. Amidst this confusion, Juárez was able to escape to Veracruz, the governor of which had invited him to establish his administration in the port. The country as a whole soon divided into two sections of approximately equal strength. The states bordering on the Gulf of Mexico were under liberal control, with the exception of the exhausted Yucatán which chose to remain neutral. The far northern states were also liberal. The central core of the country was conservative, except for the states of Michoacán and Zacatecas.

From the start, both factions had to find ways of financing their war efforts. Zuloaga, fulfilling a promise to the Church, declared the Lerdo Law null and void: the Church was to regain ownership of its disentailed property. In exchange for this, the metropolitan chapter was obliged to promise him a loan of one and a half million pesos, but as the ecclesiastical corporations had little ready cash, nine-tenths of the amount was paid in

[25] Ralph Roeder, *Juárez and his Mexico* (2 vols., New York, 1947), I, 161.

bills guaranteed by clerical property. The conservative government sold these bills at a discount to financiers who in due course acquired the clerical real estate because the Church was unable to redeem them. A discount was necessary because the liberal government had declared illegal all acts and transactions of the conservative regime. Hence the price was lowered in proportion to the risk. Other similar loans followed, including one granted by the House of Rothschild. In this way, moneylenders financed Zuloaga at the expense of the Church which was obliged to watch its wealth dispersed. Arguing that the Church was voluntarily financing Zuloaga, liberal governors and military commanders of relatively isolated areas such as Michoacán and the north decreed forced loans on the clergy which for all practical purposes amounted to confiscation of Church property. At Veracruz, the conditions were rather different. Soon after Juárez's arrival in May 1858, a shipload of rifles, consigned to a French captain, José Yves Limantour, reached the port. Of course, the constitutional government promptly requisitioned the weapons. As it could not pay for them with the limited amount of Church property left in the Gulf states, and as it had no cash available, payment was made in the form of clerical real estate in Mexico City. With the capital held by Zuloaga, all the liberal regime could do was to promise to hand over the property in the event of a liberal victory. Again, the price set for the weapons was proportional to the risk of this credit arrangement and thus Limantour, and other foreign importers, were to acquire urban property in Mexico City at a fraction of its real value.

Juárez faced a critical situation in February–March 1859 when the new conservative president and military commander, Miguel Miramón, attempted to capture Veracruz. The attempt failed, but, at almost the same time, the liberal commander of western Mexico, Santos Degollado, also failed in his attempt to seize Mexico City. After Degollado's defeat, more than a dozen liberal officers, including seven army surgeons, were taken prisoner and executed in a suburb of the capital. The conflict was becoming increasingly cruel and destructive with almost the entire country now a theatre of war. No end was in sight. The nation was divided into irreconcilable camps.

The moment had arrived for the liberals to put their aims before the nation. Thus, the constitutional government in Veracruz issued a manifesto on 7 July 1859. The document, signed by President Juárez and the two most prominent cabinet members, Ocampo and Lerdo, put all the blame for the war on the Church and a series of reforms was announced:

the confiscation of all Church wealth, both real estate and capital; the voluntary payments of parochial fees; the complete separation of Church and State; the suppression of all monasteries and abolition of novitiates in nunneries. Full freedom of worship was not proclaimed. The manifesto also recognized the need for a division of landed property, but it added that such a redistribution would take place in the future as a natural consequence of economic progress. For the moment, it promised only a law which would remove legal obstacles to the voluntary division of rural estates.

The specific laws to enact these reforms were issued during the following four weeks. The confiscated, 'nationalized' wealth, both real estate and mortgages, were to be sold to buyers of clerical properties under the Lerdo Law. Lerdo, who as Minister of Finance in the Veracruz government had drafted the confiscatory law, insisted on the continuity between the earlier disentailment and the present nationalization. The buyers who had returned the properties to the Church in areas occupied by the conservatives would, in the event of a liberal victory, recover them and then pay the government for them either in instalments extending for long periods of time or in cash at a fraction of their value. The measure was bound to attract both former and potential buyers to the liberal cause, particularly in conservative occupied central Mexico where the most valuable clerical properties were concentrated. In the areas under liberal control, most of the Church property had already been disposed of and in some states, like Veracruz, the Church had always been poor. Hence the liberal government itself obtained only a small immediate revenue from the sale of the confiscated wealth.

But the die had been cast. Now it was a life-and-death struggle of the Church and the old army against the middle class professionals, of the old world against the new. The revolutionary 'reform' laws of July 1859 drove political passions to their highest pitch, fighting increased and the demands of the Treasury became ever greater. In desperation, the constitutional government granted the United States, in exchange for 2 million dollars, transits and right of way across the Isthmus of Tehuantepec and from the Rio Grande and Arizona to the Gulf of California, as well as the right to employ its own military forces for the protection of persons and property passing through these areas. This so-called McLane–Ocampo treaty was negotiated by Melchor Ocampo who was certainly no friend of the United States, and it was signed on 14 December 1859. A liberal newspaper commented: 'Does not Señor

Juárez know that the liberal party prefers to fall anew under the double despotism of the army and the clergy before committing itself to a foreign yoke?'[26] We do not know if the liberal government was sincere in its proposed treaty or whether it was playing for time. Whatever the case, the United States Senate repudiated the treaty a few months later, thus freeing the liberals from the embarrassing position into which their extreme penury had placed them. In fact, the 2 million dollars were not needed. The war of propaganda was bearing fruit, and after the failure of Miramón's second attempt to capture Veracruz in the spring of 1860, the fortunes of the conservative armies began to decline. They began to retreat towards the capital where Miramón was trying to raise money. He now did, with the archbishop's permission, what the liberals had done against the will of the Church; in August he confiscated wrought silver from churches for coinage as well as gold and other jewels which were pawned to moneylenders. Then, in November, without either credit or funds, he confiscated 660,000 pesos which had been entrusted to the British legation on behalf of English bondholders who were going to receive part of the interest due to them for the first time since 1854. It was too late: the liberal armies were closing in on the capital.

Early in December 1860, victory was so certain that the liberal government at Veracruz finally decreed complete religious toleration. It no longer mattered what priest-led Indians might think. The liberals had won the war. On 22 December, the liberal commander, General Jesús González Ortega, a former journalist from Zacatecas, defeated Miramón in the battle for possession of Mexico City and he occupied it three days later, on Christmas day. President Juárez arrived from Veracruz three weeks later. With the cities taken by the liberals and the conservative armies scattered into rural guerrilla groups, Mexico was free to enjoy a political campaign, and the presidential contest began almost with the arrival of the president and his cabinet.

Among the liberal leaders there were four possible presidents: Melchor Ocampo, Miguel Lerdo, Benito Juárez and González Ortega. Ocampo did not seek the presidency. Considered as heir to Mora, he was satisfied with being the prophet of liberalism and hence he helped his protégé, Juárez, against Lerdo in whom he sensed a rival. Juárez may have needed such help for, even though president, he was viewed by many as second rate in comparison with Ocampo and Lerdo. Reserved and

---

unassuming, he was described later as 'not a leader who conceived and gave impulse to programmes, reforms, or ideas. That task reverted to the men who surrounded him, and he acquiesced in or rejected their leadership'.[27] As author of the revolutionary laws affecting Church wealth, Lerdo had prestige and authority, and he was popular with radical liberals. González Ortega in turn was a national hero – the man who had defeated the conservative army. These three man – Juárez, Lerdo and González Ortega – were candidates for the highest office.

At the end of January 1861, it seemed that six states favoured Juárez, six were for Lerdo and five for González Ortega; there was no information about the remaining seven states. Lerdo won in the capital and two states, only to die on 22 March. The protracted system of indirect elections had to continue with the two remaining candidates, Juárez against González Ortega, and in the final count, Juárez obtained 57 per cent of the vote, Lerdo almost 22 per cent and González Ortega over 20 per cent. It would seem that in the districts where after Lerdo's death the elections were still in progress, his supporters had given their votes to Juárez. One obvious explanation was liberal mistrust of the military. The most distinguished liberal politicians had been civilians: Zavala, Mora, Gómez Farías, Ocampo, Lerdo, Otero and de la Rosa. None of them had become president. The army, by nature conservative, was unwilling to share power with them. Excepting the transitional presidency of de la Peña, there had been no civilian head of state before Juárez. Although González Ortega was a good liberal, he was a general and therefore not to be trusted.

In June 1861, Congress declared Juárez to be president of Mexico. He was to bear the whole burden of office alone, for Ocampo had recently been captured and executed by conservative guerrillas, thus surviving his rival, Lerdo, by just over two months. Nor would Juárez ever get rid of the shadow of the army, even though it was a liberal, revolutionary force. While González Ortega was in the field fighting the conservatives, he was elected by Congress (unconstitutionally, since he should have been directly elected) president of the Supreme Court and thus next in line for the presidency. The anti-Juárez faction felt that as the president of the republic was a presumably weak civilian, some provision should be made for any possible emergency. To González Ortega's credit, it must be said that he did not attempt a military takeover

The problems facing Juárez were staggering. The sale of confiscated

[27] Frank Averill Knapp, Jr., *The life of Sebastián de Tejada, 1823–1889* (Austin, Texas, 1951), 157.

Church wealth valued at around 150 million pesos – perhaps one-fifth of the total national wealth – had begun in January 1861. To attract Mexican buyers who, as good Roman Catholics, were opposed to the confiscation, and to create a broad social base for itself, the liberal government had been accepting all kinds of paper, credits, promissory notes and depreciated internal debt bonds in payment for, or at least in part payment for, the clerical properties. Consequently, from the sale in 1861 of confiscated properties in the Federal District, worth 16 million pesos which was already a depreciated value, the government received only one million pesos in actual cash. Moreover, Veracruz financiers, like Limantour and others, had already paid for their properties in kind or cash. Finally, the government recognized as valid the purchases of ecclesiastical properties made by the powerful House of Rothschild during the conservative regime. The fact that the properties had been purchased at a fraction of their value and that many had been paid for in advance explains the extremely low revenue from the confiscation in 1861. The English bondholders, who expected some of their arrears of interest from the proceeds of the sale, received nothing. Similarly, France was pressing her claims for the Jecker bonds issued by the conservative government and recently acquired by influential politicians in France. There were all sorts of other claims for damages allegedly or actually suffered during the civil war by foreign nationals. Juárez, however, refused to accept responsibility for the acts of the conservative regime: he simply had no money. His government was obliged to suspend all payments in July. European creditors felt cheated and pressed their governments to obtain redress. On 31 October 1861, France, Great Britain and Spain signed in London a Tripartite Convention in favour of military intervention in Mexico. Their troops landed at Veracruz shortly afterwards. It soon became clear, however, that Napoleon III had ulterior motives and designs for Mexico. Hence Britain and Spain withdrew their forces, leaving the enterprise to the French.

These developments provided Mexican monarchists living in Europe, like Gutiérrez Estrada, for example, with the opportunity they had been looking for. A French occupation of Mexico would make it possible to realize their life-long dream of establishing a Mexican empire under European – this time, French – protection. And a suitable candidate for the monarchy was found in the person of the Austrian Archduke Maximilian.

Meanwhile, the French armies were advancing in Mexico. The invasion aroused genuine patriotic feelings in the country, not only among the liberals. It was not known at this point whether France was seeking to help conservatives against liberals, or in fact trying to subjugate the country. The two former conservative presidents, Zuloaga and Miramón, hesitated. As generals and former presidents, they were not enthusiastic about an empire with a foreign prince. Furthermore, they distrusted France and were devoted to their country's independence. Miramón finally offered his sword to Juárez. The issue was not liberalism against conservatism, as it had been in 1858–60, but Mexican independence against conquest by a foreign power. Certainly, in their hatred of Juárez most conservatives did accept the French as liberators from the liberal yoke, but some also found their way into the army which was fighting the invaders. For example, Manuel González (future president of Mexico 1880–4), who had been an officer in the conservative army in 1858–60, volunteered and was accepted to fight the French. Comonfort was also accepted by Juárez and he was to die on the battlefield in 1863

Temporarily repulsed by General Zaragoza in the battle of Puebla in May 1862, the French forces were reorganized and, under Marshall Forey, they embarked on a more powerful campaign. Zaragoza died and Juárez had to appoint González Ortega, whom he had kept without military assignment, to the command of the eastern armies. He surrendered in Puebla in May 1863, after a two months' siege of the city. The French were free to take the capital and from there extended their domination to other parts of the country. Aiming to continue the fight from the north, Juárez left Mexico City on 31 May, and ten days later he established his government in San Luis Potosí. He was joined by González Ortega who had managed to escape from the French while being taken to Veracruz.

The conservatives in the capital, especially the former bishop of Puebla and now archbishop of Mexico, Labastida, expected the French to do as Zuloaga had done in 1858, that is, repeal all the confiscatory laws and return the nationalized wealth to the Church. Napoleon, however, had decided to adopt the liberal programme and to the dismay of Church dignitaries, Marshal Forey recognized the validity of the nationalization and sale of ecclesiastical property. On accepting the crown of Mexico at Miramar, his castle near Trieste, on 10 April 1864, Maximilian, whose liberal background was well known, had undertaken to follow French policy in respect of the Church and the nationalization of its property. On his arrival in Mexico City in June, he found the republican government of Juárez still in control of northern Mexico and the republican guerrillas fighting the occupation forces. He attempted to bring Juárez to his side and to persuade him to submit to his empire but, of course, he failed. Nevertheless, he did succeed in winning over some of those liberals who had chosen to remain in the capital under the French occupation. He rejected the support of the conservatives and sent their best-known leader, General Miramón, abroad. Thus, he was able to form a cabinet consisting almost entirely of liberals, among them two former deputies to the constituent congress of 1856–7, Pedro Escudero y Echánove and José M. Cortés y Esparza. Escudero became Minister of Justice and Ecclesiastical Affairs and Cortés, Minister of the Interior. Foreign Affairs, Development and the new Ministry of Public Education were also in the hands of liberals. The Treasury was managed directly by the French.

Maximilian even went so far as to draft a liberal constitution. Known as the Provisional Statute of the Mexican Empire, it was signed by the emperor on the first anniversary of his acceptance of the Mexican crown. Together with a 'moderate hereditary monarchy with a Catholic prince', it proclaimed freedom of worship as one of the rights of men. As the first and foremost of these rights, 'the Government of the Emperor' guaranteed equality under the law 'to all inhabitants of the Empire',[28] a right which had only been implied in the 1857 constitution. Freedom of labour was also established. While the liberal regime had never enacted a law expressly prohibiting debt peonage, Maximilian did so on 1 November 1865. Labourers were granted the right to leave their employment at will, independently of whether or not they were in debt to their employer: all debts over ten pesos were cancelled; hours of work and child labour were restricted; corporal punishment of labourers was forbidden; and to allow competition with hacienda stores, peddlers were permitted to enter haciendas and offer their wares to peons. Finally, in a departure from the 1857 constitution, Maximilian restored to Indian villages the right to own property and granted communal lands to those villages which did not have them.

It is possible that Maximilian was seeking support among the Mexican poor – the overwhelming majority of the nation – because his authority depended so far entirely on the strength of a foreign army of occupation. But this in the eyes of most Mexicans was more important than the question of his liberal or conservative convictions. In 1858–60 the

[28] Ramírez, *Leyes fundamentales de México,* 670–80

struggle had been between Mexican liberals and Mexican conservatives. Now the issue was between Mexico and France, between the Mexican republic and a foreign monarchy. The liberal government of Juárez came to represent Mexico and the empire was seen as an instrument of a foreign power.

The conquest and the empire almost succeeded. In the final months of 1865, the advancing French armies pushed Juárez to Paso del Norte, a town on the Rio Grande across the United States border. At the same time, Juárez faced a serious internal crisis. His four-year term as president was due to expire on 1 December 1865 and it was impossible to hold elections with the French occupying most of the country. Basing himself on the extraordinary powers previously granted to him by Congress, Juárez extended his own term of office until such time as new elections again became possible. This action was no doubt unconstitutional and General González Ortega, the (also) unconstitutional president of the Supreme Court, claimed the presidency of the republic. It seemed that the days of Juárez, and even the republic, were numbered, but the general had neither the nerve nor the strength to attempt a military takeover. Juárez arrested and imprisoned him. For the moment, he weathered the storm.

In 1866 the military situation turned against the empire as a result of Napoleon's decision to withdraw his troops. They began to leave, exposing the weakness of Maximilian's position. For two years he had tried to lure the liberals into his camp and many of them had become imperial civil servants, but with the French expeditionary force about to depart he had to replace it with a Mexican army. Unable to find liberals willing to fight and, if necessary, die for his empire, he turned to the conservatives. After the departure of the French, it would once again be a war of Mexican conservatives against Mexican liberals. Maximilian appointed a conservative cabinet and welcomed the best conservative commander, Miramón, back to Mexico. Without knowing it, the conservatives and the Austrian archduke had sealed a death pact.

Republican armies closed the circle around the tottering empire which retained control of central Mexico. The eastern army moved against Puebla, and the northern army against Querétaro and it was there that Maximilian decided to make what was to be his last stand. He was defeated and became a prisoner of war, together with Generals Miramón and Mejía, the latter a conservative of Indian origins. Executions of military and civilian prisoners had been common both in the civil war of

1858–60 and during the French invasion of 1862–6. If Ocampo had been shot, why should Maximilian be spared? His royal blood made no difference. He had to come to the same end as Iturbide. Juárez intended to warn the world that an attempted conquest of Mexico, for whatever aim, did not pay. The execution of Maximilian, Miramón and Mejía was, therefore, a foregone conclusion. They were court-martialled, convicted of war crimes and faced the firing squad on 19 June 1867. After an absence of more than four years, President Juárez returned to his capital city on 15 July 1867.

In retrospect, the second Mexican empire appears to have been a tragi-comedy of errors. The conservatives had picked the wrong man. They needed a strong, conservative monarch to bolster their cause, not someone who put only obstacles in their way. They might have done better had they obtained an ultra Catholic Spanish prince. As it was, Maximilian's attempt to graft a liberal, European monarchy on a Church-dominated Latin American republic was a forlorn enterprise. He quarrelled with Miramón without winning over Juárez. His social reforms brought him into conflict with the ruling classes, particularly the large landowners. His reforms came too late to earn him popularity with the poor. In the end, he was in a country which did not want him, especially not as a gift from an invading army. In sum, the emperor who had sought to bring together liberals and conservatives, rich and poor, Mexicans and Europeans, ended by being repudiated and abandoned by almost all.

And yet, at the beginning, in 1863–4, some Mexicans did see in an empire an answer to their problems and a reasonable, even desirable alternative to the almost fifty years of anarchy and civil war that had gone before. They had lost faith in the ability of their nation to govern itself. Only a European of royal blood could command the respect of all, restrain individual ambition and be an impartial judge of their disputes. Did not the empire fulfil the Plan of Iguala of 1821 which had insisted on a European prince as the only force capable of holding the nation together? The answer, of course, is that it did, but it had come too late. Had it come immediately after independence, it might have given some stability to the new country. But now Mexico had a group of men capable of ruling, as they were soon to show, and it was these men who fought and defeated the empire.

Restored by Juárez in 1867, the liberal republic lasted until 1876 when General Porfirio Díaz, a hero of the patriotic war against the French, overthrew the civilian president, Sebastián Lerdo, a younger brother of

Miguel Lerdo and successor to Juárez after his death in 1872. Using parts of his predecessor's political machine, Díaz built one of his own which helped him to retain power for thirty-five years. He was to bring considerable stability to Mexico, making possible unprecedented economic development, but his absolute control of political offices and what to most younger contemporaries appeared to be the regime's mounting tyranny finally brought his downfall in 1911 in the first stage of the Mexican Revolution.

11

CENTRAL AMERICA FROM INDEPENDENCE TO *c*. 1870

The first half century of national independence was an unhappy time for the provinces formerly comprising the kingdom of Guatemala: Guatemala, El Salvador, Honduras, Nicaragua and Costa Rica.[1] Tensions in the economic and social structures of the late colonial period led to bitter political struggles and civil war, and the high expectations expressed by Central American leaders at the beginning of the period were soon dashed on the hard rock of reality. Economic stagnation, class antagonism, political tranny and anarchy replaced the relative tranquillity and stability of the Hispanic era. Instead of a united and prosperous independent isthmian nation, a fragmented and feuding cluster of city states calling themselves 'republics' had emerged by 1870. Nevertheless, however disappointing the rate of economic and social change, some important and necessary steps had been taken in the transition from colonialism to modern capitalist dependency.

Historians of Latin America often pass rapidly over Central American independence with the suggestion that it came about merely as a natural consequence of Mexican independence. It is true that Central America was spared the bloody wars that characterized the struggles for independence in Mexico and Spanish South America. Central American creoles did not seize control of the government following Napoleon's invasion of Spain in 1808. Peninsular rule continued in Guatemala City until 1821. And independence when it came was the result of an act of an assembly of notables who on 15 September 1821 accepted the *fait accompli* of Agustín de Iturbide's Plan of Iguala. However, during the first two decades of the nineteenth century the kingdom of Guatemala had experienced severe

---

[1] Chiapas, a province of the kingdom of Guatemala, joined Mexico at independence. Panama was a province of the viceroyalty of New Granada and became part of the republic of Gran Colombia.

economic stress and social dislocation, and significant political activity. The conflicts of the years immediately preceding independence bear directly on the issues that disrupted the Central American union during the half century after 1821.

The period 1810–14, in particular, witnessed the beginnings of the political struggles in Central America that were to last for decades. There were creole conspiracies and rebellions in El Salvador, Nicaragua and Honduras as early as 1811 and 1812 and, towards the end of 1813, in the capital itself, but the strong and efficient government of José de Bustamante y Guerra, captain general and president of the *audiencia* of Guatemala (1811–18), denied success to these movements. Meanwhile, the Cortes of Cádiz and the Constitution that it promulgated in 1812 provided political definition and substance for the emerging creole liberals who had already begun to articulate economic and social grievances. The Constitution of 1812 established freedom of the press, elections not only for city councils but new provincial bodies (*diputaciones provinciales*) and colonial representation in Spain; it pointed the way towards more representative government and more democratic procedures; it encouraged freer trade and threatened traditional *fueros* and monopolies. The political foundation of the Liberal Party in Central America and of much of its programme for the remainder of the century was laid.[2] Bustamante abhorred the Cádiz Constitution and did his best to prevent or delay its implementation. Finally, the restoration of Ferdinand VII in 1814 justified Bustamante's authoritarian dictatorship and his repression of the liberals. But his successor in 1818, Carlos Urrutia y Montoya, feeble with age and illness, first relaxed the strong-arm rule and then accepted the re-establishment of the 1812 Constitution following the Revolution of 1820 in Spain.

The 1812 Constitution had not only encouraged and strengthened liberal political arguments in Central America, but also emphasized the function of local and provincial governments in making decisions for themselves and in standing up against the traditional domination of the metropoli – Spain, Mexico or Guatemala. This regional resentment and the emergence of separatism in Central America can be documented in all of the provinces, but nowhere was it so obvious as in El Salvador. Long an integral part of the province of Guatemala, El Salvador had grown in importance in the eighteenth century as the principal producer of indigo, the kingdom's leading export. Following the destruction of Santiago de

[2] Mario Rodríguez, *The Cádiz experiment in Central America, 1808–1826* (Berkeley, 1978).

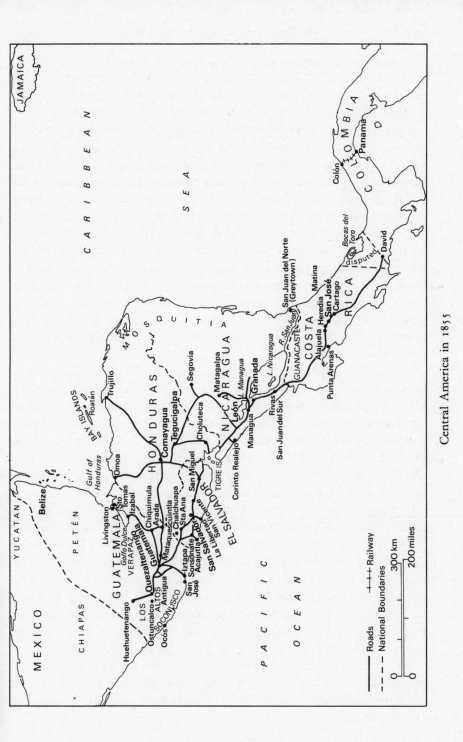

Central America in 1855

Guatemala in 1773 and its move to a new site about 40 kilometres away in 1776, San Salvador became the largest city in Central America and remained so until well after the establishment of independence. The creation of an intendancy in San Salvador in 1786 provided a degree of administrative autonomy for the first time and can be seen as the first step toward Salvadoran nationalism. Calls for ecclesiastical autonomy followed, as Salvadorans demanded their own bishop and separation from the diocese of Guatemala. The Cádiz reforms offered the Salvadoran creoles an opportunity for self-rule, and, understandably, San Salvador became a hotbed of liberal thought and action.

The resentment Salvadoran liberals felt towards what they termed the 'aristocracy' in Guatemala City, the conservative families (mostly creole) who controlled the land, the *consulado* and the *ayuntamiento*, was echoed in other provincial centres from Chiapas to Costa Rica. The restoration of the 1812 Constitution and the call for elections for the *ayuntamientos* and *diputaciones provinciales* in 1820 stimulated an increase in the level of political activity and a renewal of the political debate of 1811–14 throughout Central America.

Within the capital itself, the dialogue was between liberals and moderates and it was made public in the pages of two newspapers. *El Editor Constitucional,* directed by the fiery Pedro Molina, a physician of illegitimate parentage, without close ties to the principal families and representing the creole *letrados*, now for the first time challenged traditional institutions and the continuation of Spanish rule. Answering him was *El Amigo de la Patria*, edited by José Cecilio del Valle, who had come to the capital from a Honduran ranching family for an education and stayed to become one of the colony's leading intellectuals and a prominent attorney, widely respected among the creole elite. He had risen in position and importance during the Bustamante years as a loyal servant of that government, and his government connections caused him to counsel moderation and caution regarding independence. The leading creole families, led by the Aycinena clan, however, supported Molina's rabble-rousers, for they were now uneasy with the threats to their positions of prestige and monopoly that the return to power of the Spanish liberals promised. José del Valle, on the other hand, had the support of the colonial government, the Europeans, the opponents of free trade and the less wealthy creoles. The elections at the end of 1820 were not decisive, although Valle himself won election as *alcalde* of Guatemala City.

In February 1821 Iturbide began his rebellion in Mexico and news of his Plan of Iguala in favour of an independent monarchy spread southward. The new emphasis on local decision-making came into play, as the *ayuntamientos* in each city took it upon themselves to decide how they should react to events in Mexico. In Chiapas, the *ayuntamientos* of Comitán, Ciudad Real and Tuxtla each declared separately for the Plan respectively on 28 August and 3 and 5 September 1821 and joined independent Mexico. In Guatemala the acting Captain General, Gabino Gaínza, agreed on 14 September to the Diputación Provincial's request for a general meeting of the representatives of the principal institutions. In a stormy session the next day, creole and peninsular leaders debated the issues while a crowd outside clamoured for independence. In the end, the delegates, including most of the moderates led by José del Valle, voted in favour of independence. Virtually nothing else changed. The Spanish bureaucracy, headed by Gaínza, remained. The Guatemalan aristocracy were left in control of the government and the economy. Having escaped from the Spanish liberal regime, the creole elite no longer needed its alliance with Molina and the more radical of the local liberals; the Conservative Party was born.

It was intended that the decision taken in Guatemala City in favour of independence should apply to the entire kingdom, but the idea of local participation was now so powerful that each municipality voted separately as news travelled southward. All accepted independence from Spain, but there were variations in their approaches to the future. In San Salvador on 29 September a junta under the liberal leadership of Father José Matías Delgado proclaimed the independence of El Salvador and forced those who favoured union with Guatemala or Mexico to leave the city. Other Salvadoran towns responded differently and trouble broke out. Meanwhile, in Honduras Tegucigalpa accepted Guatemalan leadership while Comayagua insisted on independence from Guatemala as well as from Spain. Similarly, in Nicaragua conservative Granada promised to support the central government in Guatemala while León declared independence from Spain and Guatemala, although it was apparently willing to unite with Mexico! Costa Rica, remote and generally aloof from activities in the captaincy general, seceded from Spain on 27 October, leaving its position with respect to Guatemala and Mexico ambiguous while it established a provisional government completely independent of that in Nicaragua. But almost immediately its four major towns began to quarrel, as San José, Heredia and Alajuela vied for equality with Cartago, the colonial seat of power. As the national period opened, then, Central America was politically fragmented and caught up in a wave of regional and local acts of separation.

Annexation to Mexico became the first real issue clearly dividing conservatives and liberals. In general, conservatives all across Central America endorsed annexation, while liberals called for an independent republican federation. Because they controlled the apparatus of government in Guatemala and most of the other states, the conservatives succeeded in thwarting liberal efforts to resist annexation. Iturbide's dispatch of a Mexican army at the end of November furthered the annexationist cause. Violence flared in Guatemala and Nicaragua, but only in El Salvador did the republicans gain the upper hand. By the end of December 1821, 115 (104 unconditionally and 11 with certain stipulations) *ayuntamientos* had declared for incorporation into the Mexican empire. Another 32 left the matter to the provisional government while 21 declared that only a general congress could decide the issue. Only two *ayuntamientos* had opposed union absolutely, while 67 remained to be heard from. Also on the side of annexation was the powerful influence of Archbishop Ramón Casáus, who had only reluctantly accepted independence. On 5 January 1822 the provisional government declared that annexation was the overwhelming will of the country – as expressed through the *ayuntamientos* – and a few days later Gaínza, who remained titular head of state, prohibited further opposition to the decision. The provisional junta dissolved itself and Gaínza supervised a speedy election of delegates to the new congress in Mexico.

Only San Salvador and Granada rejected annexation outright, although division on the question continued in Costa Rica, where there was also sentiment for union with Colombia, and in Honduras, where the rivalry between Comayagua and Tegucigalpa continued. Led by Delgado, San Salvador turned to arms to maintain its position. Its forces, under the command of Manuel José de Arce, defeated Gaínza's Guatemalan army near Sonsonate, touching off a bloody war which was to continue intermittently for decades and was to poison chances for a successful Central American union. The arrival of a new captain-general, Vicente Filísola, with 600 Mexican troops proved decisive. Filísola took office on 22 June 1822 and immediately sought to reach a negotiated settlement. San Salvador entered into these talks apparently to buy time, for by November it was clear that the city would not submit peaceably to Mexican rule. Late that month Filísola invaded El Salvador with a force of two thousand. Frantically San Salvador sought a way out of its predicament, including a declaration of annexation to the United States. All failed, and the city capitulated on 10 February 1823. In the meantime, however, Granada continued to hold out against the annexationists in Nicaragua and in April in Costa Rica anti-Mexican troops from San José and Alajuela subdued the pro-imperial forces in Cartago.

Iturbide's empire, of course, was already doomed. While Filísola had subdued the liberals in El Salvador, liberals in Mexico had pronounced against the empire with the Plan of Casa Mata. After news arrived of the emperor's abdication, Filísola told the Guatemalan Diputación Provincial on 29 March that Mexico was in a state of anarchy. The provinces responded enthusiastically to his call for a Central American congress in accordance with the plan of 15 September 1821. Elections followed and the body which began its sessions on 24 June 1823 represented all of the states except Chiapas, which chose to remain with Mexico. Perhaps the most representative ever assembled by a Central American authority, this congress was decidedly more liberal than the previous government. Many of the conservatives were still in Mexico, and they had in any case been discredited by the collapse of the monarchy. Under the presidency of Father Delgado of El Salvador, on 1 July 1823 congress declared Central America free and independent and adopted the name *Provincias Unidas del Centro de América*, 'The United Provinces of the Centre of America'. The next day the congress became a National Constituent Assembly and set to work writing a republican constitution. Mexico recognized the United Provinces in August as Filísola and his army withdrew.

The new Central American republic began with rather naïve expressions of unity and optimism for the future after nearly two years of disunion and chaos which were now blamed on Spain, Mexico and their 'servile supporters'. Despite the sudden turn of political events in favour of the liberals, the real situation in Central America was not conducive to the success of the sort of modern, progressive nation that the framers of the 1824 Constitution envisioned. Serious economic and social problems and divisions stood in the way.

The United Provinces, even with the loss of Chiapas and excluding Belize, had a population of more than a million persons.[3] (See Table 1)

[3] Contemporary estimates of the population vary widely and are of doubtful reliability. The estimates in Table 1 reflect an analysis of these estimates together with colonial and late nineteenth-century demographic data and an estimated growth rate of about 1.3% during the first fifty years of independence, taking into consideration some variations caused by local disasters, epidemics and other circumstances.

Table 1 *Estimated Population of Central America, 1820–70*
(Thousands of inhabitants)

State	1820	1830	1840	1850	1860	1870
Costa Rica	63	72	86	101	115	137
El Salvador	248	271	315	366	424	493
Guatemala	595	670	751	847	951	1080
Honduras	135	152	178	203	230	265
Nicaragua	186	220	242	274	278	337
Central America	1227	1385	1572	1791	1998	2312

Most were illiterate peasants or peons with little voice in the future of the country. About 65 per cent of the population of Central America were Indian, 31 per cent *ladino* (*mestizo* and mulatto) and only about 4 per cent white. Individual states varied considerably from these estimates, of course. Guatemala had a larger percentage of Indians than any other state, while Costa Rica's tiny population was predominantly white. El Salvador, Nicaragua and Honduras had substantial *ladino* populations. There were some blacks, principally along the Honduran and Nicaraguan coasts, but they were for the most part outside Central American society.[4]

The economy of Central America had experienced considerable change in the two decades prior to independence, which placed additional burdens on the new republic. Briefly, in the late eighteenth century the kingdom of Guatemala had become an important exporter of Salvadoran and Guatemalan indigo. Exports beyond the isthmus from the other provinces were not very great, but Honduras and Nicaragua, and to a lesser extent Costa Rica, were important suppliers of livestock and agricultural foodstuffs to the indigo-producing regions and administrative centre of the kingdom. Growing evidence suggests that the late colonial economy was, therefore, very much tied to the international

[4] Reliable statistics on the racial composition of the population do not exist, but for the whole region, see the estimates of Severo Martínez Peláez, *La patria del criollo, ensayo de interpretación de la realidad colonial guatemalteca* (Guatemala, 1971), 397–8. Martínez Peláez says that Nicaragua was 84% *ladino* at the close of the colonial period. Alejandro Marroquín, *Apreciación sociológica de la independencia* (San Salvador, 1964), 25–8, has calculated the following percentages for El Salvador in 1807 (not including Sonsonate and Ahuachapán, which were still part of Guatemala): Spaniards 0.86%; creoles 2%; *ladinos* 53.07%; negroes and mulattos 0.1%; Indians 43.07%. It is probable that the racial composition of the Central American population did not greatly change during the period, although the process of *mestizaje* certainly continued. It is also probable that, owing to European immigration, the percentage of whites in Central America very slightly increased during the period 1821–70.

economy and that there was significant integration of the economy within the kingdom.[5]

The rapid decline of Salvadoran indigo production during the first two decades of the nineteenth century, however, brought serious economic dislocation throughout Central America. Locust plagues, attacks on Spanish shipping and competition from other indigo-producing areas with better access to European markets contributed to this significant reduction of exports and forced planters in Salvador and Guatemala to shift to producing foodstuffs, in turn cutting back purchases of livestock and grain from Honduras, Nicaragua and Costa Rica. Thus, as the colonial period closed, the kingdom was becoming less interdependent and less tied to the international market. This meant reduced living standards at a time when heavy taxes and loan demands by the Spanish government during the Napoleonic Wars were additional burdens on the Central American elites.[6]

The Guatemalan aristocracy, understandably, looked towards expanding trade, the removal of economic restrictions and new exports, notably of cochineal, as a means out of their difficult straits. Some had already turned to contraband trade, principally through British Honduras, compounding their difficulties with the Bustamante regime. At the same time they opposed economic advancement for other elements of the society and after independence the basic conservatism of the dominant class became manifest. Opposing them, especially in the provinces, were representatives of the professions and middle sectors and government bureaucrats who saw in liberalism the opportunity for greater advancement and economic opportunity. Both factions represented only a tiny percentage of the total population; the mass of Indians and *ladinos* were outside the political debates. But the economic hard times were felt not only by the elites. Indeed, the spread of poverty among the urban poor increased social tensions at the time of independence and helped to provide soldiers for the armies of both sides in the conflicts that followed.

The issues that divided liberals from conservatives at the outset of the national period were not very different from those which divided

---

[5] See Alberto Lanuza Matamoros, 'Estructuras socioeconómicas, poder y estado en Nicaragua (1821–1875)', (unpublished thesis, University of Costa Rica at San José, 1976), 83–9.

[6] R. L. Woodward, Jr, *Class privilege and economic development: the Consulado de Comercio of Guatemala, 1793–1871* (Chapel Hill, N.C., 1966), 39–41; R. S. Smith, 'Indigo production and trade in colonial Guatemala', *Hispanic American Historical Review*, 39/2 (1959), 183; Miles Wortman, 'Government revenue and economic trends in Central America, 1787–1819', *loc. cit.*, 55/2 (1975), 262–4.

Spaniards at the same time, and they had largely been delineated in debates over the Cádiz Constitution of 1812. Conservatives felt more secure with a monarchy while the liberals were republican. The Spanish Bourbons had not endeared themselves to either group sufficiently to allow monarchy to remain an institution long cherished by the conservatives, but even after the issue of monarchy *versus* republic was apparently settled in 1824, Central American conservatives retained serious scepticism about the ability of any but the educated and proper-tied to govern. A more important institution in the liberal–conservative struggle was the Church. The liberals sought to disestablish it and remove it from political and economic power, while the conservatives cherished it as a defender of their privileges and a vital element in both controlling and securing the support of the masses. Liberals sought to destroy monopolistic control of the economy and to eliminate the *fueros* of the conservatives – ecclesiastical, commercial, university, etc. Educa-tion was an issue closely related to the Church controversy, for the liberals favoured secular education with mass education as the ultimate goal, while conservatives defended an elitist educational system under the supervision of the Church. Leaders in both parties recognized the need for modernization and a rational approach to economic problems, as the utilitarian influence of Jeremy Bentham on both sides illustrates. Although the leading families of Central America were connected across the region by ties of family and marriage, differing economic and political circumstances at the local level tended to divide them along conservative or liberal lines. At the outset, there was considerable political manoeuvring, but the bitter struggles that wracked Central America after independence removed much of the middle ground and crystallized the two parties into warring camps that would characterize Central American politics for the remainder of the century.

After the declaration of independence from Mexico (1 July 1823) the liberals at first dominated the National Constituent Assembly. They moved quickly to remove class privileges. On 23 July all titles of distinction, royalty or nobility, including even the use of 'don', were abolished. The same decree included anticlerical reforms; bishops and archbishops, for example, were stripped of any title except 'padre'.[7]

---

[7] Colonial terminology was also rejected: *audiencias* and *ayuntamientos* became, respectively, *cortes territoriales* and *municipalidades*. Later, other ceremonial forms, symbols and aristocratic vestiges were abolished (21 August 1823). 'Dios, Union, Libertad', replaced 'Dios guarde a Ud. muchos

Annulment of all acts of the imperial Mexican government and peremptory dismissal of Spanish and Mexican officials soon contributed to resentment against the liberals. The first violence flared in mid-September, when Captain Rafael Ariza y Torres led a revolt, ostensibly demanding backpay for the military. It resulted in a reshuffling of the government towards more conservative interests, but then liberal troops from El Salvador arrived to support the government. Civil war was averted, but Guatemalan residents resented strongly the presence of the Salvadorans and ill-feeling persisted even after the troops left. This uprising – and a pro-Spanish revolt which the army also quicky suppressed – revealed the unsettled conditions in Guatemala and the growing hostility to the liberal assembly. Inevitably, therefore, the balance of power in the assembly began to shift as debate over the proposed constitution continued. The document that finally emerged in November 1824 was a compromise between radicals and conservatives, and José del Valle played an important part in its formulation. It blended elements of the Spanish Constitution of 1812 with the U.S. Constitution of 1789. Dedicated to the protection of 'liberty, equality, security and property' (art. 2), the 1824 Constitution guaranteed Roman Catholicism as the religion of the state 'to the exclusion of the public exercise of any other' (art. 11), outlawed slavery (art. 13), and provided extensive guarantees of individual liberties (arts. 152–76). A complex system of indirect election provided for a unicameral federal congress (arts. 23–54). All legislation had to be approved by a senate composed of two senators from each state, no more than one of whom could be an ecclesiastic (art. 92), although the congress could override senate vetoes with a two-thirds vote, except in cases concerning taxation, which required a three-fourths majority (arts. 76–86). The president had no veto and was required to execute the law once it had passed the senate (arts. 87–8). The president, who also was commander-in-chief of the armed forces, and vice president were indirectly elected for four-year terms. A supreme court, also elected indirectly, had from five to seven justices serving two-year, staggered terms (arts. 132–40). The Constitution provided for a federation of five autonomous states with state assemblies, state executives and state judicial officers, whose first duty would be to form state

años' as the official compliment closing all correspondence (4 August 1823). Alejandro Marure, *Efemérides de los hechos notables acaecidos en la República de Centro-América desde el año de 1821 hasta el de 1842* (2nd edn, Guatemala, 1895), 11–12; Isidro Menéndez, comp., *Recopilación delas leyes del Salvador en Centro América* (2nd edn, San Salvador, 1956), I, 20, 126.

constitutions consistent with the federal charter. Each state was also to have a representative council, analogous to the federal senate, to approve legislative acts and advise state governors (arts. 177–95). The Constitution went into effect immediately, even before it was ratified by the first elected congress in August 1825.[8]

The first national elections were dominated by a spirited campaign between Salvadoran liberal Manuel José de Arce and moderate José del Valle, both members of the interim governing junta. Violence erupted in several places, and the government threatened those who opposed the new constitutional system with death. When the new congress convened in February 1825, presided over by Guatemalan Dr Mariano Gálvez, liberals appeared to have triumphed, yet the election for president in April favoured the more moderate José del Valle. Receiving 41 of the 79 electoral votes actually cast, he nevertheless lacked by one vote a majority of the 82 votes authorized, and thus the election was thrown into the Congress. Arce intrigued not only to win the presidency, but also to form a broadly-based coalition which, he believed, would allow the federal government to govern successfully. To this end he gained support from conservative members with assurances that he would not insist on a separate bishop for El Salvador. The congress elected Arce by a vote of 22–5. Valle refused to accept the vice-presidency, as did the liberal radical, José Francisco Barrundiaa, the position finally going to the Guatemalan conservative Mariano Beltranena. The new republic began its existence, therefore, under the cloud of suspicion of betrayal of the wishes of the electorate and with the extreme liberals (the Barrundia faction) already disenchanted with the liberal president, who they believed had sold out to the hated '*serviles*' (conservatives).

President Arce's government never really had effective control of any of the five states which made up the federation. Each continued to go its own way. State governments organized themselves in accordance with the Constitution, but in several there was serious disagreement between liberal and conservative factions. Arce had personally led the troops in pacifying Nicaragua early in 1825, but the peace he established there was but a brief interlude in the struggle between Granada and León. Costa Rica, under the firm hand of Juan Mora, remained aloof from the federal government and achieved a degree of order and progress. Serious trouble loomed in El Salvador, where the installation of Father Delgado

---

[8] 'Constitución Federal de 1824' in Ricardo Gallardo, *Las constituciones de la República Federal de Centro-América* (Madrid, 1958), II, 103–38.

as bishop faced opposition from Archbishop Casáus and Arce's coalition federal government in Guatemala City. This was a symbolic issue, representing the powerful Salvadoran urge for independence from Guatemala. The most urgent problem faced by Arce, however, was the Guatemalan state government, dominated by the liberal '*Fiebres*' and led by Juan Barrundia. That government proceeded along radical lines, repeatedly offending the more conservative elements in the federal government with whom Arce had allied. During Arce's first year in office the rift between the two governments widened. In April 1826 Arce deposed Barrundia and in September he placed him under arrest. The remainder of the Guatemalan state government, under Lieut. Governor Cirilio Flores, fled first to San Martín Jilotepeque and later to Quezaltenango, where the state legislature enacted inflamatory liberal laws, declaring children of the clergy legal inheritors of Church property, abolishing the merchant guild (*Consulado*), and cutting the *diezmo* in half. These laws were unenforceable, but they served as a basis for much liberal legislation after 1829. The liberals' tenure in Quezaltenango was short-lived, for in October a mob attacked Flores, tearing him literally limb from limb, and the liberal government collapsed.

A new Guatemalan state government under the conservative Mariano Aycinena now co-operated with President Arce in driving the remaining liberals from the state. But Salvadoran liberals now rose to challenge the pro-Arce government in San Salvador, touching off a bloody three-year civil war. Arce commanded the federal forces, but his government depended so heavily on the state of Guatemala that Aycinena soon supplanted him in importance. Bitterness and atrocities characterized both sides in this vicious struggle that spread over much of Guatemala, El Salvador and Honduras. In the latter state, Francisco Morazán rallied the liberals and, following his defeat of federal forces at La Trinidad, Honduras (10 November 1827), emerged as the leading liberal military figure. Arce now sought conciliation, and when that failed he resigned the presidency in February 1828. Vice-President Beltranena took over, but in reality Aycinena became the principal leader against the liberals. His government drew heavily on forced loans from the clergy and local wealthy citizens, including foreign merchants, causing the latter to welcome a liberal victory. Federal troops won a bloody and costly victory in March 1828 at Chalcuapa, but thereafter the tide turned in favour of General Morazán. Completing his reconquest of Honduras and El Salvador by the end of 1828, he invaded Guatemala early in 1829, laying siege to the capital in February, when the liberals re-established a state government at Antigua. Morazán's victory at Las Charcas on 15 March was decisive, although Aycinena did not finally capitulate until 12 April.

The immediate fruits of the civil war (1826-9) were a vindictive policy toward conservative leaders and the enactment of radical liberal legislation. José F. Barrundia presided over the republic until September 1830 when elections elevated Morazán to the presidency. Morazán defeated José del Valle who, unassociated with the Arce–Aycinena government in Guatemala, was now able to return to politics, although unable to stem the liberal landslide. Juan Barrundia was reinstated briefly as governor of Guatemala, but in 1831 Mariano Gálvez won election there. Although clearly in the liberal camp, Dr Gálvez was less radical than the Barrundias, and eventually a serious split would surface between them. Morazán also had allies in office in the three central states and liberals had the upper hand in Costa Rica, but opposition in all of these states soon began to limit their effectiveness. Difficulties within El Salvador contributed to Morazán's decision to move the national capital to San Salvador in 1834.

The presidential election of 1834 reflected widespread dissatisfaction with Morazán and his programme, and José del Valle successfully challenged his bid for re-election. Unfortunately for the moderate cause, however, Valle died before taking office, and Morazán, with the second highest number of votes, constitutionally remained as president. With José del Valle, it appears, died the last hope for a moderate course. Morazán's victory under these terms left widespread bitterness and resentment among moderates and conservatives. Their frustration turned to hatred as grievances against the liberals mounted.

The case of Guatemala state best illustrates the nature of the conflicts of the 1830s and their results. Gálvez shared Morazán's belief that Central America could become a modern, progressive republic through enlightened social and economic legislation. With the leading conservatives in exile, a period of peace and order seemed assured, as, armed with extraordinary powers to deal with opposition, the Gálvez government became the pilot for Morazán's liberal programme. Convinced that Spanish colonialism was at the root of their underdevelopment, they sought to destroy Hispanic institutions and to replace them by emulating the apparent success of the United States. In practice, however, although Gálvez gained substantial acceptance of his programme among the elite, he failed to overcome widespread opposition among the lower classes of the country.

The sources of opposition were several. Liberal trade policy had damaged seriously the native weaving industry, and Gálvez's tariff modifications were too late to protect it. More serious was a new direct head tax of two pesos per capita which contributed to peasant restlessness generally. In El Salvador such a tax resulted in widespread popular rebellion in 1833, forcing suspension of the levy there, but Gálvez maintained the tax in Guatemala. Heavy demands for forced labour to build roads and other public works intensified the resentment.

Another unpopular aspect of the liberal economic programme was the policy of promoting private acquisition of public or communal lands as a means of increasing production and exports. Cochineal expansion began to increase the demand for the land and labour of Indians and *ladinos* in central and eastern Guatemala. Moreover, a number of large grants to foreigners caused considerable unrest. British commercial activity at Belize had intensified the traditional suspicion of foreigners. Spanish colonial administrations had dealt vigorously with foreign interlopers, but since independence liberal policy had welcomed them, causing apprehension among those who believed themselves to be victims of foreign competition. Foreign influence was evident in many aspects of the Gálvez programme, but the concessions made to mahogany loggers and the projects to populate the northern and eastern areas of the country with English colonists caused residents of those regions to regard the liberals as favouring foreign rather than national interests. Between March and August 1834 the Guatemalan government ceded nearly all of its public land to foreign colonization companies. As the British hold on Belize, the Miskito Shore and the Bay Islands tightened, and as Anglo-American colonizers in Texas threw off Mexican rule, many Guatemalans began to doubt the wisdom of Gálvez's colonization schemes. Ignoring or suppressing petitions from residents against the colonization contracts, however, Gálvez rejected the idea that the liberals were betraying their country to Europeans. Revolts which broke out in Chiquimula and other eastern towns in the autumn of 1835 were possibly linked to an uprising in El Salvador against Morazán. Troops suppressed the rebellion, but the inhabitants remained resentful, especially after the arrival of the first shipload of British colonists in the middle of 1836.

Another part of the liberal programme which proved offensive to the rural masses was the attack on the clergy. Anticlericalism ran especially high since the Church had backed the conservative regime of Mariano Aycinena from 1826 to 1829. Morazán's federal government exiled many anti-liberal clergy, beginning with Archbishop Casáus. Following the suppression of the regular orders and the establishment of religious liberty, the federal government prevailed on state governments to continue the assault on the traditional power and privilege of the clergy. Between 1829 and 1831 Guatemala censored ecclesiastical correspondence, seized church funds and confiscated the property of religious houses. In 1832 Gálvez stopped the collection of the tithe, ended many religious holidays, confiscated more church property, decreed the right of the clergy to write their wills as they pleased and legitimized the inheritance of parents' property by children of the clergy. Later, the Guatemalan legislature authorized civil marriage, legalized divorce and removed education from church supervision. In Indian and *ladino* villages where parishioners were already chafing at Gálvez's policies on other grounds, the priests railed against a government that challenged their authority and attacked their sacred institutions, brought Protestant foreigners into the country and threatened the very foundations of society. These rural priests were in the vanguard of the uprisings that rocked Guatemala in 1837.

Further opposition to Liberal government was provoked by the new judicial system. Persuaded that the Hispanic system of private *fueros* and multiple courts was unjust and antiquated, the liberals adopted the Edward Livingston Codes, which went into effect on 1 January 1837. José F. Barrundia promoted these codes, written for Louisiana in 1824, as a modern replacement for the system they had been abolishing piecemeal. Trial by jury was the central feature of the new system, and almost immediately problems arose in the countryside, where illiteracy was general and the deeply entrenched class structure made trial by jury impracticable. The mass of the population identified the Codes more with centralized rule from Guatemala City, with foreign influence and with anti-clericalism than with social justice. Moreover, the authoritarian manner in which the liberals introduced these and other reforms did little to improve relations between government and people. Military repression in Central America had been escalating ever since the strong-armed rule of Bustamante, but the insensitivity of both the federal and state governments in their efforts to develop the export economy, in the regulation of the morality of the inhabitants, in suppressing criticism of their own policies and in persecuting their political enemies through exile and confiscatory measures added to their unpopularity, as did the conduct of government troops.

The cholera epidemic which entered the country from Belize in 1837 turned the threatened and real grievances of the peasants in eastern Guatemala into open rebellion. In March 1837 the government quarantined infected areas and pursued other sanitary measures, undoubtedly justified but poorly understood. The peasants, already alienated from the Gálvez government, feared the vaccines and believed the priests who told them that the medicine which health officials put into the water was poison. Panic and violence resulted. Although the first major insurgency of 1837 took place at San Juan Ostuncalco, in Los Altos, where natives rioted against officials charged with effecting the Livingston Codes, the greatest trouble was in the Montaña region of eastern Guatemala. A natural leader, José Rafael Carrera, emerged who was to organize and lead the peasants to victory, and to determine the destiny of Guatemala for the next twenty-five years, until his death in 1865. Born in the capital in 1814, Carrera, a *ladino*, had served as a drummer in the conservative army during the 1826–9 civil war and later drifted into the Montaña. There he became a swineherd and gained some property after a village curate arranged a marriage with a woman of Mataquescuintla. Carrera initially commanded a patrol charged with enforcing the cholera quarantine, but he turned against the government and took his troops to the aid of peasants who were resisting a government force at Santa Rosa. Carrera's leadership turned their defeat into victory there and soon he commanded a guerrilla band that controlled much of eastern Guatemala. The cholera epidemic limited the government's ability to raise troops, but Carrera's partisans increased in numbers and effectiveness. In late June he listed his demands in a manifesto that reflected the conservative influence of the priests who advised him: 1. abolition of the Livingston Codes; 2. protection of life and property; 3. return of the archbishop and restoration of the religious orders; 4. repeal of the head tax; 5. amnesty for all exiles since 1829; and 6. respect for Carrera's orders under pain of death to violators.

Faced with popular insurgency, Gálvez formed a coalition of national unity with the conservatives, reminiscent of Arce's earlier action. He thus drove the more radical liberals led by J. F. Barrundia and Pedro Molina into an opposition faction. The divisions among the elite in the capital played into the hands of Carrera, whose ragged army extended the area of its control and terrorized the propertied classes, commerce and foreign travellers. Efforts to patch up the rift among the liberals ended in Gálvez's resignation in favour of Lieutenant Governor Pedro Valenzuela, who was more acceptable to Barrundia. But it failed to prevent Carrera's horde from over-running Guatemala City on 31 January 1838. He soon withdrew his forces from the capital and returned to his home district of Mita, but not before the beginnings of an alliance with the conservatives was born.

The economic power of the creole aristocratic class – large landowners and merchants – had been damaged but not broken by the liberal rulers. In fact, some had acquired confiscated church property and actually expanded their holdings during the 1830s. Although some members of the class remained in the liberal camp, most now supported the conservative cause. In 1833 the conservatives made a strong resurgence in the Guatemalan legislature and courted 'General' Carrera by attempting to satisfy some of his demands. The Church regained its former status; liberal military commanders were relieved of their posts; there was a move toward return to constitutional rule that allowed conservatives to gain election to office; the Livingston Codes were repealed in March. These acts reflected the popular will as voiced by the guerrilla caudillo. The preamble to a decree of 12 March, 1838, terminating all non-elected officeholders, illustrated the attention the legislature paid to this will when it acknowledged that 'a great majority of the population of the State have armed themselves to resist the administration that violated their guarantees and the fundamental pact', and justified the revolution against Gálvez, 'directed to establishing law and liberty . . . in self preservation against tyranny, [as] not only legitimate but consecrated by reason and justice'.[9]

Carrera, impatient with the slow progress of the legislature in dismantling the liberal reforms, resumed his guerrilla attacks and threatened to invade the capital once more. At the same time, conservative electoral gains and the new representative council headed by the conservative Mariano Rivera Paz put the Barrundia faction in an untenable position. In the end, Barrundia fell back on his liberal ally, Morazán, who rallied to his aid in mid-March with a thousand Salvadoran troops. Valenzuela's government had cautioned the federal caudillo against invading Guatemala, warning that it would upset the understanding with Carrera who had returned to Mita in peace. But when Carrera returned to the offensive, it forced the state to look to the federal government for help.

[9] *Boletín Oficial* (Guatemala), no. 11 (17 March 1838), 474–7.

Morazán launched an all-out campaign to track down and destroy Carrera's forces, while arresting the conservative direction of the Guatemalan government. The guerrillas responded with new ferocity. Atrocities multiplied on both sides. And by this time the federal government also faced conservative opposition in Nicaragua, Honduras and within El Salvador as well as Guatemala, while Costa Rica, now under the mildly conservative rule of Braulio Carrillo, was effectively ignoring the federation. The British consul, Frederick Chatfield, who formerly had supported Morazán, now regarded the federal cause as hopeless and sought to develop close British ties with the emerging conservative rulers. When the federal congress, recognizing and feeling these pressures, declared on 7 July 1838 that the states were 'sovereign, free and independent political bodies', Morazán returned to San Salvador to reassert his authority there.[10] He had by this time greatly weakened Carrera's influence, but had not eliminated the threat altogether.

Thus, by mid-1838 the battle lines were drawn. Carrera was the champion of the conservative cause for autonomy against Morazán and the liberals for federation. In other states the conservatives consolidated their strength and organization in alliance with the emerging popular caudillos. Thus, conservatism became closely related to local autonomy and the breakup of the Central American federation. With Morazán in San Salvador the conservatives in Guatemala quickly regained power, and on 22 July Valenzuela turned over the executive power to Rivera Paz. The new government resumed the dismantling of the liberal programme. In the country Carrera once more controlled a large area. A sudden counter-offensive in September by liberal General Carlos Salazar, however, forced Carrera to retreat into la Montaña, and when Morazán rejoined the chase, Carrera bought time by agreeing on 23 December to lay down his arms and recognize the government at Guatemala City in return for restoration of his military command in the district of Mita.

Encouraged by the apparent collapse of Carrera's guerrillas, Morazán on 30 January 1839 deposed Rivera Paz and replaced him with General Salazar. In the meantime, however, conservatives had gained power in Honduras and Nicaragua and joined forces against the liberals in El Salvador. The new liberal thrust had convinced Carrera that there could be no peace until Morazán was eliminated. On 24 March 1839 in a *pronunciamiento* from Mataquescuintla, he accused Morazán of cruelty

[10] Manuel Pineda de Mont (comp.), *Recopilación de las leyes de Guatemala* (Guatemala, 1869), I, 69.

toward the clergy and other Guatemalans, of destroying commerce, of confiscating private property and of spreading terror throughout the land. Swearing to restore Rivera Paz, he joined in alliance with the Honduran and Nicaraguan conservatives against Morazán. Within a month Rivera Paz and the conservatives once more ruled Guatemala. Carrera spent the remainder of the year mopping up in El Salvador and Honduras. Then, in January 1840, he swept into Los Altos, which in 1838 had seceded from Guatemala, and crushed the liberals there.

The inevitable showdown between Carrera and Morazán came in March 1840, when Carrera's forces routed the liberal army at Guatemala City. Morazán and a few of his officers escaped and eventually reached David in Panama, but the federation was finished. Two years later Morazán returned, reorganized his army in El Salvador with less support than he anticipated and then invaded Costa Rica, where he toppled Braulio Carrillo. Morazán's dreams of revitalizing the federation fell almost immediately before a popular insurgency that rose against him. Following a quick trial, he was executed by firing squad on 15 September 1842.

The defeat of Morazán and liberalism reflected both popular and elite disenchantment with liberal policy and a nostalgic search for a restoration of the supposed tranquillity of the Hispanic era. Also discernible is a pro-Hispanic xenophobia vaguely related to the birth of nationalism in each of the five states. The trend was most obvious in Guatemala, traditional seat of Spanish authority and tradition. However, while the conservatives had clearly strengthened their position, they were not yet dominant. In a period characterized by civil war within and between the states, the immediate masters of Central America in the 1840s were local caudillos of whom Carrera was the greatest. Carrera tried to maintain his dominance in Guatemala by playing off liberal and conservative members of the elite against each other, removing governments whenever they failed to be submissive to his bidding. The Church was the major beneficiary and his leading institutional supporter and the Jesuits and other religious orders returned to Central America. However, the liberals found that Carrera was a potential ally against the conservatives, and they were largely responsible for his accession to the presidency for the first time in 1844. Some checks on clerical privilege followed, but Carrera would never condone a full return to liberal policies, so it was inevitable that the liberals should eventually try to oust him.

New uprisings in eastern Guatemala combined with liberal opposition to force Carrera from office in 1848. The liberals were in control of Congress and Carrera's failure to end the uprising in the Montaña led him in January to offer his resignation. The conservatives persuaded him to withdraw it, but as matters worsened, he decided to accede to liberal demands for a new constituent assembly which he convened on 15 August. Addressing its opening session, he reviewed his efforts to bring peace in Guatemala, the economic growth that had occurred and his establishment of absolute Guatemalan independence in 1847. He then announced his resignation and headed for exile in Mexico, initiating at the same time the crisis that would lead to his triumphant return.

Chaos followed as Carrera watched from Chiapas. None of the series of short-term governments that followed were able to restore order or provide unified government. In mid September the conservatives regained temporary control of the Guatemalan Congress, declared Carrera a national hero and confirmed his 1847 declaration of Guatemalan independence. The liberals faced a united conservative opposition divided among themselves, as so often in this period. On 1 January 1849 Colonel Mariano Paredes took office in Guatemala City as a compromise chief of state. Closely advised by conservative statesman Luis Batres, Paredes publicly opposed Carrera's return, but privately condoned it. On 24 January Carrera announced his decision to restore peace and order in Guatemala. Liberal forces attempted to deny his return, but the Paredes government undermined their effectiveness and Carrera took Quezaltenango in April. Soon after, the government reached a peace agreement with the caudillo. Paredes remained as president, but Carrera, recommissioned a lieutenant-general, became commander-in-chief of the armed forces. Restoring order, he dealt vindictively with the liberal leaders who had opposed him. The threat of death faced those who did not flee. Thus, the liberals ceased to play a major role in Guatemalan politics for twenty years, although a few remained in the Congress and in minor offices.

After crushing rebellion in la Montaña and marching into El Salvador to assist the conservatives there (see below), Carrera once more became president of Guatemala (6 November 1851), and from 1854 president for life, a virtual monarch, with authority to designate his successor. Until his death in 1865, closely allied to the Church and the conservative aristocracy, he remained one of the most powerful caudillos in the hemisphere. He maintained friendly governments in Honduras and El

Salvador by force and also influenced the politics of Nicaragua and Costa Rica.

No Central American state escaped domination by conservative caudillos during the mid-nineteenth century, although only Guatemala had one of such durability as Carrera. In El Salvador, Honduras and Nicaragua, the turmoil among rival caudillos was especially devastating. With the liberals in disarray, some caudillos, notably Trinidad Muñoz of Nicaragua and Francisco Dueñas of El Salvador, switched parties in order to take advantage of local opportunities and circumstances.

Despite continued liberal strength in El Salvador, no leader professing Morazanista views could long escape Guatemalan intervention. Following Morazán's defeat in 1840, Carrera had placed one of his own officers, Francisco Malespín, in power. The latter's command of the military made him the dominant caudillo in El Salvador and a political force in Nicaragua and Honduras until his assassination in 1846. In addition to his ties to Carrera and the Guatemalan conservatives, Malespín worked closely with the politically active bishop of San Salvador, Jorge Viteri, and the British consul, Frederick Chatfield, so that while liberals might continue to hold political and legislative offices, conservative interests prevailed. The strength of liberalism in El Salvador, however, caused Malespín to co-operate with and use liberals (as did Carrera himself in the 1840s), which at times gave him problems with his conservative allies.

Meanwhile, Carrera's ally in Honduras, Francisco Ferrera, worked to establish conservative rule there, and he co-operated with Malespín in neutralizing the liberals in El Salvador and Nicaragua as well. Like Carrera, Ferrera came from a lower class *ladino* background and was unconnected with the leading families. As with Carrera, too, the clergy had a very great influence on his rise to power and on his way of thinking. A bitter foe of the Morazanistas, Ferrera, who had first ruled his state in 1833–5, became its first 'president' in January 1841. Although he was the leading caudillo in the country until his death in 1848, the liberals kept Honduras in a state of war much of the time. Ferrera and Malespín checked the liberals regularly. On 22 May 1845 a *coup* in Comayagua briefly gave the liberal leader, Trinidad Cabañas, control of the government for forty days. Soon back in control, Ferrera declined the presidency in 1847, but continued as minister of war under Juan Lindo, one of the more enlightened caudillos of the period and one not easily classified as liberal or conservative.

Lindo had served as first president of El Salvador (1841–2) under the protection of Malespín, where he had opposed restoration of Morazán's federation. Returning to his native Honduras he gained Ferrera's protection, although he was disliked by some of the more militaristic conservatives. Among his memorable acts as president of Honduras was his declaration of war against the United States in July 1847, in support of Mexico. In 1848 he convened a constituent assembly which established a more conservative constitution. Lindo's enlightened conservatism provided Honduras with its first real peace since independence. That peace was broken, however, when his foreign minister, General Santos Guardiola, attempted to oust him in 1850. The intervention of Trinidad Cabañas with Salvadoran liberal troops and the promise of Nicaraguan aid saved Lindo, whose conservatism was nearer that of José del Valle than that of Guardiola or Carrea. This event decidedly moved him into the liberal camp, and Lindo joined Cabañas in El Salvador in an effort to defeat Carrera in 1851. Carrera, however, won a decisive victory at San José la Arada, near Chiquimula, on 27 February 1851. In 1852 Lindo declined a third term as president and allowed the congress to elect Cabañas to succeed him. The more blatant liberalism of Cabañas and his renewed efforts to establish the Central American federation led almost immediately to an invasion from Guatemala by Guardiola, supported by Carrera, and resulted in Cabañas' defeat on 6 July 1855. Following a brief struggle for the presidency, Guardiola took possession of the office in February 1856 and held it until 1862. His unenlightened conservative rule brought some order but little progress to Honduras.

In Costa Rica, after the execution of Morazán in 1842, conservative interests generally prevailed, although the state remained politically unsettled until the strong-armed but enlightened conservative, J. Rafael Mora, seized power in 1849 and held it for a decade. By contrast Nicaragua suffered more than any of the other states from the mid-nineteenth-century civil wars between liberals and conservatives. Here the opportunistic struggles between local caudillos were more pronounced than elsewhere and the continual meddling, especially by the liberals, in the affairs of El Salvador and Honduras led to bloody and costly conflict. As conservatives consolidated their position in and around Granada, they, too, sought alliances abroad to check the persistent liberal strength of León. Nicaraguan conservatives even showed some willingness to consider reunification as a solution to the constant disorder they had experienced since independence. Fruto Chamorro, illegitimate son of an immigrant from Guatemala at the close of the colonial era, emerged as the leading conservative caudillo and established one of the most important Nicaraguan conservative clans. Liberal control of León was dealt a severe blow when José Trinidad Muñoz, renouncing his former liberal allies and supporting conservative J. L. Sandoval, took over in 1845. Sandoval and several conservative successors were almost continually besieged by liberal caudillos supported from El Salvador. In 1847 Bishop Viteri was transferred to Nicaragua where the political climate was far more favourable to him than in liberal San Salvador, and soon after Nicaragua reached a new concordat with the pope. When Muñoz returned to the liberal camp and rebelled against the government in 1851, Chamorro's forces defeated him and exiled him to El Salvador. The rise of Managua as a compromise capital between León and Granada began about this time, as several chieftains, including Chamorro in 1852, established temporary headquarters there. The conservatives generally held the upper hand during the early 1850s and followed the pattern elsewhere in Central America of emphasizing state sovereignty. They designated Nicaragua a 'republic' in 1854, changed the supreme director's title to 'president', and symbolically replaced the top stripe in the blue-white-blue liberal tricolour with a yellow stripe. Similarly symbolic was the motto of the republic's new seal: 'Liberty, Order, Labour'. A conservative constitution replaced the 1838 liberal charter. Yet the liberals refused to give up and by 1855 liberals invading from El Salvador gained control of the western part of the country and established a rival government again in León. It was at this point, as we shall see, that the filibustering expedition of William Walker arrived to play a decisive part in the conflict between liberals and conservatives in Nicaragua.

Since the independence of Central America commercial interests in North America and Europe had viewed the isthmus in terms of an interoceanic transit route. Both federal and state governments had encouraged canal schemes, but British, Dutch, American and French efforts during the first two decades after independence were ill conceived and undercapitalized. They had little effect beyond fuelling high expectations. Great Britain and the United States, however, pursued an active diplomacy designed both to insure their respective rights in any interoceanic route and to protect the interests of their subjects.

United States economic interests on the isthmus before 1850 were negligible, yet a series of U.S. agents did a remarkably good job of protecting the few Americans there, and, perhaps more importantly, they were direct carriers of the 'Jacksonian revolution' to Central America. (The French representatives had a similar ideological impact and were important noticeably in the Guatemalan revolution of 1848.)

Britain's economic and territorial interests were more substantial. British settlements at Belize and along the Miskito Shore from the Bay Islands to Costa Rica had secured for Britain a major share of Central American trade even before the close of the colonial era.[11] During the early years of independence Belize became the principal entrepot for Central American trade, while London financial houses supplied credit and loans for development to both state and federal governments. Soon after independence the English government sent George Alexander Thompson to investigate trade and canal possibilities, especially in Nicaragua. He initiated close relationships between British diplomats and Central American leaders, particularly those of the conservative party. In 1837–8 an English designer, John Baily, surveyed a canal route for the Nicaraguan government which, combined with the detailed report on canal potentials prepared by United States agent, John Lloyd Stephens, soon after, stimulated much foreign interest in the project. From 1834 to 1852 Frederick Chatfield represented the British government in Central America and worked deliberately to foster and protect British economic interests as well as trying to involve his government in more ambitious imperial schemes. Although he did not actively disrupt the Central American union, his sympathies ultimately lay with the conservatives and he became an important element in the intrigue and political manoeuvring of the 1840s as he sought guarantees for British bondholders and called in the Royal Navy when necessary to force concessions. In league with leading Guatemalan and Costa Rican conservatives, he played a significant role in the emergence of strong conservative governments in those states. Chatfield's personal secretary was Manuel F. Pavón, one of Carrera's leading advisers. Thus, as the middle states sought to restore the liberal federation, Chatfield worked to counter it with a conservative league or separate conservative sovereign states.[12]

From the outset British pretensions along the eastern coast of Central America had troubled the liberals. The Belize settlement, the ill-fated

[11] Troy S. Floyd, *The Anglo-Spanish struggle for Mosquitia* (Albuquerque, N.M., 1967).
[12] See Mario Rodríguez, *A Palmerstonian diplomat in Central America: Frederick Chatfield, Esq.* (Tucson, Ariz., 1964).

Poyais colonization adventure of Gregor MacGregor on the Honduran coast in 1823–4 and British trading posts along the Miskito coast of Nicaragua served the expansion of commerce, but they also challenged Central American sovereignty. British pursuit of fugitive slaves from Belize into Guatemalan territory was a further irritation to the liberals, who had abolished slavery immediately following independence.

In 1839 a British warship ejected Central American troops from the Bay Islands, and two years later Lord Palmerston declared that the islands were British territory, and that the British subjects who had settled there should be given some protection. This latest example of gunboat diplomacy provoked a storm of protest across Central America. The mid-century conservative governments proved more successful at resisting most British territorial ambitions and defending national independence than their liberal predecessors.

Meanwhile, close trading relations had developed between Britain and the isthmus. The Belize commercial firm headed by Marshal Bennet and John Wright took advantage of Belize's role as the principal port for Central America's exports and imports. Lacking protected deep-water ports of their own, Central Americans turned after independence to the Belize merchants to get their products to market as well as to supply them with manufactured goods. British merchants did not generally establish themselves in Central America to the extent they did in several Latin American states, but there were a few notable exceptions. Of these the most important was Bennet, who established the Guatemalan house of William Hall and Carlos Meany as a branch of his Belize firm in the 1820s. In the same decade George Skinner and Charles Klee established mercantile houses which continue to be important to the present day. Among others who served British mercantile interests during the first thirty years of independence were Thomas Manning, John Foster, Jonas Glenton and Walter Bridge in Nicaragua; William Barchard, Richard McNally, Frederick Lesperance, William Kilgour and Robert Parker, who operated with less permanent success in El Salvador; and Peter and Samuel Shepherd on the Miskito coast. The Shepherds received a massive land grant from the Miskito king in return for a few cases of whiskey and bolts of cotton chintz.

Central American imports reflected the close ties to British commerce. By 1840 nearly 60 per cent of Guatemalan imports came via the Belize settlement, while another 20 per cent came directly from Britain. Of the remaining 20 per cent, three-quarters came from Spain. The expansion of the British textile industry was important in providing markets for Salvadoran and Guatemalan indigo and cochineal. And from 1825 Britain had steadily reduced her duties on nearly all Central America's principal exports: cochineal, indigo, dyewoods, mahogany and other fine woods, hides and tortoise shells. By 1846 all Central American produce except coffee entered Britain duty free. Coffee, which had become more important than tobacco in Costa Rica after the collapse of Cuban coffee exports in the mid-1830s, soon received preferential treatment as well. Tables 2, 3 and 4 reflect the extent and expansion of British commerce during the first thirty years of independence.[13]

Belize remained the only Caribbean port of any importance, despite repeated Central American efforts to develop their own stations. Such ports as the Central Americans did maintain – Izabal, Omoa, Trujillo, San Juan del Norte, Matina – seldom harboured ships trading directly with the outside world. They served simply as transfer wharfs for the small skiffs and schooners that sailed between Belize and the Central American coast. Efforts to provide a second British entrepot at San Juan del Norte (Greytown) to serve Nicaragua and Costa Rica generally failed during the first half of the century. Most Nicaraguan and Costa Rican produce was shipped from the Pacific ports of Corinto, which gradually replaced the colonial port of Realejo in importance, or Puntarenas. Only after the completion of the Panama railway in 1855 did Central American commerce in general shift dramatically to the Pacific.

Loans added a bond of debt to that of commerce between Britain and Central America. The fiasco of the Barclay, Herring and Richardson loan of 1825 restrained investors from rushing in to Central America. Nevertheless a series of loans from British firms to the Central American states created a maze of debt problems which was not unravelled until the twentieth century. The liberals encouraged such arrangements, and

---

[13] Tables 2, 3 and 4 are based on data compiled from Customs records in the Public Record Office, London, by Robert A. Naylor, 'Tables of Commercial Statistics, 1821–1851', 'British commercial relations with Central America, 1821–1851' (unpublished Ph.D. thesis, Tulane University, New Orleans, 1958), 310–69. The tables are based on 'official values'. Naylor's tables in many cases also provide 'declared values' (generally lower) and volumes in tons, pounds or other units of measure as appropriate to the commodity. Tables 2, 3 and 4, of course, indicate only exports and imports between Central America and Great Britain and include produce of Belize and other British-held territory on the Central American east coast. Ciro F. S. Cardoso and Héctor Pérez Brignoli, *Centro-América y la economía occidental (1520–1930)* (San José, Costa Rica, 1977), 324–5, have compiled two statistical tables based on Naylor's data showing annual imports and exports between Britain and Central America. Unfortunately, there are some serious errors in their tables, especially in the one dealing with British exports to Central America, where Cardoso and Pérez have mistakenly included all British exports of foreign and English colonial goods to Jamaica as Central American imports. In addition, there are some mathematical or typographical errors in their totals.

Table 2 *Central American Imports from Great Britain and Jamaica,*
1821–50
(in thousands of £)

Years	British Exports directly to Central America	British Exports to Belize	Jamaican Exports to Central America	Totals
1821–25	6.7	1,455.9	0.0	1,462.6
1826–30	12.6	2,805.6	0.0	2,818.2
1831–35	112.3	2,937.6	74.0	3,123.9
1836–40	40.3	6,328.9	61.2	6,430.4
1841–45	76.0	4,578.1	56.4	4,710.5
1846–50	2,376.4	3,961.5	85.4	6,423.3

Table 3 *Central American Exports to Great Britain and Jamaica,*
1821–50, directly and via Belize, Peru and Chile
(in thousands of £)

| Years | British Imports from Central America | | | Jamaican Imports from C. America | Totals |
	Directly from C. America	via Belize	via Peru & Chile		
1821–25	12.8	395.9	3.3	0.0	412.0
1826–30	23.9	402.7	14.2	0.0	440.8
1831–35	105.3	1,214.5	51.0	44.9	1,415.7
1836–40	368.7	2,719.8	129.7	41.4	3,259.6
1841–45	308.1	4,133.7	435.2	6.9	4,883.9
1846–50	2,631.7	5,526.7	73.0	2.7	8,234.1

Table 4 *Principal Central American Exports to Great Britain, 1821–50*
(As percentages of total Central American exports to Great Britain)[a]

Years	Woods[b] %	Cochineal %	Indigo %	Coffee %
1821–25	73.9	7.7	15.5	0.0
1826–30	66.9	21.6	8.4	0.0
1831–35	46.3	42.6	4.2	0.3
1836–40	30.7	63.6	4.3	0.5
1841–45	18.5	67.3	1.6	12.2
1846–50	20.9	61.2	0.9	18.8

[a] Total Central American exports to Great Britain based on Table 3.
[b] Mahogany, Nicaragua wood, Brazil wood, logwood, cedar, lignum vitae, fustic. Other forest products not included. Most of these woods were imported to Britain from Belize or the Miskito Shore and thus are not a major part of the trade with the Central American republics.

although conservative governments were more wary, these transactions did not end altogether. The Carrera government, for example, in negotiating a loan with the London firm of Isaac and Samuel in 1856 to pay off its earlier debt, had to pledge 50 per cent of Guatemala's customs receipts to service the debt.

As has already been mentioned, the liberals had also encouraged English colonization efforts. From Guatemala to Panama, governments designed projects to attract European immigrants. The results were disappointing. A trickle of Englishmen came, but most of them either died, returned home or drifted into urban centres. Notable were the Gálvez government's projects in Guatemala.[14] Small grants to individual foreigners were followed by a massive concession to the Eastern Coast of Central America Commercial and Agricultural Company, a group whose origins were suspiciously linked to Gregor MacGregor's Poyais enterprise. The company agreed to develop the entire eastern part of the state from Izabal and the Verapaz into the Petén. Unfortunately, the English were more interested in exploiting mahogany stands than in agricultural colonization. In the end, the project only heightened anti-British sentiment among residents of eastern Guatemala. A similar arrangement with a Belgian company to develop the port and region of Santo Tomás eventually superseded the English grant. Carrera and the conservatives had grave doubts about the wisdom of that concession, but, through bribery and intimidation, the government approved the Belgian contract and did its best to ensure its success. It had, however, collapsed by 1852 and the lowland region remained undeveloped. One by-product of these colonization projects was the improvement in shipping service from the Caribbean coast. The English company's steamer, the *Vera Paz*, linked the Golfo Dulce with Belize, thereby increasing the commercial dependence of Guatemala on the British port. The Belgian company later provided service with Belgium on an irregular basis. By 1850 there was regular, if sometimes unreliable, steamship service to Europe from the Caribbean coast.

If the British involvement in the isthmus was greater and by 1850, thanks to Chatfield, identified with the conservative cause, the United States was becoming increasingly involved in the middle of the century and usually in support of the liberals. This became more obvious after the appointment in 1849 of E. G. Squier as American envoy to Central

---

[14] William J. Griffith, *Empires in the wilderness: foreign colonization and development in Guatemala, 1834–1844* (Chapel Hill, N.C., 1965), treats this subject in detail.

America. Anglo-American rivalry intensified and came to a head over the question of control of the transit route across the isthmus. The discovery of gold in California in 1848 greatly accelerated United States interest in the isthmus. As Americans streamed across Nicaragua via a route developed by Cornelius Vanderbilt they discovered that the British had taken control of territory on both sides of the isthmus, at San Juan del Norte (Greytown) and Tigre Island in the Bay of Fonseca. War was averted when cooler heads agreed, by the Clayton–Bulwer Treaty of 1850, to bilateral control and protection of any isthmian canal; Britain and the United States pledged themselves not to 'occupy, or fortify, or colonize, or assume or exercise any dominion over . . . any part of Central America'. While the treaty lessened the hostile atmosphere created by Chatfield and Squier, it hardly ended Anglo-American rivalry in Nicaragua at the very time when the liberal–conservative showdown was occurring there.

Among those who crossed the isthmus in 1850, probably at Panama rather than Nicaragua, was William Walker, the son of an austere family steeped in Protestant frontier religion and Jacksonian Democratic principles. Walker was a prodigious student; he had studied medicine at the universities of Nashville (later Vanderbilt), Pennsylvania, Edinburgh and Heidelberg before abandoning medicine for law in New Orleans at the University of Louisiana (later Tulane). Almost immediately, however, he turned to journalism and became editor of the liberal and controversial New Orleans *Crescent*. The untimely death of his fiancée, however, led to his abandonment of New Orleans for a fresh start in California. There he once more took up journalism, but failed either to prosper or to satisfy his restless spirit. Through associates he involved himself first in an abortive filibustering expedition into Mexico and then agreed to organize an expedition to support the hard-pressed Nicaraguan liberals.

Walker's band of 58 men landed near Realejo on 16 June 1855 and had remarkable success in assisting the liberals to several key victories. Yet the liberals also suffered reverses in the campaign, and the death – through battle or disease – of several liberal leaders enabled Walker quickly to become the dominant liberal military chieftain in Nicaragua. Granada fell to his forces in a fierce battle, following which Walker attempted to bring peace through the formation of a coalition with conservative collaborationists. He assured the Church that he had no ill will toward it and offered high office to several conservatives, including

Patricio Rivas who became president of the Republic. Some liberals, dismayed, now broke with Walker, while many conservatives refused to join the coalition. The struggle thus became one between Walker's 'democrats' and the 'legitimists'. The other Central American governments, now all under conservative rule, sent aid to the Nicaraguans opposed to Walker. Rafael Mora in Costa Rica took the lead in organizing this 'national campaign' against him. Rivas, realizing his untenable position, eventually resigned, and Walker himself succeeded him in the presidency. North Americans, mostly Mexican War veterans from the lower Mississippi Valley who had been promised land and other concessions, poured into Nicaragua to join Walker. *El Nicaragüense*, a bilingual newspaper more English than Spanish, proclaimed the liberal revolution and the establishment of a democratic regime.

The Nicaraguans and their allies – Mora's Costa Ricans, Guatemalans commanded by Mariano Paredes, Salvadorans under Gerardo Barrios and Guardiola's Hondurans – soon outnumbered Walker's forces. They first contained and then pushed back the North Americans and their remaining liberal cohorts, who suffered a cholera epidemic as well as battlefield losses. For their part the British supplied arms and other supplies to the allies through Costa Rica. The government in Washington vacillated; it never recognized Walker's regime (although the U.S. minister in Nicaragua had done so), but it was slow to take action against him. Finally a U.S. naval force arrived, in effect to rescue Walker and the few survivors of the expedition. The end came on 1 May 1857 when Walker surrendered. Returned on board a U.S. naval vessel, he received a hero's welcome in New Orleans and soon gained support for a new filibustering venture. Thwarted several times by U.S. officials, Walker finally succeeded in launching an expedition in collaboration with disgruntled British residents on Roatán who opposed Honduran sovereignty over the Bay Islands, to which Britain had agreed in 1859. Walker hoped to use Roatán as a base for a new invasion of Central America and was in touch with Trinidad Cabañas, still struggling against Guardiola in Honduras. When Walker reached Roatán, however, the British had not yet evacuated, so Walker struck directly at Trujillo. After a brief success he was captured as a result of British naval intervention, and handed over to the Honduran authorities. Following a brief trial, Walker fell before a firing squad on 12 September 1860.

The Walker episode had long-term results for Central America. The residue of anti-American and anti-British feeling remained long after to create suspicion and distrust in international relations and to encourage the xenophobia that the Conservatives had already nourished. Alliance with Walker further discredited liberals throughout Central America and allowed the conservatives to gain a stronger hold everywhere, but especially in Nicaragua. By 1860 the liberals continued to represent a serious threat only in El Salvador. Central America, although now definitively divided into five sovereign states, was solidly conservative.

In general, of course, the conservatives had better relations with Britain and Spain than with the United States or France. Spanish recognition of the Central American states and new concordats with Rome were positive achievements of conservative foreign policy. Old difficulties with the British were generally worked out amicably. The debt question was resolved through apportioning a part of it to each state, although only Costa Rica, with the smallest share, ever completed full payment. Guatemala reached apparent settlement of the Belize question in 1859, when by the Aycinena-Wyke Treaty Guatemala recognized British sovereignty there in exchange for British construction of a cart road from Guatemala City to the Caribbean. British failure to build the road eventually led to the abrogation of the treaty, as later liberal governments were unwilling to renegotiate a settlement. Honduras also settled its territorial disputes with the British by 1860, and Nicaragua made progress in the same direction, although final renunciation of British responsibility for protection of the Miskito Indians would not come until the end of the century.

Conservative domination of Central America arrested somewhat the emphasis on expanding exports and developing the country along capitalist lines which had been a feature of the liberal period. The cultural and political tone of conservative rule reflected traditional Hispanic-Catholic values, and there was a return to subsistence agriculture and a greater concern to protect Indian and *ladino* communal lands. The cities grew little, if at all, during the first half-century of independence and life remained predominantly rural. Yet the return to order after the civil wars was inevitably accompanied by an increase in agricultural production, and conservative governments could not resist the lure of increased revenue from foreign trade. Exports grew rapidly after 1840 except in Honduras which exported only livestock and foodstuffs to El Salvador and Guatemala. The dependence on natural dyestuffs of the late colonial and immediate post-independent period continued, with El Salvador and

Nicaragua the leading indigo producers and exporters. Guatemala also expanded its indigo production slightly, but depended principally on its cochineal exports. By 1845 Costa Rica's early success with coffee had begun to stimulate producers elsewhere in Central America. This became more intense after the discovery of coal-tar dyes in 1856 jeopardized the indigo and cochineal industries and eventually led to their ruin. Although dye exports continued to be the mainstay of the Salvadoran and Guatemalan export economies, coffee became increasingly important, especially in the Guatemalan highlands. By 1871, when the conservative regime finally ended there, coffee already accounted for 50 per cent of Guatemalan exports. The Civil War in the United States (1861–5) had allowed Central America to gain a larger share of the international cotton market, but only temporarily. Reliable statistics are not available for all of the states, but Tables 5, 6 and 7 (see below) illustrate the growth that occurred between 1850 and 1870.[15]

Britain remained the most important supplier of imports after 1850, even though the importance of Belize declined enormously with the development of Pacific trade after 1855. From 1850 to 1870, imports into Guatemala, as valued by customs, came from abroad in the percentages indicated in Table 8 (see below). As Table 8 also reflects, there was little trade between the Central American states. The roads were built from the capitals and producing regions to the ports, while interstate routes remained impassable. The economic interdependence that had begun to develop at the close of the colonial period was finally gone by 1870. The states were becoming more separate. Finally, while foreign involvement on the isthmus was limited when compared to other regions of Latin America, it was nevertheless highly significant from the point of view of the Central American states themselves and prepared the way for more substantial foreign domination once the liberals returned to power.

The restoration of order in most of Central America by 1860 and the emergence of coffee as a major export coincided with the resurgence of liberal efforts to control most of the Central American states. There was a restlessness among younger members of the elites, especially those

---

[15] Only fragmentary and often unreliable trade statistics have yet been compiled for most of this period in Central America. A guide to some of this material may be found in Thomas Schoonover, 'Central American commerce and maritime activity in the nineteenth century: sources for a quantitative approach', *Latin American Research Review*, 13/2 (1978), 157–69.

Table 5 *Leading Guatemalan Exports as Percentages of Total Exports,*
1851–70

Years	Value of Exports (Millons of US$)	Cochineal %	Cotton %	Coffee %
1851–55	6.2	78.4	0.0	0.0
1856–60	7.8	81.1	0.0	0.3
1861–65	7.4	56.4	8.3	11.3
1866–70	10.8	46.6	2.0	32.4

Source: R. L. Woodward, *Class privilege and economic development: the Consulado de Comercio of Guatemala, 1793–1871* (Chapel Hill, N.C., 1966), 58–63.

Table 6 *Leading Nicaraguan Exports as Percentages of Total Exports,*
1841–71

Years	Value of Exports (Thousands of US$)	Indigo %	Precious Metals %	Hides %	Cotton %	Rubber %	Woods %	Coffee %
1841	167.8	83.1	0.0	14.8	0.0	0.0	1.5	0.4
1851	1,010.0	7.9	39.6	1.2	0.0	0.0	15.8	3.0
1864	1,112.4	8.6	9.1	17.2	47.9	8.8	2.0	1.2
1865	1,155.0	16.9	12.3	8.9	47.1	4.6	2.5	2.6
1867	893.9	44.8	11.4	9.5	9.4	12.6	2.7	4.9
1870	930.3	27.0	17.9	18.0	1.7	15.7	9.7	5.4
1871	1,424.7	26.6	13.0	7.1	5.0	18.3	8.1	8.7

Source: A. Lanuza Matamoros, 'Estructuras socioeconómicas, poder y estado en Nicaragua (1821–1875)' (unpublished thesis, University of Costa Rica, 1976), 126–204.

Table 7 *Leading Salvadoran Exports, 1864–74*
(Millions of US$)

Years	Value of Total Exports	Indigo		Coffee	
		Value	% of Total Exports	Value	% of Total Exports
1864	1.7	1.13	67.4	0.08	4.8
1866	2.4	1.59	65.1	0.20	8.1
1870	?	2.62	?	0.66	?
1874	3.8	1.70	44.8	1.33	35.0

Sources: Mario Flores Macal, *Orígenes de las formas de dominación en El Salvador* (San José, 1977), 147–63; David Browning, *El Salvador. Landscape and Society* (Oxford, 1971), 162.

Table 8 *Origins of Guatemalan Imports,*
1850–70[16]
(percentage of total)

Great Britain	61
Belize	6
France	17
Germany	5
Spain & Cuba	4
U.S.A.	3
Belgium	2
Others	2
	100

connected to coffee production, and a growing general awareness that, despite modest increases in exports and economic growth, Central America lagged far behind the rapidly expanding economies of western Europe and the United States. This liberal resurgence occurred first in El Salvador. Gerardo Barrios, originally a Morazanista, had served conservative governments and co-operated with Carrera and Mora against Walker, but after he gained power in El Salvador in 1859 his liberal sentiments once more surfaced, as he symbolically ordered the remains of Morazán to be brought to San Salvador for burial with state honours. Economic, political and educational reforms followed, while he carefully avoided attacking the Church and diplomatically assured Carrera in Guatemala of his continued friendship. Carrera watched suspiciously and assembled an army on the frontier. When the inevitable anticlericalism surfaced in 1863 Carrera invaded, but Barrios repulsed him at Coatepeque. Barrios then turned against Nicaragua in an effort to end Conservative domination there, but was himself defeated. A second Carrera invasion of El Salvador in October 1863 ended Barrios's regime; he was replaced by the more reliable conservative, Francisco Dueñas. An attempt by Barrios to return two years later failed, but even under Dueñas many of the liberal reforms remained.

Carrera's death in 1865 brought new hope to the liberals throughout the region. Vicente Cerna continued conservative rule in Guatemala until the *reforma* of Miguel García Granados and Justo Rufino Barrios brought him down in 1871. In the meantime, liberals in Honduras ended Conservative rule there and co-operated with Salvadoran liberals to oust Dueñas in the same year. In Nicaragua conservatives held on to

[16] Compiled from data published in the *Gazeta de Guatemala*, 1851–71.

power until 1893, but a trend toward liberal economic policy nevertheless began soon after 1860. Costa Rica's transition to Liberal rule was
somewhat more orderly, but the pattern was not significantly different.
Mora was overthrown in 1859 and there followed a decade of domination by the Montealegre family, moderates who had been very important in the development of coffee cultivation. Although politically
conservative, certain liberal tendencies began to appear during the 1860s
in their educational, ecclesiastical and economic policies. More clearly
bringing the liberal *reforma* to Costa Rica, however, was General Tomás
Guardia, who established a liberal dictatorship in Costa Rica in 1870.

The liberal *reforma* of the 1860s in Central America challenged the
creole elites who had established neo-Hispanic regimes. After destructive civil wars and political experimentation, the leading families of the
late colonial period had largely succeeded in restoring their economic
and social hegemony. At the same time, collaboration with popular
caudillos had hastened the process of *ladino* participation in government,
so that by 1870 the white elites no longer held a monopoly of high
government office in Central America. Moreover, conservative rule had
failed to provide the progress and expansion of the export-oriented
economies at levels that significant portions of both elite and middle
sectors demanded. Despite the restoration of much of the institutional
framework of the colonial era, two new developments of the period were
caudillismo and state sovereignty, both of which would survive in Central
America long after the conservative party had ceased to be a force.

12

VENEZUELA, COLOMBIA AND ECUADOR: THE FIRST HALF-CENTURY OF INDEPENDENCE

Military and diplomatic necessity had made the vice-royalty of New Granada, the captaincy-general of Venezuela and the *audiencia* of Quito form one republic – the Republic of Gran Colombia – at independence. Its purpose was soon served, however, and its transience was apparent well before Bolívar's death in December 1830. The old imperial administrative divisions were not always clear, not always consistent in all branches of affairs, but they were supported by both common sense and local feeling. Distances were too great, provincial identity too strong, for government from Bogotá to last for long after final victory over the Spanish forces. There were no strong economic ties between the three provinces. Already by the end of the colonial period a sense of distinct identity was felt not only by the elite, but by a far wider section of opinion. As the early federalisms of the 'Patria Boba' era showed, these loyalties were more easily felt for a smaller compass than for that of the particular republic that was to emerge in 1830, but the larger entity did have some support in opinion, as well as in imperial tradition and in the geography of possible control. The common soldiers of the Venezuelan plains showed as early as 1816 what they thought of General Santander, calling this Bogotá-educated native of Cúcuta a *'reinoso futudo'*;[1] General Santander reciprocated this distrust, and both as vice-president and later in opposition to Bolívar, many of his actions and utterances looked forward to a separate New Granada. The southern frontier was more confused, but there was also a line to be drawn somewhere between Popayán and Quito. The façade of Gran Colombia had certainly been impressive – it impressed Mr Canning, it impressed the first envoys he sent out, and it impressed those who took up Colombian bond issues in the early 1820s.

---

[1] An accursed inhabitant of the *Nuevo Reino de Granada*.

Gran Colombia had obtained recognition; George IV had finally received 'the little yellow men', though he would sign no treaty that contained the word 'republic' in English. Yet the Foreign Office that had enthused over what was apparently destined to be the first nation of Spanish America was within five years watching its breakup with equanimity. The Royal Navy even lent a little assistance. The collapse of this political construction was accompanied by financial and economic crisis, a pattern that was to be often repeated in the subsequent history of the successor states. Not only did Gran Colombia's credit collapse in 1826. To foreigners and to natives alike – many of the inhabitants were just as vulnerable to early republican miscalcuation, and perhaps with more excuse – it became more and more apparent that economic and fiscal resources had been widely overestimated. Gran Colombia had sustained the war of liberation, had, one way or another, provided the men and the resources for Bolívar's armies in the South. The effort of unity had been made and the expense met in exceptional times and unrepeated ways. Nostalgia for union was for some time expressed by a few utopians and a larger number of Bolivarian officers, and by some federalist dissidents who opposed the new central authorities. In 1830, however, the realists of the hour were Generals Páez, Santander and Flores, who emerged as the respective rulers of Venezuela, New Granada and Ecuador.

The three successor republics had certain characteristics in common. They were sparsely populated: the total population of Gran Colombia was less than three million: New Granada may have had 1.1 million, Venezuela 0.9 million, Ecuador 0.5 million. All three were racially very diverse, diverse within themselves as well as differing one from another. The population in all three was overwhelmingly rural – no city in the region had forty thousand inhabitants – and in the nineteenth century both their total populations and their cities were to grow only slowly. As between the republics, communications within them were arduous and expensive. The predominantly upland population of New Granada and Ecuador lived in an enduring isolation; coastal and river navigation presented many problems before the coming of steam, and steam itself, no panacea, had to wait on the cargoes that made it economical. Within these national economies, which had been in varying degrees dislocated and decapitalized by the wars, few goods travelled far, and those that did for long bore the costs of the mule-train without the ability to sustain

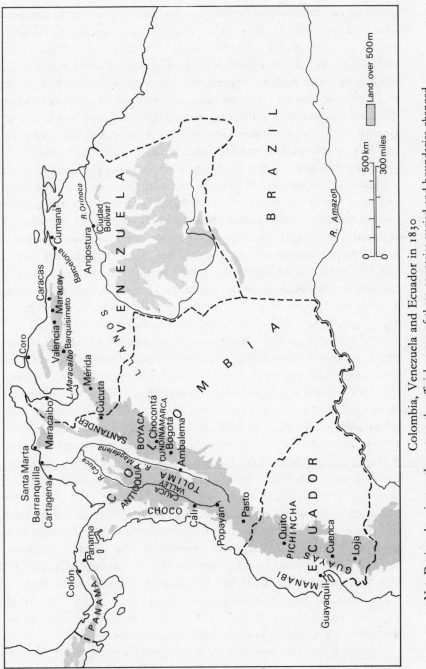

Colombia, Venezuela and Ecuador in 1830

Note During the nineteenth century the official names of these countries varied and boundaries changed.

dramatic advances. Wheel traffic ran for short distances, in few places. Few men travelled, as few goods travelled – the wars must have moved greater numbers than ever before but in most areas that mobility slowed with peace and the re-establishment of the restricted circuits of local interchange. Few had the means or the incentive or the freedom to move, and to move was often unhealthy. The pattern of settlement obeyed dictates that were not lightly ignored. Hardly anyone had travelled in Europe or the United States: General Santander would not have done so had he not been exiled, and the opportunity had not yet been forced on Generals Páez and Flores. Fortunes were modest. By Spanish colonial standards the *mantuanos* of Caracas had perhaps been rich, and Bolívar had been one of the richest of them. No other group in Gran Colombia had commanded such wealth and most had suffered in the wars. The colonial nobility had been tiny, and outside it few had been rich enough to have been menaced with official encouragement to buy titles. Republican life began in an atmosphere of republican austerity. There was nothing very self-conscious or puritanical about this, though some made a virtue out of poverty and provinciality and tried to turn it to political advantage. It was really all that these economies could sustain.

At the time of independence the economy of New Granada, the most populous of the three republics, was the least dynamic. New Granada possessed mines, the slave-worked gold deposits around Popayán and in the Choco, the few substantial mines and the myriad scattered placers of Antioquia, mostly worked by free labour, the investment-devouring silver mines of Santa Ana in Tolima. Indeed, precious metals were to remain the republic's most reliable export until the establishment of coffee in the last quarter of the century, and Antioquia's uninterrupted control over a substantial part of their production was an element in that province's commercial lead. Colombian mining was not severely damaged by the war, though it was naturally interrupted. All the same, it did not develop dramatically in the next half-century. Foreign investment in Tolima and Antioquía showed on the whole disappointing returns. Emancipation of the slaves and civil war disrupted mining in the southern part of the country. No new discoveries were made that substantially altered the contribution of gold and silver to the republic's exports, which remained during this period important, more constant than the new exports, but also constantly disappointing.

Besides gold and silver colonial New Granada had exported very little else. The botanical enthusiasts of Bourbon Spain had made discoveries that looked promising – cinchona bark and 'Bogotá tea' – and small quantities of cotton, tobacco and dye-wood, and even smaller quantities of other tropical products were exported from the northern coast. The infant *consulado* of Cartagena and the embryo journals of Bogotá speculated about such possible diversification in the last years of colonial rule. By 1830 little had been achieved.

Venezuela in contrast had been Spain's most successful agricultural colony. Venezuelan cacao was the finest in the world, and it was the region's leading export, to Europe and to Mexico. In the last years of the eighteenth century a shift began into coffee cultivation, which offered better returns on a smaller outlay. This change was intensified during the two decades of struggle after 1810, and though slavery had not disappeared and cacao continued to be grown, coffee and a system of share-cropping and free labour was now dominant. During this first cycle of coffee-production the crop was located in the hills of the central hinterland. Cotton and tobacco and hides were also exported, and mules and horses were sent to the islands. The Andean provinces to the west were at first relatively isolated, an isolation not overcome until coffee recovered from mid-century slump in the 1870s and 1880s. All the same, in comparison with New Granada, Venezuela had a stronger and more diversified export-sector. Coastal Ecuador also produced cacao, not as fine as Venezuelan but in greater quantity. Apart from hats, her other exports went only to her neighbours, chiefly in cloth of the highland *obrajes* and timber. Neither Venezuela nor Ecuador exploited mines of any great importance at this time.

The Swedish agent, Carl August Gosselman, travelling in 1837–8, provides figures for a succinct comparison of the value of exports from the three republics (see Table 1).

These sums are *absolutely* very small. (Ecuador's export earnings, at the conventional rate of conversion, are the equivalent of the annual income of the contemporary duke of Sutherland – £200,000.) They refer, of course, only to one sector of the economy, but that sector was the agent of growth and change, and government revenues depended more and more on the *aduana*, the support of order and stability.

It was not a reliable support. Neither Colombia, Venezuela nor Ecuador found in the nineteenth century a steady staple export. Nor were they very attractive to foreign investors. All three republics, sometimes together, sometimes individually, suffered the impact of price fluctuations and depressions, and weakened governments faced in-

Table 1 *Exports*
(in thousands of pesos)

Date	State	Commodity	Value	
1837	Venezuela	Coffee	1,660	
		Cacao	875	
		Cotton	616	
		Total	4,944	
1836	New Granada	Cotton	199	
		Tobacco	191	
		Gold Coins	1,579	(+ 1,000 exported clandestinely)
		Total	2,828	
1836	Ecuador	Cacao	690	
		Hats	100	
		Total	1,000	

creased malaise when a price went down, producers went bankrupt and merchants ceased to import. Venezuela's coffee planters, for example, borrowed at interest rates which had risen far above colonial levels. In the 1830s costs rose as they competed for labour and in the wake of the United States crisis of 1837–8 the price of coffee fell, and they were caught in the draconian provisions of the creditor's charter, the law 10 of 1834, which had removed the old colonial restrictions on freedom of contract, usury and foreclosure. The resulting outburst of polemical writing makes that particular crisis and its political repercussions in the 1840s relatively easy to follow, and similar patterns can be discerned at other times and in other places. Coffee remained all the same Venezuela's leading export for the rest of the century. She was second to Brazil and Java. The prices of her other exports were equally subject to brusque variations, particularly sharp in the late 1850s. The second cycle of coffee export, based on cultivation in the Andean states, showed production doubled in volume, but still subject to such fluctuations.

Colombia's first important agricultural export was tobacco. Under the colony a royal monopoly, it remained under government control until the late 1840s, but the government encouraged both increased private participation – the monopoly was expensive to run – and export.

Ambalema tobacco found markets, particularly in Germany, and for quarter of a century tobacco was the mainstay of Colombia's exports. Colombian merchants experimented with other commodities. *Quinas*, cinchona bark, were exported when this very unstable market was right, cotton enjoyed a brief fashion during the American civil war, money was lost in attempts to grow indigo. In the late 1870s the country's exports entered a prolonged crisis. They had been no more immune from fluctuation than Venezuela's, but this crisis was one of unprecedented completeness: tobacco failed as the scarce suitable land gave out and East Indian production took the German market; *quinas* from Colombia became unsaleable on a market glutted from Ceylon. For a while Colombia had almost nothing but the production of her mines. The country now turned to coffee which had first been planted on some scale in the 1860s, but recovery still looked very uncertain at the end of the century.

Ecuador's fortunes remained tied to cacao, which represented from a half to three-quarters of total exports. Ecuador was throughout the century the world's leading exporter, and the fluctuations in her foreign trade were less severe than those suffered by her former Gran Colombian partners. Cacao brought the coast commercial and financial preponderance and a steadily increasing demographic weight, from faster natural increase and from migration from the sierra. The coast also then produced most of the hats.

The attentive reader of the contemporary geographers and of the more patient and sympathetic travellers, of Agustín Codazzi, Felipe Pérez, Manuel Villavicencio, of Karl Appun, Isaac Holton and Friedrich Hassaurek, can soon begin to map that other economy which is not visible in the statistics of foreign trade, and to get a sense of a different sort of economic life. Much native artisan production showed itself well able to resist the more intense competition of imports that came with independence. Imports were after all nothing new. Neither Ecuadorian nor Colombian textiles were as rapidly or completely ruined as the protectionists of the 1830s argued that they would be. The finest quality local products, such as Chocontá saddles, were still traded throughout the three republics. Certainly, artisans protested at the lower fiscal tariffs of mid-century, but they were not all equally or drastically affected by them. Some activities expanded – Colombian hat-making is an example. High transport costs and peculiar market tastes remained. The variety of interacting local economies cannot be anything more than stated here, but an awareness of this variety does have important consequences: it helps one to understand how policies, or crises, varied in their local impact; it makes one aware of entrepreneurial activity and opportunity in areas that escaped consular notice, small, perhaps, in scale but often critical for later developments. It enables one to escape from the misleadingly stagnant connotations that hang around the too vague notion of subsistence, and from the conventional image of rural life as nothing but *hacendado* and *peón*, planter and slave, *cura doctrinero* and Indian community, with the wild horsemen somewhere out on the plains, generating by some telluric process the occasional caudillo.

Life for the great mass of the rural population of those three republics was not uniform, and it was by no means everywhere static. Substantial changes did occur in these years. These were directly and clearly brought by new export crops. Coffee in Venezuela had the liberating effects that it was later to have in Colombia. The colonial cacao plantation was worked with slave labour. Some coffee estates had slaves, but most were worked by systems of share-cropping and seasonal labour. Workers were attracted into new areas and escaped from old controls for the opportunities and hazards of a free labour market. For smaller numbers tobacco in Colombia performed a similar function, and beyond that its effects were far-reaching. This first substantial hot-country development brought steam navigation to the Magdalena, and gave Colombians their first experience of direct trade with Europe. Coastal cacao progressively altered the balance of Ecuador.

It would be quite anachronistic to suppose that any leader of Latin American independence had worked for an egalitarian rural order; promises of some land to the troops were not meant to amount to much, nor did they. But it cannot be said that the old order survived quite intact, apart from the effects of recruiting and of physical and fiscal ravaging. Slavery was not abolished outright, but it was undermined by the drafting of blacks into the armies, the end of the slave trade and the limited emancipation decreed by the Congress of Cúcuta. For long unimportant in Ecuador, its role in certain tasks in Venezuela and Colombia had been greater than numbers – 42,000 and 45,000 respectively around 1830 – suggest. But no new slave-based activity was begun in either republic, and in many areas the old authority was never effectively reasserted. Early Gran Colombian legislation had attempted to bring the Indian communities into the stream of republican progress, but these schemes were soon abandoned in the face of Indian resistance and much political and fiscal inconvenience. They were perhaps now less amenable to government interference, less subject to clerical control than they had been in late colonial times. The hold of the Church which had never been complete had been weakened. The Church's influence here followed the pattern of old settlement in the more temperate regions, the older upland towns and the more Indian areas. In Venezuela as a whole the Church was not strong: its dioceses were not rich, and it had little hold on the *pardos*, the slaves or the *libertos*. The missions in the east had been destroyed, and the more clerical western states carried as yet little weight in the nation's affairs. Most of rural Venezuela was not amenable to control through this institution. In New Granada too its strength was patchy: *mestizo* Colombia had given many colonial examples of hostility to the Church. Little of the hot country had been thoroughly catechized – Tolima, the Cauca valley, the Pacific and Atlantic coasts were never subject to the same degree of ecclesiastical control as the uplands of Boyacá, Cundinamarca and Pasto. Similar distinctions can be made within Ecuador, where García Moreno's theocratic authoritarianism enjoyed much less than universal acclaim. Much is usually made of the domination of rural life by *hacendado* and priest, but such rhetoric has ignored the many areas where the power of both had been weakened, had never existed, or was hedged about with many natural limitations – the *llanos* of Venezuela, the scattered populations of the Magdalena valley, the cattle plains of Tolima, the Cauca valley, the relative liberty of the Ecuadorian coast. Slavery, as has been stated, was in decline. It is now being increasingly realized that rural structures other than slavery were far too complex and varied to be summed up in any such simple word as peonage.

A picture of the rural population as one mostly made up of servile labourers not only ignores the surviving Indian communities and the areas of independent small settlement, but also much other non-agricultural activity such as artisan industry, mining, stock-raising, the breeding of horses and mules and the management of pack-trains – an essential activity that was the start of many a famous local fortune. Nor was a *peón* the same sort of person from one place to another, or necessarily engaged in one sort of activity all the year round. The nineteenth-century authors of sketches of local customs, *cuadros de costumbres*, delighted in distinguishing between one type and another, and in describing the full range of their habits and activities. Historians are beginning to do the same. The gain should be not only in the picturesque. It should help to resolve the paradox that such allegedly static and highly stratified societies should have proved so difficult to control.

For all three republics the nineteenth century was an era of government either seen to be unstable, or at best seen optimistically to be recently emerged from instability. All three suffered frequent civil wars and ended the century in war. Much contemporary local writing was a lament for these disappointing circumstances, the shame of these local struggles increased by memories of more glorious earlier fighting, of much the same pattern but against a different enemy. Much foreign comment was scathing and facetious about these *revolucioncitas*, attributing them to vainglory, an ill-defined militarism, office-seeking, the absence of constitutional monarchy, the defects of mixed races, or the incurable levity of the Latin mind. Much traditional historiography has been preoccupied with the course of these revolutions, with the failure of these nations for so long to emerge as coherent nation-states, without, however, making much progress either in analysing the causes of instability or assessing its importance and extent. The problem of order was a complex one. Few diplomats or foreign travellers examined it in detail, few native soldiers or politicians were able in their own writings to escape from partisan arguments, or from the desire to find a single cause. Notes of exaggeration creep, or even rush in. State power was limited at the best of times, and unreasoned emphasis on apparently national events over local developments has often exaggerated the catastrophic nature of these crises. Likewise, irregular fighting has been confused with barbarism and brutality, government bankruptcy with universal ruin, the participation of blacks and Indians with racial war. The criteria of judgement have been decidedly European. This is neither to say that they have not been shared by many South Americans, nor that disorder was something easily ignored.

The new governments were republican, and committed to republican notions of representative government. New Granada proclaimed universal manhood suffrage in 1853, Venezuela in 1853, Ecuador in 1861, though each maintained a literacy qualification. Moreover, these mid-century dispositions were of course neither everywhere effective nor irreversible. Elections were a source of legitimacy and cannot be dismissed as of no account because of widespread malpractices, but they were an imperfect source. Elections had to be 'made' by governments, and all three republics began their independent life under the domination of certain exclusive circles. Páez and his friends held Venezuela, to the exclusion of many a returning Bolivarian officer and of other meritorious patriot careers. General Santander, who was the first to see that assiduous electoral machine-building and sectarian journalism were the roads to power in New Granada, was a man of many enemies, lay, clerical and military, and who kept his enmities in good repair. General Flores was not even an Ecuadorian, and the colour of many of his troops did not blend with that of the sierra populace. All three had made their reputations in the wars, but these reputations were not unrivalled or uncontroverted.

Nor were they supported by imposing institutions. The Church had been weakened during the wars, both in its resources and in its hegemony. Sees fell empty and remained empty, clerical organization suffered partial collapse. All three republics remained Catholic, and sought to inherit the *patronato* of the Spanish crown, but diplomatic embarassments held Rome back from recognizing the new states until the 1840s. And republican Catholicism was Catholicism with a difference. General Páez made it quite clear how little church support counted in Venezuela by expelling the archbishop of Caracas in 1835. General Santander's opinions and conduct were likewise hardly calculated to appeal to clerical opinion. The Church could not be left out of account by Colombian and Ecuadorian politicians: it could provide valuable support to its friends and make dangerous opposition to its enemies. As there were many sources of friction between the Church and these post-independence governments, it cannot, however, be seen as a pillar of order. Its influence varied from region to region, from the overwhelming to the negligible. Nor did the Church itself possess a strong hierarchy, which was essential for decisive national action. A bishop was still very much the sovereign in his own diocese; the religious feelings of Pasto or Medellín were not to be controlled from Bogotá.

These were not parts of the empire where the colonial bureaucracy had been very imposing. The republican replacements were likewise modest. Cabinets were usually made up of no more than three or four portfolios – *Hacienda, Guerra y Marina, Interior, Relaciones Exteriores* – and a couple of these were often combined in the hands of one person. The number of offices was not great and patronage restricted. Many offices were unattractive, and governments found it hard to find persons willing to serve as provincial judges, *alcaldes* or even provincial governors. A few careers were spectacularly or corruptly rewarded – particularly in the Venezuela of the Monagas brothers and Guzmán Blanco. Most were not. Many of these governments were notoriously honest and austere – the administrations of Páez (1831–5, 1839–43) and Soublette (1843–7) in Venezuela, of Herrán (1841–5) and Mariano Ospina (1857–61) in New Granada, of Vicente Rocafuerte (1835–9) in Ecuador were hardly touched by financial scandal. But economy and probity did not necessarily receive rewards in the shape of political support. In the early years of these republics the numbers of those directly employed by the government, or directly and immediately influenced by its actions, remained very small, even when one includes the army.

The reason was clear and common to all. Governments lacked revenue, and economized accordingly. Again, Carl August Gosselman's sober Scandinavian calculations for the mid-1830s (Table 2), years of neither euphoria nor despair, will serve for a measure and a comparison:

Table 2 *State Revenues*

Date	State	Source	Value (in thousands of pesos)
1837	Venezuela	Import duties	968
		Export tax	168
		Others (including a *contribución extraordinaria* surcharged on the customs of 221,000 pesos)	463
		Total	1,599
1836	Colombia	Customs	907
		Tobacco monopoly	237
		Salt monopoly	225
		Others	654
		Total	2,023
1836	Ecuador	Customs	202
		cédulas personales (the Indian *tributo*)	184
		Others	194
		Total	580

The patriots had at first thought that the introduction of more advanced systems of taxation, the opening of their ports and the institution of nicely calculated fiscal tariffs would give them resources far beyond the old 'routine' of retrograde or oppressive colonial revenues. They dreamt of cadastral surveys, of the *contribución directa*. The nature of the tax-base and the unending demands of war had by the late 1820s forced them back to something very like the old system, and this could be only slowly abandoned by Gran Colombia's successor states. They were imaginative in fiscal ideas, and even capable of daring – the ending of the tobacco monopoly in Colombia was a conscious fiscal risk – but the problem was intractable. Each branch of revenue had its ceiling. Foreign credit had gone with the 1826 crash, and though efforts would be made to restore it this could not be granted much priority in most of these hard-pressed years. Neither Colombia nor Ecuador borrowed abroad again significantly in the fifty years after 1830, though Guzmán Blanco in Venezuela saw at least a personal advantage in resuming borrowing in the 1860s. Every administration had its school of financial pilot-fish, the *agiotistas*, expert in short-term loans and the manipulation of the bewildering variety of internal debt that these governments soon trailed, but the domestic money-market was rudimentary, small sums for short terms at high interest. In Venezuela Guzmán Blanco was successful in reforming and sophisticating these arrangements with the *Compañia de Crédito* in the 1870s, and the same decade saw the founding of the first Colombian banks that managed to survive, but throughout the century governments remained periodically subject to acute fiscal emergencies. All cast around for new expedients, *arbitrios*. Church wealth was sacrificed in both Venezuela and Colombia, and at the very end of the century was under Eloy Alfaro's assault in Ecuador, but the Church was not so very rich and the yield in these hard times was disappointing. The one revenue capable of rapid expansion was the customs, and all three republics came to depend on it more and more. By the 1860s it accounted for over two-thirds of Colombia's revenue, for example. Salt and alcohol monopolies, land taxes and much else were tried, and much effort and ingenuity employed in their adjustment, but strong measures could only be instituted during the very wars that greater government resources might have prevented. Even these measures hid behind their draconian exterior many compromises with victims who simply could not pay.

It is not surprising that such governments sought to keep expenses to the minimum – here European laissez-faire fashions coincided with local necessity, giving some local liberals the illusion that their microscopic administrations represented the vanguard of progress. One major item of expense which they consistently tried to cut was the armed forces. Navies were virtually abandoned. Fortresses, considered anti-republican, were allowed to decay, or even demolished. The permanent force of soldiers was everywhere after 1830 reduced to a small corps of veterans, enough to keep the arsenals and to recruit in times of emergency, but which would weigh as lightly as possible on the treasury in peacetime. The political circumstances of the dissolution of Gran Colombia favoured the reduction of armies. General Páez established his rule in Venezuela with the forces under his immediate command, and through compromise with certain locally powerful figures. The many Bolivarian officers in the armies outside Venezuela found themselves excluded. In New Granada large numbers of the officers were precisely these Venezuelans, and there were many Venezuelan troops as well. Their attempts to establish themselves locally here failed, and the Bogotá government was relieved by their departure. General Flores and forces at least part Venezuelan did establish themselves in Ecuador. Everywhere, however, by the mid-1830s numbers were small and, as few units were ever kept up to strength, smaller than those officially stated. Venezuela possessed 800 infantry and 200 cavalry. New Granada had four infantry battalions, an artillery battalion and three squadrons of cavalry, giving the comparatively heavy total of 3,300 men; however, consistent and intermittently successful efforts were made to bring this number down, and in many mid-century years the number would be less than 1,000. Ecuador officially supported 720 infantry and 360 cavalry. In all of former Gran Colombia there were therefore standing armies whose combined total was no more than 5,000 or so, often less. Even these numbers took up a large share of each republic's budget: Gosselman reported the slice as 510,000 pesos out of Ecuador's estimated revenue of 580,000; in New Granada the armed forces took 818,000 out of a budget of 2,517,000, and in Venezuela 481,000 out of 1,599,000. These high proportions should not so much be seen as signs that military considerations predominated. They derived from simple facts of political life: there was a certain minimum army required, to hold certain points. Even small armies are expensive, and troops, unlike bureaucrats, must be given pay or they will inevitably and rapidly become a menace to their surroundings and to their masters.

It was not primarily these small forces, or the regularly employed officers, who were the cause of disturbance and of that 'militarization' that many noticed *en passant* but few bothered to define. Most of these garrisons were loyal to the governments that employed them most of the time: the *cuartelazo* or barracks coup was not unknown – one started the *reformista* rebellion in Caracas in 1835, General Melo in like manner set up a rare Colombian military government in Bogotá in 1854 – but it was not characteristic of this region. Civil conflict and civil war had wider and far less simple causes – they were not what these minuscule garrisons did, but what, when circumstances grew strained, they were only too likely to fail to control.

Under the colony there had been politics of a sort – bureaucratic and *cabildo* intrigue, ecclesiastical competition – but independence brought a political life that was new in intensity, in extent, in methods and in all sorts of consequences. Republican politics were novel. To give an example, the change can be clearly seen in the Bogotano José Maria Caballero's notes and jottings in his *Diario de Santa Fé*: in 1810 a very colonial collection of observations on random occurrences and natural phenomena suddenly becomes a recognisable political diary. By 1830 all of Gran Colombia had experienced several different sorts of elections, congresses, constituent assemblies, assemblies of *padres de familia*, parties and factions with their attendant press – as well as the techniques for making elections, dissolving assemblies, overawing the press and pro-scribing political opponents. These arts were known to soldiers and civilians alike.

Participation in elections was formally restricted. There were initially limitations on the suffrage, and certain elections were indirect. There is, however, much evidence to show that informal participation was wider, and that *opinión*, the state of opinion about which governments worried, was not confined to citizens with the constitutional right to vote, or those who bothered to vote. The correspondence of the Colombian Tomás Cipriano de Mosquera, three times president (1845–9, 1863–4, 1866–7), *Gran General* and Popayán aristocrat, with his political factotum General Ramón Espina, shows much concern with the detail of working up popular opinion, and in these practices Mosquera was only following the example set by the *fons et origo* of local political practice: the British envoys to Gran Colombia were taken aback by the democratic ways of Santander, who at election times wore the popular *ruana* and drank toasts in the taverns. Timid upper-class electors often found it prudent to follow the popular opinion of their localities. Divided from the earliest days of the republic's separate existence, Colombian opinion was never easily controlled from Bogotá. Santander's energy as a correspondent and as a transparently anonymous, semi-official journalist of the *Gaceta*, his control of the administration and willingness to use it for his party's ends – these were all insufficient to secure the return of the candidate he favoured to succeed him in the election of 1836. José Ignacio de Márquez, the civilian victor, had enough support to win but not enough to govern. He had little prestige, and his support was too confined to the central uplands. He lacked sufficient national *opinión* behind him.

José Antonio Páez in Venezuela was somewhat more secure, and was able to maintain his republican reign until early 1848. But this was far from being simply based on his famous *rapport* with the *alto llano*, and it was far from being unchallenged. Many elements contributed to Páez's dominance. Military prestige and the ability to raise forces in emergency that went with that prestige were certainly important, as was seen in 1835 and 1846. But so too was Páez's skill in political manoeuvre and compromise, seen in his dealings with rivals like Generals Mariño and José Tadeo Monagas. Páez's was not the only military reputation, and others could raise troops too. Compared to his successors, Páez had a light touch: the 'conservative republic' of 1830–48 exiled some of its enemies after 1835, but the alliance of General Páez and his friends and the Caracas merchant class seemed to weigh lightly on the country while the prosperity of the 1830s lasted. Venezuela's exports recovered rapidly from the war and a mood of optimism prevailed until prices fell with the arrival of the effects of the United States crisis of 1837–8. Thereafter the extent and virulence of opposition give one a different view of this polity, a sight of the limitations of Páez's power and prestige. The heritage of colonial commerce in Caracas left merchants and landowners with more separate interests, with divisions apparently easier to exploit than elsewhere in Gran Colombia. Falling export prices exacerbated this latent conflict, and there arose against the merchant-inclined governments of these years a landowner opposition which identified with the liberal cause, and which appeared to be willing to take it to rare doctrinaire extremes. This opposition produced two journalists of genius, the ideologue Tomás Lander – in his will he was to direct that his body be mummified like Bentham's – and the versatile and well-connected demagogue, Antonio Leocadio Guzmán. The campaigns of Lander and of Guzmán can be seen to have had their effect outside as well as within the officially recognized political class. They found provincial readers, and these found listeners. The reputation of Guzmán could gather together crowds, crowds of 'artisans' and other less-definable persons. The administration could no longer control the elections to the extent that ensured a stable succession: in 1844 the Swedish diplomat, Count Adlercreutz, who himself had had first-hand experience in election-making as a mercenary Bolivarian colonel, reported to his government that the liberals had won the direct provincial elections, and that the 'oligarchic party' had only managed to bring its pressure to bear on the indirect elections for the national congress; even then, it had only been able to return mediocrities. In conditions of economic crisis, of mounting disorder, Páez lost 'the inclination and sympathies of the masses'.

Travellers from the Europe of Guizot and Louis Napoléon, Palmerston and Franz-Joseph were taken aback by the quantity of political conversation even in humble gatherings and in remote places, where these inclinations and sympathies worked themselves out, not without consequences. They were reluctant to concede much meaning to a political life lacking formal or permanent institutions, beyond a few scattered political clubs in the towns and party organizations that did not go beyond a sporadic press and a meagre network of correspondents, and in such uneducated and illiterate societies. They over-estimated the political control of landowners; power frequently brought with it land, but the reverse was much less than automatic. They underestimated the number of masterless men. Nor could they understand how local rivalries and antipathies, often of colonial origin, were caught up in new republican politics. Even had society been firmly in the control of a solidly established elite, which over much of the map was not the case, that elite would have found causes for falling out within itself. The better-known rivalries of city and city, province and province were often reproduced at less-discernible levels, down to the *veredas*, the districts of the lowly *municipio*.

The *revoluciones* and the *revolucioncitas* must be seen against this background. It is not possible in a survey of this length to give any detailed account of their causes and courses. Venezuela experienced the revolt of the *reformas*, 1835, an attempted coup by excluded Bolivarians against the prematurely civilian government of Dr José María Vargas, which placed itself under the protection of Páez; there were widespread revolts in 1846, and Páez himself fought unsuccessfully against being supplanted by his last nominee José Tadeo Monagas in 1848. The decade of rule by the Monagas family that followed was not peaceful, and culminated in the Federal War, 1859–63. Guzmán Blanco did not consolidate his power until after further fighting in 1868 and 1870. New Granada suffered an outbreak of clerical disaffection in Pasto in the south in 1839, which developed into a series of federalist declarations in other provinces, the *Guerra de los Supremos*, 1839–42. The conservative and centralist administration of Pedro Alcántara Herrán that won that war saw its men and policies progressively abandoned in the late 1840s by the succeeding government of Tomás Cipriano de Mosquera, and the conservatives lost power altogether in the elections of 1849. They revolted unsuccessfully in 1851 against the liberal government of General José Hilario López, behind whom they saw the even less reassuring figure of the popular General José María Obando. In the confused and contradictory agitation of students, artisans and Cauca valley blacks they could even discern the spectre of socialism. A brave man but a timid politician, Obando abandoned the field to the short-lived military régime of General José María Melo, which was in its turn suppressed by forces recruited and led by gentlemen of all persuasions in the short war of 1854. The conservative government that then won the elections – universal suffrage in New Granada was also counter-revolution – was then ousted by a federalist liberal rising between 1859 and 1862 led by General Mosquera. Like Venezuela, Colombia adopted an extremely federal constitution, but there the resources for a Guzmán Blanco were not to hand. Both countries saw a number of local revolts; Colombians fought major civil wars in 1876–7, and again in 1885. The long supremacy of Guzmán Blanco in Venezuela, 1870–88, seemed to indicate that certain geopolitical problems had found their solution, but the succeeding hegemony of General Joaquín Crespo, 1892–8, was not entirely peaceful. General Crespo was himself killed in battle, and like Colombia Venezuela ended the century in civil war.

In Ecuador the presence of a large Indian population in the sierra, a separate estate only intermittently concerned with white and *cholo* politics, might lead one to guess that political life was slowed by a certain passivity. This would not be a reliable conclusion. The sierra population was not always passive. Flores put down several revolts before his expulsion in 1845. Provincial rivalries were acute, all hegemonies limited in extent and capacity. The press made up for a more precarious existence and fewer readers than in Colombia or Venezuela by exceptional virulence: Ecuadorian journalism built up a tradition of violence and incitement to violence from the original massacre of those behind *El Quiteño Libre* in 1833, which reached famous heights with Gabriel García Moreno and his adversary Juan Montalvo. But the former's intense military, as well as political, activity should be stressed here. Flores did not leave Ecuador a tranquil pretorian tradition.

These wars had certain characteristics in common throughout the region, which is far from saying that they were all the same. They tended to coincide, and were more severe when they did so coincide, with periods of economic difficulty, sometimes identifiable with crises in the world economy, sometimes with particularly unfortunate local conjunctures. Economic difficulties weakened government revenue, and poor governments were less able to satisfy and enthuse their supporters and oppose their enemies. Endemic provincial dissatisfaction became more intense as needy governments kept their expenditure closer to home. In the economy at large other consequences increased the propensity for trouble. New crops, or new activities for export, such as the 1850s hide boom in the Venezuelan *llanos*, or the 1870s *quina* gathering in Santander, Colombia, brought large numbers of people into new areas and a new dependence on a fluctuating market. 'Falling back on subsistence' was not as easy as the little phrase makes it sound. For example, when the coffee price came down at the end of the 1830s it was not just the over-extended Venezuelan planter who lost, it was his now abandoned work-force, deprived of wages, now perhaps living in an unfamiliar environment, and a growing-season away from careless subsistence. Not that such people would show much initiative to revolt, but some of them would join revolts. Distress, *malestar, miseria* of this sort, not the secular poverty of the more oppressed uplands of Boyacá or Pichincha, provided a climate in which revolution could take hold. These lands were virtually unpoliced.

Another common characteristic of these wars was dictated by resources and terrain: it was hard to bring revolts to a speedy end, even when they had small beginnings. Governments had to make themselves yet more unpopular by recruiting. All three republics had militia systems, but these could not be relied on to produce troops who would serve or go long distances, and in rebellious areas they could not be relied upon at all. Recruiting was a violent and unpopular procedure. The more deferential populations would run away and hide, others would resist more dangerously, and the rebellion might appear to spread. Desertion was so common that the French traveller, Holinsky, remarked that opposing commanders in Ecuador seemed to hurry their forces into battle for fear of facing each other troopless and alone. In fact, it was not usually possible to hurry anyone anywhere. Armies could not be adequately rationed; they had to be dispersed so that they could survive, as everywhere the local surplus was limited. They had to be manoeuvred according to resources, and according to climate, not to outrun supplies and not to subject the troops to changes more brusque than they could stand. Governments occasionally enjoyed the benefit of more enthusiastic support, but on the whole relied on small forces, laboriously gathered together by their nucleus of veterans, moved with caution. Rebel systems relied more on volunteers, on the *élan* of the cause and the prospect of loot, and on the local *guerrilla*. Successful leaders had to understand the peculiarities of local warfare, both practical and psychological; what a particular region could produce or sustain in the way of resources and troops; what was the art of enthusing a particular population. The multiplication of higher ranks was not so much a reflection of a childish 'latin' delight in titles as of the need to balance local sensibilities.

It is hard to discern a standard, typical *caudillo* among these figures. Most were persons of some social standing, though the connection between property and the ability to raise troops was rarely direct – even *llaneros* like Páez and Monagas raised more men on their prestige than on their property. Even 'popular' leaders, José María Obando and Ezequiel Zamora for example, are usually found to be better connected socially than romantic admirers have made them appear; both Zamora and Obando owned a few slaves. Some had reputations made in the wars of independence; many veterans of the wars were still able and willing to take to the field in the 1860s. The range of political and military talent that appears varies in type and in origin. Zamora started life as a provincial merchant and moneylender, and found his extraordinary military ambition as a militia officer; he then indulged this penchant for combat and command in the opposition to Páez in 1846. He used guerrillas, but he was much more than a guerrilla leader – his masterpiece, the battle of Santa Inés, was an elaborate affair of entrenched ambuscades. He had perhaps a generous definition of excess, but he was a strict disciplinarian towards those who abused it; as a victor he was a model of humanity. His reputation as an egalitarian reformer rests on little more than an extraordinary *don de gente*, a gift for getting on with all classes, just as his military ascendancy came entirely from ability in the field. He was not a *llanero*, nor did he try to become one; he was not the emanation of any particular region: he won battles until he died in one: San Carlos in 1860.

José María Obando, the most popular soldier or politician Colombia produced in the last century, had bastard connections with good Popayán families, but his local reputation in the south was made first fighting for the Spanish crown and then softening the rigours of patriot occupation. He had some land in the valley of Patía, cattle country which always provided him with a hundred or so of cavalry. In the opposition to Bolívar in the late 1820s, as vice-president in 1831–2, he acquired not only notoriety as one of those accused of the assassination of Bolívar's most faithful lieutenant Antonio José de Sucre (who as the man who had ordered the sack of Pasto in 1822 was not much mourned in the south), but wider fame and popularity as one who consolidated the new republic before the return of the exiled Santander. Obando's subsequent career – the revival of the Sucre charge, civil war, exile and poverty, return and election to the presidency, failure and disgrace, alliance with his old enemy Mosquera and death in a skirmish on the eve of victory in 1861 – had a pathos which in his lifetime earned him the title of 'the American Oedipus'. With military gifts and a fine military presence Obando combined great popular attraction, heightened by the history of his persecution and exclusion by Popayán aristocrats. This appeal was not only effective in Pasto and elsewhere in Cauca, but was evident on the Caribbean coast and among the Bogotá artisans – Obando's most effective support in his brief presidency from 1853–4. But Obando was a better martyr than politician, and failed to translate this ascendancy into power. These radical reputations were matters of sentiment and affection, of prestige rather than programme.

The lives of other national military figures – not that many of them can be considered merely as soldiers – fail to conform to a common pattern. The Monagas brothers and the Sotillos were *llaneros* who kept in close touch with the *bajo llano*, the eastern Venezuelan plains. Marshal Falcón came of a landed family near Coro, in which city this kind and cultured man first became famous as an aggressive *señorito*. Guzmán Blanco was the son of the Caracas journalist Antonio Leocadio Guzmán and an aristocratic mother. The patient, worrying, commonsensical General Herrán, president of New Granada 1841–5, came from modest origins and had a long military career, some of it passed forcibly in the royalist ranks; he had, nevertheless, a very civilian mind. Gabriel García Moreno, who did a lot of fighting and who in his years of ascendancy from 1861 to 1875 was far more prone to execute opponents than the most severe general of New Granada, was the son of a Guayaquil merchant and had studied for the priesthood as far as minor orders. Tomás Cipriano de Mosquera came from a *señorial* Popayán line, and had a light-weight career as a late-independence soldier with Bolívar, a friend of his father. His appetite for power might have had something to do with this background, but it certainly cannot explain his erratic subsequent political career, or his military successes and failures; for much of the time his family looked on with alarm and disapproval.

These leaders did not make up any distinct and self-conscious caste. Not all considered themselves to be primarily soldiers, and many regarded civil war with as deep a distaste as any civilian: Falcón and Herrán were eloquent examples of the peace-loving soldier. Nor was there any greater uniformity below this level of command, as each distinct locality reacted to the breakdown of order in its own way. Some localities produced lesser commanders who gained a reputation for savagery coloured by fears of racial conflict or a repetition of past atrocities. In Venezuela there were 'el indio Rangel', 'el indio Espinosa', figures of 1846 and 1859, the Sotillo clan in the east; in Colombia, Obando's ally the 'bandit' Sarria, the *cacique* Guainas of the Páez Indians of Tierradentro, and the mulatto General David Peña of Cali, who on one famous occasion made well-born conservative ladies sweep the city streets. The Indians of the Ecuadorian sierra were not always passive victims or spectators of others' conflicts. Some of these irregulars did fight in a sanguinary way, and in some wars in some regions murderous vendettas did develop – the Barquisimeto region in the Venezuelan *Guerra Federal* is a good example. The wars confirmed and intensified local antagonisms, as the participants repeated certain inevitable patterns: what was lost in one war might be avenged in the next.

Yet it is easy to exaggerate the intensity and extent of disorder, and all too easy to exaggerate the violence of these conflicts. For logistical reasons, if for no others, as in all wars long periods passed in which nothing much happened. Armies remained relatively small, much mobilization was essentially defensive. Casualties in battle were high, and death from disease and lack of adaptation yet more common, but massacres and executions were far rarer than foreign observers deduced from the irregular nature of much of the warfare. Their conclusions seem often to be drawn from preoccupations about the violence of peoples of mixed blood, and the *frisson* produced by the sight of ragged troops with lances or *machetes*. They lumped this 'south american' fighting together with what went on in Argentina and Mexico, where conditions and practices were very different (as indeed they were in Spain). The Colombian José María Samper complained: 'Rosas is our symbol; Santa Anna, Belzú, Monagas and other terrible personages are held to be the general rule.' Of these only Monagas represented these three republics, and he was terrible only because of corruption. There are no reliable figures for the dead in these wars, and there is a strong tendency for a certain type of progressive creole writer to exaggerate the likely numbers: one suspects that Conrad's Don José Avellanos, in his *Fifty Years of Misgovernment*, painted the past of the Republic of Costaguana rather blacker and bloodier than it really was. Such authors wrote out of shame and disappointment, and often had a cosmopolitan background that did not always help them to understand the processes at work. Very few were not partisan – as always and everywhere, one side's 'energetic measures' were the other side's atrocities. One must also distinguish one conflict from another and remember that the incidence of each particular war bore harder on some provinces than others: governments might have to declare that public order was disturbed throughout their territory when that was far from being really the case.

Even short wars could be very destructive of property, particularly of cattle. The larger ones, the *Guerra Federal* in Venezuela and the contemporary Mosquera–Ospina struggle in Colombia, caused proportionately greater loss, as both governments and rebels relied on emergency exactions, armies marched from meagre surplus to meagre surplus, agriculture was abandoned and trade interrupted. The worst wars undoubtedly had severe direct economic effects. And all wars interrupted the longed-for stability: public works were abandoned, efforts to put the administration on a sound financial footing had to be forgotten, credit and reputation were lost, interest rates went higher, the speculator overshadowed the entrepreneur – where they were not combined in the same person. In such conditions governments so immediately concerned with survival could not concern themselves with much expensive continuity. The chief mourners were those who looked in these republics for the sort of government that they could not sustain.

The wars had other effects. As has been said, they confirmed and intensified, sometimes created, antagonisms that showed in more peaceful politics as well. Military mobilization was also to some extent political mobilization; those who followed a leader in war might also maintain

their attachment in peace. Wars produced heroes for parties; there was no
need to be a literate voter to admire an Obando or a Zamora. They also
decided certain important issues – a point that escapes those who are not
curious about what these wars were fought for. The *Guerra Federal* did
not have the definitively levelling effect on Venezuelan society that its
apologists hint at, but it did extinguish formal Venezuelan conservatism
– thereafter, under one colour or another, Venezuela was *liberal*. In
Colombia Mosquera's victory in the civil wars of 1859–62 was followed
by more than two decades of federal experiment, predominantly liberal-
controlled. Issues of church and state were fought out. Many involved
were deeply committed to the cause of federalism, which meant respect
for local peculiarities and needs, and escape from distant governments
unwilling or unable to perform their promises; central power is re-
established as it finds the wherewithal to have something to give.
Antonio Leocadio Guzmán's cynical assertion that his friends called
their cause federal because their opponents were centralists, and that
matters would have gone just as well the other way round, is, like much
else he said, not to be relied on. The balance of interests and regions could
sometimes only be decided by civil war. These political issues were
nowhere a simple competition for office for office's sake.

'Thank God in this well-ordered country a Diplomatic Agent can live
without taking much interest in local politics', wrote Belford Wilson,
transferred to Caracas in 1843 after some *contretemps* in Peru. He soon ran
into trouble there too, which is not surprising, for he took sides rather
clearly in the local politics he did not take much interest in. Parties were
forming, issues emerged that divided opinion, interests sought political
expression, broad liberal and conservative currents became discernible.
What decided a man, a family or a district to one current or faction or
another was not simply determined – it cannot be said that merchants
were liberals, or landowners conservatives: all such simple generalizations are too easy to disprove, and a complete account has to be built on
analysis of region, of family, of events, even of talent and inclination.
Seemingly clear-cut divisions, such as the merchant–landowner antagonism of the Venezuelan 1840s, blur on closer inspection or do not hold
for very long, as the dividing issue is resolved. Parties, however, persist,
and without denying that an analysis inspired by the methods of Sir
Lewis Namier would contribute a great deal to the understanding of
these structures too, there is much that would escape. Ownership of land
was not so easily translated into political control of the neighbourhood

or national political weight. Urban politics could be unruly, and the issues aired in the larger cities were echoed in the small towns; the artisans of Mompóx were just as concerned for their interests as the artisans of Bogotá and adopted the same democratic ideology.

Examples of the hold of liberal ideology on individual minds, and of their evolution, abound in the memoirs of the time, such as those of the increasingly sober Salvador Camacho Roldán and the always excitable aristocrat radical, Francisco de Paula Borda, who believed in Jesuit conspiracies and poisonings to the end of his days. In 1877 a moderate Colombian liberal and well-travelled merchant, Enrique Cortés, listed what he considered the lasting victories of his party: the abolition of *manos muertas* and the suppression of convents, the ending of imprisonment for debt, degrading punishments, forced labour and the death penalty; the absolute freedom of the press; municipal liberty. Less sceptical liberals would have made longer lists and would have included free trade, the expulsion of the Jesuits, the establishment of federalism and absolute separation of church and state, but Cortés was no fanatic and expressed his doubts about how long these would last. Nor did he have much illusion about the transcendental importance of the items he did record, among a population he saw as nine parts in the shadows to one part in the light. But he did see them as valuable measures achieved by his party, and he later set them against the conservative reaction of 1885.

Conservative grounds for disagreement were by no means based on archaic colonial arguments. In Colombia, the *memorias* of Mariano Ospina Rodríguez as Minister of the Interior in the early 1840s marshall conservative arguments in an impressively modern fashion. A tradition of native conservative thought not only persisted in Colombia in a way that it did not in Venezuela, where conservative argument had to re-emerge in a liberal–positivist guise, but eventually triumphed. The liberal governments of the sixties and seventies were subject to constant conservative criticism, both from the press and from the clergy, and from the example of the state of Antioquia – peaceful, relatively prosperous, strongly governed, catholic and conservative. Liberalism had to take the consequences of the collapse of the federal, free-trade radical republic between 1882 and 1885, a crisis in which 'independents' and conservatives showed themselves more pragmatic. The republic ended the century under the philosophical and political sway of Rafael Núñez, president 1880–2 and 1884–94, and Miguel Antonio Caro, president 1894–8, who together covered a wide range of conservative argument, as well as being formidable polemicists and politicians. Colombia was officially and constitutionally an island of conservatism, between the liberal confusions of Cipriano Castro in Venezuela, 1899–1908, and the radicalism of Eloy Alfaro's era in Ecuador, 1895–1912. Ideological differences were acutely felt. An *esprit fort* was needed to profess liberal beliefs in the diocese of Pasto, even under a liberal government. Conversely, Catholics in Antioquia, the Venezuelan Andes, even in the Ecuadorian sierra, did suffer from time to time from militant secularizing administrations, and responded predictably.

What was the resulting political pattern in each republic after half a century or so of independent political life? Guzmán Blanco managed to establish in Venezuela a government federal in name, increasingly centralized in practice, where the devices of the fiscal *subsidio*, the *juntas de fomento* and the *consejo federal* brought provincial rivals under increasingly tight control. Guzmán had behind him the defeat both of the conservative forces and of the leading military rivals of his own camp – and as coffee exports recovered and surpassed earlier levels, the means for such a programme. It is also hard to escape the conclusion that the experiences of the fifties and sixties had had a political and cultural effect less positive than the hypothetical levelling: there was little room for opposition, less for ideological argument. A weak Church suffered further humiliation. A tradition of adulation of the arbiter of the moment, already visible during the years of Páez, was given powerful encouragement. Páez, the Monagas brothers, Guzmán Blanco, Crespo, Castro – the successive masters of Venezuela – for all the distinct regional or class origins and tastes of each, did not *represent* those regions or classes when in power, beyond some preference for familiars. They were at the point of a civil and military balance in which, though the national government still left many aspects of regional life alone, power was still concentrated more than it was in New Granada or Ecuador. There was less correlation between social status and political power. High Caracas society never really assimilated Páez, who spent much time on his estates at Maracay and elsewhere, setting a pattern many of his successors followed. Only one of these could have claimed to be an aristocrat, and Guzmán Blanco exalted himself beyond assimilation, when he was not living far away in Paris.

New Granadan politics were not resolved in such a way. No one current extinguished the other, or came near to doing so in the entire century. Bogotá occupied a good defensive position for resisting provincial attack – it was hard for different provinces to combine against the capital and launch a simultaneous assault, and the city was situated in the midst of a dense and recruitable population – but the national government lacked the resources effective central government required. Here the 1886 constitution was a couple of decades in advance of the economy. No figure emerged from independence, which in New Granada had left the social structure relatively intact, with the political and military prestige of Páez. General Santander, perhaps Páez's equal in political skill and his superior in application, was a far more controversial figure and lacked military reputation. He could make no pretence to be above party. Colombia was to be governed by men who could put together coalitions from disparate provinces, make elections, manage congress, pay the veterans and keep everyone in a state of moderately discontented expectation. Few ascendancies lasted long – Santander was out of power by 1836, Mosquera never really established an ascendancy, the civilians Murillo Toro and Rafael Núñez only kept their influence as long as they did by making sparing use of it; both were tactful and discreet. Ideological debate was particularly keen and wide-ranging – nowhere else in Latin America did the events of 1848 in Europe find such eager followers and imitators as among the politicians, artisans, students and even soldiers of poor isolated New Granada. Nowhere else were the principles of federalism given such expression as in the Rio Negro Constitution of 1863, with its free trade in arms, its careful provisions for non-interference by the federal government in wars within the sovereign states. Reporting on Colombian political life when this period of radicalism was drawing to an end, the Chilean poet and diplomat José Antonio Soffia described how the two 'great doctrinal parties' had become more and more polarized: 'Here everything has been discussed with vehemence and passion.' To a Chilean, Colombian politics looked disorderly, overemphatic, dangerous, lower class – the best people, with some notable exceptions, did not take part, just as the modest origins of so many army officers made the army an unattractive career for the well-born. Soffia describes a competitive atmosphere, and concedes that there were issues of principle behind these excesses. He was witnessing the decadence of mid-century liberalism, and the return of conservatism in all its renewed ideological vigour. Nuñez thought that he had a recipe for 'scientific peace' – a centralized government, rapprochement with the Church, a stronger army, a restricted suffrage. . . . Two more wars after 1885 show that again ambition had outrun resources, even if the recipe was the right one. But the solution was not sought in autocracy, but in a new coalition, now to be fortified by the support of the Church. Most features of Colombian political life – the natural federalism of so much of it, the intense use of the press, the incessant electioneering, the career open to the emergent legal–journalistic–congressional talent–did not change. It is also significant that Núñez was able to change the old sovereign states into departments, but failed in his desire to alter the administrative map of the country more fundamentally. The realities of the 1886 constitution were not as central as the appearance. The liberal party did not abandon their allegiance to the old federalism until after the end of the century.

The political beginnings of Ecuador, the 'Estado del Sur de Colombia' as it was at first officially called, were more clearly pretorian. Juan José Flores married a lady of the Quito aristocracy and had a reputation for foxy intrigue, but never abandoned his reliance on his veterans and on other Venezuelans, such as the ruthless black colonel, Juan Otamendi. Opposition to the 'odious foreigner' was not long in appearing, some of it led by the Benthamite English colonel, Francis Hall, who until his violent end was one of the leaders of the liberal intellectual group gathered around the journal *El Quiteño Libre*. Nor was military discipline easily maintained – Flores faced several mutinies, and at the end of 1833 Colonel Mena's rebellion in Guayaquil led to a long-drawn-out guerrilla war in the coastal provinces of Guayas and Manabí, the *guerra de los chihuahuas*.[2] Flores sustained militarily the succeeding government of the cosmopolitan Guayaquileño, Vicente Rocafuerte, and returned to the presidency himself until 1845, when a general movement of protest against his administration arose on his attempting to raise a three-peso poll tax. Certain subsequent presidents can be seen to have governed in the Flores mould: José María Urbina, one of his former aides-de-camp, ruled from 1852–60, in part basing his power on the *tauras*, a corps of freed slaves recruited from the region of that name; Ignacio Veintemilla, the dominant figure of the late seventies and early eighties, clearly relied heavily on his 'three thousand breachleaders'. The mutiny and the *cuartelazo* were much more common in Ecuadorean politics than in Venezuela or Colombia, where examples at the national level were rare. It was also much more usual in Ecuador to use extreme measures against opponents – soldiers and civilians. Rocafuerte as well as Flores, García

---

2 So called because the leading figure in the opposition to Flores, Vicente Rocafuerte, had lived in Mexico; the *chihuahua* thereafter entered Ecuadorean folklore as the name of a firework figure that runs away when its backside is lit.

Moreno as well as Veintemilla, had their enemies shot or exiled; García Moreno ordered notorious whippings, and under Veintemilla's government the archbishop of Quito was poisoned with strychnine administered in the chalice during mass. One particularly arduous form of exile was to be sent to Brazil by way of the Napo river and the Amazon. These features of Ecuadorean strife perhaps derived from its origins under the domination of veterans of much independence fighting, many of whom were foreigners, and from the relatively miniature scale of political life. The Indian population of the *sierra*, not all so downtrodden as those who only observed it around Quito reported, remained an estate apart, effectively excluded from official political life in which in any case it had little desire to participate – paying the tribute usually exempted the Indian from recruitment. The mixed *montuvio* population of the coastal regions was more active, and in the last two decades of the century was effectively mobilized by the radical Alfaro.

Ideological divisions worked themselves out in the more personal politics of Ecuador; they also reflected local differences. Rocafuerte was one of the most prominent early liberals of Spanish America. Flores, related by marriage to the most prominent families, builder of an enormous and ramshackle Quito palace, became increasingly conservative. Urbina and Veintemilla were military radicals, their enemies said in imitation of New Granadan examples. García Moreno became internationally famous for his extreme clericalism, but his reforming energy did not make him popular with all the clergy. The liberal feelings of Guayaquil contrasted from the earliest days of the republic with the conservatism of Quito. For long friction was lessened by appalling communications. Ecuador also suffered far more than Colombia or Venezuela from diplomatic complications: Peru coveted the timber and ship-yards of Guayaquil, and President Castilla in 1860 attempted an invasion. Peruvian governments gave aid and comfort to Ecuadorean exiles. The northern frontier with Colombia was also complicated, as it did not match the old boundary of the *audiencia* of Quito. There were several invasions and counter-invasions, in which Ecuador usually came off worst. These preoccupations placed great strains on very scarce resources, as did the alarm caused by General Flores's plans to lead a Spanish-backed expedition of re-conquest after his departure in 1845. Ecuador did at times have cause to feel threatened in its very existence. There the very limited powers of the state are clearly seen in the career of García Moreno, so much of whose energy had to be devoted to survival against enemies within and without. Acute political despair led him to make overtures to France for the establishment of a protectorate – he was not the only beleaguered statesman of the region and the era to entertain such ideas.

But foreign observers – particularly such as the supercilious and ungrateful English mountaineer, Whymper, and the pessimistic U.S. minister Hassaurek, in Ecuador – were too prone to generalize their observations, and to present a picture of political instability and social stagnation. Significant social and economic changes occurred under these disadvantaged governments, and these are being uncovered by a local historiography not primarily concerned with national *fracasos*. Certain local economies and local regimes – the conservative government in Antioquia, Dalla Costa in Guayana, for example – can be seen to have had a measure of success, and a new scale of appreciation can be developed less concerned with such rare examples of progress as railways, capable of seeing the significance of a shorter road, an improved mule-track, an effort of local schooling, the differences in the maintenance of law and order from one region to another.

Contemporaries were aware of the importance of these differences and changes, and even made themselves at times ridiculous in their enthusiasm for what to strangers looked very small beer. They were also keenly aware of changes in customs. There was no mass immigration to any of these republics in the nineteenth-century, but there was a none the less significant immigration of a small number of foreigners, principally merchants, but, besides diplomats, also some engineers, artisans and doctors. These brought not only their specific skills but different patterns of behaviour, taste and fashion. After early rivalry with native merchants, those who survived the disappointments of the late 1820s frequently became naturalized in all but law. The Germans in Venezuela, even some few British in New Granada, married creole ladies, and, in the eyes of envoys anxious to avoid the endless labour of civil-war damage claims, became indistinguishable from the natives in their political and social involvement. More creoles travelled abroad, more were sent abroad for their education. Some of these returned not only with the prestige of the travelled and the fashionable but also with a new consciousness of their own national peculiarities, disadvantages and, occasionally, merits and good fortune. The Colombian, Medardo Rivas, discovered in himself a passionate tropical republicanism when he saw how Europeans laughed at Haitians. Most travellers, overwhelmed by the scale and wealth of London, were also appalled at the sight of urban poverty and prostitution, phenomena not yet so glaringly present in their own societies.

Foreign observers, on whom so much reliance has in the past been placed, could not have much sense of the pace of local change, however acute they were: their stays were usually short. But the changes of customs and attitudes are often to be found described in local *costumbrista* writing, and in Bogotá and its surroundings they were recorded by a historian whose memory for significant detail amounts to genius: José María Cordóvez Moure, 1835–1918, author of *Reminiscencias de Santa Fé y Bogotá*, an item of the 'traditional historiography' that puts so much subsequent writing to shame.

Neither Venezuela, Colombia nor Ecuador achieved during the nineteenth century what Don José Avellanos would have called 'a rightful place in the comity of nations'. A pioneer statistician, the Colombian priest Dr Federico C. Aguilar, in 1884 exposed the weakness of Colombia, for example, in his *Colombia en presencia de las repúblicas hispanoamericanas*: low per-capita exports and imports, resulting in meagre government income; few miles of railway, expensively constructed; not much movement in the ports; few schools. The contrast with Argentina, Chile and Uruguay is all too apparent, and the distance is increasing. The only position of leadership Father Aguilar can find for Colombia is the number of newspapers. The successors of Gran Colombia had attracted little foreign investment. Guzmán Blanco's guarantees did bring some to Venezuela, but at a high cost. The comparative advantages of these 'destartaladas repúblicas del norte', in a Chilean phrase, were uncertain and unimpressive.

This made, and has made, their formal *national* histories in this first half-century or so more painful to contemplate, as years of failure by the accepted indices of progress of the time. Such a simple view must yield to the detailed study of how local disadvantages of climate and topography were overcome, of how crises turned out to be less than complete, of how each cycle left something behind. It must also be apparent that the persistent habit of stern Victorian judgement, and of regard for little but the hierarchy of international commerce, is unlikely to yield many insights into the history of these countries at this time. In his *Essayo sobre las revoluciones políticas y la condición social de las repúblicas colombianas* (1861), José María Samper complained that 'The European world has made more effort to study our volcanoes than our societies; it knows our insects better than our literature, the crocodile of our rivers better than the acts of our statesmen, and it has much more learning about how quinine bark is cut, or how hides are salted in Buenos Aires, than about the vitality of our infant democracy!' The protest is still a valid one.

13

PERU AND BOLIVIA FROM INDEPENDENCE TO THE WAR OF THE PACIFIC[1]

On 28 July 1821, the Argentine general, José de San Martín, declared colonial links between Peru and Spain broken and paved the way for the political organization of the new republic. Bolívar's military campaign in 1824, which led to the destruction of the imperial army in Peru, completed the process of Peruvian independence. However, despite the wars of independence, the political, social and economic order of colonial Peru remained in many respects intact. The independence process resulted from the actions of a profoundly vulnerable Spanish and creole minority, which was intent on maintaining its former privileges under a new liberal cloak; there was a total absence of popular representation in any of the decisions taken concerning the political and economic organization of independent Peru. The very vulnerability of the dominant, though far from hegemonic, class, unable to rally behind it, on a national level, the mass of Indians and blacks, permitted the rise to power of a succession of military caudillos during the half-century after independence.

According to the *Guía de Forasteros* published in 1828, Peru had a population of one and a quarter million at the time of its independence:

Department	Inhabitants
Arequipa	136,812
Ayacucho	159,608
Cuzco	216,382
Junín	200,839
La Libertad	230,970
Lima	148,112
Puno	156,000
Total	1,248.723

[1] Translated from the Spanish by Dr Richard Southern and Dr David Brookshaw; translation revised by the Editor. The Editor wishes to thank Dr Rory Miller, Dr Luis Ortega and Dr James Dunkerley for help in the final preparation of this chapter.

The Peruvian export economy had entered a period of decline during the final years of the colonial period and the situation had worsened during the many military conflicts which had accompanied the campaign for independence. The slaves, who had constituted the basic labour force in the coastal areas, were forcibly recruited into the ranks of both the patriot and the royalist armies, with the result that the coastal sugar and cotton plantations lost one of the most important factors of production. At the same time the fall in the supply of mercury, the abolition of the *mita* (the dominant method of organizing Indian labour for the mines), the inability to deal with the permanent problem of flooding and the destruction caused by the war, all led to the marked decline of the Peruvian silver-mining industry. Output from Cerro de Pasco, which had the largest silver deposits at the time, revived during the 1830s and increased from 95,261 marks in 1830 to 219,378 marks in 1832 and to 307,213 in 1840. National silver production, however, never reached the level of the colonial period and was now exported in the form of silver coin which dramatically decreased the money supply in Peru itself. During the first two decades after independence the Peruvian economy was, therefore, mostly organized around the largely self-sufficient landed estates (haciendas) and the Indian communities *(comunidades)*. Marketable surplus was insignificant and served to supply in erratic fashion local markets. Tenuous links were maintained with international markets – mainly Britain, France, the United States and Chile – through the export of small quantities of sugar, cotton, cacao, quinine bark (which was mainly produced in Bolivia but exported through the ports of southern Peru), copper, tin and nitrates.[2] Beginning in the second half of the 1830s, in response to the growing demands of the British textile industry, significant quantities of wool, first alpaca, then sheep (and to a lesser extent vicuña and llama), began to be exported from southern Peru.[3] Given the stagnation of the export sector, at least until the late 1830s, it

---

[2] Shane Hunt, *Price and quantum estimates of Peruvian exports 1830–1962* (Princeton, Woodrow Wilson School, Discussion Paper no.33, 1973) 57–8. For estimates of Peruvian exports (excluding silver) to Britain, France, the U.S. and Chile in the period 1825–40, see Hunt, *Price and quantum estimates*, 38.

[3] Wool exports reached a peak in the 1860s and 1870s by which time Islay was, after Callao, the second most important port in Peru. However, as a port Islay never managed to create its own economic life. Its growth was closely related to the economic development of the interior of the South. For this reason, the construction of the Puno–Arequipa railway and the establishment of its terminus at Mollendo in 1874 would send Islay into sudden and complete decline. Its population, which was calculated at 1,554 inhabitants in 1862, fell to 400 in 1874. From then on, Mollendo would be the main port of entry into southern Peru, and by 1878 it already had 3,000 inhabitants. See Heraclio Bonilla, *Gran Bretaña y el Perú* (Lima, 1977), 105–7.

was necessary for Peru to export vast quantities of silver coin in order to pay for its imports from Britain. In 1825 silver coin amounted to 90 per cent of all Peruvian exports. And in 1840 it still accounted for 82 per cent of exports.[4]

At the time of independence Peru had opened its ports to world, especially British, trade. Although trade routes between Europe and Peru via the port of Buenos Aires had been opened during the last thirty years of the eighteenth century, the introduction of British goods into Peru was effected for the most part via the Magellan Straits, in the far south of the continent, turning the Chilean port of Valparaíso into a strategic link in this trade. In this sense, Peruvian ports were commercially dependent on Valparaíso, although President Santa Cruz in 1836 tried to remedy the situation by rewarding ships which sailed direct to Callao. However, the overthrow of Santa Cruz and the collapse of the Peru–Bolivian Confederation in 1839 (see below) put an end to this experiment. In 1826, goods arriving at Callao via the Magellan Straits undertook a voyage lasting 102 days in all, 90 to Valparaíso and a further 12 from there to Callao. On the other hand, the old colonial route via Panama required a total of 125 days, not so much for the maritime journey as such, but because of the long delay caused by having to cross the Panamanian isthmus. After 1840, when steamships began to make their appearance in the waters of the Pacific the time of the voyage from Europe to Peru was reduced to about 45 days. At the same time lower transport costs made it more profitable to supply the urban markets of the coast with imported agricultural produce, in particular cereals and fruits, from Chile. As a result, the highlands of the interior were increasingly cut off from the economy of the Peruvian coast.

In the first half of the nineteenth century, Peru's main trading partners were, in order of importance, Great Britain, the United States and France. Britain was by far the most significant. By 1824, there were already some thirty-six British commercial houses in Peru, twenty in Lima and sixteen in Arequipa.[5] British exports to Peru steadily increased in value from £86,329 in 1821 to £559,766 in 1825, fell to £199,086 in 1826 but had reached £368,469 in 1830.[6] Between 1820 and 1830, textiles

[4] *Ibid.*, 96. For estimates of Peru's exports to Britain in the years 1825, 1839 and 1840, see William Mathew, 'Anglo-Peruvian commercial and financial relations, 1820–1865' (unpublished Ph.D. thesis, University of London, 1964), 77.

[5] R. A. Humphreys, *British consular reports on the trade and politics of Latin America, 1824–1826* (London, 1940), 126–7.

[6] Heraclio Bonilla, Lía del Rio, Pilar Ortíz de Zevallos, 'Comercio libre y crisis de la economía andina', *Histórica* (Lima), 2/1 (1978), 3.

Peru and Bolivia after Independence

accounted for approximately 95 per cent of the value of British exports to Peru. This percentage fell noticeably immediately afterwards to an average of 50 per cent of all imports for the rest of the nineteenth century. The deluge of British textiles in the ports and markets of Peru continued, in a much more extreme way, a process which had begun with the opening of the port of Buenos Aires. That is to say, the weakened and segmented domestic markets of Peru were now captured for British products on a far greater scale, virtually putting an end to native artisan production and the Indian *obrajes* (workshops), which, because of their technological obsolescence, were unable to compete successfully with imported textiles from Britain. On the other hand, the decline in the importation of textiles, which became more noticeable after 1830, indicates that these Peruvian markets were very restricted, largely because of the self-sufficient character of the family-based economy, particularly in the case of the Indian population.

'When I took office', explained Hipólito Unanue, Peru's first minister of finance:

the treasury was empty. Agricultural lands within thirty leagues of the capital were but one vast expanse of desolation. The mines were occupied by the enemy. Callao was in enemy hands, hindering all trade. The economic resources of the people had been drained as a result of the many taxes, and they had been reduced to famine because of the total siege which they had suffered. One saw nothing but misery and desolation wherever one looked.

Three years later, in 1825, the minister declared:

During the whole time that our nation struggled, with varying degrees of success, for its independence, I was called three times to serve as Minister of Finance. On the first two occasions there were still one or two ruins left with which to repair the edifice. But now even those ruins have disappeared.[7]

Yet, in addition to the servicing of a foreign debt of 26 million pesos, the new Peruvian state had to collect some 5 million pesos every year in order to finance current expenditure, mainly the cost of the civil bureaucracy and, above all, the military. (Before 1845 Peru had no proper budget, and the exact breakdown of public expenditure is unknown. But the *memorias* of Morales y Ugalde (1827) and José María de Pando (1831) provide evidence of the considerable burden of military expenditure. In 1827 it amounted to 48 per cent of total expenditure; and in 1831 its share had risen to 59 per cent.)[8] From time to time the government resorted to cuts

---

[7] Hipólito Unanue, *Obras científicas y literarias* (Barcelona, 1914), II, 361, 370.
[8] Emilio Romero, *Historia económica del Perú* (Buenos Aires, 1949), 318; Emilio Dancuart (ed.), *Anales de la hacienda del Perú, leyes, decretos, reglamentos y resoluciones, aranceles, presupuestos, cuentas y contratos que constituyen la legislación e historia fiscal de la República* (Lima, 1902–26), II, 154–71 (henceforth cited as *Anales*).

in the bureaucracy together with the freezing of salaries. On other occasions, temporary relief was found by resorting to voluntary or forced loans from foreign and local traders, or quite simply by confiscating various local resources. In the medium term, however, it was the revenue derived from Indian tribute, from customs and from foreign loans, which enabled the government to finance its expenditure.

On 27 August 1821, San Martín, after declaring the Indians Peruvian citizens, proceeded to the abolition of the colonial tribute. However, the insolvent Peruvian state could not afford such generosity for very long. The tribute was re-established on 11 August 1826 out of the need to sustain the finances of the Republic by taxing the Indian population, and as a result of the social policy adopted early on by the Peruvian government. 'The experience of centuries has shown that the Indian tax was established with prudence and foresight', the minister of finance, José María de Pando, declared in 1830, 'and as it is such a powerful factor in the mentality of these people, firmly rooted in custom, any new departure would be dangerous.'[9] As a consequence, the old colonial tribute once again became one of the main contributors to the exchequer and remained so until its final abolition by Ramón Castilla in 1854. As a concession to the new liberal era, however, it became known as the Indian 'contribution'.

In order to collect this 'contribution', it became necessary to divide the Indian population into three fiscal categories: (a) native Indians with access to land; (b) non-native Indians (*forasteros*) with access to lesser quantities of land; and (c) landless Indians. The first category paid between five and nine pesos per year, while the two latter paid a tax which fluctuated between 2.5 and 5 pesos per year. Finally, in addition to the Indian contribution, there was until its abolition in 1840 that of the *castas*, that is to say, taxes paid by the non-Indian sectors of society and which amounted to 5 pesos and 4 per cent of the net product of their properties. The global amount originating from the Indian contribution in 1830 came to 1,039,331 pesos, while that from the *castas* totalled 431,787 pesos.[10] In view of the political and administrative instability of Peru in this period it is no surprise to find a sizeable difference between the estimated revenue from the contribution and the amount actually collected. Nevertheless, there can be no doubt that it had a considerable impact on fiscal revenue. Whereas, for example, in 1829, according to Pando's estimates, out of revenues totalling 7,962,720 pesos, 945,468

9 *Anales*, II, 154–71.   10 *Anales*, II, 49–50.

pesos originated from the contribution, between 1839 and 1845 the Indian contribution produced on average 1,757,296 pesos per year, while total revenues entering the treasury averaged 4,500,000 pesos. On the other hand, the Indian contribution produced only 830,826 pesos in 1846.[11]

The imposition of the Indian tribute had been linked historically to the ownership of land, and it was this connection which was gradually, though erratically, eroded after Independence. The liberal ideology of the Independence period was, in effect, opposed to the maintenance of institutions which might hinder the unrestricted circulation of goods and people in the market. It was because of this that the very existence of the Indian community was threatened by Bolívar's decree of 8 April 1824, which declared that the Indians had the right of ownership over their lands, and by extension, the right to sell the lands to third parties. The implicit purpose of such a decision was to create a class of prosperous independent land holders. The results, however, were different. The authorities soon began to appreciate that this measure posed a serious threat to the Indian *comunidades* and delayed its application until 1850. Nevertheless, an irreparable breach had been made in the barrier which protected the Indian community from the hacienda, and thus prepared the way for the expansion of the great landed estates once new forces began to dynamize the rural economy as a whole.

As far as customs tariffs were concerned Peruvian governments were obliged to reconcile varying interests. First, there was pressure from British interests for free trade. On the other hand, there was pressure from the weak native producers, who demanded protectionist policies and measures to halt the flood of British textiles which was threatening to ruin them. Finally, there were the financial needs of the government itself, for which customs revenue represented an important source of income. Once again, the extreme political vulnerability of the Peruvian government did not allow it to follow a consistent course in this matter. Its ambivalence is visible in the many sets of regulations – six between 1821 and 1836 – governing trade.

It is clear that until 1833 the intentions of the Peruvian government were protectionist. The provisional law of 1821 imposed a duty of 40 per cent, and the law of 1826 a duty of 80 per cent on imported foreign textiles. The third law (June 1828), known as 'the law of prohibitions', prohibited the importation of goods prejudicial to native production for

[11] *Anales*, III, 54–5; IV, 36–7.

a period of ten months, although there is evidence that this prohibition could not be enforced in practice. Neither the intentions of an unstable government, nor the desires of native producers who were politically and economically weak, could have any effect in the face of the combined pressure of British interests and the government's own financial needs. With the law of 1833, the Peruvian government began to adopt a more liberal tariff policy; it reduced the tax on textile imports to 45 per cent. This tendency towards liberalization continued with the law of 1836, passed during the Peru–Bolivian Confederation (1836–9), which further reduced the tax on imported textiles to a mere 20 per cent.

This represented a victory for British merchants trading with Peru whose influence is illustrated by the fact that the 1836 legislation did no more than sanction proposals formulated by the British trading community.[12] Equally significant, a Treaty of Friendship, Commerce and Navigation between Great Britain and Peru was signed the following year. For the Peruvian government, the law of 1836 also expressed the search for direct links with Europe, which was part of its desire to undermine the hegemony of the port of Valparaíso. The substantial reduction in customs dues and the various administrative measures taken by President Santa Cruz, notably the establishment of Arica, Cobija, Callao and Paita as free ports and the imposition of supplementary dues on goods which had passed through other ports on the Pacific coast before arriving at Callao, were all aimed to this end.[13]

The defeat of Santa Cruz in 1839 and the collapse of the Confederation were regarded as a heavy blow to the commercial interests of Europe and the United States,[14] but later trading regulations maintained the tariffs established in 1836. At the same time, the process which accelerated British commercial expansion through the massive importation of cheap textiles, and turned customs revenue into one of the main supports of public spending, ended by completely wrecking native production.

With the severing of Peru's colonial links, British investors shared the enthusiasm of manufacturers and traders; they saw a chance of investing their capital in the exploitation of Peru's legendary deposits of precious metals. In the years immediately after Independence, five companies were created for this specific purpose: The Chilean and Peruvian Association; Potosí, La Paz and Peruvian Mining Association; Pasco Peruvian

[12] William Mathew, 'The imperialism of free trade, Peru 1820–1870', *Economic History Review*, 2nd ser., 21 (1968), 566.

[13] Jorge Basadre, *Historia de la República del Perú* (5th edn, Lima, 1962–4), II, 566.

[14] Public Record Office, London, Foreign Office 61/93, Cope to Wilson, 12 October 1842.

Mining Company; Peruvian Trading and Mining Company; and the Anglo-Peruvian Mining Association. The first four had capital assets amounting to £1 million and the last one had £600,000.[15] However, illusions were very soon dispelled, and the mobilization of this capital even provoked one of the first crises in British financial capitalism in the nineteenth century. There were various reasons for this disaster, although the main one was the absence of any mechanism which might permit the mobilization of the native labour force to the mining centres. The British would have to wait until 1890 and the founding of the Peruvian Corporation for a renewed attempt at direct capital investment.

Until the war with Chile in 1879 the export of capital was normally carried out in the form of long term loans to the Peruvian government. The first loan was negotiated by San Martín in 1822. His special envoys, Juan García del Río and General Diego de Paroissien, obtained a loan of £1,200,000 from Thomas Kinder. The interest was fixed at 6 per cent, commission at 2 per cent, the cost of the bonds at 75 per cent and the repayment period at 30 years. The guarantee for this loan was to be made up of revenue from customs tariffs and silver production. Two years later, Bolívar commissioned Juan Parish to draw a new loan of £616,000 at an interest rate of 6 per cent and a cost fixed at 78 per cent. Out of this total, the sum in effect received by Peru amounted to only £200,385,[16] although she remained committed to pay back the nominal loan in full. These loans were primarily used up on maintaining the foreign army which collaborated in the Independence campaign. The stagnation of the Peruvian economy, however, did not allow the government to service the foreign debt until 1825.

Foreign sources soon dried up and the Peruvian government came to depend on internal loans for financing its expenditure not covered by the Indian contribution and customs revenue. In 1845, the internal debt was estimated at 6,846,344 pesos,[17] but included bonds contracted by the Spanish government from wealthy Lima merchants and recognized by the new regime.

The social structure of Peru in the period immediately after independence reflected the segmentation of the Peruvian economy. Rather than a national society, it is more correct to talk of regional societies, centred on the hacienda, which was the basic unit of production, with a limited

[15] Henry English, *A general guide to the companies formed for working foreign mines* (London, 1825), 8–51.
[16] *Anales*, I, 50.   [17] *Anales*, IV, 46.

capacity to sustain the population of the area. Politically, the *hacendado*, either directly or else in alliance with some local caudillo, exercised undisputed political power in each region, developing a whole system of typically client relationships in order to ensure the loyalty of his underlings. Despite their local power, landowners nevertheless lacked sufficient strength to generate and consolidate a system of political hegemony at the national level. The government in Lima was able to impose authority by lending its support to, or entering into alliance with, the political leaders of each region, without necessarily representing their interests. Until the presidency of Manuel Pardo in 1872, strictly speaking the source of each caudillo-president's power lay in the military capability of his followers. Here too, the problem was that these followers were numerous and divided through ties of personal loyalty to each military caudillo. As no president had the ability to establish general obedience, or to create a consensus which might permit a relatively stable government, the result was an acute and never ending rivalry for power in order to plunder the resources of the state.

After Simón Bolívar left Peru in September 1826 the country was plunged into a period of political confusion and anarchy. Despite the attempts made by conservative and liberal elements within the Peruvian aristocracy to give an institutional and political structure to the new nation, reflected in the passage of six constitutions before 1836, their efforts did not succeed in gathering enough social support, and the sources of political power remained firmly in the hands of regional caudillos. Group interests, regionalism and personal allegiance became key factors in power politics and, in that context, men of action supported by an armed following dominated the country's government for a decade. Prior to the setting up of the Peru–Bolivian Confederation in 1836, Peru had eight presidents over a period of ten years, but only one of them, the authoritarian and ruthless General Agustín Gamarra, managed to complete a full four-year term of office. However, after his departure, and for a period of almost two years, conspiracies and uprisings allowed several military leaders to take over the presidency only to be deposed within a matter of weeks by violent means. Early in 1835, a young commander of the Callao garrison, Felipe Salaverry, launched his own bid for power, which turned out to be successful. It seemed that, through Salaverry's heavy-handed rule, some degree of political stability was within reach, but exactly a year after he had seized power he was shot dead by a firing squad during a rebellion. The next challenger for power in Peru was General Andrés Santa Cruz, president of Bolivia (1829–39), an able and skilful politician, who, through alliances with some southern Peruvian caudillos, not only secured his control over most of Peru, but in October 1836 proclaimed the Peru–Bolivian Confederation.

Santa Cruz's scheme had some appeal within Peru. The southern interests, who had historic commercial links with Bolivia and resented Lima's dominance over the country, did in fact welcome the Confederation and supported it actively. However, both in Lima and La Paz it encountered firm opposition. The elite of the former strongly resented the partition of their country, as southern Peru became a separate state within the Confederation. For their part, Bolivians strongly disapproved of Santa Cruz's choice of Lima as the seat of the government of the Confederation. But the main threat to the Confederation came from abroad, especially from Chile, although Rosas, the Argentine dictator, also made his dislike evident. The Chilean government, whose leadership viewed the Confederation as a major threat to its independence and military and commercial hegemony on the Pacific, declared war in December 1836, to be followed by the Argentine government in May 1837. After an unsuccessful invasion in 1837, the Chileans made a second attempt in July 1838, this time with the active support and participation of a large contingent of Peruvian exiles, amongst whom the most prominent were Generals Agustín Gamarra and Ramón Castilla. In Peru itself a good section of the Lima elite, who had never been able to accept the loss of their country's independence, gave the expeditionary force active support. Amongst them, the liberals, who had always opposed Santa Cruz's political project and tough rule, and the followers of the ill-fated Salaverry, enthusiastically echoed the proclamation made by Gamarra and Castilla in which they announced their intention of restoring Peru's autonomy. In January 1839 the army of Santa Cruz was crushed at the battle of Yungay and the Confederation collapsed.

After the Chilean forces left Peru in October 1839, Gamarra became president once again and introduced a conservative constitution. However, soon the new president embarked on an invasion of Bolivia, where he was defeated and killed at Ingavi in November 1841. Once more Peru plunged into political chaos. As Bolivian troops invaded from the south, the Ecuadorians made clear their intention of doing the same from the north. The forces dispatched to fight the invaders ignored the authority of the Lima government and a new civil war broke out. Three generals became supreme rulers of Peru after Gamarra's constitutional successor was overthrown, and political turmoil was only brought to an end when in July 1844 Ramón Castilla defeated General Vivanco, thus becoming the country's new strong man. Castilla was to dominate Peru's political and institutional life until his death in 1868.

From the early 1840s to the beginning of the war with Chile in 1879 the economic and political evolution of Peru was dependent in one way or another on the exploitation of guano deposits on the coastal islands. The absence of rain along the Peruvian coastline meant that the guano which accumulated on the islands did not lose its chemical content. Archaeological evidence and the chronicles of José de Acosta, Pedro Cieza de León and Agustín de Zárate point to the use of guano in pre-Columbian agriculture. Equally, during the colonial period, agriculture on the coastal belt continued to make use of guano in order to increase the fertility of the soil. However, at no time did guano enter, at least to any significant degree, the colonial export trade. It was the changes in English agriculture during the nineteenth century which gave a fresh impulse to guano extraction. The growing use of fertilizers was one of the innovations in English farming techniques which was designed to increase productivity and meet the demands of industrial Britain. The use of Peruvian fertilizer, limited at first, became increasingly important until recession in Britain and Europe after 1873, the exhaustion of the best guano deposits, competition from synthetic fertilizers, and finally the capture of the deposits by the Chilean army during the War of the Pacific brought an end to the Peruvian guano boom.

Besides guano, Peru exported during this period copper, alpaca and sheep wool, cotton, sugar and nitrates as well as small quantities of tin, cacao, coffee and quinine bark. The export of precious metals, especially silver, is not recorded in the trade figures of the countries for which estimates of Peru's foreign trade are based – Britain, France, the U.S. and Chile. Silver production, however, of which the Cerro de Pasco mine accounted for more than half, remained stable at between 300,000 and half a million marks per annum throughout the period 1840–79.[18] Guano nevertheless enjoyed an absolute supremacy within Peru's export trade and was largely responsible for an average annual growth rate of exports of 4.5 per cent between 1840 and 1852, and 5.2 per cent between 1852 and 1878.[19]

[18] Hunt, *Price and quantum estimates*, 57–8.   [19] *Ibid.*, 67.

Estimates regarding the volume of guano exported and the income from its sale are fairly unreliable given the absence of coherent records of accounts, and the disorganized character of public administration. After growing steadily to almost 100,000 tons in 1849 it has been estimated that guano exports fluctuated during the period 1850 to 1878 from a little under 200,000 tons to 700,00 tons per annum.[20] J. M. Rodríguez, one of the compilers of the *Anales de la Hacienda Pública*, estimates that during the whole period, some 10,804,033 tons of guano were exported.[21] If £10 per ton is taken as an average price, then gross earnings from the sale of guano amount to something approaching £100 million. Moreover it is important to note that guano was never the private property of companies or families, whether foreign or native; from the beginning ownership was exercised by the Peruvian state. Peru therefore possessed the capital necessary to begin to rebuild her economy, diversify production and generate a more stable rate of growth. Nevertheless, although guano had an impact on certain sectors of the economy at certain times, its overall impact was negative.

Any analysis of the fluctuations in the value of returns from guano has to consider workers, local traders and the state. With regard to the former, namely the workers, their part in calculations concerning returned value is virtually irrelevant. Available estimates allow for a total of one thousand workers on the guano islands, whose maintenance represented only about 4 per cent of total costs. Between 1841 and 1849, when consignee contracts were monopolized by foreign merchant houses, notably Antony Gibbs and Sons, and when the position of the state was very weak in its ability to negotiate, the government took some 33 per cent of returned value. In subsequent contracts, this share rose to some 65 per cent. When competition by local traders in the marketing of guano became more significant, the income retained by the government and the local traders together fluctuated between 60 and 70 per cent of eventual sales. When, in 1869, Auguste Dreyfus (a French merchant with the support of the Société Générale in Paris) finally assumed monopoly control of the guano trade, the participation of the state in the income became even greater. To sum up, during the entire period 1840–80 the Peruvian government collected about 60 per cent of the income from guano, or between 381 and 432 million pesos, to which should be added

[20] *Ibid.*, 38–9, 43–6.
[21] J.M. Rodríguez, *Estudios económicos y financieros y ojeada sobre la Hacienda Pública del Perú y la necesidad de su reforma* (Lima, 1895), 317–19.

between 60 and 80 million pesos received by Peruvian consignees which represented a further 5–10 per cent of the income from guano. In 1846–7 income from guano accounted for approximately 5 per cent of all state revenue; in 1869 and 1875 this figure had risen to 80 per cent. However, while the resources generated by guano permitted a five-fold expansion in income between 1847 and 1872–3, expenditure increased eight times between these dates. In order to answer the question why income from guano did not have a positive effect on economic development in Peru it is important to see how revenue was spent during the guano era. More than half the income from guano was used to expand the civilian bureaucracy (29 per cent) and the military (24.5 per cent). Guano revenue was also used to expand the railway network (20 per cent), to transfer payments to foreigners and to nationals (8 per cent and 11.5 per cent) and to reduce the tax burden on the poor (7.0 per cent).[22]

One of the results of the increasing part played by guano in state revenue was the abolition of the Indian contribution during the government of Ramón Castilla. In 1854, Castilla, wishing to widen his political base, cancelled the levy to which the Indian population was subject. For the Peruvian economy as a whole, however, the abolition of the tribute led to a reduction in surplus marketable agricultural produce, which in turn led to price increases. For the majority of Indian families, the sale of this surplus was closely linked to the tribute, for only in this way were they able to find the money to bear this tax burden. Once the tribute had disappeared, there was no sense in growing and selling surplus produce, and peasant families returned to a basically self-sufficient economy. (Furthermore, with the abolition of the tribute the landowners increasingly sought to appropriate the land belonging to the Indians, as a way of maintaining access to Indian labour and control over its availability, and the state no longer had an incentive to protect the Indian community from the encroachment of the hacienda.)

Another use to which revenue from guano was put was the abolition of slavery. There were 25,505 slaves in Peru in 1854, 1.3 per cent of the total population.[23] Their manumission was carried out by means of a payment to slave-owners of 300 pesos for each freed slave. The cost of this operation involved the transfer of 7,651,500 pesos from the govern-

---

[22] Shane Hunt, *Growth and guano in nineteenth century Peru* (Princeton, Woodrow Wilson School, 1973), 64, 84, 69, 72–5, 80.

[23] Nils Jacobsen, *The development of Peru's slave population and its significance for coastal agriculture* (Berkeley, unpublished MSS. n.d.), 82.

ment to the slave-owners. The manumission of the slaves placed a considerable amount of capital in the hands of the landowners, and in some cases, as we shall see, this was used to finance the development of agriculture along the coastal belt. However, this same process of development, given the apparent impossibility of mobilizing Indian peasants from the highlands, meant that it became necessary to import vast numbers of Chinese coolies, under a system of disguised slavery, to replace the old slave labour force. Chinese immigration at the port of Callao between 1850 and 1874 amounted to 87,952; more than a quarter of that number, 25,303, arrived during the two years 1871–2.[24]

Through public expenditure guano increased internal demand and generated effects which were felt right through the Peruvian economy.[25] It has been estimated that wages increased in real terms at a rate of about 3 per cent per year during the guano period.[26] Despite these conditions, however, the structure of production did not have the capacity to respond to the incentive of demand. This failure has been attributed to the absence of an entrepreneurial class as a result of the destruction of the artisan sector, the increase in domestic costs and prices produced by guano, the choice of unfortunate projects for capital investment financed by guano and the failure of traditional institutions to create the necessary framework for strengthening production. Rather than stimulating local production, increased demand contributed to a marked increase in imports. The railways (whose construction was also financed by guano) were not completed until the end of the nineteenth century.

Another of the processes associated with the exploitation of guano was the series of loans contracted by the Peruvian government. These loans were of two types. Firstly, there were those contracted with guano traders, which were essentially mere advances to be repaid, with interest, through revenue from the sale of guano. The others were more significant, and involved a policy pursued by the Peruvian government between 1849 and 1872 of securing foreign loans guaranteed by guano sales. This policy, within reasonable limits, permitted the mobilization of foreign capital which was used to finance economic growth. However, when the servicing of the debt weakens or destroys the capacity for

[24] H. B. H. Martinet, *L'Agriculture au Pérou* (Lima, 1876), 32.
[25] Hunt, *Growth and guano, passim;* cf. Jonathan Levin, *The export economies: their pattern of development in historical perspective* (Cambridge, Mass., 1959) who explained the failure of guano to generate development in terms of the export of guano revenue in the form of profits.
[26] Hunt, *Growth and guano*, 88.

domestic capital accumulation, it can become an obstacle to growth. The Peruvian experience with its foreign debt had, in fact, disastrous consequences. It was not just a case of poor choice of financially viable projects by the government, but of a clear process of financial paralysis within the Peruvian state which led, in 1890, to the transfer of some of the country's productive resources to the control and ownership of the British creditors of Peru's foreign debt.

In 1822 and 1824, as we have seen, Peru had drawn two loans in London to the value of £1,816,000. As a result of its insolvency, it ceased paying the service on both debts two years later. In 1848, accumulated interest amounted to £2,564,532, that is to say, the total amount of the debt was now £4,380,530. When guano became Peru's main source of revenue, pressure from British bondholders and financial speculators associated with them increased in order that the service of the debt should be renewed. A final agreement was reached on 4 January 1849.[27] Repayment of the consolidated debt was to begin in 1856, for which Antony Gibbs was to deposit half of the revenue from guano sales in the Bank of England. By re-establishing the financial credibility of the Peruvian government, this operation heralded a policy of repeated foreign loans. The success of each successive loan meant the withdrawal of the bonds corresponding to the previous loan, for the exchange of which a large part of the requested loans was absorbed. In a word, they were loans to convert the debt, that is to say, to pay off previous loans.

From 1869, the railway construction programme, as we shall see, accentuated the demands of the Peruvian government for new and larger loans. Finally, in 1872 it tried to float a loan of £36.8 million, £21.8 million of which was earmarked for the conversion of the loans contracted in 1865, 1866 and 1870.

The loan of 1872 was a complete disaster. Public stock did not exceed £230,000.[28] The successive bankruptcies of Paraguay, Bolivia, and Uruguay, which were the most assiduous clients on the London market, eroded the confidence of the London lenders in the ability of Latin American countries to remain solvent, and they began to refuse fresh requests for loans. As of 1872, therefore, Peru had a foreign debt of around £35 million which carried an annual amortization charge of £2.5 million. Given the precarious nature of government finances, it was impossible to service such a large debt and, in 1876, Peru defaulted for a second time.

[27] *Parliamentary Papers* (London, 1854) LXIX, 124–6.   [28] *Anales*, IX, 35–6.

In sum, this policy of contracting huge foreign loans did nothing to finance the internal growth of the economy, but rather accustomed the state to become increasingly dependent on foreign credit, and this could only produce disastrous results when a crisis, such as that of 1872, closed off this source of foreign capital. Thus, the ground was being gradually prepared for the final collapse.

We have demonstrated the effects on the growth of internal demand which guano was able to generate through public expenditure. We have also shown the reasons why the system of production was unable to respond to this demand. A totally different picture was presented when we turn to those sectors of the economy oriented towards the overseas market, in particular to agriculture on the central and northern coastal belt. From the 1860s, the haciendas, responding to favourable international circumstances, began their process of recovery and expansion through the production of cotton and sugar. Sugar production grew at an annual rate of 28 per cent from 1862 and by 1879 sugar accounted for 32 per cent of total exports. It was produced primarily in an area situated between Trujillo and Chiclayo. In 1877 this region produced 58 per cent of sugar exports and 68 per cent a year later. The expansion of cotton production was linked to the cotton crisis in the United States. It, too, was regionally concentrated: in 1877 14 per cent of cotton exports were shipped from Piura, 38 per cent from the Department of Lima, and 42 per cent from Pisco-Ica.[29]

The expansion of export-oriented agriculture was the result of the intensive exploitation of coolie labour and a significant injection of capital. The export of cotton, for example, increased from 291 tons in 1860 to 3,609 tons in 1879, and in the same period sugar exports increased from 610 tons to 83,497 tons.[30] This would not have been possible but for the links, direct or indirect, with the benefits derived from guano. In the first place, the consolidation of the internal debt (see below) released some 50 per cent of the capital paid by the state as repayment to its internal creditors for investment in agriculture. The abolition of slavery also enabled fixed assets (the slaves) to be converted into liquid capital (the indemnity).[31] To these mechanisms one should add the credit afforded to the landowning class by the commercial and banking sectors,

[29] Hunt, *Growth and guano*, 55–6.   [30] Hunt, *Price and quauntum estimates*, 38–9, 43–6.
[31] Pablo Macera, 'Las plantaciones azucareras andinas, 1821–1875'. *Trabajos de Historia* (Lima, 1977),

which, in turn, owed their existence to the surplus capital generated by guano. The best example of this link between the surplus from guano and agrarian capital is the case of the Lurifico hacienda in the Jiquetepeque Valley, on the northern coast of Peru.[32] However, the development of export agriculture on the coast was particularly precarious, not only because of its almost total dependence on the fluctuations of the international market, but also because of its subordination to finance capital. It has been shown that in 1875 the total debts of the sugar haciendas amounted to 30 million soles, of which 17,500,000 were owed to banking institutions.[33]

In contrast to the coast, highland agriculture was relatively little affected by the guano boom, although the increased demand for foodstuffs in Lima (as well as the mining area) did contribute in some way to the expansion of cattle raising in the Central Sierra.[34] Guano also had little impact on the industrial development of Peru. Artisan industry, as we have seen, was severely hit by the massive influx of European goods. Indeed, the streets of Lima witnessed several violent demonstrations, such as those in 1858, by artisan producers.[35] The industries which existed were concentrated mainly in Lima, and concentrated mainly on the production of beer, pasta, biscuits, chocolates, butter and other processed foodstuffs. Most factory owners were immigrants whose capital no doubt came from savings and loans. In the Sierra, the most important industrial enterprise was the textile factory established in 1859 on the Lucre hacienda in the province of Quispicanchis, where the labour force was converted from serfs into wage earners.

At the beginning of the 1870s the age of guano was coming to an end. It left Peru with a huge external debt amounting to £35 million, the servicing of which required an annual repayment of about £2.5 million. Guano had stimulated internal demand, and also raised the real wages of the urban population, while at the same time galvanizing the haciendas of the central and northern coasts into a new phase of expansion. Nevertheless, and this is the crucial point, the internal market failed to develop and expand, and local production for this market failed to increase to any real degree. If it is necessary to refer to the guano period as a period of lost opportunity, it is precisely because of the inability of the military which

[32] Manuel Burga, *De la encomienda a la hacienda capitalista* (Lima, 1976), 174–8.
[33] Hunt, *Growth and guano*, 58.
[34] Nelson Manrique, *El desarrollo del mercado interno en la sierra central* (Lima, Universidad Agraria, mimeo, 1978), 68–9.   [35] Jorge Basadre, *Historia del Perú*, III, 1291.

exercised political power throughout the period and the new dominant class which emerged during the guano age to effect an alternative programme of development, based not only on the exploitation of the country's natural wealth, but also on the eradication of the colonial character of the Peruvian economy and the establishment of the necessary institutional bases to enable the country to respond adequately to the opportunities created by the export of guano.

At the time of independence in 1821, there was no ruling class in Peru with the necessary authority and legitimacy to exercise political control over the fledgling state. It was this political vacuum which caused the military to assume control. Of all the military leaders who held power, Ramón Castilla, a *mestizo*, was the most forceful and the one who possessed the greatest political and administrative skills. Between 1844 and 1868 he held a number of senior government posts, including finance, and was twice president. In matters of practical politics, his rule reflected a highly pragmatic approach, and he was always prepared to compromise. In a country so deeply divided by civil strife, Castilla, although firm in repressing uprisings, tolerated a certain degree of criticism towards his regime, allowed Congress to meet regularly and without interference and even went as far as to appoint men of diverse political persuasions to key posts. He also devoted time and effort to the normalization of the country's finances. But law and order were his main priorities and perhaps his most remarkable achievement was his success in giving Peru its first experience of stable political rule between 1845 and 1851. Once his first term as president was over, Castilla was replaced by General José Rufino Echenique, who through lack of political and administrative experience did much to undo Castilla's political work of stabilization. It was not long before the liberals felt compelled to stage another revolution, which came in early 1854, with Castilla as its leader. In a bitter confrontation, the revolutionary forces won a considerable degree of popular support and succeeded in ousting Echenique. In July 1854 Castilla began his second term as president, which lasted until 1862. Undoubtedly the best known and more important measures taken during this administration were the already mentioned ending of the Indian tribute and the abolition of slavery, which gave Castilla the title of 'Liberator' and increased his popularity. Politically, his second term of office began with a rather heated debate about the necessity of a new constitution. The initial stages of debate were won by the liberals, who secured the passing of the 1856 charter, which reduced the powers of the executive in favour of the legislature. Castilla gave only a mild and qualified support to the new constitution, but took a moderate course of action until 1858 when he dissolved Congress and organized the election of a more conservative constituent assembly. In 1860 Peru was given yet another constitution – one which better reflected Castilla's own political convictions and reinstated the presidency as the dominant political power. The texts of these two constitutions, like the famous debate on the nature of the state between the conservative Bartolomé Herrera and the liberal Pedro Gálvez which preceded them (1846–51), are notable for their total lack of relevance to the economic and social realities of mid-nineteenth century Peru and provide interesting reading only insofar as they illustrate an enormous gap which existed between the educated elite and the nation as a whole.

In 1862 General Miguel San Román succeeded Castilla as president, but died of natural causes after a brief period in office. His successor, Vice-president General Juan Antonio Pezet, had to face the difficult years of conflict with Spain over its claim to the Chincha islands (1864–6). His conciliatory policy towards the Spanish demands was considered humiliating and caused anger and resentment within the elite and the military establishment. Finally, Colonel Mariano Ignacio Prado launched an armed revolt against the president, who was deposed in November 1865. Prado took over the presidency and led the Peruvian armed forces to a convincing military victory over the Spaniards. But he had still to consolidate his position in order to remain as chief of state, and his decision to reinstate the 1856 constitution, with liberal support, only served to provoke yet another civil war, with Castilla leading those who demanded the restoration of the constitution of 1860. The seventy year old 'Liberator' died of ill-health in the early stages of the conflict, but his second in command, General Pedro Diez Canseco, took over the leadership of the movement which achieved victory early in 1868. The victorious conservative forces reinstated the 1860 constitution, and in July appointed Colonel José Balta as president of the Republic. Balta's term of office was characterized by inefficiency and corruption, and it was during his four-year rule (1868–72) that the anti-military feeling within the Peruvian elite reached its climax with the creation of the Partido Civil and the capture of the presidency by one of its leaders, Manuel Pardo, in 1872.

When guano became the Peruvian government's most important

source of revenue, not only did external creditors redouble their efforts to obtain repayment for their loans, but internal creditors also began to struggle for the recognition of their rights. At the end of Castilla's first term in office, in 1851, the consolidated internal debt already amounted to 4,879,608 pesos.[36] According to Castilla himself, the total amount of the debt could not be more than six or seven million. However, under the government of Echenique, the recognized debt totalled 23,211,400 pesos (approximately £5 million).[37] This great increase in the recognized debt was made possible through the venality and corruption of the Peruvian bureaucracy. It was precisely this abuse which provided one of the excuses for Castilla's rebellion in 1854. The commission of inquiry set up in the following year concluded that more than 12 million pesos in consolidated debt bonds in the hands of domestic creditors – merchants and landowners – were fraudulent.[38]

In 1850 the Peruvian government had signed a ten-year contract with a group of local traders for the sale of guano to Spain, France, China, the Antilles and the U.S. These traders created the Sociedad Consignataria del Guano and set about obtaining capital through the issue of shares. The result, however, was negative. A year later they were forced to restrict their activity to the United States market alone and to limit the duration of their contracts to only five years.[39] In 1860 and 1862, however, with the capital which had been paid to them as consolidation of the internal debt, they were able to replace Antony Gibbs as consignors of guano to Britain, the most important of the European markets. The Compañía Nacional Consignataria included the most powerful Lima traders, many of them beneficiaries of the process of consolidation, who were now presented with the opportunity to increase their income not only by selling guano but also by charging heavy interest on the loans made to the Peruvian government. In this way, both speculative and commercial capital gave each other mutual sustenance.

The development of the trade in guano also necessitated institutions which might facilitate the rapid mobilization of credit. Here, too, the constitution of the first directives and, above all, the immediate subscription of shares issued, would not have been possible without the control, by local capitalists, of a large part of the income produced by guano sales. In this way, a new process of fusion occurred between commercial and

---

[36] *Anales*, IV, 5.
[37] José Echenique, *Memorias para la historia del Perú (1808–1878)* (Lima, 1952), II, 199.
[38] *Anales*, V, 46.
[39] *Anales*, V, 27–8.

financial capital. In September 1862, for example, the Banco de la Providencia was organized with capital assets of 500,000 pesos. The Banco de Perú was created in May 1863 with capital assets of 10 million pesos. It was this bank which was the most closely linked to the Compañía Nacional del Guano, for its shareholders also belonged to the Guano company. Similarly, the Banco de Lima, founded in March 1869 with capital assets of 3.2 million soles, included among its shareholders some of the period's more eminent men of fortune. Finally, the Banco de Crédito Hipotecario, specialising in the issue of mortgages and long-term credit on rural and urban property, was created in 1866 with an initial capital of 1.5 million pesos.[40]

When cotton and sugar production began to expand in the 1860s, capital from guano and from the banks found new opportunities for investment in the agrarian sector. In this way, a powerful, closely linked oligarchy became firmly established. As has been seen, its wealth was derived indiscriminately from finance, trade, and land. Consequently, there were no great internal rifts within this small circle of powerful individuals, because the capital which they controlled was committed to those sectors whose prosperity depended entirely on the excellent conditions which the international market offered.

The emergence of this oligarchy of merchants, financiers and land-owners soon manifested itself in the organization of Peru's first modern political party. The creation of the Partido Civil in 1871 gave them a vehicle through which to voice their political interests, and, as a consequence of their own power and influence, to elevate Manuel Pardo to the presidency in 1872. *Civilista* ideology was expressed through opposition to government by the military, which had controlled the country virtually without interruption since 1821, and the economic orientation of the state, in particular the use made of the resources which guano had created. The basic tenets of *civilista* ideology had begun to be expressed between 1859 and 1863 in the *Revista de Lima* and had even begun to be applied before the advent of a civilian administration. It was no coincidence that one of the main contributors to the publication was Manuel Pardo. Pardo and his friends on the *Revista de Lima* understood quite clearly that Peru's future could not continue for much longer to be linked to guano, a resource which, apart from the danger of its drying up, was likely to suffer the effects of competition from other fertilizers. Moreover, they were aware of the way in which income from guano was being

---

[40] Carlos Camprubí, *Historia de los Bancos del Perú* (Lima, 1957), I, 39–40, 61–4, 85.

squandered and used unproductively. In Pardo's opinion, it was for this reason that the economic policy of the government had to be reoriented through the channelling of the few resources still generated by guano towards the completion of the national rail network. The railways would be instrumental in fostering national production by expanding markets and bringing them closer together, and by linking the Peruvian economy more efficiently to the international market. To convert guano into railways, and attract foreign capital for any additional expense, this was the main prop of the thesis presented by Pardo and the *Revista*.

What is worth underlining here is that the equation by which railways would foster production was not envisaged in terms of fostering production for the internal market. The main railways planned by Balta, and partially built during his administration, linked coastal ports with centres for raw materials. The northern railway served cotton and sugar; the central railway, silver and copper; the southern railway, wool. Consequently, once again, it was a case of using the railways to sweep away the obstacles which hindered the relative wealth of the country from being more efficiently exploited and integrated into the international market. As far as the landowners were concerned, rugged terrain and an uncompetitive system of transport based on muleteers impeded them from taking advantage of and profiting from the increasing opportunities presented by the international market. On the other hand, the completion of the rail network would also provide access to markets in the interior for monopolistic traders to place their goods at less cost. In either case, however, the programme of *civilista* politicians did not imply any real change in the traditional model of growth adopted by the Peruvian economy. It was purely and simply a case of modernizing the system of transport in order to link the Peruvian economy more efficiently to the international market. The crucial question, in this context, is whether they could have acted differently. An alternative policy would have meant removing the props responsible for the colonial character of the Peruvian economy and society, abolishing the relations of production in force on the great estates of the coastal and highland regions, doing away with the self-sufficient character of the peasant economies in order to create the basis of a healthy internal market which might, in turn, provide internal stimulus for the growth of the country's productive sectors. However, this type of growth suggested something more than railway construction. It implied the political alteration of a system and this was too great a challenge for a group which, in spite of everything, lacked both the strength to carry it out and the conviction of its need.

When Manuel Pardo took office on 2 August 1872, after the populace of Lima had foiled an attempt by the military to remain in power, he found that the state was bankrupt. The policy of railway construction, as we have seen, had helped to increase the external debt to £35 million, the amortization of which amounted to about £2.5 million, a sum equal to the entire budget. Furthermore, the servicing of the 1870 and 1872 loans absorbed *in toto* the monthly payments which Dreyfus was committed to remit to the state by virtue of the contract of 1869, and this generated a budgetary deficit of 8.5 million soles. Unlike previous decades, the situation on the London money market prevented the Peruvian government from pursuing its previous policy of raising loans, and these circumstances were made all the worse when, in 1874, Dreyfus announced that services on previous securities would only be attended to until the end of 1875. Desperate attempts by the Peruvian government to find a replacement for Dreyfus, through commercial agreements signed with the Société Générale de Paris and Peruvian Guano in 1876, eventually proved fruitless. In 1876, the Peruvian government once again entered a state of financial bankruptcy, unable to contract new foreign loans or to deal with the service on existing loans.

In such circumstances, Pardo's policies were directed primarily at reducing the budgetary deficit of 8.5 million soles. One of the measures closely examined was turning the nitrates of the desert province of Tarapacá into a new resource which might finance public expenditure. Nitrates, however, unlike guano, were a privately owned resource – by Peruvians, Chileans and other foreigners. In order to implement this policy, therefore, Pardo established a nitrate monopoly in 1873, and in 1875 expropriated the nitrate fields. Their owners received 'nitrate certificates' guaranteed by local banks. These nitrate miners thereupon transferred their operations to Chile, where they actively contributed to the war propaganda which began to rage after 1878 between Chile, Peru and Bolivia (see below).[41] Meanwhile Pardo's planned monopoly did not achieve the expected results. When foreign credit sources dried up, and guano exports began to fall, the banks and the government were forced to resort to a substantial increase in the issue of money, a process which further aggravated the crisis which had been brewing since 1872. Pardo and the civilian politicians had come to power only to be the impotent witnesses to one of Peru's greatest financial disasters, the result of a series

[41] See also Collier, *CHLA* III, chap. 14.

of policies adopted since the beginning of the guano boom, and a crisis which they had neither the capacity nor the opportunity to overcome.

From a political point of view, Pardo's administration was character-ized by mounting confrontation and stiff opposition. His attempts to reduce public spending were met by strong opposition from civilians who had become accustomed to the generosity of previous administra-tions, whilst the numerous military establishment resented the effects of this policy on their institutions. The Church strongly opposed the government's policy of promoting secular education as a function of the state. It did not take very long before disaffected politicians and military men resorted once again to traditional practices, and half-way through his administration Pardo began to face military revolts, many of which were led by Nicolás de Piérola, who campaigned vigorously against what he saw as the government's anticlericalism. Neither did the poor state of the country's economy favour the consolidation of 'civilismo'. There-fore, in 1876 Pardo, believing that the only way to solve Peru's increasing political problems, especially civil and military unrest, was a strong government headed by a military man, accepted General Prado, who could have hardly been considered a *civilista,* as his successor. Soon after being inaugurated as president Prado drifted away from the *civilistas,* who had hoped to influence him and his government. He failed, however, to attract support from Piérola's followers, and his position became increasingly unstable. Several revolts organized by both groups were defeated, but not without difficulty, and, when in Novem-ber 1878 Pardo was assassinated in obscure circumstances, Peru took a step nearer to chaos. The already fierce antagonism between Piérola's followers and the *civilistas,* who made the former morally responsible for Pardo's murder, intensified and acquired ominous characteristics; the likelihood of a confrontation became only too apparent. It was only avoided by more dramatic events.

In February 1879 Chile occupied the Bolivian port of Antofagasta and two months later declared war on Bolivia and on Peru, Bolivia's ally by secret, mutual defence treaty of 1873. After occupying the entire Bolivian littoral Chile successfully invaded the Peruvian province of Tarapacá late in 1879, the provinces of Tacna and Arica early in 1880 and the northern coast in September 1880. Lima fell in January 1881. The victories of the Chilean army and navy in the War of the Pacific brought to a climax in Peru both the financial and the political crises of the 1870s.[42]

---

[42] For a discussion of the impact of the War of the Pacific on Peru, see Heraclio Bonilla, 'The War of the Pacific and the national and colonial problem in Peru', *Past and Present,* 81, Nov. 1978, 92–118.

The present Republic of Bolivia was constituted as an independent nation on 8 August 1825, on the basis of the territory which had formed the Audiencia of Charcas. None of the new Latin American states, except perhaps Paraguay under Francia, was as isolated as Bolivia. Before the dramatic events of 1879 the country's connections with the outside world were extremely weak, amounting in effect to the continuation of two tenuous connections of colonial origin: one towards the Atlantic, the traditional route linking Potosí with Buenos Aires, lost much of its importance following the independence of the River Plate republics and the increase in transportation costs; the other towards the Pacific, probably the more important of the two, gave Bolivia access to its only port, Cobija, but only after a difficult crossing of the Atacama Desert, while trade through the Peruvian port of Arica was subject to the varying moods that governed political relations between Peru and Bolivia. In addition to this isolation from the outside world, there was a profound internal disarticulation. During the colonial period the dynamic centre of the economy of Upper Peru had been Potosí; its mineral deposits and its markets attracted the trade of entire regions like Cochabamba. With the decline of mining production, which began even before the wars of independence but which was accelerated by them, not only were these connections severed, but regions such as present-day Beni and Pando, even Santa Cruz, became internal territories practically shut in on themselves.

At the time of independence, Bolivia's population was estimated by John Barclay Pentland, the British observer, to be 1,100,000, of whom 800,000 were Indians, 200,000 whites, 100,000 *mestizos* or *cholos* (of mixed blood), 4,700 black slaves and 2,300 free blacks.[43] Probably no more than 20 per cent spoke Spanish: Quechua and Aymara were the languages of the vast majority. The largest city was La Paz with 40,000 inhabitants, followed by Cochabamba with 30,000. The economy which maintained this population was in profound crisis. In the first decades of the century Potosí had suffered a marked decline in production and population. According to Pentland, in 1827 it had scarcely 9,000 inhabitants, compared with 75,000 at the end of the eighteenth century.[44] Between 1820 and 1830 the production of the silver mines of Upper Peru fell by 30 per cent compared with 1810–20; production in the 1820s – a little under

---

43 J. B. Pentland, *Informe sobre Bolivia, 1827* (Potosí, 1975), 40–2. This is a more complete edition in Spanish of *Report on Bolivia, 1827* (Royal Historical Society, London, 1974).   44 *Ibid.*, 58.

200,000 marks per annum – was less than half that of the last decade of the eighteenth century. The factors impeding a recovery in mining activity were the destruction, flooding and abandonment of the mines during the wars, the lack of investment capital, a certain scarcity of labour following the abolition of the *mita* (although, it must be said, demand for labour was low and erratic) and the continuation in the post-colonial era of the state monopoly of the purchase of silver (at prices below the world market price) through the *Bancos de Rescate*, which severely reduced profits. At the time of independence – and for some time after – the production of the mines was low and largely the result of the utilization of discarded ore rather than deep workings.

In the agrarian sector where the basic units of production remained the haciendas and the *comunidades* (free Indian communities), the most important products were Peruvian bark (for the manufacture of quinine), coca, maize, wheat and potatoes; bark and coca were easily marketable outside the region, whereas the other products were mainly for local consumption. Pentland points out that in 1826 the value of the annual trade in coca in the city of La Paz reached £143,600, an amount equivalent to nearly 50 per cent of the value of exports of silver during the same year, whereas the value of the trade in maize and wheat was £60,000.[45]

The 'industrial' sector was represented by the *obrajes*, or workshops for the manufacture of textiles. However, as a result of the commercial reforms introduced by the Bourbons and the freedom of trade decreed at the time of independence, they could not compete with European cloth. Pentland estimated the value of textile production at £16,000, whereas in the past it had been as high as £200,000.[46]

As a result of the weakness of the productive structure, the contribution of the Bolivian economy to the international market was small and extremely precarious. Bolivian exports worth £722,750 in 1826 consisted primarily of silver and gold, followed at a great distance by Peruvian bark and tin. On the other hand, Bolivian imports in 1826 totalled £637,407. These goods were shipped in through Buenos Aires (a third) and, above all, through Arica (two-thirds). Of this total, about 70 per cent were imports from Britain, chiefly cloth. The balance was made up by goods from France, Germany and the Netherlands. There was also a very active local trade between Peru and Bolivia. The former exported, in particular, raw cotton and the wines and brandies produced

[45] *Ibid.*, 99.   [46] *Ibid.*, 100.

in the valleys of Moquegua and Tambo with a total value of £82,800. Bolivia, in turn, exported to Peru basically agricultural produce valued at £30,640, to satisfy the demand of the markets in southern Peru.[47] These official figures are, of course, conservative because of widespread contraband.

In these circumstances the Bolivian government encountered great financial difficulties. In 1825 and 1826 the average annual total of the state revenues was only £400,000, and in 1827 it was £350,000.[48] Around 60 per cent of this revenue was earmarked for military expenditure in the immediate aftermath of independence and continued at a level of 40–50 per cent throughout the period to 1879.[49] In addition the independent Bolivian state began its life owing £40,000 to Peru plus a further £140,000, the balance of the grant of £200,000 voted by the General Assembly in 1825 as compensation to the army of liberation.[50]

It is important to emphasize that the Bolivian government, in these early days, did not have recourse to foreign credit to finance its public expenditure. This was noticeably different from the practice established by the other governments of independent Latin America. Instead, the government of Antonio José Sucre (1825–8) attempted to attract domestic savings through the issue of bonds at a nominal value of £200,000, which were backed by assets owned by the state. These assets had been acquired as a result of the policy pursued by Sucre with the aim of destroying the power and influence of the regular clergy. In one of the most radical attacks on the Church in post-independent Spanish America Sucre closed down a large proportion of the religious houses, while the valuable urban and rural properties directly owned by the religious orders, or controlled by them through mortgages and *capellanías*, properties granted to the Church for pious works, were expropriated by the state. In the long run this policy served to strengthen the power of native landowners and merchants, who were able to acquire at rock-bottom

[47] *Ibid.*, 124, 121, 104.

[48] *Ibid.*, 139; William E. Lofstrom. 'The promise and problem of reform. Attempted social and economic change in the first years of Bolivian independence' (unpublished Ph.D. thesis, Cornell University, 1972), 456.

[49] In 1827 the army consisted of 2,291 Bolivian recruits and the 2,253 Colombian soldiers who accompanied the 'liberator', José Antonio Sucre. See Roberto Querejazu C., *Bolivia y los ingleses* (La Paz, 1973), 148–9. In 1828 Sucre maintained a force of 2,700 men, which was considered large by the standards of the day. For the size of Bolivian armies in the period before the War of the Pacific – never more than 5,000 men, more often less than half that number – and their cost – never less than 40% of national revenue and under Melgarejo as high as 70% – see James Dunkerley, 'Reassessing Caudillismo in Bolivia, 1825–79', *Bulletin of Latin American Research*, 1/1 (1981), 16–17.   [50] Pentland, *Informe sobre Bolivia*, 141.

prices the bonds originally issued to foreign soldiers and officers, when the latter had to leave Bolivia.[51] Another important source of the financing of public expenditure was the tax paid by the producers of silver in the *Bancos de Rescate*. At first the rate was equivalent to 10 per cent of the value of production, but later it was reduced successively to 8.5 per cent and to 5 per cent as a means of encouraging mining activity.[52] As in other Latin American countries, import duties and taxes on the internal movement of goods were also important sources of state revenue. However, in the case of Bolivia the collection of import duties was not so easy, because control of the Arica customs house was in the hands of Peru; even at its height only a third of Bolivia's foreign trade passed through Cobija. The Bolivian state had two other sources of revenue: the tithes and taxes levied on the minting of money.

Customs revenues, the tithes, taxes on mining production and the mint, and the confiscation of the properties of the religious orders were, however, together insufficient to meet the costs of public expenditure. For this reason, in Bolivia as in Peru, it was necessary to re-establish in 1826 the tribute (abolished by Bolívar in 1825) to which theoretically all Indian males aged 18 to 50 had been subject during the colonial period. The tribute had been replaced by the *contribución directa*, a general direct tax on urban and rural property and individual incomes. For the Indians, however, this represented only 3 pesos per annum, less than half the amount they were paying previously. Very soon the government realized the detrimental effect on state revenues. As a result, on 2 August 1826 Sucre signed the decree re-establishing the tribute, a decision which sanctioned the return to a fiscal structure which, as in the colonial period, divided the various strata of Bolivian society for tax purposes. Despite undergoing several vicissitudes, as we shall see, the tribute continued in existence until 1882.[53]

'I am convinced', Sucre prophetically wrote in a letter to Bolívar, 'the ground we are working is mud and sand, and that on such a base no building can subsist . . .'[54] The political history of Bolivia up to the war with Chile in 1879 shows an interminable series of barrack revolts, coups and counter-coups as a means of attaining power and despoiling the

---

[51] Lofstrom, 'Promise and problem of reform', 469–70, 259–60, 509–12.
[52] Fernando Cajías, *La Provincia de Atacama (1825–1842)* (La Paz, 1975), 218.
[53] Lofstrom, 'Promise and problem of reform', 404; Nicolás Sánchez-Albornoz, *Indios y tributos en el Alto Perú* (Lima, 1978), 191, 214.
[54] Quoted in Alcides Arguedas, *Historia general de Bolivia, 1809–1821* (La Paz, 1922), 65.

meagre resources of the state, movements undertaken by ambitious military chieftains with the complicity of some *doctores de Chuquisaca*. Against this background of political instability, even anarchy, the government of Andrés Santa Cruz (1829–39) constitutes a notable exception.

Santa Cruz, a *mestizo*, had joined the ranks of the rebels very late, but his part in the decisive battles for independence, and the favours granted to him by Bolívar, soon transformed him into one of the strong candidates to govern the destiny of independent Bolivia. It is to Santa Cruz that Bolivia owes the first attempt to achieve the efficient organization of both government and economy, and also the search for new ways to overcome the isolation of Bolivia from the outside world. The opening of the port of Cobija made it possible for the markets of southern Bolivia to be supplied with goods from abroad; these goods, transported on muleback, after a laborious crossing of the Atacama Desert, reached Potosí, Chuquisaca, Tupiza and Tarija. In view of the internal fragmentation of Bolivian territory and the almost complete absence of adequate means of internal transport, it was also essential, subsequently, to undertake the consolidation of the port of Arica as a centre for the supply of the provinces of northern Bolivia, and as a port of shipment for Bolivian exports. Despite all these achievements Santa Cruz is mainly remembered as the unsuccessful architect of Andean unity between Peru and Bolivia.

Peru and Bolivia, as we have seen, were territories with strong economic and administrative links during the colonial period. Their separation, like that of the other regions of Spanish America, was the result of the vicissitudes of the struggle for emancipation. Bolivia in the end consolidated its precarious nationhood largely through the many conflicts with its neighbours. However, this was not a clear-cut or continuous process. Ill-accustomed to an early separation which was justified neither by geography nor by economic structure, the caudillos of both countries in the post-independence era always sought to reinforce their power by utilizing the resources of the other country, and they also invoked the comradeship derived from previous military campaigns in order to obtain from the person governing the neighbouring country, in which they often found themselves exiled, the military assistance needed to reconquer power or at least to attempt to do so. This 'assistance', or the need to 'save' one of the countries from chaos, was often used as the pretext for the military expeditions undertaken from

Peru to Bolivia or vice versa. The frontier was merely an 'imaginary line', as a later president, Mariano Melgarejo, was to put it, and relations between Bolivia and Peru were inevitably conducted in a climate of mutual hostility and suspicion. When to these factors are added the difficulties involved in the shared access to the port of Arica, and the flooding of Peruvian markets with debased Bolivian currency after 1830,[55] it is not surprising that the internal politics of Peru and Bolivia should reflect the tension existing between the two countries.

Nevertheless, the threat posed by the growing economic and naval power of Chile persuaded Santa Cruz, who had briefly served as president of Peru in the 1820s, to seek a stable alliance with Peru for mutual defence and a resolution of the economic difficulties of the two nations. The pretext for the military expedition to Peru (June 1835) was, once again, the need to defend one caudillo, Orbegoso, who had been deposed by another, the turbulent Salaverry. However, the reasons for Santa Cruz's intervention were not confined to helping his fallen friend. In the justification of his acts which he wrote from exile in Ecuador, Santa Cruz argued that intervention in the affairs of Peru was a matter of life or death for Bolivia.[56]

Once victory had been attained, Santa Cruz remained in Peru to give definitive form to the new political organization which would make possible the federation of Peru and Bolivia, through the creation of three states (North Peru, South Peru and Bolivia) under his sole leadership as Protector. In this way, and in the face of the potential danger that Chile represented, the Peru–Bolivian Confederation was created on 28 October 1836 as a tardy and partial attempt to make the dreams of Bolívar come true. After the failure of this experiment, it would be 1873, once more in the face of the threat from Chile, before a similar attempt was made, this time in strictly military terms.

The fusion of Peru and Bolivia disrupted the balance of forces among the countries that had emerged from the collapse of the colonial order, and it was inevitably seen as a serious threat to their interests. This was quickly understood by Argentina and, above all, by Chile. 'United, these two States will always be more powerful than Chile in all ways and circumstances', wrote Diego Portales on 10 September 1836,[57] and on 26

[55] The debased coinage known as the *peso feble* was first issued by Santa Cruz in 1830; it represented 14% of issue in 1830–4 and 85% by 1850–9. See Dunkerley, 'Reassessing Caudillismo', 18.
[56] 'El General Santa Cruz explica su conducta pública y los móviles de su política en la presidencia de Bolivia en el Protectorado de la Confederación Perú-Boliviana' (Quito, 1840), in Oscar de Santa Cruz (ed.), *El General Santa Cruz* (La Paz, 1924), 74.

December he declared war on the Confederation on the grounds that it 'threatened the independence of other American nations'. Four months later, on 9th May 1837, Argentina, on the pretext of frontier disputes, took a similar decision.

The military response of Chile to the emergence of the Confederation was inspired not only by fear of the new coalition of forces, but also by concern at the measures taken by Santa Cruz to strengthen the commercial development of the ports of the Peruvian coast. Valparaíso had already acquired a very marked economic superiority by becoming the principal commercial link between the South Pacific and Europe; to counteract this development Santa Cruz declared Arica, Cobija, Callao and Paita free ports, and at the same time imposed additional duties on goods which had been unloaded at other ports. This was a measure directly aimed at Chilean commercial interests and which could only be resolved by force of arms. After an early campaign (1837) in which the troops of the Confederation gained the advantage, on 20 January 1839 at Yungay, a town in the northern highlands of Peru, the Chilean army led by Bulnes, and supported by Peruvian troops and officers, destroyed the fragile edifice of the Confederation. Santa Cruz at first took refuge in Guayaquil, and later (in 1843) went into exile to Europe.

The Peru-Bolivian Confederation (1836–9), which had only a brief existence and was throughout subject to frequent external and internal attacks, will be remembered only for its unfulfilled promise. The Confederation not only suffered the external attacks of Chile and Argentina, but it was assaulted from within from its very beginning. It was attacked by the besieged Bolivian commercial interests and many soldiers who believed that in this adventure they would inevitably lose out, and Peruvians did not, of course, like the idea of being 'protected' by a Bolivian. Northern Peruvians, in particular, did not believe that they had a destiny similar to that of the Andean inhabitants of the faraway south. At all events, for Bolivia the defeat of Santa Cruz at Yungay, followed by the defeat of Ingavi in November 1841 of Agustín Gamarra's expedition, a Peruvian attempt to impose hegemony over Bolivia, marked a definite end to all aspirations to restore the connections of the past and consolidated Bolivian independence, at the time still very much in the balance.

In the period following the collapse of the Confederation and Santa Cruz's withdrawal from the political scene, Bolivian regimes were too

[57] Quoted in Jorge Basadre, *Historia de la República del Perú* (5th edn, Lima, 1963), I, 401.

precarious to maintain a consistent policy, and the differences between them depended largely on the personal style of each caudillo and his ability to attract the loyalty of his followers through the distribution of patronage. Thus, while the imagination of a man such as the aristocratic José Ballivián (1841–7) made it possible for him to encourage the exploration of eastern Bolivia, to search for a more effective outlet to the Pacific, and to reorganize the educational system with the assistance of an élite of Argentine intellectuals who had been deported by Rosas, none of these endeavours was given the time or resources to succeed. After the forced resignation of Ballivián and the fleeting return to power of the southern caudillo, José Miguel Velasco, who had been president in 1828, 1829 and 1839–41 (between Santa Cruz and Ballivián) and who often arbitrated in the clashes between northern leaders, Manuel Isidoro Belzú (1848–55) set up a government of a different character, at least in its external form. It was a government that explicitly sought to base itself on the support of the urban artisans, especially the pauperized artisans of the *obrajes*, and rural masses, and at the same time it encouraged domestic production by raising the tariffs on imported cloth and re-establishing the state monopoly of Peruvian bark. Belzú, who claimed to be a reader of Proudhon and Saint Simon, addressed to his followers such speeches as the following:

Comrades, a mad crowd of aristocrats have become the arbiters of your wealth and your destiny. They exploit you unceasingly. They shear you like sheep day and night. They distribute among themselves lands, honours, jobs and positions of authority, leaving you only misery, ignorance and hard labour. Are you not equal to the rest of the Bolivians? Is this equality not the result of the equality of the human species? Why do they alone enjoy such fat inheritances, silverware, houses and farms, and not you? Comrades, private property is the principal source of transgressions and crimes in Bolivia. It is the cause of the permanent struggle between Bolivians. It is the underlying principle of the present dominant egotism. Let there be no more property, no more proprietors. Let there be an end to the exploitation of man by man. For what reason do the Ballivianists alone occupy the highest social positions? My friends, property, in the words of a great philosopher, is the exploitation of the weak by the strong; community of goods is the exploitation of the strong by the weak. Do justice with your own hands, since the injustice of men and the times deny it you.[58]

It is, in fact, very difficult to establish to what degree his adherence to the cause of the poor reflected a sincere commitment, or to what extent it was an expression of the most crude opportunism, based on the need to broaden the bases of his personal following in response to the prolifera-

[58] Quoted in Querejazu, *Bolivia y los ingleses*, 285–6.

tion of his rivals. Certainly there existed as a result of the continuous deterioration of the economy a largely impoverished mass which was responsive to the demagogic appeal of any caudillo. It has been estimated that in the decade between 1840 and 1849 alone there occurred in Bolivia sixty-five attempted coups d'état. This was hardly the most favourable climate in which to attempt to resolve the urgent problems affecting the economy and society of Bolivia.

During the first half century after independence, the Bolivian economy was fundamentally based on agriculture and stockraising and agrarian structures maintained their colonial character; that is to say, haciendas and Indian communities were, as to a great extent they are still today, the units of production in which the Indians, who comprised the bulk of the rural population, worked and lived. Until 1866, the community, or at least the use of its plots of land by the Indians, was guaranteed by the Bolivian authorities as it had been by the Spanish. In contrast to the colonial period, this policy was not now aimed at ensuring the reproduction of the Indian labour force which was essential for the functioning of the mining industry, but rather at ensuring that through the tribute the state could continuously dispose of the revenues needed to defray its current expenditure – and maintain order in the countryside. The *tributario* and the *comunitario* were, in fact, one inseparable entity. And until the 1860s nearly 40 per cent of the revenue of the Republic was derived from the tribute paid by the Indians.

José María Dalence, in his *Bosquejo Estadístico de Bolivia* [Statistical Sketch of Bolivia] (1851), calculated that out of a total population of 1,381,856 in 1846, the Indian population was 710,666 (51.4 per cent). 82 per cent of the Indians lived in the departments of the altiplano, especially La Paz, Potosí and Oruro, compared with only 6 per cent in, for example, Cochabamba. The historical reasons for this disparity are well known. Whereas the poverty of the high plateau meant that the landowners did not wish to cultivate the region and thus had no need for the Indian labour force which remained in the communities, in Cochabamba the rapid transformation of the area into the granary of Potosí caused empty lands and lands occupied by the Indians to be taken over by the landowners, who also incorporated into the estates those who were returning or escaping from the *mita*. Thus, as early as 1793 *mestizos* and whites made up 50 per cent of the population of the region. However, in addition to this regional distribution of the Indian population, estimates for 1838 show profound changes in its composition. It should be noted in the first place that the number of *tributarios* rose dramatically from 58,571 in 1770 to 124,312 in 1838 (and to 133,905 in 1858 and 143,357 in 1877). This increase took place above all in the departments of La Paz and Potosí. It is also important to emphasize that by the middle of the nineteenth century the Indian peasantry had become much more socially differentiated, a process which was reflected in an unequal access to the plots of cultivable land and also unequal participation in the payment of tribute. The number of *originarios* (original inhabitants of the community with the greatest access to land) paying tribute rose from 19,853 in 1770 to 33,308 in 1838; the numbers of tribute-paying *forasteros* ('outsiders', later arrivals with lesser landholdings) and *agregados* (like the *forasteros*, with even less or no land) together rose from 35,400 to 66,930. In addition, there was a remarkable increase in the number of tribute-paying *yanaconas* (landless Indians bound by personal service to a particular hacienda) from a total of 1,866 in 1770 to 22,227 in 1838. And a new category of *vagos*, or migrant labourers, working in the coca-plots of the Yungas, accounted for a total of 2,117 *tributarios* in 1838.[59]

It is generally held that Bolivia in the nineteenth century was the scene of a significant expansion of the big estates at the expense of the lands and people of the communities. An analysis of the register of tribute-payers, however, reveals that between 1838 and 1877 the tribute-paying population in the communities was increasing, whereas in the estates exactly the reverse was the case. In the five departments of Bolivia, the communities controlled 68 per cent of the tribute-payers in 1838, 73 per cent in 1858, and 75 per cent in 1877. Conversely, the total of tribute-payers on the estates declined continuously during this period: it was 29 per cent in 1838, 25 per cent in 1858, and 23 per cent in 1877. Furthermore, the increase in the number of *forasteros* does not appear to have affected this process. In 1838, for example, when *forasteros* and *agregados* represented 53 per cent of the total tribute-payers, 79 per cent of them lived in the communities. Finally, between 1838 and 1877, contrary to the traditional view, the estates and the communities expanded and declined together, rather than the former expanding at the expense of the latter.[60]

The reason for this remarkable stability in the agrarian structure of

---

[59] Erwin P. Grieshaber, 'Survival of Indian communities in nineteenth century Bolivia' (unpublished Ph.D. thesis, University of North Carolina, 1977), 79–80, 108, 132–7.
[60] *Ibid.*, 116, 131, 154, 291–3.

Bolivia is to be found in the economy. The decline of cities such as Potosí, Sucre and Cochabamba, combined with the small increase in the population of La Paz and Oruro, did not permit the significant increase in domestic demand needed for the more effective mobilization of the productive factors. Furthermore, the foreign market could not play a compensatory role, because during the 1840s Bolivian quinine gradually lost its access to the European market as a consequence of competition from Colombian production. It is true that in the 1860s and 1870s the renaissance of the Bolivian mining economy led to the widening of the domestic market, but demand, as will be explained below, was satisfied through other mechanisms. What happened to the Peruvian economy as a result of the expansion of cotton and sugar during the 1860s and 1870s was radically different.

This stability, however, does not mean that at various times during the nineteenth century governments did not attempt to abolish the corporate existence of the Indian communities and establish a republic of small proprietors in accordance with liberal ideology. As we have seen, such threats against the Indian communities began with Bolívar himself. In Bolivia, however, it is above all Mariano Melgarejo (1864–71) who is remembered as the author of the major assault on the property of the Indians. The growing fiscal requirements of a government constantly involved in military activity to maintain itself in power, combined with the need to reward his relations and clients, were the motives underlying Melgarejo's decision to sell the Indian community lands. The decree of 20 March 1866 declared Indians who possessed state lands to be proprietors, on condition that they paid a sum of between 25 and 100 pesos to register their individual titles. Those who did not do so within sixty days would be deprived of their property and their lands would be put up for public auction.[61] The scope of this decree was defined further in September 1868, when the National Constituent Assembly declared all community lands state property, and at the same time abolished the Indian tribute.[62]

According to Minister Lastre, in his report to the Legislative Chamber, between 20 March 1866 and 31 December 1869 the government auctioned off the lands belonging to 216 communities, or fractions of them, in the department of Mejillones (provinces of Omasuyos, Pacajes and Ingavi, Sicasica and Muñecas), 109 communities in La Paz (Yungas,

[61] Sánchez-Albornoz, *Indios y tributos*, 207.
[62] Luis Antezana, *El feudalismo de Melgarejo y la reforma agraria* (La Paz, 1970), 39.

La Unión, Larecaja, Caupolicán and Cercado), 15 in Tapacarí, Cochabamba, 12 in Yamparaes, Chuquisaca, 4 in Tarata, 3 in Oruro, and one in Potosí.[63] The total sum raised by these sales was £164,172, of which £130,144 was paid in depreciated government bonds and the balance in cash. In 1870, further sales raised a total sum of £67,637.[64] The abolition of the tribute, when combined with the dissolution of the community lands, was deprived of all significance. The Indian contribution was replaced by a personal contribution of four bolivianos and the imposition of the land tax. The former was equivalent to the five pesos that the landless Indians had always paid, while the land tax now replaced the old tribute paid by the Indians with land.[65]

The purchase of community lands with depreciated government bonds naturally did little to resolve the financial difficulties of the Bolivian state. On the contrary it was a mechanism which allowed its creditors to convert their bonds into capital, and at the same time consolidated their position within the agricultural sector. A study of Pacajes between 1866 and 1879 demonstrates that the beneficiaries of these sales were, in addition to the traditional landowners who expanded the frontiers of their estates, medium-scale proprietors, merchants, and even Indian chiefs and *mestizos*, who thus became integrated into the local and regional elites. These people, as a whole, still did not regard land as a means of production, but rather as a source of stable income and as collateral for obtaining capital for investment in medium-scale and small-scale mining undertakings.[66]

The other consequence of this process of spoliation was the massive movement of Indian protest, reflected in the risings of 1869, 1870 and 1871. The peasant population played an active part in the overthrow of Melgarejo early in 1871. Subsequently, on 31 July 1871, the Constituent Assembly declared null and void all the sales, allocations and alienations of communal lands, and at the same time promised to grant all Indians the full exercise of the rights of property. This did not mean, therefore, either the re-establishment of communal property, or the transformation of the Indian into a landless day-labourer. It has been asserted that the lands did not revert to the possession of the Indians, a view which has been challenged on the basis of the evidence obtained from four villages in

[63] Sánchez Albornoz, *Indios y tributos*, 207–8.
[64] Luis Peñaloza, *Historia económica de Bolivia* (La Paz, 1954), I, 294.
[65] Sánchez-Albornoz, *Indios y tributos*, 208–9.
[66] Silvia Rivera, 'La expansión del latifundio en el altiplano boliviano', *Avances* (La Paz), 2 (1978), 95–118.

Pacajes where the Indians did successfully reclaim their lands in 1871.[67] To what extent, however, was the case of Pacajes as a traditional centre of indigenous rebellion the exception rather than the rule? As far as the tribute was concerned, this was eliminated from the national budget, but the Indians were not exempt; its collection was entrusted to the departmental authorities until its final abolition in 1882.[68]

It is obvious that further research is needed to evaluate the results of the agrarian policy of Melgarejo and the rectification of it undertaken by Morales (1871–2). With regard to this, it should perhaps be noted that the *ley de ex-viculación* (law of disentailment) promulgated on 5 October 1874 explicitly denied the juridical existence of free Indian communities and at the same time declared that the community members would henceforth have the right of absolute ownership of the possessions of which they had hitherto had the usufruct.[69] Although we still lack the evidence necessary to measure the extent of this fresh assault on Indian communal property rights, it seems clear that this measure eliminated the legal obstacles to the expansion of the Bolivian latifundium. For this to occur, however, it was not enough to have legal authorization. What was essential was the action of what the Bolivians of the time called the forces of 'progress', that is to say mining, the international market and the railways.

The growth of the Bolivian economy from the middle of the nineteenth century was associated with the renaissance of mining activities. As in colonial times, it was the mining sector that allowed the Bolivian economy to develop a closer connection with the international market. And mining activity was at first still primarily based on the extraction and export of silver in the traditional mining zones of the altiplano. After half a century of stagnation the years between 1850 and 1873 witnessed the slow recovery of silver mining. This process was characterized by the appearance of a new group of mining entrepreneurs and later the intervention of foreign capital – and it was facilitated by new technology, especially pumping machinery worked by steam engines, and a fall in the international price of mercury. The middle and late 1870s then witnessed an impressive growth in the production of silver. Bolivia became once more one of the biggest silver producers in the world.

The resurgence of the Bolivian mining economy during the second

[67] Peñaloza, *Historia económica*, 298–9; Grieshaber, 'Survival of Indian communities', 200.
[68] Sánchez-Albornoz, *Indios y tributos*, 210–11.
[69] Ramiro Condarco Morales, *Zárate, el temible 'Willka'* (La Paz, 1965), 46.

half of the nineteenth century, unlike Potosí in the sixteenth century, was, however, unable to articulate around itself the Bolivian economy as a whole. In view of the small proportion of the labour force in mining – Huanchaca, for example, in 1877 employed only 1,567 workers[70] – as well as internal transport difficulties and the subsequent economic orientation imposed by the railways, Bolivian mining was unable (at least at that time) to contribute to the development of agriculture. On the contrary, it facilitated the expansion of Chilean exports of wheat and flour, a process which in turn transformed Cochabamba and Chayanta, which had traditionally been zones of commercial agriculture, into areas with a subsistence economy.

The inability of Bolivian mining to stimulate the development of domestic agriculture is also one explanation why the Indian population was successful for so long in maintaining its plots of land. At the same time, as happened in Peru in the case of guano, the recovery of mining undermined the importance of the Indian tribute as an instrument for financing public expenditure. Whereas between 1827 and 1866 tribute had represented an average of 37 per cent of total annual revenues, by 1886 the income derived from the collection of Indian tribute represented only 10 per cent of state revenue.[71] From the 1860s, however, the 'silver barons' were able to launch a more vigorous and more successful attack on the property and culture of the Indian population, this time in the name of progress and of the eradication of obstacles to civilization.

Around 1860 ownership of the principal mineral deposits of the altiplano was concentrated in the hands of a new elite, principally drawn from the merchants and *hacendados* of Cochabamba. For example, the Aramayo family owned the Real Socavón de Potosí, Antequera and Carguaicollo. Aniceto Arce was head of the Huanchaca company, while Gregorio Pacheco had taken over the important Guadalupe mining interests. However these proprietors, in their turn, were closely dependent on foreign capital, which exercised control over marketing and which supplied the inputs. This dependence became transformed into complete subordination in times of crisis. The case of Huanchaca, in this respect, illustrates a more general tendency.

In the 1850s the Huanchaca operations covered their costs and even generated a small profit. Nevertheless, the rate of growth was modest. The insufficient refining capacity made it impossible to derive the

[70] Grieshaber, 'Survival of Indian communities', 192–3, 222.
[71] *Ibid.*, 221.

maximum advantage from the considerable production of Pulacayo; its future development depended on the improvement of communications between the mines and the refining plants, and also on increasing the latter's capacity. For this it was necessary to have recourse to foreign capital, the influx of which was reflected in the creation of the Bolivian Huanchaca Company in 1873. This company was incorporated with a capital of £562,500 sterling, divided into three thousand shares. The control exercised by foreign capital immediately made itself evident; it was reflected in the composition of the board of directors, which was formed by the Chileans, Joaquín Dorado, Melchor Concha y Toro, Luis Warny, Hermann Fisher and the only Bolivian, Aniceto Arce, who controlled 33 per cent of the shares. At that time the participation of foreign capital was of little significance, but the reorganization of the company in 1877 facilitated the further influx of British, French and German capital. In the 1880s British capital was absolutely predominant.

British penetration into Bolivia, as elsewhere in Latin America, took two forms: first, during and immediately after independence came the export of goods and the rapid domination of markets; the second, which occurred later, consisted of the export of capital, in the form of direct investments or loans. In this connection, one factor in particular should be emphasized. The rapid saturation of the relatively small market and the precarious nature of the Bolivian economy during the first half of the nineteenth century made Bolivia a country unattractive to British interests. It was only in 1869 that the Bolivian government, through George E. Church, managed to raise a loan in London (for £1.7 million) and that transaction was rescinded shortly afterwards. Previously small loans of £187,500 and £255,549 had been raised in Peru (1865) and Chile (1868) respectively. As a result, in contrast to Peru, therefore, Bolivia in 1879 had a foreign debt of only £283,333.[72] There were few British subjects resident in Bolivia. To Stephen St John, the British envoy, Bolivia, even in November 1875, was 'one of the least interesting countries in the world.'[73] During the last third of the nineteenth century, however, the situation began to change radically. One expression of this change was the expansion of Bolivia's foreign trade. Between 1869 and 1871, for example, under Melgarejo's opening-up of the economy, British exports to Bolivia rose from £8,000 to £24,000, while Bolivian exports to Britain

---

[72] On these loans and Bolivia's foreign debt, see Peñaloza, *Historia económica*, 11, 344, 403, 405, 409, 416.
[73] Quoted in Querejazu, *Bolivia y los ingleses*, 362.

rose from £127,000 to £169,000 in the same period.[74] And an examination of the main products in this trade – no longer silver alone – reveals the growing penetration of foreign capital, especially British and Chilean, not only in the altiplano but also in the Pacific littoral.

From 1840 Chilean, British and French companies began the exploration and settlement of the Bolivian coast (the province of Atacama), with the aim of exploiting copper and, above all, the major deposits of guano. Between 1857 and 1866 nitrate deposits were discovered in the region of Mejillones in the southern Atacama, exploited by Chilean and British capital and exported to the expanding European market for fertilizers. From 1868 the port of Antofagasta, whose population like that of Cobija was over 90 per cent Chilean, became the chief port on the Bolivian coast.

The exploitation of nitrates by foreign capital led to the incorporation of the Bolivian littoral and vast areas of the Atacama Desert into international trade. In 1869 the most important concern operating in the area was Melbourne Clark and Co., a firm owned by the British subjects William Gibbs, George Smith and Melbourne Clark and the Chileans Agustín Edwards and Francisco Puelma. This served as a basis for the creation of the Compañía de Salitres y Ferrocarril de Antofagasta in 1872, a Chilean-British company registered in Valparaíso, which received generous concessions from the Bolivian government. In 1870 a new phase in the expansion of foreign capital in the Atacama region opened with the discovery and bringing into operation of the silver mines of Caracoles, linked to the outside world through the port of Mejillones. Investments made up to 1872 totalled around £2 million, and among the investors were the British subjects Gibbs, Smith and Simpson, and the Chileans Edwards, Concha y Toro, Napoleón Peró and Dorado, that is to say, those who already controlled the exploitation and exports of nitrates in the region.[75] The resident population of Caracoles was nearly ten thousand, of whom once again the vast majority were Chilean.

To mobilize credit and to avoid the exorbitant terms imposed by the merchant houses, the big mining concerns sponsored the establishment of banking institutions. The creation in 1871 of the National Bank of Bolivia fulfilled many of the requirements. The concession for its establishment was granted to Napoleón Peró, the founder of the

[74] *Ibid.*, 349.
[75] See Antonio Mitre, 'Economic and social structure of silver mining in nineteenth-century Bolivia' (unpublished Ph.D. thesis, Columbia University, 1977), 137–9.

Antofagasta Nitrate Company, while the three million pesos that formed its initial capital were subscribed by the persons who had already established an economic hegemony in the region.[76] In addition to controlling trade, nitrates, silver and banking, this group, during the 1870s, extended its control over the mining areas to the south of Potosí, first through a monopoly of marketing, and later through the supply of inputs, until finally they acquired complete ownership.

The heightened economic activity of the 1870s was abruptly interrupted when, on 14 February 1878, the Bolivian government decided to impose an additional export tax of ten centavos on every quintal of nitrate extracted since 1874 between latitudes 23°S and 24°S. The Antofagasta Nitrates and Railway Company regarded this as a clear breach of the treaty with Chile (1874) in which Bolivia had agreed not to increase taxes on Chilean companies operating in that previously disputed area in return for Chile's acceptance of 24°S as the frontier between the two countries. The authorities in Antofagasta were empowered to collect $90,000 from the Antofagasta Company; ten months later, in view of the refusal of the English manager, George Hicks, to pay this 'unjust' and 'illegal' tax, the Bolivian prefect ordered the auctioning off of the assets of the company until the amount demanded was met. Following intense lobbying by the Antofagasta Company, the Chilean response was the military occupation of Antofagasta (February 1879) and a declaration of war (April 1879) which was immediately extended to Peru, Bolivia's ally, by secret treaty, since 1873 (see above).[77] Within two months Chilean forces had occupied the Bolivian province of Atacama. By the end of the year the Bolivian army had been totally defeated. Bolivia's entire coastal territory – and a substantial part of its wealth – was permanently lost. Chile, however, had no intention of invading the altiplano; the main enemy was Peru, and Bolivia was essentially a spectator for the rest of the War of the Pacific. Politically, Bolivia's defeat led to profound changes; in particular, it brought about the end of military caudillo rule and the establishment of civilian oligarchical government, with the direct participation of the mining elite.

The reorganization of the Bolivian economy as a result of the growth of the mining sector after 1850 had transformed the class structure. The emerging group comprised those connected with the mining of silver for

---

[76] *Ibid.*, 139–40.

[77] For a fuller discussion of the nitrate issue and the origins of the War of the Pacific, see Collier, *CHLA* III, ch.14.

export, and its policy clashed with that of the old oligarchy whose power was based on control of the land and of craft industries. However, this new economic elite had failed to achieve direct access to political control of the state or policy and was obliged to patronize various caudillos in an endeavour to gain influence over government. Belzú, with his populist style, was succeeded by José María Linares (1857–61), the first civilian president, who made some initial moves towards strengthening international trade by means of a more liberal policy. In 1858 he abolished the state monopoly of Peruvian bark, reduced by 13 per cent the duty on imported *tocuyos* (coarse cotton cloth), and began to organize guarantees for the currency although he was unable to introduce a free market in silver. His overthrow by a *coup d'état* resulted in the military again achieving political control, but in practice the military were increasingly obliged to implement measures that were in harmony with the economic policy of the new dominant group. This was to some degree evident under the government of Melgarejo and more obviously so under Agustín Morales (1871–2), who, in 1872, finally decreed the free market in bullion, Tomás Frías (1872–3, 1875–6) and, above all, Adolfo Ballivián (1873–4), the son of the former president, who expressed in a more explicit fashion the interests of the group of mining entrepreneurs to which he was linked. These governments were, however, still highly unstable, as a result of the tensions existing within a still emergent dominant class and between the new dominant class and the military, and also to some extent because of the permanent mobilization of the rural and urban lower classes, the victims of the dislocation of the traditional economy. The war provided the opportunity for the civilian elite to replace the military in government. Hilarión Daza, the strong man behind Presidents Frías and Ballivián (1872–6) and president since May 1876, who had led Bolivia, unprepared, into war and to disastrous defeat, was overthrown in December 1879. He was replaced by General Narcisco Campero, supported by the mining elites, who was committed to the establishment of stable, civilian oligarchical government. It was the beginning of a new era in Bolivian politics which was to last for more than fifty years.

Peru and Bolivia, which had shared one history from the remote past until the crisis of the colonial system, had gone their separate ways after independence from Spain. Persistent internal disturbances and disputes between their armies eventually led to the failure of attempts at reunification, and at the same time encouraged a nationalism that was somewhat narrow, but not for that reason any less powerful. However, their histories ran parallel to some extent. In both countries governments were unstable. They were based on the interests of a narrow creole group which depended on the fiscal extortion of the Indian masses, while at the same time denying them any possibility of political participation. In both countries, the economies languished until the appearance of guano in Peru and the rediscovery of silver as well as the discovery of nitrates in Bolivia. However, in both countries there was an inability to formulate a policy directed towards the utilization of these resources for the development of the economy as a whole. On account of its isolation and the fact that the renaissance of its economy occurred later, Bolivia, in contrast to Peru, did not suffer the consequences of an imprudent external indebtedness; but her markets, like those of Peru, were captured by foreign products. The common misfortune which Bolivia and Peru shared in 1879 was the price that the ruling class of both countries had to pay for failing to strengthen the economy and to give greater cohesion to society during the first half-century after independence.

14

CHILE FROM INDEPENDENCE TO THE WAR OF THE PACIFIC

At a banquet in Valparaíso in 1852 the Argentine publicist Juan Bautista Alberdi proposed a toast to 'the honourable exception in South America'. In one very important respect, the story of nineteenth century Chile was, it is true, a striking exception to the normal Spanish American pattern. Within fifteen years of independence Chilean politicians were constructing a system of constitutional government which was to prove remarkable (by European as well as Latin American standards) for its durability and adaptability. This successful consolidation of an effective national state excited the envious admiration of less fortunate Spanish American republics, torn and plagued as so many of them were by recurrent strife and caudillo rule. A good part of the explanation of Chile's unusual record undoubtedly lies in what can best be called the 'manageability' of the country at the time of independence, not least in terms of the basic factors of territory and population. The effective national territory of Chile in the 1820s was much smaller than it is today. Its distinctive slenderness of width – 'a sword hanging from the west side of America' – was for obvious orographical reasons no different; but lengthways no more than 700 miles or so separated the mining districts in the desert around Copiapó, at the northern limit of settlement (27°S), from the green and fertile lands along the Bío-Bío river in the south (37°S) – the area traditionally referred to as the Frontier, beyond which the Araucanian Indians stubbornly preserved their independent way of life. The peripheral clusters of population which lay still further south, at Valdivia and on the densely-forested island of Chiloé (liberated from the Spaniards only in 1826), were remote, insignificant appendages of the republic; the same could also be said slightly later on of the struggling settlement on the Straits of Magellan established in 1843 and used as a penal colony. Leaving aside the Araucanians, who numbered perhaps

200,000, the population of Chile was still fairly small: it rose slowly from an estimated 1,000,000 at the time of independence to an official (and possibly conservative) figure of 2,076,000 in 1875. The overwhelming majority of Chileans lived and worked in the country's traditional heartland, in (or very close to) the central valley extending three hundred miles southwards from Santiago. By the standards of Argentina or Mexico, of Peru or New Granada, this was a very compact territory inhabited by a compact population.

It was in many ways a homogeneous population. Both ethnically and socially the colonial past had left indelible marks. North of the Bío-Bío, few if any Indians survived in separate communities. The tiny black and mulatto trace in the community seems to have vanished within two or three decades of the abolition of slavery (1823). Republican Chile was essentially a country in which a small creole upper class (with an aristocratic elite at its core) co-existed with the huge mass of the labouring poor, who were predominantly *mestizo* and predominantly rural. The ethnic and social divisions coincided. Politically, the struggles which followed independence reflected disagreements within the fold of the upper class rather than deeper conflicts in the body social more generally. The rural poor remained passive throughout the period and, in fact, well beyond it. This relatively simple social structure was not complicated by sharp cleavages of economic interest within the upper class or by anything very much in the way of serious regional tension. Santiago and its rich hinterland dominated the republic. The remoter northern or southern provinces, whether disaffected or not, were powerless to alter the balance in their own favour, as was shown very clearly in the civil wars of 1851 and 1859. Concepción and the south underwent a frustratingly slow recovery from the wars of independence; and although Concepción, by virtue of its role as a garrison town watching over the frontier, was able in the uncertain atmosphere of the 1820s to impose its will on the capital – as it did in 1823, with the overthrow of Bernardo O'Higgins, and again in 1829 – in normal times a determined central government in control of the army (or most of it) could not easily be dislodged.

The issues which divided the upper class Chilean politicians of the 1820s into the perhaps predictable camps of Liberal and Conservative were above all ideological and personal. The dominant figure of these years, General Ramón Freire, was a well-intentioned Liberal eager to avoid the authoritarian pattern set by his immediate predecessor, the liberator O'Higgins. The new republic drifted from one makeshift political experiment to the next. The complex and ingenious constitution devised by Juan Egaña at the end of 1823 broke down within six months, its moralistic conservatism rejected by the Liberals who surrounded Freire and who wished, as they put it, 'to build the Republic on the ruins of the Colony'. The vogue for federalist ideas which overwhelmed political circles soon afterwards owed less, perhaps, to regional aspirations than to the dogmatically radical convictions of the man of the moment, José Miguel Infante; it produced a draft constitution, numerous new laws, an atmosphere of growing uncertainty, mild disorders in several towns, and a propensity to mutiny on the part of the army. The 'anarchy' of the period has often been exaggerated by Chilean historians; it was very limited in comparison with the turmoil then occurring on the other side of the Andes. Another Liberal soldier, General Francisco Antonio Pinto, president from 1827 to 1829, briefly succeeded in organizing a government which showed signs of solidity, and a new constitution (1828), the fourth since independence, duly went into effect. It proved inadequate to stem the mounting reaction against Liberal reformism, coloured as this was by anti-aristocratic verbiage and a degree of anticlericalism. In September 1829, with the vital backing of the army in Concepción, a powerful tripartite coalition of Conservatives – the traditionalist and pro-clerical *pelucones* ('big wigs'), the followers of the exiled O'Higgins, and a tough-minded group known as the *estanqueros*[1] – launched a revolt against the Liberal regime. Freire, who sprang quixotically to its defence, was defeated in April 1830 at Lircay, the battle which ended the short civil war and ushered in more than a quarter of a century of Conservative rule.

The political settlement of the 1830s was, as has been suggested, one of the more remarkable creations of nineteenth-century Latin America. The credit for its success is usually assigned to Diego Portales, the Valparaiso trader who more than anyone was the organizing genius of the Conservative reaction. Certainly Portales's ruthless tenacity was a key factor in keeping the new regime together, though his tenure of office as chief minister was fairly brief. This in itself may have impeded the crystalliza-

---

[1] In 1824 the *estanco*, or state tobacco monopoly, was leased to the Valparaiso trading house of Portales, Cea and Co., which undertook to service the £1,000,000 loan raised in London by the O'Higgins government two years earlier. The enterprise failed, and in 1826 the contract was withdrawn, occasioning much ill-feeling. The *estanquero* group was composed of men associated with this ill-starred venture; their leader was Diego Portales.

tion of a caudillo tradition in Chilean politics, for while Portales's influence was all-important, his aversion to the trappings of power was genuine enough. 'If I took up a stick and gave tranquillity to the country', he wrote, 'it was only to get the bastards and whores of Santiago to leave me in peace.'[2] Nevertheless, his actions both in government and behind the scenes, his strict emphasis on orderly management, his, at times, harsh attitude towards the defeated Liberals and, not least, his insistence on national dignity – these fixed the tone of official policy for years to come.

The work of the Conservatives in the 1830s was later described by critics of the regime as in essence a 'colonial reaction'. That it was a reaction to the ill-starred Liberal reformism of the 1820s is clear enough. But it is perhaps more accurate to see the new political system as a pragmatic fusion of the tradition of colonial authoritarianism, still very strong in Chile, with the outward forms (and something of the spirit) of nineteenth-century constitutionalism. The Constitution of 1833, whose regular operations were not interrupted until 1891 and which survived in amended form until 1925, embodied many of the principal Conservative obsessions. It was discernibly more authoritarian than its ill-fated predecessor of 1828, and in particular very strongly presidentialist. Two consecutive five-year terms of office were permitted, a provision which led in practice to four successive 'decennial' administrations, the first being that of Portales's nominee General Joaquín Prieto (1831–41). The president's patronage, control of the judiciary and public administration, and powers over Congress were all extensive, though the legislature was left with an ultimate check on the executive through its technical right to deny assent to the budget, taxation and military establishment. The president's emergency powers, in the form of 'extraordinary faculties' or localized states of siege, were highly conspicuous: moreover, such powers were regularly used – in one variety or another they were in force for one-third of the entire period between 1833 and 1861. The centralist spirit of the constitution was equally notable. The feeble institutional relics of the federalism of the 1820s were now swept away completely. The Intendant of each province was now defined as the president's 'natural and immediate agent' – and so it was to prove in practice: the Intendants were in some way the key officials of the regime, each Intendancy becoming in a real sense the local nexus of government. The

[2] Ernesto de la Cruz and Guillermo Feliú Cruz (eds.), *Epistolario de don Diego Portales*, 3 vols. (Santiago, 1937), I, 352.

Tacna
Arica
20°S
Iquique
Territory conquered from
Peru and Bolivia, 1879–83

Antofagasta

Copiapó
Mining zone
La Serena
30°S
Coquimbo

Valparaiso
Santiago
Heartland of Chile:
Northern central
valley
Talca
Buenos
Aires
Concepción
Talcahuano
ARAUCANIA
Indian territory
until occupied,
1860–83
Valdivia
40°S
L.Llanquihue

Chiloe

PATAGONIA

50°S

0   500km
0   300miles

*Magellan
Straits*

Nineteenth-century Chile

hegemony of Santiago, already well entrenched, was thus reinforced at the expense of regional initiative.

No constitution, least of all in Spanish America, is efficacious on its own. The successful operation of the new political system depended on a number of well-tested techniques used with methodical persistence by the governments of the period. Some were more obvious than others. Repression was a recurrent tactic for three decades. By the standards of the twentieth century it did not amount to very much. The death sentence was far more often invoked than applied. The standard penalties for political dissent were incarceration, internal exile ('relegation'), or banishment abroad for a fixed period. Voluntary exile (sometimes under bond) was not uncommon, especially in the embattled decade of the 1850s. A less overt means of inculcating social discipline can be detected in the careful way in which the Conservatives restored clerical influence; until the 1850s the Church was a useful mainstay of the system. Likewise, the incipient militarism of the 1820s was curbed by a drastic purge of Liberal officers and by a comprehensive reorganization of the country's militias. By the middle of 1831 the National Guard numbered 25,000 men. It more than doubled in size later on and was a very credible counterweight to the regular army, whose peacetime establishment rarely went much above 3,000. Twice, in the mutinies of June 1837 and April 1851, the militias helped to save the regime from forcible overthrow. They also fitted very neatly into the government's control of the electoral process.

Electoral intervention runs like a constant theme through the entire period. It survived long after the repressive practices already mentioned. In fact it was a Liberal president who, when asked in 1871 by one of his ministers whether Chile would ever enjoy 'real' elections, curtly replied, 'Never!'[3] The electoral law of 1833 severely restricted the franchise, but spread the net just wide enough to include artisans and shopkeepers, many of whom formed the rank and file of the National Guard, which thus supplied a numerous voting contingent at every election. Quite apart from this invaluable support, the government resorted to any number of methods – intimidation, temporary arrest, personation, bribery – to prevent opposition voters from exercising their franchise and to secure comfortable majorities for its own candidates. The operation was co-ordinated by the Minister of the Interior, and his subaltern agents in the provinces, the Intendants, the departmental

[3] Abdón Cifuentes, *Memorias*, 2 vols. (Santiago, 1936), II, 69.

gobernadores and the *subdelegados*, were as adept as any modern Chicago ward boss (and possibly more so) in 'delivering' the vote. It is hardly surprising that seven out of the eleven congressional elections held between 1833 and 1864 (at regular three-year intervals) were either uncontested or virtually so. Even in the more tolerant political climate of the 1860s and 1870s, an opposition stood no chance whatever of electing a majority to Congress. Not until the 1890s did the executive cease to interfere directly in elections.

In its earliest years the new Conservative system both faced and survived the ultimate test of war. The relations between Chile and Peru deteriorated sharply in the early 1830s. Commercial rivalry, a brisk tariff war, and Peru's failure to repay a Chilean loan (itself part of the £1,000,000 loan raised by O'Higgins in London in 1822, on which Chile had long since defaulted) were not in themselves a sufficient cause for aggression. This was provided in 1836, when General Andrés Santa Cruz forcibly united Peru and Bolivia into a Confederation. Portales viewed the formation of this potentially powerful state as a threat to Chilean independence; it would not be an exaggeration to say that he pushed his country into war. He was himself one of its first victims. Discontent over the war brought renewed Liberal conspiracies, and the all-powerful minister was murdered by a mutinous army battalion in June 1837, an occurrence which seems to have greatly solidified support both for the war policy and for the regime in general. Portales's death delayed but did not deflect the course of events. The second of two Chilean expeditionary forces, under the command of General Manuel Bulnes, invaded Peru and defeated Santa Cruz's army at the battle of Yungay (January 1839). The Confederation dissolved. The war of 1836–9 was an example of national assertiveness which incurred strong disapproval from Great Britain and France, but it inevitably heightened the international prestige of Chile. At home, it enabled the Prieto government to adopt a more conciliatory attitude towards the opposition, while the victorious General Bulnes became the obvious successor to the presidency. Just before the election Bulnes was betrothed to a daughter of the former Liberal president, Francisco Antonio Pinto, thus confirming the apparent trend towards political relaxation.

General Bulnes's presidency (1841–51) has often been represented as an 'era of good feelings' and for much of the time this was true. In the early 1840s, indeed, Liberalism came close to being killed by kindness. But Bulnes, for all his generous bonhomie, did nothing to undermine the authoritarian framework; in certain respects (the stiff Press Law of 1846, for instance) he added to it. The revival of Liberalism as a political force towards the end of his second term owed much to the ambitions of his chief minister, Manuel Camilo Vial, whose following, well represented in Congress, went into active parliamentary opposition when Vial was dismissed (1849). The leading Liberal intellectual of the period, José Victorino Lastarria, attempted to give direction and coherence to this new opposition. Outside the congressional arena the young idealists Francisco Bilbao and Santiago Arcos, mesmerized by the French revolution of 1848, were active in trying to mobilize support among the artisans of the capital: their Sociedad de la Igualdad, with its meetings and marches, survived for much of the year 1850, until the inevitable imposition of emergency powers by the government. The main effect of this agitation, both Liberal and *igualitario*, was to frighten the Conservative party into accepting Manuel Montt as Bulnes's successor.

President Montt (1851–61) was the first civilian to govern Chile for more than a few weeks. His oddly opaque character has defied all attempts at precise historical portraiture. His talent was undeniable; so was his austere inflexibility. ('All head and no heart' was his bluff predecessor's private opinion.) Montt's election provoked three months of full-scale civil war, in which the challenge to the regime came not only from the Liberals but also, more seriously, from the southern provinces. The leader of the revolt, General José María de la Cruz, was in fact a Conservative and the cousin of ex-president Bulnes, who defeated him in a short but bloody campaign. For the moment the regime was safe. By the mid-1850s, however, Montt's authoritarian approach was inducing strains and tensions within the Conservative governing combination itself. These finally came into the open as the result of a noisy jurisdictional conflict between the government and the Church, which was now re-emerging as an independent factor in politics. In 1857 the bulk of the Conservative party defected and joined forces with what was left of the Liberal opposition. Those Conservatives who remained loyal to Montt founded a new National party, but it lacked the wider upper class support enjoyed by the nascent Liberal-Conservative Fusion. For a second time vigorous agitation led to renewed repression and so to a further armed challenge to the regime. The civil war of 1859 is chiefly remembered for the miracles of improvisation performed by the rebel army in the mining provinces of the north – the focus of the war – but once again the government won. This time, however, military victory was followed by political defeat. Montt found it impossible to impose his own choice for the succession. This would have been Antonio Varas, Montt's closest associate and a highly talented politician. An elderly, easygoing, benevolent patrician, José Joaquín Pérez, was selected in Varas's place. It was a decisive turning point.

Under President Pérez (1861–71), the last of the four 'decennial' presidents, the Chilean political system at last began to liberalize. Pérez himself, by virtue of what was called at the time 'a supreme tolerance born of an even more supreme indifference', did as much as anybody in nineteenth-century Chile to enhance the tradition of stable constitutionalism. Repression ended, even if electoral intervention did not – Pérez's ministers saw to that. The new president, though himself nominally a National, quickly summoned the Liberal-Conservative Fusion into office (1862). This alliance between former enemies proved a remarkably workable governing combination, though it naturally attracted the opposition not only of the displaced Nationals (whose loyalty to Montt and Varas won them the name of *monttvaristas*) but also of the strongly anti-clerical 'red' or 'radical' Liberals who presently became known as the Radical party. The 1860s thus saw an increasingly diversified ideological panorama, and (except electorally) the 'new politics' was allowed to grow and thrive, although as it happened, domestic rivalries were somewhat dampened down in 1865–6, when the aggressive actions of a Spanish naval squadron cruising in Pacific waters drove Chile and three of her sister republics into a short war with their former metropolis.[4] By the close of the 1860s Liberal notions of constitutional reform were occupying the forefront of the political stage. Such ideas, centred, above all, on limiting presidential power, increasingly formed common ground between the four main parties. The first amendment to the hitherto inviolate Constitution of 1833 was passed in 1871; significantly, it prohibited the immediate re-election of the president.

It was during the government of Federico Errázuriz Zañartu (1871–6) that the final transition to Liberal-dominated politics occurred. In the early 1870s 'theological questions' (as they were called) began to be taken up as political issues. They were less concerned with theology, in fact, than with the demarcation of ecclesiastical and secular functions in the national life; they generated a good deal of feeling, both pious and

---

[4] Such fighting as there was (and there was not much) took place at sea. Before withdrawing from the Pacific, however, the Spaniards subjected Valparaíso to devastating bombardment (March 1866).

impious. A dispute about private education in 1873, pitting anticlericals against the Conservatives, who were becoming more and more identifiable as the militantly Catholic party in politics, brought about the disintegration of the Fusion. The Conservatives went into opposition, and the way was thus laid open for a new dominant coalition with a Liberal focus. The clever Errázuriz conducted the necessary manoeuvres. The Liberal Alliance (1875) was the third of the great governing combinations of the period, but the least stable, since several factions of the powerful Liberal party were invariably to be found opposing as well as supporting the government. The Errázuriz presidency also saw further constitutional reforms, all tending to limit executive influence. Important changes in electoral procedure (1874) were designed to reduce official intervention, but in 1876 Errázuriz and the Alliance had no difficulty in imposing the next president in the usual manner. Their choice fell on Aníbal Pinto, the son of the Liberal president of the later 1820s.

If the outline of the Conservative settlement of the 1830s was still very much intact, its inner workings were nonetheless altering in significant ways. Party politics had developed apace since the Pérez decade; the parties themselves were acquiring rudimentary forms of organization. The Radicals, with their network of local *asambleas*, were perhaps the first group to devise a definite (if flexible) structure. The Conservatives were the first to hold a national party conference (1878). But voting on party lines in Congress was far from automatic. When in 1876 the Radical deputy Ramón Allende (grandfather of the future president) suggested that party considerations should outweigh private principle in congressional voting, the idea was greeted with several outraged reactions. Quite apart from this, it was becoming clear by the later 1870s that Congress as a whole aspired to a much greater degree of control over the executive than had been attempted or perhaps even contemplated previously. The constitution, as we have seen, was strongly presidentialist; but it was also possible, as politicians now proved, to give it a logical 'parliamentary' interpretation. Through constant use of the *interpelación* and vote of censure, congressmen made the lives of cabinet ministers increasingly tedious and arduous. This was particularly the case during Aníbal Pinto's presidency (1876–81), which coincided, as we shall see, with several parallel crises of a very acute kind. That Chilean institutions had survived the tempests of the 1850s, that they were growing noticeably more tolerant – these things were cause for pride, certainly, but there were some politicians, including Pinto, who regarded as sterile the political squabbles now often monopolizing congressional attention to the exclusion of more urgent national business, and others who wondered whether the tension between the executive and the militant legislature might not destroy the tradition of stability. 'Gentlemen of the majority, ministers', exclaimed a Conservative deputy in 1881, 'I tell you: Don't pull the string too hard, because the thing might explode!'[5]

The connection between political stability and economic progress is never entirely clear-cut. It nevertheless seems fair to argue that the considerable commercial expansion which Chile underwent between the 1820s and the 1870s owed something, at least, to the settled conditions to be found in the country, as well as to the international demand for what Chile could produce. Expansion was not, however, completely smooth. At the close of the 1850s, with the loss of certain overseas markets for wheat and flour, coupled with two poor harvests in a row and the exhaustion of some of the silver deposits in the north, there was a brief but serious recession. At other periods (notably from the end of the 1840s to the mid-1850s, and again from the end of the 1860s into the early 1870s) the growth of trade was very rapid indeed, and Chile enjoyed boom conditions. The total value of the country's external trade rose from $7,500,000 in 1825 to $74,000,000 in 1875. Government revenues increased somewhat more slowly, from $2,000,000 in 1835 to $16,400,000 in 1875; from the end of the 1830s they generally outran expenditure very comfortably.[6]

A highly cosmopolitan trading community established itself at Valparaíso in the years after independence, and the governments of the period saw trade with the maritime nations of the North Atlantic, especially Great Britain, as one of the main stimulants of progress. Indeed, the political settlement of the 1830s was accompanied by an 'economic settlement', largely carried through by the brilliant Manuel Rengifo, finance minister from 1830 to 1835 and again from 1841 to 1844. Rengifo blended liberalism with pragmatism in his economic measures, which included the simplification of the fiscal system and tariff laws, the consolidation of the public debt, and, not least, the establish-

[5] Cristián Zegers, *Aníbal Pinto. Historia política de su gobierno* (Santiago, 1969), 119. Ten years later, in the political crisis of 1891, the 'thing' did explode.

[6] The Chilean peso [$] maintained a more or less constant value throughout most of the period, being worth around 45*d.* in terms of sterling, or slightly less than an American dollar, except during the American civil war, when it was worth slightly more.

ment on a permanent basis of public warehouses (*almacenes fiscales*) at Valparaíso, where traders could store duty-free merchandise while awaiting favourable markets. That Valparaíso should be the dominant port on the Pacific coast was a cardinal maxim both for Rengifo and Portales.

Heavily dependent on customs duties for its revenues, the Chilean government had the strongest possible reason for wishing to augment the flow of trade, an aim which certainly reflected the view of the Chilean upper class as a whole. But broader considerations of national development were never entirely absent from the official mind. The state was active in many spheres, including the improvement of communications; and tariff policy did not ignore local interests other than those of exporters. The tariff reform of 1864, often presented by historians as a gadarene rush to free trade, was in many respects no more than a temporary aberration from the more standard nineteenth-century policy, which strove (rather ineffectively) to give at least a minimal degree of protection to certain domestic activities as well as to maximize trade. Nevertheless, it seems reasonably clear, given the extreme poverty of the new nation and the lack of a 'spirit of association' so frequently lamented by, *inter alia*, Manuel Montt, that even a much stronger dose of protectionism could hardly have done much to diversify economic activity or to develop an industrial base of any size. The country's options at this period were fairly narrow.

From the point of view of foreign trade, mining was by far the most important sector of the economy throughout the period. The miners of the north accumulated the largest individual and family fortunes of the time. The two thinly settled provinces of Atacama and Coquimbo, the area nowadays referred to by Chileans as the Norte Chico, constituted the most dynamic region of the country, with a population (about one-eighth of the nation's total in 1865) which rose much faster than was the case in the *hacienda*-dominated provinces of the central valley, thousands of whose people were lured to the ramshackle, rowdy and occasionally rebellious mining camps of the arid north; there were some 30,000 mineworkers there by the 1870s. Tough, enterprising, industrious, periodically volatile, fiercely proud – such was the distinctive culture of the mining zone. Its laboriously extracted riches had a vital impact on the rest of the nation, 'ennobling the central cities and fertilizing the fields of the south', as President Balmaceda was later to put it.[7] Of the three

---

[7] Roberto Hernández, *Juan Godoy o el descubrimiento de Chañarcillo*, 2 vols. (Valparaiso, 1932), II, 560.

principal metals mined in Chile in colonial times, gold did least well after independence, falling from an annual average production of 1,200 kg in the 1820s to a level of around 270 kg in the 1870s. Over the same period, by contrast, silver production rose from about 20,000 kg per annum to about 127,000 kg. (Given the persistence of smuggling, such figures are perhaps conservative). Copper, the most profitable of the three metals, was produced at an annual rate of 2,725 metric tons in the 1820s; this grew very steadily to 45,600 metric tons in the 1870s, by which time Chile regularly accounted for between one-third and one-half of the world's supply.

The allure of mineral wealth attracted numerous traders, speculators and prospectors to the northern deserts. The search for new veins of ore was incessant; the mining zone expanded slowly northwards into the Atacama desert and towards the long undefined border with Bolivia. The important early silver strikes at Agua Amarga (1811) and Arqueros (1825) were soon wholly eclipsed by the sensational discovery at Chañarcillo, south of Copiapó, in 1832. It was the single most productive mining district of the century, a veritable 'silver mountain' which yielded at least $12,000,000 in its first ten years and where by the mid-1840s there were over one hundred mines. The discovery of Tres Puntas (1848) was a further fillip to the boom, though less dramatic. The last silver rush of the period occurred in 1870, with the opening up of a major new mining district at Caracoles, across the border in Bolivia though worked almost entirely by Chileans. Copper mining depended less on new exploration than on the working of established veins of high-grade ore, but here too patient prospecting sometimes reaped a fabulous reward, as in the spectacular case of José Tomás Urmeneta, who searched for eighteen years in dire poverty before coming across, at Tamaya, his legendary deposit of copper. He was soon a millionaire, one of perhaps several dozen very rich men whose great fortunes came from the Norte Chico.

Chilean methods of mining changed only slowly and partially from the pattern established in later colonial times, which had been characterized by numerous small enterprises, individual or family entrepreneurship, simple technology and short-term marginal activity. By the 1860s, it is true, some of the larger mines – Urmeneta's at Tamaya, and José Ramón Ovalle's at Carrizal Alto, for instance – had gone in for extensive mechanization, and it is interesting that the two districts cited accounted for one-third of copper production in the 1870s. But the persistence of older practices – and a large number of small-scale operations which continued to rely, in preference to steampower, on the sturdy *barreteros* and *apires* who dug the ore and shifted it from the mine – is attested by many visitors to the north during this period. In the 1870s only some thirty-three mines in the Norte Chico used steam engines, leaving 755 which did not. Innovations in the smelting and refining of copper were a good deal more noticeable, with reverbatory furnaces (the 'English system') spreading from the 1830s onwards. Over the next two decades, in what amounted to a minor technological revolution, several large smelting plants were established on the coast, most notably at Guayacán and Tongoy in the Norte Chico and at Lirquén and Lota five hundred miles further south; these were Chile's first industrial enterprises of any size. They also processed Peruvian and Bolivian ores, and partially offset the producers' previous dependence on the smelting and refining industry of South Wales. The smelters' insatiable demand for fuel made deep inroads into the exiguous timber resources of the Norte Chico and contributed to the southward advance of the desert – that usually unremarked but basic ecological theme of Chilean history since colonial times. The main alternative to wood was coal, which was increasingly mined along the coast to the south of Concepción from the 1840s onwards. Here, domestic production was vulnerable to imports of higher-quality coal from Great Britain (or occasionally Australia), but held its own in the longer run, in part because a mixture of local and foreign coal was found to be ideal in smelting operations.

Chileans (sometimes first-generation Chileans) were outstanding among the mining entrepreneurs of this period. One or two of the copper concerns were British-owned, but these were exceptions, though foreign engineers were prominent throughout the mining zone. Men such as Urmeneta and a handful of others like him were naturally substantial capitalists in their own right, and they frequently turned their huge windfalls to good account, investing in transport and agriculture as well as in the mines, though not failing, either, to provide themselves with a suitably opulent style of life. Many of the lesser mining entrepreneurs were heavily dependent on a breed of middlemen known as *habilitadores*, who bought their ore in exchange for credit and supplies. This business was the foundation of several large fortunes, a famous example being the career of Agustín Edwards Ossandón, the son of an English doctor who settled in the Norte Chico just before independence. By the 1860s Edwards was one of the richest and most active capitalists in Chile. In 1871–2, in a well-known episode, he quietly accumulated and stockpiled vast amounts of copper, drove up the price by fifty per cent and realized a profit estimated at $1,500,000. By the time Edwards executed this audacious coup, Chile's nineteenth-century silver and copper cycle was reaching its climax. The silver mines were to maintain a high output for two more decades; but with production booming in the United States and Spain, 'Chili bars' became a decreasingly important component in the world supply of copper, no more than six per cent of which came from Chile by the 1890s. By then, of course, deserts further to the north were yielding a still greater source of wealth: nitrates.

Although mining dominated the export sector, it was agriculture which dominated most ordinary lives. Four out of five Chileans lived in the countryside in the 1860s. Here, as in so many other ways, the colonial legacy was overwhelming. Throughout the nineteenth century Chile remained a land of great estates, ownership of which conferred social status, political influence (if desired) and (less automatically before the 1850s) a comfortable income. This tradition of landownership is one of the keys to understanding Chilean history between colonial times and the mid-twentieth century. The precise number of haciendas in the mid-nineteenth century is hard to assess. The tax records of 1854 show that some 850 landowners received around two-thirds of all agricultural income in central Chile, and that of these 154 owned estates which earned in excess of $6,000 per year. (For purposes of comparison, it might be noted here that the president of the republic was paid a salary of $12,000, raised to $18,000 in 1861.) Haciendas occupied at least three-quarters of all agricultural land; most included large tracts of ground which went uncultivated from year to year. The estates were worked by a stable, resident class of *inquilinos*, or tenant-labourers, and, when necessary, by peons hired for seasonal work from outside. This type of rural labour system, as we know, was common (though with many variations) in many parts of Spanish America. When Charles Darwin rode through the Chilean countryside in the mid-1830s, he thought of it as 'feudal-like'. The Chilean *inquilino* was bound to the hacienda, allowed to cultivate his own small parcel of land in exchange for regular labour services to the landowner, by ties of custom and convenience rather than by those of law or debt. In the absence of traditional village communities of the European kind, the estate became the sole focus of his loyalty and formed his own little universe. 'Every hacienda in Chile', wrote an acute observer in 1861, 'forms a separate society, whose head is the landowner and whose subjects are the *inquilinos* . . . The landowner is an absolute monarch in his hacienda.'[8] For the tenant-labourers life was poor though not necessarily harsh; their farming methods were primitive, their diet monotonous and sometimes barely adequate and their opportunities to rise in the social scale very strictly limited. But the relative security of the hacienda could be contrasted with the plight of most of the peons outside – a destitute mass of people scraping a very precarious living by squatting on marginal land, by wandering the central valley in search of seasonal work, or in some cases by turning to cattle-rustling and banditry. From the viewpoint of the *hacendado*, there was plenty of surplus labour, as well as unused land, in the countryside. Neither was needed on a large scale before 1850 or so.

If agriculture was unproductive and unprofitable in the earlier part of this period, the reason is easy enough to identify. Local demand was quickly satisfied, while export markets were few and far between. The eighteenth-century grain trade with Peru, whose importance has probably been exaggerated by historians, was never quite re-established on the old scale following the wars of independence and the commercial rivalry of the 1830s. Between 1850 and 1880, however, the outlook for landowners improved quite radically, with haciendas responding immediately to the opening up of new markets overseas. As the only major cereal-growing country on the Pacific coast of America, Chile was well placed to take advantage of the sudden demand set up by the gold rushes in California and Australia. Exports of wheat and flour to California amounted to around 6,000 metric quintals (qqm) in 1848. Two years later no less than 277,000 qqm of wheat and 221,000 qqm of flour were shipped northwards. The boom was ephemeral – by 1855 California was self-sufficient – but it yielded high profits while it lasted, and it was responsible for consolidating a technically up-to-date milling industry in the Talca area and along Talcahuano Bay, as well as in Santiago itself slightly later on. By 1871 there were some 130 or so modern mills in Chile. (At the end of this period, further changes in the technology of milling were being pioneered in the middle west of the United States and in Europe, but these, by contrast, were slower to reach Chile.) Australia provided a second short-lived (and somewhat precarious) market for Chile in the 1850s, lucrative for a while. Landowners were well aware that geography and good luck were the causes of such windfalls, which were substantial enough: agricultural exports quintupled in value be-

[8] 'Atropos,' 'El inquilino en Chile', *Revista del Pacífico*, 5 (1861), 94.

tween 1844 and 1860. Nor was this by any means the end of the story. The experience gained in the Californian and Australian markets, combined with vital improvements in transport, enabled Chile in the 1860s to sell large quantities of grain (wheat and barley) to England: 2,000,000 qqm were exported in 1874, the peak year. Once again, however, Chile's competitive position in the international market place was more fragile than it appeared, and it was permanently undermined a few years later, when grain prices fell and new, more efficient cereal-growing countries were opened up.

The stimulus of these mid-century export booms brought some definite changes to the countryside. Most visible of these, perhaps, were the numerous irrigation canals now constructed, some of them remarkable feats of engineering. (The Canal de las Mercedes, sponsored by Manuel Montt and other *hacendados* in 1854, took thirty years to build and eventually extended seventy-five miles over very uneven terrain.) The quality of livestock was slowly improved, through the introduction of foreign breeds. With the growth of the towns, an expanding market for fruit and poultry greatly benefited nearby haciendas and the smaller (often specialist) farms known as *chacras*. Chileans had drunk their own wine since early colonial times; but the foundations of the great viticultural tradition which was later to produce the finest vintages in the western hemisphere were only laid in the 1850s, when pinot and cabernet grapes, brought from France, were grown locally for the first time. The government itself, as well as the Sociedad Nacional de Agricultura (in intermittent existence from 1838) tried to improve agricultural knowledge. Developments such as these, thus sketched, seem to convey an impression of vitality, but it is somewhat deceptive. Rural society and traditional farming methods were in no real way drastically disturbed, although it seems probable that monetary transactions in the countryside became more widespread than previously. There was relatively little in the way of high capital investment in agriculture (leaving aside irrigation works), and despite the enthusiasm of a number of progressive landowners, farm-machinery was never imported or employed on a large scale. (Oxen remained in universal use in Chile until the 1930s.) During the happy years of the export boom, landowners had ample reserves of both land and labour on which to draw. The acreage placed beneath the plough in these years may well have tripled or even quadrupled. New families from outside the haciendas were encouraged (and in many cases were no doubt eager) to swell the ranks of the *inquilinos*. The labour system itself was certainly tightened up, with greater demands being made on the tenant-labourers. Quite apart from *inquilinaje*, a variety of sharecropping practices, especially in the coastal range, were developed to help feed the export boom. The number of *minifundios* also seems to have risen. But in general it was the hacienda system itself, the basic underpinning of the nation's elite, which was most clearly consolidated by the changes of the mid-nineteenth century.

Such manufacturing as existed in Chile at the time of independence and for two or three decades thereafter was carried out by artisans and craftsmen in small workshops in the towns. In the countryside, the hacienda population largely clothed itself, though the growing import of British cottons probably had the effect over the years of reducing the extent of local weaving. The upper class was, on the whole, able to satisfy its demand for manufactured goods, including luxuries, from abroad, and was uninterested in promoting an industrial revolution. (Mining entrepreneurs were a partial exception here, and at the end of the period industrialism was viewed as a possible way forward for the country by a growing number of intellectuals and politicians.) There can be little doubt, however, that the expansion of national wealth after 1850 or so did provide certain opportunities for entrepreneurship in manufacturing, and such opportunities were sometimes seized – usually by foreigners, though these can better be regarded, perhaps, as first-generation Chileans. The first major industrial enterprises arose in connection with the export booms and were the copper smelters and flour mills mentioned already. In addition to these, the 1860s and 1870s saw the growth of small-scale factory production in such fields as textiles, food-processing, brick-making and glass-blowing. By the 1880s there were at least thirty breweries in the country. Furthermore, the needs of the new railways and of the mining industry itself stimulated the appearance of a number of small foundries and machine shops capable of repairing and in some instances even making equipment. In fact, what seems to have been a respectable metallurgical and engineering sector was developing with surprising speed by the early 1870s. There is growing evidence for supposing that the start of Chilean industrialization, often dated from the War of the Pacific, should be pushed back by about ten years.

It goes without saying that Chile's export-led economic expansion could hardly have taken place without improvements in transport and communications, which were also of obvious importance in consolidating the political coherence of the new nation. The number of ships calling at Chilean ports rose more or less constantly from the 1830s onwards, to over 4,000 per annum in the 1870s. Two 700-ton paddle steamers were brought to Chile from England in 1840 by a very enterprising American, William Wheelwright, the founder of the British-owned Pacific Steam Navigation Company. The outside world began to draw closer. From the mid-1840s it became possible, with suitable connections across the Panama isthmus, to travel to Europe in under forty days. (Sailing ships still took three or four months.) In 1868 the now well-established P.S.N.C. (whose initials later prompted several famous Chilean jokes) opened a direct service between Valparaíso and Liverpool by way of the Magellan Straits. Meanwhile, inland transport was slowly being revolutionized by the inevitable advent of the railway. The north of Chile, indeed, installed the first substantial length of track in Latin America. The line, built by Wheelwright and finished in 1851, linked Copiapó with the port of Caldera fifty miles away. It was financed by a group of wealthy miners, and it set the pattern for several later railways in the mining zone. The vital link between Santiago and Valparaíso had to wait somewhat longer. This was initially a mixed venture, the government subscribing about half the capital, but in 1858, following tiresome delays and difficulties, the state bought out most of the private shareholders; a swashbuckling American entrepreneur, Henry Meiggs, was entrusted with the completion of the line; and the last sections of the wide-gauge track were laid in 1863. Another mixed venture sponsored the third main railway, extending southwards through the central valley, a line of particular interest to cereal-growing *hacendados*. The Errázuriz government took this over in 1873, and only a few years later the line joined up with a further railway which by then had been built inland from Talcahuano and was pressing southwards into the romantic landscapes of Araucania. In 1882 there were nearly 1,200 miles of track in Chile, just over half state-owned. The state also subsidized and subsequently purchased the nascent telegraph network, construction of which began in 1852 – yet another enterprise of the indefatigable Wheelwright, to whom, in due course, a statue was raised in Valparaíso. Twenty years later the Chilean brothers Juan and Mateo Clark linked Santiago to Buenos Aires; with the laying of the Brazilian submarine cable in 1874 Chile was for the first time placed in direct touch with the Old World.

The increasing pace of economic activity during the third quarter of the nineteenth century left its mark on the country's financial and commercial institutions. Up to the 1850s the main sources of credit, for instance, had been private lenders or the trading houses. This now changed, with the appearance of the first proper banks – the Banco de Ossa and the Banco de Valparaíso, founded in the mid-1850s – and banking operations were sufficiently extensive to warrant regulation in the important law of 1860. The creation in 1856 of the notable Caja de Crédito Hipotecario funnelled credit to the countryside – in practice mainly to the big landowners. Joint-stock companies now became increasingly common, though supplementing rather than replacing the individual and family concerns and partnerships which had hitherto been the standard modes of business organization. The earliest were the railway companies; by the end of the 1870s well over 150 such enterprises had been formed at one time or another, predominantly in mining, banking and insurance, and railways. Chilean capitalism showed a markedly expansionist tendency in the 1860s and 1870s, with money flowing into the nitrate business in Bolivia and Peru as well as to the silver mines at Caracoles. Unregulated stock exchanges were operating in Valparaíso and Santiago from the early 1870s, at which point 'Caracoles fever' was driving investors into a speculative frenzy without precedent in Chilean history.

Foreign trade throughout this period was largely controlled by several dozen import-export houses centred on Valparaíso and the capital; these contributed much to the building up of the new money market, and remained influential thereafter in the developing corporate sector of the economy. Foreigners, whether as permanent residents or as transient agents of overseas trading houses with branches in Chile, were particularly prominent here, with the British leading the field. The British connection was fundamental to Chile. Investment in the country by Britons was mostly confined to government bonds – to the tune of around £7,000,000 by 1880 – but Great Britain was the destination for between one-third and two-thirds of all Chile's exports and the source of between one-third and one-half of all her imports in any given year. Imports from France also ran high, reflecting upper class tastes. As in colonial times, trade with Peru continued, but this was overshadowed by the links now being forged with the North Atlantic. The steamers, railways, telegraphs, banks and joint-stock companies all played their part in cementing Chile's solidifying association with the international economy now coming into being around the world. Politicians might occasionally denounce the British traders as the 'new Carthaginians' or even (in more popular vein) as 'infidels', but by and large their presence was welcomed as a vital element in what was confidently assumed to be the progress of the nation.

Sixty years after independence Chile was an altogether more prosperous land than would have seemed likely in 1810, as well as being more integrated economically than in colonial times. Her record in this respect contrasts forcibly with the stagnation evident in several of the other Spanish American republics. But the new prosperity was not distributed proportionately (still less evenly) to all sections of the people. The wealth of the upper class increased very strikingly, and the upper class had a fairly clear idea as to what to do with it. An American visitor in the mid-1850s observed that 'the great object of life' on acquiring wealth seemed to be to 'remove to the capital, to lavish it on costly furniture, equipage and splendid living.'[9] The gradual disappearance of older, more austere, supposedly more virtuous habits of life was lamented by writers of a moralistic cast of mind; and it is probably fair to say that the adoption of more sophisticated, European styles of living – fashions across a whole range from hats to horse-racing altered visibly between the 1820s and the 1870s – may well have deepened the psychological gulf between rich and poor; it may also be one of the keys to understanding the political liberalization which set in after 1861. The elite of Chilean society was never closed to newcomers. The new magnates of mining and finance were easily assimilated, as were the children or grandchildren of successful immigrants – though the much remarked contingent of non-Hispanic surnames in the Chilean upper class only became really conspicuous at the end of the century. (There was only one English surname in any of the cabinets before the 1880s.) The underlying coherence of this open, flexible elite was provided by a set of economic interests – in mines, land, banks and trade – which overlapped and often interlocked. The miners or traders who in different circumstances might have formed the vanguard of a *bourgeoisie conquérante* were from the start included at the highest levels of the social hierarchy, where fundamentally aristocratic outlooks and attitudes prevailed. The supreme upper class values were those concerned with family and landownership. The importance of family connections at this period cannot easily be exaggerated. It was something which often showed up in politics. President Bulnes was the son-in-law of one of his predecessors, the nephew of another and the

---

[9] [Mrs. C. B. Merwin], *Three Years in Chile* (New York, 1863), 95.

brother-in-law of one of his successors. In the century after 1830, the Errázuriz family gave the republic one archbishop, three presidents, and upwards of fifty congressmen. The attraction of rural property, likewise, integrated rather than divided the elite; landownership was the highly prized badge of aristocratic status. These powerful forces for coherence clearly encouraged continuity and stability rather than change and rearrangement in the social development of Chile.

Between the landowning upper class and the labouring poor, a small, miscellaneous 'middle band' of society grew perceptibly larger as the result of economic expansion. It consisted of the owners of the smaller businesses and farms, the growing number of clerical employees in trade, the subaltern members of the bureaucracy (which even in 1880 still numbered no more than 3,000), and the artisans and craftsmen of the towns. These last were what educated Chileans of the period meant when they used the term *clase obrera*. On the upper fringe of the middle band, frustrated would-be entrants into the best circles constituted a recognizable type, well described in some of the fiction of the time. From at least the later 1850s such people were known as *siúticos* and tradition attributes the neologism, still understood if no longer widely used, to Lastarria. Chilean artisans, for their part, were never well protected by commercial policy, but the growth of the towns (and upper class wealth) created a demand for services and products which could best be met locally, and many crafts and trades seem to have flourished, at least in a modest way. In their manners and aspirations such groups evidently took their tone from high society. Referring to the 'mechanics and retail shopkeepers' of the Santiago of 1850, a sharp-eyed visitor noted:

There is an inherent want of tidiness in their domestic life; but in public, fine dress is a passion with them, and a stranger would scarcely suspect that the man he meets in a fine broad-cloth cloak, escorting a woman arrayed in silks and jewelry, occupied no higher rank in the social scale than that of tinman, carpenter or shopman whose sole stock-in-trade might be packed in a box five feet square.[10]

The spread of mutualist associations in later years provided a greater degree of security for artisans and craftsmen. The first was founded in the printing trade in 1853 and did not last long; but by 1880, thanks to the efforts of the builder and architect Fermín Vivaceta and others, there were some thirty-nine societies of this kind enjoying legal status, foreshadowing the later emergence of trade unions.

[10] Lieut. J. M. Gilliss, U.S.N., *The United States Naval Astronomical Expedition to the southern hemisphere during the years 1849–50–51–52*, vol. I., *Chile* (Washington, 1855), 219.

A deep material and psychological chasm separated all the social groups so far mentioned from the great mass of the labouring poor in town and countryside, whose condition improved only marginally, if at all, over this period. Despite the higher number of families now being settled on the haciendas, the peons of the central valley were often obliged to look elsewhere for work. They migrated in their thousands to overcrowded and insalubrious districts in the main towns. Both *rotos* (urban labourers) and peons also flocked to the northern mining camps, and to the railway-building gangs, in Chile and overseas. When, at the end of the 1860s, the audacious Henry Meiggs (renowned for the remark that he would sooner employ five hundred Chilean *rotos* than a thousand Irishmen) embarked on grandiose railway-building schemes in Peru at least 25,000 Chileans answered his call. This outflow of labour provoked debates in Congress, with proposals to restrict emigration, while land-owners complained of a 'shortage of hands' in the countryside. In fact, there was no real shortage, and this was appreciated by those more acute Chileans who now began to subject the labouring poor to somewhat closer scrutiny than in the past.

If emigration was (briefly) a concern of Chilean legislators, the idea of immigration from Europe, as a means of 'civilizing' the lower classes, was suggested more frequently. Traces of xenophobia may have sur-vived among the poor, to be whipped up on occasion, as during the civil war of 1829–30, but in general foreigners were welcomed with open arms. ' "Foreigner" ', once said Antonio Varas, 'is an immoral word which should be expunged from the dictionary!' The census of 1875 counted 4,109 British, 4,033 German and 2,330 French residents in Chile, with people of other nationalities totalling nearly 15,000, a figure which included 7,000 Argentines. The role of the British in trade has already been noted; some prominent Chilean families came in due course from this quarter. The milling industry referred to earlier was largely estab-lished by Americans; Americans and British helped to build and then to operate the railway network; a high proportion of the industrial entre-preneurs of later years came from abroad. At a more modest level, foreigners also found a place in the expanding artisan class, notably in those trades which catered to the style of life favoured by the rich. European scholars and scientists such as the Frenchmen Claude Gay (author of a famous thirty-volume account of the country's natural and civil history) and Amado Pissis (who mapped the republic from 28°10′S to 41°58′S) did much to add to the store of Chilean knowledge; the government had a more or less systematic policy of employing such people. There was no mass immigration of the kind desired, but at the end of the 1840s the government encouraged the settlement of families from Germany in the thinly-populated southern territories around Valdivia and Lake Llanquihue. By 1860 there were more than 3,000 Germans in the south, hardy pioneers who cleared the forests and opened the land to cultivation.

This new official interest in the south spelled the beginning of the end for the independent Indian enclave of Araucania, which lay inconveniently between the new areas of settlement and the country's heartland north of the Bío-Bío. The suppression of the widespread banditry which followed independence in the southern provinces, complete by the mid-1830s, had placed the Araucanians in a somewhat more vulnerable position than previously; but for the next quarter of a century they were left largely undisturbed. As in colonial times, the army patrolled the frontier while the government in Santiago cultivated (and subsidized) a number of amiably disposed caciques. The agricultural expansion of the 1850s, however, drew settlers into the area south of the Bío-Bío, causing tension with the Araucanians. The Indian attacks on frontier settlements which followed (1859–60) raised the 'Araucanian question' as a political issue, much discussed over the next few years. The policy adopted by the Pérez government was, by establishing 'lines' of forts, to enclose the Araucanians within a diminishing belt of territory. The Indians resisted the encroaching Chilean army in a further series of assaults (1868–71), but by the end of the 1870s, with settlement spilling into the frontier, the 'lines' had drawn inexorably closer together. After the War of the Pacific, troops were sent in to 'pacify' and occupy the narrow fringe of Indian territory which remained. The long, proud history of Araucania drew to its pathetic close. The Indians themselves were given, on paper, a settlement deemed generous in the eyes of Santiago, but the pattern of land transactions on the frontier over the previous twenty years was hardly a good augury. The government strove in vain to regularize land transfers in the south, but failed to prevent the formation of new latifundia, often through chicanery and intimidation. Nor could the measures taken to protect the interests of the Araucanians against predatory landowners (great and small) be described as anything but inadequate.

The most vivid contrast, in the Chile of the 1870s, was between town and country. Civilization – that term so often used to justify the 'pacification' of Araucania – was perhaps most evident in its urban setting. Nineteenth-century Chilean urbanization (modest indeed by the standards of the twentieth century) was essentially a tale of two cities – Santiago, which grew from about 70,000 in the mid-1830s to 130,000 in 1875, and Valparaíso, which by the end of our period had reached close on 100,000. Other Chilean towns lagged far behind. During the mining booms, it is true, Copiapó enjoyed a prosperous heyday; Concepción, devastated by the earthquake of 1835, flourished again with the spread of wheat-growing and milling; and among the somnolent little towns of the central valley, Talca nurtured a well-developed sense of civic pride. But none of these places had populations of more than 20,000 in 1875. The predominance of the capital and the main port, underpinned by political and commercial hegemony, was unchallengeable. As contemporary drawings and prints show clearly, Santiago retained a definitely colonial appearance until around 1850, but the mid-century export boom quickly left its mark. By 1857 the normally sober Andrés Bello could write that 'the progress made in the last five years can be called fabulous. Magnificent buildings are rising everywhere . . .; to see the Alameda on certain days of the year makes one imagine one is in one of the great cities of Europe.'[11] The year 1857, in fact, saw the inauguration of the fine Teatro Municipal and the introduction of horse-drawn trams and gas-lamps in the streets. Architectural styles altered, French (or even English) models being preferred for the new aristocratic mansions now being built. The unusually active programme carried through by Benjamín Vicuña Mackenna, the almost legendary Intendant of the early 1870s, endowed the capital with avenues, parks, squares and the superb urban folly of the Cerro Santa Lucía, which delights *santiaguinos* to this day. Valparaíso, the first Chilean town to organize a proper fire-brigade (1851), underwent similar though less flamboyantly publicized improvements. Its business district took on a faintly British atmosphere. Both capital and port (and other towns later on) soon acquired a respectable newspaper press, which flourished with particular vigour in the more liberal political climate after 1861. The doyen of the Chilean press, *El Mercurio*, founded at Valparaíso in 1827 (and a daily from 1829), is today the oldest newspaper in the Spanish-language world.

Education in this period made slower progress than many Chileans would have wished, despite the best efforts of such presidents as Montt, whose obsessive interest in the matter was shared by his great Argentine friend Sarmiento. Illiteracy fell gradually, to around seventy-seven per

---

[11] Domingo Amunátegui Solar, *La democracia en Chile* (Santiago, 1946), 132.

cent in 1875, at which point seventeen per cent of the school-age population was undergoing some form of primary education. By 1879, too, there were some twenty-seven public *liceos* (two for girls) and a larger number of private schools providing instruction at the secondary level, along with the prestigious Instituto Nacional, where so many of the republic's leaders received their secondary (and for many years much of their higher) education. Higher studies (and especially professional training, to which women were admitted by the decree of 1877) were greatly stimulated by the formation in 1843 of the University of Chile. Modelled on the Institut de France, it was in its early years a deliberative and supervisory body rather than a teaching institution, but its standards were high. The distinct strengthening of intellectual and cultural life which now became noticeable owed much to the first rector of the university, the eminent Venezuelan scholar, Andrés Bello, who spent the last thirty-six years of a long life in Chile. Poet, grammarian, philosopher, educationist, jurist, historian, indefatigable public servant and senator – Bello had a patient and many-sided genius which inspired a host of devoted pupils and disciples. It is impossible in the space of this chapter to survey the cultural panorama of the period; but one rather singular aspect deserves to be noted. This was the primacy accorded to history, a primacy encouraged by the university and (in a small way) by the government itself. The result, between 1850 and 1900 or so, was the fine flowering of historical narrative represented, above all, in the works of Diego Barros Arana, Miguel Luis Amunátegui, Ramón Sotomayor Valdés and Benjamín Vicuña Mackenna. Of these four, Barros Arana was the most diligent and scholarly, Vicuña Mackenna the most lyrical and vivid. All can still be read with profit.

It is possible that this Chilean preference for history both reflected and reinforced the growth of national consciousness. Patriotism, to be sure, is never easy to assess. It may be doubted whether a clear sense of *chilenidad* really penetrated very far into the countryside before the 1870s. The people of the towns, by contrast, responded ardently to the victory celebrations in 1839; the *dieciocho*, the annual national holiday, though often a pretext for prolonged alcoholic indulgence, was an undeniably popular occasion; and private as well as public initiatives saw to it that statues were raised to the heroes of independence and other national figures, starting with General Freire in 1856. (Portales and O'Higgins got their monuments in 1860 and 1872 respectively). Educated Chileans were strongly inclined to see their country as superior to others in

Spanish America – and it is hard to resist the conclusion that in certain important respects they were right. 'We saved ourselves from the general shipwreck', wrote the rising Conservative politician Carlos Walker Martínez.[12] Chile as the *república modelo*, as an example to unruly, 'tropical' lands, was a recurrent theme in speeches and editorials. 'I have such a poor idea of the . . . sister republics', observed Antonio Varas in 1864, 'that . . . I regret we have to make common cause with them.'[13] Such opinions often coincided with foreign views of Chile, especially in Europe. (In April 1880 even *The Times* used the phrase 'model republic'.) European flattery was deeply pleasing to educated Chileans, many of whom believed that Great Britain and France (in particular) were leading the world up a highway of progress which in due course Chile herself was sure to follow: 'Europe's today is our tomorrow.'[14]

This mood of confidence and optimism was severely shaken by the multiple crisis of the mid-1870s. This can effectively be dated from the collapse in 1873 of the speculative bonanza induced by the Caracoles silver boom. The economic difficulties which mounted up thereafter stemmed in part from the serious international recession which began that year (the start of the 'Great Depression' which followed the long mid-Victorian boom), but they also reflected a more fundamental problem: with the appearance in the world economy of new and more efficient producers of both wheat and copper, Chile was now being displaced in her most important export markets. The springs of prosperity were running dry. Copper prices, briefly boosted by the Franco-Prussian war (as they had earlier been by the Crimean war), went into sharp decline. The value of silver exports halved within four years, though the cause often assigned to this – the shift to the gold standard by Germany and other nations – may have been exaggerated by historians. On top of all this, an alarming and untimely cycle of both flooding and drought in the central valley brought three disastrous harvests in a row. An abrupt rise in the cost of living plunged many thousands of poorer Chileans into destitution and near-starvation. There were disturbing symptoms of social unrest. The peso, stable for so long, began to depreciate, falling from 46*d*. in 1872 to 33*d*. by 1879. (It is faintly amusing to record that in this atmosphere of desperation, official hopes were briefly raised by a

[12] C. W. Martínez, *Portales* (Paris, 1879), 452.
[13] Antonio Varas, *Correspondencia*, 5 vols. (Santiago, 1918–29), v, 48.
[14] Editorial, *El Mercurio*, 18 September 1844.

Franco-American confidence trickster who claimed to be able to convert copper into gold; he was lionized and had a polka named after him.) Fearing a catastrophic run on the now largely insolvent banks, the Pinto administration took the drastic step of declaring the inconvertibility of bank-notes (July 1878), which thus became obligatory legal tender; it was the start of a century of inflation. In its efforts to solve the acute fiscal dilemma (made still more acute by the need to service a national debt which had grown perilously fast over the previous few years), the government first resorted to cuts in public spending; the National Guard, for instance, was reduced to a mere 7,000 men. As the recession deepened, many intelligent Chileans, noting their country's heavy dependence on exports, advocated a stronger protectionist dose for the embryonic industrial sector (this was partly achieved in the tariff reform of 1878) and also the imposition of new taxes on the wealthy. This latter notion, according to the British consul-general, was well regarded 'by all but those whose pockets it would chiefly affect and who, for the misfortune of their Country, just now largely compose her Legislature'.[15] In fact, Congress in 1878–9 did agree, after much argument, to levy small taxes on inheritances and property. These had little effect on the crisis, from which Chile was saved not by fiscal improvization but by blood and iron.

The menacing international tensions of the 1870s derived from long standing border disputes with Argentina and Bolivia. Neither frontier had been precisely delineated in colonial times. The Chilean presence on the Magellan Straits after 1843 had raised the question of the ownership of Patagonia, which Argentines considered theirs. Chile, in effect, abandoned her claim to all but a fraction of this huge but desolate territory in the Fierro-Sarratea agreement of 1878, accepted by Congress despite the angry crowds outside the building and a strong speech from an irate former foreign minister, who lamented that Chile would now remain 'a poor republic' instead of becoming 'a great empire'. The agreement averted the danger of war with Argentina; there had been considerable sabre-rattling on both sides of the Andes. The problem with Bolivia was more intractable, for while few vital interests had been at stake in Patagonia this was emphatically not the case in the Atacama desert, one of the principal scenes of Chilean economic expansionism. Here in the 1860s, on the Bolivian littoral, the Chilean entrepreneurs José

[15] Consul-General Packenham to the Marquis of Salisbury, Santiago, 24 February 1879. Public Record Office, London: F.O.16/203.

Santos Ossa and Francisco Puelma had pioneered the extraction of nitrate, in growing demand abroad as a fertilizer. (Chilean capital was also prominent in the nitrate business in the Peruvian desert, further north; but the industry there was nationalized by the Peruvian government in 1875). In the Atacama, thanks to generous concessions by Bolivia, the powerful Compañía de Salitres y Ferrocarril de Antofagasta, a Chilean-British corporation in which a number of leading Chilean politicians held shares, was close to constituting a state within a state. Most of the population on the littoral was Chilean. Such a state of affairs is always potentially explosive. In 1874, in an attempt to settle the frontier once and for all, Chile agreed to fix it at 24°S in return for the Bolivian promise of a twenty-five-year moratorium on the further taxation of Chilean nitrate enterprises. The additional export tax of ten centavos per quintal suddenly imposed by the Bolivians in 1878 was clearly a breach of faith. (Whether the original Bolivian concessions were imprudent or not is another matter.) The refusal of the Compañía de Salitres to pay up brought threats of confiscation. In order to forestall this a small Chilean force occupied Antofagasta (February 1879) and went on to take control of the littoral. The conflict swiftly assumed graver proportions. Peru was drawn in by virtue of a secret treaty of alliance with Bolivia, concluded six years previously. Chile declared war on both countries in April 1879.

The War of the Pacific was seen at the time (by some) as a cynically premeditated exercise in plunder, with the aim of rescuing Chile from her economic plight by seizing the mineral wealth of the northern deserts. Others detected the invisible hand of more powerful nations and the foreign trading concerns so closely enmeshed with the nitrate business. The American secretary of state, the egregious James G. Blaine, even asserted later on that it was 'an English war on Peru, with Chile as the instrument', a verdict which it is difficult to sustain from the existing evidence.[16] It must, however, be said that Chilean politicians (not least those who held or had held shares in nitrate enterprises) were aware of the advantages which might accrue from control of the deserts and were equally aware of the country's dire economic position in 1879. Insofar as there had been a public 'willingness to war' over the previous months, this had mainly been directed against Argentina. Nonetheless it may well

[16] On these points, see V. G. Kiernan, 'Foreign interests in the War of the Pacific', *Hispanic American Historical Review*, 35 (1955), 14–36, and John Mayo, 'La Compañía de Salitres de Antofagasta y la Guerra del Pacífico', *Historia*, (Santiago) 14 (1979), 71–102.

be true that the eagerness with which the outbreak of hostilities was welcomed (generally, if not universally) was in some sense an outlet for the pent-up feelings of frustration which had accumulated during the years of recession. (Chile's action in February 1879 could plausibly be described as precipitate.) But neither Chile nor her enemies were prepared for war. Their armies were small and poorly equipped. Chile had cut back her military strength during the recession, while both the Peruvian and Bolivian armies were decidedly over-officered. At sea, Chile and Peru (Bolivia had no navy) were perhaps more evenly matched; and command of the sea was the key to the war. In the end, Chile's greater national coherence and traditions of settled government probably made the vital difference. At various points during this time of mortal danger, both Bolivia and Peru were afflicted by serious political upheavals. In Chile, by contrast, congressional and presidential elections were held as usual, cabinets changed without excessive drama and energetic politicking by no means ceased: neither the Conservatives nor the disaffected Liberal group led by Vicuña Mackenna (who had made an unsuccessful bid for the presidency in 1876) were invited into the cabinet, and they made up for this by mercilessly castigating the government's numerous hesitancies and failures in the conduct of the war.

The early months, taken up with a struggle for naval mastery, were a frustrating period of reverses for Chile, but also provided the single most memorable incident of the war. On 21 May 1879, off Iquique, the decrepit wooden corvette *Esmeralda* was attacked by the Peruvian ironclad *Huascar*. Although the corvette was outclassed and doomed from the outset, the Chilean commander, Captain Arturo Prat, refused to strike his colours. He himself died in an entirely hopeless boarding operation as the *Huascar* rammed his vessel, which, after further rammings, went down. Prat's heroic self-sacrifice turned him into a 'secular saint' without compare in the admiration of his countrymen. Five months later, off Cape Angamos, the Chilean fleet cornered the *Huascar* and forced her to surrender. This victory gave Chile command of the sea and enabled her to launch an offensive on land. Soon after the battle of Angamos, an expeditionary force invaded the Peruvian desert province of Tarapacá, forcing the enemy to fall back on Tacna and Arica to the north. Early in 1880 an army of 12,000 men, commanded by General Manuel Baquedano, undertook the conquest of these provinces too, in a desert campaign culminating in the ferocious battles of Campo de la Alianza and the Morro of Arica (May–June 1880). By this time, an intervention to halt the conflict had been mooted among the powers of

Europe, but the suggestion was effectively torpedoed by Bismarck. The United States, however, succeeded in arranging talks between the belligerents, aboard a cruiser off Arica, in October 1880. The conference broke down. The Chilean government, now in control of all the main nitrate-producing areas, would almost certainly have liked to make peace, but public opinion demanded the humiliation of Peru, in strident cries of 'On to Lima!' At the end of 1880 an army of more than 26,000 men, once again under Baquedano, disembarked on the central Peruvian coast. The extremely bloody battles of Chorrillos and Miraflores (January 1881) opened the gates of Lima. The war continued in the interior of Peru for two further years, with guerrilla forces resisting the army of occupation, but nothing could disguise the fact that Chile had won a total victory. A new Peruvian government eventually accepted, in the Treaty of Ancón (October 1883), most of the victor's stiff terms for peace. Tarapacá was ceded in perpetuity, and Chile was given temporary possession of Tacna and Arica – over which there developed a long diplomatic wrangle not finally resolved until 1929. The last Chilean soldiers left Peru in August 1884. A truce with Bolivia (April 1884) allowed Chile to remain in control of the Atacama until the negotiation of a full peace settlement, which only materialized in 1904.

Victory in the War of the Pacific gave Chile very substantial international prestige. For Chileans themselves there were the inevitable temptations to hubris, not entirely resisted. The optimism so seriously shattered by the crisis of the previous decade was swiftly recaptured, with the discovery that, as Vicuña Mackenna characteristically put it, 'in the Chilean soul, hidden beneath the soldier's rough tunic or coarse poncho of native weave, there throbs the sublime heroism of the age of antiquity'.[17] In every Chilean, it seemed, there was a soldier. With the conquest of the Bolivian littoral and the southern provinces of Peru, Chile enlarged her national territory by one-third. Possession of the nitrate fields meant that the country's wealth was enormously augmented overnight – and in the nick of time, given the apparent exhaustion of the sources of Chilean prosperity in the mid-1870s. As nitrate took over from copper and silver, the material progress undergone in the half-century or so before the war soon began to look modest in comparison with the boom of the 1880s. Such sudden national windfalls need to be carefully appraised and judiciously managed. For Chile, the model republic of Latin America, the victories of peace were, perhaps, to be less assured than those of war.

[17] Eugenio Orrego Vicuña, *Vicuña Mackenna, vida y trabajos*, 3rd edn (Santiago, 1951), 376.

15

THE RIVER PLATE REPUBLICS FROM INDEPENDENCE TO THE PARAGUAYAN WAR

Argentina became independent in the second decade of the nineteenth century with few of the assets considered essential in a Latin American state. It had minerals but no mines, land but little labour, commerce but few commodities. The economy of Buenos Aires emerged from its colonial past not as a primary producer but as a pure entrepôt. The merchants of Buenos Aires made their profits not by exporting the products of the country but by importing consumer goods for a market stretching from the Atlantic to the Andes, in exchange for precious metals which had been produced or earned in Potosí. The city's rural hinterland was little developed. At the time of independence pastoral products accounted for only 20 per cent of the total exports of Buenos Aires; the other 80 per cent was silver. Until about 1815–20 land exploitation continued to be a secondary activity, and cattle estates were few in number and small in size. As for agriculture, it was confined to a few farms on the outskirts of towns, producing barely enough for the urban market.

Independence altered this primitive economy. First, the merchants of Buenos Aires were squeezed out by foreigners. With their superior resources, their capital, shipping and contacts in Europe, the British took over the entrepreneurial role previously filled by Spaniards. Unable to compete with the newcomers, local businessmen sought outlets in land and cattle. Then the province of Buenos Aires, hitherto a poor neighbour of richer cattle areas, profited from the misfortunes of its rivals. In the years after 1813 Santa Fe, Entre Ríos and Corrientes were devastated by wars of secession, while the other rich pastoral zone, the Banda Oriental, was ruined by revolution, counter-revolution and the Portuguese invasion of 1816. Buenos Aries took advantage of this opportunity, and those with capital found good returns in cattle ranching. Pasture began to expand at the expense of arable farming, the province increased its export of cattle products, and soon it came to rely upon imported grain. Finally, the trade of Buenos Aires with the interior diminished. This had always depended upon the interior's ability to earn silver from the sale of its products in the mining economies. But the competition of British imports depressed the rural and artisan industries of the interior at a time when war and secession were removing established markets in Chile and Upper Peru.

The conjuncture of British competition, the ravages of war and the decline of the interior rendered the traditional economy of Buenos Aires incapable of sustaining the ruling groups. They began, therefore, to diversify their interests, to acquire *estancias*, to establish a rural base. Land was plentiful, the soil was rich and deep, and there was normally a good supply of surface water on the pampas. The greatest danger lay on the frontier, and the frontier was uncomfortably close. The Pampa Indians, immediately to the south and west of the Río Salado, were the fiercest of all the Indians of the plains. Irredeemably savage, they lived and fought on horseback, a mobile and elusive enemy, handling the lance and the *bola* with supreme skill in their swift raids against settlements, *estancias*, personnel and property. The expansion of the *estancias* from 1815 was a disaster for the Indians. Settlers began to occupy their hunting grounds to the south of the Salado, and they retaliated by increasing their raids and enlarging their plunder. They were often joined by vagrant gauchos, deserters from the army, delinquents fleeing the justices of the peace, refugees from social or political conflicts; and their alliance was sometimes invoked in the civil wars of the time by one side or another. The new *estancieros* wanted law and order in the pampas and peace on the frontier. They also sought security of tenure.

From 1822 Bernardino Rivadavia, the modernizing minister in the provincial government of Martín Rodríguez, introduced the system of emphyteusis. Authority was given to rent public land (the sale of which was prohibited) to individuals and corporations for twenty years at fixed and extremely low rentals; the applicant simply had to measure and claim a chosen area. This simultaneously put land to productive use, especially the immense reserves of land on the expanding southern frontier, and satisfied the land hunger of prosperous families. The system favoured latifundism and land concentration. There was no limit to the area which the landowner might rent; he was then free to sell his rights and to sublet; and the commissions which determined land values and administered distribution were dominated by *estancieros*. From 1824 to 1827 a number of enormous grants were made, some individuals receiving over 10 square leagues each (66,710 acres). By 1828 almost 1,000 square leagues (over 6½ million acres) had been granted to 112 people and companies, of whom ten received more than 130,000 acres each. By the 1830s some 21 million acres of public land had been transferred to 500 individuals, many of them wealthy recruits from urban society, like the Anchorena, Santa Coloma, Alzaga and Sáenz Valiente families, the founders of Argentina's landed oligarchy.

As the pastoral economy entered a period of growth, expansion was extensive rather than intensive, for it was land, not capital, which was abundant, and there was as yet no technical innovation, no attempt to improve stock or modernize production. The number of cattle and the size of estates were all that counted. But there came a time when the pressure on grazing land and the shortage of further emphyteusis land brought the livestock sector to the limits of profitable expansion. Ranchers were pushing south once more into Indian territory in search of cheap and empty land. Government action was needed to occupy new territory and to protect it. While Rivadavia had been active in allocating land, he had done little for rural order or frontier security. Juan Manuel de Rosas, a pioneer on the southern frontier, owner of vast estates, lord of numerous peons, a militia commander who could parley with the Indians and frighten the politicians, and governor of Buenos Aires from 1829, stood for a policy of expansion and settlement and took a number of positive steps to improve the security of landholding. He organized and led the Desert Expedition of 1833 to the Río Colorado and the Río Negro, with the object of containing Indian aggression, expanding the frontier and imposing an enduring peace. His policy included diplomacy as well as force, presents as well as punishment. And it succeeded, adding to the province of Buenos Aires thousands of square miles, not desert, but land watered by great rivers. Rewards were instantaneous. The provincial government transferred large tracts of the new land to private hands in the years following 1833, especially to the senior officers of the expeditionary force itself. And as the settlers pushed southwards, they encroached once more on Indian hunting grounds. But now, in the 1840s, they were viewed by the Indians with more respect, partly because of the military reputation of Rosas, partly because of the policy of pacification by subsidy.

Rosas also introduced important and permanent modifications to the legal structure of landholding. There were three methods of land acquisition – rent, purchase and grant. Emphyteusis had now outlived its usefulness. It had facilitated land exploitation (and land concentration), but the state had profited hardly at all, for the rent was minimal. Rosas therefore decided to sell public land outright and to receive a specific revenue when he needed it. Laws of land sale in 1836–8 placed vast tracts of land on the open market. Most of it obviously went to the wealthy, the powerful, the favoured; and the names of the large purchasers were almost identical with those of the large tenants under emphyteusis, the Anchorena, Díaz Vélez, Alzaga and Arana. By 1840 3,436 square leagues (20,616,000 acres) of the province were in the possession of 293 people. Yet there was not a rush to buy land, and many would-be purchasers were deterred, either by economic recession, as during the French blockade of 1838–40, or by political insecurity. As an alternative to selling land, therefore, Rosas gave it away. Generous land grants were made to supporters of the regime, to the military who fought its wars or crushed its rebels, to bureaucrats and to favourites. Land became almost a currency and sometimes a wages and pensions fund. It was the ultimate source of patronage and, when confiscated, a terrible punishment.

By the 1840s the great plains of Buenos Aires were divided into well-stocked *estancias* and supported some 3 million head of cattle, the prime wealth of the province and the source of an export economy. They were animals of inferior grade, raised in the open range under the care of a few herdsmen; but they yielded hides and salt meat, and that was what the market demanded.

The *estancia* had to sell its products in Buenos Aires and beyond, but the infrastructure of the province was even more primitive than the estates which it served. This was a country without roads or bridges, and with tracks only on the main routes. Almost everything was done and supplied from horseback, and horses were as important a product of the *estancia* as cattle. Horses carried gauchos across the plains and armies into battle. Fishermen fished in the river on horseback; beggars even begged on horseback. But the chief method of freight transport were bullock carts, made in the workshops of Tucumán and led by hard-bitten drivers operating chiefly along the two high roads which traversed Argentina, one from Buenos Aires through San Luis and Mendoza to Chile, the other from Buenos Aires via Córdoba, Santiago, Tucumán, Salta and Jujuy to Bolivia. They travelled in trains of some fourteen carts, each drawn by six oxen with three spare, moving slowly across pampas and

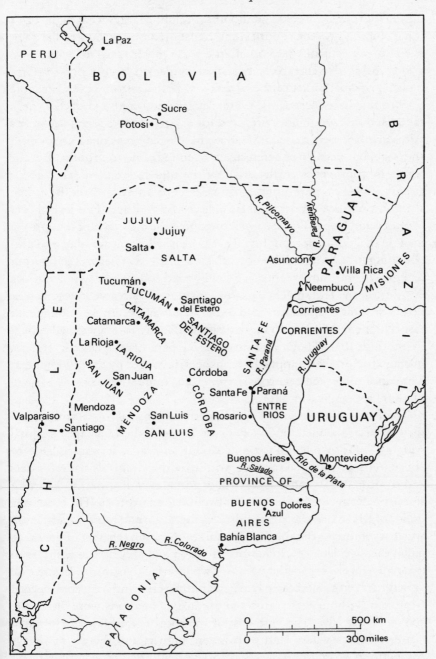

The River Plate republics, 1820–70

hills in journeys of weeks and months. Freight charges were high, £20 a ton including provincial duties, and transport alone accounted for 40 or even 50 per cent of first cost. Cattle were much easier to move than goods, being driven rapidly by expert herdsmen from ranch to port.

The principal outlet of the *estancia* was the *saladero*. These were large establishments, where cattle were slaughtered, tallow extracted, flesh salted and dried and hides prepared for export. They opened in Buenos Aires in 1810, were closed in 1817 as the alleged cause of an urban meat shortage, but began to operate again from 1819 and to proliferate at the southern approaches to the city. By the mid-1820s there were about twenty *saladeros*; they now consumed more animals than the urban slaughter-houses, exporting their hides to Europe and their jerked beef to Brazil and Cuba. The *saladero* represented the only technical improvement in the livestock economy. By the 1840s, while the number of plants operating in and around Buenos Aires was still only twenty, their output had grown enormously and each slaughtered some 200 to 400 animals a day during the season. The *saladero* constituted a sizeable investment in plant, steaming apparatus and other equipment; most belonged to associations rather than to individuals, and many foreigners had capital in the industry. They were an integral part of the *estancia* system, managed by experts, supplied by ranchers, favoured by the government. The export of jerked beef rose from 113,404 quintals in 1835, to 198,046 in 1841, to 431,873 in 1851.

The state favoured cattle-breeders at the expense of small farmers, and the country depended ultimately on imported grain. In an age of capital scarcity, inferior technology and labour shortage, it was realistic to concentrate on pastoral farming, to realize the country's natural assets and to promote its most successful exports, even if it meant diverting resources from worthy though less profitable enterprises. The economic policy of Rivadavia was to subsidize immigration and rely on a fertile soil and market forces. But the agricultural colonization schemes of the 1820s failed through lack of capital, organization and security, in contrast to the great *estancia* expansion with its own internal dynamism. In any case agriculture was subject to particular obstacles and required special treatment. Labour was scarce and expensive, methods were primitive, and yield was low. The high cost of transport forced farmers to move nearer to cities where land prices were higher; and there was always competition from foreign grain. So agriculture needed capital and protection: at this point governments hesitated, fearful of causing dearer food and losing popular support. From independence to 1825 a low-tariff policy prevailed, in favour of consumer and export interests, and in spite of farmers' complaints. But farmers were not the only critics of free trade.

The littoral provinces and those of the interior differed from Buenos Aires in a number of ways. In the first place they were less prosperous. The wars of independence and the subsequent civil wars damaged the economies of the littoral provinces – Santa Fe, Entre Ríos and Corrientes – and retarded their development. When at last they began to recover, they found Buenos Aires dominant, resolved to monoplize trade and navigation – and the customs revenue therefrom – and to dictate a policy of free trade. The negotiations for a federal pact between the provinces, therefore, were marked by bitter debates over economic policy. In the course of 1830 Pedro Ferré, representative of Corrientes and leader of the protectionist movement in the littoral, demanded not only nationaliza-tion of the customs revenue and free navigation of the rivers, but also a revision of the tariff policies of Buenos Aires. José María Rojas y Patrón, the Buenos Aires delegate, argued in reply that protection hurt the consumer without really helping the producer; if domestic industries were not competitive, nor capable of suppling the nation's needs, no amount of protection could save them. The pastoral economy depended upon cheap land, cheap money and a constant demand for hides in foreign markets. Protection would raise prices, raise costs and damage the export trade; then the mass of the people would suffer, for the sake of a small minority outside the cattle economy. Ferré rejected these argu-ments, denounced free competition, demanded protection for native industries against more cheaply produced foreign goods and called also for the opening of other ports than Buenos Aires to direct foreign trade, thus cutting distances and transport costs for the provinces. Only in this way would the littoral and the interior develop their economies, save existing investments and reduce unemployment. Buenos Aires refused to yield and the Pact of the Littoral (1831) was concluded without Corrien-tes, though it subsequently adhered to it. The fact that Corrientes took the lead in demanding protection was not a coincidence. In addition to cattle ranches it had a vital agricultural sector producing cotton, tobacco and other subtropical products, the expansion of which needed protec-tion against Paraguayan and still more Brazilian competition. But during the first government of Rosas (1829–32) fiscal policy was designed primarily to serve the cattle industry of Buenos Aires. The changes proposed in 1831 – reduced tax on salt and on transport of cattle to the city – were only meant to protect the *saladero* industry, which claimed that it was suffering from competition from Montevideo and Rio Grande do Sul. In 1833 duties on the export of hides were reduced, and the tax on salt carried in national vessels from southern provinces was abolished. But *porteño* farming, the products of the littoral and the industries of the interior, these did not receive special treatment.

The economy of the interior – the mid-west and the west – was isolated to some degree from the direct impact of independence and suffered less than the littoral from civil wars and devastation. For a few years, it is true, the north-west frontier was a war zone, and the traditional links with the markets of Upper Peru and Chile were temporarily broken. But from 1817 the Chilean economy began to function again, stimulated now by a more active overseas trade. The Argentine west was re-incorporated into the trans-Andean market, exporting mules to the mining zone, cattle to the *saladeros* and the consumers of the towns, together with other Andean products such as fruits and wines. These outlets were opportune, for after independence the competition of European wines virtually closed the east-coast market to those of Mendoza. Salta was little more than a subsistence economy, though it still fattened mules for export outside the province. Tucumán continued to produce rice and tobacco, and to manufacture sugar, aguardiente and tanned leather. But the province was a high-cost producer and situated too far from its markets to compete, for example, with Brazilian sugar. The Andean mines, too, were outside the economy. La Rioja's gold, silver, copper and iron, San Juan's gold, silver and lead, Mendoza's gold, all were dormant assets. Rivadavia's dream of mining development through British capital was never realized. Their utter remoteness, great scarcity of labour, deficient technology and almost complete lack of transport to the coast made Argentine mines too high in cost and low in yield to warrant investment. The 'industries of the interior', therefore, consisted of little more than textiles, wine and grain, none of which, in the opinion of Buenos Aires, were worth protecting.

Yet there was a protectionist interest in Buenos Aires, sometimes voiced in the assembly, sometimes expressed in public debate, which demanded measures to safeguard national industry as well as agriculture. These opinions reflected variously the anxiety of certain manufacturing enterprises, a latent but powerful resentment of foreigners, and a kind of grass-roots federalism; but representing as they did diverse minorities and interest groups rather than a broad united front, they hardly amounted to economic nationalism. Buenos Aires had a small industrial sector consisting of textile manufacturers, silversmiths, harness-makers and blacksmiths. They supplied local and lower-class needs, and sometimes the demands of the state; indeed war kept many of them in business, for it brought orders for uniforms, equipment and hardware. In 1831 Buenos Aires contained 94 leather workshops, 83 carpenters' workshops, 47 forges and iron-works and 42 silversmiths. These were mainly artisan industries but the beginnings of a factory system could be seen, some manufacturers employing a number of workers in one place, with specialization and use of machinery; this applied to textiles, hat-making, furniture and a few other activities. Few of these enterprises could compete in price and quality with foreign imports, and they constantly pressed for state intervention in their favour. In January 1836, for example, the shoe-makers of Buenos Aires petitioned the government to prohibit the import of foreign shoes, on the grounds that they could not compete with foreign manufacturers, whose low production costs, cheaper raw materials, abundant labour and modern machinery gave them an overwhelming advantage. The *estancieros*, on the other hand, including Rosas and the Anchorena, preferred free trade to protection on grounds of economic interest and in favour of the export-orientated livestock sector. They were supported by those who opposed state intervention on principle and argued that industry would only flourish when it was qualified to do so, that national manufactures which could not compete in price and quality with foreign imports were not worth protecting. The historian and journalist, Pedro de Angelis, one of the more enlightened spokesmen for the Rosas regime, strongly attacked the idea of giving protection to the provincial wine industry and the *porteño* shoe industry, on the grounds that protection would raise prices for the mass of consumers, and divert to industry labourers who would be better employed in the agrarian sector.

Nevertheless, concern for the adverse balance of payments was sufficient to keep the protectionist lobby alive, and in due course Rosas heeded the case for intervention. In the Customs Law of December 1835 he introduced higher import duties. From a basic import duty of 17 per cent, the tariff moved upwards, giving greater protection to more vulnerable products, until it reached a point of prohibiting the import of a large number of articles such as textiles, hardware and, depending on the domestic price, wheat. Rosas thus sought to give positive assistance to arable agriculture and the manufacturing industries.

Why did he do it? Did he really believe that Argentina could become more self-sufficient in industry? Was he convinced that his regime could decrease its dependence on foreign imports, resist foreign competition, and tolerate the higher living costs? Or did he act under political constraint, a need to widen the social base of his regime? There appeared to be no reason why, in 1835–6, Rosas required the support of popular or middle groups. The regime was based firmly on the *estancieros*, who remained the dominant interest in the province and the closest allies of the government. The objectives of Rosas seem to have been to sustain the existing economic structure, while protecting those minority groups who suffered most from it. The tariff of 1835, therefore, was designed to relieve distress in the industrial and farming sectors, without subverting the livestock export economy. At the same time the law had a strong inter-provincial content; it was intended to make the federalist policy credible by giving protection to the provinces as well as to Buenos Aires.

In the event national industries, *porteño* as well as provincial, failed to respond to the protection given by the customs law and the French blockade. Even under the most favourable conditions, when they could take advantage of rising scarcity prices, local manufactures proved unable to satisfy the needs of the country. If existing industries failed to expand, there was little incentive to risk scarce capital in new enterprises. The government could not afford to continue placing undue burdens on consumers, and Rosas began to have second thoughts about protection. In 1838 import duties were reduced by one-third to minimize the effects of the French blockade (see below). Then, claiming the need to procure new revenues and pointing to the shortage of certain articles, Rosas decided (31 December 1841) to allow the entry of a large list of goods previously prohibited. The argument for free trade had been proved correct: national production had not been able to take advantage of protection, the tariff had merely caused shortages and high prices, and the principal victims were the consumers and the treasury. Rosas himself appears to have lost faith in protection, which meant in effect giving artificial respiration to the weakest sector of the economy, while strangling the stronger. Very few people would have thanked him for that. Industry therefore remained on the margin of economic life confined to workshops and artisans. When the Englishman Charles Mansfield visited the River Plate in 1852–3, he travelled like a walking advertisement for British goods: his white cotton poncho, bought in Corrientes, was made in Manchester; his electro-plated spurs, bought in Buenos Aires, were made in Birmingham. The bias towards an agropecuarian economy reflected the social structure as well as economic conditions. The upper groups preferred imported manufactures, while the rest of the population did not form a consumer market for a national industry. There were few freedoms in Buenos Aires under Rosas, but free trade was one of them.

Buenos Aires lived by foreign trade, and its expanding *estancias* depended on foreign markets. In the early years after independence there was a sizeable trade gap, as exports of precious metals fell and imports of consumer goods rose, and it took two decades for livestock exports to redress the balance. In 1829 and 1832 there was still a large excess of imports over exports, and the difference had to be met by exporting specie. The result was a shortage of currency at home and its replacement by ever larger issues of paper money. The medium of international trade was letters of credit drawn on the London exchange, and British merchants came to dominate the financial market of Buenos Aires. The essential link was the trade in textiles from Britain against hides from Argentina, a trade which underwent steady if unspectacular growth, except during the years of blockade, in 1838–9 and 1845–6, when it suffered a sharp drop. From 1822 to 1837 exports from Buenos Aires rose in value from about £700,000 to £1 million; from 1837 to 1851 they doubled in value to £2 million a year. Hides formed the bulk of these exports. There was an average annual export of 798,564 cattle hides from Buenos Aires in the 1830s; 2,303,910 in the 1840s. In 1836 hides amounted to 68.4 per cent of the total value of exports from Buenos Aires; in 1851 they amounted to 64.9 per cent. If jerked beef and other cattle products are added to hides, then the livestock industry contributed 82.8 per cent of total exports in 1836, 78 per cent in 1851. The basic cause of export growth was the incorporation of more land into the economy, especially the expansion of the southern frontier after the Desert Campaign of 1833; the province of Buenos Aires now produced about two-thirds of all hides exported from the littoral provinces. A secondary cause was the blockade of Buenos Aires by foreign powers, which helped to increase the cattle stock by temporarily stopping shipment of hides, thus leaving the cattle to multiply in the pampas.

Meanwhile imports into Buenos Aires rose from a total of £1.5 million in 1825 to £2.1 million in 1850, an increase which was probably even greater in quantity than in value, owing to the falling price of manufactured goods in Europe. There was very little saving or capital accumulation. Imports of luxury and consumer goods used up any surplus capital which might otherwise have been invested. Pianos, clocks, jewelry and precious stones comprised 10 per cent of imports. Consumer goods of a luxury kind – furniture and hardware, clothes and shoes – for the quality market amounted to 32 per cent. Thus almost half of the imports were manufactured goods for the upper end of the market. Industrial raw materials such as coal, iron and other metals accounted for only 3 per cent of imports, an indication of the small degree of industrialization, the absence of technology and the low level of artisan employment.

Argentina was already developing close economic ties with Britain. In the early years of the republic British shippers carried 60 per cent of the trade in and out of Buenos Aires; by mid-century, with competition growing, British shipping in Buenos Aires was 25 per cent of the total. Most of the trade went to Britain (322 vessels and 22.8 per cent of tonnage in 1849–51) and the United States (253 vessels and 21.6 per cent), though this still left a substantial portion of trade (33 per cent) to less developed countries, Cuba, Brazil, Italy and Spain. The value of British trade to Argentina did not rise spectacularly in the first half of the nineteenth century. The average annual exports in the period 1822–5 were between £700,000 and £800,000 sterling. In 1850 the value of British exports to Argentina was still about £900,000. Yet in spite of the growing competition, the value of British trade to the River Plate up to 1837 exceeded that of all foreign countries put together; and even in 1850 it was not far short of this. Argentina relied upon British manufactures, British shipping, British markets, but it did not yet need – could not yet use – British capital and technology, it made its own economic decisions, and its independence was never in doubt. And by mid-century it was already moving towards a better balance of trade as the British market consumed more of its raw materials.

The structure of society was simple and its scale was small. Argentina, a land full of cattle, was empty of people, and its one million square miles of territory contained in 1820 a population about one-third that of contemporary London. Yet Argentina underwent steady demographic growth in the half-century after independence, from 507,951 inhabitants in 1816, to 570,000 in 1825, 1,180,000 in 1857 and 1,736,923 in 1869. In the thirty-two years from 1825 to 1857 the population roughly doubled itself. Growth was due essentially to a fall in the mortality rate: at a time when economic conditions were improving, there was no major epidemic, and the great outbreaks of cholera and yellow fever were yet to come. There was only moderate immigration in this period, though a number of Basques, French, Canarians, Italians and British entered Buenos Aires in the 1840s, once the blockades were over. The greatest population upswing was registered in the littoral provinces, which increased their share of the total from 36 per cent in 1800 to 48.8 per cent in 1869. Buenos Aires and Córdoba had over one-third of the total. Buenos Aires was an insanitary and pestilential city, without amenities, without drainage, without even a pure water supply. But it grew in numbers from 55,416 in 1822 to 177,787 in 1869, while the total of city and province combined grew from 118,646 to 495,107 in the same period.

Society was rooted in land. It was the large *estancia* which conferred status and imposed subordination. *Estancieros* or their clients dominated the administration, the house of representatives, local government and the militia. The polarization of society was absolute. There was an upper class of landowners and their associates, and a lower class comprising the rest of the population. Some social margins, it is true, were blurred. Commerce was economically important and socially respectable, and it provided the original fortunes of some of the leading families of Argentina such as the Anchorena, the Alzaga and the Santa Coloma. But the urban elite of the early nineteenth century did not acquire a separate identity or become an independent middle class. Faced with insistent British competition in the years after independence, local businessmen began to divert their capital into land and without abandoning their urban occupations to become *estancieros* and identify themselves with a new aristocracy. Meanwhile there were no others to fill the middle ranks. The entrepreneurial function came to be exercised by foreigners: British businessmen soon dominated commercial activities, while European immigrants went into artisan occupations, supplementing the roles of local craftsmen. But whereas socially the creole merchants moved upwards into the landed aristocracy, the artisans and manufacturers merged unmistakably into the lower sectors, branded by their manual occupations which were often filled by coloured people.

If there was little prospect of a native middle sector in the towns, there was even less likelihood of finding one in the countryside, where a great gulf separated the landed proprietor from the landless peon. The homogeneity of the landed class was not absolute. While some *estancieros* were owners of truly immense properties, others possessed relatively modest estates. The former were often capitalists of urban origin with some education and aspirations to higher standards of living. The latter were more likely to come from generations of country dwellers and were little removed in culture from the gauchos around them, illiterate, indifferent to material comforts and investing nothing in improvement. Yet, in spite of differences of income, culture and social style, the *estancieros* were as one compared with the peons on their estates and the gauchos of the pampas. There was strong group cohesion and solidarity among the landed class. Rosas himself was the centre of a vast kinship group based on land. He was surrounded by a closely-knit economic and political network, linking deputies, law officers, officials and military, who were also landowners and related among themselves or with their leader. Rosas used his extensive patronage to bind this small oligarchy ever closer. The Anchorena in particular were able to extend their urban and rural properties with his direct assistance, making a profit from their alleged services to the state.

At the end of the colonial period the pampas were inhabited by wild cattle, indomitable Indians and untamed gauchos. The gaucho was a product of race mixture; the components have been disputed, but there is no doubt that there were three races in the littoral, Indians, whites and blacks. By simple definition the gaucho was a free man on horseback. But the term was used by contemporaries and by later historians in a wide sense to mean rural people in general. Greater precision would distinguish between the sedentary rural dwellers working on the land for themselves or for a *patrón* and the pure gaucho, who was nomadic and independent, tied to no estate. And further refinement of terms would identify the *gaucho malo*, who lived by violence and near-delinquency and whom the state regarded as a criminal. Whether good or bad, the classical gaucho asserted his freedom from all formal institutions; he was indifferent to government and its agents, indifferent to religion and the Church. He did not seek land; he lived by hunting, gambling and fighting. The nomadism of the gaucho had many social implications. It prevented settled work or occupation. Property, industry, habitation, these were alien concepts. So too was the gaucho family. The upper sector enjoyed great family stability and drew strength from the ties of kinship. The lower sector was much weaker institutionally. This was partly an urban-rural division between two cultures; it was also a feature of the social structure. Among the gauchos and peons unions were temporary and the resulting families were only loosely joined together. Marriage was the exception, and it was the unmarried mother who formed the nucleus of the rural family, for she was the only permanent parent. Even if the father was not prone to gaucho nomadism, he had to sell his labour where he could, or else he was recruited into armies or *montoneros*.

The ruling groups in the countryside had traditionally imposed a system of coercion upon people whom they regarded as *mozos vagos y mal entretenidos*, vagrants without employer or occupation, idlers who sat in groups singing to a guitar, drinking *mate* or liquor, gambling, but apparently not working. This class was seen as a potential labour force and it was subject to many constraints by the landed proprietors – punitive expeditions, imprisonment, conscription to the Indian frontier, corporal punishment and other penalties. Legislation sought to brand *vagos y mal entretenidos* as a criminal class by definition and vagrancy itself as a crime. Applied stringently by the justices of the peace, anti-vagrancy laws were designed to impose order and discipline in the countryside, to provide a labour pool for *hacendados* and to produce conscripts for the army. The militia became in effect an open prison, into which the most miserable part of the rural population was forcibly herded. For the gaucho the years after independence were even harsher than before. Property concentration prevented the mass of the people from acquiring land, while *estancia* expansion raised the demand for labour. During the colonial period the existence of common usages in the pampas gave the gaucho access to wild cattle on the open range. But these traditional practices came to an end when *estancias* were implanted and endowed, private property spread across the plains, and cattle was appropriated by landowners. Republican laws, those of Rivadavia as well as of Rosas, attacked vagrancy and mobilized the rural population. People were forced to carry identity cards and certificates of employment; a peon caught out of his *estancia* without permission would be conscripted into the army or assigned to public works. Thus, the gaucho was forcibly converted from a free nomad into a hired ranch-hand, a *peón de estancia*.

This primitive society was not qualified for constitutional government or political participation. The *estancia* dominated economic and social life and became the model of government. *Estancieros* ruled their domains by personal authority and demanded unqualified obedience. They were a powerful and cohesive class, unrivalled by any other. Argentina did not yet possess a middle sector of commerce or industry, and there was no great concentration of peasants. The popular classes, superior in numbers, were heterogeneous in composition and divided into disparate groups, peons on *estancias*, wage labourers, small farmers or tenants, marginal gauchos and delinquents. The subordinate condition of the lower sectors, their poor expectations and their isolation in the immense plains, combined to prevent the formation of an autonomous political movement from below. On the other hand they were ideal material for military mobilization and they were easily transformed into *montoneros*, the guerrilla forces of the plains. The causes for which they fought were not class conflicts: they were sectional struggles within the upper groups, disputes between landed proprietors or among leading families, attacks upon the existing government, or clashes with neighbouring provinces. In a situation of equilibrium between factions, leaders would call on their dependants and round up their reserves of manpower the better to tip the balance against their enemies. The use of popular forces, however, did not imply popular objectives. The *estancia* could mobilize its peons either for work or for war, and a regional chieftain in turn could call upon his client *estancieros*. These struggles within the oligarchy, moreover, occurred in peculiar demographic conditions, where a relatively small population was spread thinly across the plains. While ties of kinship at the top of society were close, communications between members of the popular classes, especially in the countryside, were meagre, partly because of the great distances separating rural communities, partly because peons were tied to their estates and immobilized by the rules of the *estancia*. The masses, therefore, were ordered, recruited, manipulated, but not politicized. How was it done?

The relation of patron and client, this was the essential link. The landowner wanted labour, loyalty and service in peace and war. The peon wanted subsistence and security. The *estanciero*, therefore, was a protector, possessor of sufficient power to defend his dependants against marauding Indians, recruiting sergeants and rival hordes. He was also a provider, who developed and defended local resources and could give employment, food and shelter. By supplying what was needed and exploiting what was offered, a *hacendado* recruited a *peonada*. This primitive political structure, founded on individual power, raised upon personal loyalties, cemented by the authority of the patron and the dependence of the peon, was finally built into the state and became the model of *caudillismo*. For individual alliances were magnified into a social pyramid, as patrons in turn became clients to more powerful men, until the peak of power was reached and they all became clients of a superpatron. Thus, from his rural base a local caudillo, supported by his client *estancieros* and their dependents, might conquer the state, for himself, his family, his region. Then, as representative of a group, or a class, or a province, he would reproduce the personalism and patronage in which he had been nurtured and by which he had been raised. *Caudillismo* was the image of society, and the caudillos were its creatures.

The caudillo was first a warrior, a man qualified to lead and defend; during wars of liberation, civil wars, national wars, the caudillo was the strong man who could recruit troops, command resources, protect his people. The union of military power and personal authority was inherent in the caudillo. He responded, however, not only to military needs but also to civilian pressures. He was often the agent of an extended family, who constituted in effect a ruling dynasty; he was sometimes the representative of regional economic interests, which needed a defender against other regions or against the centre; and he was occasionally the man who succeeded in making a particular interest – the export-oriented *estancia*, for example – into a national one. With the resources of the state at his disposal, the caudillo then emerged as a distributor of patronage, allocating spoils to his clientage and earning yet further service from them; for in granting office and land, the caudillo, the super-patron, redeemed his promises to his followers and kept them in a state of political peonage.

The origins and the careers of the Argentine caudillos conformed to these prototypes. They came, in the majority of cases, from families which had been wealthy and powerful since colonial times, most of them owners of landed property, and many of them holders of military appointments. The caudillos themselves preserved this inheritance. Among the eighteen caudillos who ruled in the various provinces of Argentina between 1810 and 1870, thirteen were great landowers, one had landed property of medium size, one was the owner of a shipyard. They all held military appointments, either in the army or in the militia; and of the twelve who had been old enough to fight in the wars of independence, nine had done so. Wealth was an intrinsic qualification. Fifteen of the group were extremely wealthy, two were of medium wealth. Virtually all had some level of education. Political expectations were not good; nine died violently, three in exile. There was little evidence of social mobility in these careers. No doubt the revolution for independence allowed the creoles greater access to politics, the bureaucracy and commerce; but social structure based upon land, wealth, prestige and education remained essentially unchanged. According to the criterion of wealth, only two of the eighteen caudillos (Estanislao

López and Félix Aldao) showed any signs of moving upwards, from medium to great wealth. The rest followed the traditions of their family in wealth and prestige, and simply added to their patrimony. The occupational route they followed had familiar signposts, from *estanciero*, via the military, to caudillo.

The year 1820 was a year of anarchy. Independence from Spain had culminated not in national unity but in universal dismemberment. After a decade of conflict between Buenos Aires and the provinces, between central government and regional interests, between unitarians and federalists, the framework of political organization in the Río de la Plata collapsed. Independent republics proliferated throughout the interior, and when Buenos Aires sought to subdue them they fought back. Provincial caudillos – Estanislao López of Santa Fe, Francisco Ramírez of Entre Ríos – led their irregular gaucho hordes, the fearsome *montoneros*, against the capital. On 1 February 1820 they defeated the forces of Buenos Aires at the battle of Cepeda and proceeded to destroy all trace of central authority. Only the provincial government of Buenos Aires survived, and this too was harassed into anarchy, while persons and property lay at the mercy of petty caudillos, gauchos and Indians. Buenos Aires looked for protection to the countryside. While two of its leaders, Martín Rodríguez and Manuel Dorrego, desperately stemmed the tide, the *estancieros* of the south were asked to come to the rescue with their rural militias. They responded promptly, not least Rosas, appreciating the danger to their own interests from the seeping anarchy of the times. It was with the backing of the *estancieros* that Rodríguez was elected governor in September 1820 and made a negotiated peace with the caudillos.

The inspiration behind the Rodríguez administration was its chief minister, Bernardino Rivadavia, educated, liberal and bureaucratic. Rivadavia wanted to modernize Argentina. He sought economic growth through free trade, foreign investment and immigration. He applied the system of emphyteusis, the renting out of state land, to put the natural resources of Argentina to productive use. He had a vision of liberal institutions and a new infrastructure, in which the framework of modernization would be enlarged to comprise a great and unified Argentina, undivided by political and economic particularism. This was Rivadavia's plan, enlightened, developmental and unitarian. In truth it was more of a dream than a plan: some of its ideas were impractical, others were ahead of their time. But the entire model was rejected as irrelevant by Rosas and his associates, who represented a more primitive economy – cattle production for export of hides and salt meat – but one which brought immediate returns and was in harmony with the country's traditions. They were alarmed by the innovations of the new regime. On 7 February 1826 Rivadavia was appointed president of the United Provinces of the Río de la Plata; he had a unitary constitution and innumerable ideas. In March the city of Buenos Aires was declared capital of the nation and federalized. On 12 September Rivadavia sent to congress his proposal to divide the non-federalized part of the province of Buenos Aires into two, the Provincia del Paraná in the north and the Provincia del Salado in the south. These measures went to the heart of *estanciero* interests. The federalization of the city of Buenos Aires and its environs amputated the best part of the province and a large section of its population. It also involved nationalizing the revenues of the port, which amounted to 75 per cent of the provincial government's income, arousing the fear that the next step would be to raise alternative revenue by an income or land tax. To the world of the landowners, for whom Buenos Aires and its hinterland, port and province were one, these measures threatened division and disaster.

The policy of Rivadavia struck at too many interest groups to succeed. His immediate political opponents, the federalists, rejected unitary policy as undemocratic and, influenced by United States federalism, sought a federal solution to the problem of national organization. The *estancieros* saw Rivadavia as a danger to their economic and fiscal assets, an intellectual who neglected rural security and, while promoting urban progress of a European kind, allowed the savage Indians to roam the plains. Immigration they opposed as expensive, unnecessary and probably subversive, bringing competition for land and labour and raising the cost of both. The anti-clerical policy of the regime, designed primarily to curtail the temporal power of the Church, to extend religious freedom, and to bring Argentina into conformity with foreign expectations, was anathema not only to the clergy but to all those with conservative values, and served to unite federalists, *estancieros* and priests under the banner of *religión o muerte*. Rosas and the Anchorena took the lead in organizing resistance to Rivadavia's plans. Until now Rosas had not belonged to the federal party or associated with its leader Manuel Dorrego. But in the latter half of 1826, at the head of a network of friends, relations and clients, he allied himself to the party which he was eventually to absorb and destroy. He joined the federalists not for reasons of political ideology, which he did not possess, but because unitary policy threatened his plans of hegemony in the countryside.

Rivadavia yielded to the combined forces of his opponents and resigned from the presidency on 27 June 1827. In the ultimate analysis he did not have a constituency: he represented intellectuals, bureaucrats and professional politicians, groups which did not form an identifiable social sector. Rosas on the other hand had a specific power base, the *estancieros*, who possessed the principal resources of the country and considerable paramilitary force. But Rosas did not rule. It was the real federalists who came to power and Manuel Dorrego was elected governor on 12 August 1827. Dorrego's popularity, his independence and his refusal to take advice alerted Rosas and his friends: previous experience showed the danger of divergence between those who ruled in the *estancias* and those who governed in Buenos Aires. In the event Dorrego was overthrown, on 1 December 1828, not by his enemies within but by the unitarians from without, when General Juan Lavalle led a coalition of military returned from the war with Brazil, professional politicians, merchants and intellectuals. The December revolution was made in the name of liberal principles, against rural conservatism, caudillism and provincialism, and it was an attempt to restore the system of Rivadavia. But Lavalle gave a bonus to his enemies when he ordered the execution of Dorrego, a man of peace and moderation. This savage sentence caused revulsion in all sectors, especially among the populace. It branded the unitarians as political assassins and aggravated the anarchy of the times. It also left the way open for Rosas to lead the federal party. Backed by his *estanciero* allies and his rural hordes, Rosas reconquered power from Lavalle and the unitarians and was elected governor by a grateful assembly on 6 December 1829. It was no ordinary election, for the new governor was given dictatorial powers and a mandate to restore order.

The hegemony of Rosas, how can it be explained? He was in part a creature of circumstances. He represented the rise to power of a new economic interest, the *estancieros*. The classic elite of the revolution of 1810 were the merchants and bureaucrats. The struggle for independence created a group of career revolutionaries – professional politicians, state officials, a new military, men who lived by service to and income from the state. The merchants of Buenos Aires, emerging from the colony as the leading economic interest, were at first powerful allies of the new elite. From about 1820, however, many merchant families began to seek other outlets and to invest in land, cattle and meat-salting plants. These were the dominant social group of the future, a landowning oligarchy with roots in commerce and recruited from urban society. For the moment, however, they did not possess the executive power in the state, and the fact remained that those with economic power did not rule and those who ruled lacked an economic base. Inevitably the landowners began to seek direct political control. In defeating Rivadavia and Lavalle in 1827–9, they overthrew not only the unitarians but the existing ruling class, the career politicians, and took possession of the government through Rosas.

Conditions, therefore, created Rosas. He was the individual synthesis of the society and economy of the countryside, and when the interests of this sector coincided with those of the urban federalists, Rosas was at once the representative and the executive of the alliance. But he also had specific qualifications: his origins, career and control over events all made him a power in the land before he was even elected governor and narrowed the choice open to the *estancieros*. His personal career was unique and did not conform exactly to the model of merchant turned landowner which characterized so many of his supporters. He began on the *estancia*, learned the business from the working end, accumulated capital in the rural sector itself and advanced from there. He was a pioneer in the expansion of landowning and cattle-raising, starting some years before the big push southwards from 1820. He was a working, not an absentee, landlord, operating at every stage of cattle raising. Thus, he came into direct contact with the gauchos, delinquents, Indians and other denizens of the pampas, partly to hire them for his estates, partly to mobilize them for his militia. For Rosas was militia commander as well as *estanciero*, and he had more military experience than any of his peers. In the recruitment of troops, the training and control of militia, and the deployment of units not only on the frontier but in urban operations, he had no equal. It was the military dimension of Rosas's early career which gave him the edge over his rivals. This culminated in his role during the guerrilla war of 1829, when he raised, controlled and led anarchic popular forces in the irregular army which defeated Lavalle's professionals. Rosas, then, was a self-made caudillo.

Rosas divided society into those who commanded and those who obeyed. Order obsessed him, and the virtue which he most admired in a people was subordination. If there was anything more abhorrent to

Rosas than democracy, it was liberalism. The reason why he detested unitarians was not that they wanted a united Argentina but that they were liberals who believed in secular values of humanism and progress. He identified them with freemasons and intellectuals, subversives who undermined order and tradition and whom he held ultimately responsible for the political assassinations which brutalized Argentine public life from 1828 to 1835. The constitutional doctrines of the two parties did not interest him, and he was never a true federalist. He thought and ruled as a centralist, and he stood for the hegemony of Buenos Aires. Rosas destroyed the traditional division between federalists and unitarians and made these categories virtually meaningless. He substituted *rosismo* and anti-*rosismo*.

What was *rosismo*? Its power base was the *estancia*, a focus of economic resources and a system of social control. The domination of the economy by the *estancia* was continued and completed under Rosas. At the beginning of his regime much of the territory which eventually constituted the province of Buenos Aires was still controlled by Indians. And even within the frontier, north of the Salado, there were large areas unoccupied by whites. Rosas stood for a policy of territorial settlement and expansion. The Desert Campaign of 1833 added thousands of square miles south of the Río Negro to the province of Buenos Aires, together with new resources, new security and the confidence born of a great victory over the Indians. The land to the south, and the unoccupied or emphyteusis land in the north, gave the state a vast reserve of property which it could sell or give away. Rosas himself was one of the principal beneficiaries of this prodigious distribution. The law of 6 June 1834 granted him the freehold of the island of Choele-Choel in recognition of his leadership in the Desert Campaign. He was allowed to exchange this for sixty square leagues of public land wherever he chose. His followers were also rewarded. The law of 30 September 1834 made land grants up to a maximum of 50 square leagues altogether to officers who had participated in the Desert Campaign; while a law of 25 April 1835 granted land up to 16 square leagues for allocation to soldiers of the Andes Division in the same campaign. The military who took part in crushing the rebellion of the south in 1839 were rewarded by a land grant of 9 November 1839; generals received 6 square leagues, colonels 5, noncommissioned officers half a league, and privates a quarter of a league. Civilians too were recompensed for their loyalty.

The *boletos de premios en tierras*, or land certificates as rewards for military service, were one of the principal instruments of land distribution; 8,500 were issued by the government of Rosas, though not all were used by the recipients. No doubt this was a means by which an impecunious government paid salaries, grants and pensions to its servants. But there was also a political element present, for land was the richest source of patronage available, a weapon for Rosas, a welfare system for his supporters. Rosas was the great *patrón* and the *estancieros* were his *clientela*. In this sense *rosismo* was less an ideology than an interest group and a fairly exclusive one. For there was no sector outside the *estancieros* equipped to use these grants. Certificates of less than one league were virtually useless in the hands of soldiers or minor bureaucrats, when the existing agrarian structure averaged eight leagues per estate. But in the hands of those who already possessed estates or had the capital to buy them up cheaply, they were a powerful instrument for land concentration. More than 90 per cent of land certificates granted to soldiers and civilians ended up in the hands of landowners or those who were buying their way into land.

The trend of the Rosas regime, therefore, was towards greater concentration of property in the hands of a small group. In 1830 980 landowners held the 5,516 square leagues of occupied land in Buenos Aires province; of these, 60 proprietors monopolized almost 4,000 square leagues, or 76 per cent. In the period 1830–52 occupied land grew to 6,100 square leagues, with 782 proprietors. Of these 382 proprietors held 82 per cent of holdings above one square league, while 200 proprietors, or 28 per cent, held 60 per cent of holdings above ten square leagues. There were 74 holdings of over 15 square leagues (90,000 acres), and 42 holdings of over 20 square leagues (120,000 acres). Meanwhile small holdings accounted for only one per cent of the land in use. Among the eighty or so people who were members of the House of Representatives between 1835 and 1852, 60 per cent were landowners or had occupations connected with land. This was the assembly which voted Rosas into power and continued to vote for him. To some degree they could control policy making. They consistently denied Rosas permission to increase the *contribución directa*, a tax on capital and property, and they always prevented him from raising any revenue at the expense of the *estancieros*. In 1850, when total revenues reached 62 million pesos, chiefly from customs, the *contribución directa* provided only 3 per cent of the total, and most of this portion was paid by commerce rather than land. The administration too was dominated by landowners. Juan N. Terrero, economic adviser of Rosas, had 42 square leagues and left a fortune of 53 million pesos. Angel Pacheco, Rosas's principal general, had 75 square leagues. Felipe Arana, minister of foreign affairs, possessed 42 square leagues. Even Vicente López, poet, deputy and president of the high court, owned 12 square leagues. But the greatest landowners of the province were the Anchorena, cousins of Rosas and his closest political advisers; their various possessions totalled 306 square leagues (1,856,000 acres). As for Rosas himself, in 1830 in the group of about seventeen landowners with property over 50 square leagues (300,000 acres), he occupied tenth place with 70 square leagues (420,000 acres). By 1852, according to the official estimate of his property, he had accumulated 136 square leagues (816,000 acres).

The *estancia* gave Rosas the sinews of war, the alliance of fellow *estancieros* and the means of recruiting an army of peons, gauchos and vagrants. He had an instinct for manipulating the discontents of the masses and turning them against his enemies in such a way that they did not damage the basic structure of society. While Rosas identified culturally with the gauchos, he did not unite with them socially, or represent them politically. The core of his forces were his own peons and dependants, who were his servants rather than his supporters, his clients rather than his allies. When Rosas needed to make a critical push, in 1829, 1833 or 1835, he enlisted the gauchos in the countryside and the mob in the city. They were the only manpower available, and for the moment they had a value outside of the *estancia*. But the normal agrarian regime was very different: employment was obligatory, the *estancia* was a prison and conscription to the Indian frontier was an imminent alternative. And the gaucho forces lasted only as long as Rosas needed them. Once he had the apparatus of the state in his possession, from 1835, once he controlled the bureaucracy, the police and, above all, the regular army, he did not need or want the popular forces of the countryside. Rosas quickly recruited, equipped, armed and purged an army of the line, detachments of which were used against the countryside to round up conscripts. With the ultimate means of coercion in his hand, he ceased to rely on the irregular rural forces. The gaucho militias, moreover, were 'popular' forces only in the sense that they were composed of the peons of the countryside. They were not always volunteers for a cause, nor were they politicized. The fact of belonging to a military organization did not give the peons power or representation, for the rigid structure of the *estancia* was built into the militia, where the *estancieros* were the commanders, their overseers the officers and their peons the troops. These troops did not enter into direct relationship with Rosas; they were mobilized by their own particular patron, which meant that Rosas received his support not from free gaucho hordes but from *estancieros* leading their peon conscripts, a service for which the *estancieros* were paid by the state. The province was ruled by an informal alliance of *estancieros*, militia commanders and justices of the peace.

The severity of the rural regime reflected the emptiness of the pampas, the great population scarcity and the ruthless search for labour in a period of *estancia* expansion. The survival of slavery in Argentina was another indication of labour shortage. Rosas himself owned slaves and he did not question their place in the social structure. In spite of the May Revolution, the declarations of 1810 and the subsequent hope of social as well as political emancipation, slavery survived in Argentina, fed by an illegal slave trade which, until the late 1830s, the government openly tolerated. At the end of the colonial period the Río de la Plata contained over 30,000 slaves out of a population of 400,000. The incidence of slavery was greatest in the towns, especially Buenos Aires. In 1810 there were 11,837 blacks and mulattos in Buenos Aires, or 29.3 per cent, in a total population of 40,398, and most of the blacks were slaves. Slave numbers were depleted during the wars of independence, when emancipation was offered in return for military service, and military service often led to death. In 1822, of the 55,416 inhabitants of the city of Buenos Aires, 13,685, or 24.7 per cent, were blacks and mulattos; of these 6,611, or 48.3 per cent, were slaves. In 1838 non whites constituted 14,928 out of 62,957, or 23.71 per cent. Mortality rates were higher among non whites than among whites, and much higher among mulattos and free blacks than among slaves. Yet from 1822 to 1838 the number of non whites remained stationary, as their ranks were replenished from abroad. Rosas was responsible for a revival of the slave trade. His decree of 15 October 1831 allowed the sale of slaves imported as servants by foreigners; and an illegal slave trade from Brazil, Uruguay and Africa survived in the 1830s. It was not until 1839, when Rosas needed British support against the French, that a comprehensive anti-slave trade treaty was signed. By 1843, according to a British estimate, there were no more than 300 slaves in the Argentine provinces; and slaves who joined the federalist army, especially if they belonged to unitarian owners, gained freedom in return for military service. When, in the Constitution of 1853, slavery was finally abolished in the whole of Argentina, there were few slaves left. Meanwhile, Rosas had many blacks in his employment and many more in his political service. He seems to have been free of race prejudice, though he did not raise the non whites socially. They occupied the lowest situations: they were porters, carters, carriers, drivers and washerwomen, as well as domestic servants. They gave Rosas useful support in the streets and were part of his 'popular' following. They were deployed in a military role in Buenos Aires and the provinces where they formed a militia unit, the *negrada federal*, black troops in red shirts, many of them former slaves. But in the final analysis the demagogy of Rosas among the blacks and mulattos did nothing to alter their position in the society around them.

The hegemony of the landowners, the abasement of the gauchos, the dependence of the peons, all this was the heritage of Rosas. Argentina bore the imprint of extreme social stratification for many generations to come. Society became set in a rigid mould, to which economic modernization and political change had later to adapt. The Rosas state was the *estancia* writ large. Society itself was built upon the patron-peon relationship. It seemed the only alternative to anarchy.

Rosas ruled from 1829 to 1832 with absolute powers. After an interregnum during which instability in Buenos Aires and insubordination in the provinces threatened to restore anarchy, he returned to office on his own terms in March 1835 and ruled for the next seventeen years with total and unlimited power. The House of Representatives remained a creature of the governor, whom it formally 'elected'. It consisted of 44 deputies, half of whom were annually renewed by election. But only a small minority of the electorate participated, and it was the duty of the justices of the peace to deliver these votes to the regime. The assembly, lacking legislative function and financial control, was largely an exercise in public relations for the benefit of foreign and domestic audiences, and it normally responded sycophantically to the initiatives of the governor. While he controlled the legislature, Rosas also dominated the judicial power. He not only made law, he interpreted it, changed it and applied it. The machinery of justice no doubt continued to function: the justices of the peace, the judges for civil and criminal cases, the appeal judge and the supreme court, all gave institutional legitimacy to the regime. But the law did not rule. Arbitrary intervention by the executive undermined the independence of the judiciary. Rosas took many cases to himself, read the evidence, examined the police reports and, as he sat alone at his desk, gave judgement, writing on the files 'shoot him', 'fine him', 'imprison him', 'to the army'. Rosas also controlled the bureaucracy. One of his first and most uncompromising measures was to purge the old administration; this was the simplest way of removing political enemies and rewarding followers, and it was inherent in the patron-client organization of society. The new administration was not extravagantly large, and some of the early vacancies were left unfilled as part of the expenditure cuts which the government was obliged to make. But appointments of all kinds were reserved for political clients and federalists; other qualifications counted for little.

Propaganda was an essential ingredient of *rosismo*: a few simple and violent slogans took the place of ideology and these permeated the administration and were thrust relentlessly at the public. People were obliged to wear a kind of uniform and to use the federal colour, red. The symbolism was a form of coercion and conformity. To adopt the federal look and the federal language took the place of orthodoxy tests and oaths of allegiance. Federal uniformity was a measure of quasi-totalitarian pressure, by which people were forced to abandon a passive or apolitical role and to accept a specific commitment, to show their true colours. The Church was a willing ally, except for the Jesuits, who were re-admitted and re-expelled. Portraits of Rosas were carried in triumph through the streets and placed upon the altars of the principal churches. Sermons glorified the dictator and extolled the federal cause. The clergy became essential auxiliaries of the regime and preached that to resist Rosas was a sin. Political orthodoxy was conveyed by word as well as by deed, and the printing presses of Buenos Aires were kept fully employed turning out newspapers in Spanish and other languages containing official news and propaganda, for circulation at home and abroad. But the ultimate sanction was force, controlled by Rosas, applied by the military and the police.

The regime was not strictly speaking a military dictatorship: it was a civilian regime which employed a compliant military. The military establishment, consisting of the regular army and the militia, existed, however, not only to defend the country but to occupy it, not only to protect the population but to control it. Conscripted from peons, vagrants and delinquents, officered by professional soldiers, kept alive by booty and exactions from the *estancias*, the army of Rosas was a heavy burden on the rest of the population. If it was not an efficient military, it was a numerous one – perhaps 20,000 strong – and an active one, constantly engaged in foreign wars, interprovincial conflicts and internal security. But war and the economic demands of war, while they meant misery for the many, made fortunes for the few. Defence spending provided a secure market for certain industries and employment for their workers: the fairly constant demand for uniforms, arms and equipment helped to sustain a number of small workshops and artisan manufactures in an otherwise depressed industrial sector. Above all, the military market favoured several large landowners. Proprietors such as the Anchorena had long had valuable contracts for the supply of cattle to frontier forts; now the armies on other fronts became voracious consumers and regular customers. The army and its liabilities, however, increased at a time when revenue was contracting, and something had to be sacrificed. When the French blockade began to bite, from April 1838, not only were people thrown out of work and hit by rapid inflation but the regime saw its revenue from customs – its basic income – fall dramatically. Faced with heavy budget deficits, it immediately imposed severe expenditure cuts. Most of these fell on education, the social services and welfare in general. The University of Buenos Aires was virtually closed. When priorities were tested, Rosas did not even make a pretence of governing 'popularly'.

The contrast between military and social spending reflected circumstances as well as values. The enemy within, conflict with other provinces and with foreign powers, and the obligation to succour his allies in the interior, all caused Rosas to maintain a heavy defence budget. Some of these choices were forced upon him, others were preferred policy, yet others reflected a universal indifference towards welfare. In any case the consequences were socially retarding. In the 1840s the ministry of government, or home affairs, received on average between 6 and 7 per cent of the total budget, and most of this was allocated to police and political expenditure, not to social services. Defence, on the other hand, received absolute priority. The military budget varied from 4 million pesos, or 27 per cent of the total, in 1836, to 23.8 million, 49 per cent, during the French blockade in 1840, to 29.6 million, 71.11 per cent, in 1841. For the rest of the regime it never fell below 15 million, or 49 per cent.

This was the system of total government which sustained Rosas in power for over two decades. The majority of people obeyed, some with enthusiasm, others from inertia, many out of fear. But it was more than tyranny arbitrarily imposed. The government of Rosas responded to conditions inherent in Argentine society, where men had lived for too long without a common power to keep them all in awe. Rosas superseded a state of nature, in which life could be brutish and short. He offered an escape from insecurity and a promise of peace, on condition that he were granted total power, the sole antidote to total anarchy. To exercise his sovereignty Rosas used the bureaucracy, the military and the police. Even so there was some opposition. Internally there was an ideological opposition, partly from unitarians and partly from younger reformists; this came to a head in an abortive conspiracy in 1839 and continued to operate throughout the regime from its base in Montevideo. A second focus of internal opposition was formed by the landowners of the south of the province, whose resentment derived not from ideology but from economic interest. Already harassed by demands upon their manpower and resources for the Indian frontier, they were particularly hit by the French blockade, which cut off their export outlets and for which they blamed Rosas. But their rebellion of 1839 did not synchronize with the political conspiracy and they too were crushed. Finally, there was an external opposition to the regime, partly from other provinces and partly from foreign powers. If this could link with internal dissidents, Rosas would be in real danger. He therefore held in reserve another constraint, terror.

Rosas used terror as an instrument of government, to eliminate enemies, to discipline dissidents, to warn waverers and, ultimately, to control his own supporters. Terror was not simply a series of exceptional episodes, though it was regulated according to circumstances. It was an intrinsic part of the Rosas system, the distinctive style of the regime, its ultimate sanction. Rosas himself was the author of terror, ordering executions without trial by virtue of the extraordinary powers vested in him. But the special agent of terrorism was the *Sociedad Popular Restaurador*, a political club and a para-police organization. The Society had an armed wing, commonly called the *mazorca*. These were the true terrorists, recruited from the police, the militia, from professional cut-throats and delinquents, forming armed squads who went out on various missions, killing, looting and menacing. While the *mazorca* was a creature of Rosas, it was more terrorist than its creator: like many such death squads it acquired in action a semi-autonomy which its author believed he had to allow as a necessary means of government. Cruelty had its chronology. The incidence of terrorism varied according to the pressures on the regime, rising to a peak in 1839–42, when French intervention, internal rebellion, and unitarian invasion threatened to destroy the

Rosas state and inevitably produced violent counter-measures. Rosas never practised mass killing; selective assassination was enough to instil terror. And the peak of 1839–42 was not typical of the whole regime but rather an extraordinary manifestation of a general rule, namely, that terrorism existed to enforce submission to government policy in times of national emergency.

The system gave Rosas hegemony in Buenos Aires for over twenty years. But he could not apply the same strategy in the whole of Argentina. In the first place he did not govern 'Argentina'. The thirteen provinces governed themselves independently, though they were grouped in one general Confederation of the United Provinces of the Río de la Plata. Rosas accepted this and preferred inter-provincial relations to be governed by informal power rather than a written constitution. He refused to prepare an Argentine constitution, arguing that before the time was opportune for national organization the provinces must first organize themselves, that the progress of the parts must precede the ordering of the whole, and that the first task was to defeat the unitarians. Even without formal union, however, the provinces were forced to delegate certain common interests to the government of Buenos Aires, mainly defence and foreign policy, and also an element of legal jurisdiction, which enabled Rosas occasionally to reach out and arraign his enemies as federal criminals. Rosas, therefore, exercised some *de facto* control over the provinces; this he regarded as necessary, partly to prevent subversion and anarchy from seeping into Buenos Aires, partly to secure a broad base for economic and foreign policy and partly to acquire a national dimension for his regime. To impose his will he had to use some force, for the provinces did not accept him voluntarily. In the littoral and in the interior Rosas was seen as a caudillo who served the local interests of Buenos Aires; in these parts the loyalty of the *hacendados* and the service of their peons were not so easily procured. In many of the provinces of the interior the federal party had weaker economic roots and a narrower social base than in Buenos Aires; and in the remoter parts of the confederation Rosas could not instantly apply autocratic domination or regulate the use of terror. The unification of Argentina, therefore, meant the conquest of Argentina by Buenos Aires. Federalism gave way to *rosismo*, an informal system of control from the centre which Rosas achieved by patience and exercised with persistence.

The Federal Pact of 4 January 1831 between the littoral provinces, Buenos Aires, Entre Ríos, Santa Fe and later Corrientes, inaugurated a decade of relative stability in the east, though this could not disguise the hegemony of Buenos Aires, its control of customs revenue and river navigation, and its indifference to the economic interests of the other provinces. Rosas began to expand his power in the littoral in the years 1835–40. First, the governor of Entre Ríos, Pascual de Echagüe, moved away from the influence of the powerful Estanislao López and submitted himself unconditionally to Rosas. Then Corrientes, resentful of its economic subordination, declared war on its new metropolis; but the defeat and death of Governor Berón de Astrada at Pago Largo (31 March 1839) brought Corrientes too under the domination of Buenos Aires. Now there was only Santa Fe. Its governor, Estanislao López, was the most powerful of the provincial caudillos, experienced in the politics of the confederation and possessing a reputation equal to that of Rosas. But Rosas waited, and in 1838 López died. The subsequent election of Domingo Cullen, independent and anti-*rosista*, provoked a minor crisis, which was resolved by the triumph of Juan Pablo López, a protégé and now a satellite of Rosas. In each of the eastern provinces, therefore, Rosas succeeded gradually in imposing allied, dependent or weak governors. In Uruguay, an independent state since 1828, success did not come so easily, however. His ally, President Manuel Oribe, was overthrown in June 1838 by the rival caudillo, Fructuoso Rivera, backed by General Lavalle and acclaimed by the émigré unitarians. This was a serious challenge.

Rosas could not allow these local fires to remain unquenched, for there was danger of their being sucked into international conflagrations. The French government knew little about Rosas, but what it saw it did not like. Anxious to extend its trade and power in the Río de la Plata, and irritated by a dispute with Rosas over the status of its nationals under his jurisdiction, France authorized its naval forces to institute a blockade on Buenos Aires; this began on 28 March 1838 and was followed by an alliance between the French forces and Rosas's enemies in Uruguay. The French blockade, which lasted until 29 October 1840, harmed the regime in a number of ways. It caused the economy to stagnate and deprived the government of vital customs revenue; it de-stabilized the federal system and gave heart to dissidents in the littoral and the interior; and it led Rosas to rule with yet greater autocracy. But it had too little military muscle to be decisive. General Lavalle, assisted by the French and by other units from Montevideo, was expected to disembark at the port of Buenos Aires in support of the two rebel fronts within, the conspirators of the capital and the landowners of the south. In fact the various movements failed to synchronize. Lavalle led his forces not to Buenos Aires but to Entre Ríos, promising to free the Confederation from the tyrant and to give the provinces self-rule. But his association with the French, whom many considered aggressors against the Confederation, deprived him of support in Entre Ríos. He then turned aside to Corrientes, where Governor Pedro Ferré accepted him and declared against Rosas. But Corrientes was a long way from Buenos Aires, and by the time Lavalle's army reached striking distance it lacked money, arms and perhaps conviction. The French gave him naval support and arms, but could not supply military thrust. Lavalle entered the province of Buenos Aires on 5 August 1840 and finally appeared poised to attack Rosas. At this point his judgement, or his nerve, failed him. He paused to await French reinforcements, which did not come, and he lost the advantage of surprise. On 5 September, to the dismay of his associates and the bewilderment of historians, he withdrew towards Santa Fe, and his army, already demoralized by failure and desertion, began its long retreat towards the north.

The liberating expedition, humiliated in Buenos Aires, achieved a degree of success elsewhere. Its mere existence served to arouse Rosas's enemies in the interior. From April 1840 the Coalition of the North organized by Marco Avellaneda, governor of Tucumán, and including Salta, La Rioja, Catamarca and Jujuy, took the field under the command of General Aráoz de La Madrid in alliance with Lavalle, and threatened Rosas anew from the interior. Altogether, 1840 was a dangerous year for Rosas. Yet he survived, and at the beginning of 1841 the tide began to turn. The federal caudillos dominated Cuyo in the far west and began to strike back. Ex-president Oribe of Uruguay also fought bloodily for Rosas. On 28 November 1840 he defeated Lavalle's liberating army at Quebracho Herrado and completed the conquest of Córdoba. In the following year he destroyed the remnants of the Coalition of the North, first the spent forces of Lavalle at Famaillá (19 September 1841), then those of La Madrid at Rodeo del Medio (24 September 1841). These were cruel wars, and Rosas's generals wore down the enemy as much by terror as by battle. Lavalle himself was killed at Jujuy on 8 October 1841 on his way to Bolivia. The destruction of the unitarian forces in the interior, however, provoked rather than paralysed the littoral provinces. Their rebellion was eventually frustrated as much by their own disunity as by the energy of Oribe, who forced them to desist and disarm in December

1841. By February 1843 Oribe dominated the littoral. Rivera and the émigrés were enclosed within Montevideo, while Oribe and the *rosistas* were stationed at the Cerrito on the outskirts. And in the river the Buenos Aires fleet, completing the encirclement of the unitarians, destroyed the naval forces of Montevideo, imposed a blockade, and waited for victory. Yet the siege of Montevideo lasted for nine years.

British intervention was now the complicating factor. In the course of 1843 British naval forces broke the blockade of Montevideo and allowed supplies and recruits to reach the defenders. The action was crucial in saving the city, prolonging the war and pinning down Rosas to a long and painful siege. In addition to defending the independence of Uruguay, Britain also sought to open the rivers to free navigation: Rosas was branded as a threat to the first and an obstacle to the second. Anglo-French naval forces imposed a blockade on Buenos Aires from September 1845, and in November a joint expedition forced its way up the River Paraná convoying a merchant fleet to inaugurate direct trade to the interior. But the expedition encountered neither welcoming allies nor promising markets, only high customs duties, local suspicion, sluggish sales and the problem of returning down river. The blockade was no more effective than the expedition. This was a slow and clumsy weapon which hit trade rather than the enemy. Argentina's primitive economy made it virtually invulnerable to outside pressure. It could always revert to a subsistence economy and sit it out, waiting for pent-up trade to reopen while its cattle resources accumulated. As for the British, they simply blockaded their own trade. Rosas meanwhile gained great credit from the intervention of 1843–46. His defiance, determination and ultimate success placed him high in the pantheon of Argentine patriots. Argentina rallied round Rosas, and when the emergency was over and the British returned to seek peace and trade, they found the regime stronger than ever, the economy improving and a golden age beginning. But appearances were deceptive.

Rosas tamed the interior by relentless diplomacy and military force, establishing for himself an informal but enduring sovereignty. But he could not apply the same methods to the littoral provinces, where economic grievances coincided with powerful foreign interests. These provinces wanted trading rights for the river ports of the Paraná and the Uruguay, they wanted a share in customs revenue, and they wanted local autonomy. With outside assistance they could become the Achilles' heel of Rosas. The British had negotiated with the caudillos of Entre Ríos,

Corrientes and Paraguay for a coalition against Buenos Aires, but the governor of Entre Ríos, Justo José de Urquiza, was too careful to risk his future without the guarantee of powerful land forces. If the British could not supply these, Brazil could.

Brazil had its own account to settle with Rosas. Determined to prevent satellites of Buenos Aires becoming entrenched in Uruguay and the littoral, and anxious to secure free navigation of the river complex from Matto Grosso to the sea, Brazil was ready to move in opposition to the 'imperialism' of Rosas, or impelled by an imperialism of its own. An ally was at hand in Entre Ríos. Urquiza, like Rosas, was a rural caudillo, the owner of vast estates, the ruler of a personal fiefdom several hundred square miles in extent, with tens of thousands of cattle and sheep, and four *saladeros*. He made a fortune in the 1840s as a supplier to besieged Montevideo, an importer of manufactured goods and an exporter of gold to Europe. His private ambitions combined easily with provincial interests, and as a politician he was willing to supplant Rosas and initiate a constitutional reorganization of Argentina. He displayed, moreover, greater deference to education, culture and freedom than his rival and he had a superior reputation with the émigré intellectuals in Montevideo. In the person of Urquiza, therefore, the various strands of opposition came together, and he placed himself at the head of provincial interests, liberal exiles and Uruguayan patriots in an alliance which was backed by sufficient Brazilian money and naval forces to tip the balance against Rosas. The dictator was thus confronted not from within but from without, by the Triple Alliance of Entre Ríos, Brazil and Montevideo, which went into action from May 1851.

Buenos Aires was the privileged beneficiary of *rosismo*, but here too enthusiasm waned. Rosas was expected to guarantee peace and security; this was the justification of the regime. But in the wake of so many conflicts and so much waste he was still ready to wage war, even after 1850, relentlessly pursuing his objectives in Uruguay and Paraguay, always looking for one more victory. His army was now weak and disorganized, his military commanders were not to be trusted. By his terrorist methods and his de-politicization of Buenos Aires he had destroyed whatever existed of 'popular' support. And when, in early 1852, the invading army of the Triple Alliance advanced, his troops fled and the people in town and country did not rise in his support. On 3 February, at Monte Caseros, he was defeated: he rode alone from the field of battle, took refuge in the house of the British consul, boarded a British vessel, and sailed for England and exile.

Rosas was destroyed by military defeat. But the economic structure and the international links on which his system rested were already beginning to shift. Cattle-raising was the preferred policy of the Rosas regime. It required relatively low investments in land and technology, and, if practised on an extensive scale in large units capable of dealing with fluctuating export markets, it yielded very high profits. Investments had to be concentrated in cattle; therefore abundant, cheap and secure land was required. But cattle-raising gave a limited range of exports, mainly hides and jerked beef, for which international demand was not likely to grow. The market for hides was far from dynamic, even when continental Europe began to supplement Great Britain; and the demand for salt beef, limited to the slave economies of Brazil and Cuba, was more likely to contract than expand. The Rosas economy therefore faced present stagnation and future decline. Meanwhile, by the mid-1840s, other areas of South America were entering into competition. The *saladeros* of Rio Grande do Sul began to undercut Buenos Aires. And within the confederation the balance was no longer so overwhelmingly in Buenos Aires's favour. From 1843 the littoral provinces made the most of the peace which they enjoyed while Rosas concentrated his fighting forces on Uruguay. Cattle resources multiplied: Entre Ríos, with six million cattle, two million sheep and seventeen *saladeros*, was a new economic power. Competition was not yet critical; exports of jerked beef from Entre Ríos were still only 10 per cent of those of Buenos Aires. But there were political implications. The *estancieros* of Entre Ríos and Corrientes, profiting to some degree from the blockade of Buenos Aires, were not prepared to endure for ever the stranglehold exercised by their metropolis. Why should they sustain the commercial monopoly of Buenos Aires? Should they not by-pass its customs house and gain direct access to outside markets? To respond to these challenges the economy of Buenos Aires needed diversification and improvement. These came in the form of an alternative activity. Sheep farming had already begun to threaten the dominance of the cattle *estancia*. It was through the export of wool that Argentina would first develop its link with the world market, its internal productive capacity and its capital accumulation. Rosas thus became an anachronism, a legacy from another age.

The 'merinization' of Buenos Aires, the rise of a large sheep and wool economy, began in the 1840s and soon led to a scramble for new land. The external stimulus was the expansion of the European textile industry, which provided a secure export market. Internal conditions were also favourable, consisting of good soil and a local stock capable of improvement. In 1810 the province had a stock of 2–3 million sheep, but these were of poor quality and occupied marginal lands. By 1852 the number had grown to 15 million head, and in 1865 40 million. Wool exports increased from 333.7 tons in 1829, to 1,609.6 tons in 1840, to 7,681 tons in 1850; they then accelerated to 17,316.9 tons in 1860, 65,704.2 tons in 1870. In 1822 wool represented 0.94 per cent of the total value of exports from Buenos Aires, cattle hides 64.86 per cent; in 1836, 7.6 per cent and 68.4 per cent respectively; in 1851, 10.3 per cent and 64.9 per cent; in 1861, 35.9 per cent and 33.5 per cent; in 1865, 46.2 per cent and 27.2 per cent.

In the early years of independence *estancieros* showed little interest in improving breeds of sheep. It was left to a few Englishmen, John Harratt and Peter Sheridan in particular, to show the way: from the 1820s they began to purchase Spanish merinos, to preserve and refine the improved breeds and to export to Liverpool, encouraged by the almost total abolition of import duties on wool in England. The growing interest in sheep breeding was reflected in further imports of merinos from Europe and the United States in 1836–8, while the pampa sheep were also crossed with Saxony breeds. To improve the quality of sheep required not only the import of European breeds but also new forms of production – improvement of the grasses of the pampa, fencing of fields, building of sheds for shearing and storing wool, opening of wells. All this in turn raised the demand for labour. The gaucho was gradually replaced by the shepherd. Immigrant settlers arrived, either as hired labourers or as partners in profit-sharing schemes or as tenant farmers. Irish immigrants were particularly welcome as shepherds, but Basques and Galicians also came; and while this was not a massive immigration, it brought needed labour, skills and output. The new arrivals were often given a stake in the flocks of a sheep farmer through five-yearly contracts in which they became partners, receiving one-third of the increase and one-third of the wool in return for caring for the flock and paying expenses. An immigrant could earn enough in a few years to purchase an interest in half a flock and at the end of this time he had enough sheep and money to set up on his own. On the pampas between Buenos Aires and the River Salado sheep were beginning to drive cattle from the land; from the 1840s *estancia* after *estancia* passed into the hands of the sheep farmers. Cattle *estancias* survived, of course, either as mixed farms or on low and marshy lands whose reedy grasses were unsuitable for sheep. In general the lands which had been longest occupied, in the northern parts of the province, were the best adapted for sheep, while the new lands in the south were·more suited to the breeding of cattle. Rosas himself had always encouraged sheep rearing, if not improvement, on his own *estancias*.

The large purchases of land by foreigners, the multiplication of sheep, the appearance of more sophisticated consumer trends, all were signs of a new Argentina. The city of Buenos Aires was growing and improving, as paved streets, horse-drawn public transport and gas supplies enhanced the environment. Near the towns the enclosure of lands for agriculture and horticulture proceeded, so that within ten years after Rosas all lands over a radius of 15–20 miles around the city of Buenos Aires were subdivided and enclosed as farms or market gardens, cultivated by Italians, Basques, French, British and German immigrants, and supplying an ever-growing urban market. Railways began to connect the interior of the province with the capital, and a fleet of steam vessels placed the various river ports in daily communication with the great entrepôt. Ocean steamers arrived and departed every two or three days. Between 1860 and 1880 the total value of imports from Europe doubled, comprising mainly textiles, hardware and machinery from Britain, and luxury goods from the continent. Meanwhile foreign trade was dominated by the customary commodities, by wool, hides and salt meat, which constituted more than 90 per cent of the total value of exports.

Economic performance differed, of course, between the three major regions. Buenos Aires maintained its dominance in spite of the obstacles to growth presented by civil and foreign wars, the exactions of the state and the raids of frontier Indians. The littoral lagged some way behind, its growth uneven but its prospects promising. Santa Fe, unlike Buenos Aires, had empty lands to fill; schemes of agricultural colonization were begun, offering a harsh life for the immigrants but a profitable one for those entrepreneurs who bought up land to re-sell to the colonists. Rosario was now an active river port, poised for further development. Entre Ríos, where Urquiza himself was the greatest proprietor, had a more established prosperity, with rich cattle *estancias* and sheep farms, and trading links with Brazil and Uruguay. Foreigners now penetrated the up-river·markets more frequently. Even Corrientes, part *estancia*, part tobacco plantation, where English bottled beer was drunk on all social occasions, was emerging at last from a subsistence economy. The interior, on the other hand, was the underdeveloped region of Argentina, its production damaged by distance from the east coast and by cheap competition from Europe, its only compensating outlet being the Chilean mining market. Economic poverty and the concentration of usable land in large estates drove the poor off the soil into the hands of caudillos, who, while Buenos Aires and the littoral were moving into another age, still looked towards the past.

The defeat of Rosas did not destroy existing structures. The hegemony of the landed oligarchy survived. The dominance of Buenos Aires continued. And inter-provincial conflict simply entered another stage. The provinces conferred upon Urquiza, the victor of Caseros, the title Provisional Director of the Argentine Confederation and gave him a national role; he in turn decreed the nationalization of the customs and free navigation of the rivers Paraña and Uruguay. But Buenos Aires broke away, refused to place itself at the mercy of other provinces, some of them little more than deserts, and remained aloof from the constituent congress which Urquiza convened. The constitution, approved on 1 May 1853, reflected a number of influences – previous Argentine constitutions, the example of the United States and the bitter lessons of past conflict. But perhaps the most powerful influence was the political thought of Juan Bautista Alberdi, who advised a just balance between central power and provincial rights, and a programme of immigration, education and modernization. The constitution provided for a federal republic and incorporated the classical freedoms and civil rights. It divided power between the executive, the legislative and the judiciary. The legislature consisted of two houses, a senate to which each provincial legislature elected two members, and a chamber of deputies elected by male suffrage in public voting. While assuring local self-government to the provinces, the constitution gave countervailing authority to the federal government. The president, who was chosen by an electoral college for six years, was given strong executive powers: he could introduce his own bills, appoint and dismiss his ministers without reference to congress. The president was also empowered to intervene in any province in order to preserve republican government against internal disorder or foreign attack; to this effect he could remove local administrations and impose federal officials. The economic provisions of the constitution also addressed federal problems. Inter-provincial tariffs were abolished. The income from Buenos Aires customs house was to be nationalized and not to remain the exclusive property of the province of

Buenos Aires, which was another reason for *porteño* resistance. Urquiza was elected president for six years. But he did not preside over a nation state. A sense of national identity did not exist, or else it was not strong enough to overcome provincial and personal loyalties. While the provinces accepted the Constitution of 1853, they continued to be ruled by caudillos, even if they were called governors, and the confederation was essentially a network of personal loyalties to its president.

Argentina was now split into two states, on the one hand the city and province of Buenos Aires, ruled by its governor (from 1860 Bartolomé Mitre) and a liberal party, on the other the Argentine confederation, consisting of thirteen provinces under Urquiza and a federal party. Whereas in the past the provinces had refused to accept the domination of Buenos Aires, now Buenos Aires refused to co-operate with the provinces, or to obey a constitution which it considered a facade for *caudillismo*. And Buenos Aires could not be forced into a confederation against its wishes: it was powerful, it was rich, and its customs house was still the chief source of revenue in Argentina, the focus of foreign trade, and the property of one province. The confederation therefore established its capital at Paraná, in Entre Ríos, where Urquiza, whatever his constitutional sentiments, ruled as an old-style caudillo, though with the added role of leader of the littoral and the interior. As first president, Urquiza signed commercial treaties with Britain, France and the United States, and opened the rivers Paraná and Uruguay to free navigation for foreign trade. In normal times almost 70 per cent of imports into Buenos Aires were destined for the provinces. Now it was the policy of the confederation to free itself from Buenos Aires, trade directly with the outside world and make Rosario a new entrepôt. Urquiza was personally involved in commercial enterprises with Europe, in schemes for the establishment of import-export houses in Rosario and in the search for outside capital. But foreign shipping did not respond to the new opportunities and continued to unload at Buenos Aires: the fact remained that Rosario was not yet a sufficient market or entrepôt to justify an extra five-day journey. Further stimulus was provided in 1857 when a differential tariff was issued in the hope of tempting European trade into by-passing Buenos Aires: but even this, which only lasted until 1859, could not overcome the facts of economic life. Commercial war therefore gave way to military conflict.

By 1859 both sides were ready for a new trial by battle. Urquiza's army defeated that of Mitre at the battle of Cepeda, but Buenos Aires accepted incorporation into the confederation with great reluctance. It still had reserves of money and manpower, and in 1861 it fought back once more. The two sides met at the battle of Pavón, an encounter which was interpreted if not as a victory for Mitre at least as a defeat for the confederation, demonstrably incapable of imposing its will on the recalcitrant province. Urquiza withdrew from the battlefield, apparently convinced that if the confederation could not win quickly it would not win at all. He took his forces to Entre Ríos to guard at least his provincial interests, and left the confederation weakened and disorientated. Mitre meanwhile advanced on various fronts. He sent his military columns in support of liberal regimes in the provinces of the littoral and the interior. He negotiated with Urquiza from a position of strength and persuaded him voluntarily to dismantle the confederation. And he pressed the politicians of his own province of Buenos Aires to accept his programme of national reorganization and to proceed by negotiation rather than force.

The resultant settlement was a compromise between unitarism and federalism. Mitre accepted the constitution of 1853, with its bias towards centralism and presidential power, and was then declared national as well as provincial leader. Thus, in 1861, the idea of a federation, with Buenos Aires its centre and the interior represented there, was accepted. And Mitre, a *porteño*, a hero of the siege of Montevideo, was elected first constitutional president for the whole nation in October 1862. Now, the union of the provinces was achieved and for the first time Argentina was called Argentina and not by a clumsy circumlocution.

The opportunity for national reorganization after 1862 could have been lost had not power been held by two distinguished presidents, Bartolomé Mitre (1862–8) and Domingo F. Sarmiento (1868–74), intellectuals and men of letters as well as politicians and statesmen. Both had given many years of service towards the ideal of a greater Argentina; both now stood for three objectives, national unity, liberal institutions and modernization. In combating the confederation Mitre had fought not simply for one particular province but against fragmentation and *caudillismo*. He sought to place and keep Buenos Aires at the head of a united Argentina, and he fought on after 1862. For the caudillos did not die without a struggle. In 1863 and again in 1866–8 Mitre had to suppress rebellions in the interior. The political occasion of these insurrections was caudillo resistance to the new order. But the deeper causes were the depressed economies of the interior, the impoverishment of the provinces and their inability to sustain their populations in occupation or subsistence. Lack of work and food drove the rural peoples to the life of *montoneros*, to live in effect by banditry and booty. Forces of this kind sustained Angel Vicente Peñaloza, 'El Chacho', caudillo of wild and remote La Rioja, where one school sufficed for the entire province but where the caudillo provided personally for the welfare of his followers. When El Chacho revolted in 1863, Mitre permitted Sarmiento, governor of San Juan and a federal pro-consul in the interior, to wage a war to the death against the rebels, and the forces of Sarmiento, defending civilization with barbarism, killed their prisoners and displayed the head of El Chacho on a pole. In 1866–7 Felipe Varela, former officer of El Chacho, invaded western Argentina from Chile and raised another *montonera*, but he too was defeated and his followers mercilessly crushed by the national army. The end of the *montonera* was in sight, though it evinced further paroxysms before it was extinguished. Urquiza, reconciled now to the central state, held aloof from the provincial movements which he was supposed to patronize but now disavowed, and played his own role in supporting the new Argentina. But in the end he fell a victim to the system which he had once represented; he was assassinated in his own *estancia*, by order of a rival caudillo and former protégé, in April 1870. His killer, Ricardo López Jordán, kept alive in Entre Ríos the spirit of rebellion and the cult of *caudillismo*, until 1876. In the meantime, as president, Sarmiento, who declared that he was a *porteño* in the provinces and a provincial in Buenos Aires, had continued the work of Mitre, had defended national unity with the sword and the pen and had been even more ruthless with rebels.

In spite of provincial traditions and caudillo resistance, central power and national organization survived and took root. They were assisted by the growth of institutions with an Argentine dimension, the press, the postal service, the National Bank, the railway system. But two particular agencies promoted national identity and unity – federal justice and the national army. By law of 1862 a national judicial power was established, and in 1865–8 the Argentine Civil Code was drawn up. The supreme court and the various lower courts completed the structure of the modern state. The supreme court had power to declare unconstitutional any laws or decrees, national or provincial, in conflict with the supreme law, and thus became the interpreter of the constitution, though it was not competent to decide conflicts between the powers. The executive had the right of intervention in the provinces, a right which became more effective once it was backed by a national army. By decree of 26 January 1864 the government created a permanent army of 6,000 men distributed between artillery, infantry and cavalry. A Military Academy was established in 1869 and the formation of a professional officer corps was begun. The law of recruitment of 21 September 1872 anticipated national conscription. This was the institutional framework for the new army. But a more effective impetus was given by its operations during the rebellions of the caudillos and the War of Paraguay, when it increased its numbers and added to its experience. The army gave the president real power and enabled him to extend the executive's reach into the furthest corners of Argentina. Gradually the local oligarchies became compliant, and in return for collaboration they were offered a place in a national ruling class.

The political principles animating the presidencies of Mitre and Sarmiento were those of classical liberalism. Mitre led an identifiable Liberal Party, and after Pavón his strategy of national reorganization rested not only on the extension of federal power but also on the proliferation of liberal governments throughout the provinces, instruments of union by voluntary choice. Liberalism represented an intellectual aristocracy, survivors and heirs of the generation of 1837, now free to apply their ideas, to promote political and material progress, the rule of law, primary and secondary education, to dispel the barbarism which Sarmiento abhorred and to make the poor gaucho into a useful man. But the liberal elite held out little for the popular masses: for the gauchos and peons, who were beyond the political pale, their status to serve, their function to labour. They were represented by nothing but an epic poem, *Martín Fierro*, lamenting the departure of a noble past. The only opposition recognized by the Liberal Party was that of the federalists, who followed Urquiza and tradition and who clearly belonged to the political nation. The Liberals split into two groups during Mitre's presidency, the autonomists, who came to incorporate those federalists left leaderless by the death of Urquiza, and the nationalists, who continued to preserve pure *mitrista* principles. Meanwhile in the provinces liberalism, like federalism, was often simply another name for *caudillismo*, and political party bosses soon became known as 'caudillos'.

Modernization meant growth through exports from the rural sector, investment in a new infrastructure and immigration. Some local capital was employed in the primary sector, in cattle *estancias*, sheep farms and sugar estates. But investment depended essentially upon the import of foreign capital, mainly from Britain. Up to the early 1870s British trade to Argentina was predominantly a trade in textiles, and British investment was confined to commerce and private *estancias*. But from 1860 new trends appeared. First, several joint-stock enterprises were organized in 1861–5. These were established by British entrepreneurs with British capital and were applied to railways and banks. On 1 January 1863 the first branch of the London and River Plate Bank was opened in Buenos Aires, and in 1866 the Rosario branch went into operation. From this time iron and steel, metal manufactures and coal became more important among British exports to Argentina. The second stage comprised investment in development, encouraged by Argentina and promoted by the British who wanted to improve the market for their goods. In 1860 a loan of £2.5 million was marketed in London by Barings on behalf of the Argentine government. This was the beginning of a steady flow of capital from Britain to Argentina, much of it applied to the infrastructure, either as direct investment or as loans to the state. More substantial foreign investment had to await the period after 1870, when banks, factories and public utilities became major recipients. But one area of investment was already established, the railways, and these were essential to economic growth, bringing out agricultural exports from the vast hinterland of Buenos Aires and carrying in imported goods.

The first track was opened in 1857; this ran six miles west from Buenos Aires and was built with private local capital. During the 1860s the Northern and Southern Railways began to fan out from Buenos Aires; and in 1870 the Central Argentine Railway linked Rosario and Córdoba, and opened up the great central plains. For this line the government contracted with British capital, guaranteeing a minimum return and granting adjacent lands, necessary concessions to attract capital to an empty territory, whose value lay in future prospects rather than present performance. In twenty years 1,250 miles of track was laid in Argentina. Meanwhile communications with the outside world were improving, as steam replaced sail. The Royal Mail Company began regular service to the River Plate in 1853; Lamport and Holt in 1863; the Pacific Steam Navigation Company in 1868. The journey from England to the River Plate was cut to 22 days in a fast ship. Steamships also joined the river ports, and by 1860 a number of services were in operation. Improved docks and harbours became an urgent need, as did cable and telegraph links with Europe, and all these would soon be provided by foreign capital and technology.

The new Argentina also needed people. The growth of federal power and the hegemony of Buenos Aires in the period 1852–70 was not simply a constitutional or military process. It also represented demographic and economic forces. Argentina's population grew more rapidly after 1852, from 935,000 to 1,736,923 in 1869. The balance in favour of the coast became more pronounced. The province of Buenos Aires contained 28 per cent of the whole population in 1869; the littoral 48.8 per cent. The city of Buenos Aires increased its inhabitants from 90,076 in 1854 to 177,787 in 1869, of whom 89,661 were Argentines, 88,126 foreigners. Immigration now significantly fed population growth. After 1852 the confederation made a special effort to attract immigrants from Europe. The Constitution of 1853 gave foreigners virtually all the rights of Argentines without the obligations. In the years 1856–70 European families were brought in by the provincial government of Santa Fe to form agricultural colonies, pioneers of the 'cerealization' of the pampas. After 1862 immigration became a national policy and offices were set up in Europe, though the government did not finance the process, leaving passage and settlement to the free play of economic forces. From the late 1850s about 15,000 immigrants a year entered Argentina.

Sarmiento and others, influenced by the American model of frontier expansion, preached the virtues of agriculture and small farms, the importance of settling the immigrants in rural areas, the need to provide land for colonization and to discourage speculation and latifundism. But the actual result was different. The government viewed land as a valuable resource which could be sold or leased for fiscal purposes. Cattle and sheep raising were the basic activities of the country. The *estancieros* formed a powerful interest group, linked to the commercial leaders of the city; they regarded access to land as a vital factor for stock raising. And land speculation, either by the purchase of public land to be sold later at a profit or by subdivision and subletting of holdings, was too lucrative a business to stop. By the 1880s, therefore, most of the public land of the province of Buenos Aires, by a series of laws, had been transferred as private property to latifundists and speculators: and the pattern was repeated in other provinces. No doubt in the decades after 1850 the trend was towards smaller holdings, as the pampas became effectively occupied, land became scarce and expensive, sheep farming brought subdivision of property and new owners bought their way in and displaced the old. But this was a trend from superlatifundism to mere latifundism.

Uruguay after independence possessed a pastoral economy, an export trade, an international port and a liberal constitution. These assets were first squandered and then plundered. Uruguayans began to fight among themselves for the resources of their country. There was a fierce struggle for land, as older *estancieros* sought to secure their possessions and newcomers contended for a share. Men placed themselves under local caudillos, and these under greater caudillos, joining the *bandos*, or parties, of two rival candidates for power, the *colorados* and *blancos*. The result was the Guerra Grande, which began as a conflict between the two major caudillos, Manuel Oribe (*blanco*) and Fructuoso Rivera (*colorado*), over control of Uruguay and became, with the fall of Oribe in October 1838, an international war.

The long duration of the conflict, the presence of the *colorados* in the besieged city of Montevideo and the *blancos* in the surrounding country, brought out hitherto concealed ideological differences between the two parties. The *colorados* acquired an identity as an urban party, receptive to liberal and foreign ideas, immigrants from Europe and Brazilian support. They allied themselves with the liberal exiles from Buenos Aires against Rosas and his lieutenant Oribe, and they welcomed the intervention first of France (1838–42), then Britain and France (1843–50), when foreign interests coincided with *colorado* needs. Montevideo, therefore, was *colorado*, a European city demographically; of its 31,000 inhabitants only 11,000 were Uruguayans. European merchants dominated its trade, European loans propped up its finances (at the cost of the customs revenue), and European ideas infused its politics. But the *colorados* represented interests as well as ideas. They gained support not only from young people wanting liberty and reform, but also from immigrants hoping for land grants, from Argentine exiles using Montevideo as a base on the way back, from capitalists who owned the customs and saw the blockade of Buenos Aires as good business, and from merchants who profited from Montevideo's free access to trade and navigation of the River Plate. Rivera himself was essentially a caudillo in search of power rather than a constitutionalist. So this was an alliance of interests.

The countryside, on the other hand, was *blanco*. The *blanco* party was the party of the *estancieros*, the party of authority and tradition. It prided itself on resistance to foreign intervention, defence of 'Americanism' and alliance with the Argentina of Rosas. It was subsidized militarily and financially by Rosas, and led by a man, Oribe, who in spite of his nationalism in relation to European intervention was regarded by many as the tool of his master. The combined military forces of Rosas and Oribe were enough, if not to overcome, at least to resist the rival alliance, and the siege of Montevideo lasted from 16 February 1843 until peace was established between the Uruguayans on 8 October 1851.

In the event both parties became disillusioned with foreign intervention, Rivera with the inability of the Anglo-French allies to destroy Rosas, Oribe with Rosas's vulnerability to the rebellion led by Urquiza and both sides with the blatant exploitation of Uruguay by their respective allies. Prodded by Urquiza, the rival parties made peace in October 1851 and agreed that there was neither victor nor vanquished. Thus, they joined the rebellion against Rosas, but in a subordinate position in relation to the more powerful partners, particularly Brazil. Uruguay now made an extremely unfavourable treaty with Brazil, ceding territorial rights, granting a mortgage on the customs and allowing free (that is, untaxed) movement of cattle from Uruguay into Brazil; all this in return for a monthly subsidy, the only funds available to the Uruguayan treasury.

The Guerra Grande left Uruguay prostrate and impoverished, its livestock and *saladero* industries ruined, its government heavily in debt to national and foreign creditors, its population in decline. Private fortunes were diminished and the mass of the people destitute. And over the whole country fell the menacing shadow of Brazil. Demographically the war was a time of loss, and shortage of people was probably Uruguay's greatest problem for many years to come. The population fell from 140,000 in 1840 to 132,000 in 1852; Montevideo suffered a decline from 40,000 to 34,000. Many people, especially foreign immigrants, had abandoned the countryside to seek safety and subsistence in more prosperous parts of the Río de la Plata or Brazil, leaving a labour vacuum which retarded recuperation. Socially, while the structure of landownership had not changed, *estancias* had often changed hands. Many native landowners had been driven to seek shelter in Montevideo; their land was then neglected or plundered, it lost its cattle and its value, and the owners were forced to sell out cheaply to newcomers. From Rio Grande do Sul Brazilians surged into an empty Uruguay in the 1850s, buying their way into hundreds of *estancias*, followed by Englishmen and other Europeans. Foreigners already dominated the urban sector: in 1853, of the 2,200 merchants and artisans, 1,700 or almost 80 per cent were foreigners. Now the composition of the rural aristocracy also changed as it incorporated more and more foreigners. Secure in their titles and protected by their governments, the newcomers did not actively participate in Uruguayan politics. And the remaining native *estanciero* class was now politically homogeneous, for the *blancos*, having dominated the countryside for nine years, were now a majority, and there was no longer a struggle for land between *colorados* and *blancos*. The Guerra Grande therefore contributed to the pacification of the country-side. The rural masses, however, fared badly. The war increased their poverty and their nomadic ways, as some were conscripted and others fled from the army; now, after the war, they took reluctantly to peon status, preferring a marginal life as cowboy or rustler.

The economic consequences of war were equally grim. The basis of Uruguay's economy was the production and export of hides, jerked beef and wool. The indiscriminate slaughter of beasts, the heavy consumption of cattle by warring armies and European fleets, together with large-scale raids on *estancia* cattle by Brazilians from Rio Grande do Sul, decimated the stock of Uruguay. Cattle fell from over 6 million head in 1843 to 2 million in 1852, and many of these, wild and unimproved, were unsuitable for the export market. The *saladeros* suffered from lack of cattle and competition from Brazil for the cattle which remained; and of the twenty-four plants which functioned in 1842 no more than three or four remained in 1854. The incipient sheep industry, which in the 1830s had begun to upgrade its wool through imported stock, was stopped in its tracks. The only animals to increase during the war were the wild dogs which preyed on young cattle and became a plague of the countryside.

The cost of the war to the treasury endured long after the peace. All the resources of the state were mortgaged, either to private capitalists who had financed the *colorado* cause or to the governments of France and Brazil. In the 1850s the monthly subsidy from Brazil was virtually the only revenue of the Uruguayan government, and for this the customs remained mortgaged. Brazil became an informal metropolis and Uruguay a kind of satellite, the victim of economic penetration, financial dependence and political subordination. For Uruguay endured not only the pressure of the subsidy but also the legacy of the treaties of 1851, a Brazilian army of 5,000 (until 1855) and a Brazilian fifth column in the form of hundreds of *estancieros*, whose presence made northern Uruguay almost an appendage of Rio Grande do Sul. Uruguay was in real danger of losing its independence, at a time when Argentina, the traditional rival of Brazil in the River Plate, was pinned down by a debilitating civil war.

These were years of anarchy, isolation and nomadism in Uruguay, a time of Hobbesian insecurity. Bereft of resources and infrastructure, the state was too weak to guarantee its people their lives and possessions. As the authority of the state declined, individuals had to fend for themselves and revert to relations of personal authority and subordination characteristic of more primitive societies. The crudest *caudillismo* and clientage now prevailed.

How did Uruguay survive as a nation after the Guerra Grande and its social fabric hold together? In the end the hopelessness of their position forced *estancieros* and merchants to seek peace, to persuade the political parties to end their destructive struggle and to let economic growth take the place of conflict. From this came the policy of *fusión*, in which the parties agreed to subordinate their differences to a common object, to create a single movement animated by the ideals of peace, progress and economic recovery. And fusion was accompanied by a policy of pacts between rival caudillos to bring stability to the countryside. On 11 November 1855 Oribe made the 'Pact of Union' with Venancio Flores, the most enlightened of the *colorado* leadership. So in spite of the appearance of anarchy and the threat to fusion from periodic revolution, in fact the period after 1852 was one of relative calm in the countryside. This was the political framework in which economic recovery began, and it coincided with a decade of external peace for Uruguay and strong European demand and good prices for pastoral products during the Crimean War.

The change was seen first in demographic improvement. The population almost doubled, from 132,000 in 1852 to 221,248 in 1860. Montevideo grew from 34,000 to 57,911. Foreigners increased from 21.6 per cent of the population to 35 per cent; and in Montevideo they constituted 48 per cent. Commerce grew as internal demand for imports grew. Montevideo profited from the free navigation of the rivers and the impotence of Buenos Aires, to import and export in growing quantities, not only for itself but also for the rest of the littoral and for Rio Grande do Sul. Foreign shipping increased; foreign entrepreneurs, among them the Brazilian, Baron Mauá, extended their influence and acquired, among other assets, state bonds emanating from the war debt; foreign-controlled banks were founded.

In the countryside the cattle-breeding industry doubled its stock from 2 to 4 million in six years (1852–8), and from 4 to 8 million in 1859–62, while imported stock such as Durhams (1858), and Herefords (1864) began to upgrade the Uruguayan herds. The sheep stock, also much improved, increased from 1 million in 1852 to 3 million in 1860. A growing number of *saladeros* processed the products of the *estancia*, 160,000 head of cattle in 1858, 500,000 in 1862, and the export of hides and jerked beef surged upwards. Land prices rose by over 200 per cent in the latter half of the 1850s. But as this primitive economy rushed blindly forward it soon came up against the inevitable limits of products and purchasers.

The markets for hides and jerked beef were not dynamic, as Argentina also discovered. Jerked beef in particular had a limited outlet, the slave economies of Brazil and Cuba, and as production far exceeded demand so prices fell. Internal peace and rural abundance thus produced problems of their own and drew attention to the limitations of the economy. As boom gave way to depression, the risks involved in revolution appeared to be less daunting. The economic base was so narrow that there seemed little at stake, and the main justification for fusion and stability lost its force. Only an added dimension could make a difference, and this would come in the following decade (1860–70) with the major growth of the sheep industry. Meanwhile as Uruguay's hard-won prosperity came to an end in 1862 in a crisis of overproduction, so the fusionist assumptions were challenged and political conflict was renewed.

The state in Uruguay, as in pre-Tudor England, was weaker than its most powerful subjects. The constitution of 1830, with its president, its ministers, its congress and its civil liberties, was a facade. In the elections of 1860 Montevideo, with 60,000 inhabitants, had only 1,500 names on the civil register, and only 662 people voted. Lacking a middle or popular base, starved of revenue, without a powerful army and a modern infrastructure, the government was in no position to resist the challenge of caudillos if they had more horses, more swords and lances, and more money perhaps from foreign paymasters. Only when the state had guns and artillery, a transport system, telegraph, railways, roads and bridges (that is, from about 1875), only then could it assert itself and overcome its mighty subjects. Meanwhile, as it did not possess independent sanctions of its own, the state depended upon the good will of caudillos who had the means to sustain a government or to overthrow it. In these circumstances fusion ended and civil war was renewed. President Bernardo F. Berro (1860–4) made a brave attempt to maintain constitutionalism. But it was impossible to rule in a political vacuum, to ignore endemic *caudillismo* and factional politics. At the same time his assertion of national interests, especially against Brazil, brought a danger of intervention which he was not capable of resisting.

Brazilian settlers numbered almost 20,000 (without counting those unregistered), formed 10–15 per cent of the whole population, occupied 30 per cent of Uruguayan territory, and owned some of the best cattle property in the country. As they took root and began to spread their language and customs, they came to constitute a powerful enclave, two aspects of which were particularly worrying to the Uruguayan authorities: the concentration of their *estancias* in the frontier zone, and the tendency of the settlers to appeal to their home government against any pressure from Uruguay. The Brazilian government had reasons of its own to espouse the cause of its migrants – the search for further agricultural territory in the temperate zone, the desire to control river communications to its interior provinces, and the need to placate the immediate allies of the settlers, the magnates of Rio Grande do Sul, a peripheral province with separatist leanings. For its part, the government of President Berro attempted to control the Brazilian settlers and to impose its own law and order in the frontier territories. It took a number of positive steps to preserve Uruguayan sovereignty. It began the colonization of the frontier zone with Uruguayans, on the assumption that to populate was to defend. It sought to limit the use of slave labour on the Brazilian *estancias*. In Uruguay abolition was slow but sure, a twenty-five-year process (1825–53) comprising abolition of the slave trade, emancipation in return for military service and the gradual enactment of liberal legislation. Now the government took steps to free the slaves and semi-slaves whom Brazilian *estancieros* introduced from Rio Grande do Sul and who were thought to constitute an advantageously cheap labour supply. The Uruguayans also declined to renew the trade treaty of 1851, in order to impose duties on the passage of cattle from Uruguay to Brazil and thereby to rival *saladeros*. Finally, they placed a higher direct tax on all land and cattle in Uruguay and forced the Brazilian *estancieros* to share the tax burden of the rest of the landowning class. The cattle barons and *saladeristas* of Rio Grande do Sul opposed this campaign, for it struck at their vital interests and those of their allies and clients among the settlers in Uruguay. They demanded action from the government in Rio de Janeiro to produce a more compliant regime in Uruguay. Brazilian support for the revolution of Venancio Flores in 1863 was in part a response to the policy pursued by the Berro government.

Meanwhile Uruguay was also under pressure from Argentina. Berro remained strictly neutral in the Argentine civil war of 1861, although he and his *oribista* colleagues were politically 'federalist' and more inclined to support Urquiza than Mitre. Venancio Flores, on the other hand, fought for Mitre at Pavón and openly espoused his cause. Mitre and the *colorados* were thus bound by past alliance and present convenience. The new Argentine president would obviously prefer a Uruguayan regime which was an ally of Argentine unity to one which was a friend of federalism. Even if Argentina could not include Uruguay in its national reorganization, it might at least create a satellite Uruguay and remove a source of federalist infection.

Caught between the expansionist aims of Brazil and the menacing if uncertain intentions of Argentina, the government of Berro sought to establish a balance of power in the River Plate by forging an alliance with another nation threatened by the two giants, Paraguay, and he proposed a treaty of friendship, commerce and navigation, to save the independence of both. But Paraguay did not react positively until the end of 1864, when it was too late.

In a world of predators Berro was too honest. He did not have the power to confront Argentina and Brazil, and he did not have a strong enough base within Uruguay to resist their ally, Venancio Flores, caudillo of the *colorado* party. On 19 April 1863 Venancio Flores invaded Uruguay from Argentina. Local support was not overwhelming. Liberal *colorados* did not like assisting *caudillismo*, and Berro had a record of nonpartisan government dedicated to the national interest. But Flores had other cards to play. He enjoyed the support of President Mitre, assistance from the Argentine navy in passing men and arms across the River Uruguay, and funds from sympathizers in Buenos Aires. He was backed too by the frontier *estancieros* of Rio Grande do Sul, and hoped through them to gain the support of the emperor of Brazil. The revolution of Venancio Flores had become by 1864 an episode in a wider conflict.

Brazil and Argentina were both concerned over developments among their smaller neighbours. Each had a boundary dispute with Paraguay, and each too had other interests at stake. Brazil wanted to maintain free navigation of the River Paraguay, so that Mato Grosso would have secure exit to the sea. Regional security also presupposed a compliant Uruguay, whose ports and resources could be an asset or a threat to her neighbours. Yet the more Brazil pressed on the *blanco* government of Uruguay, the more urgently this looked for support elsewhere. In 1864 Paraguay was ready to respond.

To intervene more positively in Uruguay, Brazil needed the good will of Argentina. Mitre was disposed to give this, for he too had differences with his smaller neighbours. In Argentina, to complete the victory of union and liberalism, it was thought necessary to destroy the power of Paraguay, an enduring and perhaps infectious example of the centrifugal and conservative forces which appealed to federal caudillos. Argentina also wanted a stable, friendly and preferably liberal Uruguay, and sought this through Flores. In September 1864 Brazilian forces moved into Uruguay in support of Flores. By February 1865 Montevideo had surrendered, and Flores was established in power. He was a subordinate but not a satellite, not as long as he was allied to both Argentina and Brazil, rivals as well as allies. This was a triple alliance. As for Paraguay, it had no allies and was reduced to virtual isolation.

Paraguay reverted after independence to near-subsistence economy, trapped in an inland cul-de-sac at the end of the river system, harassed by Argentina on one side and Brazil on the other. But Paraguay was a creature of policy as well as environment. This simple society, polarized between a state ruling class and a docile peasantry, was subject to the rule of a series of dictators who imposed or inherited political and economic isolation. The first of these was Dr José Gaspar Rodríguez de Francia, a creole lawyer and philosopher, who was appointed Dictator for five years by a congress in 1814, and then Supreme Dictator for life by another in 1816, after which he ruled until his death in 1840, without a congress, a rival, or a press of any kind, but with an army to guard him and a spy system to inform him. He was accepted on his own terms because he appeared to be the only leader capable of defending Paraguay's independent identity, and to fulfil this function he demanded absolute powers. This tradition of government was continued by Carlos Antonio López, another lawyer, who ruled first as a joint consul then, from 1844, as dictator until his death in 1862. López spent much of his time establishing, promoting and rewarding his own family, reserving the ultimate prize, the succession, for his son Francisco Solano López. The relatively long reigns and the dynastic trends of these authoritarian rulers made Paraguayan government almost a monarchy in disguise.

   Francia augmented the remoteness imposed by nature, and he kept Paraguay in controlled though not total isolation, sealed off from the outside world in a posture of permanent defence against the dangers which surrounded it. His policy was a response to that of Buenos Aires, which refused to accept Paraguay's independence or to treat it as other than a rebel province; Buenos Aires sought to block river traffic and strangle Paraguay's economy, denying it free navigation by its natural outlet, the Río Paraná. As a further humiliation, down-river caudillos also preyed on Paraguayan trade, harassing, confiscating and taxing. To save Paraguay from a new dependence, Francia imposed the rule of dissociation. But he admitted those foreigners who might serve the country, and he allowed a controlled trade at two river ports. Export of *yerba*, tobacco and hardwoods was conducted through Pilar to Argentina and through Ytapúa to Brazil, against imports of arms and other manufactures, the whole trade closely supervised and taxed by the state. Otherwise Paraguay had to aim at economic self-sufficiency and submit to government monopoly. The principal products were *yerba mate* and woods, though Francia also encouraged more diversified production, tobacco, sugar and hides. Farmers were assigned a production quota of grain and cotton which they had to fulfil in order to substitute for imports. The state not only controlled the activity of private *estancias* but also entered directly into production on the extensive lands at its disposal, former crown land, ex-Jesuit land, confiscations from the Church and from political opponents, and reclamations from the wilderness. These publicly owned lands were either leased out to farmers or administered directly by state overseers, who often employed slaves. Some fifty of these '*estancias* of the state' became efficient units of production, providing commodities for export, supplies for the army and reserves of food for the poor in time of need. But in the absence of great external stimulus the economy operated at little above stagnation level and living standards remained primitive.

Society assumed a peculiar formation. The old colonial aristocracy was destroyed by Francia. The Spanish entrepreneurial class was broken by taxation, isolation and persecution. The remnants took refuge in the *estanciero* class, if refuge it was. Confiscation of estates and denial of free export outlets frustrated the development of commercial agriculture and deprived Paraguay of an *estanciero* class comparable to that in the rest of the littoral. When these classes tried to fight back, in the conspiracy of 1820, Francia crushed them in a reign of terror, executing, imprisoning, banishing. The death of the ruling class did not imply the advancement of lower sectors. In effect the state and its few servants took the place of the traditional elite, rural and commercial. Francia did not come to power as the leader of a social revolution, the saviour of the Indian peasantry against the landed aristocracy. The mass of the population, the bland and docile Guaraní people – unorganized farmers and apolitical peasantry – were passive spectators of Francia's dictatorship. They continued to live and work in a subordinate position, while government agents disposed of the labour of the Indians in Misiones. Slavery endured beyond the Francia regime, and 'slaves of the state' laboured on the government *estancias* and in public works, although the law of 1842 ended the slave trade and decreed that children born to slaves after 1842 would be free on reaching the age of twenty-five (*libertos*). According to the census of 1846, in a population of 238,862 there were 17,212 *pardos* (coloureds) of whom 7,893 were slaves and 523 *libertos*.

Francia's successor modified his policy in some important aspects. A fat and bovine *mestizo*, whose neck bulged over his collar, Carlos Antonio López made a bad impression on foreigners but not on Paraguayans. He too was a dictator, though more benevolent than Francia. He too had total power, though he used it to free political prisoners, provide a minimum of education, organize a simple judicial system and establish newspapers. He too favoured state control of land and economy, though this tended to mean control by his own family. He departed from the system of Francia, however, in two fundamentals: he ended Paraguay's isolation, and he introduced the rudiments of modernization. Already in the 1840s he allowed in a number of foreign merchants and artisans, as well as a few doctors. After 1852, following the fall of Rosas and the opening of the rivers, López began to import technology on a large scale. For the skills and equipment to give Paraguay a modern infrastructure of industry, transport and arms, he looked to Europe, particularly Britain. He sent his son Francisco Solano López at the head of a mission to buy military and naval arms and to recruit technical advisers. The party visited England, France and Spain in 1853–4. In London López contracted with A. Blythe and Company of Limehouse, a shipbuilding and engineering firm, for supplies and personnel, and Paraguay soon became one of their best customers. A steam warship was ordered, equipment and arms were purchased, engineers and technicians hired, and arrangements made for the training of Paraguayan apprentices. A whole team of British contract technicians, together with military advisers and doctors, went to Paraguay, some 200 in all including a talented young engineer, William K. Whytehead, the mastermind of the first modernization programme in South America. British machinery and equipment were used to construct a shipyard with a new wharf and dry dock, capable of building and repairing steamers; this was completed by 1860. An arsenal, with capacity for producing cannons and naval gear, was founded in

1856. Factories, an iron foundry, a telegraph system, all were installed in the course of a few years. A railway was begun in 1856 to link Asunción and Villa Rica, and a state merchant marine was inaugurated with steamships built in Paraguay. The entire operation was a monument to Paraguayan determination, British ingenuity and Guaraní labour. Yet it contained some singular features. In the first place, the process did not represent a continuous flow of investment capital into Paraguay. The government bought directly from abroad, paying hard cash for equipment and high wages to personnel. Thus, it did not engender 'dependence', but at the same time it lacked permanence. Secondly, these were essentially defence contracts rather than instruments of modernization in any long-term economic sense. While they created a new infrastructure, this was for purely military purposes, not for development. Thirdly, the structure of society was not basically changed. In a sense the Paraguayan government imported an entire middle class – engineers, architects, doctors, teachers, merchants and artisans. In the 1860s foreigners held about half of all the business licences in the country. But they left hardly a mark on Paraguayan society.

Modernization depended upon, and sought to achieve, the regional security of Paraguay. López wished to establish wider trade channels than those allowed by Francia and to open Paraguay to the modern world. He permitted trade down river to all nations, if Buenos Aires or the caudillos of the littoral could be persuaded to let it through. The results were mixed. Boundaries with Argentina and Brazil were still unsettled and remained a source of friction. Moreover, López found it difficult to make headway against Rosas, who viewed Paraguay as an errant province and restricted its use of the river system. Alliance with Corrientes and with Brazil had little success. Rosas replied by blockade, and López responded with war in 1845; but this was premature, for Paraguay did not yet possess independent military power and could go to war only as a tool of Brazil. It was these humiliating experiences which moved López to modernize his country. The fall of Rosas, in which Paraguay played no part beyond a formal alliance with Brazil, enabled it to break out of isolation. The Argentine confederation declared free navigation of the rivers in 1853. American and European powers signed treaties with López between 1852 and 1860, and the river system was opened to foreign vessels. The new trade did not bring unqualified liberation to the Paraguayan economy. In some commodities it attracted competition which damaged local production hitherto protected by isolation. In the time of Francia cotton was extensively cultivated for home consumption; but after 1852 foreign manufactures penetrated up-river, and people would no longer pay seventy five cents per yard for domestic fabric when they could purchase the imported for ten. Even North American lumber (pinewood) sold in Corrientes in competition with local wood.

Congress had granted López the right to name a temporary successor, and before he died, on 10 September 1862, he nominated his own son. Hereditary *caudillismo*, this was a new phenomenon in South America, Paraguay's exhibit in the laboratory of politics. And there was nothing temporary about this succession. Francisco Solano López had been brought up as heir apparent; within the limits of his meagre and eccentric talents, he had been educated to power, and his whole formation had been designed to make him the military leader of a new Paraguay. He admired not only British technology but also the imperial ideas of Napoleon III, and he returned from his visit to Europe with a great vision. He dreamed of a South American empire, governed from Asunción and ruled by López II, and to this end he collaborated closely with his father in the construction of a military machine and its industrial base. And when he succeeded to government, he was determined to project this new strength abroad and to make Paraguay the guardian of the balance of power in the Río de la Plata. Dr Francia's army had taken a large part of the budget, but had not numbered more than 1,500 troops in Asunción and perhaps as many on the borders. Francisco Solano López raised the standing army to 28,000 and created a menacing if crude parody of a military state.

López II continued the policy of state intervention, control of the economy, and monopoly of *yerba* and its export, in contrast to the policies of economic liberalism prevailing in Buenos Aires, where he was mockingly attacked in the Argentine press. He in turn was fiercely critical of Buenos Aires, partly in self-defence, partly on ideological grounds. In his opinion, through benevolent despotism Paraguay had achieved order, material progress and military strength. In Argentina, on the other hand, the new regime was seeking to refashion the nation in a liberal mould. But the Argentine federalists and the primitive caudillos who still survived looked upon Paraguay as a last stronghold of auton-omy and tradition against the centralist and liberal revolution. Two rival models therefore competed for supremacy in the Río de la Plata, in a mortal conflict of alternatives, constitutionalism against absolutism, liberalism against tradition, Mitre against López. And each side dreaded infection by the other.

While López was ready to resist the advance of liberal principles and economic domination from Argentina, he also faced the spread of Brazilian influence and power southwards towards the Río de la Plata. Paraguay's policy towards Brazil was a test of statesmanship. Although Dr Francia's dealings with the neighbouring giant had been generally friendly, and the Brazilians had supported Carlos Antonio López's stand against Rosas, relations had subsequently worsened. Frontier controversy convinced Carlos Antonio López that Brazil threatened the security of his country and that claims for free navigation and for disputed frontier territory were part of a wider initiative. Yet López refused to negotiate a settlement, either with Brazil or Argentina, on boundary or any other matters; at the same time he was reluctant to take the military initiative, which was the only alternative. Francisco Solano López, however, had more elementary convictions: he despised Brazilians, with an almost racialist intensity, and he believed that Argentina's national reorganization would fail. He was therefore willing to push his father's premises to their logical conclusion – war against both Buenos Aires and Brazil in defence of Paraguay's national interests and traditional values. The situation, he believed, was opportune. If he was menaced by alliances, he too had potential allies, the rural caudillos of Argentina and the *blancos* of Uruguay. And were his enemies united? A war against Paraguay was by no means a popular cause in Argentina. It was regarded by many as an illiberal expedient, whose results would be to magnify the power of the state, aggrandize the national army, and, while enabling some to profit from supplying the state, would lay intolerable burdens on the community. Brazil, moreover, was regarded as an obnoxious ally: to shed Argentine blood and spend Argentine money supporting a slave state in its imperialist ambitions was condemned by many as the height of folly. The war was therefore divisive. Moreover, it gave the provincial caudillos a chance to revert to a more primitive Argentina in opposition to Buenos Aires and in support of regionalist interests. López, however, with military superiority, did not have the skill to exploit these divisions within Argentina, or between Argentina and Brazil, and he recklessly wasted his assets.

Paraguay was the victim of Argentina, Brazil and its own ruler, although it was the latter who allowed himself to fulfil the role of aggressor. López's demands upon Brazil and Argentina for a statement of intent were ignored. He then sent an ultimatum to Brazil not to invade Uruguay. This was rejected. When Brazil invaded Uruguay, López broke off relations with her in November 1864, seized a Brazilian steamer in Asunción, and invaded the Mato Grosso. This was the first of many strategic mistakes: it might have been feasible to attack Brazil in Uruguay, but not in the heart of her own territory. In January 1865 López requested permission from Argentina to cross Misiones to reach Brazil. Permission was refused, and in March López declared war on Argentina and invaded Corrientes. This enabled Mitre to carry through the Brazilian alliance without political disaster at home. Mitre thus declared war on López, joining Brazil and the government of Flores in Uruguay. As for Argentina's own dissidents, they were now leaderlesss, for Urquiza committed himself to the war and became one of the army's principal suppliers. The overt object of the triple alliance was merely to secure free navigation of the rivers and to crush the tyrant López; and the war was presented as a crusade on behalf of civilization and liberty. This was propaganda. The treaty of alliance contained secret clauses providing for the annexation of disputed territory in northern Paraguay by Brazil and regions in the east and west of Paraguay by Argentina; and the war would not cease until the total destruction of the Paraguayan government. Basically the allies were determined to remove the focus of attraction which a strong Paraguay exercised on their peripheral regions.

For Paraguay, therefore, this was a war of survival. In any case a war against the two giants was bound to be debilitating and a severe test for an economy so narrowly based. López needed a swift victory, and if he could not win quickly he would probably not win at all. If he had stood on defence, Paraguay should have been virtually impregnable, except in the south-west and the line of the River Paraguay. As it was, he struck out indiscriminately and squandered his forces. His fleet was virtually destroyed in the battle of Riachuelo early in the war (June 1865), and the Brazilian naval and military forces were able to penetrate up river into the heart of Paraguay. Conditions deteriorated grimly for the Paraguayan people. Their supplies were cut off by the allied blockade. Their armed forces were slaughtered, many of them, including foreign advisers, by the crazed López himself, who believed he was surrounded by conspirators as well as by the enemy. The horror came to an end when López was killed at the battle of Cerro Corá on 1 March 1870.

The results were calamitous for Paraguay. The traditional view that she lost one million people is a gratuitous myth. The truth itself was bitter enough. She lost one half of her population, which dropped from 406,646 in 1864 to 231,000 in 1872. The majority of the survivors were women, children and old people. The country, so long isolated and intact, was torn open and devastated. There was a further irony. Although Paraguay eventually achieved an inferior version of the export-oriented growth typical of other parts of the River Plate, she failed in the end to undergo the process of modernization which she herself had pioneered and which was now monopolized by Argentina and Uruguay. Territorially Paraguay was also a loser, though the rivalry of Argentina and Brazil prevented worse dismemberment. She was forced to grant territory north-east of the River Paraguay to Brazil; and to Argentina she lost Misiones territory, between the Paraná and the Uruguay, and other land further west. Politically the country disintegrated. The age of the great dictators was over, and there was nothing to fill the vacuum; the exiled opposition returned, and Paraguay began a period of *golpes*, changing caudillos and unworkable constitutions. The Paraguayan version of development, therefore, had been a total waste of effort, money and lives. If it proved anything, it proved that it was impossible to create a Prussia in South America.

The other countries of the River Plate escaped the worst consequences of war. For Uruguay the 1860s was a period of economic growth. Politically, it is true, the prospect was not promising. The wartime government of Venancio Flores was not a stable one; it was a dictatorship which ended fusion and gave the *colorados* a monopoly of power, provoking an inevitable challenge from the *blancos* and other factions. Uruguay split into warring camps, and Flores and Berro were both assassinated on the same day, 19 February 1868. As central government disintegrated, and Uruguay slid helplessly into disorder and *caudillismo*, economy and society enjoyed an autonomy of their own and underwent great transformation. But while political anarchy did not automatically prevent economic growth, economic change did not immediately restore political equilibrium. There was in fact a prolonged time-lag between the growth of 1860–8 and the delayed stabilization of 1875.

The population of Uruguay rose from 221,000 in 1860 to 385,000 in 1868. Montevideo grew even faster, from 58,000 to 126,000. In the years 1860–8 some 50,000 immigrants came to Uruguay, principally Italians and Spaniards. Commercial expansion, a booming construction industry, the increase of ocean-going vessels and the activity of coastal and river shipping, all made Montevideo a growth point and a focus of immigration. Foreigners increased from 48 per cent of the total in 1860 to 60 per cent in 1868. Meanwhile in the countryside the growing sheep sector attracted settlers from many nations. The new population gave a boost to imports and exports. Imports increased from 8.2 million pesos in 1860 to 15 million in 1870; exports from 5.4 million pesos in 1860 to 12 million in 1870. The commerce of Montevideo was also stimulated by a new product, wool, bought up by warehouse owners from the rural producers and exported to Europe. The port was a supply base of the allied armies during the Paraguayan War, and from then became a permanent entrepôt, whose free trade regime encouraged transit trade and enabled it to rival Buenos Aires as a centre of distribution in the Río de la Plata.

There was a great and sudden transformation in wool production. Between 1860 and 1868 the number of sheep increased from 3 million head to 16/17 million head. The stimulus was in part internal, the favourable environment for sheep farming in Uruguay, the switch from cattle to sheep as prices for jerked beef went steadily down, the growth of middle-sized farms for which sheep were a more economical investment and the influence of foreign immigrants as sheep farmers and improvers; external stimulus was provided by strong demand from the textile industries of Britain, France and Belgium, and the absence of competition from cotton during the American Civil War. Sheepbreeding, especially of improved stock, demanded not only more labour but also a sedentary labour and one immune from *caudillismo* and revolutions. And sheep farming allowed the emergence, if not of a rural middle class, at least of smaller properties and farms, for immigrants could make progress in this sector more easily than in cattle, as in Argentina. It thus diversified the social structure of the countryside and introduced an alternative to the great cattle ranch. In 1862, among total exports wool accounted for 10.6 per cent, hides 32.9 per cent and jerked beef 11.5 per cent. In 1872 wool accounted for 24.4 per cent.

Uruguay now had three basic products, wool, hides and jerked beef. Markets, too, were diversified: hides went principally to Britain and the United States, jerked beef to Brazil and Cuba, wool to France and Belgium. If it was a dependent economy, it was not dependent on one product or one market. This diversification was a key to Uruguay's future prosperity. Economic conditions were propitious enough to attract foreign capital. Until now the influence of the Brazilian financier,

Baron Mauá, who had established the Banco Mauá in 1857, had been dominant. Now British capital entered. At the end of 1863 a branch of the Bank of London and the River Plate opened in Montevideo. Between 1861 and 1865 British and German capital established Liebig's extract of meat company at Fray Bentos. This was the first foreign investment in the meat industry, and it profited from excess cattle production, low prices and cheap labour, offering an escape from the limited outlets of Brazil and Cuba by producing a meat extract which European markets would accept, at least for their armies. In 1864–5 British capital began to lend to the state, and in the early 1870s British enterprise moved into railways and took them over.

These trends were momentarily halted by the crisis of 1868 and the civil war of 1870. The economic crisis was precipitated to some extent by the great drought of 1869–70, which savagely decimated livestock and sheep herds. But a number of other factors played their part, such as monetary instability, the great excess of imports over exports, the former stimulated by increase of population and conspicuous consumption of the upper classes, the latter hit by the fall of international prices and the decline of production in the *estancias*, which could not yet cope with improvement and modernization. In 1870 Uruguay imported 15 million pesos worth of goods and exported only 12 million. Between 1864 and 1869 imports exceeded exports by 18 million pesos. By 1875 the worst was over. Uruguay was now poised to move into a phase of modernization and development. With the promise of better things, merchants and *estancieros* wanted peace and strong government. The time for a powerful state and a national army was approaching.

Argentina differed from the Uruguayan version of development in three respects, its earlier start, its greater scale and its firmer political base. In Argentina, too, the transition from old to new was accompanied by crisis. In the mid 1860s the Paraguayan War coincided with monetary instability and a crisis in Europe to throw the Argentine economy out of gear. The markets for cattle products and for wool exports contracted and production declined; even sheep farming suffered depression. The internal causes of the crisis lay in the land and derived from an excessive expansion of the flocks in the relatively restricted areas of soft grasses suitable for sheep-raising. Over-stocking coincided with a severe drought, which was a further setback to owners of cattle and sheep. The policy of the state did not help. The law of November 1864 decreeing the sale of all public lands available within the frontier set prices which were too high and aggravated the rural crisis. So a period of expansion and land hunger was followed by a slump.

Recovery was rapid, but the experience caused a re-appraisal of Argentina's problems and prospects. Worried *estancieros* began to discuss the need for diversification of agrarian production, modernization of methods and greater capital investment. There was talk, too, of combining agriculture and livestock, investing urban capital in the rural sector, incorporating new land, establishing model farms. Innovatory ideas of this kind were characteristic of the group of *estancieros* who, in 1866, founded the Argentine Rural Society as a medium of debate and development. A mood of protectionism grew. One of the most notable, though abortive, projects of the Society was to establish the first textile factory in the country, in the hope that a national textile industry might develop, using Argentina's own raw materials and freeing her from dependence on foreign markets and foreign imports. Rural labour, its plight and its supply, became a matter of increasing concern. The insecurity, impoverishment and low status of the peon had often been attributed to Rosas and his military exactions, but there were few signs of improvement after 1852, and the demands of the Paraguayan War became a new scourge of the pampas. The need for more people was urgent and accepted. And mass immigration, which began as a drive to fill the desert, ended by swelling the towns. Argentina had come to the end of one age and the beginning of another.

Part Four

BRAZIL AFTER INDEPENDENCE

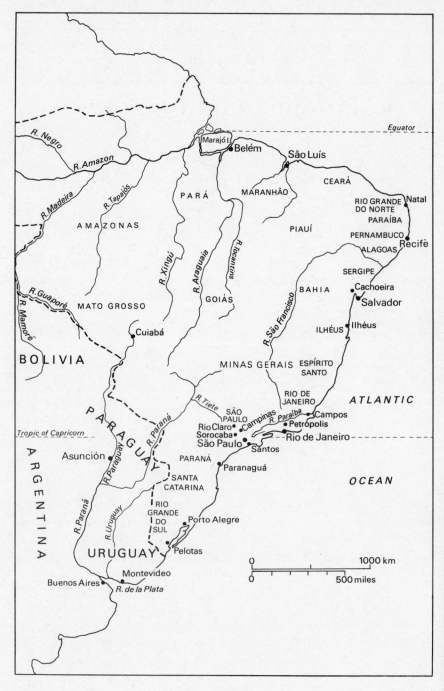

Brazil in 1830

16

BRAZIL FROM INDEPENDENCE TO THE MIDDLE OF THE NINETEENTH CENTURY

At the time of its independence from Portugal in 1822 Brazil had a population of between 4 and 5 million (if the Brazilian Indians numbering perhaps as many as 800,000 are included). This relatively small population was scattered over a vast territory of over 3 million square miles, but remained heavily concentrated in an area within 200 miles of the Atlantic coast from the provinces of the north-east (with 40–45 per cent of the total population) to Rio de Janeiro, São Paulo and the south. The only inland province with a significant population was Minas Gerais which had been the focus of the gold rush in the first half of the eighteenth century and which still accounted for 20 per cent of Brazil's population, though most of it was located in the south of the province adjoining Rio. Some provinces of the interior like Mato Grosso had populations of less than 40,000. It was an overwhelmingly rural population. The largest city was the capital, Rio de Janeiro, with around 100,000 inhabitants, while the second largest city, Salvador (Bahia), the former capital, had 60,000, and half of the provincial capitals no more than 10,000 each. Conditions of health were very poor and average life expectancy low. The general level of education was also low. Education had never been a priority of Portuguese colonial policy. As late as 1872, when the first official figures became available, only a fifth of the free population was even literate.

In 1822 less than a third of Brazil's population was white. The great majority was black or mulatto. At least 30 per cent were slaves. The best estimate of the total number of slaves is probably 1,147,515 in 1823.[1] Three-quarters of the slaves were concentrated in only five of the

---

[1] 'Memória Estatística do Império', date and author unknown, published in *Revista do Instituto Histórico e Geográfico Brasileiro*, LVIII, 1 (1959), 91–9. The total population, according to this source, was 3,960,866.

eighteen provinces – Maranhão, Pernambuco, Bahia, Minas Gerais and Rio de Janeiro – where in many areas they constituted the majority of the population. Besides supplying Brazil's additional labour needs in periods of economic expansion, the transatlantic slave trade from Africa was essential, as it always had been, to replenish the existing slave population, which did not reproduce itself. Annual imports of slaves into Brazil had risen from 15,000–20,000 at the beginning of the century to 30,000 in the early 1820s.

Slaves were to be found throughout rural Brazil in stockraising, in cereal production, in the cultivation of basic staples for local consumption and in subsistence agriculture. Minas Gerais, with an economy largely given over to cattle ranching and *pequena lavoura* since the end of the gold cycle in the middle of the eighteenth century, had the largest slave population of any single province: 170,000 in 1819. Slaves were also widely employed as domestic servants in the city of Rio, in Salvador and Recife, indeed in every town from Belém and São Luís in the north to Porto Alegre and Pelotas in the south. Urban *escravos de ganho* worked, for example, as stevedores and porters in the docks, as water and refuse carriers, as transporters of people, as masons and carpenters, prostitutes, even as beggars. Religious houses and hospitals owned slaves; the state owned, and hired, slaves for building and maintaining public works. Until the slave trade from Africa to Brazil became illegal in 1830 and the first serious efforts were made to end it slaves were both available and cheap. The existence in Brazil of an 'open frontier' with an almost limitless supply of free or cheap land together with an overall *falta de braços* (shortage of labour) also helps explain why slavery was so essential and characteristic a feature of economic and social life, rural and urban. However, as in every slave society throughout the Americas, the majority of slaves in Brazil were concentrated in single-crop, export-oriented plantation agriculture (*grande lavoura*).

Brazil had lost its near monopoly of the world's sugar supply in the middle of the seventeenth century, but sugar remained Brazil's major cash crop throughout the colonial period. The economic disruptions caused by the French Revolution and the Napoleonic Wars had given a fresh impetus to sugar planting in Brazil not only in the north-east, in the Zona de Mata of Pernambuco and the Recôncavo of Bahia where sugar had been produced since the 1530s, but also in the Campos region of Rio de Janeiro province and, most recently, in the province of São Paulo. At the time of independence sugar accounted for 40 per cent of Brazil's export earnings. Cotton, mainly grown in Maranhão and to a lesser extent in Pernambuco, came next with 20 per cent, although Brazil's share of British raw cotton imports was by now in decline. And coffee exports from Rio province which had increased from 160 *arrobas* in 1792 to 318,032 in 1817 and 539,000 in 1820, made up almost another 20 per cent of the value of Brazil's exports. The rest consisted mainly of hides, tobacco and cacao.

Since the arrival of the Portuguese court and the opening of the ports in 1808 Brazil's foreign trade, exports as well as imports, had been in the hands of foreign, especially British, but also French, German and American, as well as Portuguese merchants. Britain was now Brazil's main trading partner. The system of colonial preference effectively excluded sugar and coffee though not cotton from the British market. Nevertheless, British merchants shipped a large proportion of Brazilian produce to the European market. And Britain supplied the bulk of the manufactured goods, especially cottons, woollens, linens and hardware, imported into Brazil. The Portuguese were for the most part confined to the retail trade in foreign goods and the internal trade in Brazilian goods. Thus, whereas the productive sector of the Brazilian economy was almost completely in the hands of Brazilians, foreigners controlled the commercial sector.

In the areas of export agriculture – the north-east, Rio de Janeiro and parts of São Paulo – there had developed rural oligarchies based on plantations and slave labour. This was particularly true of older export centres like the Mata of Pernambuco, the Recôncavo of Bahia and the river valleys around São Luís in Maranhão. Here, if anywhere, was to be found the classic society of masters and slaves. Elsewhere society was more complex. The free population of Brazil was, after all, twice as large as the slave population and only a small minority of the free were planters or *estancieiros*. In the vast cattle raising areas of the interior of the north-east, from northern Minas Gerais to southern Maranhão, in Rio Grande do Sul, in the frontier areas of south and west, and in the periphery of the plantation zones throughout Brazil there existed a large intermediate stratum of small landowners and cattle ranchers, tenant farmers and squatters of varying degrees of independence. In Minas there was a substantial number of slaves, but they were not concentrated on plantations, as we have seen; and in 1823 there were already as many free blacks and mulattos as slaves. In some northern provinces, such as Ceará and Piauí (as in Santa Catarina in the south), slaves represented no more than 10 per cent of the population. In Pará 30 per cent were slaves, but there was also a large Indian population and no well-established landowning or commercial class. In the cities social stratification was, of course, even more complex. A large number of small merchants, petty officials, artisans, clerks and journeymen filled the space between the high-level bureaucrats, big merchants and capitalists on the one hand and the slaves on the other. And within the urban slave population, as we have seen, there was extraordinary occupational diversity.

The centre-south of Brazil (Minas Gerais, Espírito Santo, Rio de Janeiro, São Paulo, Santa Catarina, Rio Grande do Sul) had been somewhat integrated economically since the gold boom of the first half of the eighteenth century. The growth of the port of Rio and the expansion of sugar and coffee production in the area during the last decade of the eighteenth and the first two decades of the nineteenth century had further strengthened Rio's economic ties with Minas Gerais and the southern provinces. Minas Gerais supplied the Rio market with meat, beans and dairy produce. Rio Grande do Sul exported wheat and *charque* (dried meat) to feed the slaves and the free poor. And there was a profitable trade in mules and cattle from Rio Grande to São Paulo, Minas Gerais and Rio de Janeiro via the famous fair at Sorocaba in São Paulo. Bahia and its satellite Sergipe, Pernambuco and the neighbouring provinces of Alagoas, Paraíba, Rio Grande do Norte and Ceará and the north (Maranhão, Piauí and Pará, which then included present-day Amazonas) were mostly worlds apart from each other and from the centre-south. They had their own integrated export and subsistence economies. They were not, however, totally isolated. There was an inter-regional trade, for example the cattle trade between Bahia and the centre-south and the trade in *charque* from Rio Grande do Sul as far north as Bahia and Pernambuco. But land communications by primitive roads and by cattle and mule trails were extremely precarious. Communications between provinces were mostly by sea and by some major rivers, such as the São Francisco which linked Minas Gerais to the north-east, the Amazon crossing the northern rain forests and the Paraná on the south-west frontier. Before steam navigation it took less time to travel from Maranhão to Lisbon than to Rio de Janeiro. It could even take three weeks by sea from Recife to Rio – with a favourable wind.

Brazil in 1822 had no economic unity. Nor was there in Brazil any strong sense of national identity. The unity maintained in the transition from Portuguese colony to independent empire was political – and precarious. It would be seriously threatened when, a decade later, the alliance of forces which had brought about Brazil's independence from Portugal finally disintegrated.

The independence Brazil achieved in 1822 was incomplete. The presence of a Portuguese prince willing to assume the leadership of the movement for independence from Portugal was a crucial factor in ensuring a smooth transition to independence, political – and social – stability and national unity.[2] At the same time many leading Brazilian politicians had serious doubts about the strength of the emperor's commitment to constitutionalism and, even more serious, his willingness to sever all family and dynastic ties with the former colonial power. Although distinct these two concerns were interconnected and reinforced each other, since Pedro I's suspected absolutist convictions were easily linked by Brazilian elite and populace alike to the protection of Portugal's remaining interests in Brazil and, indeed, the fear of recolonization. The reign of Pedro I was a period of constant political tension and conflict which culminated in his abdication in April 1831.

The Constituent Assembly was the scene of the first clashes between the Brazilian political elite and Pedro I, less than a year after the declaration of independence but before, it should be remembered, Portuguese troops had been removed from Bahia, the north and the Cisplatine province. The assembly had first been summoned by the Prince Regent on 3 June 1822 but was not officially inaugurated until 3 May 1823. There the future organization of the new Brazilian state was vigorously, at times violently, debated. Even though many of the most outspoken critics of the 1822 arrangement, like Joaquim Gonçalves Lêdo who fled to Buenos Aires and Cipriano Barata who was imprisoned until shortly before the abdication of Pedro I, had been excluded, liberals, both 'moderate' and 'extreme', attempted to curb the powers of the young emperor, especially his powers to veto legislation and dissolve the legislature. For a while José Bonifácio de Andrada e Silva, the patriarch of Brazilian independence who continued to serve as Dom Pedro's adviser and first minister after independence, sided with the emperor in the interests of strong government. At the same time he tried to prevent Dom Pedro from going over completely to the 'Portuguese' faction at a time when absolutism in France, Spain and Portugal itself, where the liberal experiment was brought to an end in May 1823, was

[2] On the independence of Brazil, see Bethell, *CHLA* III, ch.4.

clearly resurgent. The resignation of José Bonifácio on 16 July 1823 is, therefore, an important episode in the political polarization which occurred in Brazil immediately after independence.

During the second half of 1823 opposition to the emperor both in the Constituent Assembly and in the press became increasingly bitter. Finally, on 12 November 1823 the assembly was forcibly dissolved and, among others, José Bonifácio and his more liberal younger brothers, Antônio Carlos Ribeiro de Andrada Machado e Silva and Martim Francisco Ribeiro de Andrada, were arrested and banished to France.[3] Dom Pedro himself immediately set up a Council of State which quickly drafted a constitution. It included a Senate (50 members) as well as a Chamber of Deputies (100 members). Senators were selected by the emperor from lists of three elected in the provinces and served for life. Deputies were to be elected – indirectly elected, first by voters, then by electors, on a limited suffrage – for four years. To be a voter it was necessary to have an annual net income from property or employment of 100 milreis (about £10 in 1830); electors had a minimum income of 200 milreis. (Deputies were required to have an income of 400 milreis, Senators 800 milreis.) The constitution confirmed the Council of State, the ten members of which were chosen by the emperor and also served for life. The emperor had veto powers over legislation. He nominated both ministers, who were responsible to him, and high court judges, and his 'moderating power', based on Benjamin Constant's *pouvoir royal* for resolving conflicts between executive, legislature and judiciary, specifically enabled him to dissolve the Chamber and to call elections. There was, finally, a high degree of political centralization: the emperor appointed provincial presidents, and the *Conselhos Gerais de Província* and the *câmaras municipais*, although elected (the *Conselhos* by indirect and the *câmaras* by direct vote), had only limited powers. The decisions of the *Conselhos Gerais* had to be approved by the Chamber of Deputies. Finally, the Catholic religion was declared the religion of the state and the emperor, as head of state, appointed bishops and dispensed ecclesiastical benefices.

The arbitrary dissolution of the Constituent Assembly in November 1823 followed by the promulgation of a new constitution in March 1824 brought to an abrupt end the honeymoon period in the relations between

---

[3] José Bonifácio returned to Brazil in July 1829 but, after serving as deputy for Bahia and after the abdication of Pedro I in 1831 as tutor to the young Dom Pedro, he was arrested in 1833 and confined to the island of Paquetá in Guanabara Bay. He died in Niterói in 1838.

Dom Pedro and important sections of the Brazilian dominant class, not only in the centre-south where the movement for independence had originated but also in the north-east. When news of the dissolution reached Bahia, on 12 December 1823, there were anti-Portuguese disturbances and threats of secession. Then in March 1824 came an armed revolt in Pernambuco led by a radical priest, Frei Caneca, and Manuel Carvalho Paes de Andrade. It was supported by Rio Grande do Norte, Paraíba and Ceará, attracted sympathy throughout the north-east, including Bahia, and led to the proclamation of an independent republic, the Confederation of the Equator. For Caneca Dom Pedro I's constitution did not define 'positively and exclusively the territory of the empire and because of this it leaves open the possibility for any future aspirations to union with Portugal'; 'it was not liberal, but totally contrary to the principles of liberty, independence and the rights of Brazil, apart from which it has been presented to us by someone who does not have the power to do so'; the Senate would become 'a new aristocracy and oppressor of the people'; the moderating power, 'a Machiavellian invention', was 'the master key to the oppression of the Brazilian nation and effectively strangles the freedom of the people'; and, finally, the constitution's centralism was particularly prejudicial to the political freedom of Brazil since it deprived the provinces of their autonomy and isolated them, each totally dependent on the central executive, subject to a type of 'Asiatic despotism'.[4] The rebellion of 1824 was put down by imperial troops after six months. The harshness with which the rebels were treated after their defeat – by specially created and unconstitutional military courts – only served to increase the gap between the emperor and the liberal opposition, moderate and radical. Frei Caneca himself, like many others throughout the north-east, and some in Rio de Janeiro, paid for his convictions with his life; he was executed by firing squad in Recife on 13 January 1825.

In addition to his autocratic methods of government and his scandalous private life (in which before and after the death of his wife Leopoldina in December 1826 his mistress Domitila de Castro Canto, the Marquêsa de Santos, figured prominently), Pedro I's close association with the Portuguese community in Rio – Portuguese bureaucrats who had come to Rio with the court in 1808, married into local landed and commercial families, acquired property themselves and chosen to stay in 1821, as well as Portuguese merchants – and his 'Portuguese' cabinets

4 Frei Caneca, *Ensaios políticos* (Rio de Janeiro, 1976), 67–75.

were by now a matter of growing concern. Particularly resented was the influence exerted by a 'secret cabinet' of his Portuguese friends among whom was his notorious drinking companion, Francisco Gomes de Silva, o Chalaça. It is not without significance that 50 per cent of the ministers were bureaucrats, civil or military, and more ministers were linked to commercial activities in the *primeiro reinado* than at any time during the empire.[5]

The negotiations over the recognition of Brazil's independence by Portugal reinforced the view that Dom Pedro was inclined to put dynastic considerations before Brazil's national interests. Under the treaty of 29 August 1825 which Sir Charles Stuart, the head of a special British mission to Brazil, negotiated on behalf of Portugal, Brazil agreed to pay Portugal compensation of £2 million, £1.4 million of which was earmarked to repay a Portuguese loan floated in London in 1823 to cover the cost of the campaign to restore Portuguese authority in Brazil. Moreover, the treaty deliberately left open the question of the succession. Pedro I did not expressly abdicate his rights of succession to the Portuguese throne, giving to many Brazilians the impression of a family deal and justifying the fear that on Dom João's death Dom Pedro would become king of Portugal and Brazil and Portugal would automatically be reunited – with Brazil possibly reduced to its former colonial status.[6]

Brazil had to pay a price for British help in securing early Portuguese – and international – recognition of its independence, but Dom Pedro was strongly criticized for paying too high a price, although it could be argued he had little choice in the matter. Brazil had, in particular, clear if unwritten obligations to come to some agreement with Britain on the slave trade question. Throughout all the diplomatic negotiations since 1822 a bargain had been implied: abolition for recognition. In any case, once Brazil and Portugal were formally separated the bulk of the slave trade to Brazil became illegal, or so George Canning, the British Foreign Secretary, argued. Portugal, whose African territories south of the equator, principally Angola, supplied the Brazilian market with an

---

[5] José Murilo de Carvalho, *A Construção da Ordem; a elite política imperial* (Rio de Janeiro, 1980), 87.
[6] João VI died in March 1826 and Dom Pedro did become enmeshed in the problems of the dynastic succession in Portugal. On 2 May he reluctantly abdicated the Portuguese throne in favour of his seven-year-old daughter. Maria da Glória married her uncle, Pedro I's younger brother, Dom Miguel, who was appointed Regent. When in 1828 Miguel dissolved the Côrtes and re-established absolutist government with himself as king, Pedro became almost obsessed with the idea of defending his daughter's right to the Portuguese throne. In 1828 Maria da Glória joined her father in Brazil. And after Dom Pedro's abdication of the Brazilian throne in April 1831 they returned together to Portugal where Dom Pedro achieved his goal just before his death in September 1834.

increasing proportion of its slaves, was bound by treaties which Britain had every intention of enforcing (by force, if necessary) not to export slaves to non-Portuguese territories across the Atlantic. After some tough negotiations conducted on the British side first by Stuart, then by Robert Gordon, Britain's minister in Rio, whom Dom Pedro was to refer to as 'that ill-mannered and obstinate Scot', a treaty was signed on 23 November 1826 under which the entire Brazil slave trade became illegal three years after its ratification. (The treaty was immediately ratified by the emperor on board a Brazilian warship sailing out of Rio harbour bound for Rio Grande do Sul, and by Britain on 13 March 1827).

Despite Canning's efforts to make it appear that the abolition of the slave trade within three years was a necessary corollary of independence arising out of obligations under existing Portuguese treaties which Brazil had no alternative but to accept – 'a positive engagement rather than . . . a demand on our part and an unconditional surrender on his [the emperor's]' – most Brazilians saw the treaty as a major sacrifice of Brazil's national interests at the insistence of a powerful foreign nation. Robert Gordon had no doubt that it had been 'ceded at our request in opposition to the views and wishes of the whole empire' and was 'in the highest degree unpopular'.[7] Moreover, the emperor had been persuaded to ignore the opinion of the Chamber of Deputies which met for the first time in May 1826 and debated two bills for the *gradual* abolition of the slave trade, one from José Clemente Pereira (Rio de Janeiro) for abolition by 31 December 1840, the other from Nicolau Pereira de Campos Vergueiro (São Paulo) for abolition after six years. When the Chamber met again in May 1827 abolition was a *fait accompli* but few deputies, even those of enlightened views, believed that it would be anything other than a disaster, above all for Brazilian agriculture but also for commerce, shipping and government revenue. Until Brazil was able to recruit free European immigrants in large numbers – 'the poor, the wretched, the industrious of Europe', José Bonifácio had called them – Brazilian agriculture, especially large-scale plantation agriculture, had no alternative to slave labour. The few attempts to promote European, mainly German and Swiss, immigration since 1808 had been rather disappointing, and strategic and military considerations continued to be more important than economic. Of the 10,000 or so Europeans who arrived in Brazil between 1823 and 1830 more than 6,000 ended up in the southern frontier province of Rio Grande do Sul.

[7] Quotations in Leslie Bethell, *The abolition of the Brazilian slave trade* (Cambridge, 1970), 54–5, 62.

To the growing list of what many Brazilians regarded as Dom Pedro's failures should be added his unpopular, expensive and ultimately unsuccessful policy in the Río de la Plata. The Banda Oriental, the source of more than a hundred years of conflict between Spain and Portugal, had been occupied by Portuguese troops in 1817 in the struggle against Artigas during the Spanish American wars of independence and incorporated into Brazil in 1821 as the Cisplatine Province. The government in Buenos Aires, which had inherited Spanish claims to the territory, was determined to reconquer it. Taking advantage of a rebellion led by Lavalleja which found broad support outside Montevideo at least, the Buenos Aires Congress on 25 October 1825 announced the incorporation of the Banda Oriental into the United Provinces of the Río de la Plata. It amounted to a declaration of war and six weeks later the emperor felt obliged to follow suit. The war went disastrously for Brazil; the imperial troops were consistently defeated. The war at sea was notable for the fact that both fleets had a British commander – Admiral Brown on the Argentine side, Admiral Norton on the Brazilian – and most of the seamen were English. In the end, largely as a result of British diplomatic mediation, the Banda Oriental was recognized in October 1828 by both Argentina and Brazil as the independent buffer state of Uruguay.

The war effort had been substantial and had placed an extra burden on the already strained national finances. It also led to a great increase in military recruitment, possibly the most hated government measure in nineteenth-century Brazil. In fact, the measure was so unpopular that the emperor decided to hire foreign troops to complement the national draft. The decision proved disastrous since not only did it fail to prevent defeat in the war, but it also resulted in the mutiny of several thousand Irish and German mercenaries in Rio in June 1828. For two days the city was at the mercy of the troops and the government had to go through the humiliation of asking for the help of British and French naval units. A last negative consequence of the war was the disruption it caused to the supply of mules and cattle from Rio Grande do Sul to São Paulo, Minas Gerais and Rio de Janeiro. The sharp rise in mule and cattle prices in the final years of the decade had an adverse effect on the economies of all three provinces.[8] For their part the ranchers of Rio Grande do Sul were

---

[8] The number of mules and cattle passing through the Sorocaba fair in São Paulo fell from 30,474 in 1822 to 21,817 in 1829, and the price of mules went up from 14$000 in 1820 to 60$000 in 1829. Maria Theresa Schorer Petrone, *O Barão de Iguape* (São Paulo, 1976), 21–8.

unhappy about the lack of adequate compensation for their efforts during the war and would add this to their list of grievances in 1835 to justify their rebellion against the central government.

It would be wrong to suggest that Dom Pedro had no support outside a narrow 'Portuguese' circle. The monarchy as an institution had great popular appeal and was still considered by most of the national elite as a powerful instrument of national unity and social stability. And Pedro I, who as the hero of independence could still draw on some goodwill, was the only member of the house of Braganza in a position to govern Brazil. It was not the case that the entire national elite had turned against the emperor: many were co-opted as ministers, senators, councillors of state; some were bought with honorific titles. During 1825–6 Pedro granted 104 titles of nobility (mostly *barão* and *visconde*), more than two-thirds of all the titles awarded during the *primeiro reinado*.[9] Among Pedro's Brazilian supporters there were diehard absolutists, and many hesitated to oppose him in case the monarchical system itself should thus be threatened. Nevertheless, there is no doubt that in the late twenties the rift between Dom Pedro and the majority of his subjects was widening. The alienation from power of the dominant groups in Minas Gerais and São Paulo and some elements in Rio de Janeiro combined with popular hatred of the Portuguese and military disaffection eventually brought him down.

Economic and financial difficulties also played their part. Coffee exports from Rio more than tripled between 1822 and 1831, it is true, but the prices of most of the country's major exports – cotton, hides, cacao, tobacco, as well as coffee – fell steadily throughout the 1820s. A small increase of 1.7 per cent in the price of sugar which still accounted for between 30 and 40 per cent of Brazil's exports was not enough to compensate.[10] The Anglo-Brazilian commercial treaty of August 1827 – the second of Britain's bills for services rendered at the time of independence – confirmed all the privileges conferred on British trade in 1810 including the 15 per cent maximum tariff on imported British goods and Britain's right to appoint judges conservators to deal with cases involving British merchants in Brazil, but offered no reciprocity. To protect West Indian produce Britain imposed duties amounting to 180 per cent ad valorem on Brazilian sugar and 300 per cent on Brazilian coffee.

[9] R. J. Barman, 'A New-World nobility: the role of titles in imperial Brazil', *University of British Columbia Hispanic Studies* (1974), 43.

[10] Carlos Manuel Pelaez and Wilson Suzigan, *História monetária do Brasil: análise da política, comportamento e instituições monetárias* (Rio de Janeiro, 1976), 51.

The limit on tariffs on British goods to 15 per cent ad valorem (extended in 1828 to all imported goods), besides obstructing the growth of manufacturing in Brazil, imposed a ceiling on revenue and exacerbated the problems the Brazilian government had in organizing state finances on a sound basis. Two years after independence Brazil had floated its first loan, for £3 million, in London to pay the Portuguese indemnity. It was followed by a second of £400,000 in 1829 to cover the servicing of the first. While the 1824 loan was negotiated at 80 per cent, the second was at 52 per cent, a clear indication of the low standing of the country's economy in the eyes of British merchant bankers. The Bank of Brazil, created by Dom João in 1808, had been in difficulties since 1821 when the king drained it of metals and the crown jewels before returning to Portugal. Dom Pedro resorted to a policy of issuing great amounts of copper coins, which contributed to the growth of inflation and opened the way for widespread counterfeiting. From 1822 to 1829 the money supply increased by 10 per cent a year, pushing up the cost of living, particularly in the major cities. The invasion of counterfeit copper coins, especially in Bahia, brought chaos to the money market and forced the government to try to substitute bills for coins in 1827. But both the bills of the Bank of Brazil and the treasury bills were not well received outside Rio and were submitted to discount rates (*ágios*) that reached 43 per cent in São Paulo in 1829.[11] The Bank was finally closed in 1829. The exchange value of the milreis also suffered a decline of almost 8 per cent a year in relation to the pound sterling between 1822 and 1830. Although beneficial to the export sector, this devaluation was responsible for an increase in the price of imported goods.[12]

Urban popular discontent added a new, explosive element to the deepening political crisis in Brazil. Independence had brought expectations of improvements, however vague they may have been. When these expectations failed to materialize, when instead living conditions deteriorated, frustration mounted. In the circumstances, this frustration found an easy target in the Portuguese, particularly those who controlled the commercial sector, and also in the emperor who still seemed not to have separated himself from his former compatriots. There were repeated demands both in Rio and other coastal cities for the expulsion of the Portuguese from the country.

A contributory factor in the transition from opposition to open

[11] See Petrone, *O Barão de Iguape*, 16.
[12] For the financial history of this period, see Pelaez and Suzigan, *História monetária*, 47–57.

rebellion was the crisis of the absolute monarchy in France. The July (1830) Revolution and the fall of Charles X had profound repercussions in Brazil and was the subject of discussions even in the Council of State. Dom Pedro himself at the end of a visit to Minas Gerais, on 22 February 1831, issued a proclamation against the *partido desorganizador* which was attacking his person and his government, taking advantage of what had happened in France. Upon the emperor's return to Rio in the middle of March there was an explosion of street clashes lasting five consecutive days and nights between his supporters, mostly Portuguese, and his opponents, in what became known as the '*Noites das Garrafadas*' (Nights of Bottle Throwing). Dom Pedro tried to assemble a group of ministers to form a liberal 'Brazilian' cabinet, but on 5 April, exercising his powers under the Constitution, he abruptly replaced it with another more to his liking, more reactionary, more 'Portuguese'. This decision was the immediate cause of what proved to be the final crisis of the first empire.

On the morning of 6 April people started gathering in several public places in the capital and by late afternoon between three and four thousand people were concentrated at the Campo de Sant'Anna, a traditional meeting place since the turbulent political events of 1821–2. A delegation of justices of the peace was sent to the emperor to urge him to reinstate the former 'Brazilian' cabinet, which he refused to do. More than twenty deputies had now joined the crowd and around 9 o'clock in the evening General Francisco de Lima e Silva, commander of the Rio garrison, agreed to try to convince the monarch to make concessions. By this time two artillery corps and one battalion of grenadiers had joined the populace and shortly after the emperor's own battalion, under the command of a brother of Lima e Silva, did the same. Although Brazilian officers, with very few exceptions, had no sympathy with radical ideas, they were willing to join the movement against the emperor, not least because they wanted the dismissal of Portuguese officers. As for the rank and file, mostly mulattos, they shared the frustrations, discontents – and nativist prejudices – of the lowest sectors of the urban population from which they were largely drawn. Indeed, their condition was often worse because they also suffered frequent delays in pay and the harsh discipline of the barracks.

In the early hours of 7 April, finding himself without military support, unwilling to yield to popular pressure ('I will do everything for the people, but nothing by the people', he is reported to have remarked) and perhaps more concerned with securing the Portuguese throne for his daughter, Dom Pedro impulsively abdicated the Brazilian throne in favour of his five-year-old son, Pedro. The news was received at the Campo de Sant'Anna amidst intense jubilation and Pedro II was immediately acclaimed emperor by the crowd. The legislature, although not officially in session, acted quickly and elected a provisional three-man regency, composed of General Francisco de Lima e Silva, Nicolau Pereira de Campos Vergueiro, a liberal senator from São Paulo, and José Joaquim Carneiro de Campos, the Marquês de Caravelas, a conservative politician and former Minister of Justice.[13] On the day of his abdication, Dom Pedro I, his family, including the twelve-year old Queen of Portugal, and his entourage boarded HMS *Warspite* at anchor in Rio bay. (The British navy was always on hand, it seems, when there was any question of transporting Portuguese or Brazilian royalty across the Atlantic.) On 13 April the *Warspite* departed for Europe.

The events of 5–7 April 1831 in which only one person had died, and then by accident, had changed the political life of the country. In a short unofficial speech on board the *Warspite*, referring to his decision to leave Brazil, Dom Pedro is reported by an English naval officer to have said: 'The Brazilians do not like me; they look upon me as a Portuguese.' He was undoubtedly right. The abdication of Dom Pedro I, the Portuguese prince who led Brazil to independence in 1822, in favour of his son, who had been born in Brazil, constituted a *nacionalização do trono* and represented the completion of the process of independence. Only in 1831 did Brazil sever her last remaining ties with Portugal. Henceforth Brazil belonged to the Brazilians – or at least to the Brazilian dominant class.

The abdication of Dom Pedro sent shock waves throughout the empire. As news of events in the capital arrived in the provinces – and in the case of the more distant provinces such as Goiás it could take up to three months for news from Rio to reach the provincial capital and even longer to reach the interior – a series of popular disturbances and military uprisings erupted. They were for the most part urban and, insofar as they had an ideological element, radical or at least nativist, but not republican. A few were restorationist. They had largely subsided – or been repressed – by the middle of 1832. One rebellion, however, in the wake of the abdication, the War of the Cabanos in Pernambuco, was rural, restorationist and lasted until 1835.

[13] The last two were replaced on 17 June by deputy José da Costa Carvalho (the future Marquês de Monte Alegre) and deputy João Bráulio Muniz.

In Rio itself the abdication crisis was followed by a series of five uprisings. Except for the last (in April 1832), which was restorationist, they were all essentially anti-Portuguese, initiated by troops, with the populace frequently joining in. One after the other, an army battalion, the police corps, the Navy artillery and two fortresses took up arms led by some radical agitators such as Major Frias de Vasconcelos and the permanent revolutionary, Cipriano Barata. In July 1831, almost the whole Rio garrison rose in arms and congregated in the Campo de Sant'Anna as they had on 6 April, where they were again joined by the populace. For ten days they kept the city in fear. The demands were almost exclusively of an anti-Portuguese nature: the deportation of 89 Portuguese, the dismissal of scores of others from public jobs and a ban on the immigration of Portuguese nationals for ten years. In Salvador, Brazil's second city, popular demonstrations had begun as early as 4 April when news of the *Noites das Garrafadas* arrived. During the next two years at least six uprisings by *tropa e povo* were registered. The most common demands were for the dismissal of the authorities, usually the military commander, and the deportation of Portuguese merchants and officials. An additional demand in Bahia was the introduction of a federal political structure, an indication of the resentment felt in the former capital at the concentration of power in Rio. In Recife, the third major city, things were not very different. One day after the arrival of the news of the abdication, troops and people organized demonstrations, picking as their main targets the absolutist society *Coluna do Trono e do Altar*, whose members and sympathizers had been in control of the government since the defeat of the 1824 revolt. The demonstrators demanded the dismissal of the military commander, of judges and several officers whose loyalty to the national cause was considered suspect. In September 1831 a more serious riot broke out. This time some slaves also joined in, apparently interpreting the news of the abdication as meaning the advent of freedom for them. Here was a good example, typical of the period, of a popular explosion without clearly defined leadership and demands. The crowd shouted *viva* Pedro II and *viva* Brazil, and *fora* (out with) the *Colunas*, the *marinheiros* (Portuguese) and the military commander. The city was completely taken over and around 42 shops and 25 taverns were looted. Many rebels got drunk and spent the night in the red light district where later on most of the looted goods were found. The government was forced to appeal to the militia and to arm civilians to put down the insurrection. Students of the Olinda law school also volunteered to help.

In the end about a hundred rebels and thirty loyal soldiers and civilians had been killed; more than a thousand arrests had been made. In November another uprising produced a list of Portuguese to be deported to which was added the demand that all single Portuguese, except artisans and capitalists, be expelled from the country and all Portuguese disarmed.

In April 1832 there was a restorationist rebellion in Recife as there was in Rio. It was led by a militia battalion made up almost exclusively of Portuguese troops. It was easily defeated, but there followed the most intriguing popular uprising of the early thirties. Known as the War of the Cabanos it was the first to take place outside the cities reaching much deeper into the foundations of society. The war lasted from 1832 until 1835 and involved small landowners, peasants, Indians, slaves and, particularly at the beginning, some *senhores de engenho*. It took place between the southern periphery of the rich sugar-producing Mata of Pernambuco and the north of the neighbouring province of Alagoas. The main leader, Vincente Ferreira de Paula, the son of a priest, was a sergeant before he deserted the army. He gave himself the title of General Commander of the Restorationist Force. Supported by Portuguese merchants in Recife and by politicians in Rio, all advocates of the restoration of Pedro I, the *cabanos* fought a guerrilla war for three years, hiding from the government troops in the thick forests of the region. At the end, the government realized that other means besides force were necessary to defeat them and the bishop of Olinda was called upon to help. He managed to convince many *cabanos* that Pedro I had already died (which he had in September 1834), that Pedro II was the legitimate emperor and that they were living a sinful life. Many turned themselves in, but the last ones, mostly slaves, were hunted down in the forest 'like deer', one by one. The leader managed to escape and organized a community of former supporters where he lived until he was arrested in 1850. In a report to the governor of Alagoas (7 July 1834), the commander of the government troops, Colonel Joaquim de Sousa, registered his shock at the physical and psychological conditions under which the rebels had lived. After the government troops were ordered to destroy all the rebels' manioc plantations and presses, the rebels had been reduced to eating wild fruits, lizards, snakes, insects and honey. The *cabanos* had hesitated in turning themselves in for fear of being tortured and skinned alive by the irreligious constitutionalists, or of being killed by their own leaders. Unable to articulate the true nature of their plight, these heroic guerrillas fought for their religion, the emperor and against what they called the *carbunários jacubinos*. Ironically, they were defeated in the end by the same person who had proclaimed the Confederation of the Equator in 1824 and was now president of the province, Manuel Carvalho Paes de Andrade.

The War of the Cabanos in Pernambuco, however, was an exceptional reaction to the abdication of Pedro I. In almost all other provinces – and of the eighteen provinces only Piauí and Santa Catarina avoided disturbances of some kind – popular demonstrations were urban and anti-Portuguese similar to those in Rio and varying in intensity according to the size of the city and the strength of Portuguese presence in government and in commerce. In general, public order was least affected in Minas and in the southern provinces of São Paulo, Santa Catarina and Rio Grande do Sul which lacked important urban centres and ports.

The First Empire was brought to an end in 1831 by a heterogeneous coalition of political and social forces. The main beneficiaries of the abdication of Dom Pedro I, and his successors in the exercise of political power under the three-man Regency, were those sectors of the Brazilian dominant class which had supported independence from Portugal in 1822, but which had increasingly opposed absolutism, extreme centralization of power – and the emperor's pro-Portuguese policies and predilections – in the decade after indepenence. These Brazilian liberals called themselves *moderados* to distinguish themselves from the extreme liberals or radicals (*exaltados* or *farroupilhas*), some of whom like Cipriano Barata and Borges da Fonseca were republicans. Drawing on the masonic tradition of social and political organization so influential at the time of independence, a *Sociedade Defensora da Liberdade e Independência Nacional* was established first in São Paulo and then, in May 1831, in Rio to which most liberal politicians and their more influential supporters affiliated, and *Defensoras* soon spread to other provinces throughout the country. (Somewhat less cohesive were the *Sociedades Federais* organized by the radicals in a number of provinces at the end of 1831. The *Sociedade Conservadora da Constituição Brasileira*, later *Sociedade Militar*, was set up in 1832 by absolutists and restorationists (*caramurus*) in the bureaucracy, the army and commerce, many though by no means all of Portuguese origin.) Among the *moderados* there was a high proportion from Minas Gerais, São Paulo and Rio. There was also a significant presence of priests among them and some graduates of Coimbra. In social terms, most were landowners and slave-owners. The most prominent leaders of the group at the time were Bernardo Pereira de Vasconcelos, a Mineiro magistrate trained at Coimbra; Diogo Feijó, a priest from São Paulo; and Evaristo da Veiga, a printer and bookseller from Rio de Janeiro and since 1827 publisher of the *Aurora Fluminense*, the most influential liberal paper. Influenced by French and American ideas, they all stood for liberal changes in the constitution in the direction of greater decentralization, but always within the monarchical framework. Some were attracted to American-style federalism. However, since most of them were linked to Rio or to the Rio economy, it was in their interest to defend national unity and to reform the existing political system to permit their participation, indeed domination, rather than destroy it. Moreover, elite consensus on the need to maintain the institution of slavery in Brazil imposed, as it always had, severe limitations on Brazilian liberalism. On the question of the slave trade no attempt was made by the liberals to reverse the Anglo-Brazilian treaty of 1826. On the contrary, taking advantage of the fact that the Brazilian slave trade was virtually at a standstill as a result of a glut on the slave market following several years of unusually heavy imports (in anticipation of the end of the trade) and uncertainty in trading circles as to what measures the British and Brazilian governments might now adopt, a law of 7 November 1831 imposed severe penalties on those found guilty of illegally importing slaves into Brazil and declared all slaves entering Brazil legally free. Few, however, believed it would actually be enforced when the demand for slaves revived (which it did in the mid-thirties): it was *uma lei para inglês ver*. Among some members of long-established rural oligarchies, pro-slavery but without strong economic ties to Rio, like, for example, the Cavalcantis of Pernambuco, who had a representative, Holanda Cavalcanti de Albuquerque, in the 'Brazilian' cabinet dismissed by Dom Pedro on 5 April, liberalism was almost identical with local rule. Holanda was an advocate of splitting up the Empire into two or three different countries, a proposal he made in 1832 and again in 1835. The fight for provincial power represented by the Cavalcantis and the fight against absolute government, best represented by urban liberals like Evaristo da Veiga and the Mineiro Teófilo Ottoni, together constituted the major drive behind the liberal reforms that were implemented between 1831 and 1835.

It came as a disappointment to committed liberals like Teófilo Ottoni that the first measures taken under the regency were not directed against the absolutist elements in society but against former allies of the 7 April, particularly soldiers. Liberals had always disliked the army: it was seen as an instrument of absolutism. In fact, the Paulistas had already suggested in 1830 the creation of a National Guard to take over its internal security duties. After the abdication liberals came to dislike the army even more, but for the opposite reason; it had apparently become an instrument of popular radicalism. A bill creating the National Guard was now rushed through the legislature in 1831 as a way of dealing with both military and popular unrest. While the bill was being discussed, the regency drafted electors (persons with a minimum income of 200 milreis a year) in Rio de Janeiro into municipal guards to whom it entrusted the policing of the city. The minister of justice, Diogo Feijó, also distributed arms to some 3,000 electors. The *Sociedade Defensora* of Rio offered its services to help patrol the city. After the popular–military revolt in Rio in July 1831, the *Sociedade Defensora* of São Paulo quickly gathered almost two thousand volunteers to come to the rescue of the central government if necessary. From Minas Gerais came also guarantees of support. After the revolt had been put down a proclamation of the regency told the people of Rio to keep calm; the government had taken measures against the 'anarchists': 'the arms are in the hands of citizens who have an interest in public order'.

Given its importance at the time and the role it played during the whole of the period of the empire, the creation of the National Guard deserves some comment. The Brazilian law of August 1831 was a copy of the French law of the same year, which had as its basic philosophy the bourgeois idea of entrusting the defence of the country to its propertied citizens. In Brazil it was at the same time a way of wresting the means of coercion from the control of the government and also a protection against the 'dangerous classes'. However, since officers were to be elected, with relatively low income requirements (200 milreis in the four major cities and 100 milreis in the rest of the country) and with no racial discrimination, the Brazilian Guard still represented an important democratic advance in relation to the colonial militias and *ordenanças* which it replaced. Moreover, it was put under the jurisdiction of the minister of justice, not the minister of war, at the national level and locally under the justices of the peace. The tasks of the Guard, which were defined in the first article of the law as being 'to defend the Constitution, the Liberty, Independence and Integrity of the Empire', were in practice the police duties of patrolling the streets, protecting public buildings, transporting prisoners and keeping order in general. In special cases, it could be taken outside the *município* as a militarized unit under army command to fight rebellions or even to help in the protection of Brazil's frontiers. Hailed by liberals as the citizens' militia, the National Guard played an important role in its initial years as a counterweight to, and substitute for, a regular army disrupted by the indiscipline and open revolt of the rank and file, and deliberately reduced by Feijó to a token force of 6,000 men. (The Rio garrison, for instance, had been completely disbanded by 1832, and the officers concentrated in one battalion.) The transformations that profoundly changed the nature of the Guard will be examined later.

A less ambiguous liberal move was the attack on the old (predominantly Portuguese) magistracy, considered, together with the army, a major pillar of the old system and frequently accused of arbitrariness and corruption. Liberal changes in the judicial structure had already begun during the reign of Dom Pedro I. In 1827 justices of the peace (*juízes de paz*), elected local magistrates, were introduced into each parish (*freguesia*) and given many administrative, judicial and police functions (at the expense of the centrally appointed and controlled *juízes de fora*). In 1830 a liberal Criminal Code strongly influenced by Benthamite utilitarianism, among other things, aimed at protecting political opposition from the arbitrary measures of government, in particular such devices as the military courts which had prosecuted the Pernambuco rebels after 1824. But only after the abdication did these liberal measures come to full fruition with the enactment, in 1832, of the Code of Criminal Procedures which strengthened the police and judicial powers of the justices of the peace; they now had the power both to arrest and to pass judgment on minor offenders. They also proposed to the municipal *câmaras* names of citizens they wished to be appointed as block inspectors (*inspetores de quarteirão*), and together with the local priest and the president of the *câmara*, made up the list of jurors. In addition, the Code created a new category of professional county judge (*juiz municipal*) who was appointed by the provincial president but from a list prepared by the local *câmara*. Finally, the Code introduced the jury system and habeas corpus, copied from American and British practices and legislation. As in the case of the National Guard, liberals had great hopes that the elected justice of the peace and the jury in particular would prove important instruments for the protection of individual liberties.

A third attack was made on those parts of the 1824 constitution considered incompatible with a liberal system. The law of the regency (1831) had already stripped the regents of several of the constitutional powers of the emperor, especially those relating to the exercise of the moderating power. The regents could not dissolve the Chamber of Deputies, grant an amnesty, bestow honorific titles, suspend guarantees for individual liberties or declare war. Except for the power to appoint ministers, senators and provincial presidents, the regents were almost completely dependent on parliament. Certainly there was no other period in the Brazilian history in which the elected legislature was so influential. However, great difficulties emerged when the constitution itself became the target of the reform movement. Most controversial were the attacks on the moderating power, the council of state and the appointment of senators for life, and the attempt to increase the powers of provincial institutions. The Senate objected strongly to most of these reforms and was locked in battle with the Chamber of Deputies for almost three years. Finally, a compromise bill was agreed which resulted in the Additional Act of August 1834. The moderating power remained intact (though not exercised under the regency) and, as could be expected, so did the Senate. But the Council of State was abolished. And although provincial presidents continued to be appointed, newly created provincial assemblies were given much greater powers than the old *Conselhos Gerais*. Moreover, a revenue-sharing system between the central government and the provinces was agreed (and implemented for the first time in the fiscal year 1836–7). In a further effort to republicanize the country, the Act introduced a popularly elected regency to replace the permanent three-man regency established in 1831. The liberal Paulista priest and minister of justice, Diogo Feijó, was elected regent in April and took office in October 1835.

A succession of liberal cabinets, in which Antônio Paulino Limpo de Abreu, Manuel Alves Branco and Holanda Cavalcanti were prominent, governed Brazil during the next two years (1835–7). With the Additional Act of August 1834 and the election of Feijó as regent in April 1835, however, the major thrust of the liberal reform movement could be said to have come to an end. Both aspects of the liberal struggle – anti-absolutism and anti-centralization – had been partly satisfied. The more radical demands for a republican government and for federalism had been defeated. It was an almost complete victory for the moderate liberals over both radicals and absolutists. This victory had been reinforced in September 1834 with the death of Pedro I in Portugal, which eliminated the *raison d'être* of the restorationist party. The divisions of political forces into *moderados, caramurus* and *farroupilhas* was coming to an end. And new political alignments were emerging, in part as a consequence of the implementation of the liberal reforms.

The transplantation of liberal ideas and institutions in Brazil did not bear the expected fruit. The reforms of 1831–4 had scarcely been implemented before disappointment and disillusion set in. The judgement of the former regent, Senator Vergueiro of São Paulo, who had been a strong supporter of the liberal reforms ('we set our political organization ahead of our social organization')[14] reflects the feelings of perhaps a majority of the Brazilian political class, especially those who had assumed power at the national level after the fall of Dom Pedro I.

If before 1831 the instruments of law and order were in the oppressive hands of the central government, they now fell into the oppressive hands of the locally powerful. In the rural areas, the elected justices of the peace were dependent on the local bosses and were themselves mostly members of the local dominant families. In major cities, less socially prominent elements were elected, but they still depended on the powerful for support in furthering their careers. It was well known, for example, that justices of the peace protected money counterfeiters and slave traders. Their ignorance of the law was a further obstacle to the proper discharge of their duties. In his famous comedy, *O Juiz de Paz na Roça*, written in 1833, Martins Pena pictures a guardsman appealing to his constitutional rights against an illegal threat of arrest, to which the justice of the peace retorts by declaring the constitution abolished. Moreover, justices of the peace were continuously involved in conflicts with professional magistrates, commanders of the national guard, priests and even the municipal *câmaras*. They could not serve as brokers in conflicts among local bosses, or between the bosses and the central government; they belonged to local factions and, since they were also able to influence the electoral process, they became a further element in local strife rather than local peace. As for the jury, although the rich themselves usually avoided serving, those who did so seldom recommended harsh sentences for fear of reprisals. Even more than the justices of the peace, the jury was responsible for the enormous increase in impunity, a fact recognized by liberals and conservatives alike. This was not only true of criminal offences (including involvement in the now illegal slave trade) but also of political crimes, such as rebellions, conspiracies, seditions, whose leaders were frequently acquitted or received light sentences. It was true not only when the powerful were brought to court (a rare enough occurrence) but also the less powerful, who seldom lacked connections with the powerful. Crimes against slaves – and women –

14 Speech in the Senate, 12 July 1841. Quoted in Visconde do Uruguai, *Ensaio sobre o Direito Administrativo* (Rio de Janeiro, 1960) 504.

were everywhere regarded for the most part as a private matter.

The national guard was relatively democratic when it was founded, as we have seen. There was even some reluctance among landowners to join the organization for fear of a defeat in the elections for the higher posts by a social inferior. Without them, however, the preservation of order, the Guard's major task, could not be achieved. Within a year, by a decree in October 1832, the government doubled the income requirement for officers, raising it to 400 milreis in the major cities and to 200 milreis elsewhere. Later the Guard came under the influence of the new provincial assemblies. They chose to interpret the Additional Act (1834) as giving them power over senior positions in the Guard. It was then tempting to use this power as a political resource, as an instrument of patronage. Almost all provincial assemblies ended up tampering with the law and introducing some sort of control over the appointment of officers. In São Paulo, for example, elections had disappeared by 1836. The notion of a citizens' militia could not work in a highly unequal and stratified society, and the National Guard had soon adapted itself to the social reality.

Some of the greatest problems emerged from the Additional Act itself. It was, as has been said, a compromise measure. More radical proposals, such as the right of provincial assemblies to elect provincial presidents and to impose import duties, had been defeated. The author of the project, Bernardo Vasconcelos, then a liberal, had already warned that to push federalism as far as the United States had done would lead to anarchy and be disastrous for the unity of the country. But, moderate as it was, the Act did give the assemblies control over provincial and municipal matters. More importantly, it gave them power over the appointment of public officials. Given the obscurity of the wording of the Act, this power became a bone of contention between the assemblies and the central government. As it turned out, they started exercising authority over almost all public employees within the provincial territory, including the *juízes de direito* – district (*comarca*) judges – who had clearly remained under central control. Some assemblies also created and appointed local mayors, transferring to them the powers of the justices of the peace. The only officials they did not interfere with were the appeal court judges (*desembargadores*), army and navy personnel, and the provincial presidents themselves. They could, however, nominate the vice-presidents who had frequent opportunities to exercise power, since the presidents were often absent in Rio serving in the national parliament.

The measures adopted by the liberals, who came to power in 1831, and the political decentralization effected after 1834, encouraged and facilitated an intensification of the struggle for power between factions within the provincial rural oligarchies. And this opened the way for social conflicts wider, deeper and more dangerous to the established order than any which had occurred in the immediate aftermath of the 1831 crisis. At the same time the fragile political unity of the empire was seriously threatened. In 1835 provincial revolts broke out in the extreme north and the extreme south of the country, Pará and Rio Grande do Sul. They were followed by revolts in Bahia (in 1837) and Maranhão (in 1838). The most radical and violent rebellions in Brazilian history, before or since, these four were merely the most serious of a series of provincial disturbances which, although their roots went deeper, significantly followed the implementation of the liberal reforms and especially the Additional Act of 1834. Their differences reflected the different conflicts and tensions within a variety of provincial social (and racial) structures. All, however, were federalist, and several, including the most serious and prolonged, were frankly secessionist or at least had distinct separatist overtones.

Pará was the scene of the first of these major provincial revolts of the 1830s. It became known as the *Cabanagem* (from *cabanos*, as the rebels, like those in Pernambuco earlier (see above), were called). The province had a little less than 150,000 people, 30 per cent of whom were slaves. There was also a large free Indian and *mestizo* population, called *tapuios*, most of them living along the great rivers of the Amazon basin. Pará had no well-established landed oligarchy and in general a much looser social structure than, for example, the provinces of the north-east. The capital, Belém, was a small city of about 12,000, but it was a commercial centre and important for its location at the mouth of the Amazon. It was the major outlet for the province's modest production of tobacco, cacao, rubber and rice. It had a substantial presence of Portuguese merchants, as well as a few British and French. Since the abdication province and capital had been plagued by conflicts between liberal Brazilian and restorationist Portuguese factions. In 1833 the provincial council refused to accept a new president appointed by the regency, arguing that he was pro-*caramuru*. Later in the same year a conflict broke out between the two factions which resulted in about 95 casualties. Many Portuguese were killed and others left the province. A new liberal president managed to maintain a semblance of government until January 1835 when a radical element among the liberals killed both the president and the military commander and started a revolt. The leadership of the rebels included justices of the peace, officers of the national guard and of the army, priests, and a *seringueiro* (rubber gatherer). One of the leaders was made president and the independence of Pará was proclaimed.

The new president appointed by the regents in Rio de Janeiro, an octogenarian marshal born in Portugal, took sixty days to arrive and did so with only 120 men whom he had collected in Maranhão. He was eventually allowed to take over the presidency, and the rebel president withdrew. But the truce was shortlived. In August 1835 a rebel army, in which the majority of the rank and file were blacks and *tapuios*, attacked the city. After nine days of house-to-house fighting, in which about 180 whites were said to have been killed, not even the support of British and Portuguese vessels stationed in the port could save the president. He decided to abandon Belém and took refuge in a Brazilian warship. He was followed by about 5,000 people, Portuguese and Brazilians, most of them 'proprietors, merchants, first class citizens', as the president described them.

The rebel president had been killed in the battle. He was replaced by Eduardo Angelim, a 21-year-old Cearense, one of the most extraordinary popular leaders of the period. Angelim tried to organize the new government, creating new military units and appointing new officers (usually promoted from the ranks). A priest served as the president's secretary, one of the few among the rebels who was able to write with any fluency. The war spread to the interior of the province and up the Amazon river. The rebels raided cities and farms for food, weapons and valuables, retreating afterwards into the forest. Few cities were able to keep them at a distance.

A naval blockade of the mouth of the Amazon and the total disorganization of production throughout the province soon weakened the rebels' position in the capital. When the new official president, General Andreia, arrived in April 1836 with fresh troops, ammunition and vessels, Angelim decided to abandon the city with 5,000 followers, leaving behind a population almost exclusively of women and, astonishingly, 95,000 milreis from the provincial treasury in the hands of the bishop. General Andreia proceeded with a ruthless campaign of repression. He arrested the rebels *en masse*, gave orders to shoot on sight those who resisted, militarized the whole province through the creation of auxiliary corps and rounded up all those over ten years of age who had no property or occupation into 'worker corps', forcing them to work either for private employers for a small wage or in public works. Violence and cruelty were widespread on both sides. Some people were seen proudly wearing rosaries made from the ears of dead *cabanos*. Around 4,000 *cabanos* died in prisons, ships and hospitals alone. In October 1836 Angelim was arrested, without resistance, by the same officer who had defeated the *cabanos* of Pernambuco the year before. Colonel Joaquim de Sousa was impressed by the poverty, dignity and honesty of the rebel leader. The last *cabanos*, many of them armed with bows and arrows, turned themselves in when a general amnesty was granted in 1840. The death toll in the rebellion has been calculated at 30,000, that is to say, 20 per cent of the total population of the province, more or less evenly divided between rebels and non-rebels. The capital Belém was almost totally destroyed. The economy had been devastated.

The *cabanos* never presented a systematic set of demands, nor did they organize any programme of government. They simply shouted slogans and war cries against foreigners, Portuguese, masons, and in favour of the Catholic religion, Pedro II, Brazilians, Pará and liberty. The secession of the province, proclaimed again in 1836, was not a central demand. A puzzling aspect is the fact that, despite the existence of a substantial number of slaves among the *cabanos*, slavery was not abolished; an insurrection of slaves was put down by Angelim. The Cabanagem was an explosion of the Indian and *caboclo* (*mestizo*) population's long-repressed hatred of the colonial power and its representatives and of the white, rich and powerful in general, released by the political mobilization of the regency period and triggered off by conflicts among sectors of the higher strata of the population. It was a popular movement, but not of the people the liberals had in mind. Evaristo da Veiga referred to the *cabanos* in the most derogatory terms – *gentalha, crápula, massas brutas* – and observed that Pará looked more like part of Spanish America than of Brazil.[15]

The second rebellion, chronologically, was quite different in nature. It became known as the *Farroupilha*, a name used to characterize the radicals after the abdication of Pedro I, and took place in the southern province of Rio Grande do Sul. The province had over 100,000 inhabitants, and the capital, Porto Alegre, had, in 1830, a population of between 12,000 and 15,000. As in Pará, slaves composed more or less 30 per cent of the total population. But Rio Grande do Sul had a very

[15] *Aurora Fluminense*, 1 January, 11 November 1835.

different social structure from the rest of Brazil. The historical circumstances of the formation of the province had led to a fusion of military status and landownership, and the militarized dominant class exercised almost total control over the subordinate groups in society. Moreover, the province had gone through an important economic transformation in the second decade of the century, moving from agriculture to livestock production. A *charque* industry also developed along the coast. The occupation of the Banda Oriental in 1817 had given a tremendous boost to the *estancieiros*. They not only bought land in what became the Cisplatine Province but also transferred vast numbers of cattle to Brazil. The loss of the Banda Oriental in 1828 had been a severe blow, although it did not stop the regular smuggling of cattle across the frontier. In fact, economic and political relations among the *estancieiros* of Rio Grande do Sul, Uruguay and the Argentine provinces of Entre Ríos and Corrientes were an important factor in the rebellion of 1835. They formed a powerful group of caudillos in search of a political organization that could best suit their interests.

The beginning of the revolt was not very different from that of the Cabanagem, in the sense that it turned around the reaction of local liberals against the formation of the *caramuru Sociedade Militar* in 1833 and against a president appointed by the regency. The president, who suspected secessionist plans among the local leaders, was overthrown in September 1835. Under the next president, himself a rich *estancieiro*, factions coalesced and in February 1836 open war broke out. In September 1836 the *farroupilhas* proclaimed the independence of the province under a republican government, although they were not able to keep control of the capital. In 1839 with the help of a small naval task force organized by the Italian revolutionary, Giuseppe Garibaldi, they invaded the neighbouring province of Santa Catarina, where a shortlived republic was also proclaimed. The fight dragged on for ten years until an armistice was agreed in March 1845.

It was a war in which a good proportion of the *estancieiros*, particularly those who had their power base and their *estâncias* in the region bordering Argentina and Uruguay, fought against the forces of the central government. But the *charque* industrialists stayed with the government as did a section of the *estancieiros*. Without going here into the classic debate as to whether or not the *farroupilhas* seriously wanted to secede from Brazil, it is important to point out those factors which favoured and those which were against secession. First of all, there were some differences between *estancieiros* and *charqueadores*. The latter depended on the Brazilian market to sell their product; the former could do without it as long as they could count on Uruguayan *charqueadas*. On the other hand, the Rio Grande *charqueadores* depended on the *estancieiros* for their raw material. From the point of view of the central government it was essential for Brazil to have both *estancieiros* and *charqueadores*. And in view of the constant threat posed by Argentina the province of Rio Grande do Sul had great strategic importance. Here was a complex network of economic and political interests, involving taxation of *charque* and its related products, both for the internal and the external markets; taxation of cattle across international borders; the price of feeding the slave population in other provinces; and strategic considerations. It seems that secession was a workable plan for the *estancieiros*, as long as they could secure an arrangement, possibly a political merger, with Uruguay together with, perhaps, some Argentinian provinces. The leader of the rebellion, Colonel Bento Gonçalves, an *estancieiro* and a mason, seemed to have definite plans for a federation with Uruguay and Argentina through his contacts with Lavalleja and Rosas. But this was a risky project, given the volatile nature of politics in the Río de la Plata area. The second most important leader of the *farroupilhas*, Bento Manuel, another colonel and *estancieiro*, changed sides three times during the struggle, starting with the rebels, going over to the government, then back to the rebels and ending the campaign with the government again. In the end it was to pay the *estancieiros* to stay with a government which would give special protection to *charque* and related products so that Rio Grande do Sul could compete successfully with Argentina and Uruguay.

These ambiguities and some concessions made by the central government, such as 25 per cent import duties on foreign *charque* introduced in 1840, together with the exhaustion of the people and the decline of the cattle industry caused by the protracted war, finally brought the struggle to an end in 1845. The failure of rebellions in other provinces – Pará, Bahia, and by this time Minas Gerais and São Paulo (see below) – prevented the *gaúchos* from extracting even the introduction of a Brazilian federation.

The third major rebellion took place in Bahia and was called the *Sabinada* from the name of its leader, Dr Sabino Barroso. It was a repetition on a larger scale of the urban upheavals of the first part of the decade, with the added dimension of a strong federalist, if not secessionist, tendency. Several of its leaders had participated in the previous rebellions. The revolt started in the army barracks of Salvador on 6 November 1837 and gained the immediate support of almost the whole garrison of the capital. Only the national guard and the navy remained loyal, but they were no match for the army and police forces which, apart from the officers, joined the rebellion *en masse*. The next day the city was taken and the provincial president fled without a shot being fired. The municipal *câmara* was summoned and proclaimed Bahia to be a 'free and independent state'.

What followed was an almost perfect replica of the war of independence: the capital was put under siege by the sugar barons of the Recôncavo, helped at sea by the imperial navy. The interior of the province outside of the Recôncavo remained quiet, frustrating the hopes of the rebels to extend the fight to the rural areas as had happened in Pará. Completely surrounded, the defeat of the rebels was only a matter of time. On 13 March 1838 a final three-day battle took place inside the capital, fought, as in Belém, from house to house. The 5,000-strong rebel army was defeated by a more experienced 4,000-strong legal force. In all, about 1,200 rebels and 600 loyalists were killed. The amnesty of 1840 saved the life of seven leaders who had been sentenced to death.

The support of some important elements among the business community and the intellectuals of Salvador gave the Sabinada a larger base of support than earlier, more purely popular upheavals in Bahia. Sabino Barroso was a journalist and a professor at the prestigious School of Medicine, one of only two in the empire. But besides the federal and republican tendencies, there is not much more information on the plans of the rebels. The initial separation from Rio seemed to have alienated some support, since this decision was later qualified: the secession was restricted to the duration of the regency. The revolution also did not take advantage of the revolutionary potential of the slave population, a legacy perhaps of the panic caused by the Bahian slave revolt of 1835 (see below). In 1837–8 a battalion of blacks was organized, but there was no general mobilization of slaves, and slavery was not abolished. The anti-Portuguese sentiment, so prominent in previous movements, had by now subsided and was barely voiced. The landed and commercial elites were afraid to join popular elements and urban intellectuals in separating the province from the rest of Brazil, much as the idea might have appealed to some of them. The resistance to the rebellion was organized by the chief of police of Salvador, who was also the scion of a powerful family of *senhores de engenho* of the Recôncavo.

The last revolt to erupt in this period was similar to the Cabanagem, although it lacked its depth and violence. Its battlefield was the southern part of the province of Maranhão, close to the border with Piauí. The area was settled by small farmers and small cattle ranchers for the most part. To the north it bordered the rich valleys of the Mearim, Itapicuru and Pindaré rivers dominated by a strong oligarchy of planters and slave-owners engaged in the production of rice and cotton. The population of the province was at the time over 200,000, of which more than 50 per cent were slaves, the highest percentage in Brazil. São Luís, the capital, was a city of over 30,000 with a strong Portuguese business sector.

The revolt became known as the *Balaiada* because one of its leaders was nicknamed *balaio* (the basket-maker). It was the one most directly linked to the liberal reforms, particularly to the Additional Act of 1834. Two factions fought for local supremacy, much in the same style as in other provinces: the liberals, called *Bentevis*, after the name of a liberal newspaper, and the conservatives, called *cabanos*. The conservative president, taking advantage of the new powers given to the provincial assemblies by the Additional Act, had a new law passed creating *prefeitos* (mayors) at the municipal level and transferring to them most of the powers of the justices of the peace. Another provincial law enabled him to appoint officers of the national guard. These measures meant the dislodgement of the *Bentevis* from the positions of power they enjoyed, and it was no surprise that they mounted a vicious campaign against the president and the new laws in their newspapers in the capital. Emotions were running high when a trivial incident triggered off the rebellion. A *cafuso* (mixed Indian and black) cowboy, Raimundo Gomes, in the service of a *bentevi* priest, who was also a rich planter, attacked a local jail to free Gomes's brother and some of his hands, unjustifiedly arrested by the sub-*prefeito*, *a cabano* enemy of the priest. Supporters poured in from several quarters and in December 1838 Gomes found himself the leader of a rebellion. Balaio joined the rebellion later. His motive was to revenge the honour of his daughter who had been raped by a police captain. A third leader Cosme, a black, self-styled Dom Cosme, Tutor and Emperor of the Bentevi Freedoms, fought a parallel revolt at the head of 3,000 runaway slaves.

The *balaios* managed to mobilize some 11,000 men and in August 1839 occupied Caxias, the second most important city of the province, which was also a liberal stronghold. There a provisional government was organized and a set of demands, including the repeal of the two provincial laws and the expulsion of the Portuguese from the province, was formulated. The central government sent a total of 8,000 troops, gathered from several provinces, under the command of Colonel Luís Alves de Lima. The back of the movement was quickly broken, not least by internal divisions between free and slave *balaios*. Colonel Lima played one against the other to good effect: Cosme arrested Gomes and was then opposed by other *balaio* leaders. By mid-1840 the rebellion had been put down. An amnesty followed, except for Dom Cosme, who was hanged in 1842. Luís Alves de Lima earned the first of a long series of titles of nobility: barão de Caxias.

The demands of the *balaios* remained very much inside the limits of the struggle between *bentevis* and *cabanos*: revocation of the law of the *prefeitos* and of the changes in the national guard; to this they added traditional anti-Portuguese measures, amnesty and pay for the rebel troops. The proclamation of one *balaio* leader, a semi-literate, ended with *vivas* for the Catholic religion, the constitution, Pedro II, the justices of the peace and the 'Holy Cause of Freedom'. Nothing of a social or economic nature was included. Despite the popular nature of most of its leadership and rank and file, the Balaiada could not escape from the ideological and political trappings of upper and middle sector conflict. It was perhaps more articulate than the Cabanagem. But it was also the product of a less polarized social structure. Many *balaois* were small farmers, cowboys and artisans; some were rich landowners. One of the proclamations mentioned the need to save 'our families and properties'. This was probably one of the reasons why there was never a good relationship between the free and slave *balaios*. But the rebels remained also isolated from the urban liberals who had created the atmosphere for the revolt. The *bentevis* of São Luís, either fearing a conservative backlash, or fearing the violence of the popular elements in the rebellion, retreated as soon as the action started. Only in Pará did urban and rural radicalisms join together. The division amongst the underdogs, slaves and free, rural poor and urban poor, was the strength of the ruling groups and frequently saved them from their own divisions.

The disappointment at the way the liberal reforms of 1831–4 had worked out in practice and the wave of rebellions that swept the country, either as a direct or indirect consequence of the Additional Act of 1834 in particular, bringing instability and threatening both internal order and the unity of the country, opened the way for the development of a new

alignment of political forces and to the formation of the two parties —
Conservative and Liberal — that would dominate politics during the
second empire.

It should be remembered that at the beginning the conservative
reaction was quite general among members of the national elite. As early
as 1835 Evaristo da Veiga's *Aurora Fluminense* as well as Vasconcelos's *O
Sete de Abril* began to criticize the liberal reforms. Still allies at the time,
they would later disagree about exactly how far and how deep the
reaction, the return (*regresso*) to order, authority and a stronger central
executive, should go. While Vasconcelos's position became more radically conservative, Evaristo remained in the middle ground, fighting for
adjustments to the liberal laws rather than major changes. The rapid
transition from absolutism to freedom, Evaristo argued, had loosened
social networks and 'we see anarchy all over the empire'. Brazil was in
danger of being plunged into the kind of political instability endemic in
the former Spanish colonies, and this could possibly lead to political
fragmentation. He conceded that the excesses of the progressive measures had caused a reaction in public opinion, and claimed that
Vasconcelos had been quick — too quick — to notice this change and had
decided to become the champion of reaction. Many would certainly
support a 'short and rational *regresso*', but Vasconcelos, he felt, had
'exaggerated beyond limits a just idea.'[16]

Pessimism had also begun to affect the recently elected regent, Diogo
Feijó, one of the bulwarks of the *moderado* faction. He was convinced that
the secession of Rio Grande do Sul was inevitable and that maybe
Pernambuco would soon follow. In the *Fala do Throno* (speech from the
throne) in 1836, he referred to widespread and growing disregard for the
authorities and warned that the country's basic institutions were threatened. A growing uneasiness was even more noticeable within the
legislature which had passed the Additional Act of 1834. Under the
leadership of Vasconcelos there emerged a strong opposition group that
soon became a majority and constituted the nucleus of the future
Conservative party. In 1837 the death of Evaristo da Veiga left Feijó
without his major supporter in parliament and in the press. Unable to
deal with the congressional opposition, not least because of his own
authoritarian character, and under pressure for not dealing with sufficient energy with the *farroupilhas* in Rio Grande do Sul, among whose
leadership there was one of his cousins, in September 1837 Feijó

[16] *Aurora Fluminense*, 6 April, 12 August, 4 September 1835.

resigned, handing the government over to the recently appointed minister of the empire (internal affairs) Pedro de Araújo Lima (the future Marquês de Olinda), a conservative senator, former president of the Chamber, and a *senhor de engenho* in Pernambuco. A new election for regent was held and the results indicated that the new conservative trend was nationwide. Araújo Lima carried fifteen of the eighteen provinces, including Minas Gerais, São Paulo and Rio Grande do Sul, and won around 45 per cent of the total vote. (In contrast, Feijó in 1835 had secured only 30 per cent of the vote and carried only eight provinces.) The elections for the new legislature had already pointed in the same direction: all the leaders of the opposition to Feijó were re-elected. Significantly, the number of magistrates in the legislature, more inclined to conservatism, rose from 24 per cent to 39 per cent, while the number of priests, most of them liberals, fell from 23 per cent to 12 per cent.[17]

Araújo Lima's opponent in the elections for regent in 1838 was Holanda Cavalcanti. (He had also stood against Feijó in 1835.) Both Araújo Lima and Holanda Cavalcanti were members of the Pernambucan sugar oligarchy. But Araújo Lima was Coimbra-educated and had been involved in national politics since independence. He had travelled to several European countries and attended a law course in France. Holanda had no higher education and often preferred to tend to the affairs of his *engenho* than to stay in Rio. Their positions regarding the political organization of the country were quite different. While Holanda was known for his advocacy of maximum decentralization, and even of secessionism, Lima, a convinced centralist, had voted against the Additional Act and had been a staunch supporter of the *regresso* from the beginning.

The *moderado* group had split. The bulk of the magistrates and bureaucrats and part of the landowning class, particularly the landed interest of Rio de Janeiro, Bahia and Pernambuco, had moved steadily to the right, leaving behind as the nucleus of what would become the Liberal party the more urban-oriented elements, a few priests, and many landowners from less traditional areas, particularly São Paulo, Minas Gerais and Rio Grande do Sul. The splinter *regressionista* group was joined by what was left of the *caramurus*, many of them entrenched in the bureaucracy and in the Senate, and the *caramurus'* traditional supporters, the Portuguese merchants of the major cities. In the government organized by Araújo Lima in 1838, reflecting the conservative majority in the

---

[17] Carvalho, *A Construção*, 83

Chamber, Vasconcelos, himself a Coimbra-educated magistrate, a
Mineiro without landed connections, was given two portfolios (empire
and justice) and was recognized as the leader of the cabinet. He was
joined by Miguel Calmon do Pin e Almeida (the future Marquês de
Abrantes), a *senhor de engenho* from Bahia, also educated at Coimbra; Rego
Barros, an army officer trained in Germany, and Maciel Monteiro, a
doctor trained in England, both linked to the Pernambucan oligarchy;
José da Costa Carvalho (the future Marquês de Monte Alegre), the
former regent; and Joaquim José Rodrigues Tôrres (the future Visconde
de Itaboraí), educated at Coimbra and linked to the coffee planters of Rio
de Janeiro. It was an alliance of magistrates and sugar and coffee planters,
well educated (for the most part in Europe, above all in Coimbra), and
with considerable experience in government.

The rationale for the new alliance was provided by Vasconcelos and
Paulino José Soares de Sousa (the future Visconde do Uruguai), another
magistrate who had started his training at Coimbra and who had family
ties with Rodrigues Tôrres (their wives were sisters). Vasconcelos and
Paulino were also the main drafters of the legislation that finally reformed the earlier liberal laws. Their basic premise was that the country
was not ready for the advanced liberal measures adopted after 1831.
Events were proving that social order and national unity could not be
maintained without a strengthening of the central government. But
while Paulino always stressed the political and administrative aspects of
the nation's problems, Vasconcelos went deeper. *O Sete de Abril*, known
to be published under his influence, discussed the need for a government
supported by the *classe conservadora*, defined as an alliance of landowners,
capitalists, merchants, industrialists and those in the arts and sciences,
people who 'in sudden changes have everything to lose and nothing to
gain'.[18] This class, according to the *Sete*, was interested in progress but
with order. *O Chronista*, the journal of the talented mulatto journalist and
protégé of Vasconcelos, Justiniano José da Rocha, agreed with this idea
and equated it with Guizot's concept of the 'legal country'.[19] The *Aurora*,
revived under a new publisher in 1838, counter-attacked, but forgot that
Evaristo himself had written in 1835 that the *moderado* party represented
'progress in order'. In a long and perceptive analysis of Vasconcelos's
political philosophy the *Aurora* described him as a follower of Bentham-

---

[18] *O Sete de Abril*, 19 November 1838. Capitalists (*capitalistas*) in the vocabulary of the day were
   financiers or big urban property owners.
[19] Quoted in *O Sete de Abril*, 7 December 1838.

ite utilitarianism, a believer only in the morality of interests, in the principle that the only motor of human action was material interests, and that the only constraint was the fear of those interests being damaged.[20] Here the *Aurora* probably came close to putting its finger on Vasconcelos's purpose: to find solid material interests on which to base the monarchy and the entire political system.

The difficulty in the late thirties and early forties was that the conservative classes in general had no consensus on what would be the best institutional framework to suit their interests, in part because these interests did not totally coincide, in part because many of their members, landowners more than merchants, were not prepared to think in terms of rule through the mediation of the state. In 1843, J. J. da Rocha was still arguing that the monarchy had no solid roots in Brazil. It was a product of reason, of the perception of its importance in maintaining order. It was still necessary to convince landowners and merchants, the aristocracy of land and wealth, that it was in their best interests to support it and be supported by it.[21] Owing to the lack of a unified perception on the part of the dominant groups, the *regresso* was far from unanimously supported in the late thirties and early forties. Besides the sugar planters of the northeast, especially Bahia, the conservative coalition relied heavily at the beginning on a group of magistrates and bureaucrats and on the coffee planters of Rio de Janeiro. The coincidence of a new economic boom based on coffee with the geographical area in which the political and administrative centre of the country was located was, as we shall see, a basic factor in the eventual success of the process of political recentralization.

The first regressionist law was the *interpretação* of the Additional Act in May 1840. It was presented as an 'interpretation', but in fact as far as the appointment and removal of public employees and the definition of their jurisdiction were concerned it substantially reduced the power of provincial assemblies. At this juncture, as a last resort, the liberal minority in the Chamber decided to promote, prematurely, the *maioridade* of the emperor in order to prevent further regressionist measures. The coming of age of the emperor was a widely accepted idea, which had been mentioned several times since 1835 as a way of bolstering the legitimacy of the central government. Although always more likely to be a conservative measure, political opportunism led the liberals to bring it forward. The

---

[20] *Aurora Fluminense*, 23 July, 17 October, 1838.
[21] *O Brasil*, 19, 21, 23, 26 September, 1843.

'parliamentary *coup d'état*' of 23 July 1840, which ended the regency of Araújo Lima and initiated the Second Empire, was supported by liberals, bureaucrats, the army and the National Guard, the people of Rio and, last but not least, the 15-year-old emperor himself. The liberal *gabinete da maioridade* which was immediately formed included two Andrada brothers (Antônio Carlos and Martim Francisco), two Cavalcanti de Albuquerque brothers (Holanda and Francisco de Paula), Antônio Paulino Limpo de Abreu, the future Visconde de Abaeté, a mineiro liberal, and Aureliano Coutinho, a courtier with a strong personal influence over the young emperor. Given the inexperience and lack of leadership of Pedro II, conflict soon broke out inside the cabinet and it collapsed at the end of March 1841. The new *gabinete conservador* kept the influential Aureliano and introduced Paulino Soares de Sousa as Minister of Justice, Miguel Calmon, a *senhor de engenho* from Bahia, Araújo Viana, the tutor of Pedro II, Vilela Barbosa, an army officer, and José Clemente Pereira, a Portuguese-born magistrate, the last two well-known former supporters of Pedro I. (The cabinet of January 1843–February 1844 included, as well as Paulino, Rodrigues Tôrres and Honório Hermeto Carneiro Leão (the future Marquês de Paraná), a young Coimbra-trained magistrate and politician from Minas Gerais who was, like Rodrigues Tôrres, a Rio *fazendeiro*.) With the help of Vasconcelos in the Senate, Paulino rushed through parliament a law re-establishing the Council of State (November 1841) and the reform of the Code of Criminal Procedures (December 1841).

The reform of the Code was the central achievement of the *regresso*. It re-established in the hands of the central government total control over the administrative and judicial structure of the empire. All judges from *desembargador* (high court judge) and *juiz de direito* (district judge) to *juiz municipal* (county judge) were to be appointed by the minister of justice. The district judges, in particular, had their powers reinforced. Only local *juízes de paz* remained independent of the central power. But this also was taken care of: the new law created *chefes de polícia* in all provincial capitals – to be appointed by the minister of justice. At the *município* and parish level, the police chiefs were represented by *delegados* and *subdelegados* who were civilians appointed by the provincial presidents on their recommendation. Most of the judicial and police attributes of the justices of the peace were transferred to the *delegados* and *subdelegados*, reducing to powerlessness the elected justices, who also lost to these 'sheriffs' the task of organizing the list of jurors and of appointing block inspectors.

The electoral boards alone remained their responsibility. Through the police chiefs, the minister could even control the appointment of jail guards throughout the country, and it was he who decided their salaries. Furthermore, the requirements for jurors were stiffened: they had to be literate and to earn 400 milreis in the major cities and 200 milreis elsewhere, which doubled the previous income requirement. Significantly, if the income came from industry or commerce, it had to be doubled again, to 800 and 400 milreis, a further indication that landowners and bureaucrats were the most favoured elements. A further centralizing measure was the appointment of provincial vice-presidents by the minister of the empire. Previously they were nominated in lists of six names by the provincial assemblies, the central government limiting itself to establishing the order in which they should serve. As a last indication of the sweeping nature of the *regresso*, the new Code required every person travelling within the empire who wanted to avoid interrogation and possible expulsion from a *município* by the local *delgado* to carry a passport. Only the National Guard survived this onslaught on the liberal measures of 1831–4, even though its loyalty when the central government had attempted, and in the case of Rio Grande do Sul was still attempting, to crush provincial rebellions had often been uncertain. It was, however, only a temporary respite, as we shall see. And the government did now begin to increase once more the size of the army.

This package of measures aiming to recentralize political power included the restoration of the exercise of the 'moderating power' which had been suspended under the regency. In a decisive move on 1 May 1842 the conservative government then dissolved the legislature elected in October 1840 during the short liberal interregnum before it had even convened, and called new elections. The liberals feared that the conservative party, taking advantage of the youth of the emperor and of the recent legislation, which had vastly expanded government patronage and control, would entrench itself in power to their permanent exclusion. Two years earlier they had recourse to the *maioridade*. Now they only had open rebellion. In May 1842, São Paulo rose up in arms, followed by Minas Gerais in June, and the rebellion spread to parts of the Paraíba valley in the province of Rio de Janeiro. The most important liberal leaders of São Paulo and Minas Gerais, including Feijó and Vergueiro in the former, Limpo de Abreu and Teófilo Ottoni in the latter, were involved. The men appointed revolutionary presidents – Tobias de Aguiar in São Paulo and Pinto Coelho in Minas Gerais – were among the richest in their provinces. Aguiar had become rich for his participation in the mule trade of Sorocaba, the focus of the rebellion, where his family had also drawn great profits from tax farming during the colonial period and the early years of the empire; he was also a colonel in the National Guard and had been president of the province under the liberal government of 1840. Pinto Coelho had made his fortune in gold mining and had recently sold a mining concern to the British for £112,500. In Rio de Janeiro, the leader of the rebels, Joaquim José de Sousa Breves, was undoubtedly the richest man in the province. He is said to have owned more than 6,000 slaves and over 30 *fazendas*, from which he harvested 100–200,000 *arrobas* of coffee a year. He was also well known for his direct involvement in the illegal slave trade. He had long been at odds with the conservative presidents of the province, especially Paulino Soares de Sousa, because of their periodic attempts to put an end to coffee tax evasions and slave trading.

In terms of leadership, the revolts of 1842 were similar to the *farroupilha* rebellion which continued in Rio Grande do Sul, but the reasons behind them were different. Paulistas and Mineiros fought mostly against the new laws of the *regresso* and against the conservative cabinet in Rio. São Paulo was also protesting against a government act early in 1842 which had prohibited the trade in mules with the gaúcho rebels, but this does not seem to have been a major cause of the rebellion, although it might have been the reason why Tobias de Aguiar joined it. Secession was mentioned in São Paulo, but the idea did not seem to have had great appeal. For one thing, the north-east of the province formed part of the Paraíba valley and its coffee economy was closely linked to the port of Rio. Moreover, the fighting spirit and capacity of the *bandeirantes* seemed to have disappeared; unlike the militarized gaúcho *estancieiros*, the paulista *fazendeiros* were easily defeated by the rather weak troops of the central government. In Minas Gerais whose Zona da Mata was also part of Brazil's coffee economy there was no talk of secession at all. And as far as Breves was concerned, the idea made no sense, since his *fazendas* were in the very heart of the Rio coffee area.

The liberal rebellions of 1842 indicate the diversity of perception within the landed class at the time regarding the political organization of the country. Landowners in all three provinces joined in; but by no means unanimously. There were landowners on both sides of the conflict (and the National Guard was also split). In São Paulo, Vergueiro, for instance, was a revolutionary, and Costa Carvalho was the loyalist president of the province. In the Paraíba valley, Breves was opposed by other coffee planters who supported the central government. The president of Rio de Janeiro province at the time was Honório Hermeto, himself a coffee *fazendeiro* in the province, who, the following year, as we have seen, would join a much strengthened conservative cabinet. Minas Gerais, which did not have as strong an export sector as Rio or São Paulo, did have quite an important network of small towns developed at the time of the gold rush. Here was the source of a more authentic form of bourgeois liberalism, best represented by Teófilo Ottoni. But even these towns, like the landowners of the province, were divided during the revolt.

The rebellion lasted a month in São Paulo and two months in Minas Gerais before it was finally crushed. Throughout the following decades, until the fall of the empire in 1889, the liberal party drew its main strength from São Paulo and Minas Gerais together with Rio Grande do Sul. São Paulo and Minas Gerais having no strong reasons to secede and Rio Grande do Sul having failed to secede they accepted the unity of the country established at the time of independence and maintained despite the turmoil of the thirties. They were not able to dispute the supremacy in national politics of Rio de Janeiro. The most liberals in São Paulo and Minas Gerais could now do perhaps was to prevent the centralization of power from going too far.

Visiting Brazil in 1842 and 1843, the Comte de Suzannet observed that Rio Grande do Sul had already seceded, that São Paulo would soon follow and that 'the unity of Brazil is only apparent. All the provinces look forward to independence. A United States style republic, this is the dream they strive to realise.'[22] Three years after the beginning of the Second Empire, this was the impression the country gave to a visitor, unsympathetic as he was. In the event, the count's predictions were proved wrong. Political as well as economic factors accounted for a different outcome. On the political side, the continued influence of Aureliano over the emperor helped to bring about another change of government. At the beginning of 1844 the liberals returned to power. Amnesty was granted to paulista and mineiro rebels who were soon back in the Chamber and in ministerial posts. The fear of a permanent monopoly of power by the conservatives was thus eliminated, and a system in which power rotated periodically between the two parties or coalitions began to take shape. Even more important, once in power, the liberals found it useful to retain the regressionist laws of 1840–1 – to

[22] Comte de Suzannet, *O Brasil em 1845* (Rio de Janeiro, 1957), 87.

enforce law and order, to exercise patronage and to win elections. Before the first legislative elections promoted by the new government they removed almost half of the *juízes de direito* in the country and several commanders of the National Guard. From 1844 to 1848, the *quinqüênio liberal*, Brazil was governed by a succession of liberal cabinets – of which the most prominent members were once more Alves Branco, Limpo de Abreu and Holanda Cavalcanti, together with José Carlos Pereira de Almeida Tôrres (visconde de Macaé) and Francisco de Paula Sousa e Melo. No serious attempt was made to undo the work of the *regresso*, to the disappointment of more consistent liberals such as Teófilo Ottoni. In disgust, the mineiro revolutionary abandoned national politics and returned to Minas, after first securing from the liberal government a forty-year licence to promote navigation on the Mucuri river.

At the same time, the political unity and stability of the empire was underpinned by the rapid growth of the coffee sector centred on Rio during the 1830s and 1840s. This not only consolidated the political authority of the Rio coffee *fazendeiros* who together with the bureaucrats and magistrates formed the backbone of the conservative party, but particularly after the 1844 tariff reform considerably strengthened the finances of the Brazilian state. The conservative cabinet led by the Visconde de Olinda (Araújo Lima) which took power in September 1848, like the cabinets of 1841 and 1843, included three out of six senior ministers linked to coffee interests in the province of Rio de Janeiro. After surviving one last liberal provincial rebellion – the *Praieira* in Pernambuco – it went on to complete the work of political centralization and even found the authority to tackle one of Brazil's most complex, intractable and pressing problems – the slave trade and relations with Britain.

During the 1830s and 1840s three products – sugar, cotton and coffee – continued to account for 75–80 per cent of Brazil's exports. It was coffee, however, which for the first time was largely responsible for Brazil's modest but steady overall economic growth. The dramatic expansion of coffee production and export was the most striking feature of Brazil's economic history in this period. Responding to the growth of demand in western Europe and the United States where the taste for coffee developed in the expanding urban centres, especially among the urban middle classes, coffee spread across the virgin highlands of the valley of the river Paraíba, which runs parallel to the coast some seventy miles inland from

Rio de Janeiro, for the most part in Rio province but also including the southeast of the province of Minas Gerais and the northeast region of São Paulo province. Soil, altitude and climate proved exceptionally favourable to the cultivation of the coffee bush in the Paraíba valley. Land values soared, landholdings were consolidated and the pattern of large plantations (*fazendas*), already so familiar in areas of sugar cultivation, was reproduced in the new and expanding coffee region of south-east Brazil.

At the time of independence coffee had already established itself as Brazil's third most important cash crop. During the five-year period 1831–5 it outstripped not only cotton but sugar to become the country's principal export accounting for 40 per cent of Brazil's total export earnings by the end of the decade and almost half by 1850 (see below Table 1). A new export cycle which was to last for more than a century begun. In this first stage almost all the coffee was grown in the Paraíba valley (80 per cent in the province of Rio de Janeiro) and exported in increasing quantities from the port of Rio (see below, Table 2). By the late forties, however, coffee was already spreading into the paulista west, from Campinas to Rio Claro, displacing sugar and at the same time, despite the difficulties of transportation over the Serra do Mar, turning Santos into a major port. In 1836/7 Campinas, for example, was exporting through Santos 153,000 *arrobas* of sugar and only 5,000 *arrobas* of coffee. In 1850–1, for the first time, Campinas exported more coffee than sugar. And in 1854/5 313,000 *arrobas* of coffee and only 12,000 *arrobas* of sugar were exported.[23]

Brazil's share of world coffee output rose from a little under 20 per cent in the 1820s to 30 per cent in the 1830s and over 40 per cent in the 1840s, by which time Brazil was by far the world's largest producer. Most of Brazil's coffee was exported to Europe, especially Germany, the Low Countries and Scandinavia, and to the United States, the largest single market. Britain, which, in any case, preferred tea, imported coffee from its colonies in the Caribbean, Central America and South Asia and preferential duties in favour of colonial produce virtually excluded Brazilian coffee from the British market. Coffee exports were largely responsible for the steady growth in Brazil's export earnings from an average of £3.8m per annum in 1822–31 to £5.4m per annum in 1832–41. And, despite falling international coffee prices, increased production was

[23] Maria Theresa Schorer Petrone, *A lavoura canavieira em São Paulo: expansão e declínio, 1765–1861* (São Paulo, 1968), 166.

Table 1 *Value of the Major Brazilian Exports in Relation to Total Exports,*
1821–1850 (%)

	Sugar (1)	Cotton (2)	Coffee (3)	(1)+(2) +(3)	Hides (4)	Others*
1821–30	30.1	20.6	18.4	69.1	13.6	17.3
1831–40	24.0	10.8	43.8	78.6	7.9	13.5
1841–50	26.7	7.5	41.4	75.6	8.5	15.9

* Tobacco, cacao, rubber, maté, etc.
Source: *Anuário Estatístico do Brasil* (Rio de Janeiro, 1939/40), 1380.

Table 2 *Exports of Coffee from Rio de Janeiro*
(in *arrobas*)

1792	160	1835	3,237,190
1817	318,032	1840–1	4,982,221
1820	539,000	1845–6	6,720,221
1826	1,304,450	1849–50	5,706,833
1830	1,958,925	1851–2	9,673,842

Source: Stanley J. Stein, *Vassouras, a Brazilian coffee*
county, 1850–1900 (Cambridge, Mass., 1957), 53.

sufficient to earn Brazil more than £1m more in the 1840s than the 1830s
(see Table 3). Total export earnings rose to an average of £5.9m per
annum in 1842–51 (and, more dramatically, to £10.9m per annum in
1852–61).[24] In view of the growth of Brazil's population during this
period (it reached over 7 million by 1850), this was not yet enough to
produce a more than modest increase in per capita incomes even in the
south-east. In the north-east, where, except for sugar in the late 1840s,
export sectors grew more slowly, stagnated or actually declined, per
capita incomes probably fell.

The Brazilian sugar boom which followed the disruption of the world
market caused by the French Revolution and the Napoleonic Wars, and
particularly the abrupt end to Saint Domingue's reign as the world's
greatest sugar producer, was short-lived. From the mid-1820s to the
mid-1840s production of sugar continued to increase, albeit relatively
slowly, in both the traditional sugar regions of the north-east, Bahia and
Pernambuco, and in São Paulo and around Campos in Rio de Janeiro
province. Overall production during the decade 1831–40 was up 50 per
cent compared with 1821–30. However, like most commodity prices,

[24] Nathaniel H. Leff, *Underdevelopment and development in Brazil* (2 vols., London, 1982), I, 80.

Table 3 *Brazilian Coffee Exports, 1821–50*

Year	Thousand of 60 kg sacks	Thousands of £ sterling	Value per sack (£ sterling)	Coffee exports as percentage of total exports
1821	129	704	5.50	16.3
1822	186	789	4.24	19.6
1823	226	878	3.89	20.1
1824	274	704	2.57	18.3
1825	224	623	2.78	13.5
1826	318	690	2.17	20.8
1827	430	774	1.80	21.1
1828	452	659	1.46	15.9
1829	459	705	1.54	20.9
1830	480	663	1.38	19.8
Decade	3,178	7,189	2.26	18.4
1831	549	964	1.76	28.6
1832	717	1,832	2.56	39.2
1833	560	1,383	2.47	42.4
1833/34	1,121	2,775	2.47	49.3
1834/35	970	2,435	2.51	45.7
1835/36	1,052	2,555	2.43	37.7
1836/37	910	2,237	2.46	40.9
1837/38	1,149	2,197	1.91	53.2
1838/39	1,333	2,494	1.87	51.3
1839/40	1,383	2,657	1.92	46.7
Decade	9,744	21,529	2.21	43.8
1840/41	1,239	2,300	1.86	42.7
1841/42	1,363	2,311	1.69	46.8
1842/43	1,444	1,909	1.32	41.6
1843/44	1,541	1,933	1.25	41.0
1844/45	1,525	1,838	1.20	37.2
1845/46	1,723	2,259	1.31	39.7
1846/47	2,387	2,465	1.03	41.9
1847/48	2,340	2,936	1.25	43.4
1848/49	2,106	2,242	1.06	38.2
1849/50	1,453	2,462	1.69	41.5
Decade	17,121	22,655	1.32	41.4

Source: Affonso de E. Taunay, *Pequena História do café no Brasil* (Rio de Janeiro, 1945), 547.

international sugar prices were falling in this period and increased production was insufficient to maintain the existing level of export earnings. With coffee export buoyant, sugar's share of total exports fell from 30.1 per cent in 1821–30 to 24 per cent in 1831–40; it then rose a little to 26.7 per cent in the following decade (see Table 1 above).

Brazil remained, after the British West Indies and Cuba, the third leading exporter of sugar with 10–15 per cent of world output in the 1830s. But at a time of rapidly expanding world demand Brazil faced increasing competition from Cuban sugar cane (exported primarily to the United States where Louisiana expanded its own production) and from European sugar beet, and gradually lost ground in the international market. The Brazilian industry, based on cheap land and cheap labour, was technically backward and capital for modernization was in limited supply. Also transportation costs, within Brazil and across the Atlantic, were relatively high. As in the case of coffee, Brazilian sugar was virtually excluded from Britain, one of the biggest markets, by colonial preference; until duties were gradually equalized after 1846 Brazilian sugar was subject to a duty of 63*s*. per cwt compared with 24*s*. per cwt on sugar from the British West Indies, East Indies and Mauritius. Continental Europe was the main market for Brazilian sugar (much of it carried in British ships directly to European ports or to London for re-export).

As for cotton, for the first time since the initial boom during the last quarter of the eighteenth century, its production and export suffered during the 1830s and 1840s an absolute decline (from which it would recover only during the American Civil War). The main foreign market was, of course, Britain. There was no colonial preference in the case of cotton but a preference for cheaper United States cotton was responsible for a decline in Brazil's share of British raw cotton imports from 20 per cent in 1801–10 to 13 per cent in 1821–30 and only 3 per cent in 1841–50. As a result cotton's share of total Brazilian export earnings fell from 20.6 per cent in 1821–30 to 10.8 per cent in 1831–40 and 7.5 per cent in 1841–50 (see Table 1 above).

'We are not so absurd as to think of becoming manufacturers yet', José Bonifácio told Henry Chamberlain, the British consul-general, in November 1822; 'we will therefore buy your manufactures and sell you our produce.'[25] In the period after independence, Britain, as we have seen, was a less important market for Brazilian produce than continental Europe. As early as 1838 the United States too was almost as important an export market as Britain. In that year, however, Britain supplied 41 per cent of Brazilian imports compared with 8 per cent from the United States. By the late forties almost half Brazil's imports came from Britain (compared with approximately 10 per cent from France, 10 per cent from the United States and 10 per cent from Portugal). Cotton goods consti-

---

[25] Quoted in C. K. Webster (ed.), *Britain and the independence of Latin America, 1812–30. Select documents from the Foreign Office archives* (2 vols., London, 1938), I, 215.

tuted over half the imports from Britain and cottons, woollens and linens together accounted for 75 per cent of the total. The remaining 25 per cent was made up of a whole range of consumer goods from hardware, earthenware and glass to hats, umbrellas and musical instruments. Prices of manufactured goods fell even faster than commodity prices during the 1830s and 1840s. Thus, the real value of Brazilian exports (expanding anyway thanks mainly to coffee) in terms of Brazil's capacity to import increased. Trade figures are notoriously difficult to assess in this period, but it has been estimated that except for three years (1831, 1837 and 1842) the Brazilian market was worth between £2m and £3m per annum to British manufacturers during these two decades, rising to £3.5m in 1851. In most years British exports to Brazil were only slightly lower, and in some years higher, than British exports to the whole of Spanish America.[26] Although importing only 5–7 per cent of total British exports and only a quarter of the value of exports to Europe and one-third of exports to the United States Brazil, after the United States and Germany, was Britain's third largest single market.

Under the Anglo-Brazilian commercial treaty of 1827, like the Anglo-Portuguese treaty of 1810, the maximum tariff on imported British goods, which were already cheap, was 15 per cent *ad valorem*. This was one important factor in Brazil's failure to develop its own manufacturing sector during Dom João's residence in Rio (1808–21) and in the period immediately after independence. Rio de Janeiro (which had a population of 200,000 by 1850) and other Brazilian cities were full of artisans' establishments making soap, candles, cotton thread, clothing, hats, snuff, cigars, furniture and ironware, but the textile and food-processing factories which were to form the basis of Brazil's early industrial growth did not appear until after 1840. Indeed there was no significant growth until the 1870s. Other factors, however, besides cheap British imports during the first half of the nineteenth century explain Brazil's late industrialization: the lack of industrial fuels, especially coal; poor transportation (no roads, canals or railways; only rivers and coastal shipping); limited amounts of capital, domestic or foreign, and a rudimentary banking system; outdated commercial legislation hindering the establishment of joint stock companies; a labour market dominated by slavery; low levels of education and the almost total absence of scientific or technical training; the small size of the market for manufactured goods in a society in which the majority were either slaves or free poor with only

[26] D. C. M. Platt, *Latin America and British trade 1806–1914* (London, 1972), 30.

limited purchasing power; the self-sufficiency of many plantations; the absence of a national market (only loosely articulated regional and local markets); the prevalence of *laissez-faire* ideas amongst both Brazilian landowners and the merchants of the coastal cities; and the failure of government in any way to encourage the growth of industry.

A more direct consequence of the 15 per cent maximum tariff on British imports (indeed *all* imports because of Brazil's most favoured nation treaties with her other trading partners) was the strict limit it imposed on Brazilian government revenues, 80 per cent of which by the 1840s came from customs duties. (See Table 4.) Government expenditure in this period – a period of external and internal wars – was on average 40 per cent above government revenue. The amount of paper money in circulation was therefore expanded. And further loans were raised in London in 1839 and 1843.

Thus the Anglo-Brazilian commercial treaty of 1827 which, like the anti-slave trade treaty of 1826, had been negotiated during the period of Brazil's weakness and dependence on Britain following her declaration of independence from Portugal and negotiations for its recognition, proved increasingly irksome to Brazilians. It irritated in particular the conservatives who were in power, as we have seen, during the years 1837–40 and 1841–4. In the first place, they resented the extra-territorial privileges it conferred on Britain, especially the right to appoint judges conservators, which they considered incompatible with Brazilian sovereignty. Secondly, the treaty was with justification held largely responsible for Brazil's not inconsiderable financial difficulties. And by the 1840s there were the first signs of an awareness in some circles that, by providing protection for home manufacturing, higher tariffs could be an instrument of economic change as well as a valuable source of revenue. Certainly the low duties on British goods contrasted most unfavourably with the virtually prohibitive duties on Brazilian produce entering the British market. Unless Britain modified its commercial policy and lowered duties on Brazilian sugar and coffee, permitting a more balanced trade between Britain and Brazil, there was every reason for Brazil to seek to raise duties on British manufactured goods. An early attempt to revise the 1827 treaty and put Anglo-Brazilian commercial relations on a more equal footing – the Barbacena mission to London in 1836 – had failed. The treaty, however, was due to expire in November 1842, fifteen years after its ratification, or so it seemed. (In the event Britain invoked an article of the treaty under which it could continue in force until

Table 4 *Customs Duties and total Government*
Revenues, 1830–50

Years	Rio's customs as % of total customs	Total customs as % of total revenues
1830/31	44	47
1831/32	54	42
1832/33	55	57
1833/34	55	59
1834/35	53	50
1835/36	53	59
1836/37	53	77
1837/38	54	74
1838/39	55	78
1839/40	57	78
1840/41	58	84
1841/42	60	82
1842/43	56	80
1843/44	54	79
1844/45	50	78
1845/46	51	80
1846/47	49	78
1847/48	49	78
1848/49	54	79
1849/50	49	81
1850/51	50	82

Source: Amaro Cavalcanti, *Resenha financeira do ex-Império
do Brasil em 1889* (Rio de Janeiro, 1900), 330.

November 1844.) There was widespread feeling throughout Brazil that it should not be renewed without radical revision.

In Britain there was at this time growing pressure for free trade and, in particular, for lower duties on imported foodstuffs. In the case of sugar there was one complicating factor: slavery. Brazilian (and Cuban) sugar was slave-grown. The West India interest could defend colonial preference on more respectable grounds than economic self-interest. The abandonment of fiscal discrimination against slave-grown sugar would, besides ruining the West Indies, stimulate production, and therefore the demand for slaves, in Brazil and Cuba and undermine Britain's efforts to bring about the abolition of the slave trade and slavery throughout the world. At the end of 1841 the British government decided to submit proposals for a new Anglo-Brazilian commercial treaty similar to the one in existence (with its favourable tariffs on British manufactures) but with important and striking additions: Britain would reduce import duties on

Brazilian sugar; in return Brazil as well as fulfilling existing treaty commitments to suppress the slave trade would declare free all children born of slave mothers at an early date (to be determined by negotiation) and consider the emancipation of all slaves at the earliest possible moment.

A special mission to Brazil in 1842 led by Henry Ellis found both the press and public opinion in Rio 'absurdly violent and impertinent' in their opposition to 'enslaving Brazil with treaties'. It did not take Ellis long to realize that his principal objective – to persuade the Brazilian government to take the steps necessary to make the abolition of slavery in Brazil certain 'at no distant period' – was 'quite out of the question'.[27] Without a Brazilian concession on slavery there could be no British concession on sugar. And without the latter there could be no renewal of the existing commercial treaty. When he consulted British merchants in Rio Ellis found to his surprise that they no longer attached much importance either to their judicial privileges in Brazil or to the 15 per cent preferential tariff; these had been useful in the past when Britain was establishing its position in the Brazilian market but, provided there was no positive discrimination against British goods, Britain's economic superiority over its nearest rivals would ensure the continuation of Britain's pre-eminence in Brazil. Ellis, however, could not even secure a treaty which simply guaranteed that British merchants and their goods would be treated on a par with those of other nations. In return for most favoured nation status for British manufactures, the Brazilian negotiators demanded that Brazilian sugar, coffee, tobacco and other agricultural produce should enter Britain at duties no more than 10 per cent higher than those levied on colonial produce and where possible on equal terms. As for the abolition of slavery, Honório Hermeto Carneiro Leão, conservative Foreign Minister at the time, made it absolutely clear that this was 'a question for the future and not for the present'. Negotiations broke down in March 1843, having generated in Brazil a fresh wave of ill-feeling against Britain. They were renewed in London later in the year, but again without success. At the insistence of Brazil the 1827 treaty was thus terminated in November 1844.

There was a certain amount of apprehension in British manufacturing and commercial circles about the consequences for British trade of the failure to replace the 1827 treaty with at least a most favoured nation treaty. In December 1843, anticipating the ending of the treaty, the

[27] Quotations in Bethell, *Abolition*, 232.

conservative government in Brazil appointed a Tariff Commission to prepare new tariffs on imported goods and gave it instructions that revealed a new concern for the protection of national industries against foreign competition. The highest tariffs (60 per cent) were to be imposed on articles that were or could be produced inside the country. Machines for the infant textile industry, on the other hand, were to be free of all duties. (Decree of 17 May 1843.) Then, in February 1844, the liberals returned to power. The new tariffs announced by the Minister of Finance, Manuel Alves Branco, in August 1844 were somewhat less protectionist. Only tobacco and related products were taxed at 60 per cent. Cotton cloth and thread were taxed at only 20 per cent, which had little or no adverse effect on British imports. (Decree of 12 August 1844.) National industries, however, continued to be favoured with free imports of machines and raw materials, and with exemption from military service for their employees. (Decree of 8 August 1846.) And towards the end of the decade in a further effort to diversify the economy, the government began to lend money to industrialists such as Irineu E. de Sousa, the future barão de Mauá, who was to become the most dynamic businessman of the empire. (Decree of 2 October 1848.) Limited as they were, these measures indicate a broadening of state action and an attempt to diversify and expand economic activity in Brazil. Nevertheless, the main purpose of the increase in most tariffs from 15 per cent to 20 per cent or 30 per cent in 1844 was fiscal rather than protectionist. Government revenues increased 33 per cent from 1842/3 to 1844/5. And by 1852/3 they were double what they had been in 1842/3.[28]

For the Conservative government in Britain the ending of the 1827 treaty in 1844 had one positive advantage. The treaty had guaranteed to Brazilian sugar the benefit of any reduction in the duties on foreign sugar entering the British market. Sir Robert Peel, who had already in two stages reduced the duties on coffee from 15*d.* per lb foreign and 6*d.* per lb colonial to 6*d.* foreign and 4*d.* colonial (an example of British inconsistency – if coffee, why not sugar?), now lowered the duty on *free-grown* foreign sugar (from Java, for example) to 34*s.* per cwt while leaving that on slave-grown sugar at 63*s.* And a year later the duty on colonial sugar was reduced to 14*s.* per cwt and that on foreign free-grown sugar to 23*s.* per cwt. In 1846, however, following the repeal of the Corn Laws and the fall of Peel's government, the Whig Prime Minister Lord John Russell proposed the reduction of the differentials in favour of colonial sugar

[28] Amaro Cavalcanti, *Resenha financeira do ex-Império do Brasil em 1889* (Rio de Janeiro, 1900), 328.

over five years (later amended to eight years) until the final equalization
of the duties on sugar 'of all sorts, of whatever growth and whencesoever
imported'. (The duties on coffee were also to be equalized by 1851.)
British discrimination against Brazilian sugar – and coffee – was thus
gradually ended in the years after 1846. The Sugar Duties Act undoubtedly stimulated the sugar industry in Brazil, mainly in the north-east.
Production in Pernambuco, for example, rose from 42,000 tons in 1844/5
to 51,000 tons in 1846/7 and 73,000 tons in 1848/9.[29] Sugar's share of total
exports rose from 22 per cent in 1841–5 to 28 per cent in 1846–50.
Exports of coffee also continued to rise; they were 40 per cent higher in
1846–50 than in 1841–5, but in the case of coffee the lowering of British
import duties had only a marginal impact on Brazilian production. As
some British abolitionists had feared, the demand for slaves in Brazil
intensified during the late 1840s, although there were many reasons for
this besides the ending of discriminatory duties on slave-grown produce
entering the British market. And the Whig government in which Lord
Palmerston was Foreign Secretary having, as they put it, abandoned the
policy of 'fiscal coercion' had not the slightest intention of giving up the
struggle to end the slave trade by means of 'physical coercion'.

The question of the Brazilian slave trade which continued long after it
had been declared illegal by treaty with Britain in 1826 (effective from
March 1830) and by Brazilian legislation (November 1831) dominated
relations between Brazil and Britain during the 1830s and 1840s. In 1831,
and several years after, very few slaves were in fact imported into Brazil,
largely because, in anticipation of the abolition of the trade, 175,000 had
been imported during the three years 1827–30. (For slave imports into
Brazil after 1831, see Table 5.) There was a temporary falling off in
demand which was reflected in low prices. The end of the legal slave
trade coincided, however, with the rapid expansion of coffee throughout
the Paraíba valley. From the outset coffee *fazendas* were worked by
slaves, most of them imported from Africa. Slaves cleared the forests,
planted the bushes, harvested and processed the beans, maintained the
plantation and served in the Big House. Moreover, even when a slave
labour force was established, the rate of slave mortality in Brazil was so
high that it required regular replenishment from across the Atlantic.
'America', wrote the French émigré, Charles Auguste Taunay, in his

---

[29] David Albert Denslow, Jr, 'Sugar production in Northeastern Brazil and Cuba, 1858–1908'
(unpublished Ph.D. thesis, Yale University, 1974), 9.

Table 5 *Slave Imports into Brazil,*
1831–1855

Years	Slaves	Years	Slaves
1831	138	1844	22,849
1832	116	1845	19,453
1833	1,233	1846	50,324
1834	749	1847	56,172
1835	745	1848	60,000
1836	4,966	1849	54,061
1837	35,209	1850	22,856
1838	40,256	1851	3,287
1839	42,182	1852	800
1840	20,796	1853	—
1841	13,804	1854	—
1842	17,435	1855	90
1843	19,095		

Source: Foreign Office memorandum, 4 August 1864, in Leslie Bethell, *The abolition of the Brazilian slave trade* (Cambridge, 1970) 388–93, Appendix: estimate of slaves imported into Brazil, 1831–55.

Manual do Agricultor Brazileiro (1839), 'devours the blacks. If continued importation were not supplying them, the race would shortly disappear from our midst.'[30] The demand for slaves in Brazil, therefore, especially in the coffee regions of the centre-south, soon revived, prices rose and the Brazilian slave trade was gradually reorganized after 1830 on an illegal – and highly profitable – basis.

Successive Brazilian governments under the regency proved unwilling or unable to enforce the 1831 anti-slave trade law. They were for the most part weak and short-lived, lacking adequate financial, military or naval resources and preoccupied with political and constitutional issues and the various provincial revolts which threatened to destroy the unity and stability of the country. Law enforcement at the local level was in any case in the hands of elected justices of the peace and officers of the National Guard, few of whom were above accepting bribes and most of whom were themselves landowners or closely linked by family and interest to the landed class which had a stake in the revival and expansion of the illegal slave trade. With rare exceptions they connived at illegal slave landings. When a slave trader was apprehended he was brought

[30] Quoted in Stanley J. Stein, *Vassouras. A Brazilian coffee county, 1850–1900* (Cambridge, Mass., 1957), 227.

before a local jury and invariably acquitted. Once clear of the coast illegally imported slaves were beyond the reach of the law; *fazendeiros de café* and *senhores de engenho* exercised virtually supreme authority on their own estates.

For one short period only, in 1835, was there a discernible reaction against the slave trade. This followed the major insurrection of the Malês (African Muslims) – the most serious urban slave uprising of the nineteenth century – in Bahia on 24/25 January 1835. It was in the event easily repressed, though with great violence. Around 40 blacks, slaves and freedmen, were killed. Hundreds were prosecuted and punished. Eighteen were sentenced to death, of whom 5 were actually executed. Other sentences included deportation to Africa, forced labour and physical punishment: some slaves were punished with up to 1,000 lashes. As a direct consequence of events in Bahia a drastic measure was introduced in 1835: all slaves who killed or gravely injured their masters or overseers would be punished by death. The requirement under the Criminal Code that where the sentence was death the verdicts of juries should be unanimous was changed; a two-thirds majority was sufficient and the sentence was to be carried out immediately, without appeal. Thus, internal security and white domination were quickly reinforced. Even so, the Bahia slave revolt, combined with threats of similiar revolts elsewhere, served to remind white Brazilians of the dangers inherent in the annual importation, legal or illegal, of thousands of African slaves. In the opinion of the liberal editor Evaristo da Veiga each new slave introduced into the country was another barrel of gunpowder added to the Brazilian mine.[31] And even when the fear of slave rebellion receded, the fear of 'Africanization' remained.

Nevertheless, the illegal slave trade gradually established itself during the mid-1830s with little or no interference from the Brazilian local authorities along the coast, until it eventually reached and passed its pre–1826 level. By the end of 1836 slave prices were falling for the first time in five years. The conservative government of September 1837 headed by Bernardo Pereira de Vasconcelos, a vociferous campaigner against the 1826 treaty and the law of 1831, resisted the growing demand from *municípios* in Rio de Janeiro, Minas Gerais and São Paulo for the repeal of anti-slave trade legislation, but made no effort to enforce it. And most of the limited anti-slave trade measures adopted by previous liberal governments were abandoned. Even ministers known to oppose the trade could

[31] *Aurora Fluminense*, 20, 27 March, 4 April 1835.

see little point in instituting proceedings against those involved in it since, as the Brazilian Foreign Minister told the British chargé d'affaires in February 1838, 'it may be safely predicted from experience, that no court of justice will be found to give sentence against them'.[32] During the three years 1837–9 at least 35,000 and probably as many as 45,000 slaves per annum were illegally imported into Brazil, mainly from the Congo, Angola and Mozambique. 80–90 per cent of them were landed along the coast to the north and south of Rio de Janeiro between Campos and Santos and in the capital itself, the majority clearly destined for the coffee *fazendas* of the Paraíba valley.

Brazilian governments before and after 1837 not only resisted persistent pressure from the British legation in Rio (which virtually assumed the role of an abolitionist society in Brazil) to introduce and enforce more effective anti-slave trade legislation, but also refused to concede to Britain the powers it needed if the British navy, particularly the West African squadron, were to suppress the trade on the high seas. In 1831 Brazil had agreed that the Anglo-Portuguese treaty of 1817, under which British naval vessels had the right to visit, search and, when their suspicions were confirmed, detain ships illegally trading in slaves between Africa and Brazil (at that time north of the equator only), should be extended to cover the entire Brazilian slave trade now that it was illegal south of the equator as well and should continue in force for fifteen years from March 1830. Captured Brazilian ships were to be sent for adjudication before Anglo-Brazilian mixed commissions in Sierra Leone or Rio de Janeiro. The treaty of 1817, however, lacked 'equipment' and 'break up' clauses, which were vital to the effectiveness of the West African squadron; that is to say, ships equipped for the slave trade but without slaves actually on board could not be visited, searched and captured, and slave vessels condemned by the mixed commission could not be destroyed to prevent their returning to the trade. All negotiations with Brazil for the strengthening of the treaty – and they were carried on year after year – ended in failure. Yet, even if they had been successful and if as a result the anti-slave trade operations of British warships had been less circumscribed, the West African squadron in the 1830s lacked the necessary numbers – and, it should be said, the speed – to prevent the growth of the Brazilian trade. At the same time a stronger maritime police force would have been similarly frustrated.

In 1839 the Whig government in Britain, and more particularly the

[32] Quoted in Bethell, *Abolition*, 84.

Foreign Secretary Lord Palmerston, adopted tougher measures to curb the Brazilian slave trade which was now growing at an alarming rate. These included: the so-called Palmerston Act which unilaterally extended the powers of the British navy to intercept slavers flying the Portuguese flag, with or without slaves on board, and to send them to British vice-admiralty courts for condemnation; confirmation of the ruling by British mixed commissioners in both Rio and Freetown that the treaty of 1817 as it stood, taken in conjunction with the treaty of 1826, permitted British cruisers to search and seize Brazilian vessels intending to trade in slaves; the strengthening of the West African and Cape squadrons which still had the primary responsibility for the suppression of the slave trade; the decision to allow British warships on anti-slave trade patrol to cruise inshore, to enter African waters and rivers and to blockade key points on the African coast. (The South American squadron also became more active at this time, but there were relatively few ships available to patrol the Brazilian coast and they had to be careful to avoid unnecessary interference with legitimate coastal trade and to show some token respect for Brazilian sovereignty in Brazilian territorial waters. Even so clashes with the local Brazilian authorities were not always avoided.) Partly as a result of these British initiatives – and a marked increase in the number of slave ships captured by the British navy – slave imports into Brazil during the three years from the middle of 1839 to the middle of 1842 fell to less than half their recent level (see Table 5 above). The somewhat more determined effort to restrict the slave trade which some Brazilian authorities made during the liberal interregnum (July 1840–March 1841) may have contributed to its relative decline. More significant was the temporary glut on the market following the huge imports of the late thirties.

It was against this background of reduced slave imports in the early forties and the recognition by some, at least, that the slave trade, indeed slavery itself, was in the long run doomed that the conservative government of March 1841 (a government, as we have seen, closely tied to coffee interests in Rio province) began to concern itself with alternative sources of labour. The budget allocation for European immigration had been terminated in 1830, and during the regency almost nothing had been done to foster immigration. Even fewer immigrants arrived in the 1830s – none in fact during the first half of the decade – than in the 1820s. (See Table 6.) Those who did come did not choose to travel thousands of miles in order to work alongside African slaves on sugar or coffee

Table 6 *European Immigrants entering*
Brazil, 1820–55

Year	Immigrants	Year	Immigrants
1820	1,790	1838	396
1821	0	1839	389
1822	0	1840	269
1823	0	1841	555
1824	468	1842	5,568
1825	909	1843	694
1826	828	1844	0
1827	1,088	1845	2,364
1828	2,060	1846	435
1829	2,412	1847	2,350
1830	117	1848	28
1831	0	1849	40
1832	0	1850	2,072
1833	0	1851	4,425
1834	0	1852	2,731
1835	0	1853	10,935
1836	1,280	1854	18,646
1837	604	1855	11,798

Source: Computed from several sources in George P. Browne, 'Government immigration policy in imperial Brazil, 1822–1870', unpublished Ph.D. thesis, Catholic University of America, 1972, 328.

plantations. A budget allocation for immigration was reintroduced for 1841–2. But this was not enough. The fundamental problem was how to keep such free, immigrant labour as could be enticed to Brazil on coffee plantations organized for slave labour when, in the first place, vast expanses of public land were freely available (i.e. how to prevent an immigrant from becoming a landowner by the simple process of occupying public land), and, secondly, there was competition from the periphery of the coffee region for scarce labour.

In August 1842 a project drafted by Vasconcelos and modelled on E. G. Wakefield's plans for the colonization of Australia, first published in *A Letter from Sydney* (1829), was put before the Council of State. Its purpose was twofold. First, landownership would be regulated and regularized. The system of *sesmarias* (royal grants of public land) had been terminated in 1822–3 and not replaced. As a result, private land titles, always confused, were now in a state of chaos, which undermined the authority of the central government and promoted local conflict and violence. *Sesmarias* (most of which had expanded beyond their original legal boundaries) would be revalidated and *posses* (the landholdings, large and small, of squatters) would be legalized. Properties would be measured, registered and sometimes reduced in size, all at the cost of the owners. Secondly, Vasconcelos's project aimed to promote the immigration of *trabalhadores pobres, moços e robustos* and at the same time tie them to the coffee plantations. Public land would in future only be sold and at prices deliberately set above the market value. If land had to be bought and was made expensive, so the argument went, immigrants (who already had to repay part of the cost of their transportation) would be forced to work a few years before they could buy their own plot. And the income from the sale of public land together with an annual land tax would generate the funds necessary to subsidize the importation of free labour.

A bill along these lines was introduced into the Chamber by Rodrigues Tôrres in June 1843. 'We want', he said, 'to keep free workers, who come to us from other parts of the world, from being able to arrive in Brazil and, instead of working for the landowners for some time at least . . . finding crown lands immediately.'[33] The bill was strongly supported by the representatives of the coffee growers of the Paraíba valley, the main beneficiaries. But deputies from other provinces were not convinced of the urgency of the need for European immigrants and were reluctant to pay the price the initiative, largely for the benefit of Rio province, would cost. Reaction was particularly strong among mineiro and paulista deputies. In Minas Gerais and São Paulo there were many *posseiros*, owners of vast and non-legalized tracts of land. They objected to the land registration – and its cost. And the land tax caused an uproar. Some deputies predicted civil war if the bill were passed. On 16 September 1843 it was nevertheless approved with minor amendments by the Chamber in which the conservatives had a large majority and was sent to the Senate. But there it remained throughout the *quinqüênio liberal* until at the end of the decade another conservative cabinet, which included Rodrigues Tôrres, managed to pass it into law, although only after introducing important modifications.

In the meantime the slave trade had already begun to revive once again after several years of reduced activity. And in March 1845, on the advice first of the foreign affairs sub-committee of the Council of State (consist-

---

[33] Quoted in Warren Dean, 'Latifundia and land policy in nineteenth-century Brazil', *Hispanic American Historical Review*, 51 (November, 1971), 614.

ing of three leading conservatives, the Marquês de Monte Alegre (José da Costa Carvalho), Vasconcelos and Honório) and then of a full meeting of the Council presided over by the young emperor, the Brazilian government fifteen years after 1830 chose to terminate the anti-slave trade treaty of 1817 under which the British navy exercised the right of search and the Anglo-Brazilian mixed commissions adjudicated on captured Brazilian vessels. It was not simply a question of freeing the slave trade from British interference in the interest of the Brazilian coffee planter. (The Brazilians insisted – not very convincingly – that left to themselves they could and would suppress the trade.) In pursuing the slave traders the British had acted arrogantly and at times violently. The continuation of the trade was now linked in the public mind with national sovereignty as well as economic survival. The treaty – and any attempt to negotiate a new treaty – was extremely unpopular. As early as October 1842 Justiniano José da Rocha had written in *O Brasil*: 'If there is today a generalized and highly popular idea in the country it is that England is our most treacherous and persistent enemy.'[34]

The Conservative government in London was in no mood to abandon the struggle against the Brazilian slave trade. The Prime Minister Peel and the Foreign Secretary Lord Aberdeen were already under attack from Palmerston for allowing the trade to recover after 1842. And having failed to renew or replace the commercial treaty of 1827 (see above) they could not afford a second retreat in the face of pressure from Brazil, a weak and formerly dependent state, particularly since by placing it 'beyond the reach of the only means of repression which have hitherto been found effective', it was bound to lead to a further increase in the slave trade. On the other hand, an opportunity to discard the treaty of 1817 which had always been less than satisfactory and had given rise to interminable wrangles was not entirely unwelcome – provided it was possible to find an equal, and preferably more effective, alternative. Now the treaty of 1826 remained in full force but lacked any specific provision for search and seizure. Under its first article, however, the Brazilian slave trade was to be 'deemed and treated as piracy'. And it was in the word piracy that the British found what they needed. In August 1845 the Slave Trade (Brazil) Act, known in Brazil as *o bill Aberdeen*, authorized the British navy to treat Brazilian slave ships as pirate vessels and send them for condemnation in British vice-admiralty courts.

The Aberdeen Act was based upon an interpretation of the 1826 treaty

[34] *O Brasil*, 1 October 1842.

which was and remained controversial even in England. (In his *Explorations of the Highlands of the Brazil* (1869) Richard Burton called it 'one of the greatest insults which a strong ever offered to a weak people'.) News of the passage of the Act inevitably produced in Rio, the British minister reported, '(an) excited state of public feeling . . . argument, virulence, invective in the public press'.[35] Palmerston who returned to the Foreign Office in June 1846 was not known for his sensitivity to foreign opinion. The Aberdeen Act was in his view a less drastic measure than the circumstances justified. He was, moreover, sensitive to the charge made by critics of the government at home that the Sugar Duties Act which the Whigs had introduced would undo all the good work of the Aberdeen Act. If the Brazilian slave trade continued to grow, he warned, Britain would resort to 'still sharper measures of coercion'.[36]

The five years 1845–50 were the most successful the West African and Cape squadrons had ever known. Over 400 ships engaged in the Brazilian slave trade alone were captured and sent to vice-admiralty courts (half of them to St Helena, the rest to Sierra Leone and the Cape of Good Hope). Yet the slave trade grew. Indeed, during the late forties, with demand and therefore prices high, it exceeded all previous levels: at least 50–60,000 slaves per annum were imported into Brazil, 1846–9. (See Table 5 above.) Two-thirds were landed along the 200-mile stretch of coast north and south of Rio, the rest in the capital itself, where it was still possible openly to visit auctions of newly imported slaves, in Bahia and Pernambuco, and, a new development, south of Santos, especially near Paranaguá. The trade was more highly organized than ever. For the first time steamships were employed – their engines 'the best England could manufacture'. The trade had become big business and traders like Manuel Pinto da Fonseca and José Bernardino de Sá who ten years earlier had served in small provision stores now commanded impressive financial resources and wielded considerable political influence. 'They are the nabobs of the Brazils', a British naval officer wrote. 'They form the dazzling class of the parvenus millionaires.'[37] In January 1847 barão de Cairú, the Brazilian Foreign Minister, is reported by James Hudson, the British minister, to have said: '[Fonseca] and scores of minor slave dealers go to the Court – sit at the tables of the wealthiest and most respectable citizens – have seats in the Chamber as our Representatives and have a voice even in the Council of State. They are increasing in vigilance, perseverance, audacity – those whom they dare not put out of

---

[35] Quoted in Bethell, *Abolition*, 265.   [36] *Ibid.* 295.   [37] *Ibid.* 289.

the way, they buy . . . with such men to deal with, what am I to do, what can I do?'[38]

No liberal government in Brazil between 1844 and 1848 was sufficiently strong nor in power long enough to conceive, much less secure parliamentary support for, and execute, new anti-slave trade measures. The more far-sighted political leaders were disturbed by the proportions the trade had now reached, even if in some cases they were primarily concerned at the consequences for Brazilian society of the continued importation of 'milhares de defensores das instituições de Haiti'. They were also conscious that a country whose flag was not respected on the high seas and some of whose laws were enforced by foreign agents could hardly regard itself as fully independent and sovereign. The majority of Brazilian politicians in the Council of State, the Senate and the Chamber, however, positively favoured the slave trade (and in some cases as planters and slave-owners themselves were indirectly engaged in it) or else, in view of its importance to the Brazilian economy, preferred to leave well alone. In 1848 the last of the liberal administrations led by Francisco de Paula Sousa e Melo finally came round to the idea of introducing new legislation into the Chamber, but discussion of a bill to replace the law of 1831 was deferred until the following session not due to begin until January 1850. It was left to the conservative government which took power in September 1848 to grasp this, the most prickly of all Brazilian nettles.

In Britain during the late forties there was mounting opposition, principally among northern manufacturers and merchants and Free Traders, but also among the abolitionists themselves, to Britain's self-appointed role as the world's anti-slave trade policeman. The suppression system was expensive; it had an adverse effect on political relations, and therefore commercial relations, with, for example, Brazil; and it had failed. Britain in the words of William Hutt, M.P. for Gateshead, should 'leave to a higher authority . . . the moral government of the world'. Even *The Times* in October 1849 questioned whether 'the difference between what the slave trade is and what it would be if our squadron were withdrawn is worth what it costs us to keep the squadron where it is'.[39] The leaders of both Whigs and Peelites – Palmerston, Peel, Aberdeen, Russell – were, however, determined to resist any attempt to weaken much less dismantle the system for the suppression of the slave trade based on British naval power. What the 'coercionists' badly needed

[38] *Ibid.* 290.   [39] *The Times*, 24 October 1849.

was a signal success and what better than the final suppression of the Brazilian slave trade. There were rumours in 1849 that Palmerston was preparing to take more extreme measures and for the first time on the Brazilian side of the Atlantic. The decade ended without a solution to the slave trade question, but it was becoming increasingly clear, both in Brazil and in Britain, that a solution would not be long delayed.

In September 1848, after four and a half years of Liberal rule, the Emperor Dom Pedro II invited Pedro de Araújo Lima, Visconde de Olinda, the former regent (1837–40), to form a Conservative cabinet. Almost immediately on their return to power the Conservatives were faced with a liberal armed revolt in the provinces, as they had been in 1841–2. This time the trouble arose not in São Paulo and Minas Gerais, now firmly tied to the central government in Rio, but in Pernambuco. What proved to be the last major provincial uprising of the period erupted there towards the end of 1848. Known as the *Praieira* from Rua da Praia, where a liberal newspaper was published, it presented some features which were common to earlier provincial rebellions, but also some that were specific to Pernambuco.

At first sight, the socio-economic structure of Pernambuco was not very different from that of Bahia, for instance. In both cases, a large urban centre was surrounded by a sugar belt controlled by a rich oligarchy of planters. On the periphery of this belt – and beyond it – a rich variety of lesser planters, farmers and cattle growers could be found. The tradition of political struggle in the two provinces, however, was quite different. In Bahia, the conservative Recôncavo was always able to keep in check the urban radicalism of the capital, while the vast interior remained quiet. In Pernambuco, ever since the rebellions of 1817 and 1824, both urban radicals and the planter class as a whole had been involved in provincial politics. Even the rural poor of the periphery had been mobilized in the War of the Cabanos (1832–5). The division of political forces between liberals and conservatives in the late 1830s and early 1840s resulted in complicated alliances in Pernambuco. The sugar oligarchy of the Zona da Mata split, with the prominent Cavalcanti clan forming the liberal wing and being joined by urban journalists and agitators and by landowners in the periphery of the Mata.

With the fall of the conservative government in Rio in 1844, the liberal Praia rose to power in Pernambuco. Making use of the legislation introduced by the conservatives, Praia presidents made sweeping changes in the police and National Guard, substituting their supporters for the conservatives. When a further shift in national politics – the formation of the conservative cabinet of Araújo Lima, himself per-nambucano – brought the conservatives back to power in Pernambuco in 1848, they tried to dismantle the political base built by the *praieiros*. It was this which sparked off liberal armed rebellion in November 1848, although the situation had been tense since June (when anti-Portuguese riots had broken out in Recife leaving five Portuguese dead and another forty wounded). The struggle took place mostly in the southern periph-ery of the Mata, and in the so-called Dry Mata to the north of Recife. Twenty sugar *engenhos* were the basis for the recruitment and provision-ing of the liberal troops. In February 1849 the northern and southern armies of the rebels – some 2,500 troops – joined forces to attack Recife. But they failed to gain the support of the urban populace and were defeated, leaving 500 dead in the streets. The fight continued in the interior for some time and guerrilla bands survived until early 1850 under the protection of planters, but without posing a serious threat to the government.

The most radical of the rebels' demands – federalism, abolition of the moderating power, the expulsion of the Portuguese and nationalization of the retail trade and, a novelty, universal franchise – were formulated by urban leaders, particularly Borges da Fonseca, Pedro I's old republi-can opponent. However, despite the considerable impact made by the French revolution of 1848, a republican government was not included in the demands. And, once again, slavery remained untouched. Despite the intense urban agitation, the struggle ended up being mostly limited to a dispute among sectors of the landowning class. The reasons for this division are not entirely clear. Certainly, there was resentment against the small group of families that controlled the fertile lands of the humid Mata, although the Cavalcantis themselves controlled one-third of the *engenhos* in this area. The British Sugar Duties Act (1846) may also have played a part. While as a direct consequence of the Act sugar production in Pernambuco increased by 70 per cent between 1844/5 and 1848/9, as we have seen, prices went down from US $78 per ton to US $64. The richer and long-established sugar producers were certainly better pre-pared to face the difficulties of overproduction. Smaller producers, and those who had abandoned cotton or cattle for sugar attracted by the initial increase in prices, were bound to be the ones most hurt. Also the expansion in sugar production led to encroachment by the big landowners on the land of smaller planters, squatters and free peasants, turning their sympathies toward the *praieiros*.

The defeat of the liberal Praieira in 1848–9, together perhaps with the defeat of liberals all over Europe during these years, reinforced the conservative government in Rio de Janeiro and consolidated conservative power throughout Brazil. The result of the elections for the Chamber of Deputies in 1849 was virtually a clean sweep for the conservatives; the liberals won only one seat. And in 1850 the conservatives put the final touch to the process of political centralization they had initiated in 1837: the National Guard was brought under tighter central government control. The elective principle established in 1831 was eliminated. Officers were now to be appointed either by provincial presidents or directly by the central government, and they in turn appointed their non-commissioned officers.[40] Moreover, officers were required to have the income of electors (which was now 400 milreis, about £46), and had to pay for their commissions a sum equal to one month's salary of the equivalent rank in the army. This in practice limited access to the officer corps to a minority among the guardsmen. At first sight, this measure could be interpreted as a move against local bosses. But it would be more accurate to see it, like other centralizing laws, as a compromise between the central government and the landowners. It indicated, on the one hand, that the government was not able to maintain order in the interior without the help of the landowners; on the other hand, it revealed the incapacity of the latter to solve their disputes without the arbitration of the government. The reform represented a further move to co-opt the ruling sectors into the political system in exchange for the recognition and legitimation of their social power.

The Brazilian government which came to power in September 1848, especially after October 1849 when the Marquês de Monte Alegre replaced Olinda as president of the Council of Ministers, proved to be by far the strongest since independence. Like the conservative governments of 1837–40 and, more especially 1841–4, it represented an alliance between, on the one hand, state bureaucrats and magistrates and, on the other, landowners, above all coffee *fazendeiros* in Rio de Janeiro province. Its dominant figures were Paulino Soares de Sousa (Foreign

---

[40] At the same time a decree of 6 September 1850 regulated promotion in the army on the basis of merit and length of service. According to John Schulz, 'The Brazilian army in politics, 1850–1894' (unpublished Ph.D. dissertation, Princeton University, 1973), 53–8, in eliminating promotion by personal influence and status, this was a crucial step in the professionalization of the army.

Affairs) and Joaquim José Rodrigues Tôrres (Finance) together with Eusébio de Queiroz Coutinho Matoso da Câmara (Justice), who had been born in Angola, the son of a judge, and who had married into a rich 'capitalist' family in Rio. In the Council of State the government had the powerful support of, among others, Bernardo Pereira de Vasconcelos (until his death from yellow fever in May 1850) and Honório Hermeto Carneiro Leão.

All these men, except Eusébio, had been prominent members of previous conservative governments which in defiance of Britain had permitted the illegal slave trade to flourish. Yet this government, like to some extent the last liberal government, seemed ready to get to grips with this most intractable of problems. Apart from Spain and its colony Cuba, Brazil was now isolated internationally on this question. Before long Brazilian agriculture would have to adapt itself to the end of the slave trade. And if the Brazilians did not want Britain to put a stop to the trade – and there was every evidence that Britain remained more determined than ever to do so, even if it meant transferring its anti-slave trade naval operations to the Brazilian coast – they would one day have to suppress it themselves. Moreover, no self-respecting Brazilian government with any claim to authority could permit the continuation of such widespread contempt for the law. There was one further consideration: Brazil was increasingly anxious about the situation in the strategically sensitive Río de la Plata region where the independence of Uruguay and the territorial integrity of the empire itself were believed to be threatened by Juan Manuel de Rosas. In the event of war with Buenos Aires – and the ground was being prepared for an alliance with the anti-Rosas faction in Uruguay and General Urquiza in Entre Ríos – Brazil would require at least the benevolent neutrality of Britain and that could only be secured by a settlement of the slave trade question. Thus, in a number of respects the larger interests of the Brazilian state were beginning to demand that some action be taken against the Brazilian slave trade. Towards the end of 1849 the Minister of Justice advised the Rio police chief that new measures to end the slave trade were being prepared and would be introduced into the Chamber the following year.

At about the same time a number of British ships of the South American squadron were transferred from the Río de la Plata to the coast of Brazil specifically for anti-slave trade duties. In terms of the number of slaves captured, January 1850 was the most successful month the British navy had ever had on the Brazilian side of the Atlantic. Before the

Brazilian government was able to take any action – in May in his *Relatório*
to the Chamber Eusébio de Queiroz promised to bring forward a bill –
Britain itself then took what proved to be a decisive step leading to the
final suppression of the Brazilian slave trade. On 22 April 1850, a month
after 154 members of the House of Commons – almost twice as many as
in a similar debate in 1848 – had voted against the continuation of
Britain's efforts to suppress the foreign slave trade by force, the Foreign
Office advised the Admiralty that under the Aberdeen Act of 1845
British warships need not confine their anti-slave trade operations to the
high seas: they could enter Brazilian territorial waters and even Brazilian
ports. On 22 June Rear Admiral Reynolds, commander of the South
American squadron, instructed his ships accordingly. There followed a
series of incidents up and down the Brazilian coast of which the most
serious was an exchange of shots between HMS *Cormorant* (Captain
Schomberg) and the fort at Paranaguá.

When news of the incident at Paranaguá reached Rio it provoked a
major political crisis. There was some talk of war. But Brazil had no
moral or material means to resist this blatant violation of its sovereignty.
Moreover British 'hostilities' if continued and extended would paralyse
trade, damage the economy, undermine state finances, inflame the slave
population, threaten internal stability and unity and weaken Brazil's
position in the coming confrontation with Rosas. (The scale of the recent
naval action and the degree of deliberate planning which lay behind it
was exaggerated.) On 11 July a meeting of the Council of State decided
that the Brazilian government had no choice but to push through its own
plans to curb the slave trade even though they would appear, as indeed to
a large extent they were, a capitulation to British aggression. It was too
late now for spontaneous action. On 12 July Eusébio finally introduced
into the Chamber his bill to strengthen the 1831 law, in particular by
establishing special maritime courts to deal with cases of slave trading
which was declared to be equivalent to piracy. It passed quickly through
the Chamber and the Senate, and became law on 4 September 1850. The
emperor, now 25 years old and beginning to play a more decisive role in
government, resisted a last-minute bid by conservative diehards to force
a change of ministry.

The Brazilian government's task was made somewhat easier by the
fact that the slave trade was in a considerably weakened state in the
second half of 1850, thanks partly to the efforts of both the West African
and South American squadrons, but more particularly because of an-

other glut after years of heavy imports. Between January and June only 8,000 slaves had in fact been imported along the coast from Campos to Santos, the lowest figure for more than five years. The coffee planters' apparently insatiable demand for slaves was, however temporarily, satisfied. Eusébio de Queiroz, the minister responsible for the law of 1850, pointed out that many landowners had become deeply indebted to, and in many cases had mortgaged their properties to, the most prominent slave dealers. The latter, the majority of whom were foreign and, worse still, Portuguese, were also by now resented for their ostentatious wealth and their political influence. The 1850 law was deliberately directed at those who shipped, imported and sold rather than those who illegally purchased slaves. And it was speedily and effectively enforced by the provincial presidents, provincial chiefs of police and county *delegados*, district and county judges, the National Guard, the army, the navy and the special courts. There were only nine successful landings of slaves in Brazil (a total of 3,287 slaves) during 1851 and only two of these – both in Bahia – occurred during the last four months of the year. There were to be only three further known landings (two in 1852 and one in 1855). The Brazilian slave trade had been brought to a complete standstill. (See Table 5 above.)

More impressive still, the trade was not allowed to revive, as it had in the 1830s, when the excess of imports had been absorbed, the market recovered and prices began to rise once more, offering the prospect of enormous profits to the slave traders. The price of slaves in the coffee *municípios* of Rio de Janeiro almost doubled between 1852 and 1854, but all attempts to re-establish the trade, one as late as 1856, failed. Of course, the British claimed that just as the British navy had been primarily responsible for ending the trade in the first place – 'the achievement which I look back on with the greatest and the purest pleasure was forcing the Brazilians to give up their slave trade, by bringing into operation the Aberdeen Act of 1845', wrote Palmerston in 1864[41] – the permanent threat of a resumption of naval hostilities in Brazilian waters was what kept it closed. (The Aberdeen Act, the 'Sword of Damocles', was not actually repealed until 1869.) More significant perhaps was the fact that for the first time since independence a government in Rio de Janeiro had the authority and the necessary muscle to enforce its will throughout the country.

The problem of the future supply of labour to the Brazilian coffee

[41] Quoted in Bethell, *Abolition*, 360.

plantations posed by the ending of the transatlantic slave trade was partly
solved in the short run by the internal slave trade and ultimately by
European immigration. Already in 1847, encouraged by the liberal
government at the time, Nicolau Vergueiro had been the first Brazilian
landowner to experiment with the *parceria* system (a form of
sharecropping), importing first German and later Portuguese *colonos*
(contract labourers, virtually indentured servants) to work on his plantations, recently converted from sugar to coffee, at Limeira (São Paulo). In
August 1850 the conservative government revived the 1843 land (and
immigration) bill which had been opposed by the Mineiros and Paulistas
and blocked in the Senate during the period of liberal rule. This time it
was quickly approved in both houses and became law on 18 September
1850 – two weeks after the passage of the new anti-slave trade law.
Changes were introduced to eliminate some of its more controversial
aspects and to adapt it to new circumstances. The land tax, for example,
was dropped. The bill was still viewed by some deputies as highly
detrimental to the landowning class; one mineiro deputy was even able to
find communist overtones in it. In the event the new law proved virtually
unenforceable; its major purpose, the regularization of land titles by
means of demarcation and registration, was to a great extent frustrated.
Nevertheless, the law indicates the growing concern of the government
with the long-term problem of labour supply. And the number of
European immigrants arriving in Brazil did increase, albeit slowly, after
1850. (See Table 6 above.)

The conservative government also turned its attention to Brazil's
future economic development. Brazil, the provincial president of Rio de
Janeiro, Manuel de Jesus Valdetaro, had written to the Minister of the
Empire in May 1848, had paid in full its 'tribute of blood on the fields of
civil discord', and now, 'weary of struggling and chasing after political
reforms, [the country] seems to be concentrating the lion's share of its
vitality on the exploitation of the abundant resources of its soil and in the
development of its material interests'.[42] In June 1850 Brazil was given its
first Commercial Code, which integrated and updated a variety of laws
and regulations dating back to the colonial period. Of particular importance in the Code was the definition of the different types of business
company and the regulation of their operations. The timing was opportune since within a few months substantial amounts of capital were
released from the slave trade. The country experienced for the first time a
fever of business activity and speculation, particularly in Rio de Janeiro.

[42] Quoted in Thomas Flory, *Judge and jury in Imperial Brazil 1808–1871* (Austin, Texas, 1981), 181.

While in the previous twenty years only seventeen enterprises had been authorized by the government, in the next ten years this number jumped to 155 and included banks, industries, steam navigation companies, railways, colonization companies, mining enterprises, urban transportation companies.[43] Despite the speculative nature of many of these initiatives, they do indicate a new mood in the country, a move from a dominant concern with political matters towards economic endeavours. The end of the slave traffic, the land and immigration law, the Commercial Code, these were all moves in the direction of capitalist modernization, in so far as they were all attempts to introduce and organize a market for the mobilization of labour, land and capital. Soon British capital would also be brought in to be invested in railways and urban transport, and British banks would be established forging new links with external capitalist economies.

At the beginning of the 1850s, nearly thirty years after independence, Brazil enjoyed political stability, internal peace from north to south and a certain prosperity based primarily on exports of coffee. Externally, Britain had been given satisfaction on the slave trade question and Rosas was defeated in February 1852. A state, or at least a working system of political domination, had been built. The dominant class had reached relative agreement on fundamental issues; during the next ten years liberals and conservatives served together in the same administrations (a period known as the *conciliação*). National unity had been maintained through difficult times. But had a nation also been forged? The answer must be qualified.

In a total population of seven and a half million, including the Brazilian Indians,[44] 25–30 per cent were still slaves and a much larger percentage, indeed the overwhelming majority, were, to use an expression of the time, non-active citizens, that is, Brazilians without

---

[43] Liberato de Castro Carreira, *História financeira e orçamentária do império do Brasil* (Rio de Janeiro, 1889), 378–9.

[44] Near the coast most Indian tribes lived in poverty and near extinction. On the Amazon and its main tributaries, especially the Rio Negro, a period of economic decline during the first half of the nineteenth century had provided a respite for the surviving tribes, many of whom had been contacted in the eighteenth century and were now less harassed. Two recently pacified tribes were, however, involved in the Cabanagem, the provincial revolt which erupted in Pará in 1835: the Mura on the side of the rebels, the Mundurucú on the side of the authorities. In the Tocantins–Araguaia basin and the interior of Maranhão and Piauí this was a period of frontier expansion. A number of Gê-speaking tribes accepted peaceful contact: Appinagé, Cherente and Krahô on the Tocantins; eastern Timbira in Maranhão; and some groups of northern Kayapó on the lower Araguaia. The Chavante retreated westwards and became increasingly hostile, and there were attacks in Goiás by the elusive Canoeiros. Some groups of the Bororo of central Mato Grosso fought settlers, but other tribes were generally peaceful – for example, Terena and Guató of the

either the legal rights, or the level of literacy and education, or the socio-economic conditions, which would enable them to participate in a meaningful way in the political life of the country. Ironically, the factors that had probably contributed most to the development of a sense of national identity were anti-Portuguese and anti-British feelings. The former permeated most of the social and political protests of the regency and was still prominent during the Praieira rebellion; the latter became predominant after 1839 as Britain stepped up its international crusade to suppress the slave trade. When the Comte de Suzannet visited Rio de Janeiro in the early forties, he was struck by the generalized hatred of foreigners, particularly the Portuguese and the British, and by the ease with which all the troubles of the country were blamed on them. Another Frenchman who settled as a businessman in Rio de Janeiro in the early fifties, Charles Expilly, made a similar observation. Immediately upon his arrival, he was advised by a German who had been living in the city for some time only to praise what he found there to avoid being considered an enemy of the country. 'Ce sentiment d'un inintelligent patriotisme est poussé à l'excès au Brésil', he concluded.[45] But it was still mostly a negative feeling, limited to certain sectors of the population. Even leaving aside the regional differences and the deep social and racial divisions, there was still in Brazil too little communication between the provinces, too little economic integration, too little sharing in the government of the country for a positive sense of national identity yet to have developed.

Paraguay, Apiaká of the Arinos, the surviving southern Kayapó and Guaran of south Brazil, Karajá of the Araguaia near Bananal. The laws authorizing the enslavement of the so-called Botocudo of Espírito Santo and eastern Minas Gerais and the Kaingang were repealed in October 1831. But many of these Indians continued to resist. Others responded to good treatment by the former French officer, Guy de Marlière, on the Rio Doce.

Missionary 'catechism' was again seen as the answer to the Indian problem, after the disastrous failure of Pombal's lay directors in the late eighteenth century. Generally speaking, however, the Italian Capuchin missionaries who arrived in the 1840s, especially after the Indian legislation of 1845, were a pathetic failure, unable to cope with the rigours of central Brazil and Amazônia and worse at communicating with Indians than their Jesuit and Franciscan predecessors had been in the colonial era.

It was in this period that Brazilian Indians were seen for the first time by non-Portuguese European naturalists and scientists. The most important were: Johann Baptist von Spix and Carl Friedrich Philip von Martius, who laid the foundations of Brazilian anthropology; Georg Heinrich von Langsdorff, accompanied by Hércules Florence, in Mato Grosso, 1825–9; the Austrian Johann Natterer who made ethnographic collections on the Amazon and upper Rio Negro, 1828–35; Prince Adalbert of Prussia (accompanied by Count Bismarck) on the Xingu, 1842–3; Francis, Comte de Castelnau on the Araguaia-Tocantins and upper Amazon in the 1840s; Henry Walter Bates and Alfred Russell Wallace who arrived on the Amazon in 1848; and Richard Spruce who arrived in 1849.

The authors are grateful to Dr John Hemming for the information on which this note is based.
[45] Charles Expilly, *Le Brésil tel qu'il est* (Paris, 1862), 34.

17

BRAZIL FROM THE MIDDLE OF THE NINETEENTH CENTURY TO THE PARAGUAYAN WAR

In the early 1850s Brazil's population numbered a little over seven and a half million. It was concentrated, as it always had been, along the eastern seaboard. Forty per cent lived in three south-eastern provinces – Rio de Janeiro, Minas Gerais and São Paulo – and the capital city of Rio de Janeiro with its 180,000 residents. The north-east, the principal area of settlement in colonial times, still accounted for 44 per cent. Black and mulatto slaves probably numbered between two and two and a half million, that is, between a quarter and a third of the population. By 1872, at the time of the first national census, Brazil's total population had increased to ten million. The proportion in the north-east had declined to 40 per cent while the city of Rio had grown to 275,000. Twenty years after the end of the slave trade the number of slaves had fallen to one and a half million (15 per cent), and a larger proportion of the slave population was to be found in the provinces of Rio de Janeiro, São Paulo and Minas Gerais. The rapid growth of coffee exports in the south-east, along with a relative decline of sugar, explains the regional shift in population from 1850 to 1870. Rio de Janeiro's commercial class prospered as the coffee trade linked planters to the international economy. Labour, however, whether slave or free, rural or urban, received little of the increased wealth. And planters and merchants subtly combined outright force with benevolent protection to maintain worker dependency. The government of the empire, responsive to the class interests of planters and merchants, had become an instrument in their efforts to maintain political and social control. During these twenty years political leaders also succeeded in co-opting those who once opposed central authority, while moving, sometimes grudgingly, toward the middle ground between conservatism and reform. A stable polity resulted, but loyalties to particular regions, defined by export crops, remained strong.

747

Sugar continued to have an important place in the Brazilian economy in the early 1850s and sugar exports, though lagging behind coffee, easily surpassed in value cotton, hides, tobacco and other products. Sugar exports increased by 50 per cent from 1841–5 to 1871–5 (see Table 1). But world production meanwhile quadrupled, and Brazil's share of the world market fell from approximately ten to five per cent. All regions of Brazil produced sugar for domestic consumption but, apart from a small centre around Campos in the province of Rio de Janeiro, almost all the sugar Brazil exported came from the narrow strip, 50 to 100 miles deep, along the coast of the provinces of the north-east, especially Bahia and Pernambuco. Contemporaries often attributed the relative stagnation of sugar production in the north-east to technological backwardness. Certainly sugar production in Brazil seemed primitive by the international standards of the day. Every two to three years slaves used hoes to dig up the old cane and plant fresh shoots in the deep clay soil. Eventually planters set them to work on new lands and abandoned the old; with an abundance of land it made little sense to fertilize the soil. Once a year slaves slashed the ripened cane and piled it into bundles to be carried to the mill on oxcarts or mules. At the mill, metal or metal-covered rollers crushed the cane to extract the juice. In 1854 80 per cent of the mills in the province of Pernambuco relied upon oxen or horses, while 19 per cent used waterwheels and only 1 per cent were steam driven; by contrast, in 1860 70 per cent of Cuban mills operated with steam power. The cane juice was then boiled in a succession of huge cauldrons to remove the water. Heat came from burning wood, thus contributing to deforestation. When the sugar began to crystallize, workers poured the syrup into conical clay moulds from which the dark brown molasses drained, leaving a damp raw sugar. Further refining took place principally in Europe and North America.

The failure to adopt the latest technology, however, sprang from experience and solid judgement. Milling improvements could not overcome the advantage of proximity to markets enjoyed by Cuban cane and European beet producers. Some millowners in Bahia who did take steps to modernize their mills – most notably João Maurício Wanderley, later barão de Cotegipe – found it nearly impossible to secure encouraging financial returns. For others the abundance of land and forest resources discouraged investment in agricultural development: when cane fields could be so readily extended into virgin lands it made sense to neglect the

Table 1 *Major Exports of Brazil (by decade), 1841–80*

Product	1841–50		1851–60		1861–70		1871–80	
	Value (in £1000)	%	Value (in £1000)	%	Value (in £1000)	%	Value (in £1000)	%
Coffee	22,655	46.99	49,741	53.67	68,004	50.38	112,954	59.49
Sugar	14,576	30.23	21,638	23.35	18,308	13.56	23,540	12.40
Cotton	4,103	8.51	6,350	6.85	27,293	20.22	19,070	10.04
Hides	4,679	9.70	7,368	7.95	8,958	6.64	11,106	5.85
Tobacco	974	2.02	2,679	2.89	4,567	3.38	6,870	3.61
Rubber	214	0.44	2,282	2.46	4,649	3.44	10,957	5.77
Cacao	537	1.11	1,033	1.11	1,388	1.03	2,438	1.28
Maté	477	0.99	1,583	1.71	1,817	1.35	2,945	1.55
Totals of Leading Exports	48,215	99.99	92,674	99.99	134,984	100.00	189,880	99.99

Source: Brazil, Instituto Brasileiro de Geografia e Estatística, *Anuário Estatístico do Brasil*, Ano 5 (1939–40), 1381.

fertilization of older fields. Loan capital sought less risky opportunities elsewhere, raising the cost of money. Furthermore, traditional practices brought in a reassuringly substantial income to the few largest planters, who thus maintained a comfortable social and political dominance.

As in colonial days, Brazilian sugar planters could be divided into two main categories: those who owned mills as well as land and those who merely owned land. The former, the *senhores de engenho*, towered over the cane farmers (*lavradores*) in economic and social importance, but managed to persuade the latter to share their outlook in opposition to that of tenants, free wage workers and slaves. The cane farmers supplied cane to the millowners either on contract, being paid for their cane in cash, or in exchange for half the sugar produced. Often the cane farmers, having borrowed excessively from the millowners, lost their land and found themselves reduced to tenantry. Among the *senhores de engenho* themselves sharp divisions separated a few into a virtual oligarchy. For one *município* (county) in the province of Pernambuco, it has been calculated that 15 per cent of the millowners accounted for 70 per cent of all plantation land. Just nine inter-related families owned almost all the properties. Henrique Marques Lins and his sons or sons-in-law owned thirty plantations and he and his clan not surprisingly occupied the most powerful political positions locally. In 1863 a journalist claimed the *município* was Lins's 'fief' and all the other families just 'so many slaves'.[1]

During the 1830s coffee had overtaken sugar as Brazil's leading export and by 1850 coffee accounted for nearly half of all Brazilian export earnings (see Table 1 above). Coffee cultivation had spread throughout the Paraíba valley, and by the middle of the century it had displaced sugar west of the city of São Paulo. Coffee exports grew from 9.7 million sacks (132 pounds each) in the 1830s, to 26.3 million sacks in the 1850s and 28.8 million in the following decade. It is important, however, to remember that there were commodities exported from other tropical or sub-tropical regions which were significantly more valuable than coffee: the cotton exported from the south of the United States in the 1850s, for example, brought in five times as much revenue as Brazilian coffee.

The sons of the original pioneers who had carved their estates out of the virgin forest of the Paraíba valley continued energetically to direct the process of deforestation either on inherited estates or in newer areas. Although some historians have stressed how they prized status and power over profit, newer evidence suggests the bulk of these planters were sound businessmen who carefully weighed the risks and advantages of each investment. By 1870 the careful observer could note the first signs of stagnation in the Paraíba valley: an ageing slave population, old coffee bushes not being replaced and a preference for investing capital elsewhere rather than in fertilizing the worn-out soils. From the middle of the century many had been attracted to the centre-west of São Paulo province. The hills there were not as steep, and yet a gently rolling terrain insured good drainage and slanting sunlight on the bushes. Still using the same agricultural methods, planters found the reddish soils of São Paulo even more fertile than that of the Paraíba valley. Land seemed to stretch endlessly westward. Although at first the costs of transportation across the escarpment to the sea ate up the profits of those located beyond a certain distance from the coast, planters confidently believed that railroad builders would eventually overcome that barrier – which they did in 1868. Nevertheless, before 1870 the major source of coffee remained the Paraíba valley, that is to say, the province of Rio de Janeiro and the north-east of São Paulo province.

At the centre of a coffee *fazenda*, the master's house faced slave quarters and processing sheds. These adobe and timbered structures

---

[1] Quoted by Peter L. Eisenberg, *The sugar industry in Pernambuco: modernization without change, 1840–1910* (Berkeley, 1974), 138–9.

stood solidly around large beaten-earth or bricked coffee-drying patios. At harvest time (July–November) slaves gathered the cherry-like fruit of the coffee bushes into large baskets for carrying down the hillsides to these patios. There they spread out the berries to be dried by the sun, raking them together at dusk to protect them from the dew. When the fruit blackened, a water-driven wooden mortar removed the dry shells and hulled the green coffee beans. Using laborious hand methods slaves then separated out the dirt and imperfect beans and sacked the coffee for shipment.

The public domain here, as in other settled areas, had long been alienated through royal land grants dating from colonial times or through legal and customary rights of squatters large and small. But with the spread of export agriculture, subsistence farmers quickly found their claims disputed by the more powerful and wealthy planters or yielded to attractive financial offers and moved elsewhere. Even the royal grants had often overlapped. Neither public officials nor private owners carried out systematic surveys or registered their properties. The land law of 1850, calling for the sale (rather than gift) of all public lands in the future and systematic surveys of existing holdings to be paid for by all who wished their titles confirmed promised to end a chaotic situation. But although many landowners did make formal initial depositions as called for by the law, their claims consisted of listing the names of their bordering neighbours; they made no measurements, did not resolve their conflicting claims and soon forgot further provisions of the law. Even today titles remain confused.

In addition to coffee and sugar, only cotton among Brazil's other export crops was important in this period. Although long-staple cotton – native to Brazil – had figured significantly in Brazil's exports at the turn of the century, its exportation declined steadily after the invention of the cotton gin made possible the use of the shorter staple variety so abundantly grown in the south of the United States. Most Brazilian cotton was produced in the less humid, slightly higher regions of the north-east, back from the coast thirty to one hundred miles. In 1863–4 Pernambuco led in cotton exports with 30 per cent of the total, and Maranhão followed next with 21 per cent. Other provinces of the north-east – especially Alagoas and Paraíba – supplied 45 per cent. As a result of the Civil War in the United States, Brazil enjoyed a sudden if ephemeral surge in cotton exports (see Table 1 above). From 21 million pounds exported in 1860–1, exports rose to 92 million pounds five years later, reaching somewhat higher levels in the early 1870s. Even some coffee areas of São Paulo province switched briefly to short-staple cotton.

At the end of the Civil War a number of southerners migrated to Brazil hoping to recreate slave-worked cotton plantations. But in Brazil cotton was predominantly produced by small proprietors; it required less capital investment for its processing before export than did coffee or sugar. In São Paulo they planted it in the less fertile areas, often along with beans and corn in the same field. Following practices used in the north-east, they burned off the bush before planting to kill off the pests and return nutrients to the soil rapidly, if wastefully. Although larger planters used ploughs and other agricultural machinery, most continued to rely on hoes as they did for food crops and coffee. Cultivation or weeding also proceeded laboriously with hoes rather than with horse-drawn tools and was, therefore, done less frequently than recommended by agricultural experts. When prices began to weaken many marginal producers abandoned the crop. Meanwhile, however, the growth of Brazilian textile manufacturing provided a new, domestic market for cotton.

Tobacco, in contrast to its prominent role in colonial times, accounted for only 3 per cent of Brazil's export earnings in the period 1850–70. It predominated in the region of Cachoeira, across the bay from Salvador. Like cotton, tobacco was raised on relatively small tracts and family farms with few slaves. The leaves were picked, one by one, as they ripened and hung to dry on outdoor racks. In Salvador factory workers made cigars, and there and in Rio de Janeiro they prepared snuff. Tobacco grown in Minas Gerais, usually twisted into ropes, could be bought by the foot for use in the preparation of hand-rolled cigarettes.

In the Amazon region Indians and their mixed-race descendants, collectively called *caboclos*, gathered cacao from trees that grew wild in the forest and sold it to small entrepreneurs. By the 1860s landowners using slave labour experimented with it in southern Bahia. Workers broke open the soft shells of the ripened large yellow or green fruit and drained the brown seeds of their surrounding thick white liquor, allowing them to dry either in the sun or in raised drying sheds. The manufacture of chocolate took place in Europe.

Brazilian rubber began to attract increasing attention following the discovery of the vulcanization process in 1839. Exports rose from 388 tons in 1840 to 1,447 tons ten years later, 2,673 tons in 1860, and 5,602 tons in 1870, just before the real 'rubber rush' began. In the Amazon rainforest *caboclos* tapped the wild rubber trees and stiffened the latex over a wood fire forming it into large balls. Itinerant peddlers traded implements and food for this rubber, often on credit at onerous rates. Landowners, who needed settled labourers for their agricultural enterprises, resented the mobility rubber-gathering allowed, not yet sensing the opportunities for wealth the trade would later bring.

In the southern provinces of Paraná, Santa Catarina, and Rio Grande do Sul *cabaclos* also gathered maté from wild bushes. They cropped the leaves and tender shoots, toasted them in baskets over slow-burning fires, and then used primitive wooden mortars to crush the leaves into a coarse powder. After being bagged, maté was exported to the neighbouring countries to the south. Some maté, marketed within Brazil, was not toasted but merely dried and sold as leaves to be brewed as tea. Despite the rising exports of maté, cacao and rubber, these crops together accounted for less than 6 per cent of Brazil's exports between 1851 and 1870.

Cattle were raised in Brazil both for hides (largely exported) and for meat (principally consumed within the country). Foreign observers described three distinct cattle regions, each with a specific culture. In the arid *sertão* of the north-east, away from the humid coastal strip and westward even of the cotton areas, cattle raising had been a major occupation since the sixteenth century. Although the region has a sufficient average amount of rain, it tends to fall in torrential downpours, leaving the land most of the time with insufficient moisture for regular agriculture except on a small scale. Occasional droughts sear the land making it inhospitable even to cattle. The *mestizo* population, relatively nomadic, dressed in a characteristic style of leather chaps, hats, and jackets to protect themselves from the cactus and other prickly growth. The region supplied cattle to the sugar zone, both for fresh meat and as oxen to drive the mills or pull the heavy carts laden with cane or chests of sugar.

Another region, the rolling *cerrados* of Minas Gerais, had cattle as the mainstay of its economy. This land of grass and scattered gnarled trees had, in the eighteenth century, supplied meat to the gold and diamond panners and to the turbulently rich cities that sprang up in the mining region. In the nineteenth century cattlemen turned their attention to supplying fresh meat to Rio de Janeiro, a city rapidly growing in size and wealth because of rising coffee exports. Cattle drives down the escarpment to the fattening pastures in the lowlands became a common sight along the roads leading to the city.

It was in the province of Rio Grande do Sul, however, that cattlemen emerged as the most prosperous in nineteenth-century Brazil. The south's grassy plains especially favoured such activity although the province's resources could not match the even more luxurious pampas of Uruguay and Argentina. After some early experimentation with wheat growing, the early settlers (in contrast to more recently arrived European immigrants) had turned to cattle. By 1863–4 Rio Grande do Sul exported nearly seven-tenths of Brazil's hides. It also produced 'jerked' or salted beef, sold for consumption on coffee and sugar plantations to the north. In *saladeros* slaves soaked the meat in brine and dried it in the sun. It would then last for months or even years.

Besides eating meat, Brazilians derived their proteins from a mixture of beans and rice or beans and maize. Coarse manioc meal made from the cassava root also supplied daily calories. Bacon occasionally enriched the diet. Except for dried beef from Rio Grande do Sul and imported wheat flour and codfish, a local population drew supplies from nearby producers. Planters doubtless used surplus labour during non-harvest seasons to produce food, and small owners and peasants sold their surplus to planters or city residents. Participants in the expanding coffee economy, both rural and urban, drew much of their food from farming regions of Minas Gerais. Immigrant settlements in Rio Grande do Sul also produced enough beans and corn to ship out of the province. Brazil increasingly imported some food to meet the demands of urban centres and even plantation needs. Generally, however, local self-sufficiency was the rule. Certainly many more Brazilians laboured at producing food for domestic consumption than at raising export crops.

Although every kind of agricultural activity in all regions of Brazil counted on some slave labour, as did stock raising, cereal production, even rubber and maté gathering – and, of course, slaves worked as artisans and domestics – it was the major cash crops of sugar and coffee that accounted for Brazil's heavy reliance on black slaves. Everywhere, the central question for the slaveowner was how best to make the slave do the master's will. Because the answer to that question varied, slavery comprised a number of working relationships. The bulk of field slaves laboured in regimented gangs under the watchful eye of an overseer who did not hesitate to use the whip, the stocks, or other punishments, to get sixteen or even eighteen hours of work per day out of those he drove. The centuries-long experiences with exceedingly cheap slaves led most planters to pay insufficient attention to slave welfare in food, clothing and housing. Other slave-owners, however, whether out of charitable impulse or good business sense, perceived that fullest control could be exerted through a combination of harsh discipline for the recalcitrant and paternalistic benefits for the docile and compliant. The Paraíba planter, Francisco Peixoto de Lacerda Werneck, barão do Patí do Alferes, for instance, included elaborate instructions on the proper care of slaves in his *Memória* (1847) on how to set up a coffee estate. The guiding purpose of a planter's solicitude, he implied, was to ensure a slave's willing obedience. When such techniques failed, however, he did not hesitate to 'lay bare the flesh'.[2] Benevolence acquired purpose only insofar as it sprang from the master's ability to exert maximum force.

Slaves in other activities encountered similar juxtapositions of controlling devices. For, even among plantation slaves, by no means all were engaged in raising and harvesting coffee and sugar or in processing these crops. They also worked at the myriad other artisan jobs demanded by the operation of a large estate. Towns were few and distances between them great, so a large planter with extensive holdings often preferred to maintain skilled slaves of his own to repair equipment, construct his warehouses, manufacture slaves' clothes, or even decorate his plantation house. Smaller landowners came to the plantation to rent the labour of these skilled slaves. Slaves also rendered domestic service and, as planters' wealth from exports increased, did so in greater numbers. An imposing house, frequently filled with guests and the centre of social and political life, required numerous servants. On the other hand, a declining export economy, as in the province of Minas Gerais, for example, also released a substantial number of slaves for domestic service as well as food production. House slaves and artisans enjoyed more comfortable living conditions than did the field slaves: better clothes, perhaps even shoes, and often the same food as that of the master. They might also acquire a certain conversational polish, even occasionally learn to read, and stood a greater chance of being freed for exceptionally loyal service than field hands. Their proximity to the master, however, lessened the space they could call their own and made their every move readily observed. It has even been argued that violence did more to recognize the humanity of a slave than did that all-enveloping paternalism.

Planters differed on how best to provide food for their slaves and this

[2] Francisco Peixoto de Lacerda, barão do Paty do Alferes, *Memoria sobre a fundação de uma fazenda na provincia do Rio de Janeiro, sua administraçaõ, e épochas em que devem fazer as plantações, suas colheitas, etc. etc.* (Rio de Janeiro, 1847); ibid. to Bernardo Ribeiro de Carvalho, Fazenda Monte Alegre, 31 March 1856, Werneck Papers, Arquivo Nacional (Rio de Janeiro), Seção de Arquivos Particulares, Códice 112, Vol.3, Copiador 1, fl.352.

difference had implications for the relations between master and slave. Some preferred to feed their slaves directly, while others allowed them provision grounds on which to raise foodstuffs. The former believed it better to keep slaves steadily at work on the main task – producing coffee and sugar – and to buy supplies from small landowners and squatters operating in the interstices of the plantation system or from free retainers working on the planters' land. Coffee *fazendeiros* in the Paraíba valley often had slaves produce foodstuffs in relatively new groves where beans and maize, planted between the rows of coffee bushes, benefited from the frequent cultivation while receiving plenty of sunlight. Others, especially those with mature coffee groves, chose to rid themselves of the responsibility of feeding their slaves and probably noticed that slaves worked for them more willingly six days a week if on the seventh they provided for themselves and their families. From the slaves' point of view we may guess some preferred the security of being fed by the master, while others enjoyed the relative freedom of their own plots, despite the unceasing toil and greater uncertainty and anxiety.

Efforts to control slaves – whether through force or benevolence – did not meet with uniform success. The very multiplicity of techniques directed to this end bears witness to the difficulty of making one man's will determine another's action. The slaves' response to those efforts consisted not only or even principally in rebellious behaviour, but in the failure to carry out instructions, in 'laziness' and sloppy work. Even obedience could be accompanied by a demeanour that made clear the existence of another will. The *jongos* or slave ditties remembered by ex-slaves reveal a clear consciousness of their plight.[3] And the murder of a master occurred with sufficient frequency to make slave-owners fear it. Flight could be another response. Advertisements for runaway slaves filled many columns of the daily newspapers in cities like Rio de Janeiro, Salvador and Recife. Often the runaways joined forces in the forest to form small *quilombos* or maroon communities where up to twenty or more fugitives planted manioc and corn, surviving for months, even years, They raided plantations for additional supplies and sometimes displayed considerable political acumen in selecting their targets.

Slaves also found it possible to create their own families and forge other social ties to both slave and free while shaping a pattern of shared understandings to be passed on to the next generation. Many documents

[3] See Stanley J. Stein, *Vassouras. A Brazilian coffee county, 1850–1900* (Cambridge, Mass., 1957), 208–9.

reveal the purchase of freedom for a slave by a father, mother, husband or lover. Wills left by freedmen bespeak their close emotional connections to former fellows in slavery. Isolated letters between slaves at distant plantations poignantly capture both the anguish of forced separation and the steadfastness of affection. Slaves passed on their culture not only in everyday family life, but also by practising traditional rituals (however modified they may have been). In special holiday dances or *batuques* participants learned the secrets of skilful drumming (and drum making) along with a set of inherited beliefs. The vitality in Brazil today of religious practices that derive from memories of Africa suggests a continuing effort to create and safeguard a cultural patrimony.

Not only did bondsmen find some opportunities for independence, the boundary between them and free workers was not always clearcut. Some historians have even seen in provision grounds elements of a peasant economy. Certainly slaves sometimes sold their excess production, by rights to the master but sometimes to the owner of a country store who did not hesitate to purchase small amounts of 'stolen' coffee as well. Thus, chattel slaves themselves came to own some property and exchange it for cash. Indeed, some planters used cash as an incentive for extra work, paying a monetary reward, for instance, for any basket of coffee harvested beyond a certain minimum. In this way the distinction between slave labour and wage labour tended to blur. Moreover, there was a real possibility that the individual slave might move from slavery to freedom. By which means, incidentally, the culture of slaves became the culture of the free poor.

The frequency with which Brazilian slave-owners granted freedom to individual slaves surprised foreign visitors in the nineteenth century. High interest rates combined with the long delay in recovering the cost of rearing slave children to working age had long encouraged the freeing of children at birth, especially girls who would not fetch a high price even once reared. The need for free workers to fill certain labour requirements, such as that of supervising slaves, further encouraged the practice. Perhaps most importantly, manumission, even of adult men, served as one more tool by which good behaviour could be encouraged through the example of a few whose exceptional loyalty and obedience had been thus rewarded. The hope of possible freedom may also have lessened the number of those slaves who ran away, killed their masters, or, out of despair, committed suicide. Sometimes owners granted freedom on the condition of continued faithful service for a specified number of years.

Society valued manumission and rewarded with praise the generosity of the planter who granted freedom. It was often argued with some basis in law that a slave who could pay his purchase price should be freed by right. The freed black did not threaten the social order for he or she could easily be absorbed into one of the many layers at the lower end of the social structure. Free blacks and mulattos accounted for 74 per cent of all blacks and mulattos by 1872, 44 per cent of the total population. There is some evidence, however, that the frequency of manumissions declined once no more slaves could be purchased in Africa.

The long established custom of occasional manumission did not undermine the institution of slavery as long as more slaves could be purchased. During the 1830s and 1840s slaves had been imported from Africa, albeit illegally, at an unprecedented rate, most of them destined for the coffee *fazendas* of the Paraíba valley. The transatlantic slave trade had finally been ended in 1850–1, but it was followed by the growth of the internal slave trade. The deportation in 1850 of the most notorious Portuguese slave traders merely opened the way for other slave merchants in the cities of Rio and Santos to continue as middlemen, selling slaves brought from the north-east. North-eastern sugar planters, with a declining share of the world market, began to sell slaves southward to the thriving coffee regions. During the ten years from 1852 the number of slaves arriving annually from other provinces at Rio de Janeiro port averaged 3,370.[4] Others were supplied overland. Although numbers are small compared to the yearly average of 41,400 imported from Africa between 1845 and 1850, they helped feed the still insatiable demand for workers on coffee plantations. Between 1864 and 1874 the number of slaves in the north-eastern, mainly sugar-producing, region declined from 774,000 (45 per cent of all Brazilian slaves) to 435,687 (28 per cent) while the coffee regions increased their slave population from 645,000 (43 per cent) to 809,575 (56 per cent) and São Paulo province more than doubled its slaves from 80,000 to 174,622.

The institution, nevertheless, did enter its long period of decline in the 1850s. With the end of the transatlantic slave trade, the number of slaves overall could not be maintained. The earlier reliance on levies from Africa had produced a sharply unbalanced sex ratio among slaves: only

---

[4] Estimates of their number differ. Cf. Robert Conrad, *The destruction of Brazilian slavery, 1850–1888* (Berkeley, 1972), 289, with Sebastião Ferreira Soares, *Notas estatísticas sobre a produção agrícola e carestia dos gêneros alimentícios no império do Brasil*, facsim. ed. (Rio de Janeiro, 1977), 135–6, Eisenberg, *Sugar Industry*, 156 n., and Herbert S. Klein, *The middle passage: comparative studies in the Atlantic slave trade* (Princeton, 1978), 97.

one-third of those transported to Brazil were females. In part because of the preference for freeing girls, the number of child-bearing women among slaves born in Brazil remained relatively low as well. The high interest rates that encouraged manumission of children also discouraged the care of pregnant women or new-born infants. Harsh working and living conditions no doubt also meant high mortality for men and women. Poor clothing, inadequate housing and insufficient food (most of it of poor quality), as well as overwork, accounted for a good part of the decline in the slave population. Epidemics of yellow fever, smallpox and cholera that marked the decade of the 1850s especially ravaged already debilitated slaves. No reliable count exists for slaves in 1850, but these have been estimated to have numbered between two and two and a half million. By 1864 Agostinho Marques Perdigão Malheiro, a careful student of slavery, put their number at only 1,715,000 and the official census of 1872 (which did not include children born after September 1871) at 1,510,806.

Meanwhile, as slaves became more regionally concentrated, Brazilian elites began to divide on the issue of slavery. The percentage of slaves among agricultural workers in the sugar counties of Pernambuco reached only 14 per cent by 1872, whereas in the coffee counties of Rio de Janeiro province it held at 46 per cent. Landowners in the north-east became steadily less wedded to the institution of slavery as they sold off their bondsmen and turned increasingly to free, though dependent, labour. Meanwhile, by the late 1860s, as the railway over the escarpment in São Paulo neared completion and wealthy coffee *fazendeiros* acquired western lands and organized railway companies to link them to the trunk line, they clearly saw that unless a new labour system were adopted, their hopes for the future would be frustrated. Finally, although the salt-meat factories in southern Brazil used slaves, the region as a whole and especially the cattlemen were not particularly tied to slavery. In the province of Rio de Janeiro, however, as well as in the older section of São Paulo province along the upper reaches of the Paraíba and in parts of the province of Minas Gerais there was still a firm commitment to slavery and a determination to see it continue as the dominant labour system in Brazil. Slaves, however, became more restive now that a larger proportion of them were Brazilian-born, often mulattos, and the promise of manumission seemed to decline.

Even before the end of the slave trade from Africa an attempt had been made to substitute slaves with indentured servants from Europe.

Nicolau Pereira de Campos Vergueiro (1778–1859) had drawn a good bit of his fortune from a slave-importing business in Santos during the 1830s and 1840s. He had also invested in several plantations in the *paulista* highlands and had distributed imported slaves to his neighbours as well as using them on his own properties. In 1847 he persuaded the imperial and provincial governments to issue interest-free loans with which he funded recruiters to travel through the Germanies and Switzerland then being ravaged by the potato famine. The first indentured servants went to his own plantation where he installed them in wattle-and-daub shacks and assigned them coffee bushes to plant, cultivate and harvest on a share-cropping basis. Soon neighbouring planters began to engage immigrant workers through his firm. And other Santos merchants successfully followed his example. Within a few years, however, the experiment was abandoned. Immigrant workers who found their correspondence censored, their egress from the plantation blocked and their debts mounting as a result of the planters' book-keeping manipulations proved unwilling to submit to such slave-like discipline. In 1856 a group of Swiss workers on one of Vergueiro's estates, frightened by threats to the life of their spokesman, Thomas Davatz, armed themselves while awaiting an official investigation into charges that Vergueiro had defrauded them; he, however, claimed they plotted a rebellion with the help of slaves, receiving direction from a Swiss 'communist' living in São Paulo city.[5] The incident exemplifies the difficulty of exerting control over free Europeans in ways inherited from slavery. The continuing ease of buying slaves from the north-east and the availability of more tractable free Brazilians served to discourage similar efforts and to postpone serious attempts to attract European agricultural workers for another thirty years.

The relationship between rural employers and Brazilian-born free workers bore a strong resemblance to slavery. Among the free, for instance, was a social type known as the *agregado* – a kind of retainer – commonly to be found in the sugar zone of the north-east as well as in the coffee regions of Rio de Janeiro and São Paulo. An *agregado* depended upon someone else, especially for housing or at least a space in which to live. He or she could be a family member, even a respected parent, sister, or brother who lacked an independent source of income; more often, however, the *agregado* was a poverty-stricken agricultural worker, or

---

[5] Quoted in Warren Dean, *Rio Claro. A Brazilian plantation system, 1820–1920* (Stanford, 1976), 102. Also see advertisement for a 'runaway settler' in *Correio Mercantil*, 10 Dec. 1857, 3.

single mother, sometimes a freed slave, to whom the landowner granted the right to raise subsistence crops on some outlying patch of the large estate. In exchange the *agregado* proffered occasional services, but especially loyalty. For men, that could frequently mean armed struggle in electoral disputes or against neighbouring and rival landowners. The *agregados'* claim upon security remained tenuous, and landowners could eject them without hesitation. In turn *agregados* too were free to move if they could find another protector, and landowners sometimes complained of how *agregados* would abandon one patron for another 'without the least apology'.[6] In the city the *agregado's* contribution to the family economy customarily resembled that of an apprentice or domestic servant. Whether in the city or in the country, the patron's care on the one hand and loyalty and service on the other dominated the relationship. The occasional cash payment for labour or surplus crops and the uncertainty of the tie to a particular landowner nevertheless suggests the partial penetration of monetary considerations and increasingly fluid social relations.

In the cotton- and food-producing area of the north-east, between sugar-producing coast and cattle-raising interior, the landlords – owning smaller tracts than on the coast – frequently peopled their estates almost entirely with *agregados* and relied on them for labour rather than on slaves. When, in late 1874, significant numbers of peasants rose up briefly in an apparently leaderless revolt called the Quebra Quilos against the payment of new taxes on the grain and vegetables they brought to market and against the local merchants who took advantage of the introduction of the metric system to alter prices, these interior landowners acquiesced as long as the notarial offices containing land records were not disturbed. In contrast, *agregados* from the coastal sugar region marched in under the leadership of mill owners to put down the revolt. The psychological weight of dependence varied markedly from region to region.

Whether as *agregados* or hired hands who worked for cash, agricultural labourers received minimum compensation for their work. Rural wages in this period have not been systematically studied, but evidence suggests they barely exceeded subsistence. Most of the free lived outside the market economy, in abject poverty, barefoot, unhealthy and undernourished. Small landowners – some of whom also worked part-time for cash – fared little better. Securing land became significantly more difficult after the passage of the 1850 land law which attempted to end the practice

[6] See quotation in Eisenberg, *Sugar Industry*, 148.

of squatting. Those who held land did so only insecurely and perched precariously between the estates of the wealthy. They had to forge alliances with the powerful and offer deference in exchange for security and protection.

A Brazilian planter relied on an astute combination of force and promised rewards or protection in order to manipulate both his workers, free or slave, and his dependent neighbours. Through careful attention to his honour and social status – sometimes requiring conspicuous consumption or displays of open-handed generosity – he attempted, on the whole successfully, to legitimize the deference he received from others lower down the social hierarchy. The efforts made by the planter to bolster and maintain his authority within the self-contained social system of the *fazenda* have sometimes misled observers into discounting his economic rationality. Most planters probably felt no tension between the roles of paternalistic seigneur and capitalist entrepreneur. They understood the complex internal structure of Brazil's export economy, and worried over their profit and loss accounts vis à vis Brazilian middlemen and foreign export houses. They were aware of Brazil's role in the international division of labour and kept a sharp eye on world commodity prices. They also made the Brazilian economy as a whole – the development of railways, the growth of the banking system, the level of imports as well as exports, even the beginnings of manufacturing – a vital part of their concern.

Before the railway, the most common means of transporting goods and people overland was by mule. Through the Paraíba valley muleteers contracted with the planters to carry the coffee to small coastal towns whence coffee was shipped to Rio de Janeiro on small sailing vessels. Or they led their muletrains into Rio directly, where the animals dirtied the already filthy streets. Two sacks of coffee, each weighing 60 kg, could be transported by one mule down the steep, winding trails to the coast. To get that far the mules had to overcome the obstacle of the escarpment, sometimes descending 2500 feet in the space of 5 miles. Heavy rainfall on the escarpment caused everyone to complain of the government's failure to improve mountain roads beyond laying a few large flat stones at the steepest curves. Mules often sank into the bogs, drenching the coffee, and delaying the descent for hours until the mules could be pulled out. Across the flatter terrain of the north-east slow-moving oxcarts, their fixed axles filling the air with a high-pitched moan, carried the heavy chests of sugar to the coast.

Muleteers, often independent small businessmen, bought the mules at a cattle fair in southern São Paulo province from drivers who herded them northward from Rio Grande do Sul. Besides transporting export crops, muleteers linked the interior towns northward, connecting coffee-rich São Paulo and Rio de Janeiro with sugar-producing Bahia and Pernambuco and, even beyond, with Piauí, Maranhão and Pará. Some bought land and became planters themselves. While ocean trade-oriented port cities more toward Europe than toward each other, their hinterlands were woven together by a network of intersecting muletrain routes.

Coffee planters of the Paraíba valley took an active interest in road building, but could marshal only limited resources. The major mule tracks through the region had been cut by the pioneering planters and subsequently some large landowners took up subscriptions for improvements or sought government subsidies for the construction of bridges. Principally, however, they concerned themselves with assuring access from their own *fazenda* to the main routes. The first road for wheeled vehicles to cross the southern escarpment linked Rio de Janeiro to the summer retreat of the royal family in Petrópolis. In the 1850s a privately owned stagecoach company extended that route into the coffee region, opening its macadamized surface to use by horse-drawn wagons. A much less satisfactory road linked Santos to São Paulo where muletrains remained the rule until replaced by the railway.

Lack of capital proved the major obstacle to building railways in Brazil. Despite the prosperity of coffee producers, there was insufficient capital in this period to allow them either to finance construction themselves or even to attract foreign investors who remained more interested in expanding overland networks elsewhere, say, in the United States. Only in 1852, when the Brazilian government offered a guaranteed return on capital, did investors find Brazilian prospects attractive. Even this benefit, however, did not draw overseas profit-seekers to the first project to connect the port of Rio across the escarpment to the Paraíba valley. Coffee planters launched the enterprise (the Dom Pedro II Railway) but relied on the public treasury for half the investment. The company foundered nevertheless, and the government assumed the entire bill for the line's construction. Its first section was completed in 1858 and the rails reached the Paraíba river in the early 1860s. The construction in 1868 of the São Paulo Railway, a highly profitable short line connecting the port of Santos to the plains beyond the coastal ridge in São Paulo, proved in the long run to be even more important for coffee exports. Relying on a series of inclined planes, this British-owned railway surmounted major technical difficulties and opened up the way for the spread of Brazilian railway lines across the emerging coffee-producing districts of the province of São Paulo. Also during the fifties and sixties British investors built other railways in the north-east, most notably the Recife and São Francisco, the Great Western of Brazil and the Bahia and São Francisco, unconsciously encouraging sugar planters to open up new lands rather than fertilize the old. Brazil delayed for a long time the construction of any kind of railway network that would connect major cities to each other rather than rural regions to a port. With their heavy investment in fixed routes railways tended to draw each region in upon itself economically, weakening those ties across the interior upon which muleteers had relied for their trade.

The Brazilian planter controlled production, but British and American businessmen predominated in the export trade, both of coffee from Rio de Janeiro and Santos and of sugar from Recife and Bahia. From the mid-forties to the late eighties, the twenty largest export firms in Rio de Janeiro – handling four-fifths of the coffee exports – were all foreign-owned. Phipps Brothers (British), Maxwell, Wright & Co. (American) and Edward Johnston & Co. (British) dominated coffee exports. The most important Brazilian and Portuguese houses trailed far behind. British export firms controlled the sugar trade even more fully, perhaps because the bulk of Brazil's sugar exports went to Great Britain.

Between the planter and the exporter stood a series of other middle-men, most of whom were Brazilians or, at least, Portuguese. In Rio de Janeiro city, for instance, one to two hundred coffee factors (*comissários*) linked the plantation to international trade. The factor stored coffee in his warehouse as soon as it arrived in town, whether on muleback or by rail. As the planter's agent, he sought the best price for the coffee, charging a percentage of the sale as his fee. Still acting as an agent, the factor purchased jerked beef, grains or manioc flour to feed plantation slaves, and iron implements, coffee-hulling equipment, or even bags for sacking coffee. As the coffee planter became more prosperous, the factors' bills also listed luxury goods, dresses and hats from Paris, wine and butter, crystal and china, pianos and books.

In all these activities, including the delivery of slaves, the factor derived his principal importance by channelling credit. Foreign manufacturers and local merchants supplied him goods and slaves on credit which he then passed on to the planter. Or else the factor paid cash, in effect lending it to the planter. Planters hoped to replenish their accounts with their agents during the harvest season, but when production fell off they relied on him to carry them over until the next year. Sometimes factors extended short-term loans into mortgages. Factors were essential to planters' hopes for securing financing while they awaited the next crop, or over the long term.

Although coffee planters occasionally voiced complaints against the dealings of their agents, they rarely did so and for one simple reason: planter and factor were often relatives, even more frequently partners, and sometimes only a double role played by the same person. Earlier historians presumed a merchant–planter hostility, relying on isolated examples to verify it; but recent research has shown that at least a sixth of all partners in Rio factorage firms were interior coffee planters; and, furthermore, that numerous other merchants, though living in the city, owned plantations.[7] Still others married the daughters of planters, thus making their sons both planters and factors. Planters joined merchants, and even some foreigners, in the commercial associations of Recife, Bahia and Rio, lobbying together to protect their shared interests in the export trade. When factors did clash with planters it was more often with lesser ones than with the truly wealthy.

One example will serve to demonstrate the marriage of trade and land. Antonio Clemente Pinto (1795–1869) arrived from Portugal as a boy without a *real* to his name to begin life in Rio as an office boy. Through hard work, business acumen and luck he succeeded in the business world, first as a slave trader and then as a coffee factor. Next, he bought land and by 1850 could be counted among the largest landowners in the province of Rio de Janeiro, receiving the title of barão de Nova Friburgo in 1857. He lent money to other planters as well as investing in railways. His home in the then fashionable Catete district in the city of Rio, elaborately decorated by immigrant architects and designers, later became Brazil's presidential palace. Pinto's estate was appraised at nearly £800,000 (well over U.S.$3.5 million) at then current exchange rates. He left fourteen coffee *fazendas*, over two thousand slaves, his factorage firm and several town houses, one stocked with some fifteen hundred bottles of imported wine.

[7] Joseph E. Sweigart, 'Financing and marketing Brazilian export agriculture: the coffee factors of Rio de Janeiro, 1850–1888' (unpublished Ph.D. thesis, University of Texas at Austin, 1980), 66–98.

Only a short step separated factorage from banking. Capital derived from profits on coffee growing had long been lent by one planter to another: within the family, to trusted neighbours, or in the calculated hope of eventual foreclosure on desired properties. As partners in factorage firms which extended commercial credit, the planter had become accustomed to calculate risk and judge the vagaries of the money market. By the 1850s planters joined coffee factors as major investors in several banks. Investors deposited funds they would previously have loaned to slave traders. Almost all these banks concentrated on commercial loans, lending principally to factors who held planters' obligations as security. Some banks were also authorized to issue currency, especially from 1857 to 1860 when banking law was briefly liberalized. Financial opinion blamed either the lingering effect of this liberalization or its subsequent restriction for the financial crisis of 1864, which bankrupted several important banking firms. Three British banks set up in 1862 escaped the crisis and went on to prosper. Only in the next decade, when altered laws made it easier to recover on defaulted loans, did mortgage banks begin to lend money directly to planters. Always, however, the lack of firm land titles made slaves important as security; as slaves grew older and could not be replaced, planters found it ever harder to raise funds for long-term modernization or expansion. Not slavery, but the promised end of slavery seemed to threaten export prosperity.

Credit financed imports and most of those came from Great Britain. In the late 1840s Britain supplied half the goods imported into Brazil; the next most important supplier, the United States, accounted for only one-tenth. By 1875 the French had supplanted the Americans, but the British still led the way. Seventy per cent of the British imports from 1850 to 1870 consisted of textiles and half the remainder of other consumer goods. Capital goods and raw materials – hardware and other irongoods, coal, cement and machinery – accounted for only 15 per cent. Most imports arrived at Rio de Janeiro (54 per cent from 1845 to 1849), while Bahia (19 per cent) and Recife (14 per cent) trailed far behind. Foreigners, especially the British, owned most of the importing houses. Foreign firms sold either to Brazilian wholesalers or, more often, to retailers and, through the *comissários*, to the landowners themselves. They ensured that plantation slaves were dressed in British cottons and wielded British hoes.

Any measure to restrict imports – such as protective tariffs urged by some would-be industrialists – encountered the firm opposition of those policy-makers who wished to keep the price of imports low and thus diminish the cost of producing exports. On the other hand, planters and merchants shared a common interest in the effective performance of certain governmental functions which required revenue, preferring that this revenue come from import tariffs rather than from any other source. Taxes on imported goods accounted for approximately 60 per cent of governmental revenues in the third quarter of the nineteenth century, while only 16 per cent came from export taxes. In 1844 the government had found itself free at last from the limitation of the tariff to 15 per cent under the Anglo-Brazilian treaty of 1827. A new tariff raised the rates to 30 per cent in general, and in some cases to 60 per cent. Although principally fiscal in purpose, it had a moderately protective effect and for a while helped traditional craftsmen withstand a swelling flood of imported manufactures. However, the minister of finance in the new conservative administration which took office in 1848, Joaquim José Rodrigues Torres, the future visconde de Itaboraí (1802–72), himself a coffee planter, named a commission to study and revise the tariff. The report, published in 1853, enthusiastically urged the virtues of free trade. Citing a host of authorities, mostly British, its authors displayed a strong commitment to the principle that governments should not restrict international trade. Brazil should concentrate, they said, on what it did best: growing coffee. Nevertheless, the need for governmental revenue slowed steps toward free trade until the tariff of 1857 and the even more liberal tariff of 1860 significantly lowered duties. The costs of the Paraguayan War (1864–70), requiring additional revenues, brought a somewhat higher rate into effect, but without protectionist purpose.

In any case, most manufacturing consisted of craft shops. Skilled and unskilled workers in groups of 10 to 20 laboured in these small establishments making hats, shoes, saddles, bindings for books, rope, and furniture. They also worked in breweries and snuff factories and prepared vegetable oil or canned foodstuffs. Soap and candles were also manufactured locally. Brazilians or foreign entrepreneurs had established ten foundries in Rio by 1861, although their number decreased subsequently as it became easier to import machinery and spare parts. As transportation to the interior improved, textiles hand-loomed there became uneconomical in competition with imported cloth. Above all, the concentration of wealth in the hands of a few hampered economic development: the presence of slavery and the highly skewed distribution of wealth among the free considerably restricted the market for consumer goods.

Nevertheless, two Brazilian cotton mills established in the 1840s, protected by the tariff, prospered by mid-century. In 1850 one mill in the immediate hinterland of Rio de Janeiro, at the foot of the Orgão Mountains, had fifty looms, 2012 spindles and employed 116 workers. A mill in Bahia in 1861 used 4160 spindles and 135 looms. By 1866 a total of nine cotton mills, five of them in Bahia, produced a growing supply of textiles, requiring 800 workers on 350 looms and 14,000 spindles. Almost all depended on water power. By 1875 there were thirty mills, one-third of them in Bahia and the remainder in Rio de Janeiro, São Paulo, and Minas Gerais. Still, they produced a very small proportion of Brazil's consumption.

The Paraguayan War greatly stimulated industrial production in the late 1860s. Government procurement of war *matériel* did so directly, but two other factors contributed: the inflation caused by government deficits and the inadvertent protection provided by higher general tariffs to fund the war effort. Businessmen complained, nevertheless, that the government preferred to buy shoddy imported uniforms, for example, than to foster the expansion of Brazilian factories.

Before the war one entrepreneur particularly stood out by the variety of his concerns and the flamboyance of his business activity, if not by the success of his ventures. Irineu Evangelista de Sousa, barão, later visconde de Mauá (1813–89), born in Rio Grande do Sul, began work as an errand boy for a British importer in Rio de Janeiro at the age of thirteen. An uncle had secured him the position, but thereafter he seemed to rely principally on his own skills, both entrepreneurial and political. By the time he was twenty he was a partner in the firm and, at twenty-four, sole manager. Encouraged by the 1844 tariff and inspired by his earlier visit to England's industrial towns, he set up an iron foundry to supply the government with pipes for draining a swampy part of the city of Rio. By 1850 he employed 300 workers. Upon this establishment, Mauá built a business empire. Soon he successfully bid for the supply of gas to Rio and manufactured the necessary pipes and lamps. Next, he purchased and expanded a shipyard where he eventually constructed 72 small vessels, most of them steam. He then created a shipping company to ply the Amazon River and a tug-boat firm in Rio Grande do Sul. By 1857 he had more than doubled his workers to 667, including 85 slaves he owned outright, 75 more whom he rented and 300 foreigners.

The tariff reduction in 1857 forced Mauá to compete with foreign-made products and he then paid more attention to his banking activities and other investments. He had since 1840 been a partner in a Manchester commercial bank along with his British business partner. In 1851 he created his first bank in Brazil; a later Mauá bank had branches not only throughout southern Brazil but also in Uruguay and Argentina. He saw banks as allies of railways in which he also invested large sums. Indeed, he built the very first railway in Brazil (1854), although it was only fourteen kilometres long, really went nowhere, and, as he himself said, served only as a 'sample cloth' of what railways were and what they could do.[8] More important were Mauá's heavy investments in the São Paulo Railway and his recklessly large advances to its building contractor whose bankruptcy seriously undermined his own financial standing. The crisis that ruined several commercial banking firms in Rio in 1864 further drained Mauá's resources. His simultaneous involvement in Uruguayan politics as the chief financier of a shaky government brought him to his knees; the next financial crisis in Brazil (1875) forced him finally into an expected bankruptcy.

In all his activities Mauá was to some degree a client of the planter-dominated government and, like all clients, found his interests easily sacrificed when it suited the patron. The government's failure to extend credits to a beleaguered Mauá did not spring, however, from hostility to his commercial background on the part of a seigneurial planter class, as some have alleged, but from the planters' ability to use the system to defend their business interests with more acumen than he.

Economic decision-making increasingly centred in the port cities. Coffee factors and other merchants, bankers, fledgling industrialists, managers of insurance companies, agents of shipping lines and bureaucrats high and low, along with the accompanying shopkeepers, hoteliers, lawyers, doctors and teachers, filled the ranks of the urban upper and middle classes. Their employees or slaves – stevedores, maids, construction workers, water carriers, seamstresses, salesmen, accountants, and clerks – further extended the urban complex. By 1872 the city of Rio de Janeiro had a population of over a quarter of a million and both Recife and Salvador had over 100,000. Not big cities by international standards, they seemed enormous in contrast to other Brazilian cities or to themselves at earlier times.

---

[8] Quoted by Alberto de Faria, *Mauá – Ireneo Evangelista de Souza, barão e visconde de Mauá, 1813–1889* (2nd edn, São Paulo, 1933), 165.

Slaves supplied much of the labour in these expanding urban centres. Male slaves bore the curtained chairs on which fine ladies went about. At the port they loaded coffee sacks onto waiting ships. They also carried them through the streets to warehouses; and their heavy loads were said to cripple a man's hips and knees within ten years. Foreign travellers often commented on the widespread use of slaves in craft shops. A city such as Recife or Salvador, and much more so the metropolitan centre of Rio de Janeiro, demanded an almost endless range of work from silversmiths, carpenters, masons, painters, shoemakers and hatters, slave as well as free. Domestic slaves, principally women, were employed not only by the upper class but also by those of middling income, to carry water, fetch food from the marketplace, wash clothes at the public fountains, or empty the garbage and night-soil at the beach.

Two practices approximated urban slavery to wage labour. Slaves often did not work for their owner directly, but for someone else to whom they were rented. The practice lent a flexibility to slave labour often ignored by later theorists. The employer in this case had only a cash nexus to his worker and would prefer to find another labourer than to expend unusual effort or resources in exerting personal authority through force or favours. Some slaves hired themselves, returning to their master a fixed sum each month. These slaves found their own work, contracting out their skills or strength as best they could, but keeping for themselves any amount they earned over and above what the master demanded. They arranged for their own housing, took care of all their personal needs and sometimes even hired others – slave or free – to work for them in fulfilling contracts.

With the increasing demand for slaves in the expanding coffee sector, urban slaves decreased in number and in proportion to the urban population as a whole. Scores of city slave-owners tempted by the high prices paid by planters sold their slaves for work on the plantations, turning instead to free workers to supply their labour needs. Of the 30,000 female domestic servants of Rio de Janeiro in 1870 only 43 per cent were slave.[9] Slaves also gave way to wage-labourers in cotton manufacturing. Of the cotton-mill workers, a large proportion were free women and children, 'drawn', said one contemporary, 'from the poorest classes, a few from the direst misery'.[10] Simultaneously, immigrants

[9] Sandra Lauderdale Graham, 'Protection and obedience: the paternalist world of female domestic servants, Rio de Janeiro, 1860–1910' (unpublished Ph.D. thesis, University of Texas at Austin, 1982), 10, 18.

[10] Quoted in Stanley J. Stein, *The Brazilian cotton manufacture: textile enterprise in an underdeveloped area, 1850–1950* (Cambridge, Mass., 1957), 54.

Table 2 *Immigrants to Brazil, 1846–75*

Year	Portuguese	German	Italian	Other	Total
1846–50	256	2,143	5	2,399	4,925
1851–55	25,883	5,213		7,936	39,078
1856–60	43,112	13,707		25,813	82,669
1861–65	25,386	7,124	3,023	15,354	50,970
1866–70	24,776	5,648	1,900	13,689	46,601
1871–75	32,688	5,224	4,610	37,716	81,314
Total	152,101	39,058	9,533	102,907	305,557

Source: Imre Ferenczi, comp., *International Migrations*, ed. Walter F. Willcox (New York: National Bureau of Economic Research, 1929), 549–50.

pushed out of Portugal by unemployment, but unwilling to work in the coffee fields under harsh conditions identified with slavery, sought urban employment in Brazil. A little over 300,000 immigrants arrived during the 30-year period 1846–75 (an average of 10,000 per annum); half of them were Portuguese (see Table 2). By 1872 there were more Portuguese immigrants in Rio de Janeiro than there were slaves.

The city opened up opportunities lacking in the countryside not only for slaves but for the free. Cities allowed for some small increase in the impersonality of human relationships, more social mobility and a greater variety of acceptable behaviour. Blacks could more readily create and transmit their customs, language, music, family traditions, in short, their culture. Female domestic servants, although closely supervised, might enjoy stolen moments of liberty in their daily rounds; they certainly moved about the city with more familiarity and less restraint than did many of their mistresses hemmed in by the restrictive customs of a jealous male-dominated society. Relationships between workers and employers, nevertheless, hinged on favours provided in exchange for loyal service whether from slaves or free persons, Brazilian or Portuguese. Hierarchical social values permeated even urban life. City craft-shop owners or merchants, for example, lived in close proximity to their employees: typically, workers slept at the back of the shop and the employer and his family resided upstairs. Even the factory owner, like a paternalistic planter, supplied food, clothing and shelter, along with training. Employers wished to control the use of whatever free time remained to workers, watching over their coming and going, their casual relationships, in short, over every aspect of their behaviour. Free workers often received no wage at all but merely daily necessities and perhaps a cash bonus at the end of the year depending upon their good behaviour (thus again closing the gap between slave and free). If in the cities there was less overt violence against recalcitrant free workers than against slaves, they could nevertheless be constantly threatened with dismissal and a consequent loss not only of wages but of housing and protection. The scarcity of alternative urban opportunities transformed such threats into a disguised violence. Even as urban slavery declined, cash wages only slowly displaced the obligations of dependence. And while fewer and fewer urban dwellers felt committed to the maintenance of slavery, slaves continued to be part of the urban scene until abolition in 1888.

Although with the growth of cities groups alien to, and even hostile towards, landowners eventually emerged, in 1870 the latter still exercised clear authority in most political decisions. Certainly, if the alleged dichotomy between merchants and landowners is recognized as more an historian's creation than a past reality and it is noticed that insofar as it existed it only occasionally led to conflicting interests, landowners and merchants together can be said to have played the dominant role in the political system. Manufacturers before 1870 did not form an important or independent political force and many of them were themselves merchants engaged in the export and import trade. The non-propertied, slave and free, although, of course, the vast majority, exercised little influence upon the state except through the age-long processes of passive resistance. Some historians have alleged that a bureaucratic-political class or estate stood as a counterweight to the landowners, but most politicians and bureaucrats at this time either held land themselves or were connected to landowning interests through family ties. Others, through their links to merchant and financial interests, had interests essentially in harmony with those of the propertied class. Even those landowners who did not feel they received a fair share of the system's benefits were on the whole content to let the wealthiest sectors exercise power in order to maintain social order, so essential for their own continued control over slaves and the lower classes and for the political stability that Brazilian publicists never tired of contrasting with the disturbances allegedly endemic in Spanish America. The values that justified the social hierarchy also reinforced the authority of the propertied within the political system.

A constitutional monarch reigned in Brazil. The cabinet was responsible both to him and to a parliament consisting of a Senate of a little over fifty members and a Chamber of Deputies of around 120. The emperor, with advice from a Council of State, appointed Senators from among the three candidates who received the most votes in each province. Senators served for life. Deputies were chosen by indirect elections at least every four years. Pedro II (1825–91), then a young child, had succeeded to the throne on the abdication of his father Pedro I (1798–1834) in 1831. By 1850, now 25 years old, he no longer relied upon the narrow coterie of advisers which had guided his first steps as ruler, but he still exercised the powers vested in him by the constitution of 1824 with great caution, much more sensitive than his father to the realities of economic and political power in Brazil. He proved useful in adjudicating disputes among members of the dominant class. Despite a stream of instructions addressed to cabinet members generally advocating moderate reform, they only occasionally heeded his advice. He was never able – and rarely wished – to impose basic changes that would threaten the interests of the propertied who sustained his authority. He took pains never to discredit his office by acts of personal immorality or moments of levity. A sober, often sombre man, Pedro II attended to the minutiae of government, not because he wielded vast power, but because he exercised so little. By his constant meddling in details, however, he inadvertently drew the blame for Brazil's failure to undertake major change.

For the emperor's presence loomed visibly large. The nation invariably returned representatives to parliament who supported the cabinet in power. This was true despite the façade of liberal measures protecting the rights of political opponents, maintaining freedom of the press and attempting to ensure the honest counting of the vote. Only the emperor, by dismissing one prime minister and summoning a rival, could bring in another party to control the machinery of government. Since both political parties – Conservative and Liberal – drew support from virtually the same social and economic constituency – and in some cases alternating support from identical voters – Pedro II did not thus threaten any dominant social group or economic interest. Rather, he responded to the rhythms impelling or restraining modest shifts in the direction sought by the political and bureaucratic leaders closely in touch with regional concerns.

A Council of State, consisting of twelve senior politicians, appointed by the emperor for life, advised him on the exercise of his 'moderative power'. In choosing them the emperor, by custom, relied on nominations from the prime minister. The emperor turned to the Council, in turn, for advice in the exercise of his right to appoint and dismiss the ministers. Each cabinet had either to gain the confidence of the legislature as well, or to ask the emperor to dismiss parliament and call new elections which he would do after consultation with members of the Council of State. Legislation required the emperor's approval, and he would normally consult the council before granting it. Finally, the Council of State acted as a court to consider those cases involving disputes between branches of government and suits brought against the government, thus exercising a judicial review over the constitutionality of laws and decrees.

The prime minister, called President of the Council of Ministers, selected his cabinet members with a careful eye to balancing competing political ambitions, regional strengths and parliamentary skills and contacts.[11] The cabinet guided the policies of the government. It drew up the budget for submission to parliament, and, in practice, it prepared proposed legislation for debate. Most importantly, it named all other administrative officers, appointed, subject to some restrictions, all judges and bishops, and granted most military promotions.

The appointment of the presidents of each province stood out as most decisive. Although responsible for carrying out the directives issued by the cabinet and ensuring compliance with the laws of the empire, the provincial presidents' chief function, in fact, was to produce electoral returns favourable to the cabinet. For that task they relied on patronage as their most important instrument. Provincial presidents distributed positions as rewards for past – and future – political loyalty. The cabinet relied heavily upon the presidents for political information and sound judgement. Despite their crucial role, however, presidents had a very short term of office. They served at the pleasure of the prime minister, and in his constant re-shuffling of the national bureaucracy, he moved presidents from province to province, brought them to Rio to fill key positions, promoted them to cabinet posts, or shoved them into minor sinecures when he considered them inadequate. A significant number of presidents simultaneously served in parliament and therefore departed from their provincial capitals for Rio de Janeiro at the beginning of each

---

[11] José Murillo de Carvalho, 'Elite and state-building in imperial Brazil' (unpublished Ph.D. thesis, Stanford University, 1974), 190, shows that during the period 1853–71, 26 per cent of the cabinet ministers came from Bahia and Pernambuco, another 26 per cent came from the city and province of Rio de Janeiro, 18 per cent from Minas Gerais and São Paulo, 24 per cent from other provinces and 6 per cent from outside Brazil, presumably from Portugal.

session, leaving the day-to-day administration of the province in the hands of vice-presidents.

The provincial presidents' chief agents both in enforcing the law and gathering political intelligence were the provincial chiefs of police and their police commissioners (*delegados*), also appointed by the central government. Deputy commissioners (*subdelegados*) and block inspectors (*inspetores de quarteirão*) – twenty-five houses to a block – carried the authority of the central government, at least theoretically, into every small locality. Aside from the chief, however, police officials did not receive government salaries, but derived their personal income from their ordinary, private activities; in short, in the countryside most were landowners who cherished such positions in order to exert added authority, especially over local rivals. Henrique Marques Lins, the wealthy Pernambucan sugar planter, secured the position of police commissioner for one son-in-law and placed a brother-in-law as his deputy. Three other police officials in that county owned between them nine plantations. In the cities presidents preferred lawyers and judges but occasionally found it advantageous to name military officers to these positions. By relying on ordinary citizens to carry out its orders, the government kept open the lines of communication and recognized the power and importance of the locally prominent.

Just as from ancient times the Portuguese king ruled principally as judge, so distinctions between judicial authority and law enforcement or police functions were blurred. Since the passage of a controversial law in 1841, local police commissioners held judicial powers. They not only pressed charges, but also assembled evidence, heard witnesses and presented the county judge (*juiz municipal*) – also centrally appointed – with a written record of the inquiry from which the judge derived his verdict. Locally elected justices of the peace (*juízes de paz*) who had earlier held police authority now mattered only as organizers of electoral boards. For ordinary citizens, police commissioners now became the focus of authority. Mercy could temper the severity of the law, especially for the politically compliant; but no doubt remained that such benevolence could as easily be withheld.

In contrast to the police commissioners, judges, who shared a common education in either of Brazil's two law schools (often starting in one and finishing in the other), hoped for advancement within a professional hierarchy. Although they might own land, slaves, or businesses, they received a salary from the government and endured frequent removals from place to place. District Judges (*juízes de direito*) enjoyed tenure for life but normally remained at one location only for four years. At the end of that period they could either be re-assigned for another term or be 'promoted' to a court of higher rank but not always at a more attractive place. After a second term they faced, once again, the likelihood of a move. At any time, a district judge could lose his position by being named chief of police; after serving in such a position even for a short time, he would be returned to the bench but no longer necessarily at his old location. He could also be retained without a seat, receiving his salary while awaiting a vacancy. District judges were recruited from the ranks of county judges. The latter could be shifted around even more readily and, at election time, their placement resembled moves in an elaborate chess game.

All public servants who wished to keep their posts attended to winning elections for the party then in power in Rio de Janeiro. Elections were indirect and the suffrage limited. In addition to women and slaves whose exclusion from access to the ballot box was taken for granted, the law barred men under 25 years of age, beggars, vagrants, personal and domestic servants, as well as all those whose income from property did not reach 200 *reis* per year. Much debate concentrated on how income should be defined and proved, but anyone could vote if his name appeared on the list of qualified voters. This fact – as well as the decision whether a potential voter were really the person so named – depended entirely on the electoral boards. If challenged regarding income or indentity, a prospective voter needed only to present the sworn statements of three witnesses to prove his case; contrary depositions, however, could as easily deny him the right to vote. If there were witnesses on both sides – as, of course, there usually were – the electoral board decided according to its best lights. From 1846, membership on the board depended upon the results of the previous elections. Voting was only for electors (except in the case of county councilmen who were directly elected). The electors then met in district electoral colleges to choose deputies to parliament, members of the provincial assemblies, and to nominate senators when a vacancy occurred. The most voted for elector in each parish became justice of the peace and presided over the electoral board at the next election; all the board's other members were also electors.

The electoral process provided ample opportunity for pressure both from the central government and from local oligarchs. Citizens did not vote secretly. Because most voters were illiterate, they deposited in the ballot box a list of candidates for electors received from a local patron. The police commissioner maintained order at election time; sometimes this meant keeping 'trouble-makers' – that is, opposition voters – away from the polls. The election, if challenged, could be thrown out either by the county judge or provincial president. The electors themselves, like the local potentates in general, had much to gain by supporting the government candidate and much to lose if he were defeated. Consequently, elections for parliament invariably returned a majority who favoured the cabinet then in power; sometimes the government's support in the Chamber of Deputies was nearly unanimous. In 1855 the creation of single-member instead of province-wide electoral districts enabled minority interests to gain some representation in parliament, since the government could not give its full attention to all areas, although even this opening narrowed again with changes in the electoral law in 1860 (see below).

A politician who aspired to national prominence, perhaps eventually to be prime minister, demonstrated his strength by rewarding supporters with local appointive offices. Since cabinet members or their direct appointees could fill virtually any local position – whether judicial, police, educational or tax-gathering – an elaborately articulated column of patronage formed the backbone of the political system.[12] Ultimately, patronage linked court and village to connect even the *agregados* to a national system of personal obligations. Through politics, local potentates defended a clientelistic and paternalistic social structure and projected it into the next generation. A slave-owner or his son participated in order to obtain bureaucratic appointments, sinecures, livings, or commissions for his family and for the vast network of dependants and clients each family member carried with him. The state, to be sure, was not simply the 'executive committee' of the economically powerful, first, because the latter were not themselves agreed upon particular ends and

---

[12] Among the positions to be filled through political patronage were those of the Church. Following colonial precedent, the government proposed to the Vatican the names of those to fill the archbishopric of Bahia and the eight other bishoprics. Parish priests were similarly nominated to the bishops and promotions or transfers depended on political commitment. Although the Church could summon loyalties in its own right, it meshed with other institutions through the structure of patronage. The state collected and kept the tithe and paid only modest salaries to churchmen. Other ordained clergy sought employment as chaplains on *fazendas* or for wealthy lay brotherhoods in the cities. Patrons, whether private or public, expected deference from the clergy as from their other clients. Whereas in earlier times churchmen actively engaged in rebellions, by the middle of the century they preached order and obedience to constituted authority. Only in the 1870s did some churchmen question whether this authority resided in the emperor or the pope.

means and, secondly, because the safeguarding of the overall system sometimes required actions that offended the interests of powerful groups. But the state reinforced the hegemony of the propertied by reproducing within itself the paternalistic order of deference on the one hand and favours on the other.

In maintaining and consolidating national unity, the empire drew on the political and administrative skills of a relatively small group of men of similar backgrounds, education and experience. Recent research has shown that of those cabinet ministers whose social backgrounds could be identified from biographical dictionaries, 54 per cent were connected to landowning interests and another 14 to business. Seventy-two per cent had been trained in law, either in the case of the first generation at the University of Coimbra in Portugal or at the Brazilian law faculties in Recife and São Paulo.[13] To enter such faculties candidates needed both an expensive secondary education and connections to men of influence. Another path into the political elite lay through the military academy, more open to talented youth from modest backgrounds; but this route became less common after 1850. After graduation, the aspiring politician sought placement in ever more diverse geographic locations, broadening his contacts while also making him always more obligated to repay the patronage of older, more established figures. From district attorney to county and district judgeships and then on to provincial presidencies, the mobile candidate demonstrated his administrative abilities and political steadfastness. Election to the Chamber of Deputies and Senate finally put him into the pool from which cabinet ministers were chosen. As the landed, slave-owning class participated actively in politics at all levels, including the highest, it forged links across provincial and regional boundaries. Despite the sectional loyalties that arose from focusing on distinct export crops and the increasing orientation toward port cities which the railways encouraged, their fundamental political unity was strengthened in the middle decades of the nineteenth century. A common loyalty to the crown served as symbolic expression of this unity.

Yet within a narrow range disagreements surfaced of course. Although there was much truth in the saying that 'nothing resembles a Conservative more than a Liberal in power', some differences emerged, if for no other reason than that the Liberals were not as often in power. Some political leaders of the era – a minority – placed slightly greater emphasis on individual liberty than on public order and preferred

---

13 Carvalho, 'Elite and state-building', 97–8, 132.

provincial or local autonomy to central authority. Yet even on these divisions, though they loomed at particular moments, the positions of individuals varied so much over time that one suspects they were merely rhetorical stands for momentary political advantage, rather than firm convictions. Certainly none of these divisions addressed the legitimacy of the system as a whole. Politicians in Rio Grande do Sul, São Paulo and Minas Gerais, and from the cities, more often tended to identify with the Liberal party than did those from the coffee-rich Paraíba valley, but numerous examples could be found to the contrary. Those who desired, for diverse reasons, to move towards an end of slavery typically sided with the Liberals, but the Conservatives actually passed the few emancipationist laws and Liberals proved easily divided on the issue, since their constituents, like those of the Conservatives, included slave-owners.

To speak of parties is somewhat misleading, for parliamentary agglomerations lacked unity and did not depend on disciplined electorates, nor represent ideologically defined movements. Several important leaders abandoned the Liberals to join the Conservatives and vice versa. Out in the districts party labels were adopted with little consistency, and much local-level struggle occurred within and not between the so-called parties. Village factions, entwined by family and the ancient ties of patrons and clients, vied for electoral victory in order to receive positions of local authority. No particular political philosophy distinguished one group from another. Their elected representatives, once in parliament, formed unstable alliances with each other. Contemporaries, however, continued to think of Liberals and Conservatives in terms of their nineteenth-century British counterparts.

A search for accommodation, a fear of party strife and an effort to head off extreme reformist demands characterized national politics from 1853 to 1868. The sequence of cabinets makes clear that, at most, a successful politician could advocate only gradual and measured change. Acceptable reforms must be bestowed by those above and never result from demands of those below. Based as it was on slavery, society appeared inherently unstable to contemporaries; paternalistic measures combined with firmness served to keep it stable.

Since 1837, as coffee emerged to give the nation a new economic centre of gravity, there had been a steady movement away from the liberalism of the previous decade and a reaction towards the restoration of the power of the central government. The institution in 1841 of centrally appointed police commissioners holding extensive judicial authority was the culmination of that process and remained the touch-stone for subsequent Liberal-Conservative differences. Unsuccessful Liberal revolts in 1842 and 1848 played into the hands of those who saw excessive provincial autonomy and individual liberty threatening social order with anarchy. The triumph of the Conservatives in the elections of 1849 – only one Liberal won a seat in parliament – provided the basis for strengthening still further the Conservative tenor of the cabinet named in September 1848 headed by the well-known Conservative and former regent, Pedro de Araújo Lima, visconde de Olinda (1793–1870). Paulino José Soares de Sousa, later visconde de Uruguai (1807–66) and his wife's brother-in-law Joaquim José Rodrigues Tôrres, later visconde de Itaboraí,[14] joined Eusébio de Queiroz Coutinho Matoso da Câmara (1812–68) in government. All three had close ties either directly or through marriage to slave-holding coffee-planters of Rio de Janeiro province. Known as the *Saquaremas* (from the name of the *fazenda* where they often met) they believed in a strong central government, which they or their friends could count on dominating. The firm control exercised by this Conservative cabinet enabled it to pass and enforce a number of measures that had once been too controversial to tackle, notably the suppression of the international slave trade and the land law of 1850. The cabinet also pushed through parliament in 1850 a Commercial Code, which had been debated for fifteen years. By newly codifying commercial relations regarding partnerships, contracts and bankruptcies, as well as creating business-run courts to adjudicate commercial conflicts, the measure helped businesses within Brazil to mesh with the international economy. Not long after, parliament empowered the government to guarantee interest on the capital invested in railways, a measure which bolstered the efforts of the planters to link Brazil more closely to overseas markets. The creation of a semi-official Bank of Brazil expanded government control of the currency by replacing privately owned regional banks of issue. Itaboraí also initiated attempts towards lowering import duties. Finally, reform of the National Guard in 1850, by eliminating the election of its officers, placed it tightly under the command of the national government. This cabinet thus completed the process of centralizing authority in a government now firmly managed by the coffee-planters of Rio de Janeiro.

[14] For the sake of simplicity, upon second and subsequent reference to individuals titles will be used even if only acquired later.

Once central government had been solidly established it proved possible to conciliate warring political factions by granting space within the system to conforming Liberals. In 1853 the Conservative Honório Hermeto Carneiro Leão, visconde and later marquês de Paraná (1801–56), presided over a government of conciliation (*conciliação*) which included, for instance, both the distinguished mineiro, Antonio Paulino Limpo de Abreu, visconde de Abaeté (1798–1883), who had been a leader in the 1842 Liberal revolt in Minas Gerais and, as Minister of War from 1855, Luís Alves de Lima e Silva, marquês and future duque de Caxias (1803–80), who derived his prestige principally from his military exploits while suppressing regional revolts. Eusébio, Itaboraí and Uruguai found themselves excluded. The relatively young João Maurício Wanderley, future barão de Cotegipe (1815–89), who tried to modernize his Bahia sugar mills, similarly believed the way to preserve the old order generally was to modify it. José Maria Paranhos, future visconde de Rio Branco (1817–80), and Luis Pedreira do Couto Ferraz, visconde de Bom Retiro (1818–86), had both been Liberals but could now be counted as progressive Conservatives. José Tomás Nabuco de Araújo (1813–78), although considered a Conservative at this time, already leant toward the Liberal party which he would later direct: deeply committed to individual freedom, and somewhat anticlerical, he had doubts about the value of the monarchy and advocated the gradual emancipation of slaves, yet simultaneously felt that Brazil could be changed only slowly if it were to avoid the destructive disorder of social revolution.

One of the cabinet of *conciliação*'s most important measures, in the event, was the creation in 1855 of single-member electoral districts. By allowing the Liberals a chance to elect some members of parliament, despite Conservative control of the electoral system in general, it drew Liberals into peaceful participation and signalled the possibility of their once again attaining power. As a result of this law a sizeable minority of Liberals were elected in 1856. In response to their presence the new cabinet led by Olinda included as Treasury Minister the Liberal leader, Bernardo de Sousa Franco (1805–75). He finally pushed through the lower tariff first proposed by his Conservative predecessor in 1851, thus combining his ideological predispositions with support for the interests of export-oriented land owners. His pet project was the reform of the banking law, creating banks of issue and thus increasing the currency in circulation. On this issue planters divided as did merchants, depending on their particular circumstance as debtors or creditors. The measure proved short-lived, however. Eusébio, Itaboraí and Uruguai (the *Saquaremas*) all attacked it in the Senate. In a cabinet reshuffle in 1858, the journalist Francisco de Sales Tôrres Homen, later visconde de Inhomirim (1822–76), replaced Sousa Franco.

The appointment of Inhomirim signalled a renewed endorsement of conservatism. He had once been a Liberal, indeed a virulent critic of the emperor and had collaborated with the Liberal revolts of 1842, suffering exile as a result. He had since mellowed and been wooed back into the mainstream of national political life. Through a newspaper he edited he had ardently defended the moderately conservative policies of the *conciliação* cabinet. Sousa Franco's banking policy then provoked his ire and he became its most articulate critic, both in the press and in parliament. As Minister of Finance, Inhomirim proceeded to undo Sousa Franco's measures. He also opposed the efforts of Mauá to establish unregulated joint-stock companies. Finally, he began work on a severely restrictive company law which, when passed in 1860, forced all would-be companies first to obtain government approval. The next Conservative cabinet of 1859–61 not only pushed through that restrictive company law but reversed the direction of electoral reform by enlarging the area of electoral districts with three candidates instead of one chosen from each. Regional chieftains thus gained strength against local factions, and the representation of local interests and minority viewpoints became more difficult.

The elections of December 1860 halted the conservative drift. Middle-of-the-road (conciliation) Conservatives, disaffected by those retrograde measures, joined forces with the Liberals who, since their partial victories of 1856, had modest patronage to dispense. The campaign developed as a particularly heated one, especially in the city of Rio, hot-bed of dissident opinion and focus of national attention. One old Liberal leader, Teófilo Ottoni (1807–69), a veteran of the struggles in Minas Gerais of 1842, adopted a white handkerchief as his symbol when campaigning in Rio's parishes to the loud acclaim of the urban populace. The result of the election, while continuing the Conservative majority in parliament, also led to the seating of several fiery Liberals. Thirty years later Joaquim Nabuco, the first major historian of the empire, wrote that the 1860 election reversed the conservative trend begun in 1837 and marked the turn of the tide toward a reformism that would culminate in the overthrow of the monarchy in 1889. For the time being, however, accommodation continued to characterize cabinet-level politics.

The election of 1860 split both Conservative and Liberal 'parties'. The more progressive among the elected Conservatives joined with a number of Liberals to form a parliamentary league. The Progressive League, as it was sometimes called, intended to revoke the legislation of December 1841 and remove judicial powers from police authorities. The *saquaremas* still felt such a measure would threaten the order they had so carefully created, while at the other extreme some Liberals considered such measures far too moderate. They regarded such a reform as merely the first step toward a revision of the entire Constitution which would end, or at least restrict, the emperor's 'moderative power', require senators to stand for election at regular intervals, allow provincial presidents to be elected rather than appointed, and make elections for deputy direct. None of these far-reaching reforms could make headway in the 1860s.

These new divisions in parliament led to an early defeat for the Conservative cabinet named in 1861. League support for a motion of no-confidence proved crucial, but when a League member – former Conservative Zacarias de Góis e Vasconcelos (1815–77) – was named prime minister, proposing only modest changes in the 1841 law, the Liberals abandoned him, and he too was forced to resign. A compromise cabinet unwilling to move in any direction proved not much stronger, but managed to hang on for lack of an alternative until forced to call fresh elections in 1863.

The new parliament, meeting in January 1864, reflected two changes in the intervening period. The Progressive League had drafted a moderate programme of reform specifically excluding major alterations to the Constitution, but calling for the separation of judicial from police authority. Meanwhile, Conservative leaders had decided that the provisions of the 1841 laws were no longer a necessary condition for their own survival or for the stability of the empire. As these tendencies became clearer, the 'purer' Liberals found themselves isolated. The centre had again emerged victorious. Zacarias once more became prime minister.

From a wealthy family in Bahia, Zacarias had been elected to parliament in 1850 as a Conservative and soon joined the Itaboraí cabinet. As a student and then professor at the Recife law school, however, Zacarias had already been much influenced by his reading of John Stuart Mill and Jeremy Bentham: he increasingly believed the individual should be protected from state control, became an opponent of the 1841 law, and in 1860 published a stinging critique of the 'moderative power' of the emperor. Still, he did not question the larger framework of government, wished only cautious reforms and later, in fact, emerged as a staunch defender of Church prerogatives. A sharp-tongued speaker, he had a special gift for making enemies through his sarcasms and cruel jibes. Liberals from Rio Grande do Sul hastened to attack him when he appeared to lack forcefulness in pursuing Brazilian diplomatic goals in Uruguay. He fell from power after seven months as Brazil moved toward war, first with Uruguay and then with Paraguay.

The Paraguayan War, a major international conflict, had other effects besides preventing Zacarias from pushing through moderate reforms. It exposed the contradiction between the façade of polished discourse among political elites and the exploitative realities faced by most Brazilians. It also exacerbated tensions within the Brazilian military. Yet, by sharpening divisions within Brazil, it eventually advanced the cause of reform, especially with regard to slavery. Zacarias would be at the centre of that later storm, when he once again became prime minister in 1866. Initially, however, the War drew attention away from internal change.

First the Portuguese, then the Brazilians, had a long history of involvement in the affairs of the Banda Oriental of the Río de la Plata (Uruguay). The Portuguese had established themselves at Colônia do Sacramento in 1680 and only withdrew in 1776. Portuguese armies retook the region in 1816 and from 1821 until the creation of the independent state of Uruguay in 1828 the area had been a Brazilian province. Then, preoccupied with ensuring their own unity during the 1830s and 1840s, Brazilians had not been able to withstand the expanding influence in Uruguay of Juan Manuel de Rosas, the Argentine caudillo.[15] Meanwhile, the cattlemen of Rio Grande do Sul had extended their herds and lands on both sides of the border, frequently taking their young cattle to the better pastures of Uruguay and later driving them back to Rio Grande do Sul for slaughter. Having given up their ten-year struggle to create an independent state of their own in 1845, they looked to the central government to protect their interests in Uruguay. The Conservative and centralizing *saquarema* faction, in power in Rio from 1848, happily co-operated. As foreign minister, visconde de Uruguai also hoped eventually to open a secure passage for Brazilian ships to guarantee free navigation up the River Paraguay to the province of Mato Grosso. In pursuit of the goal of reasserting Brazilian influence to the south, Brazil allied itself in 1851 with a Uruguayan faction opposed to Rosas' influence and – with Justo José Urquiza, a restless caudillo in north-eastern

---

[15] The politics of the River Plate Republics and the origins of the Paraguayan War are discussed in detail in Lynch, *CHLA* III, chap. 15.

Argentina – committed Brazilian troops under the command of Caxias to the attempt (soon successful) to overthrow Rosas and install in his place in Buenos Aires a progressive, European-oriented, cosmopolitan government.

Uruguay continued, however, to be torn by internecine struggle. And whichever government was in power in Montevideo had to contend with at least 20,000 resident Brazilians who owned some 400 estates with lands totalling almost a third of the national territory. Constant civil war between *Blancos* and *Colorados*, the two 'parties' of Uruguay, meant many Brazilians nursed grievances and pressed monetary claims against successive Uruguayan governments. Furthermore, the Brazilians wished to move cattle from one estate to another or to drive them to market across the frontier into Rio Grande do Sul without paying taxes. All Uruguayan governments considered these revenues necessary to finance the costs of maintaining order. Mauá's firm had meanwhile virtually become Uruguay's official bank. Brazilian cattlemen in the area blamed Mauá for the taxes the government levied to pay off its debts to him, while he saw as excessive their claims for damages which threatened to force the government to default. Moreover, the Uruguayans, having abolished slavery in 1853, threatened to free the slaves Brazilians brought into the country. A clash was inevitable.

Some Brazilian Liberals who in the mid-1860s participated in the Progressive League owed political debts in Rio Grande do Sul. They were thus committed to pressing Brazilians' claims against Uruguay. One way of doing so was to back the faction then out of power – the *Colorados* – as they sought, with Argentine support, to overthrow the *Blanco* government in Montevideo. The *Blancos*, meanwhile, correctly perceiving the threat posed by both Brazil and Argentina, sought to ally themselves with Paraguay's dictator, Francisco Solano López.

López, to whom the guaraní-speaking Paraguayans were fiercely loyal, had inherited from his father leadership of a nation which had remained largely isolated from the rest of the world. He sensed the encroaching threat of Brazilian and Argentine power and feared the definitive loss of disputed territory claimed by Paraguay on both borders. He responded only too willingly to appeals for help from some Uruguayans, but did not announce his intentions clearly enough to make Brazilian and Argentine leaders understand that he considered any threat to Uruguay a threat to Paraguay and to himself. Nevertheless, when in June 1864 Argentine and Brazilian ministers met in Montevideo to work out what they thought would be a settlement of the internal Uruguayan struggle, they informally agreed on joint action should Paraguay come to the rescue of the defeated *Blancos*.

The terms of this agreement proved a self-fulfilling prophecy. By their action López felt confirmed in his conviction that Brazil and Argentina planned to divide Paraguay between them. When the settlement in Uruguay did not hold, Brazilian troops moved into Uruguay (September 1864) to enforce Brazil's claims to reparations for damages to Brazilian citizens and to install the *Colorados* in power. Paraguay responded by seizing Brazilian ships on the Río Paraguay and invading Brazilian territory. Mistakenly counting on the support of Urquiza in north-eastern Argentina, López ordered his troops to cross Argentine territory and thus found himself at war with that country too. Secret clauses of the treaty signed in May 1865 by Brazil, Argentina and Uruguay called, among other things, for the transfer of disputed Paraguayan territory to Argentina and Brazil, as well as for the opening of Paraguayan rivers to international trade and the deposition of López. When these provisions leaked to the press, an international outcry ensued, but the allies did not abandon their aims.

The war has been presented by some historians as the result of the mad schemes of a megalomaniac Paraguayan tyrant. In fact it resulted from the step-by-step escalation of conflicting interests, complicated by a series of mistaken but understandable judgements on all sides. López not irrationally feared Paraguayan dismemberment and the end of his nation's existence, which he understood to depend on an equilibrium of power in the region. He seriously miscalculated his own strength and the support he could get from Urquiza, apparently doubting that the Argentine caudillo had really made his peace with Buenos Aires in 1862. Leaders in Buenos Aires quite reasonably feared the rise of Urquiza in the north-east in an alliance with López and the *Blancos* of Uruguay. In López's fear of Brazil he was encouraged by the belligerent statements of some Brazilian parliamentarians and the contingency planning of Brazil's diplomats. He believed he had made clear his views that Brazilian intervention in Uruguay meant war. Brazil wanted the *Colorados* in power in Uruguay so as to advance the interests of its citizens and to assert its own power in the region. Brazilians did not believe López would actually go to war, but were confident that, should he do so, Brazil would easily win and thus rid itself of troublesome border questions while guaranteeing the free navigation of the Río Paraguay. Wrongheadedness on all sides had provoked war.

From the start the war went badly for the Paraguayans. Brazilian troops, having installed a compliant government in Montevideo, moved quickly to the Paraguayan front. By September 1865 the Brazilians had cleared foreign troops from Rio Grande do Sul. But Brazil, anxious to assert its hegemony in the region, then spurned Paraguayan efforts toward peace. The Paraguayans fought ever more steadfastly once the theatre of battle moved into their own territory. Allied troops suffered a major defeat at Curupaití in September 1866. The Argentine general and president Bartolomé Mitre, who had exercised a loose command over allied troops, now turned his attention to opposing dissidents in Argentina where the war had proved unpopular, especially among provincial caudillos. Brazil carried on alone, stubbornly insisting on overthrowing López himself, and the war dragged on for another four tragic years.

The war exposed several tensions within Brazilian society. Brazil's determination to pursue the war with Paraguay after Brazilian territory had been cleared of Paraguayan troops and to overthrow and kill López himself bespoke a deep national anxiety. Brazilian leaders justified their action on the grounds that they had to bring civilization to that barbaric country and to free the Paraguayans from tyranny. They frequently ridiculed the racial heritage of Paraguay and hinted at a concept of white supremacy. Perhaps Brazilian politicians doubted the degree of their own 'civilization' and feared disparaging comparisons with the European nations with which they so closely identified. Brazilians were surrounded by slaves, but felt an increasing sense of guilt regarding their enslavement. The ferocious pursuit of the war by Brazil seems to have been an opportunity to work out a gnawing self-doubt.

An opera first performed just as the Paraguayan War ended indirectly reveals some of those racial doubts. Antonio Carlos Gomes (1836–96) based his opera on a romantic novel by José de Alencar (1829–77) titled *O Guaraní*. Set in the sixteenth century, both novel and opera glorified the noble savage and racial mixture between Portuguese and Indians, but ignored the African background of the bulk of the Brazilian population. A search for a mythology encasing Brazilian themes within European forms – the opera had an Italian libretto and first played at La Scala – reflects not only the divorce between upper and lower classes but the alienation of the intelligentsia from a country in which 79 per cent of the adult free population did not know how to read or write. Even Antonio de Castro Alves (1847–71), usually remembered for the moving denunciation of the slave trade he included in his first book of poems in 1870, nevertheless endowed black protagonists with 'white' qualities, even

altering their physiognomy to make them acceptable as heroic characters. Slaves struggled not against flesh-and-blood masters but against
vague, sinister, impersonal forces. A Europeanized high culture in this
export economy revealed an understandable reluctance to confront the
shattering implications of a reality marked by personal oppression
witnessed daily on plantation or city street.

The Paraguayan War also brought to a head conflicts within the
Brazilian armed forces. The landed class had taken measures to ensure
their dominance over public instruments of force by creating in 1831 a
National Guard in which they were the officers. As a centralizing
measure, the Conservative cabinet in 1850 had made all positions as
officers in the National Guard appointive rather than elective, but these
appointments continued to go almost exclusively to large landowners.
Typical was the case of Henrique Marques Lins, the wealthy north-
eastern sugar planter, who commanded the county National Guard and
whose fifteen company captains included eight who between them
owned sixteen plantations. The regular army officer corps, however, was
also restructured and to some extent professionalized in 1850. A career
open to talent through the military academies became possible for those
who could neither afford the costly secondary education needed to enter
law school nor count on the necessary contacts. The seeds were thus
sown for the eventual growth of a certain class hostility between military
officers and civilian politicians, although its flowering came only in the
1880s and later.

In the period before the Paraguayan War, the very highest military
officers still customarily came from or established close connections with
elite families. Caxias, for instance, was the brother of a leading financier
of the empire and was himself an active Conservative political leader who
had been elected to the Senate in 1845, serving in three cabinets, twice as
prime minister. As a political leader he defended the interests of the
dominant land- and slave-owning class. Younger, middle-ranking officers, however, especially those enjoying rapid promotion during the
war, did not share Caxias's easy familiarity with the powerful.

Since even the officers of the National Guard recognized they were
usually unsuited for leadership in actual combat, it was common at times
of national emergency to suspend such officers for indeterminate periods
and appoint army officers in their stead. During the Paraguayan War,
especially at the beginning, there were not enough army officers to go
around, and National Guard commanders whose experience had been

limited to parading in fancy uniforms on Sundays suddenly found themselves in charge of troops under fire. As the war dragged on however, the percentage of troops drawn from the National Guard fell from 74 per cent in 1866 to 44 per cent in 1869. The regular officer corps grew accordingly. Not surprisingly army officers had all their prejudices about their National Guard counterparts confirmed during the war. After the war the Rio Branco cabinet ended all compulsory service in the National Guard, made Guard officers purely honorific without command authority and denied them the right to recruit soldiers for the army or to exercise policing functions. Landowners acquiesced, partly because they welcomed the opportunity to turn over to others the task of fighting wars and partly because they correctly understood that their local authority remained secure and their national power did not depend on the direct command of military force.

Finally, the war with Paraguay exacerbated partisan political strife, provoked the return of the Conservatives to power (in 1868) and contributed to the break-up of the middle-of-the-road Progressive League. When Zacarias, the somewhat cautious Progressive reformer, fell from power in mid-1864 he had been replaced by Francisco José Furtado (1818–70), also a Progressive though more committed to reform than Zacarias. He was not, however, as able a politician. His appointment of the Conservative visconde do Rio Branco as emissary to Montevideo alienated the Liberal members of parliament. Then, when Paraguayan troops invaded Brazilian territory, the logical choice to lead Brazilian forces would have been Caxias. As a Conservative party stalwart and regular defender of the law of 1841, however, he appeared to Liberals as the personification of all they opposed. The Furtado government nevertheless approached him at this time of crisis. He replied that since he would rely principally on National Guard troops from Rio Grande do Sul, the provincial president there could not be the incumbent who had been appointed to carry out the political will of the Liberal-Progressives. The Minister of War agreed, but when Liberal members of parliament learned of this kow-towing to the Conservative leanings of Caxias, they raged, and Furtado hesitated. The Minister of War resigned and Furtado chose a well-known personal enemy of Caxias to hold that portfolio. Caxias, not surprisingly, now altogether refused to lead the Brazilian military effort. The controversy brought down the Furtado cabinet in May 1865, and its successor, still Progressive-Liberal in composition, determined to manage without Caxias.

Brazilian troops at first fared reasonably well without him and by October 1865 López seemed to be heading for an early defeat. Two generals and an admiral closely identified with the Liberals led the Brazilian troops. But the defeat at Curupaití (September 1866) changed everything. The need for a strongly unified Brazilian command became ever more evident. Meanwhile, the Progressive cabinet in Rio split over the old issue of repealing the 1841 law; as a result, in August 1866 Zacarias once again became prime minister.

At this time Zacarias demonstrated genuine political skill by winning over Caxias's support while not losing that of the Liberals. He offered the Liberals a stunningly radical proposal: major steps toward the emancipation of the slaves. In the Speech from the Throne which Zacarias drafted for delivery in May 1867 he had the emperor announce that measures towards this end would be taken up as soon as the fighting ended. Considerations other than political tactics led in the same direction. Some leaders feared British pressure for the abolition of slavery combined with a slave uprising.[16] Sectors of the new coffee elite, especially the planters of São Paulo, increasingly doubted whether slaves could continue to supply their labour needs. And there were some signs of growing urban middle class opposition to slavery. By moving toward emancipation, Zacarias won the firm support of many Liberals despite his appointment of Caxias as sole commander of Brazil's military efforts. Once Caxias finally got things in order on the war front and began winning battles in early 1868, however, the Conservatives felt they should be the main beneficiaries. They intrigued to bring about a rift between Caxias and the prime minister. Although their efforts proved unsuccessful at first, Zacarias did resign in the middle of the year over the emperor's choice, on the advice of the Council of State, of a by now notably anti-Liberal Inhomirim as senator. Both contemporaries and later commentators have disagreed, however, as to the motives behind

---

[16] The British minister to Brazil in the early 1860s, William Christie, had stridently called on Brazil to undertake a series of measures leading to the final end of slavery. In 1863 he ordered the seizure by British ships of several Brazilian vessels outside the port of Rio de Janeiro, ostensibly as reprisals for Brazil's failure to comply with some of his minor demands, but evidently to suggest British willingness to use force in the matter of slavery. The lesson was not lost on the Brazilian government. In 1867, for instance, José Antonio Pimenta Bueno, visconde de São Vicente, in submitting a proposal to the Council of State to free the children of slave mothers, indicated the need to thus avoid 'British pressure'. See Richard Graham, 'Os fundamentos da ruptura de relações diplomáticas entre o Brasil e a Grã-Bretanha em 1863: "A questão Christie"', *Revista de História*, 24: 49 and 50 (1962), 117–38, 379–402; and Richard Graham, 'Causes for the abolition of Negro slavery in Brazil: an interpretive essay,' *Hispanic American Historical Review*, 46/2 (1966), 123–37.

his resignation. For Joaquim Nabuco, the historian, the choice of Inhomirim as senator merely provided a pretext for the resignation of Zacarias; the real issue was Caxias's hostility to the cabinet. With the subsequent importance of civil-military relations in Brazil, this interpretation has gained wide currency. But there is much evidence, including the speeches of Zacarias himself, to support the view that Zacarias resigned because he believed conservative members of the Council of State opposed the speed with which he was moving toward the end of slavery.[17] Even the moderate Zacarias had gone too far too fast; the brakes must be applied. The choice for Zacarias's successor bears out this view.

Zacarias was replaced as prime minister in 1868 by Itaboraí, the archconservative *saquarema* coffee planter. Members of the new cabinet included Paulino José Soares de Souza Filho (1834–1901), a son of the visconde de Uruguai, as well as Cotegipe, emerging leader of the Bahian Conservatives, Rio Branco and the novelist-politician, José de Alencar. The Council of State, having thus thrown its weight behind a Conservative reaction, backed Itaboraí's call for new elections when the Liberal chamber refused to endorse him. The government as usual had no difficulty in securing an overwhelming victory.

In response to these events Progressive-Liberals like Furtado and Zacarias joined their Liberal colleagues in parliament such as Nabuco de Araújo and even radical liberals like Teófilo Ottoni in organizing a Reform Club under the leadership of Nabuco. In May 1869 it issued a manifesto calling for thorough-going reform of the Constitution. They called for the repeal of the law of 1841 which gave the police judicial powers, greater autonomy for the judiciary, an end to the National Guard and to forced recruitment into the army, a limited tenure for senators, reduction of the power of the Council of State and the gradual emancipation of the slaves. Their manifesto nevertheless remained a cautious document despite the bravado of its last words, 'Reform or Revolution!'[18] In November of the same year another group issued a Radical Manifesto which, besides including these goals and others for which Liberals had long struggled, included direct elections and the extension of the suffrage, the election of provincial presidents and local police officials, the end of the emperor's moderative power and the

---

[17] Brazil. Congresso. Senado, *Annaes*, 15 and 18 July, 1870, 94–142.
[18] Américo Brasiliense de Almeida Mello (ed.), *Os programas dos partidos e o 2° império. Primeira parte: exposição de princípios* (São Paulo, 1878), 42.

Council of State, and the immediate abolition of slavery. Among the signatories of this document many went on in December of the following year to sign in Rio de Janeiro the Republican Manifesto calling for the end of the empire.

Once the war with Paraguay ended with the death of Solano López in March 1870 and in the face of mounting criticism of the Itaboraí cabinet from a new reform-minded generation of young politicians, intellectuals, businessmen and progressive planters, the more enlightened leaders of the Conservative camp realized the time had come for major concessions in order to avert more serious dissidence. Even Itaboraí accepted a proposal to end public slave auctions. The fear that a Liberal cabinet would sometime use the 1841 law to elect a wholly Liberal parliament persuaded some Conservatives of the advantages of its repeal. The emperor, as always, put his weight behind the cause of reform. After a five-month interim cabinet, visconde do Rio Branco became prime minister in March 1871. His Liberal start in political life, his participation in the *conciliação* cabinet, his experience as a diplomat during the Paraguayan War, all augured well for moderate reform. Few, however, could have been prepared for the series of far-reaching measures which Rio Branco pushed through in quick succession with impressive political skill. He separated police and judicial functions, simultaneously strengthening the tenure of judges and removing from the police commissioners their judicial duties, thus finally undoing the law of 1841. He reduced the powers of the National Guard: henceforth professional police and, when insufficient, the army itself would be used to maintain public order. Most important of all, he persuaded the Council of State to do an about-face and back his effort to push through the Law of Free Birth (1871), granting freedom to all children subsequently born to slave women and setting up a fund for the emancipation of adults. While not dispossessing planters of their present property, he thus attempted to persuade slaves that continued obedience could win freedom. By these measures Rio Branco, a Conservative prime minister, against the opposition of the right-wing *saquarema* faction of his own party, satisfied the bulk of the Liberals. By his farsightedness and disinterested statesmanship, he disarmed the critics of the empire, postponing more far-reaching change to the end of the next decade. Once again Brazilian political leaders had searched for – and found – a middle position so essential to the maintenance of order in a hierarchical yet potentially unstable social system based on slavery.

Much of the intellectual energy of these two decades centred on the nature of the state and the correct exercise of political power. In a country where a successful career as lawyer or judge fulfilled the aspirations of so many literate men, the jurist headed the intellectual elite. Visconde de Uruguai himself, retiring from political and diplomatic activity in 1857, turned his attention to preparing two magisterial studies of Brazilian jurisprudence: *Ensaio sobre o direito administrativo* (1862) and *Estudos práticos sobre a administração das províncias no Brasil* (1865). His powerful defence of the conservative viewpoint doubtless influenced many subsequent generations of law-school students, bureaucrats and politicians. Somewhat more emphasis on individual freedom characterized the treatise on public law and the Brazilian constitution published in 1857 by José Antonio Pimenta Bueno, marquês de São Vicente (1803–78), but he also asserted the essential virtue of the Brazilian system of government. Both authors grasped the importance of the effort to construct a stable regime accomplished in Brazil by the middle of the century, and both merely advocated minor refinements. Much the same was true of *Escravidão no Brasil: ensaio histórico, jurídico, social*, Agostinho Marques Perdigão Malheiro's study of the laws of slavery, published in 1866 and 1867.

The creation of a new civil code to replace the one inherited from Portugal preoccupied a succession of jurists. Candido Mendes de Almeida (1818–81), who in 1870 published his massive and erudite edition of the existing Philippine Code (in force since 1603), provided the basis – principally through the footnotes referring to alterations worked by law and custom – for the elaboration of a new code. The Liberal Nabuco de Araújo set to work on a draft. Although not complete at the time of his death in 1879 his version remained the basis of discussion until the enactment of a new code in 1916.

The constitutional system also suffered a number of brilliant attacks, most effectively from the pen of Zacarias in 1860 in his pamphlet-book on the nature and limits of the moderative power. Rising above political party, the Liberal Aureliano Cândido Tavares Bastos (1839–75) addressed many major issues, above all regionalism; he laid the groundwork for the eventual emergence of federalism as a major force in Brazilian political life. Despite their reform efforts, however, Zacarias, Tavares Bastos and others like them continued to accept the essential structure of the imperial system even as they tried to modify it.

Essentially moderates, they sought a consensus within the ruling class in order to preserve a slave-based society.

The stability which so concerned both Conservatives and Liberals mainly sprang not from political institutions, however, but from social relationships based upon the exchange of loyal service for protection and favours. As surely as Pedro II enacted the part of father for the entire nation, so did *senhores de engenho*, coffee *fazendeiros*, or industrialists, for their workers. In turn, real fathers retained clear authority over wives and children, as they did over other relatives, servants, *agregados* and slaves. And in every case, benevolent care gloved outright force. In political life elaborate systems of patronage made it possible to grant benefits – especially authority over others – to those who steadfastly supported the existing structure. Favours not only won compliance from those expected to obey, but assuaged the sensibilities of those charged with enforcement. The expansion of foreign trade based on coffee exports in this period increased the resources available to the state and enabled it truly to fulfil a paternal role. Thus, the state simultaneously maintained its legitimacy and that of the hierarchical social order. For many Brazilians who still prize social hierarchy these two decades (1850–70) represent a golden age in which government was both liberal and stable.

Part Five

CULTURAL LIFE

THE LITERATURE, MUSIC AND ART
OF LATIN AMERICA
FROM INDEPENDENCE TO *c*.1870

It is difficult to make sense of the cultural history of Latin America in the nineteenth century without an understanding of the age of revolutionary struggle and independence with which it begins. This would be true even if the Latin American experience at the time had not itself been so firmly inserted within the context of international events following the revolutions of 1776 and 1789, the incipient industrial revolution in Europe and the spread of liberalism following the century of enlightenment. The historical transition from European colony to independent republic (or, in the case of Brazil, from colony to independent empire), corresponds broadly to the beginning of a transition from neo-classicism, which itself had only recently replaced the baroque, to romanticism in the arts. Triumphant romanticism is the characteristic mode of the new era, particularly in literature – though the continuing influence of neo-classicism in the other arts, especially painting and architecture, is much more persistent than is generally appreciated. Hugo's equation of liberalism in politics with romanticism in literature applies more forcefully, though even more contradictorily, in Latin America than in Europe, where much of the romantic impulse was in reality an aristocratic nostalgia for the pre-scientific, pre-industrial world. This brings the historian, at the outset, up against an enduring problem in using labels for the arts in Latin American cultural history. Terms such as neo-classicism and romanticism are often inaccurate approximations even in Europe where they originated, yet critics frequently assume that they designate entire historical periods of artistic development, rather than denote the formal and conceptual contradictions of historical processes as these are reproduced in art. In Latin America these same labels can at times appear to become completely disembodied, losing all direct concrete relation to historical determinants, giving rise to a persistent perception among

Americanist artists of a conflict in which America's 'natural' and spontaneous realities are repeatedly constrained and oppressed by Europe's
coldly rational 'cultural' forms.

Spain was the nation which had given Europe the picaresque novel and
Don Quijote, but was also the colonial power whose Holy Inquisition
had prohibited the writing and diffusion of prose fiction in its American
territories and, especially, of all works about the native Americans, the
Indians. It was therefore both appropriate and profoundly ironic that the
first outstanding literary work of the independence period in Spanish
America should have been a picaresque novel, *El periquillo sarniento*
(1816), by the Mexican José Joaquín Fernández de Lizardi (1776–1827),
a satirical survey of opportunism and corruption which looked for the
first time at the structure and values of contemporary Mexican society,
using the themes and expression of popular culture in a clear
emancipatory gesture characteristic of the novel's generic function at
that time. Lizardi, self-styled *El Pensador Mexicano* (the title of his first
newspaper, 1812), was a journalist, politician, bureaucrat and man of
letters, and the close relationship between journalism and literature
forged by his generation continues in the continent to this day. In addition
to his newspaper articles, he published innumerable satirical pamphlets
and broadsheets demanding freedom of expression and claiming for the
still adolescent press the role of orientating public opinion and taste:
'Public opinion and the freedom of the press are the muzzle and leash for
restraining tyrants, criminals and fools.'[1] Ironically enough, Lizardi
appears to have wrapped his ideas in fictional guise not out of an artistic
vocation but in order to avoid censorship and imprisonment or worse,
but his characteristically heterogeneous works give us our most complete picture of those turbulent and ambiguous times. It is tempting to
link him with the Argentine Bartolomé Hidalgo (1788–1823), whose
cielitos and gaucho dialogues on contemporary politics during the revolutionary period convey vividly the language and mentality of the age.
Lizardi's educated wit and Hidalgo's popular humour were, however,
the exception. The staple fare of the neo-classic period was a diet of
heroic hymns, patriotic odes, elegies, madrigals, epigrams, fables, and
comedies and tragedies framed by the poetics of Horace, Boileau and

---

[1] From his last newspaper, the *Correo Semanario de México* (1826), quoted by Carlos Monsiváis, *A
ustedes les consta. Antología de la crónica en México* (Mexico, 1980), 19. All translations in the text are
the author's.

Luzán. Divorced from the emotions and conventions which created and conditioned such works, it is difficult for the modern reader to identify with them; yet most of the literary expression of the revolutionary period is clothed in such forms. Among writers neo-classicism gradually came to be associated with the more conservative versions of Enlightenment doctrine and with the authoritarian outcome of the French Revolution, in view of its association with the contemporary cultural policies of the Portuguese and Spanish empires. Little wonder, then, that writers were searching for something new. What they found was a European romantic movement at first sight tailor-made for them, whose combination of political passion and private sentimentality would make a particularly lasting impact on Latin American literature and art generally precisely because it corresponded to the early decades in the history of the new republics. Germán Arciniegas has gone so far as to assert: 'The republics that were born romantically in the New World constitute the greatest achievement, the masterwork of the Romantic spirit.'[2] And another modern critic, Luis Alberto Sánchez, individualized the idea by declaring that Simón Bolívar himself was an intrinsically romantic spirit who became the focal point of Spanish American artistic expression: 'How long might it have taken for our romanticism to emerge without the stimulus of a man and a writer like Bolívar? And to what extent would Bolívar have been able to realise himself without the literary and romantic aura which surrounded him?'[3]

The pre-independence and independence period in Spanish America was an age of travellers, intellectuals, journalists, poets and revolutionaries. Many men were all these things by turns or at one and the same time, and they embodied the Americanist concept by living, learning, working and fighting in other men's countries, like Byron, who called his yacht *Bolívar* and longed to go to America, and Garibaldi, who did go, and who wore an American poncho as a mark of rebellion to the end of his days. The interwoven lives of men like the Mexican Father Servando Teresa de Mier (1765–1827), the Venezuelans, Francisco de Miranda (1750–1816), Simón Rodríguez (1771–1854), Bolívar (1783–1830) and Andrés Bello (1781–1865), or the Guatemalan, Antonio José de Irisarri (1786–1868), are as remarkable in their peripatetic majesty as anything the Enlightenment or revolutionary periods in Europe have to show. The Ecuadorean José Joaquín Olmedo (1780–1847) expressed the Bolivarian dream in

[2] Germán Arciniegas, *El continente de siete colores* (Buenos Aires, 1965), 391.
[3] Luis Alberto Sánchez, *Historia comparada de las literaturas americanas* (Buenos Aires, 1974), II, 230.

verse: 'Unite, oh peoples,/ to be free and never more defeated,/ and may the great chain of the Andes make fast/ this union, this potent bond.' The dream dissolved, as is known ('we have ploughed the sea'), but its memory echoes still both in contemporary politics and literature. In those early days, before even the provisional boundaries of the new republics had been finally determined, many writers anticipating the new order – which would be *criollo* and bourgeois in intention, if not yet in reality – would have approved the 1822 declaration by José Cecilio del Valle (1780–1834), a Honduran who was also an ardent Central-Americanist: 'From this day forth America shall be my exclusive occupation. America by day, whilst I write; America by night, whilst I think. The proper object of study for every American is America.' After the revolutionary period the Americanist theme lived on, but circumscribed and directed now by nationalism, as men and republics came down, albeit reluctantly, to earth.

In the meantime, however, a number of writers were already seeking a new expression to communicate their new perspective on American reality. A writer like Lizardi, for example, although undoubtedly more innovatory than most, still really belonged to the Enlightenment and appeared to see his immediate task, not unreasonably, as that of helping his countrymen to catch up by filling in the gaps in their knowledge and correcting the errors of the past and present rather than constructing the new republican culture that was on the horizon. Had everyone attended to the foundations as he did, more castles – or, rather, government palaces – might have been built on the ground instead of in the air. The theatre was vigorous for a time in many regions, with a predominance of dramas in which morality and patriotism fused almost to the point of synonymity, but none of the plays of that period are ever performed today. Only lyric poetry managed to effect tolerable adaptations to the changing circumstances, so that a small number of poems by Olmedo, Bello or the young Cuban, José María Heredia (1803–39), are as close to the hearts of educated Latin Americans today as are a few well-known paintings of Bolívar, Sucre and San Martín and the scenes of their triumphs in battle. These, however, are no more than isolated landmarks in a vast and mainly uninhabited landscape.

The most characteristic poet of the era is José Joaquín Olmedo, whose lasting fame was secured by his celebratory *La victoria de Junín. Canto a Bolívar* (1825). It is one of the very few serious works which deals with the independence struggles as such. Olmedo was quite unable to find a suitable form for his romantic subject, but perhaps this is appropriate. At any rate, the famous cannon thunder of the opening verses is memorable, though it provides the first of many examples of Latin American literary works which have no lived experience of the reality they are attempting to communicate. In that opening salvo we have Olmedo, who was not present at the battle, purporting to recreate it by 'firing away', as Bolívar himself felt obliged to point out, 'where not a shot was heard'. Sarmiento would later write romantic – and enduringly influential – evocations of the Argentine pampa without ever having seen it, and his twentieth-century apostle, Rómulo Gallegos, would emulate him by writing *Doña Bárbara* (1929) having spent a total of five days on the Venezuelan llanos where his apparently authoritative novel was to be set. In this respect, however, the classic predecessor of them all was Chateaubriand, who set *Atala* (1801) on the banks of the Mississippi, although – or perhaps because – he had never travelled that far. No wonder some critics say, not altogether fancifully, to judge by the writings of artists and intellectuals, that America has been more dreamed about than lived.

Neither Olmedo nor his more important contemporary, the Venezuelan Andrés Bello, introduced any innovations in versification or style and their poetry remained essentially neo-classical: measured, harmonious, exemplary and impersonal. What had changed were the themes or, more precisely, the attitude towards them. Those new themes were American nature, virginal again as the Spaniards had conceived it at the time of the conquest (for now it belonged to new masters); the Indian, viewed for the moment not as a barbarian or forced labourer, but as a noble savage ripe for redemption; and political and cultural liberation inaugurating a new social order. Bello would have been one of Latin America's great men had he never written a word of poetry (in this regard he is similar to José Bonifácio de Andrada e Silva in Brazil), but he did. His *Alocución a la poesía* (1823) correctly assumed the eventual triumph of the revolutionary forces and effectively inaugurated nineteenth-century literary independence in Spanish America. It was later used by the Argentine writer, Juan María Gutiérrez, as the introductory work in his *América poética* (Valparaíso, 1846), the first important anthology of Latin American poetry. The *Alocución* was in some respects closer to Virgil or to Horace than to Victor Hugo, but it clearly perceived the great themes of the American future, calling on poetry to 'direct its flight/ to the grandiose scenarios of Columbus' realm/ where the earth is clothed still in its most primitive garb'. Nevertheless, Bello's own rather ponderous verse (more eloquent than poetic, in Pedro Henríquez Ureña's phrase) was itself an indication that this world of nature, mother of poetry, would remain largely unexplored during the nineteenth century, a 'poetry without poets', to plagiarize Luis Alberto Sánchez's verdict on the state of the Latin American novel a century later. What Bello was effectively demanding, of course, was what would later be called *nativismo* or *criollismo*, both forms of literary Americanism which would indeed gradually emerge from the later romantic movement. In his second major poem, *La agricultura de la zona tórrida* (1826), the descriptions of the American landscape and its vegetation recall the Guatemalan priest Rafael Landívar's earlier evocation (*Rusticatio Mexicana*, 1781) or the Brazilian José Basílio da Gama's *O Uraguai* (1769), and anticipate the equally admirable *Memoria sobre el cultivo del maíz en Antioquia* (1868) by the Colombian Gregorio Gutiérrez González (1826–72) towards the end of the romantic era. For a long time, however, despite Bello's passionate plea, and despite innumerable beautiful anthology pieces now largely forgotten by criticism, Latin America's natural regional landscapes would be merely 'backcloths', 'settings', not truly inhabited by the characters of literature. There was to be little internalization of landscape, except in Brazil, where both social and literary conditions were different and where Portuguese traditions obtained. At the same time it must be said that much dismissive criticism of nineteenth-century Spanish American poetry and prose as descriptive or one-dimensional is itself unthinking and superficial. Peninsular Spanish literature had little or no tradition of natural observation, and the European travellers to the New World at this time were only more successful in evoking its landscapes and inhabitants because their works implicitly communicated the necessarily limited view of the outsider. Latin Americans themselves were secretly searching not for reality but for emblematic images – the Indian, the gaucho, the Andes, the tropical forests – in literature and painting, just as they had to search for them as themes for their national anthems, flags or shields.

Bello and Olmedo were both mature men approaching middle age when they wrote their famous poems and were too set in the Enlightenment mould to discard their neo-classical formation. They were both fortunate, however, to witness what Olmedo called the triumph of the Andean condor over the Spanish eagle in the southern continent. Other revolutionaries did not live to see that day. One of the most revered is the young Peruvian Mariano Melgar (1791–1815), a rebel executed by the

Spaniards. After a classical education, he wrote love poems which are still recited in Peru, including impassioned Inca-style *yaravíes* which made him, according to Henríquez Ureña, 'the first poet to give voice in a consistent fashion to Indian feeling in Spanish poetry'.[4] In his famous 'Ode to Liberty', he saw the intellectual and the people united in the romantic new world to come: 'Cruel despotism,/ horrid centuries, darkest night,/ be gone. Know ye, Indians who weep,/ despised sages, the world entire,/ that evil is no more, and we have taken/ the first step towards our longed for goal . . ./ And those who called my land/ an "obscure country",/ seeing it so fertile in wonders/ now say, "Truly, this is indeed a new world".' Melgar did not live to see that world, but his youthful and passionate poetry make him a genuine precursor of it.

Different but also tragic was the poet of frustrated independence, the Cuban José María Heredia, the most authentically lyrical poet of the period and the first great poet of absence and exile (see especially 'Vuelta al sur' and 'Himno del desterrado', both from 1825). Critics disagree about his literary definition, but many view him as a precursor and some as even the initiator of Latin American romanticism. His precociousness, political failure and tragic destiny have encouraged such a view, which, despite his clearly neo-classical point of departure, is persuasive. *En el teocalli de Cholula* (1820), which he wrote at the age of 17, and *Niágara* (1824), inspired partly by Chateaubriand, have become literary symbols of Latin America's natural majesty as also of historical imminence. When it became clear that Cuba was not to share in the exhilaration of a triumphant independence struggle, Heredia, moving to the United States, Venezuela and Mexico, gradually gave himself up to despair. In 'La tempestad' (1822), he was already lamenting, 'At last we part, fatal world:/ the hurricane and I now stand alone'; and, in 'Desengaños' (1829), he at once reproves his passive compatriots and acknowledges his own surrender to despair and domesticity ('the novel of my fateful life,/ ends in the arms of my dear wife'). He was not to know that those who did see political liberation would themselves be lamenting its dissipation in many of the new republics until well after mid-century.

Brazil's evolution was less turbulent, but more productive. As the only Portuguese colony in the New World, Brazil arrived earlier at a distinctively national conception of its literary identity, in a movement which, coinciding with the high-point of neo-classical *arcadismo* or pastoral literature, spread from Minas Gerais to Rio de Janeiro and then

[4] Pedro Henríquez Ureña, *Las corrientes literarias en la América hispánica* (Mexico, 1949), 112.

to Pernambuco from about 1770 to 1820. Brazil, moreover, had been the theatre of one of the earliest responses to advanced European and North American thought in the shape of the Inconfidência Mineira (1788–9). By far the greatest writer of the period, however, was José Bonifácio de Andrada e Silva (1763–1838), tireless promoter of Brazil's literary independence and patriarch of its relatively peaceful political independence in 1822. He was an Enlightenment figure who distinguished himself in scholarship and scientific research, whilst occupying a number of important administrative posts in Portugal and Brazil. His literary career followed a path from Virgilian classicism to an almost Byronic romanticism, though possibly his most representative works are his patriotic verses. A man with some of the qualities of both a Miranda and a Bello, he was perhaps the most widely read and productive man of letters of the era in Latin America.

The period from the 1820s to the 1870s saw a violent and often incoherent struggle to restructure the Latin American societies. The interests of the rural sector, its regional caciques and oligarchs predominated, but the project of the era was clearly urban and bourgeois. Liberalism was espoused, slavery abolished everywhere but Brazil and Cuba, education was revolutionized and culture gradually refurbished on national lines. All the arts except literature languished or declined at first in most regions, because they required a level of wealth, investment and stability lacking in Spanish America generally – the Brazilian case was very different – until the 1870s or later. Relatively few important buildings were erected and few paintings or musical compositions were officially commissioned before mid-century, other than the traditional religious works for churches. The academies founded in some large cities in the last years of the colonial period remained immersed in the most unimaginative versions of classical doctrine and style. The political functions of art were not immediately perceived, except in Brazil, where continuity of monarchical and aristocratic perspective allowed the reconstruction of Rio de Janeiro to be undertaken, mainly in French neoclassical style. Literature, however, retained all its traditional social functions and acquired new ones. Most of the best-known writers of the nineteenth century would be men of action. Yet when these patriots and revolutionaries found time to look around them, they found themselves in a vast, barbarous continent which was less welcoming than Bello, for example, had remembered when he dreamed about it through the mists of his London exile. It was an empty, overwhelmingly rural and agricultural continent, whose only significant industry was mining. In 1850 the total population was only 30 million scattered among twenty countries. Most cities remained in appearance much as they had in colonial times; apart from Rio de Janeiro, which had almost 200,000 inhabitants, only Mexico City, Havana and Salvador (Bahia) had populations of more than 100,000.

Since the project of the era was to build new republics with new cultures, it is appropriate to begin with architecture. The end of the eighteenth century had seen the triumph of neo-classical architecture throughout the western world. It was to be particularly welcome in Latin America in the early nineteenth century because of its misleading identification with the French Revolution (its identification with Napoleon's empire received less emphasis, at least from liberals), whilst the baroque became identified with Spain and Portugal, perhaps unreasonably since the discord between structure and ornamentation which characterizes its Latin American versions may itself be interpreted as a sign of rebellion. The baroque style, at any rate, had unified Latin American art. As the continent became more accessible – perhaps vulnerable would be a better word – to contemporary European influences other than those of Spain and Portugal, neo-classicism in architecture and painting, and later romanticism in other fields, gave art a secular function, and reinforced this unity.

In a few Spanish American cities, particularly those like Buenos Aires which had little distinguished colonial architecture, the independence struggle gave an impetus to architectural innovation which would symbolize the rejection of Spanish colonialism. Many buildings in Buenos Aires were constructed according to non-Hispanic principles, and French, Italian and British architects were frequently employed. Nevertheless, it is essential to recognize that this process was already under way at the end of the colonial period. Neo-classicism's cooler, more rational lines were already visible in, for example, the Palacio de Minería in Mexico City built by the Spaniard Manuel Tolsá (1757–1816), also known as the sculptor of the equestrian statue of Carlos IV on the Paseo de la Reforma, in the churches and great houses constructed in the Bajío region of Mexico by Tolsá's pupil, Francisco Eduardo Tresguerras (1759–1833), in the dome and towers designed for the metropolitan cathedral in Mexico City by Damián Ortiz de Castro (1750–1793) and in Santiago's Moneda Palace built in the last years of the eighteenth century by the Italian architect, Joaquín Toesca (1745–99). At the same time, it is equally important to acknowledge that the continuing existence of colonial architecture, dominant in strictly quantitative terms, and the place it has held in conservative minds, meant that Spanish American architecture after independence, taken as a whole, remained unavoidably provincial (as it did until the 1930s). Unlike Brazil, most of the new republics were too impoverished to undertake a great process of reconstruction in the so-called anarchic period between the 1820s and the 1860s. Nevertheless, what innovation did take place was in general accord with neo-classical taste, symbolizing the adoption by the new rising elites of European rationalism and positivism, and pointing the way in the process to the specific economic and political future of Latin American societies as perceived at the time. Nothing shows more clearly than architecture what the nineteenth-century project was all about, for nothing materializes more dramatically the selection of the Enlightenment and France as the Latin American cultural and ideological model, frequently translated, it has to be said, into the Versailles of Louis XIV and the Paris of Napoleon. If any reconstruction of colonial culture is inevitably the view from the monastery or the fortress, the edifice containing Latin America's nineteenth-century culture would remain, in effect, despite the apparent predominance, first of romanticism and then of modernism, a neo-classical academy, and the impact of this on Latin American art would be enduring. (In Mexico the Academia de San Carlos, founded in 1785, survived to serve as one of the pillars of institutionalized artistic activity there until well into the twentieth century.) If the baroque spoke of an identity, however contradictory, between church and state, neo-classicism symbolized bourgeois liberties and civil society, the growth of secular education and a general process of integration into the wider European world order. For this reason European educationalists like Lancaster and Thompson were invited to Caracas and Buenos Aires by Bolívar and Rivadavia as early as the 1820s, at the same time as droves of French and Italian architects arrived to build new neo-classical edifices alongside colonial structures, much as the Spaniards had once built on top of pre-Columbian monuments. As early as 1816 during the residence of Dom João in Rio de Janeiro, a French Commission on Fine Art led by Joachim Lebreton (1760–1819) arrived to advise on future construction and, in effect, to lay down a blueprint for artistic policy for the rest of the century. Auguste-Henri-Victor Grandjean de Montigny (1776–1850) was the principal architect; he designed the Academy of Fine Arts in Rio and many other buildings. Later Louis Léger Vauthier built the theatres of Santa Isabel in Recife, Belem de Pará and São Luís de Maranhão. Italian architects and other artists remained influential in most Spanish American republics until the 1870s, when French models finally triumphed, but as early as 1823 it was a French architect, Prosper Catelin (1764–1842), who completed the façade of the cathedral in Buenos Aires in neo-classical style seventy years after it had been started; and another Frenchman, François Brunet de Baines (1799–1855), founded the first school of architecture in Chile, though it was a Chilean, the famous writer and thinker Benjamín Vicuña Mackenna (1831–1886), who later redesigned the city centre and earned the name 'the Chilean Haussmann'.

The transition from the American baroque's peculiar combination of the sacred and the paganistic – concealing many tensions and contradictions even as it flaunted them – to neo-classical rationalism and positivism was also a transition to an architecture which was actually severely hierarchical in its symbolism, and this permitted – indeed, it imposed – an increasingly tyrannical academicism in Latin American art which would in the long run become reactionary and archaic, and was not finally to be shaken until the First World War a century later. It is partly for this reason that artists in many fields have been led to believe that the baroque – shaped by instinct and intuition – is the true vehicle and expression for the Latin American *mestizo* character, and that colonial art is therefore closer to Latin American reality. This is highly problematical, needless to say, but it seems evident that baroque ornamentation gives more scope for hybridization and syncretism than any version of the classical.

The French Artistic Mission in Rio dismissed the work of the incomparable Brazilian architect and sculptor, Aleijadinho (1738?–1814), as a 'curious gothic antique'. His true worth would go unrecognized for more than a century, and the values of foreign experts determined the course of Brazilian architecture and the plastic arts for most of the nineteenth century, illustrating another general problem for the art historian. The vertebral division in Latin American art from the early nineteenth century until the present day is between Americanist–nativist and European–cosmopolitan currents, a distinction which has frequently caused more difficulties than it has resolved. In the last century, however, there was another side to this problem. Within Latin American art itself, unlike the situation during the colonial period, there opened up a particularly wide – indeed, a virtually unbridgeable – gap between academic art (*arte culto*) and popular art (*arte popular o semiculto*). The latter, of course, was not perceived as having any history, for it was only in the 1840s that some Europeans, under the spell of romanticism, began to conceive of the concept of folklore. Latin Americans would take a long time to assimilate such lessons and spent most of the nineteenth century attempting to suppress or conceal their own uncultivated and implicitly shameful folk art and music, until the moment when strong regionalist movements finally emerged and socialism made its first tentative appearance on the Latin American stage. If we look at the case of painting, for example, in Mexico it was later artists like Diego Rivera who recognized the full worth of popular engravers like Posada or Gahona, just as it was Frida Kahlo who rehabilitated the popular tradition of *pulquería* wall painting; in Peru, likewise, it was artists, not critics, who most lovingly recalled the contribution of 'El mulato Gil' (José Gil de Castro, 1785–1841) to Peruvian and Chilean post-independence culture and the contribution of the great popular artist, Pancho Fierro (1803–79), later in the century. Latin American art criticism was overwhelmingly provincial and subjective, concentrating almost exclusively on historical, biographical and generally 'literary' aspects, with very little aesthetic insight in evidence. Almost all art criticism appeared in newspapers and most of the critics were poets and writers, so that purely plastic criteria were effectively ignored. The great writer, thinker and future president of Argentina, Domingo Faustino Sarmiento (1811–88), was one of the first art critics in the continent and almost certainly the earliest in Argentina, whilst Vicuña Mackenna takes precedence in Chile. The first exhibitions in Buenos Aires were held in 1817 and 1829, but for the next half century such events were few and far between in most other cities.

Despite the predominance of neo-classicism in architecture and, at first, through the influence of the academies, in the plastic arts, the quest for a national art and literature was, as we have seen (remembering Bello and, later, Sarmiento), a grand continental theme from the moment of independence; but the ideal was a very long time in the achieving. For most of the nineteenth century Latin American painting was almost exclusively descriptive. Brazilian painting, for example, which had been particularly backward during the colonial period (unlike music, sculpture and architecture), set out to take a more determinedly nationalist course after independence in 1822, but nationalism as channelled through French and Italian tutors not infrequently produced a merely insipid version of a supposed 'universalist', in fact thoroughly Europeanized, art. Academic painting encouraged the depiction of historical personages and events in the style of David and Ingres. The imperial government invited teachers to Brazil from Paris and Rome and sponsored young artists to travel and study in Europe. The most important of the artistic immigrants was Nicolas Antoine Taunay (1755–1830), who came with the French Artistic Mission and painted many portraits and landscapes, including *O morro de Santo Antônio em 1816*. As well as his famous scenes of slave life, Jean-Baptiste Debret (1768–1848) painted portraits of João VI, the *Sagração de D. Pedro I*, and the *Desembarque de D. Leopoldina, primeira Imperatriz do Brasil*. Brazilian painting proper only really began in the 1840s, when Jean Léon Pallière Grandjean de Ferreira, who was a grandson of Grandjean de Montigny, returned to Brazil after spending most of his early life in France and galvanized the artistic world with the latest European techniques. Manuel de Araújo Pôrto Alegre (1806–79), barão de Santo Angelo, equally well known as a poet, was a notable disciple of Debret, best known for his *Coroação de D. Pedro II*. But this was court painting at its least audacious, and in the works of even the most accomplished later artists like Vítor Meireles (1832–1903), Pedro Américo (1843–1905), José Ferraz de Almeida Júnior (1850–99) and Rodolfo Amoêdo (1857–1941), the dead hand of European academicism reaches well into the Brazilian republican period after 1889.

In other countries also the most significant phenomenon of the first half-century after independence was the arrival of a succession of artists from Europe, intrigued by the colourful types, scenes, customs and landscapes of the newly liberated continent. Artists like Vidal, Fisquet, Nebel, Verazzi, Menzoni and, above all, the German Johann-Moritz Rugendas (1802–58) and the Frenchman Raymond-Auguste Quinsac de Monvoisin (1790–1870), went to work, teach and write, and exerted an influence out of all proportion to their real status in their own countries or in the history of art. Frequently they sent their works back for reproduction or for sale to collectors of the picturesque. In Chile, for example, artists like the English naval officer, Charles Wood (1793–1856), who painted marine views around Valparaíso, Rugendas, who lived there from 1834 to 1845 after visiting Brazil and Mexico and was a friend of Andrés Bello, Monvoisin, who was also there in the 1840s, and E. Charton de Treville (1818–78), between them provided most of the scenes which thereafter illustrated Chilean histories of the period. Not until the 1870s did significant native-born artists appear. In Mexico the most influential painters of the period were the conventional Catalan Pelegrín Clavé (1810–80), brought to Mexico by Santa Anna in 1846 to reorganize the Academy, and the Italian Eugenio Landesio (1810–77), known for romantic landscapes such as *Chimalistac, Valle de México*, and *Vista de la Arquería de Matlala*, exhibited in 1857, and also tutor to Mexico's most important nineteenth-century artist, José María Velasco (1840–1912). Such travelling foreign artists were in many cases the first to record Latin American life in the early republican period, and it took some time in a number of countries before national artists – for example, Ramón Torres Méndez (1809–85) in Colombia, Martín Tovar y Tovar (1828–1902) in Venezuela – were able to adopt the genres and styles which these frequently more romantically inclined Europeans had laid down.

The only way in which most artists, other than popular painters, could conceive of their search for a national art was through *costumbrist* painting. In Argentina the first important national painter was Carlos Morel (1813–94), who painted portraits of Rosas and his mother but was best known for his scenes of gauchos, Indians and local customs in the late 1830s and early 1840s, with titles like *La carreta, Payada en una pulpería, La familia del gaucho*, or *Cacique pampa y su mujer*. These works, many of which first appeared in his 1844 album *Usos y costumbres del Río de la Plata*, have been reproduced on innumerable occasions. In such pictures, and those of other Argentine painters like Carlos Pellegrini (1800–75), we see a varied, colourful, social and natural world constrained in painting which is ultimately one-dimensional. These were artists viewing their own reality – though of course the underlying point here is that it was not yet truly their own reality – partly through European eyes. Yet they were generally well in advance of the men of letters, largely because they moved in much wider social circles than the salon life to which writers of the period were often confined. Indeed, as in peninsular Spain and other parts of Europe, many *costumbrista* poets and writers who reproduced the picturesque and the picaresque learned their skills of observation primarily from their contemporaries among the painters. A case in point was the leading Argentine romantic, Esteban Echeverría (1805–51), who was in the same art class as Carlos Morel when they were both students, and may well have been inspired to write his brutal novella *El matadero* (1838) partly as a result of a picture by the English painter, Emeric Essex Vidal.

Portraiture had developed only slowly during the eighteenth century, but expanded rapidly during the first sixty years of the nineteenth century. Neo-classicism encouraged an austere, voluminous style of portrait painting, as exemplified in the works of travellers like Rugendas. Indeed, most artists made a living painting portraits of the rising bourgeoisie, although of course the trade declined abruptly after about 1860 with the spread of the daguerrotype, at which point many painters like Morel and Prilidiano Pueyrredón (1823–70) in Argentina also became photographers. Pueyrredón, son of the famous general, was, unlike most painters, a member of the social elite and spent much time in Europe, where he was influenced both by David and Delacroix. He produced a vast output of more than two hundred paintings, of which more than half were portraits in oils. The most famous was his portrait of Manuelita Rosas dressed in Federal red (1850), but he also painted outstanding portraits of his father (1848), his friend, Don Miguel J. de Azcuénaga (1864), both also from life, as well as pictures of Rivadavia and Garibaldi. Typical of men of the age, Pueyrredón was in fact a trained engineer and architect who was responsible for many of the public buildings erected in and around Buenos Aires between 1854 and 1864 after his return from a second sojourn in Europe. He also produced such well-known landscapes as *Un alto en el camino* (1861) and *San Isidro* (1867), and numerous scenes of native customs.

Only with the gradual triumph of romanticism in the plastic arts and literature, however, were painters like Pueyrredón in Argentina, Almeida Júnior in Brazil, Velasco in Mexico and Juan Manuel Blanes (1830–1901) in Uruguay able to begin the move out of academic, descriptive or merely *costumbrist* painting in the direction of a more specifically individualistic and to that extent – at this stage – national style. In the second half of the century, when romanticism had been more profoundly absorbed and had itself in turn given way to Courbet's naturalism, a few painters, often influenced by the findings of archae-ological expeditions (those of J. L. Stephens and E. G. Squier, for example), made the first faltering attempts to gain inspiration from a historically grounded but formally romantic return to aboriginal roots. Francisco Laso (1823–69) of Peru, for example, seems to foreshadow *indigenismo* in his attempt to travel this road by uniting individual and national identity in pictures like *El habitante de la cordillera* (1855).

In music the national concept was barely reflected at all until well after mid-century, at a time when conservatories and other formative institutions had developed or were being newly founded. Before that it was largely left to the chapel-masters of the great cathedrals, such as José Maurício Nunes Garcia (1767–1830) and Francisco Manuel da Silva (1795–1865) in Brazil, or José Antonio Picasarri (1769–1843) in Argentina, to lay the foundations of national musical life, often forming schools of music, philharmonic societies and ensembles, and thereby ensuring that patriotic or nativist currents' did not take art music too far from its religious base in the continent. In Mexico the musical scene was dominated in the post-independence period by José Mariano Elízaga (1786–1842), known in that most patriarchal century as the 'father of Mexican music'. San Martín is said to have had a fine singing voice and to have intoned Parera's *Marcha patriótica* to the massed crowds in Santiago de Chile in 1818, whilst in later years Juan Bautista Alberdi wrote numerous salon pieces for piano. In Brazil Pedro I himself wrote the Brazilian Hymn of Independence, as well as an opera whose overture was performed in Paris in 1832. By that time the minuet and mazurka, polka and waltz had arrived in Latin America, rapidly became acclimatized and then gave birth to local versions and variations.

But if every educated man and woman had an interest in music, its public performance and development were securely in the hands of foreigners after the chapel-masters had had their day. In Chile, exceptionally, German influences were strong; but there as elsewhere, Italian opera had been popular since the early eighteenth century and continued to dominate the scene, initially through Rossini and Bellini. When new theatres were opened it was usually with opera in mind, since the performance of symphonic and chamber works only really became feasible, even in the larger republics, in the last quarter of the century. Opera apart, the main musical fare consisted of piano and song recitals, and light musical theatre, particularly the Spanish *género chico* of *zarzuelas* and *sainetes*, usually performed by Spanish touring troupes.

Argentina and Brazil are the most interesting countries in terms of music during this period. In Argentina as elsewhere, patriotic music in particular flourished alongside the more vernacular *cielitos*. At the same time European salon music grew rapidly in social acceptance after 1830, in somewhat ironic counterpoint to the rural music of the gaucho *payadores* and their pampa *gatos*, *vidalitas* and *tristes*. Yet despite the aura of barbarous spontaneity which appears to have surrounded such folk music at the time, its European heritage is obvious, and the gauchos, for all their alleged savagery as denounced in contemporary literature, were not remotely as beyond the pale as the Indians and negroes who predominated in other nations. In this sense it is not surprising that the River Plate region, even before the waves of European immigration in the last quarter of the century, should have largely followed European trends in developing its musical culture. Buenos Aires, moreover, was always an especially welcoming host to Italian operas, which appeared regularly from the 1820s – Rossini's *Barber of Seville* was premiered in 1825 – until by 1850 some two dozen operas were being mounted regularly in Buenos Aires each year. More than a dozen theatres opened in the city during the nineteenth century, including, in 1857, the Teatro Colón, which would in time make Buenos Aires a world opera capital.

In Brazil, where the development of culture moved through successive organic rather than revolutionary transformations, Italian opera was even more effectively acclimatized. The transfer of the Portuguese court to Rio de Janeiro in 1808 and the establishment of an independent empire in 1822, whilst initially stifling such creativity as had been apparent in the late eighteenth century, provided for a more stable and continuous evolution over the ensuing decades than was possible elsewhere. The mulatto priest, José Maurício Nunes Garcia, although primarily an outstanding composer of sacred music, including an admired Requiem Mass (1816), is credited with having written, in 1809, Brazil's first opera, *Le du gemelle*. In the 1840s his pupil Francisco Manuel da Silva reformed the orchestra of the Imperial Chapel and galvanized musical activity in the capital; he established the national conservatory in 1847. In 1856 Manuel de Araújo Pôrto Alegre, the celebrated poet and painter, provided the Portuguese text to music by Joaquim Giannini, an Italian professor at the conservatory, to produce *Véspera dos Guararapes*; and in 1860 Elias Alvares Lôbo went further, himself composing the music for an opera *A noite de São João*, staged at the new Opera Lírica Nacional, with a libretto based on narrative poems by the most important novelist of the era, José Martiniano de Alencar (1829–1877). The following year saw a still more significant event, the performance of *A noite do castelo*, the first work by Antônio Carlos Gomes (1836–96), destined to be nineteenth-century Latin America's most successful composer, above all with *Il Guarany* (1870), based on Alencar's already famous novel *O Guarani* (1857). It remains the only Latin American opera in the international repertory to this day.

Only negligible attention has been paid to the history of the theatre in nineteenth-century Latin America, and the casual observer might conclude that there were few if any theatres, playwrights or plays. This is far from being the truth, although it is true that theatres were mainly confined to national or provincial capitals and that the standard of artistic achievement appears to have been generally low. Moreover, as we have seen, most theatres were opened with opera or light musical comedy in mind. Nevertheless, the theatre was a central focus of literary activity at a time when literature was still far from acquiring the essentially private character it has assumed today, occupying the same place in the construction of the imagination as the cinema and television now. Thus, when the young Sarmiento arrived in Santiago de Chile for the first time in 1841, he conceived it as a 'theatre' full of unknown personages in which he was called upon to act.

Taking Mexico City as an example, there were already two theatres in operation in the 1820s, one of which served to finance the hospital while the other was built on the site of a cockpit and continued to be associated with this activity in the popular mind. A play entitled *México libre* was produced at the Coliseo Nuevo in 1821, the year of Iturbide's triumph, in which Mars, Mercury and Liberty together defeated Despotism, Fanaticism and Ignorance on Mexican soil, while in the succeeding years of the decade dramas with titles like *El liberal entre cadenas* and *El despotismo abatido* were performed. Most of the leading impresarios and actors were Spaniards, a tradition only temporarily interrupted by their expulsion after 1827. Manuel Eduardo de Gorostiza (1789–1851), a doughty liberal campaigner and outstanding dramatist – *Contigo pan y cebolla* (1823) is his best known work – was one of the unfortunate exiles of the period. Censorship was still prevalent, despite independence, though most of its motivation remained religious and moralistic rather than political. By 1830 in Mexico City, as in Buenos Aires and Rio de Janeiro, the opera had become the favourite pastime of the upper classes. The city was also visited by French ballet troupes, foreign conjurers and balloonists, exotic performing animals and, in due course, other diversions such as Daguerre's diorama in 1843 and wrestling in 1849. Almost all such events took place in or directly outside the theatres. The age of the impresario had dawned, and show business was just around the corner. By the end of the 1830s European romantic drama had arrived, above all in the shape of Hugo's plays, and as early as 1840 Mexican imitations such as *El torneo* by Fernando Calderón (1809–45), or *Muñoz, visitador de México* by another young romantic, Ignacio Rodríguez Galván (1816–

42), were appearing, while the *costumbrist* works of the Spaniard Manuel Bretón de los Herreros were soon filling theatres in Mexico as they would elsewhere in Spain and Latin America for over half a century.

Needless to say, during the nineteenth century and particularly the romantic period up to the 1880s, the theatre was not only an artistic phenomenon but an important focus of social activity, and theatre criticism often seemed as much concerned with the behaviour of the audience and the state of the auditorium as with the drama and its performance. Most of the plays and authors have long since been forgotten, but in its day the romantic theatre, both historical and *costumbrist*, was a closer reflection of contemporary reality than either the novel or poetry. In 1845, for example, the recognition of the independence of Texas by the United States inspired a Mexican drama entitled *Cómo se venga un texano*. At the same time the continuing influence of Spain in theatrical and musical tradition must not be overlooked. In the 1850s the *zarzuela* was revived in the Peninsula and transferred to Spanish America, proving particularly popular in Mexico. José Zorrilla, whose *Don Juan Tenorio* was staged in Mexico in 1844, only six months after the first performance in Spain, spent much time in the Mexican capital. Many other foreign touring companies and star performers visited Latin American countries with increasing regularity throughout the nineteenth century, sometimes at great personal risk, and a number of them died of diseases such as cholera and yellow fever.

In the 1850s four more theatres opened in Mexico City and the Teatro Nacional in 1858 saw the first performance of an opera by a Mexican composer – this was in fact the only Mexican thing about it – *Catalina de Guisa* by Cenobio Paniagua (1821–82). Soon afterwards a comic opera treating national customs, *Un paseo a Santa Anita*, was launched and became an overnight sensation, the forerunner to the *revistas* so important in later Mexican popular theatrical history. After Juárez's triumph in 1861 theatre censorship was removed and specifically Mexican works were positively encouraged. The two leading dramatists of the period were Juan A. Mateos (1831–1913) and Vicente Riva Palacio (1831–96), Juárez's close collaborator, who was also an excellent short-story writer. Riva was the author of the famous satirical song. *Adiós, mamá Carlota*, which heralded the expulsion of the French in 1867, an event also celebrated by Felipe Suárez's romantic drama *El triunfo de la libertad*, about a Mexican guerrilla fighter who arrives in the nick of time to save the honour of La Patria, his Mexican sweetheart. The following year *La*

Patria became the title of another play, by the poet Joaquín Villalobos, whose central character was an Indian maiden of that name aided jointly by Father Hidalgo and Minerva to defeat the French invaders.

Only Peru could approach Mexico's abundance of theatrical activity during this period, with two particularly outstanding playwrights, the conservative Felipe Pardo (1806–68), author of *Los frutos de la educación* (1829), and Manuel Ascensio Segura (1805–71), author of the celebrated *El sargento Canuto* (1839) and *Ña Catita* (1856). They represented two integral aspects of Lima society and both in their different ways foreshadowed Ricardo Palma's sharp but cynical observation (see below). Brazilian theatre had few really outstanding names in the nineteenth century, although in Brazil as elsewhere most well-known poets and novelists also wrote for the stage, including opera. One romantic playwright who deserves to be remembered is the founder of Brazilian comedy, Luís Carlos Martins Pena (1815–48), although the poet Gonçalves de Magalhães is, historically speaking, the true originator of Brazilian theatre. Martins Pena's comedies of manners – *O juiz de paz da roça* (1833, staged 1838) is the best example – though light and superficial, were also accomplished and entertaining. Unlike the theatre of the Spanish American republics, they were the product of a relatively stable society, where veiled criticism was not considered dangerous, and were based on a vigorous representation of all the social classes of Rio. Pena was very successful at giving the public exactly what it appeared to want. As Samuel Putnam rather cruelly puts it, 'His countrymen saw themselves and their daily lives in all their mediocrity mirrored in his creations, had a chance to laugh at their own reflections, and went away satisfied.'[5]

There can be little doubt, however, that despite its social importance, the theatre in Mexico, Peru, Brazil, or the rest of Latin America, was the least distinguished of the literary genres. Let us then turn to those other forms of literary expression, and in particular to the impact of the romantic movement in the continent. It is logical to remain with Brazil, since that country undoubtedly saw the most complete and 'European' version of the movement, although perhaps lacking some of the more dramatic features precisely because Brazil's relations with the outside world were generally less turbulent than those of most Spanish American nations. Independence was achieved with few heroics in 1822 (even the monarchy survived), which meant that the transition from neo-classi-

---

[5] Samuel Putnam, *Marvelous journey: a survey of four centuries of Brazilian writing* (New York, 1948), 161.

cism to romanticism was less abrupt and much less contradictory than in Spanish America. As a result, Brazil's classicalist tendency has been more persistent over time, harmonizing more fluently in this period with a romanticism which itself was on the whole more sentimental and less agonized, with little to show in terms of revolutionary impulse. The various parts of fragmented Spanish America have been forced to speak to one another, in however sporadic and spasmodic a fashion, and this has produced an Americanist dimension more profound and enduring in that part of the continent than in Brazil, which has on the whole pointed largely in the direction of Europe, with few deviations. By contrast Brazil, itself of continental proportions, experienced a far more complex regionalist dialectic than most Spanish American nations.

The first flowering of romanticism in Brazil was in poetry, beginning in 1836, when Domingos José Gonçalves de Magalhães (1811–82), a member of the *Niterói* group resident in Paris, published there his *Suspiros poéticos e saudades*, while another, Manuel de Araújo Pôrto Alegre, who was also a painter, as we have seen, published *A voz da Natureza*. Gonçalves de Magalhães did not give himself over to the new virile romanticism of Hugo as much as to the sentimentality of the Chateaubriand who had written *Atala* and *Le Génie du christianisme*. An aristocrat abroad, his talents were largely imitative and much of his rhetoric remained arcadian rather than romantic, but his contemporaries felt that here in intention was a new poetry with its combination of religiosity and langorous scepticism, of exultation and melancholy.

Probably the greatest Brazilian romantic poet was Antônio Gonçalves Dias (1823–64), who produced four collections of poetry between 1846 and 1857 (the first prefaced with lines from Goethe and Chateaubriand), a drama *Leonor de Mendonça* (1847), and one of the earliest Indianist poems of Latin America, *Os timbiras* (1848) (the latter prompting Gonçalves de Magalhães to produce his own influential *Confederação dos tamoios* in 1856). For many Brazilian critics this composer of opulent, pantheistic hymns to the tropics, at once nostalgic and assertive, patriotic, Americanist and Indianist, combining fluency and formal elegance, is the greatest of all Brazilian poets. Certainly he is the leading poet of Brazilian nationality, notably for his repeatedly quoted 'Canção do exílio', written in Coimbra: 'My land has palm trees,/ wherein sings the sabiá bird;/ he sings a sweeter note by far than ever here is heard./ Our sky has more stars,/ our bushes have more flowers,/ our forests have more life in them,/ more loves that life of ours.' Gonçalves Dias died in a shipwreck within sight of land, retrospectively underlining the characteristic *saudade* of his great poems. His important 'O canto do guerreiro' is similar to Longfellow's *Song of Hiawatha*; other works even recall Hernández's later *Martín Fierro*. He is characteristic of Brazilian romanticism, but his greatness bursts its limitations to become, as so many critics have said, the first truly Brazilian voice.

After Gonçalves Dias, romantic *indianismo* and *paisagismo* gained momentum. The aristocratic background of many Brazilian poets permitted a more patriarchal, Hugoesque style than most Spanish Americans were able to adopt, within a generally nationalistic perspective. The Indian stood in reality for a defeated and largely eliminated culture, and was therefore quite safe to adopt as the basis of a nationalist myth. He is far more in evidence in Brazilian literature before 1870 than the negro, on whom the economy still largely rested. Landscape was another romantic concern, but genuine interest in the rural world and the real conditions of its inhabitants was glaringly absent. Instead a certain mysticism and fatalism, which many critics have chosen to see as a projection of some Brazilian national character, was much in evidence, a sense that God and nature had determined man's destiny within the vast cosmic expanse of Brazil. One of the most representative romantic poets was Francisco Adolfo de Varnaghen (1816–78), author of *Epicos brazileiros* (1843), editor of the famous anthology *Florilégio da poesia brasileira* (1850), and an important promoter of national historiography; another was the errant Luís Nicolau Fagundes Varela (1841–75).

However, a succeeding generation of romantic poets (it is customary for critics to speak of four such generations) were entirely lacking in any sense of religiosity. They formed the Satanic school, a 'lost generation', according to Samuel Putnam, writers of a 'homicidal literature', in Afrânio Peixoto's words,[6] sufferers long before anyone in Spanish America from the *mal de siècle* or *taedium vitae* of decadent romanticism, much given to alcohol and other artificial paradises, for whom both nationalism and Americanism were empty concepts. The nearest equivalent in the Spanish-speaking countries would probably be the Mexican, Manuel Acuña (1849–73), who committed suicide aged 24 when the more normal tradition among young romantic poets in his country was to die for political causes. Most of these young Brazilian poets also died before their time. The most characteristic of them was the child prodigy of Brazilian romanticism, Manuel Antônio Alvares de Azevedo (1831–

---

[6] Afrânio Peixoto, *Noções de história da literatura brasileira* (Rio de Janeiro, 1931), 161.

52), who was like Byron or Baudelaire at their most morbid. Called the 'poet of doubt', he proposed his own epitaph: 'He was a poet, he had dreams, he loved.' These writers were more individualistic and aesthetically oriented than their more complacent, patriarchal forerunners, though much of their work was in reality, as critics have pointed out citing one of Azevedo's best known works, a long dark 'night in a tavern'. Nonetheless, another of them, Casimiro José Marques de Abreu (1839–60), became one of the most lastingly popular of Brazilian poets as the author of verses for lovesick adolescents.

Quite a different phenomenon was another short-lived romantic poet, Antônio de Castro Alves (1847–71), Brazil's greatest social poet of the era and, for some, a finer poet even than Gonçalves Dias. He was known as a *condoreiro* or condor poet, of lofty wingspan and high ambitions, unmistakably Hugoesque in range but innately Brazilian in sentimental orientation. His first impact on public consciousness was in 1867 with his drama *Gonzaga ou a revolução de Minas*, based on the life of the great mineiro poet of the late eighteenth century, Tomás Antônio Gonzaga. Castro Alves's poetry was public and private by turns, declamatory and intimate, Hugoesque or Byronic. A mulatto from Bahia, he filled his work with compassion and tropical sensuality. Erico Veríssimo has justly said of him that while other romantic poets were picking at their own sores, Castro Alves attended to the wounds of his suffering compatriots, not least the black slaves, and the indignant 'O navio negreiro' remains his single best-known poem. *Espumas flutuantes* (1871) was the only collection in book form to appear during his lifetime.

Castro Alves reminds us that the nineteenth century was the century of *Uncle Tom's Cabin*. It was also the century of *The Last of the Mohicans*. In Brazilian fiction the Indianist motif was represented most comprehensively and lastingly by the country's greatest romantic novelist, José Martiniano de Alencar. There had, however, been two memorable novels before Alencar's first triumph in the late 1850s. One was the famous *A moreninha* (1844) by Joaquim Manuel de Macedo (1820–82), a naive and touching novel still much read and loved by Brazilian women today, and the first truly popular work of Brazilian literature. The other, entirely different at first sight, was *Memórias de um sargento de milícias* (1853), by Manuel Antônio de Almeida (1831–61). At first reading the work appears to have been produced decades before its time, possessed of a startling objective realism; critics have noted, however, that its underlying impulse, though well-disguised, was romantic; it looked back fondly through a *costumbrist* prism to the good old days of João VI's residence in Brazil at the beginning of the century. Another more visibly romantic novelist was Antônio Gonçalves Teixeira e Sousa (1812–61), a mulatto best known for *A Independência do Brasil* (1847), but also the author of novels of a kind then being written all over the rest of Latin America, after the style of Alexandre Dumas and Eugène Sue, with titles like *Fatalidades de dois jovens* (1856), or *Maria ou a menina robada* (1859). They were immediate precursors of Alencar's works, typical of the romantic movement in their obsessive emphasis on young lost lovers (with an exotic tinge always available through an emphasis on their racial differences), in the treatment of wild sylvan settings, and with a gothic frisson evoked by themes of incest, cannibalism or headhunting. A novelist influenced, like Alencar himself, by the more serious Walter Scott was João Manuel Pereira da Silva (1817–98). Like most other major Brazilian writers of the time, he was able to reside in Europe, notably Paris, for long periods, and there he wrote *Jerónimo Corte Real* (1839), set in the sixteenth century, and his *História da fundação do Império brasileiro* (1864–68).

José de Alencar, an aristocratic politician from a Pernambucan family, who also wrote a number of plays and much poetry, including the Indianist *Os filhos de Tupan* (1867), was, however, the unrivalled master of Brazilian romantic fiction. He set out, almost like a Balzac, to cover the entire range of Brazilian historical periods and themes. No novelist of the era from Spanish America can match his achievement in terms of breadth, narrative fluency and grasp of detail. Curiously, though, as in the case of Gonçalves Dias, it is for his Indianism that he is remembered today. Like Fenimore Cooper, with whom he is sometimes unconvincingly compared, he owed a large debt to Walter Scott, and as much to Chateaubriand, though he was more skilful than the latter in terms of detail and general management of action, and not inferior in his symphonic mastery of prose which is sonorous and rhythmical. Sentimental, platitudinous, but unmistakably accomplished, his works are probably the highpoint of nineteenth-century Indianism in Latin America and of the romantic novel as a whole, reminiscent of Hugo, Lamartine and Chateaubriand, with his powerful use of emotion, lyrical landscapes and high moral tone. In addition, he frequently used Brazilian popular idiom and regional themes. The best-known novels include *O Guarani* (1857), *Iracema* (1865), about a beautiful Indian girl who falls tragically in love with a Portuguese soldier, *O gaúcho* (1870), *Ubirajara* (1875), *O*

sertanejo (1875), and the posthumous *Lembra-te-de-mim* (1887). *O sertanejo*
went further than his previous works in detailing popular customs, but
these remained divorced from their true social and economic content.
His characters were spiritual rather than social beings, and a novelist
from a later era, José Lins do Rego, commented unkindly but rather
appropriately that Alencar 'moved them about as if they were trees'.[7]

Just as Brazil's historical experience during the first three quarters of
the nineteenth century was different from that of the Spanish American
republics, so her romantic movement developed differently, both more
complete and less dramatic than the movements in the sister states, where
political and social upheaval produced a literature with more
imperfections in which the passionate, affirmative and committed current in romanticism was stressed. Furthermore, there can be little doubt
that the melancholy and misty religiosity of Brazilian romanticism
derived from the aristocratic background of many of the poets involved,
nor that its muted pessimism was shaped unconsciously by the fear that
the social order which gave them their stable way of life, based as it was
on slavery, was slowly but surely drawing to its end.

The romantic phenomenon, viewed as a movement, appeared earlier
and more vigorously in Argentina than elsewhere. Indeed, such was the
importance of Argentine literature up to the 1870s that, perceived
through the standard histories, Spanish American literature as a whole
can often seem to be almost reducible to the history of literature in that
one republic, with even Mexico and Peru in subordinate roles.
Echeverría, Mármol, Varela, López, Mitre, Sarmiento, Alberdi,
Gutiérrez, gauchesque poetry: there appears to be an unbroken dialogue,
a continuity, even in its conflictiveness, typical of western European
literatures. Only Brazil's less convulsive but even more organic development can compare in this regard. Indeed, it is arguable that Argentine
and River Plate literature (with close ties to Chilean literature up to 1850)
is one history, and that of all the other Spanish American republics
another during this period. This is particularly striking because of course
what was now Argentina had been a distant outpost, a zone of strictly
secondary importance during most of the colonial period. Now, however, Argentina, with less of the heritage of Spanish colonialism and with
its political and literary elites most strongly influenced by England and
France, became almost inevitably the home of nineteenth-century Spanish American literature until the time of *modernismo*, which in Argentina

[7] Quoted by Putnam, *Marvelous journey*, 148.

came curiously late perhaps precisely because that nation had its own authentic literary-social trajectory to develop.

It was in Argentina where a number of enduring themes in Latin American cultural history emerged most emphatically. Thus, in Argentina, from the very start, the opposition between a civilized Europe and a barbarous America was established, with Buenos Aires perceived as a far-flung outpost of civilization marooned in a savage, empty continent. The theme is well expressed in an 1843 poem by L. Domínguez, 'El ombú', which laments the unmarked grave of 'one of those brave men/ worthy of glory and fame/ who, because they were born out here/ left no memory of their name'. Such concepts are essential to an understanding of the Argentine literary mentality to this day. The perceived emptiness encouraged the development of two further themes, both of them conducive to a romantic cast of mind – solitude and distance – and both appear even in the titles of some of Latin America's great works of literature. They are themes which have emerged wherever white Europeans have settled vast areas with sparse aboriginal populations (Australia comes particularly to mind). Rómulo Gallegos, in all the novels he wrote about the previous century, above all *Canaima* (1935), evoked that 'unfinished world' of Genesis, a world not only uncompleted by God but by man: uncharted, unsettled, undeveloped, unknown. The entire continent awaited exploration by the emotions and the senses – the project of romanticism – and by scientific empiricism – the project of positivism – though not ideally, perhaps, in that order. Unfortunately intellectuals tended to act as though each of the new nations really was as empty as it seemed, a cultural vacuum, a ghostly blank sheet of paper bequeathed not by Spain or Portugal but by the French Enlightenment, on which they could write whatever future they saw fit. The *conquistadores* had dreamed of El Dorado; nineteenth-century intellectuals dreamed of utopias. They were bitterly disappointed in those early decades and nowhere more so than in Argentina, where the expectations were highest. The dilemmas were acutely perceived by the brilliant young thinker and writer Juan Bautista Alberdi (1810–84), at that time a journalist who modelled himself on the Spanish writer Mariano José de Larra. In 1838 Alberdi wrote:

The revolution has taken us abruptly out of the arms of the middle ages and has placed us quite unprepared alongside the nineteenth century. These two civilizations have married in our country, but they live ill-wed, as one might expect. The young century, sparkling with elegance and youthful energy, cannot but smile ironically all the while at its silly, decrepit and ridiculous wife. Such heterogeneous arrangements are to be found in every situation, in every misadventure of our society.[8]

The leader of the rebel intellectual generation in post-independence Argentina, founder of the Generación Joven and the Asociación de Mayo in 1837 and 1838, and author of the seminal *Dogma socialista* (1837), was Esteban Echeverría, who wrote the first self-consciously romantic poems in the Spanish language. He had spent the period 1826–30 in Paris, during the years of Vigny's *Cinq mars* (1826), and Hugo's *Cromwell* (1827) and *Hernani* (1830), and then almost literally imported the movement back into Argentina with his other baggage. In Europe he had read Schiller, Goethe and, above all, Byron, realizing that the new movement was, in Pedro Henríquez Ureña's words, 'a spiritual revolution which paved the way for each national or regional group to find its own expression, the complete revelation of its own soul, in contrast to the cold, ultra-rational universality of classicism'.[9] Although Echeverría had little instinct for poetry, his temperament undoubtedly predisposed him to the new movement, as a fragment from his reflections, 'On my thirtieth birthday . . .' (1835), will reveal: 'Between the ages of eighteen and twenty-six my passions and emotions became gigantic, and their impetuosity, bursting all limits, shattered into fragments against the impossible. An insatiable thirst for knowledge, ambition, glory, colossal visions of the future . . . all these things I have felt'. In 1894 the critic García Mérou commented that the defining characteristics of Echeverría's works, typical of his generation, were 'the protests and complaints of those who aspire to a higher destiny, but fail to attain it'.[10]

On his return to Buenos Aires he found a nation wracked by the struggle between unitarians and federalists. Rosas, already governor of Buenos Aires province, was soon to become dictator. By that time Echeverría had published his poems *Elvira o la novia del Plata* (1832) and *Los consuelos* (1834), and was preparing his best-known poetic work, the narrative *La cautiva* (1837), about a passionate heroine who braves the dangers of the savage pampa in an effort to save her lover from bloodthirsty Indians. His real talent, however, as the remarkable and now classic novella *El Matadero* (1838) shows, was for vigour and clarity in prose writing, although in his own day he was celebrated particularly

[8] 'Del uso de lo cómico en Sud América', *El Iniciador* (Buenos Aires), no. 7 (15 July 1838), quoted in Juan Carlos Ghiano, *'El matadero' de Echeverría y el costumbrismo* (Buenos Aires, 1968), 69.
[9] Henríquez Ureña, *Las corrientes literarias*, 121.   [10] Ghiano, *'El matadero'*, 11

for his rather wooden and ultimately cerebral romantic poetry. This is characteristic of the entire era: until the end of the century Argentine critics remained convinced that national achievement in poetry was far superior to the quality of prose writing, whereas quite the opposite was actually the case. When the liberal revolution of 1839 failed, Echeverría's band were forced to flee, mostly to Montevideo. He devoted himself to his writings, a broken man – impotent rage, as we have seen, character-izes the literary work of most of the *proscritos* at this time – and died a year before Rosas was finally defeated at Caseros. His impact on his contemporaries was immense, and is visible in the early works of Juan María Gutiérrez (1809–78), whose *Los amores del payador* appeared in 1833, and equally in *Santos Vega* (1838) by Bartolomé Mitre (1821–1906), one of the great men of the century in Argentina.

In the year of Echeverría's death, one of his young disciples, José Mármol (1817–71), completed his long novel *Amalia*, parts of which had been appearing since 1844. It was the outstanding fictional work of the era, though other interesting novels were also being written: Mitre's *Soledad* (1847), *Esther* (1850) by Miguel Cané (1812–63), *La novia del hereje o la Inquisición de Lima* (1840) by Vicente Fidel López (1815–1903), and Gutiérrez's *El capitán de Patricios* (1843), most of them composed in exile and only published much later. They were mainly pale copies of Walter Scott, and Argentina's own lack of historical tradition made it difficult for writers far from home to produce convincing works of fiction based on such a model. The period also saw the emergence of Argentina's first important female novelist, Juana Manuela Gorriti (1818–92), who married the Bolivian politician Manuel Isidoro Belzú and produced a number of early romantic Indianist works such as *La quena* (Lima, 1843). Mármol's *Amalia*, however, was more interesting than any of its contemporary rivals. It is Latin America's first novel about dictatorship. Its one-word title, a woman's name, is characteristic of the era, with its hyperbolic individualism and the identity it presupposes between indi-vidual, nation and history. Unlike most romantic novels after Scott, *Amalia* deals with the immediate past, although, as Mármol explained in the prologue, it was written as if distant in time to make its point of view immediately accessible to future generations. It dramatizes the heroic struggle of two young men against Rosas's regime embodied in the Mazorca. The beautiful Amalia, a young widow, is the beloved of one and cousin of the other: all are children of heroes of the wars of independence. When first we see Amalia in her scrupulously tasteful home, furnished entirely in European style, she is reading Lamartine's *Méditations*, whilst outside is Rosas's world of asphyxiating terror. Unfortunately, only the villains come alive – Rosas's depiction is unforgettable – whereas the heroes are aristocratic supermen whose idealized behaviour and eventual fate, despite some exciting episodes, leave the modern reader cold. As a document of the times, however, even in its ideological bias, *Amalia* is invaluable. By chapter five, Mármol has diagnosed his fellow countrymen as: 'ignorant by education, vengeful by race, excitable by climate . . . a wild horse rampaging from Patagonia to Bolivia, kicking out at civilization and justice whenever they try to put a brake on its natural instincts'. The image is suggestive, similar to Echeverría's view of Rosas's bloodthirsty supporters in *El matadero* and an anticipation of Sarmiento's portrayal of the gaucho in *Facundo*. Yet Mármol's own narrative clearly demonstrates that his fellow intellectuals were largely ignorant of the true condition of the Argentine Republic, which Rosas understood only too well. The caudillo's popularity with the lower orders was intolerable to the representatives of liberal civilization – whom he enraged still further by dubbing them 'filthy, savage unitarians' – and history incubated a long dialectic which would see the whole phenomenon repeated and magnified with the rise and fall of Perón.

Mármol had been imprisoned whilst still a student for distributing propaganda against Rosas, and it was in prison that he wrote his first poems, although most of his work was produced in exile. After being forced to escape from Montevideo also in 1844, Mármol began his Byronic *Cantos del peregrino*, often considered, despite its unevenness and imperfections, one of the outstanding works of romantic poetry in Spanish. The poet reflected as he sailed the stormy seas: 'Glory longs for bards, poetry for glories,/ Why is there no harmony, voice and heart all gone?/ Europe sends forth no more lyres nor victories,/ Songs died with Byron, glories with Napoleon'. Mármol's annual poetic maledictions against Rosas, written each 25th of May from exile, have become anthology pieces and count among the most violent diatribes ever written in the language ('Savage of the pampa vomited by Hell . . ./ Ah, Rosas, we cannot celebrate May/ without sending you our dread, eternal curse'). Unlike Echeverría, Mármol lived on to respectability in more peaceable days, renounced writing and became, like so many famous Argentine writers after him, director of the National Library.

Clearly, one of the principal reasons for the intensity of literary activity among nineteenth-century Argentines was the intensity of the nation's political life, and in particular the bitterness of a whole generation of intellectuals who felt cheated by the Rosas dictatorship of their right to rule. Argentina was therefore an early and leading producer of writers from exile, writer politicians and political writers, a seemingly permanent Latin American phenomenon ever since. Most of the great authors of the century, accordingly, were also great journalists. In 1852 Mitre, in *Los Debates*, quoted Lamartine's famous dictum:

Each age has its own dominant, characteristic passion: a source of life, if well understood, a source of death when unrecognized. The great passion of our time is a passion for the future, a passion for social perfectibility. The instrument of this passion for bringing about a moral world is the press, the prime civilizing instrument of our epoch.

Mitre, of course, would later found *La Nación* (1870). Many of the writers who had opposed Rosas would gain power after his demise, above all Mitre himself (president, 1862–8) and Domingo Faustino Sarmiento (president, 1868–74). Sarmiento's ideological adversary, Alberdi, the 'citizen of solitude', as Rojas Paz called him in a celebrated biography, never attained real power but his *Bases* were nevertheless instrumental in the elaboration of the 1853 Constitution.

As we have seen, the exiled Argentine rebels took refuge mainly in Montevideo, until Rosas besieged it, and then in Santiago de Chile. It was there, in a much more stable, prosaic and conservative environment – already characteristically a home of realism rather than romanticism – that the famous polemics of 1842 took place, between Andrés Bello and Sarmiento, over the appropriate form of a Latin American linguistic identity, and between Sarmiento's friend Vicente Fidel López and Bello's disciple José Joaquín Vallejo, 'Jotabeche' (1809–58), over romanticism in literary creation. The debates soon became generalized and moved on to overtly political ground, when Sarmiento began to equate grammar with conservatism of every stripe. José Victorino Lastarria (1817–88), a leading Chilean intellectual for the next forty years, was one of the prime movers of the debate, declaring that literature should be 'the authentic expression of our nationality'. It was at this time also that Francisco Bilbao (1823–65), author of the explosive *Sociabilidad chilena* (1844), and Vicuña Mackenna were making their mark in the Santiago intellectual milieu, where most young men were still under the distant spell of Fígaro, the great Spanish poet and journalist Mariano José de Larra. Bello, who had perhaps not expected such buffetings in the Chilean capital, retired wounded from the fray and set about preparing his famous *Gramática* (1847). Once the tutor of Bolívar, although less of an influence than the passionate Simón Rodríguez, he had lived in London from 1810 to 1829, editing epoch-making magazines and composing his famous poems, and had then moved to Chile, where he had become the first rector of the university and perhaps the most widely and consistently enlightened writer in Spanish in the nineteenth century: his contributions to law, literature, criticism and philosophy were all outstanding, and he was the dominant influence in the cultural reorganization of the Chilean republic. Such Latin American patriarchal sobriety as he and Olmedo represented, was as much British as Hispanic. Bello even managed to domesticate Hugo when he translated him later in life.

Sarmiento is at first sight Bello's polar opposite, except in his breadth of achievement. He remains one of a handful of undeniably great literary figures of nineteenth-century Latin America, despite the fact that he almost never wrote works of a purely literary character. He was not interested in following 'models', for 'inspiration' was one of the wellsprings of his existence; at the same time, like Echeverría, he was more comfortable writing about political and philosophical concerns, however passionately expressed, than imaginative literature, and he wrote exclusively in prose. So important is he that the dates of his birth (1811) and death (1888) are frequently used as the boundaries of the Spanish American romantic movement as a whole, especially since the year of his death coincides with the publication of Rubén Darío's *Azul*, the inaugural work of *modernismo*. *Facundo: civilización y barbarie* (1845), produced in exile in Chile, although primarily a work of sociology or 'essay in human geography', is one of only a handful of nineteenth-century works that can still be read for pleasure today. In it a personality imbued with the romantic spirit of self-affirmation is able to identify itself with the present and future of a national territory and, paradoxically, to sound more like the dictator and gauchos he is almost literally loving to hate, and less like that idealized cerebral world of European culture which, the more he exalts it, the more ethereal and unreal it sounds and the more abstract and unsatisfying his text becomes. Most astonishing of all is Sarmiento's certainty: he really seems to *know* that the future belongs to him (Rosas's downfall is accurately predicted in the text), and is palpably talking about a material world over which he intends to take power. At the same time, there is nothing aristocratic about him: he uses the concept of civilization as a club with which to beat his enemies, not as a fan to waft away the unpleasant smell of the masses. His works have none of the abstract distance with which writers like Martínez Estrada, Mallea or Murena would gaze on that same territory a hundred years later. Sarmiento was a dreamer, but also an intensely practical man. He was profoundly interested in the natural sciences (transformation and cultivation of the land) and in education (transformation and cultivation of the people). He founded the first teacher training school in Latin America in Santiago in 1842, and that capital's first serious newspaper, *El Progreso*, in the same year. When Bello argued for a renovated classical mode of language at this time, Sarmiento retorted that 'a correct purist style can only be the fruit of a completely developed civilization', and himself wrote vigorously and spontaneously, like the self-taught romantic he was. He gives the characteristic note to Spanish American – as opposed to Brazilian or European – romanticism: the epic of challenge, construction, achievement. Indeed his texts, vigorous as they are, are only a pale reflection of his continuously active, tempestuous life. There were many tragic figures in the period after Spanish American independence, as we have seen: Heredia, Melgar, Echeverría, Acuña. And there were plenty of sentimentalists, for example, the Colombian Jorge Isaacs, who was really more like a Brazilian of the era. But Sarmiento is the true man of his century. Byron, then, becomes less relevant after the 1840s, except to Brazil's Satanic Generation; even Chateaubriand becomes secondary, though still enormously important – especially in Brazil – and the inspiration of a number of seminal works. The fundamental figures are Victor Hugo in poetry and drama, and Walter Scott in narrative fiction.

If Sarmiento was a man of the future, at a time when other romantic writers had set out to portray the landscapes of the continent in poetry, or to depict the types and customs of its inhabitants, part of the contradictory romantic impulse was to the past. Walter Scott and Washington Irving had initiated the tradition of the historical romance, which Dumas and Sue had continued and, by vulgarizing it, made one of the most enduring forms of popular literature. Its true significance is sometimes misunderstood, however. When the romantics exhume the past it is not always from a merely conservative impulse of nostalgia; it can also be to provide their own post-mortem on it, in which case they are rewriting history according to the bourgeois view of the world. Similarly when they divine the soul of the people in myth and folklore, it is to take possession of that excessively fluid and combustible mass by representing it. In the prologue to his romantic novel *Soledad* (1847), Mitre remarked:

South America is the poorest part of the world in the matter of original novelists. This is why we should like the novel to put down deep roots in America's virgin soil. Our people are ignorant of their history, their barely formed customs have not been studied philosophically. . . . The novel will popularize our history, taking hold of the events of the conquest and colonial period, and our memories of the wars of independence.

Fifteen years earlier Heredia had written a prescient *Ensayo sobre la novela* (1832) on the relation between history and fiction, in which he drew an essential distinction between the historical novel and the sentimental novel.

Thus the development in nineteenth-century Spanish America of two sub-categories of the historical romance, the *leyenda* and the *tradición*, may not always correspond to the more conservative wing of romanticism, as was normally the case in the European context. The lapse of the Spanish realist tradition after the sixteenth and seventeenth centuries and the absence of either a satisfactory historical tradition or of a national store of myths, legends and popular traditions, left the Latin American writer in each new republic in a position where there was no choice but to improvise. If his instincts were concrete, he would turn to the *cuadro de costumbres*; if mystical and sentimental, to the *leyenda*, usually a narrative in prose or poetry about the mysterious past, some local religious miracle or strange natural phenomenon. Eventually the tendency would find its classic expression in the *tradición*, a genre invented by the Peruvian Ricardo Palma. Although the Latin American historical novel proper derives mainly from Scott, Dumas and Sue, the *cuadros de costumbres*, *leyendas* and *tradiciones*, all embryonic forerunners of the short story, were modelled primarily on the works of Spanish writers like the Duke of Rivas, Larra and Zorrilla (the 1843 anthology *Los españoles pintados por sí mismos* was the highpoint of the movement), and only in the more accomplished cases on the critical realism inherent in the French *roman de moeurs*. Although these Spanish writers were aristocratic by birth or inclination, the genres they developed underwent important modifications when transplanted to American soil. At the same time, it is true that each work must be examined on its own specific terms: some were modern in spirit, but archaic in subject matter; others appeared to be exploring contemporary customs, but from a reactionary standpoint. The search for national authenticity often degenerated into mere picturesqueness or local colour and moral superficiality. Where contemporary realist fiction (Balzac and his imitators), which came late both to Spain and Latin America, would attempt to typologize and individualize at one and the same time, *costumbrist* writers would tend to typify and stereo-type, and although they frequently reproduced the dialect and idiom of popular culture, their intention was often to satirize and caricature whilst avoiding true social comment and overlooking misery and oppression.

It is not surprising that the *leyendas* and *tradiciones* are to be found primarily in the more traditional 'colonial' regions of the former Spanish empire. Two of the pioneers, for example, are Guatemalan: José Batres Montúfar (1809–44), known as 'Don Pepe', creator of the influential *Tradiciones de Guatemala*, whose best-known book is the very entertaining *El relox*, reminiscent of Byron's lighter work; and Antonio José de Irisarri, best known for his semi-autobiographical *El cristiano errante* (1845–7), who had shown himself a master of satire and slander in similar short pieces. Other Guatemalans worthy of mention are Juan Diéguez Olavarri (1813–66) and José Milla y Vidaurre ('Salomé Jil', 1822–82), author of *Don Bonifacio* (1862), a narrative in verse, *La hija del Adelantado* (1866), and the famous *Historia de un Pepe* (1882), in which the tenacious influence of Scott, Dumas and Sue was visibly giving way – at last – to other more realist models at the close of the romantic era.

Mexico produced many accomplished exponents of the romantic historical novel, but none of them achieved either true greatness or genuine continental significance. Manuel Payno (1810–94) was one of the first, with the novel *El fistol del diablo* (1845), and also one of the longest-lived, spanning the entire romantic period and beyond. The poet Juan Díaz Covarrubias (1837–59) wrote the characteristically entitled *Gil Gómez, el insurgente o la hija del médico* (1858), in the year before he was executed by the forces of reaction. Vicente Riva Palacio composed a series of lurid novels about the Inquisition, with titles like *Calvario y tambor* (1868) or *Monja y casada, virgen y mártir* (1868). Since Riva was such a close collaborator of Juárez, his works were nationalist, anti-Spanish and anti-clerical in orientation, with definite symptoms of a nascent desire to recuperate the indigenous past. In Mexico the dialectic between civilization and barbarism was from the beginning viewed in terms far more complex and ambiguous than in the Río de la Plata. The Indian question was never couched in such simplistic and dramatic terms as in Argentina, and the redemptionist current was visible rather earlier than in Brazil. Ignacio Ramírez, 'El Nigromante' (1818–79), while not a novelist, was a seminal literary figure of the era; but the greatest influence of all on Mexican literary life in the Reform period and after was Ignacio Altamirano (1834–93), himself an Indian like Juárez, author of the romantic *costumbrist* novel *Clemencia* (1869), the nostalgic and much loved *La Navidad en las montañas* (1871), and the adventure novel, *El Zarco* (written 1888, published 1901), a tale of banditry set in the early 1860s. The theme had already been broached in *Astucia* (1866) by Luis G. Inclán (1816–75), and was treated again in Payno's lastingly popular *Los bandidos de Río Frío* (1891). As in Spain, the bandit is a favourite figure in Mexican fiction, not only because, like the pirate, he was exalted by the romantics, but because he corresponded to a significant social reality. Altamirano, however, was more important as a cultural promoter than as a novelist. He it was who initiated the famous *Veladas Literarias* late in 1867, inviting all the leading writers and critics of the time; and who in 1869 founded the magazine *El Renacimiento*, which began the conscious search for a national culture and a nationalist literature. Mexico had 'still not heard the Cry of Dolores', in her literature, proclaimed Altamirano, and his call for national renovation was to echo down the following decades and into the 1920s, although Altamirano himself was really one of the last of the romantics rather than the transition to something genuinely new.

Cuban romantic fiction was passionate, as one might expect of novelists convulsed by the conflicting pressures of Spanish colonialism at its most ruthless and the national struggle for liberation. Gertrudis Gómez de Avellaneda (1814–73), who spent most of her turbulent life in Spain, wrote *Sab* (1841), a courageous if sentimentalized abolitionist novel, one of the first American anti-slavery works since Lizardi's *El periquillo sarniento*, which contains a memorable condemnation of the system. Anselmo Suárez Romero (1818–78) began his novel *Francisco* in 1832, but it was published, posthumously, only in 1880. It told the story of two slaves in love who commit suicide when that love cannot be realized, a plot typical of the romantic era and repeated with numerous variations both in Cuba and elsewhere. Similar in its orientation (and in its publishing history) was Cuba's best-known nineteenth-century novel, *Cecilia Valdés o la Loma del Angel*, by Cirilo Villaverde (1812–94), begun in 1839, finally completed only in 1879 and eventually published in 1882. In nineteenth-century Cuba writers could never be confident that their works could or would be safely published.

The greatest writer of prose fiction in nineteenth-century Spanish

America, though a late arrival – confirming the thesis that it was only around 1870 that the romantic movement there found its definitive focus – was the Peruvian Ricardo Palma (1833–1919), creator of the *Tradiciones peruanas*, which he began to produce in embryonic form in the 1850s but only published regularly between 1870 and 1915. He is a nineteenth-century classic, at once characteristic and unique, whose masters are really Cervantes and Quevedo and whose irony allows him both to preserve and to undermine colonial tradition. Faintly anti-aristocratic and anti-clerical, attacking injustice with humour and satire rather than denunciation, Palma's stories are consistently entertaining, communicating the love of their author for his native city, warts and all, with a subtle mix of everyday language, Spanish proverbial sayings and Peruvian vernacular dialogue. Manuel González Prada called them a 'bitter-sweet falsification of history', whilst Eugenio María de Hostos protested that so much erudition should go to waste on mere diversions in which the critique of colonialism was almost invisible. Nonetheless, Palma's works clearly imply a shift from the early *costumbristas*, who at bottom were in reality providing a critical parody of the new classes emerging after independence. The *leyenda*, predecessor to the *tradición*, had been an unmistakably romantic form, treated in verse by Zorrilla and in prose by Bécquer within peninsular tradition. Palma's *tradición* was in effect a combination of the *leyenda* and the *cuadro de costumbres*, radically updated in the direction of the short story, which in Brazil appeared through Machado de Assis as early as the 1860s but in Spanish America did not properly emerge until well into the *modernista* period. His works helped to recover, albeit in a distorted mirror, a lost colonial past, laid the bases of a national literature, and, indeed, became a precursor both of Borges's incomparable 'fictions' and of the so-called magical realist current in twentieth-century Latin American narrative. He evidently hoped that his fictionalized historical fragments would actually *become* Peruvian 'traditions', connecting national history and folklore through the genre of literary romance. In the introduction to his early *tradición*, 'Un virrey y un arzobispo', first published in 1860, he had written:

In America traditions have hardly any life. America still has the freshness of the recent discovery and the value of a fabulous but as yet barely exploited treasure. . . . It is up to our young people to ensure that traditions are not lost altogether. This is why we ourselves pay such close attention to tradition, and to attract the interest of the people, we think it appropriate to clothe each historical narrative in the garb of romance.

Palma's first series of definitive *Tradiciones peruanas* appeared in 1872. He later became an important member of the literary establishment and long-time director of the National Library from 1884 to 1912.

What the *leyendistas* had been attempting to solve with their newly developed genre, and what Palma did partially resolve, was the problem of finding an American form for American subject matter. As the Peruvian was composing his small literary jewels, the Colombian Jorge Isaacs (1837–95) managed to find a persuasive mould for the romantic novel, just before it finally became entirely archaic. The result was *María* (1867), the most successful of all Spanish American romantic works. It is a novel in the line of Rousseau's *La Nouvelle Héloïse*, Bernardin de Saint Pierre's *Paul et Virginie*, Lamartine's *Graciela*, or Constant's *Adolphe*. The most direct influence on Isaacs, however, was Chateaubriand: the characters of the novel themselves spend much time reading *Atala* and *Le Génie du christianisme*, fittingly enough, for in later Spanish American fiction many a heroine can be found, bathed in tears, reading *María*, which remains a powerful force today in popular fiction, drama and cinema. A close Brazilian equivalent is Alfredo d'Escragnolle Taunay's enduringly popular *sertão* romance *Inocência* (1872). With Chateaubriand in mind, Efraín, the narrator of *María*, says of his beloved that 'she was as beautiful as the poet's creation and I loved her with the love that he imagined'. In reality the novel was largely compensatory. Isaacs had mismanaged the family estate El Paraíso (which has the same name in the novel) after the death of his father during Colombia's plague of civil wars, and wrote most of it in a tent high in the tropical forests at a camp called La Víbora, earning a living as an inspector of roads. The work combines the nostalgic adolescent purity of one branch of romanticism with the willed desire for innocence of the liberal sector within a landed, slave-owning aristocracy. The result is a tropical pastoral symphony, gentle, tragic, tearful: objectively false but emotionally true. What was new was that Isaacs had based his novel not on other works of literature, as one might imagine, but on largely autobiographical experiences and on a real setting, the beautiful Cauca valley, whilst ruthlessly suppressing all but the most indirect social dimension to the work. (Isaacs, a converted Jew and embattled landowner, a liberal and a conservative by turns, was heavily involved in civil and military campaigns, but there is no trace of such things in the novel.) As the Colombian critic, Mejía Duque, has said, 'for thousands of readers *María* goes on living with the warmth common to the sweetest dreams and the most tenacious myths'.[11]

It was at this time that *Indianismo*, that version of historically inclined romanticism which exalted the Indian of the pre-conquest era whilst ignoring his contemporary descendants (the movement which defended them would begin later and be called *Indigenismo*), reached its zenith in Spanish America, as it had somewhat earlier in Brazil with Alencar. It may seem paradoxical that Spanish Americans were only able to achieve in the 1870s what French novelists had done in the wake of the Enlightenment, but that is how long it took them to distance themselves sufficiently from their own reality to achieve aesthetic perspective – and then only to see their American compatriots as distantly in time as the Europeans had in space almost a century before. It is a still more striking fact, as we have seen, that until the very last years of the century the Indian was given a heroic role only in countries like Brazil, where he was not the major social 'problem', or like the Dominican Republic, where he had long before been exterminated. Lins do Rego would later comment caustically that 'Alencar, by way of fleeing Brazil, sought out the jungle; by way of escaping from the Brazilian, he discovered the Indian'. Certainly the Indian who appears in nineteenth-century Latin American literature is invariably the childlike noble savage of the fifteenth and sixteenth centuries, used as a symbol of liberation after nineteenth-century independence, and not the downtrodden and malnourished figure who has worked on virtually feudal estates up and down the continent to this day. As Henríquez Ureña said, the living Indian was not considered poetical.

In 1879 the Ecuadorean Juan León Mera (1832–94) published his celebrated exoticist novel *Cumandá*, subtitled 'a drama among savages', which was full of sexual titillation including the almost obligatory danger of incest between unwitting relatives, and set among the head-hunting Jivaro Indians of the Amazon jungle. Like *María*, this was a late-flowering, voluptuous bloom, a highpoint of American Indianism. In the Dominican Republic, meanwhile, the conservative José Joaquín Pérez had produced a series of narrative poems, *Fantasías indígenas* (1877), exalting the Indians of the early colonial period, whilst between 1879 and 1882 Manuel J. Galván (1834–1910) published his long novel *Enriquillo*, set in the same period, and now recognized as one of the great historical

---

[11] Jaime Mejía Duque, 'Jorge Isaacs: el hombre y su novela', in Mirta Yáñez (ed.), *La novela romántica latinoamericana* (Havana, 1978), 373–442 (p.442).

works of the last century for its grasp of detail and its progressive critical perspective. In 1888 the Uruguayan Juan Zorrilla de San Martín (1855–1931), published *Tabaré*, the most famous verse narrative of the nineteenth century, about the son of a Spanish woman and an Indian chief. Zorrilla, both Catholic and romantic, mourned the passing of the Indian race through his tragic romance, but without conviction; his verse, however, already showed traces of the symbolist current which distinguished Darío's *Azul*, published that same year. Zorrilla later became the 'national poet of Uruguay' and was commissioned to write his *La epopeya de Artigas* in 1910 for the independence centenary.

Romanticism, as we have seen, launched first an Americanist, and then a Nationalist project, but succeeded on the whole only in producing a narrowly provincial, descriptive literature which rarely advanced beyond Spanish *costumbrismo*. Very late in the day, writers like Alencar, Isaacs and Mera brought the movement to its highest artistic point, but at the cost of carefully excluding all traces of social or historical realism. It was in the 1870s, and more particularly in the 1880s, that romanticism began to bifurcate into a realist narrative strand arising out of the *cuadro de costumbres* and historical novel, and a more rigorously specialized poetic strand in which the emotional exuberance of romantic poetry and the carefully chiselled artifice of the *tradición* combined to produce a more precise, musical and artistic modernist movement. Before this moment, the outstanding works, like Echeverría's *El matadero* or Sarmiento's *Facundo*, had been strange, anarchic creations, frequently a product of unforeseen hybridizations and fusions. One of the greatest of all such works was the gauchesque poem, *Martín Fierro* (1872) – with its sequel, the *Vuelta de Martín Fierro* (1879) – by the Argentine writer José Hernández (1834–86). Although it is customary to categorize gauchesque poetry separately, it is clear that this River Plate phenomenon is a nativist current among others, and part of the romantic impulse to commune with the spirit of the folk. It emerged very early – with the first manifestations of romanticism itself, during the emancipation period – and not in the latter part of the nineteenth century with *Indigenismo* and other such movements. This can be explained by the precociousness of Argentine and Uruguayan romanticism, which from the start saw the rural songs and music of the gauchos as adaptable to art literature, in the same way that the *romances viejos* had been imitated by urban poets at court in sixteenth-century Spain. Gauchesque poetry, accordingly, was written not by gauchos but by educated city dwellers.

Its origins, however, lay back in the eighteenth century, in oral tradition, and it was Bartolomé Hidalgo who, at the time of independence, captured it for written literature and history, reminding Argentinians and Uruguayans of the gaucho contribution to the defeat of the Spaniards and giving permanent impetus to the *criollista* tendency. After all, the existence of the gaucho, however much Sarmiento and his contemporaries may have considered him a barbarian, made it all the more easy to render the Indian invisible to literature, before he was finally exterminated at the end of the period under review.

It was Hilario Acasubi (1807–75) who most decisively perceived the potential in the gaucho theme for producing a national literature based on rural life, with rustic speech and popular songs. His best known works are *Paulino Lucero*, begun in 1838 and full of anti-Rosas sentiment (not at all characteristic of the real gauchos), and *Santos Vega* (1850, published 1872). Even more urban in its perspective was *Fausto* (1866), by Estanislao del Campo (1834–80), a city man who, on returning to Argentina from exile, saw in the rural gaucho a somewhat comic symbol of Argentine nationhood. The work recreates an ingenuous gaucho's impression of Gounod's *Faust*, which had recently been performed in the celebrated Teatro Colón, then in its first decade of operation. Del Campo's poem is sophisticated, entertaining and very characteristic of Argentine literary tradition.

Unlike most important Argentine writers of the nineteenth century, Hernández himself had been a *rosista* until Rosas fell in the poet's eighteenth year. He had also led the life of a gaucho, and in 1882 he published a knowledgeable *Instrucción al estanciero*. He was for much of the time at odds with post-Rosas Argentina, not least during the presidency of Sarmiento. His poem, *Martín Fierro*, is a popular epic with an individual voice, one of the greatest achievements of romantic poetry in Spanish. Like *Don Quixote*, it manages to evoke the landscapes in which it is set without actually needing to describe them. Hernández is so closely attuned to gaucho culture that the reader is persuaded by the picturesque dialect he invents for his narrative, even though, as Borges has remarked, no gaucho ever spoke as Martín Fierro does. The poem provides an implicit critique of the direction being taken by Argentine society and, indeed, of the Europeanized writers who were setting the pace. Hernández, instead, evokes the solitude and extension of the pampas, the everyday heroism of its inhabitants, and the simple Hispanic romanticism of the horse, the road and the horizon, all framed by a song sung to guitar, which would have so many literary miles to travel in both South and North America over the century to come. It is the single most important work of Argentine literature, viewed from the nationalist perspective. Leopoldo Lugones in 1913 called it the 'Argentine national epic'. At the same time, its elegiac quality is clearly evident, for the freedom of the prairies had been increasingly circumscribed by the advance of civilization and private property since independence. Moreover, it was the gaucho, and the rural population in general, who were to suffer most directly from the wave of immigration which, when the poem was composed, was only just beginning. Hernández' definitive expression of a gaucho nationalist mythology retrospectively re-emphasized the importance of Sarmiento's *Facundo*, as well as of other gauchesque poets since Hidalgo, and prepared the ground for Gutiérrez's *Juan Moreira* (1879) and Güiraldes's *Don Segundo Sombra* (1926).

From the 1860s, then, the age of realism had slowly begun to dawn in Latin America. Even Hernández' sober and stoical gaucho demonstrated that. Men still looked back with envy or nostalgia to the heroic days of the independence era, but for the most part were beginning to feel that such heroics were not for them. If romanticism, on the whole, seemed to have been a partially negative reaction to the rationalism of the Enlightenment, realism demonstrated anew the Enlightenment's decisive contribution to the shaping of the western mind, and the growth of industrialization and urbanization in Europe had reinforced the trend. The result in Latin America was a fairly unproblematical development out of the historical and *costumbrist* modes of romanticism into realism or, more frequently, its variant, naturalism. One might even say that these schools were the more cosmopolitan, more specifically urban counterpart to a *costumbrism* that had been – and, in the many areas where it continued to flourish, still remained – unvaryingly provincial, leading to a further distinction to be made when we reach the twentieth century, between a regionalism which is the attempt by city-based novelists to rehabilitate life in the interior from within a progressive perspective on artistic nationalism, and a *criollismo* which embodies the conservative impulse to keep both society and literature very much as they are for as long as possible.

Looking back, the independence and post-independence periods set the national rather than continental patterns for Latin American culture. It

was not only a time of passionate upheaval followed by national intro-
spection – imposed partly by willed choice and more by immovable
circumstance – but also one when the integration of the independent
republics into the rapidly evolving international economic system had
still barely begun. Although the period 1780 to 1830 had seen many Latin
American intellectuals travel to Europe (and the United States), few
other than Brazilian aristocrats were able in the decades after 1830 to gain
first-hand experience of the continent whose philosophical ideas and
artistic modes they nonetheless continued, inevitably, to adopt and
imitate. This is perhaps the true explanation for the aridity and alleged
'inauthenticity' of much Latin American artistic expression between the
1820s and the 1870s (with the partial exception of Brazil): not so much
that the European forms did not fit Latin American reality, as is usually
said, though this certainly remains an important theoretical consideration; more that the Latin American writers and artists themselves were
not fully able to inhabit those forms; and if through lack of lived
experience, they could not master foreign forms, they were hardly likely
to be able to apply them to their own autochthonous reality with any
conviction. This dual character of their inauthenticity derived from a
two-fold failure of assimilation. The more 'authentic' a Latin American
artist actually was – that is, the less he was affected by Europe – the more
inauthentic his works were likely to seem, with occasional exceptions
like José Hernández. The decisive sea-change would come only after
modernismo (*parnasianismo* – *simbolismo* in Brazil) from the 1880s to the
1910s, because for the most part that movement merely reversed the
process: with the improvement in communications (which itself derived
from the closer integration of Latin America into the international
economic system) writers became more proficient with the tools of
literature – language and ideas – by sharing the experiences of the
Europeans they were bent on imitating, but were for the most part too
alienated from their own reality, either because they actually lived in
Europe or were, sometimes literally, dying to go there, to apply the new
tools to native materials. The latter process got fully under way only in
the 1920s. Having said this, it is important not to repeat the
commonplaces of most criticism of Latin American art by dismissing
implicitly or explicitly all that does not conform to 'European' taste in
literary and artistic expertise and production, particularly since so many
of the shortcomings perceived in that art derive precisely from the effort
to mimic those distant models. Moreover, European art itself would

look very different if its story were told without reference to the concepts of 'masterpieces' or 'works of genius'. Latin America's historical reality has always produced Latin America's proper cultural expression: if so much of that art, particularly in the nineteenth century, now seems to have deformed or disguised Latin American realities, then that in itself is a Latin American reality for which artists alone cannot be held responsible. If critics or historians are 'disappointed' by what they find in the art and literature of Latin America of this period, it behoves them to explain what they were expecting to find, and on what assumptions. Even more than in other contexts, it is their task and their duty to grasp the movement and direction of Latin America's cultural history, which has always been, for every artist, at once a search for personal, national and continental self-expression which will lead the way from a colonial past to some freer, better future. Nowhere are the hopes and disillusionments of that quest better exemplified than in the early national period.

BIBLIOGRAPHICAL ESSAYS

ABBREVIATIONS

ESC	*Estudios Sociales Centroamericanos*
HAHR	*Hispanic American Historical Review*
HM	*Historia Mexicana*
JIAS	*Journal of Inter-American Studies and World Affairs*
JLAS	*Journal of Latin American Studies*
LARR	*Latin American Research Review*
TA	*The Americas*

I. THE ORIGINS OF SPANISH AMERICAN INDEPENDENCE

Most of the documentary compilations and narrative sources throw more light on the course of independence than on its origins, but some data on the latter will be found in *Biblioteca de Mayo* (17 vols., Buenos Aires, 1960–3); *Archivo del General Miranda* (24 vols., Caracas, 1929–50); *Biblioteca de la Academia Nacional de la Historia* (82 vols., Caracas, 1960–6); *Colección documental de la independencia del Perú* (30 vols., Lima, 1971). Mexico and northern South America attracted the attention of a distinguished contemporary observer, Alexander von Humboldt, whose *Ensayo político sobre el reino de la Nueva España*, ed. Juan A. Ortega y Medina (Mexico, 1966), and *Viaje a las regiones equinocciales del Nuevo Continente* (5 vols., Caracas, 1956) illuminate conditions in the late colonial period. For an example of liberal economic writings in Buenos Aires, see Manuel Belgrano, *Escritos económicos*, ed. Gregorio Weinberg (Buenos Aires, 1954).

The Spanish background has a large bibliography, of which the following is a small selection: Gonzalo Anes, *Economía e ilustración en la*

España del siglo XVIII (Barcelona, 1969) and *Las crisis agrarias en la España moderna* (Madrid, 1970); Josep Fontana Lázaro, *La quiebra de la monarquía absoluta 1814–1820* (Barcelona, 1971); *La economía española al final del Antiguo Régimen.* III. *Comercio y colonias,* ed. Josep Fontana Lázaro (Madrid, 1982). The Enlightenment can be studied in Richard Herr, *The eighteenth-century revolution in Spain* (Princeton, 1958), and its impact in America in R. J. Shafer, *The economic societies in the Spanish world (1763–1821)* (Syracuse, 1958); see also M. L. Pérez Marchand, *Dos etapas ideológicas del siglo XVIII en México a través de los papeles de la Inquisición* (Mexico, 1945). José Carlos Chiaramonte (ed.), *Pensamiento de la Ilustración. Economía y sociedad iberoamericanas en el siglo xviii* (Caracas, 1979), provides a survey of the state of the subject and a selection of primary texts.

Applied enlightenment, or imperial reform, and American responses to it can be approached through Stanley J. and Barbara H. Stein, *The colonial heritage of Latin America* (New York, 1970), 86–119, and then studied in more detail in John Lynch, *Spanish Colonial Administration, 1782–1810. The intendant system in the viceroyalty of the Río de la Plata* (London, 1958); J. R. Fisher, *Government and society in colonial Peru. The intendant system 1784–1814* (London, 1970); and Jacques A. Barbier, *Reform and politics in Bourbon Chile, 1755–1796* (Ottawa, 1980). The attempt to reform *repartimientos* and control local economic interests is dealt with in Brian R. Hamnett, *Politics and trade in southern Mexico 1750–1821* (Cambridge, 1971), and in Stanley J. Stein, 'Bureaucracy and business in the Spanish empire, 1759–1804: Failure of a Bourbon reform in Mexico and Peru', *HAHR*, 61/1 (1981), 2–28. Military reform is given precise definition in Christon I. Archer, *The army in Bourbon Mexico 1760–1810* (Albuquerque, 1977), Leon G. Campbell, *The military and society in colonial Peru 1750–1810* (Philadelphia, 1978), and Allan J. Kuethe, *Military reform and society in New Granada, 1773–1808* (Gainesville, 1978). Clerical immunity and its erosion by reform and revolution are studied in Nancy M. Farriss, *Crown and clergy in colonial Mexico 1759–1821. The crisis of ecclesiastical privilege* (London, 1968). Aspects of renewed fiscal pressure are explained in Sergio Villalobos R., *Tradición y reforma en 1810* (Santiago, 1961) for Chile, and for Mexico in Asunción Lavrin, 'The execution of the Law of Consolidación in New Spain's economy. Aims and Results', *HAHR*, 53/1 (1973), 27–49.

The violent reaction to taxation and other burdens has been studied in a number of works on the rebellions of the eighteenth century. Joseph

Perez, *Los movimientos precursores de la emancipación en Hispanoamérica* (Madrid, 1977) identifies the major movements and their character. Leon G. Campbell, 'Recent research on Andean peasant revolts, 1750–1820', *LARR* 14/1 (1979), 3–49, provides a critical survey of primary and secondary material for the region of 'Inca nationalism'. Segundo Moreno Yáñez, *Sublevaciones indígenas en la Audiencia de Quito, desde comienzos del siglo XVIII hasta finales de la colonia* (Bonn, 1976), describes Indian protest and riot in the region of Quito, 1760–1803, against a background of agrarian structure. Indian and *mestizo* movements in Upper Peru are the subject of René Arze Aguirre, *Participación popular en la independencia de Bolivia* (La Paz, 1979). Individual rebellions are studied in Boleslao Lewin, *La rebelión de Tupac Amaru y los orígenes de la emancipación americana* (Buenos Aires, 1957); Alberto Flores Galindo (ed.), *Antología-Túpac Amaru II* (Lima, 1976); Scarlett O'Phelan Godoy, 'El movimiento Tupacamarista: fases, coyuntura económica y perfil de la composicion social de su dirigencia', *Actas del Coloquio Internacional Tupac Amaru y su Tiempo* (Lima, 1982), 461–88; John Leddy Phelan, *The people and the king. The Comunero Revolution in Colombia, 1781* (Madison, 1978); Carlos E. Muñoz Oraá, *Los comuneros de Venezuela* (Mérida, 1971).

The problems of economic causation continue to exercise historians. Tulio Halperín Donghi (ed.), *El ocaso del orden colonial Hispanoaméricana* (Buenos Aires, 1978), brings together a number of studies of a socio-economic character dealing with crises in the colonial order. Spanish thinking on colonial trade is the subject of Marcelo Bitar Letayf, *Economistas españoles del siglo XVIII. Sus ideas sobre la libertad del comercio con Indias* (Madrid, 1968), while policy and practice are described in E. Arcila Farías, *El siglo ilustrado en América. Reformas económicas del siglo XVIII en Nueva España* (Caracas, 1955), and Sergio Villalobos R., *El comercio y la crisis colonial. Un mito de la independencia* (Santiago, 1968). The role of colonial trade in Spanish economic development is discussed in Jordi Nadal and Gabriel Tortella (ed.), *Agricultura, comercio colonial y crecimiento económico en la España contemporánea. Actas del Primer Coloquio de Historia Económica de España* (Barcelona, 1974). Quantitative studies of *comercio libre* and its fate during the Anglo-Spanish wars are provided by Antonio García-Baquero, *Cádiz y el Atlántico (1717–1778)* (2 vols., Seville, 1976) and *Comercio colonial y guerras revolucionarias* (Seville, 1972), and by Javier Ortiz de la Tabla Ducasse, *Comercio exterior de Veracruz 1778–1821* (Seville, 1978). John Fisher, 'Imperial "Free Trade" and the Hispanic economy, 1778–1796', *JLAS* 13/1 (1981), 21–56, gives a precise measurement of trade from Spain to America under *comercio libre*, while the next phase is studied by Javier Cuenca Esteban, 'Statistics of Spain's colonial trade, 1792–1820: Consular Duties, Cargo Inventories, and Balance of Trade', *HAHR* 61/3 (1981), 381–428, and by the same author, 'Comercio y hacienda en la caída del imperio español, 1778–1826', in Fontana, *Comercio y colonias*, 389–453.

Economic conditions within Spanish America in the late colonial period are the subject of basic new research. The mining sector and its position in the socio-economic structure of Mexico is studied in David A. Brading, *Miners and merchants in Bourbon Mexico, 1763–1810* (Cambridge, 1971). For mining in Peru, see J. R. Fisher, *Silver mines and silver miners in colonial Peru, 1776–1824* (Liverpool, 1977), and for Upper Peru Rose Marie Buechler, *The mining society of Potosí 1776–1810* (Syracuse University, 1981). Enrique Tandeter, 'Forced and free labour in late colonial Potosí', *Past and Present*, 93 (1981), 98–136, demonstrates the importance of *mita* labour to the survival of Potosí production. Enrique Florescano, *Precios del maíz y crisis agrícolas en México (1708–1810)* (Mexico, 1969), examines rising maize prices, agrarian crisis and rural misery on the eve of the Mexican insurgency. Humberto Tandrón, *El real consulado de Caracas y el comercio exterior de Venezuela* (Caracas, 1976), illustrates the tension between agricultural and commercial interests and the clash between Venezuelan and Spanish viewpoints, while problems of another export economy and its hinterland are studied by Michael T. Hamerly, *Historia social y económica de la antigua provincia de Guayaquil, 1763–1842* (Guayaquil, 1973). Susan Migden Socolow, *The merchants of Buenos Aires 1778–1810. Family and commerce* (Cambridge, 1978) analyses the formation, economic role and social position of the *porteño* merchant group, while the little-known history of artisans is investigated by Lyman L. Johnson, 'The silversmiths of Buenos Aires: a case study in the failure of corporate social organisation', *JLAS*, 8/2 (1976), 181–213.

Social structure of the pre-independence period involves problems of class, creoles and race. Historians have recently tended to emphasize economic interests, social perceptions and political groupings rather than simple creole-peninsular conflict as an explanation of independence: see Luis Villoro, *El proceso ideológico de la revolución de independencia* (Mexico, 1967), for a survey of social classes in Mexico; further refinement of analysis is provided by David A. Brading, 'Government and elite in late colonial Mexico', *HAHR*, 53 (1973), 389–414, and by Doris M. Ladd, *The Mexican nobility at independence 1780–1826* (Austin, 1976).

Venezuelan structures are explained by Germán Carrera Damas, *La crisis de la sociedad colonial venzolana* (Caracas, 1976), and Miguel Izard, *El miedo a la revolución. La lucha por la libertad en Venezuela (1777–1830)* (Madrid, 1979); while the growing tension between whites and coloureds is described by Federico Brito Figueroa, *Las insurrecciones de los esclavos negros en la sociedad colonial* (Caracas, 1961), Miguel Acosta Saignes, *Vida de los esclavos negros en Venezuela* (Caracas, 1967), and I. Leal, 'La aristocracia criolla venezolana y el código negrero de 1789', *Revista de Historia*, 2 (1961), 61–81. The influence of the revolution in Saint-Domingue can be studied in Eleazar Córdova-Bello, *La independencia de Haití y su influencia en Hispanoamérica* (Mexico-Caracas, 1967). Creole demand for office and the Spanish 'reaction' are measured by Mark A. Burkholder and D. S. Chandler, *From impotence to authority. The Spanish crown and the American Audiencias 1687–1808* (Columbus, 1977).

Incipient nationalism has not been systematically studied. J. A. de la Puente Candamo, *La idea de la comunidad peruana y el testimonio de los precursores* (Lima, 1956), and Nestor Meza Villalobos, *La conciencia política chilena durante la monarquía* (Santiago, 1958), discuss various aspects of the subject, as does David Brading, *Los orígenes del nacionalismo mexicano* (Mexico, 1973). A synthesis is suggested by John Lynch, *The Spanish American Revolutions 1808–1826* (London, 1973), 24–34, 335–8.

2. THE INDEPENDENCE OF MEXICO AND CENTRAL AMERICA

The bibliography on Mexico's struggle for independence is vast, perhaps the largest in Mexican studies. Published documentary collections are rich; only the most notable can be mentioned here. The fundamental set is Juan E. Hernández y Dávalos, *Colección de documentos para la historia de la guerra de independencia de México* (6 vols., Mexico, 1877–82). Almost as useful are Genaro García, *Documentos históricos mexicanos* (7 vols., Mexico, 1910–12) and *El Clero de México y la guerra de independencia*, vol. 9 in *Documentos inéditos o muy raros para la historia de México* (Mexico, 1906); Joaquín García Icazbalceta, *Colección de documentos para la historia de México* (Mexico, 1925) and *Nueva colección de documentos* (5 vols., Mexico, 1886). And for Morelos there is Luis Castillo Ledón, *Morelos, documentos inéditos y poco conocidos* (Mexico, 1927). Equally important are the histories written by participants and observers. The classic work is Lucas Alamán, *Historia de Méjico desde los primeros movimientos que prepararon su independencia en el año de 1808 hasta la época presente* (5 vols., Mexico, 1849–

52). Other very useful works are Carlos María Bustamante, *Cuadro histórico de la revolución mexicana* (2 vols., 2nd edn, Mexico, 1843–4); Anastasio Zerecero, *Memorias para la historia de las revoluciones en México* (Mexico, 1869); Servando Teresa de Mier, *Historia de la revolución de Nueva España* (Mexico, 1822); José María Luis Mora, *México y sus revoluciones* (3 vols., Paris, 1836); and Henry George Ward, *Mexico in 1827* (2 vols., London, 1828). Francisco de Paula de Arrangoiz y Berzábal, *Méjico desde 1808 hasta 1867* (4 vols., Madrid, 1871), is derivative and generally follows Alamán.

Though always a subject of great fascination to scholars, Mexican late colonial and independence studies have undergone much recent revision. Some of the most significant new works that trace the political history are Timothy E. Anna, *The fall of the royal government in Mexico City* (Lincoln, Nebraska, 1978) and *Spain and the loss of America* (Lincoln, 1983); the very different interpretation of Romeo Flores Caballero, *La contrarevolución en la independencia: los españoles en la vida política, social y económica de Mexico 1804–1838* (Mexico, 1969); another study of the royalists and their resistance to independence, Brian R. Hamnett, *Revolución y contrarevolución en México y el Perú: liberalismo, realeza y separatismo (1800–1824)* (Mexico, 1978); the basic study of Hidalgo, Hugh M. Hamill, Jr, *The Hidalgo Revolt: prelude to Mexican independence* (Gainesville, 1966); on Morelos, Anna Macías, *Génesis del govierno constitucional en México, 1808–1820* (Mexico, 1973); Jaime E. Rodríguez O., *The emergence of Spanish America: Vicente Rocafuerte and Spanish Americanism, 1808–1832* (Berkeley, 1975); and Luis Villoro, *El proceso ideológico de la revolución de independencia* (Mexico, 1967). Important new institutional and social studies include Christon I. Archer, *The army in Bourbon Mexico, 1760–1810* (Albuquerque, 1977) and 'The army of New Spain and The Wars of Independence, 1790–1821', *HAHR*, 61/4 (1981), 705–14; Michael P. Costeloe, *Church wealth in Mexico, 1800–1856* (Cambridge, 1967); N. M. Farriss, *Crown and clergy in colonial Mexico, 1759–1821: the crisis of ecclesiastical privilege* (London, 1968); Doris M. Ladd, *The Mexican nobility at independence, 1780–1826* (Austin, 1976); and Javier Ocampo, *Las ideas de un día: el pueblo mexicano ante la consumación de su independencia* (Mexico, 1969). Providing much new knowledge about the economic and social condition of late colonial Mexico are David A. Brading, *Miners and merchants in Bourbon Mexico, 1763–1810* (Cambridge, 1971); Enrique Florescano, *Precios del maíz y crisis agrícolas en México (1708–1810)* (Mexico, 1969); Brian R. Hamnett, *Politics and trade in southern Mexico, 1750–1821* (Cambridge, 1971); Enrique Florescano and Isabel Gil, *1750–1808: la época de las reformas borbónicas y del crecimiento económico* (Mexico, 1974); and John Tutino, 'Hacienda social relations in Mexico: the Chalco region in the era of independence', *HAHR*, 55/3 (1975), 496–528. David A. Brading's *Los orígenes del nacionalismo mexicano* (Mexico 1973) is perhaps the most thoughtful study on the origins of creolism. All these works alter earlier views of the meaning and process of independence, especially clarifying social, economic and class structures.

At the same time, a number of older works remain invaluable for their contributions, largely in the fields of narrative history and institutional studies. These include Nettie Lee Benson (ed.), *Mexico and the Spanish Cortes, 1810–1822: eight essays* (Austin, Texas, 1966), and *La diputación provincial y el federalismo mexicano* (Mexico, 1955); Luis Castillo Ledón, *Hidalgo, la vida del héroe* (2 vols., Mexico, 1948–9); Donald B. Cooper, *Epidemic diseases in Mexico City, 1761–1813* (Austin, Texas, 1965); Mariano Cuevas, *Historia de la iglesia en México* (5 vols., El Paso, Texas, 1928); Lillian Estelle Fisher, *The background of the revolution for Mexican independence* (Boston, 1934), and *Champion of reform, Manuel Abad y Queipo* (New York, 1955); Enrique Lafuente Ferrari, *El Virrey Iturrigaray y los orígenes de la independencia de México* (Madrid, 1941); John Rydjord, *Foreign interest in the independence of New Spain* (Durham, N.C., 1935); William Spence Robertson, *Iturbide of Mexico* (Durham, N.C., 1952); Wilbert H. Timmons, *Morelos of Mexico, priest, soldier, statesman* (El Paso, Texas, 1963); and María del Carmen Velázquez, *El estado de guerra en Nueva España, 1760–1808* (Mexico, 1950). An important reference work, dealing with the rebels, is José María Miquel i Vergés, *Diccionario de insurgentes* (Mexico, 1969). For a Soviet historian's view see M. S. Al'perovich, *Historia de la independencia de México, 1810–1824* (Mexico, 1967).

While not as vast or complex as the historiography of Mexican independence, Central American historiography has also been fascinated by independence and its impact, though the story there is one of a relatively bloodless political movement. Some published collections of documents are useful. Notable among them are Carlos Meléndez, *Textos fundamentales de la independencia Centroamericana* (San José, 1971); Rafael Heliodoro Valle, *Pensamiento vivo de José Cecilio del Valle* (2nd edn, San José, 1971), and *La anexión de Centro América a México* (6 vols., Mexico, 1924–7). The two important periodicals edited during the independence era have been reprinted: Pedro Molina's *El Editor constitucional* (3 vols., Guatemala, 1969), and José del Valle's *El Amigo de la Patria* (2 vols., Guatemala, 1969). Notable histories written in the nineteenth century are Lorenzo Montúfar, *Reseña histórica de Centro América* (7 vols., Guatemala, 1878–88), and Alejandro Marure, *Bosquejo histórico de las revoluciones de Centro América* (Guatemala, 1837).

Important works on the background to independence include Oscar Benítez Porta, *Secesión pacífica de Guatemala de España* (Guatemala, 1973), and Jorge Mario García Laguardia, *Orígenes de la democracia constitucional en Centroamérica* (San José, 1971). The best recent general treatment of Central American independence is Ralph Lee Woodward, Jr, *Central America: a nation divided* (New York, 1976), chapter 4; this work also contains the most complete general bibliography. Also notable are chapters on independence in Franklin D. Parker, *The Central American republics* (London, 1964) and Thomas L. Karnes, *The failure of union: Central America, 1824–1975* (rev. edn, Tempe, 1976). The most important monographs are Andrés Townsend Ezcurra, *Las Provincias Unidas de Centroamérica: Fundación de la república* (Guatemala, 1958; 2nd rev., edn, San José, 1973); Louis E. Bumgartner, *José del Valle of Central America* (Durham, N.C., 1963); Mario Rodríguez, *The Cádiz Experiment in Central America, 1808–1826* (Berkeley, 1978), which provides the most complete study of the influence of Spanish liberal constitutionalism; and Ralph Lee Woodward, Jr, *Class privilege and economic development: the Consulado de Comercio of Guatemala, 1793–1871* (Chapel Hill, N.C., 1966). See also by R. L. Woodward, 'Economic and social origins of the Guatemalan parties (1773–1823)', *HAHR*, 45/4 (1965), 544–66. Other recent works on the independence period worthy of mention include Francisco Peccorini Letona, *La voluntad del pueblo en la emancipación de El Salvador* (San Salvador, 1972); Chester Zelaya, *Nicaragua en la independencia* (San José, 1971); Ricardo Fernández Guardia, *La independencia: historia de Costa Rica* (3rd edn, San José, 1971). Rafael Obregón, *De nuestra historia patria: los primeros días de independencia* (San José, 1971); and Héctor Samayoa, *Ensayos sobre la independencia de Centroamérica* (Guatemala, 1972). On the Mexican intervention and annexation, see H. G. Peralta, *Agustín de Iturbide y Costa Rica* (2nd rev. edn, San José, 1968); also Nettie Lee Benson and Charles Berry, 'The Central American delegation to the First Constituent Congress of Mexico, 1822–1824', *HAHR*, 49/4 (1969), 679–701, and Miles Wortman, 'Legitimidad política y regionalismo. El

Imperio Mexicano y Centroamérica', *HM*, 26 (1976), 238–62. Separation from Mexico and creation of the Federation is treated in Pedro Joaquín Chamorro y Zelaya, *Historia de la Federación de la América Central* (Madrid, 1951), and in the very useful work of Alberto Herrarte, *La unión de Centroamérica* (San José, 1972). See also two articles by Gordon Kenyon, 'Mexican influence in Central America', *HAHR*, 41/2 (1961), 175–205, and 'Gabino Gaínza and Central America's Independence from Spain', *The Americas*, 12/3 (1957), 241–54. On the independence of Yucatan, see Paul Joseph Reid, 'The Constitution of Cádiz and the independence of Yucatan', *TA* 36/1 (1979), 22–38. Biographies of prominent individuals include César Brañas, *Antonio de Larrazabal, un guatemalteco en la historia* (2 vols., Guatemala, 1969), and Enrique del Cid Fernández, *Don Gabino de Gaínza y otros estudios* (Guatemala, 1959). A book that brings together a number of biographies of the chief figures of independence is Carlos Meléndez (ed.), *Próceres de la independencia Centroamericana* (San José, 1971).

3. THE INDEPENDENCE OF SPANISH SOUTH AMERICA

The independence movement of Spanish South America has long been a favourite topic among conservative historians while attracting rather few innovative scholars either in Latin America or in other countries. Nevertheless, thanks to the efforts of both traditional academicians and official agencies, the student of the period has available an unusually wide array of printed source collections. These range from the classic and misleadingly titled *Memorias del general O'Leary* (Caracas, 1879–88), only three of whose 32 volumes are in fact devoted to the memoirs of Bolívar's Irish aide, Daniel F. O'Leary, to the recent *Colección documental de la independencia del Perú* (Lima, 1971–), which is an amalgam of official documents, newspapers of the period, writings of 'ideologues', memoirs and travel accounts. A gratifying number of newspapers have also been reprinted in their own right, of which perhaps the most important examples are the *Gaceta de Buenos Aires* (6 vols., Buenos Aires, 1910–15) and *Gaceta de Colombia* (5 vols., Bogotá, 1973–5), each spanning roughly a decade. Every country except Paraguay, Bolivia and Ecuador has produced one or more major source compilations, and even they have some lesser ones.

Few top-ranking patriot leaders left autobiographical memoirs, and of those who did only José Antonio Páez produced one that is still a major source, though certainly to be used with care: *Autobiografía* (2nd rev. edn, 2 vols., New York, 1871). More valuable are the memoirs left by foreign adventurers like O'Leary (*Bolívar and the War of Independence* Robert F. McNerney, Jr, trans. and ed., Austin, 1970) and William Miller, who served both San Martín and Bolívar (John Miller (ed.), *Memoirs of General Miller in the service of the Republic of Peru* (2nd edn, 2 vols., London, 1829). Equally helpful, particularly on the scene behind the lines of battle or after the fighting was over in a given area, are the accounts of foreign non-participants. William Duane, *A visit to Colombia in the years 1822 and 1823, by Laguayra and Caracas, over the cordillera to Bogotá, and thence by the Magdalena to Cartagena* (Philadelphia, 1826), and Charles Stuart Cochrane, *Journal of a residence and travels in Colombia, during the years 1823 and 1824* (2 vols., London, 1825) for Gran Colombia, Maria Callcott, *Journal of a residence in Chile during the year 1822; and a voyage from Chile to Brazil in 1823* (London, 1824), for Chile, and the brothers John P. and William P. Robertson, *Letters on South America; comprising travels on the banks of the Paraná and Río de la Plata* (3 vols., London, 1843) for the Río de la Plata well exemplify this genre.

The secondary literature is mostly less impressive. The pertinent chapters of the survey of John Lynch, *The Spanish-American revolutions: 1808–1826* (London, 1973) give an excellent overview; no other general account is remotely as good. There does not even exist a really satisfactory biography of Bolívar, which might serve as general narrative of the struggle in much of South America, although vast numbers have been written. Probably the most useful are Gerhard Masur, *Simon Bolívar* (rev. edn, Albuquerque, New Mexico, 1969) and Salvador de Madariaga, *Bolívar* (London, 1951), of which the former is somewhat pedestrian and the latter tendentiously critical. San Martín has fared better, thanks to the classic study by Argentina's first 'scientific' historian, Bartolomé Mitre, *Historia de San Martín y de la emancipación sudamericana* (2nd rev. edn, 4 vols., Buenos Aires, 1890), and the conscientious work of such twentieth-century Argentine scholars as José Pacífico Otero, *Historia del libertador José San Martín* (4 vols., Buenos Aires, 1932) and Ricardo Piccirilli, *San Martín y la política de los pueblos* (Buenos Aires, 1957). There are adequate if hardly definitive studies of several secondary figures: for example, John P. Hoover, *Admirable warrior: Marshal Sucre, fighter for South American independence* (Detroit, 1977). On the whole, however, what has been written on the heroes of independence in a biographical vein, whether pietistic or debunking, is somewhat superficial.

Historians who have not been intent on following a single military figure from one battleground to another have seldom dealt with more than one country. For Venezuela, the best one-volume survey is no doubt the Spanish historian, Miguel Izard's *El miedo a la revolución; la lucha por la libertad en Venezuela 1777–1830* (Madrid, 1979), whose title reveals its central thesis that the creole elite wanted at all costs to avoid a real revolution. A stimulating brief interpretation is Germán Carrera Damas, *La crisis de la sociedad colonial venezolana* (Caracas, 1976), but it is best appreciated by someone who already has a general grasp of the period as obtained from Izard, from a Bolívar biography, or from the competent studies of the Venezuelan academic historian Caracciolo Parra-Pérez: *Mariño y la independencia de Venezuela* (4 vols., Madrid, 1954–6) and *Historia de la primera república de Venezuela* (2nd edn, 2 vols., Caracas, 1959). The literature on Colombian independence is less abundant than that on Venezuela. Nevertheless, the pertinent volumes of the *Historia extensa de Colombia* issued by the Academia Colombiana de Historia – particularly Camilo Riaño, *Historia militar; la independencia: 1810–1815* (Bogotá, 1971), Guillermo Plazas Olarte, *Historia militar; la independencia: 1819–1828* (Bogotá, 1971), and Oswaldo Díaz Díaz, *La reconquista española* (2 vols., Bogotá, 1964 and 1967) – give a reasonably complete account of the struggle in New Granada, while for the years of Gran Colombian union there is David Bushnell, *The Santander regime in Gran Colombia* (Newark, Del., 1954).

In Ecuador disproportionate attention has been devoted to the first Quito junta, and on it the available literature is mainly of interest to a few specialists. Peruvian historians traditionally have been less fascinated with independence than their Gran Colombian or Platine neighbours, but Peru's independence sesquicentennial of 1971 righted the balance at least somewhat. That occasion inspired not just the multi-volume collection noted above but some interesting leftist revisionism, such as Virgilio Roel Pineda, *Los libertadores* (Lima, 1971), and the wide-ranging interpretative volume of Jorge Basadre, *El azar en la historia y sus límites* (Lima, 1973). More recently, Timothy Anna has contributed *The fall of the royal government of Peru* (Lincoln, Nebraska, 1979), a provocative analysis that speaks well of Viceroy Abascal but reflects little credit on anyone else. Chilean scholars, for their part, regularly produce fine monographic articles and special studies on aspects of independence, even though the topic does not absorb the attention of current scholars to the same extent as it absorbed that of Chile's great nineteenth-century historians. The ideological dimensions, for example, have been well treated in Walter Hanisch Espíndola, *El catecismo político-cristiano; las ideas y la época: 1810* (Santiago, 1970), as well as in Jaime Eyzaguirre, *Ideario y ruta de la emancipación chilena* (Santiago, 1957). Eyzaguirre's *O'Higgins* (6th rev. edn, Santiago, 1965) is the best-known modern biography of the Chilean liberator. The most important single study of Chilean independence in recent years is Simon Collier, *Ideas and politics of Chilean independence, 1808–1833* (Cambridge, 1967).

Bolivian authors have emphasized the junta experience of 1809 as have the Ecuadorians, and with not much of permanent value resulting. The best account of Bolivian independence continues to be Charles Arnade, *The emergence of the Republic of Bolivia* (Gainesville, Florida, 1957). For Paraguay there is even less, and Uruguayan writings on Artigas, though abundant, are somewhat monotonous. An honourable exception is the examination of his social and agrarian policies in Lucía Sala de Touron, Nelson de la Torre and Julio C. Rodríguez, *Artigas y su revolución agraria, 1811–1820* (Mexico, 1978), which reflects both a Marxist perspective and industrious documentary research. Also valuable is John Street, *Artigas and the emancipation of Uruguay* (Cambridge, 1959). But Argentine independence, on balance, continues to receive the most adequate treatment. The tradition begun by Mitre was ably continued in the first part of the present century by such figures as Ricardo Levene in his *Ensayo histórico sobre la Revolución de Mayo y Mariano Moreno* (4th edn, 3 vols., Buenos Aires, 1960). More recently, the literature on Argentine independence has been enriched by a plethora of both right- and left-wing revisionism (e.g., Rodolfo Puiggrós, *Los caudillos de la Revolución de Mayo* (2nd rev. edn, Buenos Aires, 1971)); by competent topical treatments of cultural developments (e.g., Oscar F. Urquiza Almandoz, *La cultura de Buenos Aires a través de su prensa periódica desde 1810 hasta 1820* (Buenos Aires, 1972)), and economic policy (e.g., Sergio Bagú, *El plan económico del grupo rivadaviano (1811–1827)* (Rosario, 1966)); and by Tulio Halperín Donghi, *Politics, economics and society in Argentina in the revolutionary period* (Cambridge, 1975), whose very title suggests a breadth of approach not to be found in most older writings.

Although the analysis of social alignments and economic interests is still not the dominant tendency in work done on Spanish American independence, it has in fact attracted a growing number of scholars. A brief introduction is provided by the trail-blazing essays of Charles Griffin, *Los temas sociales y económicos en la época de la Independencia* (Caracas, 1962). There are some good specialized studies on socio-economic aspects, of which one or two have been cited above, and there are a number of suggestive articles, such as that of Mary L. Felstiner, 'Kinship politics in the Chilean independence movement', *HAHR*, 56/1 (1976) 58–80, who shares with Halperín-Donghi an interest in problems of elite behaviour. Marxist historians by definition offer some sort of socio-economic emphasis, and several of them have also written on independence. But other than Germán Carrera Damas in his *Boves: aspectos socio-económicos de su acción histórica* (2nd rev. edn, Caracas, 1968), and *La crisis de la sociedad colonial venezolana* (Caracas, 1976), the Uruguayan rediscoverers of Artigas's agrarian populism, and Manfred Kossok, 'Der iberische Revolutionzyklus 1789 bis 1830: Bemerkungen zu einem Thema der vergleichenden Revolutionsgeschichte', *Jahrbuch für Geschichte von Staat, Wirtschaft und Gesellschaft*, 6 (1969), 211–38, they have mainly tended to offer either a mechanical economic determinism or a propagandist effort to co-opt Bolívar and similar heroes for present-day causes. In the latter respect, naturally, they have not lacked company among non-Marxists. Nor, apart from Griffin, is there any overview of social and economic aspects of independence that cuts across geographic boundaries.

Continental overviews are more readily available concerning the position of the Church, as in Rubén Vargas Ugarte, *El episcopado en los tiempos de la emancipación sudamericana* (2 vols., Buenos Aires, 1945), and Pedro Leturia, *Relaciones entre la Santa Sede e Hispanoamérica* (3 vols., Rome, 1959–60), a major contribution on Hispanic America and the Vatican, two volumes of which are devoted to the independence period. But the latter falls as much in the area of foreign relations, where a great part of the literature almost inevitably treats Latin America as a whole vis-à-vis given outside powers.

4. THE INDEPENDENCE OF BRAZIL

The first chronicle of the events of the entire period 1808–31, though concentrating on the years 1821–31, is John Armitage, *History of Brazil from the arrival of the Braganza family in 1808 to the abdication of Dom Pedro the first in 1831*, published in London in 1836 when the author, who had gone to Rio de Janeiro as a young merchant in 1828, was still only 29. Intended as a sequel to Robert Southey's monumental *History of Brazil* (1810–19), the first general history of Brazil during the colonial period, Armitage's *History* has been used and justly praised by every historian of the independence period in Brazil. Of the many contemporary accounts perhaps the best known and most valuable is Maria Graham, *Journal of a Voyage to Brazil and Residence there during part of the years 1821, 1822, 1823* (London, 1824). The author was resident in Brazil from September 1821 to March 1822 and again from March to October 1823, that is to say, immediately before and immediately after independence. Indispensable for the period of Dom João's residence in Brazil (1808–21) is Luiz Gonçalves dos Santos [1767–1844], *Memórias para servir à história do Reino do Brasil* [1825] (2 vols., Rio de Janeiro, 1943).

The traditional historiography of Brazilian independence is dominated by four great works, all essentially detailed accounts of political events: Francisco Adolfo de Varnhagen, *História da Independência do Brasil* (Rio de Janeiro, 1917); Manoel de Oliveira Lima, *Dom João VI no Brasil 1808–21* (1909; 2nd edn, 3 vols., Rio de Janeiro, 1945), the classic study of the Portuguese court in Rio, and *O Movimento da Independência* (São Paulo, 1922); and Tobias do Rego Monteiro, *História do império. A elaboraçao da independência* (Rio de Janeiro, 1927). And for the story of the independence of Bahia, Braz do Amaral, *História da independência na Bahia* (Salvador, 1923).

Caio Prado Júnior was the first historian to analyse the internal tensions and contradictions in the process leading to Brazilian independence. See, in particular, *Evolução política do Brasil* (São Paulo, 1933 and many later editions); *Formação do Brasil contemporâneo: Colônia* (São Paulo, 1963) which has been translated as *The colonial background of modern Brazil* (Berkeley, 1967); and the introduction to the facsimile edition of *O Tamoio* (São Paulo, 1944). Octávio Tarquínio de Souza, *José Bonifácio* (Rio de Janeiro, 1960) and *A vida do Dom Pedro I* (3 vols., 2nd edn, Rio de Janeiro, 1954), are important biographies.

Among more recent general works on Brazilian independence, especially worthy of note are Sérgio Buarque de Holanda (ed.), *História geral da civilização Brasileira*, Tomo II, *O Brasil Monárquico*, vol.1 *O Processo de emancipação* (São Paulo, 1962); Carlos Guilherme Mota (ed.), *1822: Dimensões* (São Paulo, 1972); and, above all, José Honório Rodrigues, *Independência: revolução e contrarevolução* (5 vols., Rio de Janeiro, 1975): I, *A evolução política*; II, *Economia e sociedade*; III, *As forças armadas*; IV, *A liderança nacional*; V, *A política internacional*. By far the most important and provocative single essay on Brazilian independence is Emília Viotti da Costa, 'Introdução ao estudo da emancipação política do Brasil' in Carlos Guilherme Mota (ed.), *Brasil em Perspectiva* (São Paulo, 1968); revised English version 'The political emancipation of Brazil' in A. J. R. Russell-Wood (ed.), *From colony to nation. Essays on the independence of Brazil*

(Baltimore, 1975). See also two essays by Emília Viotti da Costa on José Bonifácio: 'José Bonifácio: Mito e História', *Anais do Museu Paulista*, 21 (1967), which was revised and republished in *Da monarquia à república: momentos decisivos* (São Paulo, 1977); and 'José Bonifácio: Homem e Mito', in Mota (ed.), *1822*. On the independence movement in Rio de Janeiro the essay by Francisco C. Falcón and Ilmar Rohloff de Mattos, 'O processo de independência no Rio de Janeiro' in Mota (ed.), *1822* is particularly interesting. And on the movement in Bahia, see Luis Henrique Dias Tavares, *A independência do Brasil na Bahia* (Rio de Janeiro, 1977), and F. W. O. Morton, 'The conservative revolution of independence: economy, society and politics in Bahia, 1790–1840' (unpublished D.Phil. thesis, Oxford, 1974).

On relations between Portugal and Brazil and the development of Brazil in the late eighteenth century, see Mansuy-Diniz Silva, *CHLA* I, chap.13 and Alden, *CHLA* II, chap.15. The outstanding recent work on the late colonial period, in particular on economic policy-making and on the trade between Brazil, Portugal and England, is Fernando A. Novais, *Portugal e Brasil na crise do antigo sistema colonial (1777–1808)* (São Paulo, 1979). On the balance of trade, see also José Jobson de A. Arruda, *O Brasil no comércio colonial* (São Paulo, 1981). The influence of the Enlightenment on colonial Brazil is examined in Maria Odila da Silva, 'Aspectos da ilustração no Brasil', *Revista do Instituto Histórico e Geográfico Brasileiro* 278 (1968), 105–70. Also see Carlos Guilherme Mota, *Atitudes de inovção no Brasil (1789–1801)* (Lisbon, 1970) and E. Bradford Burns, 'The intellectuals as agents of change and the independence of Brazil, 1724–1822' in Russell-Wood (ed.), *From colony to nation*. The best study of the *Inconfidência mineira* (1788–9) is to be found in Kenneth R. Maxwell, *Conflicts and conspiracies. Brazil and Portugal 1750–1808* (Cambridge, 1973). See also his essay 'The generation of the 1790s and the idea of Luso-Brazilian empire' in Dauril Alden (ed.), *Colonial roots of modern Brazil* (Berkeley, 1973). There are several studies of the *Inconfidência baiana* (1798): Luis Henrique Dias Tavares, *História da sedição intentada na Bahia em 1798: a 'conspiração do alfaiates'* (São Paulo, 1975); Alfonso Ruy, *A primeira revolução social brasileira, 1798* (2nd edn., Salvador, 1951); Kátia Maria de Queirós Mattoso, *A presença francesa no movimento democrático baiano de 1798* (Salvador, 1969); and chapter IV of Morton, 'Conservative revolution'. There is a modern edition of the *Obras econômicas* of José Joaquim da Cunha de Azeredo Coutinho with an introduction by Sérgio Buarque de Holanda (São Paulo, 1966). For a commentary, see E. Bradford Burns, 'The role of Azeredo Coutinho in the enlightenment of

Brazil', *HAHR* 44/2 (1964), 145–60.

The transfer of the Portuguese court from Lisbon to Rio de Janeiro (1807–8) has been thoroughly studied by Alan K. Manchester, *British preeminence in Brazil. Its rise and decline* (Durham, N.C., 1933), chap.III; 'The transfer of the Portuguese court to Rio de Janeiro', in Henry H. Keith and S. F. Edwards (eds.), *Conflict and continuity in Brazilian society* (Columbia, S.C., 1969); and 'The growth of bureaucracy in Brazil, 1808–1821', *JLAS*, 4/1 (1972). On the opening of Brazilian ports to foreign trade (1808), besides Manchester, *British preeminence*, see Manuel Pinto de Aguiar, *A abertura dos portos. Cairú e os ingleses* (Salvador, 1960) and José Wanderley de Araújo Pinho, 'A abertura dos portos – Cairú', *Revista do Instituto Histórico e Geográfico Brasileiro*, 243 (April–June 1959). Manchester, *British preeminence* remains the best study of the Anglo-Portuguese treaties of 1810 and of Portuguese expansionism in the Banda Oriental. Early attempts at encouraging industrial growth in Brazil are examined in Nícia Vilela Luz, *A luta pela industrialização do Brasil, 1808–1930* (São Paulo, 1961) and Alice P. Canabrava, 'Manufacturas e indústrias no período de D. João VI no Brasil' in Luis Pilla, *et al.*, *Uma experiência pioneira de intercambio cultural* (Porto Alegre, 1963). The French artistic mission is the subject of Affonso d'Escragnolle Taunay, *A missão artística de 1816* (Rio de Janeiro, 1956; Brasília, 1983). There has been only one modern study of the revolution of 1817 in Pernambuco: Carlos Guilherme Mota, *Nordeste, 1817. Estruturas e argumentos* (São Paulo, 1972), which concentrates on the ideological aspects of the struggle. Still useful is the account by one of the leading participants: Francisco Muniz Tavares, *História da revolução de Pernambuco em 1817* (3rd edn, Recife, 1917). On the armed forces during this period, besides volume III of Rodrigues, *Independência*, there is an interesting case study of Bahia, F. W. O. Morton, 'Military and society in Bahia, 1800–21', *JLAS*, 7/2 (1975). The Portuguese Côrtes, and especially the role of the Brazilian representatives, is the subject of two essays: George C. A. Boehrer, 'The flight of the Brazilian deputies from the Côrtes Gerais in Lisbon, 1822', *HAHR*, 40/4 (1960), 497–512, and Fernando Tomaz, 'Brasileiros nas Côrtes Constituintes de 1821–1822' in Mota (ed.), *1822*. The most recent work on the constituent Assembly is José Honório Rodrigues, *A Constituinte de 1823* (Petrópolis, 1974). The question of the continuation of the slave trade and Brazilian independence has been studied by Leslie Bethell, *The abolition of the Brazilian slave trade* (Cambridge, 1970), chapters 1 and 2. See also his article, 'The independence of Brazil and the abolition of the

Brazilian slave trade: Anglo-Brazilian relations 1822–1826', *JLAS*, 1/2 (1969). On Anglo-Brazilian relations in general, and British recognition of Brazilian independence, Manchester, *British preeminence* remains the best study. But see also Caio de Freitas, *George Canning e o Brasil* (2 vols., São Paulo, 1960).

5. INTERNATIONAL POLITICS AND LATIN AMERICAN INDEPENDENCE

The basic source for British relations with Latin America during the independence period is C. K. Webster (ed.), *Britain and the Independence of Latin America, 1812–1830: select documents from the Foreign Office archives* (2 vols., London, 1938; repr. New York, 1970), the introduction to which provides a valuable overview of British policy. This can be followed in more detail through its successive phases in J. Lynch, 'British policy and Spanish America, 1783–1808', *JLAS*, 1 (1969); C. M. Crawley, 'French and English influences in the Cortes of Cadiz, 1810–1814', *Cambridge Historical Journal* 6 (1939); J. Rydjord, 'British mediation between Spain and her colonies, 1811–1813', *HAHR*, 21 (1941); C. K. Webster, *The foreign policy of Castlereagh, 1812–1815* (London, 1931), and *The foreign policy of Castlereagh, 1815–1822* 2nd edn (London, 1934); and H. Temperley, *The foreign policy of Canning, 1822–1827* (London, 1925; repr. London, 1966). Leslie Bethell, *George Canning and the emancipation of Latin America* (The Hispanic and Luso Brazilian Councils, London, 1970), gives a brief re-evaluation of Canning's role. W. W. Kaufmann, *British policy and the independence of Latin America, 1804–1828* (New Haven, 1951; repr. London, 1967) offers an interesting, though idiosyncratic, interpretation of the whole period, based on printed sources.

British commercial relations are discussed in D. B. Goebel, 'British trade to the Spanish colonies, 1796–1823', *American Historical Review*, 43 (1938); R. A. Humphreys, 'British merchants and South American independence', *Proceedings of the British Academy*, 51 (1965); J. F. Rippy, 'Latin America and the British investment "boom" of the 1820s', *Journal of Modern History*, 19 (1947); and the first part of D. C. M. Platt, *Latin America and British Trade, 1806–1914* (London, 1972). They are documented in R. A. Humphreys (ed.), *British consular reports on the trade and politics of Latin America, 1824–1826*, Camden Society, third series, vol. 53 (London, 1940).

The local implementation of British policy in the southern hemisphere may be followed through the selection of dispatches from British naval commanders printed in G. S. Graham and R. A. Humphreys (ed.), *The Navy and South America, 1807–1823*, Publications of the Navy Records Society, vol. 104 (London, 1962). British activities in relation to Brazil and Argentina may be traced in the earlier chapters of A. K. Manchester, *British preeminence in Brazil: its rise and decline* (Chapel Hill, N.C., 1933; repr. New York, 1964); Leslie Bethell, *The abolition of the Brazilian slave trade: Britain, Brazil and the slave trade question, 1807–1869* (Cambridge, 1970); H. S. Ferns, *Britain and Argentina in the nineteenth century* (Oxford, 1960); and V. B. Reber, *British mercantile houses in Buenos Aires, 1810–1880* (Cambridge, Mass., 1979); in J. Street, 'Lord Strangford and Río de la Plata, 1808–1815', *HAHR*, 33 (1953); and in J. C. J. Metford, 'The recognition by Great Britain of the United Provinces of Río de la Plata', and 'The Treaty of 1825 between Great Britain and the United Provinces of Río de la Plata', *Bulletin of Hispanic Studies* 29 (1952) and 30 (1953).

There is little in English on northern South America, but material from British archives is printed in Spanish translation in C. Parra-Pérez (ed.), *Documentos de las cancillerías europeas sobre la Independencia venezolana* (2 vols., Caracas, 1962) and C. L. Mendoza, *Las primeras misiones diplomáticas de Venezuela* (2 vols., Caracas, 1962). There is much information on British relations at local level in Carlos Pi Sunyer, *El General Juan Robertson: un prócer de la Independencia* (Caracas, 1971) and at metropolitan level in the same author's *Patriotas Americanos en Londres* (Caracas, 1978). D. A. G. Waddell, *Gran Bretaña y la Independencia de Venezuela y Colombia* (Caracas, 1983), is a study of contacts between British authorities and both patriots and royalists.

Anglo-Mexican negotiations are discussed in the light of Mexican archive material in Jaimé E. Rodríguez O., *The emergence of Spanish America: Vicente Rocafuerte and Spanish Americanism, 1808–1832* (Berkeley, 1975), as are Mexico's early dealings with other European powers. The period before 1810 is explored in J. Rydjord, *Foreign interest in the independence of New Spain* (Durham, N.C., 1935; repr. New York, 1972).

United States relations are fully documented in W. R. Manning (ed.), *Diplomatic correspondence of the United States concerning the independence of the Latin-American Nations* (3 vols., New York, 1925), and comprehensively discussed in A. P. Whitaker, *The United States and the independence of Latin America, 1800–1830* (Baltimore, 1941; repr. New York, 1962). C. C. Griffin, *The United States and the disruption of the Spanish Empire, 1810–1822*

(New York, 1937; repr. 1968) is valuable for American relations with Spain. D. Perkins, *The Monroe Doctrine 1823–1826* (Cambridge, Mass., 1927) is still the standard work on its subject, though E. R. May, *The making of the Monroe Doctrine* (Cambridge, Mass., 1975) places new emphasis on the influence of American domestic politics. American relations with particular countries may be followed in W. R. Manning, *Early diplomatic relations between the United States and Mexico* (Baltimore, 1916; repr. New York, 1968), in E. B. Billingsley, *In defence of neutral rights: the United States navy and the wars of independence in Chile and Peru* (Chapel Hill, N.C., 1967), and in the appropriate chapters of H. F. Peterson, *Argentina and the United States, 1810–1960* (New York, 1964); L. F. Hill, *Diplomatic relations between the United States and Brazil* (Durham, N.C., 1932; repr. New York, 1969); and E. T. Parks, *Colombia and the United States, 1765–1934* (Durham, N.C., 1935; repr. New York, 1968).

Anglo-American rivalry is investigated at local level in J. F. Rippy, *Rivalry of the United States and Great Britain over Latin America, 1808–1830* (Baltimore, 1929; repr. New York, 1972); at metropolitan level in B. Perkins, *Castlereagh and Adams: England and the United States, 1812–1823* (Berkeley, 1964); and in a perceptive essay by R. A. Humphreys, 'Anglo-American rivalries and Spanish American emancipation', *Transactions of the Royal Historical Society*, Fifth Series, 16 (1966).

The standard work on French policy is W. S. Robertson, *France and Latin American independence* (Baltimore, 1939; 2nd edn, New York, 1967). H. Temperley, 'French designs on Spanish America in 1820–25', *English Historical Review* 40 (1925) deals with a controversial period. Russian relations have been the subject of a recent study by R. H. Bartley, *Imperial Russia and the struggle for Latin American independence, 1808–1828* (Austin, 1978). The policy of the central European powers is well covered in M. Kossok, *Historia de la Santa Alianza y la Emancipación de América Latina* (Buenos Aires, 1968), and illustrated in K. W. Körner, *La independencia de la América Española y la diplomacia Alemana* (Buenos Aires, 1968) with documents from a variety of European archives. W. S. Robertson, 'Metternich's attitude towards Revolutions in Latin America', *HAHR*, 21 (1961) provides a few basic facts. J. L. Mecham, 'The papacy and Spanish American independence', *HAHR*, 9 (1929) is a succinct survey.

6. HAITI AND SANTO DOMINGO, 1790–*c*.1870

Among contemporary works, Médéric L. E. Moreau de Saint-Méry, *Description topographique, physique, civile, politique et historique de la partie française de l'isle de Saint Domingue* (2 vols., Philadelphia, 1797–8; 3 vols., Paris, 1958), and Bryan Edwards, *An historical survey of the French colony in the island of St. Domingo* (London, 1797) offer the most comprehensive view of the economic, social and political problems of colonial Saint-Domingue in the years immediately before the French Revolution. The best and most comprehensive work on the Haitian Revolution continues to be C. L. R. James, *The Black Jacobins: Toussaint L'Ouverture and the San Domingo Revolution* (New York, 1938; 2nd rev. edn, 1963). Other, less satisfactory, works include José L. Franco, *Historia de la revolución de Haiti* (Havana, 1966), and T. O. Ott, *The Haitian Revolution, 1789–1804* (Knoxville, 1973). A book now out of fashion because of its racism, though still retaining some interest, is T. Lothrop Stoddard, *The French Revolution in San Domingo* (Boston, 1914; reprint, 1982). Among the many biographies of Toussaint Louverture two are now classics: Victor Schoelcher, *Vie de Toussaint-Louverture* (Paris, 1889), and Horace Pauléus Sannon, *Histoire de Toussaint-Louverture* (3 vols., Port-au-Prince, 1920–33). There are contrasting accounts of the military side of the Revolution. The one favourable to Toussaint is Alfred Nemours, *Histoire militaire de la Guerre d'Indépendance de Saint-Domingue* (2 vols., Paris, 1925–8). From the French point of view there is Henry de Poyen-Bellisle, *Histoire militaire de la Révolution de Saint-Domingue* (Paris, 1899), from the Spanish, Antonio del Monte y Tejada, *Historia de Santo Domingo*, volumes III and IV (Santo Domingo, 1890–2), and from the British, Sir John Fortescue, *History of the British Army*, volume IV (London, 1906). An important recent study is David P. Geggus, *Slavery, war and revolution. The British occupation of Saint-Domingue 1793–1798* (Oxford, 1982).

For the impact that the Haitian Revolution had upon Spanish Santo Domingo, several works are worthy of note: see, for example, Emilio Rodríguez Demorizi (ed.), *Cesión de Santo Domingo a Francia* (Ciudad Trujillo, 1958) and *La era de Francia en Santo Domingo* (Ciudad Trujillo, 1955), Joaquín Marino Incháustegui Cabral (ed.), *Documentos para estudio: Marco de la época y problemas del Tratado de Basilea de 1795 en la parte española de Santo Domingo* (2 vols., Buenos Aires, 1957), and Manuel Arturo Peña Batlle, *El Tratado de Basilea* (Ciudad Trujillo, 1952). The Haitian invasions of Santo Domingo are dealt with in Emilio Rodríguez Demorizi (ed.), *Invasiones Haitianas de 1801, 1805 y 1822* (Ciudad Trujillo, 1955). On Spain's efforts to recover the part of Santo Domingo ceded to France in 1795, see Miguel Artola, 'La guerra de reconquista de Santo Domingo 1808–1809', *Revista de Indias*, 11 (1951), 447–84. For a modern synthesis of this period in the history of Santo Domingo, see Frank Moya Pons, *Historia colonial de Santo Domingo* (Santiago de los Caballeros, 1974).

Haiti's evolution during the years that followed independence were chronicled by several of the British and North American visitors to the island during this period. Four of these accounts continue to be the most trustworthy contemporary sources for the period: Jonathan Brown, *The History and Present Condition of St. Domingo* (2 vols., Philadelphia, 1837; repr. London, 1972) with its ample reporting of Haitian social customs and of the evolution of the Haitian political system, which Brown termed, on consideration, 'a republican monarchy resting on its bayonets'; John Candler, *Brief Notices of Hayti, with its conditions, resources, and prospects* (London, 1842; repr. London, 1972) which contains valuable information upon the government of Boyer; James Franklin, *The Present State of Hayti (Saint Domingo)* (London, 1828; repr. London, 1972) which is excellent for its assessment of the evolution of Haiti's economy and Haitian agriculture in the times of Pétion and Christophe; and, lastly, Charles Mackenzie, *Notes on Haiti, made during a residence in that republic* (2 vols., London, 1830; repr. London, 1972), which comprises notes that the author collected in Haiti as British consul there (1826–7), in which he presents useful statistics and enlightened observations on the economic and social differences between the two parts of the island. The traditional Haitian account of its early independent history is to be found in the monumental work of Beaubrun Ardouin, *Etudes sur l'histoire d'Haiti* (11 vols., Paris, 1853–60; 2nd edn, Port-au-Prince, 1958); this is indispensable for any knowledge of Boyer's régime, but not always wholly to be relied upon, since it reflects the official point of view and the ideology of Haiti's mulatto élite. There are few modern works, but see Hubert Cole, *Christophe, king of Haiti* (New York, 1967); Leslie F. Manigat, *La Politique agraire du gouvernement d'Alexandre Pétion, 1807–1818* (Port-au-Prince, 1962); David Nicholls, *Economic development and political autonomy. The Haitian experience* (Montreal, 1974) and 'Rural protest and peasant revolt in Haiti (1804–1869)', in M. Cross and A. Marks (eds.), *Peasants, plantations and rural communities in the Caribbean* (Guilford and Leiden, 1979), 29–53. See also the series of articles by Benoît Joachim largely drawn from his thesis 'Aspects fondamentaux des relations de la France avec Haiti de

1825 à 1874: le néocolonialisme à l'essai' (unpublished thesis, University of Paris, 1968), notably 'La Reconnaissance d'Haiti par la France (1825): naissance d'un nouveau type de rapports internationaux', *Revue d'Histoire Moderne et Contemporaine*, 22 (1975), 369–96, 'L'Indemnité colonial de Saint-Domingue et la question des repatriés', *Revue Historique*, 246 (1971), 359–76, and 'Commerce et decolonisation: l'expérience franco-haitienne au XIXᵉ siècle', *Annales: Economies, Sociétés, Civilisations*, 27 (1972), 1497–1525.

The traditional Dominican account of the period can be found in volumes II and III of José Gabriel García, *Compendio de la historia de Santo Domingo* (4 vols., Santo Domingo, 1893–1906). The Haitian occupation of Santo Domingo during the period of Boyer's rule is the subject of Frank Moya Pons, *La dominación Haitiana, 1822–1844* (Santiago de los Caballeros, 1973). Moya Pons studies the political impact of the changes Boyer tried to introduce in the agricultural structure of the former Spanish sector, and the economic decline of Haiti due to the agrarian policy of the mulatto governments of those years. On Boyer's fall and the proclamation of its independence by the Dominican Republic there are contemporary studies by Thomas Madiou, *Historie d'Haiti: années 1843–1846* (4 vols., Port-au-Prince, 1847–8 and 1904), and by Romuald Lepelletier de Saint-Rémy, *Saint-Domingue, étude et solution nouvelle de la question haitienne* (2 vols., Paris, 1846; Santo Domingo, 1978). See also H. Pauléus Sannon, *Essai historique sur la révolution de 1843* (Lescayes, Haiti, 1905). The events of 1843–4 have been the subject of hundreds of articles in the Dominican Republic, but we still lack the great synthesis which is needed to sum up the materials published in several collections of documents, especially Emilio Rodríguez Demorizi, 'La Revolutión del 1843: apuntes y documentos para su estudio', *Boletin del Archivo General de la Nación*, 25–6 (1943) and *Correspondencia del Cónsul de Francia en Santo Domingo* (2 vols., Ciudad Trujillo, 1944–7), as well as *Correspondencia de Levasseur y de otros agentes de Francia relativa a la Proclamación de la República Dominicana, 1843–1844* (Ciudad Trujillo, 1944) which the Dominican Government published upon the centenary of independence.

For the Haitian government after 1843, and on Faustin Soulouque especially, Gustave d'Alaux, *L'Empereur Solouque et son empire* (Paris, 1856) continues to be useful, but should be used with caution: it is reportedly really the work of Maxime Raybaud, consul-general of France in Haiti. Sir Spenser Buckingham Saint John, *Hayti, or the Black Republic* (London, 1884; repr. 1972) has a very informative explanation of Haiti's economic decadence in the second half of the nineteenth century, although its point of view is totally anti-Haitian. On the Dominican Republic and Dominican-Haitian relations after 1844 Emilio Rodríguez Demorizi has published a long series of documentary volumes, some of which are prefaced by important introductions; the most useful are *Documentos para la historia de la República Dominico* (3 vols., Ciudad Trujillo, 1944–7), *Guerra Dominico-Haitiana* (Ciudad Trujillo, 1957), *Antecedentes de la anexión a España* (Ciudad Trujillo, 1955), and *Relaciones Dominico-Españolas (1844–1859)* (Ciudad Trujillo, 1955). In 'Datos sobre la economía dominicana durante la Primera República', *Eme-Eme Estudios Dominicanos*, 4 (1976), Frank Moya Pons reconstructs the economic evolution of Santo Domingo in the years following independence, from the reports of the British consuls of the period. On Santo Domingo's annexation by Spain, and the Haitian reaction to it, see Ramón González Tablas, *Historia de la dominación y última guerra de España en Santo Domingo* (Madrid, 1870), the (critical) war memoirs of an officer in the Spanish army who served in Santo Domingo, and from the Commander-in-Chief of the Spanish troops during Santo Domingo's 'War of Restoration', José de la Gándara y Navarro, *Anexión y Guerra de Santo Domingo* (2 vols., Madrid, 1884). The Dominican version of the period is given by Gregorio Luperón, *Notas autobiográficas y apuntes históricos* (1895–6; 3 vols., Santiago de los Caballeros, 1939), the work of one of the outstanding generals in the struggle against the Spaniards. See also Manuel Rodríguez Objío, *Gregorio Luperón e Historia de la Restauración* (2 vols., Santiago de los Caballeros, 1939), written by another participant in the War. Pedro María Archambault, *Historia de la Restauración* (Paris, 1938) is a modern but 'traditional' account of the war. More recent and satisfactory is Jaime de Jesús Domínguez, *La anexión de Santo Domingo a España, 1861–1863* (Santo Domingo, 1979). For the Dominican Republic in the second half of the nineteenth century, Harry Hoetink, *El pueblo Dominicano: 1850–1900. Apuntes para su sociología histórica* (Santiago de los Caballeros, 1972); Eng. trans. *The Dominican people: 1850–1900* (Baltimore, 1982) offers an intelligent examination of the social, economic and institutional changes that occurred.

Either because of the relative size of the island of Hispaniola, or because of the primitive state of its historiography, or perhaps because documentation on some periods is still scarce, the best treatments of the histories of Haiti and Santo Domingo often appear within general works, whose titles should not mislead the reader into thinking they are superficial accounts. For example, James G. Leyburn, *The Haitian People* (New Haven, 1941; rev. edn. 1966 with a lengthy introduction by Sidney W. Mintz and an updated bibliography) has still not been surpassed as the best ethno-historical introduction to the study of Haitian society. See also Dantès Bellegarde, *La Nation haitienne* (Paris, 1938; revised version, *Histoire du peuple haïtien: 1492–1952*, Port-au-Prince, 1953), the work of an outstanding Haitian intellectual, and T. Lepkowski, *Haiti* (2 vols, Havana, 1968–9), the work of a Polish historian. A recent history of Haiti containing an abundance of fresh data is Robert Debs Heinl, Jr. and Nancy Gordon Heinl, *Written in Blood: the story of the Haitian People, 1492–1971* (New York, 1978), a book marred, however, by the manifest antipathy of the authors towards all Haitian politicians. A recent major work by the English historian, David Nicholls, *From Dessalines to Duvalier: race, colour and national independence in Haiti* (Cambridge, 1979) displays much greater perception. The most recent and comprehensive history of the Dominican Republic is Frank Moya Pons, *Manual de historia dominicana* (Santo Domingo, 1977). A book excellent for its period, though anti-Haitian in tone, and still providing a useful introduction to the history of the Republic, is Sumner Welles, *Naboth's Vineyard: the Dominican Republic, 1844–1924* (2 vols., Washington, 1966) which was first published in 1928 as a history of the relations of the Dominican Republic with the United States. But for a more comprehensive view of the subject, see Charles Callan Tansill, *The United States and Santo Domingo, 1789–1873* (Gloucester, Mass., 1967). For Haiti's relations with the United States, see Rayford W. Logan, *The diplomatic relations of the United States with Haiti, 1776–1891* (Chapel Hill, N.C., 1941) and Ludwell Lee Montague, *Haiti and the United States, 1714–1938* (Durham, N.C., 1940). Finally, two efforts to study the history of both peoples in parallel should be mentioned. Jean Price Mars, *La République d'Haiti et la République Dominicaine: les aspects divers d'un problème d'histoire, de géographie et d'ethnologie* (2 vols., Port-au-Prince, 1953), contains an interpretation dictated by intense resentment at the Dominicans for not having wanted to stay united to Haiti. Rayford W. Logan, *Haiti and the Dominican Republic* (London, 1968) provides an interesting synthesis that is accurate, but lacks the brilliance of his earlier work on U.S.-Haitian relations.

7. CUBA FROM THE MIDDLE OF THE EIGHTEENTH CENTURY TO C. 1870

Hugh Thomas, *Cuba or the pursuit of freedom* (London, 1971), is a general history of Cuba since 1762. Raymond Carr, *Spain 1808–1939* (Oxford,

1966), is the best general history of Spain for this period. A history of U.S.–Cuban relations to 1895, coloured by twentieth-century guilt, is Philip Foner, *A history of Cuba and its relations with the U.S.* (2 vols., New York, 1962–3). Ramiro Guerra y Sanchez, *Sugar and society in the Caribbean: an economic history of Cuban agriculture*, trans. Marjorie Urquidi (New Haven, 1964) and Fernando Ortiz, *Cuban counterpoint: tobacco and sugar*, trans. Harriet de Onís (New York, 1947), are brilliant and suggestive essays by great Cuban writers. H. S. Aimes, *A history of slavery in Cuba 1511–1868* (New York, 1907), is a workmanlike, if occasionally misleading, work of scholarship by a North American historian. Planter society is well analysed in Roland Ely, *Cuando reinaba su majestad el azúcar: estudio histórico-sociológico de una tragedia latinoamericana* (Buenos Aires, 1963), a major work of historical reconstruction largely based on the papers of the Drake and Terry families, and by Franklin W. Knight, *Slave society in Cuba during the nineteenth century* (Madison, 1970). See also a recent article by Knight, 'Origins of wealth and the sugar revolution in Cuba, 1750–1850', *HAHR*, 57/2 (1977), 236–53. The sugar industry is best studied from a technical point of view in Manuel Moreno Fraginals, *El ingenio*, 1 (Havana, 1964), Eng. trans. *The Sugarmill. The socioeconomic complex of sugar in Cuba 1760–1860* (New York, 1976). The slave trade to Cuba in the nineteenth century, and its abolition, has been adequately covered in David Murray, *Odious commerce: Britain, Spain and the abolition of the Cuban slave trade* (Cambridge, 1980), while the Spanish side of the abolition of both the slave trade and slavery has been analysed in Arthur F. Corwin, *Spain and the abolition of slavery in Cuba 1817–1886* (Austin, 1967). See also Raúl Cepero Bonilla, *Azúcar y abolición* (Havana, 1948). Among other recent studies of slavery in Cuba are: Herbert Klein, *Slavery in the Americas: a comparative study of Virginia and Cuba* (Chicago, 1967) – which suffers from a disposition to believe Spanish slave laws meant what they said – Gwendolyn Hall, *Social control in slave plantation societies: a comparison of Saint Domingue and Cuba* (Baltimore, 1971), Verena Martinez-Alier, *Marriage, class and colour in nineteenth-century Cuba. A study of racial attitudes and sexual values in a slave society* (Cambridge, 1974), and J. Peréz de la Riva, *El Barracón. Esclavitud y capitalismo en Cuba* (Barcelona, 1978). On U.S. attitudes to Cuba in the middle of the nineteenth century, besides Foner, see Basil Rauch, *American interests in Cuba, 1848–1855* (New York, 1948) and Robert E. May, *The southern dream of a Caribbean empire, 1854–61* (Baton Rouge, 1973).

8. ECONOMY AND SOCIETY IN POST-INDEPENDENCE SPANISH AMERICA

Roberto Cortés Conde and Stanley J. Stein (eds.), *Latin America. A guide to economic history 1830–1930* (Berkeley, 1977), is a comprehensive survey of existing secondary literature which concentrates on Argentina, Brazil, Chile, Colombia, Peru and Mexico. Ciro F. S. Cardoso and Héctor Pérez Brignoli, *Historia económica de América Latina* (2 vols., Barcelona, 1979), is a general economic history of Latin America which includes a valuable chapter (vol. II, chapter 4) on the post-independence period. See also Tulio Halperín Donghi, *Historia contemporánea de América Latina* (Madrid, 1969), chapters 3 and 4, and *The aftermath of revolution in Latin America* (New York, 1973), especially chapter 2.

There are a number of valuable studies of the commercial and financial relations between the new Spanish American states and Britain in the period after independence: for example, D. C. M. Platt, *Latin America and British trade, 1806–1914* (London, 1973), Leland H. Jenks, *The migration of British capital to 1875* (New York, 1927; reissued London, 1971), and J. Fred Rippy, *British investments in Latin America, 1822–1949* (Minneapolis, 1959). Sergio Villalobos R., *El comercio y la crisis colonial, un mito de la Independencia* (Santiago, 1968), examines the case of Chile, carrying to extremes Platt's scepticism about the real impact of the opening of trade which accompanied political emanicaption, from a perspective which is not exclusively Chilean.

On the whole, however, studies at the national or regional level predominate for this period. This can be partially explained by the fact that general studies inspired by the theme of dependence or reaction to dependence, so abundant over the last ten years, concentrate their attention on the colonial period or on the period after 1870. This is the case, for example, of Stanley and Barbara Stein, *The colonial heritage of Latin America* (New York, 1970), or Marcello Carmagnani, *Formación y crisis de un sistema feudal. América Latina del siglo XVI a nuestros días* (Mexico City, 1976).

A pioneering study of the impact of the Wars of Independence on the economy and society of Spanish America is Charles C. Griffin, 'Economic and social aspects of the era of Spanish American independence', *HAHR*, 29/2 (1949), 170–87, an essay revised and expanded in *Los temas sociales y económicos en la época de la Independencia* (Caracas, 1962). The impact of the political and military crisis on rural society is studied for Venezuela in Germán Carrera Damas, *Materiales para el estudio de la cuestión agraria en Venezuela (1800–1830)* (Caracas, 1964), and for Uruguay in L. S. de Touron, N. de la Torre and J. G. Rodríguez, *La revolución agraria artiguista* (Montevideo, 1969), of which there is an abridged version entitled *Artigas y su revolución agraria, 1811–1820* (Mexico, 1978). The impact on society as a whole is studied, for Mexico, by Luis Villoro in *La revolución de independencia: ensayo de interpretación histórica* (Mexico, 1953), in a more arbitrary fashion for Colombia in the relevant sections of Indalecio Lievano Aguirre, *Los grandes conflictos sociales y económicos de nuestra historia* (4 vols., Bogotá, 1966), and for Argentina, in Tulio Halperín Donghi, *Politics, economics and society in Argentina in the revolutionary period* (London, 1975). R. A. Humphreys (ed.), *British consular reports on the trade and politics of Latin America, 1824–1826* (London, 1940), covers in considerable detail the situation in the different ports, and reflects the impact on them and the new nations generally of the still recent political and military crisis. An attempt to trace the social and economic development of a nation under the twin impact of the commercial and the political/military crisis can be found in Jonathan C. Brown, *A socioeconomic history of Argentina 1776–1860* (London, 1979).

On the new economic and social order and political reconstruction after independence, once again the most important contributions concern specific countries. David Bushnell, *The Santander Regime in Gran Colombia* (Newark, Delaware, 1954), is an exemplary study of the administrative difficulties of the new state in the face of problems by no means exclusive to Colombia. Miron Burgin, *The economic aspect of Argentine federalism, 1820–52* (Cambridge, Mass., 1946), reexamines the themes studied somewhat impressionistically, but nonetheless perceptively, by Juan Alvarez in his *Estudio sobre las guerras civiles argentinas* (Buenos Aires, 1914). An equally impressionistic but much more positive study on Chile is provided by Francisco Encina in a book which was destined to exert considerable influence both inside and outside that country: *Nuestra inferioridad económica* (Santiago, 1911). There are very few studies of social change during the second quarter of the nineteenth century. John V. Lombardi, *The decline and abolition of negro slavery in Venezuela, 1820–1854* (Westport, Conn., 1971), is worthy of mention and for Mexico, Jean Meyer, *Problemas campesinos y revueltas agrarias (1821–1910)* (Mexico, 1973). For Cuba, both Franklin W. Knight, *Slave society in Cuba during the nineteenth century* (Madison, 1970), and Manuel Moreno Fraginals, *El ingenio* (Havana, 1964; English trans., *The sugarmill*, New

York, 1978), concentrate their attention on this period. The vast travel literature of the period is listed in Bernard Naylor. Worthy of special mention is H. G. Ward, *Mexico in 1827*, (2 vols., London, 1828), a systematic study by a well-informed and acutely aware, if not disinterested, observer. To this should be added the critical analyses by locally born authors: for example, José Antonio Saco's outstanding *Memoria sobre la vagancia en la isla de Cuba* (Havana, 1832), and Mariano Otero, *Ensayo sobre el verdadero estado de la cuestión social y política que se agita en la República Mexicana* (Mexico, 1842). The literature on the post-1850 period and the foundations of a new order in Spanish America is more extensive, but almost more scattered and heterogeneous. A few national studies which have implicit relevance to the whole of Latin America deserve mention. A study of the formation of a dominant group during an export boom, such as *Guano y burguesía en Perú* (Lima, 1974), by Heraclio Bonilla, is, without a doubt, an exception, as was the whole Peruvian experience at this time. The impact of the new order, as felt to the fullest by the peasantry, is the subject of T. G. Powell, *El liberalismo y el campesinado en el centro de México (1850–1876)* (Mexico, 1974), which offers a less negative view than usual of the relations between the peasantry and the first exponents of liberalism, and Arnold J. Bauer, *Chilean rural society from the Spanish Conquest to 1930* (London, 1975). Another aspect of liberal reform, the confiscation of church property, is studied in Jan Bazant, *Alienation of Church wealth in Mexico. Social and economic aspects of the liberal revolution, 1856–1875* (Cambridge, 1971). Frank Safford, *The ideal of the practical: Colombia's struggle to form a technical elite* (Austin, Texas, 1976), provides a subtle view of reformism which distances itself from the standard view of liberalism. H. S. Ferns, *Britain and Argentina in the XIXth Century* (Oxford, 1960) provides a convincing study of the transition to the age of the railway, in a country which, perhaps more than any other, would feel its impact. This period witnessed the publication of exhaustive descriptions of the geography and socio-economic characteristics of the new countries, along the lines of the pioneer study by Agostino Codazzi, published in 1842 under the title *Resúmen de la geografía de Venezuela*. In Colombia, the 'Comisión Geográfica', also directed by Codazzi, produced Manuel Ancízar's *Peregrinación de Alpha por la provincia del Norte de la Nueva Granada, en 1850 y 1851* (Bogotá, 1853). In Peru, there was the monumental work by the Italian geographer, Antonio Raimondi, *El Perú* (3 vols., Lima, 1874–80); in Chile, the even more ambitious *Historia física y política de Chile* (Paris–Santiago, 1844–71) by the French botanist Claude Gay, of which the two volumes on *La agricultura*, published in 1862 and 1865, are of particular interest; in Argentina, the *Description géographique et statistique de la Confédération Argentine* (3 vols., Paris, 1860–73), by Jean-Antoine-Victor Martin de Moussy.

On individual Spanish American countries, see *CHLA*, III, bibliographical essays 10–15.

9. POLITICS, IDEOLOGY AND SOCIETY IN POST-INDEPENDENCE SPANISH AMERICA

Tulio Halperín Donghi offers many imaginative insights into the post-independence period in *Historia contemporánea de América Latina* (Madrid, 1969), chapters 3 and 4, and *The aftermath of revolution in Latin America* (New York, 1973).

There is no single work on the constitutional history of all the Spanish American states. A significant work on early constitutional formation in Mexico is Nettie Lee Benson, *La diputación provincial y el federalismo mexicano* (Mexico, 1955), and a recent contribution on Central America is Mario Rodriguez, *The Cadiz experiment in Central America, 1808–1826* (Berkeley, 1978). David Bushnell's *The Santander Regime in Gran Colombia* (Newark, Delaware, 1954) is a model monograph on the early administrative and political formation of a Spanish American state.

A general view of elite ideologies in the nineteenth century may be found in Leopoldo Zea, *The Latin American mind* (Norman, Okla., 1949). Works on particular countries which shed light on Spanish America as a whole include Simon Collier, *Ideas and politics of Chilean independence, 1808–1833* (Cambridge, 1967); Jaime Jaramillo Uribe, *El pensamiento colombiano en el siglo xix* (Bogotá, 1964); Charles Hale, *Mexican liberalism in the age of Mora, 1821–1853* (New Haven, 1968). See also an interesting article by Hale, 'The reconstruction of nineteenth-century politics in Spanish America: a case for the history of ideas', *LARR*, 8/2 (1973), 53–73.

The political polarization in the middle of the nineteenth century is treated for Mexico in Hale's *Mexican liberalism* and in Moisés González Navarro, *Anatomía del poder en México, 1848–1853* (Mexico, 1977), the latter a loosely-constructed work, but one rich in suggestive detail. On Colombia, see Robert L. Gilmore, 'Nueva Granada's socialist mirage', *HAHR*, 36/2 (1956), 190–210; Germán Colmenares, *Partidos políticos y clases sociales* (Bogotá, 1968); and J. Leon Helguera, 'Antecedentes sociales de la revolución de 1851 en el sur de Colombia (1848–1851)', *Anuario Colombiano de Historia Social y de la Cultura*, 5 (1970), 53–63. On

Chile, see a contemporary account, Benjamín Vicuña MacKenna, *Historia de la jornada del 20 de abril de 1851: una batalla en las calles de Santiago* (Santiago, 1878) and a recent monograph, Luis Alberto Romero, *La Sociedad de la Igualdad. Los artesanos de Santiago de Chile y sus primeras experiencias políticas, 1820–1851* (Buenos Aires, 1978).

Valuable works on social and economic aspects of political alignments are Tulio Halperín Donghi, *Politics, economics and society in Argentina in the revolutionary period* (Cambridge, 1975); Miron Burgin, *Economic aspects of Argentine Federalism, 1820–1852* (Cambridge, Mass., 1946); François Chevalier, 'Conservateurs et libéraux au Mexique: essaie de sociologie et géografie politiques de l'Independance à l'intervention française', *Cahiers d'Histoire Mondiale*, 8 (1964), 457–74; David A. Brading, *Los orígenes del nacionalismo mexicano* (Mexico, 1973). Frank Safford, 'Bases of political alignment in early republican Spanish America', in Richard Graham and Peter H. Smith (eds.), *New Approaches to Latin American history* (Austin, Texas, 1974), 71–111, offers a critical review of this topic.

On issues affecting the Church in Spanish American politics, J. Lloyd Mecham offers a country-by-country survey in *Church and state in Latin America* (Chapel Hill, N.C., 1934; 2nd edn, 1966); the first edition offers some material on the nineteenth century that is deleted in the second edition. More recent works examining the role of the Church in the economy as well as in politics are Michael P. Costeloe, *Church wealth in Mexico* (Cambridge, 1967) and Jan Bazant, *Alienation of Church wealth in Mexico. Social and economic aspects of the liberal revolution, 1856–1875* (Cambridge, 1971). Arbold Bauer's more general analysis, 'The Church and Spanish American agrarian structure 1765–1865', *The Americas*, 28/1 (1971), lucidly develops some of the ideas imbedded in Bazant's work.

There is a voluminous literature on *caudillismo*, particularly if all the biographies of caudillos are included. For many of these, see the bibliographical essays on individual countries in this period. General analyses of the phenomenon may be found in Charles E. Chapman, 'The age of the caudillos: a chapter in Hispanic American History', *HAHR*, 12/3 (1932), 281–300; Hugh M. Hamill, Jr (ed.), *Dictatorship in Spanish America* (New York, 1965); Robert L. Gilmore, *Caudillism and militarism in Venezuela, 1810–1910* (Athens, Ohio, 1964); Eric R. Wolf and Edward C. Hansen, 'Caudillo politics: a structural analysis', *Comparative Studies in Society and History*, 9/2 (1967), 168–79; Fernando Díaz Díaz, *Caudillos y caciques* (Mexico, 1972); and Malcolm Deas, 'Algunas notas sobre la historia del caciquismo en Colombia', *Revista de Occidente*, 63 (1973), 118–40. One of the most useful contributions is the analysis of a single case

(Martín Güemes in the province of Salta, Argentina) by Roger Haigh, 'The creation and control of a Caudillo', *HAHR*, 44/4 (1964), 481–90. Most of the analyses of political instability in the period after independence also have something to say about *caudillismo*. Two classic works are Francisco García Calderón, *Latin America: its rise and progress* (New York, 1913) and L. Cecil Jane, *Liberty and despotism in Spanish America* (London, 1929). The most important recent contributions are two essays by Richard M. Morse, 'Toward a theory of Spanish American government', *Journal of the History of Ideas*, 15 (1954), 71–93, and 'The heritage of Latin America', in Louis Hartz (ed.), *The founding of new societies* (New York, 1964), 123–77.

On individual Spanish American countries, see *CHLA*, III, bibliographical essays 10–15.

10. MEXICO FROM INDEPENDENCE TO 1867

Ernesto de la Torre Villar *et al.* (eds.), *Historia documental de México* (2 vols., Mexico, 1964) is an important documentary collection. F. Tena Ramírez (ed.), *Leyes fundamentales de México 1808–1973* (5th rev. edn, Mexico, 1973), reproduces all the constitutions and their drafs as well as the most important laws and decrees. For economic and social aspects of the period from around 1800 to 1852, L. Chávez Orozco (ed.), *Colección de documentos para la historia del comercio exterior de México*, in two series: series I in 7 vols. (Mexico, 1958–62); series II in 4 vols. (Mexico, 1965–67) should be consulted; it covers much more ground than the title indicates. Documentation on the Juárez era can be found in J. L. Tamayo (ed.), *Benito Juárez, documentos, discursos y correspondencia* (14 vols., Mexico, 1964–70), and Secretaría de la Presidencia (ed.), *La administración pública en la época de Juárez* (3 vols., Mexico, 1973). For foreign relations, see L. Díaz (ed.), *Versión francesa de México. Informes diplomáticos 1853–1867* (4 vols., Mexico, 1963–7), and L. Díaz (ed.), *Versión francesa de México 1851–67. Informes económicos* (consular reports) (2 vols., Mexico, 1974).

There are a number of general works which include substantial treatment of Mexican history in the period after independence. Most notable among older works are Lucas Alamán, *Historia de México, 1808–1849* (5 vols., Mexico, 2nd edn, 1942–8), vol. V, Vicente Riva Palacio (ed.), *México a través de los siglos* (Mexico, 1889; facsimile edn, Mexico, 1958), Vols IV and V; Francisco de Paula de Arrangoiz, *México desde 1808 hasta 1867* (4 vols., Mexico, 1871–2; 2nd edn, 1974). More recently Luis González y González (ed.), *Historia general de México* (4 vols., El Colegio de México, Mexico, 1976), Vol. III (1821–1910), and Jan Bazant, *A concise history of Mexico from Hidalgo to Cárdenas* (Cambridge, 1977), chapters 2 and 3, have provided valuable syntheses. Still useful is Justo Sierra, *Evolución política del pueblo mexicano*, now available in English as *The political evolution of the Mexican people* (Austin, Texas, 1970).

On particular aspects of the period, Charles A. Hale, *Mexican liberalism in the age of Mora 1821–1853* (New Haven, 1968) is essential for the study of ideas. J. Bazant, *Historia de la deuda exterior de México 1823–1946* (Mexico, 1968), replaces the older book by Edgar Turlington, *Mexico and her foreign creditors* (New York, 1930). Michael P. Costeloe, *Church and state in independent Mexico. A study of the patronage debate 1821–1857* (London, 1978), is an excellent study of church-state relations. R. W. Randall, *Real del Monte, a British mining venture in Mexico* (Austin, Texas, 1972), is one of the few books on mining. Robert A. Potash, *El Banco de Avío de México 1821–1846* (Mexico, 1959), is essential for the history of manufacturing and government banking. For background on the Yucatán Caste War, there are three well-researched articles by Howard F. Cline: 'The "Aurora Yucateca" and the spirit of enterprise in Yucatán, 1821–1847', *HAHR*, 27 (1947), 30–60; 'The sugar episode in Yucatán. 1825–1850', *Inter-American Economic Affairs*, 1/4 (1948), 79–100; 'The Henequén episode in Yucatán', *Inter-American Economic Affairs*, 2/2 (1948), 30–51. See also Moisés González Navarro, *Raza y Tierra* (Mexico, 1970), and N. Reed, *The Caste War of Yucatán* (Stanford, 1964). On agrarian structures and the history of the hacienda, see Charles H. Harris III, *A Mexican family empire. The latifundio of the Sánchez Navarros 1765–1867* (Austin, Texas, 1975); J. Bazant, *Cinco haciendas mexicanas. Tres siglos de vida rural en San Luis Potosí, 1600–1910* (Mexico, 1975), a summary of parts of which was published in English in K. Duncan and I. Rutledge, *Land and labour in Latin America. Essays on the development of agrarian capitalism in the 19th & 20th centuries* (Cambridge, 1977); Herbert J. Nickel, *Soziale Morphologie der mexikanischen Hacienda* (Wiesbaden, 1978), one of the best hacienda studies so far published; David A. Brading, *Haciendas and ranchos in the Mexican Bajío* (Cambridge, 1978). Finally, on the difficult question of church wealth and its disposal, see M. P. Costeloe, *Church wealth in Mexico* (Cambridge, 1967), and J. Bazant, *Alienation of church wealth in Mexico. Social and economic aspects of the liberal revolution 1856–1875* (Cambridge, 1971; 2nd revised edn in Spanish, *Los bienes de la iglesia en México*, Mexico, 1977). Charles R. Berry, *The reform in Oaxaca, 1856–76. A micro-history of the liberal revolution* (Lincoln, Nebraska, 1981) is a detailed regional study of the question. There are two collections of essays on aspects of the economic and social history of Mexico in the nineteenth century edited by Ciro F. S. Cardoso: *Formación y Desarrollo de la Burguesía en México. Siglo XIX* (Mexico, 1978) and *México en el siglo XIX (1821–1910). Historia económica y de la estructura social* (Mexico, 1980).

For the period 1821–35, contemporary descriptions include J. Poinsett, *Notes on Mexico* (London, 1825) and H. G. Ward, *Mexico in 1827* (2 vols., London, 1828). Günther Kahle, *Militär und Staatsbildung in den Anfängen der Unabhängigkeit Mexikos* (Cologne, 1969), is a pioneer study of the formation of the Mexican army through the amalgamation of guerrilla fighters for independence and former royalist officers. Michael P. Costeloe, *La primera república federal de México 1824–1835* (Mexico, 1975), is a study of political parties, based on research in the press and pamphlets. Also worthy of note are R. Flores C., *Counterrevolution: the role of the Spaniards in the independence of Mexico 1804–1838* (Lincoln, Nebraska, 1974); H. D. Sims, *La expulsión de los españoles en México, 1821–1828* (Mexico, 1974), which contains valuable statistical information; and Brian R. Hamnett, *Revolución y contrarevolución en México y el Perú* (Mexico, 1978), for the difficult first years of independent Mexico.

The Texas revolution and the Mexican war have naturally received a great deal of attention from U.S. and Mexican historians, contemporary and modern. See R. S. Ripley, *The war with Mexico* (2 vols., New York, 1849, reprinted 1970); R. Alcaraz, *et al.*, *The other side: or notes for the history of the war between Mexico and the United States* (trans. and ed. by A. C. Ramsey, New York, 1850), in which 15 prominent Mexicans describe the war; Carlos E. Castañeda (ed. and trans.), *The Mexican side of the Texan revolution 1836* (Washington, D.C., 1971) contains accounts by five chief Mexican participants, including Santa Anna; J. F. Ramírez, *Mexico during the war with the United States*, ed. by W. V. Scholes, trans. by E. B. Sherr (Columbia, Mo., 1950); G. M. Brack, *Mexico views Manifest Destiny 1821–1846, An essay on the origins of the Mexican War* (Albuquerque, N.M., 1975), a sympathetic account, well documented from Mexican newspapers and pamphlets; Charles H. Brown, *Agents of Manifest Destiny. The lives and times of the Filibusters* (Chapel Hill, N.C., 1980), a very useful study of these adventurers.

For the period after 1848 there are two studies of the later years of Santa Anna: F. Díaz D., *Caudillos y caciques* (Mexico, 1972) and M. González Navarro, *Anatomía del poder en México 1848–1853* (Mexico, 1977). On liberal politics, see W. V. Scholes, *Mexican politics during the*

Juárez Régime 1855–1872 (2nd edn, Columbia, Mo., 1969) and Richard N. Sinkin, *The Mexican Reform, 1855–1876. A study in liberal nation-building* (Austin, Texas, 1979); on French intervention, J. A. Dabbs, *The French Army in Mexico 1861–1867, a study in Military government* (The Hague, 1963); and on the empire, Alfred Jackson Hanna and Kathryn Abbey Hanna, *Napoleon III and Mexico. American triumph over monarchy* (Chapel Hill, N.C., 1971).

A number of political biographies are worthy of note: W. S. Robertson, *Iturbide of Mexico* (Durham, N.C., 1952) which is heavily based on archival materials (see also *Memoirs of Agustín de Iturbide* (Washington, D.C., 1971)); J. E. Rodríguez, O., *The emergence of Spanish America. Vicente Rocafuerte and Spanish Americanism 1808–1832* (Berkeley, 1975), a fine biography of an Ecuadorean liberal who took part in the struggle for the Mexican republic; Wildrid H. Callcott, *Santa Anna* (Norman, Oklahoma, 1936) and O. L. Jones Jr, *Santa Anna* (New York, 1968) which should be read together with A. F. Crawford (ed.), *The Eagle. The autobiography of Santa Anna* (Austin, Texas, 1967); Thomas E. Cotner, *The military and political career of José Joaquín de Herrera 1792–1854* (Austin, Texas, 1949); Frank A. Knapp, *The life of Sebastián Lerdo de Tejada 1823– 1899* (Austin, Texas, 1951) and C. G. Blázquez, *Miguel Lerdo de Tejada* (Mexico, 1978); I. E. Cadenhead, Jr, *Benito Juárez* (New York, 1973), which to a considerable extent replaces the older and more voluminous biography by R. Roeder, *Juárez and his Mexico* (2 vols., New York, 1947); also by Cadenhead, *Jesús González Ortega and Mexican national politics* (Texas Christian University Press, 1972); finally, Joan Haslip, *The crown of Mexico, Maximilian and his Empress Carlota* (New York, 1971), a comprehensive biography, both personal and political, of the two tragic figures.

11. CENTRAL AMERICA FROM INDEPENDENCE TO *c.*1870

A comparison of Lázaro Lamadrid, 'A survey of the historiography of Guatemala since 1821. Part 1 – The nineteenth century', *TA*, 8/2 (1951), 189–202; W. J. Griffith, 'The historiography of Central America since 1830', *HAHR*, 40/4 (1960), 548–69; and Griffith, 'Central America', in C. C. Griffin (ed.), *Latin America, a guide to the historical literature* (Austin, 1971), 403–21, reflects the rapid growth of historical publications in the mid-twentieth century. The following essay is concerned principally with works published since Griffin and will be most useful when employed together with the guides mentioned above and the extensive bibliographical essay in R. L. Woodward, Jr, *Central America, a nation divided* (2nd edn, New York, 1985), 278–312, as well as with appropriate sections of the *Handbook of Latin American Studies*.

While earlier general works continue to have utility, Woodward, *Central America*, and Ciro Cardoso and Héctor Pérez, *Centroamérica y la economía occidental (1520–1930)* (San José, 1977) incorporate much of the recent scholarship on the first half-century of independence, especially for the economic and social history. Edelberto Torres Rivas, *Interpretación del desarrollo social centroamericano* (San José, 1971) has provided much of the inspiration for serious recent historical research in the social sciences in Central America. Histories of individual states that reflect recent scholarship have been few, but exceptions are Alastair White, *El Salvador* (New York, 1973); Narda Dobson, *A history of Belize* (London, 1973); O. N. Bolland, *The formation of a colonial society: Belize from conquest to crown colony* (Baltimore, 1977); and David Luna, *Manual de historia económica* (San Salvador, 1971). For reference, although uneven in quality, the *Historical Dictionary* series published in Metuchen, N.J., are useful: Philip Flemion, *El Salvador* (1972); H. K. Meyer, *Nicaragua* (1972) and *Honduras* (1976); R. E. Moore, *Guatemala*, rev. edn (1973); and Theodore Creedman, *Costa Rica* (1977). Also useful are the first volumes in the World Bibliographical Series (Oxford: Clio Press): R. L. Woodward, *Belize* (1980) and *Nicaragua* (1983), and Woodman Franklin, *Guatemala* (1981).

Several recent studies deal with specific aspects of the post-independence period: D. R. Radell, *Historical geography of Western Nicaragua: the spheres of influence in León, Granada and Managua, 1519–1965* (Berkeley, 1969); David Browning, *El Salvador, landscape and society* (Oxford, 1971); Alberto Sáenz M., *Historia agrícola de Costa Rica* (San José, 1970); Carolyn Hall, *El café y el desarrollo histórico-geográfico de Costa Rica* (San José, 1976); Constantino Láscaris, *Historia de las ideas en Centroamérica* (San José, 1970); Carlos González, *Historia de la educación en Guatemala*, 2nd edn (Guatemala, 1970); Otto Olivera, *La literatura en publicaciones periódicas de Guatemala: siglo XIX* (New Orleans, 1974); Arturo Castillo, *Historia de la moneda de Honduras* (Tegucigalpa, 1974); Samuel Stone, *La dinastía de los conquistadores* (San José, 1975); Cleto González Víquez, *Capítulos de un libro sobre historia financiera de Costa Rica*, 2nd edn (San José, 1977); and R. L. Woodward, Jr, *Privilegio de clases y el desarrollo económico: el consulado de comercio de Guatemala, 1793–1871* (San José, 1981), which contains extensive documentary appendices not included in the 1966 English edition.

Among the most noteworthy articles based on new research and new methodologies recently published in Central American journals are: Ciro Cardoso, 'La formación de la hacienda cafetalera en Costa Rica (siglo XIX)' *ESC*, 2/6 (1973), 22–50; Carlos Araya, 'La minería y sus relaciones con la acumulación de capital y la clase dirigente de Costa Rica, 1821– 1841', *ESC*, 2/5 (1973), 31–64, and 'La minería en Costa Rica, 1821– 1843', *Revista Historia* (Costa Rica), 1/2 (1976), 83–125; Héctor Pérez, 'Economía y sociedad en Honduras durante el siglo XIX. Las estructuras demográficas', *ESC*, 2/6 (1973), 51–82; Guillermo Molina, 'Estructura productiva e historia demográfica (Economía y desarrollo en Hondu- ras)', *Anuario de Estudios Centroamericanos*, 3 (1977), 161–73; and Alberto Lanuza, 'Nicaragua: territorio y población (1821–1875)', *Revista del Pensamiento Centroamericano*, 31/151 (1976), 1–22, 'Comercio exterior de Nicaragua (1821–1875)', *ESC*, 5/14 (1976), 109–36, and 'La minería en Nicaragua (1821–1875)', *Anuario de Estudios Centroamericanos*, 3 (1977), 215–24. R. L. Woodward, Jr has reviewed the literature on the demogra- phic history of the period in 'Crecimiento de población en Centroamérica durante la primera mitad del siglo de la independencia nacional', *Mesoamérica* 1/1 (1980), 219–31. Although he overlooks some of the work already done, Thomas Schoonover, 'Central American commerce and maritime activity in the nineteenth century: sources for a quantita- tive approach', *LARR*, 13/2 (1978), 157–69, provides some guidance in this area.

Among recent works dealing with the establishment of Central American independence, clearly the most important is Mario Rodríguez, *The Cádiz Experiment in Central America, 1808–1826* (Berkeley, 1978). While Louis Bumgartner, *José del Valle of Central America* (Durham, N.C., 1963) remains the definitive work on that important political figure, Ramón López, *José Cecilio del Valle, Fouché de Centro América* (Guatemala, 1968) offers some new insights, and Rafael H. Valle, *Pensamiento vivo de José Cecilio del Valle*, 2nd edn (San José, 1971), is an excellent anthology of his writings and synthesis of his ideas. The role of the first Central American Constituent Assembly is dealt with in detail by Andrés Townsend, *Las Provincias Unidas de Centroamérica: fundación de la República* (San José, 1973) in a substantial amplification of his 1958 book of the same title. Two revisionist articles on the Federation period are Philip Flemion, 'States' rights and partisan politics: Manuel José Arce and the struggle for Central American Union', *HAHR*, 53/4 (1973), 600–18, and Mauricio Domínguez, 'El Obispado de San Salvador: foco de desavenencia político-religiosa', *Anuario de Estudios Centroamericanos*, 1 (1974), 87–133. Francisco Morazán's *Memorias*, written following his defeat in 1840 and published in Paris in 1870, were reprinted in Tegucigalpa in 1971, and a collection of his personal papers have appeared in W. J. Griffith, 'The personal archive of Francisco Morazán', *Philological and Documentary Studies*, II (Publication 12, Middle American Research Institute, Tulane University, New Orleans, 1977), 197–286. For the post-independence period, T. L. Karnes, *The failure of union: Central America, 1824–1975*, rev. edn (Center for Latin American Studies, Arizona State University, Tempe, 1976), is identical to his earlier work, and Alberto Herrarte, *El federalismo en Centroamérica* (San José, 1972), is a condensation of his *Unión de Centroamérica* (Guatemala, 1964). F. D. Parker, *Travels in Central America, 1821–1840* (Gainesville, Fla., 1970), deals with a number of the perceptive travel accounts of this period. Reflecting substantial new research are the articles on Guatemala by Mario Rodríguez, Miriam Williford, R. L. Woodward, Jr and W. J. Griffith, in *Applied Enlightenment: 19th-century liberalism* (Publication 23, Middle American Research Institute, Tulane University, New Orleans, 1972). Griffith's article in that volume, 'Attitudes toward foreign colonization: the evolution of nineteenth-century Guatemalan immigration', expands upon the ideas earlier presented in his *Empires in the wilderness* (Chapel Hill, N.C., 1966). See also Williford's 'The educational reforms of Dr. Mariano Galvez', *JIAS*, 10/3 (1968), 461–73. For the diplomatic history of the period, in addition to Mario Rodriguez's excellent *Palmerstonian diplomat in Central America: Frederick Chatfield, Esq.* (Tucson, Arizona, 1964), see R. A. Humphreys, 'Anglo-American rivalries in Central America', in *Tradition and revolt in Latin America* (London, 1969), 154–55; David Waddell, 'Great Britain and the Bay Islands, 1821–61', *The Historical Journal*, 2/1 (1959), 59–77; C. L. Stansifer, 'Ephraim George Squier: diversos aspectos de su carrera en Centroamérica', *Revista Conservadora del Pensamiento Centroamericano*, 20/98 (1968); Cyril Allen, *France in Central America* (New York, 1966), which concentrates on canal agent Felix Belly; and Andrés Vega Bolaños, *Los atentados del superintendente de Belice* (Managua, 1971), which focuses on British activities of 1840–2. José Ramírez describes the career of an early Nicaraguan diplomat in his *José de Marcoleta: padre de la diplomacia nicaragüense* (2 vols., Managua, 1975). Chester Zelaya and L. F. Sibaja treat Costa Rican acquisition of Guanacaste in *La anexión del partido de Nicoya* (San José, 1974). Zelaya has also elucidated the career of J. F. Osejo in *El Bachiller*

Osejo (2 vols., San José, 1971). Traditional liberal condemnations of Rafael Carrera have been challenged by Luis Beltranena, *Fundación de la República de Guatemala* (Guatemala, 1971), and Keith Miceli, 'Rafael Carrera: defender and promoter of peasant interests in Guatemala, 1837–1848', *TA*, 31/1 (1974), 72–95, as well as by R. L. Woodward, 'Liberalism, conservatism and the response of the peasants of La Montaña to the government of Guatemala, 1821–1850', in *Plantation Society in the Americas*, 1/1 (1979), 109–30. See also Pedro Tobar Cruz, *Los montañeses: la facción de los Lucíos y otros acontecimientos históricos de 1846 a 1851* (Guatemala, 1971). An important memoir of the period has been republished in Francisco Ortega, *Cuarenta años (1838–1878) de historia de Nicaragua*, 2nd edn (Managua, 1974).

The Anglo-American rivalry for a transoceanic route and the William Walker episode continue to attract historical writings at all levels. Enrique Guier, *William Walker* (San José, 1971), offers nothing new but is a competent work, while Frederic Rosengarten, *Freebooters Must Die!* (Wayne, Penn., 1976) combines a lively account with many contemporary illustrations and maps. More scholarly are the works of David Folkman, *The Nicaragua route* (Salt Lake City, 1972); R. E. May, *The southern dream of a Caribbean empire, 1854–1861* (Baton Rouge, 1973); and Germán Tjarks *et al.*, 'La epidemia del cólera de 1856 en el Valle Central: análisis y consecuencias demográficas', *Revista de Historia* (Costa Rica), 2/3 (1976), 81–129. Alejandro Bolaños has begun to publish a series of works on the Walker period based on the enormous volume of materials he has been accumulating. Of the first volumes to appear, perhaps the most interesting is his *El filibustero Clinton Rollins* (Masaya, Nic., 1976), in which he exposes Rollins, supposedly an associate of Walker, as the pseudonym of H. C. Parkhurst and his accounts of Walker as fiction.

For the close of the period, Wayne Clegern, author of *British Honduras: colonial dead end* (Baton Rouge, 1967), suggests a transitional role for the Vicente Cerna administration in 'Transition from conservatism to liberalism in Guatemala, 1865–1981', in William S. Coker (ed.), *Hispanic-American essays in honor of Max Leon Moorhead* (Pensacola, Florida, 1979), also published in Spanish in *Revista del Pensamiento Centroamericano*, 31/151 (1976), 60–5. There are studies of major figures in Costa Rica and El Salvador during this period: Carlos Meléndez, *Dr. José María Montealegre* (San José, 1968), and Italo López, *Gerardo Barrios y su tiempo* (2 vols., San Salvador, 1965). Finally, valuable contemporary impressions of the period have been reprinted: Francisco Lainfiesta, *Apuntamientos para la historia de Guatemala, período de 20 años corridos del 14 de abril de 1865 al 6 de abril de 1885* (Guatemala, 1975), and Pablo Levy, *Notas geográficas y económicas sobre la República de Nicaragua*, 2nd edn (Managua, 1976).

12. VENEZUELA, COLOMBIA AND ECUADOR: THE FIRST HALF-CENTURY OF INDEPENDENCE

General

For Gran Colombia see D. Bushnell, *The Santander Régime in Gran Colombia* (Newark, N.J., 1954); J. M. Restrepo, *Historia de la revolución de la República de Colombia en la América meridional* (8 vols., Bogotá, 1942–50); R. M. Baralt and R. Díaz, *Resumen de la historia de Venezuela desde el año de 1797 hasta el de 1830* (2 vols., Bruges, 1939). Also very useful for its collapse are two volumes by C. Parra-Pérez: *Mariño y la independencia de Venezuela* (4 vols., Madrid 1954–60), vol. IV, and *La monarquía en la Gran Colombia* (Madrid, 1957). Valuable accounts of the whole area are C. A. Gosselman, *Informes sobre los estados sudamericanos en los años de 1837 y 1838* (Stockholm, 1962) and M. M. Lisboa, Barão de Japura, *Relación de un viaje a Venezuela, Nueva Granada y Ecuador* (Caracas, 1954), an account of a journey in 1852–3. A useful contemporary constitutional series of studies is J. Arosemena, *Estudios constitucionales sobre los gobiernos de la América Latina* (2nd edn, 2 vols., Paris, 1878).

Venezuela

J. V. Lombardi, *et al.*, *Venezuelan History: a comprehensive working bibliography* (Boston, Mass., 1977), is indispensable.

The following collections of documents also serve the period well: P. Grases and M. Pérez Vila (eds.), *Pensamiento político venezolano del siglo XIX* (15 vols., Caracas, 1960–2); T. E. Carillo Batalla, comp., *Historia de las finanzas públicas en Venezuela* (10 vols., Caracas, 1969–73); *Las fuerzas armadas de Venezuela en el siglo xix* (12 vols. to date, Caracas, 1963–); C. Gómez R. (ed.), *Materiales para el estudio de la cuestion agraria en Venezuela (1829–1860). Enajenación y arrendamiento de tierras baldías* (Caracas, 1971); R. J. Velásquez (introd.), *Decretos del poder ejecutivo de Venezuela por el Despacho del Interior y Justicia, 1831–1842* (Caracas, 1973); A. L. Guzmán, *Causa célèbre por su iniquidad la de supuesta conspiración del redactor de 'El Venezolano' Antonio L. Guzmán en 1846* (6 vols., Caracas, 1884).

Contemporary memoirs and diaries are not as abundant as they are in Colombia, but see J. A. Páez, *Autobiografía* (2 vols., Caracas, 1973); J. M. de Rojas, *Tiempo perdido* (Caracas, 1967); W. Dupuy (ed.), *Sir Robert Kerr Porter's Caracas Diary, 1825–1842* (Caracas, 1966); L. Level de Goda, *Historia contemporánea de Venezuela política y militar, 1858–1886* (Caracas, 1976); C. Parra-Pérez (ed.), *La cartera del Coronel Conde de Adlercreutz* (Paris, 1928). There is much of interest in B. Bruni Celli (comp.), *José María Vargas – obras completas* (7 vols. in 10, Caracas, 1958–66); J. A. Cova (ed.), *Archivo del Mariscal Juan Crisóstomo Falcón* (5 vols., Caracas, 1957–60) is confused and disappointing; R. R. Castellanos V., *Guzmán Blanco íntimo* (Caracas, 1969), contains selections from a large surviving archive; see also his *Páez, proscrito y peregrino* (Caracas, 1976).

The most useful biographical studies are C. Parra-Pérez, *Mariño y las guerras civiles* (3 vols., Madrid, 1958–60); R. Díaz Sánchez, *Guzmán. Elipse de una ambición de poder* (2 vols., Caracas, 1968) – both these are well-documented 'lives and times'. F. Brito Figueroa's *Tiempo de Ezequiel Zamora* (Caracas, 1975), invited the scrupulously researched and ironically understated riposte of A. Rodríguez's *Ezequiel Zamora* (Caracas, 1977); the earlier lives of this figure by M. Landaeta Rosales and L. Villanueva (both reprinted, Caracas, 1975) are still worth reading, as is J. R. Pachano, *Biografía del Mariscal Juan C. Falcón* (2nd edn, Caracas, 1960). See also J. A. de Armas Chitty, *Fermín Toro y su época* (Caracas, 1966) R. A. Rondón Márquez, *Guzmán Blanco, 'el Autócrata Civilizador'* (2 vols., Caracas, 1944).

Of the older histories F. González Guinán, *Historia contemporánea de Venezuela* (2nd edn, 15 vols, Caracas, 1954), still contains much that is not easily found elsewhere; J. Gil Fortoul, *Historia constitucional de Venezuela* (5th edn, 3 vols., Caracas, 1967), and E. González, *Historia de Venezuela, t. III: 1830–1858* (Buenos Aires, 1944), are both lucid. J. S. Rodríguez, *Contribución al estudio de la guerra federal en Venezuela* (2nd edn, 2 vols., Caracas, 1960), and L. Alvarado, *História de la revolución federal en Venezuela* (vol. 5 of *Obras Completas*, 8 vols., Caracas, 1953–8) are both still essential. Of the 'positivists', the most rewarding is L. Vallenilla Lanz, a new edition of whose works is promised. The writings of P. M. Arcaya are also still valuable.

The evolution of Venezuelan historiography can be traced in G. Carrera Damas (comp.), *Historia de la historiografía Venezolana. Textos para su estudio* (Caracas, 1961). A recent general history is John V. Lombardi, *Venezuela* (Oxford, 1982).

An introduction to the recent historiography of nineteenth-century

Venezuela is provided in the essays of M. Pérez Vila, R. P. Matthews, B. A. Frankel, M. B. Floyd and N. Harwich in M. Izard, *et al.*, *Política y economía en Venezuela, 1810–1976* (Caracas, 1976). The best short survey of the century by a single author is J. A. de Armas Chitty, *Vida política de Caracas en el siglo XIX* (Caracas, 1976). A guide to parties and factions, which include some provincial political activity, is M. V. Magallanes, *Los partidos políticos en la evolución histórica venezolana* (Caracas, 1973). M. Watters, *A history of the Church in Venezuela, 1810–1930* (New York, 1933) is likely to remain the standard survey of its subject. Among other recent monographs and articles, J. V. Lombardi, *The decline and abolition of negro slavery in Venezuela, 1820–1854* (Westport, Conn., 1971), goes well beyond its immediate subject; R. P. Matthews, *Violencia rural en Venezuela, 1840–1858, antecedentes socio-económicos de la Guerra Federal,* (Caracas, 1977), sheds more light on the Llanos than on the Federal War; R. L. Gilmore's *Caudillism and militarism in Venezuela, 1810–1910* (Athens, Ohio, 1964), seems uncertain about the precise nature of its subject. See also B. A. Frankel, *Venezuela y los Estados Unidos, 1810–1888* (Caracas, 1977); R. W. Butler, 'The origins of the Liberal Party in Venezuela, 1830–1848' (unpublished Ph.D. thesis, University of Texas, 1972); L. F. Snow Jr, 'The Páez Years – Venezuelan Economic Leglislation, 1830–1846' (unpublished Ph.D. thesis, University of North Carolina, 1970); G. E. Carl, *First among equals: Great Britain and Venezuela, 1810–1910* (Ann Arbor, 1980); J. V. Lombardi and J. A. Hanson, 'The first Venezuelan coffee cycle, 1830–1855', *Agricultural History*, 44 (1970); D. Bushnell, 'La evolución del derecho de sufragio en Venezuela', *Boletín Histórico,* 39 (1972); A. Lemmo B., *La educación en Venezuela en 1870* (Caracas, 1961).

The most famous early republican geography is A. Codazzi, *Resumen de la geografía de Venezuela (Venezuela en 1841)* (3 vols., Caracas, 1940). Outstanding travel books which described the country in this period are K. F. Appun, *En los trópicos* (Caracas, 1961); E. B. Eastwick, *Venezuela or Sketches of Life in a South American Republic* (London, 1868); P. Rosti, *Memorias de un viaje por América* (Caracas, 1968). A complete list is provided by M. L. Ganzenmuller de Blay, *Contribución a la bibliografiá de viajes y exploraciones de Venezuela* (Caracas, 1964).

The paintings of Anton Goering have been reproduced in *Venezuela de hace un siglo* (Caracas, 1969): no. 52 conveys more about an army than could be put into many words.

The following statistical compilations are available: M. Izard, *Series estadísticas para la historia de Venezuela* (Mérida, 1970); A. A. Moreno, comp., *Las estadísticas de las provincias en la época de Páez* (Caracas, 1973); M.

Landaeta Rosales, *Gran recopilación geográfica, estadística e histórica de Venezuela* (2 vols., Caracas, 1889. 2nd edn, Caracas, 1963); R. Veloz, *Economía y finanzas de Venezuela, 1830–1944* (Caracas 1945).

Colombia

There is unfortunately no Colombian equivalent to J. V. Lombardi and his team's working bibliography of Venezuelan history. The work of Colombia's first bibliographer, I. Laverde Amaya, *Apuntes sobre bibliografía colombiana con muestras escogidas en prosa y verso* (Bogotá, 1882) is still a valuable guide to the authors of this period. The following works are widely available: G. Giraldo Jaramillo, *Bibliografía de bibliografías colombianas* (2nd edn, corrected and updated by R. Pérez Ortiz, Bogotá, 1960); the same author's *Bibliografía colombiana de viajes* (Bogotá, 1957); S. Bernal, *Guía bibliográfica de Colombia de interes para el antropologo* (Bogotá 1970), invaluable for local history; H. H. Orjuela, *Fuentes generales para el estudio de la literatura colombiana, guía bibliográfica* (Bogotá, 1968); E. Ortega Ricaurte, *Bibliografía académica, 1902–1952* (Bogotá, 1953); M. G. Romero, *et al.*, *Papeletas bibliográficas para el estudio de la historia de Colombia* (Bogotá, 1961).

The following printed personal archives are particularly recommended: R. Cortázar (comp.), *Cartas y mensajes del General Francisco de Paula Santander* (10 vols., Bogotá, 1953–6) and *Correspondencia dirigida al general Francisco de Paula Santander* (14 vols., Bogotá, 1964–1967); L. A. Cuervo (comp.), *Epistolario del doctor Rufino Cuervo* (3 vols., Bogotá, 1918–22); J. L. Helguera and R. H. Davis (eds.), *Archivo epistolar del General Mosquera* (3 vols. to date, Bogotá, 1966–); H. Rodríguez Plata, *José María Obando íntimo: archivo – epistolario – comentarios* (Bogotá, 1958); S. E. Ortiz and L. Martínez Delgado (comps.), *Documentos y correspondencia del general José María Obando* (4 vols., Bogotá, 1973); E. Lemaitre (intro.), *Epistolario de Rafael Núñez con Miguel Antonio Caro* (Bogotá, 1977); G. Hernández de Alba (ed.), *Epistolario de Rufino José Cuervo con Luis María Lleras y otros amigos y familiares* (Bogotá, 1970); G. Hernández de Alba, *et al.* (comps.), *Archivo epistolar del General Domingo Caycedo* (3 vols., Bogotá, 1943–7).

S. Camacho Roldán, *Escritos varios* (3 vols., Bogotá, 1892–5), M. Samper, *Escritos político-económicos* (4 vols., Bogotá, 1925–7), and R. Núñez, *La reforma política en Colombia* (7 vols., Bogotá, 1946–50), are fundamental commentaries on Colombia in the nineteenth century. An isolated diplomatic report of great sensitivity is contained in R. Donoso, 'José Antonio Soffia en Bogotá', *Thesaurus* (Bogotá) 31/1, 1976.

For memoirs, see J. M. Restrepo, *Autobiografía* (Bogotá, 1957), and *Diario político y militar* (4 vols., Bogotá, 1954); J. M. Cordóvez Moure, *Reminiscencias de Santa Fé y Bogotá*, ed. E. Mujica (Madrid, 1962); F. de P. Borda, *Conversaciones con mis hijos* (3 vols., Bogotá, 1974); A. Parra, *Memorias* (Bogotá, 1912); S. Camacho Roldán, *Memorias* (2 vols., Bogotá, 1945); J. M. Samper, *Historia de una alma* (Bogotá, 1971); J. M. Obando, *Apuntamientos para la historia* (2 vols., Bogotá, 1945); J. Posada Gutiérrez, *Memorias histórico-políticas* (4 vols., Bogotá, 1929). For contemporary accounts of civil war see A. Cuervo, *Cómo se evapora un ejército* (Bogotá, 1953); M. Briceño, *La revolución, 1876–1877; recuerdos para la historia* (Bogotá, 1947); J. M. Vargas Valdés, *A mi paso por la tierra* (Bogotá, 1938); V. Ortiz, *Historia de la revolución del 17 de abril de 1854* (Bogotá, 1972).

Biographies: C. Cuervo Márquez, *Vida del doctor José Ignacio de Márquez* (2 vols., Bogotá, 1917); E. Posada and P. M. Ibáñez, *Vida de Herrán* (Bogotá, 1903); E. Gómez Barrientos, *Don Mariano Ospina y su época* (2 vols., Medellín, 1913–15), continued as *Veinticinco años a través del Estado de Antioquía* (2 vols., Medellín, 1918); A. and R. Cuervo, *Vida de Rufino Cuervo y noticias de su época* (2 vols., Paris, 1892); J. M. Arboleda Llorente, *Vida del Ilmo. Señor Manuel José Mosquera, Arzobispo de Santa Fé de Bogotá* (2 vols., Bogotá, 1956); A. J. Lemos Guzmán, *Obando*, (Popayán, 1959); I. Lievano Aguirre, *Rafael Núñez* (Bogotá, 1944); G. Otero Muñoz, *La vida azarosa de Rafael Núñez* (Bogotá, 1951).

G. Arboleda, *Historia contemporánea de Colombia* (6 vols., Bogotá, 1918–35) is the most complete of older works, but unfortunately runs only to 1861. Valuable for the later years of the century is E. Rodríguez Piñeres's *El Olimpo Radical, 1864–1884* (Bogotá, 1950).

A comprehensive and magnificently documented study of its subject is J. L. Helguera, *The first Mosquera administration in New Granada, 1845–99* (unpublished Ph.D. thesis, University of North Carolina, 1958). For mid-century see G. Colmenares, *Poder político y clases sociales* (Bogotá, 1965), and for intellectual development, J. Jaramillo Uribe, *El pensamiento colombiano en el siglo XIX* (Bogotá, 1964). An introduction to party struggles is J. L. Helguera, 'Liberalism versus conservatism in Colombia, 1849–1885; in F. B. Pike (ed.), *Latin American History: Select Problems* (New York, 1969).

On economic history the fundamental work remains L. Ospina

Vásquez, *Industria y protección en Colombia, 1810–1930* (Medellín, 1955), which is to be preferred to the not always reliable W. P. McGreevey, *An economic history of Colombia, 1845–1930* (Cambridge, 1971). F. Safford, *The ideal of the practical* (Austin, Texas, 1975), which explores many themes *via* a consideration of technical education, his unpublished Ph.D. thesis 'Commerce and enterprise in Central Colombia, 1821–1870' (Columbia University, 1965) and the essays in his *Aspectos del siglo XIX en Colombia* (Medellín, 1977) are all essential. So too are J. P. Harrison, 'The Colombian tobacco industry from government monopoly to free trade, 1778–1876' (unpublished Ph.D. thesis, University of California, 1951); R. C. Beyer, 'The Colombian coffee industry: origin and major trends. 1740–1940' (unpublished Ph.D. thesis, University of Minnesota, 1947); J. J. Parsons, *Antioqueño colonization in Western Colombia* (Berkeley, 1968); R. Brew, *El desarrollo económico de Antioquía desde la independencia hasta 1920*, (Bogotá, 1977). On transport see R. L. Gilmore and J. P. Harrison, 'Juan Bernardo Elbers and the introduction of steam navigation on the Magdalena River', *HAHR*, 28 (1948); H. Horna, 'Francisco Javier Cisneros: a pioneer in transportation and economic development in Colombia' (unpublished Ph.D. thesis, Vanderbilt University, 1970). J. Friede, *El indio en la lucha por la tierra* (Bogotá, 1944), and O. Fals Borda, *El hombre y la tierra en Boyacá* (Bogotá, 1975) treat aspects of highland agricultural development in the south and centre respectively. V. Restrepo, *Estudio sobre las minas de oro y de plata en Colombia* (Bogotá, 1882), is still the best source for republican mining up to the date of its publication. For Indian communities, see A. García, *Legislación indigenista de Colombia* (Mexico, 1952). For general reference, A. Pardo Pardo, *Geografía económica y humana de Colombia* (Bogotá, 1972). M. Urrutia and M. Arrubla, *Compendio de estadísticas históricas de Colombia* (Bogotá, 1970), contains series on population, wages, prices, foreign trade, tobacco, coffee and presidential elections.

For nineteenth-century geography, the reports of A. Codazzi are in Comisión Corográfica, *Geografía física y política de la provincias de la Nueva Granada* (2nd edn, 4 vols., Bogotá, 1957–8); F. Pérez, *Geografía general de los Estados Unidos de Colombia* (Bogotá, 1883), derives from the same source and M. Ancízar, *Peregrinación de Alpha* (Bogotá, 1956), from the same travels. R. Gutiérrez, *Monografías* (2 vols., Bogotá, 1920–1) contains much useful material from the 1880s.

Other valuable accounts are J. Stewart, *Bogotá in 1836–7* (New York, 1838); I. Holton, *New Granada: twenty months in the Andes* (New York,

1857): E. Rothlisberger, *El Dorado* (Bogotá, 1963); F. Von Schenk, *Viajes por Antioquia en el año 1880* (Bogotá, 1952); A. Hettner, *Viajes por los Andes Colombianos, 1882–1884* (Bogotá, 1976).

The series of watercolours reproduced in *Album de la Comisión Corográfica* – *suplemento de 'Hojas de cultura popular colombiana'*, are an extraordinary record of types, scenes and activities in the middle of the nineteenth century.

Ecuador

The problems of Ecuadorian historiography are set out in A. Szászdi, 'The historiography of the Republic of Ecuador', *HAHR*, 44/4 (1964); in the short article and shorter bibliography by J. Maiguashca in E. Florescano (ed.), *La historia económica en América Latina* (2 vols., Mexico, 1972), and M. T. Hamerley, 'Quantifying the nineteenth century: the ministry reports and gazettes of Ecuador as quantitative sources', *LARR*, 13/2, 1978. C. M. Larrea's *Bibliografía científica del Ecuador* (Madrid, 1952) lists 9,300 items, but many in the historical sections are virtually unobtainable.

Three short histories provide an introduction: G. Cevallos García's textbook *Historia de Ecuador* (Cuenca, 1967); O. E. Reyes, *Breve historia general del Ecuador* (2 vols., Quito, 1942); E. Ayala, *Lucha política y origen de los partidos en Ecuador* (Quito, 1978).

I. Robalino Dávila's *Orígines del Ecuador de hoy* (collected edition, 6 vols. to date, Puebla, Mexico, 1966–) is a series of well-documented politico–biographical studies running from the ascendancy of Flores to the career of Alfaro; a conservative bias is increasingly apparent and the volume on García Moreno is much more successful than the treatment of Alfaro. The series still represents the most ambitious effort of traditional historiography, and is much less partisan than J. L. R. [J. M. Le Gouhir y Rodas], *Historia de la república del Ecuador* (3 vols., Quito, 1920–38), a Jesuit work still useful for its documentation. J. Tobar Donoso, *Monografías históricas* (Quito, 1937) and his *La iglesia ecuatoriana en el siglo XIX: de 1809 a 1845* are also valuable. *Cultura*, Vol. II, No. 6, January–April 1980, a journal published by the Banco Central del Ecuador, Quito, is entirely devoted to 'El Ecuador en 1830: ideología, economía, política'.

There is no biography of Flores and no proper study of Rocafuerte's activities in Ecuador. On García Moreno, see Vol. IV of Robalino Dávila's *Orígines*, and R. Patee, *Gabriel García Moreno y el Ecuador de su tiempo* (3rd edn, Mexico, 1962). On Montalvo, see O. E. Reyes, *Vida de Juan Montalvo* (2nd edn, Quito, 1943). Veintemilla's years produced a spirited defence from his niece Marieta: M. Veintimilla, *Páginas del Ecuador* (Lima 1890), and a reply from Flores's son Antonio: A. Flores, *Para la historia del Ecuador* (2 vols., Quito, 1891). On Alfaro, see F. Guarderas, *El viejo de Montecristi: biografía de Alfaro* (Quito, 1953); A. Pareja Diez-Canseco, *La hoguera bárbara (vida de Eloy Alfaro)* (Mexico, 1944). For the late nineteenth century church, see F. González Suárez, *Memorias íntimas* (Guayaquil–Quito, n.d.), introductory essay by H. Rodríguez Castelo.

The collections of García Moreno's writings are listed in Robalino Dávila's biography; the largest published collection of his letters is that edited by W. Loor, *Cartas de García Moreno* (4 vols., Quito, 1953–5), but it is far from complete. E. Alfaro's *Obras escogidas* provide a taste of his thinking (2 vols., Guayaquil, 1959).

There are few modern monographs. Most notable is M. T. Hamerley, *Historia social y económica de la antigua Provincia de Guayaquil, 1763–1842* (Guayaquil, 1973).

There is interesting information on the history of the sierra in Comité Inter-americano de Desarrollo Agricola (CIDA), *Tenencia de la tierra y desarrollo socio-económico del sector agrícola – Ecuador* (Washington, D.C., 1965), a study directed by R. Baraona, and in A. Rubio Orbe, *Leglislación indigenista del Ecuador* (Mexico, 1954).

C. M. Larrea's bibliography lists travellers and geographical studies. The earliest comprehensive national geography is M. Villavicencio, *Geografía de la república del Ecuador* (New York, 1858). Of foreign observers, two of the more accessible and informative are F. Hassaurek, *Four years among Spanish-Americans* (New York, 1867) and A. Holinsky, *L'Equateur – Scènes de la vie Américaine* (Paris, 1861).

13. PERU AND BOLIVIA FROM INDEPENDENCE TO THE WAR OF THE PACIFIC

For the entire period from independence to the War of the Pacific, Jorge Basadre's great work, *Historia de la República del Perú* (5th edn, 10 vols., Lima, 1962–4), undoubtedly constitutes the most important source of reference. His earlier works, *Perú, problema y posibilidad* (Lima, 1931), and *La multitud, la ciudad y el campo* (Lima, 1947), have not only maintained their freshness but were responsible for pioneering the study of Peru's history. Apart from Basadre's classic works, another summary of this period written by Emilio Romero, *Historia económica del Perú* (Buenos Aires, 1949) contains information which is still of value. More recently, Ernesto Yepes del Castillo, *Perú 1820–1920. Un siglo de desarrollo capitalista* (Lima, 1972) has provided an overall interpretation of the nineteenth century, while Julio Cotler, in *Clases, estado y nación en el Perú* (Lima, 1978) discusses and explains the persistence of the colonial character of Peruvian society and the state after 1821. A useful general history in English is Frederick B. Pike, *The modern history of Peru* (London, 1967). Heraclio Bonilla, *Un siglo a la deriva* (Lima, 1980, chaps. I and II), and Shane Hunt, *Price and quantum estimates of Peruvian exports 1830–1962* (Princeton, Woodrow Wilson School, Discussion Paper 33, 1973) have suggested the division of the nineteenth century into economic periods, on the basis of the country's export performance.

The years between 1821 and 1840 were decisive in the process of disengagement from the colonial system and in the emergence of a new national order. However, nobody has yet undertaken a general study of this period. Heraclio Bonilla, *Gran Bretaña y el Perú. Los mecanismos de un control económico* (Lima, 1977), examines the conditions and effects of the British presence in post-independence Peru. The unique economic and social characteristics of the Andean region have been dealt with in John F. Wibel, 'The evolution of a regional community within the Spanish empire and the Peruvian nation: Arequipa, 1780–1845' (unpublished Ph.D. thesis, Stanford University, 1975) and Alberto Flores-Galindo, *Arequipa y el Sur Andino, siglos XVIII-XX* (Lima, 1977). Relations between the communities and haciendas and the process of decomposition and recovery within the former during this period are the subject of Christine Hünefeldt, *Lucha por la tierra y protesta indígena* (Bonn, 1982). Two general works on the army and on the Church contain useful information on this period. Víctor Villanueva, *Ejército peruano: del caudillaje anárquico al militarismo reformista* (Lima, 1973) and Jeffrey Klaiber, *Religion and Revolution in Peru, 1824–1976* (Notre Dame, Ind., 1976). On the Peru-Bolivian Confederation, that is to say, the failed attempt to unite the two countries, the following are worth consulting: L. C. Kendall, 'Andrés Santa Cruz and the Peru-Bolivian Confederation', *HAHR*, 16 (1936), 29–48; Robert Burr, *By reason or force. Chile and the balancing of power in South America, 1830–1905* (Berkeley, 1965); Carlos Ortiz de Zevallos Paz Soldán, *Confederación Perú–Boliviana, 1835–1839* (2 vols, Lima, 1972–4).

Jonathan Levin, *The export economies. Their pattern of development in historical perspective* (Cambridge, Mass., 1960), inaugurated the modern debate on the impact of guano on the Peruvian economy. Levin's thesis that the guano boom produced in Peru a typical enclave economy was questioned by Hunt in *Growth and guano in nineteenth century Peru* (Princeton University, Woodrow Wilson School, 1973). On the other hand, William M. Mathew, in 'Anglo-Peruvian commercial and financial relations, 1820–1865' (unpublished Ph.D thesis, University of London, 1964), and in 'Peru and the British guano market, 1840–1870', *Economic History Review*, 2nd series, 23 (1970), has shown, by basing himself on the private papers of Antony Gibbs & Sons, the mechanics by which guano was marketed, and the considerable autonomy enjoyed by the Peruvian government. See also by W. M. Matthew, 'The imperialism of free trade, Peru 1820–1870', *Economic History Review*, 2nd series, 21 (1968); 'The first Anglo-Peruvian debt and its settlement, 1822–49', *JLAS* 2/1 (1970); 'Foreign contractors and the Peruvian government at the outset of the guano trade', *HAHR*, 52/4 (1972); 'A primitive export sector: guano production in mid-nineteenth century Peru', *JLAS*, 9/1 (1977); 'Antony Gibbs & Sons, the guano trade and the Peruvian government 1842–1861', in D. C. M. Platt (ed.), *Business imperialism 1840–1930* (Oxford, 1977); and *The House of Gibbs and the Peruvian guano monopoly* (London, 1981).

The attitude of the ruling class regarding the policy to be pursued with resources from guano, and the process by which the international crisis of 1872 affected Peruvian finances, are themes examined in Juan Maiguashca, 'A reinterpretation of the Guano age, 1840–1880' (unpublished D.Phil. thesis, University of Oxford, 1967). See also R. Miller and R. Greenhill, 'The Peruvian government and the nitrate trade, 1873–1879', *JLAS*, 41 (1973). Heraclio Bonilla *Guano y burguesía en el Perú* (Lima, 1974) examines the collapse of the Peruvian economy during the guano period in terms of the characteristics of the ruling class and the limitations of the internal market. Alfonso Quirós, in 'La consolidación de la deuda interna' (unpublished bachelor's degree dissertation, Universidad Católica de Lima, 1980), has questioned the idea that the 'consolidation of the internal debt', that is to say, the fraudulent payment of guano revenue to large numbers of the state's local creditors, was responsible for the economic recovery of the Peruvian elite. The role of guano in the growth of productive capital for export agriculture has been examined in the following: Pablo Macera, 'Las plantaciones azucareras andinas, 1821–1875', *Trabajos de Historia* (Lima) 4 (1977); Manuel Burga, *De la encomienda a la hacienda capitalista* (Lima, 1976); Juan R. Engelsen, 'Social aspects of agricultural expansion in coastal Peru, 1825–1878' (unpublished Ph.D. thesis, University of California, Los Angeles, 1977). In contrast to the direct links with agriculture on the coast, the agrarian sector of the Andean highlands grew independently of the effects of guano. The reasons for this are analysed in Florencia E. Mallon, *The defense of community in Peru's Central Highlands. Peasant struggle and capitalist transition, 1860–1940* (Princeton, 1982), Nelson Manrique, *El desarrollo del mercado interno en la sierra central* (Lima, 1978), and Martha Giraldo and Ana Lizia Franch, 'Hacienda y gamonalismo, 1850–1920' (unpublished Master's dissertation, Universidad Católica de Lima, 1979). Other changes associated with the overall effects of guano were the mobiliza- tion of capital and the creation of the banking system, the importation of Chinese workers in massive numbers and the construction of the Peruvi- an rail network. On the banks, Carlos Camprubí Alcazar, *Historia de los bancos del Perú, 1860–1879* (Lima, 1957) vol. 1, is still useful. On the Chinese 'coolies', Watt Stewart's pioneer work, *Chinese bondage in Peru. A history of the Chinese coolie in Peru, 1849–1874* (Durham, N.C., 1951), can be supplemented by a more recent, albeit more general study, by Arnold J. Meagher, 'The introduction of Chinese laborers to Latin America: the coolie trade, 1847–1874' (unpublished Ph.D. dissertation, University of California at Davis, 1975). A study of the railways has not yet been undertaken. The only work of any relevance is Watt Stewart's biography of the American contractor who put down the first lines: *Henry Meiggs: a Yankee Pizarro* (Durham, N.C., 1946). It is now well known that guano produced wealth and poverty at the same time. Gigantic price increases in cities like Lima in the early 1870s caused one of the first important mass uprisings. Its composition and objectives are the subject of a careful study by Margarita Giesecke, *Masas urbanas y rebelión en la historia: golpe de estado, Lima 1872* (Lima, 1978).

The demographic history of the period has been largely ignored. Although some important research is being carried out on the whole Cuzco region, the only basic work of reference currently available is George Kubler, *The Indian caste of Peru 1795–1940* (Washington, D.C., 1950).

An interesting discussion of the politics of this period and especially the role of the state can be found in Ronald H. Berg and Frederick Stirton Weaver, 'Towards a reinterpretation of political change in Peru during the first century of independence', *JAIS*, 20/1 (1978), 69–83, and Stephen M. Gorman, 'The state, elite and exports in nineteenth century Peru', *JIAS* 21/3 (1979), 395–418.

Many books of differing quality have been produced on the war with Chile. Henri Favre was the first scholar to draw attention to the need to examine the conflict from a new perspective: 'Remarques sur la lutte des classes au Pérou pendant la Guerre du Pacifique', in *Littérature et société au Pérou du XIX siècle à nos jours* (Grenoble, 1975). The war is also the starting point for analysing problems such as the issue of national identity and the colonial tradition in modern Peru. Heraclio Bonilla, 'The War of the Pacific and the national and colonial problem in Peru', *Past and Present*, 81 (1978), set out the guidelines for a re-examination of both issues. The most important work since then is Nelson Manrique, *Campesinado y nación: la sierra central durante la Guerra del Pacífico* (Lima, 1981).

The bibliography on Bolivian history between 1825 and 1879 is unfortunately still very weak. General works which offer coverage of this period include Herbert S. Klein, *Bolivia. The evolution of a multi-ethnic society* (Oxford, 1982); J. Valerie Fifer, *Bolivia: land, location and politics since 1825* (Cambridge, 1972) and Luis Peñaloza, *Historia económica de Bolivia* (2 vols., La Paz, 1946–7). *Estudios Bolivianos en homenaje a Gunner Mendoza L.* (La Paz, 1978) is an interesting collection of essays on various aspects of Bolivian history.

The transition from colony to republic is the subject of William F. Lofstrom, 'The promise and problem of reform: attempted social and economic change in the first years of Bolivian independence', (unpublished Ph.D. thesis, Cornell University, 1972); Charles Arnade, *The emergence of the Republic of Bolivia* (Gainesville, 1957); and Alberto Crespo *et al.*, *La vida cotidiana en La Paz durante la Guerra de la Independencia* (La Paz, 1975). The state of the country's resources at the time of independence were described in J. B. Pentland, 'Report on Bolivia 1827', ed. J. Valerie Fifer, Royal Historical Society, London, *Camden Miscellany*, 35 (1974). There is a more complete version in Spanish: J. B. Pentland, *Informe sobre Bolivia, 1827* (Potosí, 1975) is a unique and indispensable collection of demographic and economic data on Bolivia in the middle of the nineteenth century. Fernando Cajías, *La provincia de Atacama, 1825–1842* (La Paz, 1975), is a valuable regional study. On the survival of the Indian tribute system, see Nicolás Sánchez-Albornoz, *Indios y tributos en el Alto Perú* (Lima, 1978). The standard work on Santa Cruz, who dominated the political life of Bolivia in the post-independence period, is

Alfonso Crespo, *Santa Cruz, el cóndor indio* (Mexico, 1944). Also see Oscar de Santa Cruz (ed.), *El General Santa Cruz, Gran Mariscal de Zepita y el Gran Perú* (La Paz, 1924). Manuel Carrasco, *José Ballivián, 1805–1852* (Buenos Aires, 1960), is a biography of the third most important of the early presidents (after Sucre and Santa Cruz). An interesting discussion of Bolivian politics in this period can be found in James Dunkerley, 'Reassessing Caudillismo in Bolivia, 1825–79', *Bulletin of Latin American Research*, 1/1 (1981). The complicated relations between Great Britain and Bolivia at this time have been described, in a rather heavy-handed way, by Roberto Querejazu C., *Bolivia y los ingleses* (La Paz, 1973). An important contribution on mining in the nineteenth century has been made by Antonio Mitre in 'Economy and social structure of silver mining in nineteenth century Bolivia' (unpublished Ph.D. thesis, Columbia University, 1977), and *Los patriarcas de La Plata* (Lima, 1981). On the survival of Indian communities in the nineteenth century, Erwin P. Grieshaber, 'Survival of Indian communities in nineteenth century Bolivia' (unpublished Ph.D. thesis, University of North Carolina, 1977), and 'Survival of Indian communities in nineteenth century Bolivia: a regional comparison', *JLAS*, 12/2 (1980), 223–69 are important. A useful monograph on Melgarejo's policies is Luis Antezana, *El feudalismo de Melgarejo y la reforma agraria* (La Paz, 1970). Relations between haciendas and communities in the highlands are examined in an important article by Silvia Rivera C., 'La expansión del latifundio en el altiplano boliviano', *Avances*, 2 (1978), 95–118.

14. CHILE FROM INDEPENDENCE TO THE WAR OF THE PACIFIC

Historical scholarship of the traditional kind in Chile tended to focus less on the post-independence period than on the colonial era and the wars of independence. While recent research has helped to fill some of the gaps in our knowledge, a good deal of basic work (not least on the economic and social side) remains to be done. Simon Collier, 'The historiography of the "Portalian" period in Chile (1830–91)', *HAHR*, 57 (1977), 660–90, provides a general discussion of the literature to the mid-1970s.

The most extensive description of the period as a whole is to be found in Francisco Antonio Encina, *Historia de Chile desde la prehistoria hasta 1891* (20 vols., Santiago, 1942–52), IX–XVII. This huge and idiosyncratically conservative work has not lacked critics. It is instructive, when using it, to consult the relevant passages of Ricardo Donoso's sustained attack, *Francisco A. Encina, simulador* (2 vols., Santiago, 1969–70). The years from independence to 1833 are covered in great detail in Diego Barros Arana, *Historia general de Chile* (16 vols., Santiago, 1884–1902), XI-XVI. Narratives of specific presidencies include Ramón Sotomayor Valdés, *Chile bajo el gobierno del general don Joaquín Prieto* (2nd edn, 4 vols., Santiago, 1900–4), Diego Barros Arana, *Un decenio de la historia de Chile 1841–1851* (2 vols., Santiago, 1905–6), Alberto Edwards, *El gobierno de don Manuel Montt* (Santiago, 1932), and, on the administrations between 1841 and 1876, Agustín Edwards, *Cuatro presidentes de Chile* (2 vols., Valparaiso, 1932). The classic account of the War of the Pacific is Gonzalo Bulnes, *La guerra del Pacífico*, (3 vols., Santiago, 1911–19). Numerous documents on the war were collected soon after it ended, as a gesture of national pride, in Pascual Ahumada Moreno (ed.), *Guerra del Pacífico: recopilación completa de todos los documentos oficiales, correspondencias y demás publicaciones referentes a la guerra* (9 vols., Valparaiso, 1884–90). This apart, there are few printed documentary collections for this period comparable to those available for colonial times and the war of independence. Congressional debates, however, were printed as *Sesiones del Congreso Nacional* from 1846 onwards. Congressional documents (and certain debates) prior to that date have been collected in Valentín Letelier (ed.), *Sesiones de los cuerpos legislativos de la República de Chile, 1811–1845* (37 vols., Santiago, 1887–1908).

On the politics of this period in general, the stimulating essay by Alberto Edwards, *La fronda aristocrática* (7th edn, Santiago, 1972), can be recommended for its many acute insights; the ideological battles of the time have been chronicled by the doyen of mid-twentieth century Chilean historians, Ricardo Donoso, in *Las ideas políticas en Chile* (3rd edn, Buenos Aires, 1975); a promising line of inquiry has been opened up in Gabriel Marcella, 'The structure of politics in nineteenth century Spanish America: the Chilean oligarchy, 1833–1891' (unpublished Ph.D. thesis, Notre Dame University, 1973). Valuable short accounts which extend the discussion into the economic and social field include Sergio Villalobos R., Fernando Silva V., Osvaldo Silva G. and Patricio Estellé M., *Historia de Chile* (4 vols., Santiago, 1974–6), III-IV, written by Sergio Villalobos R. and Fernando Silva V.; Brian Loveman, *Chile, the legacy of Hispanic capitalism* (New York, 1979), 116–96; and Julio César Jobet, *Ensayo crítico del desarrollo económico-social de Chile* (Santiago, 1955), 31–75. Luis Vitale, *Interpretación marxista de la historia de Chile* (3 vols., Santiago,

1967–71), III, offers a further perspective on the period up to 1859.

No satisfactory study fully covers the economic history of nineteenth century Chile, and for reviews of the available literature the reader is directed to Sergio Villalobos R., 'La historiografía económica de Chile: sus comienzos', *Historia* (Santiago), 10 (1971), 7–56, and Carmen Cariola and Osvaldo Sunkel, 'Chile', in Roberto Cortés Conde and Stanley J. Stein (eds.), *Latin America. A guide to economic history 1830–1930* (Berkeley, 1977), 275–363. Markos Mamalakis, *The growth and structure of the Chilean economy* (New Haven, 1976), 3–85, deals with the period 1840–1930 in a single sweep. José Gabriel Palma, 'Growth and structure of Chilean manufacturing industry from 1830 to 1935' (unpublished D.Phil. thesis, Oxford, 1979), contains valuable insight on the economic history of the period. The long-neglected theme of agriculture has been taken up in Arnold J. Bauer's first-class study, *Chilean rural society from the Spanish Conquest to 1930* (Cambridge, 1975), which, despite the title, largely focusses on this period. Landowners' ideas have been examined in Gonzalo Izquierdo, *Un estudio de las ideologías chilenas: La Sociedad de la Agricultura en el siglo XIX* (Santiago, 1968). Much more needs to be known about copper and silver mining, but L. R. Pederson, *The mining industry of the Norte Chico, Chile* (Evanston, Ill., 1966), 160–229, is an excellent introduction. The story of nitrates to the end of the War of the Pacific can be followed in Oscar Bermúdez, *Historia del salitre desde sus orígenes hasta la Guerra del Pacífico* (Santiago, 1963), the classic work, and Thomas F. O'Brien, 'Chilean elites and foreign investors; Chilean nitrate policy 1880–82', *JLAS*, 11/1 (1979), 101–21, and *The Nitrate Industry and Chile's critical transition 1870–1891* (New York, 1982). See also his 'The Antofagasta company: a case study in peripheral capitalism', *HAHR*, 60/1 (1980). Tariff policies in the early part of the period have been examined in John L. Rector, 'Merchants, trade and commercial policy in Chile, 1810–1840' (unpublished Ph.D. thesis, Indiana University, 1976), 88–112, and in the later part in William F. Sater, 'Economic nationalism and tax reform in late nineteenth century Chile', *TA*, 33 (1976), 311–35. The classic work on the ups-and-down of the merchant navy is Claudio Véliz, *Historia de la marina mercante de Chile* (Santiago, 1961). Railway-building and its economic context are well covered in Robert B. Oppenheimer, 'Chilean transportation development: the railroads and socio-economic change in the Central Valley' (unpublished Ph.D. thesis, University of California at Los Angeles, 1976) and, especially good on regional issues, John Whaley, 'Transportation in Chile's Bío-Bío region, 1850–1915' (unpublished Ph.D. thesis, Indiana University, 1974). The best description of monetary problems prior to 1878 is to be found in Pierre Vayssière, 'Au Chili: de l'économie coloniale à l'inflation', *Cahiers des Amériques Latines*, 5 (1970), 5–31. No detailed study of the recession of 1858–61 yet exists, but the more severe crisis of the 1870s is dealt with in William F. Sater, 'Chile and the world depression of the 1870s', *JLAS*, 11/1 (1979), 67–99, and Luis Ortega, 'Change and Crisis in Chile's economy and society, 1865–1879' (unpublished Ph.D. thesis, London University, 1979) which also presents valuable evidence on the topic of industrial growth in this period.

Social history, however broadly defined, has not been well served as yet, and some of the gaps in our knowledge here are huge. Bauer, *Chilean rural society*, contains much valuable information on the rural labouring classes. Artisans and craftsmen up to the 1850s have been studied in Luis Alberto Romero, *La Sociedad de la Igualdad. Los artesanos de Santiago de Chile y sus primeras experiencias políticas* (Instituto Torcuato di Tella, Buenos Aires, 1978). Systematic investigations of the urban lower classes, the mine-workers of the north and the upper class elite itself are urgently required. Jean-Pierre Blancpain, *Les allemands au Chili, 1816–1945* (Cologne, 1974), a magnificent piece of research, provides a fine description of the German settlements in the south after 1850. John Mayo, 'British interests in Chile and their influence, 1851–1886' (unpublished D.Phil. thesis, Oxford University, 1977) examines aspects of the British presence, so important to Chile in this period. See also, his 'Before the nitrate era: British commission houses and the Chilean economy, 1851–80', *JLAS*, 11/2 (1979), 263–303. The decline and fall of the Araucanian Indian enclave is well examined in Jacques Rossignol, 'Chiliens et Indiens Araucans au milieu du XIXe siècle', *Cahiers du Monde Hispanique et Luso-Brésilien*, 20 (1973), 69–98, as well as in the older work of Tomás Guevara, *Historia de la civilización de la Araucanía* (3 vols., Santiago, 1900–2) vol. III of which carries the story through to the 1880s. See also, Leonardo León S., 'Alianzas militares entre los indios araucanos y los grupos indios de las pampas: la rebelión araucana de 1867–1872 en Argentina y Chile', *Nueva Historia*, 1/1 (London, 1981), 3–49.

Urban histories are in general deficient for this period. On Santiago, two works by René León Echaiz, *Historia de Santiago* (2 vols., Santiago, 1975), and *Nuñohue* (Buenos Aires, 1972), the latter dealing with the eastern suburbs, can best be seen as useful introductions, but not much more. The progress of education has been usefully summarized in Fernando Campos Harriet, *Desarrollo educacional 1810–1960* (Santiago, 1960). On the 'uses of history' see Allen Woll, *A functional past. The uses of history in nineteenth century Chile* (Baton Rouge, 1982). There have been no detailed recent investigations of the role of the Catholic Church, and the study of freemasonry has not advanced since the standard account was published: Benjamín Oviedo, *La masonería en Chile* (Santiago, 1929), written from a masonic standpoint. Work on the demographic history of the nineteenth century is still in its infancy, but is likely to develop in the near future: Robert McCaa, 'Chilean social and demographic history: sources, issues and methods', *LARR*, 13/2 (1978), 104–26, gives an intelligent survey of the problems. A good case study is Ann Hagerman Johnson, 'The impact of market agriculture on family and household structure in nineteenth century Chile,' *HAHR*, 58 (1978), 625–48.

Chile's international position and the development of her diplomacy can best be followed in Robert N. Burr, *By reason or force. Chile and the balancing of power in South America, 1830–1905* (Berkeley, 1965), and in the general account, Mario Barros, *Historia diplomática de Chile, 1541–1938* (Barcelona, 1970), 63–440.

The Oficina Central de Estadística was founded as early as 1843, and the government, slightly later on, was assiduous in collecting statistical information, not least in the *Anuario estadístico* published from 1861 onwards. Commercial statistics were published from 1844, as were the censuses of 1854, 1865 and 1875. Statistical material from this period, however, has to be used with critical caution. For a detailed list of Chilean government publications, see Rosa Quintero Mesa (ed.), *Latin American serial documents. No.7, Chile* (New York, 1973). Markos Mamalakis (ed.), 'Historical statistics of Chile, 1840–1965', 4 vols. (Yale University Economic Growth Centre, mimeo) provides useful material.

In addition to the standard bibliographical aids, two Chilean sources deserve to be indicated here. The publications of the period itself are systematically listed in Ramón Briseño (ed.), *Estadística bibliográfica de la literatura chilena* (3 vols., Santiago, 1965–6). Briseño's original two volumes were published in 1862 and 1879. Vol. III contains additions and amendments by Raúl Silva Castro. Invaluable work has lately been done by the journal *Historia* (Santiago) in keeping a detailed record of all materials published on Chilean history in recent years. These are listed in the journal's regular 'Fichero bibliográfico'. The first such bibliographies were reprinted in Horacio Aránguiz Donoso (ed.), *Bibliografía histórica (1959–1967)* (Santiago, 1970). Subsequent 'ficheros' have been published in *Historia*, 10 (1971), 11 (1972–3), 12 (1974–5), 13 (1976) and 14 (1979).

15. THE RIVER PLATE REPUBLICS FROM INDEPENDENCE TO THE PARAGUAYAN WAR

The bibliography of nineteenth-century Argentina can be approached through Joseph R. Barager, 'The historiography of the Río de la Plata area since 1930', *HAHR*, 39 (1959), 588–642, and James R. Scobie, *Argentina. A city and a nation* (New York, 1964), 248–74. A more specialist work is Julio O. Chiappini, *Bibliografía sobre Rosas* (Rosario, 1973).

Public documents are reproduced in a number of collections. The formal policy reviews of the executive are given in H. Mabragaña, *Los Mensajes, 1810–1910* (6 vols., Buenos Aires, 1910); for the governors of Buenos Aires a better version is provided by Archivo Histórico de la Provincia de Buenos Aires, *Mensajes de los gobernadores de la provincia de Buenos Aires 1822–1849* (2 vols., La Plata, 1976). Basic legislative, constitutional and inter-provincial texts are to be found in Emilio Ravignani (ed.), *Asambleas constituyentes argentinas* (6 vols., Buenos Aires, 1937–9). The main documentation concerning Rosas is that of Adolfo Saldías (ed.), *Papeles de Rosas* (2 vols., La Plata, 1904–7), which can be supplemented by two convenient compilations of his thought and policy, Andrés M. Carretero, *El pensamiento político de Juan M. de Rosas* (Buenos Aires, 1970) and Arturo Enrique Sampay, *Las ideas políticas de Juan Manuel de Rosas* (Buenos Aires, 1972). Aspects of the opposition to Rosas are documented in Gregorio F. Rodríguez (ed.), *Contribución histórica y documental* (3 vols., Buenos Aires, 1921–2), and Archivo Histórico de la Provincia de Buenos Aires, *La campaña libertadora del general Lavalle (1838–1842)* (La Plata, 1944). Amidst other and smaller collections the monumental writings of Argentina's three most eminent figures of politics and letters stand out, beginning with Juan B. Alberdi, *Obras completas* (8 vols., Buenos Aires, 1876–86) and *Escritos póstumos* (16 vols., Buenos Aires, 1895–1901). Bartolomé Mitre, *Archivo del General Mitre: documentos y correspondencia* (28 vols., Buenos Aires, 1911–14), can be supplemented by *Correspondencia literaria, histórica y política del General Bartolomé Mitre* (3 vols., Buenos Aires, 1912) and *Correspondencia Mitre–Elizalde* (*Documentos para la historia argentina*, 26, Buenos Aires, 1960).

Domingo F. Sarmiento, *Obras completas* (52 vols., Santiago, 1887–1902), is an indispensable source for Argentine history, together with *Sarmiento–Mitre: correspondencia, 1846–1868* (Buenos Aires, 1911), *Facundo* (La Plata, 1938), and *Epistolario entre Sarmiento y Posse, 1845–1888* (2 vols., Buenos Aires, 1946–7).

The subject is rich in narrative sources, and the following is no more than a brief selection. Sir Woodbine Parish, *Buenos Ayres and the Provinces of the Río de la Plata* (2nd edn, London, 1852), a work first published in 1838, is an objective and scholarly account by the former British chargé d'affaires. William MacCann, *Two thousand miles' ride through the Argentine provinces* (2 vols., London, 1853), brings the economy and the people of the pampas to life. One of the first approaches to quantification is provided by Victor Martin de Moussy, *Description géographique et statistique de la Confédération Argentine* (3 vols., Paris, 1860–4). Thomas Joseph Hutchinson, *Buenos Ayres and Argentine gleanings* (London, 1865), is a less accurate account, by the British consul at Rosario, but takes the story to 1862–3. Wilfred Latham, *The States of the River Plate* (2nd edn, London, 1868), is an amplified version of a book first published in 1866 and written from the author's 'home in the campo', a large sheep farm.

General histories are headed by the Academia Nacional de la Historia, *Historia de la nación Argentina* (2nd edn, 10 vols., Buenos Aires, 1939–50), with its sequel, *Historia argentina contemporánea, 1862–1930* (Buenos Aires, 1963–). These are composite works, uneven in quality. Tulio Halperín Donghi, *Argentina: de la revolución de independencia a la confederación rosista* (Buenos Aires, 1972) is analytically superior, as is his masterly essay introducing *Proyecto y construcción de una nación (Argentina 1846–1880)* (Caracas, 1980), a selection of texts from major writers of Argentina's age of nation-building. Haydée Gorostegui de Torres, *Argentina: la organización nacional* (Buenos Aires, 1972), gives a balanced account of the period 1852–74.

Study of the economy can begin with Jonathan C. Brown, *A socioeconomic history of Argentina, 1776–1860* (Cambridge, 1979), which combines synthesis, original research and a sense of chronology. Miron Burgin, *The economic aspects of Argentine federalism 1820–1852* (Cambridge, Mass., 1946), is still unsurpassed for data and interpretation. Juan Carlos Nicolau, *Rosas y García (1829–35). La economía bonaerense* (Buenos Aires, 1980), concentrates on financial and fiscal policy. The basic institutional account of landowning is Miguel A. Cárcano, *Evolución histórica del régimen de la tierra pública, 1810–1916* (3rd edn, Buenos Aires, 1972), first published in 1917. The land policy of Rivadavia is identified by Emilio A. Coni, *La verdad sobre la enfiteusis de Rivadavia* (Buenos Aires, 1927). Further details on land acquisition and concentration are provided by Jacinto Oddone, *La burguesía terrateniente argentina* (3rd edn, Buenos Aires, 1956), but for more accurate data see Andrés M. Carretero, 'Contribución al conocimiento de la propiedad rural en la provincia de Buenos Aires para 1830', *Boletín del Instituto de Historia Argentina 'Doctor Emilio Ravignani'*, 2nd series, 13/22–23 (1970), 246–92, and *La propiedad de la tierra en la época de Rosas* (Buenos Aires, 1972). Cattle-raising can be studied in Horacio C. E. Giberti, *Historia económica de la ganadería argentina* (Buenos Aires, 1961), and the processing plants in Alfredo J. Montoya, *Historia de los saladeros argentinos* (Buenos Aires, 1956) and *La ganadería y la industria de salazón de carnes en el período 1810–1862* (Buenos Aires, 1971). Aspects of early industrial developments are covered in José M. Mariluz Urquijo, *Estado e industria 1810–1862* (Buenos Aires, 1969), a collection of texts; Juan Carlos Nicolau, *Antecedentes para la historia de la industria argentina* (Buenos Aires, 1968), and *Industria argentina y aduana, 1835–1854* (Buenos Aires, 1975); and Clifton Kroeber, *The growth of the shipping industry in the Río de la Plata region, 1794–1860* (Madison, 1957). Foreign trade and its participants are studied in a useful article and two important books: Juan Carlos Nicolau; 'Movimiento marítimo exterior del puerto de Buenos Aires (1810–1854)', *Nuestra Historia*, 12 (1973), 351–61; H. S. Ferns, *Britain and Argentina in the nineteenth century* (Oxford, 1960); Vera Bliss Reber, *British merchant houses in Buenos Aires, 1810–1880* (Cambridge, Mass., 1979). For the wool cycle and the economy in transition, see José Carlos Chiaramonte, *Nacionalismo y liberalismo económicos en la Argentina 1860–1880* (Buenos Aires, 1971), and the now classic H. Gibson, *The history and present state of the sheepbreeding industry in the Argentine Republic* (Buenos Aires, 1893).

Society in its demographic aspect is well described by Ernesto J. A. Maeder, *Evolución demográfica argentina de 1810 a 1869* (Buenos Aires, 1969), while for a shorter period population change is measured by Susana R. Frías, César A. García Belsunce, *et al.*, *Buenos Aires: su gente, 1800–1830* (Buenos Aires, 1976), based on censuses of the city of Buenos Aires. These should be supplemented by George Reid Andrews, *The Afro-Argentines of Buenos Aires, 1800–1900* (Madison, 1980). On immigration, see Juan Antonio Oddone, *La emigración europea al Río de la Plata* (Montevideo, 1966). New research on the life and labour of the Irish is provided by Juan Carlos Korol and Hilda Sabato, *Cómo fue la inmigración irlandesa en la Argentina* (Buenos Aires, 1981). The most powerful social group is studied by María Sáenz Quesada, *Los estancieros* (Buenos Aires, 1980). Gauchos, peons and vagrants are placed in their historical context by Gastón Gori, *Vagos y mal entretenidos* (2nd edn, Santa Fe, 1965), and Ricardo Rodríguez Molas, *Historia social del gaucho* (Buenos Aires, 1968). Rubén H. Zorrilla, *Extracción social de los caudillos 1810–1870* (Buenos Aires, 1972), discusses the social base of *caudillismo*.

Political history can be divided into three periods, comprising Rivadavia, Rosas and national organization. On the first, Ricardo Piccirilli, *Rivadavia y su tiempo* (2nd edn, 3 vols., Buenos Aires, 1960) is a work of scholarship, and Sergio Bagú, *El plan económico del grupo Rivadaviano 1811–1827* (Rosario, 1966) a cogent interpretation with documents. The enormous bibliography on Rosas is a hindrance rather than a help to understanding. Adolfo Saldías, *Historia de la Confederación Argentina: Rosas y su época* (Buenos Aires, 9 vols., 1958), a work first published in 1881–87 from official Rosas sources, is a useful chronicle of events. Roberto Etchepareborda, *Rosas; controvertida historiografía* (Buenos Aires, 1972), is a modern survey of the 'problems'. Enrique M. Barba, *Cómo llegó Rosas al poder* (Buenos Aires, 1972), explains the conquest of power. Among the *rosista* historians, Carlos Ibarguren, *Juan Manuel de Rosas, su vida, su drama, su tiempo* (Buenos Aires, 1961), first published in 1930, provides a well-documented political biography; and Julio Irazusta, *Vida política de Juan Manuel de Rosas, a través de su correspondencia* (2nd edn, 8 vols., Buenos Aires, 1970), supplies much detail and documentation. Ernesto H. Celesia, *Rosas, aportes para su historia* (2nd edn, 2 vols., Buenos Aires, 1968), is hostile but well researched. Benito Díaz, *Juzgados de paz de campaña de la provincia de Buenos Aires (1821–1854)* (La Plata, 1959), studies a vital agency of the regime. On the foreign blockades and other forms of intervention, see John F. Cady, *Foreign intervention in the Río de la Plata 1838–50* (Philadelphia, 1929), and Nestor S. Colli, *La política francesa en el Río de la Plata: Rosas y el bloqueo de 1838–1840* (Buenos Aires, 1963), as well as the work by Ferns already cited. The international context of the fall of Rosas is explored by the *rosista* historian José María Rosa, *La caída de Rosas: el Imperio de Brasil y la Confederación Argentina (1843–1851)* (2nd edn, Buenos Aires, 1968). For a recent history of Rosas, his power base and his policy, see John Lynch, *Argentine dictator: Juan Manuel de Rosas 1829–1852* (Oxford, 1981).

In the period of national organization the transitional figure is Urquiza: see Beatriz Bosch, *Urquiza y su tiempo* (Buenos Aires, 1971).

Older accounts of the decade after Rosas are now superseded by James R. Scobie, *La lucha por la consolidación de la nacionalidad argentina, 1852–1862* (Buenos Aires, 1964). The great constitutional statesmen have attracted a number of biographies, of which Jorge M. Mayer, *Alberdi y su tiempo* (Buenos Aires, 1963) is outstanding. Sarmiento receives scholarly attention from Ricardo Rojas, *El profeta de la pampa: vida de Sarmiento* (Buenos Aires, 1945), and José S. Campobassi, *Sarmiento y su época* (2 vols., Buenos Aires, 1975).

The history of Uruguay in the nineteenth century has an established framework of political narrative and documentation in Eduardo Acevedo, *Anales históricos del Uruguay*, vols. 2 and 3 (Montevideo, 1933), which should be supplemented for the mid-century by Juan E. Pivel Devoto, *El fin de la Guerra Grande* (Montevideo, 1953). An excellent analysis of economy, society and politics is provided by José Pedro Barrán, *Apogeo y crisis del Uruguay pastoral y caudillesco 1838–1875* (Historia Uruguaya, 4, Montevideo, 1974). On the rural structure, see José Pedro Barrán and Benjamín Nahum, *Historia rural del Uruguay moderno. Tomo 1 (1851–1967)* (Montevideo, 1967), a work of basic scholarship. Juan Antonio Oddone, *Economía y sociedad en el Uruguay liberal 1852–1904. Antología de textos* (Montevideo, 1967), is a collection of documents preceded by a valuable introduction. For an analysis of the social structure see Carlos M. Rama, *Historia social del pueblo uruguayo* (Montevideo, 1972).

The best approach to understanding the history of Paraguay in the nineteenth century is provided by John Hoyt Williams, *The rise and fall of the Paraguayan Republic, 1800–1870* (Austin, 1979), a work of research and interpretation. Richard Alan White, *Paraguay's autonomous revolution 1810–1840* (Albuquerque, N.M., 1978), takes a new, though partial, look at Francia. For a Paraguayan view, see Julio César Chaves, *El supremo dictador. Biografía de José Gaspar de Francia* (4th edn, Madrid, 1964). The same author has written the history of Francia's successor, *El Presidente López. Vida y gobierno de Don Carlos* (2nd edn, Buenos Aires, 1968); see also Juan F. Pérez Acosta, *Don Carlos Antonio López, 'Obrero Máximo'* (Buenos Aires, 1948). For the demographic and developmental history of the period, see John Hoyt Williams, 'Observations on the Paraguayan Census of 1846', *HAHR*, 56 (1976), 424–37, and 'Foreign Técnicos and the modernization of Paraguay, 1840–1870', *Journal of Interamerican Studies and World Affairs*, 19/2 (1977), 233–57. The latter subject is explored in further detail by Josefina Pla, *The British in Paraguay (1850–*

70) (London, 1976). On the Paraguayan War, Pelham Horton Box, *The origins of the Paraguayan War* (Urbana, Ill., 1929) is still worth reading, but should be supplemented by Efraím Cardozo, *Vísperas de la guerra del Paraguay* (Buenos Aires, 1954) and *El Imperio del Brasil y el Río de la Plata* (Buenos Aires, 1962). The same author's *Hace cien años* (8 vols., Asunción, 1967–72), is a useful chronicle of events based on contemporary Paraguayan newspapers. For a history of the war in English see Charles Kolinski, *Independence or death. The story of the Paraguayan War* (Gainesville, Florida, 1965), though Ramón J. Cárcano, *Guerra del Paraguay* (3 vols., Buenos Aires, 1938–40), still has value as a work of reference. There is an expert survey of Paraguayan bibliography by John Hoyt Williams, 'Paraguayan historical resources. Part Four. A selective Paraguayan historiography', *TA*, 34 (1978), 1–20.

16. BRAZIL FROM INDEPENDENCE TO THE MIDDLE OF THE NINETEENTH CENTURY

Two volumes of the *História geral da civilização brasileira* (ed. Sérgio Buarque de Holanda) cover the period 1822–48: Tomo II, *O Brasil monárquico*: Vol. 1, *O processo de emancipação* (São Paulo, 1962) and vol. 2, *Dispersão e Unidade* (São Paulo, 1964). The only general history in English, sensible and well organized, but somewhat superficial and now out of date, is C. H. Haring, *Empire in Brazil. A New World experiment with monarchy* (Cambridge, Mass., 1958). Still valuable is Stanley J. Stein, 'The historiography of Brazil, 1808–1889', *HAHR*, 40/2 (1960), 234–78. For the period 1822–31 Tobias do Rego Monteiro, *História do império: O primeiro reinado* (Rio de Janeiro, 1939), remains the most detailed account of political events. An indispensable contemporary account is John Armitage, *History of Brazil from the arrival of the Braganza family in 1808 to the abdication of Dom Pedro the first in 1831* (2 vols., London, 1836). Other important nineteenth-century accounts include João Manuel Pereira da Silva, *História do Brasil de 1831 a 1840* (Rio de Janeiro, 1878), Manuel Duarte Moreira de Azevedo, *História Pátria: O Brasil de 1831 a 1840* (Rio de Janeiro, 1884) and Heinrich Handelmann, *Geschichte von Brasilien* (Berlin, 1860; Portuguese translation, *História do Brasil*, Rio de Janeiro, 1931).

Nícia Vilela Luz, 'Brazil' in Stanley J. Stein and Roberto Cortés Conde (eds.), *Latin America. A guide to economic history, 1830–1930* (Berkeley, 1977), 163–272 is a useful guide to the secondary literature on Brazilian economic history. There are two general economic histories of Brazil, both now classics, which touch on this period: Caio Prado Júnior, *História econômica do Brasil* (6th edn, São Paulo, 1959), and Celso Furtado, *Formação econômica do Brasil* (Rio de Janeiro, 1959): English translation, *The economic growth of Brazil. A survey from colonial to modern times* (Berkeley, 1963). The most comprehensive (and provocative) recent study of Brazil's economic history after independence is Nathaniel H. Leff, *Underdevelopment and development in Brazil*, Vol. I, *Economic structures and change 1822–1947*; Vol. II, *Reassessing the obstacles to economic development* (London, 1982). On the beginnings of the coffee boom, see Stanley J. Stein, *Vassouras. A Brazilian coffee county, 1850–1900* (Cambridge, Mass., 1957), Warren Dean, *Rio Claro. A Brazilian plantation system, 1820–1920* (Stanford, 1976), and, still useful, Affonso d'Escragnolle Taunay, *História do café* (15 vols., Rio de Janeiro, 1939–43). On sugar, see Maria Teresa Schorer Petrone, *A Lavoura Canavieira em São Paulo: expansão e declínio, 1765–1861* (São Paulo, 1968), and Peter L. Eisenberg, *The sugar industry in Pernambuco: modernisation without change, 1840–1910* (Berkeley, 1974). For two different views on the impact made by British imperial preference, especially the sugar duties, on Brazilian economic development or underdevelopment, see Paulo Nogueira Batista, Jr, 'Política tarifária britânica e evolução das exportações brasileiras na primeira metade do século XIX', *Revista Brasileira de Economia* (34/2 (1980), 203–39, and Roberta M. Delson, 'Sugar production for the nineteenth century British market: rethinking the roles of Brazil and the British West Indies', in A. Graves and B. Albert (eds.), *Crisis and change in the international sugar economy, 1860–1914* (forthcoming). The outstanding work on Anglo-Brazilian commercial and financial (as well as diplomatic and political) relations in the first half of the nineteenth century is Alan K. Manchester, *British preeminence in Brazil. Its rise and decline* (Durham, N.C., 1933). Brazil's failure to industrialize in the period after independence is examined in the early chapters of Nícia Vilela Luz, *A luta pela industrialização no Brasil* (São Paulo, 1961). On the financial history of the period, see Carlos Manuel Pelaez and Wilson Suzigan, *História monetária do Brasil* (Rio de Janeiro, 1976). On government income and expenditure in particular, Liberato de Castro Carreira, *O orçamento do império desde a sua fundação* (Rio de Janeiro, 1883), and *História financeira e orçamentária do império do Brasil* (Rio de Janeiro, 1889) remains indispensable. See also Amaro Cavalcanti, *Resenha financeira do ex-império do Brasil em 1889* (Rio de Janeiro, 1890). A recent monograph which breaks new ground by examining internal trade, and in particular the organization of Rio de

Janeiro's food supply, is Alcir Lenharo, *As tropas da moderação (O abastecimento da Corte na formação política do Brasil, 1808–1842)* (São Paulo, 1979).

The most wide-ranging study of the political system of the empire is José Murilo de Carvalho's Ph.D. thesis, 'Elite and state building in imperial Brazil' (Stanford University, 1974). The first part, revised and expanded, has been published in *A construção da ordem. A elite política imperial* (Rio de Janeiro, 1980). See also his article, 'Political elites and state building: the case of nineteenth century Brazil', *Comparative Studies in Society and History*, 24/3 (1982). Two other important recent contributions are Fernando Uricoechea, *The patrimonial foundations of the Brazilian bureaucratic state* (Berkeley, 1980) which examines in particular the National Guard, and Thomas Flory, *Judge and jury in imperial Brazil, 1808–1871. Social control and political stability in the new state* (Austin, Texas, 1981), which examines the political and administrative role of the judges. On the National Guard, see also Jeanne Berrance de Castro, *A milícia cidadã: a Guarda Nacional de 1831 a 1850* (São Paulo, 1977). There is no study of the army in this period, but see the early chapters of John H. Schulz, 'The Brazilian army in politics, 1850–1894', (unpublished Ph.D. thesis, Princeton University, 1973). João Camilo de Oliveira Torres, *A democracia coroada (teoria política do império do Brasil)* (Rio de Janeiro, 1957) remains valuable for the political history of the empire. Indispensable as a reference work is *Organizações e programas ministeriais. Regime parlamentar no império* (2nd edn, Arquivo Nacional, Rio de Janeiro, 1962). The electoral legislation of the period can be found in Francisco Belisário Soares de Souza, *O sistema eleitoral no império* (1892: Brasília, Senado Federal, 1979). Also useful are José Honório Rodrigues (ed.), *O Parlamento e a evolução nacional* (8 vols., Senado Federal, Brasília, 1972), which covers the period 1826–40, José Honório Rodrigues (ed.), *Atas do Conselho de Estado* (14 vols., Senado Federal, Brasília, 1973) and Tavares de Lyra, *Instituições políticas do Império* (Senado Federal, Brasília, 1979).

There are a number of biographies of leading politicians in this period, notably those written by Octávio Tarquínio de Sousa: *José Bonifácio* (Rio de Janeiro, 1945), *A vida de D. Pedro I* (3 vols., Rio de Janeiro, 1952), *Bernardo Pereira de Vasconcelos e seu tempo* (Rio de Janeiro, 1937), *Evaristo da Veiga* (São Paulo, 1939) and *Diogo Antônio Feijó (1784–1843)* (Rio de Janeiro, 1942), republished as vols. 1–7 of *História dos fundadores do Império do Brasil* (10 vols., Rio de Janeiro, 1957–8).

An excellent well-documented recent study of the political mobilization at the beginning of the regency is Augustin Wernet, *Sociedades políticas (1831–1832)* (São Paulo, 1978).

On the provincial revolts of the 1830s and 1840s, besides the various regional histories in the *História geral da civilização brasileira*, II, 2, and chapters 3 and 4 of Caio Prado Júnior, *Evolução política do Brasil* (São Paulo, 1933), a number of works deserve mention. The best available study of the War of the Cabanos is Manuel Correira de Andrade, *A Guerra dos Cabanos* (Rio de Janeiro, 1965) which is partly summarized in 'The social and ethnic significance of the War of the Cabanos', in Ronald H. Chilcote (ed.), *Protest and resistance in Angola and Brazil: comparative studies* (Berkeley, 1972). A recent study by Dirceu Lindoso, *A utópia armada. Rebeliões de pobres nas Matas do Tombo Real* (Rio de Janeiro, 1983), emphasizes the ideological and cultural aspects of the war. See also, Manuel Correia de Andrade, *Movimentos Nativistas em Pernambuco: Setembrizada e Novembrada* (Recife, 1971), for the smaller rebellions in Pernambuco during the regency. Astolfo Serra, *A Balaiada* (Rio de Janeiro, 1946), and Luiz Vianna Filho, *A Sabinada (A República Bahiana de 1837)* (Rio de Janeiro, 1938), remain the best studies of these movements. On the Sabinada, see also F. W. O. Morton, 'The Conservative revolution of independence: economy, society and politics in Bahia, 1790–1840' (unpublished D.Phil. thesis, Oxford, 1974, ch. XI). Although very disorganized, Domingos Antonio Rayol, *Motins políticos ou história dos principais acontecimentos políticos da Província do Pará desde o ano de 1821 até 1835* (3 vols., Belém, 1970), is still the best study of the Cabanagem. The best-documented study of the Farroupilha is Alfredo Varela, *História da Grande Revolução* (6 vols., Porto Alegre, 1925). Walter Spalding, *A revolução Farroupilha. História popular do Grande Decênio* (São Paulo, 1939), is also valuable. A recent study which emphasizes the economic roots of the rebellion is Spencer L. Leitman, 'Socio-economic roots of the Ragamuffin War: a chapter in early Brazilian history' (unpublished Ph.D. thesis, University of Texas at Austin, 1972), published as *Raízes sócio-econômicas da Guerra dos Farrapos* (Rio de Janeiro, 1979). The only recent work on the liberal revolts in Minas Gerais and São Paulo is Victor M. Filler, 'Liberalism in imperial Brazil: the regional rebellions of 1842' (unpublished Ph.D. thesis, Stanford University, 1976). For the view of a participant, see José Antônio Marinho, *História do movimento político que no ano de 1842 teve lugar na província de Minas Gerais* (Conselheiro Lafaiete, 1939). Apart from the Farroupilha, the Praieira is the best studied rebellion of the period. There are two important recent studies: Izabel

Andrade Marson, *Movimento Praieiro, 1842–1849; imprensa, ideologia e poder político* (São Paulo, 1980), which stresses ideology, and Nancy Priscilla Naro, 'The 1848 Praieira revolt in Brazil' (unpublished Ph.D. thesis, University of Chicago, 1981), which examines the political and economic aspects of the revolt.

Useful information on the population of Brazil (as well as on slavery and immigration) in the decades after independence can be found in T. W. Merrick and D. Graham, *Population and economic development in Brazil, 1808 to the present* (Baltimore, 1979). See also Maria Luiza Marcílio, 'Evolução da população brasileira através dos censos até 1872', *Anais de História* 6 (1974), 115–37. The best study of immigration before the beginnings of mass European immigration is George P. Browne, 'Government immigration policy in imperial Brazil 1822–1870' (unpublished Ph.D. thesis, Catholic University of America, 1972). A critical view of Senator Vergueiro's free labour policies by a German-Swiss *colono*, which tells us much about rural São Paulo in the middle of the nineteenth century, is Thomas Davatz, *Memórias de um colono no Brasil (1850)*, edited with an introduction by Sérgio Buarque de Holanda (São Paulo, 1941). Land policy, and especially the origins of the law of 1850, is examined in Warren Dean, 'Latifundia and land policy in nineteenth century Brazil', *HAHR* 51/4 (1971), 606–25; José Murilo de Carvalho, 'A modernização frustrada: a política de terras no Império', *Revista Brasileira de História*, 1/1 (1981), and Emília Viotti da Costa, 'Política de Terras no Brasil e nos Estados Unidos' in *Da Monarquia à república: momentos decisivos* (São Paulo, 1977). More generally, Ruy Cirne Lima, *Pequena História Territorial do Brasil. Sesmarias e Terras Devolutas* (Porto Alegre, 1954), remains useful. On urban growth in this period, see the works by Richard Morse, Emília Viotti da Costa, Eulália Maria Lahmeyer Lobo and Kátia M. de Queirós Mattoso cited in bibliographical essay 17. The bibliography on slavery in nineteenth-century Brazil is also discussed in bibliographical essay 17. In addition there is an unpublished Ph.D. thesis on urban slavery in Rio de Janeiro during the first half of the century: Mary C. Karasch, 'Slave life in Rio de Janeiro, 1808–50' (University of Wisconsin, 1971). Another important Ph.D. thesis is João José Reis, 'Slave rebellion in Brazil. The African Muslim uprising in Bahia, 1835' (University of Minnesota, 1983). The slave trade question in Anglo-Brazilian relations and the final abolition of the slave trade in 1850–1 are thoroughly examined in Leslie Bethell, *The abolition of the Brazilian slave trade. Britain, Brazil and the slave trade question, 1807–1869* (Cambridge,

1970). The best diplomatic history of the period is still João Pandiá Calógeras, *A política externa do império* (3 vols., São Paulo, 1927–33), vol. II, *O primeiro reinado*, vol. III, *Da regência à queda de Rosas*.

An important source for the social history of Brazil in the period after independence are the accounts of the many European travellers, scientists and artists who visited the country: for example, Maria Graham, Auguste de Saint-Hilaire, Jean Baptiste Debret, Johann-Moritz Rugendas, Alcide d'Orbigny. They are listed in Bernard Naylor, *Accounts of nineteenth century South America* (London, 1969). See also Gilberto Freyre, *Sobrados e mucambos. Decadência do patriarcado rural e desenvolvimento do urbano* (2nd edn, 3 vols., Rio de Janeiro, 1951; English translation *The mansions and the shanties: the making of modern Brazil* (New York, 1963)), a continuation into the nineteenth century of his more famous *The masters and the slaves*; and his 'Social life in Brazil in the middle of the nineteenth century', *HAHR*, 5/4 (1922), 597–630. A pioneer work which makes good use of judicial records is Patricia Ann Aufderheide, 'Order and violence: Social deviance and social control in Brazil, 1780–1840' (unpublished Ph.D. thesis, University of Minnesota, 1976).

17. BRAZIL FROM THE MIDDLE OF THE NINETEENTH CENTURY TO THE PARAGUAYAN WAR

Rubens Borba de Moraes and William Berrien (eds.), *Manual bibliográfico de estudos brasileiros* (Rio de Janeiro, 1949) is essential; although uneven in its coverage, its annotated entries and historiographical essays provide a base from which the historian can build using the *Handbook of Latin American Studies*. Still useful is Stanley J. Stein, 'The historiography of Brazil, 1808–1889', *HAHR*, 40/2 (1960), 234–78. Among aids for the researcher on mid-nineteenth-century Brazil, Cândido Mendes de Almeida's splendid *Atlas do império do Brasil* (Rio de Janeiro, 1868) deserves special mention.

Two broad interpretive studies of Brazilian history that give prominent attention to the social and political circumstances of mid-century are Raymundo Faoro, *Os donos do poder* (2nd edn, Porto Alegre and São Paulo, 1975), and Florestan Fernandes, *A revolução burguesa no Brasil* (Rio de Janeiro, 1975). Both are concerned to trace the connection between social structure and political institutions and events. Both are heavily influenced by Weberian typologies, although Fernandes also includes a certain amount of Marxist thought in his scheme. Less ambitious and more mechanically Marxist is Nelson Werneck Sodré, *História da burguesia brasileira* (Rio de Janeiro, 1964). Caio Prado Júnior's *História econômica do Brasil* (5th edn, São Paulo, 1959), is not so rigid as is Sodré in the economic interpretation of society and politics.

The first historian of the empire, who still exerts great influence on our understanding of the period, was Joaquim Nabuco whose biography of his father, *Um estadista do império* (2 vols., 2nd edn, São Paulo and Rio de Janeiro, 1936), first published in 1897–1900, dealt chronologically with politicians and political events without neglecting the larger social setting within which they acted. Nabuco's conservative, pro-imperial point of view can be contrasted with the critical stance adopted in 1909 by Euclides da Cunha in *À margem da história* (2nd edn, Oporto, 1913); da Cunha felt much more clearly than Nabuco the empire's failure to change. A defence of the empire that plays down the role of the emperor and stresses the responsiveness of the system to the shifting tempers of social and economic elites is José Maria dos Santos, *A política geral do Brasil* (São Paulo, 1930).

Another political history, this one built around the theme of legislation regarding slavery and the slave trade, is Paula Beiguelman's *Formação política do Brasil*, I: *Teoria e ação no pensamento abolicionista* (São Paulo, 1967). C. H. Haring prepared the only chronological account of the entire period in English, *Empire in Brazil* (Cambridge, Mass., 1958). Based as it was on his reading of standard works up to that time, it can be used to measure the changes in the understanding of the empire during the next ten to fifteen years, when contrasted with the various essays in Sérgio Buarque de Holanda (ed.), *História geral da civilização brasileira*, Tomo II: *O Brasil monárquico*, vols. 3, 4 and 5 (São Paulo, 1967–1972).

Two Brazilian scholars – one a political scientist, the other a sociologist – have produced impressively detailed studies of political life in nineteenth-century Brazil: José Murilo de Carvalho used biographical dictionaries and some other printed sources to construct a composite picture of the political elite in his *A construção da ordem* (Rio de Janeiro, 1980) – a translation of the first part of his unpublished doctoral thesis, 'Elite and state building in imperial Brazil' (Stanford University, 1974); Fernando Uricoechea went to the manuscript sources to explore the values and social relationships displayed in the life of the National Guard in his *The patrimonial foundations of the Brazilian bureaucratic state* (Berkeley, 1980). A less sophisticated, but nevertheless still useful, description of political institutions during the empire is João Camilo de Oliveira Torres, *A democracia coroada* (Rio de Janeiro, 1957). His conservative, pro-monarchical point of view is also found in Affonso d'Escragnolle Taunay's two studies of members of the houses of parliament: *O senado do império* (São Paulo, 1942) and 'A Câmara dos Deputados sob o império', *Anais do Museu Paulista*, 14 (1950), 1–252. The Council of State – part legislature, part court – has been ably studied by José Honório Rodrigues in *O Conselho de Estado: o quinto poder?* (Senado Federal, Brasília, 1978). Although most of Thomas Flory's *Judge and jury in imperial Brazil* (Austin, Texas, 1981) deals with the period before 1850, the final chapter (pp. 181–200) is a fine discussion of changes in the place of magistrates within the social, political and ideological system of Brazil to 1871. Also provocative is Eul-Soo Pang and Ron L. Seckinger's 'The Mandarins of Imperial Brazil', *Comparative Studies in Society and History*, 14/2 (1972), 215–44. There has been no significant study of the provincial presidents who so importantly shaped the course of the empire's political history, and the only study of elections was first published in 1872: Francisco Belisário Soares de Souza, *O sistema eleitoral no império* (2nd edn, Senado Federal, Brasília, 1979).

Of the many biographies of the Emperor Pedro II the best remains Heitor Lyra's *História de Dom Pedro II, 1825–1891* (2nd rev. edn, 3 vols., Belo Horizonte and São Paulo, 1977). Mary W. Williams presented a romanticized account in her *Dom Pedro the Magnanimous* (Chapel Hill, 1937). Of the triumvirate – Eusébio, Itaboraí and Uruguai – who defined what we could call the far right at mid-century, only the last has received a worthy biography: José Antônio Soares de Souza, *A vida do visconde do Uruguai (1807–1866) (Paulino José Soares de Souza)* (São Paulo, 1944). The more creative conservatives at the centre-right – Rio Branco and Cotegipe – have been more fortunate: see, for example, José Wanderley Pinho, *Cotegipe e seu tempo: primeira phase, 1815–1867* (São Paulo, 1937), which was unfortunately not continued by the author; José Maria da Silva Paranhos, 2nd baron Rio Branco, *O visconde do Rio Branco* (2nd edn, Rio de Janeiro, 1943); and, more interestingly interpretive, Lídia Besouchet, *José Ma. Paranhos, visconde do Rio Branco. Ensaio histórico-biográfico* (Rio de Janeiro, 1945). At the centre-left stood Nabuco de Araújo, whose biography by his son Joaquim Nabuco was mentioned earlier. Teófilo Ottoni defended the most reformist measures of the period; see Paulo Pinheiro Chagas, *Teófilo Ottoni, ministro do povo* (2nd rev. edn, Rio de Janeiro, 1956).

Alongside the debates in parliament, pamphlets formed the central pieces of political discourse in the nineteenth century. Many of these have been reprinted. See, for example, Raymundo Magalhães Júnior, *Três panfletários do segundo reinado: Francisco de Sales Torres Homem e o 'Líbelo do povo'; Justiniano José da Rocha e 'Ação, reação, transação'; Antonio Ferreira Vianna e 'A conferência dos divinos'* (São Paulo, 1956).

On the Paraguayan War the literature is still unsatisfactory except on its military aspects. John Hoyt Williams, *The rise and fall of the Paraguayan Republic, 1800–1870* (Austin, Texas, 1979), provides the necessary background, while Pelham Horton Box, *The origins of the Paraguayan War* (Urbana, 1930) examines its immediate causes. The point of view of Paraguay is ably presented by Efraím Cardozo, *El imperio del Brasil y el Río de la Plata* (Buenos Aires, 1961). The best military history of the war is Augusto Tasso Fragoso, *História da guerra entre a Tríplice Aliança e o Paraguai* (5 vols., Rio, 1956–60). The Brazilian military itself is provocatively discussed in Nelson Werneck Sodré, *História militar do Brasil* (Rio de Janeiro, 1965).

A study of Brazil's economic history for the period must begin with the chapter on Brazil by Nícia Villela Luz in Stanley J. Stein and Roberto Cortés Conde (eds.), *Latin America: a guide to economic history, 1830–1930* (Berkeley, 1977), 163–272. Celso Furtado presents a general interpretive survey in *The economic growth of Brazil: a survey from colonial to modern times*, translated by Ricardo W. de Aguiar and Eric Charles Drysdale (Berkeley, 1963). Furtado's knowledge of Keynesian economic theory enlightens rather than beclouds his treatment. A contrasting Marxist perspective can be found in Caio Prado Júnior's account, already mentioned. Older, but still useful is J. F. Normano, *Brazil, a study of economic types* (Chapel Hill, N.C., 1935). Nathaniel H. Leff, *Underdevelopment and development in Brazil* (2 vols., London, 1982) is somewhat tendentious, but full of useful data.

Particular sectors of the economy have not been studied in sufficient detail. Notable on the sugar economy is Peter L. Eisenberg, *The sugar industry in Pernambuco: modernization without change, 1840–1910* (Berkeley, 1974), although Eul-Soo Pang argues an alternative point of view in 'Modernization and slavocracy in nineteenth century Brazil', *Journal of Interdisciplinary History*, 9/4 (1979), 667–88. The classic account regarding coffee, which includes the transcription of many documents, is the *História do café* prepared in fifteen volumes by Affonso d'Escragnolle Taunay (Departamento Nacional do Café, Rio de Janeiro, 1939–43). It is said that the author was paid by the word and wrote as many of these as he could; fortunately, he also prepared a summary entitled *Pequena história do café no Brasil (1727–1937)* (Departamento Nacional do Café, Rio de Janeiro, 1945). A more lively and still briefer account can be found in Odilon Nogueira de Matos, *Café e ferrovias: a evolução ferroviária de São Paulo e o desenvolvimento da cultura cafeeira* (2nd edn, São Paulo, 1974). On coffee, see also the books by Richard Graham, Stanley J. Stein, Warren Dean and Emília Viotti da Costa cited below. The coffee trade is examined by Joseph Sweigart 'Financing and marketing Brazilian export agriculture: the coffee factors of Rio de Janeiro, 1850–1888' (unpublished Ph.D. thesis, University of Texas, Austin, 1980). In contrast to the many studies on coffee and sugar, there are relatively few on the production of other crops or on the cattle economy. Still useful, after more than a century, however, is the work of Brazil's first statistician, Sebastião Ferreira Soares, especially his *Notas estatísticas sobre a produção agrícola e a carestia dos gêneros alimentícios no Império do Brasil,* (2nd edn, Rio de Janeiro, 1977). Also see a chapter on the economy of Rio Grande do Sul in José Hildebrando Decanal and Sergius Gonzaga (eds.), *RS: Economia & política* (Porto Alegre, 1979), and the first part of Barbara Weinstein's *The Amazon rubber boom, 1850–1920* (Stanford, 1983). Also see Alice Canabrava's discussion of the brief period of cotton production in São Paulo province, *Desenvolvimento da cultura do algodão na província de São Paulo* (São Paulo, 1951).

There are a number of works on transport in nineteenth-century Brazil. Almost folkloric, but with some useful data on muletrains is José Alípio Goulart, *Tropas e tropeiros na formação do Brasil* (Rio de Janeiro, 1961). Much more detailed, and at times even erudite, is José B. Sousa's book on ox-carts, *Ciclo do carro de bois no Brasil* (São Paulo, 1958). The early history of railways in Brazil is discussed in Richard Graham, *Britain and the onset of modernization in Brazil, 1850–1914* (Cambridge, England, 1968). Subsequent works include the book by Odillon Nogueira de Matos, already mentioned, and Robert H. Mattoon, Jr, 'Railroads, coffee, and the growth of big business in São Paulo, Brazil', *HAHR*, 57/2 (1977), 273–95.

Richard Graham, *Britain and the onset of modernization* also explores foreign control of the export and import business. Ana Célia Castro, *As empresas estrangeiras no Brasil, 1860–1913* (Rio de Janeiro, 1979), provides a brief summary of foreign investments. To place this trade and investment in a larger context, consult D. C. M. Platt, *Latin America and British trade, 1806–1914* (New York, 1972), as well as Irving Stone's two articles: 'British long-term investment in Latin America, 1865–1913', *Business History Review*, 42/3 (1968), 311–39 and 'La distribuzione geografica degli investimenti inglesi nell'America Latina (1825–1913)', *Storia Contemporanea*, 2/3 (1971), 495–518. These works suggest the need for revisions in J. Fred Rippy, *British investments in Latin America, 1822–1949* (Minneapolis, 1959).

First steps toward modern manufacturing in Brazil are closely tied to the figure of Mauá. Unfortunately, no satisfactory account of his life has yet been written. Anyda Marchant's *Viscount Mauá and the empire of Brazil* (Berkeley, 1965) does not seek to explain entrepreneurial success or failure, attributing Mauá's problems – as he did – to the personal enmity of others. Her omission of all footnotes advances scholarship no further than did Alberto de Faria, *Mauá: Ireneo Evangelista de Souza, barão e visconde de Mauá* (3rd edn, São Paulo, 1946). The best study of textile mills, really a collection of provocative essays, is Stanley J. Stein's *The Brazilian cotton manufacture: textile enterprise in an underdeveloped area, 1850–1950* (Cambridge, Mass., 1957).

Slavery shaped Brazilian life both in the cities and the countryside. It has consequently been the subject of a large number of studies. Robert Conrad, *Brazilian slavery* (Boston, Mass., 1977) is a useful bibliography. Leslie Bethell has written the major study of the end of the slave trade: *The abolition of the Brazilian slave trade* (Cambridge, 1970). For the abolition of slavery itself, see Robert Conrad, *The destruction of Brazilian slavery, 1850–1888* (Berkeley, 1972), Robert Brent Toplin, *The abolition of slavery in Brazil* (New York, 1972) and, above all, Emília Viotti da Costa, *Da senzala à colônia* (São Paulo, 1966), the major work on slavery and abolition in São Paulo. All works on Brazilian slavery respond in one way or another to the views of Gilberto Freyre on the plantation system as expressed, for instance, in his *The mansions and the shanties*, translated by Harriet de Onis (New York, 1963). In sharp contrast to his favourable view of the paternalistic relationship between master and slave stands Stanley J. Stein's brilliant *Vassouras. A Brazilian coffee county, 1850–1900* (Cambridge, Mass., 1957). A similar approach focused on a region that turned to coffee only later is Warren Dean, *Rio Claro. A Brazilian plantation system, 1820–1920* (Stanford, 1976). See also Amilcar Martins Filho and Roberto B. Martins, 'Slavery in a non-export economy: Nineteenth century Minas Gerais revisited', *HAHR*, 63/3 (1983), 537–68, and the comments upon it, pp. 569–90. For a survey of the different approaches to the subject, see Richard Graham, 'Brazilian slavery re-examined: a review article', *Journal of Social History*, 3/4 (1970), 431–53. Maria Sylvia de Carvalho Franco notes the importance of free men to slave society in her *Homens livres na ordem escravocrata* (2nd edn, São Paulo, 1974). An impressively detailed quantitative analysis is Robert W. Slenes, 'The demography and economics of Brazilian slavery, 1850–1888' (unpublished Ph.D. thesis, Stanford University, 1975).

The issues of population, urban life and land-tenure have not received the attention they deserve. Maria Luiza Marcílio notes the various estimates for Brazil's population at mid-century in 'Evolução da população brasileira através dos censos até 1872', *Anais de História*, 6 (1974), 115–37. Richard Morse makes stimulating suggestions regarding the relationship of villages, rural estates and cities in his 'Cities and society in nineteenth-century Latin America: the illustrative case of Brazil', in Richard Schaedel, Jorge Hardoy and Nora Scott Kinzer (eds.), *Urbanization in the Americas from its beginnings to the present day* (The Hague, 1978). See also Emília Viotti da Costa, 'Urbanização no Brasil no século XIX', in *Da monarquia à república: momentos decisivos* (São Paulo, 1971). Rich statistical information on the city of Rio de Janeiro is included in Eulália Maria Lahmeyer Lobo, *História do Rio de Janeiro (do capital comercial ao capital industrial e financeiro)* (2 vols., Rio de Janeiro, 1978). Sandra Lauderdale Graham explores the urban setting and cultural values of domestic servants in 'Protection and obedience: the paternalist world of female domestic servants', Rio de Janeiro, 1860–1910, (unpublished Ph.D. thesis, University of Texas, Austin, 1982). Kátia M. de Queirós Mattoso discusses the social and economic life of Salvador (Bahia) in *Bahia: a cidade do Salvador e seu mercado no século XIX* (São Paulo, 1978). Urban women are the subject of June E. Hahner's *A mulher brasileira e suas lutas sociais e políticas, 1850–1937*, translated by Maria Theresa P. de Almeida and Heitor Ferreira da Costa (São Paulo, 1981). On the 1850 land law, see the essays by Warren Dean, José Murilo de Carvalho and Emília Viotti da Costa cited in bibliographical essay no. 16.

The literary history of the period is ably surveyed in the relevant sections of Antônio Cândido de Mello e Souza, *Formação da literatura brasileira* (2 vols., São Paulo, 1959). He is careful to suggest the connections between the larger society and trends in literature. More attentive to stylistic criticism is José Guilherme Merquior, *De Anchieta a Euclides: breve história da literatura brasileira, I* (Rio de Janeiro, 1977). A quick reference work is Alfredo Bosi's *História concisa da literatura brasileira* (São

Paulo, 1970), while much greater detail can be found in Afrânio Coutinho (ed.), *A literatura no Brasil*, Vol. 1, Tomo 2: *Romantismo* (2nd edn, Rio de Janeiro, 1968). José de Alencar, Brazil's most famous mid-century novelist – also a politician – has been the subject of several biographies; see, for instance, Raimundo Magalhães Júnior, *José de Alencar e sua época* (2nd edn, Rio de Janeiro, 1977).

Philosophy and music are other topics that provide an insight into the nineteenth-century ethos. João Cruz Costa, *A history of ideas in Brazil*, translated by Suzette Macedo (Berkeley, 1964), like the work of Antônio Cândido, relates intellectual life to social and economic change. The ideas of political thinkers are explored in Nelson Saldanha, *O pensamento político no Brasil* (Rio de Janeiro, 1979). Finally, Gerard Béhague, *Music in Latin America, an introduction* (Englewood Cliffs, New Jersey, 1979), makes important observations on Antônio Carlos Gomes, the composer whose *Il Guarany* excited the opera world in 1870.

18. THE LITERATURE, MUSIC AND ART OF LATIN AMERICA
FROM INDEPENDENCE TO C. 1870

The study of artistic production in nineteenth-century Latin America is in a disconcertingly incomplete state. To take the case of literature, for example, on which there is a vast, if widely scattered bibliography, many of the most elementary tasks remain to be completed. With the exception of Brazil, Argentina and Peru, histories of Latin America's national literatures are incomplete, and the inter-relation of national and continental patterns has not been satisfactorily established. Paradoxically, the extraordinary expansion of interest in contemporary Latin America and its culture during the past two decades, when Latin American artists in a wide range of fields have come to international attention, threatens to obscure or even obliterate all that has gone before. Almost no one, since the mid 1960s, has set out to become a specialist on colonial or nineteenth-century literature and culture. The historian of the nineteenth century must for the most part rely on many of the same textual and critical materials that would have been used a quarter of a century ago, albeit with a number of invaluable additions, above all in the bibliographical field.

Of general works on cultural history, Pedro Henríquez Ureña, *Historia de la cultura en la América hispánica* (Mexico, 1947; English translation with a supplementary chapter by G. Chase: *A concise history of*

Spanish American culture, New York, 1947), although little more than an annotated checklist, remains perhaps the most useful. More exuberant, less balanced but also invaluable, is G. Arciniegas, *El continente de siete colores* (Buenos Aires, 1965; English translation, *Latin America: a cultural history*, New York, 1966). M. Picón Salas, *De la conquista a la independencia* (Mexico, 1958; English translation, *A cultural history of Spanish America from conquest to independence*, Berkeley, 1960), is as stimulating today as when it was written. Specifically on Brazil, F. de Azevedo, *A cultura brasileira* (Rio de Janeiro; English translation, *Brazilian culture*, New York, 1950) remains indispensable. See also Nelson Werneck Sodré, *Sintese da cultura brasileira* (Rio de Janeiro, 1970).

The history of Latin American architecture is relatively underworked, and the nineteenth century, usually viewed as a sterile transition from the glories of the colonial period to the adventures of the modern age, is particularly neglected. An understanding of the pre-Columbian and colonial background is essential. See especially D. Angulo Iñíguez, *Historia del arte hispanoamericano* (3 vols, Barcelona, 1950), P. Keleman, *Baroque and Rococo in Latin America* (New York, 1951), and, above all, G. Kubler and M. Soria, *Art and architecture in Spain and Portugal and their American dominions, 1500–1800* (Baltimore, 1959). And for a fuller discussion, see *CHLA II* bibliographical essay 17. The most accessible outline history is L. Castedo, *A history of Latin American art and architecture from Precolumbian times to the present* (New York, 1969). R. Segre (ed.), *América Latina en su arquitectura* (Mexico and Paris, Siglo XXI and Unesco, 1975), is a useful attempt at an historical synthesis.

Authoritative works on painting and sculpture in this period are very thin on the ground. But see Castedo and Angulo Iñíguez, cited above. D. Bayón (ed.), *América Latina en sus artes* (Mexico and Paris, 1974), gives a structured historical overview. On national developments, see M. Romero de Terreros, *Paisajistas mexicanos del siglo XIX* (Mexico, 1943), R. Tibol, *Historia general del arte mexicano* (Mexico, 1964), and B. Smith, *Mexico: a history in art* (London, 1979); M. Ivelic and G. Galaz, *La pintura en Chile desde la colonia hasta 1981* (Valparaiso, 1981); R. Brughetti, *Historia del arte en la Argentina* (Mexico, 1965), A. Matienzo, *Carlos Morel, precursor del arte argentino* (Buenos Aires, 1959) and A. D'Onofrio, *La época y el arte de Prilidiano Pueyrredón* (Buenos Aires, 1944); J. M. dos Reis Jr, *História da pintura no Brasil* (São Paulo, 1944).

On music the three best-known works in English are N. Slonimsky, *Music of Latin America* (New York, 1945), G. Chase, *A guide to Latin*

American music (New York, 1955), and G. Béhague's invaluable recent history, *Music in Latin America: an introduction* (New Jersey, 1979). Most useful of all, perhaps, is the *New Grove dictionary of music and musicians* (20 vols, Macmillan, London, 1980), to which Béhague has again contributed extensively, a fully comprehensive encyclopaedia which includes both continental and national sections on Latin America covering indigenous, folk and art music, with innumerable individual composer entries. O. Mayer-Serra's *Música y músicos de Latinoamérica* (Mexico, 1947) remains essential.

On individual republics, see O. Mayer-Serra, *Panorama de la música mexicana* (Mexico, 1941), R. M. Stevenson, *Music in Mexico* (New York, 1952) and G. Saldívar, *Historia de la música en México* (Mexico, 1954); A. Carpentier, *La música en Cuba* (Mexico, 1946); J. I. Perdomo Escobar, *Historia de la música en Colombia* (Bogotá, 1938); E. Pereira Salas, *Historia de la música en Chile* (Santiago, 1957), and S. Claro and J. Urrutia Blondel, *Historia de la música en Chile* (Santiago, 1973); M. G. Acevedo, *La música argentina durante el período de la organización nacional* (Buenos Aires, 1961), V. Gesualdo, *Historia de la música en la Argentina* (Buenos Aires, 1961), and R. Arizaga, *Enciclopedia de la música argentina* (Buenos Aires, 1971); L. H. Correia de Azevedo, *Bibliografia musical brasileira, 1820–1950* (Rio de Janeiro, 1952), R. Almeida, *História da música brasileira* (Rio de Janeiro, 1942).

There is a vast bibliography on Latin American literature, though surprisingly few works which are both accessible and useful on the period in question here. A basic bibliographical resource is S. M. Bryant, *A selective bibliography of bibliographies of Latin American literature* (Texas, 1976), with 662 entries. A well-organized general survey is W. Rela, *Guía bibliográfica de la literatura hispanoamericana desde el siglo XIX hasta 1970* (Buenos Aires), whilst J. Becco, *Fuentes para el estudio de la literatura hispanoamericana* (Buenos Aires, 1968), is a helpful minimal list. A. Flores, *Bibliografía de escritores hispanoamericanos. A bibliography of Spanish American writers, 1609–1974* (New York, 1975), provides perhaps the most useful practical guide to criticism on individual writers.

In view of the lack of definitive critical editions of nineteenth-century works, it would be fruitless to attempt a guide in the space available. This bibliography is accordingly devoted above all to secondary sources. One might mention here, however, the Biblioteca Ayacucho, published in Caracas since 1976 under the late Angel Rama, which has reissued numerous historic works unavailable in some cases for decades. Recent anthologies include *Pensamiento de la Ilustración*, J. C. Chiaramonte (ed.) (1979); *Pensamiento político de la emancipación, 1790–1825*, J. L. and L. A. Romero (eds.) (2 vols, 1977); *Poesía de la independencia*, E. Carilla (ed.) (1979); *Tradiciones hispanoamericanas*, E. Núñez (ed.) (1979); and *Poesía gauchesca*, A. Rama (ed.) (1977).

There are few English translations of works of this period, and those that exist are frequently the efforts of enthusiasts rather than specialists. For an overview of what is available, see W. K. Jones, *Latin American writers in English translation: a classified bibliography* (Washington, D.C., 1944), B. A. Shaw, *Latin American literature in English translation: an annotated bibliography* (New York, 1976); and the following anthologies: W. K. Jones (ed.), *Spanish American literature in translation. A selection of prose, poetry and drama before 1888* (New York, 1966), J. Englekirk, *et al.*, *An anthology of Spanish American literature* (2 vols, 2nd edn, New York, 1968), and A. Flores (ed.), *The literature of Spanish America* (6 vols, New York, 1966ff). Examples of translated works from the period are Almeida's *Memoirs of a militia sargeant* (translated by L. J. Barrett, Washington, D.C., 1959), Sarmiento's *Life in the Argentine Republic in the days of the tyrants* (translated by Mrs H. Mann, New York, 1868), Alencar's *Iracema, the honey-lips* (translated by I. Burton, London, 1866), Palma's *The knights of the cape* (translated by H. de Onís, New York, 1945), Taunay's *Innocence* (translated by H. Chamberlain, New York, 1945), Altamirano's *El Zarco, the bandit* (translated by M. Allt, London, 1957), Galván's *The cross and the sword* (translated by R. Graves, London, 1957), and Villaverde's *Cecilia Valdés* (translated by S. G. Gest, New York, 1962).

The outstanding synthesis of Latin American literary development to 1940 is still Pedro Henríquez Ureña, *Las corrientes literarias en la América hispánica* (Mexico, 1949), which included Brazil and appeared first in English as *Literary currents in Hispanic America* (Cambridge, Mass., 1945). Also valuable is Luis Alberto Sánchez, *Historia comparada de las literaturas americanas* (4 vols, Buenos Aires, 1976), in which the veteran Peruvian critic drew on a lifetime's experience. Two useful works on the period to 1820 are M. Hernández Sánchez-Barba, *Historia y literatura en Hispanoamérica, 1492–1820* (Madrid, 1978), and L. Iñigo Madrigal (ed.), *Historia de la literatura hispanoamericana*. Vol. 1: *Época colonial* (Madrid, 1982). Vol. 2 on the nineteenth century has not yet appeared, but promises to be fundamental.

There are a number of well-known general histories. J. Franco, *An introduction to Spanish American literature* (Cambridge, 1969), and *Spanish American literature since independence* (London, 1973), remain useful outline introductions in English, as does D. P. Gallagher, 'Spanish American literature', in P. E. Russell (ed.), *Spain: a companion to Spanish studies* (London, 1976), 429–71. The best of the general works in Spanish include R. Lazo, *Historia de la literatura hispanoamericana*, Vol. I: *El período colonial* (Mexico, 1965), and Vol. II: *El siglo XIX, 1780–1914* (1967), E. Anderson Imbert, *Historia de la literatura hispanoamericana* (2 vols, Mexico, 1954, also available in English), and A. Zum Felde, *Indice crítico de la literatura hispanoamericana* (2 vols, Mexico, 1959). Among the many works specifically on fiction, K. Schwartz, *A new history of Spanish American fiction* (2 vols, Miami, 1972), is particularly helpful for the independence and post-independence periods. On drama, see F. Dauster, *Historia del teatro hispanoamericano, siglos XIX y XX* (Mexico, 1966).

The outstanding authority on the literature of the independence period in Spanish America is E. Carilla: *La literatura barroca en Hispanoamérica* (New York, 1972), *La literatura de la independencia hispanoamericana: neoclasicismo y romanticismo* (Buenos Aires, 1964), brief but much cited, *El romanticismo en la América hispánica* (Madrid, 1958), and *Estudios de literatura hispanoamericana* (Bogotá, 1977), which includes important studies of a number of early nineteenth-century authors. On romanticism, see M. Suárez-Murias, *La novela romántica en Hispanoamérica* (New York, 1963), particularly useful on minor novelists, M. Yáñez (ed.), *La novela romántica latinoamericana* (Havana, 1978), a collection of well-known studies of key texts, R. Lazo, *El romanticismo: lo romántico en la lírica hispánica* (Mexico, 1971), and C. Meléndez, *La novela indianista en Hispanoamérica, 1832–1889* (San Juan, Puerto Rico, 1961). J. Brushwood, *Genteel barbarism: experiments in analysis of nineteenth-century Spanish-Americal novels* (Lincoln, Nebraska, 1981), examines eight well-known texts. Works of social contextualization include E. L. Tinker, *The horsemen of the Americas and the literature they inspired* (Texas, 1967), P. Verdevoye, '*Caudillos*', '*caciques*' *et dictateurs dans le roman hispano-américain* (Paris, 1978), with essays on Irisarri, Mármol, *et al.*, F. Fox-Lockhart, *Women novelists in Spain and Spanish America* (Metuchen, New Jersey, 1979), G. Brotherston, 'Ubirajara, Hiawatha, Cumandá: national virtue from American Indian literature', *Comparative Literature Studies*, 9 (1972), 243–52, and A. Losada's pathbreaking *La literatura en la sociedad de América Latina. Perú y el Río de la Plata, 1837–1880* (Frankfurt, 1983).

On Mexico, see J. Jiménez Rueda, *Letras mexicanas en el siglo XIX*

(Mexico, 1944), and, above all, a number of works by J. L. Martínez: *La expresión nacional. Letras mexicanas del siglo XIX* (Mexico, 1955), *La emancipación literaria de México* (Mexico, 1954), and 'México en busca de su expresión', in *Historia general de México*, vol. 3 (El Colegio de México, 1976). Also indispensable are R. E. Warner, *Historia de la novela mexicana en el siglo XIX* (Mexico, 1953), J. L. Read, *The Mexican historical novel, 1826–1910* (New York, 1939), J. S. Brushwood, *The romantic novel in Mexico* (Columbia, Miss., 1954), S. Ortiz Vidales, *Los bandidos en la literatura mexicana* (Mexico, 1949), and L. Reyes de la Maza, *Cien años de teatro mexicano, 1810–1910* (Mexico, 1972). On Cuba, see J. J. Remos, *Proceso histórico de las letras cubanas* (Madrid, 1958), and M. Henríquez Ureña *Historia de la literatura cubana* (2 vols, New York, 1963); and on Guatemala, D. Vela, *Literatura guatemalteca* (2 vols, Guatemala, 1944–5), and O. Olivera, *La literatura en publicaciones periódicas de Guatemala, siglo XIX* (New Orleans, 1974). On Venezuela, see M. Picón Salas, *Formación y proceso de la literatura venezolana* (Caracas, 1940), and R. Díaz Sánchez, *Paisaje histórico de la cultura venezolana* (Buenos Aires, 1965); and on Colombia, D. McGrady, *La novela histórica en Colombia, 1844–1959* (Bogotá, 1962). On Peru, see M. J. Watson Espiner, *El cuadro de costumbres en el Perú decimonónico* (Lima, 1980), and L. A. Sánchez, *Introducción a la literatura peruana* (Lima, 1972).

On Chile, see R. Silva Castro, *Panorama literario de Chile* (Santiago, 1962), A. Torres-Rioseco, *Breve historia de la literatura chilena* (Mexico, 1956), F. Alegría, *La poesía chilena: orígenes y desarrollo del siglo XVI al XIX* (Mexico, 1954), N. Pinilla (ed.), *La polémica del romanticismo en 1842* (Santiago, 1945), and an invaluable recent work, B. Subercaseaux, *Cultura y sociedad liberal en el siglo XIX. Lastarria: ideología y literatura* (Santiago, 1981).

There is a vast bibliography on Argentina, where, unusually and for well-known historical reasons, the nineteenth century is better studied than the twentieth. Particularly useful on this period are R. Rojas, *Historia de la literatura argentina: ensayo filosófico sobre la evolución de la cultura en el Plata* (9 vols, Buenos Aires, 1957), an unrivalled classic, J. C. Ghiano, *Constantes de la literatura argentina* (Buenos Aires, 1953), and E. Carilla, *Estudios de literatura argentina: siglo XIX* (Tucumán, 1965). Works of more specific orientation include A. Prieto, *et al.*, *Proyección del rosismo en la literatura argentina* (Rosario, 1959), H. E. Frizzi de Longoni, *Las sociedades literarias y el periodismo, 1800–1852* (Buenos Aires, 1947), R. H. Castagnino, *Contribución documental a la historia del teatro en B. A. durante la época de Rosas, 1830–1852* (Buenos Aires, 1945), J. Cruz, *Teatro romántico argentino* (Buenos Aires, 1972), with texts by Mármol and Mitre, F. Chávez, *La cultura en la época de Rosas: aportes a la descolonización mental de la Argentina* (Buenos Aires, 1973), R. Cortázar (ed.), *Indios y gauchos en la literatura argentina*. On Uruguay, see L. Ayestarán, *La primitiva poesía gauchesca en el Uruguay, 1812–1838* (Montevideo, 1950), and W. Rela, *Historia del teatro uruguayo, 1808–1968* (Montevideo, 1969). On Paraguay, see J. Plá, *El teatro en el Paraguay: de la fundación a 1870* (Asunción, 1967).

On Brazil, Afrânio Coutinho, *Introdução à literatura no Brasil* (Rio de Janeiro, 1955; translated as *An introduction to literature in Brazil*, New York, 1969), is perhaps the most satisfactory general presentation. Also in English, see particularly E. Veríssimo's chatty *Brazilian literature: an outline* (New York, 1945), and S. Putnam's celebrated *Marvelous journey: a survey of four centuries of Brazilian writing* (New York, 1948). C. Hulet (ed.), *Brazilian literature* (3 vols, Washington, D.C., 1974), is an invaluable critical anthology with texts in Portuguese and commentary in English. Other essential works are Sílvio Romero's classic pioneering *História da literatura brasileira* (2 vols, Rio de Janeiro, 1888), A. Cândido, *Brigada ligeira* (São Paulo, 1945) and *Formação da literatura brasileira, 1750–1880* (2 vols, São Paulo, 1959), N. Werneck Sodré, *História da literatura brasileira: seus fundamentos econômicos* (Rio de Janeiro, 1940; rev. edn, São Paulo, 1982), and A. Bosi, *História concisa da literatura brasileira* (São Paulo, 1972). On romanticism, see particularly F. Cunha, *O romantismo em Brasil* (Rio de Janeiro, 1971), D. Salles, *Do ideal às ilusões* (Rio de Janeiro, 1980), and J. G. Merquior, *O fantasma romântico* (Petrópolis, 1981). For social themes, D. Driver, *The Indian in Brazilian literature* (New York, 1942), and M. Garcia Mendes, *A personagem negra no teatro brasileiro, 1838–1888* (São Paulo, 1982). A recent work, David T. Haberly, *Three sad races. Racial identity and national consciousness in Brazilian literature* (Cambridge, 1983), includes chapters on Gonçalves Dias, José de Alencar and Castro Alves.

INDEX